Volume I

Food Processing and Preservation

Highlights

- Food Processing and Preservation: An Overview
- Engineering Properties of Food
- Process and Instrumentation Control
- Heat and Mass Transfer in Food Industry
- Automation in Food Industry
- Unit Operations: An Overview
- Ambient Temperature Processing
- Pulse Electric Field, Ultrasound and Hurdle Technology
- Thermal and Non-thermal Processing
- Processing by Application and Removal of Heat
- Microwave, Ohmic and Radio Frequency Heating

Contents at a Glance

VOLUME II

VOLUME I

Volume I

Food Processing and Preservation

DS Warris

CBS Publishers & Distributors Pvt Ltd

New Delhi • Bengaluru • Chennai • Kochi • Kolkata • Mumbai
Bhopal • Bhubaneswar • Hyderabad • Jharkhand • Nagpur • Patna • Pune
Uttarakhand • Dhaka (Bangladesh) • Kathmandu (Nepal)

Disclaimer

Science and technology are constantly changing fields. New research and experience broaden the scope of information and knowledge. The author has tried his best in giving information available to him while preparing the material for this book. Although, all efforts have been made to ensure optimum accuracy of the material, yet it is quite possible some errors might have been left uncorrected. The publisher, printer and the author will not be held responsible for any inadvertent errors, omissions or inaccuracies.

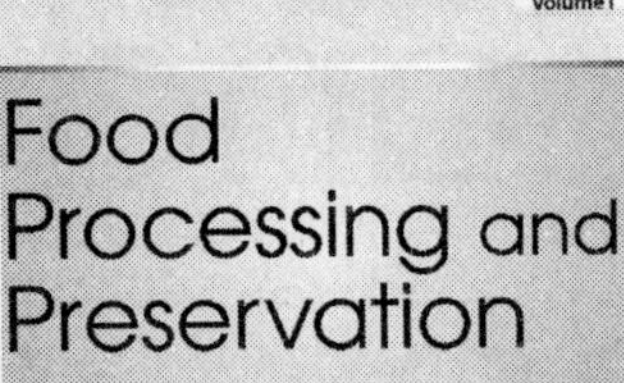

ISBN: 978-93-89688-59-7

First Edition: 2020

Published by Satish Kumar Jain and produced by Varun Jain for

CBS Publishers & Distributors Pvt Ltd

4819/XI Prahlad Street, 24 Ansari Road, Daryaganj, New Delhi 110 002, India.

Ph: 23289259, 23266861, 23266867 Website: www.cbspd.com

Fax: 011-23243014 e-mail: delhi@cbspd.com; cbspubs@airtelmail.in.

Corporate Office: 204 FIE, Industrial Area, Patparganj, Delhi 110 092

Ph: 4934 4934 Fax: 4934 4935 e-mail: publishing@cbspd.com; publicity@cbspd.com

Branches

- **Bengaluru:** Seema House 2975, 17th Cross, K.R. Road, Banasankari 2nd Stage, Bengaluru 560 070, Karnataka
  Ph: +91-80-26771678/79 Fax: +91-80-26771680 e-mail: bangalore@cbspd.com
- **Chennai:** 7, Subbaraya Street, Shenoy Nagar, Chennai 600 030, Tamil Nadu
  Ph: +91-44-26680620, 26681266 Fax: +91-44-42032115 e-mail: chennai@cbspd.com
- **Kochi:** 68/1534, 35, 36, Power House Road, Opp. KSEB, Kochi 682018, Kerala
  Ph: +91-484-4059061-65 Fax: +91-484-4059065 e-mail: kochi@cbspd.com
- **Kolkata:** 6/B, Ground Floor, Rameswar Shaw Road, Kolkata-700 014, West Bengal
  Ph: +91-33-22891126, 22891127, 22891128 e-mail: kolkata@cbspd.com
- **Mumbai:** 83-C, Dr E Moses Road, Worli, Mumbai-400018, Maharashtra
  Ph: +91-22-24902340/41 Fax: +91-22-24902342 e-mail: mumbai@cbspd.com

Representatives

• **Bhopal**	0-8319310552	• **Bhubaneswar**	0-9911037372	• **Hyderabad**	0-9885175004	• **Jharkhand**	0-9811541605
• **Nagpur**	0-9421945513	• **Patna**	0-9334159340	• **Pune**	0-9623451994	• **Uttarakhand**	0-9716462459
• **Dhaka (Bangladesh)**	01912-003485	• **Kathmandu (Nepal)**	977-9818742655				

Printed at Mudrak, Noida, UP, India

Preface

The increasing global demand for processed foods has led to a greater prominence of the food industry, its specific needs and processing challenges. Consequently, in recent times the role of the engineer in the food industry has gained considerable prominence. In contrast to other more traditional processing industries, the raw materials or ingredients that are used tend to be of greater complexity in nature. While processing conditions are also more moderate in that temperatures even in hottest ovens may not exceed 200°C and pressures rarely exceed one or two bar, the materials themselves are highly complex in composition, textural and flavour characteristics. During their handling and processing, many changes to their properties occur. The extent of these changes is often a strong function of their process history. In the food industry, one plant is frequently required to perform one purpose. To produce a product which is constituent and desirable to the consumer's expectations in terms of appearance, texture and taste all year round from raw materials which may be derived from different sources or suppliers together with seasonal variability, requires a sound understanding of the physical and chemical properties of the food materials being processed and the detailed understanding of the function of various units operations. In all of this, food safety is paramount. Understanding the nature and sources of contamination is essential, and its control critical to ensure that the processed foods are safe to eat. Product safety is as critical as process safety. Over the past couple of decades, the role of the engineer in the food industry has gained considerable prominence. The food processing industry is extremely complex, diverse and evolved. With the consumer market becoming even more sophisticated and demanding, there is a continual need for process innovation. Even allowing for the demands of the consumer for product consistency and quality, the consumer expects excitement, novelty, value for money and a product that is safe in tamper-proof packaging. For the food process engineer, the challenge is to use process plant and associated equipment which is sufficiently flexible to respond to any changes in demand.

The complexity and challenges of food processing engineering is best illustrated by considering the mixing criteria used in the food industry. Process engineers will be more familiar with the handling and mixing of robust components with the aim of achieving homogeneity in which liquids have low viscosity or exhibit straightforward Newtonian behaviour and where scale-up is based on simple power-to-volume ratios. In contrast, the criteria for food mixing involve ingredients which have complex components with each exhibiting very different chemical and physical properties. They often have high viscosities and exhibit non-Newtonian behaviour. Consumers are increasingly demanding foods which are nutritious and healthy such as fortified organic and minimally processed foods. There is also a considerable demand for foods which are highly processed such as sausages, burgers, baked beans and dehydrated foods, and foods which have long shelf-life and total sterility such as canned and bottled foods with packaging that is tamper-proof yet can be easily opened. Production runs are becoming ever shorter as tastes and fads change. While food processing may be classified into either chemical, physical or biological operations, there are many major issues affecting food process engineering including molecular genetics with the use of GMOs, the use of animal cloning, new regulatory procedures, ethical issues, public concerns, planetary considerations and a number of major socio-economic considerations. The underlying requirements for technological progress in food processing are a minimum of risks acceptable for the benefits, gains, as well as a full public understanding. The role of the food process engineer is critical in all of this.

This reference textbook on *Food Processing and Preservation* is divided in two volumes. This volume is divided into four sections and comprises 1 to 28 chapters.

Section I discusses general considerations and engineering aspects. Chapter 1 is devoted to food processing and preservation: an overview. Chapter 2 deals with engineering properties of food. The engineering properties of foods are important and they can be classified as thermal, optical, electrical, mechanical, etc. Most of these properties indicate changes in the chemical composition and structural organisation of foods ranging from the molecular to the macroscopic level. Chapter 3 concentrates on process and instrumentation control. This chapter discusses the basics of instrumentation concepts of measurement and control and food processes, respectively. This chapter will also present a short description of the various food processing. Chapter 4 focuses on heat and mass transfer in food industry. Heat transfer is the exchange of thermal energy between physical systems. Mass transfer is the net movement of mass from one location, usually meaning stream, phase, fraction or component, to another. Chapter 5 discusses automation in food industry. The food industry presents many unique challenges to complete automation, the industry has been successful in putting many automatic processes into place. Chapter 6 explains unit operations: an overview. Unit operations common to many food products include cleaning, coating, concentrating, controlling, disintegrating, drying, evaporating, fermentation, forming, heating/cooling (heat exchange), materials handling, mixing, packaging, pumping, separating, and others.

Section II discusses ambient temperature processing. Chapter 7 is devoted to size reduction. Size reduction is the unit operation in which the average size of solid pieces of food is reduced by the application of grinding, compression or impact forces. When applied to the reduction in size of globules of immiscible liquids (for example oil globules in water) size reduction is more frequently referred to as homogenisation or emulsification. Chapter 8 deals with mixing and forming. The term 'mixing' essentially refers to operations reducing the non-uniformities in the spatial distribution of composition, properties, or temperature within bulk material. In the context of food processing, this is a necessary step.

Chapter 9 concentrates on separation and concentration of food components. Filtration is one of the most common methods for the downstream processing of fermentation products and it is used at all production scales. Chapter 10 focuses on food irradiation which is the process of exposing food to ionising radiations to destroy micro-organisms, bacteria, viruses or insects that might be present in the food. Chapter 11 concentrates on pulse electric field, ultrasound and hurdle technology. Some important aspects in pulsed electric field technology are the generation of high electric field intensities, the design of chambers that impart uniform treatment to foods with minimum increase in temperature, and the design of electrodes that minimise the effect of electrolysis. Ultrasound has been emerged as a revolutionary technology in the field of food industry. Its use is continuously increasing in various steps of processing of food products. Hurdle technology is an efficient technique for improving the quality of food and to enhance its shelf life. The main objective of this technology is food preservation, storage of food products and enhancement of their shelf life thereby giving us good quality products. Chapter 12 explains thermal and non-thermal processing which is the heart of food processing.

Section III discusses processing by application and removal of heat. Chapter 13 is devoted to blanching of foods which is a unit process prior to freezing, canning or drying in which fruits and vegetables are heated for the purpose of inactivating enzymes, modifying texture, nutritional value. Chapter 14 deals with pasteurisation which is the mild heat treatment in which food is heated below 100°C. Chapter 15 concentrates on sterilisation which involves exposing foods to a temperature generally exceeding 100°C for a period sufficient to inhibit enzymes and all forms of micro-organisms, including bacteria. Chapter 16 focuses on evaporation and crystallisation. Evaporation is the process of a substance in a liquid state changing to a gaseous state due to an increase in temperature and/or pressure. Evaporation is a fundamental part of the water cycle and is constantly occurring throughout nature. Evaporators are widely used in the food processing industry to remove a portion of the water from food products. This reduces bulk and weight for subsequent processing, increases solids content (as for jams and molasses), helps preserve the product, provides convenience to the end consumer and concentrates colour or flavour. Chapter 17 explains extruder. Extrusion technologies are novel and versatile manufacturing technique in food industry for conveying and shaping fluid forms of processed raw materials like doughs and pastes. It was found that the extrusion process is continuous in nature. In order to obtain the desired output, the process variables should be standardised.

Chapter 18 is devoted to drying. Drying is a method of food preservation that works by removing water from the food, which inhibits the growth of micro-organisms and hinders quality decay. Drying food using Sun and wind to prevent spoilage has been practised since ancient times. Chapter 19 deals with smoking. Smoking is the process of flavouring, browning, cooking, or preserving food by exposing it to smoke from burning or smoldering material, most often wood. Meat, fish, and lapsang souchong tea are often smoked. Chapter 20 focuses on food frying. Frying is a popular method used in food preparation and manufacturing. During frying, several physical and chemical changes occur in foods that impart desirable characteristics. Chapter 21 concentrates on microwave, ohmic and radio frequency heating. Microwave ovens have become an indispensable appliance in the 21st century household in countries like the United States and Canada, as well as many European countries. Ohmic heating, the innovative method of food processing technology, which supersede retort, and aseptic packaging. Radio frequency (RF) heating is an advanced and emerging technology for food application because of its higher penetration depth, heat distribution and low energy consumption. Chapter 22 discusses chilling. Chilling is the unit operation in which the temperature of a food is reduced to between 1 and 8°C. It is used to reduce the rate of biochemical and microbiological changes, and hence to extend the shelf life of fresh and processed foods. Chapter 22 explains freezing. The spectacular growth of the frozen food industry has been largely due to favourable economics of process, convenience of preparation, and the high quality of processed products. The range of frozen products includes fruits, vegetables, juices, meats, dairy products, and bakery goods. Modern freezing systems cause minimal changes in the quality attributes of products during processing.

Section IV discusses processing and preservation of fruits, vegetables and meat products. Chapter 24 is devoted to apples and apple processing. Various methods of processing of dried and speciality apples along with their nutritional values and quality control aspects are discussed in detail. Chapter 25 deals with cherry, strawberries, raspberries and grape juice processing. Chapter 26 concentrates on miscellaneous fruits. This chapter discusses various important fruits such as oranges, tangerines, plums, prunes, cranberry, blueberry, currant, gooseberry, grapefruits, lemons, limes, bananas, guava, lychee, mango, papaya and avocados, etc. Chapter 27 focuses on vegetables. Vegetables are parts of plants, which can be consumed either, raw or processed in some way. Chapter 28 explains meat, fish and egg products. These are the most valuable livestock product and for many people serves as their first-choice source of animal protein.

Diagrams, figures, tables and index supplement the text. All topics have been covered in a cogent and lucid style to help the reader grasp the information quickly and easily.

It may not be wrong to hold that the present reference textbook of *Food Processing and Preservation* is a complete treatise on this subject. It is essential reading for BTech (environmental biotechnology/ microbiology/food biotechnology/microbiology/biomedical and biochemical engineering) and students pursuing BSc/MSc course in biotechnology and microbiology. Besides students, this book will prove useful to industrialists and consultants in the respective fields.

The reference textbook also caters to the requirement of the syllabus prescribed by various universities for undergraduate and postgraduate courses in the above subjects. It has been prepared with meticulous care, aiming at making the book error-free. Constructive suggestions are always welcome from users of this book.

DS Warris

Contents

SECTION I

General Considerations and Engineering Aspects

Chapter 1

Food Processing and Preservation: An Overview

INTRODUCTION

Food technology has evolved into an interdisciplinary area of applied science and engineering based on chemical engineering and food science. India is primarily based on agriculture. The demand for uniform and high quality food round the year even at remote places from production centre has led to improved food processing technologies.

Food items are being processed for various reasons. Since times immemorial, grains have been dried after harvest to increase their shelf life. Initially, foods were processed primarily to improve digestibility, palatability and to ensure a continuous supply. In India pickles, *murabbas* and *papads* are examples of preserved products made from certain vegetables/fruits/grains. With passage of time, improved transportation, communication and increasing industrialisation, the needs of consumers have become more diverse and there is now increasing demand for convenient foods, 'fresh' and 'more natural' foods, 'safer and healthier' foods and foods with adequate shelf life. Consumers expect better-quality foods with retention of nutrients, many a time having specific functional properties and taste/texture/consistency, while being shelf-stable and easy to package, store and transport. This has served as a stimulus to scientists to develop methods and techniques to process foods in a manner that the food products will meet the requirements and demands of the consumers. All of us eat readymade foods. These range from biscuits, bread, pickles/papads to foods such as ready-to-eat curries, meal items, snacks, etc. Such foods and others are manufactured using a variety of processes and technologies. For some, simple traditional methods are still used while newer processes and technologies are employed to produce processed foods in bulk.

It is well known that simple diets based largely on staple foods such as cereals are often deficient in certain nutrients leading to deficiency diseases. Therefore, food fortification is done by adding the nutrient that is lacking in the food stuffs or condiments to ensure that minimum dietary requirements are met. Some examples are iodised salt, folic acid added to flour, vitamin A added to oils/fats. Increasing prevalence of diseases like heart disease and diabetes and concern about wellness, has made it necessary for scientists to alter the nutrient content of foods, for example reducing the Calorie content of processed foods in several ways such as using artificial sweeteners. Likewise fat from ice creams is replaced by specially treated proteins which give ice cream the smooth texture associated with fat but the energy value is reduced. Also, consumer perceptions about food have changed. The demand for foods free of chemicals, pesticides and preservatives, yet having a longer shelf life and retaining their natural flavour and appearance, is rapidly increasing. All this has increased the importance of food processing and technology as a discipline and there is a huge demand for food technologists.

Food processing: It is the set of methods and techniques used to transform raw ingredients into finished and semi-finished products. Food processing requires good quality raw materials from either plant and/or animal source to be converted into attractive, marketable and often long shelf-life food products.

IMPORTANCE OF FOOD PROCESSING AND PRESERVATION

The food processing is a branch of manufacturing wherein raw materials are transformed into intermediate foodstuffs or edible products through the application of scientific knowledge and technology. Various processes are used to convert bulky, perishable and sometimes inedible food materials into more useful, concentrated, shelf-stable and palatable foods or potable beverages. Changes in the products often reduce preparation time for the cook. Most of the time, processing of foods adds value to the resultant product by increasing storability, portability, palatability and convenience. Professionals in the food processing need to be knowledgeable about general characteristics of raw food materials, principles of food preservation, processing factors which influence quality, packaging, water and waste management, good manufacturing processes and sanitation procedures. Let us briefly examine the need, principles, methods and modernisation of food processing.

Foods are subject to physical, chemical and biological deterioration. Food deterioration is associated with spoilage, development of off-flavours, deterioration of textures, discoloration and loss of nutritional value in varying degrees, reducing aesthetic appeal and rendering it unfit/unsafe for consumption. A number of factors can lead to food deterioration or spoilage, e.g. pests, infestation by insects, inappropriate temperatures used for processing and/or storage, excessive exposure to light and other radiations, oxygen, moisture. Food is also contaminated by micro-organisms (bacteria, fungus and moulds) or chemicals such as pesticides. Food can also be spoiled due to degradation by naturally present enzymes (a specific class of protein molecules that act as biological catalysts to accelerate chemical reactions). In addition, physical and chemical changes in certain constituents of food from plant and animal sources occur soon after harvesting or slaughtering, altering the food quality.

Therefore food processing and preservation are required to preserve food in edible and safe form. Methods by which food is preserved from spoiling after harvesting or slaughtering date back to prehistoric times. The oldest methods were sun drying, controlled fermentation, salting/pickling, candying, roasting, smoking, baking and using spices as preservatives. These tried and tested techniques are still used although, with the advent of industrial revolution, new methods have been developed. Food processing incorporates and unifies the general characteristics of different classes of foods and principles of food science, chemistry, food microbiology, nutrition, sensory analysis and statistics including good manufacturing practices as per regulations.

Many food processing operations are designed to extend the shelf life of the food products. The concepts associated with food processing are reducing/eliminating microbial activity and other factors that influence food spoilage. The principle micro organisms that cause food spoilage are bacteria, fungi, yeasts and moulds. Just recollect that you studied in biology how they grow typically very rapidly under congenial conditions. Factors influencing microbial growth are nutrient availability, moisture, pH, oxygen levels and the presence or absence of inhibiting substances, e.g. antibiotics. The activity of enzymes inherently present in foods also depends on pH and temperature. Oxidative enzymes in fresh fruits and vegetables continue to use oxygen to metabolise, reducing the shelf life of fruits and vegetables. So the basic concepts in food processing methods to prevent food spoilage are:

1. Application of heat.
2. Removal of water moisture.
3. Lowering of temperature during storage.
4. Reduction of pH.
5. Controlling the availability of oxygen.

Processed foods can be classified on the basis of extent and type of processing as follows:

1. Minimally processed foods: These are processed as little as possible in order to retain the quality of fresh foods. Generally the processes used are cleaning, trimming, shelling, cutting, slicing and storage at low, i.e. refrigeration temperatures.
2. Preserved foods: The methods of preservation used do not change the character of the product substantially, e.g. frozen peas and frozen vegetables, dehydrated peas, dehydrated vegetables, canned fruits and vegetables.
3. Manufactured foods: In such products, the original characteristics of the raw products are lost and some basic methods of preservation are used, often using various ingredients such as salt, sugar, oil or even chemical preservatives. Examples are pickles, jams, marmalades, squashes, papads, wadis.
4. Formulated foods: These are products prepared by mixing and processing of individual ingredients to result in relatively shelfstable food products such as bread, biscuits, ice cream, cakes, kulfi.
5. Food derivatives: In industry, components of foods may be obtained from the raw product through purification, e.g. sugar from sugarcane or oil from oil seeds. In some cases, the derivative or the component may be processed further, e.g. conversion of oil to vanaspati (the process is called hydrogenation).
6. Functional foods: These are foods that can have a beneficial effect on human health, e.g. probiotics, lycopene.
7. Medical foods: These are used in dietary management of diseases, for example, low sodium salt, lactose–free milk for persons with lactose intolerance.

TECHNIQUES TO PREVENT FOOD FROM SPOILING

The term food preservation refers to any one of a number of techniques used to prevent food from spoiling. It includes methods such as canning, pickling, drying and freeze-drying, irradiation, pasteurisation, smoking, and the addition of chemical additives. Food preservation has become an increasingly important component of the food industry as fewer people eat foods produced on their own lands, and as consumers expect to be able to purchase and consume foods that are out of season.

The vast majority of instances of food spoilage can be attributed to one of two major causes: (i) the attack by pathogens (disease-causing micro-organisms) such as bacteria and moulds, and (ii) oxidation that causes the destruction of essential biochemical compounds and/or the destruction of plant and animal cells. The various methods that have been devised for preserving foods are all designed to reduce or eliminate one or the other (or both) of these causative agents. For example, a simple and common method of preserving food is by heating it to some minimum temperature. This process prevents or retards spoilage because high temperatures kill or inactivate most kinds of pathogens. The addition of compounds known as BHA and BHT to foods also prevents spoilage in another different way. These compounds are known to act as antioxidants, preventing chemical reactions that cause the oxidation of food that results in its spoilage. Almost all techniques of preservation are designed to extend the life of food by acting in one of these two ways.The search for methods of food preservation probably can be traced to the dawn of human civilisation. People who lived through harsh winters found it necessary to find some means of insuring a food supply during seasons when no fresh fruits and vegetables were available. Evidence for the use of dehydration (drying) as a method of food preservation, for example, goes back at least 5000 years. Among the most primitive forms of food preservation that are still in use today are such methods as smoking, drying, salting, freezing, and fermenting.

Early humans probably discovered by accident that certain foods exposed to smoke seem to last longer than those that are not. Meats, fish, fowl, and cheese were among such foods. It appears that compounds present in wood smoke have antimicrobial actions that prevent the growth of organisms that cause spoilage. Today, the process of smoking has become a sophisticated method of food preservation with both hot and cold forms in use. Hot smoking is used primarily with fresh or frozen foods, while cold smoking is used most often with salted products. The most advantageous conditions for each kind of smoking—air velocity, relative humidity, length of exposure, and salt content, for example—are now generally understood and applied during the smoking process. For example, electrostatic precipitators can be employed to attract smoke.

PRESERVATION PROCESSES

Types of Preservation Processes

Preservation processes include:

1. Heating to kill or denature micro-organisms (e.g. boiling).
2. Oxidation (e.g. use of sulphur dioxide).
3. Toxic inhibition (e.g. smoking, use of carbon dioxide, vinegar, alcohol, etc.).
4. Dehydration (drying).
5. Osmotic inhibition (e.g. use of syrups).
6. Low temperature inactivation (e.g. freezing).
7. Ultra high water pressure (e.g. fresherised, a kind of 'cold' pasteurisation, the pressure kills naturally occurring pathogens, which cause food deterioration and affect food safety.).
8. Combinations of these methods.

Drying

One of the oldest methods of food preservation is by drying, which reduces water activity sufficiently to prevent or delay bacterial growth.

Refrigeration

Refrigeration preserves food by slowing down the growth and reproduction of micro-organisms and the action of enzymes which cause food to rot.

Freezing

Freezing is also one of the most commonly used processes commercially and domestically for preserving a very wide range of food including prepared food stuffs which would not have required freezing in their unprepared state. For example, potato waffles are stored in the freezer, but potatoes themselves require only a cool dark place to ensure many months' storage. Cold stores provide large volume, long-term storage for strategic food stocks held in case of national emergency in many countries.

Vacuum packing

Vacuum-packing stores food in a vacuum environment, usually in an air-tight bag or bottle. The vacuum environment strips bacteria of oxygen needed for survival, slowing spoiling. Vacuum-packing is commonly used for storing nuts to reduce loss of flavour from oxidation.

Salt

Salting or curing draws moisture from the meat through a process of osmosis. Meat is cured with salt or sugar or a combination of the two. Nitrates and nitrites are also often used to cure meat and contribute the characteristic pink colour, as well as inhibition of *Clostridium botulinum.*

Sugar

Sugar is used to preserve fruits, either in syrup with fruit such as apples, pears, peaches, apricots, plums or in crystallised form where the preserved material is cooked in sugar to the point of crystallisation and the resultant product is then stored dry. This method is used for the skins of citrus fruit (candied peel), angelica and ginger.

Artificial food additives

Preservative food additives can be antimicrobial, which inhibit the growth of bacteria or fungi, including mould or antioxidant, such as oxygen absorbers, which inhibit the oxidation of food constituents.

Pickling

Pickling is a method of preserving food in an edible anti-microbial liquid. Pickling can be broadly categorised as chemical pickling for example. In chemical pickling, the food is placed in an edible liquid that inhibits or kills bacteria and other micro-organisms. In fermentation pickling, the food itself produces the preservation agent, typically by a process that produces lactic acid. Fermented pickles include sauerkraut, nukazuke, kimchi, surströmming, and curtido. Some pickled cucumbers are also fermented. In commercial pickles, a preservative like sodium benzoate or EDTA may also be added to enhance shelf life.

Lye

Sodium hydroxide (lye) makes food too alkaline for bacterial growth. Lye will saponify fats in the food, which will change its flavour and texture. Lutefisk uses lye in its preparation, as do some olive recipes. Modern recipes for century eggs also call for lye. Masa harina and hominy use agricultural lime in their preparation and this is often misheard as 'lye'.

Canning and bottling

Canning involves cooking food, sealing it in sterile cans or jars, and boiling the containers to kill or weaken any remaining bacteria as a form of sterilisation.

Jellying

Food may be preserved by cooking in a material that solidifies to form a gel. Such materials include gelatine, agar, maize flour and arrowroot flour.

Potting

A traditional British way of preserving meat (particularly shrimp) is by setting it in a pot and sealing it with a layer of fat.

Jugging

Meat can be preserved by jugging, the process of stewing the meat (commonly game or fish) in a covered earthenware jug or casserole. The animal to be jugged is usually cut into pieces, placed into a tightly-sealed jug with brine or gravy, and stewed. Red wine and/or the animal's own blood is sometimes added to the cooking liquid.

Irradiation

Irradiation of food is the exposure of food to ionising radiation, either high-energy electrons or X-rays from accelerators or by gamma rays (emitted from radioactive sources as Cobalt-60 or Caesium-137). The treatment has a range of effects, including killing bacteria, moulds and insect pests, reducing the ripening and spoiling of fruits, and at higher doses inducing sterility.

Pulsed electric field processing

Pulsed electric field (PEF) processing is a method for processing cells by means of brief pulses of a strong electric field. PEF holds potential as a type of low temperature alternative pasteurisation process for sterilising food products.

Modified atmosphere

Modifying atmosphere is a way to preserve food by operating on the atmosphere around it. Salad crops which are notoriously difficult to preserve are now being packaged in sealed bags with an atmosphere modified to reduce the oxygen (O_2) concentration and increase the carbon dioxide (CO_2) concentration.

Burial in the ground

Burial of food can preserve it due to a variety of factors: lack of light, lack of oxygen, cool temperatures, pH level, or desiccants in the soil. Burial may be combined with other methods such as salting or fermentation.

Controlled use of micro-organism

Some foods, such as many cheeses, wines, and beers will keep for a long time because their production uses specific micro-organisms that combat spoilage from other less benign organisms. These micro-organisms keep pathogens in check by creating an environment toxic for themselves and other micro-organisms by producing acid or alcohol.

High pressure food preservation

High pressure food preservation refers to high pressure used for food preservation.

PRINCIPLES OF FOOD PRESERVATION

Food preservation operates according to three principles, namely:

1. Prevention or delay of microbial decomposition.
   - Asepsis: Process of keeping micro-organisms out of food and its surroundings.
     Proper packaging of the product.
     Maintenance of sanitary conditions.
   - Removal of micro-organisms.
     - o Washing.
     - o Trimming ingredients.
     - o Discarding dirt.
     - o Filtering clear liquid.
   - Hindering the growth and activity of micro-organisms.
     - o Low temperature-freezing.
     - o Drying-reduces moisture.
     - o Maintenance of anaerobic conditions—removal of air, e.g. hotdogs, bacon.
     - o Use of chemicals—preservatives.
   - Killing micro-organisms by heat or irradiation.
     Micro-organisms are killed by heat.
2. Prevention or delay of self-decomposition of foods.
   - Destroying or inactivating food enzymes.
     - o Blanching is an example of this kind of prevention.
     - o Low temperature.
     - o Chemical preservatives.
     - o Drying.
   - Preventing oxidation with the use of antioxidants.
     - o Oxygen speeds up decomposition of food antioxidants deprives food from oxygen.
     - o Butter, margarine and other fatty foods.
3. Prevention of damage because of external factors such as insects, rodents, dust, odour, fumes, and mechanical, fire, heat or water damage.
   - Styrofoam boxes, cartons, and shock absorbing materials.
   - Sealed tight, vacuum-packed.

Chapter 2

Engineering Properties of Food

INTRODUCTION

The engineering properties of foods are important, if not essential, in the process design and manufacture of food products. They can be classified as thermal (specific heat, thermal conductivity, and diffusivity), optical (colour, gloss, and translucency), electrical (conductivity and permittivity), mechanical (structural, geometrical, and strength), and food powder (primary and secondary) properties. Most of these properties indicate changes in the chemical composition and structural organisation of foods ranging from the molecular to the macroscopic level. Both modern and more conventional measurement methods allow computation of these properties, which can provide information about the macrostructural effects of processing conditions in fresh and manufactured foods. Mathematical models have been fitted to data as a function of one or several experimental parameters, such as temperature, water content, porosity, or other food characteristics. Most engineering properties are significantly altered by the structural differences between foods. Several microscopy, scanning, and spectrometric technologies permit close visualisation of changes in structure at different levels without intrusion. Microstructure studies have increased understanding of several changes detected in foods resulting from treatment in emerging and conventional unit operations, by relating these changes to engineering property characterisation data and models. In the future, structure–property modelling could lead to the synthetic production of natural materials with improved characteristics, provided advances in genetic engineering and biotechnology are incorporated into the food engineering field.

The word engine, derived from the words engineer and engineering, comes from the Latin word for talent, ingenium. From the onset of the Industrial Revolution to the beginning of the twentieth century, the term was used almost exclusively to describe power machines. Those who designed, built, and operated these machines became known as engineers, and their profession, or expertise, as engineering. In today's technological world, the meaning of the term has expanded to include not only such disciplines or activities as chemical, medical, polymer, or food engineering, but also genetic engineering and social engineering. Although these disciplines have little to do with engines, they heavily rely on the ingenuity from which the term was originally conceived. It is difficult to define what exactly constitutes an engineering property of a certain food. In general, however, any attribute affecting the processing or handling of a food can be defined as an engineering property. Since many properties are related, there is usually an arbitrary element in their classification. Traditionally, they are divided into the following categories:

- Thermal properties such as specific heat, conductivity, diffusivity, and boiling point rise, freezing point depression.
- Optical properties, primarily colour, but also gloss and translucency.
- Electrical properties, primarily conductivity and permittivity.
- Structural and geometrical properties such as density, particle size, shape, porosity, surface roughness, and cellularity.
- Mechanical properties such as textural (including strength, compressibility, and deformability) and rheological properties (such as viscosity).
- Others, including mass transfer related properties (diffusivity, permeability), surface tension, cloud stability, gelling ability, and radiation absorbance.

Nearly all of the above properties are manifestations of a food's chemical composition and structural organisation over several orders of length scales—from the molecular to the macroscopic. A change in either composition or structure usually results in a simultaneous change in several properties. Hence it is difficult, if not impossible, to control a single property in isolation. Moreover, properties can be intrinsic, and primarily controlled by the material itself (for example, structural properties like density) and response properties, varying according to the external conditions to which the food is exposed (including colourimetric properties like hue).

Food materials or biological materials in general can display large compositional variations, inhomogeneities, and anisotropic structures. Composition can change due to seasonal variations and/or environmental conditions, or in the case of processed foods, properties can be affected by process conditions and material history. For example, North Atlantic fish show dramatic compositional changes in their protein and moisture contents throughout the seasons. Cereals that are puffed up under different moisture and temperature conditions can vary widely in density and cell-size distribution, and exposure of such products to moist atmospheres, sometimes for short periods only, can have dramatic effects on their crispness. Therefore, in many cases the data found in published lists for engineering properties of foods can only be considered as approximate values. Nevertheless, these tabular values are still very useful since a safety factor is added to almost all calculations or designs of food processes and/or operations. An understanding of what affects the engineering properties of foods is essential for their proper interpretation and successful utilisation. Therefore, one should always pay attention to the conditions under which the reported properties were determined, especially when response properties are involved.

Early physical property analyses of food products required constant uniform values and were often oversimplified and inaccurate. Now-a-days, computational engineering techniques, such as the finite element method, are much more sophisticated and can be used to evaluate non-uniform properties (for example, thermal properties) that change with time, temperature, and location in food products that are heated or cooled. Improvements measuring the compositions of foods are now allowing predictions of engineering properties that are more accurate than previously, since they can be predicted from existing numerical and empirical models of the food's composition, temperature, and porosity. There has always been a tendency to make general correlations in predicting properties of food materials for use in process design equations. A myriad of mathematical functions have already been fitted to experimental data, and models are bringing order to experience with the goal of clarifying which components or interactions are important in a food system. The engineering properties of foods topic covers different sets of engineering properties that are described in greater detail in specific articles, each with wide applications to food engineering and useful for product characterisation and equipment design in food manufacture. Basic definitions, common methods, parameter dependence, modelling, and food engineering applications will dictate the basic pattern followed within most sections. The final section will define how engineering properties and microstructure are related, because foods are complex in both structure and composition, this being the main reason for variability during property determination.

THERMAL PROPERTIES

Most processed and fresh foods receive some type of heating or cooling during handling or manufacturing. Design and operation of processes that involve heat transfer require special attention due to the heat-sensitivity of foods. Thermal properties of foods are related to heat transfer control in specified foods and can be classified as thermodynamic properties (enthalpy and entropy) and heat transport properties (thermal conductivity and thermal diffusivity).

Thermophysical properties not only include thermodynamic and heat transport properties, but also other physical properties involved in the transfer of heat, such as freeze and boiling point, mass, density, porosity, and viscosity. These properties play an important role in the design and prediction of heat transfer operations during the handling, processing, canning, storing, and distribution of foods.

Heat can be transferred in three different ways: by radiation, conduction, or convection.

- Radiation is the transfer of heat by electromagnetic waves (as in a microwave oven).
- Conduction is the transfer of thermal energy due to molecular oscillations (for example, heating of food by direct fire through metal containers).
- Convection is the transfer of heat by bulk movement of molecules in heated fluids such as liquids or gases (for example, air in heated oven or in tank during juice evaporation).

Although all three types of heat transfer can take place simultaneously, generally only one is predominant, depending on the state of the food and the heating system. In many heat transfer processes associated with storage and processing, heat is conducted through the product, heat is transferred by forced convection between the product and a moving fluid (for example, hot air during tray drying), which surrounds or comes in contact with the product.

Basic definitions of thermal properties of foods related to conduction within the product, with reference to properties associated with forced convection through the surface (such as surface heat transfer coefficient), will be mentioned in this section. Measuring techniques will be briefly described, as well as parameters involved during processing applications.

In liquid foods, boiling refers to water evaporation, in which water changes from the liquid phase to steam or vapour phase, and water vapour pressure equals the external pressure. Liquid foods contain high molecular weight solids that cause the boiling point to be elevated above that of pure water. The boiling point rise, ΔTr, is known as the increase in boiling point over that of water in a given liquid food. As the vapour pressure of most aqueous solutions is lower than that of water at the same temperature, the boiling temperature (boiling point) of the solution is higher than that of pure water.

During freezing, water in the food changes to ice while heat is removed by a refrigeration system. During heat removal, the unfrozen water will still contain dissolved food solids. The presence of dissolved solids will depress the initial freezing point a certain amount ΔT_f below the expected solidification temperature for pure water. Freezing point depression is defined as the temperature reduction ΔT_f. Both the boiling point rise and the freezing point depression of a food are related to its solutes concentration.

Thermal Variations in Properties and Methods of Determination

Precision and accuracy of measurement are important factors in determining thermal properties variations. In commercial heating or cooling applications, computer techniques now-a-days provide accuracies of 2–5 per cent for most heat-transfer calculations, which provide much lower relative errors than practical boundary condition determinations (for example, air temperature and velocities).

Several methods are known for measuring specific heat and C_p and thermal conductivity κ experimentally. C_p measurement of foods can be determined by methods of mixtures and differential scanning calorimetry (DSC). For methods of mixtures, a calorimeter of known specific heat is used and C_p is determined from a heat exchange balance. In the DSC method, the sample is put in a special cell where the temperature is increased at a constant heating rate. The specific heat of the food is obtained from a single heat thermogram, which relates heat flow as a function of time or temperature. Two experimental methods to determine κ are the Fitch method and the line source method. In the Fitch method, a solid slab of a certain food receives heat from one layer and conducts it to a copper plug. Conductivity κ is obtained from the food's temperature as a function of heat conduction time. The line source method is based on the use of a thermal conductivity probe to measure a temperature–time relation on a thin cylindrical food piece to which constant heat is applied.

Thermal diffusivity α is usually either determined by direct experimental methods or estimated. Several direct methods for α determination can be based on a one-dimensional heat conduction equation where geometrical boundary conditions are defined. For instance, an apparatus can be used where the sample is located in a special cylinder and immersed in a water bath at constant temperature. Thermocouples located at the center of the sample (axis) and surface of cylinder measure temperature at different heating times. Transient temperature variations are used for the analytical solution. Indirect methods, although they might yield more accurate diffusivity values, require more time and instrumentation for the three-parameter determination (ρ, κ, and C_p).

Boiling point elevation ΔT_r at a certain external pressure can be determined from a thermodynamic equation using the latent heat of vaporisation and molar fraction of the food. However, the use of these equations requires knowledge of the proportions of specific components of the foods that cause changes in the boiling points. In many cases, estimates for specific components present in higher concentrations can be used. Sometimes reference liquids under the same vapour pressure conditions can be compared with the food, and charts can be used to determining boiling points at different saturation concentrations. On the other hand, freezing points T_f in foods can be directly determined from the freezing curve (or cryoscope) method without using component concentrations. ΔT_f value can be derived from the temperature plateau after initial temperature depression (or supercooling) on a time-temperature plot. Furthermore, DSC can also be used to determine the onset, peak, and end of freezing.

Foods show extended variability in composition (mainly water, proteins, carbohydrates, fat, ash, and fibre) and structure, and can be turned into even more complex composite materials when heated together, as in the case of many canned and packed foods, pastry, confectionery, and a wide variety of prepared foods. Thermophysical properties depend on the chemical composition of the structure, determined by the physical arrangement and phase distribution of a system. Thus, heat transfer by conduction may take place in several forms depending on the tortuosity of the material, which may vary at different locations. As porous materials contain a gaseous phase, the value of the thermal conductivity, specific heat C_p, and thermal diffusivity α will depend on the internal and external pore space represented by its porosity. Thermophysical properties are significantly influenced by changes in water content and temperature. During drying, the transfer of heat into food products is accompanied by simultaneous diffusion of water through the product to the surrounding air, provoking differences in thermophysical properties at different regions of the food. Pore size and distribution not only affect heat transfer because of air retention, but also because of the affinity pores have to retain water. The smaller the pore diameter, the greater the surface tension forces, and the more affinity it has for water. Specific heat C_p of foods is drastically influenced by water content. For example, specific heat has been found to vary exponentially with water content in fruit pulps at above ambient temperatures. Furthermore, nonaqueous components show lower C_p. The specific heats of oils and fats are usually about one-half the specific heat of water, while the specific heat of dry materials in grains and powders is approximately one-third to one-fourth that of water. As a result of solute water interactions, the C_p of each individual component in a food differs from the C_p of a pure component, and usually changes with the concentration of soluble solids. The same occurs with thermal conductivity κ, where water shows greater relative magnitudes in comparison to other food constituents. Thus, both κ and C_p increase with increased moisture content. It is common to find a linear relation between thermal conductivity and moisture content at ambient conditions.

The effect of temperature on thermophysical properties is not easy to establish because solids (or semisolids), liquid foods, and food emulsions undergo structural changes. Thermophysical properties of foods change dramatically during the freezing process. Specific heat changes are difficult to predict when free water becomes solid. Bound water or unfrozen water has a different C_p than bulk-frozen water, and ice has a C_p of about one-half that of liquid water. Thus, C_p below freezing is approximately half that of C_p above freezing. Continuous changes in the fraction of frozen water as temperature varies below the freezing point explain this similarity. In fact, specific heat can be utilised to predict the state of water in frozen foods. Thermal conductivity, however, has been found to be high when temperatures allow water to be in liquid or solid state at very low or high temperatures. Yet when temperatures are within the range of –10 to 0°C, shows its lowest values. Freezing point depression has been modelled with the initial freezing point as a function of water content using linear and quadratic equations.

Some thermophysical property models for food systems have been developed as a function of water content or temperature. Additionally, as composition greatly differs between one food and another, other models are linear combinations of water, fat, protein, carbohydrate and/or ash content, and temperature. C_p has been measured at different temperatures in fresh and dried fruits, meats, cereal grains and cereal products, oils and fats, powders, and other dry foods. Although linear correlations of C_p with concentration are known in liquid foods, variations are often neglected for engineering calculations at near room temperature.

General correlations also predict thermal conductivity κ, of food materials for use in process design equations. Linear, quadratic, and multiple correlations of moisture, temperature, and composition can be found for κ in food materials. Some models consider that different components of foods (for example, fibres) are arranged in layers either parallel or perpendicular to the heat flow. In products such as meats, heat is usually transferred parallel to fibres and κ is dependent on the direction of the heat flow. More general in nature are the randomly distributed models, which consider that the food is composed of a continuous phase with a discontinuous phase dispersed within (solid particles being in either regular or irregular array). In porous materials, porosity must be included in the model because air has a κ much lower than that of other food components. Models including density or porosity, and pressure, have been developed in fruits and vegetables, meat and meat products, dairy products, cereals, and starch.

Several models for predicting α in foods have also appeared in literature, however, most are product specific and a function of water content or temperature. Although the influence of carbohydrates, proteins, fat, and ash on thermal diffusivity has been also investigated, it was found that temperature and water content are the major factors affecting α. Above freezing temperatures, diffusivity varies linearly with temperature or water composition in some foods, while this is not valid at below-freezing temperatures.

Food Processing Applications

Food thermal properties play an important role in the quantitative analysis of food processing operations. Heat exchanged and resulting temperature–pressure relations must consider the minimisation of reactions such as browning, vitamin loss, and oxidation reduction in order to preserve the acceptability and nutritional value of the food. Thermal properties are useful when evaluating capacities of drying systems, or studying the effect of product shrinkage or internal cracking with the aid of mathematical and numerical drying models. Enthalpy and specific heat are required to calculate the heat load in food processing operations. Specific heat measurement allows evaluation of the structure of foods (for example, fat polymorphism in chocolate).

During processing involving heat, temperature within a food changes continuously, varying not only the food C_p but also the κ. When conduction of heat is involved, thermal conductivity is important to predict or control the heat flux and processing times. In a processing system, it is necessary to predict the time end-point of processing to ensure the efficiency of the equipment. It is also desirable to heat and cool foods as rapidly as possible to improve the economics of the process by increasing the capacity and delivering a better quality product. All processing-time prediction models need the thermal conductivity data of food where energy transfer is involved. The speed of heat propagation or diffusion through the material is also related to processing times. Therefore, thermal diffusivity can also participate in processing-time estimation of processes like canning, cooling, freezing, and frying.

The equilibrium freezing point can be used for the prediction of thermophysical properties because of the discontinuity exhibited at that point. Accurate freezing point data can also be used to calculate other colligative properties such as effective molecular weight, water activity, bound, free, and frozen water, and enthalpy below freezing point. Knowledge of freezing point is important for analysing freezing and thawing times of frozen foods. Freezing point data can be used to ascertain chemical purity with regard to whether a sample differs from a natural or desired condition. The increase in boiling point or boiling point rise (ΔT_r) of liquid foods is a property of interest in evaporators or other types of heat exchanger equipment design and operation.

It is worth mentioning the role of the surface heat transfer coefficient, as it is one of the important parameters necessary to design and control food processing equipment where fluids (air, nitrogen, steam, water, or oil) participate. Although it is not a property of a food, it is used to quantify the transfer rate of heat by convection from a liquid or a gas (especially boiling liquids and condensing vapours) to the surface of the foods. It plays an important role when evaluating the effectiveness of heat transfer in processes where hot water or steam is applied through the evaluation of the overall resistances during heat transfer.

OPTICAL PROPERTIES

Optical properties are those material properties resulting from physical phenomena occurring when any form of light interacts with the material under consideration. In the case of foods, the main optical property considered by consumers in evaluating quality is colour, followed by gloss and translucency or turbidity among other properties. 'Colour' is the general name applied to all sensations arising from the activity of the retina, and is related to visual appearance of food (shape, size, surface and flesh structure, and defects).

Optical properties are related to consumer judgment on food appearance and produce some kind of visual effect. Among these, colour, gloss and translucency can be defined as follows.

- Gloss is the name given to light specularly reflected from a plain smooth surface. It can be defined by a goniophotometric curve, which represents the intensity of light reflected at the surface at different angles of incidence and viewing.
- Colour is essentially a beam of light composed of irregularly distributed energy emitted at different wavelengths. Depending on the type of illumination, the same material can show different light qualities and produce different sensations. Foods, along with other materials, have colour properties, which depend exclusively on their composition and structure.
- Translucency of foods is defined using an opaque-to-transparent scale. In liquid foods, light passing through changes its path randomly (in other words, is scattered) when interacting with suspended particles. Although light can be transmitted or reflected, the human eye only experiences translucency as a sensory attribute distinct from colour. Many food products (such as cloudy fruit and vegetable juices) are neither fully opaque nor fully transparent, but are translucent.

Methods and Applications

The colour perceived when the eye views a food is related to the following three factors: the spectral composition of the light source, the chemical and physical characteristics of the food, and the spectral sensitivity properties of the eye. To evaluate the colourimetric properties of a food, two of these factors must be standardised. Although the human eye can give fairly uniform results, it can be replaced by some instrumental sensor or photocell to provide even more consistent determinations. Visual colourimeters facilitate visual comparisons and eliminate differences in interpretation between operators.

In practice, visual measurement of colour entails comparing the colour problem with reference colours available in printed charts under well-defined and favourable conditions for good, reproducible comparisons. Light source, geometry of viewing, and colour of background are the most important factors to control. Description of colour for purchase specifications of food commodities or packaging materials involves colour tolerances, which are defined in one, two, or three dimensions in colour space to avoid variability of the human eye. Several systems of colour analysis have been created. The most used are the CIE, Munsell, Hunter, and Lovibond systems.

- In the CIE system, spectral curves indicate how the eyes of normal observers respond to various spectral light types in the visible portion of the spectrum. The system is based on the fact that any colour can be matched as a suitable mixture of red, green, and blue. These primary combinations are called *tristimulus* values of colour. A certain colour can be defined by chromacity coordinates x and y, and by the luminous transmittance or lightness. A chromacity diagram defines different colour points that define the standard colour of a food. The US Department of Agriculture uses chromacity coordinates to define specifications of colour standards for a variety of products.
- In the Munsell system, all colours are described by three attributes: hue (or type of colour), lightness (relative to the proportion of light emitted), and saturation or purity (associated with clear to dark perception). The hue scale is based on ten hues distributed on a circumference (scaled 1 to 10), the lightness ranges from black to white (0 to 10) and is distributed on a perpendicular line, the purity

is of irregular length beginning with 0 for the central gray to the limit of purity obtainable by available pigments in the Munsell book of colour. The Hunter system is also a three-dimensional system using parameters L^*, a^*, and b^* in each dimension: L^* is the lightness (nonlinear), a^* is redness or greenness, and b and b^* is yellowness or blueness. Combination of L^*, a^{**} can be converted to a single colour.

- The Lovibond system is a standard method generally used to determine the colour of vegetable oils. It involves visual comparisons of light transmitted through a glass couvette using colour filters. Vegetable oils are usually expressed in terms of red to yellow. The Lovibond index can also be used to measure colour in wines and juices. Computer software packages have been developed that easily convert light transition spectra into CIE, Munsell, Hunter, and Lovibond colour indices.

Colour can be measured instrumentally with colourimeters, which may be broadly classified as tristimulus colourimeters and spectrophotometers. The difference between spectrophotometers and colourimeters is that the former measures intensity of light through the completely visible spectrum, and colourimeters are designed to measure only some parameters related to sensory colours. Colourimeters are very useful in the quality control of foods, and give results normally correlated with visual measurements. A Munsell colourimeter consists of a circular rotating platform where several coloured disks are mixed in different proportions to provide a range of shades to match the colour of a certain food product. It is widely used in the food industry for quality control of a number of solid products like tomatoes, fruits, and peanut butter. Tristimulus colourimeters measure both related scales of Munster, Hunter, or CIE systems, which are numerically related. The quality of output for this type of instrument mainly depends on the correct combination of light source, filter, and photocell to obtain a good reproduction of visual response.

Glossmeters measure intensity of light reflected at three angles of incidence and reflection, and normally give results in the form of indices, obtained by comparing the sample reflectance to that of a highly reflective flat glass, used as a calibration standard. These indices are easy to interpret, in contrast to more difficult goniophotometric curves used in the past for classification. Translucency can be the measurement of the reflection of a thin sample against both a white and black background. From these measurements, the value of reflection from an opaque layer is calculated as a ratio between absorption and scattering to measure scattered light. Additional information on the visual appearance of turbid products such as orange juice can be obtained.

Processing can affect food product colour through changes in its physical state and/or pigment content. Colour measurement techniques can improve the understanding on processing changes and reaction kinetics in foods. Applications of colour measurement for food processing research are many and varied. For instance, colour measurement techniques are used for recording desirable colour changes in canning salmon with higher oil content, defining translucency of the tissues and green pigment degradation after blanching treatment of green peas, studying browning kinetics, or determining the influence of particle sizes in the final colour of powders. Characterisation of the colour of ingredients can also help to predict the colour of the final product—for example, control of raw strawberries for processing into jam. In red wine, the percentage of brown component and the relative loss of anthocyanin can be followed by reflectance measurement during storage.

Glossiness of a product is a property of the smoothness of its surface. When this characteristic is desired, manufacturers try to improve it, as in the case of fruits covered with wax to make them more visually appealing. Translucency is also worth consideration in some liquid foods, such as fruit juices. Its measurement can be determined by considering the contributions of both absorbed and scattered light when traversing these products. For a few clear liquid foods, such as oils and beverages, colour is mainly a matter of transmission of light. Other foods are opaque and derive their colour mostly from reflection. Optical properties can be used to perform quality control and continuous inspection during processing operations. Major requirements for a quality control system are ease of calibration and use, stability, precision, speed, cheapness, and industry-wide applicability. A complete colour description requires the use of three dimensions, and a control automatic system may be based on this complete specification. Specifications may be set to provide an idea of fruit ripeness, milk or cream discolouration during sterilisation, degree of roasting of coffee grains, or browning of apples slices during storage. Continuous colour measurements are used in tasks involving colour sorting (or electronic sorting) by using in-line systems.

Colour sorting is used for a very wide range of food materials in screening defects. Visible, infrared, and ultraviolet laser beams can provide continuous inspection through scanning of product size, symmetry, damage, irregular shape, fill level, and label placement by adding automatic software in connection with mechanical devices. For example, during conveying of pre-fried potato chips, optical devices detect any with defects (for example, black spots), and automatically deploy an air nozzle to deflect their path from the conveyor belt.

ELECTRICAL PROPERTIES

There are two main electrical properties in food engineering: electrical conductivity and electrical permittivity. Electrical properties are important when processing foods involving electric fields, electric current conduction, or heating through electromagnetic waves. These properties are also useful in the detection of processing conditions or the quality of foods.

Electrical Conductivity and Permittivity

Electrical conductivity is a measure of how well electric current flows through a food of unit cross-sectional area A, unit length L, and resistance R. It is the inverse value of electrical resistivity (measure of resistance to electric flow) and is expressed in SI units S/m in the following relation:

$$\sigma = L/(AR)$$

Electrical permittivity is a dielectric property used to explain interactions of foods with electric fields. It determines the interaction of electromagnetic waves with matter and defines the charge density under an electric field. In solids, liquid, and gases the permittivity depends on two values:

- The dielectric constant ε', related to the capacitance of a substance and its ability to store electrical energy.
- The dielectric loss factor ε'', related to energy losses when the food is subjected to an alternating electrical field (i.e. dielectric relaxation and ionic conduction).

The electrical conductivity of foods has been found to increase with temperature (linearly), and with water and ionic content. Mathematical relationships have been developed to predict the electrical conductivity of food materials: for example, for modelling heating rates through electrical conductivity measurements, or for probability distribution of conductivity through liquid-particle mixtures. Electrical conductivity shows different behaviours during ohmic and conventional heating. At freezing temperatures, electrical conductivity increases with temperature, as ice conducts less well than water. Starch transitions and cell structural changes affect electrical conductivity, and fat content decreases conductivity. As in thermal properties, the porosity of the food plays an important role in the conduction of electrons through the food.

In foods, permittivity can be related to chemical composition, physical structure, frequency, and temperature, with moisture content being the dominant factor. Dielectric properties (ε', ε'') are primarily determined by their chemical composition (presence of mobile ions and permanent dipole moments associated with water and other molecules) and, to a much lesser extent, by their physical structure. The influence of water and salt (or ash) content largely depends on the manner in which they are bound or restricted in movement by other food components. Free water and dissociated salts have a high dielectric activity, while bound water-associated salts and colloidal solids have low activity. Power dissipation is directly related to the dielectric loss factor ε'' and depends on the specific heat of the food, density of the material, and changes in moisture content (for example, because of vaporisation). Permittivity also depends on the frequency of the applied alternating electric field. Frequency contributes to the polarisation of molecules such as water. In general, dielectric constant increases with temperature, whereas loss factor may either increase or decrease depending on the operating frequency. Both the dielectric constant ε' and loss factor ε'' decrease significantly as more water freezes.

Reasonable comprehensive tabulations of electrical properties data are available for foods in electronic and printed form.

Methods and Applications

The conductivity of a material is generally measured by passing a known current at constant voltage through a known volume of the material and by determining resistance. The total conductivity is then calculated simply by taking the inverse of the total resistivity. Basic measurements involve bridge networks (such as the Wheatstone bridge circuit) or a galvanometer. There are other devices that measure electrical conductivity of foods under ohmic or conventional heating conditions, using thermocouples and voltage and current transducers to measure voltage across and current through the samples.

Known methods for measuring dielectric properties are the cavity perturbation, open-ended coaxial probe, and transmission line methods. Since modern microwave network analysers have become available, the methods of obtaining dielectric properties over with frequency ranges have become more efficient. Computer control of impedance analysers and network analysers has facilitated the automatic measurement of dielectric properties over wide frequency ranges, and special calibration methods have also been developed to eliminate errors caused by unknown reflections in the coaxial-line systems. Distribution functions can be used in expressing the temperature dependence of dielectric properties.

Electrical properties are important in processing foods with pulsed electric fields, ohmic heating, induction heating, radio frequency, and microwave heating. Conductivity plays a fundamental role in ohmic heating, in which electricity is transformed to thermal energy when an alternating current (ac) flows through food. As it has potential use in fluid pasteurisation, it is important to know the effective conductivity or the overall resistance of liquid-particle mixtures. Furthermore, liquid-particle mixtures can be pasteurised using pulsed electric field technology, where products with low electrical conductivity are better and more energy-efficient to process. Electrical conductivity can be used for acidity studies, therefore, and for monitoring processes where acidity increases, as in fermentations. Crystallisation processes (for example, in sugar solutions) can also be monitored with conductivity measurements, as conductivity has been found inversely proportional to viscosity, which in turn follows supersaturation closely. Conductivity measurements have also been used to measure moisture contents in materials, particularly grain products.

The electrical field inside the food is determined by the dielectric properties and the geometry of the load, and by the oven configuration. These properties are also useful in detection processing conditions, or the quality of foods. The major uses for dielectric properties are measuring and heating applications. Permittivity and moisture are closely correlated when the water content is high. Properly designed electrical instruments can be used to determined moisture content or water activity. Knowledge of dielectric properties in partially frozen material is critical in determining the rates and uniformity of heating in microwave thawing. As the ice in the material melts, absorption of energy increases tremendously. Thus, the portions of material that thaw first absorb significantly more energy and heat at increasing rates, which can lead to localised boiling temperatures while other areas are still frozen. Salt affects the situation through freezing point depression, leaving more water unfrozen at a given temperature.

Dielectric properties are also important in the selection of proper packaging materials and cooking utensils, and in the design of microwave and radio frequency heating equipment, because they describe how the material interacts with electromagnetic radiation. Studies of heating uniformity and temperature elevation rate involve dielectric properties. Typical features of power density patterns of a load are large internal hot and cold areas, internal focusing effects, and the edge-heating phenomenon. For example, when a raw egg is heated it may explode because the power density near its center is much higher than in other parts, causing violent shattering as the interior becomes superheated. The dielectric properties of materials are very important in evaluating the penetration depth of energy (in other words, the distance at which the power drops 37 per cent of its value in the material) that can be achieved in a certain food.

MECHANICAL PROPERTIES

The mechanical properties mainly result from the structure, physical state, and rheology. They can be subdivided into two groups: structural and geometrical properties, and strength properties. Structural and geometrical properties include mass–volume–area-related properties (density, shrinkage, and porosity), and morphological properties (surface area, roundness, and sphericity). Strength properties are related to solid and semi-solid stress and deformation, and intervene in food texture and rheological characterisation. These properties are needed for process design, estimating other properties, characterising foods, and quality determination.

Structural and Geometrical Properties

Density

This is defined as mass per unit volume (the SI unit of density is kg/m^3). Indeed, there are different forms of density such as true, material, particle, apparent, and bulk that can be used, depending on its application in process calculations or product characterisation. The volume measurement method is what determines the difference between them. True and material densities are calculated by excluding volumes occupied by internal and external pores within the food, while particle, apparent, and bulk densities are determined from less accurate measurement methods that include pore volume. A material's volume can be measured by buoyant force, liquid, gas or solid displacement, or gas adsorption, or by estimating the material's geometric dimensions. The buoyant force method for apparent or particle volume determination utilises sample weight differences in air and water, while the liquid displacement method measures the increase in liquid volume when the material is immersed in a non-wetting fluid such as mercury or toluene. A gas pycnometer is a gas displacement device that uses high-pressure air differences in a sample cell connected to a manometer to determine material volume. Apparent or particle density can be determined by coating particles in order to include internal pores in the volume measured. For solid displacement, sand or glass beads can be used instead.

In most engineering designs, solids and liquids are assumed to be incompressible—in other words, density changes moderately with changes in temperature and pressure. In food engineering, the density of solid and liquid foods changes with temperature and pressure and is dependent on temperature and composition. In the case of liquid foods, no generic equations exist to predict the density. In the literature most of the density data is correlated empirically as a function of temperature, water, solids, and fat content. Different types of nonlinear correlation, such as exponential, quadratic, and cubic, are used to relate density and moisture content.

Porosity

Porosity indicates the volume fraction of void space or air space inside a material. Volume determination is relative to the amount of internal (or closed) or external (or open) pores present in the food structure. Therefore, like density, different forms of porosity are also used in food processing studies, namely open pore, closed pore, apparent, bulk, and total porosities. Porosity can be measured by direct and microscopic methods, or can be estimated from density data. Porosity in foods is mainly predicted from empirical correlations, which are valid for individual foods under given processing conditions. Fundamental models exist that are based on the conservation of mass and volume, as well as a number of terms that account for interaction of components and formation or collapse of air or void phase during processing.

Shrinkage

This is the reduction in volume or geometric dimensions during processing. When post-processing volume is larger than initial volume, it is termed as expansion. Two types of shrinkage isotropic and anisotropic are usually observed in the case of food materials. Isotropic shrinkage is described as the uniform shrinkage of the materials under all geometric dimensions, whereas anisotropic (or non-uniform) shrinkage develops in different geometric dimensions. The former is common in fruits and vegetables while the latter is known in animal tissue, such as in fish. Shrinkage occurs as a result of moisture loss (during drying), ice formation (during freezing), and formation of pores (by drying, puffing, extrusion, and frying). The glass transition theory is one of the concepts proposed to explain the process of shrinkage, collapse, fissuring, and cracking during drying. The methods of freeze-drying and hot-air drying can be compared on the basis of this theory.

Pore disruption and structure hardening, as well as moisture transport mechanisms, counterbalancing internal forces, and environmental pressure, are some of the causes for reduction or collapse in a food structure. Expansion can be caused by gas generation, which is mainly a result of water evaporation and subsequent pore formation within the food structure. More work is needed to develop a fundamental understanding of how pores are formed, or of the collapse mechanism during processing, and their impact on product characterisation. Most of the density, shrinkage, and porosity prediction models for liquid and solid foods are empirical in nature. Recent models have been developed to predict porosity during air-drying based on drying temperature, moisture content, initial porosity, and product type.

Two types of surface areas are used in process calculations and product characterisation—the outer or boundary surface of a particle or object, and the total surface area of a porous object, or the pore surface area. It is very common to estimate the surface area from its geometric dimensions in the case of a Euclidian geometric object. A Euclidian geometry always has characteristic dimensions and assumes surfaces to be smooth (in other words, with no external pores), such as in spheric, cubic, and ellipsoidal geometries. Many natural patterns are either irregular or fragmented, to such an extreme degree that Euclidian or classical geometry is no help in describing their form. Fractal analysis is used instead to characterise and estimate the surface areas of these shapes. Native and physically or chemically transformed food particles can be characterised by fractals to predict the efficiency of the transformation process and food particle properties, such as adsorption capacity, solubility, puffing ability, chemical reactivity, and emulsifying ability to optimise food ingredient selection for product development and process design. Like fractal analysis, neural networks or artificial intelligence may have potential in modelling surface, shape, and other mechanical properties of foods. Morphological properties such as roundness and sphericity are also used to characterise a food's shape. Roundness is a measure of the sharpness of the corners of a solid. Sphericity indicates how the shape of an object deviates from a sphere. Sphericity is defined from the volume, surface area, or geometric dimensions of an object. Sphericity and shape factors are also needed in heat and mass transfer calculations.

Size, shape, sphericity, volume, surface area, density, and porosity are important physical characteristics of many food materials in handling and processing operations. Fruits and vegetables are usually graded according to size, shape, and density. Impurities in food materials can be separated by density differences between impurities and foods. Values for surface areas of fruits and vegetables are needed in investigations related to respiration rate in heat transfer calculations for heating or cooling. Density and the shape factor of food materials are also necessary for predicting the freezing and thawing rate. Volume change and porosity are important parameters in estimating diffusion coefficients for shrinking systems. Porosity and tortuousity are used to calculate effective diffusivity during the mass transfer process.

Rheology and Texture

Mechanical properties are intertwined with rheology when including strength properties. Mohsenin defines mechanical properties as 'those having to do with the behaviour of the material under applied forces.' Rheology has been defined as 'a science devoted to the study of deformation and flow,' or as 'the study of those materials that govern the relationship between stress and strain.' 'Stress' is defined as force components acting on a body per unit cross-sectional area or area of the deformed specimen (SI units in Pa). 'Strain' is the change in size or shape (SI units in mm or percentage) of a body in response to the applied force (at a certain time or during continuous change as stress is applied). Rheologically, the behaviour of a material is expressed in terms of stress, strain, and time effects. Therefore, properties that deal with the motion of the material as a result of an applied force can be included as mechanical forces.

Rheological tests express stress–strain relationships and study strain rate dependency. Ideal solids deform in an elastic Hookean manner, while ideal liquids flow in a viscous Newtonian manner, in each case the behaviour is independent of the strain rate. Nonetheless, foods are strain-rate dependent. They usually contain some solid and liquid attributes and, rheologically, are termed viscoelastic bodies. In addition, many possess structural elements that 'yield' or rupture when forces are applied, thus changing the stress–strain behaviour not only with the applied rate of strain, but also with the applied amount of strain. Foods are anisotropic in nature and their mechanical properties may vary in the direction of the stress application. There are three stresses that are commonly applied to characterise foods mechanically: compressive (directed toward the material), tensile (directed away from the material), and shearing (directed tangentially to the material). Shear stress is the most prevalent with fluids or viscous materials. Since strain is the response of the material to stress, compressive shear and tensile strains can be found. When small deformations are exerted under compression, foods can show a straight line in the stress strain plot, and its slope is called the 'Young modulus of elasticity.' Rheologically, a material can deform in three ways: elastic, plastic, or viscous, it can be denoted by a spring friction element and a dashpot arranged in series or parallel, respectively, in rheological models.

Different mechanical situations define how stress can act on a food: static (constant stress or strain), dynamic (varying stress or strain), or impact (stress exerted and removed after a very short period of time). Impact during mechanical handling is the most common cause of mechanical damage to foods. Behaviour under static or dynamic stresses governs the extent of potential mechanical injury (for example, during hopper storage or discharge) and can provide valuable information on the design of handling machinery. In cases like these, definitions of creep (when constant stress is applied to a body increasing in strain as a function of time) or stress relaxation (when constant strain is applied to a body) play a role. Solid foods are mechanically characterised by compression tests or impact tests. Universal testing machines give curves of normal force versus deformation, shear forces, creep, and stress relaxation measurements.

The most important mechanical-rheological behaviour of fluid or viscous foods is the flow behaviour, which can be basically defined as Newtonian, pseudoplastic, and Bingham, indicating viscosity of the material and its dependence on shear rate. In processing, flow properties can influence pumping requirements, flow of fluid through pipes, or even extrusion properties. Flow properties can be determined using any variety of available rheometers or viscometers.

The mechanical properties of foods intersect not only with rheological behaviour but also with the texture of foods. In fact, mechanical properties form the basis for food's sensory properties related to texture (in other words, properties involved with material resistance to mastication). Furthermore, sensory terms that characterise texture of a food can include the rheological principles of stress, strain, and time effects. Both the mechanical properties and texture of food relate to the mechanical work that occurs in food processing operations, as they do when they later interact in the consumers mouth. For instance, during both mastication and industrial size-reduction processes (for example, slicing, grinding, mashing, pressing), it is desirable to weaken the structure so that it will properly disintegrate when forces are applied.

In this way, texture can be defined as those physical characteristics arising from the structural elements of the food that are sensed primarily by the feeling of touch, related to deformation, disintegration, and flow of the food under a force, and measured objectively by functions of mass, time, and length. This indicates that texture studies include structure (molecular, microscopic, and macroscopic) and the manner in which structure reacts to applied forces. It also emphasises that texture is a multidimensional property comprising a number of sensory characteristics.

For instance, the Texture Profile Analysis widely used in industry defines mechanical parameters such as hardness, fracturability, cohesiveness, springiness, chewiness, gumminess, and resilience. Compression tests evaluate texture by compressing the food in one direction and unrestraining it in the other two dimensions to evaluate hardness or strength in solid foods. The puncture test is the oldest one used for food texture determination, and involves the measurement of force necessary to penetrate the test material with a punch. Sometimes puncture tests imitate the failure involved in mastication and can measure the firmness of a fresh fruit. The introduction of computer readout and analysis of force-time plots obtained with Universal Testing Machines allow reading of the maximum forces from the force–time graphs, measuring of slopes, and calculation of areas under the curve, among other features. Highly complex analyses of force–time plots have now become routine.

Structure may refer to the often-complex organisation and interactions of food components under the influence of external and internal physical forces. Structure also refers to the size and shape of the components of the food, as well as how they interact to form an organisation. Thus, texture properties can predict deformation mechanisms after stress application, effects of heating in baked products, thawing or freezing mechanisms in meats, or changes in the hardness of fleshy fruit tissues during ripening, through structural microscopy studies. Surface structure microscopy can complement the characterisation of the strength properties through traditional qualitative methods such as scanning electron microscopy or confocal laser scanning, among other microstructural methods.

PROPERTIES OF FOOD POWDERS

Food powders are particle systems that can be used as food products or ingredients. Particle characterisation—description of primary properties of food powders in a particulate system—underlies all work in particle technology. Primary particle properties such as particle shape, particle density, porosity, and particle size, control secondary or bulk properties such as mechanical compressibility, cohesion, angle of repose, flowability, segregation, and attrition, among others. Various methods assess both primary and bulk properties of food powders for quality control or process characterisation. Powder properties contribute to the understanding of operations like grinding, filtration, sedimentation, centrifugation, spray or freeze-drying, conveying, dosing, hopper storage, mixing, and many others where particles are present as an initial or final product.

Primary Properties

Several single particle characteristics influence a powder's mechanical properties. These include particle size, particle shape, surface roughness, density, hardness, and adsorption properties. Of these features, particle size is the most important. The 'size' of a powder or particulate material is relative. For a particulate material to be considered powder, its approximate median size (50 percent of the material is smaller than the median size and 50 per cent is larger) should be less than 1 mm. It is also common practice to talk about 'fine' and 'coarse' powders, several attempts have been made to standardise particle nomenclature. SI units for particle size are micrometers (or microns) or millimeters depending on the size range. The selection of a relevant characteristic particle size measurement depends on particle shape, which is rarely spherical. Among varied shapes, particles may be compact, plate-like, or needle-like. The term 'diameter' refers to the characteristic linear dimension. Particulate food materials are mostly organic in origin and possess diverse individual structures, ranging from extreme degrees of irregularity (ground materials like spices) to an approximate sphericity (starch) or well-defined crystalline shapes (granulated salt). Many definitions have been established to define individual particle diameter.

More important than individual size is the size distribution among the particles. Particle size distribution is directly related to material behaviour and/or physical properties of products. Bulk density, compressibility, and flowability of a food powder are highly dependent on particle size and its distribution. In quality control or system property description, measurement of the particle size distribution in food powders becomes paramount. Different types of methods such as sieving, microscope counting techniques, sedimentation, and stream scanning are available for measuring particle size distribution. Particle density and porosity have been discussed previously, and all of the above-mentioned classifications apply to particulate systems as well. Other definitions to take into account are the 'loose bulk density' measured after a powder is freely poured into a container, or 'compact density' after it is allowed to compress by mechanical pressure, vibration, and impact.

In particle technology, density measurement is important in separation processes (in other words, sedimentation and centrifugation) and in pneumatic and hydraulic transport of powders and particulates, or for processing condition definitions. In particular, dehydration or agglomeration processes can significantly affect the extent and nature of pore formation, and hence the true particle density of the material. During mixing, transportation, storing, and packaging particulate material, it is also important to know the primary properties of bulk material.

Secondary Properties

Bulk density control is a major objective of many food processes, especially when spray drying and grinding. Under low compressive loads (for example, during powder storage on hoppers), bulk density can be related to normal stress. Bulk density and normal stress have been associated in empirical logarithmic or semi-logarithmic relationships, from which a constant slope value is defined as mechanical compressibility. A simultaneous decrease in a powder's loose bulk density and increase in compressibility indicate greater attractive and cohesive interactions among powders. Mechanical compressibility can also be determined from stress–strain data using Universal Testing Machines or compaction tests, which put the bulk sample in a vertically vibrating system. Compaction tests simulate density changes during handling and transportation.

Binding and frictional interactions among particles when forming a static heap can give an idea of flowability among particles when variations in composition or moisture content occur. The angle that a powder heap forms with the horizontal is denominated angle of repose. More cohesive powders form higher angles while lower angles represent greater flowability to some degree. If determined under pertinent conditions, this magnitude can provide useful information in the design of conveyors or bin discharge. It is also widely used in the food ingredient industry for bulk quality control.

Flow properties determine how a powder will behave in bins, hoppers, feeders, and other handling equipment. They deal with difficulties associated with withdrawing material from storage hoppers without interruption and at the required rate. Flowability is the ease at which a powder flows through a chute or hopper. Flow of powders is approached differently from known rheological evaluations of flow in fluids. In powders, interactions are studied from the shear stresses needed to make the powder flow under specified normal stress conditions. Shear cells are used according to standard procedures such as Jenike's method. Some powders may not flow because of particle interlocking or friction among particles, which contributes to stabilising structures in hoppers during storage. Others possess additional inter-particle forces such as electrostatic, van der Waals, or solid-liquid bridging, providing increased compact strength and cohesion among particles and decreasing flowability even more.

Mechanical and chemical interactions among powders depend on the powder's composition, moisture content, surface mechanical characteristics, particle history (for example, from production to storage), particle shape and size, and the manner in which the particles interact geometrically. Food powder particles can also stick together and form stable structures or cakes that can prevent flow due to mechanical forces resulting from variations in temperature and composition (especially moisture and fat content). Caking is the unwanted, spontaneous agglomeration process that produces mechanically stable lumps in powders, where both size distribution and strength of the agglomerates can vary dramatically.

This phenomenon is commonly found in foods with low molecular weight compounds and increased moisture such as fruit powders, sugars, or coffee, and it may occur in different drying processes during powder production.

Many food powders (for example, instant beverages or dry soup mixes) are mixtures of two or more particles of different composition. During conveying, mixing, discharging, charging, bulk storage, and packaging of powders, another undesirable phenomena termed *segregation* might occur. This is the unwanted separation of fine particles from coarse particles induced by motion during different handling and storage activities, and occurs almost exclusively in free-flowing mixtures. Different indices can give an idea of the level of segregation in a mixture. Another phenomenon that is more product-related is powder *attrition*, involving the breakdown of particles. In food powders, it is more frequent in agglomerates, mainly because of their multi-particulate structure. Food agglomerates possess brittle characteristics that make the product susceptible to vibration, compressive, shear, or even convective forces applied to the particles during processing. During impact, breakage of brittle particles can occur, as in instant coffee or milk agglomerates. In such cases, density changes can be attributed, at least partly, to progressive changes in particle size distribution and not only to their spatial rearrangement. Indices that characterise attrition effect on agglomerates and brittle powders have also been developed.

ROLE OF FOOD MICROSTRUCTURE IN ENGINEERING PROPERTIES

Most engineering properties of foods, including the above-described thermal, optical, electrical, and mechanical properties, are significantly altered by structural differences between foods and within them. By researching a food's structure, behaviour of properties under different processing conditions can be explained, and different structure–property relationships determined. Food microstructure studies help to explain the external manifestation of the arrangement of structural elements beyond the resolution of the naked eye. The food engineer's task in structural characterisation is to find the scaling laws that translate microstructural data into macrostructural behaviour in relation to engineering properties.

Food processing may be viewed as a controlled effort to preserve, transform, destroy, or create structure. Microscopy and related techniques make it possible to visualise and identify food components or changes in structure closely without interfering in the food sample's structural arrangements. Formation, rearrangement, or stabilisation of new food structures achieved through processing can be better understood from a qualitative microscopic perspective. However, quantitative characterisation of interacting forces or energies involved in the whole structure formation and stabilisation through microstructural analysis is still far from being attained.

Structural Characterisation of Foods

Food processing can be defined as the controlled incorporation of materials and energy into a food. From a structural point of view, it combines different restructuring operations mixing molecules and assemblies until a product is created. Changes in engineering properties of foods can be better explained by following changes in structure. Moreover, visual perception of microstructural phenomena can verge upon the understanding of mechanical, electrical, optical, or thermal changes induced by processing of food.

Structure is the spatial arrangement of structural elements (water and oil droplets, gas cells, fat crystals, strands, granules, micelles, and interface) and assemblies (fibres, proteins, cell walls, cells, and tissue), and their interaction governs values for porosity and density. The scale of observation is important in setting up the engineering problem or in finding a solution, since food elements are viewed differently at different scales. Relationships between engineering properties and structure reflect the interactions occurring at the molecular, ultrastructural, microstructrural, and macrostructural level during food processing. Structure–property relationships describe the way in which physico-chemical, functional, technological, and even some nutritional properties of foods are related to their structure. In engineering, microstructure can integrate structural information and data generated by other physico-chemical methods to derive structure–property relationships in foods. Within this framework some general uses can be mentioned:

- To obtain physical and morphological information on the system under study at a relevant scale.
- To understand how natural food materials are assembled at different size scales and organisation levels, and identify alternatives for disassembling them.
- To determine the type of breakdown occurring in a food and define compression mechanisms of different types of foods.

- To monitor the controlled destruction of structure during food processing (for example, release of valuable components, development of new structural compounds).

The molecular and supramolecular architecture constituting food structure is continually and increasingly being unravelled by combining powerful analytical techniques such as microscopy, thermal and mechanical analysis, and advanced spectroscopy. A significant number of analytical and microscopy techniques have become available for explaining microstructural phenomena in medicine, biology, and materials science. Technologies already applied include direct light, confocal laser scanning, fluorescence, transmission and scanning electron, scanning probe, and atomic force microscopy as well as microspectrophotometry, immunolabelling, and X-ray analysis.

Direct microscopic observation of controlled experiments on a stage mounted under the microscope can provide structural information at a resolution about 10^3 times smaller than the human eye can perceive. Advanced computer imaging technologies, fluorescent probe developments, and computer designed optics have all been integrally linked with improved analytical light confocal laser scanning microscopes for high-resolution volumetric imaging, used for optically sectioning a sample without intrusion. Fluorescence microscopy is useful in food science since it can detect substances in low concentrations, and thus allows the visualisation of materials not possible by other light microscopy methods.

The prevailing need for food scientists to view a wide spectrum of structural organisation resulted in the scanning electron microscope (SEM) method, which combines the best features of the light and transmission electron microscope with a magnification of 500000 times. A wide range of similar microscopes can provide images of surface topography of a specimen at submicron levels, allowing the examination of surfaces of uncoated 'wet' specimens at ambient conditions.

Commercial equipment is now available that allows 'miniaturisation' heating and cooling (freezing) of thin samples or solutions at controlled rates and visualisation through charged-coupled device (CCD) cameras linked to a TV monitor and VCR. Scanning probe microscopy and related high-resolution techniques can scan specimen surfaces at the molecular level, by scanning with a sharp probe closely over the sample surface and measuring some function of distance between the material and probe. They can provide estimates of distance and determine spatial distribution of specific structures (for example, particular macromolecules or elements). Microspectrophotometry is applied to quantitative cytochemistry for determination of nucleic acids, proteins, enzymes, pigments, and hormones. Immunolabelling techniques, the use of probes (antibodies or lecithins) that bind to specific sites on individual molecules, is now a standard method in most histology laboratories. An X-ray microanalysis approach routinely provides results with a spatial resolution in cubic μm and complements information obtained from the above-mentioned techniques.

The development of food materials science requires understanding of the physical properties or function of biopolymeric microstructures. Several techniques used in mechanical and polymer science may be coupled with microscopy simultaneously to observe a structure and measure rheological behaviour, thermal transitions, and mechanical properties. Micromanipulation techniques borrowed from biology may well be adapted to assess the engineering properties of cells of tissues. Computer-mediated image analysis can help quantify many of the features revealed by microscopic examination of foods: sizes and shapes of cellular components, thickness of cell walls or particle networks in gels, pore size, and size distributions in gels, relative proportions of various phases, and other properties.

The food engineer views microstructure as an opportunity to return to the traditional engineering concept of assembling building blocks by combining heat, mass, and momentum transfer. Food engineers now have the tools to identify picogram quantities of almost any chemical species, to probe the motility of food molecules, and to look inside them with minimal intrusion and in real time for evaluation of almost any food property and the different structural levels present. In the future, structure–property relationships may, with the help of biotechnology and genetic engineering, contribute to synthesising natural materials with improved characteristics.

Practical Implications

Foods are dynamic systems where structures vary during storage, distribution, and preparation depending on factors such as composition, acidity, internal pressures, interacting phases, and environmental conditions such as relative humidity, external pressure, or temperature. Modelling and optimisation of engineering properties in current and future food processes will depend not only on better mathematical algorithms or faster and more powerful computers, but also on a clearer comprehension of the underlying phenomena at appropriate relevant scales. During processing, microstructural changes can occur without changing the main composition of a food, they may go unnoticed by the naked eye but be detected using engineering property techniques.

Food microstructure, phase transitions, density, and porosity strongly affect the thermal and transport properties of foods. In mass or heat transfer processes, where diffusion is the main mechanism, the architecture and properties of the intervening elements may explain the magnitude of effective diffusivity. However, other effects such as shrinkage may also contribute to a low instant diffusivity. The study of heat and transport phenomena of foods and biological materials can be advanced through structure visualisation in combination with physical measurements. Heat and mass transfer should be understood at the tissue, cellular, and subcellular levels, so that mechanisms prevailing during processing (such as dehydration and extraction) are clearly identified and modelled. For example, confocal laser scanning microscopy revealed, with minimal intrusion and three-dimensional resolution, that cells in the crust of a fried potato strip remain largely intact and oil free, while oil forms an egg-box arrangement surrounding these cells. Thus, the architecture of a processed solid food can be assisted by models that define diffusion coefficients and include individual properties of the phases. Furthermore, correlations can be made for specific heat and thermal conductivity. In fact, structural conductivity has been modelled in heterogeneous biphasic materials.

The microstructural arrangement of food chemical components affects heat conduction during drying operations. Microstructure can be utilised to develop moisture distribution profiles in drying studies. Furthermore, other common phenomena such as radial cracking and formation of channels during drying (for example, through spherical starch granules) can be characterised. Microstructural studies provide complementary information for the optimisation of freezing rates. Freezing involves simultaneous immobilisation of water as ice and temperature reduction. Along with ice crystallisation, extensive microstructural changes occur inside organised tissues. The rate of freezing will determine the sensory quality of foods, as small crystals can be formed at a faster rate. For example, small crystal formation has a tremendous impact on the sensory evaluation of ice cream. The density and shape factor of food materials are also necessary for predicting the freezing and thawing rates.

Porosity, pore distribution, and cellularity can also be assessed with microstructural information in mechanical, thermal, and electrical property studies. Quantifications of pore distributions can be accomplished by image processing/image analysis using either an image from a microscope, or in the case of macroporous foods, an image directly captured by a video camera and macrolense. Volume change and porosity are important parameters in estimating diffusion coefficients of shrinking systems. In cellular materials, compression functions depend on the type of cell wall collapse occurring, which can be brittle or plastic (as in gels). Techniques that quantify the ruggedness of products such as fractal analysis are used to estimate the surface areas of these shapes. Fractals, in combination with micro-structural studies, can predict the efficiency of the transformation process and food particle properties (such as solubility, puffing ability, emulsifying ability) used to optimise food ingredient selection for product development.

Mechanical properties in food microstructure are explained by understanding the main mechanisms leading to structure formation, which can be studied using the most appropriate microscopy techniques and supported by other experimental data. Surface structure microscopy can enhance the characterisation of the strength properties through traditional qualitative methods such as transmission light microscopy, scanning electron microscopy, and transmission electron microscopy. Furthermore, the kinetics of structural changes can be inferred from rheological or mechanical responses. Mathematical models should be derived based on available structural data and previous findings, which allow predictions of properties for any changes in structure (for example, that induced by change in formulation).

Through structural microscopy studies, texture properties can predict deformation mechanisms after stress application, effects of heating in baked products, thawing or freezing mechanisms in meats, or changes in the hardness of fleshy fruit tissues during ripening. Controlled destruction of biological materials, such as by pressing or reducing particle size, is needed to release valuable components, microstructural characteristics often dictate the type of breakdown of the material. During roller pressing or milling of fruit pulps or powder cakes, microstructural studies define the rotating directions or speeds of metal rollers in order to obtain the desired product in optimal conditions (for example, faster extraction rates from broken and damaged surface cells). Many foods like meats or vegetables have cellular or fibrous structures that determine mechanical properties. Biochemical microstructural changes in meats (for example, during rigor mortis and cooling) can be monitored by following the stress of a slightly stretched sample. Strain hardening of flesh can also be traced to combined microstructural and molecular changes.

During extrusion, macro- and microstructures are formed by diverse frictional and other mechanisms involving heat release or application. Microscopy, gel permeation, chromatography, and viscosity measurements have demonstrated fragmentation of the starch granule during extrusion as a result of shear at the subcellular level. Distinctive desirable textures controlled by die design and extruder operating conditions can be assured from studies that combine mechanical strength properties and microstructural characterisation. Understanding the nonlinear interactions between the levels becomes essential to controlling the texture of food.

In rheology, deviations from ideal Newtonian behaviour in complex fluids can be traced back by defining the role of macromolecules or particles and their interactions through structural modelling of flow conditions over time. Viscosity will depend on solid-like networks, shear-induced deformation, and transient superstructures at different shear rates. Microscopic image analysis tools can be adapted to represent different shear and normal stresses to express flow at different points of a fluid. Nondestructive methods such as dynamic oscillatory rheometry or mechanical spectroscopy are particularly suitable for this purpose.

Powder flowability is determined by particle deformability and surface roughness (or friction). Flow properties in powders can also be monitored with microstructural surface characterisation techniques. Surface topography is also important in determining friction in sliding conveyors and between particles, or attrition in the breakdown of powders. Attrition mechanisms of food powders have been assessed through the detection of crack propagation paths detected by scanning electron microscopy.

Electrical properties can also be used to evaluate desirable or undesirable characteristics of some foods. Some examples that can be correlated with microstructural modelling are measurement of heat damage to artificially dried shelled corn, testing the degree of injury and death suffered by plant tissues, detecting frost hardness in some food materials, or determining egg quality and freshness of fish. Optical properties are also related to microstructure due to the compositional chromatic elements of foods. Their distribution within a food can be monitored through hierarchical studies at different levels on the structure and location of these components.

Advances in genetic engineering and biotechnology will forge a new path where naturally synthetic components and raw food materials with modified properties will be fabricated at the molecular and microstructural level. The application of 'nanotechnology' will allow the manufacture and positioning of specific molecules or functional groups within food microstructures.

Chapter 3

Process and Instrumentation Control

INTRODUCTION

In the food industry, numerous approaches are involved in every step, from research to trade, where engineering techniques are mandatory. The objective is to help those practically involved with those engineering approaches to make food processing more scientific and engineered. In the broad perspective of food processing measurement and control, a food scientist is also an instrumentation engineer and *vice versa*.

This chapter discusses the basics of instrumentation concepts of measurement and control and food processes, respectively. This chapter will also present a short description of the various food processing. Industries and the process parameters, as well as their importance in quality control. The basic structures of process input-output variables and basic principles of feedback control systems are also presented. These basic concepts will be especially useful in understanding the various measurement and control techniques, etc.

Food processing is a vast sector of the industrial world. A major percentage of cereals, vegetables and fruits are processed for human consumption and preservation for future use.

The specifications of ingredient materials for best results are termed standards. The standards used by a manufacturer depend on the product in which the material is to be used and on the manufacturing process. There is no universally set standard for each material. Setting a standard for ingredient material requires vast experience in handling and the manufacturer might set its own specifications. Nevertheless, some broad outlines can be given for dictating the specifications in the following categories:

1. Identity: This is a precise definition of originality of the material. Only microscopic tests can determine these attributes.
2. Purity and composition: The aspects of this standard can have the following factors:
   (a) Chemical: This gives assay requirements such as percentage of moisture, fat, protein, antioxidants, additives and so on.
   (b) Physical: This specifies the requirements such as size, colour, weight, viscosity, density and so on.

3. Microbiological: This refers to microbiological organisms responsible for health, safety significance and sanitary conditions. Tests conducted to measure sanitary conditions are called filth tests.
4. Packaging: This refers to the net weight and quantity of the packaging material.
5. Storage: This standard depicts the conditions for cold storage outside the factory. Warehouse conditions such as temperature and relative humidity are major concerns of this category.

During the processes of cooking, canning and sterilisation and filling of fruits and vegetables, several process parameters must be measured and controlled, including the following:

1. pH, temperature and timing during thermal heating of canned fruits and vegetables.
2. Moisture content, fat, protein, antioxidants, pH, colour, brix and flavour of the product.
3. Filling weight and filling temperature for canning.
4. Temperature and humidity control during storage trials.

PROCESS INSTRUMENTATION AND CONTROL

There has been considerable development in the field of instrumentation in the last few decades. The reason for this rapid growth is that its principles are based on multidisciplinary facts and the applications are also multidisciplinary in nature. As technology advances in different fields, instrumentation also advances technologically. There is always an increasing need for precise, efficient measurement schemes in industrial environments.

Industrial control and automation are meaningless without a proper instrumentation scheme. Therefore, technological advancement requires advancement in both instrumentation and control. A judicious amalgamation of instrumentation and control can only contribute to the industrial needs for improving quality, increasing productivity, increasing efficiency, reducing manufacturing costs and material waste, saving energy and so on.

Industrial Process as a Manufacturing Unit

An industrial process is a manufacturing unit in which a series of continuous or regularly occurring actions take place in a predetermined or planned manner to produce the desired product. The product changes from the raw material stage to the final product stage within a certain span of time. During this transition, there might be more than one form of physical or chemical change of property of the material. On the other hand, there can be addition or removal of materials in quantity. The physical and chemical changes that take place in the materials or components in an industrial process are mainly responsible for the quality of the final product. The causes of the physical and chemical changes are the variations of some parameters that get reflected in some other parameters. These parameters are called process parameters or process variables. It is evident that the process action mainly depends on the process variables, so careful attention to the process variables is very much essential to knowing the state of the process action. The process variables that indicate the correctness of the process action are the process outputs or system outputs. The process variables that can change the process action are the process inputs or system inputs. This concept of process input and output variables is explained by an example of a tea dryer illustrated by a block diagram in Fig. 3.1.

The industrial process of black tea manufacturing that takes place inside the tea dryer is a physical and chemical change of state of the fermented tea. In a chain type of dryer, fermented tea is fed through a hopper onto a moving chain conveyer, which circulates the tea at a constant speed from the top left side to the bottom right side of the dryer. Hot air is injected from the bottom left side to dry the tea.

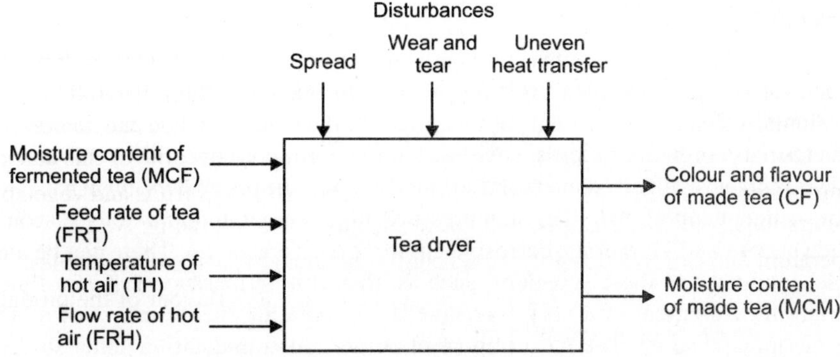

Fig. 3.1: Block diagram of a tea dryer.

Chemical change of the tea is a complex process that is difficult to model. If we consider only the physical change of drying of the tea in this process, fermented tea is the raw material and black tea is the product. The quality of the final product can be defined by the process output variables (controlled) such as grade, colour and moisture content. The feed rate, moisture content of the fermented tea and the temperature of the hot air are the manipulated input variables. These variables have independent, direct influence on the output variables. However, not all input variables are always highly responsible for the quality of the product. For example, in a tea dryer, the density of the fermented tea does not have a direct influence or might have a low gain influence on the product quality.

At this point we can identify the flow rate of the black tea as productivity of the final product rather than defining it as quality. Not all process input or output variables affect the quality of the product. Some process output variables might not indicate the quality of the product in a process. The flow rate of the black tea is a similar kind of output variable. Therefore, sufficient process knowledge is required to identify the actual process outputs that represent the quality of the final product. Similarly, some input variables might not affect the quality of the product in a process. A process can thus be represented by a system with manipulated input variables and controlled output process variables. The manipulated input variables control the quality of the final product and the controlled output variables carry the signature of the quality of the product. A process can be classified on the basis of numbers of input and output variables. For example a system can be a single-input, single-output (SISO) or a multiple-input, multiple-output (MIMO) system (Fig. 3.2). Most food processing generally consists of a combination of SISO and MIMO intermediate systems (Fig. 3.3).

Fig. 3.2: Models of process systems: (a) SISI model, and (b) MIMO model.

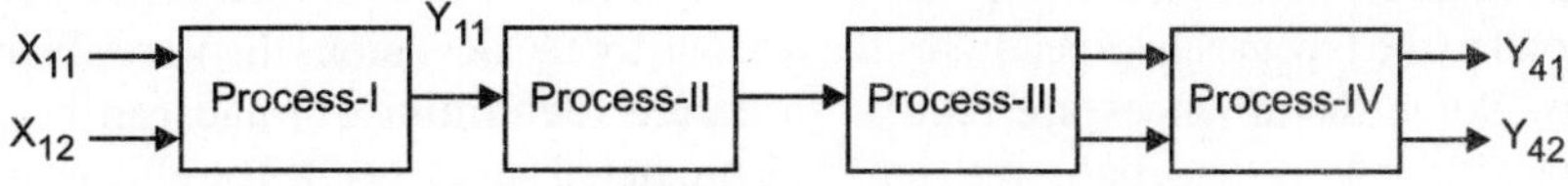

Fig. 3.3: Block diagram of a multiprocess system.

Process Parameters

Industrial processes to be handled by measurement and instrumentation can vary widely, from a simple oven at a biscuit factory to a complex brewing process. In this case, the parameters to be measured, controlled, or monitored can range from the temperature of the oven at the biscuit factory to the various process parameters of a brewing process, such as: temperature, pressure, flow rate, level, pH, colour, flavour, volatile compounds, mineral content and so on. Moreover, the parameters might have to be measured under different stringent conditions, like: high pressure, high temperature, noxious gaseous conditions, large-magnitude shocks and vibrations, corrosive environments and so on. There can be a good number of combined subconditions of these situations, such as: temperature measurement of a fluid under high pressure, pressure measurement of a very corrosive fluid, vibration measurement of a machine under radio-active emission and so on. The most important point in instrumentation under such conditions is to develop special sensors or to select the right equipment for error-free measurement of the process parameters of interest.

Batch and Continuous Processes

Production of a particular commodity involves well-defined multiple process operations in a pre-determined sequence, procedure and time. If the raw materials are treated in the stages of operations continuously with a single stream of product flow, the process is called a continuous process. If the product flow is discontinuous, meaning the raw materials or ingredients are treated with a time lag between stages, the process is called a batch process. However, it is difficult to have a purely batch process or a purely continuous one. Some batch processes demand continuous control of some variables and some continuous processes require some batch processing stages at the end of the schedule like batch sorting, batch packaging and so forth.

In the past, most of the chemical and petroleum-based products were manufactured in batch mode. Later it was felt that if there is a large demand for single product and a system is inherently suited (physically or chemically), a continuous process is more efficient than a batch process. If these conditions are not fulfilled or the product does not become cost-effective to produce using continuous process machinery, batch mode continues to be quite popular. Apart from this inherent advantage, batch mode processes have other beneficial qualities, such as: processing flexibility, multiple uses of equipment and higher safety in handling hazardous ingredients or products because of short processing duration. One added advantage of batch mode processing is easy controllability. A continuous mode process will have much more complex cross-correlation between process parameters than a batch mode process.

Process Instrumentation and Control

As defined earlier, a process carries out a single or a series of operations in a sequential manner leading toward a particular goal or object. The process is governed by the controlled variables, which is the desired output. A manipulated variable is a parameter that is varied by the controller to adjust the output to the desired quality or quantity. In a process, control is the technique of setting the outputs if there is deviation from the desired level, the manipulated input variables are adjusted to minimise the deviation. In a process, the causes of deviation of the output variables from a streamlined behaviour can be either internal or external to the process. Irrespective of the reasons for the deviations, they are always categorised as disturbances. Some disturbances are regular in nature (deterministic) and can be predicted and compensated for within the system, but some cannot be predicted (stochastic). The effects of unpredictable disturbances can only be compensated for by a feedback control system.

In a closed-loop feedback control system, the difference between the output of the system and the set point or desirable input is used as a measure for the repair to be performed. The difference is called the error, which is used to adjust the controllable input variable. To understand a manual control system, imagine the control of an electric heater by a human operator. The operator controls the temperature under a specific condition, for example, the maximum and minimum limits. The operator looks at the thermometer and if the temperature is above the specified limit, he or she switches the power off and thereby decreases the temperature. When the temperature decreases below the minimum limit, the operator switches the power on and the temperature rises again. This is a manual control approach in which the human operator works as a controller.

In another situation, consider an electric oven temperature that is controlled within a certain limit using a simple thermal switch. When the temperature of the oven crosses the limit, the thermal switch disconnects electric power to the oven, working as a controlled switch. If the temperature drops below the limit, the thermal switch operates to continue the power supply to the oven, thereby increasing the temperature. The set point of the temperature limit is imposed on the thermal switch, that is, the thermal switch is adjusted as per the temperature limit. In this example the thermal switch works both as a sensor and feedback controller. This feedback controller is basically an on-off controller that simply switches the input to the system to on or off state when the output goes below or above the set point, respectively. Figure 3.4 shows the block diagram of a feedback control system and Fig. 3.5 shows the temperature controller. There are few other types of traditional controllers, such as proportional, derivative and integral controllers that vary the input according to some function of the error signal. The advantage of a feedback control system is that a deviation of the output from the set point can be minimised by proper controller design. The output of a process generally fluctuates or deviates from the quality limit due to disturbances or variations in the process parameters. If feedback control is adopted, such deviations can be eliminated or minimised easily.

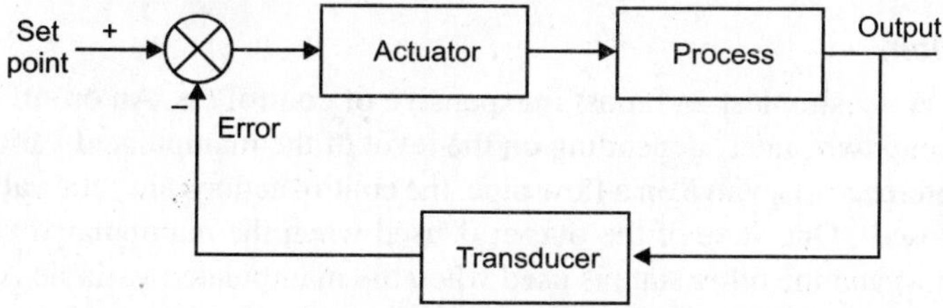

Fig. 3.4: A feedback control system.

In contrast to manual control, in automatic control, measurement and adjustment are made automatically and continuously. Manual control can be used in simple and linear processes in which disturbances are fewer, the process is not fast and minimal monitoring is required. In situations in which process variables change too rapidly for the operator to take action, automatic control is compulsory. Thus in an alternative arrangement for the heater control example, the temperature can be measured by a suitable sensor, then the signal is processed and fed to a controller for adjusting the process input. A simple electronic circuit to follow simple control laws can be realised by the controller. For complex control schemes the controller is realised using a microprocessor or a personal computer.

In industry, controllers are generally used to perform a particular kind of control action or a combination of two or more actions. The type of control action produced is called the control mode. The selection of

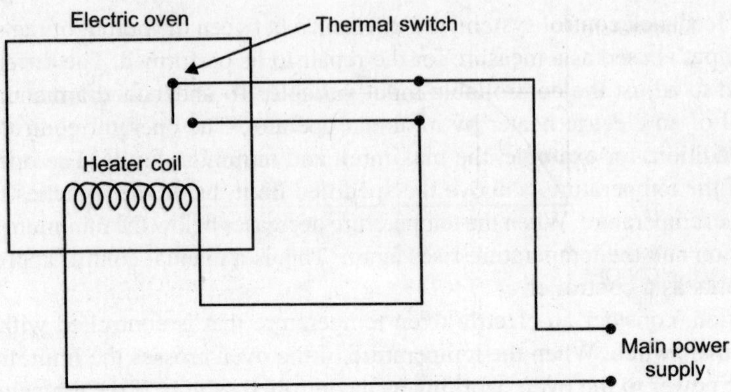

Fig. 3.5: Schematic diagram of a temperature-controlled electric oven.

a particular kind of control action depends on the complexity of the control parameters for which it is required, behaviour of the process variables and cost effectiveness. The different modes of traditional control actions are as follows:

1. On-off or two-position control.
2. Proportional control (P).
3. Proportional plus integral control (PI).
4. Proportional plus derivative (rate) control (PO).
5. Proportional plus integral plus derivative control (PID).

Traditional control schemes are not always successful in nonlinear, complex systems where advanced and intelligent control laws are found to be more convenient.

On-off control action

An on-off controller is the simplest and most inexpensive of controllers. An on-off controller results in an output action, in only two states, depending on the level of the manipulated variable. Describing the control action with reference to a valve on a flow pipe, the control actions are: 'the valve is fully open' and 'the valve is fully closed'. One state of the output is used when the manipulated variable is above the desired level (set point) and the other state is used when the manipulated variable is below the set point level. Consider an on-off control action for a temperature-controlled batch retort used for closing and heat sterilisation operation of cans to achieve microbiological stability in canning. As soon as the temperature crosses the set level, the steam entry valve is turned off. This causes the temperature to come down to the set level because the valve is still in the off position. Cycling of temperature and switching of the valve, on and off, continues simultaneously, as shown in Fig. 3.6. The range of temperature variation and the rate of switching are two very important features of an on-off controller. They are dependent on the process response and characteristics.

The range of temperature variation determines the precision of the controller and a high rate of switching causes mechanical disturbances to the final control elements like actuators, valves, relays and so on. Therefore, a simple on-off controller causes output to cycle rapidly as temperature crosses the set point. To eliminate this disadvantage, an on-off differential gap is introduced to the control action. This function causes the heater to turn off when the temperature exceeds the set point by a certain amount,

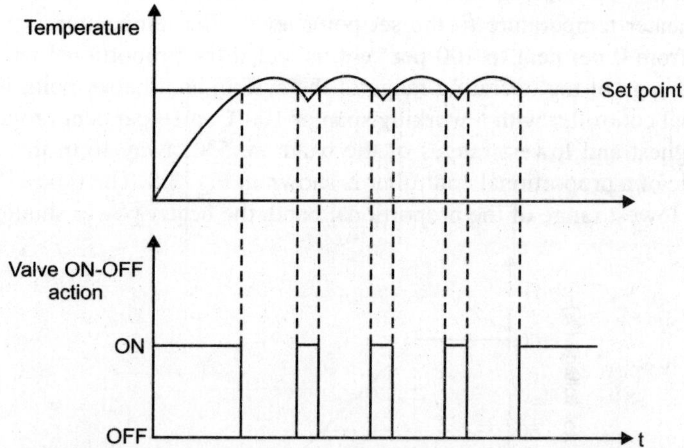

Fig. 3.6: ON–OFF control action of temperature controller.

which is generally half the gap. The gap prevents the controller from cycling rapidly. The representation of the differential gap for an on-off controller is shown in Fig. 3.7. As the temperature gradually increases from level A and reaches B through F, the heater turns off, dropping to point C. The temperature continues up to D and then decreases to point E, where the heater once again turns on. The temperature might slightly drop up to point G, then again reaches B through F, repeating the cycle. Incorporation of the differential gap in an on-off controller considerably reduces oscillations of the controlled output.

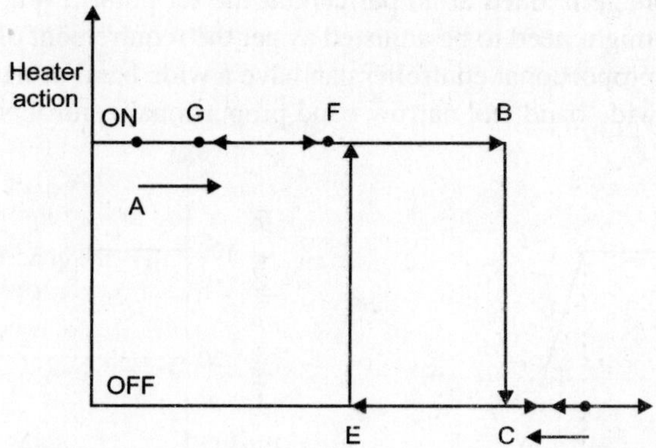

Fig. 3.7: Representation of the control action due to the differential gap.

Proportional control action

In a proportional controller, the manipulated variable is proportionately adjusted according to the variation of the actual output from the desired output. In the case of a temperature-controlled electric heater, the electrical power to the heater is adjusted proportionately to the deviation of temperature from the set level. The electrical voltage to the heater is decreased by an amount proportional to the temperature by which it exceeds the set level. The voltage is increased similarly when the temperature decreases from the set level.

This brings the heater temperature to the set point level. The temperature range, over which the voltage is adjusted from 0 per cent to 100 per cent, is called the proportional band. This is normally expressed as a percentage of the operating range of the system and the set point is centered at 50 per cent. In a proportional controller with a working span of 100°C, a 10 per cent proportional band would be 10°C and the highest and lowest ranges of the band are 5°C away from the set point level. The transfer characteristic of a proportional controller is shown in Fig. 3.8. The figure illustrates that below 100°C, which is the lowest range of the proportional band, the heater power should be 100 per cent.

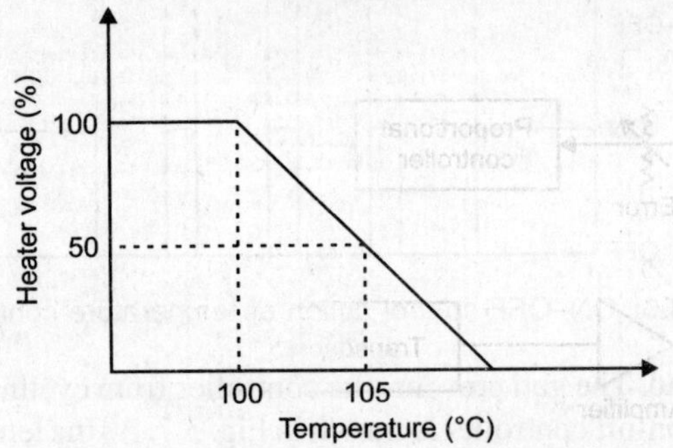

Fig. 3.8: Transfer characteristic of a proportional controller.

On the other hand, above the highest range of the proportional band (i.e. 110°C), the heater voltage should be zero. The voltage to be applied to the heater therefore can be determined from the characteristic graphically. The heater voltage is fixed at 50 per cent at the set point level. There is every possibility that the proportional band might need to be adjusted as per the requirement of the process response and characteristics. Hence the proportional controller can have a wide band or narrow band of control. The transfer characteristics of wide band and narrow band proportional controllers are shown in Fig. 3.9.

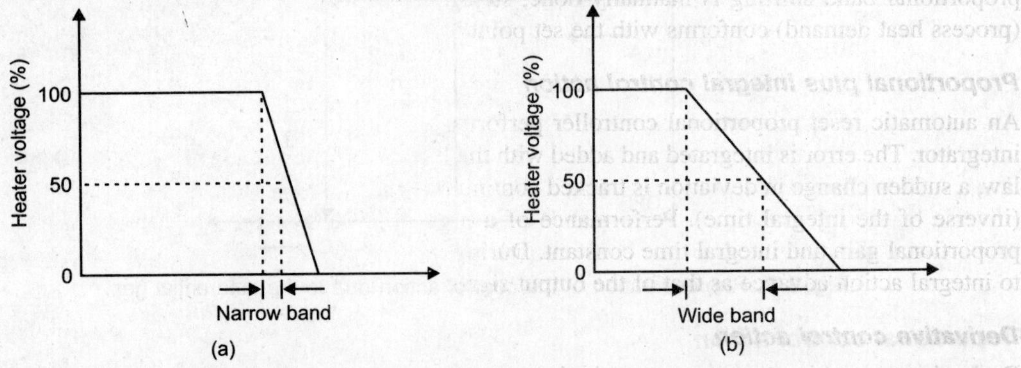

Fig. 3.9: Transfer characteristic of (a) a narrow band and (b) a wide band proportional controller.

In a narrow band proportional controller, a small change in temperature causes a large manipulated output. The performance of a proportional controller can be expressed in terms of the controller gain as

$$\text{Gain} = 100\%/\text{proportional band (per cent)}$$

Hence, the gain of a narrow band proportional controller is higher than that of a wide band controller. A proportional controller is suitable for a system where deviation of output is not large and is not sudden. A proportional controller can be incorporated in a closed-loop feedback control system illustrated in Fig. 3.10. The output signal is sensed by a sensor and amplified before comparison with the set point level. The error signal is positive when the output is below the set point level, negative when the output is above the set point and zero when the output is adjusted to make it equal to the set point. The proportional output is 50 per cent when the error signal is zero.

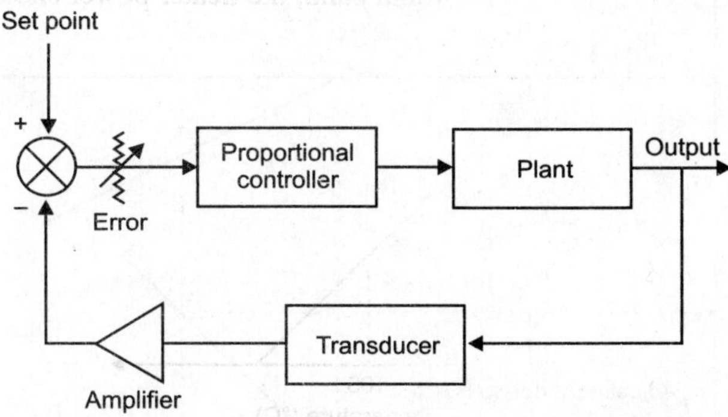

Fig. 3.10: Block diagram of a proportional controller.

In practical situations, the heat input for attaining set point temperature never equals 50 per cent of the maximum available. Therefore, the output temperature oscillates before coming to an equilibrium condition. The temperature difference between the stabilised and set point level is called the offset. The offset temperature value becomes less in a narrow band proportional controller. For fine-tuning of a controller the offset must be removed. This can be done manually or automatically. Manual reset is a traditional method in which a potentiometer is used to nullify the offset electrically. The amount of proportional band shifting is manually done, step by step, until the manipulated input to controller (process heat demand) conforms with the set point level of temperature.

Proportional plus integral control action

An automatic reset proportional controller performs a reset operation with the help of an electronic integrator. The error is integrated and added with the error signal. Due to the integral term in the control law, a sudden change in deviation is tracked continuously, at a certain rate, determined by the reset rate (inverse of the integral time). Performance of a proportional controller is expressed by two terms: proportional gain and integral time constant. During integral time, equal parts of the output signal due to integral action advance as that of the output signal due to proportional action.

Derivative control action

Derivative control incorporates a term in the control law, which is first derivative of the error signal. It facilitates the shift of the proportional band either up or down to compensate for rapidly changing outputs. The controller tracks the set point level at a rate proportional to the rate of change of the error signal. If the output makes a sudden jump, the derivative action immediately brings the output toward the set point level. If the output changes gradually at a constant rate, the output tracks the set point at a similar rate to the proportional action. In this control action, a derivative time constant can also be defined in a similar manner. The derivative action does not have any limit of occurrence, unlike integral action. The derivative action can occur even outside the proportional band. The speed of correction is proportional to the amount of deviation, but this incorporates oscillations in the system output. The timing diagram of a proportional plus derivative control action is shown in Fig. 3.11.

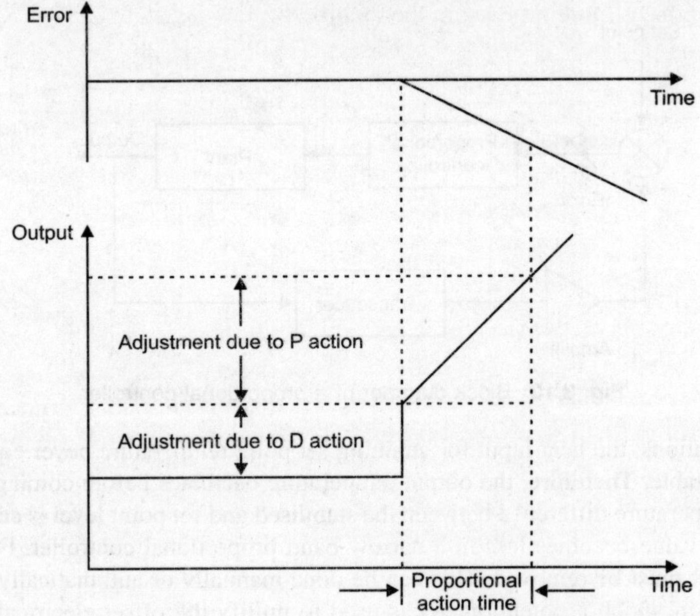

Fig. 3.11: Typical characteristics of proportional plus derivative controller.

PID controller

Combination of these three modes of control action is advantageous for controlling complex processes. This mode of control is best suited for cases where the output fluctuations are large and sudden and the system has a lag.

Selection of Controller

Selection of a controller for a particular application requires attention to several factors. It has been found that the simplest controller that meets the requirement of the process is the best and least expensive. Although a better controller might be employed in a process that needs precise tuning of the output, a simple controller can be adequate in a process that permits a comparatively wide range of outputs.

Selection of a controller depends on the following factors:

1. Process response curve.
2. Physical system analysis.
3. Past experience.
4. Experimental testing.

A process response curve is a plot between the process outputs with time when a steady input is applied. The process response curve for a first-order thermal system is shown in Fig. 3.12. The essential characteristics of a thermal process response curve are the time constant and the rate of temperature increase. The controllability of a process depends on these two factors. If the curve becomes steeper, the controllability of the process becomes difficult. If the output temperature (T_p) starts increasing as soon as the input is applied, there is no propagation delay or dead time. This relates to the time constant (t). Such a system is easy to control. In a more complicated situation, when a heater is modified with thick metal plates, it introduces more time lag in the thermal system.

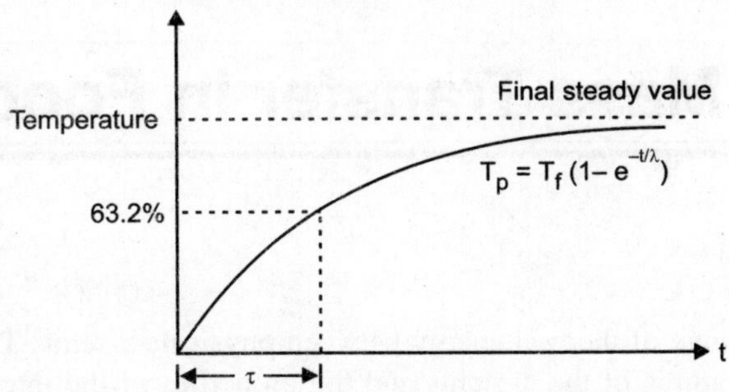

Fig. 3.12: Response of a first-order thermal system.

This will introduce a second time constant, which results in a second-order system that is more difficult to control than a first-order system. The size of the process compared to the output requirement is also a major factor in selecting the controller. An oversized process does not give stable output, whereas an undersized one gives slow response. Analysing controllability and process output stability requirements will help in selecting the controller. Thorough knowledge about the process response in the past is also an important clue. Experimental verification of the process response by computer simulation of the process is also a faithful method of selection of a controller. However, there are obviously some guidelines for controller selection, as follows:

1. A proportional controller is used where:
   - Load analysis is insignificant.
   - Offset can be permitted.
   - A narrow proportional band is permitted.
2. Integral control is used where:
   - Offset cannot be permitted.
   - Process has a lag.
3. Derivative control is used where:
   - Sudden and large deviation of output takes place.
   - There are severe plant lags.

Chapter 4

Heat and Mass Transfer in Food Industry

INTRODUCTION

Heat transfer is the exchange of thermal energy between physical systems. The rate of heat transfer is dependent on the temperatures of the systems and the properties of the intervening medium through which the heat is transferred. The three fundamental modes of heat transfer are conduction, convection and radiation.

Mass transfer is the net movement of mass from one location, usually meaning stream, phase, fraction or component, to another. Mass transfer occurs in many processes, such as absorption, evaporation, adsorption, drying, precipitation, membrane filtration, and distillation. Mass transfer is used by different scientific disciplines for different processes and mechanisms.

HEAT AND MASS TRANSFER IN FOOD PROCESSING

Heat transfer in food processing is complicated by the occurrence of simultaneous heat and mass transfer in drying and frying, free convection heat transfer in thermal sterilisation of cans, and phase change in freezing and thawing. Air drying, freeze drying, spray drying, and steam drying are accompanied by moisture transfer, which also undergoes phase change (evaporation). Heat transfer, together with moisture and vapour transfer, controls these processes. Other phase change operations, such as evaporation and condensation, are commonly used in the food industry, mainly to concentrate liquid foods such as milk and juices. Food is dried with hot air or superheated steam, fried in hot oil and usually sterilised in cans or pouches with steam. Heat is transferred from the heating fluid to the surface of the material by free or forced convection. With solid food, heat is transferred by conduction while vapour is transported by diffusion or other mechanisms through the pores of the food. For liquid food in containers, natural convection rather than conduction dominates heat transfer. Thawing of products such as meat is usually done in a hot air environment or by using hot water. However, microwave and radio frequency may also be used to assist in thawing of meat. Microwaves and radio frequency waves have the ability to penetrate deep inside the food, producing heat within the material. Vacuum microwave drying is sometimes applied for heat sensitive food so that evaporation occurs at temperatures well below 100°C thus minimising serious damage caused by high temperature applications.

DESCRIPTION OF HEAT TRANSFER

Heat transfer and mass transfer are kinetic processes that may occur and be studied separately or jointly. Studying them apart is simpler, but both processes are modelled by similar mathematical equations in the case of diffusion and convection (there is no mass-transfer similarity to heat radiation), and it is thus more efficient to consider them jointly. Besides, heat and mass transfer must be jointly considered in some cases like evaporative cooling and ablation.

The usual way to make the best of both approaches is to first consider heat transfer without mass transfer, and present at a later stage a briefing of similarities and differences between heat transfer and mass transfer, with some specific examples of mass transfer applications. There are complex problems where heat and mass transfer processes are combined with chemical reactions, as in combustion, but many times the chemical process is so fast or so slow that it can be decoupled and considered apart, as in the important diffusion-controlled combustion problems of gas-fuel jets, and condensed fuels.

Heat transfer is the flow of thermal energy driven by thermal non-equilibrium (i.e. the effect of a nonuniform temperature field), commonly measured as a heat flux (vector), i.e. the heat flow per unit time (and usually unit normal area) at a control surface. The aim here is to understand heat transfer modelling, but the actual goal of most heat transfer (modelling) problems is to find the temperature field and heat fluxes in a material domain, given a previous knowledge of the subject (general partial differential equations, PDE), and a set of particular constraints: boundary conditions (BC), initial conditions (IC), distribution of sources or sinks (loads), etc. There are also many cases where the interest is just to know when the heat-transfer process finishes, and in a few other cases the goal is not in the direct problem (given the PDE + BC + IC, find the T-field) but on the inverse problem: given the T-field and some aspects of PDE + BC + IC, find some missing parameters (identification problem), e.g. finding the required dimensions or materials for a certain heat insulation or conduction goal.

Heat-transfer problems arise in many industrial and environmental processes, particularly in energy utilisation, thermal processing, and thermal control. Energy cannot be created or destroyed, but so-common it is to use energy as synonymous of exergy, or the quality of energy, than it is commonly said that energy utilisation is concerned with energy generation from primary sources (e.g. fossil fuels, solar), to end-user energy consumption (e.g. electricity and fuel consumption), through all possible intermediate steps of energy vaporisation, energy transportation, energy storage, and energy conversion processes. The purpose of thermal processing is to force a temperature change in the system that enables or disables some material transformation (e.g. food pasteurisation, cooking, steel tempering or annealing). The purpose of thermal control is to regulate within fixed established bounds, or to control in time within a certain margin, the temperature of a system to secure its correct functioning.

As a model problem, consider the thermal problem of heating a thin metallic rod by grasping it at one end with our fingers for a while, until we withdraw our grip and let the rod cool down in air, we may want to predict the evolution of the temperature at one end, or the heat flow through it, or the rod conductivity needed to heat the opposite end to a given value. We may learn from this case study how difficult it is to model the heating by our fingers, the extent of finger contact, the thermal convection through the air, etc. By the way, if this example seems irrelevant to engineering and science (nothing is irrelevant to science), consider its similarity with the heat gains and losses during any temperature measurement with a typical 'long' thermometer (from the old mercury-in-glass type. to the modern shrouded thermocouple probe). A more involved problem may be to find the temperature field and associated dimensional changes during machining or cutting a material, where the final dimensions depend on the time-history of the temperature field.

Everybody has been always exposed to heat transfer problems in normal life (putting on coats and avoiding winds in winter, wearing caps and looking for breezes in summer, adjusting cooking power, and so on), so that certain experience can be assumed. However, the aim of studying a discipline is to understand it in depth, e.g. to clearly distinguish thermal-conductivity effects from thermal-capacity effects, the relevance of thermal radiation near room temperatures, and to be able to make sound predictions. Typical heat-transfer devices like heat exchangers, condensers, boilers, solar collectors, heaters, furnaces, and so on, must be considered in a heat-transfer course, but the emphasis must be on basic heat-transfer models, which are universal, and not on the myriad of details of past and present equipment. Heat transfer theory is based on thermodynamics, physical transport phenomena, physical and chemical energy dissipation phenomena, space-time modelling, additional mathematical modelling, and experimental tests.

Thermodynamics of Heat Transfer

Heat transfer is the relaxation process that tends to do away with temperature gradients (recall that $\nabla T \rightarrow 0$ in an isolated system), but systems are often kept out of equilibrium by imposed boundary conditions. Heat transfer tends to change the local state according to the energy balance, which for a closed system is:

$$\text{What is heat } (\equiv \text{heat flow})?\ Q \equiv \Delta E - W \rightarrow Q = \Delta E|_{V,\ \text{non-dis}} = \Delta H|_{p,\ \text{non-dis}} \quad \ldots(4.1)$$

i.e. heat, Q (i.e. the flow of thermal energy from the surroundings into the system, driven by thermal nonequilibrium, not related to work or to the flow of matter), equals the increase in stored energy, ΔE, minus the flow of work, W. For non-dissipative systems (i.e. without mechanical or electrical dissipation), heat equals the internal energy change if the process is at constant volume, or the enthalpy change if the process is at constant volume, both cases converging for a perfect substance model (PSM, i.e. constant thermal capacity) to $Q = mc\Delta T$. However, it is worth to keep in mind that:

- Heat is the flow of thermal energy driven by thermal non-equilibrium, so that 'heat flow' is a redundancy. Heat must not be confused with stored thermal energy, and moving a hot object from one place to another must not be called heat transfer. But, in spite of all these remarks, it is common in normal parlance to say 'heat flow', to talk of 'heat content', etc.
- Heat is an energy flow, defined by (4.1) just for the case of mass-impervious systems (i.e. $Q \equiv W_{adiab} - W$). When there are simultaneous energy and mass flows, heat flow must be considered at a surface with no net mass flow.
- Heat input to a system, may not necessarily cause a temperature increase. In absence of work, a heat input always increases internal energy [$Q = \Delta E$ for $W = 0$ in (4.1)], but this increment may be 'sensible' (i.e. noticeable as a temperature increase), or 'latent' (e.g. causing a phase change or other endothermic reaction at constant temperature).
- A temperature increase in a closed system is not necessarily due to a heat input, it can be due to a work input [e.g. $\Delta E = mc\Delta T = W$ for $Q = 0$ in (4.1)], either with dissipation (e.g. internal stirring), or without (isentropic compression).
- The First Law (4.1) shows that, for a steady state without work exchange, the heat loss by a system must pass integrally to another system, i.e. for the interface, $Q \equiv Q_{net} = Q_{in} - Q_{out} = 0$ for $\Delta E = W = 0$.
- The Second Law teaches that heat always flows from the hotter system towards the colder one. Even when we want to extract heat from a cold system like in refrigeration, we must procure a

colder working substance for heat to flow down the temperature gradient to the working fluid (later to be compressed to a higher temperature than that of the heat sink, to finally dispose of the thermal energy again by letting heat to flow down the temperature gradient to the ambient).

In Thermodynamics, sometimes one refers to heat in an isothermal process, but this is a formal limit for small gradients and large periods. Here, in Heat Transfer, the interest is not in heat flow, Q, but on heat flow-rate, $\dot{Q} = dQ/dt$, that should be named just heat rate, because the 'flow' characteristic is inherent to the concept of heat, contrary for instance to the concept of mass, to which two possible 'speeds' can be ascribed: mass rate of change, and mass flow rate. Heat rate, thence, is energy flow rate at constant volume, or enthalpy flow rate at constant pressure:

$$\text{What is heat flux } (\equiv \text{heat flow rate})? \quad \dot{Q} \equiv \frac{dQ}{dt} = mc\left.\frac{dT}{dt}\right|_{\text{PSM,non-dis}} \equiv KA\Delta T \qquad \ldots(4.2)$$

where, the global heat transfer coefficient K (associated to a bounding area A and the average temperature jump ΔT between the system and the surroundings), is defined by, the inverse of K is named global heat resistance coefficient $M \equiv 1/K$. Notice that this is the recommended nomenclature under the SI, with $G = KA$ being the global transmittance and $R = 1/G$ the global resistance, although U has been used a lot instead of K, and R instead of M. In most heat-transfer problems, it is undesirable to ascribe a single average temperature to the system, and thus a local formulation must be used, defining the heat flow-rate density (or simply heat flux) as $\dot{q} \equiv dQ/dA$. According to the corresponding physical transport phenomena explained below, heat flux can be related to temperature difference between the system and the environment in the classical three modes of conduction, convection, and radiation:

$$\text{What is heat flux density } (\approx \text{heat flux})? \quad \dot{q} \equiv K\Delta T \begin{cases} \text{Conduction} & \dot{\vec{q}} = -k\nabla T \\ \text{Convection} & \dot{q} \equiv h(T - T_\infty) \\ \text{Radiation} & \dot{q} = \varepsilon\sigma(T^4 - T_0^4) \end{cases} \qquad \ldots(4.3)$$

These three heat-flux models can also be viewed as: heat transfer within materials (conduction), heat transfer within fluids (convection), and heat transfer through empty space (radiation).

Notice that heat (related to a path integral in a closed control volume in thermodynamics) has the positive sign when it enters the system, but heat flux, related to a control area, cannot be ascribed a definite sign until we select 'our side'. For heat conduction, (4.3) has a vector form, stating that heat flux is a vector field aligned with the temperature-gradient field, and having opposite sense. For convection and radiation, however, (4.3) has a scalar form, and, although a vector form can be forged multiplying by the unit normal vector to the surface, this commonly-used scalar form suggest that, in typical heat transfer problems, convection and radiation are only boundary conditions and not field equations as for conduction (when a heat-transfer problem requires solving field variables in a moving fluid, it is studied under Fluid Mechanics). Notice also that heat conduction involves field variables: a scalar field for T and a vector field for $\dot{\vec{q}}$, with the associated differential equations relating each other (because only short-range interactions are involved), which are partial differential equations because time and several spatial coordinates are related. Another important point in (4.3) is the non-linear temperature-dependence of radiation, what forces to use absolute values for temperature in any equation with radiation effects. Conduction and convection problems are usually linear in temperature (if k and h are T-independent), and it is common practice working in degrees Celsius instead of absolute temperatures.

Finally notice that (4.1) and (4.2) correspond to the First Law (energy conservation), and (4.3) incorporates the Second-Law consequence of heat flowing downwards in the T-field (from hot to cold).

Physical Transport Phenomena

Heat flow is traditionally considered to take place in three different basic modes (sometimes superposed): conduction, convection, radiation.

- Conduction is the transport of thermal energy in solids and non-moving fluids due to short-range atomic interactions, supplemented with the free-electron flow in metals, modelled by the so-called Fourier's law, $\vec{q} = -k\nabla T$, where k is the so-called thermal conductivity coefficient. Notice that Fourier's law has a local character (heat flux proportional to local temperature gradient, independent of the rest of the T-field), what naturally leads to differential equations. Notice also that Fourier's law implies an infinite speed of propagation for temperature gradients (thermal waves), which is nonsense, thermal conduction waves propagate at the speed of sound in the medium, as any other phenomena small perturbation. In crystalline solids, packets of quantised energy called phonons serve to explain thermal conduction (as photons do in electromagnetic radiation).
- Convection, in the restricted sense used in most Heat Transfer books, is the transport of thermal energy between a solid surface (at wall temperature T) and a moving fluid (at a far-enough temperature T_∞), modelled by a thermal convection coefficient h as in the second line of (4.3), named Newton's law, in this sense, heat convection is just heat conduction at the fluid interface in a solid, whereas in the more general sense used in Fluid Mechanics, thermal convection is the combined energy transport and heat diffusion flux at every point in the fluid. Notice, however, that what goes along a hot-water insulated pipe is not heat and there is no heat-transfer involved, it is thermal energy being convected, without thermal gradients. Related to fluid flow, but through porous media is percolation, a special case concerns heat transfer in biological tissue by blood perfusion (i.e. the flow of blood by permeation through tissues: skin, muscle, fat, bone, and organs, from arteries to capillaries and veins), the cardiovascular system is the key system by which heat is distributed throughout the body, from body core to limbs and head.
- Radiation is the transport of thermal energy by far electromagnetic coupling, modelled from the basic black-body theory (fourth-power-law of thermal emission), $M_{bb} = \sigma T^4$, named Stefan-Boltzmann law (proposed by Jozef Steafan in 1879 and deduced by his student Ludwig Bolzmann in 1884), σ being a universal constant $\sigma = 5.67 \cdot 10^{-8}$ W.m^{-2}.K^{-4}, modified for real surfaces by introducing the emissivity factor, ε ($0<\varepsilon<1$). Radiation is emitted as a result of the motion of electric charges in atoms and molecules (by thermal vibrations or external forces), and radiation is absorbed by matter increasing the atomic motion of electric particles. Notice that (4.3) only applies to radiation heat transfer when the surface absorptance to radiation coming from the environment at temperature T_0 is equal to surface emissivity at temperature T, what is usually not the case if both temperatures are of different orders of magnitude. If absorption at a surface is not total, part of the incident radiation may be reflected or transmitted behind (scattered, in general). Heat transfer by thermal radiation is not only important at high temperatures, even at room temperatures, $T \approx 300$ K, the equivalent linear coefficient of heat transfer is $K = 4\sigma T^3 = 6.1$ W/(m^2·K), comparable to a typical natural convective coefficient in air of $h = 10$ W/(m^2·K).

The three heat-transfer modes above-mentioned, often appear at the same time on a thermal problem, but seldom with the same importance, what allows for simple one-mode analysis in many instances. A combined case that appears in many cases is the heat flow by convection from one fluid to another fluid separated by an intermediate solid wall (single, as in pipes, or double, as in modern window panes), in such cases, dealing with an overall heat-transfer coefficient, K, is very helpful (one has just to apply (4.2), e.g. typical values for a modern house may be: $K = 0.5$ W/(m^2·K) for walls, $K = 0.6$ W/(m^2·K) for the roof, $K = 0.7$ W/(m^2·K) for the floor, and $K = {}^3$ W/(m^2·K) for a double-pane window.

Notice finally that isothermal surfaces are usually assumed in convection- and radiation- heat-transfer problems, and that the temperature field is only solved in heat conduction problems (except when big computation codes are used to solve the whole fluid mechanics problem, namely in CFD).

Thermal Conductivity

The thermal conductivity, k, of a given isotropic material at given conditions, is the proportionality constant defined by Fourier's law, $\dot{q} = -k\nabla T$. For non-isotropic materials, k is no-longer a scalar magnitude but a tensor.

Measuring k is based on measuring heat flux against temperature gradient in steady-state set-ups, or on measuring thermal diffusivity in transient processes. Measuring k in liquids is very difficult because test sizes are restricted to avoid heat convection, and it is even harder to measure k in gases because, not only convection must be avoided, but thermal radiation too. Many times, conductivity-values at different temperatures are needed, but notice that measuring k always implies a temperature difference to generate the heat flow, which cannot be too small without compromising uncertainty in the measure, thus all k-values are more or less averaged values.

A summary of the different approaches followed to measure thermal conductivities is presented below, quoting the formulation to be used, which is covered in detail separately under Heat Conduction modelling. Steady state methods to measure thermal conductivity of materials (most accurate, but slow and expensive):

- Planar geometry. A slab (or a long isolated bar for good conductors) is kept between a guarded heater at one side of the sample (e.g. an electrical heater mat insulated on the other side, or in a symmetric configuration), and a guarded cooler on the other side of the sample (e.g. cooling water, or a thermoelectric refrigerator). If the heat flow is unidirectional, the conductivity is given by $k = (\dot{Q}/A)/(\Delta T/L)$, but, as it is very difficult to measure $\dot{Q}$ without losses, a reference-k material is used to measure k by comparison. Most accurate values for poor conductors are obtained in a multilayer set-up like H-T-R1-T-S-T-R2-T-C, where H stands for the heater, T stands for an aluminium disc with embedded thermocouples, R1 and R2 stand for two reference-material discs (preferably with a similar conductivity as the sample), S stands for the sample, and C for the cooler. Very thin materials like films and foils are tested by stacking several sample layers together.
- Cylindrical geometry. A cylindrical sample with a central heater and a cooler on the outside is used. The conductivity is given by $k = [(\dot{Q}/L)/(2\pi\Delta T/\ln(R_{ext}/R_{int}))]$ but, as above, a reference-k material can be used to measure k by comparison.

Unsteady methods to measure thermal conductivity of materials (not so accurate, but quicker (half a minute instead of half an hour), cheaper, and yield thermal diffusivity directly):

- Planar geometry. The most used variant of this method is the quasi-steady state method. A disc-shape sample (a thin slab may do) is sandwiched between a planar wall of a metal container with a well-stirred bath at a fixed temperature, T_w, and a small copper disc of mass m_{Cu}, and area A_{Cu}, well-insulated on all sides except that in contact with the sample. Assuming linear quasi-steady heat transfer through the sample, its conductivity is obtained by the copper energy-balance,

$k = \left[(m_{Cu}c_{Cu}L/A_{Cu}t)/(\ln(T_{Cu}(t)-T_w)/(T_{Cu,initial}-T_w)\right]$, accuracy can be enhanced by optimisation of sample and copper thicknesses. Another planar method is based on the time lag between two thermocouples on each side of a thin sample, when a short light-pulse is shined on one side, this is known as flash method, and, although already introduced in the 1950s, still lacks accuracy, the thermal diffusivity of the sample is usually estimated as $a = 0.14\,L^2/t_{1/2}$, where L is sample thickness, and $t_{1/2}$ is the time it takes for the rear thermocouple to reach half of the maximal temperature increase (temperature falls afterwards, due to heat losses, axially and laterally).

- Cylindrical geometry (also known as line heat source method). The method is based on the temperature rise at radius R within the sample, after a centred line heater of given power is switched on. The most used variant of this method is the singular case with R=0, i.e. when temperature rise is measured just at the axis, where the heater is also located, a line-heat-source probe holds both a heater and a thermometer, either inside a narrow tube, or on the outside of a tube or a rod (internal placement makes the probe more robust, but external placement yields more accurate data). The conductivity of the sample is obtained by fitting the straight portion of the $T(t)$ versus ln$t$ plot, and using $k = (\dot{Q}/(4\pi))/(dT/d(\ln t))$ (the curved initial and final portions should be discarded). The sample diameter D must be large enough, $D^2/(at)>10$, and probe diameter d narrow enough, say $d/D<10$, and even so, uncertainties are typically around 5%.
- Spherical geometry (also known as thermistor method). The method is based on measuring the temperature rise of a thermistor of radius R, encapsulated in a nearly-spherical bead, embedded within the sample, and used as a point source of constant power, $\dot{Q}$. The thermal diffusivity of the sample material is obtained from $\dot{Q} = \left[(4\pi Rk + 4R^2\sqrt{\pi k\rho c/t}(T_R(t)-T_\infty)\right]$, i.e. by linear fitting of the thermistor temperature versus the inverse of the square root of time. This method required calibration with a medium of known thermal conductivity to find the effective bead radius, R, and even so, uncertainties are typically around 20%, mainly due to heat losses through the connectors..

Heat Equation

The heat-transfer equation is the energy balance for heat conduction through an infinitesimal non-moving volume. To deduce it, we start from the energy balance (4.2) applied to a system of finite volume:

$$\left.\frac{dH}{dt}\right|_p = \dot{Q} \rightarrow \int_V \rho c\frac{\partial T}{\partial t}dV = -\int_A \vec{\dot{q}}\cdot\vec{n}\,dA + \int_V \phi\,dV \qquad \ldots(4.4)$$

where, ϕ is some energy release rate per unit volume (e.g. by nuclear or chemical reactions), sometimes written as $\dot{q}_{gen}$. Equation (4.4) can be read as 'the time-increment of enthalpy within de volume is due to the heat input through the frontier plus the energy dissipation in the interior', the minus sign coming from the choice of $\vec{n}$ as the normal outwards vector. When the Gauss-Ostrogradski theorem of vector calculus is used to transform the area-integral to the volume-integral, and (4.4) is applied to an infinitesimal volume within the system, one gets:

$$\int_V \rho c\frac{\partial T}{\partial t}dV = -\int_A \vec{\dot{q}}\cdot\vec{n}\,dA + \int_V \phi\,dV = \int_V \nabla\cdot\vec{\dot{q}}\,dV + \int_V \phi\,dV \xrightarrow{V\to 0} \rho c\frac{\partial T}{\partial t} = \nabla\cdot\vec{\dot{q}} + \phi \qquad \ldots(4.5)$$

Finally, considering Fourier's law (4.3) and constant material properties (density ρ, thermal capacity c, conductivity k, and their combination, the thermal diffusivity:

$$a \equiv \frac{k}{\rho c} \qquad \ldots(4.6$$

one gets the so-called heat equation:

$$\rho c \frac{\partial T}{\partial t} = k\nabla^2 T + \phi, \text{ or } \frac{\partial T}{\partial t} = a\nabla^2 T + \frac{\phi}{\rho c} \qquad \ldots(4.7)$$

The heat equation (4.7) is the most well-known parabolic partial-differential equation (PDE) in theoretical physics, ϕ being a non-homogeneous term. The heat equation is also known as diffusion equation, and it has solutions that evolve exponentially with time to the steady state. At steady state, the heat equation becomes an elliptic PDE named Poison's equation, which, without the non-homogeneous term, becomes Laplace equation, $\nabla^2 T = 0$. Besides parabolic and elliptic PDE, the third type is the hyperbolic PDE $\partial^2\Psi/\partial t^2 - c^2\partial^2\Psi/\partial x^2 = 0$, typical of wave-like phenomena.

A more general heat equation takes account also of the effect of relative motion between the material system and the coordinate system with a velocity $\vec{v}$, which, in a fix reference frame (Eulerian reference frame) takes the form:

$$\frac{\partial T}{\partial t} = a\nabla^2 T + \frac{\phi}{\rho c} - \nabla \cdot (\overrightarrow{Tv}) \qquad \ldots(4.8)$$

although we will only consider such motions when analysing moving heat sources in a stationary solid (to change to a reference frame moving with the source), of application to machining, grinding, cutting, sliding, welding, heat treatment, and so many materials processing. The most general heat equation (e.g. to be used in computational fluid dynamics (CFD), must include in the energy release term ϕ, viscous dissipation and the dilatation work due to the time-variation of pressure along a fluid line, if any, although both are usually negligible energy contributions. To solve the heat equation, besides the parameters explicitly appearing in it (a, ϕ, ρ, c...), appropriate bounding conditions for the variables are required, i.e. initial conditions for time and boundary conditions for the space variables.

Modelling Space, Time and Equations

Space-time modelling may refer to the consideration of continuous or discrete processes in space and time, but space-time modelling in heat transfer usually refers to the consideration of processes as steady or nonsteady, zero-dimensional, one-dimensional, two-dimensional or three-dimensional geometry, planar, cylindrical or spherical, etc. So important this modellisation is, that heat transfer books, and in particular the heat conduction part, is usually divided in different chapters for the different space-time models: steady onedimensional conduction, unsteady one-dimensional conduction, steady two-dimensional conduction, etc.

As in many other engineering problems, the steady state solution is usually analysed first, in heat-transfer problems, leaving transient effects for a more advanced phase, but many undesirable events may occur during transients. Here in this context, thermal shock (e.g. breaking a glass by pouring hot water) and local overheating (e.g. charring shoes and cloth before getting warm), can be mentioned.

Every step in problem-solving may have an associated mathematical modelling, from geometrical definition and materials properties, to results and conclusions. We want now to consider the main mathematical tools used to formulate and solve heat-transfer problems, traditionally divided into classical analytical methods (partial differential equations in a continuum, developed in the 19th century), and modern numerical methods (discrete set of algebraic equations applied to small elements of the system, developed in the late 20th century, like the finite element method FEM, the finite difference method FDM, or the boundary element method BEM. In both cases there are imposed bounding conditions (BC), which, in heat transfer, are the initial conditions (heat equation is 1st order in time) and boundary conditions (heat equation is 2nd order in space variables), the latter are usually classified as:

- First kind boundary conditions, when the temperature is known at the boundary.
- Second kind boundary conditions, when the temperature-gradient is known at the boundary. It often happens that, on the whole boundary of a closed system, conditions of a first kind apply to some parts, and of the second kind to the others.
- Third kind boundary conditions, when the temperature-gradient at the boundary is a known function of the temperature there.
- Fourth kind boundary conditions, when neither the temperature-gradient nor the temperature-gradient are known at the boundary, but are functions of other boundary conditions in the problem (i.e. the boundary at hand is an intermediate boundary in a much larger system).

In practice, all real problems are of the third and fourth kind, because it is really difficult to force a constant temperature at a boundary (thermostatic baths and blocks are often used for the purpose), and even more difficult to guarantee a constant heat flux.

By the way, continuous field theory (as used in Fluid Mechanics, Elasticity, or Electromagnetism) is a simplifying recourse to modelling the influence of many discrete microscopic particles on other manyparticles systems (i.e. the goal of Thermodynamics). Classical field theory started with Newton's Law of Gravitation, followed with Euler's Law of fluid motion (later expanded to Navier-Stokes equation), and Fourier's heat equation, and peaked with Maxwell's electromagnetism equations. But Fourier was the first to solve a multi-dimensional field equation (a PDE), inventing Fourier's series and separation of variables to solve the heat equation.

APPLICATIONS OF HEAT TRANSFER

Heat transfer theory may be used to compute heating/cooling times in heat transfer problems, or to compute temperature fields and heat fluxes, or to compute required dimensions or properties for heat insulation or conduction. In some special cases, the goal is to find the value of a parameter in a thermal problem that produces branching solutions, as in the onset of Bénard-Marangoni convection when heating a thin liquid layer from below (bifurcation analysis).

Heat-transfer problems may arise in typical thermal applications, like heating and cooling, e.g. the defrosting problem in refrigeration and air conditioning, due to thermal insulation of the ice layer (frosty ice conductivity can be as low as that of wood), admits several solutions, all of them controlled by heat transfer. Any temperature-measure involves some heat transfer problem. Besides, many other heat-transfer problems come from non-thermal pursuits, for instance:

- Cooling electronic equipment: Microprocessor computing power is limited by the difficulty to evacuate the energy dissipation (a Pentium 4 CPU at 2 GHz in 0.18 μm technology must dissipate 76 W in an environment at 40°C without surpassing 70°C). Most electronics failures are due to overheating by improper ventilation or fan malfunction. Bipolar junctions in silicon wafers fail to keep the energy gap between valence and conduction electrons above some 400 K, but at any working temperature there is some dopant diffusion and bond-material creep, causing some random failures, with an event-rate doubling every 10°C increase, depending on the reliability demanded, bipolar junctions are usually limited to work at 90–100°C. Electrical powers up to a few watts can usually be dissipated by natural convection to ambient air, and up to few hundred watts by forcing air with fans (cheap, but noisy and wasteful), and liquid cooling is usually needed beyond 1 kW systems.

- Cooling rubbing parts: In a mechanical transmission, the oil loses its lubricating capacity if overheated, in a hydraulic coupling or converter, the fluid leaks under the pressure created. In an electric motor, overheating causes deterioration of the insulation. In an overheated internal combustion engine, the pistons may seize in the cylinders.
- Lamp design: The size of an incandescent lamp is governed by heat transfer (the filament needs a bulb to keep away from oxygen, but the bulb-size is large in glass bulbs to avoid glass softening by high temperatures, and small in halogen lamps to be hot enough to maintain the halogen cycle inside (to avoid deposition at a cold bulb), in spite of the little size for the electrical resistance R that must be fed at low voltage for the same power $P = VI = V^2/R$).
- Materials processing like casting, welding, hot shaping, crystal growth, etc. Materials machining is limited by the difficulty to evacuate the energy dissipation. And not only engineering materials: food processing and cooking, dish washing, cloth washing, drying and ironing, and many other house-hold tasks, are dominated by heat transfer.
- Energy conversion devices, like solar collectors, combustors, nuclear reactors, etc.
- Environmental sciences like meteorology, oceanography, pollutant dispersion, forest fires, urban planning, building, etc.

Relaxation Time

The two usual limits for thermal interaction in Thermodynamics are the isothermal process and the adiabatic process, the former corresponding to the limit of very slow heat transfer due to an infinitesimal temperature difference along an infinite time, and the latter corresponding to a quick process with negligible heat transfer. In Heat Transfer, however, we are interested on finite-time process, and a basic question is to know the thermal inertia of the system, i.e. how long the heating or cooling process takes, usually with the intention to modify it, either to make the system more permeable to heat, more insulating, or more 'capacitive', to retard a periodic cooling/heating wave.

When the heat flow can be imposed, as when heating water with a submerged electrical resistor, the minimum time required is obtained from the energy balance, $dH/dt = Q = mc\Delta T/\Delta t$, e.g. to heat 1 kg of water from 15 to 95°C with a 1000 W heater, the minimum time is $\Delta t = mc\Delta T/\dot{Q} = 1{\cdot}4200{\cdot}(95-15)/1000 = 336$ s (the actual value in practice depends on the way of heating, the geometry of the vessel, and the way temperature is measured, typically, 30% more time is required with highly efficient types of heaters like a microwave oven or induction heaters, and up to 100% more time with inefficient heaters as external electrical resistors).

For the case where the heat flux is not imposed but a temperature gradient is imposed, an order-of magnitude analysis of the energy balance, $dH/dt = \dot{Q} \rightarrow mc\Delta T/\Delta t = KA\Delta T$, shows that the relaxation time is of the order $\Delta t = mc/(KA)$, and, depending on the dominant heat-transfer mode in K, two extreme cases can be considered: solids in well-stirred fluids (convection dominates, and evolution is driven by conduction), and highly conducting solids (convection-driven case).

Conduction Driven Case (Convection Dominates)

Problems where the thermal conductance from a solid system to a surrounding fluid, $K = h$, is much larger than the thermal conductance within the solid, $K \approx k/L$, i.e. where $Bi \equiv hL/k \to \infty$ (Bi is a non-dimensional parameter called Biot number). In this case, the boundary condition imposes a constant temperature on the body surface, and the time Δt it takes for heat to penetrate to the centre of the body, of characteristic length L (volume divided by surface), i.e. the relaxation time may be guessed from (4.2–4.7):

$$\Delta t \approx \frac{\Delta H}{\dot{Q}} \approx \frac{mc\Delta T}{KA\Delta T} \approx \frac{mc\Delta T}{kA\dfrac{\Delta T}{L}} \approx \frac{\rho L^3 c}{kL^2\dfrac{1}{L}} = \frac{\rho c L^2}{k} = \frac{L^2}{a} \qquad \ldots(4.9)$$

where, the ΔT from initial to final states of the system has been assumed to be of the same magnitude of the representative ΔT from the system to the surroundings (although the former is not uniform and the latter is not constant but decreases with time). Thus, the time it takes for the centre to reached a midtemperature representative of the forcing is L^2/a, i.e. increases with the square of the size, decreases with thermal diffusivity, and is independent of temperature.

Convection Driven Case (Conduction Dominates)

Problems where the thermal transmittance within the system, $K=k/L$, is much larger than the thermal transmittance to the surroundings, $K=h$, (i.e. where $Bi \equiv L/k \to 0$). In this case, the temperature within the body can be assumed spatially uniform and the relaxation time may be guessed from (4.2–4.7):

$$\Delta t \approx \frac{\Delta H}{\dot{Q}} \approx \frac{mc\Delta T}{KA\Delta T} \approx \frac{mc}{hA} \approx \frac{\rho L^3 c}{hL^2} = \frac{\rho c L}{h} \qquad \ldots(4.10)$$

where, as before, the ΔT from initial to final states of the system has been assumed to be of the same magnitude of the representative ΔT from the system to the surroundings. The difference now is that the convective coefficient with the environment is not a material property but depends a lot on the motion outside, and that now the relaxation time is directly proportional to the size L and not its square function.

Heat Flux

Thermodynamics is concerned with heat accounting $Q=\Delta E-W$, but Heat Transfer is focussed on rates, so that one question is to know the relaxation time for a given amount of heat, and another question is the flow-rate function considered here (yet, a third one would be to find the materials and geometry that satisfy a prescribed flow-rate or relaxation time).

Typical heat-flux problems mostly consist on finding the heat flux corresponding to prescribed temperatures at the boundaries of a given geometry and known material. In many circumstances, the simple steady state, one-dimensional planar geometry, may be a good approximation, and in other cases the uniform-temperature approximation is acceptable, for more complicated problems, the heat-flux problem must be found concurrently with the temperature field.

Temperature Field

Although in many thermal problems (and even in some heat transfer problems) temperature is assumed uniform in a system (as in the hot-potato problem just explained, and in many heat convection and radiation problems), temperature is never uniform in practice (equilibrium systems are just limit models, we live in a non-equilibrium world). The heat equation (4.4), with the appropriate initial and boundary conditions, can provide a spatial temperature distribution at every time. Many times, particularly in thermal control problems, only the extreme temperatures are sought. Living beings have very short temperature ranges (human cannot support body temperatures outside T=(310±4) K, and typical electrical batteries deteriorate outside T=(300±30) K. Refractory materials are those material able to withstand high temperatures (say >1500 K), without failure by fusion or decomposition, they are usually classified according to chemical behaviour, as acid refractories (fireclay), neutral refractories (coal, graphite, refractory metals and metal carbides), and basic refractories (metal oxides).

Dimensioning for Thermal Design

The goal of most heat transfer modelling is to find the temperature field and heat fluxes in a material domain, given a set of constraints: general heat equation (e.g. set as a partial differential equation, PDE), boundary conditions (BC), initial conditions (IC), distribution of sources or sinks (SS), etc. In a few cases the goal is not in the direct problem (given the PDE+BC+IC+SS, find the temperature field), but on the inverse problem: given the T-field and some aspects of PDE+BC+IC+SS, find some missing parameters remaining (identification problem).

Perhaps the very simplified, yet very important, problem of one-dimensional steady heat transfer between two bodies, separated by a solid layer, can make more clear the several different goals in heat transfer: heat fluxes, T-fields, material characterisation, and dimensioning:

- $Q = kA\,(T_1 - T_2)/L$, i.e. find the heat flux for a given set-up and T-field.
- $T_1 = T + QL/kA)$, i.e. find the temperature corresponding to a given heat flux and set-up. Notice that our thermal sense (part of the touch sense) works more along balancing the heat flux than measuring the contact temperature, what depends on thermal conductivity of the object; that is why Galileo masterly stated that we should ascribe the same temperature to different objects in a room, like wood, metal, or stone, contrary to our sense feeling.
- $k = \dot{Q}\,L/(A\Delta T)$, i.e. find an appropriate material that allows a prescribed heat flux with a given T-field in a given geometry.
- $L = kA\,(T_1 - T_2)\,/Q$, i.e. find the thickness of insulation to achieve a certain heat flux with a given T-field in a prescribed geometry.

THERMAL DESIGN AND THERMAL ANALYSIS

Thermal Design

Design is an intricate multidisciplinary top-down activity. Thermal design, in heat-transfer problems, aims at providing a suitable configuration (materials, components, geometry, arrangement), amongst different possibilities, trying to optimise the cost/benefit. For instance, a thermal designer may be asked to provide solutions to keep a computer CPU dissipating 70 W without becoming hotter than 70°C, amongst the different possibilities, the most common one now-a-days is to leave some free-room nearby and blow air with a fan (with the associated noise and dissipation increase), but using a heat-pipe to efficiently-connect the internal chip with an external ample sink is already taking over (e.g. in laptops), high-power-dissipation devices may demand liquid cooling loops or even phase change loops (which might be expandable in some cases, similar to animal sweating). Thermal design requires a broad knowledge of the subject (and related subjects), and is left to a later stage in training, except for simple 'design' problems where the configuration is already given and only a parameter of the configuration is to be optimised. The most common endeavour for beginners is to solve well-defined thermal problems, i.e. to perform some heat transfer analysis to find temperatures, heat fluxes, or relaxation times.

Thermal Analysis

To solve a heat-transfer problem in practice, to find the temperature field and heat fluxes, like for any other engineering task, there are not magic recipes, but sound understanding of the subject matter. The practitioner should not compile a set of graphics, tables and formulas, much less the student. On the contrary, they should master the principles of heat transfer, and have an idea of the different tools available. Several steps are usually taken to solve a heat-transfer problem:

1. Mathematical modelling of the physical problem. This is the most creative phase in solving a problem. Sometimes, physical analogies help to build the mathematical model. The electrical analogy consists on taking thermal resistances as resistors, thermal capacities as capacitors, heat sources as intensity sources, the thermal environment as electrical ground, and applying Kirchhoff's law to the network. It is important, however, to keep in mind that analogies are just analogies, not identities, and care is needed to avoid stretching them beyond their applicability.
2. Mathematical solution of the mathematical problem. Although it is just a mathematical burden, engineers must be aware of the available methods of solution, and their pros and cons, in order to direct the previous idealisation towards feasible, available, affordable, efficient and solvable problems. The two basic approaches are:
   - Analytical solutions, which gives a whole and concise parametric solution, but only in extremely idealised problems (only of academic interest or to check numerical simulations).
   - Numerical solutions, which gives particular solutions to any practical problem, but without an overview of the influence of the parameters (several particular cases must be solved to have an idea of the influences).
3. Analysis of the results (analytical or numerical) and physical interpretation. In some circumstances, particularly with new or complicated problems, some experimental tests, where the temperature field and heat fluxes are metered in an instrumented sample, are required to provide evidence of the goodness of the mathematical modelling.

In actual practice, heat-transfer problems are solved numerically by using a large commercial computer package, usually an integrated fluid-thermal-structural CFD-package, or at least with inputs and outputs compatible with main commercial packages for mechanical and structural analysis.

Mathematical Modelling

The mathematical modelling is the idealisation of the physical problem until a well-defined set of (mathematical) constraints, representing the main features, is established. Mathematical modelling is required not only in analytical work but also in actual heat-transfer practice, where a large commercial computer package is used, the user has to identify and approximate the actual geometry of the system, has to select the most appropriate terms from the list of supplementary effects in the PDE, must approximate the boundary conditions according to specific package procedures, and, most important of all, the user has to give knowledgeable feed-back on possible weaknesses and improvements, since heat-transfer analysis, as any other engineering activity, is an iterative process that must be refined as needed, effort proportional to expected utility (a common error of beginners, both at school and at work, is to spend too much effort and time pursuing very precise numerical solutions to 'what if' preliminary problems that are discarded soon afterwards, or even before being finished). Mathematical modelling is the most creative part in the whole process of solving heat-transfer problems. Modelling usually implies approximating the geometry, materials properties, and the heat transfer equations.

Modelling the Geometry

In thermal problems, the first task is to identify the system under study. On one side, the geometry is idealised, assuming perfect planar, cylindrical or spherical surfaces, or a set of points and a given interpolation function. Besides the edges or boundaries (which are usually fixed, as in Fig. 4.1, except in some special cases like the Stefan problem of moving phase-change), further information is needed to know if the region or domain of interest lies inside, outside, or in between boundaries. Additionally, several numerical methods of solving heat-transfer problems, make use of a subdivision of the domain in small sub-domains called elements, and procedures are needed to carry out an automatic meshing and the associated numbering. Location procedures are also needed to know to which element a given point belongs, which are the neighbour elements, and so on.

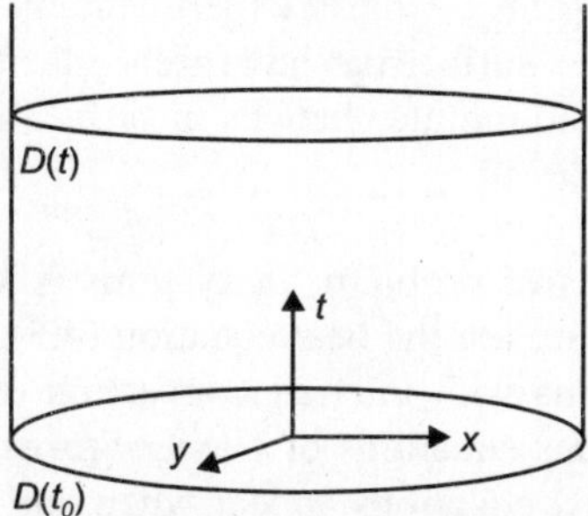

Fig. 4.1: The space-time domain is divided in the spatial domain or boundary, *D* (that may be one-, two- or three-dimensional, and is usually assumed independent of time in thermal problems, $D(t)=D(t_0)$, and the time domain (that is one-dimensional, with a clear start, $t=t_0$, and a clear bias, $t>t_0$).

The most complicated case occurs when boundary conditions are imposed on free-moving boundaries, i.e. surfaces with a priori unknown locations which separate geometric regions with different characteristics, as in heat-transfer problems with phase change, e.g. freezing of liquids or moist solids, casting, or polymerisation. This type of moving-boundary-value problems is known as Stefan problem, because Jozef Stefan was the first, in 1890, to analyse and solve it, when studying the rate of ice formation on freezing water, although a similar problem was first stated in 1831 in a paper by Lamé and Clapeyron. Phase-change materials are very efficient thermal-energy stores, either to accommodate heat input to heat output, or even to get rid of large amounts of thermal energy by ablation. In the normal case of phase-change accumulators, only the solid/liquid phase-change is considered, and with some buffering space to avoid large pressure build-up, this void fraction, plus the usual metal mesh used to increase thermal conductance, makes thermal modelling complicated.

Modelling Materials Properties

Once the system is defined, its materials properties must be idealised, because density, thermal conductivity, thermal capacity, and so on, depend on the base materials, their impurity contents, actual temperatures, etc. Most of the times, materials properties are modelled as uniform in space and constant in time, for each material, but, whether this model is appropriate, or even the right selection of the constantproperty values, requires insight. Unless experimentally measured, thermal conductivities from generic materials may have uncertainties of some 10%. Most metals in practice are really alloys, and thermal conductivities of alloys are usually much lower than those of the components, it is good to keep in mind that conductivities for pure iron, mild steel, and stainless steel, are (80, 50, 15) W/(m·K), respectively. Besides, many common materials (like graphite, wood, holed bricks, reinforced concrete), are highly anisotropic, with directional heat conductivities, particularly all modern composite materials. And measuring k is not simple at all: in fluids, avoiding convection is difficult, in metals, minimising thermal-contact resistance is difficult, in insulators, minimising heat losses relative to the small heat flows implied is difficult, the most accurate procedures to find k are based on measuring thermal diffusivity $a=k/(\rho c)$ in transient experiments.

Unless experimentally measured, convective coefficients computed from generic correlations may have uncertainties of some 10%, whereas those taken from 'typical value' tabulations are just coarse orders of magnitude, e.g. when it is said that typical h-values for natural convection in air are 5.20 W/(m^2·K) and one assumes h=10 W/(m^2·K). Unless experimentally measured on the spot, absorptance coefficients and emissivities of a given surface can have great uncertainties, which in the case of metallic surfaces may be double or half, due to minute changes in surface finishing and weathering.

Modelling the Heat Equations

The equations defining a heat-transfer problem, in systems where thermal conduction is the only heattransfer mechanism in the interior, are the heat equation (4.5), and its bounding conditions (initial and boundary conditions). In systems with internal convection, the above equations must be solved concurrently with the fluid mechanics equations of Navier-Stokes. In systems with internal radiation, very complicated integral-differential equations appear when one considers spectral absorptances and multidirectional dispersions. Here we restrict the rest of the analysis to conductive systems, with convective and/or radiative effects entering only as boundary conditions.

Perhaps the key point to remember when actually doing the mathematical modelling of thermal problems is that it is nonsense to start demanding great accuracy in the solution when there is not such accuracy in the input parameters and constraints. Without specific experimental tests, there are big uncertainties even in materials properties, like thermal conductivity of metal alloys, entrance and blocking effects in convection, and particularly in thermo-optical properties.

Analysis of Results

The analysis of the results may be quite different in the case of a closed analytical solution than for the case of a numerical solution. In the last case, the interpretation of the numerical solution to judge its validity, accuracy and sensitivity to input parameters can be quite involved. The direct solution usually gives just the set of values of the function at the nodes, what is difficult to grasp for humans in raw format (a list of numbers or, for regular meshes, a matrix). Some basic post-processing tools are needed for:

- Visualisation of the function by graphic display upon the geometry or at user-selected cuttings. Unfortunately many commercial routines, besides the obvious geometry overlay, only present the function values as a linear sequence of node values and don't allow the user to select cuts. Additional capabilities as contour mapping and pseudo-colour mapping are most welcome.

- Computation of function derivatives (and visualisation). Some times only the function is computed, and the user is interested in some special derivatives of the function, as when heat fluxes are needed, besides temperatures.
- Feedback on the meshing, refining it if there are large gradients, or large residues in the overall thermal balance. It is without saying that the user should do all the initial trials (what usually takes the largest share of the effort) with a coarse mesh, to shorten the feedback period.
- Precision and sensitivity analysis by running some trivial cases (e.g. relaxing some boundary condition) and by running 'what-if' type of trials, changing some material property, boundary condition and even the geometry.

HEAT TRANSFER AND SOLID FOODS

Table 4.1 gives an overview of heat transfer processes related to solid food. This table also introduces the different mechanisms of transfer which will be dealt with in this chapter.

Convection

Convection is the most common means of heat transfer used for heating solid foodstuffs. This means that heat is transferred between a fluid and the solid interface. The heat transfer medium is in most cases air, water or an air/moisture mixture. Oil is also used, for instance, in deep fat frying. The dimensionless parameters may be used for calculating the heat transfer between solid foods and a gas or a liquid. The dimensionless relationships have their limitations as it is only the mean values that are obtained. The heat transfer coefficients, for example, vary with time during the process and with location on the product surface.

Simultaneous heat and mass transfer during convection

For all solid foodstuffs containing water which are processed by convection heat transfer, there is a coupled heat and mass transfer and the purpose of the process is to attain a certain degree of moisture (depending on the aim of the process). The consequence of this is that the rate-controlling step differs between processes. This is also illustrated in Table 4.1.

The coupled heat and mass transfer through the boundary layer may be described as follows. It is supposed that the surrounding medium is air or air mixed with vapour. It is also supposed that there are no temperature, humidity or velocity gradients in the air bulk. Heat is transferred to the solid material and is used to evaporate water on the surface, to superheat this vapour and to heat the product with the help of the thermal properties of the food. The heating process may be divided into four periods from the mass transfer point of view. These periods are the preheating period, the constant-rate period and the first and the second falling-rate periods which are dependent on the mass flux.

During the preheating period the surface temperature of the foodstuff is heated from the initial temperature to the wet-bulb temperature of the air. During this period water vapour will condense on the surface until the dewpoint temperature is reached due to the mechanisms responsible for the condensation of water in air. Heat is released and aids further heat transfer. Thus, as this is a very effective transfer mechanism, the surface temperature will rise rapidly to the dewpoint. As the dewpoint temperature and the wet-bulb temperature are relatively close, this period is short. During the preheating period there will be a slight gain in weight of the product due to the condensation of water on the surface, i.e. there is some mass transfer to the product.

Table 4.1: Heat transfer process in solid foodstuffs.

Process	*Transfer mechanism*	*Heat transfer*	*Temp. of media (°C) media*	*Fluid velocity (m/s)*	*Products*	*Aim of process*	*Governing transfer mechanism*
Drying	Convection Conduction Radiation	Air Metal	30–300	< 5	Fish, fruit, vegetables	Decrease water content	Internal mass transfer rate
Baking	Convection	Air	150–250	2–10	Meat, bread	Decrease a_w on surface	Internal heat transfer rate
	Radiation	Electromagnetic waves				Certain time-temperature dose	
Deep fat frying	Convection	Oil	150–200	–	Meat, fish, potatoes	Decrease a_w on the surface Certain time-temperature dose at the center	Internal heat transfer rate
Reheating	Convection Microwaves	Air Electromagnetic energy (915 MHz, 2450 MHz)	110–150	Low	Meat, ready-to-serve-foods	Heat the product to eating temperature	Internal heat transfer rate
Cooling	Convection Conduction	Water Air Metal	0–8	Low	Almost all foods	Cool the product to below a certain low temperature above 0°C, regulated by law	External heat transfer rate or internal
Boiling Blanching	Convection	Steam Water	80–100	–	Vegetables, meat, fish	Certain time-temperature dose at the center	Internal heat transfer rate
	Microwave	Electromagnetic energy (915 MHz, 2400 MHz)					

(Cont'd...)

Process	*Transfer mechanism*	*Heat transfer*	*Temp. of media (°C) media*	*Fluid velocity (m/s)*	*Products*	*Aim of process*	*Governing transfer mechanism*
Sterilisation	Conduction	In package Metal	100–150		Meat, fish, vegetables	Certain time-temperature dose at the thermal center to kill micro-organisms	Internal heat transfer rate
	Convection	Air Steam	100–150	≤ 5			
	Microwaves	Electromagnetic energy					
Pasteurisation	Conduction	Packages Metal	70–90	–	Meat, fish, vegetables	Certain time-temperature dose to kill micro-organisms	Internal heat transfer rate
	Microwaves	Electromagnetic energy					
Freezing	Convection	Air, N_2 CO_2	–20– (–40)	< 5	Meat, fish, vegetables	Lower temperature to about –20°C for storage	Heat of solidification
	Conduction	Metal surface					
Thawing	Convection	Water Air	5–20	< 5	Meat, fish, vegetables	Heat above 0°C	Heat of melting
	Microwaves						

When the wet-bulb temperature is reached on the surface the constant rate period starts. During this period water is evaporated directly from the surface and transported through the boundary layer to the surrounding air. First the water that condensed during the preheating period evaporates and secondly water that is transported from the interior to the surface is vapourised and transferred to the surroundings. This means that during this period the transport from the surface to the air is much slower than the transport inside the product, i.e. there is a decrease in mass transfer rate when the water reaches the surface. During the constant-rate period the mass transfer is totally governed by the resistance caused by the boundary layer on the surface. The surface temperature during this period is equal to the wet-bulb temperature of the air. All heat is used to evaporate water from the surface of the product. After the preheating period evaporation takes place from the heated moist food and vapour is forced to pass the boundary layer.

Conduction

In some solid-food processes conduction is used for heat transfer, i.e. the foodstuff is placed in contact with either heated or chilled solid surfaces. These surfaces may be made of different materials. They are heated via electrical elements, condensing steam or chilled by melting ice depending on the process temperature. The processes concerned are, e.g. frying, cooling, freezing and drying.

The advantage of using conduction as a method of heat transfer compared with convection, especially via air, is that it makes the process more effective and faster. The heat transfer coefficient is higher. Conductive heat transfer is limited by the geometry of the foodstuff. It is often difficult to process configurations other than flat slices. In solid foodstuffs in which liquid or vapour are mobile, the mass transport behaviour is the same regardless of the external heat transfer mechanism.

Contact frying is used for frying meat and fish products. The purpose of this process is the same as for roasting meat, i.e. to produce a crust on the surface and to cook the product. Heat is transferred from solid matter in direct contact with the products. Sometimes the heat is transferred via a thin film of fat. The thickness of this film varies and local air and/or vapour bubbles may be present. Heating normally takes place from one side only at a time, i.e. the product has to be turned over at certain time intervals. In some cases double-sided frying is used. The different periods correspond to: (i) heating of the surface to 100°C, (ii) the crust formation period, and (iii) the period when the surface temperature decreases and the center temperature reaches its final value. For these processes period (i) is short due to the high heat transfer coefficient.

Fluidised beds

A fluidised bed consists of particles flowing in an upward stream of fluid. The system behaves like a liquid and by inclining the bed slightly the surface of the bed will still be essentially horizontal but the particles can be made to move towards the exit end. In food processing fluidised beds are mainly used in drying and freezing. Calculations of such processes are complicated by the fact that the function of the gas is not only to fluidise the particles but also to transfer heat and water.

There is a minimum, critical fluid velocity below which there is no movement of the particles. When the velocity is increased the bed starts to expand, at still greater velocities the particles will reach a turbulent type of flow. There is also an upper limit above which particles begin to leave the bed with the fluid. In a gas-fluidised bed part of the gas passes through the bed as bubbles. These bubbles are maintained through the bed and on leaving the bed they create a phenomenon which gives an impression that the bed is boiling.

Cooling of food products

Natural or free convection is an important feature during cooling of agricultural products. Natural convection is caused by density differences in a fluid, in this case air, surrounding the product. The density differences are a result of differences in temperature at different positions in the (silo) product. The temperature difference may be induced either by conductive heating via the container surfaces or by cold air entering the silo from the bottom. Further, natural convection may be superimposed on forced convection if air is forced through the silo. Many agricultural food products generate heat during storage and a temperature difference occurs resulting in natural convection.

Methods of Measuring Convective Heat Transfer Coefficients

Heat and mass transfer coefficients may be estimated in different ways. As shown earlier, the effect of the mass transfer to and from the solid foodstuff differs from process to process. Methods of measuring the heat transfer coefficient may be divided into three categories:

1. Steady-state measurement of the surface temperature.
2. Measurement of transient temperature as a body cools or heats.
3. Measurement of heat flux at the surface of the body.

The heat flux is measured using either an electrical resistance heater placed at the center of the body or an induction coil. The surface temperature is calculated by averaging the surface temperatures in the system. The heat transfer coefficient is then calculated by means of Newton's law of cooling. This method will give the best estimate of surface heat transfer coefficients if the conditions of the test can be kept constant and no mass transfer occurs. It is, however, extremely difficult to use this method for food products as their physical properties change continuously during the process. It is also difficult to obtain reliable measurements of the surface temperature.

The second category of methods is that based on transient temperature measurements. This means that the temperature variation in the product is measured after an initial change in the ambient temperature. This category contains essentially two different types of methods. In one of these the temperature of the object is assumed to be uniform. The third category, i.e. measurement of heat flux at the surface of the body, necessitates using a sensor that can detect heat flux at the surface. Also, the surface temperature is measured as a function of time. However, the mere presence of a measuring device alters the surface of the body, thus making the readings approximate.

Heat Transfer Within Solid Foodstuffs

Conduction heat transfer

Heat transfer within a solid foodstuff is controlled by the heat conduction in the food solid, the surface temperature and the thermal properties of the food. The thickness is the most important variable in the heat transfer calculations, so it should be accurately measured and controlled. This is often difficult because food products change their dimensions as a result of shrinking, swelling, etc. The boundary conditions are often limited by 100°C, the boundary between crust and crumb. In heat transfer calculations it is often adequate to maintain the surface temperature at 100°C for the whole process.

Heat and mass transfer in foods

Heat transfer within solid food is, in almost all cases, coupled to a transport of water especially for processes where the product is not packaged. In this section, therefore, simultaneous heat and mass transfer are discussed in more detail with respect to parallel pure heat transmission. In the extreme case this means a drying operation, but in operations where only heating is intended some transfer of water also takes place, e.g. leakage in boiling and blanching. The simultaneous appearance of both heat and mass transfer makes the theoretical treatment more complicated and a complete analytical solution to the problem is not available. The fact that the physical properties of the material vary with varying temperature and moisture content adds to the complexity of the problem. Therefore, simplifications have to be made and different models are presented, each of which is specific with regard to the material and the boundary conditions.

An alternative shrinking-core model may be described in the following way for any solid foodstuff. This model is used for operations where a dry shell or a crust is formed on the product surface.

The flow of water inside the evaporation zone is assumed to take place only in the liquid phase. The driving potentials are the moisture gradient and the effect of denaturation of proteins ('drip'). It is assumed that there is no vapour flow. Drip means that, when the proteins denature, the structure will change and water will be exuded from the product. The flow of water derives from both the internal part (crumb) and the evaporation zone. The amount of water removed from the crumb depends on the product properties. Heat transfer in the crumb is due to conduction.

As described earlier, some heat and mass transfer models assume that the content in the dry shell is in equilibrium with the vapour pressure at the corresponding temperature according to the sorption isotherm. If heat conduction in the product is high compared with the heat transfer coefficient, the temperature is uniform in the whole shell and the water content is constant throughout the shell. In the baking of bread and roasting of meat the intention is to form a dry brown shell on the surface, the crust. Mass transport inside the evaporation zone (the crumb) takes place mainly as a result of concentration differences and in the form of liquid. Heat transported to the crumb in a meatloaf is used to heat the product. In the baking of bread a porous structure is formed in the crumb due to volume changes. Large pores filled with water and water vapour are formed. Due to temperature differences in these, some water is transported towards the center. Water is evaporated at the higher temperature and condensed at the lower temperature. If this mechanism was not present in bread the heat transport would be lower and similar to that in an insulating material. The heat transport in bread is relatively fast. The water content at the center of the dough is sometimes lower than at the center of the baked product.

Heat transfer in solid foods by means of microwaves

Microwave heating is used in industry for the partial thawing of frozen blocks of meat (915 MHz) and in smaller quantities, for different cooking and drying applications (both 2450 and 915 MHz). The power used is generally between 20 and 100 kW. The penetration depth of microwaves is limited to a few centimeters in most thawed and moist foods. Thus calculations of the combined heat transfer of the microwave energy and of conventional conduction and convection will be needed to predict and explain microwave heating of solid foods.

Freezing and thawing

The freezing process may be divided into three periods:

1. Precooling.
2. Change of phase.
3. Tempering.

The corresponding periods in thawing are:

1. Tempering.
2. Change of phase.
3. Heating.

In freezing of solid foods the phase change period starts at different times in different volume elements of the product due to temperature gradients that occur during the precooling period. The phase starts at the surface and moves towards the center.

The duration of the phase-change period is longer for the thawing process than for freezing. This is due to the fact that the thermal diffusivity in the thawed part of the product is much lower than in the frozen part, i.e. when thawing heat has to be transported through a part of thawed product before reaching the phase-change zone. The tempering period during freezing starts when the latent heat is negligible compared with heat conduction in the product. In this period the temperature decreases considerably. In solid food products there is no distinct solidification or melting point as there is for example in pure water. In foodstuffs such as meat this temperature may be identified by a plot of percentage frozen water versus temperature.

When the surface has reached the final freezing point the second phase-change period starts. During this period the product has a layer of frozen material and a layer of mixed frozen and unfrozen material. When the ice front has reached the center of the product the tempering period starts. This last period ceases when the final temperature is reached in the whole product. The mass transfer during freezing is of minor importance and the rate-controlling process during freezing is the transport of the ice front through the product, i.e. the phase-change periods.

Heat Transfer and Liquid Foods

There are many processes responsible for heat transfer in food products such as convection, conduction, infrared radiation, ultraviolet radiation, microwave radiation, electric resistance and friction. During conventional practical processes only convection and conduction are responsible for the equilibration of temperature gradients once they are created by the heat transfer, from internal heat generation or external heat supply. Conductive heat transfer consists of motion on a molecular level, while convective heat transfer is achieved through several phenomena, which differ in degree of efficiency.

Chapter 5

Automation in Food Industry

INTRODUCTION

The food industry has traditionally lagged behind other industries in adopting new technology, and plant automation is no exception. However, rapid advances in computer technology and heightened expectations of consumers and regulatory agencies for improved food quality and safety have forced the food industry to consider automation of most manufacturing processes. Though the food industry presents many unique challenges to complete automation, the industry has been successful in putting many automatic processes into place.

The next significant development will be to integrate these 'islands of automation' into an overall system of plant automation, from receiving vision, expert systems, computer integrated manufacturing, flexible manufacturing systems, systems engineering, etc. have enabled integration of many batch operations into an overall manufacturing system design to provide on-line and continuous control capability. This trend will continue at an even faster pace in the next several years.

The automation of manufacturing plants has been actively pursued for more than 50 years. And it will continue to be so, even more aggressively, during the next 50 years. The increased zeal in industrial automation is mainly due to the explosive growth in computer hardware and software technology. As computers invade almost every aspect of our daily lives, the public at large has come to expect a high level of automation in every facet of the manufacturing processes.

The extent of industrial automation depends a great deal on the type of industry. The automobile and semiconductor industries represent the most mature in adopting plant automation principles with nearly all processes having been automated and fairly well integrated. At the other end of the spectrum is perhaps the food industry, representing lower levels of automation, which has traditionally lagged behind in adopting technological advances. The current level of automation in the food industry has been described as 'islands of automation'. Nonetheless, the food industry now ranks among the fastest growing segments for plant automation. For example, the food industry is among the top ten in using machine vision technology, a key component in plant automation. However, most systems are isolated, batch-type operations that target a specific task. In order for automation to be successful, it must be integrated into the overall manufacturing system design and provide on-line, continuous control capability.

NEED FOR AUTOMATION

The need to automate industrial processes is driven by several key requirements for competitive success and, in some industries, viability of the manufacturing plants. They can be listed as those needing to improve productivity, product quality, and profitability. This is shown in Fig. 5.1.

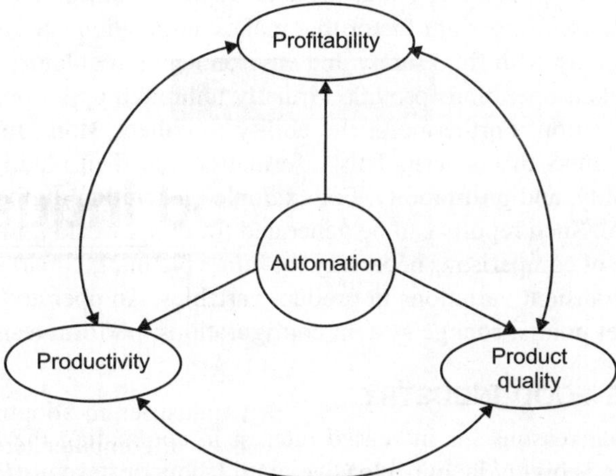

Fig. 5.1: Plant automation can improve productivity, product quality, and profitability.

Improved Productivity

Plant productivity may be defined as the quantity of end products manufactured per unit of operating parameters – plant size, number of workers, time of operation, etc. Therefore, productivity is directly related to how efficiently the input resources are utilised in translating them into marketable end products. This is possible because automation allows for efficient scheduling of work flow and labour use. The ability to maintain good records and information about past processes can clearly highlight areas that can be targeted for a more efficient allocation of resources.

One plant reported a 30 per cent increase in plant productivity by using three discrete microprocessor-based controllers designed to perform all continuous loops involving complex, integrated algorithms, valve interlocking, and some sequencing. Similar controls can also be used to optimise formulations, production scheduling, and process modelling.

Improved Product Quality

Quality assurance is one of the most important goals of any industry. The ability to manufacture high quality products consistently is the basis for success in the highly competitive food industry. High quality products encourage customer loyalty and results in an expanding market share. Quality assurance methods used in the food industry have traditionally involved human visual inspection. Such methods are tedious, laborious, time-consuming, and inconsistent.

As plant productivity increased and quality tolerance tightened, it became necessary for the food industry to employ automatic methods for quality assurance and quality control. In fact, this aspect of food manufacture is one of the areas that has received the most attention in terms of automation. Thanks to advances in computer vision technology, substantial changes have been implemented in food plants to facilitate automatic food quality evaluation.

Improved Profitability

Increased profit is perhaps most important from the perspective of management. Improved profitability not only adds to shareholder value but also allows management to invest strategically in expanding plant operations, increasing product lines, further improving product quality, etc. As discussed previously, automation helps to improve productivity and product quality. Both of these contribute directly to improved profitability. Another important factor that makes automation extremely critical for the food industry is the need to comply with food safety and environmental regulatory agencies.

Computer-controlled plant operations provide virtually unlimited opportunities to maintain records of all events in plant operation. Furthermore, the ability to collect, store, retrieve, and process data allows plants to identify areas of concern. This information can then readily be used for improved productivity, product quality, and profitability. For example, generating ingredient usage reports helps in active inventory control. Such reports can be generated for daily, weekly, monthly, and yearly use to give a quantitative picture of comparisons necessary for future planning. Smart systems can also monitor and record periodic and transient variations in product variables. An operator can use these records to monitor real time, alter set points, change system configurations, perform testing, etc.

UNIQUENESS OF THE FOOD INDUSTRY

One of the most important reasons for increased interest in automating the food industry is its cost structure. Food processing is highly labour-intensive, with labour costs at anything up to 50 per cent of the product cost. Improving productivity and reducing labour costs will therefore have a significant impact on profitability. Much of the manual work in food processing requires rapid, repetitive, and monotonous movement and, consequently, low levels of motivation are often found. This leads to poor quality control and a high incidence of industrial accidents. The repetitive nature of the work has resulted in a substantial medical cost to the industry. Automating repetitive tasks will improve quality control and efficiency and reduce the high level of accidents.

One of the most important obstacles in the automation of food manufacturing is the biological variation in size, shape, and homogeneity of the raw materials. Some materials (e.g. dairy) lend themselves readily to automatic processing because the raw material (milk) can be handled in bulk. Accordingly, the dairy industry is among the most automated. But materials such as fruits, vegetables, meat, etc. need to be handled on a more individual unit basis. This has hampered automation tremendously. Thus, food industry automation requires a level of flexibility uncommon to other mature industries.

Additional problems are due to the lack of complete physical and chemical characterisation of foods. Even when complete information is available, the raw material or the end product can change. Changes in the raw material arise from the introduction of new varieties and/or variations in agronomic conditions. The end product can change due to continual reformulation of product lines to gain market share. Application of computer vision technology is substantially changing the quality evaluation tasks in the food industry. In addition to a products physical characteristics, factors such as microbiological and biochemical concerns place additional limitations on handling and processing procedures employed. The mechanical, thermal, and sensory properties of food materials also require specific limits on the nature and extent of processing steps. These constraints complicate process automation.

Materials that are not well defined in size or shape are often presented in a random, unconstrained orientation. They must often be handled carefully to prevent damage and thus challenge the capabilities of current technology. Therefore, there are few examples of ‘hard’ automation – types that give little or no allowance for variability. For example, automatic equipment for peeling fruit still relies heavily on standard shapes and sizes. Some excellent examples of automation include processing and packaging of fresh eggs and dairy products. Although most baking is done in automatic ovens, baked products are still manually graded and packaged. In the poultry industry, automation is possible as long as the birds are graded into different weight classes. Development in this industry can offer automatic slaughtering, plucking, washing, decapitating, and eviscerating of poultry carcasses at a fairly high rate. Another commercial operation is automatic fish processing. An automated butchering system separates the edible loin portions of transverse tuna slices. Each slice is scanned by a computer vision system, and control signals are transmitted to a cutting arm that then separates the edible portion. Vision systems have also been successfully used in automating sweet corn processing.

Food plant floors are rather hostile to electronics and computers. Temperature extremes, vibration, dust and, especially wash down, can all interfere with the operation of computer hardware. Lower levels of hardware such as controllers are not generally affected by these problems because they are specifically designed for plant use. However, computers are more prone to damage. Processors wanting computers on plant floors should either buy units specifically adapted for ruggedness, which cost two to three times that of regular units, or else locate all computing equipment in an industrial enclosure away from the plant floor. Obviously, cost and convenience should be weighed carefully to avoid expensive computer downtime when proper precautions are not taken.

TOOLS OF AUTOMATION

Computer Vision Systems

Computer vision is the science that develops the theoretical and algorithmic basis by which useful information about an object or scene can be automatically extracted and analysed from an observed image, image set, or image sequence. An image can be defined as a spatial representation of an object or scene. A digital monochrome image is a two-dimensional (2-D) light intensity function denoted by $I(x,y)$, where the value or amplitude of intensity I at spatial coordinates x and y is typically proportional to the radiant energy received in the electromagnetic band, to which the sensor or detector (camera) is sensitive in a small area around the point (x,y). As far as the computer is concerned, the image is a matrix x,y of numeric values, each representing a quantised image-intensity value. Each matrix entry is known as a pixel (short for picture element). The total number of pixels in an image is determined by the size of the 2-D array used in the camera. The intensity of the monochrome image is known as the gray level. The influence of an object's size, shape, position, orientation, and other attributes from the spatial distribution of gray levels requires the capability to infer which pixels belong to the object and which do not. Then, from the pixels belonging to the object, it requires the capability to identify those object features of interest. Many algorithms and processing methods have been developed to translate the gray levels of a pixel in a manner that accentuates desired features. In general, a machine vision system is used to measure some aspect of the results of the manufacturing process (e.g. shape, size, texture, location) that is indicative of the accuracy, efficiency, or quality of the process.

The measured parameters can then be used as feedback in a real time control loop that optimises the manufacturing process through variations in process parameters (speed, temperature, flow rate, etc.). The essential steps in such a process are image acquisition, image processing, and image understanding (Fig. 5.2). The image-processing step involves several key operations such as pre-processing, segmentation, and feature extraction. The image-processing step relies heavily on the knowledge of the product being evaluated and the nature of the defect or quality attributes of interest. Together, they facilitate image understanding and enable final decisions to be made.

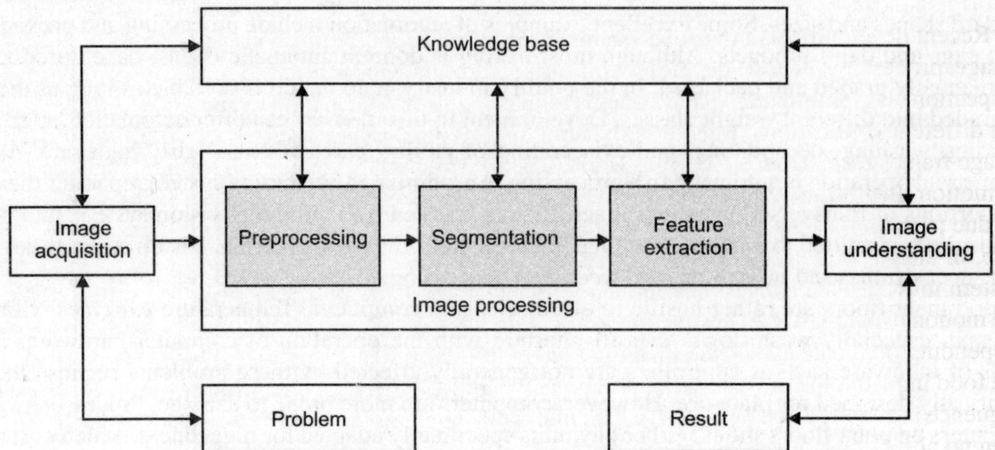

Fig. 5.2: Essential steps in computer vision system application.

Computer vision applications currently range from simple inspection to vision-guided robotic assembly. Most practical applications can be grouped into six general categories:

- Gauging – performing precise dimensional measurements.
- Verification – qualitatively ensuring that one or more desired features are present and/or undesired features are absent.
- Flow detection – finding and discriminating unwanted features of unknown size, location, and shape.
- Identification – determining the identity of an object from symbols, including alphanumeric characters.
- Recognition – determining the identity of an object from observed features.
- Locating – determining the location and orientation of an object.

Some key requirements in selecting appropriate computer vision follow:

- Speed of operation – the system must operate in real time, i.e. at production line speed.
- Robustness – the ability to function properly in a food plant environment.
- Tolerance – the ability to tolerate acceptable variations in the product.
- Accuracy – the ability to identify required features with a high level of accuracy.
- Flexibility – the ability to allow for changes in set points, operating algorithms, controls, etc.
- Reliability – the ability to perform a variety of inspection tasks consistently and repeatedly over a long period of time.

Due to advances in electronics and computer technology, vision systems can be installed in almost all food plants for a cost-effective quality evaluation/control operation. However, vision systems must be carefully designed around the particular characteristics of products being inspected so that they perform reliably under plant conditions. Significant research and analysis is necessary to determine the best method for enhancing and detecting product defects. This means pre-testing a large number of representative products with required defects or features.

Recent developments in vision systems include colour image processing and three dimensional (3D) image processing. These developments offer additional benefits, especially for more challenging inspection tasks. Computer vision systems for analysing on-line or moving scenes are also being designed for different applications. Input to a dynamic or moving scene analysis is in the form of a sequence of image frames taken from a changing world. The camera used to acquire the image sequence may also be in motion. Each frame represents an image of the scene at a particular instant. Changes in a scene may be due to motion of the camera or the objects, illumination changes, or changes in an object's structure, size, or shape. It is usually assumed that changes in scene are due to camera and/or object motion. A system must detect changes, determine motion characteristics of the observer and objects, characterise the motion using high level abstraction, recover the structure of the objects, and recognise moving objects. Depending on the design of the imaging system, different image processing techniques are required. In the food industry, the most common design is that of a stationary camera and moving objects. If a frame sequence is acquired at a rate such that no dramatic change takes place between two consecutive frames, then no abrupt change in motion can be observed for most physical objects. This is the basis for nearly all on-line applications currently available in the food industry. The important factor, then, is to set the image acquisition rate fast enough to minimise image blur so that an analysis of image data can take place frame-by-frame. Real time image processing boards and real time processors are available to assist in on-line real time computer vision applications.

For a continuous stream of material flowing along a conveyor belt, a computer vision system can be designed using a line-scan camera for image acquisition. A line-scan camera contains a one-dimensional array of photosensitive sites. The line-scan camera is suitable for fairly rapidly moving object scenes. In addition to higher speeds, linescan cameras offer high resolution and the ability to handle infinitely long image scenes. A new breed of cameras, known as time-delay and integrated cameras, are line-scan cameras, which use charge couple device image sensor technology to gain speed or increase sensitivity up to 100-fold (that of conventional cameras) while providing exceptional spatial resolution.

General requirements for on-line applications are throughput, speed, accuracy, consistency, durability, diversification, flexibility, and adaptability. Considerations of these conditions and constraints must be taken into account at all stages of system design and development. Speed of evaluation is perhaps the most striking requirement. It has been estimated that an on-line apple grading system may need to examine at least 3600 points/min. Several commercial systems are being used to examine 3.5 million pieces of fruit (apples, oranges, etc.) in an 8 hr day. Another on-line fill-height inspection system has been reported to handle speeds of up to 1400 bottles/min. Computer vision technology is becoming an integral part of the food industry's move towards automation. The presence of a machine vision system on a production line has come to represent an unmistakable demonstration of an industry's commitment to quality.

Chapter 6

Unit Operations: An Overview

INTRODUCTION

The number of different food products and the operations and steps involved in their production are indeed very great. Further, each manufacturer introduces departures in methods and equipment from the traditional technology for that product, and processes are in a continual state of evolution. The processes used by the food industry can be divided into common operations, called unit operations. Examples of unit operations common to many food products include cleaning, coating, concentrating, controlling, disintegrating, drying, evaporating, fermentation, forming, heating/cooling (heat exchange), materials handling, mixing, packaging, pumping, separating, and others. These operations are listed alphabetically, not in the order of their natural sequence or importance.

Most unit operations are utilised in the making of a variety of food products. Heat exchanging or heating, for example, is used in the manufacture of liquid and dry food products, in such diverse operations as pasteurising milk, sterilising foods in cans, roasting peanuts, and baking bread. Because of the dependence of the unit operation on a physical principle or a small group of associated principles, quantitative relationships in the form of mathematical equations can be built to describe them. The equations can be used to follow what is happening in the process, and to control and modify the process if required. Important unit operations in the food industry are fluid flow, heat transfer, drying, evaporation, contact equilibrium processes (which include distillation, extraction, gas absorption, crystallisation, and membrane processes), mechanical separations (which include filtration, centrifugation, sedimentation and sieving), size reduction and mixing. These unit operations, and in particular the basic principles on which they depend, are the subject of this chapter, along with the materials being processed. Two very important laws which all unit operations obey are the laws of conservation of mass and energy.

CONSERVATION OF MASS AND ENERGY

The law of conservation of mass states that mass can neither be created nor destroyed. Thus in a processing plant, the total mass of material entering the plant must equal the total mass of material leaving the plant, less any accumulation left in the plant. If there is no accumulation, then the simple rule holds that 'what goes in must come out'. Similarly all material entering a unit operation must in due course leave.

For example, if milk is being fed into a centrifuge to separate it into skim milk and cream, under the law of conservation of mass the total number of kilograms of material (milk) entering the centrifuge per minute must equal the total number of kilograms of material (skim milk and cream) that leave the centrifuge per minute. Similarly, the law of conservation of mass applies to each component in the entering materials. For example, considering the butter fat in the milk entering the centrifuge, the weight of butter fat entering the centrifuge per minute must be equal to the weight of butter fat leaving the centrifuge per minute. A similar relationship will hold for the other components, proteins, milk sugars and so on.

The law of conservation of energy states that energy can neither be created nor destroyed. The total energy in the materials entering the processing plant, plus the energy added in the plant, must equal the total energy leaving the plant. This is a more complex concept than the conservation of mass, as energy can take various forms such as kinetic energy, potential energy, heat energy, chemical energy, electrical energy and so on. During processing, some of these forms of energy can be converted from one to another. Mechanical energy in a fluid can be converted through friction into heat energy. Chemical energy in food is converted by the human body into mechanical energy. Note that it is the sum total of all these forms of energy that is conserved. For example, consider the pasteurising process for milk, in which milk is pumped through a heat exchanger and is first heated and then cooled. The energy can be considered either over the whole plant or only as it affects the milk. For total plant energy, the balance must include: the conversion in the pump of electrical energy to kinetic and heat energy, the kinetic and potential energies of the milk entering and leaving the plant and the various kinds of energy in the heating and cooling sections, as well as the exiting heat, kinetic and potential energies.

To the food technologist, the energies affecting the product are the most important. In the case of the pasteuriser, the energy affecting the product is the heat energy in the milk. Heat energy is added to the milk by the pump and by the hot water passing through the heat exchanger. Cooling water then removes part of the heat energy and some of the heat energy is also lost to the surroundings.

The heat energy leaving in the milk must equal the heat energy in the milk entering the pasteuriser plus or minus any heat added or taken away in the plant.

Heat energy leaving in milk = initial heat energy
+ heat energy added by pump
+ heat energy added in heating section
– heat energy taken out in cooling section
– heat energy lost to surroundings.

The law of conservation of energy can also apply to part of a process. For example, considering the heating section of the heat exchanger in the pasteuriser, the heat lost by the hot water must be equal to the sum of the heat gained by the milk and the heat lost from the heat exchanger to its surroundings.

From these laws of conservation of mass and energy, a balance sheet for materials and for energy can be drawn up at all times for a unit operation. These are called material balances and energy balances.

Using a material balance and an energy balance, a food engineering process can be viewed overall or as a series of units. Each unit is a unit operation. The unit operation can be represented by a box as shown in Fig. 6.1. Unit operations may include numerous different activities. The unit operation of mixing, for example, includes agitating, beating, blending, diffusing, dispersing, emulsifying, homogenising, kneading, stirring, whipping, and working. We may want to mix to beat in air, as in making an egg white foam or to blend dry ingredients, as in preparing a ton of dry cake mix, or we may wish to mix to emulsify, as in the case of mayonnaise or to homogenise to prevent fat separation in milk. We may wish to mix and develop a bread dough, which requires stretching and folding, referred to as kneading. One of the key

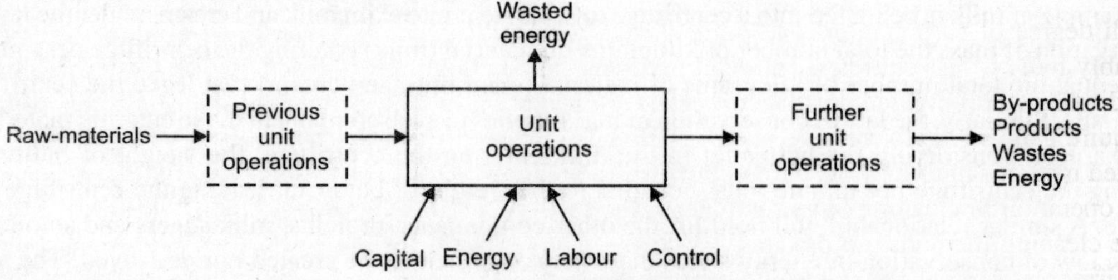

Fig. 6.1: Unit operation.

elements to food processing is the proper selection and combination of unit operations into more complex integrated processing systems. These operations and processes consume great quantities of energy.

COMMON UNIT OPERATIONS

Materials Handling

Materials handling includes such varied operations as hand and mechanical harvesting on the farm, refrigerated trucking of perishable produce, box car transportation of live cattle, and pneumatic conveying of flour from rail car to bakery storage bins. Throughout such operations emphasis must be given to maintaining sanitary conditions, minimising product losses (including weight loss of livestock), maintaining raw material quality (e.g. vitamin content and physical appearance), minimising bacterial growth, and timing all transfers and deliveries so as to minimise holdup time, which can be costly as well as detrimental to product quality. The movement of produce from farm to processing plant and/or raw materials through the plant may take many forms. Oranges, for example, are moved by truck trailers to juice plants, where they are graded and washed. There is a limit to the size the trucks may be and the length of time the fruit may be held since fruits and vegetables are alive, respire, and can cause the temperature of a batch to rise to the point where complete spoilage may occur.

Bulk dry sugar delivered to confectionery and other types of food plants is conveyed from the truck to storage bins by a pneumatic lift system. Storage must not be for a period of time not at a temperature and humidity that will allow the sugar to cake. Transfer of sugar in the plant must avoid dusting and the buildup of static electricity to prevent possible explosion of the highly combustible sugar particles.

This method of materials handling has the additional advantages of preventing loss of desirable volatiles from the spices, irritation to personnel; and flavour exchange between different spices. The use of a wide variety of screw conveyors, bucket conveyors, belt conveyors, and vibratory conveyors in food plants needs no elaboration here beyond the obvious recognition that conveying and handling equipment for eggs in the shell must be different than for less fragile products.

Cleaning

Foods by the nature of the way they are grown or produced on farms in open environments often require cleaning before use. Cleaning ranges from simple removal of dirt from egg shells with an abrasive brush to the complex removal of bacteria from a liquid food by passing it through a microporous membrane. Grains must be cleaned of stones before use. Cleaning can be accomplished with brushes, high-velocity are steam, water, vacuum, magnetic attraction of metal contaminants, mechanical separation, and so on, depending on the product and the nature of the dirt. The cleanliness of water used in the soft drink bottling industry must exceed many of the standards found adequate for drinking water.

If a high degree of carbonation is to be achieved, then the water used in making the drink must be remarkably free of dust particles, colloidal particles, and certain inorganic salts, since these minimise carbon dioxide solubility and promote excessive escape of gas bubbles. To adequately clean this water may require that city water receive such additional treatments as controlled chemical flocculation of suspended matter, sand filtration, carbon purification, microfiltration, and deaeration. This is no longer the unit operation of cleaning but a total cleaning process.

Some cleaning methods are dictated by surface characteristics of the product. Because pineapples have an irregular surface, the scrubbing action of high-pressure water jets is used. Just as different food materials require special cleaning, the surfaces of food processing equipment need thorough and frequent attention. The cleaning of equipment, as well as a facility's walls and floors, must take into consideration the chemical and physical properties of both the surface to be cleaned and the type of soil. Many types of soil can be removed with mildly alkaline detergents, but strong alkali may be required for more tenacious deposits and heavy deposits of fats and oils or built-up protein deposits. Alkaline films and hard-water scales may require mildly acid detergents. Strong acids are highly corrosive to several metals, fabrics, wood, rubber, and concrete floors. Strong alkalis also are corrosive to various metals and to glass. For these reasons, moderately alkaline and neutral detergents find wide application in the food industry. Food plant operators generally call on detergent manufacturers for expertise in establishing highly effective cleaning procedures since these further depend on detergent concentration, temperatures of application, order of application where more than one cleaning aid is used, and other variables.

Separating

The unit operation of separating can involve separating a solid from a solid, as in the peeling of potatoes or the shelling of nuts, separating a solid from a liquid, as in the many types of filtration or a liquid from a solid, as in pressing juice from a fruit. It might involve the separation of a liquid from a liquid, as in centrifuging oil from water or removing a gas from a solid or a liquid, as in vacuum removal of air from canned food in vacuum canning. One of the commonest forms of separating in the food industry is the hand sorting and grading of individual units as in the case of vegetables and fruit. However, because of the high cost of labour, mechanical and electronic sorting devices have been developed. Difference in colour can be detected with a photocell and off-colour products rejected. This can be done at enormous speeds with automatic rejection of discoloured or mouldy nuts or kernels of grain the flow past the photocell. In the case of peanuts to be made into peanut butter, each peanut individually passes through a light beam that activates a jet of air to blow the discoloured peanuts from the main stream when an off-colour changes the amount of reflected light. Light shining through eggs can detect blood spots and automatically reject such eggs. Automatic separation according to size is easily accomplished by passing fruits or vegetables over different size screens, holes or slits.

The skins of fruits and vegetables may be separated using a lye peeler (Fig. 6.2). Peaches, apricots, and the like are passed through a heated lye solution. The lye or caustic softens the skin to where it can be easily slipped from the fruit by gentle action of mechanical fingers or by jets of water. Differences in the density of the fruit and skin can then be used to float away the removed skin.

To separate corn oil from corn kernels, the germ portion of the corn first is separated from the rest of the kernel by milling, then the oil is separated from the germ by applying high pressure to the germ in an oil press. Similarly, pressure is used to squeeze oil out of peanuts, soyabeans, and cottonseeds. The last traces of oil can be removed from the pressed cake by the use of fat solvents. There then remains the separation of the oil from the solvent.

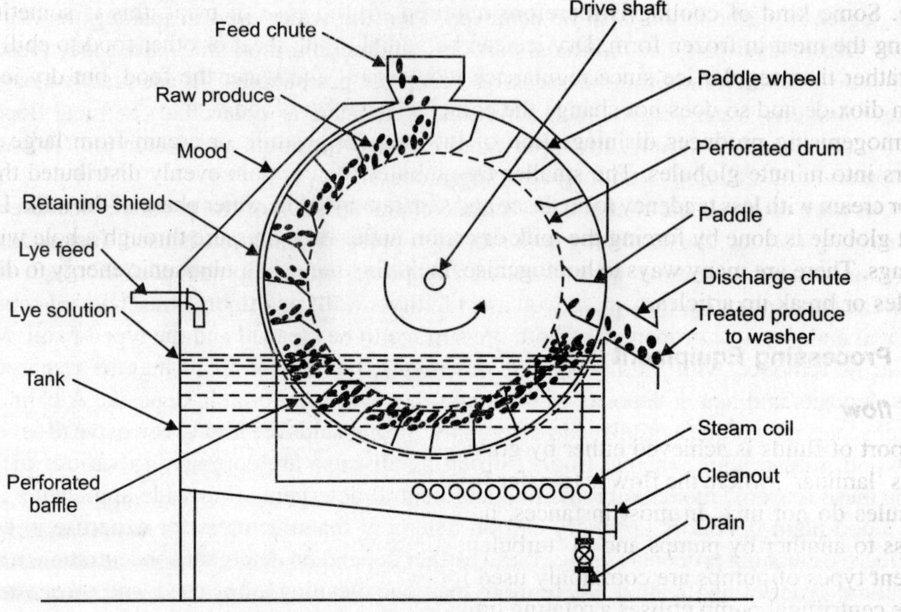

Fig. 6.2: Fruit and vegetable lye peeler.

Crystallisation is used to separate salt from sea water or sugar from sugar cane juice. Here, evaporation of some of the water causes supersaturation, and crystals form. Since crystals are quite pure, this is also considered a purification process. The crystals are then separated from the suspending liquid by centrifugation.

Newer methods of separation include several techniques involving manufactured membranes with porosities or permeabilities capable of separations and fractionations at the colloidal and macromolecular size level. Ultrafiltration uses membranes of such porosity that water and low-molecular-weight salts, acids, and bases pass through the membrane but larger protein and sugar molecules are retained. This selective separation process, carried out at ambient temperatures, avoids the heat damage to sensitive food constituents that is often associated with water evaporation at high temperatures. Further, removal of acids and salts with the water prevents their concentration, which would otherwise be detrimental to sensitive retained solids.

Disintegrating

Operations which subdivide large pieces of food into smaller units or particles are classified as disintegrating. It may involve cutting, grinding, pulping, homogenising and so on. Although the dicing of vegetables is done on automatic machines, the cutting of meat still largely represents a time-consuming, hand-labour operation. This is because skill is required to separate specific cuts of meat, and the value of the cuts can be sharply reduced by a sloppy job. However, automatic knives with a 'brain' are being researched and developed. In another application, cutting of bakery products can be done cleanly and precisely with fine jets of high-pressure, high-velocity water. Laser beams also can replace knives in some cutting applications. Disintegrating by grinding, as in the preparation of hamburger or hash, always is associated with heating of the product due to friction created in the grinding process. This can be damaging to the food product. It can partially denature proteins or it can give burned flavours to ground coffee. Some kind of cooling is therefore required. In the case of meat, this is sometimes done by grinding the meat in frozen form. Dry ice can be added to the meat or other food to chill it. Dry ice is used rather than regular ice since regular ice would melt and water the food, but dry ice goes off as carbon dioxide and so does not change the composition of the food.

Homogenising produces disintegration of fat globules in milk or cream from large globules and clusters into minute globules. The smaller fat globules then remain evenly distributed throughout the milk or cream with less tendency to coalesce and separate from the water phase of the milk. Disintegrating the fat globule is done by forcing the milk or cream under high pressure through a hole with very small openings. There are many ways to homogenise, including the use of ultrasonic energy to disintegrate fat globules or break up articles.

Food Processing Equipment

Fluid flow

Transport of fluids is achieved either by gravity flow or through the use of pumps. In gravity flow the flow is 'laminar', where the flow is transfer from the fluid to the wall between adjacent layers. Adjacent molecules do not mix. In most instances, however fluids are transported from one unit operation or process to another by pumps and in 'turbulent' flow where there is mixing of adjacent particles. Two different types of pumps are commonly used for different purposes.

The centrifugal pump utilises a rotating impeller to create a centrifugal force within the pump cavity, so that the fluid is accelerated until it attains its tangential velocity close to the impeller tip. The flow is controlled by the choice of impeller diameter and rotary speed of the pump drive. The capacity of a centrifugal pump is dependent upon the speed, impeller length and the inlet and outlet diameters. Product viscosity is an important factor affecting centrifugal pump performance. If the product is sufficiently viscous, the pump cavity will not fill with every revolution and the efficiency of the pump will be greatly reduced. Centrifugal pumps are used to transport fluid and for cleaning operations. Centrifugal pumps may be high speed or low speed, with high speed pumps being used for cleaning (CIP).

A positive pump generally consists of a reciprocating or rotating cavity between two lobes or gears and a rotor. Fluid enters by gravity or a difference in pressure and the fluid forms the seals between the rotating parts. The rotating move of the rotor produces the pressure to cause the fluid to flow. Because there is no frictional loss, positive pumps are used where a constant rate of flow is required (timing pump), for high viscosity fluids or for transporting fragile solids suspended in a fluid (such as moving cottage cheese curd from a vat to a filler). Some of the liquid pumps for fluid flow are shown in Fig. 6.3.

Mixing

An agitation device may be placed in a tank for a number of purposes. The mixing device may need to produce bulk circulation in the tank, a controlled velocity at some surface of the tank or a controlled rate of shear. Two major purposes of mixing are either heat transfer or ingredient incorporation. Different mixer configurations will be used to achieve different purposes. The efficiency of mixing will depend upon: Design of impeller-diameter of impeller-speed-baffles.

Mixing equipment: Many forms of mixers have been produced from time to time but over the years a considerable degree of standardisation of mixing equipment has been reached in different branches of the food industry. Possibly the easiest way in which to classify mixers is to divide them according to whether they mix liquids, dry powders or thick pastes.

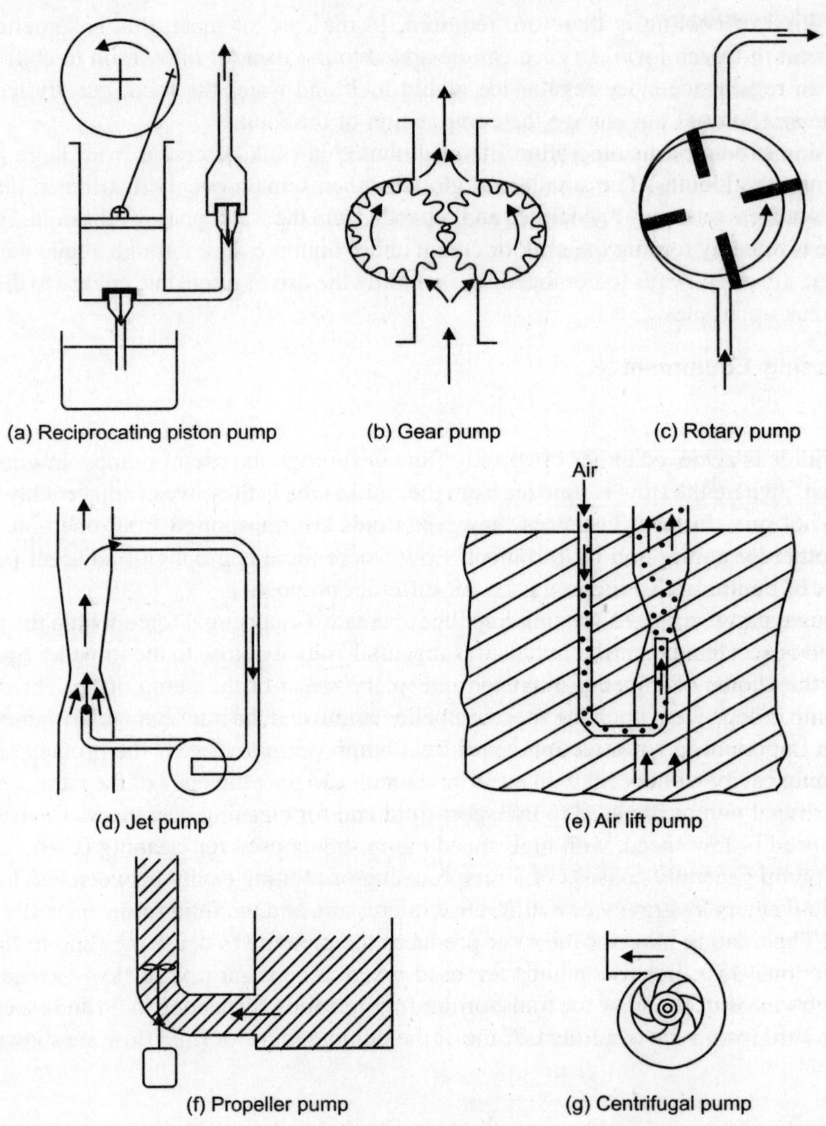

(a) Reciprocating piston pump (b) Gear pump (c) Rotary pump

(d) Jet pump (e) Air lift pump

(f) Propeller pump (g) Centrifugal pump

Fig. 6.3: Liquid pumps.

***Liquid mixers*:** For the deliberate mixing of liquids, the propeller mixer is probably the most common and the most satisfactory. In using propeller mixers, it is important to avoid regular flow patterns such as an even swirl round a cylindrical tank, which may accomplish very little mixing. To break up these streamline patterns, baffles are often fitted or the propeller may be mounted asymmetrically. Various baffles can be used and the placing of these can make very considerable differences to the mixing performances. It is tempting to relate the amount of power consumed by a mixer to the amount of mixing produced, but there is no necessary connection and very inefficient mixers can consume large amounts of power.

Powder and particle mixers

The essential feature in these mixers is to displace parts of the mixture with respect to other parts. The ribbon blender, for example, shown in Fig. 6.4a consists of a trough in which rotates a shaft with two open helical screws attached to it, one screw being right-handed and the other left-handed. As the shaft rotates sections of the powder move in opposite directions and so particles are vigorously displaced relative to each other. A commonly used blender for powders is the double-cone blender in which two cones are mounted with their open ends fastened together and they are rotated about an axis through their common base. This mixer is shown in Fig. 6.4b.

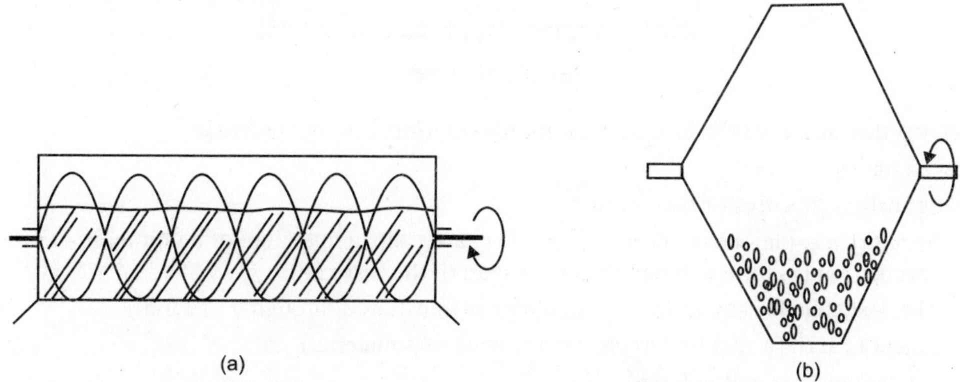

Fig. 6.4: Mixers (a) ribbon blender, and (b) double-cone mixer.

Dough and paste mixers

Dough and pastes are mixed in machines that have, of necessity, to be heavy and powerful. Because of the large power requirements, it is particularly desirable that these machines mix with reasonable efficiency, as the power is dissipated in the form of heat, which may cause substantial heating of the product. Such machines may require jacketing of the mixer to remove as much heat as possible with cooling water. Perhaps the most commonly used mixer for these very heavy materials is the kneader which employs two contra-rotating arms of special shape, which fold and shear the material across a cusp or division, in the bottom of the mixer. The arms are of so-called sigmoid shape as indicated in Fig. 6.5.

They rotate at differential speeds, often in the ratio of nearly 3:2. Developments of this machine include types with multiple sigmoid blades along extended troughs, in which the blades are given a forward twist and the material makes its way continuously through the machine.

Another type of machine employs very heavy contra-rotating paddles, whilst a modern continuous mixer consists of an interrupted screw which oscillates with both rotary and reciprocating motion between pegs in an enclosing cylinder. The important principle in these machines is that the material has to be divided and folded and also displaced, so that fresh surfaces recombine as often as possible.

Heat transfer

Heat is either transferred into a product (heating) or removed from a product (cooling). Heating is used to destroy micro-organisms to provide for a healthful food, prolong shelf-life through the destruction of certain enzymes and to promote a product with acceptable taste odour and appearance.

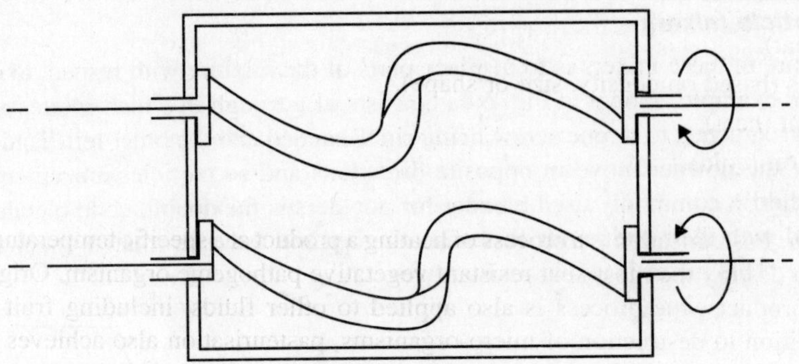

Fig. 6.5: Kneader.

The factors that influence the heat transfer into or out of the product include:

1. Heat exchanger design.
2. Heat transfer properties of the product:
   (a) Specific heat (amount of heat required to change the temperature of a unit mass of product a specific temperature without change in state of the material).
   (b) Thermal conductivity (rate by which heat is transferred through a material).
   (c) Latent heat (heat required to change the state of a material).
3. Density (weight per unit volume).
4. Method of heat transfer:
   (a) Conduction (transfer from molecule to molecule through the material).
   (b) Radiation (transfer from electromagnetic radiation of a body due to the vibration of its molecules).
   (c) Convection (transfer through movement of mass).
5. Viscosity (related to the amount of force required to move the fluid product).

A variety of heat exchanges are utilised in the food industry, which include:

1. Plate heat exchanges.
2. Tubular heat exchanges.
3. Swept surface heat exchangers.

Plate heat exchanges pass fluid over a plate where a heating or cooling medium is being passed up or down on the other side of the place. The thin film makes for rapid heat transfer and is the most efficient method of heat fluids of low viscosity. Tubular heat exchanges general are compose of a tube within a tube, in which product and heating or cooling medium are flowing in opposite (countercurrent) directions. This a low cost method of heating or cooling and is applicable to fluids of higher viscosities that generally passed through a plate heat exchanger. Swept surface heat exchanges have blades that scrape the surface of the heat exchanger and bring new product continuously to the heat or cooling surface. These are utilised for fluids of very high viscosity. An ice cream freezer is an example of a swept surface heat exchanger.

Common unit processes that include heat transfer as a unit operation include:

1. Pasteurisation (heat).
2. Sterilisation (heat).

3. Drying (heat).
4. Separations (based on density, size or shape).
5. Evaporation (heat).
6. Refrigeration (cold).
7. Freezing (cold).

Pasteurisation: Pasteurisation is a process of heating a product at a specific temperature for a controlled period of time to destroy the most heat resistant vegetative pathogenic organism. Originally developed for fluid dairy products, the process is also applied to other fluids, including fruit juices and juice products. In addition to destruction of micro-organisms, pasteurisation also achieves almost complete destruction of undesirable milk enzymes — such as lipase.

Pasteurisation was originally conducted in jacket vats equipped with an agitator to give complete mixing and the ability to heat and cool. For milk vat pasteurisation required a heat treatment of 145°F for 30 minutes, with the air space above the product being heated to a higher temperature to insure all molecules of the product were adequately pasteurised. The component parts of a vat pasteuriser are the tank body, heating/cooling channels, inlet port, outlet valve with leak detector, agitator and drive motor, product indicating thermometer, recording devices, air space heater and indicating thermometer, steam inlet and outlet, cooling water inlet and outlet.

Next plate heat exchanger were used with a higher temperature and shorter time (161.5/15 seconds) being used to achieve the same bacterial destruction. This is called HTST pasteurisation. To improve efficiency the cold milk is used to partially cool the pasteurised milk and the hot milk partially heats the cold milk in a processed call regeneration. The component parts of an HTST pasteuriser include the balance tank, cold side of regenerator, timing pump, heating section, holding tube, flow diversion valve, hot side of regenerator, cooling section, controls.

Ultra high temperature (UHT) pasteurisation is achieved with plate heat exchanges operating at temperatures of at least 190°F for 2 seconds. The same principles are used as for HTST, except that higher temperatures are used and the equipment is designed for very rapid heating and cooling.

Sterilisation: The primary object of sterilisation is to destroy the most heat resistant pathogenic spore forming organism:

1. Flame steriliser—conveyor, preheater, gas jets.
2. Still retort—retort body, product basket, steam inlet, water inlet, pressure gage, pressure relief valve.
3. Hydraulic cooker—a continuous steriliser, where the cans are rotating during the sterilisation process.
4. Still retort—a type of batch steriliser used for canning food, where the cans are not in motion during the sterilisation process.

Baking: Baking is the process by which moisture is removed from wheat based (or other cereal grain), products. Batch or continuous oven are utilised to heat the products resulting in an increase in volume of the product, gelatinisation or starch of protein elation to set the final structure of the product. Baking is an essential process for bread, cakes, cookies and crackers. A rotary oven is a fairly simple device which has a cabinet, oven trays, heating element, thermostat and temperature controls. Many commercial ovens are continuous in that the product moves though the oven on a continuous belt.

Concentration: Concentration can be achieved through evaporation and through reverse osmosis. Evaporation generally involves heating the fluid in a vessel under vacuum to cause a change in state of water from liquid to vapour and then recovers of water by passing the vapour through a condenser. The component parts of the evaporator include an enclosed vessel with product inlet, manhole, heating rings, finished product outlet, condenser, steam inlet, vacuum and condenser pump. In some product evaporation causes the loss of flavour volatiles and this case, a low temperature unit is added to recover the flavour volatiles so that they can be added back to the product. To reduce operating costs, multiple effect evaporators are utilised, which have two or more evaporators placed in series to provide a means for the continuous concentration of a fluid product. This increases the efficiency of the evaporation process.

Reverse osmosis (RO) is a process where the fluid is passed through a semi-permeable membrane with very small pores that permit only the transfer of water. Most systems consist a membrane cast on a solid porous backing—usually in the form of a tube. High pressure is applied to force the water (called permeate) through the membrane the concentrated fluid (called retentate) is retained in the tubing. The rate of water removal decreases as the fluid is concentrate, until it is no longer economically feasible to remove more water. Concentration is often used as a pre-step to drying to reduced the amount of water that needs to be removed in drying and reducing drying costs. Evaporation can achieve higher solids economically than can reserve osmosis. RO is preferred over evaporation for heat sensitive fluids.

Drying: Three common methods of drying are: (i) sun or tray drying, (ii) spray, drying, and (iii) freeze drying. Sun or tray drying is least expensive, followed by spray drying and freeze drying. The drying method of choice is generally based on the characteristics of the product.

Products that are already solid lend themselves to sun or tray drying. These include fruits and vegetables. The products may be dried by exposure to sun or place in trays and dried in a current of warm or hot air. Products that are very heat sensitive are freeze dried. Commercially only instant coffee is widely freeze dried. Some freeze dried fruits are beginning to reach the market, but these are in limited quantities. In freeze drying the moisture is removed without a phase change (sublimation). A freeze drying is comprised of a dryer cabinet, drying chamber with: Heating/cooling shelves, trays and door, vacuum pump, condenser, controls and digital readout.

The most common drying method is spray drying, which is applicable to fluid products. The bulk density (weight per unit volume) is controlled to a large extent by the solids that are sent to the dryer. A spray drying has an air inlet, air heater, drying chamber, inlet atomiser, cyclone chamber, cyclone separator, dry product collection vessel, hot air inlet and outlet, drying fan and motor, controls. There are several different designs of spray nozzles through which the fluid is atomised into the heated air. These generally are either centrifugal nozzles or high pressure spray nozzles. The type of nozzles will vary with the product being dried. For some products that are very hydroscopic, the dried product may be partially re-wetted and the redried. This produces agglomerated products that are easily dispsered in solution. Spray dried powders with a surfactant is also a method for improving dispersion.

Another method, no longer in common use, is roller drying—where the product is allowed to flow over a hot, rotating drum and the dried product is scraped off. This is a low cost method of drying, but creates a lot of heat damage to the product.

Freezing: Lowering the temperature below the freezing point of the product stops micro-organisms from growing and reduces the activity of enzymes. Vegetables and some fruits are heat treated (blanched) before freezing to eliminate enzymes. One of the most common frozen foods is ice cream. An ice cream freezer can be operated either in batch or continuous mode. A batch ice cream freeze consists of a freezer cylinder, dasher assembly with scraper blades, counter rotating agitator, mix inlet, ice cream outlet gate, motor. A continuous ice cream freezer consists of an inlet pump, air injector assembly, freezer cylinder, dasher assemble with scraper blades, outlet pressure gage, ice cream back pressure regulating valve, refrigeration unit inside cabinet. The continuous freezer provides much better control of drawing temperature and overrun than batch machines and is the machine of choice for commercial ice cream operations. The product from these machines is placed in low temperature freezers to freeze out additional water and produce the packaged products found in super markets. Soft serve machines are generally some modification of the batch freezer and the product is served directly from the machine without further hardening. For frozen fruits and vegetables, the products are generally frozen in the package and generally is blast freezers, where the product is moved through the freezer in a continuous manner.

Separations: Separations can be achieved on the basis of density or size and shape. Separations that are based on density differences include the separation of cream from milk, recovery of solids from suspensions, and removal of bacterial from fluids.

1. Cream Separator: Milk can be separated into skim milk and cream based on the density difference between fat and non-fat solids of milk. A cream separator is used to obtain the cream from milk and is a disc type centrifuge in which the fluid is separated into low and high density fluid streams that permits the separate collection of cream and skim milk. The machine consists of a regulating cover with float, cream outlet cover, skim milk outlet cover, bowl assembly with inlet, cream outlet, skim outlet, spindle, disc stack and cream disc with cream adjusting screw skim milk outlet, motor, adjusting screw.
2. Clarification: Sediment and micro-organisms can be removed centrifugally in a clarifier, which is generally a disc-type centrifuge that employs forces of 5 to 10 thousand times gravity and forcing the denser material to the outside. By periodically opening the bowl, the solids can be continuously removed from the remainder of the fluids. A centrifugal machine call a Bactofuge was used in Europe to reduce the bacterial count by two log cycles in fluid foods. This same principle has been used to recover yeast cells from spent fermentation broths and to continuously concentrate bakers cheese from whey.
3. Membrane processes: Reverse osmosis (RO), ultrafiltration (UF) and microfiltration (MF) are processes that use membranes with varying pore sizes to affect separation on the basis of size and shape. Reverse osmosis has membranes with the smallest pore and is used to separate water from other solutes. Ultrafiltration has membranes with larger pores and will retain proteins, lipids and colloidal salts, while allowing smaller molecules to pass through to the permeate phase. Microfiltration, with pores >0.1 micron, is used to separate fat from proteins and to reduce micro-organisms from fluid food systems.
4. A typical ultrafiltration plant is comprised of a: feed tank, circulating pump, membrane housing, membranes, product inlet, permeate outlet, retentate outlet, controls. The components for RO and ME are similar expect for the pumps that are required.

Size reduction

Size reduction can be through the use of high shear forces, graters, cutters or slicers. Emulsions with very small fat globule droplets are frequently made with a homogeniser which is a high shear positive pump that forces fluid though a very small orifice at very high pressure to form or reduce the size of an emulsion. The positive pump uses a reciprocating or rotating cavity between two lobes, gears or between a stationary cavity and a rotor. The fluid forms the seal between the rotating parts. The components of a homogeniser consist of a suction manifold, suction check valves, plungers and cylinders, discharge check valves, discharge manifold, discharge pressure gage, 1st and 2nd stage homogenising valves, plunger seals.

Typical equipment for size reduction in meat products and their component parts include:

1. Grinder which forces pieces of meat out through small openings consists of a motor, product tray, grinder screw and die.
2. Bacon slicer—product holder, cutting blade, conveyor belt and slicer arm.
3. Sausage stuffer—inlet, stuffer body, stuffer drive assembly, product feeder, product outlet and product horn.
4. Vertical chopper—bowl, cutting blade, motor and cover.

Powdered products are frequently ground into fine particles through ball mills.

Fermented products

Useful micro-organisms are used to preserve a number of food products, which include:

1. Yeast fermentations:
   (a) Beer
   (b) Wine
   (c) Champagne
   (d) Bread
2. Lactic acid fermentations:
   (a) Cultured buttermilk
   (b) Yogurt
   (c) Cheese
   (d) Sourkraut
   (e) Pickles
   (f) Fermented sausages

All fermentations results from the action of micro-organisms growing on carbohydrates in the product and producing some material (alcohol or acid) which minimises the growth of undesirable organisms and preserves the product.

The equipment used for fermentation varies as a function of the product. Generally, a fermentation vessel is used—which may be open or closed. Modern beer, wine and cheese operations utilise closed vessels for the initial fermentation, where careful sanitation practices can be employed to present contamination. Cultures used for the fermentations are prepared under close sanitary control.

SECTION II

Ambient Temperature Processing

Chapter 7

Size Reduction

INTRODUCTION

Size reduction is the unit operation in which the average size of solid pieces of food is reduced by the application of grinding, compression or impact forces. When applied to the reduction in size of globules of immiscible liquids (for example oil globules in water) size reduction is more frequently referred to as homogenisation or emulsification.

BENEFITS OF SIZE REDUCTION IN FOOD PROCESSING

Size reduction has the following benefits in food processing:

1. There is an increase in the surface-area-to-volume ratio of the food which increases the rate of drying, heating or cooling and improves the efficiency and rate of extraction of liquid components (for example fruit juice or cooking oil extraction.
2. When combined with screening, a predetermined range of particle sizes is produced which is important for the correct functional or processing properties of some products (for example icing sugar, spices and cornstarch).
3. A similar range of particle sizes allows more complete mixing of ingredients (for example dried soup and cake mixes).

Size reduction and emulsification have little or no preservative effect. They are used to improve the eating quality or suitability of foods for further processing and to increase the range of products available. In some foods they may promote degradation by the release of naturally occurring enzymes from damaged tissues, or by microbial activity and oxidation at the increased area of exposed surfaces, unless other preservative treatments are employed.

Different methods of size reduction are classified according to the size range of particles produced:

1. Chopping, cutting, slicing and dicing:
   - Large to medium (stewing steak, cheese and sliced fruit for canning).
   - Medium to small (bacon, sliced green beans and diced carrot).
   - Small to granular (minced or shredded meat, flaked fish or nuts and shredded vegetables).

2. Milling to powders or pastes of increasing fineness (grated products > spices > flours > fruit nectars > powdered sugar > starches > smooth pastes).
3. Emulsification and homogenisation (mayonnaise, milk, essential oils, butter, ice cream and margarine).

Size Reduction of Solid Foods

In all types of size reduction there are three types of force used to reduce the size of foods:

1. Compression forces.
2. Impact forces.
3. Shearing (or attrition) forces.

In most size reduction equipment, all three forces are present, but often one is more important than the others. When stress (force) is applied to a food the resulting internal strains are first absorbed, to cause deformation of the tissues. If the strain does not exceed a certain critical level named the elastic stress limit (E), the tissues return to their original shape when the stress is removed, and the stored energy is released as heat.

The amount of energy that is needed to fracture a food is determined by its hardness and tendency to crack (its friability) which in turn depends on the structure of the food. The fewer the lines of weakness in a food, the higher is the energy input needed to cause fracturing. Harder foods absorb more energy and consequently require a greater energy input to create fractures.

Compression forces are used to fracture friable or crystalline foods, combined impact and shearing forces are necessary for fibrous foods, and shearing forces are used for fine grinding of softer foods. It is thought that foods fracture at lower stress levels if force is applied for longer times. The extent of size reduction, the energy expended and the amount of heat generated in the food therefore depend on both the size of the forces that are applied and the time that food is subjected to the forces.

Other factors which influence the energy input are the moisture content and heat sensitivity of the food. The moisture content significantly affects both the degree of size reduction and the mechanism of breakdown in some foods. For example, before milling wheat is 'conditioned' to optimum moisture content and maize is thoroughly soaked and wet milled in order to obtain complete disintegration of the starchy material. However, excessive moisture in a 'dry' food can lead to agglomeration of particles which then block the mill and very dry foods create excessive dust which causes a health hazard, and is extremely inflammable and potentially explosive. Substantial amounts of heat are generated in high-speed mills. The heat sensitivity of the food determines the permissible temperature rise and the necessity to cool the mill. In cryogenic grinding, liquid nitrogen or solid carbon dioxide are mixed with foods (for example spices) before milling, to cool the product and to retain volatiles or other heat sensitive components. Solid carbon dioxide is also used to cool meat during size reduction in the manufacture of sausagemeat.

Equipments used in food processing

This section describes selected equipment used to reduce the size of both fibrous foods to smaller pieces or pulps, and dry particulate foods to powders. Most meats, fruits and vegetables fall into the general category of 'fibrous' foods. Meats are frozen or 'tempered' to just below their freezing point to improve the efficiency of cutting. Fruits and vegetables have an inherently firmer texture and are cut at ambient or chill temperatures. All types of cutters require the blade to be forced through the food with as little resistance as possible. Knife blades must be kept sharp, to both minimise the force needed to cut the food and to reduce cell rupture and consequent product damage and reduced yield. In moist foods, water acts as a lubricant, but in some sticky products, such as dates or candied fruits, food grade lubricants may be needed to cut them successfully. In general blades are not coated with non-slip materials, such as 'Teflon' or poly-tetra-fluoro-ethylene (PTFE) as these may wear off and contaminate the product, and are instead mirror-polished during manufacture.

Improved cutting introduction of ultrasonic cutters cutting

They are readily automated and have the following benefits:

- Quality of the cut face is visually excellent.
- The product is virtually undisturbed.
- The required cutting force is significantly reduced.
- Multi-layered products or hard particles contained in a soft matrix can be cut.
- The blade is self-cleaning.
- Crumbs and debris are significantly reduced.
- It is cost effective, having low running costs.
- Less sharp blades are needed and longer intervals between sharpening, compared to conventional blades.

The technique is particularly suitable for products that are difficult to cut using other methods (for example, sticky confectionery, hot bread and soft cake) and is increasingly used for bakery products of all types, frozen pies, ice cream, and fresh meats, fish and vegetables.

Size reduction of fibrous foods

There are four main types of size reduction equipment, classified in order of decreasing particle size as follows:

1. Slicing and flaking equipment
2. Dicing equipment
3. Shredding equipment
4. Pulping equipment.

Slicing and flaking equipment

These are high speed slicers for both cutting bread precisely from corner to corner and for slicing fillings. The food is held against the slicer blades by centrifugal force and each slice falls away freely. This eliminates the problems found in earlier cutters, where multiple knife blades caused compression of the food and damage as it passed between the blades. High speed cutters are used to slice bacon and 'wafer thin' cooked meats at up to 2000 slices per minute and vegetables at up to 6 T/hr. Newer designs are computer controlled and can be programmed easily by operators to bulk slice and stack a range of products including cheeses, pizza toppings, cooked meats, cucumber and tomato, and then apply them onto sandwich bread. Meats are also cut using circular rotary knives with a blade at right angles to the path of the meat. An 'intelligent' cheese cutter weighs and measures each block to determine the maximum number of portions that can be cut to the required weight with the minimum amount of waste.

Harder fruits such as apples are simultaneously sliced and de-cored as they are forced over stationary knives fitted inside a tube.

Dicing equipment

For dicing, vegetables, fruits and meats are first sliced and then cut into strips by rotating blades. The strips are fed to a second set of rotating knives which operate at right angles to the first set and cut the strips into cubes.

Shredding equipment

Typical equipment is a modified hammer mill in which knives are used instead of hammers to produce a cutting action. A second type of shredder, known as the *squirrel cage disintegrator*, has two concentric cylindrical cages inside a casing. They are fitted with knife blades along their length and the two cages rotate in opposite directions. Food is subjected to powerful shearing and cutting forces as it passes between them.

Pulping equipment

This uses a combination of compression and shearing forces for juice extraction from fruits or vegetables, for cooking oil production and for producing pure´ed and pulped meats. For example a rotary fruit crusher consists of a cylindrical metal screen fitted internally with high-speed rotating brushes or paddles.

Grapes, tomatoes or other soft fruits are heated if necessary to soften the tissues, and pulp is forced through the perforations of the screen by the brushes. The size of the perforations determines the fineness of the pulp. Skins, stalks and seeds are discarded from the end of the screen. Other types of pulper, including roller presses and screw presses, are used for juice expression or cold extraction of cooking oils. A *bowl chopper* is used to chop meat and harder fruits and vegetables into a pulp (for example for sausagemeat or mincemeat preserve).

A horizontal, slowly rotating bowl moves the ingredients beneath a set of high-speed rotating blades. Food may be passed several times beneath the knives until the required degree of size reduction and mixing has been achieved.

Ball Mills

These have a slowly rotating, horizontal steel cylinder which is half filled with steel balls 2.5–15 cm in diameter. At low speeds or when small balls are used, shearing forces predominate. With larger balls or at higher speeds, impact forces become more important. They are used to produce fine powders, such as food colourants. A modification of the ball mill named a *rod mill* has rods instead of balls to overcome problems associated with the balls sticking in adhesive foods.

Disc Mills

There are a large number of designs of *disc mill*, each employing shearing forces for fine grinding or shearing and impact forces for coarser grinding. For example:

- Single-disc mills in which food passes through an adjustable gap between a stationary casing and a grooved disc, which rotates at high speed.
- Double-disc mills which have two discs that rotate in opposite directions to produce greater shearing forces.
- Pin-and-disc mills which have intermeshing pins fixed either to the single disc and casing or to double discs. These improve the effectiveness of milling by creating additional impact and shearing forces.

Hammer Mills

These have a horizontal cylindrical chamber, lined with a toughened steel breaker plate. A high-speed rotor inside the chamber is fitted with swinging hammers along its length. Food is disintegrated mainly by impact forces as the hammers drive it against the breaker plate. Hammer mills are widely used for crystalline and fibrous materials including spices and sugar.

The above mills can be operated in three modes:

1. Free flow of materials through the mill in a single pass.
2. The exit from the mill is restricted by a screen and food remains in the mill until the particles are sufficiently small to pass through the screen apertures (under these 'choke' conditions, shearing forces play a larger part in the size reduction).
3. Recirculation through the mill of all material or larger pieces until sufficient size reduction has been achieved.

Roller Mills

Roller mills are widely used to mill wheat. Two or more steel rollers revolve towards each other and pull particles of food through the 'nip' (the space between the rollers). The main force is compression but, if the rollers are rotated at different speeds, or if the rollers are fluted, additional shearing forces are exerted on the food. The size of the nip is adjustable for different foods and overload springs protect against accidental damage from metal or stones.

Effect on foods

Size reduction is used in processing to control the textural or rheological properties of foods and to improve the efficiency of mixing and heat transfer. The texture of many foods (for example bread, hamburgers and juices) is controlled by the conditions used during size reduction of the ingredients. There is also an indirect effect on the aroma and flavour of some foods. The disruption of cells and resulting increase in surface area promotes oxidative deterioration and higher rates of microbiological and enzymic activity. Size reduction therefore has little or no preservative effect. Dry foods (for example grains or nuts) have a sufficiently low a_w to permit storage for several months after milling without substantial changes in nutritional value or eating quality.

Sensory characteristics: There are small but largely unreported changes in the colour, flavour and aroma of dry foods during size reduction. Oxidation of carotenes bleaches flour and reduces the nutritional value. There is a loss of volatile constituents from spices and some nuts, which is accelerated if the temperature is allowed to rise during milling. In moist foods the disruption of cells allows enzymes and substrates to become more intimately mixed, which causes accelerated deterioration of flavour, aroma and colour. Additionally the release of cellular materials provides a suitable substrate for microbiological growth and this can also result in the development of off-flavours and aromas. The texture of foods is substantially altered by size reduction, both by the physical reduction in the size of tissues and also by the release of hydrolytic enzymes. The type and duration of size reduction and the delay before subsequent preservation operations are closely controlled to achieve the desired texture.

Nutritional value: The increase in surface area of foods during size reduction causes loss of nutritional value due to oxidation of fatty acids and carotenes. Losses of vitamin C and thiamin in chopped or sliced fruits and vegetables are substantial (for example 78% reduction in vitamin C during slicing of cucumber). Losses during storage depend on the temperature and moisture content of the food and on the concentration of oxygen in the storage atmosphere. In dry foods the main loss in nutritional value results from separation of the product components after size reduction.

Size Reduction in Liquid Foods

The terms emulsifiers and homogenisers are often used interchangeably for equipment used to produce emulsions: emulsification is the formation of a stable emulsion by the intimate mixing of two or more immiscible liquids, so that one (the dispersed phase) is formed into very small droplets within the second (the continuous phase). Homogenisation is the reduction in size (to 0.5–30 μm), and hence the increase in number, of solid or liquid particles in the dispersed phase by the application of intense shearing forces. Homogenisation is therefore a more severe operation than emulsification. Both operations are used to change the functional properties or eating quality of foods and have little or no effect on nutritional value or shelf life. Examples of emulsified products include margarine and low-fat spreads, salad cream and mayonnaise, sausagemeat, ice cream and cakes.

The action of homogenisers reduces the size of droplets in the dispersed phase and emulsifying agents that are present in, or added to, a food form micelles around each droplet. This reduces the interfacial tension between the phases and prevents the droplets from coalescing (the higher the interfacial tension between the continuous and dispersed phases, the more difficult it is to form and maintain a stable emulsion). Emulsifying agents therefore lower the energy input needed to form an emulsion.

Naturally occurring proteins and phospholipids act as emulsifying agents, but in food processing synthetic agents (including esters of glycerol or sorbitan esters of fatty acids) are more effective and these are normally used. Synthetic emulsifying agents are classified into polar and non-polar types. Those that contain mostly polar groups bind to water and therefore produce o/w emulsions.

Polar emulsifying agents are also classified into ionic and non-ionic types. Ionic types have different surface activities over the pH range, owing to differences in their dissociation behaviour. The activity of nonionic emulsifiers is independent of pH. Careful selection of the type of emulsifying agent is therefore needed to create the required emulsion in a given food system. Stabilisers are polysaccharide hydrocolloids which dissolve in water to form viscous solutions or gels. In o/w emulsions, they increase the viscosity and form a three-dimensional network that stabilises the emulsion and prevents coalescence. Microcrystalline cellulose and related cellulose powders are able to stabilise w/o emulsions.

Equipments

The five main types of homogeniser are:

1. High-speed mixers
2. Pressure homogenisers
3. Colloid mills
4. Ultrasonic homogenisers
5. Hydroshear homogenisers and microfluidisers.

High-speed mixers: High-speed mixers use turbines or propellers, to pre-mix emulsions of low-viscosity liquids. They operate by a shearing action on the food at the edges and tips of the blades.

Pressure homogenisers: Pressure homogenisers consist of a high-pressure pump, operating at 10000–70000 × 10^3 Pa, which is fitted with a homogenising valve on the discharge side. When liquid is pumped through the small adjustable gap (up to 300 μm) between the valve and the valve seat, the high pressure produces a high liquid velocity (80–150 ms^{-1}). There is then an almost instantaneous drop in velocity as the liquid emerges from the valve. These extreme conditions of turbulence produce powerful shearing forces and the droplets in the dispersed phase become disrupted. The collapse of air bubbles (termed cavitation) and impact forces created in some valves by placing a hard surface (a breaker ring) in the path of the liquid, further reduce the globule size. In some foods, for example milk products, there may be inadequate distribution of the emulsifying agent over the newly formed surfaces, which causes fat globules to clump together. A second similar valve is then used to break up the clusters of globules. Pressure homogenisers are widely used before pasteurisation and ultra high-temperature sterilisation of milk, and in the production of salad creams, ice cream and some soups and sauces.

Colloid mills: Colloid mills are essentially disc mills with a small clearance (0.05–1.3 mm) between a stationary disc and a vertical disc rotating at 3000–15 000 rpm. They create high shearing forces and are more effective than pressure homogenisers for high-viscosity liquids. With intermediate-viscosity liquids they tend to produce larger droplet sizes than pressure homogenisers do. Numerous designs of disc, including flat, corrugated and conical shapes, are available for different applications. Modifications of this design include the use of two counter-rotating discs or intermeshing pins on the surface of the discs to increase the shearing action. For highly viscous foods (for example peanut butter, meat or fish pastes) the discs may be mounted horizontally as in the *paste mill*. The greater friction created in viscous foods may require these mills to be cooled by recirculating water.

Ultrasonic homogenisers: Ultrasonic homogenisers use high-frequency sound waves (18–30 kHz) to cause alternate cycles of compression and tension in low-viscosity liquids and cavitation of air bubbles, to form emulsions with droplet sizes of 1–2 μm. The two phases of an emulsion are pumped through the homogeniser at pressures of 340–1400 × 10^3 Pa. The ultrasonic energy is produced by a vibrating metal blade. The frequency of vibration is controlled by adjusting the clamping position of the blade. This type of homogeniser is used for the production of salad creams, ice cream, synthetic creams, baby foods and essential oil emulsions. It is also used for dispersing powders in liquids.

Effect on foods

Viscosity or texture: In many liquid and semi-liquid foods, the desired mouthfeel is achieved by careful selection of the type of emulsifying agent and stabiliser and by control over homogenisation conditions. In milk, homogenisation reduces the average size of fat globules from 4 m to less than 1 m, thereby giving the milk a creamier texture. The increase in viscosity is due to the higher number of globules and adsorption of casein onto the globule surface.

In solid food emulsions the texture is determined by the composition of the food, the homogenisation conditions and post-processing operations such as heating or freezing. Meat emulsions (for example sausage and pate´) are o/w emulsions in which the continuous phase is a complex colloidal system of gelatin, proteins, minerals and vitamins, and the dispersed phase is fat globules. The stability of the continuous phase is determined in part by the water-holding capacity (WHC) and fat-holding capacity (FHC) of the meat proteins. The quality of the emulsion is influenced by:

- The ratios of meat:ice:water:fat
- Use of polyphosphates to bind water
- The time, temperature and speed of homogenisation.

The emulsion is set by heat during subsequent cooking. Cream is an o/w emulsion that is mechanically agitated (churned) to cause a partial breakdown of the emulsion when it is made into butter. During this stage, air is incorporated to produce a foam. Liquid fat is released from globules at the surfaces of air bubbles, and this binds together clumps of solid fat to form butter 'grains'. These are then mixed at low speed (worked) to disperse water as fine droplets throughout the mass and to rupture any fat globules remaining from the cream. Although butter is thought of as a w/o emulsion, the complete inversion of the o/w emulsion of cream does not take place. The final product has a continuous phase of 85% fat which contains globules and crystals of solid fat and air bubbles. The dispersed phase (15%) consists of water droplets and buttermilk. The stability of butter is mostly due to its semi-solid nature which prevents migration of bacteria trapped in water droplets, and not due to the action of an emulsifying agent.

In ice cream and cake batters, the emulsion is formed as a liquid, and the texture of the final product is partly determined by subsequent unit operations of freezing and baking respectively. Ice cream is a thick o/w emulsion which has a complex continuous phase of ice crystals, colloidal milk solids, dissolved sugar, flavouring, colouring and stabilisers, and a solid–air foam. The dispersed phase is milk fat.

Freezing partially destabilises the emulsion to produce a degree of clumping of fat globules, which improves the texture. Commercial ice creams usually have a softer texture than home-made products due to faster freezing, which produces smaller (40–50 μ) ice crystals, the overrun, and emulsifiers (e.g. esters of mono- and diglycerides) and stabilisers (e.g. alginates, carrageenan, gums or gelatin), which cause a larger proportion of the aqueous phase to remain unfrozen. This prevents lactose crystallisation and reduces graininess. As a result, less heat is needed to melt the ice cream and it does not therefore feel excessively cold when eaten.

Cake batters are similarly o/w emulsions, in which the continuous phase is colloidal starch, a solution of sugar and flavours, and a foam produced during mixing. The dispersed phase is added fats or oils.

Colour, aroma, nutritional value and shelf life

Homogenisation has an effect on the colour of some foods (for example milk) because the larger number of globules causes greater reflectance and scattering of light. Flavour and aroma are improved in many emulsified foods because volatile components are dispersed throughout the food and hence have greater contact with taste buds when eaten. The nutritional value of emulsified foods is changed if components are separated (for example in butter making), and there is improved digestibility of fats and proteins owing to the reduction in particle size. The nutritional value of other foods is determined by the formulation used and is not directly affected by emulsification or homogenisation. However, the additional unit operations (for example chilling, freezing and baking), which are necessary to extend the shelf life, may cause changes to nutritional value. In all food emulsions, degradative changes such as hydrolysis or oxidation of pigments, aroma compounds and vitamins, and microbial growth on the finely dispersed material, are minimised by careful control over the processing, packaging and storage conditions. In many countries, special regulations are in force to control hygienic standards during preparation of food emulsions (particularly meat and dairy emulsions) owing to the risk of dispersing pathogenic bacteria throughout the food.

Chapter 8

Mixing and Forming

INTRODUCTION

The term 'mixing' essentially refers to operations reducing the non-uniformities in the spatial distribution of composition, properties, or temperature within bulk material. In the context of food processing, this is a necessary step. Variety of equipments are commercially available for use in specific mixing operations, such as dispersing flavour into solutions or solids, homogenising a suspension of particulates, forming pastes, and dissolving gases in aqueous solutions. These types of equipment are invariably very complex in design and the mechanisms by which homogeneity is brought about are not fully understood. This chapter highlights the characteristic features of food mixing, and provides an overview of the methods used to assess mixture quality and the types of equipment used for different processing operations. The scale of scrutiny determines whether a mixture can be considered as homogeneous or not. When a product contains several different phases, it is inevitable that it will appear segregated at a sufficiently small scale of scrutiny. The key consideration for any processor is to ensure that the product maintains homogeneity when examined on the consumer's scale of scrutiny. Mixing or dispersing ingredients is an essential step in most food processing operations. Ingredients can be used in any physical state of matter - solid, liquid or even gas. They can be dissolved to form a single uniform phase, or dispersed homogeneously to form multiphase mixtures. Today, a large majority of processed ready-to-eat products are indeed multiphase dispersions: solids dispersed in liquids (e.g. baked beans), emulsions (e.g. soups), or bubbly dispersions. Mixing is therefore recognised as one of the most widely practiced food processing operations. A wide variety of mixing equipment is in use, and novel mixing technologies are constantly emerging on the industrial scene. Despite the wide existence of a variety of mixers effectively used thus far, the mixing mechanisms operating within these devices are hardly understood. Consequently, it is extremely difficult to relate operating conditions with product quality on a firm scientific basis, and process design and control can only be achieved with the help of expensive practical trials.

IMPORTANCE OF FOOD MIXING

- Mixing involves a whole spectrum of materials from dry free-flowing powders to thin, viscous liquids and viscous pastes such as dough.

- More often than not, mixing involves too many components existing in different physical states, which have widely differing and time-dependent properties.
- Energy requirements for dispersing each component can also differ widely. For instance, emulsification requires high energy, whereas dispersion of delicate particulate matter in shear sensitive liquids requires relatively lower energy levels (e.g. dispersion of nuts into chocolate or whole fruits into yogurt).
- Mixing particulates also involves other characteristics: mixing and segregation occur simultaneously, and particulates are often polydisperse. Particle-liquid dispersion either involves particles dispersed into liquid bulk, or relatively low amounts of liquids dispersed with high volumes of particles (e.g. dispersion of flavours). Furthermore, when particles are dispersed into liquids, the rheological and interfacial properties of the continuous phase can change as mixing progresses. Moreover, segregation of blended components can also occur during discharge from the mixer: design of discharge is therefore critical.
- Food mixing can involve dispersion of air or gas bubbles into liquids and pastes. Bubble incorporation in processes (e.g. the manufacture of ice creams, sponge cakes, meringues, and bubbly chocolate confectionery) is so widely practiced that air and gases are increasingly being recognised as 'food ingredients'.
- In contrast, bubble incorporation, which inevitably accompanies the mixing of viscous recipes (e.g. sauces and salad cream), is undesirable, since it can result in inconsistent filling of packages and acceleration in spoilage. De-aeration or bubble exclusion can be classified as a food mixing operation since the end product results in a greater level of homogeneity.
- An idiosyncratic feature of food mixing (like many other food processing operations) is that it is rarely a process where mixing is the sole intended effect. A multitude of physico-chemical processes occurs simultaneously in the mixer environment, and the effectiveness of mixing can only be assessed in the context of end product quality.
- Finally, the effect of mixing can continue well after the mixing action has ceased, and it could be quite some time before the end point is reached. In such situations, on-line monitoring and process control can be very challenging.

It is therefore evident that the state of any mixture is the result of several highly complex mixing mechanisms operating in parallel. At this stage, it is desirable to discuss the ways of describing mixtures.

ASSESSMENT OF MIXEDNESS

Scale of Scrutiny

Although mixing normally aims to achieve an almost uniform distribution of components, the degree of uniformity must be assessable. An obvious method is to measure the concentration of each component and express it in terms of appropriately defined relative concentration. A problem at once arises. Since such assessments depend on sample size, what then should the scale of scrutiny be? It is inevitable that, as the scale of scrutiny decreases, a given component will appear more segregated. It is necessary that any practical process should achieve homogeneity on a pre-determined scale of scrutiny. From a producer's perspective, this scale may correspond to the volume of unit packages.

However, this does not necessarily correspond to the consumer's scale of scrutiny, which could be much smaller. One example used concerns the mixing of nutrients to form a cake for animal feeding. If the primary concern were to ensure that each animal receives the correct amount of nutrients daily, then the appropriate scale of scrutiny would be the volume corresponding to the daily intake of cake. However, if the criterion is to control the nutrient intake on a weekly basis, then the scale of scrutiny should be chosen according to the weekly consumption of cake. In the latter case, significant variations in nutrient concentration between daily feeds might exist, but averaged over the entire week, the nutrient intake would satisfy the overall requirement. It is therefore important to produce a product that is homogeneous based on the consumer's scale of scrutiny.

FOOD MIXING IN THE INDUSTRIAL PROCESSES

Many foods have to be preceded by a mixing process in order to achieve characteristics that are important for the final product such as texture, homogeneity, composition and temperature. Mixing can start as early as the preparation of ingredients and can be continuously used until the end of the process. It has been one of the most used steps for food preparation for a long time. Even if it is a very basic step it has not been understood in its totality because of its wide variety of uses. Food mixing can go from nano-emulsions to large particle suspensions, highly viscous pastes to dry powders with or without the incorporation of gas.

The ingredients being mixed directly influence the equipment type that should be used depending on the mixing scenario (solid-solid mixing [powders or textural effects], solid-liquid mixing [coffee, sugar] or liquid-solid mixing [butters, pastes and dough], liquid-liquid mixing [emulsions: margarines and spreads] and gas-liquid mixing [fermentation or chlorination]). It is important to consider a balance between the equipment and ingredients properties in order to obtain an effective size of production without using a large quantity of time and energy consumption, this would relapse in a better process and energy efficiency. Another important parameter for sizing the equipment is the rheology. In the food industry hygienic design and suitability of cleaning are very important issues to consider because of the consequences that could result from a poor hygienic standard, for example the contamination of the product by microbial growth. For the mixing of fluids some of the most important equipment items used are: the paddle mixer, anchor mixers, turbine mixers (different impellers), propeller mixers and the new generation of static mixers.

All these types of fluid mixing equipments are used for different applications: to prevent scorching, to promote heat transfer (jacketed kettles), mass transfer, phase dispersion, low or high viscosities or the combination of two or more of these items. Mixing of solids is more difficult than liquids because of its tendency to segregate and the different sizes, shapes and densities. The equipment for solids could be divided in two sections: Diffusive mixers (random motion of particles by the effect of gravity or vibration) and convective mixers (mechanical agitation). The most common diffusive mixers are the drum blender, the double-cone tumbler and the V-shaped tumbler, for convective mixing, the most common equipment pieces are the paddle mixer and the trough mixers that have a ribbon mixer, a very common solid mixer, in its category. Different mixers are used for solid mixing. There are some complex foods like dough and paste-like products that need to have intensive mixing. The equipment for these types of operations are built to deliver high rotational momentum even with low rotational speed giving us a considerable energy input per unit mass. The mechanical energy applied to these types of products is transformed into heat and this is the reason why a cooling jacket is often provided in order to prevent overheating. Some machines for kneading are: the planetary mixers, horizontal dough mixers, sigma blade mixers and cutter mixers. 'The quality of mixing depends on the effective energy input by unit mass or unit volume fluid.' The power number, the Reynolds number and the Froude number are important power correlations in the field of mixing. These are the numbers that help to know and understand all the important forces taking place in each case of mixing, relating the dimensions, type and operating conditions. The Froude number contains the gravitational forces, the Reynolds number contemplates the inertial and viscous forces and the power number relates the power (torque) with the diameter of the impeller, speed shaft and density of the liquid. The Reynolds number is a very important parameter because it helps to understand the flow regime and it also helps to determine if the power number is constant or not. The Froude number is just important if the Reynolds number is over 300 and if the vessel is not baffled (only where vortex formation takes place).

Mixing in the food industry is used mainly to obtain homogeneity with the best possible equipment and the best relation of the power correlations. Food mixing has not been totally developed because of the constant change in products with different additives, functional ingredients and changing stringent labelling, and because of the many purposes of the 'mixing' equipment, for example, the modification of the structure of food or the development of texture in order to get better sensory characteristics. The fact that some viscoelastic products should retain the gas produced during the process and some other products should avoid gas dispersion, make the situation more complicated. With the development of Computational Fluid Dynamics (CFD), it is easier to explain fluid flow as well as heat and mass transfer phenomena leading to better equipment design and process control for the mixing process. Finally it is necessary to underline the most important differences between the chemical mixing and the food mixing: cleanliness and sanitation, where official regulations are involved, and the adaptation of the general mixing in order to prevent degradation or unwanted cooking, for example the material of the equipment parts that are going to be in contact with the product should be made of stainless steel or other materials that could stand vigorous cleaning and sanitising. Food mixing can happen between liquid-liquid, gas-liquid, and solid-liquid. This section focuses on emulsions, one of the most complicated liquid-liquid mix, and gas-liquid mixing due to its wide application and the reappearance and creation of products based on air as the most abundant ingredient.

Emulsions

One of the biggest groups of mixing is Liquid-Liquid mixing, containing emulsions as an important part of it due to its complexity. Many products in the food industry are emulsions or have been produced via an emulsion. Emulsions are not just complex in their structure but also in their composition as well as in their dynamic. An emulsion consists of two immiscible liquids, with one of the liquids dispersed as small spherical droplets in the other. Some examples of food emulsions are milk, butter, desserts, soups, mayonnaise, salad creams, and sauces. The main objectives of the food industry are to get a homogeneous fluid as well as to use the basic principles and techniques to improve the food quality keeping the price low. High-quality emulsions can be produced by choosing the right emulsifier, the most suitable process to produce the emulsion, proper packaging, and storage. The quality itself is affected by the properties of the emulsion, which is strongly influenced by concentration, distribution, and size of the droplets. There are a large variety of emulsions because of the diversity of ingredients that can be used. The physio-chemical and organoleptic properties of an emulsion are defined by its structure, type, concentration as well as the interactions between its components. Usually emulsions are polydisperse systems, which mean that the diameter of the droplets varies from droplet to droplet. If necessary, monodisperse emulsions may also be produced. Even if the properties of every single component of an emulsion are known, the actual behaviour of the emulsion cannot be predicted. This is because of complex interactions between its ingredients as well as between the droplets. Those droplet-interactions are responsible for the rheology, stability, appearance, and many other characteristics of the emulsion. If the temperature, the pH or the concentration of emulsifier change or if some salt is added, the properties of the emulsion can change immensely. Therefore the important parts of an emulsion are: the emulsifier, the type of emulsion and its stability and the equipment used to achieve the required properties.

The emulsifiers are so-called surface-active molecules, which are absorbed by the surface of the droplet right after its formation, and keep them from reunifying. There are natural and synthetic emulsifiers. The natural ones are just a few, the synthetic ones are made of natural emulsifiers by treating them with chemicals. Many emulsifiers are amphilic molecules, which mean that they consist of a polar and a non-polar part. This enables them to form a connection between the immiscible liquids. If there is just a lipophilic, then there will be no dispersion at all. A slightly dispersed solution is created by increasing the ratio of the hydrophilic and decreasing the one of the lipophilic which produces a water-in-oil emulsion. When the portion of the hydrophilic rise, the emulsion changes from water-in-oil to an oil-in-water emulsion and finally to a colloidal solution.

Even though the emulsifiers decrease the interfacial tension between both liquids, it does not improve the disruption, which is accomplished through mechanical agitation. In the food industry, it is normal to take a combination of a couple of emulsifier, so that multiple functions are covered. The use of this kind of combined emulsifier enables, for example, a cake to be soft, moist and fluffy at the same time. Usually the emulsifiers in the food industry are small surfactants, phospholipids, proteins and polysaccharides. Some of them are based on mono-glycerol and its derivates.

Furthermore the type of emulsion and its stability have to be considered. Emulsions can be classified by their relative distribution of the oily and aqueous phase. Besides the classic emulsion of water-in-oil (W/O) and oil-in-water (O/W), there are so-called 'multiple emulsions' such as water-in-oil-in-water (W/O/W) and oil-in-water-in-oil (O/W/O). In the W/O/W emulsion, the dispersed phase consists of a water-in-oil emulsion, which has then been 'emulsified' in an aqueous phase.

Many food emulsions not only contain an aqueous and oily phase and an emulsifier, but also other substances such as vitamins, fatty acids, proteins and sugar for example. The stability of an emulsion is the most important property which means that the emulsion's properties's do not change over time. The diameter of the droplets is supposed to be constant and therefore physically stable. Without any emulsifier a mixture of oil and water will separate immediately when the mixing process stops. By the usage of an emulsifier, the mixture can be kinetically stabilised for a certain period of time and the emulsion is 'kinetically trapped'. The stability of an emulsion can be negatively influenced by chemical reactions such as oxidation. This phenomenon can be inhibited by adding antioxidants. Instability can also be caused by other external factors such as light. If the viscosity of the continuous phase is increased, the droplets are not able to move easily, so that the stability of the emulsion is enhanced. To raise the viscosity, thickening or gelling agents may be used. 'Among the principle food stabilisers are alginates, cellulose derivate, gelatine, pectin, starch and other jelly forming substances.'

The mixing of immiscible liquids with an appropriate emulsifier can be carried out by using intense mechanical agitation such as high speed blenders and high pressure valve homogenisers. Emulsion can also be produced by forcing the liquid, the dispersed phase, either through a membrane or a micro-structured system, or by using ultra sound. Here the droplets will be detached by the flow of the continuous phase. Another type of equipment is homogenisers. Homogenisation is the diameter reduction of droplets in an already existing emulsion by applying high shear forces and often high pressure (up to 70 MPa). High-pressure homogenisation is widely used in the food industry, especially for the production of fine dispersed emulsions. As an example, in the dairy industry high-pressure homogenisation is used to prevent milk from creaming. Salad dressings, sauces, and soups are emulsified by a homogeniser. To mix highly viscous immiscible liquids there are mixers, which are characterised by their ability to deliver a high rotational moment at a low speed. Thereby energy is often converted into a lot of heat, so that the process is usually cooled. Planetary and sigma-blade mixers are examples for those kind of agitators. In these agitators, the shear force is intense and because of this reason, enormous changes in the structure of the emulsion takes place. Emulsions are an enormous part of the food industry. For example, 'Milk is transformed into a vast array of dairy products: fluid milks and creams, evaporated and dried products, yogurt and fermented milk products, butter, ice cream, and cheese.' Raw milk is an oil-in-water emulsion with approximately 4% fat present in the dispersed phase. The droplets are sized between 1–4 μm and are surrounded by a membrane, which helps to stabilise them. If the milk were not homogenised, the fat droplets would cream. In mayonnaise, on the other hand, an acidified aqueous phase is mixed with oil to an emulsion by using egg yolk and phospholipids as emulsifier. There are a lot of reasons why emulsions are complex and the diameter, the size distribution as well as the density of the droplets changing during homogenisation are some of the most representative.

Gas-Liquid

Besides liquid-liquid mixing, gas-liquid mixing plays an important role in the food industry. Gas-Liquid mixing is explained because of its wide application and the new development of products based on air as the most abundant ingredient. Gas incorporation is an important process in the food industry, as many foods such as bread, beer, champagne, ice cream and even some chocolates contain bubbles. 'The inclusion of bubbles in foods permits creation of very novel structures.' Gas incorporation is also important for foods such as cheese and yogurt for bacteria growth. Foams are common in many food products such as beer, breakfast cereal, and ice cream. The two principal methods for mixing gas into liquids are mechanical agitation under positive pressure and steam-induced mixing. The method of mixing the phases is not the only important part of the Gas-Liquid mixing also the amount of gas incorporated should be analysed. Gas hold up is seen to be the gauge of the level of bubbles in liquid foods. 'Gas-hold up values in bubble-containing liquid foods range from 15% to 20%, for example, in milkshakes, to over 90% in extruded products such as popcorn and rice cakes.' Using agitation under positive pressure is a very common method and can be seen in almost every kitchen with an electric whisker. This process effectively beats air into the material to produce bubbles in the liquid 'larger air bubbles are initially incorporated from the head space and their sizes diminish as agitation proceeds.' Another common positive pressure gas liquid device is a carbonator. A carbonator relies on mass transfer principles and allows close contact between the gas (carbon dioxide) and the liquid. Other important factors to influence the degree of carbonation include the pressure of the system, gas solubility, time and area of contact.

Steam-induced mixing is applied to such products as cereals, puffed rice and popcorn. The structure of these products are formed by introducing pellets into a toasting oven, where the material is exposed to a temperature of up to 300°C for up to 90 seconds. This extreme heat causes the trace amount of water in the porous structure to evaporate into steam, which then forces its way out of the pellet creating the expanded product .Steam-induced mixing can also be found in every coffee shop. Steam is injected into the milk and air is entrained in the headspace of the coffee cup.

Gas incorporation is an important to the field of food mixing because so many products use air for visual looks and product shaping. Methods of completing these tasks include mechanical agitation under positive pressure. This includes carbonators which are used to carbonate such things as soda and beer. Steam-induced mixing is used for such things as puffed rice, popcorn, and many kinds of coffee.

Sanitation

Although the interactions between liquids, solids and rheology in all mixing situations are important, it is necessary to emphasise the difference between general mixing and the mixing in food industry, sanitisation. The cleanliness of the equipment is crucial in maintaining product quality. In simple mixers, such as a paddle type mixer, the sanitation issues that arise are relatively simple. Other than basic cleaning and drying of the mixing paddles, the main issue that arises is the placement of the bearings and grease fittings. To ensure the quality of the product, bearings and fittings must be placed away from the product stream, in case leakage occurs. When it is impractical for such placement, the bearings are required to be sealed in a casing, which must be periodically checked for leaking. As the mixers become more complex, sanitation problems become more complex. Mixers such as reel-type mixers and twin screw mixers experience problems because build up occurs at the side walls and at the end of the mixers. There are two cleaning procedures that are used for more complex equipment, cleaning out of place and cleaning in place.

Cleaning out of place (COP) operation requires the mixer be disassembled to properly expose all soiled surfaces that may compromise product quality. Each individual component of the mixer is rinsed, cleaned, sanitised, dried, and reassembled. Common practice dictates that tubing and equipment parts be machine cleaned using turbulent fluid flow and brushes, while permanent equipment, such as tanks and holding vessels, are manually cleaned using high pressure nozzles, detergents and sanitisers. Since COP operation requires the equipment to be disassembled into its individual components, it is quite intensive labour and therefore it has obvious negative economic consequences. For this reason centralised cleaning in place, or CIP, are being investigated to replace COP systems.

CIP operation allows the mixers to be cleaned in place by passing strong hot cleaning solutions at high velocities through the equipment. In order to ensure proper sanitation inspection of the equipment is still required, and thus mixers are designed so they can be easily dissembled with simple tools. A typical CIP system contains a central metering pump, a detergent source, and a piping system to distribute the cleaning solution. Rinsing, cleaning, and sanitising fluids circulate along the path of the product and provide the detergents and mechanical action needed to remove any contaminants. In the food industry two types of CIP systems are prevalent: single use and reuse systems. In a single use system, the detergents and sanitisers are run through the system for only one cleaning cycle and are then discarded. Advantages of these systems are that they tend to be fairly inexpensive and require very little space. Reuse CIP systems are more expensive and require more floor space because they recycle the cleaning fluids by storing them between subsequent cycles. Converting from COP to CIP is thought to be one of the greatest advances in food plant design, as it causes a significant decrease in the labour needed for sanitation processes, which increases economic return. Since CIP systems are more efficient and cost friendly than COP systems, they are slowly becoming more common in the food industry.

The main focus of food mixing is to ensure the homogeneity of the product. The equipment used and the mixing power correlations are important to know in order to properly understand mixing applications in the food industry and the complexities faced by each. Additionally, the problem of contamination/ cleanliness of the equipment can effect the entire production (batch), which can cause changes in the properties of the product or even lead to the complete degradation of the product.

Chapter 9

Separation and Concentration of Food Components

INTRODUCTION

Foods are complex mixtures of compounds and the extraction or separation of food components is fundamental for the preparation of ingredients to be used in other processes (for example cooking oils from oilseeds or gelatin from connective tissue), or for retrieval of high value compounds, such as enzymes. Other types of separation methods are used to sort foods by separating them into classes based on size, colour or shape, to clean them by separating contaminating materials, or to selectively remove water from foods by evaporation or by dehydration. This chapter discusses various methods of separations such as filtration, centrifugation, adsorbent, membrane filtration, etc.

FILTRATION

Filtration is one of the most common methods for the downstream processing of fermentation products and it is used at all production scales. Basic principle in filtration is to separate the suspended particles or larger molecular mass components from bulk liquid with porous medium. Filtration is applicable as a separation method when molecular sizes of substances in process stream differ significantly. Several parameters affect effectivity of filtration processes, such as pore size, pressure and temperature. Filtration processes and equipment are often classified by pore size, direction of flow in relation to filter, type of filter and geometry of filters. Typically in the field of bioprocess technology, the highest equipment and operating cost exist in the downstream processing of fermentation products. Manufacturing costs, including capital and operational expenses, of downstream processing part can be up to 50% of the overall costs. Often the situation is that operational costs exceed clearly all other expenses and thus any improvements in the efficiency of downstream processing can have significant effects in the profitability of the process.

Theory of Filtration

Filtration is one of the most common methods for the downstream processing of fermentation products and it is used at all production scales. Basic principle in filtration is to separate the suspended particles or larger molecular mass components from bulk liquid with porous medium. Driving force can be pressure difference, vacuum, concentration gradient, valence or electrochemical affinity.

In principle, filtration and membrane separation technologies can be used in four different ways: (i) clarifying the cells from the fermentation broth and conditioning the cells for mechanical or chemical disruption, (ii) clarifying the products from homogenate of cellular debris after the disruption process, (iii) clarifying extracellular product from the culture after fermentation, and (iv) concentration and diafiltration of a clarified product for chromatography.

Filtration materials can be classified in depth filters, screen filter and membranes. Depth filters and screen filter are commonly used in dead-end filtration, while membranes are used in tangential flow filtration. Depth filters do not have a precise pore size or structure and thus they are not absolute. This means that particles with wider range in size will permeate through the filter. Components that are larger than the apertures of the filter will be trapped on the surface of the filter. In the case of smaller particles, random entrapment and adsorption of matter occurs within the structure of the media. Depth filter may also have an electric charge which aids in the entrapment of smaller particles. Depth filters have thicker construction and higher porosity. This leads to some advantages, such as higher flow rate and dirt loading capacity when compared to screens and membrane filters. They are also cheaper than many screens and membrane filters. Depth filters are manufactured from fibrous materials, woven or nonwoven polymeric material or inorganic materials.

MEMBRANE FILTRATION

A membrane is a thin layer of semi-permeable material that separates substances when a driving force is applied across the membrane. Membrane processes are increasingly used for removal of bacteria, micro-organisms, particulates, and natural organic material, which can impart colour, tastes, and odours to water and react with disinfectants to form disinfection by-products. As advancements are made in membrane production and module design, capital and operating costs continue to decline. The membrane processes discussed here are microfiltration (MF), ultrafiltration (UF), nanofiltration (NF), and reverse osmosis (RO).

Membrane materia: Normally, membrane material is manufactured from a synthetic polymer, although other forms, including ceramic and metallic 'membranes,' may be available. Almost all membranes manufactured for drinking water are made of polymeric material, since they are significantly less expensive than membranes constructed of other materials.

Membranes constructed of polymers that react with oxidants used in drinking water treatment should not be used with chlorinated feed water. Mechanical strength is another consideration, since a membrane with greater strength can withstand larger trans-membrane pressure (TMP) levels, allowing for greater operational flexibility and the use of higher pressures.

Membranes with bi-directional strength may allow cleaning operations or integrity testing to be performed from either feed or filtrate side of the membrane. Membranes with a particular surface charge may remove particulate or microbial contaminants of the opposite charge due to electrostatic attraction. Membranes can also be hydrophilic (water attracting) or hydrophobic (water repelling). These terms describe how easily membranes can be wetted, as well as its ability to resist fouling to some degree.

MF and UF membranes may be constructed from a wide variety of materials, including cellulose acetate, polyvinylidene fluoride, polyacrylonitrile, polypropylene, polysulphone, polyethersulphone, or other polymers. Each of these materials has different properties with respect to the surface charge, degree of hydrophobicity, pH and oxidant tolerance, strength and flexibility.

NF and RO membranes are generally manufactured from cellulose acetate or polyamide materials, and their various advantages and disadvantages. Cellulose membranes are susceptible to biodegradation and must be operated within a narrow, pH range of 4 to 8 but they do have some resistance to continuous low-level oxidants. Chlorine doses of 0.5 mg/L or less may control biodegration and biological fouling without damaging the membrane. Polyamide membranes, by contrast, can be used under a wide range of pH conditions and are not subject to biodegradation. Although these membranes have very limited tolerance for strong oxidants, they are compatible with weaker oxidants such as cholramines. These membranes require significantly less pressure to operate and have become the predominate material used for NF or RO applications.

Membrane modules: Membrane filters are usually manufactured as flat sheet stock or as hollow fibers and then formed into on of several different types of membrane modules. Module construction typically involves potting or sealing the membrane material into an assembly, such as with hollow-fiber module. These types of modules are designed for long-term use over the course of a number of years. Spiral-wound modules are also manufactured for long-term use, although these modules are encased in a separate pressure vessel that is independent of the module itself.

Microfiltration

Microfiltration (MF) is a well-known separation process, which is capable of removing particle sizes of micro-scale (from 0.02 μm up to 10 μm) in contaminated liquid or gas streams by a semi-permeable membrane of certain pore size. The separable size of particle has different specifications depending on the study, but the scale is similar. The most prominent process designs for MF include in-line (dead-end) filtration and cross-flow (tangential) filtration. In in-line filtration the feed stream is forced completely through the membrane which results in particle accumulation on membrane surface and a particle free permeate. In cross-flow filtration the feed is circulated across the membrane surface which results in particle free permeate and in retentate concentrated in particles. The membranes utilised in MF can be divided in two classes: In depth and screen membranes. The difference between them is the pore size and particle capture site. In depth membranes have small pores that capture the particles on the surface on the membrane and screen membranes have larger pores which capture the particles in the membrane interior. The membranes are usually fitted in special cartridges, which enable folding of the membranes and thus larger surface area. Modern cartridge filter units have multiple cartridges installed.

MF processes in industry usually consist of two cartridge filters (pre filter and final filter) consisting of two or more membranes, a feed-pump and pressure difference measuring and control equipment. The prefilter is the main filtering unit, which captures the largest of particles and the final filter is used to capture the residual fine particles. The main purpose of prefilter is to prevent plugging of the fine filter and thus extend its operation time. By measuring and controlling the pressure difference across the filters their stage of plugging can be controlled: Pressure difference rises as the filters are covered with particles until the preset value of pressure difference is met and the filters are changed. To extend filter life some modern cross-flow filter a back-flushing (long flow reversal) or -pulsing (short reversal) method is used. In back-flushing the filter membrane is flushed opposite to filtrate flow direction with water or solvent in order to remove particles from filter.

Ultrafiltration

Ultrafiltration (UF) is a separation process that makes use of filters with pore size between 1 and 20 nanometers. Membrane permeability in UF is however often specified by molecular weight cut-off

(MWCO) rather than by pore diameter. The separation is often done using hydraulic pressure of 2 to 10 atmospheres to force low molecular weight solutes through membrane. UF membranes are designed to provide high retention of proteins and other macromolecules by small pore size and sometimes by electrostatic interactions. Amino acids generally pass through UF membranes, while proteins are too large to pass through. UF is typically used for protein concentration and buffer exchange, processes which were earlier performed using size exclusion chromatography. However, UF is practical only when separating molecules whose molecular weights differ by at least a factor of ten as the membranes often have significant variance in pore size. At industrial scale, UF processes are generally carried out as fed batch operations followed by batch operation. Membrane material is typically composite regenerated cellulose in industrial scale, but also regenerated cellulose, polysulphone and polyethersulfone can be used. Membranes can be either anisotropic or isotropic. Anisotropic filters have a thin skin with small pores on top of a thicker, highly porous layer that provides mechanical strength. Isotropic, self-supporting filters have homogenous structure that allows them to be cleaned by backflushing. Anisotropic filters are geometrically generally flat sheets while isotropic filters are hollow fibers.

Industrial significance and general applications

Both ultrafiltration and microfiltration are applied in dairy industry. Microfiltration can be applied in dairy industry for bacteria removal or protein extraction process for manufacturing. Microfiltration can be used in cheese making process to extract proteins for the manufacture of whey protein isolates and micellar casein products. Another MF application in dairy industry is treatment of dairy effluents and waste streams. Those effluents represent a risk of pollution, and cross-flow microfiltration is used for bacteria removal, which provides a lower-temperature approach for microbial growth control. That leads to extended shelf life of the products. Microporous membranes can be also applied on testing for micro-organisms, clinical and general laboratory applications and in the cold sterilisation of fluids. In the cold sterilisation of the fluids the membranes are used to remove micro-organisms from the fluid with the dead-end flow. The required pore size is 0.2–0.45 μm.

Ultrafiltration method has three group of applications: concentration, desalting and fractionation. Concentration will decrease the solvent volumes during isolation and purification. The solvent is removed through the membrane. Ultrafiltration is used for decreasing the solvent volumes during isolation and purification, replacing older techniques such as evaporation, precipitation, gel filtration and dialysis.

When ultrafiltration is used for desalting, small molecules quantitatively passes through the membrane along with the solvent and macromolecules are retained by the membrane. The simplest desalting method is to replace the solvent that had passed through the membrane with contaminant free solvent.

Fractionation is the separation of molecules with different size. The dilute mixture of components with higher and lower molecular weights is filtered through the membrane, and the component with higher molecular mass (retentate) is rejected when the component with smaller molar mass (filtrate) passes the membrane. Ultrafiltration method is applied on deproteinisation of blood and urine samples. The advantage of ultrafiltration method in deproteinisation is that UF can be used for all analyses without any change of the solute concentration. Furthermore, ultrafiltration method adds no ions to the sample, unlike the standard technique.

Thus, filtration is effective and relatively cheap method for separating or concentrating products in downstream processing. It can be applied at several different points in downstream processing and combined with other separation techniques. Filtration is also often relatively easy process to scale up and the equipment doesn't take as much space as many other separation processes. However, it is not always applicable as it requires the molecules in incoming stream to have significant difference in their molecular weight.

CENTRIFUGATION

Centrifugation is one of the most important and widely applied research techniques in food procesing, biochemistry, cellular and molecular biology, evaluation of suspensions and emulsions in pharmacy and in medicine. Current research and clinical applications rely on isolation of cells, subcellular organelles, and macromolecules, often in high yields. A centrifuge uses centrifugal force (g-force) to isolate suspended particles from their surrounding medium on either a batch or a continuous–flow basis.

Many particles or cells in a liquid suspension, given time, will eventually settle at the bottom of a container due to gravity. However the length of time required for such separations is impractical. Other particles, extremely small in size, will not separate at all in solution, unless subjected to high centrifugal force. When a suspension is rotated at a certain speed or revolutions per minute (rpm), centrifugal force causes the particles to move radially away from the axis of rotation. The force on the particles (compared to gravity) is called Relative Centrifugal Force (RCF). For example, an RCF of 500 × g indicates that the centrifugal force is 500 times greater than earthly gravitational force. Centrifugation is a process which involves the use of the centrifugal force for the sedimentation of heterogeneous mixtures with a centrifuge, used in industry and in laboratory settings. This process is used to separate two immiscible liquids. More-dense components of the mixture migrate away from the axis of the centrifuge, while less-dense components of the mixture migrate towards the axis. Pharmacists, chemists and biologists may increase the effective gravitational force on a test tube so as to move rapidly and completely cause the precipitate (pellet) to gather on the bottom of the tube. The remaining solution is properly called the 'supernate' or 'supernatant liquid'. The supernatant liquid is then either quickly decanted from the tube without disturbing the precipitate, or withdrawn with a Pasteur pipette.

As enunciated by Sir Isaac Newton in his first law of motion, a freely moving body (such as a ball) tends to travel in a straight line, and if directed along a curved path by some restraining force (such as would result were a hand-held string tied to it) it will exert a force against the directing or restraining force in its continual effort to fly off onto a straight tangential course. It is a familiar observation that an object revolving in a circle exerts a force away from the centre of rotation. This force, which is the outward pull of the ball on its string, is the centrifugal force. Also, there is general appreciation of the fact that the amount of this force can be increased by increasing either the angular velocity of rotation, the mass of the object, or the radius of the circle through which the object moves. Perhaps not so generally appreciated is the fact that whereas the centrifugal force is directly proportional to the radius and to the mass, it is proportional to the square of the angular velocity. For example, doubling the mass of the rotating object will increase the centrifugal force by a factor of 2, but doubling the number of revolutions per minute (rpm) will increase the centrifugal force by a factor of 4 (equals 2 times 2), similarly, increasing the speed by a factor of 10 will increase the force by a factor of 100 (equals 10 times 10). Centrifugal force is expressed by the basic relation $F = mv^2/R = 4\pi^2 mn^2R$, F is the centrifugal force, m the mass, R the radius, v the speed, and n the number of revolutions per second.

Centrifuge is any device that applies a sustained centrifugal force, that is, a force due to rotation. Effectively, the centrifuge substitutes a similar, stronger, force for that of gravity. Every centrifuge contains a spinning vessel, there are many configurations, depending on use. A perforated rotating drum in a laundry that throws off excess water from clothes, for example, is a type of centrifuge. A similar type is used in industry to separate fluids from solid matter after crushing.

Basics of Centrifugation

The Earth gravitational force is sufficient to separate many types of particles over time. A tube of anticoagulated whole blood left standing on a bench top will eventually separate into plasma, red blood cell and white blood cell fractions. However, the length of time required precludes this manner of separation for most applications. In practice, centrifugal force is necessary to separate most particles. In addition, the potential degradation of biological compounds during prolonged storage means faster separation techniques are needed.

Principles of centrifugation

Particles having a size above 5 μm sediment at the bottom due to gravitation force. Such a suspension can be separated by simple filtration techniques. If the size of particles is less than 5 μm they undergo Brownian motion. In such suspension a stronger centrifugal force is applied to separate the particles.

Considering a body of mass m rotating in a circular path of radius r at a velocity of v (Fig. 9.1). The force acting on the body in a radial direction is given by:

$$F = mv^2/r$$

where, F = centrifugal force, m = mass of body, v = velocity of the body, r = radius of circle of rotation.

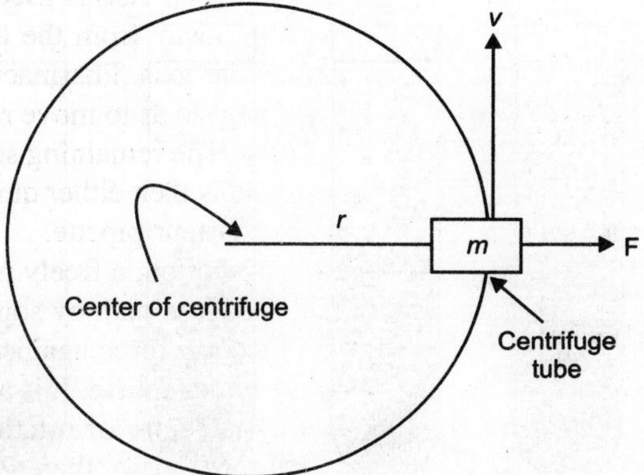

Fig. 9.1: Illustration of the principle of centrifugation.

The gravitational force acting upon the same body G = mg

where, G = gravitational force, g = acceleration due to gravity.

The centrifugal effect is the ratio of the centrifugal force and gravitational forces so that

$$C = F/G = mv^2/mgr = v^2/gr \qquad ...(9.1)$$

Since, $v = 2\pi$ rn where n = speed of rotation (rpm)

$$C = F/G = (2\pi\ rn)^2/g\ r = 4\pi^2\ r^2n^2 = 2\pi^2/g\ D\ n^2 = kD\ n^2 \qquad ...(9.2)$$

where, $k = 2\pi^2/g$ = constant D = maximum diameter of the centrifuge. D can be measured from the center of the centrifuge to the free surface of the liquid or to the tip of the centrifuge tube.

From the equation $C = kDn^2$ it can be concluded that

Centrifugal effect ∝ diameter of centrifuge

Centrifugal effect ∝ (speed of rotation)^2

Applications of principle of centrifugation

If the particles of suspensions are very small then high centrifugal effect will be required to separate the particles. To separate such suspensions the size of the centrifuge is kept smaller but it is rotated at very high speed (rpm). If a large amount of material is to be separated and a low centrifugal effect is sufficient to separate the suspension then the diameter (D) of the centrifuge is increased and speed (n) is kept low.

Types of Centrifugation Separations

There are two types of centrifugal techniques for separating particles, differential centrifugation and density gradient centrifugation. Density gradient centrifugation can further be divided into rate-zonal and isopycnic centrifugation.

Differential centrifugation

The simplest form of separation by centrifugation is differential centrifugation, sometime called differential pelleting (Fig. 9.2). Particles of different densities or sizes in a suspension will sediment at different rates, with the larger and denser particles sedimenting faster. These sedimentation rates can be increased by using centrifugal force. A suspension of cells subjected to a series of increasing centrifugal force cycles will yield a series of pellets containing cells of decreasing sedimentation rate.

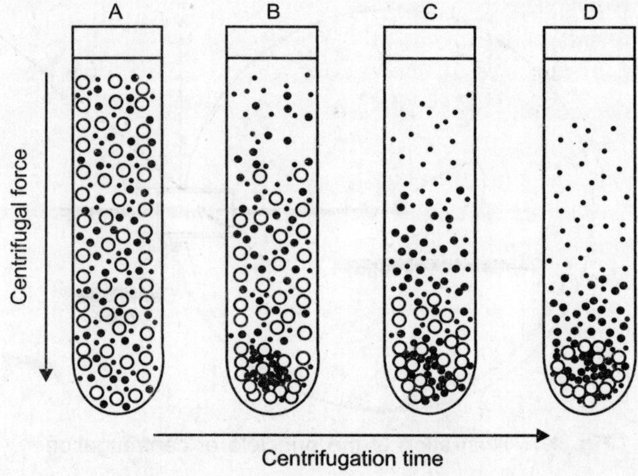

Fig. 9.2: Differential centrifugation.

Particles of different densities or size will sediment at different rates with the largest and most dense particles sedimenting the fastest followed by less dense and smaller particles. Differential pelleting is commonly used for harvesting cells or producing crude subcellular fractions from tissue homogenate. For example, a rat liver homogenate containing nuclei, mitochondria, lysosomes, and membrane vesicles that is centrifuged at low speed for a short time will pellet mainly the larger and more dense nuclei. Subsequent centrifugation at a higher centrifugal force will pellet particles of the next lower order of size (e.g. mitochondria) and so on. It is unusual to use more than four differential centrifugation cycles for a normal tissue homogenate. Due to the heterogeneity in biological particles, differential centrifugation suffers from contamination and poor recoveries. Contamination by different particle types can be addressed by resuspension and repeating the centrifugation steps (i.e. washing the pellet).

Density gradient centrifugation

Density gradient centrifugation is the preferred method to purify subcellular organelles and macromolecules. Density gradients can be generated by placing layer after layer of gradient media such as sucrose in a tube with the heaviest layer at the bottom and the lightest at the top in either a discontinuous mode. The cell fraction to be separated is placed on top of the layer and centrifuged. Density gradient separation can be classified into two categories, rate–zonal (size) separation and isopycnic (density) separation.

Rate-zonal centrifugation: In rate-zonal centrifugation the problem of cross-contamination of particles of different sedimentation rates may be avoided by layering the sample as a narrow zone on top of a density gradient. In this way the faster sedimenting particles are not contaminated by the slower particles as occurs in differential centrifugation. However, the narrow load zone limits the volume of sample (typically 10%) that can be accommodated on the density gradient. The gradient stabilises the bands and provides a medium of increasing density and viscosity.

Sample is layered as a narrow zone on the top of a density gradient. Under centrifugal force, particles move at different rates depending on their mass. The speed at which particles sediment depends primarily on their size and mass instead of density. As the particles in the band move down through the density medium, zones containing particles of similar size form as the faster sedimenting particles move ahead of the slower ones. Because the density of the particles is greater than the density of the gradient, all the particles will eventually form a pellet if centrifuged long enough.

Isopycnic centrifugation: In isopycnic separation, also called buoyant or equilibrium separation, particles are separated solely on the basis of their density. Particle size only affects the rate at which particles move until their density is the same as the surrounding gradient medium. The density of the gradient medium must be greater than the density of the particles to be separated. By this method, the particles will never sediment to the bottom of the tube, no matter how long the centrifugation time.

Starting with a uniform mixture of sample and density gradient (Fig, 9.3A) under centrifugal force, particles move until their density is the same as the surrounding medium (Fig. 9.3B).

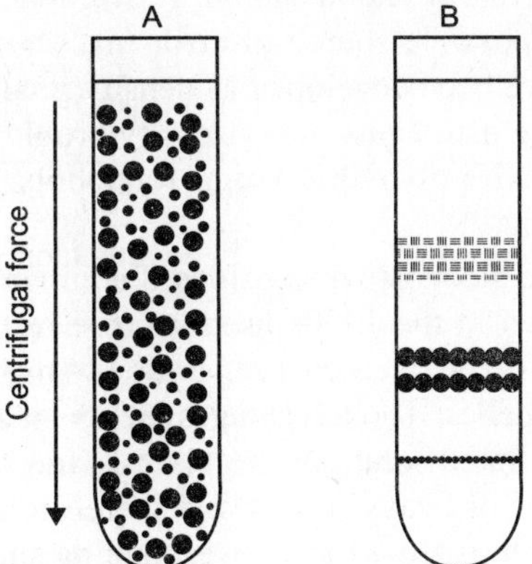

Fig. 9.3: Isopycnic centrifugation.

Upon centrifugation, particles of a specific density sediment until they reach the point where their density is the same as the gradient media (i.e. the equilibrium position). The gradient is then said to be isopycnic and the particles are separated according to their buoyancy. Since the density of biological particles is sensitive to the osmotic pressure of the gradient, isopycnic separation may vary significantly depending on the gradient medium used. Although a continuous gradient may be more suited for analytical purposes, preparative techniques commonly use a discontinuous gradient in which the particles band at the interface between the density gradient layers. This makes harvesting certain biological particles (e.g. lymphocytes) easier.

Selection of suitable density gradient medium: The primary function of density gradient centrifugation is to separate particles, either on the basis of their buoyancy density or their rate of sedimentation. For rate-zonal separations, the function of the gradient is to provide a gradient of viscosity which improves particle resolution while stabilising the column from convection currents. For isopycnic separations, the important feature is that the maximum density of the gradient media is higher than that of the particles.

Properties of ideal density gradient media: An ideal density gradient media should have sufficient solubility to produce the range of densities required, should not form solution of high viscosity in the desired density range, should not be hyperosmotic or hypoosmotic when the particles to be separated are osmotically sensitive, solutions of the gradient should be adjustable to the pH and the ionic strengths that are compatible with the articles being separated, should not affect the biological activity of the sample, should be nontoxic and not metabolised by cells, not interfere with assay procedures or react with the centrifuge tubes, should exhibits a property that can be used as a measure of concentration, should be easily removed from the purified product, autoclavable and possess reasonable cost. No single compound can satisfy all of the above criteria.

Most media are capable of producing the range of densities required and being easily removed from the particles of interest. The effect of osmolality on biological particles requires special consideration. The osmolality of most mammalian fluids is 290–300 number of osmoles (mOsm). This is the osmolality of balanced salt solutions (e.g. 0.850–0.9% NaCl) and most common media. High osmolality solutions not only remove water from the interior of membrane-bound particles, they also remove water bound to macromolecules like DNA. Loss of water from cells will reduce their size and increase their density, thereby affecting their buoyancy and rate of sedimentation. The osmotic effect on cells and macromolecules may be reversible, though it is a possible source of error that should be avoided. Over the years, a variety of different compounds have been developed as density gradient media in order to enhance the separation process and to overcome osmolality and viscosity problems. There are five main classes of density gradient medium. These are polyhydric (sugar) alcohols, polysaccharides, inorganic salts, iodinated compounds, colloidal silica.

Polyhydric alcohols: Polyhydric alcohols are considered nonionic gradient media. Some of the first centrifugation techniques developed in the 1950s used sucrose in the purification of cell organelles. Sucrose gradients are widely used for the rate-zonal separation of macromolecules and for the isopycnic separation of viruses and cell organelles. The advantages are its stable nature, inertness, and low cost. The disadvantages are that concentrated solutions are viscous and hypertonic. Reagent-grade sucrose may be contaminated with RNAses or heavy metals and therefore are unsuitable for DNA and RNA purification. Glycerol solutions are less dense than corresponding sucrose solutions. However, glycerol solutions of the same density of sucrose solutions are much more viscous. Glycerol helps to preserve the activity of certain enzymes and it can be removed through vacuum. Examples are sucrose organelles, membrane vesicles, viruses, proteins, ribosomes, polysomes glycerol mammalian cells (infrequent), proteins sorbitol nonmammalian subcellular particles.

Polysaccharides: These include: Ficoll®, polysucrose and dextrans Mammalian cells (sometimes in combination with iodinated density gradient media), mammalian subcellular particles (infrequent).

Inorganic salts (ionic metal Salts): Ionic gradient media, comprised of concentrated heavy metal salts, are almost exclusively used for isopycnic separations of nucleic acids. Cesium chloride and cesium sulphate are the most widely used heavy metal salts with gradient densities of up to 1.91 g/cm^3. Other useful salts include sodium iodide, sodium bromide and the rubidium salts. The steepness and shape of the ionic density gradient formed depends on the centrifugal force and type of rotor respectively. Ionic gradient media are highly ionic and non-viscous with high osmolarities. It should be kept in mind that the density of the sample is highly dependent on the sample's hydration, which in turn depends on the dehydration power of the ionic gradient media. Examples are: CsCl, DNA, viruses, proteins Cs_2SO_4 DNA, RNA, KBr and Plasma lipoproteins.

Nonionic iodinated density gradient media: The iodinated aromatic compounds, originally devised for X-ray contrast applications, solve the more serious deficiencies of the other classes of gradient media. Iodinated gradient media have much lower osmolarities and viscosities than sucrose at any concentration. Polysaccharides such as Ficoll® are even more viscous than sucrose at all densities. Ionic gradient media, such as cesium chloride, have higher densities and lower viscosities than other density gradient media. However, their use is restricted due to the high osmolarities and ionic strength which affect the hydration of osmotically sensitive particles and can disrupt or otherwise modify the integrity of biological particles. For example, diatrizoate mainly is used as a component of commercial lymphocyte isolation media. Nycodenz®, Histodenz™ Mammalian cells, organelles, membrane vesicles, viruses Iodixanol Mammalian cells, organelles, membrane vesicles, viruses, plasma lipoproteins, proteins, DNA Colloidal silica media Percoll® Mammalian cells, organelles, membrane vesicles (infrequent).

Classification of Industrial Centrifuges

Perforated bowl or filter types.

1. Batch type:
   - Top – driven
   - Under – driven
2. Semicontinuous
3. Continuous

Solid – bowl or sedimentation types.

1. Vertical:
   - Simple bowl
   - Bowl with plates
2. Horizontal:
   - Continuous decanters

Batch type top driven centrifuge

Construction of batch type top driven centrifuge: This consists of a rotating basket suspended on a vertical shaft and driven by a motor from top. The sides of the basket are perforated and are also covered with a screen on the side. Surrounding the basket is a stationary casing that collects the filtrate.

Working batch type top driven centrifuge: Top driven centrifuge is a batch-type machine (Fig. 9.4). The material (suspension) is put into the basket. Then power is applied. The basket accelerates to its maximum speed. The particles and liquid are thrown by centrifugal force to the wall of the basket. The liquid passes out through the screen and the solid particles retained on the screen as deposit. After a definite time the power is turned off, a brake brought to rest. The discharge valve at the bottom of the basket is raised, and the deposited solid is cut from the side of the basket into the opening.

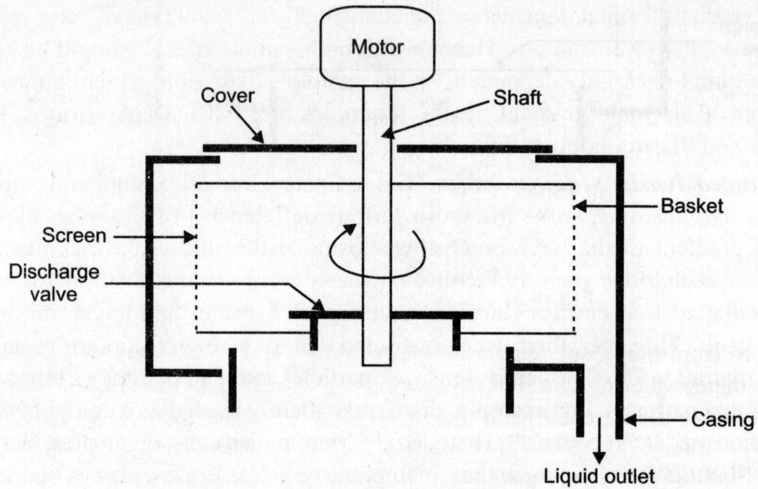

Fig. 9.4: Top-driven batch centrifuge.

Uses

1. Crystal can be separated from mother-liquor.
2. Liquids can be clarified by removing unwanted solids dirt from oils.

Batch type under driven centrifuge

Construction batch type under driven centrifuge: Batch type under driven centrifuge consists of a rotating basket place on a vertical shaft and driven by a motor from bottom. The sides of the basket are perforated and are also covered with a screen on the inside. Surrounding the basket is a stationary casing that collects the filtrate.

Bottom-driven batch centrifuge: Bottom-driven batch centrifuge is shown in Fig. 9.5. When power is applied the basket accelerates to its maximum speed. The particles and liquid are thrown by centrifugal force to the wall of the basket. The liquid passes out through the screen and the solid particles retained on the screen as deposit. After a definite time the power is turned off, a brake applied, and the basket brought to rest. The cover at the top of the basket is raised, and the deposited solid is cut from the side of the basket and collected.

Types of Centrifuges

Centrifuges achieve separation by means of the accelerated gravitational force achieved by a rapid rotation. This can either replace normal gravity in the sedimentation of suspension or provide the driving force in the filtration through a filter medium of some kind. The most common application is separation

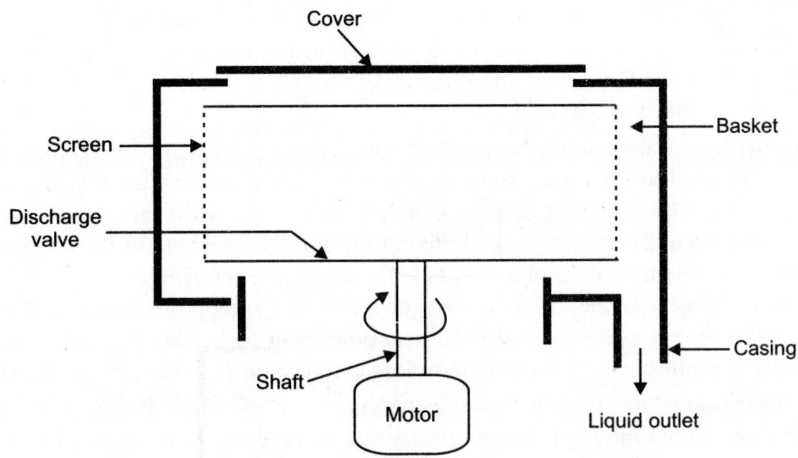

Fig. 9.5: Bottom-driven batch centrifuge.

of solid substances from high concentrated suspensions. Used in this way for the treatment of sewage sludge it enables the dewatering with the production of more or less consistent sediment depending on the nature of the sludge to be treated, and the accelerated thickening of low concentration sludge.

Principle of centrifuges

The separation is similar in principle to that achieved in a gravity separation process. The driving force is higher because is resulting from the rotation of the liquid: in the case of sedimentation, where the driving force is resulting from the difference in density between the solids particles and the liquid, the separation is achieved with a force from 1000 to 20000 times that of gravity.

Types of centrifuges

Most centrifuges rotate thanks to some kind of motor drive. The types of centrifuge used for sedimentation include: hydrocyclone, tubular bowl, chamber bowl, imperforate basket, disk stack separator and decanter. Sedimenting centrifuges were invented for liquid solid separation and not for handling solids. It soon became apparent that these machines had wider applications, which would involve the presence of solid impurities, leading to use for separating solids from liquids.

Hydrocyclone: The simplest device to use centrifugal force to achieve separation is the hydrocyclone. It not really a centrifuge: the centrifugal separation is produced by the motion of the slurry, induced by the tangential introduction of the feed material. Its principle of operation is based on the concept of the terminal settling velocity of a solid particle in a centrifugal field.

The feed enters tangentially into the cylindrical section of the hydrocyclone and follows a circulating path with a net inward flow of fluid from the outside to the vortex finder on the axis. The centrifugal field generated by the high circulating velocities creates an air core on the axis that usually extends on the spigot opening at the bottom of the conical section through the vortex finder to the overflow at the top. In order for this to occur the centrifugal force field must be several times larger than the gravitational one. Particles that experience this centrifugal field will tend to move outwards relative to the carrier fluid because of their relatively greater density. The larger, heavier pqarticles will migrate rapidly to the outside walls of the cylindrical section and will then be forced to move downward to the inside of the conical wall. Small particles will, on the other hand, be dragged inward by the fluid as it moves towards the vortex finder. The solid separation occurs in the passage of the suspension along the barrel of the hydrocyclone, to form thickened slurry at the outer wall, which than leaves the hydrocyclone as a continuous stream from its discharge nozzle.

Tubular bowl centrifuge: The tubular bowl centrifuge has been used for longer than most other designs of centrifuge. It is based on a very simple geometry: It is formed by a tube, of length several times its diameter, rotating between bearings at each end. The process stream enters at the bottom of the centrifuge and high centrifugal forces (let to separate out the solids). The bulk of the solids will adhere on the walls of the bowl, while the liquid phase exits at the top of the centrifuge. As this type of system lacks a provision of solids rejection, the solids can only be removed by stopping the machine, dismantling it and scraping or flushing the solids out manually. Tubular bowl centrifuges have dewatering capacity, but limited solids capacity. Foaming can be a problem unless the system includes special skimming, etc.

Chamber bowl centrifuge: The chamber bowl centrifuge is a number of tubular bowl arranged co-axially. It has a main bowl containing cylindrical inserts that dived the volume of the bowl into a series of annular chambers, which operate in series. Feed enters the center of the bowl and the suspension passes through each chamber in turn, at increasing distances from the axis. The solids settle onto the outer wall of each chamber and the clarified liquid emerges as an overflow from the largest diameter chamber. This device provides also a classification of the suspended solids: the coarse particles deposit in the inner chamber and the increasingly fine particle deposit on the subsequent chambers. The removal of sedimented solids requires the stopping of rotation for manual cleaning.

Disk stack separator: The simplest design is a closed bowl, containing the disk stack, with any solids present collecting at the outer part of the bowl, from which they have to be removed manually after stopping rotation. The solids are discharged from the bowl by a number of methods, including the basic use of nozzles, which are open continuously, allowing thick slurry to discharge. In the more complicated design valved nozzles open automatically when the solid depth in the bowl reaches a certain value, and then close again when most of the solids have been discharged. In the most complicated design the bowl is opened: its shell splits circumferentially for a short period, with the opening also controlled by solids depth in the bowl.

Imperforate basket centrifuge: The imperforate basket centrifuge is used when if the solid content of the suspension is higher. It consists of a simple drum-shaped basket or bowl, usually rotating around a vertical axis. The solids accumulate and compress as effect of the centrifugal force, but they are not dewatered. The residual liquid is drained out when the rotation of the bowl is stopped. The layer of solids is removed manually by scraping or shoveling. Unloading can be achieved semi automatically first by use of a skimmer pipe to remove the residual liquid and then by lowering a knife blade into the solid and so cutting it out from the bowl. This allows avoiding the switching off of the machine.

Decanter: The decanter centrifuge is the only sedimentation centrifuge designed from the start to handle significant solid concentration in the feed suspension. At the same time it can achieve quite good degrees of clarification of the liquid concentrate. Although a complicated piece of machinery it embodies a simple principle. They consist basically of a horizontal cylindrical bowl rotating at a high speed, with a helical extraction screw placed coaxially. The screw perfectly fits the internal contour of the bowl, only allowing clearance between the bowl and the scroll.

The differential speed between screw and scroll provides the conveying motion to collect and remove the solids, which accumulate at the bowl wall.

Advantages of decanter: The prime beneficial characteristic of the decanter is its ability to remove separated solids from the separation zone on a fully continuous basis.

By comparison with:

- Gravity sedimentation: the decanter can achieve separations that would be very difficult in a clarifier or lamella separator and it produces drier solids.
- Hydrocyclones: the decanter has a much higher liquid capacity, can handle much higher slurry concentrations and producer much drier solids.
- Tubular bowl centrifuges: the decanter offers higher capacities, the ability to handle concentrate slurries, and continuous operation.
- Imperforate basket centrifuges: the decanter operates continuously, can handle much higher solids concentrations, and produces much drier solids.
- Disk stack centrifuge: the decanter is truly continuous in operation, can handle much higher solids concentrations in the feed slurry and produces drier solids. The advantages of the decanter are its wide range of potential use, coupled with its continuous operation, its ability to accept a wide range of feed concentrations, and its availability in a wide range of feed capacities.

Applications of decanter centrifuge: The decanter centrifuge can be used for most types of liquid/ solid separation. It can be used for the classification of solids in liquid suspension or for the clarification of liquids. It can also be used in the recovery of a valuable solid from its suspension in the liquid and it can wash the recovered solid from its mother liquor. The decanter can also dewater slurries to a high level of dryness and it can finally be operated so as to act as a thickener, producing clear liquid and more concentrated slurry.

Cream Separation by Centrifugation

The cream separation is a very important unit operation in dairy industry. The cream or fat is taken out of milk for standardisation purpose. Besides, cream is also required to prepare some value added products as ghee, butter, etc. Cream is usually separated from milk by the centrifugation process.

Sometimes gravity separation may be too slow because of the closeness of densities of the particle and the fluid, or because of the association forces holding components together, as in emulsions like whole milk. In that case centrifugation helps in separation of the components on the basis of differences in their densities.

- The centrifuge increases the forces on particles many fold.
- Thus the particles that do not settle readily or at all in gravity settlers can often be separated from fluids by centrifugal force.
- The relative settling velocities of small particles are not changed, but the disturbing effects of Brownian motion and free convection currents are overcome.

The equipment using this principle of separation is known as a centrifuge. The centrifuges are used for:

- Separation of immiscible liquids.
- Clarification of liquids by removal of small amounts of solids.
- For removal of solids from liquids.

Centrifuges are also used for centrifugal filtration, where the centrifugal force is used (not the pressure difference) to separate the solids through a filter medium. As can be observed from Fig. 9.6, for cream

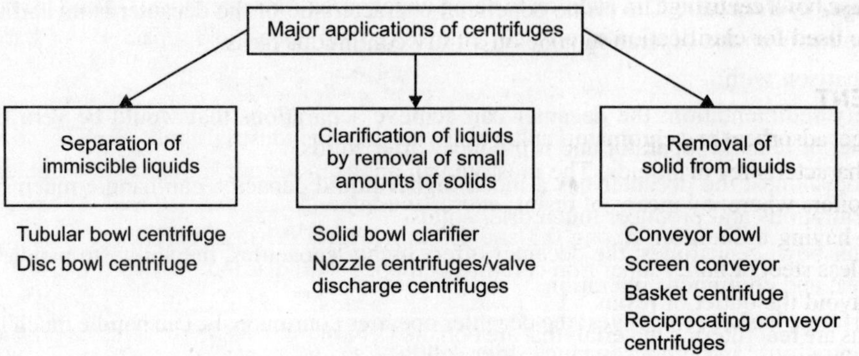

Fig. 9.6: Major applications of the centrifuges

separation, two types of centrifuges are used, namely, the tubular bowl centrifuge, and the disc bowl centrifuge.

Tubular Bowl Centrifuge

The basic characteristic features of a tubular bowl centrifuge are as follows:

- It consists of a vertical cylinder (or bowl), typically 0.1–0.15 m in diameter and 0.75 m long.
- Rotates inside a stationary casing (15000–50000 rev/min depending on the diameter).
- Tubular bowl centrifuges, which develop about 13000xg force, are also known as super centrifuges.
- Feed liquor is introduced continuously at the base of the bowl and the two liquids are separated and discharged through a circular weir system into stationary outlets.
- Some narrow centrifuges known as ultra centrifuges have a diameter of 75 mm and very high speeds of about 60000 rev/min.

Disc Bowl Centrifuge

The characteristic features of a disc bowl centrifuge are as follows:

- It consists of a conical bowl (0.2–1.2 m diameter), which contains a stack of inverted metal cones.
- The cones rotate at 2000–7000 rev/min.
- There is a fixed clearance between cones: 0.5–1.27 mm, and they have matching holes which form flow channels for liquid movement.
- Feed is introduced at the base of the disc stack.
- Due to the centrifugal force, the denser fraction moves towards the wall of the bowl, along the underside of the discs. The lighter fraction moves towards the centre along the upper surfaces.
- Both liquid streams are removed continuously by a weir system at the top in a similar way to the tubular bowl system.
- Disc bowl and tubular centrifuges can have capacities even up to 150000 l/hr.
- Better separation is obtained by the disc bowl centrifuge due to the formation of thinner layers of liquid.
- Periodic cleaning of deposited solids is required.

- The disc bowl centrifuge, in addition to being widely used for separation of cream from whole milk, is also used for clarification of oils, coffee extracts and juices, and separation of starch-gluten.

ADSORBENT

Ion exchange, adsorbent and chromatographic resins are used in industrial applications to modify physico-chemical characteristics of liquids. The most known applications are softening or demineralisation of water for boilers where, by means of resins, encrusting mineral salts are removed. The resins appear as little beads having a diameter among 0.3 and 1.2 mm with a density higher than water and are used inside stainless steel or hard rubber iron columns equipped with distributors which allow the passage of fluids and avoid the outlet of resins.

The resins are real filtering materials that are obtained by polymerisation processes at high temperatures which give to the micro spheres a high physico-chemical stability. The regulations for the application of these products in food industry fix the maximum monomer release allowed. The manufacturer is committed to issue the conformity certificate. Ion exchange resins are mainly used to reduce ashes content (demineralisation) and to recover organic acids in food liquids.

Adsorbent resins are suitable for the adsorption of specific organic molecules from food and non-food liquids allowing the selective recovery. Chromatographic resins are suitable for separation of organic and inorganic molecules. The plants are built by engineering companies who know processes and resins performances.

Many times new applications are involved,where the process is developed thanks to the accomplishment of laboratory tests and pilot plant trials. In particular, adsorbent resins, are new products which can replace crystallisation and distillation steps.The appropriate knowledge of the resins allows the intervention on liquids in order to solve process problems, giving a value-added to the production and for new products carrying out.

Resins Description

Gel type strongly acidic cation resins

In food industry they are mostly applied for demineralisation of liquids that contain organic stuff which is required to be left in solution.The percentage of Divinylbenzene (DVB) used during production changes the physico-chemical characteristics of the polymer and its performances.

Porous type strongly acidic cation resins

In food industry they are mostly applied for demineralisation of sugar solutions with density higher than water. The percentage of DVB used during production changes the physico-chemical characteristics of the polymer and its performances. Porous type strongly acidic cation resins are also available in highly uniform screen grade version.

Weakly acidic cation exchange resins

In food industry they are mostly applied for partial demineralisation of liquids with density similar to water.They have a high exchange capacity but they cannot completely decationise. The percentage of DVB used during production changes the physico-chemical characteristics of the polymer and its performances.

Weakly basic anion exchange resin.

In food industry they are applied for demineralisation and decolourisation of sugar solutions with density higher than water. The percentage of DVB used during production changes the physico-chemical characteristics of the polymer and its performances.Weakly basic anion exchange resins are also available in highly uniform screen grade version.

Gel strongly basic anion exchange resin

In food industry they are mostly applied for demineralisation of liquids containing organic stuff which is required to anion exchange resins.The percentage of DVB used during production changes the physico-chemical characteristics of the polymer and its performances.

Porous type strongly basic anion exchange resins

In food industry they are applied for demineralisation of sugar solutions with density higher than water. They have a lower exchange capacity compared to weakly basic anion exchange resins. The percentage of DVB used during production changes the physico-chemical characteristics of the polymer and its performances.

Adsorbent resins

There are several applications in food industry oriented to removal of undesired organic substances and to recovery of valuable organic substances. These are products in constant development, therefore the new and unknown applications are many. Adsorbent resins reversibly adsorb polar organic molecules as polyhydric phenols, organic acids, etc. and according to the eluant it is possible the recovery. Based on the polymeric matrix, type styrenic or acrylic, they show different degree of hydrophobicity.

Strong cation gel type chromatographic resin

In food industry they are mostly applied for demineralisation and separation of sugars. They are products in constant development,therefore the new and unknown applications are many. The percentage of DVB used during production changes the physico-chemical characteristics of the polymer.

Chromatographic columns

They consist of a cylindrical body in stainless steel with a rounded bottom welded on the top. A stainless steel plate put on the bottom of the cylindrical body is the support for the resins. For the distribution of the fluids are used collectors equipped with distributors with fissures smaller than the resin beads diameter to avoid the outlet. The fluids distribution system is very important and it is essential to avoid the creation of preferential ways in the resin bed. Chromatographic processes in food industry are carried out at high temperatures, therefore the columns are insulated. The most updated chromatographic processes (Improved Simulated Moving Bed) are carried out in four or more rooms built in one or more columns. On the cylindrical part and on the bottom there are manholes and portholes necessary for maintenance interventions of internal parts and for the vision of the resin during working.

Description of Resins Processes

General description of traditional demineralisation process

Demineralisation with cation and anion resins: Traditional demineralisation process by means of ion exchange resins is applied on food liquids when it is necessary to remove mineral salts and organic molecules with positive or negative charges. The liquid goes through the anion and cation columns in series, respecting defined working parameters which allow the ion exchange. The resins reduce to the lowest levels the saline content of the liquids, drastically decreasing the conductivity.

Biological treatment of regeneration eluates: Regeneration eluates of traditional plants for fruit juices demineralisation need an aerobic biological treatment before being discharged. The plant essentially consists of a deposition tank where are piped all the regeneration waters which are pumped at a steady flow to the oxidation tanks. In these tanks the main water treatments are: oxidation/nitrification and denitrification. The waters are piped from oxidation tanks to a clarifier and the separation between biological active mud and treated water. A final physico-chemical plant, composed by a floater and a system for reagents dosage, eliminates the polluting substances left in solution. The treated water from the floater goes to the final discharge well and floated mud is sent to mud dehydration plant.

General description of adsorbtion process

Removal of undesired organic substances: Adsorbent resins allow the selective removal of undesired organic substances from food liquids and from waste waters. There are different kind of adsorbent resins distinguished by a specific hydrophobic capacity, by a particular size and volume of the pores. Being polymers without functional group, they do not make any ion exchange with mineral salts but adsorb organic molecules exploiting van der Waals' forces. The suitable adsorbent resins is selected according to the molecule to be removed. They are new product in constant development which allow the product's quality improvement and the recovery of liquids with disagreeable taste or smell. The suitable operating system is selected according to the liquid to be treated. The adsorption phase is made at a specific low flow rate. The regeneration is made with NaOH at 2–4% in the measure of 50–80 g of NaOH at 100%/l resin. During this phase it is obtained a regeneration eluate with NaOH and organic substances that need a biological treatment before being discharged.

Recovery of valuable organic substances: Adsorbent resins selectively adsorb organic molecules in a reversible way. There are various kind of adsorbent resins distinguished by a specific hydrophobic capacity, by a particular size and volume of the pores. The suitable adsorbent resins is selected according to the molecule to be removed. The adsorption phase is made at specific low flow rates. The recovery of adsorbed organic substances is made with alcohol or with organic solvents and according to the concentration of the eluant it is possible to make a further selective recovery. They are products in constant development which allow the realisation of new natural extracts on industrial scale, to reach high purities and to replace crystallisation phases. The suitable operating system is selected according to the liquid to be treated. Regeneration eluate constituting the product contains alcohol or solvent recoverable by distillation. In this process there are no eluates to be treated.

General description of chromatographic process

Chromatographic process in column, by means of chromatographic grade resins, is mostly applied for sugars separation and for sugary juices demineralisation. In this process are not applied reagents for regeneration and the resins work as a separation vehicle of atoms and molecules. Each molecule in solution has a specific affinity with the resin and thanks to this property the separation takes place. For example, beet molasses is rich in sugar and mineral salts which are recovered by means of ionic exclusion chromatographic process. In this case it is applied a chromatographic resin that is more similar to sugars compared to mineral salts and polyphenols. The process is developed at high temperatures, the concentrated molasses is put inside the column at fixed specific flow rates and then demineralised water is injected to move the product from the resin bed. From the bottom of the column will be recovered in sequence a first fraction of mineral salts and polyphenols and in a second fraction purified sugars. This process is applied also where there are 2 or more molecules in solution to be separated using suitable resins. Up-to-date chromatographic systems with four or eight columns allow to obtain high purity grade and low dilutions of the recovered fractions. The most fine and uniform resins have shown the best performances.

Co-current system

Co-current system is suggested when it is necessary to treat liquids with suspended solid material since it is easier to wash the resins. During the cycle the liquid goes through the columns from the top to the bottom, transferring to the resins all the mineral salts and organic molecules with positive or negative charge (organic acids, amino acids, etc.). The resins have a fixed exchange capacity and the volumes of cation and anion are calculated according to the specific exhaustion flow rate and are balanced according to the analysis of the liquid to be treated. The higher is the density and mineral salts content, the lower will be the specific exhaustion flow rate. During these phases are produced acid and basic regeneration eluates containing salts removed from the product, the excess of the product and the excess of regenerants.

During treatment of food fluids are obtained eluates with high organic content that normally need a biological treatment before being discharged. In this process, it is used a higher quantity of regenerant compared to counter current and fixed bed or floating bed systems, since the lower part of the resin bed is the last to be involved. Normally these operations are carried out automatically, by means of a programmable logic controller (PLC) that calculates opening and closing of pneumatic valves. When the resins are regenerated and drained, the production starts. The resins are immersed in demineralised water and during inlet and outlet of the product in the plant there are dilutions which, due to the empty spaces, in this system are very high.

Industrial Applications: Grapes Sugar Production

Description of the process

Grape sugar, commonly called must, is submitted to a demineralisation process by means of ion exchange resins for the production of grape sugar, composed of about 50% fructose and about 50% glucose. Red or white must contains about 200 g/l of sugars, organic acids, polyphenols, amino acids and mineral salts. During demineralisation the mineral cations and amino acids are exchanged by cation resin, the mineral anions and organic acids by anion resin. This last, reversibly adsorbs polyphenols and the outcoming product is a transparent water solution containing about 200 g/l of sugars. The concentration of these sugars is commonly expressed in 'Brix' (1° Brix = 10 g/l). The conductivity of starting must is around 2500 μS/cm given by the presence of mineral salts, etc. demineralised and decolourised must has a conductivity below 10 μS/cm. It is mostly used to raise alcoholic content of wines but also as diet sweetener. Grape sugar is commercialised at 70° Brix to reduce transportation cost impact and is commonly called rectified concentrated must (RCM), concentrated rectified must.

Organic acids recovery (tartaric/malic acid)

During demineralisation of grapes must, weak anion resin exchanges organic acids and adsorbs polyphenols. In grapes, are mostly present tartaric acid and malic acid which are exchanged by the anion resin. Before proceeding with regeneration, it is made the extraction of organic acids using sulphuric acid and water. Strong acids have the property to move the weaker acids from the resins since they are more similar. About 10% less of sulphuric acid is used compared to organic acids exchanged by the resin so as to make the movement of solution losing a minimum quantity of organic acids. It is proceeded with the injection in the column of sulphuric acid at 10–15% followed by demineralised water. From the bottom of the column it is collected a solution containing 30–35 g/l of tartaric acid and malic acid with a portion of polyphenols released by weak anion resin. In order to purify the acids, the solution is passed on adsorbent resin. The organic acids are concentrated and used as they are in wine-making industry, otherwise they are separated by means of precipitation of calcium tartrate and commercialised in food industry.

Description of the process

The alcoholic solutions obtained from malt fermentation are submitted to demineralisation and decolourisation process with ion exchange and adsorbent resins to produce a clear alcoholic solution without mineral salts, amino acids, polyphenols, organic acids, aldehydes and ketones. The alcoholic solution of malt contains from 140 to 190 ml/l of alcohol. This process is an efficacious alternative to distillation,mineral cations and amino acids are exchanged by cation resin,mineral anions and organic acids by anion resin. Adsorbent resin, after demineralisation, reversibly adsorbs polyphenols and the outcoming product is clear and odourless.

A column with disposable activated carbons as final is placed safety filter. The conductivity of starting solution is around 2000 μS/cm due to the presence of mineral salts, etc. demineralised and decolourised product has a conductivity less than 20 μS/cm and is applied for low alcoholic content beverages. Description of the process.

Whey coming from cheese production is submitted to a demineralisation process by means of ion exchange resins for the production of demineralised powder whey enriched (with proteins). Whey contains approximately 50 g/l lactose, proteins, beta-carotene, amino acids, organic acids and mineral salts. During demineralisation, mineral cations and amino acids are exchanged by a cation resin, the anions and organic acids by a special anion resin with a minimum loss of protein. The latter reversibly adsorb beta-carotene. The outcoming product is a water solution containing about 50 g/l of lactose with proteins. In order to reach good performances is crucial the choice of suitable resins. The conductivity of starting whey is around 2500 μS/cm given particularly from the presence of mineral salts. Demineralised whey has a conductivity less than 20 μS/cm and is concentrated at 60 °Brix to be powdered. It is applied for the production of milk for babies and as ingredient in food industry.

Industrial Applications: Demineralised Power Whey Production

Description of the process

Whey is filtered through ultra filtration membranes which allow the separation of proteins from other components. Concentrated proteins are commercialised for the production of ricotta (soft white unsalted cheese) or as WPI (whey protein concentrated). The permeate contains about 50 g/l of lactose, proteins, beta-carotene, amino acids, organic acids and mineral salts. During demineralisation, mineral cations and amino acids are exchanged by a cation resin, mineral anions and organic acids by an anion resin. The latter reversibly adsorbs betacarotene. The outcoming product is a water solution containing about 50 g/l of lactose. The conductivity of starting permeate is around 2500 μS/cm given particularly from the presence of mineral salts. Demineralised permeate has a conductivity less than 20 μS/cm and is constituted by lactose in solution that is concentrated and crystallised. Due to the very low salt content the production of mother waters is reduced to the minimum. In some cases it is preferred to decolourise the permeate with an adsorbent resin and make crystallisation but with a high production of mother waters. Lactose finds several applications as ingredient in food and pharmaceutical industry.

Industrial Applications: Liquid Date Sugar Production

Description of the process

Date juice is submitted to a demineralisation and decolourisation process by means of ion exchange and adsorbent resins for the production of liquid sugar composed by approximately 50% of fructose, about 45% glucose, about 5% saccharose and water. Date juice contains about 200 g/l of sugars, organic acids, polyphenols, amino acids and mineral salts. Due to the quantity and the quality of polyphenols contained in the juice, demineralisation it is necessary to decolourise the juice with an adsorbent resin regenerable with NaOH. Then, cation resin exchanges amino acids and cations whereas organic acids and mineral anions are exchanged by anion resin.

The outcoming product is a water solution containing about 200 g/l of sugars, the concentration is normally expressed in °Brix (1° Brix = 10 g/l). The colour of juice is expressed in ICUMSA, in the starting product is around 3000 and conductivity around 3500 µS/cm given particularly from the presence of mineral salts. The concentrated date sugar is commercialised at 60–70 Brix (600–700 g/l sugars), has a conductivity less than 50 µS/cm and 100–150 ICUMSA (International Commission for Uniform Methods of Sugar Analysis). It is mostly applied as diet sweetener for preparation of beverages and canned fruit.

Industrial Applications: Demineralised Orange Juice Debittering

Description of the process

Orange juice is submitted to debittering process by means of adsorbent resin. The molecules in charge of bitter taste, Limonine, Naringine, etc. are selectively removed from orange juice with the purpose of obtaining a sweet product without added sugars. In orange juice there are many types of polyphenols and organic molecules, by means of a specific adsorbent resin it is possible to selectively intervene so as not to spoil the organoleptic characteristics of the juice. In these processes, the juices goes through the resin bed at a specific very low flow rate. The concentration of dry substance in the juice is around 80 g/l of which 90% sugars. The pulp content must not be higher than 1% otherwise, in the columns, the increase of differential pressure avoids the juice passage. Normally, above the filters are installed some quartzite safety prefilters are installed above the filters.

Industrial Applications: Separation of Fructose/Grapes Glucose

Description of the process

Concentrated grapes sugar at 65° Brix contains 250 g/l glucose and 360 g/l fructose. With chromatographic technology it is possible to separate the two sugars using a cation chromatographic resin in calcium form. The process is performed at 65°C to reduce viscosity of sugar liquid. A fixed quantity of solution at a specific flow rate is sent to the plant and some demineralised water elutes the resin's sugars. The resin is more similar to fructose and from the bottom of the column will be collected in sequence the first fraction full of glucose and the second one full of fructose maintaining unchanged the chemico-physical characteristics of sugar molecules.

In 4 columns systems the production is made continuously. If the 2 fractions are collected separately separated sugars at required purity degree are obtained. The higher is the purity, the higher will be the water quantity to be applied. With modern multiple columns chromatographic systems the dilution effect is mostly reduced.

Description of the process

Adsorbent resins are able to adsorb the anthocyanins present in red grapes juice and to release them in alcoholic solutions. Grape juices previously filtered slowly go through the adsorbent resin releasing the colouring organic substances mainly composed of anthocyanins, catechins and proanthocyanins. From the bottom of the column it is collected a transparent grape juice that normally is applied for the production of grape sugar. When the resin is loaded of natural colouring (anthocyanins) it is washed with demineralised water to remove sugars and then regenerated with an alcoholic solution higher than 50°. The deep red eluate is collected and, by means of a distillation tower, alcohol it is separated from natural colouring in water solution. The concentrated colouring solution is powdered and commercialised as natural colouring. With the same technology it is possible to extract tannins from white grapes juices.

Food Applications of Resins

- Apple juice demineralisation.
- Polyphenols recovery from apple peels extract.
- Patulin removal from apple juice.
- Pineapple juice demineralisation.
- Pineapple juice deodourisation and decolourisation.
- Demineralisation and decolourisation of date juice.
- Demineralisation and purification of alcoholic malt solution.
- Grape juice demineralisation.
- Grape juice decolourisation.
- Anthocyanins recovery from grapes juices.
- Tannins recovery from grapes juices.
- Anthocyanins recovery from washing water of grapes peels.
- Proanthocyanidins purification from grapes seeds.
- Tartaric acid decationisation.
- Heavy metals removal from grapes juices.
- Debittering of orange/lemon peels extract.
- Citrus juices debittering.
- Citrus juices deacidification.
- Anthocyanins recovery from red oranges.
- Pomegranate juice decolourisation.
- Ellagic acid recovery from pomegranate juice.
- Anthocyanins recovery from wooden fruits/onion/cabbages.
- Deodourisation of anthocyanins extract from red anions/cabbages.

- Betacyanine/betaxantine recovery from red beet.
- Pinitol recovery from carob juice.
- Epigallocatechins separation from green tea.
- Glycyrrhizic acid purification.
- Betain recovery from molasses.
- Milk whey demineralisation.
- Milk whey decolourisation.
- Lactose decalcification.
- Lactose demineralisation.
- Lactose hydrolysis.
- Proteins separation of milk whey.
- Demineralisation-decolourisation of citric acid.
- Demineralisation-decolourisation of lactic acid.
- Extraction/Purification amino acids (Glutamic, Lysine, Tryptophan).
- Decalcification of saccharose from beet.
- Alkalinisation of saccharose from beet.
- Demineralisation of saccharose from beet.
- Demineralisation of hydrogenated syrups (Sorbitol, Mannitol, Maltitol, Xylitol).
- Quentin Process.
- Saccharose hydrolysis.
- Sugar cane decolourisation.
- Saccharose extraction from beet molasses - chromatography.
- Saccharose extraction from cane molasses - chromatography.
- Glucose/fructose separation - chromatography.
- Dextrose purification - chromatography.
- Maltose purification - chromatography.
- Sorbitol purification - chromatography.
- Mannose purification - chromatography

Chapter 10

Food Irradiation

INTRODUCTION

The technology of food irradiation is gaining more and more attention around the world. In comparison with heat or chemical treatment, irradiation is more effective and appropriate technology to destroy food borne pathogens. Radiation technique makes the food safer to eat by destroying bacteria which is very much similar to the process of pasteurisation. Radiation does not leave the food items radioactive for two seasons.

First, the gamma rays from cobalt-60 used in food radiation are not energetic enough to make it radioactive.

Second, as the food never comes into contact with the source directly, it is not possible for the food to become contaminated with radioactive material. In the changing scenario of world trade, switching over to radiation processing of food assumes great importance.

Radiation will be moving fast to the status of a 'wonder technology' to satisfy the sanitary and phyto sanitary requirements of the importing countries. Food once irradiated, can be prone to re-contamination unless appropriately packed Therefore, if radiation treatment is intended to control microbiological spoilage or insect infestation, prepackaging becomes an integral part of the process. India has been practicing various methods of food preservation from time immemorial such as sun drying, pickling and fermentation. These methods were supplemented with more energy consuming techniques like refrigeration, freezing and canning, however had its merits and demerits. The quest was ever on for newer methods of food preservation with least change in sensory qualities.

Preservation of food items is a prerequisite for food security. The seasonal nature of production and the long and unmanageable distances between the production and consumption centers and the rising gap between demand and supply have posed great challenges to conventional techniques of food preservation and thereby to food security. The hot and humid climate of the country is quite favourable to the growth of numerous insects and micro-organisms which destroy stored crops and cause spoilage of food. In the changing scenario of world trade, switching over to radiation processing of food assumes great importance. Radiation processing can be used for disinfestations of pests and disease-causing organisms from a range of products including fruits and vegetables.

RADIATION AS A PRESERVATION TECHNIQUE

Radiation is one of the latest methods in food preservation. Radiation technique makes the food safer to eat by destroying bacteria which is very much similar to the process of pasteurisation. In effect, radiation disrupts the biological processes that lead to decay and the ability to sprout. Being a cold process, radiation can be used to pasteurise and sterilise foods without causing changes in freshness and texture of food unlike heat. Further, unlike chemical fumigants, radiation does not leave any harmful toxic residues in food and is more effective and can be used to treat packaged commodities too.

Food irradiation is a technology that can be safely used to reduce food losses due to deterioration and to control contamination causing illness and death. Food irradiation uses radiant energy electron beams, gamma rays or X-rays to rid food of harmful micro-organisms, insects, fungi and other pests, and to retard spoilage. It does not make food radioactive. Irradiation kills pathogens and makes them incapable of reproduction.

There are several processes that are collectively referred to as Food Irradiation. The object of each process is to kill or impair the breeding capacity of unwanted living organisms or to affect the product morphology in a beneficial way that will extend shelf-life. Each process has an optimal dose of ionising energy (radiation) dependent on the desired effect. The dose of radiation is measured in grays (Gy). A gray is a unit of energy equivalent to 1 joule per kilogram. This unit of measure is based on the metric system. Thus, 1 kilogray (kGy) is equal to 1000 grays (Gy). All three forms of ionising energy have the same effect, gray for gray. Some of the major processes are.

Pasteurisation (Pathogen Reduction)

Irradiation is used to effectively eliminate disease causing organisms including bacteria and parasites. (e.g. Irradiating ground beef to make it safe from *E. coli* O157:H7. Irradiating live oysters to make them safe from *vibrio*).

Sterilisation

Irradiation is used at a very high dose to eliminate all organisms so that refrigeration is not required (shelf stable). (e.g. Certain foods are sterilised for NASA astronauts.)

Sanitation

Irradiation is widely used to reduce organisms for spices, herbs and other dried vegetable substances. (e.g. Irradiating spice blends that are added to meat for hot dogs and other Ready to Eat products that may not be cooked again.) the population of spoilage causing organisms, including bacteria and mold. On certain fruits and tubers, irradiation delays ripening and/or sprouting. (e.g. Irradiating berries to reduce mold. Irradiating fresh fruits to extend their market reach. Irradiating potatoes, onions and garlic to impair cell division and hence allow them to go through the off season without sprouting.)

Disinfestation

Irradiation is used to stop reproduction of both storage and quarantine insect pests.(e.g. Irradiating foreign produced mangoes to eliminate the seed weevil, which is a quarantined pest, for import to the US. Irradiating papaya is to eliminate fruit flies, which are quarantined pests, for import from Hawaii or foreign countries into the US mainland.) All three forms of irradiation are referred to as a cold process. Although all of the radiation energy is converted to heat during treatment, the process typically increases the product temperature by about 1°C (Benebion.).

Types of Radiation Sources

Three principal types of radiation source can be used in food irradiation according to the Codex Alimentarius General Standard (Food and agriculture organisation, world health organisation, 1984):

1. Gamma radiation from radionuclides such as 60Co or 137Cs8.
2. Machine sources of electron beams with energies up to 10 MeV.
3. Machine sources of brems strahlung (X rays) with electron energies up to 5 MeV.

Because of their greater penetrating capability, rays and X rays may be used for processing of relatively thick or dense products. For situations where only a shallow penetration is needed and where rapid conveyor speeds can be used, high power electron beams may provide a higher output at lower cost per unit of product when large amounts of product are involved.

Gamma rays

The rays used in food processing are obtained from large 60Co radionuclide sources. This type of radiation is essentially monoenergetic (60Co emits simultaneously two photons per disintegration with energies of 1.17 and 1.33 MeV). Using analytical techniques such as the point kernel or Monte Carlo methods, it is possible to compute the dose distribution in irradiated food products even when very complicated source geometries such as extended plaque sources are used. The resulting depth dose distribution in the food products usually resembles an approximately exponential curve. Irradiation from two sides (two sided irradiation), obtained either by turning the process load or by irradiation from two sides of a plaque source, is often used to increase the dose uniformity in the process load.

Electrons

Electrons emitted by accelerators have fairly narrow spectral energy limits (usually less than ±10% of the nominal energy). The energy of the electrons reaching the product is further controlled by the bending magnets of the beam handling system, if applicable. The range of an electron in a medium is finite (unlike that for photons) and is closely related to its energy.

Bremsstrahlung (X rays)

Bremsstrahlung irradiator design principles are essentially the same as those for electron irradiators .An extended source of X rays is achieved by distributing the primary electron beam over a target (X ray converter) of sufficient size. In contrast to the radionuclide sources, which emit nearly monoenergetic photons, bremsstrahlung (X ray) sources emit photons with a broad energy spectrum.

The effectiveness of processing of food by ionising radiation depends on proper delivery of absorbed dose and its reliable measurement. For food destined for international trade, it is of the utmost importance that the dosimetry techniques used for dose determination are carried out accurately and that the process is monitored. Food packed in crates or boxes is placed on conveyor belts and moved into the heart of the irradiator, where it is exposed to the radiation source.

Electron beam irradiators can cleanse packaged food at the end of food-processing production lines. High-energy waves pass through the food, exciting the electrons in both the food and any pests or pathogens. When the electrons absorb enough energy, they break away from their atoms, leaving positively charged centers behind. Irradiation disrupts the molecular structure, kills or reduces the number of bacteria and yeasts, delays the formation of mold, and sterilises or kills parasites, insects, eggs and larvae. Levels of absorbed radiation are currently measured in kilo grays (kGy).

Food Irradiation Applications

The scientific community has defined three levels of food irradiation.

Applications at low dose levels (10 Gy – 1 kGy)

Sprouting of potatoes, onions, garlic, shallots, yams, etc. can be inhibited by irradiation in the dose range 20–150 Gy. Radiation affects the biological properties of such products in such a way that sprouting is appreciably inhibited or completely prevented. Physiological processes such as ripening of fruits can be delayed in the dose range 0.1–1 kGy. These processes are a consequence of enzymatic changes in the plant tissues. Insect disinfestations by radiation in the dose range 0.2–1 kGy is aimed at preventing losses caused by insect pests in stored grains, pulses, cereals, flour, coffee beans, spices, dried fruits, dried nuts, dried fishery products and other dried food products. A minimum absorbed dose of about 150 Gy can ensure quarantine security against various species of tephretid fruit flies in fresh fruits and vegetables, and a minimum dose of 300 Gy could prevent insects of other species from establishing in non-infested areas. In most cases irradiation either kills or inhibits further development of different life-cycle stages of insect pests. The inactivation of some pathogenic parasites of public health significance such as tapeworm and trichina in meat can be achieved at doses in the range 0.3–1 kGy.

1. Inhibition of sprouting 0.05–0.15 Potatoes, onions, garlic, root ginger, yam, etc.
2. Insect disinfestations and parasite disinfection 0.15–0.5 Cereals and pulses, fresh and dried fruits, dried fish and meat, fresh pork, etc.
3. Delay of physiological processes (e.g. ripening) 0.25–1.0 Fresh fruits and vegetables.

Applications at medium dose levels (1–10 kGy)

Radiation enhances the keeping quality of certain foods through a substantial reduction in the number of spoilage causing micro-organisms. Fresh meat and seafood, as well as vegetables and fruits, may be exposed to such treatments with doses ranging from about 1 to 10 kGy, depending on the product. This process of extending the shelf life is sometimes called radurisation.

Pasteurisation of solid foods such as meat, poultry and sea foods by irradiation is a practical method for elimination of pathogenic organisms and micro-organisms except for viruses. It is achieved by the reduction of the number of specific viable non-spore-forming pathogenic micro-organisms such that none is detectable in the treated product by any standard method, for which doses range between 2 and 8 kGy. The product will usually continue to be refrigerated after the radiation treatment. This process of improving the hygienic quality of food by inactivation of foodborne pathogenic bacteria and parasites is sometimes called radicidation. This medium dose application is very similar to heat pasteurisation, and is hence also called radiopasteurisation.

- Extension of shelf-life 1.0–3.0 kGy fresh fish, strawberries, mushrooms, etc.
- Elimination of spoilage and pathogenic micro-organisms 1.0–7.0 kGy Fresh and frozen seafood, raw or frozen poultry and meat, etc.
- Improving technological properties of food 2.0–7.0 kGy Grapes (increasing juice yield), dehydrated vegetables (reduced cooking time), etc.

Applications at high dose levels (10–100 kGy)

Irradiation at doses of 10–30 kGy is an effective alternative to the chemical fumigant ethylene oxide for microbial decontamination of dried spices, herbs and other dried vegetable seasonings. This is achieved by reducing the total microbial load present in such products including pathogenic organisms. Radiation sterilisation in the dose range 25–70 kGy extends the shelf life of precooked or enzyme inactivated food products in hermetically sealed containers almost indefinitely. This is valid independent of the conditions under which the product is subsequently stored as long as the package integrity is not affected. This effect is achieved by the reduction of the number and/or activity of all organisms of food spoilage or public health significance, including their spores, to such an extent that none are detectable in the treated product by any recognised method. This process is analogous to thermal canning in achieving shelfstability (long term storage without refrigeration) and is sometimes called radappertisation:

- Industrial sterilisation (in combination with mild heat) 30–50 Meat, poultry, seafood, prepared foods, sterilised hospital diets.
- Decontamination of certain food additives 10–50 Spices, enzyme preparations, natural gum, etc. and ingredients (Technical reports series No. 409 2002).

Packaging

Food once irradiated, can be prone to recontamination unless appropriately packed. Therefore, if radiation treatment is intended to control microbiological spoilage or insect infestation, prepackaging becomes an integral part of the process. Technical functions of packaging are well known. These include prevention of moisture uptake or loss, maintenance of an atmosphere other than air, protection from mechanical damage or simply keeping the food clean.

Since packaging materials are also exposed to radiation during the treatment, these materials must also satisfy additional requirements such as resistance to radiation with respect to its functional properties. In addition, it should not transmit toxic substances into food nor impart any off odour to the products. Of the several packaging materials currently available such as cellulose, glass, metals and organic polymers, plastics offer unique advantages over the use of conventional rigid containers from the point of view of flexibility, low cost, light weight and low weight to volume ratio. Increasingly, packaging materials for use in aseptic processing lines in the food, pharmaceutical and cosmetic industry are now being sterilised by ionising radiation. The packaging requirements of a particular food are significantly influenced by the desired objective of the radiation treatment.

Packaging materials used for irradiated food are broadly classified into two categories depending on the type of radiation treatments.

- Processes requiring doses less than 10 kGy, such as extension of shelf-life of food.
- Processes requiring doses from 10–60 kGy, for storing such items as meat and poultry for long periods without refrigeration.

Irradiation of food is one of the most effective ways of food preservation to inactivate micro-organisms and destroy insect pests. Effective irradiation treatment on food is associated with an effective packaging material, which performs all the technical functions of packaging along with resistance to radiations. Though several packaging materials like glass, cellulose, metals and organic polymers are available for this purpose, plastics offer unique advantages over the conventionally used rigid containers in terms of flexibility, low cost, light weight, and low weight to volume ratio. Multi-laminate packaging structure of polymers like nylon, EVOH, PVC, cellophane, PE and Polyester are used as a prominent barrier material in packaging of irradiated food.

Irradiation of food is one of the most effective ways of food preservation to inactivate micro-organisms and destroy insect pests. Effective irradiation treatment on food is associated with an effective packaging material, which performs all the technical functions of packaging along with resistance to radiations

OTHER APPLICATIONS OF RADIATION IN FOOD PROCESSING

The major benefits achieved by radiation processing of food include: (i) inhibition of sprouting of tubers and bulbs, (ii) disinfestation of insect pests in agricultural commodities, (iii) delayed ripening and senescence of fruits and vegetables, (iv) destruction of microbes responsible for spoilage, and (v) elimination of pathogens and parasites of public health concern.

Sprouting of potatoes, onions, garlic, shallots, yams, etc. can be inhibited by irradiation in the low dose range of 0.02–0.2 kGy. Physiological processes such as ripening of fruits can be delayed in the dose range of 0.2–1 kGy. These processes are possible consequence of inhibition of enzymatic activities in plant tissues induced by radiation. Radiation enhances the keeping quality of certain foods through a substantial reduction in the number of spoilage causing micro-organisms. Fresh meat and seafood may be exposed to such treatments with dose range of 1–7 kGy depending on the product.

This process of extending the shelf life is called radurisation. The process of improving the hygienic quality of food by inactivation of foodborne pathogenic bacteria and parasites is called radicidation. This utilises medium dose of 2–8 kGy and is similar to heat pasteurisation, and hence called radio-pasteurisation. Irradiation at high doses of 10–30 kGy is an effective alternative to the chemical fumigants like ethylene oxide for microbial decontamination of dried spices, herbs and other dried vegetable seasonings. This is achieved by reducing the total microbial load present in such products including pathogenic organisms. Radiation sterilisation is achieved by the reduction of the number and/or activity of all organisms of food spoilage or public health significance including their spores to such an extent that none are detectable in the treated product by any recognised method. This process is analogous to thermal canning in achieving shelf-stability (long term storage without refrigeration) and is called radappertisation.

Effect of Radiation Processing on Food Quality

Irradiation produces little or no chemical changes in food. The physical properties of food are also not affected by irradiation. The majority of changes due to radiation processing of food are similar to those by other preservation methods such as the thermal (heat) food processing. The radiolytic products and free radicals produced in the irradiated food are identical to those present in the foods processed by cooking and canning. None of these changes known to occur have been found to be harmful. The highly sensitive scientific tests/techniques utilised for the past 50 years have not revealed any new chemical product in the radiation-processed foods. The safety and wholesomeness of the technology was endorsed in the early nineties by the international organisations including the WHO, FAO, IAEA, and the Codex Alimentarius Commission. The FSSAI has also endorsed this technology.

The irradiation process involves passing of food through a radiation field allowing the food to absorb the desired radiation energy restricting the irradiated food never to come into direct contact with the radioactive material and keeping the food radioactive-free. There is no evidence to suggest that free radicals or radiolytic products jeopardise safety of the radiation-processed food. Irradiation is quite effective against living organisms but does not cause any significant loss of macronutrients in foods. Proteins, fats and carbohydrates undergo little change in nutritional value, however, the use of higher doses of radiation may induce some changes in the sensory properties depending upon the nature of food which limits the radiation dose employed. Other trace components such as essential amino acids, minerals, essential fatty acids, trace elements remain unaffected under practical irradiation, but in some cases vitamins such as vitamin C and vitamin B1 get partially lost. However, very little change in vitamin content is observed in food exposed to doses up to 1 kGy2.

Methods to Detect Irradiated Food

There are certain analytical methods that can discriminate between irradiated and non-irradiated foods. Such analytical methods detect physical, chemical and microbiological changes occurring as a consequence of food irradiation. The most useful and widely used methods include electron spin resonance spectroscopy (ESR), luminescence methods (thermo-luminescence TL), and photo stimulated luminescence (PSL). These analytical methods have been adopted as standard methods for detection of irradiated foods by Codex Alimentarius Commission.

Recent R&D Findings in India Indicating Additional Applications of Radiation Processing

The shelf-life extension of 10 d was achieved for the button mushroom (*Agaricus bisporus*) by γ-irradiation (2 kGy) and low temperature (10°C) storage. Sugarcane juice was preserved for 35 d by addition of the permitted preservatives, γ-irradiation (5kGy) and storage at 10°C. Safety of the leafy vegetables can be ensured by radiation processing with extended shelf-life of more than two weeks. A combination process including radiation treatment can ensure safety and also extend the shelf-life of sweet corn kernels more than one month. Dried water chestnut can be preserved by radiation processing for more than one year. Safety of herbals and tea can also be ensured by radiation treatment. The misconceived notion about the safety concern of the irradiated food has remained a stumbling block in wider adoption of this technology worldwide. Enormous research efforts have been directed towards biological testing of irradiated foods for the evaluation of their safety and wholesomeness. Some recent studies included long term exposure studies with irradiated foods and meat products in bacterial and human cell line models, which have shown that there is no genotoxic effect of irradiated foods and such foods, are safe for consumption.

Shelf-stable Special Purpose Foods developed in India using Radiation Processing

Several new ready-to-eat (RTE) shelf-stable food products have also been developed for the benefits of the special groups of consumers such as the persons affected by natural calamities, defense personnel, and immune-compromised patients. Many food items were developed in India using the radiation processing during IAEA CRP (D6.20.09) on 'The Development of Irradiated Foods for Immuno-Compromised Patients and other Potential Target Groups'. Also the radiation doses, treatment and storage conditions were standardised for these products. The products include Naso-Gastric Liquid Feed formulation (NGLF), Low Cost Enteral Food (LCEF), Intermediate Moisture (IM) Papaya Cubes, Irradiated honey, Stuffed Baked Food (SBF, Local name: Litti), Methi Paratha, Puran Poli, Vegetable pulav, and RTE meat products (Chicken tikka, Chicken pahadi kabab, Chiken paratha, Chikenpulav, and Baked chiken dumpling). The products have been reported to retain wholesomeness and quality attributes. Two of these products (NGLF, and LCEF) have been developed by Food Technology Division, BARC in association with the Tata Memorial Hospital mainly for the immune-compromised patients. Other products are for use during natural calamities and by the defense personnel deployed to remote places. These products are equally good for routine consumption by other individuals.

Challenges

Despite all these developments, irradiation is still an issue of concern for consumers, particularly in food items. A greater effort is required to convince the consumers with scientific and accredited information about food irradiation. Expansion and strengthening the collaboration between various agencies viz., Food Corporation of India, Ministry of Food Processing, National Disaster Management

Authority, Defense authorities, hospitals, and commercial as well as institutional food suppliers is necessary. This will ensure the eventual adoption and integration of the irradiated foods into the supply chains and will help promote commercialisation and widespread use of the technology. It is also required to develop appropriate outreach and education materials for the targeted audiences including family members, medical professionals, private investors, community groups, NGOs, regulatory agencies, and financial and legal industries. The private entrepreneurs should be encouraged to establish more food irradiation facilities to ensure the large scale availability of the irradiated food in the market so that consumers will have an option.

Food Safety

The microbial contamination of food takes place at every stage of food processing including the: (i) primary production stage (due to manure, soil, irrigation-water, worker, etc.), (ii) processing stage (worker, conveyer belt, washing water), and (iii) retail marketing or consumption stage (cross-contamination, cutting bed, improper storage). Several microbes including the bacteria (*Clostridium botulinum*, *E. coli* O157:H7, *L. monocytogenes*, *Salmonella spp*., *Shigella spp*., *Staphylococcus spp*., *Vibrio cholerae and Yersinia enterocolitica*), viruses (Norovirus and Hepatitis A) and protozoa (*Cryptosporidium* spp. and *Cyclospora* spp.) have been reported to be associated with major fruits and vegetables leading to the outbreaks worldwide. The leafy greens including spinach are the most likely agricultural produce causing the food-borne illnesses as the internalisation of pathogenic bacteria has been reported in such produce. In order to address the safety concern of the microbial contaminated leafy greens, the US FDA has issued the Final Rule on the Approval of Irradiation of Spinach and Iceberg Lettuce. The proposition that *E. coli* testing of the imported fresh fruits and vegetables should be mandatory was unanimously opined by the scientific panel on Contaminants or Biological Hazards of the Food Safety and Standards Authority of India (FSSAI) in New Delhi. Recently, the US FDA (2013) has also released a draft on risk assessment of the levels of contaminants in spices. Nearly, 12% of the spices imported by the US were found to be contaminated with insects and rodent excrement and ~6.6% of the spices were contaminated with *Salmonella*. Other pathogens included *Clostridium perfringens*, *Shigella* and *Staphylococcus aureus*. Considering the impact of microbial and parasitic contamination of foods on consumer's health, food safety needs to be ensured at the retail and also at the consumer level. Here, food irradiation can be a boon for consumers and have a phenomenal impact on the safety assurance in the global food supply. In conjunction with good manufacturing practices, food irradiation has well established safety potential. This provides a strong scientific background for implementation of radiation processing of foods as an effective means to improve their safety. So far, more than 60 countries have approved irradiation as a sanitary and phytosanitary method for many food products.

Packaging

Food once irradiated, can be prone to recontamination unless appropriately packed. Therefore, if radiation treatment is intended to control microbiological spoilage or insect infestation, prepackaging becomes an integral part of the process. Technical functions of packaging are well known. These include prevention of moisture uptake or loss, maintenance of an atmosphere other than air, protection from mechanical damage or simply keeping the food clean.

Since packaging materials are also exposed to radiation during the treatment, these materials must also satisfy additional requirements such as resistance to radiation with respect to its functional properties. In addition, it should not transmit toxic substances into food nor impart any off odour to the products.

Of the several packaging materials currently available such as cellulose, glass, metals and organic polymers, plastics offer unique advantages over the use of conventional rigid containers from the point of view of flexibility, low cost, light weight and low weight to volume ratio. Increasingly, packaging materials for use in aseptic processing lines in the food, pharmaceutical and cosmetic industry are now being sterilised by ionising radiation.

The packaging requirements of a particular food are significantly influenced by the desired objective of the radiation treatment.

- Packaging materials used for irradiated food are broadly classified into two categories depending on the type of radiation treatments. Processes requiring doses less than 10 kGy, such as extension of shelf-life of food.
- Processes requiring doses from 10–60 kGy, for storing such items as meat and poultry for long periods without refrigeration.

Irradiation of food is one of the most effective ways of food preservation to inactivate micro-organisms and destroy insect pests. Effective irradiation treatment on food is associated with an effective packaging material, which performs all the technical functions of packaging along with resistance to radiations. Though several packaging materials like glass, cellulose, metals and organic polymers are available for this purpose, plastics offer unique advantages over the conventionally used rigid containers in terms of flexibility, low cost, light weight, and low weight to volume ratio. Multi-laminate packaging structure of polymers like nylon, EVOH, PVC, cellophane, PE and Polyester are used as a prominent barrier material in packaging of irradiated food.

Irradiation of food is one of the most effective ways of food preservation to inactivate micro-organisms and destroy insect pests. Effective irradiation treatment on food is associated with an effective packaging material, which performs all the technical functions of packaging along with resistance to radiations.

RADIATION PROCESSING

Ionising radiation has high energy which is enough to break the molecular bonds and ionise atoms. As a result, materials exposed to this radiation undergo modification in their physical, chemical and biological properties. At present, the principal industrial applications of this radiation are sterilisation of health care products including pharmaceuticals, irradiation of food and agriculture products (for various end objectives, such as disinfestation, shelf life extension, sprout inhibition, pest control and sterilisation, etc.) and materials modification (such as chain scission, polymer cross linking and gemstone colourisation, etc.)

A significant impetus was given to the radiation processing industry with the advent of nuclear reactors, which have the capability to produce radioisotopes. Cobalt-60, the gamma ray emitter is widely used as the radiation source for industrial use mainly because it is readily available from simple nuclear reactions in nuclear reactors and is non-soluble in water. In recent times, the use of electron accelerators as a radiation source (and sometimes equipped with X ray converter) is increasing. However, gamma irradiators standout when it comes to irradiation of non-uniform and high density (thicker) materials. This is due to the deeper penetration of gamma in a given material.

HYGIENISATION

Availability of hygienic, safe and nutritious food is essential for sustainable human development. Food security is an important element of economic stability and self reliance of a nation. Though the need to preserve food has been felt by mankind since time immemorial, it is even stronger in today's context.

The rising population and increasing gap between demand and supply, agro-climatic conditions, inadequate, post-harvest practices, seasonal nature of produce, and long distances between production and consumption centers underscore the need to devise improved conservation and preservation strategies. The climatic conditions in India are quite favourable for the growth of insect pests and micro-organisms that destroy stored crops and cause spoilage of food. Spoilage also occurs due to biochemical and physiological changes in stored foods. During the course of harvesting, handling and storage, food could be easily contaminated with harmful pathogens and parasites, which could lead to food borne illness.

As in the other parts of the world, India also uses traditional and conventional methods of food preservation. These include:

- Pickling
- Fermentation
- Drying (Sun drying and mechanical drying)
- Refrigeration
- Freezing
- Canning

Each of these methods has advantages and limitations and search has always been for newer methods of food preservation.

PURPOSE OF RADIATION PROCESSING

Radiation processing of food involves controlled application of the energy of short wave length radiations of the electromagnetic spectrum, which includes radiowaves, microwaves, infrared, visible and ultraviolet light. These short wave length radiations are also known as ionising radiations and include gamma rays, accelerated electrons, and X-rays.

Radiation processing of food can achieve different objectives in different foods. Some of the major benefits of radiation processing of food are:

- Insect disinfestation of dried stored products.
- Phytosanitation to overcome quarantine barriers in fruits and vegetables.
- Inhibition of sprouting in tubers, bulbs and rhizomes.
- Delay in ripening and senescence of fruits.
- Enhancement in shelf–life by destruction of spoilage microbes.
- Elimination of pathogens and parasites.

The dose of radiation is measured in the SI units known as Gray (Gy). One Gray (Gy) dose of radiation is equal to 1 joule of energy absorbed per kg of food material. In radiation processing of food the doses are generally measured in terms of KGy (1000 Gy) [The old unit of absorbed dose was rad (1 Gy=100 rad)]. On the basis of the dose of radiation the application of radiation to food processing is generally divided into three main categories:

Process dose	*(kGy)*
I. Low dose applications (<1 kGy)	
Sprout inhibition of tubers, bulbs, rhizomes	0.02–0.2 kGy
Delay in ripening of fruits	0.2–1.0 kGy
Insect disinfestation of cereals, legumes and their products	0.25–1.0 kGy

II. Medium dose applications (1–10 kGy)

Shelf life improvement of meat, fish, fruits and vegetables	1.0–3.0 kGy
Elimination of pathogens in various foods	1.0–7.0 kGy
Hygienisation of spices	6.0–14.0 kGy

III. High dose applications (>10 kGy)

Sterilisation of packaged food and hospital diets	5.0–25.0 kGy

BENEFITS OF RADIATION PROCESSING OF FOOD

- Radiation processing is a cold process and therefore, unlike heat, it can be used on agricultural commodities without changing their fresh-like character.
- Radiation processing does not alter significantly nutritional value, flavour, texture and appearance of food.
- Radiation using Cobalt-60 cannot induce any radioactivity in food and does not leave any harmful or toxic radioactive residues on foods as is the case with chemical fumigants.
- Due to the highly penetrating nature of the radiation energy, it is very effective method.
- Pre-packaged foods can be treated for hygienisation and improving shelf-life.
- The radiation processing facilities are environment friendly and are safe to workers and public around.

LIMITATIONS OF RADIATION PROCESSING OF FOOD

- Radiation processing is a need based technology and cannot be applied to all kinds of foods.
- Radiation processing cannot make a bad or spoiled food look good.
- It cannot destroy already present pesticides and toxins in foods.
- Amenability of a particular food commodity to radiation processing has to be tested in a laboratory.
- Only those foods for which specific benefits are achieved by applying appropriate doses and those duly permitted under the Atomic Energy (Radiation Processing of Food and Allied Products) Rules, 2012 can be processed by radiation.

WHOLESOMENESS AND NUTRITIONAL ADEQUACY OF RADIATION PROCESSED FOODS

Wholesomeness and nutritional adequacy of radiation processed foods have been studied extensively all over the world for more than four decades. All the aspects of toxicology, nutritional adequacy and wholesomeness of radiation processed foods have been studied in detail. These include:

- Radiological safety.
- Safety of chemical changes.
- Microbiological safety.
- Toxicological safety.
- Nutritional adequacy.

It is not possible by the rules of physics to induce radioactivity in foods with Cobalt-60 gamma radiation. Hence the question of (residual) radioactivity in the material does not arise. Chemical changes in relation to formation of free radical are not unique to the irradiation process and do not lead to any toxicity. Micro flora of food after irradiation at low or medium doses may undergo selective reduction which is also encountered with other processes like heat. This does not pose any health risk if foods are processed by irradiation following Good Manufacturing Practice (GMP) and Good Irradiation Practices (GIP). Irradiation does not induce any changes in micro-organisms that potentiate their risks. On the contrary it reduces the fitness of the surviving micro-organisms. Studies have shown that irradiation does not change the main nutrients in food. As is also the case with other processing techniques, vitamins do show varied sensitivity to radiation. Vitamins A, E, C, K and B_1 in foods are relatively sensitive to radiation, while riboflavin, niacin, and vitamin D are more stable. The change induced by irradiation depends upon the dose of radiation, type of food, conditions of irradiation and packaging. Very little change in vitamin content is observed in food exposed to doses upto 1 kGy. Numerous studies on laboratory animals in the various laboratories around the world have shown that the consumption of radiation processed foods does not pose any health risks. Studies carried out on human volunteers also have shown no adverse effects of consumption of radiation processed foods.

DETECTION OF RADIATION PROCESSED FOODS

It is not possible to detect the process of irradiation carried out on food by sight or smell, or even by simple chemical tests. This only shows that food does not undergo discernible change after radiation processing. It is possible to detect some of the changes in radiation processed foods using sophisticated methods such as electron spin resonance (ESR), Thermoluminiescence (TL) or gas chromatography coupled with mass spectrometry (GCMS). The search is however on for development of simple and quick methods for detection of radiation processed foods.

GOOD IRRADIATION PRACTICES (GIP) IN RADIATION PROCESSING OF FOODS SPROUT INHIBITION OF BULB AND TUBER CROPS

Bulbs, tubers, and rhizomes undergo a natural process of sprouting during storage and transport. Due to sprouting the commodities lose weight, appearance and thus marketability. The crops permitted for radiation processing as per PFA rules include potato, onion, shallots (small Madras onion), and fresh ginger. The sole purpose of radiation processing here is to inhibit sprouting during storage and transport. The radiation may not destroy rot causing microbes, and would thus control only sprouting in these commodities which is a physiological process.

Onion: Only varieties suitable for radiation processing and long term storage should be used. The bulbs should be of uniform maturity. The onion should be harvested after the foliar fall-over is complete and dry. The bulb should preferably be topped 3–5 cm above the neck. The bulbs for radiation processing should be fully mature, sound, firm, and well covered with dry scales. The effectiveness of sprout inhibition caused by radiation processing may vary with variety, soil, and climatic conditions. Proper curing of onion prior to radiation processing is essential.

Curing may be done by field drying or artificial drying. Radiation processing carried out soon after harvest is the most effective. Post- processing storage should be as best as for the commodity not processed by irradiation would normally demand. The onion could be stored in well ventilated storage structures to remove heat of respiration. Onions stored in net bags or open crates may also need proper ventilation for air circulation. Onions can be stored upto 4–6 months at ambient temperatures with adequate ventilation. Radiation processing may cause a brownish discolouration of the inner bud or growth centre which is generally inconsequential to most uses of onion.

Potato: Only varieties of proven storage ability and suitable for radiation processing should be used. The tubers should be dry and fully mature prior to radiation processing. Immature potato has a weakly developed skin (periderm) and should not be used. After harvesting, potato may be held for a period upto four weeks at ambient temperature to allow maturing. Potato should be stored in well ventilated structures protected from light in order to prevent greening and solanine (a toxic glycoalkaloid) production. Potato after irradiation processing is best stored at 10–15°C. Processing should be done soon after the harvest when the tubers are naturally dormant. Since natural wound healing process of potato is inactivated by irradiation, the post-processing storage and handling is important. The handling should be minimised and the storage should be properly ventilated. Potato can be stored upto 4–6 months under above conditions. In certain varieties a little darkening may be observed after cooking.

Ginger, garlic, and shallots (small onions): Conditions of maturity at harvest, curing, post-harvest storage, irradiation and post-processing storage as applicable to the commodities of this class also apply these commodities. In all the commodities irradiated for sprout inhibition, procedures such as screening, sorting, grading and packaging, are applicable as for the normal commodity under the best of the farming or trading practices.

DELAY IN RIPENING OF BANANA AND MANGO

The purpose of radiation processing of banana and mango is to extend their normal shelf-life by delay in their ripening. Other possible effects of radiation processing such as reduction of spoilage micro-organisms or insect disinfestation may be secured, but is not the primary purpose here. Fruits to be processed should be freshly harvested. Only sound, clean fruits free of any mechanical injury or physiological disorder and without indication of microbial spoilage or insect disinfestation should be used for radiation processing. Radiation processing cannot make up for the initial poor quality of fruits. The fruits should be harvested under cool and dry conditions and stored under good ventilation. The maturity of fruit at the time of harvest is a critical factor. The fruits should be harvested at the hard mature state and should not have entered climacteric state marked by ethylene evolution and respiratory outburst. Radiation processing of immature fruit is to be avoided as such fruits fail to ripen normally. Similarly, radiation processing of fruits after the onset of ripening may accelerate the ripening process rather than delaying it.

Banana: Bananas are harvested in mature green state, given fungicide treatment, and appropriately packed prior to processing by radiation treatment. Irradiation should be carried out with a minimum delay after harvesting. A minimum delay of 7–8 days could be achieved at ambient temperature after processing by radiation. Best results are obtained when the fruits after radiation processing are stored at lower temperatures.

Mango: Mango should be picked in mature green stage with a specific gravity index of more than 1.0. Fruits should be thoroughly dried before packaging and processing by radiation. Hot water treatment at 45°C for 2–5 min could be given prior to radiation processing to obtain the best results. Radiation processing of immature fruits should be avoided. A delay in ripening of 7–14 days could be obtained at ambient temperature after processing. However, the best results are obtained when fruits are stored at lower temperatures.

MICROBIAL DECONTAMINATION AND DISINFESTATION OF SPICES

The specific purpose of the radiation processing of spices, herbs and dry vegetables are to eliminate or reduce microbial load, eliminate pathogenic microbes, and insect disinfestation. Use of chemical fumigants has several disadvantages and therefore is being phased out all over the world. The radiation processing offers several advantages. Unlike fumigants it does not leave harmful residues and it is safe for the environment and workers. It is a cold process and at the same time it is highly effective. The usual considerations regarding the quality and good manufacturing practices would apply to all these commodities, as radiation processing cannot be used to correct quality deficiencies. These commodities being of agricultural origin get contaminated with micro-organisms and insects. The quantity and quality of the biological burden on spices vary with the nature of material, conditions of climate, harvesting, processing, handling, storage and the transport employed by the persons dealing in commodity. A dose of 10 kGy can inactivate all stages of storage insects, eliminate pathogenic bacteria, and bring down the load in the range of 0–100 colony forming units (cfu)/g, which is below the acceptable safe levels by a magnitude of 10–100.

Only pre-packaged spices, herbs and dry vegetables can be processed by radiation. In order to avoid recontamination and re-infestation after processing, the product should be properly packed and sealed. Packaging material impervious to insect pests should be used to prevent re-infestation. It is useful to pack the commodity in its final distribution form. Adequately packed spices, herbs and dry vegetables after radiation processing can be stored at ambient temperature for long period upto 1 year or even more. Both whole and ground spices can be processed in bulk provided they are packed in appropriately lined, air tight packaging.

INSECT DISINFESTATION OF CEREAL GRAINS, GRAIN PRODUCTS, PULSES AND PULSE PRODUCTS

Dry cereal grains such as rice, wheat products such as atta, semolina, sooji or rawa, pulses (legumes) and pulse products can be infested with insects. Storage insects severely damage these commodities resulting in huge economic losses. Insect activity also increases moisture content of the commodity and promotes microbial activity. The initial moisture content of the commodity is crucial for the quality of these commodities and hence must be strictly controlled as a part of the good manufacturing practices. Packaging material that cannot be penetrated by insects should be used to avoid post-processing infestation. It is possible to carry out grain processing but this should be coupled with storage in insect proof silos or containers.

INSECT DISINFESTATION OF DRY FRUITS AND RAISINS

Insect infestation of dry fruits and raisins is a major problem during storage. Radiation processing of these commodities can destroy metamorphic stages of storage insects and prevent their emergence and subsequent damage. As for other radiation disinfested commodities, packaging material that cannot be penetrated by insects should be used to avoid post-processing infestation.

INACTIVATION OF PATHOGENS AND PARASITES AND ENHANCEMENT OF SHELF-LIFE OF MEAT AND POULTRY

Raw meat products, such as chopped or comminuted meat, mechanically deboned meat and poultry meat, whether fresh or frozen, can be processed by radiation. The purpose of radiation processing is to inactivate pathogenic micro-organism present in meat and thereby make it safer for human consumption. The process can also inactivate protozoan and helminthes parasites present in these meats. The radiation processing is also carried out for assurance of quality and extension of shelf-life fresh meats by reducing the population of spoilage microbes.

Relevant international codes for hygienic, good manufacturing practices and prescribed microbiological standards in these commodities should be adopted. These include slaughtering of only healthy animals, hygienic dressing operations, prompt and effective reduction of product temperature to 4°C or below, and appropriate cutting, trimming and deboning, and grinding (if required) operations. The low product temperatures should be maintained during transport and storage. In case of frozen meats the final product temperature should be below 0–20°C. Packaging should be done prior to processing by radiation and should be functionally protective. There are mechanisms other than bacterial action which cause meat spoilage. Additional measures, such as vacuum and inert packaging, may be required to prevent these changes during storage of meat. To avoid the risk of botulism the packaged material should always be stored below 4°C.

CONTROL OF PATHOGENS AND MICROBIAL LOAD IN FISH AND SHRIMP

Frozen fish and shrimp may be contaminated with pathogenic bacteria. Radiation processing can inactivate pathogenic bacteria in pre-packed frozen fish and shrimp. In case of fresh fish and shrimp radiation processing can bring down the microbial load and extend the Shelf-life when kept under refrigeration. It can also inactivate the pathogens present in these foods. The fish or shrimp should be dressed, handled and stored as per the good manufacturing practices. In case of frozen fish or shrimp the freezing should be carried out on product produced under good manufacturing practices. Quick freezing should be practiced. Packaging should be adequate and functionally protective and should be approved for the purpose. Additional measures, such as vacuum packaging may be applied for preventing non-bacterial spoilage. In order to prevent risk of botulism, fresh fish should be stored at temperature below 3°C. Frozen products should be maintained below –20°C during radiation processing and post-processing storage and transport.

DISINFESTATION OF DRIED FISH

Dried fish can be infested with storage insects. These insects feed on the fish tissue and cause damage and economic losses. Radiation processing can be used as an effective means of disinfestation of dry fish. Although mould growth can cause spoilage of these foods, doses employed for insect disinfestation may not control it. Therefore, mould growth should be prevented by using other measures such as salting and using preservatives. Good manufacturing practices should be followed in maintaining the initial quality of fish before and during drying and also during pre-process handling and packaging. Packaging should be done in packaging material impervious to insect. Improved packaging under vacuum and inert atmosphere can give better product quality. The moisture level should be maintained below 14% during pre- and post-processing storage. Radiation processed dry fish can be stored up to 6–9 months at ambient temperatures without changes in quality.

REQUIREMENTS FOR PACKAGING/ STORAGE

Where packaging is essential to prevent post-treatment recontamination the food should be packaged before treatment. Package size, especially with bulk packs should be such that they should be amenable to efficient handling. The choice of the packaging material and the nature of the container for specific food is usually determined by the purpose they are required to serve such as prevention of moisture loss or moisture uptake, to provide an atmosphere devoid of air, or to avoid mechanical damage to food. Foods processed for microbial decontamination must be packed in sealed packages which do not allow entry of micro-organisms and insect pests. Also, where disinfestation is the purpose, the packaging material should be impervious to insect penetration from outside. Flexible plastic containers because of their low density are highly suitable for packing foods processed by radiation. Films over 76 /lm thick are satisfactory for preservation of radiation processed products. Only those packaging materials approved under PFA Rules should be used. It should be noted that the quality and shelf-life retention is best maintained with the best of the packaging material used.

RE-IRRADIATION

Except for foods with low moisture content (cereals, pulses, dehydrated foods and other such commodities irradiated for the purpose of controlling insect re-infestation) radiation processed food shall not be re-processed by radiation. Generally, food is not considered as having been re-irradiated when (a) the food prepared from materials which have been processed at low dose levels, e.g. about 1 kGy, is processed again by radiation for another technological purpose, (b) the food containing less than 5% of radiation processed ingredient is again processed by radiation, or when (c) the full dose of ionising radiation required to achieve a desired effect is applied to the food in more than one installment as part of processing for a specific technological purpose. The cumulative overall average dose absorbed should not exceed 10 kGy as a result of first and second radiation processing. These aspects form the special requirement for radiation processing. Re-irradiation would be permissible only as per the PFA rules.

QUALITY ASSESSMENT OF INCOMING PRODUCT FOR RADIATION PROCESSING

Food and food ingredients of all types coming in for processing in a facility should be processed as per good manufacturing practices (GMP). These include hygiene during harvesting and post-harvest processing (curing, bleaching, drying, cleaning, grinding, packing, transportation and storage). The incoming product would be subjected to quality control inspection at the facility for radiation processing. The facility may ask for a certificate of quality from the manufacturer of food for processing by radiation carried out under a loan licence under PFA rules.

CONSUMER RESPONSE TO RADIATION PROCESSED FOODS

Consumer acceptance is a major factor in commercialisation of radiation processing technology. A number of surveys have been conducted nationally and internationally to study the response of consumers to radiation processed food. These surveys as well as limited market trials have demonstrated that consumers are receptive towards radiation processed food. A review on consumer attitudes and market response to food processed by radiation has shown that though consumers express concern about food processed by radiation, when presented with correct information, the acceptance is improved.

To evaluate the public perception on radiation processed foods in India, a questionnaire was prepared. The target groups of consumers were contacted in various scientific seminars and BARC staff canteens, covering a wide spectrum of urban consumers. More than 1500 consumers participated in these trials. They were served snack items such as *'vadas'*, *'bhajias'* made from radiation processed potato (0.1 kGy) and onion (0.06 kGy), respectively. After tasting the snacks, consumers were requested to answer the questionnaire. Apart from the personal data, they were asked whether they knew about radiation processing of food before, whether they liked the food, would they eat/buy radiation processed food in future and other remarks, if any. Data collected was statistically analysed. An overwhelming majority of the participants did not find any difference in the food items prepared from radiation processed commodities. In another study sensory evaluation of radiation-processed spices was carried out by housewives in Anushaktinagar (DAE staff quarters), college canteens and quantity cookery laboratory of SNDT Women's University, Mumbai. A good percentage of participants preferred radiation processed (and stored) spices. It has been observed that a majority of urban consumers have an open mind to radiation processed food. A small percentage of consumers were apprehensive about the technology. From the general comments made by the consumers, it appears that they were concerned about safety, cost, nutritional value and quality of radiation processed foods. Providing factual information about the benefits of radiation processing of foods in terms of improved shelf-life, quality, toxicological safety and nutritional adequacy would lead to increased consumers' confidence.

TYPICAL RADIATION PROCESSING FACILITY

In a typical gamma radiation processing facility, food processing is carried out inside a radiation processing chamber which is shielded by 1.5–1.8 m thick concrete walls. Pre-packed food material placed in suitable containers is sent into the irradiation chamber with the help of an automatic conveyor. The conveyor goes through a concrete wall labyrinth, which prevents radiation from reaching the work area and the operator room. When the facility is not in use the radiation source is stored under 6 m deep water. The water shield does not allow radiation to escape from the stored source into the radiation chamber, thus permitting free access to personnel for carrying out plant maintenance. For treating food, the source is lifted and brought to the irradiation position, above the water level after activation of all safety devices. The goods in aluminium carriers and tote boxes are mechanically positioned around the source rack and are turned, so that the contents are irradiated on both the sides. The absorbed dose is determined by the residence time of the carrier or tote box in irradiation position. Absorbed dose is checked by placing dose meters at various positions in a tote box or carrier which in turn will depend upon the source strength. Food can be processed by radiation only in those facilities which are authorised by the Atomic Energy Regulatory Board and Licensed by the Competent Authority.

MAJOR COMPONENTS OF A RADIATION PROCESSING FACILITY

- A source of gamma radiation (Cobalt-60).
- A radiation processing cell (irradiation cell).
- Product conveyors and control mechanisms.
- Safety devices and interlocks.

SITING OF IRRADIATORS

Site selection is an important aspect of setting up of a radiation processing facility. Geological features of the site that could affect the integrity of radiation shields should be evaluated. Areas of potential or actual surface or subsurface subsidence, uplift or collapse should be taken into consideration while assessing the suitability of site. Other factors that are not necessarily due to natural features (e.g. underground mining) that could result in instability should also be considered. The minimum levels of subsoil ground water should not cause flooding of irradiator, or influence pool water level or cause damage to structure. In areas with potential for seismic disturbance, gamma irradiators may be equipped with a seismic detector which on being activated by any disturbance will trigger appropriate control mechanism to shield the source automatically. In locating the irradiator a minimum distance from the boundary wall of the irradiator as mentioned below should be maintained:

1. Ammunition storage, explosive dumps, civil and military air fields: 2 km.
2. Residential area and public places: 30 m.

GAMMA RADIATION SOURCE

Source strength and throughput: Throughput of a food item in a radiation facility using Cobalt-60 source or other power sources may be related to the dose requirements of a process and source strength by the following equation:

$$\text{Throughput (kg/h)} = \frac{\text{Power in kW of source} \times 3600}{\text{Dose in kGy}} \times \text{E (Efficiency of irradiator)}$$

where, E is the efficiency of the radiation energy utilised in the process expressed in fraction. MCi or 37.5 PBq of Cobalt-60 = 15.0 kW of power.

Internal design: The source design must satisfy the specifications prescribed by the competent authority. After construction, shielding should be evaluated thoroughly. Shielding design requires the expertise of specialists. The shielding properties of materials are well documented. Access to irradiation cell and reliability of the interlocks are the other areas of design. It is essential to put radiation level monitors at the product monitor exit. A radiation monitor is also needed in the water treatment system. Other important aspects to be considered are fire protection, design of electrical power systems, ventilation requirements, water treatment systems, etc.

Source sealing: The radioactive material is properly encapsulated and stored. Each sealed source has at least two encapsulations. The material of encapsulation is either SS-304L or of equivalent metallurgical properties. The encapsulation facilitates efficient transfer of decay heat to the outermost surface during storage and use. The source may be either a single sealed source or several sealed sources forming an integral source unit. The sealed sources are classified in accordance with AERB/SS/3 (Rev.1).

Source storage: The source frame remains in its shielded position except when moved to irradiation position by the operator following the procedure specified by the manufacturer in the operating manual. The maximum radiation level at any accessible location outside the radiation cell should not exceed 1 μSv/h. The structure of the storage area should have adequate mechanical strength to support the source transport container. Means are provided for continuously removing decay heat from radiation source at all times while the source is stored. This may be achieved by either forced ventilation or water circulation. In the first case adequate means are provided to control and monitor the source coolant.

Water pool: The materials of construction of the water pool should be resistant to corrosion. The inner surface of the pool should be lined with either stainless steel or ceramic tiles so as to prevent seepage of water. The loss of water through the pool surface should not exceed 0.1% of its total volume in 24 hr. Depth of water is such that when filled with water up to its normal level, the radiation level outside the pool for sources of maximum design capacity should not exceed 1 μSv/h. Means are to be provided to monitor water level in the pool at three locations corresponding to maximum, normal and low levels. Means are also provided to automatically replenish water when the level falls below the low level.

Pool water quality: The pool water should be demineralised and free from turbidity, fungal growth or any other dissolved solid matter and should all have an electrical conductivity not exceeding 10 μ mho/cm. The quality of water is maintained by means of an online clean up system.

Pool guard: A radiation resistant physical barrier should be provided over the pool to prevent accidental fall of persons or objects into the pool. This arrangement may be removed to facilitate source loading/ unloading and other controlled servicing operations.

RADIATION PROCESSING CELL

Radiation shielding: The maximum radiation level at any occupied location outside the walls and above the ceiling of the cell should not exceed 1 μSv/hr. This is accomplished by enclosing the cell with concrete walls (1.5 m to 1.8 m thick).

Access control: Entry into radiation processing chamber or irradiation cell is through a personnel access door. The radiation incident on the personnel access door should undergo at least three scatters. The safety and accidental entry is ensured through multiple interlocks.

Cell ventilation: The irradiation cell is provided with ventilation through air entry and exhaust fans and the cell is maintained under negative pressure. There are at least six air changes per hour to prevent the concentration of O_3, NO_x and other toxic gases exceeding their corresponding safe levels. Gas detectors should be provided in installations where NO_x concentrations are likely to be significant. Time delay interlock should be provided to prevent personnel entry into the cell immediately after the source has returned to its fully shielded position in case of all categories of irradiators.

Fire safety: Heat and smoke sensors with audio visual display are installed in the radiation processing cell. An automatic fire extinguishing system with means to prevent accidental operation may be provided. Chemical substances that could adversely affect the integrity of the source should not be used in the fire extinguishing system. Power supply to the cell and the cell ventilation system should automatically be cut off in the event of fire or presence of smoke inside the cell.

OPERATING SYSTEMS

The processing may be carried out by either moving the source close to the product or by positioning the product close to the fixed source. In the first case the source movement may be either vertical or horizontal. Motive power to the source movement system and the product positioning system may be electrical, pneumatic, or hydraulic and this power should be cut off during any servicing or maintenance operation.

Source frame: The integral sources are firmly fixed in a rigid frame such that the sources do not get dislodged from the frame under normal use and accident conditions. The material of the source frame should not corrode or deteriorate in its storage. Tools and implements required for positioning and removing the sources should be capable of being operated from outside radiation shields.

Maintenance of source frame: The source frame should be capable of being moved from its shielded position to the irradiation position by at least two wire ropes of identical specifications. Wire ropes used for moving the source frame should conform to the specifications as per the Bureau of Indian Standards.

The source frame should automatically return to its fully shielded position in the event of any one of the following: (i) power failure (ii) smoke/fire alarm (iii) snapping or loosening of wire ropes (iv) ground motion in excess of threshold of seismic detector (v) emergency stop from the control panel (vi) disengagement of the door latch bar (vii) actuation of entry control device at product entry/exit ports (viii) failure of cell ventilation (ix) product carriers jammed (x) pressure plate sensing (xi) reduction of compressed pressure or lower level of oil in hydraulic system and (xii) fall of pool water level in the source pool.

Product movement: The product movement system should be such that any malfunction of the system leads to termination of radiation processing and lowering the source in shelved position. All components of this system shall be designed for fail safe operation. Means should be provided at product entry/exit ports to prevent inadvertent entry of any person in the radiation processing cell during operation. Means should also be provided to terminate operation from inside the cell. Such a device should be conspicuously labelled and marked. Actuation of this device should cause visual or audible warning in control room.

Control console: All operations of the irradiator should be performed from the control console by qualified operators. The selection and status of critical equipments should be displayed on the control console. An on-demand display of other parameters is to be provided. Control and display for routine operations is physically separated and distinctly marked from the control and display. for emergency operations. There shall be a clear and permanent display of the following process parameters on the control panel:

Radiation level	: Normal/Abnormal
Cell Ventilation	: On/Off
Position of product carrier, container, etc.	: Clear/Jammed
Personnel access door	: Open/Closed
Water level	: High/Normal/Low

Apart from normal parameters, emergency situations and abnormal conditions should also be displayed on the panel by means of audio or visual indications. The control console should have a programmable logic circuit with provisions for auto diagnosis and indication of an abnormal situation. Permanent display of source position should also be provided on the personnel entry door in a prominent manner.

Safety interlocks: The following mechanisms should be electrically mechanically or hydraulically interlocked with source position so as to interrupt/terminate the irradiation process when any of these are actuated.

These interlocks shall be of fail-safe design.

- Personnel access door and cell radiation level.
- Personnel access door and water level.
- Personnel access door.
- Personnel access door and ventilation system.
- Product movement system.
- Smoke/fire alarms and power supply to the cell.
- Tensions in wire ropes of source handling system.
- Roof plug, if any.
- Alarm from seismic detector, if any.
- Pressure plate sensing.

Power failure: Means should be provided to ensure that the irradiation process is automatically terminated in the event of loss of power supply exceeding ten seconds. Diesel generators should be provided to resume power operation in the event of persistent loss of on-line power.

Quality assurance: An adequate quality assurance programme including appropriate quality control measures shall be established for the design and operation of irradiation plants. The quality assurance program shall meet the requirements of IS 9000 or IS 14000. Records of all quality assurance procedures should be maintained for the entire life of the irradiator. Loading and unloading of sources, transport of sources and packaging and transport of radioactive sources should be in accordance with the provision of the AERB Safety Code SC/TR/01.

Installation of sources in the source frame: The source loading and unloading operations may be carried out either from inside the irradiation cell or from outside the cell through a loading port. The source transport container may be brought to the cell either through an opening on the cell roof or through product entry/personnel entry route. When an opening is provided on the cell roof, the opening should be kept closed by a shield plug during operation of the irradiator. Operation of the irradiator is automatically prevented If the roof plug, if any, is not properly fixed in its place. Loading of sources from outside the cell is through individual source channels clearly marked and identified from the loading port. Every source position on the loading port and transport should have a shutter action which is interlocked with the selection and alignment of relative channels. Actual source transfer (either from the loading or the transport flask) should be possible only after ensuring selection and correct alignment of the relative channel positions and verified by trial operations.

SYSTEMS TO ENSURE SAFETY AND RELIABILITY

Safety philosophy: Radiation processing facility should have a comprehensive safety philosophy having the following features:

Defence in depth: This ensures provision of several levels of protection and minimal need for human intervention. This concept applies to access control, shielding and confinement of radioactivity, control of the facility by automatic activation of safety systems and by operator action. The levels of defence in depth can be identified. The first level aims at preventing deviations from normal operation. The aim of the second level is to detect and respond to deviations from normal operations. The objective of the third level is to mitigate the consequences of an accident. The facility is operated only if all the levels of defence are functioning.

Redundancy: Redundancy lies in using more than the minimum number of items needed to accomplish a given function. This principle helps to improve the reliability of safety systems. Redundancy enables the failure or unavailability of one system to be tolerated without loss of function. An instance in point is the provision of three or four interlocks when two are sufficient.

Diversity: Provision of diversity improves reliability. This concept is to be applied very discretely. One has to weigh the benefits with the disadvantages of making the operation complicated.

Independence: Reliability of the system can be enhanced by maintaining independence among redundant systems and components.

Safety analysis: The facility should demonstrate how the design and operational procedures will contribute to the prevention of accidents and mitigation of the consequences. The formal safety analysis has a very useful role. Several conditions may be examined in the analysis:

- Loss of access control.
- Malfunctions and failures of structures, systems and components.
- Loss of control over the source movement system.
- Loss of system or component integrity, including the shielding source encapsulation and pool integrity.
- Electrical distribution faults, from very localised faults to complete loss of external energy sources.
- Failure resulting from external causes such as storm, floods, earthquakes or explosions.
- Failure of personnel to observe safe procedures.
- Breakdown of procedures for preventing access to the facility by unauthorised persons.
- Breakdown of administrative procedures leading to unsafe practices.

RESPONSIBILITIES OF DESIGNERS AND MANUFACTURERS

The following information should be provided to the operating organisation by the manufacturers:

- Detailed description of design and operation of irradiator, safety systems, and control circuits
- List of components identified as per the following classification:
  Group A : Replaceable by manufacturer or with his explicit consent
  Group B : Replaceable to exact specifications
  Group C : Replaceable without restrictions
- Site specific data as given in site selection criteria
- Operating and maintenance procedures including type and frequency of checks for various systems
- Safety analysis report of the facility
- Test procedures and reports establishing conformance of each component system, subsystem, and its operation in accordance with its design and relevant standard specifications.
- Schedule of tests and checks on various component systems, subsystems, and procedures to accomplish these.
- Instructions and procedures to be followed in emergency situations.
- Reports on the pre-commissioning tests and their results

The following information regarding sources shall be maintained by the source manufacturer and operating organisations:

- Identification and model number of each source, source activity as on date of installation, and its location in the source frame.
- Source classification designation certificate issued by the competent authority.
- Bend test certificate.
- Leak test certificate by the manufacturer.
- Contamination test certificate issued by manufacturer.
- Special form radioactive certificate issued by the competent authority.
- Any other information as specified by the competent authority.

TRAINING OF MANPOWER FOR OPERATION AND INSPECTION

The operating organisation shall ensure that those of their employees who are engaged in work with ionising radiation receive such information, instructions and training as it will enable them to conduct that work in accordance with the requirements of their written instructions.

- The nature of ionising radiation.
- The health hazards from exposure to such irradiation.
- The basic principles of radiation protection (shielding, etc.).
- The basic understanding of working and operation of radiation measuring devices (meters, detectors, etc.).
- A clear understanding of the plant safety systems and their operations.

Training must be updated regularly and whenever staff changes occur. Suitable training should be imparted at an institution or industry where the technology is well established. Trained operators should have a certificate from the training institute which should be updated and endorsed from time to time.

Written administrative instructions governing the responsibility on the use of radiation processing plant and the associated radiation safety programme should be provided to the authorised personnel. These instructions should be fully understood by all the authorised personnel.

Qualified operators - responsibilities: Because qualified operators usually have the closest association with the radiation processing plant, day to day responsibility for the safe operation is generally theirs. Operator training, experience, attitude and competence will establish the degree of safety associated with operation of the irradiation plant. Each individual who operates or maintains plant shall have a responsibility to ensure that the laid down safety procedures are observed and should hold an appropriate certificate of competence and approved training which is recognised by the competent authority.

DOSIMETRY AND PROCESS CONTROL

Control of food processing in all types of facilities involves the use of accepted methods of measuring the absorbed radiation dose, the distribution of that dose in the product package, and of monitoring of the physical parameters of the process. Dosimetry for food irradiation is analogous to temperature monitoring in thermal processing, with dose meters being the analogs of thermocouples in that they are employed to provide an accurate measure of the rate of energy delivery, total energy delivered or absorbed and the over dose ratio. There are several types of dose meters, the most common ones being based on a chemical change that is linear within a practical dose range. Dosimetry is the keystone of the proper radiation processing. Careful dosimetry is required to ensure that a technologically useful dose has been applied, while maintaining the best possible dose uniformity ratio. Therefore, prior to commissioning of the plant, extensive dosimetric calibrations of the irradiator are carried out and followed during the processing by routine dosimetry. Because it is not possible to distinguish irradiated from non-irradiated products by sight, smell or taste, it is important that appropriate indicator devices which undergo radiation induced colour change be attached to each container/package, and that physical barriers be employed in the radiation plant to keep processed and non-processed products separated from each other.

DOCUMENTATION AND RECORD KEEPING

Documentation and record keeping is an essential function of a food irradiation facility, and must be maintained in a complete and reliable manner. Records are kept to provide information on various aspects of a facility operation which include:

- Facility characteristics, maintenance, etc.
- Personnel and environmental safety.
- Food product receipt, treatment and shipment.
- Government licensing, authorisation, etc.
- Personnel qualifications, training, performance, safety, etc.
- Customer relations.

INSPECTION OF RADIATION PROCESSING FACILITIES

- Checking that the operation meets all the conditions laid down in the licence and that the plant is well maintained.
- Reviewing the logs and records, the results of various tests, maintenance and monitoring programs.
- Checking that the recommendations made after a previous inspection have been taken into account.

- Conducting periodic audits to ensure that the quality assurance programme is being properly carried out.
- Updating of emergency plans, conducting a survey of the availability of emergency equipment and witnessing the emergency drills.
- Preparing reports on regulatory inspection activities.
- Carrying out regulatory inspections during decommissioning to ensure that the facility is decommissioned safely and is maintained in a safe and secure condition.

STATUTORY REQUIREMENTS AND REGULATORY APPROVALS

Both the safety of foods processed by radiation and the safety of radiation processing facilities have undergone intense scrutiny by the scientific institutions as well as law enforcing agencies around the world. The Government of India has enacted rules and regulations and provided guidelines and standards to ensure high degree of product and process safety. The safety of food processed by radiation is regulated under the Prevention of Food Adulteration Act (PF A) Rules, 1955, enforceable by the local Food and Drug Administration (FDA).

Chapter 11

Pulse Electric Field, Ultrasound and Hurdle Technology

INTRODUCTION

Pulsed electric field (PEF) processing is a emerging method of food preservation that uses short bursts of electricity for microbial inactivation (cell-lysis) and causes minimal or no detrimental effect on food quality attributes. PEF can be used for processing liquid and semi-liquid food products. Pulsed electric field (PEF) processing is a novel, non-thermal preservation method that has the potential to produce foods with excellent sensory and nutritional quality and shelf-life. High intensity pulsed electric field (HIPEF) processing involves the application of pulses of high voltage (typically 20–80 kV/cm) to foods placed between 2 electrodes. PEF treatment is conducted at ambient, sub-ambient, or slightly above ambient temperature for less than 1 s, achieved by multiple short duration pulses typically less than 5 μs and energy loss due to heating of foods as well as undesirable changes in the sensory properties of the food is minimised. For food quality attributes, PEF technology is considered superior to traditional heat treatment of foods because it avoids or greatly reduces the detrimental changes of the sensory and physical properties of foods. Although some studies have concluded that PEF preserves the nutritional components of the food, effects of PEF on the chemical and nutritional aspects of foods must be better understood before it is used in food processing.

Some important aspects in pulsed electric field technology are the generation of high electric field intensities, the design of chambers that impart uniform treatment to foods with minimum increase in temperature, and the design of electrodes that minimise the effect of electrolysis. The large field intensities are achieved through storing a large amount of energy in a capacitor bank (a series of capacitors) from a DC power supply, which is then discharged in the form of high voltage pulses. Studies on energy requirements have concluded that PEF is an energy efficient process compared to thermal pasteurisation, particularly when a continuous system is used.

Consumer demand has increasingly required processed food to have a more natural flavour and colour, with a shelf-life that is sufficient for distribution and a reasonable period of home storage before consumption. This can be achieved by minimal processing methods that preserve foods but also remain to a greater extent their nutritional quality and sensory characteristics by reducing the reliance on heat as the main preservative action. This minimal processing destroys micro-organisms, and in some cases enzymes, and there are no substantial increases in product temperature. There is therefore little damage to pigments, flavour compounds and vitamins and in contrast to heat processing, the sensory characteristics and nutritional value of foods are not degraded to a significant extent. The resulting products have higher quality and consumer appeal in markets where the retention of natural sensory characteristics can command premium prices.

The use of an external electrical field for a few microseconds induces local structural changes and a rapid breakdown of the cell membrane. Based on this phenomenon, called electroporation, many applications of high intensity pulsed electric fields (HIPEF) have been studied in the last decades. In the area of plant and microbial genetics pulsed electric fields are applied to cause an electroporation of cell membranes to infuse foreign material such as DNA into the cell. This process of reversible pore formation has to be controlled to maintain viability of the organisms during the application of the PEF. Due to the reversible permeabilisation, the cells repair their membranes through resealing the electropores immediately after the PEF treatment. At higher treatment intensity PEF can be utilised for the inactivation of micro-organisms by an irreversible breakdown of the cell membrane. HIPEF consists of a number of components including a power source, capacitor tank, a switch, treatment chamber, voltage current and temperature sensors and aseptic packaging equipment. Generation of different voltage waveforms in PEF: exponential pulses, square pulses, bipolar pulses and oscillatory pulses.

Formation of pores and cell membranes by HIPEFs is not entirely understood. Zimmermann and others, applying the dielectric rupture theory, concluded that membrane rupture is caused by an induced transmembrane potential approximately 1V larger than the natural potential of the cell membrane. The reversible or irreversible rupture (or electroporation) of a cell membrane depends on factors such as intensity of the electric field, number of pulses, and duration of pulses. The plasma membranes of cell become permeable to small molecules after being exposed to an electric field, permeation then causes swelling and the eventual rupture of the cell membrane. HIPEF processing system is associated with minimum energy utilisation and greater energy efficiency than thermal processing. In apple juice treatment, energy utilised in PEF is 90% less than the amount of energy used in high temperature and short time processing methods (HTST).

HISTORY AND ENGINEERING ASPECTS OF PEF PROCESSING

Historical Background of PEF Processing

The bactericidal effect of an electric current had already been tested at the end of the nineteenth century, but the lethal effects found by applying direct or low-frequency alternating current resulted from thermal or electrochemical effects. In the 1920s a process called Electropure was introduced in Europe and the USA. Being one of the first attempts to use electricity for milk pasteurisation, it was performed by the application of a (not pulsed) 220 V alternating current within a carbon electrode treatment chamber. About 50 plants were in operation until the 1950th, but due to rising energy costs and competition with mild novel thermal preservation technologies such as UHT, these (ohmic heating) plants have been replaced. Apart from thermal effects based on the mechanism of ohmic heating, lethal effects of electrochemical reactions such as the hydrolysis of chlorine were found when subjecting food to discharges with a voltage of 3–4 kV. Pulsed discharges of high voltage electricity across two electrodes for microbial inactivation were first investigated in the 1950th, resulting in a process called electrohydraulic treatment.

The electrodes were submerged in the liquid medium within a pressure vessel, electric arcs were generated by high voltage pulses forming transient pressure shock waves up to 250 MPa and ultraviolet light pulses. Experiments conducted by Doevenspeck revealed that pulsed electric fields can be applied for disruption of cells in food material and were further developed and expanded to the inactivation of micro-organisms and wastewater treatment. Based on this work, the 'Elcrack' process for the disintergration of animal material such as fish or meat and the 'Elsteril' process for liquid media decontamination were developed by Krupp Maschinentechnik GmbH, Germany. The application of electric fields for electroplasmolysis of apple mash was first reported by Flaumenbaum, in which an increase in juice yield of 10–12 per cent was found and the products were described to be lighter in colour and less oxidised than after a heat or enzymatic pre-treatment.

Important early patents in the application of PEF for treatment were applied by Krupp in Germany, developing the Elcrack and Elsteril processes, for inactivation of vegetative micro-organisms in milk and fruit juices with an electric field strength up to 30 kV/cm, but heating due to high energy dissipation and consequently high costs of operation inhibited a successful industrial application. Later patents were applied by PurePulse Technologies, San Diego, USA with electric fields in the range from 10 to 25 kV/cm and the microbial showing an increase of shelf-life of about one week. Engineering aspects of PEF processing: (i) bench-top unit, (ii) lab-scale pulser and (iii).treatment chamber.

MECHANISM OF ACTIONS IN PEF PROCESSING

It is generally accepted that the primary effect of PEF on biological cells is related to local structural changes and the breakdown of the cell membrane, which is a highly important component of the biological cell as it acts as a semi-permeable barrier responsible for mass transfer and plays an important role in the synthesis of RNA and DNA, protein and cell wall components as well as many other complex metabolic activities. Disruption of intracellular organelles and other structural changes have also been described. When the overall potential exceeds a critical value of about 1V, depending upon the compressibility, the permittivity and the initial thickness of the membrane, the electrocompressive force causes a local dielectric rupture of the membrane inducing the formation of a pore, acting as a conductive channel. Taking into account a membrane thickness of 5 nm, this translates to a dielectric strength of 2000 V/cm. A drastic increase in permeability re-establishes the equilibrium of the electrochemical and electric potential differences of the cell plasma and the extracellular medium. Alternative concepts are based on molecular reorientation and localised defects within the cell membrane which are expanded and destabilised by exposure to an electric field. The presence of small fluctuating hydrophobic pores in the lipid matrix was suggested to be the initial structural basis of electroporation.

PULSED ELECTRIC FIELD PROCESSING

Present Status of Pulsed Electric Field Technology

The extent of improvement in a food processing company achieved by an emerging technology generally reflects the interest in that technology by the food industry. The method of high intensity pulse electric field used to inactivate micro-organisms has been under research for nearly 45 years, initiated with the first patent received by Doevenspeck. During this time span the technology has proved to be most effective in the activation of vegetative bacteria, yeasts, and molds, while bacterial spores are much more tolerant. Additionally, the synergistic effect to PEF technology in combination with other mild preservation methods is one of the interests popular in recent years. The use of antimicrobials as nisin or other bacteriosins has been proposed as having lethal effects on electroporation. Among all liquid products, PEF technology has been most widely applied to apple juice, orange, juice, milk, liquid egg, and brine solutions. A significant inactivation of staphylococcus aureus inoculated skim milk treated by PEF was also reported. The ability of PEF to increase permeabilisation means it can be successfully used to enhance mass and heat transfer to assist drying of plant tissues. As started before, PEF technology commonly focused on processing pumpable and homogenous liquid foods free of particles and air. In the case of solid foods the mixture is mixed with air, contributing to the low electric conductivity of the product, hence, not limiting the maximum applicable electric field intensity. Some studies conducted on model foods, viscous foods such as yoghurt and rice pudding or particulate foods such as pea soup with plastic beads, reported successful result for PEF application on solid or semi-solid foods.

APPLICATIONS OF PEF TECHNOLOGY IN FOOD PROCESSING

The applications of PEF as a food processing tool is gaining popularity, since it represents a nonthermal alternative to conventional pasteurisation methods. The PEF treatment, being a nonthermal process, may also have no significant detrimental effect on heat-labile components present in foods such as vitamins. The major disadvantage of PEF operation is the initial investment.

Micro-organism Inactivation

PEF has been mainly applied to preserve the quality of foods, such as to improve the shelf-life of bread, milk, orange juice, liquid eggs, and apple juice, and the fermentation properties of brewer's yeast.

1. Processing of apple juice: Simpson and others reported that apple juice from concentrate treated with PEF at 50 kV/cm, 10 pulses, and pulse width of 2 μs and maximum processing temperature of 45°C had a shelf-life of 28 day compared to a shelf-life of 21 day of fresh-squeezed apple juice. There were no physical or chemical changes in ascorbic acid or sugars in the PEF-treated apple juice and a sensory panel found no significant differences between untreated and electric field treated juices.
2. Processing of orange juice: Zhang and others evaluated the shelf-life of reconstituted orange juice treated with an integrated PEF pilot plant system. The PEF system consisted of a series of co-field chambers. Temperatures were maintained near ambient with cooling devices between chambers. Three waveshape pulses were used to compare the effectiveness of the processing conditions. Their results confirmed that the square wave is the most effective pulse shape.
3. Processing of milk: Fernandez-Molina and others studied the shelf-life of raw skim milk (0.2% milk fat), treated with PEF at 40 kV/cm, 30 pulses, and treatment time of 2 μs using exponential decaying pulses. The shelf-life of the milk was 2 week stored at 4°C, however, treatment of raw skim milk with 80°C for 6 s followed by PEF treatment at 30 kV/cm, 30 pulses, and pulse width of 2 μs increased the shelf-life up to 22 d, with a total aerobic plate count of 3.6-log cfu/ml and no coliform. The processing temperature did not exceed 28°C during PEF treatment of the raw skim milk.
4. Processing of eggs: Earliest studies in egg products were conducted by Dunn and Pearlman in a static parallel electrode treatment chamber with 2-cm gap using 25 exponentially decaying pulses with peak voltages of around 36 kV. Tests were carried out on liquid eggs, on heat-pasteurised liquid egg products, and on egg products with potassium sorbate and citric acid added as preservatives. Comparisons were made with regular heat-pasteurised egg products with and without the addition of food preservatives when the eggs were stored at low (4°C) and high (10°C) refrigeration temperatures. The study showed the importance of the hurdle approach in shelf-life extension.

5. Processing of green pea soup: Vega-Mercado and others exposed pea soup to 2 steps of 16 pulses at 35 kV/cm to prevent an increase in temperature beyond 55°C during treatment. The shelf-life of the PEF-treated pea soup stored at refrigeration temperature exceeded 4 week. There were no apparent changes in the physical and chemical properties or sensory attributes of the pea soup directly after PEF processing or during the 4 week of storage at refrigeration temperatures.
6. Processing of beer: Inactivation and sub-lethal injury of the beer spoilage organism *Lactobacillus plantarum* in a model system using different pulsed electric field (PEF) strengths (10–19 kV/cm) and total energy inputs (13–42 kJ/kg) were investigated.

Spore inactivation

Compared to vegetative cells, microbial spores are resistant to extreme ambient conditions such as high temperatures and osmotic pressures, high and low pHs, and mechanical shocks. Their resistance is associated not only with their small size (which make them more difficult to destroy than larger cells), but also dehydration and mineralisation. Yin and others reported that inactivation up to 2 log cycles of *B. subtilis* spores with pulse durations of 1, 2, 4, and 6 μsec at frequencies of 3000, 1500, 750, and 500 Hz, respectively, with an applied electric field strength of 30 kV/cm at 36°C.

Enzyme inactivation

Enzymatic activity is altered by PEF, though, in general, enzyme inactivation by PEF requires stronger electrical condition to achieve significant reductions than microbial inactivation. This fact is important because some enzymes are useful for the food industry, thus PEF would allow the destruction of micro-organisms while maintaining the activity of some enzymes.

PROBLEM AND CHALLENGES IN PEFS PROCESSING

A task still challenging for electro-engineers is the development of equipment with reliable, industrial scale generation of high-strength electric field pulses. Javier Raso and Volker Heinz reported important things which are that, from 2000 to the present, great advances have been achieved in the commercialisation of PEFs applications. However translating the technical parameters into affordable and effective PEF system within legal regulation is not easy. Currently, commercial PEF systems are available that include both bench-top and industrial systems, as those provided by Pure-pulse Technologies, Inc.

The present challenge is to increase treatment capacity with the use of feasible high power systems, by optimising the overall PEF system design in light of critical process parameters. In the last few years problems due to electrochemical reactions at the electrode/medium interfaces have been discussed, indicating that there is a challenge to replace commonly used stainless steel electrodes by other materials or to modify pulse generator systems to reduce the amount of electrochemical reactions. An overview of possible electrochemical reactions at a steel electrode may cause harmful to human being.

Application of carbon electrodes may be one solution to overcome this problem and application of shorter pulses or switching systems without leak current have also been discussed to avoid electrochemical reactions. Apart from a reduction in electrode life time the release of particles and heavy metals from the electrode may cause toxicity problems.

Reyns and others reported the generation of bactericidal and mutagenic compounds by a PEF treatment, even if they operated with 300 pulses at a pulse width of 2 s and 26.7 kV/cm, treatment intensity much higher than required for liquid food preservation.

Researchers all over the world still have many possible project development designs that need to be focused on the better understanding of the technology. The project must be related to aspects of the PEF product and process that have not been addressed yet and are of relevance to implementation at a commercial level. The result obtained up to now are not enough for a complete generalisation of different aspects dealing with the quality, microbiology, and nutritional characteristics of the products as well as their processing conditions.

The establishment of unknown destruction kinetics of many microbial pathogens (especially *Clostridium botulinum*) and the identification of the proper indicator organisms for each specific product that consider the handling and storage conditions of raw products and finished products are examples of where microbiological experience will be major contribution. The uniformity of the delivered treatment and the means to assess the process are still challenging food and electrical engineers. The impact of processing conditions such as temperature, pH, moisture, and lipid content on the safety and quality aspects of new products leaves an area that is still open to food chemists.

Furthermore, the implementation of the hurdle technology and the use of food additives suggest even more new alternatives. It is not clear yet if the food industry will fully accept PEF as a processing technology. Nevertheless, its tremendous potential to replace or compliment conventional methods, which provides the basis for ongoing studies on PEF that can be regarded as both meaningful and worthy of consideration to all those in the field of food processing.

APPLICATIONS OF PULSE ELECTRIC FIELD

Processing of Milk

Fernandez-Molina and others studied the shelf-life of raw skim milk (0.2% milk fat), treated with PEF at 40 kV/cm, 30 pulses, and treatment time of 2 µs using exponential decaying pulses. The shelf-life of the milk was 2 week stored at 4°C, however, treatment of raw skim milk with 80°C for 6 s followed by PEF treatment at 30 kV/cm, 30 pulses, and pulse width of 2 µs increased the shelf-life up to 22 d, with a total aerobic plate count of 3.6-log cfu/ml and no coliform. The processing temperature did not exceed 28°C during PEF treatment of the raw skim milk.

Dunn and Pearlman conducted a challenge test and shelf-life study with homogenised milk inoculated with *Salmonella* Dublin and treated with 36.7 kV/cm and 40 pulses over a 25-min time period. *Salmonella* Dublin was not detected after PEF treatment or after storage at 7–9°C for 8 d. The naturally occurring milk bacterial population increased to 107 cfu/ml in the untreated milk, whereas the treated milk showed approximately 4×10^2 cfu/ml.

Further studies by Dunn indicated less flavour degradation and no chemical or physical changes in milk quality attributes for cheesemaking. When *Escherichia coli* was used as the challenge bacteria, a 3-log reduction was achieved immediately after the treatment.

Qin and others reported that milk (2% milk fat) subjected to 2 steps of 7 pulses each and 1 step of 6 pulses with an electric field of 40 kV/cm achieved a shelf-life of 2 week at refrigeration temperature. There was no apparent change in its physical and chemical properties and no significant differences in sensory attributes between heat pasteurised and PEF treated milk.

Calderon-Miranda studied the PEF inactivation of *Listeria innocua* suspended in skim milk and its subsequent sensitisation to nisin. The microbial population of *L. innocua* was reduced by 2.5-log after PEF treatments at 30, 40 or 50 kV/cm. The same PEF intensities and subsequent exposure to 10 IU nisin/ml achieved 2-, 2.7- or 3.4-log reduction cycles of *L. innocua*. It appears that there may be an additional inactivation effect as a result of exposure to nisin after PEF. Reina and others studied the inactivation of *Listeria monocytogenes* Scott A in pasteurised whole, 2%, and skim milk with PEF. *Listeria monocytogenes* was reduced 1- to 3-log cycles at 25°C and 4-log cycles at 50°C, with no significant differences being found among the 3 milks. The lethal effect of PEF was a function of the field intensity and treatment time.

Processing of Eggs

Some of the earliest studies in egg products were conducted by Dunn and Pearlman in a static parallel electrode treatment chamber with 2-cm gap using 25 exponentially decaying pulses with peak voltages of around 36 kV. Tests were carried out on liquid eggs, on heat-pasteurised liquid egg products, and on egg products with potassium sorbate and citric acid added as preservatives. Comparisons were made with regular heat-pasteurised egg products with and without the addition of food preservatives when the eggs were stored at low (4°C) and high (10°C) refrigeration temperatures. The study showed the importance of the hurdle approach in shelf-life extension. Its effectiveness was even more evident during storage at low temperatures, where egg products with a final count around 2.7 log cfu/ml stored at 10°C and 4°C maintained a low count for 4 and 10 d, respectively, versus a few hours for the heat pasteurised samples. Other studies on liquid whole eggs (LWE) treated with PEF conducted by Qin and others and Ma and others showed that PEF treatment decreased the viscosity but increased the colour (in terms of β-carotene concentration) of liquid whole eggs compared to fresh eggs. After sensory panel evaluation with a triangle test, Qin and others found no differences between scrambled eggs prepared from fresh eggs and electric field-treated eggs, the latter were preferred over a commercial brand. In addition to colour analysis of eggs products, Ma and others evaluated the density of fresh and PEF-treated LWE (indicator of egg protein-foaming ability), as well as the strength of sponge cake baked with PEF-treated eggs. The stepwise process used by Ma and others did not cause any difference in density or whiteness between the PEF-treated and fresh LWE. The strength of the sponge cakes prepared with PEF-treated eggs was greater than the cake made with non-processed eggs. This difference in strength was attributed to the lower volume obtained after baking with PEF-treated eggs. The statistical analysis of the sensory evaluation revealed no differences between cakes prepared from PEF processed and fresh LWE.

Processing of Various Food Products

Green pea soup

Vega-Mercado and others exposed pea soup to 2 steps of 16 pulses at 35 kV/cm to prevent an increase in temperature beyond 55°C during treatment. The shelf-life of the PEF-treated pea soup stored at refrigeration temperature exceeded 4 week, while 22 or 32°C were found inappropriate to store the product. There were no apparent changes in the physical and chemical properties or sensory attributes of the pea soup directly after PEF processing or during the 4 week of storage at refrigeration temperatures.

Apple juice

Simpson and others reported that apple juice from concentrate treated with PEF at 50 kV/cm, 10 pulses, pulse width of 2 μs and maximum processing temperature of 45°C had a shelf-life of 28 d compared to a shelf-life of 21 d of fresh-squeezed apple juice. There were no physical or chemical changes in ascorbic acid or sugars in the PEF-treated apple juice and a sensory panel found no significant differences between untreated and electric field treated juices. Vega Mercado and others reported that PEF extended the shelf-life at 22–25°C of fresh apple juice and apple juice from concentrate to more than 56 d or 32 d, respectively. There was no apparent change in its physico-chemical and sensory properties.

Grape juice

Juice extraction from Chardonnay white grape using pulse electric field with two pressure conditions was studied. A PEF treatment of 400 V/cm was applied. The PEF pretreatment increased the juice yield by 67–75% compared to the control sample without any treatment.

Sugar

The juice yield of pretreated samples was higher (74.5% at 5kV, 20 pulses) than heat treated (73.2%) and untreated sugar cane (65.5%). The energy consumption for disintegration of sugar cane (17 kJ/kg at 5 kV and 20 pulses) was 10 times less when compared to heat treatment (171 kJ/ kg). Additionally the cell disintegration using occurred faster (less than 2 min with 1Hz pulses frequency and 80 pulses) than thermal disintegration (20 min at 70°C). PEF was used as an intermediate in the cold juice extraction from sugar beet cossettes using a pilot scale multi-plate and frame pressing equipment and a pulse generator. A yield of about 80% in juice per initial mass of cossettes was achieved before washing. Purity of juices was higher following PEF treatment compared to those juices without to PEF treatment (96–98% and 90–93% respectively.

Meat and fish

The electro-permeabilisation of cell membranes, leading to a drastic increase in mass transfer rates, can be utilised to enhance drying rates of cellular tissue. An increase in mass transfer rates, resulting in faster water transport to the product surface and therefore reduction of drying time after a pretreatment will lead to drastic saving of energy and better utilisation of production capacities during convective air drying. Taking into account the low energy input required for a PEF treatment of plant or animal tissue (2–20 kJ/kg), it is evident that there is a potential to reduce the total energy input for product drying.

Thus, PEF inactivates vegetative micro-organisms including yeasts, spoilage micro-organisms and pathogens, and it can be used to pasteurise fluids such as juices, milk and soups without using additives. This technology can substitute for conventional heat pasteurisation or it can operate at room temperature to retain quality and heat-sensitive vitamins. PEF can be used as continuous process but, after processing, products have to be packaged hygienically and kept cool during storage. Using some of antimicrobial substances prolongs the shelf life of foods within pulsed electric fields. An application of PEF for food preservation provides the tremendous potential to preserve high quality products at lower temperatures and short residence time to retain the fresh-like character and nutritional value of the products.

ULTRASONIC PROCESSING AND ITS USE IN FOOD INDUSTRY

Ultrasound are sound waves having frequency beyond the audible range of human capacity (~20 kHz). It has a variety of applications with many advantages as compared to conventional methodologies used in food industries. Ultrasound is similar to 'normal' (audible) sound based on physical properties. Ultrasound is one of the emerging technologies that were developed to minimise processing, maximise quality and ensure the safety of food products. It is one of the new technologies which increases and ensures quality and reduces the time of processing and cost of the food products. So ultrasound is used in food technology for processing, preservation and extraction steps. It makes use of physical and chemical phenomena which marks the difference with conventional techniques. It offers great advantage in various fields like productivity, yield, better quality, less time and being environmental friendly.

Ultrasound has been emerged as a revolutionary technology in the field of food industry. Its use is continuously increasing in various steps of processing of food products. Ultrasonic is a fast growing area of research, which has been found to be used increasingly in the food industry for analysis as well as modification of various food products. The use of ultrasound in food industry involves various novel ideas and methods which are interesting as compared to conventional methods or techniques. This introduces us to the food processing methods which are alternatives to conventional ones. The use of ultrasound is an active subject within the food industry for both of the research and development. When the ultrasound propagates through a material it induces compressions and decompressions (rarefactions) in the particles of the medium, due to which high amount of energy is produced. Sound is a mechanical wave that travels in a straight line and also it requires a medium through which it travels. Ultrasound is a wave with a frequently exceeding the upper limit of human hearing which is greater than 20000 Hz (Hertz). In ultrasound, the sound ranges can be broadly divided into two different categories. The one is low energy, high frequency diagnostic ultrasound in the MHz range and another one is high energy, low frequency, power ultrasound in the kHz range. So it is possible that ultrasound can be used for processing. The basic principle behind working of ultrasound is that it utilises interaction between high-frequency sound waves and matter to obtain information about the composition, structure and dimensions of materials through which it propagates. Ultrasound has mainly two distinct categories of frequency ranges. They are high frequency, low energy diagnostic ultrasound in MHz range and low frequency high energy power ultrasound. Low energy (low intensity, low power) ultrasound has frequencies greater than 100 KHz with intensities down 1W.cm^2. These can be used as monitoring of food products while processing and storage with high quality and safety. It is used for evaluation of the composition of meat products, poultry and fish of raw and fermented stages. It is also used for the quality check or control of fruits, vegetables, cheese, oil, bread, cereals, etc. High energy (high intensity, high power) ultrasound has frequencies between 20 and 500 kHz with intensities more than 1W.cm^2. These are disruptive in nature and have effect on mechanical, physical or biochemical properties of foods. This is used for controlling microstructures and modification, emulsification, defoaming of food products. It also has role in freezing, thawing, microbial inactivation, drying, etc. Ultrasound is sound waves which have frequency beyond the hearing capacity of human ears (~20 kHz). Ultrasound is one of the emerging technologies that was developed to reduce the cost and time of processing. It ensures the quality and safety of food products.

Few animals use ultrasound for navigation (dolphins) or hunting (bats) tracking the back-scattering sound waves. Ultrasound techniques are emerging technology for modifying food products which are relatively cheap, energy saving and simple. Low power (high frequency) ultrasound mainly monitors the physico-chemical properties and composition of the components of food and products during various steps of processing and storage which helps to control the properties and quality improvement.

At the contrary high power (low frequency) ultrasound includes physical, mechanical and biochemical changes through various processes like cavitation which are used in various operations such as extraction, drying, freezing, emulsification and also inactivates the pathogenic bacteria on the surfaces of food products. It is also used for the quality control of fresh vegetables and fruits in both pre- and postharvest, cheese during processing, commercial cooking oils, bread and cereal products, bulk and emulsified fat based food products, food gels, aerated and frozen foods. Other applications include the detection of honey adulteration and assessment of the aggregation state, size and type of protein. High power ultrasound with frequency higher than 20 kHz has mechanical, chemical and/or biochemical effects, which are used to modify the physico-chemical properties and enhance the quality of various food systems during processing. Conventional food processing methods use may involve losses of some compounds, low production efficiency, time- and energy-consuming procedures (prolonged heating and stirring, use of large volumes of water, etc.). These shortcomings have led to the use of new sustainable 'green and innovative' techniques in processing, pasteurisation and extraction, which typically involve less time, water and energy, such as ultrasound assisted processing, supercritical fluid extraction and processing, extrusion, microwave processing, controlled pressure drop process, pulse electromagnetic field, high pressure and subcritical water extraction. Alternatives to conventional processing, preservation and extraction procedures may increase production efficiency and contribute to environmental preservation by reducing the use of water and solvents, elimination of wastewater, fossil energy and generation of hazardous substances.

Ultrasound has significant effect in the food industry in case of rate of various processes. By this technique food processes can be finished in very less time of seconds or minutes with good reproducibility. It reduces the processing cost and simplify the work giving high purity to the final product as compared to conventional processes. Ultrasound in food technology is used for various processes like processing preservation and extraction. It uses different physical or chemical phenomena which are fundamentally different as compared to conventional methods. It has advantages in terms of productivity, yield, quality and also is environmentally friendly. Ultrasound is used for positive effects in food processing such as improvement in mass transfer, food preservation, assistance of thermal treatments and manipulation of texture and food analysis. Ultrasound has its various effects on different systems. On solids it effects through vibrational energy for cutting and melting, in liquids it effects by the production of intense cavitation and in gases it affects by producing high-intensity acoustic fields.

Power Ultrasound Generation and Equipment

It is electricity driven ultrasonic system, which is most commonly used in the food processing industry. It has basic components: power generator, the transducers (converting the electrical power to mechanical vibrations). Two major types of ultrasound transducers are magnetostrictive trasducers and piezoelectric transducers. The main form of ultrasound is diagnostic ultrasound which is mainly used as an analytical technique. It is mainly used for quality assurance, process control and non-destructive inspection. It is applied to determine food concentration, viscosity and composition, etc. It is used to measure flow rate, flow level in food packaging.

Magnetostrictive Transducer

It provides a large driving force because the system is of an extremely robust construction. However, about 40 per cent of the electrical energy will be lost as heat and thus external cooling is required. Its maximum operating frequency is restricted to 100 kHz.

Piezoelectric Transducer

It has higher electro mechanical conversion and over 95 per cent electrically efficient. Also it can be operated over the whole ultrasonic range.

Ultrasound Phenomena or Methods in Food Preservation

Ultrasound is involved in process development. Unlike other non-thermal processes it can be easily tested in lab or bench-top scale which generates reproducible results for scale-up. The effects, however, are not severe enough for a sufficient destruction of micro-organisms when using ultrasound alone. This can be achieved by combining ultrasound with heat or pressure or both.

Applications using combination with other preservation methods are:

- Ultrasonication (US): It is the application of ultrasound at low temperature and require high energy. It is mainly used for heat sensible products. This method requires long treatment time to inactivate stable enzymes.
- Manosonication (MS): It is combined method in which ultrasound and pressure are applied together. Moderate pressures at low temperatures are combined in this. Upon combination inactivation efficiency is higher than ultrasound alone.
- Thermosonication (TS): This method is the combination of ultrasound and heat. It produces a greater effect on inactivation of micro-organisms than heat alone.
- Manothermosonication (MTS): It is combined method of heat, ultrasound and pressure. This method inactivates several enzymes at lower temperatures in a shorter time than thermal treatments. Micro-organisms that have high thermotolerancecan be inactivated by manothermosonication.

Fundamentals of Ultrasound

1. Ultrasonic Disintegration of Cell Structures: It is used for the extraction of intracellular materials, e.g. starch from the cell matrix. Ultrasonic disintegration can easily be tested in any scale. It can be used at lab scale for 1ml to approximately 5 L. At bench top scale it can be used at approximately 0.1 to 20 L/minute. Production scale in this case starts at 20 L/minute.
2. Protein and enzyme extraction: Extraction of enzymes and proteins which are stored in cells and sub cellular particles are also processed by ultrasound. It is unique and effective application of high intensity ultrasound. It has potential benefit in the extraction and isolation of novel potentially bioactive components.
3. Extraction of lipids and proteins: Lipids are extracted from plant seeds, such as soyabeans (e.g. fluor or defatted soyabeans) or other oil seeds. In this case destruction of cell walls facilitates the pressing (cold or hot) and reduces the residual oil or fat in the pressing cake. This technique is applicable to citrus oil from fruits, oil extraction from ground mustard, peanut, herb oil, canola, soy and corn, etc.
4. Microbial and enzyme inactivation: It is mainly used in the microbial and enzyme inactivation of fruit juices and sauces. Thermal treatment can cause undesirable alterations of sensory attributes, i.e. texture, flavour, colour, smell and nutritional qualities like vitamins and proteins. Ultrasound is an efficient non-thermal (minimal) processing alternative.
5. Ultrasonic dispersion and deagglomeration: Ultrasonic cavitation generates high shear that breaks particle agglomerates into single dispersed particles. Ultrasonic laboratory devices are used for volumes from 1.5 ml to approximately 2 L. It is involved in the process development and production for batches from 0.5 to approximately 2000 L or flow rates from 0.1 L to 20m^3/hr.
6. Synergies of ultrasound with temperature and pressure: Ultrasonication is often more effective when combined with other anti-microbial methods such as thermo-sonication, i.e. heat and ultrasound, mano-sonication, i.e. pressure and ultrasound and mano-thermo-sonication, i.e. pressure, heat and ultrasound.
7. Sonication of bottles and cans for leak detection: Ultrasound is used in bottling and filling machines for the online container leak testing of bottles and cans. The instantaneous release of carbon dioxide is the decisive effect of ultrasonic leakage of containers filled with carbonated beverages.

8. Liberation of phenolic compounds and anthocyanins: It is done from grape and berry matrix, in particular from bilberries and black currants into juice after thawing, mashing and enzyme incubation.
9. Chemical and biochemical effects: ultrasound is used for bactericidal action, effluent treatment, modification of growth of living cells, alteration of enzyme activity and sterilisation of equipment.

Use of high intensity ultrasound in food processing

The basics of ultrasound applications are mainly three different methods:

- Direct application with the product.
- Coupling to the device.
- Using ultrasonic bath submergence.

Few application of ultrasound in food processing is as follows:

Drying

Acoustic drying has great potential and have commercial importance. It is used from so long time and has been a topic of interest for many years. Conventional method of dehydrating food products is done by hot air. This method is an economical process but the main problem of this is interior moisture retaining. In this method, the main problem is high temperatures can damage the food, which may affect the colour, taste and nutritional value of the food products. At the contrary ultrasonic osmotic dehydration technology obtain higher water loss and solute gain rates by using lower solution temperatures. So by using this probability of oxidation or degradation is reduced in the foodstuff. The colour, flavour and nutritional value also remain unaffected by using this technology. So by this treatment a reduction in subsequent conventional freeze-drying times and rehydration properties is observed.

The drying which is enhanced sonically can be carried out at lower temperatures due to which probability of oxidation or degradation reduces in the material. This method of drying is useful in case of heat sensitive material. Ultrasonic dehydration involves lower solution temperatures for acquiring higher water loss and solute gain rates. In this case because of application of low temperatures and less time periods for dehydration, the colour, flavour and nutritional value of products remain unaltered. While in conventional methods the high temperatures may cause damage to the product by changing the colour, taste and the nutritional value of products. It has also been used prior to the drying of vegetables like pretreatment. It reduces subsequent conventional and freeze-drying times in rehydration processes.

Filtration

In the food industry, to produce solid-free liquid or to isolate solid from its mother liquor, the separation of solids from liquids is an important step. In this case two specific effects is involved:

- Agglomeration of fine particles in the nodes of the acoustic waves.
- Generation of sufficient vibrational energy to keep the particles partly suspended and therefore leave more free 'channels' for solvent elution.

Acoustic filtration also called as ultrasonically assisted filtration is successfully used to increase the vacuum filtration of difficult mixtures to separate like coal slurry. But the main problem in filtration is deposition of solid materials on the surface of filtration membrane. Ultrasound is useful in the filtration processes because it can increase the flux by breaking the concentration polarisation and cake layer on the surface of membrane without creating an affect on the permeability of membrane. This method is mainly applied to extract the fruit juice and drinks from the pulp. From another studies it is clear that high-power acoustic or ultrasound is used for to remove the cake which is accumulated in the filtration processes.

Depolymerisation

This is one of the oldest applications of ultrasound which is involved in the degradation of polymers. The depolymerisation mainly involves two possible mechanisms:

- By collapsed cavitation bubble mechanical degradation of the polymer.
- Chemical degradation.

Chemical method involves reaction between the high energy molecules and the polymer. The high energy molecules like hydroxyl radicals are produced from cavitation phenomenon. Ultrasound has important potential for the conversion of raw materials like carbohydrates which are polymeric in nature to useful less weight molecules or its simpler components. In food industry, the area in which the use of ultrasound is active is to depolymerise starch. So due to its progress in sonochemical engineering it may play a big role in the carbohydrate industry.

Defoaming: Foam is a colloidal system and dispersion of gas in liquid. They are thermodynamically unstable and have density approaching that of the gas. The distance between individual bubbles are very small. Foam has applications in a variety of industrial processes, e.g. cosmetics and food production, etc. But the intensive foaming or persistent foams are undesirable in various processes. This is so because it may lead to problems like loss of products, decrease in productivity, etc. In history foam has been controlled by the use of mechanical breakers, lowering the temperature and by the addition of chemical antifoams. High intensity ultrasonic waves have a distinctive method of foam breaking because they does not need high air flow, prevent chemical contamination and also it is operated under sterile conditions or in a contained environment. So because of this it is an appropriate choice for implantation in the pharmaceutical and food industries. This defoaming system for ultrasound has been developed on a different and new type of ultrasonic generator. In this on a rotation system a focused airborne emitter is placed which is controlled by electricity. So when the transducer rotates a complex movement is created which covers a large defoaming area with different rotation speeds. Under the acoustic beam most of the bubbles break almost instantaneously.

Demolding and extrusion

When the industrial cooking of foods is done, it leads to adhesion of the products to the cooking vessel or mold. If this product is removed easily it makes cleaning easy and also container is reusable in less time. But the cooked product is difficult to remove from the mold because of product adhesion to the mold by cooking. To counteract this difficulty the molds are fabricated with a surface coating of white grease, thin layer of silicone or PTFE (Polytetrafluoroethylene). So to replace them over a span of time is expensive and also not absolutely successful. So in these days this problem is solved by using mechanical methods such as knocking vibration for the removal of adhered products. The alternative solution to the earlier conventional methods is achieved by coupling the mold or vessel to a source of ultrasound to release the food products. So by using this technique the cleaning of residual material from the mold become easy and is done automatically.

Extrusion is also a similar property of ultrasound which is its ability to release material from a surface, by virtue of reducing drag. In this ultrasound is provided by energy input by ultrasonic excitation of the metal tubes, so the food is extruded. The ultrasonic source is attached to tube at right angle for providing radial vibration. So this process improves the fluidity of sticky or highly viscous materials through tube by reducing the drag resistance. It also has property of modification of structures of food products.

Degassing/deaeration

A liquid contains gases in the mixed form for example a liquid may contain oxygen, carbon dioxide and nitrogen gas. Degassing in an ultrasonic field is done when acoustic waves cause rapid vibration of gas bubbles and adjacent bubbles move within the liquid and coalesce. Degassing in ultrasonic field becomes highly visible phenomenon when an ultrasonic cleaning bath is used with tap water used regularly inside. It occurs when the acoustic waves bring the rapid vibration of gas bubbles and these bubbles grow to sizes which rise up through the liquid, against gravity, until they reach the surface. During the processing of carbonated drinks, its main role is to remove or displace the air from the liquid surface. So by doing this damages caused by bacteria and oxygen are avoided. Mainly this technique is used to degas carbonated beverages such as beer before bottling. Deaeration process by ultrasound involves coupling a transducer to the bottle's outside which leads to degassing. So by using this the advantages like decrease in the number of broken bottles and wasting of beverages are obtained as compared to conventional method of mechanical agitation. Ultrasonically assisted degassing is useful in case of aqueous systems but is difficult in case of viscous liquids to remove gas for example like melted chocolate.

Defrosting/thawing

Freezing is a technique which is widely used for increasing the shelf life of various food products. But if thawing conditions are optimised it can be successful. Acoustic thawing is a promising technology in the food industry if optimum frequencies and acoustic power are chosen. To thaw frozen food products is a slow process and is also very inconvenient and costly process. Thawing is a slow process so also involves damaging food stuffs by the contamination of micro-organisms through chemical and physical changes with time. So it is important to quick thawing at low temperature for the good food quality and to escape excessive dehydration of food. The work on the relaxation mechanism showed that when a frequency in the relaxation frequency range of ice crystals in the food was applied, the more acoustic energy could be absorbed by frozen foods. So it was observed that the thawing process in this relaxation frequency was faster than the process using only conductive heating. So it is believed that acoustic thawing is a good technology in the food industries if the acoustic power and frequencies are optimum. So acoustic thawing has advantages like cutting the time or shortening the thawing time so reducing drip loss the improvement in the product quality.

Freezing and crystallisation

Ultrasound play a role in the crystal formation too. The ultrasound which ranges from 20 to 100 kHz is very helpful in crystallisation process. These two processes are linked because both of these involve initial nucleation followed by crystallisation. When ultrasound is exposed to the medium it enhances both the nucleation rate and rate of crystal growth by the production of various number of nucleation sites in the medium. The basics to this is because the cavitation bubbles behaves as nuclei for crystal growth.

Freezing or cooling is a technique of food preservation which is used from a long time ago by preserving food in natural ice or over winter storage. During freezing the water content present in the food material get converted into ice crystals. While in case of conventional freezing the problems like non-uniform crystal development and destruction or texture because of the continuous formation of small ice crystals. These crystals kept growing in size and hence break some of the cell walls which leads to the destruction of cell structure and drip loss on thawing. So due to problems like non-uniform crystal development, loss in sensory food quality in case of conventional methods new innovative technologies such as air blast, immersion freezing, cryogenic freezing, fluidised-bed freezing, high pressure freezing and their combinations are now the most widely and commonly used method in the food industry. When ultrasound is applied, even conventional cooling provides much more rapid and seeding, due to which dwell time is reduced. Sonication is thought to enhance both the nucleation rate and rate of crystal growth in a saturated or supercooled medium by producing a large number of nucleation sites in the medium throughout the ultrasonic exposure.

This may be due to cavitation bubbles acting as nuclei for crystal growth and/or by the disruption of seeds or crystals already present within the medium thus increasing the number of nucleation sites. When temperature or pressure is slightly decreased, crystallisation can occur in an uncontrolled manner due to which severe problems occur. So this technique has advantages in food industry because of efficient heat transfer throughout the cooling process.

Brining, pickling and marinating

Pickling and marinating are the techniques which are used with a variety of vegetables and meat products. Most commonly used salt-brining or pickling fermentation has mainly three limitations

1. For brining, a high quantity of sodium chloride is used which may require the desalting process for the use of food products.
2. The process is difficult to control during fermentation.
3. By soaking methods the products may get soften, bloated or structural damage may occur.

So to eradicate these limitations there is a need for alternative technologies. Ultrasound reduces pickling time of products particularly the foods which have crunchy texture. Also the products contain low sodium content so there is no need for desalting. This process provides a product which is uniformly salted. Brining involves two main mass transfer processes: water migration happens from the meat to the brine and the solute migration happens from the brine to the meat. Ultrasound energy can be used with combination for the methods like brining or marinating raw foodstuffs by submerging it in the brine or marinade. So the salting time is mainly reduces by this technology. It was found that the water and NaCl contents of samples after treatment were higher in sonicated than non-sonicated samples. In the cheese industry, the effect of ultrasound on mass transfer during cheese brining has been investigated.

Cutting

Ultrasonic is used since the early 1950s, it is mainly used for the accurate cutting of brittle materials like ceramics, glass and in aerospace industry for carbon fibre composites. It is used because it has improved food processing by providing a new way to cut or slice. So by using this maintenance costs and product waste is minimised. It involves a knife-type blade which is attached to a shaft linked to an ultrasonic source. The cutting tool can be considered as acoustic horn which is a part of ultrasonic resonating device. These tools can be of different or many shapes. The ultrasonic cutting depend on the condition and type of food, e.g. thawed or frozen.

The most widely used application of ultrasound is the cutting of fragile food products. It also play a great role in improvement of hygiene because due to vibration the product adherence on the blade is prevented and so there is less development of micro-organisms on the surface. This is because of the property of ultrasound in the 'auto or self-cleaning' of blade. So there is also less wastage of food products as compared to conventionl method. Hence the foodstuffs retain a better standardised weight.

Cooking

In conventional cooking method either by frying or boiling the exterior of the food may be overcooked as compared to the interior. This may reduce the quality of the product. Ultrasound has the ability to provide improved heat transfer characteristics so there is no problem such like the conventional method. So this technology have been utilised in the cooking. So cooking by ultrasound leads to greater cooking speed. It also provide an energy efficient and rapid method which also improves the textural attributes of food. The post-cooking moisture content is also preserved by using this. The use of high-intensity ultrasound thus has the potential to increase the water-binding properties of meat. So ultrasound is useful in cooking of moist meats and hence is useful in the food industries for food processing. A patent describes a cooking vessel in which ultrasound is applied to a hot oil to provide better and more even overall frying and it is claimed to reduce energy consumption.

Meat tenderisation

The traditional method of meat tenderisation is mechanical pounding. But this method makes poor quality of meat. Power ultrasound is one of the method which is very useful in this technique. Ultrasound act by using two methods:

1. By the breakage of integrity of muscular cells.
2. By increasing the rate of enzymatic reactions by using biochemical effect.

Ultrasonic tenderisation can be achieved with poultry meat, veal and beef. So ultrasound is used for producing processed meats. Meat products are present in the recombined form such as beef rolls. These meat pieces are held together by a protein gel which is formed by the myofibrillar proteins released during processing. Tumbling the meat pieces by sonication or adding salt help in tenderisation of meat. So the samples which are treated with these are superior in quality. So ultrasound help in improving physical properties of meat products which includes tenderness, water-binding capacity and cohesiveness.

Sterilisation/pasteurisation

Conventional thermal pasteurisation and sterilisation are the widely used techniques till date for inactivating micro-organisms and enzymes in the food products. But these methods take great time for the processing and may lead to loss of nutrients, development of undesirable flavour and deteriorating the quality of food products. By the use of ultrasound such processes can be improved on the basis of the effects of cavitation. At a great high acoustic power inputs, it break cells but at lower intensity a cell can be inactivated.

The ultrasound is effective in the dairy industry for the processes like pasteurisation. It is found effective for killing the micro-organisms like *E. coli*, *Pseudomonas*, etc. and it does not have detrimental effect on the total protein or casein content of milk. The microbes are killed mainly by thinning of cell membranes and by the production of free radicals.

Ultrasound is also effective to inactivate the enzyme which are responsible for deteriorating the fruit and vegetable juice. These enzymes are mainly pectinmethylesterase, polyphenoloxidases and peroxides, etc. The use of ultrasound in pasteurisation continues to be of great interest to the dairy industry. It has proved effective for the destruction of *E. coli*, *Pseudomonas fluorescens* and *Listeria monocytogenes* with no detrimental effect on the total protein or casein content of pasteurised milk. The mechanism of microbial killing is mainly due to the thinning of cell membranes, localised heating and production of free radicals. Investigation on ultrasound effectiveness have also shown the inactivation of enzymes such as pectinmethylesterase, polyphenoloxidases and peroxidases responsible for deterioration of fruit and vegetable juice and various enzymes pertinent to milk quality. So various treatments like thermo-sonication (TS) and manothermosonication (MTS) inactivate various enzymes. Ultrasound with combination to heat has potential to accelerate the rate of sterilisation by taking less time and also reducing damage as well as intensity of thermal treatments.

Emulsification/homogenisation

It is a technique of delivering the hydrophobic bioactive compounds into different food products. Acoustic emulsifications have different improvement over the conventional methods. The emulsion produced from this technique has sub-micron distribution. These emulsions are more stable as compared to conventional ones. In this case there is no need of adding surfactants. This method utilise less energy than the older conventional methods. Ultrasonic emulsification is developing area for in-time treatment. It is used in food industry for various products like fruit juices, mayonnaise and tomato ketchup, etc. It is also comparable like microfluidity for generating sub-micron dispersions.

Ultrasound in Food Preservation

Ultrasound processing is one of these new methods. While its application in food processing is relatively recent, it has been proved that high-intensity ultrasonic waves can rupture cells and denature enzymes, and that even low-intensity ultrasound is able to modify the metabolism of cells. In combination with heat, ultrasonication can accelerate the rate of sterilisation of foods, thus lessening both the duration and intensity of thermal treatment and the resultant damage. The advantages of ultrasound over heat sterilisation include: the minimising of flavour loss, greater homogeneity, and significant energy savings.

Applications of ultrasound

Applications of ultrasound in food preservation can be divided into two main categories depending upon its area of utilisation.

Directly related to food

Micro-organism inactivation: It has been shown that micro-organisms do not all react in the same way to ultrasound treatment. Factors affecting the effectiveness of microbial inactivation are:

- Amplitude of ultrasound waves.
- Exposure or contact time.
- Volume of food processed.
- Composition of food.
- Treatment temperature.

Spore inactivation: Microbial spores are resistant to extreme conditions such as high temperatures and osmotic pressures, high and low pHs, and mechanical shocks. Those bacterial spores that survive heat treatment may severely restrict the shelf-life of thermally processed foods because of spoilage and poisoning.

Enzyme inactivation: To prevent denaturation, an enzyme has to keep its native conformation. Hydrophobic interactions, hydrogen bonding, vander Waals interactions, ion paring, electrostatic forces and steric constraints stabilise the three-dimensional molecular structure of globular proteins.

Indirectly related to food

One of the major long-established industrial applications of power ultrasound is in surface cleaning and it has proved to be an extremely efficient technology.

Ultrasound is particularly useful in surface decontamination where the inrush of fluid that accompanies cavitational collapse near a surface is non-symmetric.

Ultrasound-assisted Extraction

UAE in comparison to non-conventional extraction techniques

Ultrasound-assisted extraction (UAE) is an emerging potential technology that can accelerate heat and mass transfer and has been successively used in extraction field. Ultrasound waves after interaction with subjected plant material alter its physical and chemical properties and their cavitational effect facilitates the release of extractable compounds and enhances the mass transport by disrupting the plant cell walls. UAE is a clean method that avoids the use of large quantity of solvent along with cutting down in the working time. Ultrasounds are successively employed in plant extraction field. Ultrasound is well known to have a significant effect on the rate of various processes in the chemical and food industry.

Application of UAE in food research

The use of ultrasound can enhance the extraction process by increasing the mass transfer between the solvent and plant material. Ultrasound in the use of plant extraction has benefits in increased mass transfer, better solvent penetration, less dependence on solvent used, extraction at lower temperatures, faster extraction rates and greater yields of product.

Application of UAE in food industry

For the food industry the use of ultrasound assistance is becoming increasingly important. The mains matrix of ultrasound assisted extraction is vegetable (seeds and herbs). Compounds extracted will be use as immediately (liquor) or as food and cosmetic additives (essential oil, molecule with special activity). Ultrasonic food processing involves a vibrating knife producing a nearly frictionless surface to which food products do not stick nor deform. The surface cleanly cuts or slits products including fillers such as nuts, raisins, dried fruit or chocolate morsels without displacement or plowing.

Advantages of ultrasonic food processing

- Wider cutting temperature range.
- Cuts cleanly through various densities and consistencies of products with filler materials.
- Cuts edges cleanly without pinching or feathering for higher yield in packaging.
- Cutting speeds can be increased substantially.
- Cleaner, repeatable and more consistent slits and cuts.
- Greatly reduced normal down time for clean up.
- Does not smear the cut surface.
- Ease of use - uncomplicated and user friendly. As simple as flipping the switch on or off.
- Flexibility in adapting the Ultrasonics cutting equipment to existing conventional slitting and cutting equipment.

Food industries using ultrasonic food processing

- Cheese
- Fish
- Prepared meats
- Vegetable
- Bakery and snack foods
- Candy and confectionery
- Health bars

Ultrasound is a nonthermal processing technique that can be used in a broad range of applications. This technology can increase process efficiency through enhanced yields, increased throughput and reduced processing costs as well as modify biomaterial structure. The range of applications of ultrasonic processing in the food and other industries is expanding rapidly. Innovation-driven research organisations and companies are investing more in the development of novel processes and the improvement of existing processes to increase process efficiencies, product quality or to design products with new functionalities. Most ultrasonic systems require a liquid (often water) to couple and deliver energy.

- Reduced environmental footprints.
- Shortened processing times.
- Higher product yields.
- Reduced processing costs and/or maintenance costs.
- Improved or new products with enhanced textures, colours and flavours.

In most cases, ultrasound does not cause detrimental effects on food quality attributes and it enhances retention of fresh flavours and pigments, resulting in products with more appealing flavour, taste, colour and brightness. Ultrasound has also proven to be a powerful tool for targeted, product-specific texture modulation.

Thus, ultrasound has many applications in the food industries. But it can provide more benefit when coupled with other methods of food preservation. While it has considerable advantages over pre-existing technologies. So from the applications and advantages of ultrasound it is evident that ultrasonic processing is one of the new technologies which has huge future in the food industry. By using ultrasound, full reproducible food processes can now be completed in seconds or minutes with high reproducibility, reducing the processing cost, simplifying manipulation and work-up, giving higher purity of the final product, eliminating post-treatment of waste water and consuming only a fraction of the time and energy normally needed for conventional processes. The advantages of using ultrasound for food processing, includes: more effective mixing and micro-mixing, faster energy and mass transfer, reduced thermal and concentration gradients, reduced temperature, selective extraction, reduced equipment size, faster response to process extraction control, faster start-up, increased production, and elimination of process steps.

HURDLE TECHNOLOGY

In recent years, food preservation and food security have become an important factor of concern. In modern era of food processing, the demand for fresh and good quality food products has led to the emergence of hurdle technology. Hurdle technology is an efficient technique for improving the quality of food and to enhance its shelf life. The main objective of this technology is food preservation, storage of food products and enhancement of their shelf life thereby giving us good quality products. In the present contribution a brief introduction is given about hurdle technology, its aspects and widespread applications in different food products for their efficient preservation. Most common hurdles for food preservation are shown in Fig. 11.1.

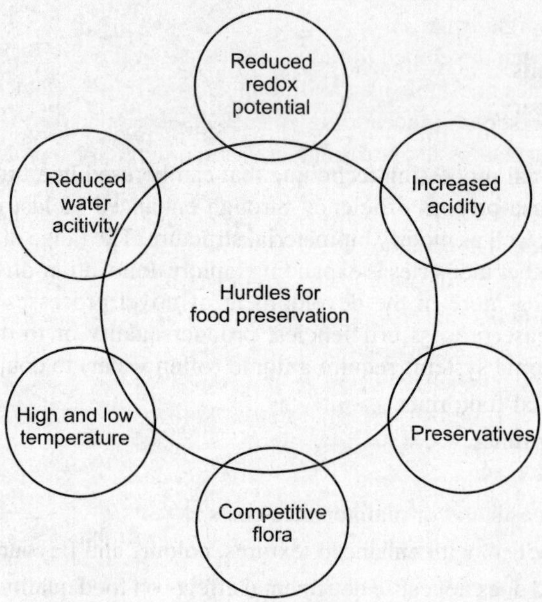

Fig. 11.1: Most common hurdles for food preservation.

Due to the inadequate technologies for post harvested food preservation more than 50% of the harvested food is often lost due to spoilage in developing countries. It has been reported by FAO of United Nations that one third of the total harvested food of the world is lost before it is consumed. The current consumer demands natural and fresh food which urges the food manufacturers to establish a new preservation technique. Statistics shows that 95% of the investment for agriculture resources has been allocated for production while only 5% for the preservation of food. In the majority of the cases micro-organisms are responsible for the spoilage or poisoning. Despite the availability of a range of preservation techniques like freezing, blanching, pasteurisation, canning, etc. spoilage and poisoning of food materials by micro-organisms is still a major cause for food spoilage. The microbial safety and stability of most foods are based on an application of preservation factors called as hurdles and the technique applying the different hurdles is known as hurdle technology. Hurdle technology is a concept that was developed to address the consumer demand for more natural and fresh foods. Hurdle technology as an intelligent combination of hurdles which secures the microbial safety and stability as well as retains the organoleptic, nutritional quality and economic viability of food products.

Some of the hurdles such as temperature (high or low), water activity (a_w), preservatives (nitrite, sorbate), competitive micro-organisms (lactic acid bacteria) and acidity (pH) have been empirically used for years to stabilise meat, fish, milk and vegetables. Various novel hurdles that are being applied in various food products includes nano-thermosonication, ultrahigh pressure, photodynamic inactivation, modified atmosphere packaging of both non-respiring and respiring products, edible coatings, ethanol, milliard reaction products. The basic concept is to apply combinations of existing and novel preservation techniques (hurdles) in order to eliminate the growth of micro-organisms.

Therefore, while the aim of effective food preservation is to control all forms of quality deterioration, the overriding priority is always to minimise the potential for the occurrence and growth of food spoilage and food poisoning micro-organisms.

Hurdle technology has been developed to reduce the usage of preservatives in foods, and consists of the combined effect of hurdles to establish an additional antimicrobial effect, thus improving the quality of the food. This modern preservation technology has been developed for the consumers who demands healthy and fresh foods that retains its nutritional and organoleptic properties as well.

Aspects of Hurdle Technology

The hurdle technology affects the physiology and growth of micro-organisms in food. There are mainly 4 major mechanisms by which hurdle technology affects the growth of micro-organisms in foods:

Homeostasis: It is the process that maintains the stability of the living cells internal environment in response to the changes in external environment. Some of the examples of homeostasis in the body are regulation of temperature and balance between acidity and alkalinity (pH). These factors are prerequisite feature of living cells and this applies to higher organisms as well as micro-organisms. The concept behind homeostasis is already known in higher organisms but this knowledge should be incorporated in micro-organisms important for the poisoning and spoilage of foods. Disturbing the homeostasis of the micro-organisms by various hurdles eventually results in the death of the spoilage causing microbes thereby protecting the food product from microbial spoilage.

Metabolic exhaustion: This aspect of hurdle technology deals with auto sterilisation of food. This was firstly observed in the experiment carried out on liver sausages inoculated with *Clostridium sporogens* and stored at 37°C. Later this behaviour of some bacterial spores was regularly observed in shelf stable meat products during storage time period. It has been observed that the spore counts in hurdle technology treated food products actually decreases during storage especially at ambient temperature. The microbes in the hurdle treated stable products uses their energy for homeostasis thereby becoming metabolically exhausted. This leads to auto sterilisation of food products. Thus, the microbiologically stable product becomes safer for storage at normal room temperatures.

Stress reactions: Some microbes acquire resistance or may become more virulent under stress conditions as they synthesise stress shock proteins. The synthesis of stress shock protein is affected by several factors like pH, water activity, ethanol, heat, etc. The different responses of microbes under stress conditions might hamper the food preservation. Exposure to multiple stresses simultaneously activates the energy utilising synthesis of several stress shock proteins, in turn making the microbes metabolically weak. Therefore, multitarget preservation of foods could be an efficient approach towards reducing the synthesis of stress shock proteins and in food preservation.

Multitarget preservation of food: It is a very important aspect for efficient and effective preservation of targeted food material. Hurdles applied in the targeted food material might not just have effects on microbial stability but they could act synergistically. Synergistic effect could be achieved in the targeted food, if the hurdles affects different targets such as pH, a_w, Eh, enzyme systems simultaneously within the microbial cell and thus disturb the homeostasis of the microbes rendering it difficult for the microbes to synthesise different stress shock proteins and to maintain their homeostasis. Therefore the application of several hurdles simultaneously would lead to an optimal microbial stability and effective food preservation. Applications of Hurdle technology in different products: Hurdle Technology is a novel concept which has several applications in the preservation of various food products such as. Basic aspects behind the concept of hurdle technology are shown in Fig. 11.2.

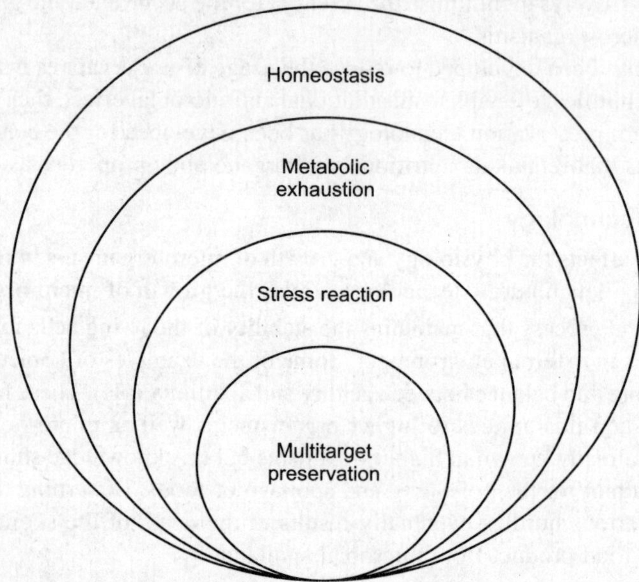

Fig. 11.2: Basic aspects behind the concept of hurdle technology.

Dairy products: Hurdle technology has been applied in many dairy products to enhance their shelf life. Shelf stable paneer can be prepared by applying various hurdles such as pH, aw, preservatives and modified atmosphere packaging (MAP). The quality and shelf life of hurdle treated paneer extended from one to twelve days at ambient temperature and six to twenty days at refrigeration temperature without affecting its physico-chemical and sensory properties.

In another study, the shelf life of paneer curry was increased using hurdle technology. The product has been treated with certain modified control hurdles like aw, pH and preservatives. The hurdle treated paneer was found to have better quality than heat sterilised product. Another product brown peda , a traditional Indian heat desiccated milk khoa based product have also been prepared and preserved through hurdle technology. Panjagari and others studied the effect of conventional cardboard boxes, modified packaging and vacuum packaging techniques on the sensory, physico-chemical, biochemical, textural and microbiological characteristics of brown peda during its storage for forty days at 30°C and observed a stable shelf life due to low moisture content, higher amount of sugar and severe heat treatment applied during its preparation. Hurdle treated brown peda could be best preserved up to forty days at room temperature (30±1°C) without any quality loss.

Fruits and vegetables: Several hurdles are considered to be important in the preservation of various vegetables and fruits like carrot, pineapple, coconut and papaya to enhance their stability and shelf life. Shelf-stable grated carrot products are developed using hurdle technology. Vibhakara and others used several hurdles such as antimicrobials, partial dehydration and packaging in polymeric bags to develop grated carrotsthat can remain fresh and microbiologically safe for more than 6 months at ambient temperature.

Hurdle technology can also be applied to develop shelf stable RTE (Ready-To-Eat) intermediate moisture pineapple with increased shelf life. Osmotic dehydration, infrared drying and gamma radiation can successfully reduce the microbial load in pineapple slices increasing its shelf life up to 40 days. Gunathilake applied hurdle technology in the preservation of fresh scrapped coconut. Additives such as humectants, acidulants and preservatives were used. The shelf life of hurdle treated coconut gratings was increased by one month at ambient temperature and by three months at refrigerated temperature (5+2°C). Hurdle technology applied in various products is shown in Fig. 11.3.

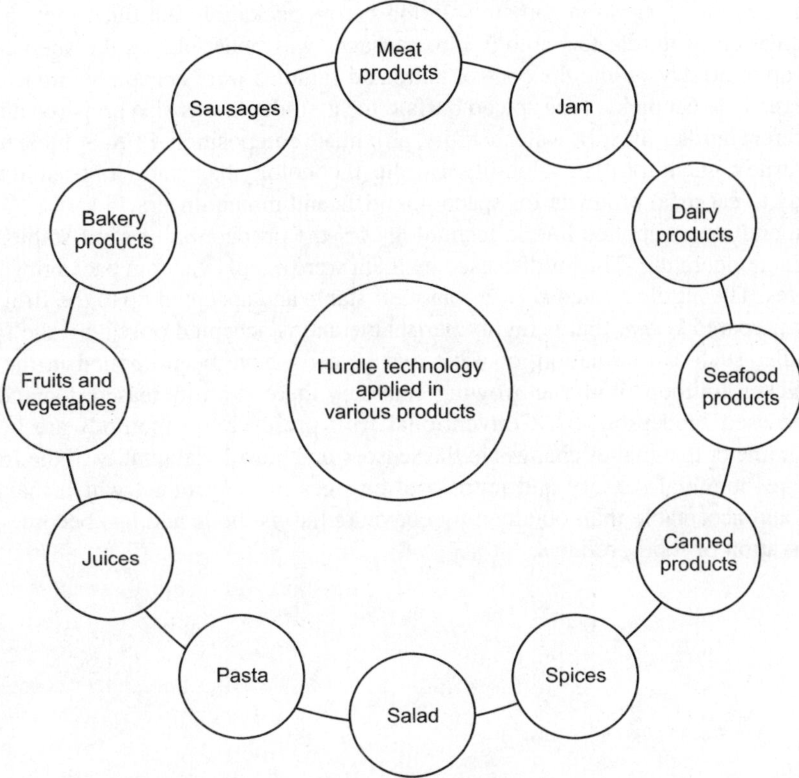

Fig. 11.3: Hurdle technology applied in various products.

Minimally processed shelf stable high moisture grated papaya is also prepared by hurdle technology using different hurdles like mild heat treatment, a_w, pH reduction, and the addition of preservatives. This combined methods technology developed microbiologically safe and nutritionally intact papaya that is shelf stable at ambient temperature for more than five months.

Fruit derived products: Several conventional hurdle strategies are effectively used along with the novel ones for the preservation of various fruit products. Some of the hurdles applied in fruit processing includes UV light, pulsed light (PL), ultrasound (US), and high hydrostatic pressure (HHP). Sankhla and others preserved sugarcane juice by using several potential hurdles like heat treatment, preservatives, irradiation and various packaging materials. The applicability of these hurdles shows great enhancement in the level of product safety and stability and thus it can therefore be recommended for preservation of all kinds of food material. Hurdle or combined technology is also applied in the preservation of high moisture fruit products such as peach, pineapple, papaya, mango and banana. The technology is based on the combination of heat treatment, aw and addition of antimicrobials.

In meat and meat products: Hurdle technology has been applied to a number of meat products. Thomas and others studied the effect of different hurdles such as (pH, a_w, vacuum packaging and post package treatment) in pork sausages at refrigerated temperature. The combined effect of these hurdles on pork sausages resulted in the inhibition of the growth of yeast and molds up to 12 days, while the dipping of sausages into potassium sorbate solution before packaging inhibited their growth up to 30 days. Implementation of hurdle technology into sausages was beneficial as the shelf life of sausages was increased up to 30 days while the control untreated samples were acceptable up to 18 days.

Shelf stable ready to eat pickle type spiced buffalo meat products was also prepared and preserved by controlling different hurdles like pH, water activity, proximate composition, FFA, Soluble hydroxyproline, TBA values, nitrite content, protein solubility. Hurdle Technology has made it possible to deliver shelf stable and ready to eat meat products for space scientists and mountaineers.

Karthikeyan and others applied hurdle technology for the production of shelf stable caprine *keema* stable at ambient temperature. The hurdles used by them were a_w, pH vacuum packaging, heat treatment and preservatives. The hurdle treated *keema* was shelf stable and accepted up to the fifth day unlike the conventionally prepared *keema* that is highly perishable and is accepted only until the first day.

Several hurdles such as marination, cooking and glycerol have been applied in the production of shelf stable chicken lollipop. With the growing economy there is an increased demand for fresh and minimally processed food products. Conventional fruit preservation methods are based on single preservation parameter that makes changes in the sensory and nutritional quality of the fruit. The hurdle technology makes minimal sensory and nutritional changes in the product which makes the product more valuable and acceptable than obtained by conventional methods and has become a boon for the efficient preservation of food products.

Chapter 12

Thermal and Non-thermal Processing

INTRODUCTION

Thermal processing is relatively a more recent technique used for fruit preservation, but it has proven to be one of the most effective. The significant progress achieved in the microbiology of food spoilage, understanding of thermal destruction kinetics of micro-organisms and heating behaviour of packaged foods led to scientific approaches in thermal process calculations. The intervening period also saw significant developments in the manufacturing of thermal processing equipment in the form of improved versions of retort systems. Next in the line of process equipment were continuous systems for thermal sterilisation of food cans and glass jars and systems for handling high-temperature short time (HTST) processes in batch or continuous modes in still or rotary autoclaves. Developments such as aseptic processing and packaging, thin profile processing, fully automated agitating retorts and retort systems based on different media have revolutionised the food industry in the last few decades. New processes such as combined methods technology are continually being introduced, especially for heat-sensitive products, such as delicate fruits and fruit juices, to preserve overall colour, flavour and other quality attributes. Fruits, in general, are commodities with special organoleptic properties which must be carefully preserved when establishing operating conditions for a thermal process.

THERMAL PROCESS CONSIDERATIONS

Canning is the most commonly used technique to heat-sterilise foods in order to prevent microbiological and enzymatic spoilage. A variety of foods are canned such as meats, fish, poultry, fruits, vegetables, dairy and vegetable products. Heat processes used for these foods are dependent on the type of food, its chemical composition and types of micro-organisms that cause spoilage or public health concern, in addition to properties related to container material, shape and size as well as the properties related to the heating medium. Any thermal process for a food should be designed to achieve three basic objectives, the most important being to reduce the number of micro-organisms to statistically small levels, whether they are of public health concern or of the spoilage type which cause off-flavours and odours. The second objective is to create an environment in the container which would suppress the growth or activity of spoilage type micro-organisms by utilising one or more of the following methods: (i) oxygen removal, (ii) pH control, and (iii) control of storage temperature. The third objective is to assure an adequate or thermetic seal of the container to prevent recontamination following processing and during storage. Thermal processing is not intended to completely sterilise the packaged food. Such an approach might produce a stable product, but it will be at the expense of severe destruction of product quality. The success of thermal processing depends on selectively destroying the micro-organisms of spoilage and public health concern while creating an environment around the product to minimise the growth and activity of other micro-organisms.

In order to determine the extent of heat treatment, several factors must be known: (i) The type and the heat resistance of the target micro-organism, spore or enzyme present in the food, (ii) The pH of the food, (iii) The storage conditions following the process, (iv) The heating conditions, and (v) The thermophysical properties of the food and container shape and size.

Thermal Resistance of Micro-organisms and Enzymes

Target micro-organisms and enzymes for thermal destruction in a food vary according to the type of food and its composition. Thus, these target components and their respective thermal resistance determine the thermal process itself. The first step in designing the thermal process is to verify the type of test micro-organism or enzyme upon which the process should be based. Several factors should be considered in this aspect. For example, thermetic conditions that are used to package foods with extremely low oxygen levels (under vacuum) provide an atmosphere which does not support the growth of micro-organisms that require oxygen (obligate aerobes) to cause food spoilage or public health problems. Further, the spores of obligate aerobes are less heat resistant than the microbial spores that grow under anaerobic conditions (facultative or obligate anaerobes). The growth and activity of these anaerobic micro-organisms are largely pH dependent. Consequently, the most important factor affecting microbial spoilage is acidity and heat processing requirements for various foods depend mainly on pH. From a thermal processing standpoint, foods are categorised into three pH groups: (i) high-acid foods (pH < 3.7), (ii) acid or medium-acid foods (3.7 < pH < 4.5), and (iii) Low-acid foods (pH> 4.5).

The pH classification of thermally processed foods is extremely important, especially for the determination of processing requirements and specific criteria. The establishment of the resulting thermal process is generally based on *Clostridium botulinum*, which is a highly heat-resistant, rodshaped, spore-forming, anaerobic pathogen. The mere presence of the pathogen alone in a product does not constitute a health hazard, however, concern in this respect is warranted if the spores are permitted to germinate in favourable conditions for growth and produce a deadly botulism toxin. It has been generally recognised that *C. botulinum* does not grow and produce toxin below a pH of 4.6, which is the pH of most fruits and fruit products. Berries and most fermented foods are included in this category because they are considered high-acid foods (pH < 3.7). Consequently, the designated pH to separate the low acid group from the acid group is set at 4.5 such that in the medium-and high-acid foods (pH < 4.5), *C. botulinum* would not pose any potential threat. On the other hand, in the low-acid foods (pH> 4.5), the most heat-resistant spore former, *C. botulinum*, may cause foodborne illness and death following production of the fatal toxin.

This can easily occur under anaerobic conditions that prevail inside a sealed container, provided, of course, the pathogen is not destroyed by the heat treatment. There are other micro-organisms for example, *Bacillus stearothermophilus, Bacillus thermoacidurans* and *Clostridium thermosaccolyaticum,* that are more heat resistant than *C. botulinum*. These are generally thermophilic in nature (optimal growth temperature ~50 to 55°C) and hence are of little concern if the processed cans are stored at temperatures below 30°C. The phrase minimal thermal process defined as 'the application of heat to food, either before or after sealing in a thermetically sealed container, for a period of time and at a temperature scientifically determined to be adequate to ensure the destruction of micro-organisms of public health concern.' For low-acid foods, *C. botulinum* is designated the micro-organism of public health concern.

Due to its high heat resistance, temperatures of 115 to 125°C are commonly employed for the processing of these foods. Thermal processes for acid foods and medium-acid foods are usually based on the destruction of heat resistant spoilage-type vegetative bacteria, yeasts or moulds or the inactivation of enzymes at temperatures below 100°C. Thus, thermal processes for such foods are normally carried out in boiling water.

If not inactivated following thermal processing, several heat-resistant enzymes in fruits (including peroxidase, pectinesterase, lipoxygenase, catalase and polyphenoloxidase) may cause undesirable quality changes in the final canned fruit product during storage, especially related to colour, texture and flavour attributes. For the thermal processing of acid foods (including pasteurisation), the inactivation of these enzyme systems is often used as a basis because they usually possess a higher thermal resistance than the micro-organisms present in the food. As peroxidase is known to have a very high heat resistance, its destruction is often used as an adequate marker for the destruction of all heat-resistant enzymes present in the food. Nevertheless, the heat resistance of enzymes varies with the fruit, its variety, pH and TSS (total soluble solids).

Despite the established processing criteria for acid foods and high-acid foods, fruits that receive a heat treatment such as blanching or cooking have recently been designated as potentially hazardous by the food and drug Administration. All fruits are subject to a variety of conditions during growth, harvest and distribution, all of which provide sources of microbial contamination. Although most raw fruits possess a protective barrier that prevents penetration of potentially pathogenic microbes, it is recognised that thermal processing may destroy this barrier, allowing potential pathogens to penetrate the produce and to grow in conditions conducive to their growth. In order to prevent contamination and foodborne illnesses, it is recommended that chlorinated water be used to remove soil from produce and that proper refrigeration, storage and shipping conditions be maintained.

Fruit Canning Operations

Raw material selection

The quality of processed fruit depends largely on the quality of incoming fruit and this in turn depends on how the fruit is harvested, handled and stored. Harvesting at the proper maturity is an important step in thermal processing of fruits. Plums, grapes, whole olives, gooseberries, brandied peaches and maraschino cherries are harvested and processed in the 'firm-ripe' stage. Exceptions include bananas, pears and some apples that, when harvested at a mature stage, produce a higher quality processed product than those harvested at the 'soft-ripe' stage. However, most types of fruits are canned in the 'mellow-ripe' stage to capture maximum natural nutrients, flavour, aroma and colour. Different ingredients may be added such as spices, salt, sugar, colours, flavours and nutrients (e.g. vitamin C) to compensate for the underdeveloped full natural flavour, aroma and nutrient loss. Fruits that are needed to produce juices, purees, preserves, marmalades and sauces are processed in the 'soft-ripe' stage because flavour and aroma are more important than fruit texture.

Washing

Fruits are washed with water to remove dust, dirt and mould spores that will affect their colour, aroma and flavour. Fruits that are peeled, such as peaches, pears, apples and apricots, are seldom washed before peeling. On the other hand, washing after peeling removes vitamins and minerals and should be kept to a minimum.

Sorting/Grading

This operation ensures the removal of inferior and/or damaged produce. An inspection belt may be used in addition to trained personnel who detect poor quality produce unsuitable for canning. Sugar content may be measured using high-resolution magnetic resonance and quality evaluation at this stage may also include the glycoside content of raw stone fruits such as cherries, peaches and apricots, which may be associated with cyanogenesis in the final canned product. Acceptable fruits are then size-sorted, where they are mechanically passed over a screen with different sizes of holes or slits. Undersized fruit may be sorted out and used as concentrate or for baby food. Fruits with aesthetic defects may be used for juices and concentrates.

Blanching during Thermal Processing

The blanching of fruits or a 'partial cook' is an important step in the canning process, especially with respect to overall final quality evaluation. The product is usually immersed in hot water (88 to 99°C) or exposed to live steam. It is an energy-intensive unit operation and can account for as high as one third of the total energy required for processing. Most of the water-soluble nutrients, such as ascorbic acid, are lost in this operation.

During the blanching process, it is imperative that certain enzymes that have the potential to cause flavour and textural changes be inactivated. The process involves a brief heat treatment applied to most vegetables but also to some fruits in order to inactivate oxidative enzyme systems such as catalase, peroxidase, polyphenoloxidase, ascorbic acid oxidase and lipoxygenase. When the unblanched tissue is disrupted or bruised and exposed to air, these enzymes come in contact with substrates, causing softening, discolouration and the production of off-flavours. Since this action can potentially occur during the period prior to heat processing, it is most often standard practice to blanch fruits in order to prevent quality deterioration.

Although the primary purpose of blanching is enzyme inactivation, especially with preservation techniques such as freezing and dehydration, there are several other benefits: blanching initially cleanses the product, decreases the microbial load and preheats the product before processing. The mild heat treatment also softens the fruit, which facilitates compact packing in the can. At the same time, intercellular gases in the raw fruit are expelled, preventing excessive pressure buildup in the container and allowing for an improved heat transfer during heat processing. Consequently, a higher vacuum can be achieved in the final product as well as a reduction in internal can corrosion.

For fruits that are blanched, the most common methods are conventional water and steam blanching. Water blanching is generally of the immersion type or could be a spray as the product moves on a conveyor. Steam blanching often involves belt or chain conveyors upon which the product moves through a tunnel containing live steam. Other methods less frequently used include hot gas blanching and microwave blanching. Adequacy of blanching is usually assessed based on inactivation of one of the heat-resistant enzymes (peroxidase or polyphenol oxidase.

Prevention of Fruit Browning

Some fruits cannot be subjected to blanching due to delicate tissues that may be disrupted during the process. They undergo alternate treatments that are used to prevent the oxidative browning which can occur due to exposure to oxygen, especially during peeling and slicing operations. Oxidative browning is caused by the action of oxidase with catechol tannins and is an important problem, especially in fruits such as peaches, apples, bananas, cherries, nectarines, apricots, grapes and persimmons. Pineapples, tomatoes and melons are not as prone to browning. The most common means of preventing browning in fruits are the following:

SO_2 or sulphite treatment

A 2000 to 4000 ppm SO_2 solution (sodium or potassium metabisulphite) may be used to dip the fruits for approximately 2 to 5 minute. SO_2 may also be used as a gas dissolved in water (sulphurous acid) for dipping or in the gaseous form in fumigation chambers as is commonly done for grapes to control fungal growth prior to dehydration. The Food and Drug Administration has recommended a maximum residual sulphur dioxide level of 300 ppm in fruit juices and 2000 ppm in dried fruit.

Acids

Acids used to raise acidity (acidifying antioxidants) include citric, fumaric, tartaric, acetic, phosphoric, ascorbic and citraconic acid. For example, acidification with citric acid is especially important for sliced fruit. The cut surfaces may be protected from browning by immersion into a 1 to 2 per cent solution of citric acid.

Antioxidants

Ascorbic acid is a commonly used antioxidant in most fruit juices and canned fruits. Prestano and Manzano found ascorbic acid to be an effective inhibitor of peroxidase in selected fruits such as kiwi. It may be used on its own, in dry sugar/citric acid/ascorbic acid mixes or in syrups. Citric acid is sometimes necessary because it acts as a stabiliser for the ascorbic acid. Usually, very small amounts are used that do not affect the taste of the final canned product. Ascorbic acid acts to reduce quinones, which are generated by polyphenol oxidase-catalysed oxidation of polyphenols, back to phenolic compounds, preventing their conversion to brown pigments.

Sugars

Although the main purpose of sugar is to sweeten the fruit, it is also used to prevent browning in peeled and sliced fruit, whether it is in dry or syrup form. It acts in inhibiting oxidation by partially excluding air in the tissues. This ability seems to increase with pH. In many cases, the sugar is mixed with ascorbic acid and citric acid as an effective agent against loss of texture, colour and flavour.

Peeling/Preparation

Many different types of equipment are used in peeling and/or coring fruits. Some peeling and coring methods are advantageous for only certain kinds of fruits due to their structure or physical resistance to bruising.

Lye peeling

Lye peeling is a common method of peeling for various fruits such as peaches, nectarines, apricots and pears. Lye is an aqueous solution of approximately 10 to 15 per cent caustic soda (sodium hydroxide) or potassium hydroxide. The operation requires an ample water supply, lye and a heat source. The lye peeler is a heated tank containing the hot lye solution (60 to 90°C) that allows for the passage of fruit at a specific rate. The caustic lye solution dissolves the fruit skin. Several variables should be controlled at all times, namely lye concentration and temperature, product holding time and agitation in the caustic solution. Larger fruits require more water than smaller fruits during lye peeling. Following the treatment, the fruits are subjected to a water wash with pressure sprays to remove the peel and remove the lye from the surface. An acid dip is used (citric acid) after washing to neutralise any remaining traces of caustic soda. This method is advantageous in that there is a relatively low loss in usable fruit tissue as compared to other methods and it is economical.

Mechanical peeling

Mechanical peelers are also very popular with fruits, especially apples and pears. The fruit should be free of bruises and other blemishes in order to ensure the efficient operation of the peeling and coring (if necessary) operation. Either the fruit is made to rotate against a stationary knife or vice versa. The operation may consist of a continuous system to peel, core and slice in a high-speed, continuous manner.

Peeled fruits are washed with high-pressure water and then mechanically cored. Coring is usually done before slicing. If there is a delay after peeling and coring, fruit may be held in a 2 to 3 per cent salt solution to prevent browning, treated in one of the ways previously mentioned. Examples of fruits that usually require peeling before canning include peaches, apples, tomatoes and pears. Generally, fruits that are not peeled prior to canning retain more nutrients as compared to peeled fruits.

Filling

Filling of the cans is usually done by automatic machines, although it may be done by hand for very soft fruits that have a tendency to bruise easily. Mechanical fillers are adjusted to dispense each can a predetermined volume of fruit from a chamber and add a given amount of syrup or juice. These quantities must be uniform in order to ensure accurate and constant fill weights for the final product.

Some fruit products undergo a 'hot fill' whereby they enter the can at a sufficiently high temperature (approximately 80 to 85°C). This preheating of the contents before filling, which drives much of the dissolved gases in the product, may be done for the removal of air and the production of a vacuum. In such cases, a headspace is not necessary. Generally, these products are not processed at high sterilisation temperatures and hence space is not needed for the expansion of the can contents, which may cause a strain on the seal. Canned applesauce is an example of a 'hot-fill' product.

Some fruit products require a headspace in the can, especially those that are processed in an agitating retort. The heads pace bubble in the can is crucial for the movement of the contents during agitation. The amount of heads pace in a can is important, insufficient space may cause can ends, to bulge, whereas excessive space can cause underprocessing and even collapse of cans during processing as well as lead to can corrosion during storage due to insufficient vacuum.

Type of pack

Fruits are available for canning in a variety of forms: whole fruit, slices, halves, sauce, purée, juice or in mixed fruit packs such as fruit cocktail. Peaches are usually canned as halves, slices or in fruit cocktail. Pears canned as halves or slices are also known as 'grade pack,' which is used to distinguish them from pears added to fruit cocktail. This unit operation involves the addition of prepared fruit and the covering liquid, when necessary, into the can.

Type of covering liquid

During thermal processing of canned fruits, heat is first transferred from the heating medium (steam or water) to the container surface and then to the covering liquid. The covering liquid may include syrups, water, mixtures of fruit juices and water or fruit juice alone. Heat from the covering liquid is then transferred to the fruit product. Besides facilitating the heat transfer to fruits, the covering media also serves to sweeten the product and improve the quality characteristics (odour and colour), as well as to fortify the nutrients. The most common syrups used in canned fruit products are sucrose syrup (cane or beet sugar), corn syrup, invert sugar syrup, dextrose and high-fructose corn syrup.

Can lacquer

Fruits such as apricots, grapefruit, peaches, pears and pineapples need an acidresisting lacquer that is mostly used for high-acid foods. Highly coloured fruits such as boysenberries, raspberries, strawberries and red plums also require it, as do cans for jams made from fruits high in anthocyanin pigments.

Exhausting and Vacuum

The primary reason for exhausting and vacuum is to create an anaerobic environment in the can that would inhibit microbial spoilage. Vacuum treatment also removes occluded gases from fruit tissue, which is necessary in order to increase its specific gravity. Generally, three methods of can exhausting are used in order to remove headspace gas and produce a vacuum.

The conventional technique is thermal exhausting, which involves the passage of cans through a steam chamber or exhaust box. The steam replaces the air inside the can and it is sealed while still hot. Vacuum is created in the can following condensation of the steam. This process is very energy intensive due to excessive steam requirements.

High-speed mechanical vacuum sealing is also commonly used for fruits. In this method, cans filled cold with fruit and syrup are passed into a clincher that clinches the cans (first operation roll seam) but does not form an airtight seal. The cans are then subjected to a vacuum for only a short period of time. This practice will remove only the free headspace air but not all dissolved gases within the product. An advantage of this method is that it eliminates the need for exhausting of cans as a separate unit operation and saves processing space.

Can Seaming and Closing

Can container should be closed immediately after filling to prevent excessive cooling of the surface of the product. Modern can seaming machines operate at speeds as high as 300 cans per minute. Liquid products may be sealed in cans at speeds of up to 1600 per minute. The double seaming operation is critical for the assurance of an thermetic seal and good keeping quality of the final product during storage. Faulty seaming can result in deformations in the can during processing and eventually recontamination. Glass jars are closed with a screw cap.

Cooling

After thermal processing, the contents of the can should be cooled to an average temperature of about 35 to 40°C. Storage at higher temperatures will cause loss of normal colour and darkening or pink discolouration (stack burn). If cans are cooled too far below the average temperature, they will remain wet and rusting may result due to insufficient surface drying. Water used for cooling should be noncorrosive, low in bacterial and yeast content and chlorinated for measurable free-chlorine residual detected at the discharge end of the cooler. The cooling water should also be chlorinated with 2 ppm of available chlorine to preclude infection of the can contents by spoilage micro-organisms.

Labelling and Storage

Following cooling, cans are labelled for identification purposes. Adequately processed cans usually ensure an acceptable canned fruit quality on the retail market for at least 1 year. Storage temperature has been found to be the most important variable in the maintenance of an acceptable product with minimal flavour, colour and textural and nutritive changes.

QUALITY CONTROL OF CANNED FRUITS DURING THERMAL PROCESSING

The colour, flavour and texture of fruits are affected by thermal processing. In the thermal processing of fruits, sacrificing colour and flavour are inevitable in order to provide longer shelf life and more convenience. Because heat preservation is the most destructive method of fruit processing, the processor's goal should be to minimise flavour and colour changes while ensuring a safe product. Canned fruits should be regularly examined for four parameters that have the potential to change following a thermal treatment: pH, added colour, metallic contamination and vacuum. Commercial juices such as grapefruit, pear and orange may be analysed for bacterial contamination during processing using D-alanine.

Textural properties of fruits are important as they can predict the overall acceptability of the fruits for consumption. Texture loss in thermally processed fruits can be attributed to degradation of pectic substances. Fruits selected for thermal processing should be firm enough to withstand high temperatures, although substances such as calcium lactate may be added to grapefruit sections in juice or syrup to decrease firmness loss.

During processing, the juice of the fruit will dilute the syrup. Consequently, the density of the final syrup (the 'cutout' syrup) will be lower than that of the added syrup. For example, a syrup added before processing with a 40° Brix will usually 'cut out' at 22 to 25° Brix. The cutout syrup will depend upon various factors: strength of the added syrup, the type of fruit, its ripeness, soluble solids content and the ratio of fruit to syrup.

In order to preserve the colour of processed fruit, selection of fruit with optimal pigmentation is recommended. Undesirable compounds such as melanoidins and melanins are formed in browning reactions. The major pigments in fruits are chlorophylls, carotenoids and anthocyanins. Chlorophylls are lipid soluble pigments that disappear during fruit ripening. Carotenoids are subdivided into xanthophylls and carotenes. Xanthophylls are yellow (as in Golden Delicious apples and bananas) and carotenes are red (such as lycopene, the major pigment in watermelon and pink grapefruit flesh) and orange (the B-carotene found in orange and apricots). Anthocyanins are water soluble pigments responsible for the red, blue and purple of many fruits, flowers and vegetables. All these pigments related to colour are destroyed during thermal processing. The chlorophylls are degraded to brown pheophytins, the carotenoids are converted to epoxides and the anthocyanins are rapidly degraded.

During heat processing, anthocyanins react quite readily with the metal walls of nonlacquered cans. Thus, it is necessary to lacquer the cans to protect both the product and the can, as the colour will usually pass out into the syrup during processing. There are two types of discolouration associated with anthocyanins. The first type occurs when leucoanthocyanins are converted to anthocyanins during canning. This causes the characteristic pink discolouration of pears and the excess red colour in peaches. Other fruits that undergo pink discolouration include guava, lychee and banana. The second type involves enzymic browning, which can be prevented by blanching and the addition of ascorbic acid, citric acid and malic acid. Heat processing may also cause the formation of various zinc complexes such as in canned kiwifruit slices. The products are graded on a variety of quality factors such as flavour and aroma, tenderness and maturity, colour, consistency of texture, appearance of packing media, uniformity of size and shape and freedom from defects and foreign matter. The appropriate grade must appear on the main part of the label. The standards for grades usually vary for each commodity. They include the definition of the product, the style of pack (whole, halves, quarters, slices, dices, pieces or mashed) and the grade. Examples of quality factors include colour uniformity, freedom from decay and defect, maturity based on soluble solids content, firmness and shape. The above factors vary depending on the type of fruit.

ADVANCED THERMAL PROCESSING TECHNOLOGIES

Advanced thermal processing technologies are aimed at optimising both food quality and process time. It is well known that the destruction rates (D values) of most common spoilage and pathogenic micro-organisms during thermal processing are more sensitive to changes in temperature than to changes of other quality factors, thus, in theory, the use of high temperatures cannot only help achieve a shorter process time but can also promote better food quality. However, this theory is based on the assumption that the temperature distribution inside the food during processing is uniform and rapidly changing. For liquid foods, especially for those with low viscosity such as milk and fruit beverages, this assumption can be easily realised with the application of various types of heat exchangers and pumps. However, for solid foods, especially those stored in larger containers, neither rapid change nor uniformity is easy to achieve since heat is transferred by conduction, which has a limited heat transfer rate.

Therefore, different thermal processing methods have been developed based on the characteristics of foods and packages. For example, the traditional HTST or ultra high temperature (UHT) techniques, with processing temperatures in the range of 130 to 145°C, are used for liquid foods. Such techniques are not appropriate for solid foods since they heat slowly and a large temperature gradient exists between the product at the container surface and that at the center, therefore, by the time the required sterility is achieved in the center, the product bulk on the outer regions gets over-processed, resulting in greater quality destruction. Thus, the product quality is unfavourably affected with HTST or UHT processing techniques. The concept used to improve quality and shorten process time for solid foods is called thin profile processing: reducing package thickness by employing thinner containers such as retortable pouches or thin profile semirigid containers and then applying an optimal temperature profile for a given package size. On the other hand, in agitation retort processing, the product packaged in a given container is agitated during processing to induce mixing of the container liquid and particulate foods. In aseptic processing all three concepts are combined. In the following text, these typical advanced thermal processing techniques are further discussed.

Critical Factors that Affect Thermal Processing

Among the major critical factors that affect thermal processing of retort containers are the following:

1. Minimum headspace.
2. Product consistency.
3. Maximum filling or drained weight.
4. Initial temperature.
5. Processing temperature.
6. Processing time.

7. Temperature distribution.
8. Container orientation.
9. Residual gas in headspace and in food.
10. Processing and racking systems.
11. Processing medium.
12. Product heating rates.
13. Materials from which the pouch rack is constructed.
14. Divider sheet hole sizes and spacing.

Products packed in retortable flexible containers include meats, sauces with or without particulates, soups, fruits and vegetables, speciality items like potato salad, bakery products and pet foods. Generally, any product currently packaged in cans or glass jars may also be packaged in flexible containers.

NON-THERMAL PROCESSING TECHNOLOGIES

Consumer requirements for foods are constantly changing. Today consumers demand foods that are both fresh and natural. Therefore the steps used to process foods should be designed to preserve their natural quality. Hence non-thermal processing techniques such as high-pressure processing (HPP), pulsed electric field and ozone treatment have been attracting more attention from food scientists and engineers in recent years not only because of their food preservation capabilities but also because of their potential to achieve some interesting functional effects.

High-Pressure Processing (HPP)

New and alternative food processing methods and novel combinations of existing methods are continually being investigated by the industry in pursuit of producing better quality foods more economically. HPP offers one such technique for the pasteurisation of foods or for modification of their functional properties to develop and commercialise high-pressure processing equipment.

High-pressure technology has traditionally been used in nonfood areas on a relatively large scale for the production of ceramic, carbide and steel components and superalloys, where inert gases or water are used as the pressure medium. As liquid compression results in a small volume change, high-pressure machines using water do not present the same operating hazards as machines using compressed gases. Furthermore, the application of hydrostatic pressure to food results in instantaneous and uniform transmission of the pressure throughout the product independent of the product volume. The hydrostatic treatment is unique in that the effects do not follow a concentration gradient nor do they change as a function of time.

Other advantages include the absence of chemical additives and operation at low or ambient temperatures so that the food is essentially raw. Presumably, hydrostatic pressure is a physical treatment that will not cause extensive chemical changes in the food system. Once the desired pressure is reached, it can be maintained without the need for further energy input. Liquid foods can be pumped to treatment pressures, held and then decompressed aseptically for filling as with other aseptic processes.

Principles and advantages of HPP

There are two principles that underlie the development of an HPP system. The first is the Le Chatelier-Braun principle that governs the influence of high pressure on biomolecules. This principle implies that under equilibrium conditions any event (such as a chemical reaction, phase transformation, molecular transformation, etc.) that is accompanied by a decrease in volume is reinforced by an increase in applied pressure, while an event accompanied by an increase in volume is suppressed by a pressure increase. Generally, high pressure affects noncovalent bonds (such as hydrogen, ionic and hydrophobic bonds) substantially as such bonds are usually very sensitive to pressure, it follows that low-molecular-weight food components (i.e. those responsible for nutritional and sensory characteristics) are not affected by pressure whereas high-molecular-weight components (whose tertiary structure is important for functionality determination) are pressure-sensitive. Some specific covalent bonds, however, are modified by pressure.

The second principle that plays a key role in HPP systems is Pascal's law or the isostatic rule, which states that the transmittance of pressure is uniform and instantaneous. This makes HPP independent of the size and also shortens processing time. Moreover, overprocessing, which is a major concern for the thermal processing method, is prevented. Compared with conventional thermal processing, HPP has a number of unique advantages

First, it can produce much higher quality 'fresh-like' foods because HPP destroys micro-organisms at lower temperatures and most of the quality components are not affected.

Second, HPP is environmentally friendly since it requires only electrical energy for pressure build up. Moreover, HPP can easily be combined with other treatments such as heating, supercritical CO_2 and other methods to increase its efficiency.

Advantages of HPP

HPP has many advantages:

1. It does not break covalent bonds, therefore, the development of flavours alien to the products is prevented, maintaining the natural qualities of the products.
2. It can be applied at room temperature thereby reducing the amount of thermal energy needed for food products during conventional processing.
3. Because HPP is isostatic (applied uniformly throughout the food), the food is preserved evenly throughout its mass without any particles escaping treatment.
4. High pressure is not time- or mass-dependent, it reduces processing time by acting instantaneously.
5. HPP is independent of the size and geometry of the food.
6. The process is environment-friendly since it requires only electrical energy and there are no waste products.

Limitations of HPP

However, much like any other process. HPP also has certain limitations.

These are:

1. Food enzymes and bacterial spores are very resistant to pressure and very high pressure is required for their inactivation.
2. Residual enzyme activity and the presence of dissolved oxygen results in enzymatic and oxidative degradation of certain food components.
3. Most pressure-processed foods need low-temperature storage and distribution to retain their sensory qualities.

Applications of HPP

HPP has been applied in various areas of the food industry such as food preservation (pasteurisation and sterilisation), starch gelatinisation, enzyme inactivation (blanching), osmotic drying enhancement, pressure-shift freezing and thawing enhancement. Generally, HPP has been shown to be more effective against vegetative bacteria. However, more recently, by combining higher pressures from 700 to 1000 MPa and higher temperatures from 70 to 90°C, HPP has been successfully applied to the sterilisation of low-acid foods. High pressure has also been used to improve the functionality of foods. For example, pressurisation of rice grains at 400 MPa or higher significantly increased their water uptake. Because high-pressure processing affects only noncovalent bonds, food quality factors such as colour, flavour and nutrients are minimally affected. Strawberry jams prepared by high pressurisation at pressures from 4000 to 6000 kg/cm^2 not only maintain their original, fresh fruit colour and flavour but also retain up to 95 per cent of the vitamin C originally present in the fresh fruit. Pressure-processed jams were preferred to heat-processed jams. However, high pressure may cause unwanted browning of fresh foods through activation of enzyme reactions.

SECTION III

Processing by Application and Removal of Heat

Chapter 13

Blanching of Foods

INTRODUCTION

Blanching is a unit operation prior to freezing, canning, or drying in which fruits or vegetables are heated for the purpose of inactivating enzymes, modifying texture, preserving colour, flavour, and nutritional value, and removing trapped air. Hot water and steam are the most commonly used heating media for blanching in industry, but microwave and hot gas blanching have also been studied. Different hot water and steam blanchers have been designed to improve product quality, increase yield, and facilitate processing of products with different thermal properties and geometries. More recently, energy conservation and waste reduction have driven further improvement of equipment design. Although blanching seems a simple operation, heat transfer to a conveyed bed of product and its effects on product properties are very difficult to accurately model with predictive mathematics. Processing conditions are usually set up to inactivate enzymes, but other quality parameters, such as colour and texture, are commonly monitored. For a given product, typically mass flow rate is fixed, temperature is measured, and heating media flow rate is adjusted to ensure that the temperature is kept at the set point.

This chapter discusses blanching principles and equipment, effects of blanching on product quality, blanching indicators, and energy and waste considerations.

PRINCIPLES OF EQUIPMENT

The design of blanching systems depends on the product, the process following it, and the final use of the product. Blanching is carried out as a pretreatment for freezing, canning, and drying. Most vegetables are blanched prior to freezing to inactivate enzymes that cause the development of off-flavours and off-colours during frozen storage. Some exceptions include onions, leeks, and peppers because they lose flavour and colour on blanching. Blanching removes trapped air (e.g. in broccoli florets) and metabolic gases within vegetable cells and replaces them with water, forming a semicontinuous water phase that favours a more uniform crystal growth during freezing. Gas removal is the main benefit of blanching before canning because it allows easier can fill, reduces strain on can during heating, and reduces can corrosion. Although, in this case, enzyme inactivation also takes place, it is not relevant because any remaining activity is destroyed on retorting. Blanching facilitates peeling and dicing, and is also accompanied by microbial load reduction. Fruits are usually not blanched, or blanched under mild (low temperature) conditions prior to freezing because blanching produces undesirable texture changes. Before drying, fruits and vegetables are sometimes blanched. After blanching, vegetables are quickly chilled by spraying with cold water, or by conveying them to a flume of cold water that often serves to transport them to the next part of the process. Blowing cold dry air has also been used to take advantage of evaporative cooling, using the water adhered to the surface of the product.

Water Blanching

Water blanching is performed in hot water at temperatures ranging typically from 70°C to 100°C. However, low-temperature long-time (LTLT) blanching and combinations of LTLT with high-temperature short-time (HTST) blanching have also been studied. Water blanching usually results in a more uniform treatment, allowing processing at lower temperatures. There are water blanchers that use a screw or a chain conveyor to transport the product inside the tank, where hot water is added. Others use a rotary drum to immerse and convey the product. Water is usually heated indirectly with steam in a heat exchanger, therefore steam quality does not need to be 'food-grade.' Water blanching requires longer processing times, results in increased leaching of minerals and nutrients such as vitamins, and produces effluents with large biological oxygen demand (BOD).

Steam Blanching

In steam blanchers, a product is transported by a chain or belt conveyor through a chamber where 'food-grade' steam at approximately 100°C is directly injected. Usually temperature in the headspace is measured and the flow rate of steam is controlled. Steam blanching is usually used for cut and small products, and requires less time than water blanching because the heat transfer coefficient of condensing steam is greater than that of hot water. However, because of the high-temperature gradients between the surface and the center of the product, larger products or pieces of product can be 'overblanched' near the surface and 'underblanched' at the center. To increase heat transfer efficiency, forced convection blanchers have been designed. These blanchers are made of nested chambers that allow recirculating steam with a fan that interconnects both chambers. The fan forces the flow of steam through a packed bed of product conveyed by a mesh belt. This technology allows higher product bed depths and higher product throughput. Another technology, individual quick blanching (IQB), was developed to minimise product treatment nonuniformities. In IQB, a single layer of product is conveyed through the steam chamber and each 'individual' piece of product immediately enters in contact with the steam.

Steam blanching is more energy-efficient and produces lower BOD and hydraulic loads than water blanching. In addition, nutrient leaching is reduced compared to water blanching.

Microwave Blanching

Studies on radiofrequency and microwave vegetable blanching date back to the 1940s. Among the first important findings were retention of ascorbic acid and carotene, and very short processing time compared to conventional water or steam blanching. These early studies used batch ovens, making the cooling step difficult. Continuous ovens developed later overcame that issue. However, most studies on microwave blanching have been carried out using commercially available home microwave ovens. These studies are difficult to compare due to the variability in equipment performance and are difficult to extrapolate to industrial conditions. Recent studies used different products and improved instrumentation such as fibre optic temperature probes and infrared imaging to further demonstrate heat penetration and efficacy of the technology. Microwave technology has been combined with water blanching to further reduce heating time. Despite the tremendous potential of microwave blanching to improve product quality and minimise waste production, industrial implementation may take several years for several reasons. In general, the use of microwave ovens in industry is limited. At present, high-value products are the most likely users for this technology. Once it has shown its value, it might draw the freezing and canning industry. Substitution of existing water or steam blanchers is unlikely to occur. The vegetable industry would be reluctant to replace pieces of equipment before full depreciation and especially if their market niche is stable. Finally, it remains to be shown that the shorter processing times of microwave ovens will result in reduced operating costs and higher value products, thereby compensating for equipment cost.

Gas Blanching

Hot gas blanching using combustion of flue gases with addition of steam to increase humidity and prevent product dehydration has been studied. This type of blanching has the advantage of reducing waste production, is comparable to conventional blanching with respect to nutrient retention, but often results in product weight loss. This approach is not currently used in industry and needs further research.

ENERGY AND WASTE CONSIDERATIONS

In the freezing industry, blanching is the operation with the second largest energy consumption after freezing itself. Heat losses can be estimated from the difference between the actual steam consumption and this proposed ideal estimate. Decrease in energy losses has been performed by insulating blancher walls and improving blancher seals. However, in steam blanchers, steam loss through product inlet and outlet ports is still a problem. Product retention time at a constant product feed rate (and therefore equipment size) is determined by the rate of heat transfer from the heating medium to the product. The rate of heat transfer depends on the thermal conductivity of the product, heat transfer coefficient, and temperatures gradients between the heating medium and the product.

Blanchers are designed to handle a variety of products by adjusting feed rate. Blanching produces approximately 40% of total plant effluent BOD in vegetable processing. Each vegetable produces different amounts of wastes because different products have different compositions, shapes, and surface areas. In addition, organic matter diffuses at different rates depending on the product. For example, leaching is faster in cut product through the cut sections than in wholesome products such as peas or lima beans where a membrane acts as a diffusion barrier. To reduce BOD and hydraulic waste loads, in many cases, water blanchers have been substituted by steam blanchers.

When water blanching is required, it has been recommended to recirculate water streams to saturate them, thus preventing further leaching of organic matter, resulting in an overall decrease in BOD and a potential increase in nutrient retention. Microwave blanching may play an important role in further reducing BOD load, but as mentioned above, this technology has not reached industrial applications for blanching and its energy efficiency relative to conventional blanching needs to be demonstrated.

EFFECTS ON FOOD QUALITY AND BLANCHING INDICATORS

Flavour, texture, and colour are quality parameters that are typically assessed for fresh products, immediately after blanching and after a given storage time. These studies allow determining the efficacy of the process in retaining or improving food quality and depend on each process. As discussed above, food quality is greatly affected by the type and extent of blanching. The quality parameters commonly used to evaluate the effects of blanching are discussed below.

Flavour

Blanching indirectly and directly affects the flavour of many products by inactivation of enzymes responsible for off-flavour development. The most notable is lipoxygenase (LOX) in several vegetables. Sometimes blanching increases flavour retention, and sometimes it removes undesirable bitter flavours from the product. Headspace volatiles assayed mostly by gas chromatography have been correlated to flavour attributes defined in sensory panels.

Texture

Blanching can result in undesirable softening of vegetable tissues. However, calcium can be added to reduce the softening. A combination of low-temperature blanching and calcium addition has also been shown to be effective in firming canned vegetables. The latter is due to the activity of pectin methyl esterase that produces pectin with a reduced degree of methylation that readily interacts with calcium. Texture assessment of the effects of blanching includes sensory characterisation of firmness, crispness, and crunchiness, and instrumental measurements such as cutting energy and maximum shear force.

Colour

Blanching can have both direct and indirect effects on colour. The former is exemplified by the destruction of pigments, such as chlorophyll, by heat. A good example of an indirect effect is in potato processing, in which the reducing sugar content can be adjusted via water blanching, affecting colour development during later, more intensive heating steps where the Maillard reaction takes place. Colour assessment in the food industry is commonly performed visually by comparison to standards. Instrumental methods based on reflectance (e.g. Hunter colorimeter) are also frequently used.

Nutritional Value

Generally, blanching produces a decrease in the nutritional value of foods. Nutrients leach out from the product especially during water blanching. In addition, vitamins are degraded by heat. Vitamin C (ascorbic acid) is, by far, the most commonly assayed nutrient in blanching probably because its high solubility and heat susceptibility make it a conservative indicator of nutrient retention. Vitamins B_1 and B_2, carotenes, and dietary fibres have also been assayed.

Quality Indicators

Peroxidase and catalase are the most commonly assayed enzymes for blanching before freezing because they are more resistant to heat than most enzymes, and there are simple rapid assays to measure their activity. However, for many vegetables such as corn, peas, and green beans, LOX, a less heat-resistant enzyme, was found to be the enzyme responsible for the development of off-flavours. Although food processors are aware of this, it is only recently that some rapid methods to measure LOX activity have been developed.

Blanching is an old and well-established practice in the food industry. Early technological improvements focused on increasing product quality. Later, process efficiency in terms of product throughput, energy efficiency, and waste effluent reduction has been the main concern. Targeting the right enzyme indicator would reduce blanching time and tackle all these priorities: improving product quality (increasing retention of nutrients and other fresh like quality attributes), reducing energy consumption, and reducing waste production. However, implementation of this requires modification of existing equipment to allow either faster product conveying or shorter pieces of equipment.

FUNCTION OF BLANCHING

Blanching serves a variety of functions, one of the main ones being to destroy enzymic activity in vegetables and some fruits prior to further processing. A few vegetables, e.g. onions and green peppers, do not require blanching to prevent enzyme activity during storage, but the majority suffer considerable loss in quality if they are not blanched or if they are underblanched. To achieve adequate enzyme inactivation, food is heated rapidly to a preset temperature. The blanching process also reduces the microbial load of vegetables and renders packaging into containers easier. To evaluate the effectiveness of blanching, indicator enzymes such as catalase and peroxidase are traditionally used. The reason for using indicators is that blanching is not a process of indiscriminate heating: too little heating is ineffective, whereas heating too much negatively impacts the freshness of certain vegetables. The choice of an indicator depends on the vegetable being processed. For example lipoxygenase may be an ideal indicator for peas and beans. The problem with using peroxidase as a universal indicator is that it sometimes overestimates heat requirements, which may vary from one product to another. Effect of blanching method on ascorbic acid losses in selected vegetables are shown in Table 13.1.

Table 13.1: Effect of blanching method on ascorbic acid losses in selected vegetables.

Treatment	*Loss (%) of ascorbic acid*		
	Peas	*Broccoli*	*Green beans*
Water blanch-water cool	29.1	38.7	15.1
Water blanch-air cool	25.0	30.6	19.5
Steam blanch-water cool	24.2	22.2	17.7
Steam blanch-air cool	14.0	9.0	18.6

Blanching prior to freezing has the advantage of stabilising colour, texture, flavour and nutritional quality, as well as helping destroy micro-organisms. Blanching, however, can cause deterioration of taste, colour, texture, flavour and nutritional quality, because of heating. There are three ways of blanching produce: water, steam or microwave. Blanchers need to be energy efficient, give a uniform heat distribution and time and have the ability to maintain the quality of the produce while destroying enzymes and reducing microbial load. Blanching using water is done at 70–100°C for a specific time frame, giving a thermal energy transfer efficiency of about 60 per cent, versus 5 per cent for steam blanchers. The time-temperature combination is very important in order to inactivate enzymes while maintaining the quality of the vegetables. Effects of blanching on plant tissues include alteration of membranes, pectin demethylation, protein denaturation and starch gelatinisation. Microwave blanching gives a result similar to that of water blanching, but the loss of vitamins is higher than in steam and water methods.

Advantages and limitations of steam and hot-water blanchers are shown in Table 13.2.

Table 13.2: Advantages and limitations of steam and hot-water blanchers.

Equipment	*Advantages*	*Limitations*
Steam blanchers	Smaller losses of water soluble components and higher product yield Smaller volumes of effluent and lower disposal costs than water blanchers, particularly with air cooling instead of water	Limited cleaning of foods so washers are also required Uneven blanching if food is piled too high on the conveyor Some loss of mass from the food

(Cont'd...)

Equipment	*Advantages*	*Limitations*
	Better energy efficiency Better retention of product colour, flavour and texture	Larger, more complex equipment with higher maintenance costs More difficult to clean
Hot-water blanchers	Lower capital cost than steam blanchers More uniform product heating Use less floor space	Large volumes of dilute effluent result in higher costs for both purchase of water and effluent treatment Risk of contamination of foods by thermophilic bacteria Turbulence may cause physical damage to some products

Blanching is an example of unsteady-state heat transfer, involving convective surface heating by steam or hot water and conduction of heat from the surface to the interior of the food. Mass transfer of material into and out of the food is also important for the yield of product and nutrient losses. Steam blanching times for selected vegetables are shown in Table 13.3.

Table 13.3: Steam blanching times for selected vegetables.

Product	*Size (mm)*	*Blanching times*
Broad beans	20–25	90–120
Broccoli, cut	30	120–180
Brussels sprouts	25	150–180
	40	240–300
Cabbage, cut	13	60–90
Carrots, diced	10	50–70
Carrots, sliced	6	90–120
Carrots, whole, baby	50	240–300
Cauliflower florets	20–50	180–240
Corn on the cob	–	480–720
Green beans, cut	13–30	70–90
Leeks, cut	13	150–180
Lima beans	20–30	60–90
Mushrooms, sliced	4	60–90
Mushrooms, whole	25	180–240
Peas	10	45–60
Potatoes, diced	10	60–90
Potatoes, whole	25	240–300

Newer Blanching Methods

There have been many studies of microwave blanching (e.g. corn kernels, mushrooms, turnip greens and peanuts. Most have confirmed the advantages over conventional blanchers of faster heating and reduced energy costs, which lead to reduced processing times and lower nutrient losses. The main disadvantages of microwave blanching are the higher cost of the equipment compared to conventional blanchers, nonuniform energy distribution, and difficulties in predicting and monitoring the heating pattern.

Microwave blanching has been used commercially in Europe and Japan, but not widely. It is reviewed by Dorantes-Alvarez and Parada-Dorantes and Ramesh and others. It is not yet used commercially for blanching, but studies have indicated its potential for mushroom blanching. Icier and others applied ohmic blanching to pea pure´e and found that peroxidase was inactivated in a shorter time than using water blanching. Similar results were found in ohmically blanched artichokes. Guida and others found that ohmic blanching (at 24 V cm^{-1} and 80°C) inactivated peroxidase and polyphenoloxidase in artichoke heads more quickly than hot-water blanching at 100°C and better preserved their colour and texture. Lespinard and others studied ultrasonic-assisted blanching of mushrooms and concluded that a combined treatment with conventional blanching could reduce the processing time and retain the colour of the blanched product.

High-humidity hot-air impingement blanching (HHAIB) is a thermal technology that is under development. It combines the advantages of steam blanching and hot-air impingement technologies to produce a uniform, rapid and energy-efficient blanching process that causes minimum loss of water-soluble nutrients. It uses jets of high-humidity hot air that impinge on the product surface at high velocity to achieve a high rate of heat transfer. Studies by Xiao and others found that HHAIB pretreatment accelerated drying and improved the whiteness of yam slices, and Bai and others found that the process inactivated polyphenoloxidase and maintained the quality of Fuji apple and grapes respectively.

Pan and others evaluated the feasibility of using medium- and far-infrared heating in a catalytic infrared blancher/dryer for blanching and drying fruits and vegetables without water or steam. Pear cubes, baby carrots, sweetcorn and French fries were blanched with a radiation energy intensity of 5.7 kW m^{-2} for between 1 and 3.5 min to inactivate peroxidase. When pear cubes were dried with radiant energy after blanching, the time was reduced by 44% and the texture and appearance of the dried pears was superior, compared to those produced by steam blanching and hot-air drying. This catalytic infrared processing system is commercialised for drying, peeling, toasting and disinfecting foods in addition to blanching. There have been a number of studies of high-pressure blanching which have demonstrated greater nutrient retention than conventional blanching but Cheftel and others concluded that there is insufficient inactivation of enzymes at high-pressure low temperatures and it is unlikely that this process will replace commercial thermal blanching.

Effect on Foods

The heat received by a food during blanching inevitably causes some changes to sensory and nutritional qualities. Blanching causes physical and metabolic changes within food cells that result in cell death. Heat damages cytoplasmic and other membranes, which become permeable and result in loss of cell turgor. Water and solutes pass into and out of cells, resulting in nutrient losses. Heat also disrupts subcellular organelles and their constituents become free to interact within the cell. Overblanching can cause excessive softening and loss of flavour in the food, but the heat treatment is less severe than, e.g. in heat sterilisation, and the resulting changes in food quality are less pronounced.

Blanching removes intercellular gases from plant tissues, which together with removal of surface dust, alters the wavelength of reflected light of the food and hence brightens the colour of some vegetables. The time and temperature of blanching also influence changes to food pigments according to their D-value. Changes in colour and flavour caused by blanching are described in more detail by Selman.

Sodium carbonate (0.125% w/w) or calcium oxide may be added to blancher water to protect chlorophyll and to retain the colour of green vegetables, although the increase in pH may also increase losses of ascorbic acid. Holding foods such as cut apples and potatoes in dilute (2% w/w) brine prior to blanching prevents enzymic browning. When correctly blanched, most foods have no significant changes to flavour or aroma. The time–temperature conditions needed to achieve enzyme inactivation may cause an excessive loss of texture in some types of food (e.g. some varieties of potato) and in large pieces of food. To reduce this, calcium chloride (1–2% w/w) is added to blancher water to form insoluble calcium pectate complexes and thus maintain firmness in the tissues. In canned foods, blanching softens vegetable tissues, which facilitates filling into containers. The removal of intercellular gases from plant tissues by blanching also assists the formation of a partial vacuum in the head-space of containers.

This prevents expansion of air during processing and so reduces strain on the container seams. Removal of oxygen also reduces oxidative changes to the product during storage. The heat received by a food during blanching inevitably causes some changes to sensory and nutritional qualities. Some minerals, water-soluble vitamins and other water-soluble components are lost during blanching. Losses are mostly due to leaching, thermal destruction and to a lesser extent, oxidation. The amount of vitamin loss depends on a number of factors including:

- The variety of food and its maturity.
- Methods used in preparation of the food, particularly the extent of cutting, slicing or dicing.
- The surface-area-to-volume ratio of the pieces of food.
- Method of blanching and cooling.
- Time and temperature of blanching (lower vitamin losses at higher temperatures for shorter times).
- The ratio of water to food (in both water blanching and cooling).

Fat-soluble components (e.g. β-carotene) are largely retained. Puupponen-Pimia and others studied the effect of blanching on 20 common vegetables. They found that changes were plant species-dependent, but in general dietary fibre components were either not affected or increased slightly, carotenoids and sterols were not affected, and minerals were stable although there were some leaching losses of soluble minerals. Phenolic antioxidants and vitamins were more heat-sensitive and significant losses of antioxidant activity (20–30%) were found in many vegetables. Phenolic compounds and other phytochemicals are water-soluble and therefore susceptible to leaching, but blanching inactivates enzymes that cause their oxidation. However, chemical degradation can occur during storage, depending on the available oxygen and exposure to light. Typical vitamin losses are 15–20% for riboflavin, 10% for niacin and 10–30% for ascorbic acid and >50% for folic acid. There is a 30% loss of thiamine in spinach due to blanching before freezing and losses of 9–60% in the frozen product. Losses of ascorbic acid are used as an indicator of the severity of blanching and therefore of food quality. Rickman and others also report studies in which asparagus had the smallest losses during blanching and freezing, with retention averaging 90%, but note that losses of ascorbic acid can vary widely, from 10–80%, with average values ~50%, depending on the cultivar and processing conditions.

Effect on Micro-organisms

Blanching reduces the numbers of contaminating microorganisms on the surface of foods and hence assists in subsequent preservation operations. This is particularly important in heat sterilisation, as the time and temperature of processing are designed to achieve a specified reduction in cell numbers. If blanching is inadequate, a larger number of microorganisms are present initially and this may result in a larger number of spoiled containers after processing. The effect of blanching on microorganisms has been described by a number of authors including, e.g. Breidt and others who found that blanching whole cucumbers for 15 s at 80°C reduced bacteria by 2–3 log cycles.

Chapter 14

Pasteurisation

INTRODUCTION

Pasteurisation is most important in all dairy processing. It is the biological safeguard which ensures that all potential pathogens are destroyed. Extensive studies have determined that heating milk to 63°C (145°F) for 30 minutes or 72°C (161°F) for 15 seconds kills the most resistant harmful bacteria. In actual practice these temperatures and times are exceeded, thereby not only ensuring safety but also extending shelf life.

Most milk today is pasteurised by the continuous high-temperature short-time (HTST) method (72°C or 161°F for 15 seconds or above). The HTST method is conducted in a series of stainless steel plates and tubes, with the hot pasteurised milk on one side of the plate being cooled by the incoming raw milk on the other side. This 'regeneration' can be more than 90 per cent efficient and greatly reduces the cost of heating and cooling. There are many fail-safe controls on an approved pasteuriser system to ensure that all milk is completely heated for the full time and temperature requirement. If the monitoring instruments detect that something is wrong, an automatic flow diversion valve will prevent the milk from moving on to the next processing stage. Higher temperatures and sometimes longer holding times are required for the pasteurisation of milk or cream with a high fat or sugar content.

Pasteurised milk is not sterile and is expected to contain small numbers of harmless bacteria. Therefore, the milk must be immediately cooled to below 4.4°C (40°F) and protected from any outside contamination. The shelf life for high-quality pasteurised milk is about 14 days when properly refrigerated.

Extended shelf life can be achieved through ultrapasteurisation. In this case, milk is heated to 138°C (280°F) for two seconds and aseptically placed in sterile conventional milk containers. Ultrapasteurised milk and cream must be refrigerated and will last at least 45 days. This process does minimal damage to the flavour and extends the shelf life of slow-selling products such as cream, eggnog, and lactose-reduced milks. Ultrahigh-temperature (UHT) pasteurisation is the same heating process as ultrapasteurisation (138°C or 280°F for two seconds), but the milk then goes into a more substantial container—either a sterile five-layer laminated 'box' or a metal can. This milk can be stored without refrigeration and has a shelf life of six months to a year. Products handled in this manner do not taste as fresh, but they are useful as an emergency supply or when refrigeration is not available.

Pasteurisation is the process of heating the product to a predetermined temperature and holding it until all or nearly all objectionable micro-organisms, which may be present, are killed.

PASTEURISATION REQUIREMENTS FOR MILK

Pasteurisation by heating and time treatments are a compromise among bacterial killing along with a number of other factors such as taste, phosphate inactivation, cream line reduction, etc. The target micro-organism for milk processing is Micobacterium tuberculosis (TB germ). Table 14.1 shows how the pasteurisation process has been standardised considering these factors. Accordingly, the methods of pasteurisation can be given as in Table 14.2.

Table 14.1: Standardisation of pasteurisation requirements for milk.

Requirement	*30 min*	*15 sec*
Kill TB germ	138°F	158°F
Phosphate inactivation	142°F	160°F
Pasteurisation requirement	145°F (63°C)	161°F (72°C)
Creamline reduction	146°F	162°F

Table 14.2: Methods of pasteurisation for milk.

Methods	*Treatment*
Long hold batch type/Vat pasteurisation	63°C–30 min
High temperature short time (HTST) pasteuriSation	72°C–15 s
Ultra high temperature (UHT) pasteurization	88°C–3 s

However, the time and temperature combination maintained in a dairy plant may vary from the above Table values depending on the initial microbial load and other considerations.

LONG HOLD OR VAT PASTEURISATION

The long hold or vat pasteurisation is a batch type method where the pasteurisation is carried out at 63°C for 30 min. The basic operations involved in a vat pasteuriser are given in Fig. 14.1.

Types of vat pasteurisers (Classification based on flow of heating medium).

1. Spray type.
2. Flooded type.
3. High velocity flooded type.

General requirements

The following are the requirements for a successful batch pasteurisation process.

- Rapid heating: Generally the circulation of heating medium is started as soon as filling of the vat is begun, thus shortening the heating time.
- Immediate cooling: In some designs the cold water is circulated over the outside of the inner lines as soon as the holding period is completed, so a part of cooling can be done in the vat itself.
- Heating medium should be only a few degrees warmer than milk to prevent formation of milk stones on heating surfaces and cause minimum injury to cream line or flavour.

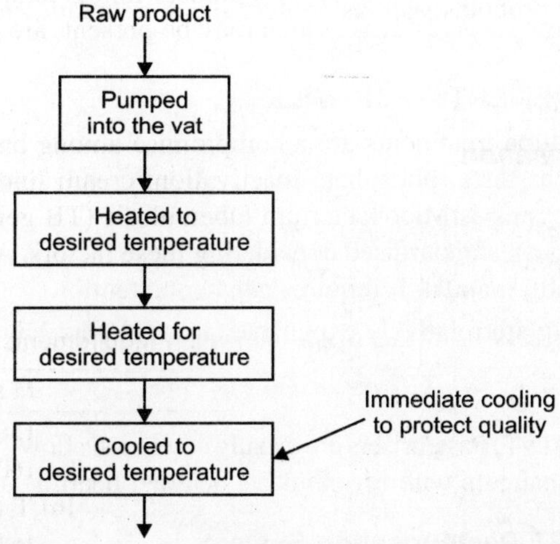

Fig. 14.1: Basic operations in a vat pasteuriser.

- Agitation of milk within a certain degree helps in improving the heat transfer.
- Agitation is easier in case of hot fluid than cold ones.
- Agitation should not develop foam and it should not injure the cream line.
- Viscosity of the fluid greatly affects the type of agitator.
- Less viscous materials require small diameter high speed agitator. Highly viscous materials require slow speed large surface blade type agitators.

For vat pasteurisers, an electric or air operated control can be connected with a timing clock so that the heat is shut off when the proper milk temperature has been reached and a bell rings when the proper length of holding time has elapsed. Also temperature of heating water can be controlled during the holding period. Pasteuriser controls is shown Fig. 14.2.

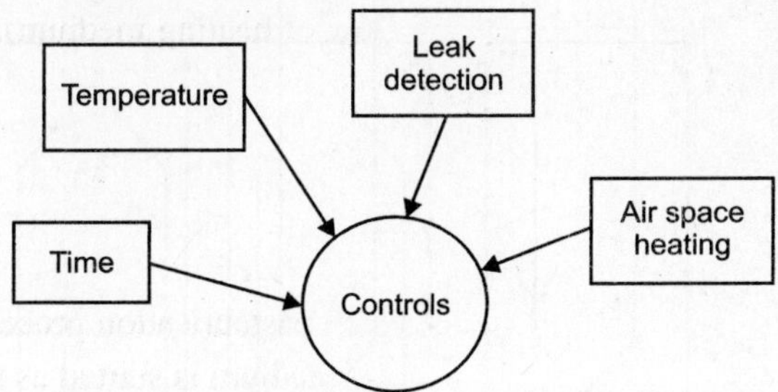

Fig. 14.2: Pasteuriser controls.

Advantages of pasteurisation

- Well suited for small plants, low volume products
- Variety of products can be handled.

- Well suited for cultured products such as bottle milk, sour cream, etc.
- Simple controls
- Low installation cost

Disadvantages of pasteurisation

- Batch type
- Slow process
- As the controls are mostly manual, it requires constant attention.
- Both heating and cooling are relatively expensive (as we do not have heat regeneration).

HTST PASTEURISATION

High temperature short time (HTST) pasteurisers are usually continuous flow systems using heat exchangers. Generally plate type heat exchangers with regenerative heating, heating and cooling systems are used.

Basic Components of HTST Pasteurisation System

The HTST pasteurisation process and its basic components are shown in Fig. 14.3. First from a constant level tank, milk is pumped by a booster pump into a heat exchanger to heat it with the help of pasteurised milk to about 60°C. As the pasteurised milk is used for heating the raw milk and there is no external heating source, we call that a regenerative heater. The regenerator reduces the actual heat requirement for pasteurisation and hence is very important for the overall cost effectiveness of the system. Then the milk enters into the heater where the temperature of milk is raised to the actual pasteurisation temperature. The milk then passes through the holder, where the milk temperature is maintained for the specific time so that pasteurisation is completed. Then the pasteurised milk goes to the regenerator so that it gives away some heat to the raw milk. It is also simultaneously cooled so that the refrigeration requirement is

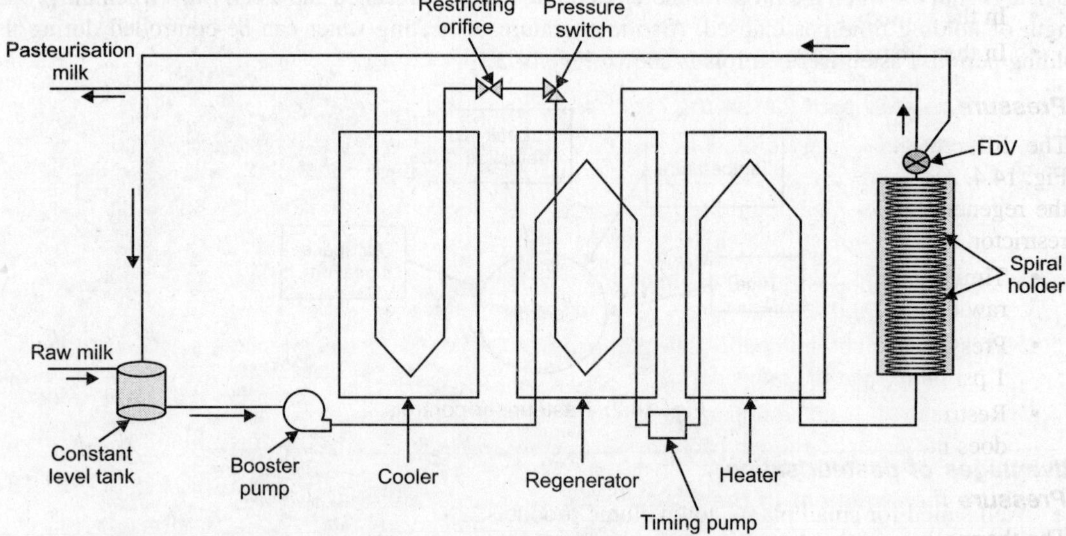

Fig. 14.3: HTST pasteurisation process.

reduced. After the regenerator, the pasteurised milk goes to a chiller, where the milk temperature is reduced to about 4–5°C. For HTST pasteurisation, the following controls are very important.

- Flow rate
- Temperature
- Pressure

Control for flow rate

- The flow rate is regulated by a metering or timing pump.
- A positive displacement pump of rotary or piston type is used.
- Often variable speed drives are used to change the rate of flow when desired.
- Pump must be sized and perfectly driven such that flow rate does not exceed the actual, i.e. the holding time is not below legal minimum.

Control for temperature

- Control of temperature includes means for maintaining a uniform product temperature at or above the legal minimum at a safe value.
- It should divert the flow back to the system if the temperature at the end of holder is below legal minimum.
- Usually a safety thermal limit recording controller is used. (It makes a continuous record of the temperature and marks the time when the flow diversion valve operates).

Control for pressure

The pressure control is important in the following three sections.

- In the regenerators
- In the flow diversion valve
- In the diverted milk lines (for homogenisation, etc.)

Pressure related problem in the regenerator

The different causes and effects of pressure related issues in a pasteurisation system are given in Fig. 14.4. As it can be seen, the centrifugal booster pump takes care of the pressure related problems in the regenerator. Besides, there are three more devices as the timing pump, pressure switch and the restrictor, the functions of which are given below:

- Timing pump: It assures that the pasteurised product side is always under higher pressure than the raw side in the regenerator.
- Pressure switch: It will allow the pump to run only when the pressure in pasteurised side is at least 1 psi more than the raw side.
- Restrictor: It is an additional device to satisfy the minimum 1 psi difference if the cooler section does not produce enough back pressure on the pasteurised side.

Pressure management in the flow diversion valve

The thermal limit recorder not only makes a record of the temperature of the milk, but also indicates, records and controls the action of the flow diversion valve.

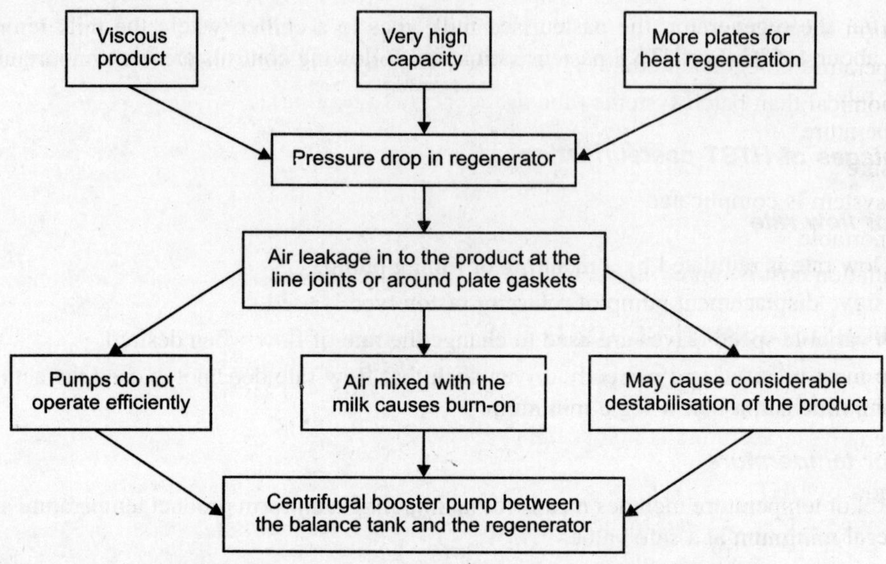

Fig. 14.4: Use of booster pump in a pasteurisation system.

Pressure management in diverted milk line

- The other pressure management is needed on the diverted milk line, since it may affect the holding time during diversion.
- If the holding time during diverted flow is shorter than that in forward flow, a restricting orifice should be placed in the divert line.

Main parts of HTST pasteuriser

The main parts of HTST pasteuriser are as follows:

- Constant level tank
- Regenerator
- Booster pump
- Timing pump
- Heater
- Holder
- Flow diversion valve
- Pressure switch
- Restricting orifice
- Cooler

Important accessories

- Leak detector valves at all inlet and outlet pipes.
- Air space heaters (Air space heating is done by introducing steam above the level of the product).

Advantages of HTST pasteurisation

- Uniform treatment.
- Temperature is regulated at close limits and overheating is prevented.
- Economical than batch systems (due to regenerative heating).

Disadvantages of HTST pasteurisation

- The system is complicated.
- Not portable.
- Installation cost is more.

ULTRA HIGH TEMPERATURE (UHT) PASTEURISATION

As we have discussed previously, the UHT pasteurisation process involves heating the milk at a temperature of 88°C for 3 sec. The equipment is much the same as the HTST units and the controls are also similar, but the operating temperature is higher. The holder is much smaller for smaller pasteurising time.

Advantages of UHT

- Better texture of milk due to short holding time.
- Greater bacterial destruction is possible.

When UHT treatment is needed for greater bacterial destruction or its beneficial effect on the body and texture of ice cream, then the treatment may be given following regular pasteurisation.

Pasteurisation and homogenisation

- Since nearly all fluid milk and ice cream mix etc. are homogenised, homogenisers are integrated to the continuous pasteurisation process.
- As the homogenisation temperature must be at least 60°C, the homogeniser must be located either between the regenerator and heater or after the heater.
- The equipment, when installed, should not reduce the holding time below the legal minimum either when they are operating or when they are at rest.
- The capacity of the homogeniser can seldom be synchronised exactly with the timing pump unless a vented cover or other relief valve is employed, and then the pump operates at slightly greater capacity than the homogeniser.
- The usual practice now a day is to use homogeniser having 3–8% greater capacity than the maximum flow rate of the system. They are equipped with a recirculation, by-pass loop from the discharge line to the suction feed line.
- Here the timing pump regulates the flow rate of the system at all the times.

Like homogenisers, clarifiers and separators may also be integrated into the lines of HTST and UHT systems.

Uperisation (Ultra-pasteurisation)

This is another method of pasteurisation and the unit operations involved in the process are given in Fig. 14.5.

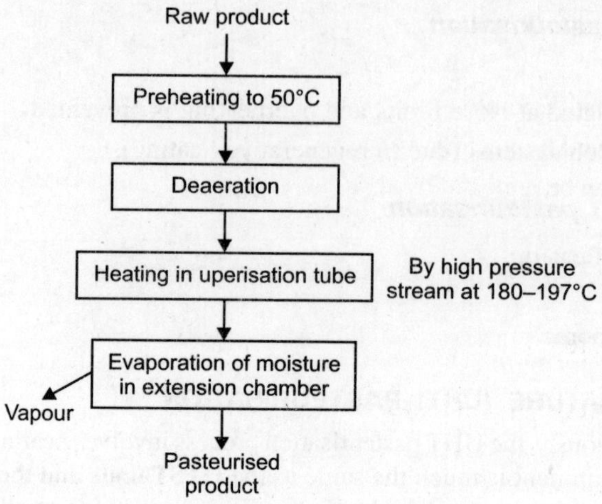

Fig. 14.5: Uperisation process.

The process involves heating the milk with high pressure steam at 180–197°C. The milk is heated to 150°C for less than 1 sec to obtain the desired effect of pasteurisation.

Vacreation

- The process of heat treatment under vacuum in stainless steel chamber is known as vacreation.
- Vacreation is normally done for cream used in manufacture of butter.

The purpose of vacreation is to:

- Kill bacteria.
- Inactivate enzyme.
- Remove undesirable odours and flavours.
- Deaeration to expel dissolved air and finely dispersed bubbles. The system consists of a product feed pump, steam pressure controller, a temperature recorder controller, vacuum controller, milk inlet controller, concentration ratio controller. The equipment is called 'Vacreator' (trade name adopted from Protech engineering, NZ). Care and maintenance of pasteurising equipment.
- Keep all surfaces clean.
- Routine preventive maintenance and adjust controls.
- Proper care and lubrication of gasket.
- Lubrication of motor, pump and other necessary equipments.
- Thermometers and control equipments should be checked for accuracy. Replace if out of tolerance.

Flavour treating system of milk

The milk may contain flavours, which are mainly as follows:

- Flavour which is made of volatile component.
- Weed and feed flavour.

When it is desired to remove flavour, the following methods are adopted.

- Aeration
- Vacuum flashing or distillation.
- Steam injection followed by vacuum washing.

The volatile substances can be removed by aeration. The fat and soluble flavours are removed by steam washing method.

Types of flavour treating equipment

Vacuum alone type:

- Deaeration with no vaporisation of the product.
- Vaporising unit.

Steam vacuum unit:

- Temperature control steam supply type.
- Excess steam supply type/steam washing.

The vaporising unit is placed immediately after the flow diversion valve.

Efficiency of Pasteurisation

The HTST pasteurisation standard can be designed to achieve a five-log reduction, killing 99.999% of the number of viable micro-organisms in milk. This is considered adequate for destroying almost all yeasts, molds, and common spoilage bacteria and also to ensure adequate destruction of common pathogenic, heat-resistant organisms (including *Mycobacterium tuberculosis*, which causes tuberculosis, but not *Coxiella burnetii,* which causes Q fever). As a precaution, modern equipment tests and identifies bacteria in milk being processed. HTST pasteurisation processes must be designed so the milk is heated evenly, and no part of the milk is subject to a shorter time or a lower temperature.

Even pasteurisation without quality control can be effective, though this is generally not permitted for human consumption; a study of farms feeding calves on pasteurised waste milk using a mixture of pasteurisation technologies (none of which were routinely monitored for performance) found the resulting pasteurised milk to meet safety requirements at least 92% of the time. An effect of the heating of pasteurisation is that some vitamin, mineral, and beneficial (or probiotic) bacteria is lost. Soluble calcium and phosphorus levels decrease by 5%, thiamine (vitamin B_1) and vitamin B_{12} (cobalamin) levels by 10%, and vitamin C levels by 20%. These losses are not significant nutritionally.

Verification

Direct microbiological techniques are the ultimate measurement of pathogen contamination, but these are costly and time-consuming (24–48 hr), which means that products are able to spoil by the time pasteurisation is verified. As a result of the unsuitability of microbiological techniques, milk pasteurisation efficacy is typically monitored by checking for the presence of alkaline phosphatase, which is denatured by pasteurisation.

B. tuberculosis, the bacterium that requires the highest temperature to be killed of all milk pathogens is killed at ranges of temperature and time similar to those that denature alkaline phosphatase. For this reason, presence of alkaline phosphatase is an ideal indicator of pasteurisation efficacy.

Phosphatase denaturing was originally monitored using a phenol-phosphate substrate. When hydrolysed by the enzyme these compounds liberate phenols, which were then reacted with dibromoquinonechlorimide to give a colour change, which itself was measured by checking absorption at 610 nm (spectrophotometry). Some of the phenols used were inherently coloured (phenolpthalein, nitrophenol) and were simply assayed unreacted. Spectrophotometric analysis is satisfactory but is of relatively low accuracy because many natural products are coloured. For this reason, modern systems use fluorometry which is able to detect much lower levels of raw milk contamination. According to the United States Centers for Disease Control between 1998 and 2011 79% of the dairy related outbreaks were due to raw milk or cheese products. They report 148 outbreaks, 2,384 illnesses (284 requiring hospitalisations) as well as 2 deaths due to raw milk or cheese products during the same time period.

Consumer Acceptance

Although pasteurisation has been practiced for a long time, some consumers contend that they should have the right to buy and sell unpasteurised milk if they want to. Some consumers also point out that government-enforced pasteurisation law has been used as a tool for large business to shut out competition from smaller producers.

Products that are Commonly Pasteurised

- Beer
- Canned food
- Dairy products
- Eggs
- Milk
- Juices
- Low alcoholic beverages
- Syrups
- Vinegar
- Water
- Wines

Objectives of Pasteurisation

- To make the product safe for human consumption by destroying the pathogenic organism, which may be present.
- Improves preservation quality by destroying almost all spoilage organisms.
- Helps to retain good flavour over a longer period of time.

Chapter 15

Sterilisation

INTRODUCTION

Sterilisation can be defined as any process that effectively kills or eliminates transmissible agents (such as fungi, bacteria, viruses and prions) from a surface, equipment, foods, medications, or biological culture medium. In practice sterility is achieved by exposure of the object to be sterilised to chemical or physical agent for a specified time. Various agents used as steriliants are: elevated temperature, ionising radiation, chemical liquids or gases etc. The success of the process depends upon the choice of the method adopted for sterilisation. Variables that affect sterilisation include:

1. The dryness of devices to be processed.
2. The temperature and humidity of the processing area.
3. Whether or not the devices were properly prepared and loaded into the steriliser.
4. Whether or not the sterilising agent is properly delivered into the system.
5. The steriliser's condition and maintenance protocol.
6. Whether or not the correct sterilisation method and cycle were used.

METHODS OF STERILISATION

The various methods of sterilisation are:

1. Physical method: (i) thermal (heat) methods, (ii) radiation method and (iii) filtration method.
2. Chemical method: (i) gaseous method.

Heat Sterilisation

Heat sterilisation is the most widely used and reliable method of sterilisation, involving destruction of enzymes and other essential cell constituents. The process is more effective in hydrated state where under conditions of high humidity, hydrolysis and denaturation occur, thus lower heat input is required. Under dry state, oxidative changes take place, and higher heat input is required.

This method of sterilisation can be applied only to the thermostable products, but it can be used for moisture-sensitive materials for which dry heat (160–180°C) sterilisation, and for moisture-resistant materials for which moist heat (121–134°C) sterilisation is used. The efficiency with which heat is able to inactivate micro-organisms is dependent upon the degree of heat, the exposure time and the presence of water. The action of heat will be due to induction of lethal chemical events mediated through the action of water and oxygen. In the presence of water much lower temperature time exposures are required to kill microbe than in the absence of water. In this processes both dry and moist heat are used for sterilisation.

Dry Heat Sterilisation

Examples of dry heat sterilisation are:

1. Incineration
2. Red heat
3. Flaming
4. Hot air oven

It employs higher temperatures in the range of 160–180°C and requires exposures time up to 2 hr, depending upon the temperature employed. The benefit of dry heat includes good penetrability and non-corrosive nature which makes it applicable for sterilising glasswares and metal surgical instruments. It is also used for sterilising non-aqueous thermostable liquids and thermostable powders. Dry heat destroys bacterial endotoxins (or pyrogens) which are difficult to eliminate by other means and this property makes it applicable for sterilising glass bottles which are to be filled aseptically.

Hot-air oven

Dry heat sterilisation is usually carried out in a hot air oven, which consists of the following: (i) an insulated chamber surrounded by an outer case containing electric heaters, (ii) a fan, (iii) shelves, (iv) thermocouples, (v) temperature sensor, and (vi) door locking controls.

Operation

(i) articles to be sterilised are first wrapped or enclosed in containers of cardboard, paper or aluminium, (ii) then, the materials are arranged to ensure uninterrupted air flow, (iii) oven may be pre-heated for materials with poor heat conductivity, and (iv) the temperature is allowed to fall to 40°C, prior to removal of sterilised material.

Moist Heat Sterilisation

Moist heat may be used in three forms to achieve microbial inactivation:

1. Dry saturated steam – autoclaving.
2. Boiling water/steam at atmospheric pressure.
3. Hot water below boiling point.

Moist heat sterilisation involves the use of steam in the range of 121–134°C. Steam under pressure is used to generate high temperature needed for sterilisation. Saturated steam (steam in thermal equilibrium with water from which it is derived) acts as an effective sterilising agent. Steam for sterilisation can be either wet saturated steam (containing entrained water droplets) or dry saturated steam (no entrained water droplets). Autoclaves use pressurised steam to destroy micro-organisms, and are the most dependable systems available for the decontamination of laboratory waste and the sterilisation of laboratory glassware, media, and reagents. For efficient heat transfer, steam must flush the air out of the autoclave chamber. Before using the autoclave, check the drain screen at the bottom of the chamber and clean if blocked. If the sieve is blocked with debris, a layer of air may form at the bottom of the autoclave, preventing efficient operation. Autoclaves should be tested periodically with biological indicators like cultures of *Bacillus stearothermophilus* to ensure proper function. This method of sterilisation works well for many metal and glass items but is not acceptable for rubber, plastics, and equipment that would be damaged by high temperatures.

Autoclaves, or steam sterilisers essentially consist of following:

1. A cylindrical or rectangular chamber, with capacities ranging from 400 to 800 litres.
2. Water heating system or steam generating system.
3. Steam outlet and inlet valves.
4. Single or double doors with locking mechanism.
5. Thermometer or temperature gauge.
6. Pressure gauges.

Operation

For porous loads (dressings) sterilisers are generally operated at a minimum temperature of 134°C, and for bottled fluid, sterilisers employing a minimum temperature of 121°C are used. Ensure that there should be sufficient water in the autoclave to produce the steam. The stages of operation of autoclaves include air removal, steam admission and sterilisation cycle (includes heating up, holding/exposure, and cooling stages).

Gaseous sterilisation

The chemically reactive gases such as formaldehyde, (methanol, H.CHO) and ethylene oxide $(CH_2)_2O$ possess biocidal activity. Ethylene oxide is a colourless, odourless, and flammable gas. The mechanism of antimicrobial action of the two gases is assumed to be through alkylations of sulphydryl, amino, hydroxyl and carboxyl groups on proteins and amino groups of nucleic acids. The concentration ranges (weight of gas per unit chamber volume) are usually in range of 800–1200 mg/L for ethylene oxide and 15–100 mg/L for formaldehyde with operating temperatures of 45–63°C and 70–75°C respectively.

Both of these gases being alkylating agents are potentially mutagenic and carcinogenic. They also produce acute toxicity including irritation of the skin, conjunctiva and nasal mucosa.

Ethylene oxide steriliser: An ethylene oxide steriliser consists of a chamber of 100–300 litre capacity and surrounded by a water jacket. Air is removed from steriliser by evacuation, humidification and conditioning of the load is done by passing sub-atmospheric pressure steam, then evacuation is done again and preheated vaporised ethylene oxide is passed. After treatment, the gases are evacuated either directly to the outside atmosphere or through a special exhaust system.

Ethylene oxide gas has been used widely to process heat-sensitive devices, but the aeration times needed at the end of the cycle to eliminate the gas made this method slow.

Low temperature steam formaldehyde (LTSF) steriliser: An LTSF steriliser operates with sub atmospheric pressure steam. At first, air is removed by evacuation and steam is admitted to the chamber.

Liquid sterilisation

Peracetic acid liquid sterilisation: Peracetic acid was found to be sporicidal at low concentrations. It was also found to be water soluble, and left no residue after rinsing. It was also shown to have no harmful health or environmental effects. It disrupts bonds in proteins and enzymes and may also interfere with cell membrane transportation through the rupture of cell walls and may oxidise essential enzymes and impair vital biochemical pathways.

In a low-temperature liquid chemical sterile processing system, several steps must be followed for effective sterilisation:

1. Pre-cleaning of the devices is necessary because many devices have small connected lumens.
2. Leak testing is done to ensure there are no leaks that could allow fluid to enter/leak the ampoules/vials and cause damage.
3. The appropriate tray/container must then be selected, and if the device has lumens, the appropriate connector is attached.
4. The sterilant concentrate is provided in a sealed single- use cup and requires no pre-mixing or dilution.

The disadvantages of this method of sterilisation are that the devices must be immersible, must fit in the appropriate tray, and must be able to withstand the 55°C temperature the process uses.

Hydrogen peroxide sterilisation: This method disperses a hydrogen peroxide solution in a vacuum chamber, creating a plasma cloud. This agent sterilises by oxidising key cellular components, which inactivates the micro-organisms. The plasma cloud exists only while the energy source is turned on. When the energy source is turned off, water vapour and oxygen are formed, resulting in no toxic residues and harmful emissions. The temperature of this sterilisation method is maintained in the 40–50°C range, which makes it particularly well-suited for use with heat-sensitive and moisture-sensitive medical devices. The instruments are wrapped prior to sterilisation, and can either be stored or used immediately.

There are five phases of the hydrogen peroxide processing cycle:

1. A vacuum phase creates a vacuum in the chamber and the pressure drops to less than one pound per square inch. This phase lasts about 20 minutes.
2. In the injection phase, the aqueous hydrogen peroxide is introduced into the vacuum chamber and is vaporised into a gas, which creates a rise in pressure due to the increase of molecules.
3. During the diffusion phase the hydrogen peroxide vapour spreads throughout the chamber and the increased pressure drives the sterilant into the packs, exposing the instrument surfaces to the sterilant and killing the micro-organisms.
4. During the plasma phase the radio frequency energy is applied, stripping the electrons from some of the molecules and producing a low-temperature plasma cloud. Following this reaction, the activated compounds lose their high energy and recombine to form oxygen and water.
5. The purpose of the venting phase is to introduce filtered air into the chamber and return the chamber to atmospheric pressure so that the door can be opened. It lasts about one minute.

Radiation sterilisation

Many types of radiation are used for sterilisation like electromagnetic radiation (e.g. gamma rays and UV light), particulate radiation (e.g. accelerated electrons). The major target for these radiation is microbial DNA. Gamma rays and electrons cause ionisation and free radical production while UV light causes excitation. Radiation sterilisation with high energy gamma rays or accelerated electrons has proven to be a useful method for the industrial sterilisation of heat sensitive products. But some undesirable changes occur in irradiated products, an example is aqueous solution where radiolysis of water occurs.

Radiation sterilisation is generally applied to articles in the dry state; including surgical instruments, sutures, prostheses, unit dose ointments, plastic syringes and dry pharmaceutical products. UV light, with its much lower energy, and poor penetrability finds uses in the sterilisation of air, for surface sterilisation of aseptic work areas, for treatment of manufacturing grade water, but is not suitable for sterilisation of pharmaceutical dosage forms.

Gamma ray steriliser: Gamma rays for sterilisation are usually derived from cobalt-60 source, the isotope is held as pellets packed in metal rods, each rod carefully arranged within the source and containing 20 KCi of activity. This source is housed within a reinforced concrete building with 2 m thick walls. Articles being sterilised are passed through the irradiation chamber on a conveyor belt and move around the raised source.

Ultraviolet irradiation: The optimum wavelength for UV sterilisation is 260 nm. A mercury lamp giving peak emission at 254 nm is the suitable source of UV light in this region.

Electron accelerator

There are two types of electron accelerator machines, the electrostatic accelerator which produces electrons with maximum energies of 5 MeV, and the microwave linear accelerator which produces electrons with maximum energies of 10 MeV. Higher energies cause better penetration into the product but there is a risk of induced radiation.

A high energy electron beam is generated by accelerating electrons from a hot filament down an evacuated tube under high potential difference, and then additional energy is imparted to this beam in a pulsed manner by a synchronised travelling microwave. Articles to be sterilised are arranged on a horizontal conveyor belt and are irradiated from one or both sides.

Filtration sterilisation

Filtration process does not destroy but removes the micro-organisms. It is used for both the clarification and sterilisation of liquids and gases as it is capable of preventing the passage of both viable and non viable particles.

The major mechanisms of filtration are sieving, adsorption and trapping within the matrix of the filter material. Sterilising grade filters are used in the treatment of heat sensitive injections and ophthalmic solutions, biological products and air and other gases for supply to aseptic areas. They are also used in industry as part of the venting systems on fermentors, centrifuges, autoclaves and freeze driers. Membrane filters are used for sterility testing.

Application of filtration for sterilisation of gases: HEPA (High efficiency particulate air) filters can remove up to 99.97% of particles >0.3 micrometer in diameter. Air is first passed through prefilters to remove larger particles and then passed through HEPA filters. The performance of HEPA filter is monitored by pressure differential and airflow rate measurements.

There are two types of filters used in filtration sterilisation

Depth filters: Consist of fibrous or granular materials so packed as to form twisted channels of minute dimensions. They are made of diatomaceous earth, unglased porcelain filter, sintered glass or asbestos.

Membrane filters: These are porous membrane about 0.1 mm thick, made of cellulose acetate, cellulose nitrate, polycarbonate, and polyvinylidene fluoride, or some other synthetic material. The membranes are supported on a frame and held in special holders. Fluids are made to transverse membranes by positive or negative pressure or by centrifugation.

Application of filtration for sterilisation of liquids: Membrane filters of 0.22 micrometer nominal pore diameter are generally used, but sintered filters are used for corrosive liquids, viscous fluids and organic solvents. The factors which affects the performance of filter is the titre reduction value, which is the ratio of the number of organism challenging the filter under defined conditions to the number of organism penetrating it. The other factors are the depth of the membrane, its charge and the tortuosity of the channels. The merits, demerits and applications of different methods of sterilisation are given in Table 15.1.

Table 15.1: Merits, Demerits and Applications of Different Methods of Sterilisation.

Methods	*Mechanism*	*Merits*	*Demerits*	*Applications*
Heat sterilisation	Destroys bacterial endotoxins	Most widely used and reliable method of sterilisation, involving destruction of enzymes and other essential cell constituents	Can be applied only to the thermostable products	Dry heat is applicable for sterilizing glasswares and metal surgical instruments and moist heat is the most dependable method for decontamination of laboratory waste and the sterilisation of laboratory glassware, media, and reagents
Gaseous sterilisation	Alkylation	Penetrating ability of gases	Gases being alkylating agents are potentially mutagenic and carcinogenic	Ethylene oxide gas has been used widely to process heat-sensitive devices
Radiation sterilisation	Ionisation of nucleic acids	It is a useful method for the industrial sterilisation of heat sensitive products	Undesirable changes occur in irradiated products, an example is aqueous solution where radiolysis of water occurs	Radiation sterilisation is generally applied to articles in the dry state; including surgical instruments, sutures, prostheses, unit dose ointments, plastics
Filtration sterilisation	Does not destroy but removes the micro-organisms	It is used for both the clarification and sterilisation of liquids and gases as it is capable of preventing the passage of both viable and non viable particles	Does not differentiate between viable and non viable particles	This method is sterilising grade filters are used in the treatment of heat sensitive injections and ophthalmic solutions, biological products and air and other gases for supply to aseptic areas

Tests for Sterility

Tests for sterility are carried out by two methods:

1. Membrane filtration method.
2. Direct transfer/inoculation method.

The membrane filtration method is used as the method of choice wherever feasible.

Media used in sterility testing

Fluid Thioglycollate Medium (Medium 1) and Soyabean-Casein Digest Medium (Medium 2) are the two media generally used for tests for sterility.

Medium 1 (fluid thioglycollate medium)

Composition:

Pancreatic digest of casein	15.0 g
Yeast extract (water-soluble)	5.0 g
Glucose monohydrate/anhydrous	5.5 g/5.0 g
Sodium chloride	2.5 g
L-Cystine	0.5 g
Sodium thioglycollate	0.5 g
0.1% resazurin sodium solution (freshly prepared)	1.0 mL
Granulated agar (moisture not more than 15%)	0.75 g
Purified water	1000 mL
Polysorbate 80	5.0 mL
pH after sterilisation (measured at room temperature):	7.1± 0.2

Method of preparation: The pancreatic digest of casein, yeast extract, glucose, sodium chloride, L-cystine, agar and water are mixed in the proportions given above and heat until dissolved. Sodium thioglycollate is dissolved in the solution. The specified quantity of Polysorbate 80 is added if this ingredient is to be included. If necessary, 1 M sodium hydroxide or 1 M hydrochloric acid is added so that after the solution is sterilised its pH will be 7.1± 0.2. If the solution is not clear, mixture is heated to boiling and filtered while hot through moistened filter paper. Resazurin sodium solution is added and mix.

Medium 2 (Soyabean-casein digest medium)

Composition:

Pancreatic digest of casein	17.0 g
Papain digest of soybean meal	3.0 g
Glucose monohydrate/anhydrous	2.5 g /2.3 g
Sodium chloride	5.0 g
Dipotassium hydrogen phosphate (K_2HPO_4)	2.5 g
Purified water	1000 mL
Polysorbate 80	5.0 mL
pH after sterilisation (measured at room temperature):	7.3±0.2

Method of preparation: The ingredients are mixed in the proportions given above with slight warming. The solution is cooled to room temperature. The specified quantity of Polysorbate 80 is added if this ingredient is to be included. If necessary, sufficient 1 M sodium hydroxide or 1M hydrochloric acid so that after the solution is sterilised its pH will be 7.3± 0.2. If the solution is not clear it is filtered through moistened filter paper. Alternative media types may be appropriate where the nature of the product or method of manufacture can result in the presence of fastidious organisms (e.g. vaccines, blood products). Validation studies should indicate that alternative media are capable of supporting the growth of a wide range of micro-organisms in the presence of the product.

Method of Membrane Filtration

Procedure

The filter should be a membrane filter disc of cellulose esters or other suitable plastics, having a nominal average pore diameter not exceeding 0.45 μm. The membrane should be held firmly in a filtration unit which consists of a supporting base for the membrane, a receptacle for the fluid to be tested, a collecting reservoir for the filtered fluid, and the necessary tubes or connections. The apparatus is so designed that the solution to be filtered can be introduced and filtered under aseptic conditions. It permits the aseptic removal of the membrane for transfer to medium or it is suitable for carrying out the incubation after adding the medium to the apparatus itself.

Cellulose nitrate filters are recommended for aqueous, oily and weakly alcoholic solutions and cellulose acetate filters for strongly alcoholic solutions. The entire unit should be sterilised by appropriate means with the membrane filter and sterile airways in place. The method of sterilisation should not be deleterious to the membrane, e.g., weaken it or change the nominal average pore diameter. The sterile airways should provide free access to the sterilising agent. After sterilisation, the apparatus should be free of leaks to the atmosphere except through the sterile airways.

Method of Direct Transfer

Procedures

Liquids and soluble or dispersible solids: Appropriate quantities of the preparation to be examined are added directly into Medium 1 and Medium 2. Approximately equal quantities of the preparation should be added to each vessel of medium. The test vessels of Medium 1 is incubated at 30–35°C and the vessels of Medium 2 is incubated at 20–25°C. The volume of Medium 1 should be such that the air space above the medium in the container is minimised. The volume of Medium 2 should be such that sufficient air space is left above the medium to provide conditions that permit the growth of obligate aerobes. Unless otherwise prescribed, in no case should the volume of material under test be greater than 10% of the volume of the medium alone, i.e., 90% medium and 10% product. If a large volume of product is to be tested it may be preferable to use concentrated media, prepared so as to take the subsequent dilution into account. Where appropriate the concentrated medium may be added directly to the product in its container. Wherever possible solid articles such as devices should be tested by immersion in or filling with culture media. Immerse all parts of each article in sufficient medium contained in one vessel to completely cover all parts. The volume of Medium 1 should be such that the air space above the medium in the container is minimised. The volume of Medium 2 should be such that sufficient air space is left above the medium to provide conditions that permit the growth of obligate aerobes. Place half the articles into Medium 1 and the remaining half into Medium 2. Incubate the test vessels of Medium 1 at 30–35°C and the vessels of Medium 2 at 20–25°C.

Ointments and oily preparations: Ointments and oily preparations may be tested by the method of Direct Transfer if testing by the method of Membrane Filtration is not feasible, i.e. when a suitable solvent is not available

Incubation and examination of sterility tests: All test vessels of Medium 1 are incubated at 30– 35°C. The vessels of Medium 2 are incubated at 20–25°C. All test and control vessels, other than the subcultured vessels referred to below, must be incubated for at least 14 days unless microbial contamination is detected at an earlier time.

If turbidity, precipitate, or other evidence of microbial growth during incubation is seen: the suspected growth is examined microscopically by Gram stain; attempts are made to grow single colonies using appropriate microbiological methods; colonies of each type of micro-organism present are examined for colonial morphology and cellular morphology by Gram stain; attempts are made to identify the isolates, as far as the genus, and preferably species.

Interpretation of the test results: If microbial growth is not evident in any of the vessels inoculated with the product, the sample tested complies with the test for sterility, if microbial growth is evident the product does not comply with the test for sterility unless it can be clearly demonstrated that the test was invalid for causes unrelated to the product being examined. If the test is declared to be invalid it may be repeated with the same number of units as in the original test. If there is no evidence of growth in any vessels inoculated with the product during the repeat test the product passes the test for sterility. This interpretation applies even if growth occurs in negative product control vessels. If there is evidence of growth in the test vessels the product fails the test for sterility. Further testing is not permitted under any circumstances.

Evaluation of Sterilisation Method

Sterile products possess several unique properties, such as freedom from micro-organism, pyrogens, particulates and high standards of purity and quality. This ultimate goal in the manufacture of sterile products can be attained by evaluation of sterilisation procedure. The sterilisation processes are likely to be subjected to the most detailed and complex validation procedures.

The judgment of sterility has relied on official sterility test. A validated manufacturing procedure is one which has been proved to do what it purports to do. The proof of evaluation is obtained through the collection and evaluation of data, preferably beginning, from the process development phase and continuing through the production phase. Evaluation of processing includes equipments, process, personnel, material, etc.

The principle involve in the evaluation of sterilisation process are:

1. To build sterility into product.
2. Perform a maximum level of probability.
3. Establish specification and performance characteristic.
4. To provide greater assurance of support of the result.
5. Specific methodology, process and equipment.
6. Final product testing using validated analytical method.
7. Verification, calibration and maintenance of equipments used in the processes.

Evaluation of sterilisation methods are done to ensure that the product produce by design process should be of best quality. The process control and finished product testing alone are not sufficient to assure product quality. When testing a specified portion of the total product and if the specified portion passes the test of sterility, it cannot assure that the total product is sterile.

Evaluation of sterilisation methods provides a high degree of assurance which indicates a specific process will consistently produce a product that will meets it predetermined specifications and quality assurance. So this action proves that any procedure, process, equipments, material activity or system actually leads to the expected result and produce quality product. This concept of evaluation has been expended to encompass a wide range of activities from analytical methods used for quality control of drug substance and drug products. The purpose of evaluation of any material equipment is achieved by means of a validation protocol which details the test to be carried out; frequency of testing and results expected that is the acceptance criteria.

Process of Microbial Destruction

Microbial destruction methods such as heat, chemical, and radiation sterilisation are used. Upon exposure of such treatment, micro-organisms die according to logarithmic relationship between concentration or population of the living cells and the time exposure or radiation dose. The relationship between microbial population and time may be linear or non linear. The D value or time required or dose required for one log reduction in microbial population may be calculated from these plots.

D value

It is the rate of killing of micro-organism. It determines the time required to reduce the microbial population by one decimal point, i.e. it is the time required for 90% reduction in the microbial population. Hence the time or dose it takes to reduce thousand microbial cells to hundred cells is the D value. D value is important in the validation of sterilisation process for several reasons:

1. It is specific for each micro-organism in environment subjected to specific sterilising agent or condition.
2. The knowledge of D value at different temperature in heat sterilisation is necessary for the calculation of Z value.
3. The D value is used in the calculation of biological factor F.
4. Extra-polation of D value predicts number of log reduction of microbial population.

D value is affected by several parameters which are as follows:

1. The type of micro-organism used as biological indicator
2. The formulation component and characteristics
3. The surface on which the micro-organism is exposed
4. The temperature, gas concentration and radiation dose

D value is determined by:

1. Survival curve method: The survival curve method is based on plotting the log number of the surviving organism verses independent variable such as time, gas concentration or radiation dose
2. Fraction negative method: In this method, sample containing similar spore population are treated in an identical environment and the number of sample still showing microbial growth after treatment and incubation are determined.

Data obtained by survival curve method are plotted semi logarithmically. Data points are connected by least square analysis.

$$\text{Log N} = a + bt$$

where, N is number of surviving organism, t is time, a is γ intercept and b is slope of line as determined by linear regression. D value is the reciprocal of linear slope

$$D = 1/b$$

Z value

This term is exclusively used in the validation of heat sterilisation process. The Z value is the reciprocal of slope resulting from the plot of the logarithm of D value verses the temperature at which the D value was obtained. The Z value may be defined as the temperature required for one log reduction in the D value. The accepted standard (Z value) for steam sterilisation of Bacillus stearothermophilus spores and dried heat sterilisation for Bacillus subtilis are 10°C and 22°C respectively. These plots are important because one can determine D value of the indicator micro organism at any temperature of interest. The magnitude of slope indicates the relative degree of lethality as temperature is increased or decreased.

F value

The F value measures equivalent time, not clock time that a monitored article is exposed to the desired temperature, e.g. 121°C. F value is calculated from following equation:

$$F = \Delta t \sum 10^{(T-T_0)/Z}$$

where, Δt is the time interval for the measurement of product temperature t.

T is reference temperature.

To is 121°C for steam sterilisation.

Evaluation and in Process Monitoring of Sterilisation Procedures

Dry heat sterilisation

Physical indicator: In this process temperature record chart is made of each sterilisation cycle with dry heat sterilisation. This chart forms the batch documentation and is compared against a master temperature records. The temperature should be taken as the coolest part of the loaded steriliser, further information on heat distribution and penetration within steriliser can be gained by the use of thermocouple place at selected site in the chamber or injected into test packs or bottles.

Chemical indicator: It is based on the ability of heat to alter the chemical or physical characteristics of variety of chemical substances. This change should take place only when satisfactory condition for sterilisation prevails. Thus conforming that sterilisation cycle has been successfully completed. Chemical indicators generally under go melting or colour change.

Biological indicator: The biological indicators are the standardised bacterial spore preparations which are usually in the form of suspension in water or culture medium or of spore dried on paper or plastic carriers, they are placed in steriliser. After the sterilisation process the aqueous suspension/spores are on carriers are aseptically transferred to an appropriate nutrient medium, which is then incubated and occasionally seen for the growth. *Clostridium* species is generally used for dry heat sterilisation indicator (Table 15.2).

Table 15.2: Dry heat sterilisation.

Indicators	*Sterilisation methods*	*Principle*	*Device*	*Parameter monitored*
Physical	Dry heat	Temperature recording charts	Temperature recording charts	Temperature
Chemical	Dry heat	Temperature sensitive coloured solution	Browne's tube	Temperature, Time
		Temperature sensitive chemical	A temperature sensitive white wax concealing a black marked	Temperature
Biological	Dry heat	Temperature sensitive microbes	*Bacillus subtilis*	D value

Moist heat sterilisation

Physical indicator: In this process temperature record chart is made of each sterilisation cycle with dry heat sterilisation. This chart of the batch documentation is compared against a master temperature records. The temperature should be taken as the coolest part of the loaded steriliser, further information on heat distribution and penetration within steriliser can be gained by the use of thermocouple place at selected site in the chamber or injected into test packs or bottles.

Chemical indicator: It is based on the ability of heat to alter the chemical or physical characteristics of variety of chemical substances. This change should take place only when satisfactory condition for sterilisation prevails. Thus conforming that sterilisation cycle has been successfully completed chemical indicator generally under go melting or colour change.

Biological indicator: Spores of *B. Steareothermophylus* in sealed ampoules of culture medium are used for moist heat sterilisation monitoring and these may be incubated directly at 55°C, thus may eliminate the need of aseptic transfer (Table 15.3).

Table 15.3: Moist Heat Sterilisation.

Indicators	*Sterilisation methods*	*Principle*	*Device*	*Parameter monitored*
Physical	Moist heat	Temperature recording charts	Temperature recording charts	Temperature
Chemical	Moist heat	Temperature sensitive coloured solution	Browne's tube	Temperature, Time
		Steam sensitive chemical	A device which is impregnated into a carrier material.	Saturated steam
Biological	Moist heat	Temperature sensitive microbes	*Bacillus Stearothermophilus*	D value

Aseptic transfer is also avoided by use of self contained units where the spores strip and the nutrient medium are present in the same device ready for mixing after use.

The bacterial spores should have following qualities

1. It should be non pathogenic.
2. Should posses above average resistant to the particular sterilisation process.

Gaseous sterilisation

Physical indicator: Gas concentration is measured independently of pressure rise, often by reference to weight of gas used.

Chemical indicator: The chemical indicator used here are Royach Sacket, the indicator paper impregnated with reactive chemical which undergoes a distinct colour change on reaction. Chemical indicators are valuable monitors of the condition prevailing at the coolest of most in accessible part of a steriliser.

Biological indicator: As with chemical indicator they are usually packed in dummy packs located at strategic sites in the steriliser. Alternatively for gaseous sterilisation, these may also be placed in tubular helix device. The species of bacteria generally used for gaseous sterilisation are *B. subtilis var.niger* and *B. subtilis var. golbigii.* One of the long-standing criticisms of biological indicator is that the incubation period required is very long in order to find satisfactory results (Table 15.4).

Table 15.4: Gaseous sterilisation.

Indicators	*Sterilisation methods*	*Principle*	*Device*	*Parameter monitored*
Physical	Gaseous	Temperature recording charts	Temperature recording charts	Temperature
Chemical	Gaseous	Reactive chemical	Indicator paper impregnated with reactive chemical.	Gas concentration, Temperature, Time
		Capillary principle	Based on same migration along wick principle	Gas concentration, Temperature, Time
		Temperature sensitive chemical	A temperature sensitive white wax concealing a black marked	Temperature
Biological	Gaseous	Temperature sensitive microbes	*Bacillus subtilis*	D value

Radiation sterilisation

Physical indicator: In radiation sterilisation a plastic or perspex dosimeter which gradually darkens in proportion to the radiation it absorbs give an accurate measure of the radiation dose and is considered to be the best technique currently available for the radiation sterilisation process.

Chemical indicator: Chemical dosimeter acidified with cerric ammonium sulphate or cerric sulphate solution. These responds to irradiation by dose change in the applied density. Those are considered best and accurately measure relation dose.

Biological indicator: These are consist of standardised bacterial spore preparation which are usually in the form of suspension in water or culture medium or of spore dried on paper or plastic carriers , they are placed in steriliser. After the sterilisation process the aqueous suspension/spores are on carriers are asepticaliy transferred to an appropriate nutrient medium, which is then incubated and periodically observed for the growth. *Clostridium* species is generally used for dry heat sterilisation indicator (Table 15.5).

Table 15.5: Radiation sterilisation.

Indicators	*Sterilisation methods*	*Principle*	*Device*	*Parameter monitored*
Physical	Radiation	Recording charts	Recording charts	Radiation dose
Chemical	Radiation	Radio chromic chemicals	Plastic device impregnated with radio sensitive chemicals which undergo colour changes at relative low radiation doses	Only indicate exposure to radiation
		Dosimeter device	Acidified ferric ammonium sulphate solutions responds to irradiation by dose related changes in their optical density	Accurately measures radiation doses
Biological	Radiation	Radiation sensitive microbes	*Bacillus pumilus*	D value

Filtration sterilisation

Physical indicator: Sterilising filters are subjected to a bubble point pressure test. This is a technique for determining the pore size of a filter, and may also be used to check the integrity of certain types of filters. The principle of the test is that the wetted filter in its assembled unit is subjected to an increasing air or nitrogen gas pressure difference. The pressure difference recorded when the first bubble of gas breaks away from the filter is related to maximum pore size.

When the gas pressure is further increased slowly there is general eruption of bubble over the entire surface. The pressure difference here is related to the mean pore size. Pressure difference below the expected value would signify a damage or faulty filter.

Biological indicator: Filtration sterilisation require a different approach from biological monitoring, the test effectively measure in the ability of a filter to produce a sterile filtrate from a culture of suitable organism *S. marcesence*, a small gram negative rod shape bacterium. *B. diminuta* used as a biological indicator having a dimension 0.5 micrometer and 0.3 micrometer respectively has been used for filters of 0.45 micrometer and 0.22 micrometer. The extent of the passage of this organism through membrane filter is enhanced by increasing the filtration pressure. Thus successful sterile filtration depends markedly on the challenge condition. Such test are used as the part of filter manufacture characterisation and quality assurance process, and users initial validation procedure. They are not employed as a test of filter performance in use (Table 15.6).

Table 15.6: Filtration sterilisation.

Indicators	*Sterilisation methods*	*Principle*	*Device*	*Parameter monitored*
Physical	Filtration sterlisation	Forcibly passing of solution through the membrane	Bubble point pressure test	Pressure
Biological	Filtration sterlisation	Retention of bacteria	*P. diminuta*	Size of micro-organism

Chapter 16

Evaporation and Crystallisation

INTRODUCTION

Evaporation is the process of a substance in a liquid state changing to a gaseous state due to an increase in temperature and/or pressure. Evaporation is a fundamental part of the water cycle and is constantly occurring throughout nature. Evaporation is the process by which water changes from a liquid to a gas or vapor. Water boils at 212°F (100°C), but it actually begins to evaporate at 32°F (0°C), it just occurs extremely slowly. As the temperature increases, the rate of evaporation also increases.

Evaporators are widely used in the food processing industry to remove a portion of the water from food products. This reduces bulk and weight for subsequent processing, increases solids content (as for jams and molasses), helps preserve the product, provides convenience to the end consumer and concentrates colour or flavour.

Many types of evaporators are in use, most with certain common features:

- A heat source (normally steam) that evaporates the water.
- An evaporation vessel where water is driven out of the product as vapour.
- A vapour separation vessel, where vapour and product are separated.
- A vacuum system that draws water vapour out of the separation vessel.

This vacuum also reduces pressure in the evaporation vessel, which reduces the boiling point.

Evaporators may operate singly or several may operate in series. Each one is referred to as an effect and in multiple-effect systems, the product output from one effect is the feed for the following effect. Similarly, higher-temperature vapour driven out of the product in one effect is used to heat lower-temperature product in another. Efficiency is gained by using multiple-effect systems.

EVAPORATORS

Types of Evaporators

In the evaporation process, concentration of a product is accomplished by boiling out a solvent, generally water. The recovered end product should have an optimum solids content consistent with desired product quality and operating economics. It is a unit operation that is used extensively in processing foods, chemicals, pharmaceuticals, fruit juices, dairy products, paper and pulp, and both malt and grain beverages. Also it is a unit operation which, with the possible exception of distillation, is the most energy intensive.

The more common types of evaporators include:

- Batch pan
- Forced circulation
- Natural circulation
- Wiped film
- Rising film tubular
- Plate equivalents of tubular evaporators
- Falling film tubular
- Rising/falling film tubular

Batch Pan

Next to natural solar evaporation, the batch pan (Fig. 16.1) is one of the oldest methods of concentration. It is somewhat outdated in today's technology, but is still used in a few limited applications, such as the concentration of jams and jellies where whole fruit is present and in processing some pharmaceutical products. Up until the early 1960's, batch pan also enjoyed wide use in the concentration of corn syrups.

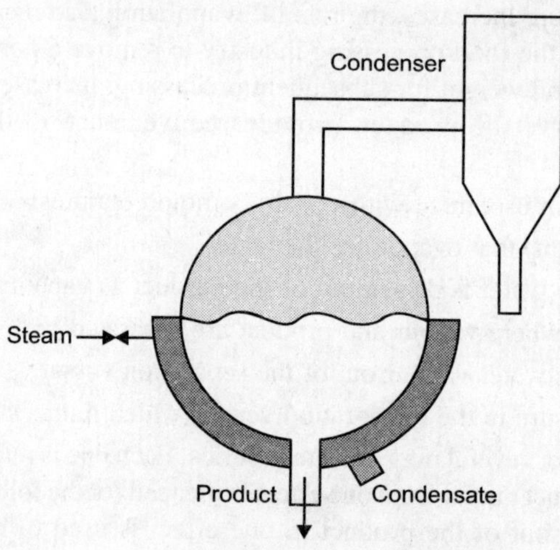

Fig. 16.1: Batch pan.

With a batch pan evaporator, product residence time normally is many hours. Therefore, it is essential to boil at low temperatures and high vacuum when a heat sensitive or thermodegradable product is involved. The batch pan is either jacketed or has internal coils or heaters. Heat transfer areas normally are quite small due to vessel shapes, and heat transfer coefficients (HTC's) tend to be low under natural convection conditions. Low surface areas together with low HTC's generally limit the evaporation capacity of such a system. Heat transfer is improved by agitation within the vessel. In many cases, large temperature differences cannot be used for fear of rapid fouling of the heat transfer surface. Relatively low evaporation capacities, therefore, limit its use.

TUBULAR EVAPORATORS

Natural Circulation

Evaporation by natural circulation is achieved through the use of a short tube bundle within the batch pan or by having an external shell and tube heater outside of the main vessel (Fig. 16.2). The external heater has the advantage that its size is not dependent upon the size or shape of the vessel itself. As a result, larger evaporation capacities may be obtained. The most common application for this type of unit is as a reboiler at the base of a distillation column.

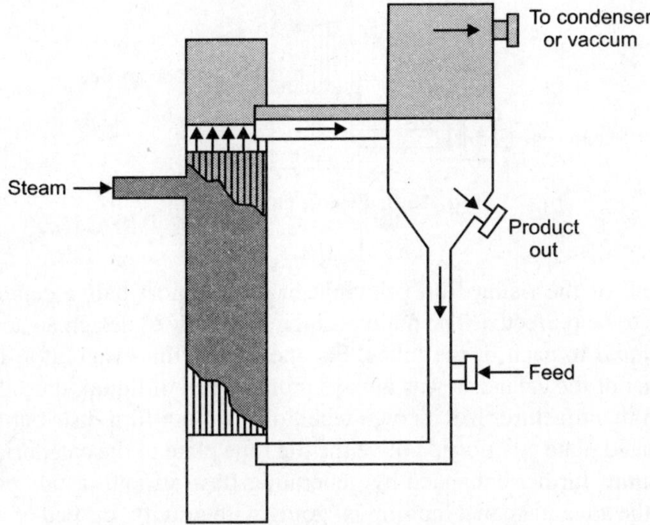

Fig. 16.2: Evaporation by natural circulation.

Rising Film Tubular

Considered to be the first 'modern' evaporator used in the industry, the rising film unit dates back to the early 1900's. The rising film principle was developed commercially by using a vertical tube with steam condensing on its outside surface (Fig. 16.3). Liquid on the inside of the tube is brought to a boil, with the vapour generated forming a core in the center of the tube. As the fluid moves up the tube, more vapour is formed resulting in a higher central core velocity that forces the remaining liquid to the tube wall. Higher vapour velocities, in turn, result in thinner and more rapidly moving liquid film. This provides higher HTC's and shorter product residence time.

The development of the rising film principle was a giant step forward in the evaporation field, particularly in product quality. In addition, higher HTC's resulted in reduced heat transfer area requirements and consequently, in a lower initial capital investment.

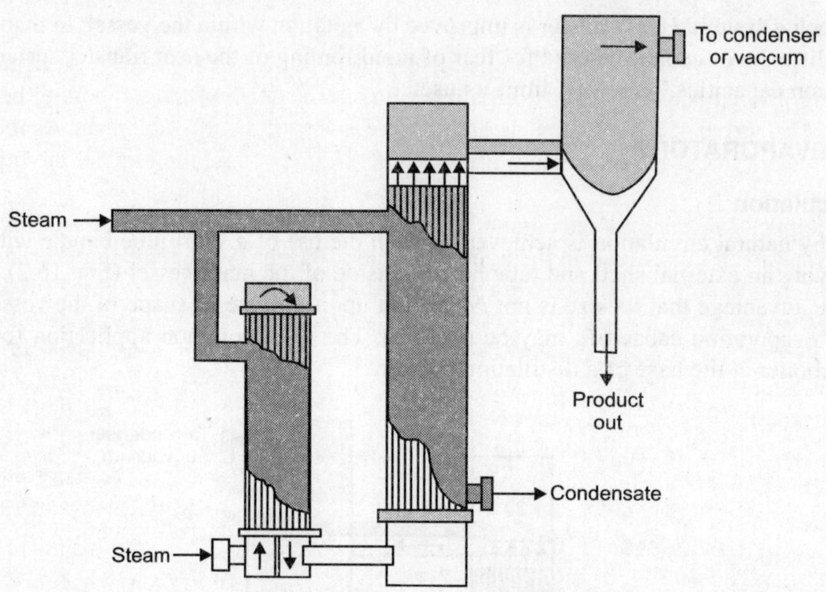

Fig. 16.3: Rising film tubular.

Falling Film Tubular

Following development of the rising film principle, it took almost half a century for a falling film evaporation technique to be perfected. The main problem was how to design an adequate system for the even distribution of liquid to each of the tubes. For the rising film evaporator, distribution was easy since the bottom bonnet of the calandria was always pumped full of liquid, thus allowing equal flow to each tube. While each manufacturer has its own technique, falling film distribution generally is based around use of a perforated plate positioned above the top tube plate of the calandria. Spreading of liquid to each tube is sometimes further enhanced by generating flash vapour at this point. The falling film evaporator does have the advantage that the film is 'going with gravity' instead of against it. This results in a thinner, faster moving film and gives rise to an even shorter product contact time and a further improvement in the value of HTC.

To establish a well-developed film, the rising film unit requires a driving film force, typically a temperature difference of at least 25°F (14°C) across the heating surface. In contrast, the falling film evaporator does not have a driving force limitation—permitting a greater number of evaporator effects to be used within the same overall operating limits. For example, if steam is available at 220°F (104°C), then the last effect boiling temperature is 120°F (49°C); the total available ΔT is equal to 100°F (55°C).

In this scenario a rising film evaporator would be limited to four effects, each with a ΔT of 25°F (14°C). However, using the falling film technique, it is feasible to have as many as 10 or more effects.

Rising/Falling Film Tubular

The rising/falling film evaporator has the advantages of the ease of liquid distribution of the rising film unit coupled with lower head room requirements. The tube bundle is approximately half the height of either a rising or falling film evaporator, and the vapour/liquid separator is positioned at the bottom of the calandria.

Forced Circulation

The forced circulation evaporator was developed for processing liquors which are susceptible to scaling or crystallising. Liquid is circulated at a high rate through the heat exchanger, boiling being prevented within the unit by virtue of a hydrostatic head maintained above the top tube plate. As the liquid enters the separator where the absolute pressure is slightly less than in the tube bundle, the liquid flashes to form a vapour.

The main applications for a forced circulation evaporator are in the concentration of inversely soluble materials, crystallising duties, and in the concentration of thermally degradable materials which result in the deposition of solids. In all cases, the temperature rise across the tube bundle is kept as low as possible, often as low as 3–5°F (2–3°C). This results in a recirculation ratio as high as 220 to 330 lbs (100 to 150 Kg) of liquor per pound (kilogram) of water evaporated. These high recirculation rates result in high liquor velocities through the tube which help to minimise the build up of deposits or crystals along the heating surface. Forced circulation evaporators normally are more expensive than film evaporators because of the need for large bore circulating pipework and large recirculating pumps. Operating costs of such a unit also are considerably higher

Wiped Film

The wiped or agitated thin film evaporator has limited applications due to the high cost and is confined mainly to the concentration of very viscous materials and the stripping of solvents down to very low levels. Feed is introduced at the top of the evaporator and is spread by wiper blades on to the vertical cylindrical surface inside the unit. Evaporation of the solvent takes place as the thin film moves down the evaporator wall. The heating medium normally is high pressure steam or oil. A high temperature heating medium generally is necessary to obtain a reasonable evaporation rate since the heat transfer surface available is relatively small as a direct result of its cylindrical configuration.

The wiped film evaporator is satisfactory for its limited applications. However, in addition to its small surface area, it also has the disadvantage of requiring moving parts such as the wiper blades which, together with the bearings of the rotating shaft, need periodic maintenance.

Plate Type Evaporators

To effectively concentrate an increasing variety of products which differ by industry in such characteristics as physical properties, stability, or precipitation of solid matter, equipment manufacturers have engineered a full range of evaporation systems. Included among these are a number of plate type evaporators.

Plate evaporators initially were developed and introduced by APV in 1957 to provide an alternative to the tubular systems that had been in use for half a century. The differences and advantages were many. The plate evaporator, for example, offers full accessibility to the heat transfer surfaces. It also provides flexible capacity merely by adding more plate units, shorter product residence time resulting in a superior quality concentrate, a more compact design with low headroom requirements, and low installation cost. These APV plate evaporation systems are made in four arrangements—rising/falling film, falling film, paravap, and forced circulation and may be sized for use in new product development or for production at pilot plant or full scale operating levels.

Applications of Plate Type Evaporators

Although plate evaporators can be used on a broad range of products, the main application has been with products that are heat sensitive and therefore benefit from the high HTC's and low residence time.

Products that are being processed in this evaporator include: Apple juice, Coffee, Pear juice, Amino acids, Fruit purees, Pectin, Beef broths, Gelatin, Pharmaceutical products, Beet juice, Grape juice, Pineapple juice, Betacyclodextrin, Lime juice, Skim milk, Caragenan, Liquid egg, Sugars, Cheese whey, Low alcohol beer, Vegetable juices, Chicken broth, Mango juice, Whey protein, Citrus juice, Orange juice, Whole milk.

Rising/Falling Film Plate

This is the original plate type evaporator. The principle of operation for the rising/falling film plate evaporator (RFFPE) involves the use of a number of plate packs or units, each consisting of two steam plates and two product plates. These are hung in a frame which resembles that of a plate heat exchanger. The first product passage is a rising pass and the second, a falling pass. The steam plates, meanwhile, are arranged alternately between each product passage.

Rising/Falling Film Plate

This is the original plate type evaporator. The principle of operation for the rising/falling film plate evaporator (RFFPE) involves the use of a number of plate packs or units, each consisting of two steam plates and two product plates. These are hung in a frame which resembles that of a plate heat exchanger. The first product passage is a rising pass and the second, a falling pass. The steam plates, meanwhile, are arranged alternately between each product passage.

The product to be evaporated is fed through two parallel feed ports and is equally distributed to each of the rising film annuli. Normally, the feed liquor is introduced at a temperature slightly higher than the evaporation temperature in the plate annuli, and the ensuing flash distributes the feed liquor across the width of the plate. Rising film boiling occurs as heat is transferred from the adjacent steam passage with the vapours that are produced helping to generate a thin, rapidly moving turbulent liquid film.

During operation, the vapour and partially concentrated liquid mixture rises to the top of the first product pass and transfers through a 'slot' above one of the adjacent steam passages. The mixture enters the falling film annulus where gravity further assists the film movement and completes the evaporation process. The rapid movement of the thin film is the key to producing low residence time within the evaporator as well as superior HTC's. At the base of the falling film annulus, a rectangular duct connects all of the plate units and transfers the evaporated liquor and generated vapour into a separating device.

The plate evaporator is designed to operate at pressures extending from 10 psig (1.7 barg) to full vacuum when using any number of effects. However, the maximum pressure differential normally experienced between adjacent annuli during single effect operation is 15 psi (1 bar). This, and the fact that the pressure differential always is from the steam side to the product side, considerably reduce design requirements for supporting the plates. The operating pressures are equivalent to a water vapour saturation temperature range of 245°F (118°C) downwards, and thus are compatible with the use of nitrile or butyl rubber gaskets for sealing the plate pack.

Most rising/falling film plate evaporators are used for duties in the food, juice and dairy industries where low residence time and a temperature lower than 195°F (90°C) are essential for the production of quality concentrate. Also, increasing number of plate evaporators are being operated successfully in both pharmaceutical and chemical plants on such products as antibiotics and inorganic acids. These evaporators are available as multi-effect and/or multi-stage systems to allow relatively high concentration ratios to be carried out in a single pass, non-recirculating flow.

The rising/falling film plate evaporator should be given consideration for various applications that:

- Require operating temperatures between 80–212°F (26 to 100°C).
- Have a capacity range of 1000–35000 lbs/hr (450 to 16000 kg/hr water removal.
- Have a need for future capacity increase since evaporator capabilities can be extended by adding plate units or by the addition of extra effects.
- Require the evaporator to be installed in an area that has limited headroom as low as 13 ft (4m).
- Where product quality demands a low time/temperature relationship.
- Where suspended solid level is low and feed can be passed through 50 mesh screen.

Falling Film Plate

Incorporating all the advantages of the original rising/falling film plate evaporator system with the added benefits of shorter residence time and larger evaporation capabilities, the falling film plate evaporator has gained wide acceptance for the concentration of heat sensitive products. With its larger vapour ports, evaporation capacities are typically up to 60000 lbs/hr (27000 kg/hr).

The falling film plate evaporator consists of gasketed plate units (each with a product and a steam plate) compressed within a frame that is ducted to a separator. The number of plate units used is determined by the duty to be handled. One of the important innovations in this type of evaporator is the patented feed distribution system. Feed liquor first is introduced through an orifice into a chamber above the product plate where mild flashing occurs. This vapour/liquid mixture then passes through a single product transfer hole into a flash chamber which extends across the top of the adjacent steam plate. More flash vapour results as pressure is further reduced and the mixture passes in both directions into the falling film plate annulus through a row of small distribution holes. These assure an even film flow down the product plate surface where evaporation occurs. A unique feature is the ability to operate the system either in parallel or in series, giving a two-stage capability to each frame. This is particularly advantageous if product recirculation is not desirable.

In the two-stage method of operation, feed enters the left side of the evaporator and passes down the left half of the product plate where it is heated by steam coming from the steam sections. After the partially concentrated product is discharged to the separator, it is pumped to the right side of the product plate where concentration is completed. The final concentrate is extracted while vapour is discharged to a subsequent evaporator effect or to a condenser.

EVAPORATION SYSTEMS

Process

The APV Paravap evaporation system is designed for the evaporation of highly viscous liquids. The system is often used as a finishing evaporator to concentrate materials to high solids following a low solids multi-effect or MVR film evaporator. The main components of the system are a plate heat exchanger, vapour liquid separator, condenser and a series of pumps. It is designed to operate as a climbing film evaporator with the evaporation taking place in the plate passages. Compared with forced circulation evaporators, the pumping costs are significantly reduced.

Under normal operating conditions the feed is introduced at the bottom of the plates. As the feed contacts the plate surface, which is heated by either steam or hot water, the feed starts to evaporate. The narrow gap and corrugations in the plate passages cause high turbulence and a resulting partial atomisation of the fluid. This reduces the apparent liquid viscosity and generates considerably higher HTC's than would occur in a shell and tube heat exchanger under similar conditions. It is particularly effective with non-Newtonian viscous liquids.

A clear advantage when processing temperature sensitive products is gained with a Paravap because most duties do not require liquid recirculation. For most duties the conventional gasketed plate heat exchanger is specified. However, for duties where the process fluid could attack the gasket, APV can offer the welded plate pair exchanger which eliminates elastomer gaskets on the process side.

The Paravap is usually operated in single effect mode although some systems are operating with double effect. Since most systems are not physically large, the equipment can often be fully preassembled on a skid prior to shipment. Preassembly reduces installation time and, in most cases, significantly lowers the overall project cost.

The Paravap evaporation system is particularly effective in processing the more viscous products. Often the Paravap can be used in place of a wiped film or thin film evaporator with a substantial reduction in cost. For duties where severe fouling can occur on boiling heat transfer surfaces, the process should be performed in an APV Forced Circulation Evaporator.

Some typical duties that are performed in a Paravap include:

- Sodium hydroxide.
- Concentration of sugar solutions to extremely high solids content.
- In one case a solids concentration of 98% was achieved.
- Removal of water from soaps.
- Finishing concentrator on certain fruit purees such as banana and apple.
- Concentration of high solids corn syrups.
- Removal of solvents from vegetable oils.
- Concentration of fabric softeners.
- Lignin solutions.
- High concentration gelatin.
- High concentration chicken broth.

APV FORCED CIRCULATION EVAPORATOR SYSTEMS

Process

The APV Forced Circulation Evaporator System is designed for the evaporation of liquids containing high concentrations of solids. In particular, the system is used as a finishing evaporator to concentrate materials to high solids following a low solids multieffect or MVR film evaporator.

The main components of the system are a plate heat exchanger, vapour liquid separator, condenser and a series of pumps. It is designed to operate as a forced circulation evaporator with the evaporation being suppressed in the heating section by back pressure. This back pressure can be generated by a liquid head above the exchanger or by using an orifice piece or valve in the discharge from the evaporator.

The evaporation then occurs as the liquid flashes in the entrance area to the separator. The suppression of boiling, together with the high circulation rate in the plate heat exchanger, result in less fouling than would occur in other types of evaporators. This increases the length of production runs between cleanings.

In addition, the narrow gap and corrugations in the plate passages result in far higher heat transfer rates than would be obtained in shell and tube systems. For most duties the conventional gasketed plate heat exchanger is specified. However for duties where the process fluid could attack the gasket, APV can offer the welded plate pair exchanger which eliminates elastomer gaskets on the process side.

The APV forced circulation evaporator system can be used either as a single or multiple effect evaporator. Since many systems are not physically large, the equipment can often be fully preassembled on a skid prior to shipment. Preassembly reduces installation time and, in most cases, significantly lowers the overall project cost. Because of the large range of viscosities that can be handled in a forced circulation evaporator, this form of evaporator can economically handle a wider range of duties than any other evaporator. In particular, due to the high turbulence and corresponding high shear rates, the APV Forced Circulation Evaporator is excellent at handling Non-Newtonian fluids with high suspended solids content.

Some typical duties that are performed in an APV forced circulation evaporator include:

- Concentration of wash water from water based paint plants to recover the paint and clean the water.
- Removal of water from dyestuffs prior to drying.
- Finishing concentrator on waste products from breweries and distilleries.
- Concentration of brewer's yeast.
- Concentration of kaolin slurries prior to drying.
- Recovery of solvents in wastes from cleaning operations.
- Evaporation of solvents from pharmaceutical products.
- Crystallisation of inorganic salts.
- Cheese whey.

EVAPORATOR TYPE SELECTION

The choice of an evaporator best suited to the duty on hand requires a number of steps. Typical rules of thumb for the initial selection are detailed below.

Mode of Evaporation

The user needs to select one or more of the various types of evaporator modes that were described in the previous section. To perform this selection, there are a number of 'rules of thumb' which can be applied.

- Falling film evaporation:
  - o Either plate or tubular, provides the highest heat transfer coefficients.
  - o Is usually the mode chosen if the product permits.
  - o Will usually be the most economic.
  - o Is not suitable for the evaporation of products with viscosities over 300 cp.
  - o Is not suitable for products that foul heavily on heat transfer surfaces during boiling.
- Forced circulation evaporators:
  - o Can be operated up to viscosities of over 5000 cp.
  - o Will significantly reduce fouling.
  - o Are expensive; both capital and operating costs are high.

- Paravap evaporators:
  - o Are suitable for viscosities up to 10000 cp for low fouling duties.
  - o Are suitable for very high viscosities, i.e. over 20000 cp, usually the only suitable evaporation modes are the wiped film and thin film systems

Film Evaporators—Plate or Tubular

- Plate evaporators:
  - o Provide a gentle type of evaporation with low residence times and are often the choice for duties where thermal degradation of product can occur.
  - o Often provide enhanced quality of food products.
  - o Require low headroom and less expensive building and installation costs.
  - o Are easily accessed for cleaning.
  - o Provide added flexibility, since surface area can easily be added or removed.
- Tubular evaporators:
  - o Are usually the choice for very large evaporators.
  - o Are usually the choice for evaporators operating above 25 psia (1.7 bar).
  - o Are better at handling large suspended solids.
  - o Require less floor space than plate evaporators.
  - o Have fewer gasket limitations.

Forced Circulation Evaporators—Plate or Tubular

- Plate systems will provide much higher HTC's for all duties. With viscous products, the plate exhibits vastly improved performance compared with a tubular.
- Tubular systems must be selected when there are particulates over 2 mm diameter.

EVAPORATOR CONFIGURATIONS FOR ENERGY CONSERVATION

Conservation of energy is one major parameter in the design of an evaporator system. The larger the evaporation duty, the more important it is to conserve energy. The following techniques are available:

Multi-Effect Evaporation

Multi-effect evaporation uses the steam produced from evaporation in one effect to provide the heat to evaporate product in a second effect which is maintained at a lower pressure (Fig. 16.4). In a two effect evaporator, it is possible to evaporate approximately 2 kgs of steam from the product for each kg of steam supply. As the number of effects is increased, the steam economy increases. On some large duties it is economically feasible to utilise as many as seven effects.

Increasing the number of effects, for any particular duty, does increase the capital cost significantly and therefore each system must be carefully evaluated. In general, when the evaporation rate is above 3000 lbs/hr (1350 kg/hr), multi-effect evaporation should be considered.

Thermo Vapour Recompression (TVR)

When steam is available at pressures in excess of 45 psig (3 barg) and preferably over 100 psig (7 barg), it will often be possible to use thermo vapour recompression. In this operation, a portion of the steam

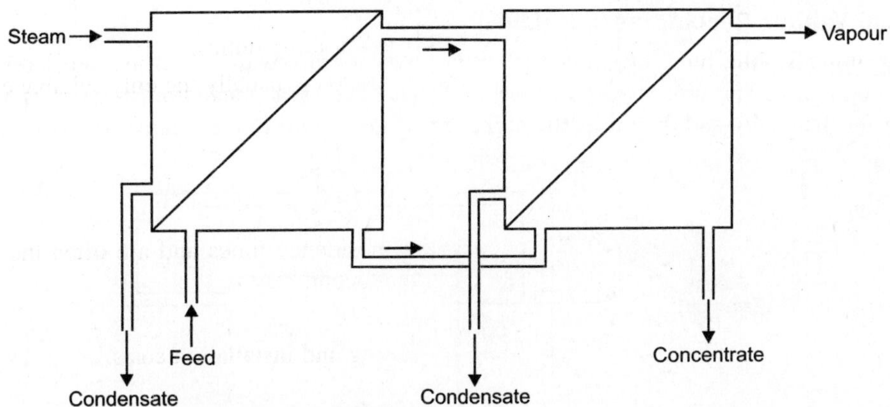

Fig. 16.4: Multi-effect evaporation maintained at a lower pressure.

evaporated from the product is recompressed by a steam jet venturi and returned to the steam chest of the evaporator. A system of this type can provide a 2 to 1 economy or higher depending on the product the steam pressure and the number of effects over which TVR is applied.

TVR is a relatively inexpensive technique for improving the economy of evaporation. TVR can also be used in conjunction with multi-effect to provide even larger economies (Fig. 16.5) are the economies that can be achieved.

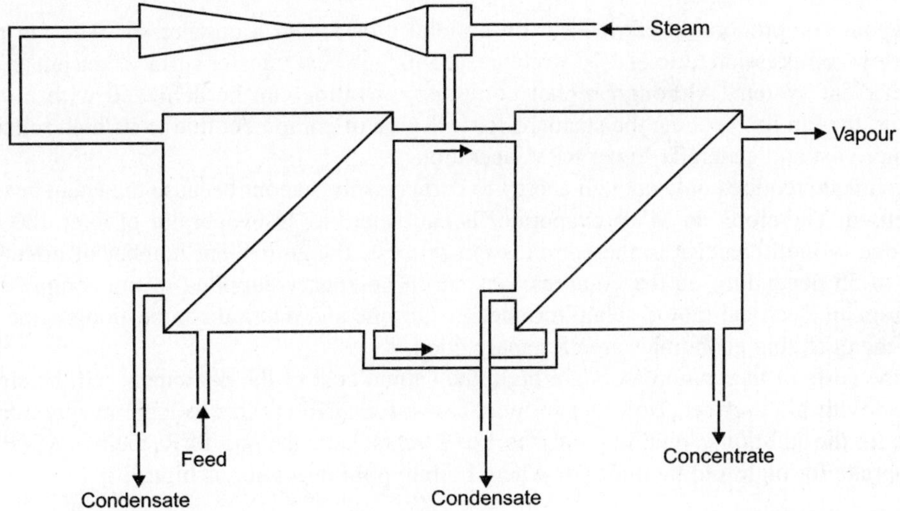

Fig. 16.5: Thermo vapour recompression showing multi-effect evaporation.

Thermocompressors are somewhat inflexible and do not operate well outside the design conditions. Therefore if the product is known to foul severely, so that the heat transfer coefficient is significantly reduced, it is best not to use TVR. The number of degrees of compression is too small for materials that have high boiling point elevation.

Mechanical Vapour Recompression (MVR)

Thermodynamically, the most efficient technique to evaporate water is to use mechanical vapour thermorecompression. This process takes the vapour that has been evaporated from the product, compresses the vapour mechanically and then uses the higher pressure vapour in the steam chest (Fig. 16.6).

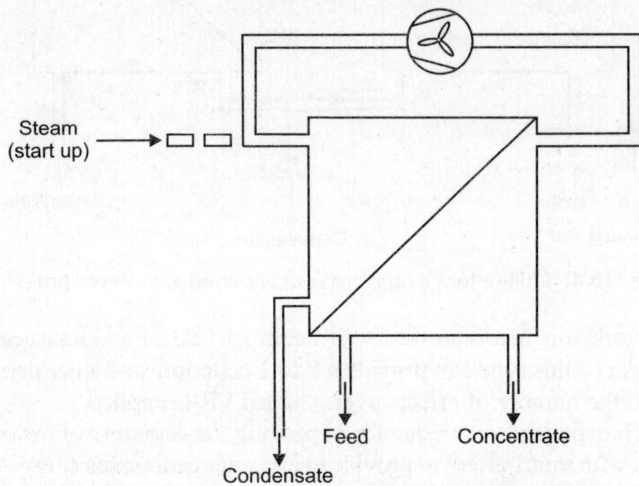

Fig. 16.6: Mechanical vapour recompression.

The vapour compression is carried out by a radial type fan or a compressor. The fan provides a relatively low compression ratio of 1:30 which results in high heat transfer surface area but an extremely energy efficient system. Although higher compression ratios can be achieved with a centrifugal compressor, the fan has become the standard for this type of equipment due to its high reliability, low maintenance cost and generally lower RPM operation.

This technique requires only enough energy to compress the vapour because the latent heat energy is always reused. Therefore, an MVR evaporator is equivalent to an evaporator of over 100 effects. In practice, due to inefficiencies in the compression process, the equivalent number of effects is in the range 30 to 55 depending on the compression ratio. The energy supplied to the compressor can be derived from an electrical motor, steam turbine, gas turbine and internal combustion engine. In any of the cases the operating economics are extremely good.

Since the costs of the compressors are high, the capital cost of the equipment will be significantly higher than with multi-effect. However in most cases, for medium size to large evaporators, the pay back time for the addition capital will only be 1 to 2 years. Like the one TVR, the two MVR system is not appropriate for high fouling duties or where boiling point elevation is high.

Combination of Film and Forced Circulation Evaporators

The most economic evaporators utilise falling film tubulars or plates, with either TVR or MVR. However with many duties, the required concentration of the final product requires a viscosity that is too high for a film evaporator. The solution is to use film evaporation for the pre-concentration and then a forced circulation finisher evaporator to achieve the ultimate concentration, e.g. a stillage or spent distillery wash evaporator.

The material would typically be concentrated from 4% to 40% in a falling film evaporator and then from 40% to 50% in a forced circulation evaporator. Usually the finisher would be a completely separate evaporator since the finisher duty is usually relatively low. In the duty specified above, almost 98% of the evaporation would take place in the high efficiency film evaporator. For cases where the finisher load is relatively high, it is possible to incorporate the forced circulation finisher as one of the effects in a multi-effect evaporator. However this is an expensive proposition due to the low coefficients at the high concentration.

RESIDENCE TIME IN FILM EVAPORATION

Since many pharmaceutical, food and dairy products are extremely heat sensitive, optimum quality is obtained when processing times and temperatures are kept as low as possible during concentration of the products. The most critical portion in the process occurs during the brief time that the product is in contact with a heat transfer surface which is hotter than the product itself. To protect against possible thermal degradation, the time/temperature relationship therefore must be considered in selecting the type and operating principle of the evaporator to be used.

For this heat sensitive type of application, film evaporators have been found to be ideal for two reasons. First, the product forms a thin film only on the heat transfer surface rather than occupying the entire volume, greatly reducing residence time within the heat exchanger. Second, a film evaporator can operate with as low as 6°F (3.5°C) steam-to-product temperature difference. With both the product and heating surfaces close to the same temperature, localised hot spots are minimised. As previously described, there are rising film and falling film evaporators as well as combination rising/falling film designs. Both tubular and plate configurations are available.

Comparison of Rising Film and Falling Film Evaporators

In a rising film design, liquid feed enters the bottom of the heat exchanger and when evaporation begins, vapour bubbles are formed. As the product continues up either the tubular or plate channels and the evaporation process continues, vapour occupies an increasing amount of the channel. Eventually, the entire center of the is filled with vapour while the liquid forms a film on the heat transfer surface.

The effect of gravity on a rising film evaporator is twofold. It acts to keep the liquid from rising in the channel. Further, the weight of the liquid and vapour in the channel pressurises the fluid at the bottom and with the increased pressure comes an increase in the boiling point. A rising film evaporator therefore requires a larger minimum ΔT than a falling film unit. The majority of the liquid residence time occurs in the lower portion of the channel before there is sufficient vapour to form a film. If the liquid is not preheated above the boiling point, there will be no vapour. And since a liquid pool will fill the entire area, the residence time will increase. As liquid enters the top of a falling film evaporator, a liquid film formed by gravity flows down the heat transfer surface. During evaporation, vapour fills the center of the channel and as the momentum of the vapour accelerates the downward movement, the film becomes thinner. Since the vapour is working with gravity, a falling film evaporator produces thinner films and shorter residence times than a rising film evaporator for any given set of conditions.

Tubular and Plate Film Evaporators

When compared to tubular designs, plate evaporators offer improved residence time since they carry less volume within the heat exchanger. In addition, the height of a plate evaporator is less than that of a tubular system.

Film evaporators offer the dual advantages of low residence time and low temperature difference which help assure a high product quality when concentrating heat sensitive products. In comparing the different types of film evaporators that are available, falling film designs provide the lowest possible ΔT, and the falling film plate evaporator provides the shortest residence time.

DESIGNING FOR ENERGY EFFICIENCY

Although the concentration of liquids by evaporation is an energy intensive process, there are many techniques available, as detailed in previous sections, to reduce the energy costs. However, increased energy efficiency can only be achieved by additional capital costs. As a general rule, the larger the system, the more it will pay back to increase the thermal efficiency of the evaporator. The problem is to select the correct technique for each application. The main factors that will affect the selection of the technique are detailed below.

Evaporation Rate

The higher the capacity of the evaporator, the more the designer can justify complex and expensive evaporation systems in order to provide high energy efficiency. For evaporator design purposes, the capacity is defined as the evaporation rate per hour. However, in some applications such as seasonal fruit juice processors, the equipment is only operated for part of the year. This means that an expensive evaporator is idle for part of the year. The economic calculation has to include annual operating hours.

For low capacities the designer is less concerned about energy efficiency. If the evaporation rate is below 2200 lb/hr (1000 kg/hr), it is difficult to justify multi- effect evaporation. Usually a single-effect evaporator, often with thermo vapour recompression (TVR), is the system of choice at this capacity.

In many cases, mechanical vapour recompression (MVR) is the most efficient evaporator. However, these systems operate at a low temperature difference, which results in high heat transfer area. Also MVR requires either a centrifugal compressor or a high pressure fan which are expensive equipment items. These cannot usually be justified for low capacity evaporators.

Steam/Electricity Costs

For medium to large duties, a selection has to be made between multi-effect and MVR. A critical parameter that will affect this selection are steam costs relative to electricity costs. Providing process conditions are favourable, MVR evaporation will be more economic, particularly in areas where the electricity cost is low, such as localities around major hydro generating plants. However if low cost steam is available, even at pressures as low as atmospheric, then multi-effect evaporation will be usually more economic due to the lower capital cost.

Steam Pressure

The availability of steam at a medium pressure of about 100 psig (7 barg), permits the efficient use of TVR either on a single or multi-effect evaporator. TVR can be applied across one, two or even three effects. This is the simplest and least costly technique for enhancing evaporator efficiency. The effectiveness declines significantly as the available steam pressure is reduced.

Material of Construction

The majority of evaporators are made in 304 or 316 stainless steel. However there are occasions that much more expensive materials of construction are required, such as 904 L, 2205, nickel, Hastelloy C, titanium and even graphite.

These expensive materials skew the economic balance, with the capital cost becoming more significant in the equation. Typically MVR would become less economic as the material cost increases, due to the size of the heat exchangers required.

PHYSICAL PROPERTIES

There are a number of physical properties that can severely influence the selection of an evaporator.

Boiling Point Elevation

A boiling point elevation of over 5°F (3°C) essentially eliminates MVR evaporators from consideration. This can be partially circumvented by using MVR as a pre concentrator. Once the concentration is sufficient to produce significant boiling point elevation, the final evaporation would be performed in a steam driven finisher.

Product Viscosity

High product viscosity of over 300 to 400 cp usually eliminates falling film evaporators in favour of forced circulation. Forced circulation requires a higher temperature difference, which eliminates MVR. TVR is used on some duties.

Product Fouling

Both MVR and TVR are not particularly suitable for duties where severe fouling of heat transfer surfaces occurs over a short time period. The performance of these evaporators will fall off more rapidly than with a multi-effect system. Forced circulation evaporators with suppressed boiling usually perform better with high fouling than film evaporators.

Temperature Sensitive Products

Many products, particularly in the food industry, are prone to degradation at elevated temperatures. The effect is usually made worse by extended residence time. This problem limits the temperature range for multi-effect systems. For example on a milk evaporator, the temperature is limited to a maximum of 160°F (71°C). Since a typical minimum boiling temperature is 120°F (49°C), there is a limited temperature difference to perform the evaporation. This type of duty is suitable for MVR since the evaporation occurs at essentially the same temperature. Although a lower operating temperature increases the size of the major equipment, MVR is the most economic solution for large capacity dairy evaporators. In many cases the selection of the energy conservation technique is obvious. However, for many applications it is necessary to evaluate a number of techniques in detail before a decision can be made.

MECHANICAL VAPOUR RECOMPRESSION EVAPORATORS

Mechanical vapour recompression (MVR) evaporation provides an extremely energy efficient technique for the concentration of solids in water. Usually the capital cost of an MVR system is higher than a comparable steam driven evaporator. However, as the capacity of the system increases the relative cost difference decreases. Although MVR evaporators are seldom chosen for small duties, the concept is often used for medium to large capacity evaporators.

MVR Defined

The basic principle of MVR is to remove the steam that is evaporated from the product, compress it in a mechanical device, and use the higher pressure steam, which has a corresponding higher saturation temperature, to provide the heating medium for the evaporation. No steam input is required once the system is operating. The small difference in enthalpy between the vapours on the condensing and boiling sides is the theoretical energy required to perform the evaporation. Essentially, the process reuses the latent heat of the vapours. The theoretical thermal efficiency of MVR can exceed that of a 100 effect evaporator, although there are a number of practical limitations, such as compressor and motor efficiencies which lower the achievable efficiency. The mechanical device can be a centrifugal compressor for applications with high compression ratios, or a fan for lower compression ratios. For either device, the drive can be an electric motor, steam turbine, internal combustion engine or gas turbine.

Thermodynamics of MVR

The process is best explained by reference to the Mollier—enthalpy/entropy diagram for steam. The vapour evaporated from the product is represented on the Mollier diagram at point A. The actual values in US and metric units are presented on Table 1a and 1b. The vapour enters the compressor at point A. The vapour is then compressed to the higher pressure, at constant entropy at point B. The compressor, which in this case is a fan, has inefficiencies which results in an increase in entropy above that of the entropy at inlet. This is represented by point C. Vapour at point C is at the required pressure for the steam jacket of the condenser. However, it is superheated and must be cooled in order to condense in the evaporator. This cooling can be performed on the heat transfer surface of the evaporator. However, since desuperheating HTC's are usually low, the desuperheating is usually performed by the introduction of a spray of condensate into the vapour duct. This condensate vaporises as the vapour is cooled back to the saturation temperature, and generates more vapour. This condition is represented by point D. At this point most of the vapour is condensed in the evaporator. However, there is an excess of vapour, which is required for heat loss and/or preheat duties. Any balance is condensed or vented.

WASTE WATER EVAPORATORS

As the world has become more concerned about the environment, there has been an increase in the application of evaporator systems to waste water treatment. These types of evaporators essentially reduce the volume of the waste by removing and recovering most of the water in the waste. In some applications, the concentrate contains product of value, which can be sold or further processed in a dryer to a solid product. In cases where the product has no value, the concentrate can be dried and the resulting product buried in a landfill. Since the condensate from these evaporators is usually quite pure, the water that is recovered can be used as boiler feed, as rinse fluid for cleaning or merely disposed into the sewer or directly into a river.

As with the processing of any waste product, there are usually severe cost restraints since, unless forced by regulation, few organisations wish to spend valuable capital on waste treatment processes. The equipment therefore has to have both low capital and operating costs.

The key points in the design of a waste water evaporator are:

- Flow rate: this is usually quite high for these evaporators.
- Solids concentration in the feed: this is usually quite low.
- Product concentration and the viscosity of the product at that concentration.
- Problems with possible volatile components in the feed.
- Corrosive nature of the feed: since may waste water evaporators have high concentration ratios, the effects of corrosion can be enhanced in the final stages of evaporation.

- Potential for fouling: this can be very serious in many cases.
- Boiling point elevation.

Because of the large duties, mechanical vapour recompression (MVR) evaporation is usually the choice. However if boiling point elevation is high, the MVR would be limited to the pre concentration and would require a separate steam powered single or multieffect finisher to arrive at the final concentration. The presence of volatile components in the feed, such as ethanol, can also limit the application of MVR. In this case, it is usually necessary to remove the volatile components in a stripper column. In a multieffect evaporator the stripper column can be placed between effects, which allows recovery of the heat needed to operate the stripper.

Brewery/Distillery Effluents

The effluents from brewery and distillery plants are often processed with evaporators to recover the water and produce a concentrated syrup, which can be sold in liquid form, or added to the spent grains prior to drying. In this case the solids have value as animal food.

Both MVR and multi-effect evaporators have been used for these types of duty. Normally falling film tubular calandrias would be used for the pre evaporator with forced circulation plate or tubular evaporators as the finisher. As in most applications the viscosity of the product at the evaporation temperature controls the point at which the material has to be processed in a forced circulation system.

The problem with these applications is that the product, which can be called stillage, spent wash, spent grains or pot ale, is extremely variable. In particular the viscosity characteristics of the concentrated liquids depend on the raw material grain. Waste water produced from plants using corn (maize) as the feed stock are relatively easy to process. However, waste water from plants which use wheat or barley as the feedstock will be far more viscous at elevated concentrations. In some cases, the viscosity characteristics will be so bad that even a forced circulation evaporator will only be able to concentrate to 35% solids. This usually means treating the feed with enzymes prior to evaporation so that a solids concentration of 45% solids can be achieved.

The higher the viscosity, the more frequently the evaporator will have to be cleaned. The accepted run time in the industry is 6 to 8 days. To achieve this, it is usually necessary to provide high recirculation around the calandrias to provide a high wetting rate and prevent burn on. On the finisher, it is occasionally necessary to provide duplex heat exchangers, so that one can be cleaned while the other is in operation.

EVAPORATOR CONTROL

The control of most chemical/industrial evaporator systems is quite simple. However, with hygienic evaporators the control is somewhat more complicated due to the need to start up, operate, shut down and then clean at quite frequent intervals. As a result sophisticated control is more likely to be needed on hygienic systems.

On almost all evaporation systems there are only two basic objectives:

- To concentrate a liquid to a pre-defined solids content.
- To process a pre-defined feed rate of raw material.

Theoretically this can be achieved with only two control loops. However in practice there are additional loops for level control and pressure control. Product concentration has been measured using refractive index, density and viscosity techniques. Over the last ten years, the use of mass flow meters for density measurement has become the standard. This type of meter provides an accurate measurement (usually out to the 4th decimal place) of both flow and density. The density measurement, which is easily converted to a solids content, can then be used to control either product removal rate from the evaporator, steam flow, or feed flow.

There are two techniques used to control evaporators, and the choice is based on the design of the evaporator. In applications where liquid recirculation is required to maintain sufficient wetting in the final stage of the evaporator, the product concentration control is simple and accurate. The procedure is to set the steam flow rate at the design value, remove product based on density in the recirculation loop, and adjust the feed flow to maintain liquid levels in the evaporator. When a higher throughput is required, then the steam rate is increased. This technique provides excellent control of the product concentration with conventional analog controllers.

For heat sensitive products, it is best to avoid recirculation whenever possible. In the case of once-through-flow in the final stage, there is no recirculation loop in which to install the transmitter and to delay discharge of product when not on specification. In this case, the method is to set the feed flow rate to the desired value and then change the energy input to produce the product concentration required. The energy input may be the steam rate or the power into the MVR. This technique does not control product quality particularly accurately, since response is slow. However it is satisfactory for most purposes, and the user can always apply more sophisticated PLC control when necessary.

Almost all evaporators will have to be cleaned at some time. Some chemical evaporators may run for months between cleaning cycle. Also with non-hygienic duties, the only requirement is to clean the heat transfer surface sufficiently to restore design performance.

In the case of hygienic evaporators, the concern is not only plant operation, but also contamination from bacteria. Typically, a hygienic evaporator will be cleaned every day.

Dairy evaporators, which are designed and constructed to 3A standards, are subject to one of the highest cleaning standards. The inspector will expect that the equipment be cleaned completely with no residue left on any surfaces. The potential labour costs to start up, shut down and go through a complex cleaning cycle, on a daily basis, are very high. A fully automatic system is therefore required to perform all these operations. These functions are ideally performed by a PLC.

Usually PLC control offers maximum throughput, maximum efficiency, constant product, and minimises startup and shutdown times. It also minimises CIP time while maximising CIP effectiveness. Most PLCs offer historical data collection so that management can continue to improve and maximise the evaporator system's performance.

PRODUCTION OF HIGH QUALITY JUICE CONCENTRATES

Changes in our lifestyles over the past twenty years have been dramatic. Not the least of these changes has been our dietary habits—influenced not only by our perceived values of diet related to general health, but also by changes in food processing technology across a very wide spectrum.

Storage of fruit before processing begins a gradual process of change from the fresh product. Breaking or peeling of fruit releases some of the natural essences even at atmospheric temperatures, and natural biochemical processes commence which affect colour and enzyme components, pectin and other characteristic properties of the fruit. The aim of food manufacturers is to produce a juice or concentrate which closely resembles the original 'fresh from the fruit'. Of all the ways we can influence this, time and temperature are paramount.

Evaporation

Evaporation is by far the most prevalent process used for the production of concentrates. It provides a highly energy efficient means of removing water and is well suited to recovering 'essence' components during the process. The problem for the equipment designer has always been one of providing a cost-effective system having low energy requirements, with acceptable concentrate quality, and along the way collecting essences in sufficiently useable quantity and quality. The ultra short time FFPE (Falling Film Plate Evaporator) was introduced by APV in the early 1970's. The patent covered a two-plate per unit design—one steam and one product—in which the product could be fed first to one half of the plate then returned in series to the other side of the plate for improved wetting without recirculation.

The most difficult design area of any falling film evaporator is the liquid distribution system which ensures an even flow of liquid over the total evaporating surface. This was achieved by an ingenious three stage process involving small pressure losses and flash vapour.

Time/temperature are markedly influenced by single pass operation in an evaporator by avoiding the use of recirculation. In the FFPE, with its two-stage design and longer flow path, recirculation is avoided on all triple effect and over systems, and even on double-effect under some temperature conditions.

This design could still be improved, however, and the FFSR (Falling Film Long Evaporator) is the current development in the plate evaporator technology. This is a divided plate design like the FFPE, but has a 50% longer flow path. This creates thinner films off the plate, with improved wetting characteristics. A special arrangement of the support pipes improves cleaning in place (CIP) of the plate, by using a disparate positioning on the plate. The FFLE is current state-of-the art technology, producing concentrates of high quality on a wide range of juices.

Essence Recovery

Distillation

Essences can be recovered by full distillation techniques with high yield on products less sensitive to temperature, such as apple and grape.

Partial condensation

The loss of, or damage to, essences from fruit commences at the moment of picking. It increases after extraction, and with any form of heating and flash vapour release. The partial condensation aroma recovery unit has provided effective and economic ways of capturing the elusive flavour components for storage and reuse with reconstituted juices or for use in the cosmetic and other industries.

The partial condensation aroma recovery unit makes use of the fact that if juice is heated in a closed system, then released into a region of pressure below the saturation point, flash vapours released will strip aroma compounds from the liquid phase into volatiles which travel with the vapours. There will be some essence components which do not volatalise and remain in the juice throughout the process, but a substantial percentage of the aromas is liberated.

If the vapours from the first 'strip' are withdrawn from the first stage of evaporation in a multi-effect system, they will be more than enough in quantity to ensure a high percentage recovery of aromas. These will go with the vapour to the heating side of the next evaporator effect to provide the energy for further evaporation. In the process, only part of the vapour is condensed. A portion, perhaps 10 or 15%, is allowed to pass through the heating side uncondensed, and then ducted to the aroma recovery system.

Because of the different boiling points of aroma compounds, most of the essences remain with the uncondensed portion. In the aroma recovery unit, a further selective condensing process takes place, which removes more of the water vapour to leave a concentrated essence. This essence is chilled and collected together with recovered components from a final vent scrubber system. It can then be stored for later use or added back to aseptically processed concentrate during the cooling stage. The temperature at which the first strip takes place varies according to the fruit. Some tropical fruits, like pineapple, are move sensitive, and temperatures above 60°C should be avoided. For apple and less sensitive fruits, temperatures in the 80s or 90s can provide higher yields without thermal degradation of the essence.

EVAPORATOR SYSTEMS

Energy Efficiency Measures

Several changes can be made to evaporator systems to improve their efficiency. Here are some of them:

- Installation of additional effects will generally improve the efficiency of an evaporator system. There is a practical limit to how many effects can be used, as each evaporation vessel must have a lower pressure than the previous effect.
- Preheating feed product reduces the heat required to achieve boiling in the evaporation vessel. This requires addition of a heat exchanger appropriate to the characteristics of the feed.
- Vapour recompression takes advantage of the significant heating value of the vapour driven out of the product. Vapour can be reused in the same evaporator by increasing its temperature and pressure close to those of the steam injected into the heat exchanger. This can be done using a steam jet or a compressor.

Operations Tips to Improve Energy Efficiency

The following list provides operating practices that can reduce energy consumption in your evaporators:

- Optimise the venting rate of non-condensable gases to reduce steam waste while maintaining appropriate evaporation vessel pressure. Non-condensable gases in the evaporation vessel increase pressure, which increases the boiling point and heat requirements.
- Maintain the optimum pressure profile as provided in the evaporator's design. Excess pressure inhibits evaporation by raising the boiling point.
- Condensed steam can be used to preheat feed product or used in the next effect of a multi-effect system. It can also be fed back to the boiler to offset the use of cold makeup water.
- Pre-concentration of the feed will reduce the energy required to operate an evaporator. For some applications, pre-concentration with separation membranes can save up to 90 per cent of energy consumption.

Maintenance Tips to Improve Energy Efficiency

Regular maintenance will help ensure that equipment serves a long, useful life and also operates efficiently. The following suggestions will help keep your evaporators operating efficiently:

- Prevent air leaks into the evaporators to minimise venting rates. Air is a noncondensable gas and has to be vented to keep evaporation vessel pressure from increasing.
- Clean heat transfer surfaces to allow the most efficient use of energy to evaporate water from the product.

- Inspect and repair or replace wet or damaged insulation as it is found. Also, make sure insulation is the appropriate thickness.
- Keep the vapour separation vessel clean to maintain product yields and pressure profiles.
- Prevent water leaks into the system to avoid diluting the product, which defeats the process.

CRYSTALLISATION IN FOODS

In the food industry, controlling crystallisation is a key factor in quality as it relates to texture, with some foods requiring the promotion of crystallisation and others its prevention. In the first publication to focus specifically on this process as it applies to food, Crystallisation in Foods covers fundamental principles in ice, sugar, and lipid crystallisation, and their applications. Crystallisation in Foods is a valuable resource for food engineers and other scientists working with crystallisation in foods, particularly in the dairy, confectionery, frozen foods, and baked goods industries.

Crystallisation is a typical downstream processing method for high quality products with high purity requirements. It is an established method used in the initial recovery of organic acids and amino acids, and more widely used for the final purification of a diverse range of compounds. Crystallisation is based on supersaturation, and crystal growth and nuclei formation processes are important aspects on this phenomena. The most common crystallisation techniques are evaporative and vacuum cooling crystallisation. Elimination of moisture is a very important step for the product to go through, since moisture is responsible for corrosion and instability of the product.

Mechanism of Crystallisation

Crystallisation is a natural phenomena that is utilised in different artificial separation and purification processes. It is also considered as a typical polishing process in bioseparation. Those processes responsible for the production of 108 T/year of different materials, including sodium and aluminium sulphates, sodium chloride and sucrose worldwide. Purification of organic liquids using crystallisation is more favourable than distillation. Crystallisation process require low temperature and low energy consumption. Compared to distillation the lateral enthalpy of crystallisation is lower than in distillation (evaporation enthalpy). Industrially crystallisation is responsible for about 70% of solids produced.

Crystals formation can be achieved from liquid and vapour phase. Supersaturation is a key parameter in crystallisation, since the more the dissolved materials in the solution the higher probability of crystal formation. Nuclei formation and crystal growth are the two stages in any crystallisation process. The rates of those two stages determine the capacity and residence time of a crystalliser. Which makes crystallisation a rate process.

Nuclei formation can be divided into two different cases, primary nucleation and secondary nucleation. Primary nucleation happens in crystal free systems, when concentration of solution reaches metastable limit. It can be homogenous which is spontaneous, or heterogenous which depends on the presence of foreign particles. Industrial perspective homogenous are very rare, because there is almost always some foreign object, like the dust, which makes crystallisation heterogenous. Secondary nucleation is a process which start to happen when there is a presence of crystals in a supersaturated liquid, beyond metastable limit. The rate of the secondary nucleation depends on the generation of the near solid phase, cluster removal and growth to form new solid phase. Most common sources for this kind of nucleation are crystal-crystal and crystal-impeller contact. Factors affecting this phenomenon are degree of agitation, degree of saturation, cooling and presence of impurities. This happens in lower supersaturation levels which makes it the main nucleation style in industry.

Crystal growth rate is the pace of transporting molecules from the solution to the critical sized crystal surface which cause the formation of crystal lattice. Surface tension of the solution and relative crystal velocity are few of the factors that affect crystal growth rate, in addition to pressure, temperature and Reynolds number. There is also nucleation rate which effects on crystal growth rate. This ratio depends on amount of nucleons which take part for crystal forms and attrition rate, what tells how easily crystals breaks and how small those broken crystals then reacts.

Classification of Crystallisation

Crystallisation has two methods: evaporative, and cooling crystallisation. These techniques are commonly used, due to their tendency for larger crystals formation. The basic principle behind these techniques is the change of temperature, which affects the evaporating/cooling rate. Supersaturation also depends on heating/cooling power, and component individual solubility. The heat effects on crystallisation process can be evaluated with either heat or enthalpy balance of process.

Crystallisers can be divided into continuous and batch crystallisers. There is possible to do crystallisation in a multiple stages. Batch processes are normally basic jacketed tanks, where different style impellers can be used. There are methods for crystal size controlling for batch crystallisation, like seeding techniques, programmed cooling and ultrasound. Seeding is the most used technique of these, and its purpose is to prevent new nuclei forming in batch process, by adding tiny seeds in the tank. This decreases time which is crystallisation takes, because now crystals don't have to form in randomly interactions, recrystallisation can start immediately.

The most used continuous crystallisation methods are forced circulation (FC), draft tube baffle (DTB) and fluidised bed (Oslo) crystallisation. With forced circulation technique you can have large or small capacity, with small or long retention time and it's very stable process. DTC method is used for producing many organic products, due its large crystal forming and its usability for soft and fragile crystals, for example amino acids.

When choosing crystallisation method, starting point is of course characters of the feed system equilibrium and production capacity. Most of the cases the focus is producing large those crystals, because those are easier to handle, more purified and there is positive impact product's marketability. After choosing the usable crystallisation method, the operation conditions have to be selected to achieve larger crystal size. These operation methods are control of supersaturation is important that it does not exceed metastable region, maximise growth rate and optimise mixing energy input so secondary nucleation is minimised. After essential mass and energy balance calculations, there should be potential crystalliser type in our mind for chosen process. When designing and testing these crystallisation equipments, kinetic and population parameters of planned process should be optimised to get final product which satisfies a customer.

In crystallisation the purity and size of the crystals can be controlled which makes it very common in different sectors of the industry. High supersaturation prerequisite is considered one of its drawbacks, since a decrease in concentration can cause the ability to recover pure materials to decrease. Another disadvantage is the requirement for large amount of solvents during the process and crystal wash. Furthermore, consecutive crystallisations are needed to achieve more pure crystals.

THEORETICAL BACKGROUND

Crystallisation is the process of forming a crystalline material from a liquid, gas or amorphous solid. The crystals thus formed have highly regular internal structure, the basis of which is called the crystal lattice. Since the formation of such a highly ordered structure prohibits foreign molecules from being incorporated into the lattice, a solid product of high purity is obtained. The simultaneous formation and purification of a solid product makes crystallisation an important operation in the process industry.

All crystallisation processes are aimed at creating a supersaturated solution or melt. The supersaturation is the driving force under whose inuence new crystals are formed and present crystals grow. For most substances, the solubility increases with increasing temperature, with sodium chloride being a notable exception.

In cooling crystallisation, the supersaturation is created by a decrease in temperature. Depending on how the solution is cooled, a different end product is obtained. The simplest way of performing a cooling crystallisation is to let a warm solution cool to the surrounding room temperature. Obviously, the cooling rate will be highest in the beginning, when there is a large temperature difference between the solution and its surroundings, and it will be lowest at the end of the crystallisation. The seed crystals will not be able to grow fast enough to consume the supersaturation created in the beginning. As a consequence, we are likely to shoot into the labile region and have nucleation. Therefore, we can expect our end product have a rather wide distribution of crystal sizes.

Chapter 17

Extruder

INTRODUCTION

Extrusion technologies are novel and versatile manufacturing technique in food industry for conveying and shaping fluid forms of processed raw materials like doughs and pastes. In 1797, Joseph Bramah from England used extrusion principle to develop hand operated piston press to extrude seamless lead pipe. Extrusion is a process of shaping by forcing softened and plasticised materials through dies or holes by pressure. Food ingredients of various types may be processed by extrusion and are referred to as extrudates. Earlier extrusion methods were simple conveying devices and became sophisticated in the last decade. Presently, processing steps include conveying, mixing, shearing, separation, heating or cooling, shaping, co-extrusion, venting volatiles and moisture, flavour generation, encapsulation and sterilisation. Extrusion application of food industry includes ready to eat breakfast cereals, baby foods, pet foods and confectionary products. It was found that the extrusion process is continuous in nature. In order to obtain the desired output, the process variables should be standardised.

FOOD EXTRUDER

Food extruder is equipment used for the shaping and restructuring process for food ingredients. Extrusion processing equipment has become popular in many food industries throughout the world. The screw is the heart of the extrusion process and its design and speed of rotation greatly influence the extrusion operation. The screw has got three functions: conveying, shearing, heating and mixing. The feeder section accepts moistened granular feed materials and conveys them down the length of the screw to the exit. As the feed materials move along the screw, they encounter great friction, restriction or compression, causing them to completely fill the channel or the space existing between the screw flights. The energy necessary to make the viscous materials flow is supplied by a large drive motor turning the screw. Dies are provided at the exit to attain desired shape of the material and is cut into desired length using a cutter attachment fitted at the end of the discharge. Extruders come in several designs, dependent upon their application. Some extruders are designed simply to convey the raw materials, while others are designed to mix and knead them; most, however, are designed to impart mechanical and thermal energy to the raw materials to bring about desired physico-chemical changes.

Extruders can be broadly categorised on the basis of.

Method of Operation of Extruders

- Cold extruders.
- Hot extruders (extrusion cooking).

Method of Construction of Extruders

Single- or twin- screw extruders

The most commonly used extruders are single and twin-screw. Extruders with more than two screws have been used in the plastics industry but not in food processing.

Extruders are composed of five main parts (Fig. 17.1):

1. Pre-conditioning system.
2. Feeding system.
3. Screw or worm.
4. Barrel.
5. Die and the cutting mechanism.

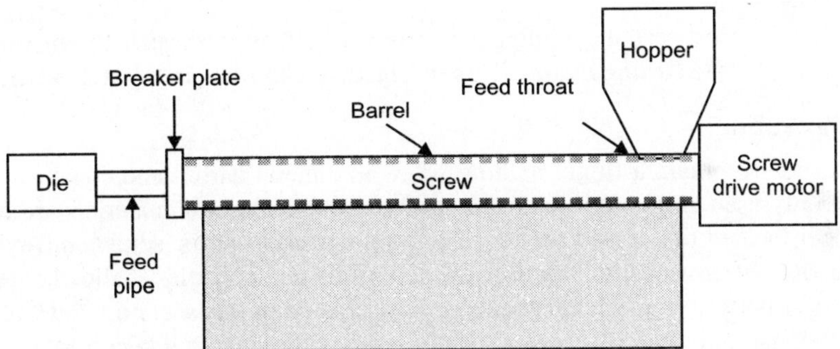

Fig. 17.1: Different parts of extruder.

Also, they can vary with respect to screw, barrel and die configuration. The selection of each of these items will depend on the raw material used and the final product desired.

Pre-conditioning

Pre-conditioning with steam or water has always been an important part of the extrusion process. Pre-conditioning is not applied to all extrusion processes. In general, this step is applied when moisture contents around 20 to 30% and long residence times of the material are used. Preconditioning favours uniform particle hydration, reduces retention times within the extruder and increases throughput, increasing the life of the equipment, due to a reduction in the wearing of barrel and screw components, also reducing the costs of energy involved in the process.

Feeding system

It is necessary to guarantee a constant and non-interrupted feeding of the raw materials into the extruder for an efficient and uniform functioning of the extrusion process.

Screw

The screw of the extruder is certainly its most important component, not only to determine cooking degree, gelatinisation and dextrinisation of starch and protein denaturation, but also to ensure final product quality screws can be mono-piece (composed of a unique piece) or multipiece (composed of various elements) screw elements can vary in number and shapes, each segment is designed for a specific purpose. Some elements only convey raw or pre-conditioned material into the extruder barrel, while other segments compress and degas the feedstock. Others must promote kneading, backflow and shear.

Barrel or sleeves

The barrel is divided into feeding, kneading an The sleeves surrounding the screw can be solid, but they are often jacketed to permit circulating of steam or superheated oil for heating or water or air for cooling, thus enabling the precise adjustment of the temperature in the various zones of the extruder.

Die

The die presents two main functions: give shape to the final product and promote resistance to material flow within the extruder permitting an increase in internal pressure. The die can present various designs and number of orifices.

Cutting Mechanism

The cutting mechanism must permit obtaining final products with uniform size. Product size is determined by the rotation speed of the cutting blades. This mechanism can be horizontal or vertical.

Single screw extruder

Single screw extruders contain a single rotating screw in a metal barrel, and come in varying patterns. The most commonly used single scews have a constant pitch. The raw materials are fed in a granular form at the hopper located in the feed section. The rotating action of the screw conveys the material to the transition section. In the transition section, the screw channel becomes shallower and the material is compacted. A major portion of mechanical energy is dissipated in this section, which results in a rise in temperature of the material. Starch becomes gelatinised, and the material becomes more cohesive. It is transported further by the metering section and pushed through the die opening. The barrels of single-screw extruders usually have helical or axial grooves on inner surfaces. This helps to convey and mix the material more effectively.

Twin screw extruder

Twin-screw extruders are composed of two axis that rotate inside a single barrel; usually the internal surface of the barrel of twin-screw extruders is smooth. However, this type of extruder is little used in the food industry, even though they present more efficient displacement properties. When the material enters the barrel, the ingredients are thoroughly mixed before further processing in the other zones of the extruder. In this initial step, the screw is designed with a large screw channel depth to provide enough space between the root of the screw and the barrel for sufficient mixing to take place, and often, the screws are reverse-threaded to permit intensive mixing and longer residence times before delivery. In the next zone, the diameter of the root increases rapidly while the channel depth becomes shallower in order to provide material cooking, thus increasing the pressure applied to the product, and the starchy content of food is gelatinised and the proteinaceous material denatured.

Comparison of single and twin screw extruders

The main difference between single and twin screw extruder is the conveying mechanism. In a single screw extruder, the conveying action is the result of the friction effects; the friction between screw and the product and the friction between barrel and product. The single screw extruder needs the barrel wall for the good conveying action. The product may co-rotate along with the screw. Whereas, in a twin screw extruder, the product is enclosed between the intermeshing screws and barrel and is conveyed positively towards the die. Due to such positive displacement action, the product is prevented from co-rotating with the screw. In twin screw extruder the friction at the barrel is of less importance. A single-screw extruder is the simplest food manufacturing device and is very economic to operate. Jianshe and Andrew suggested that single-screw extruders are only suitable for manufacturing of foods that contain less than 4% fat, 10% sugar and 30% water. The presence of high contents of fat, sugar and moisture will significantly reduce the friction between food material and the inner barrel surface and, therefore, impair the mixing and flow of food. Twin-screw extruders consist of two intermeshing screws either co-rotating or counter-rotating against each other. They have much higher mixing capability than single-screw extruders. One significant advantage of twin-screw extruders is the much extended product range. Food that contain 20% fat, 40% sugar and 65% moisture and can be handled by a twin-screw extruder.

Advantages of extrusion cooking

A wide range of products, many of which cannot be produced easily by any other process, is possible by changing the ingredients, extruder operating conditions and dies. Lower processing cost of extrusion and higher productivity than other cooking and forming processes. Extruder can operate continuously with high throughput product quality: Extrusion cooking involves high temperatures applied for a short time, retaining many heat sensitive components of a food. The whole process is environmental friendly, as low-moisture process, extrusion cooking does not produce significant process effluents, reducing water treatment costs and levels of environmental pollution.

Disadvantages of extrusion cooking

Single-screw extruders have relatively poor mixing ability, they are usually supplied with premixed material which often has been preconditioned with added steam and water. Since the single-screw extruder has only one shaft, it will not self-clean as completely at the end of the operation. 'Wet extruders' have higher capital investment than 'dry extruders'.

Physico-chemical Changes during Extrusion

The most used raw materials in the extrusion process are starch and protein based materials. The structure of the extruded products may be formed from starch or protein polymers. Most products, such as breakfast cereals, snacks and biscuits are formed from starch, while protein is used to produce products that have meat-like characteristics and that are used either as full or partial replacements for meat in ready meals, dried foods and many pet food products.

Major changes occurs during extrusion process are:

- Changes in starch.
- Changes in proteins.
- Changes in lipid.
- Changes in fibre.

Raw materials

In general, the chemical or physico-chemical changes in biopolymers that can occur during extrusion cooking include: binding, cleavage, loss of native conformation, fragmention, recombination and thermal degradation. The structure of an extruded product is created by forming a fluid melt from a polymer and blowing bubbles of water vapour into the fluid to form a foam. The bubbles rapidly expand as the super heated water is released very quickly at atmospheric pressure.

Changes in starches

The major difference between extrusion processing and conventional food processing is that in the former starch gelatinisation occurs at much lower moisture contents (12–22%). Once inside the extruder, and at relatively high temperatures, the starch granules melt and become soft, besides changing their structure that is compressed to a flattened form. The application of heat, the action of shear on the starch granule and water content destroy the organised molecular structure, also resulting in molecular hydrolysis of the material. The starch polymers are then dispersed and degraded to form a continuous fluid melt. The fluid polymer continuum retains water vapour bubbles and stretches during extrudate expansion until the rupture of cell structure. The starch polymer cell walls recoil and stiffen as they cool to stabilise the extrudate structure. Finally, the starch polymer becomes glassy as moisture is removed, forming a hard brittle texture.

Changes in protein

Proteins are biopolymers with a great number of chemical groups when compared to polysaccharides and are therefore more reactive and undergo many changes during the extrusion process, with the most important being denaturation. During extrusion, disulphide bonds are broken and may reform. Electrostatic and hydrophobic interactions favour the formation of insoluble aggregates. The creation of new peptide bonds during extrusion is controversial. High molecular weight proteins can dissociate into smaller subunits. Enzymes, also proteins, lose their activity after being submitted to the extrusion process due to high temperatures and shear.

Changes in lipids

Fats and oils can be described as lipids. Lipids have a powerful influence in extrusion cooking processes by acting as lubricants, because they reduce the friction between particles in the mix and between the screw and barrel surfaces and the fluid melt.

Changes in fibres

Research has shown that cooking fibres by extrusion can produce changes in their structural characteristics and physico-chemical properties, with the main effect being a redistribution of insoluble fibre to soluble fibre. This effect would be the result of the rupture of covalent and noncovalent bonds between carbohydrates and proteins associated to the fibre, resulting in smaller molecular fragments, that would be more soluble.

Influence of Extrusion Cooking on Moisture and Temperature

In the extrusion process of expanded products with low moisture, the expansion of the final product is inversely related to the moisture of the raw material and directly related to the increase in extrusion temperature; however, the effect of moisture is more significant. In high moisture extrudates, expansion occurs when the product exits the die, but the structure collapses before the necessary cooling, resulting in a dense and hard product. Another important parameter for extrudate expansion is process temperature. Products do not expand if the temperature does not reach 100°C. Expansion increases with the increase in temperature when moisture content of the material is close to 20%, due to lower viscosity, permitting a more rapid expansion of the molten mass, or due to an increase in water vapour pressure. At low extrusion temperatures, expansion is reduced because starch is not completely molten. Radial expansion degree is proportional to temperature up to a certain value, decreasing at much higher temperatures. The reduction of expansion at very high temperatures is attributed to an increase in dextrinisation, weakening starch structure.

Influence of Extrusion Cooking on Various Parameters

Three main factors of extruded product on consumer view are:

- Product quality.
- Nutritional quality.
- Microbiological quality.

Influence on product quality

Extrusion-cooking has an important influence on product quality, emphasising features like expansion, texture, shelf-life, colour and flavour. Products obtained with high temperatures and short extrusion process times normally present a porous, open structure, what confers to them a 'crunchy' texture. Colour in extruded products is influenced by temperature, raw material composition, residence time, pressure and shear force.

Effect of extrusion on nutrition quality

The effects of extrusion cooking on nutritional quality are ambiguous. Benefits include destruction of antinutritional factors, gelatinisation of starch, increased soluble dietary fibre and reduction of lipid oxidation. Starch digestibility is largely dependent on complete gelatinisation. High starch digestibility is essential for specialised nutritional foods such as infant and weaning foods. Creation of resistant starch by extrusion may have value in reduced calorie products. The nutritional value of vegetable proteins is generally enhanced by mild extrusion cooking conditions due to the increase in digestibility, probably a result of protein denaturation and the inactivation of enzyme inhibitors present in raw materials, by the exposure of new active sites for enzyme attack.

Influence on microbiological quality

One of the most important consumer requirements is the microbiological safety of food products. Most conventional extruded products such as snack foods and breakfast cereals are safe to eat because the raw materials are subjected to high temperatures (higher than 130°C) and the water activity temperatures (0.1–0.4) of the product is low because the product is dried to a moisture content of less than five per cent. Although it is well known that most vegetative organisms, yeast and molds are destroyed under typical extrusion conditions (55–145°C). Figure 17.2 shows a typical extrusion processing. The process begins with characterising and receiving the raw ingredients. The raw ingredients used are crucial to the product consistency at the end of the processing line. The raw ingredients then undergo mixing and/or pre-conditioning, which can be done with the equipment such as ribbon blenders and preconditioners to ensure uniformity as they enter the extruder. However, mixing and preconditioning is optional for certain products.

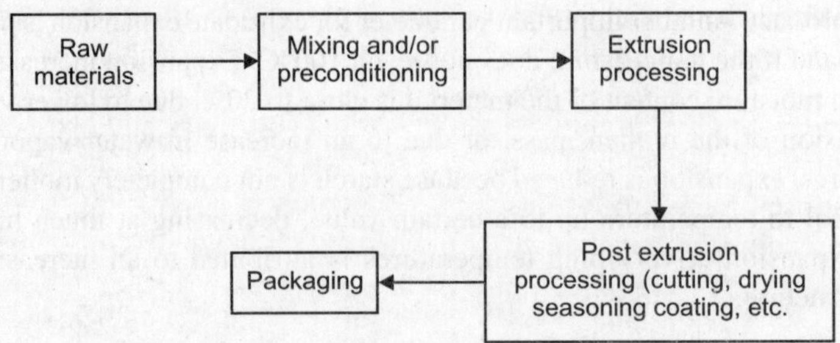

Fig. 17.2: A typical extrusion processing.

Extrusion processing then follows, which is the main cooking step where the raw ingredients are transformed into the cooked and formed products. Post-extrusion processing operations, such as cutting the extruded products into appropriate sizes, drying the products to the desired moisture, as well as seasoning or coating to provide the desired flavour and taste to the products before they go on to packaging. Along with these major sets of processing, there may be additional steps depending of the type of products being produced and their intended uses.

Within the extrusion processing step, the food ingredients are subjected to high shear, temperature, and pressure for a short period of time. This helps to transform the ingredients from solid powders to a melt state inside of the extruder. The melted ingredients are then forced through a die at the end of the extruder into the atmosphere. The melt coming out of the extruder encounters a sudden drop in pressure, resulting in rapid expansion as well as a decrease in temperature, helping it to transform into a cooked product. The final quality and texture of the extruded product depends on various factors, including the ingredient mixture and its properties, extrusion processing conditions, and post-processing conditions. Because of the great flexibility of extrusion processing, it has found very diverse applications in the food industry, some of which can be seen in Table 17.1.

Table 17.1: Applications of extrusion cooking.

Bread crumbs	Degermination of spices
Precooked starches	Flavor encapsulation
Anhydrous decrystallisation of sugar to make confectioneries	Enzymatic liquefaction of starch for fermentation into ethanol
Chocolate conching	Quick-cooking pasta products
Pre-treated malt and starch for brewing	Oilseed treatment for subsequent oil extraction
Stabilisation of rice bran	Preparation of specific doughs
Gelatin gel confectioneries	Destruction of aflatoxins or gossypol in peanut meal
Caramel, licorice, chewing gum	Precooked soy flours
Corn and potato snack	Gelation of vegetable proteins
Coextruded snacks with internal filling	Restructuring of minced meat
Flat crispbread, biscuits, crackers, cookies	Preparation of sterile baby foods
Pre-cooked flours, instant rice puddings	Oilseed meals
Cereal-based instant dried soup mixes or drink bases	Sterile chees processes
Transformation of casein into caseinate	Animal feeds
Pre-cooked instant weaning foods or gruels	Texturised vegetable proteins

Extrusion processing is beneficial largely because of its applicability in various food processes, its flexibility, its reduced cost benefits, high production rate, and quality products compared to other ordinary food processes.

Versatility

Extrusion can be utilised for plenty of different food products and easily be modified by changing control parameters to adjust for materials that are challenging or conditions that are unattainable with general food processing.

Reduced cost

Extrusion processing has a lower cost range compared to other food processes. Its one-step, continuous system requires little labour, and the energy consumption of the extruder is relatively low.

High output

Owing to a continuous extrusion process, the extruder serves a high productivity system, which can provide higher efficiency for the food manufacturing process.

Product quality

Extrusion can increase starch and protein digestibility by gelatinising and denaturing, respectively. It also blocks and reduces contaminant microorganisms.

Extruder Parts

The major parts of an extruder include the feeder, barrel, screw(s), and die, although many more parts can be added for increased product versatility. The feeder is used for continuously feeding the mixture into the extruder at a constant rate to ensure consistency. Feeders often feed the material in either gravimetrically or volumetrically and it is possible to use more than one feeder at a time for different ingredients. The barrel encases the screw or a set of screws. Often, the barrel is jacketed for heating and for cooling. The heating can also be accomplished by providing electrical heating units on the barrel or by steam. The inner layer of barrels is often smooth in twin-screw systems while it may be grooved or fluted in single screw systems. The barrel may also have various injection ports or additional feeding ports along it. Injection ports may be used for water or other liquid ingredients while added feeding ports may have additional powder ingredients being forced in through the side of the barrel so they experience less cooking by by-passing a large section of the extruder. The role of the screws is to assist in imparting shear to the ingredient mixture and forcing the dough of the mixed ingredients out from the extruder through the die. The screws are also responsible for the buildup of pressure that occurs at the end of the extruder as well as added mixing of the ingredients. The die functions to hold the material in the screws, providing time for the screws to impart shear energy onto the sample. The die also controls the final shape of the product and can be varied tremendously. The last essential part of the extruder is the motor, which provides the energy needed to rotate the screws. Other optional parts may include a preconditioner, which can be used to pre-hydrate the ingredient mix and in some cases pre-cook the materials before feeding into the extruder. A die cutter is also frequently used to help cut the final extrudates coming out of the die.

Extrusion as MIMO System

Extrusion can be considered as a multiple input and multiple output (MIMO) system. Various extrusion processing parameters can be broadly classified into three categories: (i) independent parameters (input parameters), (ii) system parameters (dependent parameters) and (iii) product properties (output parameters).

Independent parameters

Independent parameters are the parameters that the extruder operator has direct control over. These include the raw material (ingredient) properties and the extrusion operation parameters such as feed rate, barrel temperatures, screw configurations, screw speeds, die dimensions, and others. By modifying the independent parameters, the operator can achieve changes in the system parameters and final product properties.

System parameters

System parameters are the ones that the extruder operator does not have direct control over, but the operator can influence them by changing the independent parameters. The mean residence time, residence time distribution, back pressure, motor torque, and specific mechanical energy being applied to the material are the system parameters that can be measured. These impact the final product properties, but can only be modified indirectly through varying the independent parameters.

Product properties

Product properties are parameters that help describe the final extruded product quality. This can include, physical properties (expansion ratio, density, etc.), chemical properties (water absorption and solubility, etc.) and sensory properties (crispness, crunchiness, texture, etc.). Describing extrusion processing with the MIMO system helps to control the extrusion process to manufacture food products consistently.

Direct-Expanded Food Products

The most common food products that are manufactured by direct expansion phenomenon include puffed snacks, breakfast cereals, and others. The majority of these direct-expanded products have a higher percentage of carbohydrates. The major source of these carbohydrates include cereal grains (such as corn, rice, and wheat), plant tubers (such as potato), and pulses (such as peas), among others. It is well researched that among the different biopolymers, starch expands the most in extrusion. Proteins generally tend to inhibit expansion due to their inherent nature to denature and texturise during extrusion processing. Fibres (specifically the insoluble fibre) are known to inhibit expansion as they do not go through phase change when s ıbjected to heat and shear like the starches and proteins. As the melt material exits the dies, the expansion process is initially caused by a sudden drop in pressure. This causes the liquid water in the melt to convert to steam. The steam then accumulates into small pockets and expands outward in all directions, causing products to expand radially and longitudinally from the die. After the initial expansion, the product continues to cool, resulting in a decrease in expansion, predominantly in the cells around the edge of the formed extrudate. Various extrusion conditions, as well as ingredients, can be used to process and change the type of structures being formed. Direct expanded products provide a great opportunity for the food industry to deliver nutritious and fun foods to consumers. Consumer demand for higher quality food products that have a great texture and high nutrient value is increasing. Extrusion processing has proven to be a very practical and economical processing tool to produce various food products that the consumers enjoy. With its ease and flexibility, extrusion has a great promise to continue to be a valuable processing technology for the food industry. As research continues in extrusion, more methods on how to utilise it effectively, and alter it further, will continue to drive the technology forward and expand the scope of possible products that can be produced.

RECENT DEVELOPMENTS IN DAIRY, BREAKFAST CEREAL AND PET FOOD INDUSTRY

Extruders permit the production of many foods of nutritional importance. The ability of extruders to blend diverse ingredients to make novel foods.

Some of the recent application of extruders are given below:

1. Dairy
2. Breakfast cereal
3. Pet foods

Extrusion in dairy industry

Milk protein posses health benefits and desirable functional properties. When protein is subjected for mechanical shear, considerable changes in the molecular structures of the protein is seen. This changes leads to a formation of new protein-based food product known as 'Texurisation'. Texturisation stretches and shears the protein to form a new fibre-bundle like structure which withstands - hydration, cooking and other procedures.

Extrusion for breakfast cereals

Basic processes of making breakfast cereals include flaking, oven, gun puffing, baking, shredding and direct expansion (extrusion cooking), which convert raw and dense grains (7.7 kg/100 cm^3) into friable, crunchy or chewable products with the density of 0.6 to 1.6 kg/100 cm^3. But extrusion process combines all the above processes and presents advantages over the conventional processes. Meat analogues increase in vegetarians, lead to a preparation of protein incorporated meat extenders and meat analogues which can be obtained from extrusion process. Vegetable protein posses a charecteristic appearance and texture similar to fibrilar structure of meat.

Thus, meat extenders are obtained from thermoplastic extrusion at low moisture contents (20–35%) and meat analogues are obtained at high moisture contents (50–70%). The main vegetable proteins used to prepare meat analogues are legumes, soyabeans, common beans and peas.

Extrusion cooking of cereals with fish

Research on extrusion of fish muscle started in the 1980's. A number of studies have reported successful incorporation of fish flesh or fish powder into starch-based materials by extrusion processes to produce nutritious extruded products that were acceptable by consumers. Choudhury and others undertaken several studies to develop dry expanded snack food products from fish mince and starchy ingredients using single and twin-screw extruders and they found that incorporation of fish hydrolysates along with cereals improve the nutritional quality of extrudates. Rice flour and varying amounts (10–35%) of deboned minced carp were coextruded resulting in a precooked blend which had a shelf life of six months stored at room temperature. Rhee and others successfully developed a snack food by extrusion of minced catfish with corn and defatted soya flour. Gry standardised conditions for best extrusion using cod mince, wheat flour and potato flour. Murray and others reported that texture of the extruded product was improved by the addition of fish which also reduced the temperature required for optimal texturisation during extrusion. During twin-screw extrusion of rice flour and pink salmon blends, the influence of location and spacing of reverse screw and kneading elements on specific mechanical energy input and product attributes were studied by Binoy and others. Thermal and physico-chemical properties of rice flour fish mince based extruded products were studied by Dileep and others. The advantages of developing fish-based extruded products will help in supplying nutritious and balanced diets to undernourished people in developing countries. Clayton and Das suggested that fish with cereal flours offers shelf stable foods with better nutritional quality.

Pet foods and animals foods

Extrusion is not only used to prepare food for humans but also used to prepare semi-moist and dry expanded pet foods, aquatic food, and foods for laboratory animals. Whereas, dog and cat foods are directly extruded and dried. Feed for ornamental fish, high-grade complete feeds to maintaining the health, foods for exotic species in aquariums can also be made from extrusion process. This permits better utilisation of available cereal grains, vegetable and animal proteins.

To sum up, extruders permit the production of many foods of nutritional importance. The ability of extruders to blend diverse ingredient in novel foods can be exploited in the development of functional foods. Traditional snacks or breakfast cereal can be enhanced by the addition of extra fibre or whole grain flour as ingredients. During extrusion, transformed into palatable cereal based products that also promote beneficial physiological effects. Consumers are discriminating, Consumers want healthy nutrition, Consumers want fair prices. Rightly so! extrusion systems meet the current, constantly changing requirements – flexibly, efficiently and economically.

Chapter 18

Drying

INTRODUCTION

Drying is a method of food preservation that works by removing water from the food, which inhibits the growth of micro-organisms and hinders quality decay. Drying food using Sun and wind to prevent spoilage has been practised since ancient times. Water is usually removed by evaporation (air drying, Sun drying, smoking or wind drying) but, in the case of freeze-drying, food is first frozen and then the water is removed by sublimation. Bacteria yeasts and molds need the water in the food to grow. Drying effectively prevents them from surviving in the food.

METHODS OF DRYING

There are many different methods for drying, each with their own advantages for particular applications. Some of the important methods of drying are given below:

1. Drum drying.
2. Freeze drying.
3. Shelf dryers.
4. Spray drying.
5. Sunlight.
6. Commercial food dehydrators.
7. Household oven.

Drum Drying

Drum drying is a method used for drying out liquids, for example, milk is applied as a thin film to the surface of a heated drum, and the dried milk solids are then scraped off with a knife. Powdered milk made by drum drying tends to have a cooked flavour, due to caramelisation caused by greater heat exposure. Compared to spray drying, drum drying is a more intense heat treatment which results in more denatured proteins. The powder is less soluble as a result. The temperature uniformity of the heated roller/drum is poor so spray drying results in better quality milk powder.

Other products such as drum drying can be used are for example starches, breakfast cereals, baby food, instant mashed potatoes to make them cold water soluble.

Freeze Drying

Freeze drying (also known as lyophilisation or cryodesiccation) is a dehydration process typically used to preserve a perishable material or make the material more convenient for transport. Freeze drying works by freezing the material and then reducing the surrounding pressure and adding enough heat to allow the frozen water in the material to sublime directly from the solid phase to the gas phase.

Freeze drying process

There are four stages in the complete drying process: pre-treatment, freezing, primary drying, and secondary drying.

Pretreatment: Pretreatment includes any method of treating the product prior to freezing. This may include concentrating the product, formulation revision (i.e. addition of components to increase stability and/or improve processing), decreasing a high vapour pressure solvent or increasing the surface area. In many instances the decision to pretreat a product is based on theoretical knowledge of freeze-drying and its requirements, or is demanded by cycle time or product quality considerations. Methods of pretreatment include: Freeze concentration, solution phase concentration, formulation to preserve product appearance, formulation to stabilise reactive products, formulation to increase the surface area, and decreasing high vapour pressure solvents.

Freezing: In a lab, this is often done by placing the material in a freeze-drying flask and rotating the flask in a bath, called a shell freezer, which is cooled by mechanical refrigeration, dry ice and methanol or liquid nitrogen. On a larger scale, freezing is usually done using a freeze-drying machine. In this step, it is important to cool the material below its triple point, the lowest temperature at which the solid and liquid phases of the material can coexist. This ensures that sublimation rather than melting will occur in the following steps. Larger crystals are easier to freeze-dry. To produce larger crystals, the product should be frozen slowly or can be cycled up and down in temperature. This cycling process is called annealing. However, in the case of food or objects with formerly-living cells, large ice crystals will break the cell walls (a problem discovered, and solved, by Clarence Birdseye), resulting in the destruction of more cells, which can result in increasingly poor texture and nutritive content. In this case, the freezing is done rapidly, in order to lower the material to below its eutectic point quickly, thus avoiding the formation of ice crystals. Usually, the freezing temperatures are between –50° and –80°C. The freezing phase is the most critical in the whole freeze-drying process, because the product can be spoiled if badly done. Amorphous materials do not have a eutectic point, but they do have a critical point, below which the product must be maintained to prevent melt-back or collapse during primary and secondary drying.

Primary drying: During the primary drying phase, the pressure is lowered (to the range of a few millibars), and enough heat is supplied to the material for the water to sublime. The amount of heat necessary can be calculated using the sublimating molecules latent heat of sublimation. In this initial drying phase, about 95 per cent of the water in the material is sublimated. This phase may be slow (can be several days in the industry), because, if too much heat is added, the material's structure could be altered. In this phase, pressure is controlled through the application of partial vacuum. The vacuum speeds sublimation, making it useful as a deliberate drying process. Furthermore, a cold condenser chamber and/or condenser plates provide a surface(s) for the water vapour to resolidify on. This condenser plays no role in keeping the material frozen, rather, it prevents water vapour from reaching the vacuum pump, which could degrade the pump's performance. Thus, the condenser temperatures are typically below –50°C (–60°F). It is important to note that, in this range of pressure, the heat is brought mainly by conduction or radiation, the convection effect is considered to be inefficient.

Secondary drying: The secondary drying phase aims to remove unfrozen water molecules, since the ice was removed in the primary drying phase. This part of the freeze-drying process is governed by the material's adsorption isotherms. In this phase, the temperature is raised higher than in the primary drying phase, and can even be above 0°C, to break any physico-chemical interactions that have formed between the water molecules and the frozen material. Usually the pressure is also lowered in this stage to encourage desorption (typically in the range of microbars or fractions of a pascal). However, there are products that benefit from increased pressure as well. After the freeze drying process is complete, the vacuum is usually broken with an inert gas, such as nitrogen, before the material is sealed. At the end of the operation, the final residual water content in the product is extremely low, around 1 to 4 per cent.

Properties of freeze-dried products: If a freeze-dried substance is sealed to prevent the reabsorption of moisture, the substance may be stored at room temperature without refrigeration, and be protected against spoilage for many years. Preservation is possible because the greatly reduced water content inhibits the action of micro-organisms and enzymes that would normally spoil or degrade the substance.

Freeze drying also causes less damage to the substance than other dehydration methods using higher temperatures. Freeze drying does not usually cause shrinkage or toughening of the material being dried. In addition, flavours, smells and nutritional content generally remain unchanged, making the process popular for preserving food. However, water is not the only chemical capable of sublimation, and the loss of other volatile compounds such as acetic acid (vinegar) and alcohols can yield undesirable results.

Freeze-dried products can be rehydrated (reconstituted) much more quickly and easily because the process leaves microscopic pores. The pores are created by the ice crystals that sublimate, leaving gaps or pores in their place. This is especially important when it comes to pharmaceutical uses. Freeze drying can also be used to increase the shelf-life of some pharmaceuticals for many years.

Applications of freeze drying: Freeze drying is used to preserve food, the resulting product being very lightweight. The process has been popularised in the forms of freeze-dried ice cream, an example of astronaut food. It is also widely used to produce essences or flavourings to add to food. Because of its light weight per volume of reconstituted food, freeze dried product is also popular and convenient for hikers. More dried food can be carried per the same weight of wet food, and has the benefit of 'long-life' compared to wet food that will go off. The hikers then reconstituted the food with water available at point of use. Instant coffee is sometimes freeze-dried, despite the high costs of the freeze-driers used. The coffee is often dried by vapourisation in a hot air flow, or by projection on hot metallic plates. Freeze-dried fruit is used in some breakfast cereal. Culinary herbs are also freeze-dried, although air-dried herbs are far more common and less expensive.

Freeze drying equipment

There are essentially three categories of freeze-driers: The rotary evaporator freeze-drier, the manifold freeze-drier, and the tray freeze-drier. Rotary freeze-driers are usually used with liquid products, such as pharmaceutical solutions and tissue extracts. Manifold freeze-driers are usually used when drying a large amount of small containers and the product will be used in a short period of time. A manifold drier will dry the product to less than 5 per cent moisture content. Without heat, only primary drying (removal of the unbound water) can be achieved. A heater must be added for secondary drying, which will remove the bound water and will produce a lower moisture content.

Tray freeze-driers are more sophisticated and are used to dry a variety of materials. A tray freeze-drier is used to produce the driest product for long-term storage. A tray freeze-drier allows the product to be frozen in place and performs both primary (unbound water removal) and secondary (bound water removal) freeze-drying, thus producing the driest possible end-product. Tray freeze-driers can dry products in bulk or in vials. When drying in vials, the freeze-drier is supplied with a stoppering mechanism that allows a stopper to be pressed into place, sealing the vial before it is exposed to the atmosphere. This is used for long-term storage, such as vaccines. Improved freeze drying techniques are being developed to extend the range of products that can be freeze dried, to improve the quality of the product, and to produce the product faster with less labour.

Spray Drying

Spray drying is a method of producing a dry powder from a liquid or slurry by rapidly drying with a hot gas. This is the preferred method of drying of many thermally-sensitive materials such as foods and pharmaceuticals. A consistent particle size distribution is a reason for spray drying some industrial products such as catalysts. Air is the heated drying media, however, if the liquid is a flammable solvent such as ethanol or the product is oxygen-sensitive then nitrogen is used.

All spray dryers use some type of atomiser or spray nozzle to disperse the liquid or slurry into a controlled drop size spray. The most common of these are rotary nozzles and single-fluid pressure swirl nozzles. Alternatively, for some applications two-fluid or ultrasonic nozzles are used. Depending on the process needs drop sizes from 10 to 500 micrometres can be achieved with the appropriate choices. The most common applications are in the 100 to 200 micrometre diameter range. The dry powder is often free-flowing. The hot drying gas can be passed as a co-current or counter-current flow to the atomiser direction. The co-current flow enables the particles to have a lower residence time within the system and the particle separator (typically a cyclone device) operates more efficiently. The counter-current flow method enables a greater residence time of the particles in the chamber and usually is paired with a fluidised bed system.

Alternatives to spray dryers are:

1. Freeze dryer: A more-expensive batch process for products that degrade in spray drying. Dry product is not free-flowing.
2. Drum dryer: A less-expensive continuous process for low-value products, creates flakes instead of free-flowing powder.
3. Pulse combustion dryer: A less-expensive continuous process that can handle higher viscosities and solids loading than a spray dryer, and that sometimes gives a freeze-dry quality powder that is free-flowing.

Spray dryer

A spray dryer is a device used in spray drying. It takes a liquid stream and separates the solute or suspension as a solid and the solvent into a vapour. The solid is usually collected in a drum or cyclone. The liquid input stream is sprayed through a nozzle into a hot vapour stream and vapourised. Solids form as moisture quickly leaves the droplets. A nozzle is usually used to make the droplets as small as possible, maximising heat transfer and the rate of water vapourisation. Droplet sizes can range from 20 to 180 μm depending on the nozzle.

Spray dryers can dry a product very quickly compared to other methods of drying. They also turn a solution, or slurry into a dried powder in a single step, which can be advantageous for profit maximisation and process simplification.

Micro-encapsulation: Spray drying often is used as an encapsulation technique by the food and other industries. A substance to be encapsulated (the load) and an amphipathic carrier (usually some sort of modified starch) are homogenised as a suspension in water (the slurry). The slurry is then fed into a spray drier, usually a tower heated to temperatures well over the boiling point of water. As the slurry enters the tower, it is atomised. Partly because of the high surface tension of water and partly because of the hydrophobic/hydrophilic interactions between the amphipathic carrier, the water, and the load, the atomised slurry forms micelles. The small size of the drops (averaging 100 micrometres in diameter) results in a relatively large surface area which dries quickly. As the water dries, the carrier forms a hardened shell around the load.

Load loss is usually a function of molecular weight. That is, lighter molecules tend to boil off in larger quantities at the processing temperatures. Loss is minimised industrially by spraying into taller towers. A larger volume of air has a lower average humidity as the process proceeds. By the osmosis principle, water will be encouraged by its difference in fugacities in the vapour and liquid phases to leave the micelles and enter the air. Therefore, the same percentage of water can be dried out of the particles at lower temperatures if larger towers are used. Alternatively, the slurry can be sprayed into a partial vacuum. Since the boiling point of a solvent is the temperature at which the vapour pressure of the solvent is equal to the ambient pressure, reducing pressure in the tower has the effect of lowering the boiling point of the solvent.

The application of the spray drying encapsulation technique is to prepare 'dehydrated' powders of substances which do not have any water to dehydrate. For example, instant drink mixes are spray dries of the various chemicals which make up the beverage. The technique was once used to remove water from food products, for instance, in the preparation of dehydrated milk. Because the milk was not being encapsulated and because spray drying causes thermal degradation, milk dehydration and similar processes have been replaced by other dehydration techniques. Skim milk powders are still widely produced using spray drying technology around the world, typically at high solids concentration for maximum drying efficiency. Thermal degradation of products can be overcome by using lower operating temperatures and larger chamber sizes for increased residence times.

Spray drying applications

1. Food: Milk powder, coffee, tea, eggs, cereal, spices, flavourings.
2. Pharmaceutical: Antibiotics, medical ingredients, additives.
3. Industrial: Paint pigments, ceramic materials, catalyst supports.

Solar Drying Technology for Food Preservation

Preserving fruits, vegetables, grains, and meat has been practiced in many parts of the world for thousands of years. Methods of preservation include: canning, freezing, pickling, curing (smoking or salting), and drying. Food spoilage is caused by the action of molds, yeasts, bacteria, and enzymes. The drying process removes enough moisture from food to greatly decrease these destructive effects.

***Moisture content*:** The moisture content of fresh foods ranges from 20 to 90 per cent. Foods require different levels of dryness for safe storage. For example: the moisture content of rice must be reduced from 24 to 14 per cent of the total weight. Therefore, drying 1000 kg of rice requires the removal of 100 kg of water. Safe storage generally requires reducing the moisture content to below 20 per cent for fruits, 10 per cent for vegetables, and 10–15 per cent for grains. If food is properly dried, no moisture will be visible when it is cut.

***Moisture absorption*:** The length of time required to dry food depends upon how quickly air absorbs moisture out of the food. Fast drying primarily depends upon three factors: the air should be warm, dry, and moving. The dryness of air is measured in terms of relative humidity (RH). If air is at 100 per cent relative humidity, it has absorbed 100 per cent of the water it can hold at that temperature. If air has a RH near 100 per cent, it must be heated before it will be able to absorb moisture out of food.

***Energy requirements*:** The amount of energy that must be added in order to dry produce depends on the local climate. Air drops in temperature as it absorbs moisture from food, and thus supplies some energy for drying. Therefore, if the air is warm and dry enough, food will dry slowly without additional heating from fuel or the Sun. However, additional heat shortens the drying process and yields a higher quality product. Under typical conditions 100 kg of maize might be dried with roughly 3 kg of kerosene, or with 10 kg of biomass such as wood or rice husks. Alternatively, a 6 m^2 solar collector will dry the maize over three sunny days, if the relative humidity is low. The size of solar collector required for a certain size of drier depends on the ambient temperature, amount of Sun, and humidity.

Solar drying essentials

***Solar drier components*:** Solar driers may be viewed as three main components—a drying chamber in which food is dried, a solar collector that heats the air, and some type of airflow system. The drying chamber protects the food from animals, insects, dust, and rain. It is often insulated (with sawdust, for example) to increase efficiency. The trays should be safe for food contact, a plastic coating is best to avoid harmful residues in food. A general rule of thumb is that one m^2 of tray area is needed to lay out 10 kg of fresh produce. The solar collector (or absorber) is often a dark coloured box with a transparent cover. It raises the air temperature between 10° and 30°C above ambient. This may be separate from the drier chamber, or combined (as with direct driers). Often the bottom surface of the absorber is dark to promote solar absorption, and occasionally charred rice chaff serves this purpose. Glass is recommended for the absorber cover, although it is expensive and difficult to use. Plastic is acceptable if it is firm or supported by a rib such that it does not sag and collect water.

Solar driers use one of two types of airflow systems, natural convection utilises the natural principle that hot air rises, and forced convection driers force air through the drying chamber with fans. The effects of natural convection may be enhanced by the addition of a chimney in which exiting air is heated even more. Additionally, prevailing winds may be taken advantage of. Natural convection driers require careful use, stacking the product too high or a lack of Sun can cause air to stagnate in the drier and halt the drying process. The use of forced convection can reduce drying time by three times and decrease the required collector area by 50 per cent. Consequently, a drier using fans may achieve the same throughput as a natural convection drier with a collector six times as large. Fans may be powered with utility electricity if it is available, or with a solar photovoltaic cell. For comparison, one study showed that the installation of three small fans and a photovoltaic cell was equivalent to the effect of a 12 m chimney.

***Drying process*:** Producing safe, highquality dried produce requires careful procedures throughout the entire preservation process. Foods suffer only a slight reduction in nutrition and aesthetics if dried properly, however, incorrect drying can dramatically degrade food and brings the risk of food poisoning.

A process similar to the following seven steps is usually used when drying fruits and vegetables (and fish, with some modifications):

1. Selection (fresh, undamaged produce)
2. Cleaning (washing and disinfection)
3. Preparation (peeling, slicing, etc.)
4. Pre-treatment (e.g. sulphurising, blanching, salting)
5. Drying
6. Packaging
7. Storage or export

Only fresh, undamaged food should be selected for drying to reduce the chances of spoilage and help insure a quality product. After selection, it is important to clean the produce. This is because drying does not always destroy micro-organisms, but only inhibits their growth. Fruits, vegetables, and meats generally require a pretreatment before drying. The quality of dried fruits and vegetables is generally improved with one or more of the following pretreatments: anti-discolouration by coating with vitamin C, de-waxing by briefly boiling and quenching, and sulphurising by soaking or fumigating. Fish is often salted. A small amount of chemical will treat a large amount of produce, and thus the cost for these supplies is usually small.

However, potential problems with availability and the complexity of the process should be considered. The best pretreatment procedure may be determined through a combination of experimentation and consulting literature on the subject.

After selection, cleaning, and pretreatment, produce is ready to place in the drier trays. Solar driers are usually designed to dry a batch every three to five days. Fast drying minimises the chances of food spoilage. However, excessively fast drying can result in the formation of a hard, dry skin — a problem known as case hardening. Case hardened foods appear dry outside, but inside remain moist and susceptible to spoiling. It is also important not to exceed the maximum temperature recommended, which ranges from 35° to 45°C depending upon the produce. Learning to properly solar dry foods in a specific location usually requires experimentation. For strict quality control, the drying rate may be monitored and correlated to the food moisture content to help determine the proper drying parameters.

After drying is complete, the dried produce often requires packaging to prevent insect losses and to avoid re-gaining moisture. It should cool first, and then be packaged in sanitary conditions. Sufficient drying and airtight storage will keep produce fresh for six to twelve months. If possible, the packaged product should be stored in a dry, dark location until use or export. If produce is to be exported, it must meet the quality standards of the target country. In some cases this will require a chemical and microbiological analysis of dried samples in a laboratory. Food drying requires significant labour for pretreatment (except for grains), and minimal involvement during the drying process such as shifting food to insure even drying. Solar drying equipment generally requires little maintenance.

Capabilities of solar driers: Solar drying can preserve a variety of fruits, vegetables, grains, and some meat. It can also be used for cash crops such as coffee, herbs, cashew, and macadamia. Solar driers exist for treating timber, although they are not discussed here. Fruits are ideal for preservation by drying since they are high in sugar and acid, which act to preserve the dried fruit. Vegetables are more challenging to preserve since they are low in sugar and acid. Drying meat requires extreme caution since it is high in protein, which invites microbial growth. Fish drying, for example, requires thorough cleaning of the drier after each batch.

Lists are available explaining which foods are suited to drying. For example, apples, apricots, coconuts, dates, figs, guavas, and plums are fruits that dry quite easily, while avocados, bananas, breadfruit, and grapes are more difficult to dry. Most legumes are easily dried, as well as chilies, corn, potatoes, cassava root, onion flakes, and the leaves of various herbs and spices. On the other hand, asparagus, beets, broccoli, carrots, celery, various greens, pumpkin, squash, and tomatoes are more difficult to dry successfully.

Classification and selection of driers

***Classification of food driers*:** Drying techniques may be divided into six general categories based on the way the food is heated (summarised in Table 18.1). Open-air or unimproved, solar drying takes place when food is exposed to the Sun and wind by placing it in trays, on racks or on the ground. Although the food is rarely protected from predators and weather, in some cases screens are used to keep out insects, or a clear roof is used to shed rain. Direct Sun driers enclose food in a container with a clear lid, such that Sun shines directly on the food. In addition to the direct heating of the solar radiation, the greenhouse effect traps heat in the enclosure and raises the temperature of the air. Vent holes allow for air exchange. Indirect Sun driers heat fresh air in a solar collector separate from the food chamber, so the food is not exposed to direct sunlight.

Table 18.1. Classification of food driers.

Classification	*Description*
Open-air	Food is exposed to the Sun and wind by placing in trays, on racks or on the ground. Food is rarely protected from predators and the weather
Direct Sun	Food is enclosed in a container with a clear lid allowing Sun to shine directly on the food. Vent holes allow for air circulation
Indirect Sun	Fresh air is heated in a solar heat collector and then passed through food in the drier chamber. In this way the food is not exposed to direct sunlight
Mixed mode	Combines the direct and indirect types, a separate collector preheats air and direct sunlight adds heat to the food and air
Hybrid	Combines solar heat with another source such as fossil fuel or biomass
Fueled	Uses electricity or fossil fuel as a source of heat and ventilation

This is of particular importance for foods which loose nutritional value when exposed to direct sunlight. Mixed mode driers combine the aspects of direct and indirect types, a separate collector preheats air and then direct sunlight adds heat to the food and air. Hybrid driers combine solar energy with a fossil fuel or biomass fuel such as rice husks. (It is interesting to note that a harvest of 1000 kg of rice yields 200 kg of husks, and requires burning only 25 kg of husks to be dried). Fueled driers use conventional fuels or utility supplied electricity for heat and ventilation.

***Comparing solar drying with other options*:** A first step when considering solar drying is to compare it with other options available. In some situations open-air drying or fuelled driers may be preferable to solar. If either of these is already used in a certain location, solar drying will only be successful if it has a clear advantage over the current practice.

The above comparison will assist in deciding among solar, open-air, and fueled driers. The local site conditions will also play an important role in this decision. Some indications that solar driers may be useful in a specific location include:

1. Conventional energy is unavailable or unreliable (making fuel driers unattractive).
2. Plenty of sunshine.
3. Dry climate (relative humidity below 60 per cent).
4. Quality of open-air dried products needs improvement.
5. Land is extremely scarce (making open-air drying unattractive).
6. Introducing solar drying technology will not have harmful socio-economic effects.

In addition to local conditions, the type of product to be dried plays a role in the decision process. For example, in some locations traditional open-air drying may be suitable for coffee, whereas fruit would largely be lost to predators. High-value cash crops often require consistent high quality without risking lost produce, and thus the use of fuel driers may be best.

The uses of solar dried products might include: self-consumption, local sale, large markets. and export. Therefore, the potential market for solar dried foods is often another important consideration. Preservation always slightly reduces nutrition and aestheucs, and therefore dried foods are only desirable if fresh is not available. Even where fresh is not available, consumer acceptance may be problematic if dried foods are not already on the market.

Existing infrastructure may be available to facilitate marketing dried produce. The expected market price will influence how much can be invested in a drier. Unfortunately, higher quality from solar driers doesn't always bring higher market prices than open-air drying. In some cases local markets are not willing to pay extra for higher quality solar dried products.

In some cases a centralised operation is more economical than numerous small driers, due to economies of scale. The appropriate amount of centralisation is different for simple natural convection driers than for more sophisticated forced convection driers.

Natural convection may be more effective with multiple small driers rather than one large unit. This is because the construction of small driers is simpler, and independent operation allows more flexibility. However, for forced convection driers, economies of scale favour centralisation to maximise use of the ventilation equipment.

***Some useful criteria for selecting a solar drier*:** If the use of solar driers appears favourable, the next step is to consider which type of solar drier to use.Choosing a solar drier is a subjective decision, and is heavily dependent upon local conditions and the product to be dried. The following aspects should be considered when selecting a drier:

1. Can the drier be made from locally available materials and skills?
2. What are the purchase and maintenance costs?
3. What is the drying capacity?
4. What range of foods can be dried?
5. What is the drying time required?
6. What is the quality of the dried product?
7. Is the drier adaptable to local conditions?

Solar drying has the potential to improve the quality of life in some areas. Once a particular drier has been chosen, it may be purchased (if available) or constructed. Experience shows that the best configuration of a solar drier is different for each location, and therefore successful food drying usually requires a period of experimentation and adjustments at the local site.

DRYING OF FRUITS

Botanically, a fruit is 'a ripened ovary' usually developing as part of the plant that contains the ovules that become the seeds of the plant. Fruits are essentially dessert foods. Artificial drying of fruit is an important method of preservation and production of a wide variety of products. Storage technologies are now available to keep fruit fresh over extended periods of time without appreciable change in the original physical form of the fruit. Drying, on the other hand, changes the physical and biochemical form of the fruit leading to shrinkage and change of colour, texture, taste and so on. If the water activity is reduced to appropriate levels (depending on the fruit variety and sugar content), the dried product can have a shelf life exceeding 1 year if properly packaged.

Fruit may be dried as a whole (e.g. grapes, various berries, apricot, plum, etc.), in sliced form (e.g. banana, mango, papaya, kiwi, etc.), in puree form (e.g. mango, apricot, etc.), as leather or as a powder by spray or drum drying. Depending on the physical form of the fruit (e.g. whole, paste, slices), different types of dryers must be used for drying.

Fruits are characterised by the following features, which must be taken into account when selecting the type of dryer as well as the operating conditions:

1. Very high initial moisture content.
2. High temperature sensitivity (colour, flavour, texture, nutritional value subject to thermal deterioration).
3. High susceptibility to microbial attack.
4. High sugar content (problems of stickiness, fermentation, etc.)
5. Presence of a 'skin' on some fruits that has poor permeability for water or moisture (e.g. grapes, blueberries).

The drying of fruit is necessarily a very slow process carried out under gentle drying conditions, leading to large dryers for a given throughput. Where feasible, solar drying often provides the most cost-effective drying technique although open Sun drying is practiced widely in California and the tropical countries. Pretreatment of the feed to speed the drying process and use of additives to avoid biochemical damage during the extended drying period are often necessary. The type of treatment and additives used depends on the species of fruit being dried. No generalisation can be made.

Drying Characteristics of Fruits

Properties of fruits

Fruits are highly hygroscopic materials. The water contained in a fruit is bound to the solid matrix such that the vapour pressure it exerts is lower than that for pure water at the same temperature. Sorptional equilibrium data for water vapour-foodstuff systems are used to describe the hygroscopic properties of a product. This information is required in numerous processes involving foods. In drying, desorption equilibrium moisture content determines the final moisture content to which a material can be dried using the specified drying conditions.

Density and thermal properties

The design and optimisation of any process in which the transfer of heat is involved requires knowledge of the density, as well as of the thermal properties, of the materials being processed. The density of fresh fruits is typically in the range 865 to 1067 kg/m^3, whereas for frozen fruits it is between 625 and 801 kg/m^3. In addition, fruits being materials of biological origin, their chemical compositions are not fixed but vary with parameters like variety, maturity or the location where they are grown.

Shrinkage

Considerable changes in the physical structure of the product, such as reduction in volume and decrease in internal porosity can be found during drying. Shape and size changes during drying modify both dimensions and transport properties of individual particles and also thickness and porosity of the packed bed in the dryer. In practice, however, this phenomenon is also dependent on drying conditions. There are few reported models for shrinkage and most of them fit the data only under specific operating conditions.

Mass transfer

Diffusion coefficients are often used to characterise mass transfer during drying. A rigorous and realistic approach to the phenomena taking place in biological multi phase materials (e.g. fruits) during air-drying was developed by Crapiste. This theory was defined in terms of a reduced dimensionless coordinate that follows the movement of the non-aqueous material due to shrinkage.

Dielectric properties

Moist solids such as foodstuffs are classified as 'lossy dielectric materials'. Such materials absorb electromagnetic energy and convert it into heat.

Radiation

Specifically for infrared (IR) drying, knowledge of the material properties may be the clue to accomplish a safe efficient process because radiation properties of both the radiator and the material to be dried must be matched in order to obtain the most efficient results. Again, quality parameters determine the suitability of radiant heating. The material to be dried by IR should have low reflectivity in order to minimise the power required to heat it. In drying thick moist materials such as foodstuffs, it is necessary to have a reasonable level of transmissivity in order to avoid excessive heating and thermal damage to the product surface. It is important to point out that, if the absorptivity of a material is low, its transmissivity is high and *vice versa*.

Properties like absorptivity and transmissivity of moist materials are not readily found in the literature. In addition to the dependency with wavelength and thickness, these properties also depend on the water content. The variation of absorptivity of moist materials with wavelength is difficult to estimate without experimental data.

Foodstuffs, for example, are complex mixtures of different large biochemical molecules and polymers, inorganic salts and water and the absorption bands of each of these constituents are not the same. Generally, many fully wet materials have their minimum absorptivity at those wavelengths where water has its maximum transmissivity, this points out the important role that water plays in radiation absorption. For many materials, transmissivity is generally higher at lower wavelengths.

As drying proceeds, the material being dried undergoes a change in its radiation properties, increasing its reflectivity and, consequently, lowering its absorptivity at low water contents. It is then possible to adequately change the temperature of the emitter in order to improve the absorption of radiation during drying. Further, transmissivity decreases with increase of layer thickness, while absorptivity is increased.

Quality Considerations

Special attention on quality is required in processes dealing with foodstuffs. As mentioned by Karel, the quality of a dehydrated product depends strongly on the quality of the raw materials, but their processing and storage must be carried out, minimising any undesirable change in quality.

The quality characteristics may be separated into two major groups sensory and hidden. Colour, gloss, size, shape, defects, texture, flavour and aroma belong to the former group and the nutritive value and the presence of adulterants and toxic components belong to the latter group. Attention has recently been focused on degradation of nutraceutical compounds during drying. Such is the case for tomato drying, in which the deterioration of lycopene has been extensively studied.

The whole process of drying involves also the treatment of foodstuffs before and after dehydration—for example, transport, peeling, cutting and storage—so quality restrictions have to be taken into account in all these sub-processes. The important changes occurring in a foodstuff due to dehydration are the influence of drying on micro-organisms, enzymatic and chemical conversions and physical changes. The estimation of these changes as a function of the wide, diverse range of conditions that can be expected for individual foods is extremely complicated.

Specific Drying Systems

Conventional hot-air drying

In this type of drying, the heat needed for drying is provided by convection with hot air in contact with the product. The most common of these dryers used for fruits are: kiln, cabinet, tunnel and continuous belt. The kiln dryer is basically an oven heated by gas burners in which the product is placed in slotted trays. This equipment is operated in a batch mode and is still widely used to dry slices of apples and several other fruits. It takes from 6 to 8 hr to dry a batch of slices or rings of apples to a final moisture content of 14 to 40 per cent.

The cabinet dryer is also a type of batch equipment, but there is a forced flow of air along or through the trays where the material is placed. This air is heated indirectly, generally by steam coils, after entering the cabinet. The operation can be controlled and the drying is more uniform in this case than in the kiln dryer. This unit is more suitable for small-scale operations of pieced fruits and although the cost of the equipment is low, its operating (labour) cost is high. The thermal efficiency is low as well.

The tunnel dryer is the most commonly used equipment to dry fruits. It is similar to the cabinet dryer but the trays are made to move along a tunnel in which hot air flows in parallel or counter flow to the product. This type of dryer is efficient yet simple. It is more suitable to industrial application because they can handle larger production rates. This method is often used to dry apricots, peaches, pears, apples, figs, dates and so on. Fruits should first be selected for their ripeness (ripe or slightly overripe fruits are required) and after wards washed, peeled and cut into chunks. The fruit pieces are pressed until a smooth puree is obtained. In order to obtain the desired texture and to avoid fruit darkening, water and ascorbic acid are added to the puree. The fruit puree is poured into trays that are placed in a kiln or cabinet dryer at 60°C (maximum temperature to avoid case hardening) until the fruit leather is dry.

Microwave drying

Conventional drying of foods is a slow process. Attempts to enhance this process have been made, but only few of them are applied presently in the industry. Microwave heating increases the temperature of the interior, wetter parts of the solid. In addition, moisture transport to the evaporation surface is also enhanced by an internal pressure gradient.

Microwave heating has three main advantages: (i) a penetrating quality that leads to uniform drying (conventional drying may cause damage to the surface of the product, it is dry and uses high temperatures compared to the interior), (ii) selective adsorption by liquid water, which leads to a uniform moisture profile within the particle, and (iii) ease of control due to the rapid response of such heating.

Advantages: (i) and (ii) increase the quality of the final product and make it easier to be rehydrated. But on the other hand, such equipment is complicated and expensive and unfortunately, no industry uses it for fruit dehydration.

Work done on the finish drying of fruits demonstrated a synergistic effect between hot-air and microwave drying. Apple, mango and pineapple were investigated recently for microwave drying under vacuum. The rate of drying and the core temperature were measured in this work. The experimental results showed that the geometry of the samples and the power used have a strong influence on the microwave drying rate of fruits, as well as on product quality.

Osmotic dehydration

Hot-air drying notably reduces the quality of the processed foodstuffs (changes in colour, shape, losses of aroma and nutrients, etc.). Osmotic dehydration is an alternative technology to reduce the water content, as well as to improve the quality of the final product. This process is being used in industry to dehydrate fruits, vegetables, meat and fish, but the industrial application is still limited. Osmotic dehydration involves the immersion of cut foods in concentrated solutions of sugars and salts. A flux of water out of the food and of other solutes into the foodstuff develops due to the difference in osmotic pressure. The product thus loses some water to the external solution.Smith and others first applied osmotic dehydration for reduction of weight by up to 50 per cent of apples prior to vacuum drying. The osmotic dewatering rate can be enhanced by increasing the concentration of the osmotic solution or the temperature.

Explosion puffing

The incorporation of explosion puffing into a hot-air dehydration process facilitates faster dehydration and leads to a final product with a highly porous structure that is capable of rapid rehydration. This process has long been applied to rice and wheat breakfast cereals and now is being applied to fruit and vegetables. Explosion puffing has been successful with apples, blueberries and banana slices.

The process starts with conventional hot-air drying of the fruit pieces until a certain water content is attained. Then the pieces are placed in a closed chamber, the gun, where the pressure is increased by means of superheated steam. After some time, the pressure is suddenly released by opening the lid of the gun. Due to the high temperature and the sudden decompression, the water in the particles flashes explosively. Then the solids are placed again in the air drying equipment to be dried to the desired final water content. Due to the highly porous structure after puffing, the drying time is reduced notably.

Heat pump dryers

Drying of heat-sensitive products (e.g. fruits and vegetables) requires large amounts of low-temperature heat. Use of high-grade energy sources (e.g. gas, oil, electricity, etc.) for such tasks leads to low energetic efficiencies. Heat pumps can take advantage of the energy of high-grade energy sources. Indeed, benefits of heat pumps increase as the target air temperature for heating approaches the ambient temperature. Several different configurations are possible to couple heat pumps with conventional convective dryers. They may be single-pass or of a recirculating type. Industrial drying of fruits is a technology based both on engineering and empiricism. Experimental evaluation of the effects of dryer operating variables on the drying kinetics (which govern the dryer size), as well as the quality of the product, are keys to successful design and economic drying of fruits.

Energy consumption is often a secondary consideration to quality, but it is possible to enhance efficiency without compromising on quality through a fundamental understanding of the phenomena involved. Drying of biological materials such as fruits is extremely complex since it is accompanied by biochemical and physical changes that govern product quality, such as colour, flavour, shape, size, taste, etc. Extensive laboratory and pilot testing is needed before a full-scale dryer can be designed without prior experience with the same feedstock.

Chapter 19

Smoking

INTRODUCTION

Smoking is the process of flavouring, browning, cooking, or preserving food by exposing it to smoke from burning or smoldering material, most often wood. Meat, fish, and lapsang souchong tea are often smoked. Smoking can be done in four ways: cold smoking, warm smoking, hot smoking, and through the employment of 'liquid smoke'. However, these methods of imparting smoke only affect the food surface, and are unable to preserve food, thus, smoking is paired with other microbial hurdles, such as chilling and packaging, to extend food shelf-life.

SELECTING FOODS TO BE SMOKED

Virtually any meat, poultry, game or seafood can be smoked, as can hard cheeses, nuts, vegetables, and sausages.

1. Prepare items:
   - Trim excess fat.
   - Fish should be gutted and cleaned of gills and all blood, large fish are often filleted.
   - Poultry should be trussed.
   - Larger cuts of meat should be boned and cut into smaller pieces.
   - The rind should be removed from cheese.
2. Cure items (optional):
   - Dehydrates - low moisture prevents bacteria growth and allows smoke to penetrate the item.
   - Adds flavour.
   - Prevents botulism.
   - Enhances colour.
   - Smaller, thinner pieces cured, larger pieces brined.
3. Rinsing:
   - Stops the curing process.

- Removes excess saltiness and excess surface fat.

4. Dry foods well:
   - Removes excess surface moisture to form a skin (pellicle).
   - A wet surface will not readily absorb smoke.
   - Removes excess surface fat.
   - Forms the pellicle.
5. Smoking process:
   - Smoke is a seasoning - don't overdo it.

Smoke is the complex production of very complicated compounds that occur during the thermal decomposition of wood (chips or sawdust). This process primarily occurs between a temperature range of 390°F and 750°F. Although at the point of generation smoke is a gas, it rapidly separates into a vapor and a particle state. It is the vapor phase that contains the components largely responsible for the flavour and aroma that smoke imparts to foods. More than 300 different compounds have been isolated from wood smoke, but not all of these compounds occur in smoked meat products. The components most commonly found are phenols, organic acids, alcohols, carbonyls, hydrocarbons, and some gaseous components such as carbon dioxide, carbon monoxide, oxygen, nitrogen, and nitrous oxide.

Smoke is Applied to Meat for the Following Reasons

- For preservation: Phenolic compounds and formaldehyde have antimicrobial action, this affects only the surface of the meat as smoke does not penetrate deeply into items.
- Acids: Smoke emits a number of acids which cling to the meat and form an outside layer or skin. The acids help the coagulation of the surface meat, and also help preserve the meat by preventing the growth of surface mold and bacteria.
- Add aroma and flavour: Phenols, carbonyl compounds and organic acids contribute the smoky taste. Excessive smoke flavour can become bitter.
- Develop appealing colour: Carbonyl compounds combine with free amino groups combined with meat protein to form furfural compounds that are dirty brown in colour and translucent, when added with the reddish colour of the cooked cured meat, you see a reddish brown colour that is characteristic of smoked products.
- Creation of new food products: The addition of a smoky taste results in a product with a longer shelf life and pleasing colour.
- Protection from oxidation: Smoke will protect the food from lipid oxidation and eliminate any stale fat tastes.
- Formation of a protective skin on meats and emulsion-type sausages: Acids in smoke help coagulate the protein on the surface of the meat.

Smoked Pork Chops

Yield: 6 Portions

Ingredients	Amounts
Pork chops, one-inch thick	6 ea.
Wood chips	2 cup

Cilantro, fresh chopped	
Salt and pepper	½ cup
Olive oil	1 oz

Method

1. Fabricate 1-inch thick pork chops and remove excess fat.
2. Moisten the wood chips in cold water.
3. Marinate pork chops with spices, herbs and pepper for 1 hour.
4. Pan-smoke the chops, for 3 to 5 minutes until they reach a light yellow colour. Grill the chops, finishing on a rack in the oven at 375°F if needed.
5. Repeat twice, using different woods for smoking.

Hot-Smoked Swordfish

Yield: 6 Portions

Ingredients	Amounts
Sword or tuna fish, thick steaks	1½ lb.
Marinade	
Lemon juice	1 ea.
Salt	1½ tsp.
Worcestershire sauce	1 oz.

Method

1. Combine all ingredients for the marinade.
2. Rub marinade over half of the fish, refrigerate for 1–2 hr. Leave the other half of the fish plain.
3. Blot-dry with paper towels and hot-smoke until desired doneness.
4. Repeat twice, using different woods for smoking.

Tea and Spice Smoked Chicken

Yield: 1 chicken

Ingredients	Amounts
Chicken, whole	1 ea.
For smoking the chicken	
Dry black tea leaves	¼ cup
Brown sugar	¼ cup
Raw rice	1/3 cup
Szechwan brown peppercorns	1 Tbsp.
Star anise	3 ea.
Cinnamon sticks, broken into small bits	2 ea.
Brown sugar, for smoking the second side of the chicken	¼ cup
Sesame oil	2 Tbsp.

Method

1. Combine the smoking ingredients and spread evenly in the bottom of the pan.
2. Pan-smoke the chicken for 10–15 minutes. Turn the chicken over and continue to pan smoke the chicken for an additional 5–8 minutes. If necessary, finish the chicken in 375°F oven until an internal temperature of 170°F has been reached. Rub the outside of the chicken with the sesame oil.
3. Repeat the process twice, using different tea (e.g. orange pekoe or green tea) for smoking.

PAN-SMOKED CHICKEN BREAST WITH ARTICHOKE AND MUSTARD SAUSE

Yield: 10 servings

Ingredients	Amounts
Chicken breast, boneless, skinless	2 ¼ lb.
Olive oil	2 tsp.
Shallots, diced	1 oz.
Chicken Stock	10 oz.
Fond de Veau Lié	10 oz.
Mustard, whole-grain	2 oz.
Mustard, Dijon	1 oz.
Balsamic vinegar	3 Tbsp.
Artichoke hearts, cooked, quartered	10 ea.
Kalamata olives, pitted, halved	3 oz.
Tarragon, chopped	2 Tbsp.

Method

1. Trim and cut the chicken into ten 3½ oz portions. Lightly pound the chicken to an even thickness.
2. Place the chicken on a rack in a roasting pan containing a thin layer of hardwood chips. Cover with a tight-fitting lid and place over low direct heat. Pan smoke for 6 to 8 minutes. Remove the breasts form the pan and cool. Refrigerate until needed.
3. To make the sauce, heat the oil in a small saucepan. Add the shallots and sauté until translucent. Add the stock and reduce by half. Stir in the fond de veau lié, mustards, and vinegar. Simmer until reduced to a sauce consistency. Add the remaining ingredients and heat thoroughly. Keep warm.
4. For each serving: Place 1 portion of smoked chicken on a rack in a roasting pan in a 375° F oven and bake until internal temperature of 165°F is reached, about 10 minutes. Slice the chicken on a bias and serve on a pool of 3 fluid oz of the sauce.

Smoke-Roasted Chicken Breast with BBQ Sause

Yield: 10 servings

Ingredients	Amounts
Chicken breast portions	10 (6 oz.)
Salt	As req.
Pepper	As req.

Marinade	
Vegetable oil	10 fl. oz.
Cider vinegar	5 fl. oz
Worcestershire sauce	1 fl. oz.
Brown sugar	1 Tbsp.
Dry mustard	2 tsp.
Tabasco sauce	1 tsp.
Garlic powder	1 tsp.
Onion powder	1 tsp.
Garlic, minced	¼ oz.

Method

1. Rinse chicken, pat dry, season with salt and pepper, and place in shallow hotel pan.
2. Combine the ingredients for the marinade and pour over the chicken, turning to coat evenly. Marinate under refrigeration for 3 hr or up to overnight.
3. Place the chicken on a rack and set it in a pan over lightly dampened hardwood chips. Cover tightly and heat in a 450°F oven until the smell of the smoke is apparent. Smoke for 3 minutes from that point. Transfer the chicken to a baking pan and finish baking (without smoke) in a 350°F oven until done, about 8 to 10 minutes more (170°F for breast meat).
4. Serve at once with additional barbecue sauce if desired.

Smoke Roasted Strip Loin of Beef

Yield: 6 Portions

Ingredients	Amounts
Sirloin	4 lbs.
Dry rub	
Garlic powder	1 Tbsp.
Onion powder	1 Tbsp.
Salt, kosher	3 Tbsp.
Sugar	4 Tbsp.
Cumin, ground	2 Tbsp.
Black pepper, fresh cracked	2 Tbsp.
Cayenne	1 Tbsp.
Paprika	4 Tbsp.
Chili powder	2 Tbsp.

Method

1. Combine all and mix well to evenly distribute the spices.
2. Trim the sirloin of excess fat and connective tissue.
3. Rub the dry spice mixture all around the sirloin strip and allow to sit for 15 minutes before smoke roasting.

4. Smoke roast the sirloin strip over low heat as instructed by the manufacturer of the gas or charcoal grill.
5. Cook to an internal temperature of 120–125°F for medium rare.
6. Remove from the grill and allow to rest for 20 minutes to allow the juices to settle.
7. Slice and serve.

Smoke Roasted Pork Loin with Grilled Apples

Yield: 6 Portions

Ingredients	Amounts
Pork loin, boneless	3 lb.
Brine	2 qt.
Apples, granny smith	6 ea.
Apple cider or apple juice	½ cup
Sugar	¼ cup
Cinnamon	To taste
Nutmeg	To taste
Vinegar, apple cider	1 Tbsp.

Method for the pork

1. Set-up a gas or charcoal grill to medium heat following the manufactures instructions. For a gas grill, follow manufactures instructions regarding the use of wood chips. For a charcoal grill, bank the charcoal to two sides. Clean and preheat the grill racks.
2. Cure the pork loin for 8–12 hr in the brine. Remove, rinse and allow to air dry under refrigeration for several hours, until the surface is very dry.
3. Smoke roast over medium heat to an internal temperature of 155°F. Remove and allow to sit for 20 minutes before slicing.

Method for the apples

1. Peel and core the apples. Slice them into rings ¾″ thick. Season a section the grill racks with oil over the charcoal. Allow to reheat and grill the apples covered until almost tender turning occasionally. Remove and allow to cool.
2. In a food processor puree ½ of the apples with the apple cider vinegar to desired consistency. If a thicker applesauce consistency is desired use less apple juice. For a sauce like consistency add more apple juice or cider. Add the sugar and season to taste with the cinnamon, nutmeg and vinegar.
3. Slice the remaining apples ¼ inch thick, across the ring and add to the sauce.
4. Heat and serve with the pork loin.

TYPES OF SMOKING

Cold Smoking

Cold smoking differs from hot smoking in that the food remains raw, rather than cooked, throughout the smoking process. Smokehouse temperatures for cold smoking are typically done between 20 to 30°C

(68 to 86°F). In this temperature range, foods take on a smoked flavour, but remain relatively moist. Cold smoking does not cook foods, and as such, meats should be fully cured before cold smoking. Cold smoking can be used as a flavour enhancer for items such as cheese or nuts, along with meats such as chicken breasts, beef, pork chops, salmon, scallops, and steak. The item is often hung in a dry environment first to develop a pellicle, then it can be cold smoked up to several days to ensure it absorbs the smokey flavour. Some cold smoked foods are baked, grilled, steamed, roasted, or sautéed before eating.

Cold smoking meats is not something that should be attempted at home, according to the US National Center for Home Food Preservation:

'Most food scientists cannot recommend cold-smoking methods because of the inherent risks.' Cold smoking meats should only be attempted by personnel certified in HACCP, or Hazard Analysis and Critical Control Points, to ensure that it is safely prepared.

Warm Smoking

Warm smoking exposes foods to temperatures of 25–40°C (77–104°F).

Hot Smoking

Hot smoking exposes the foods to smoke and heat in a controlled environment such as a smoker oven or smokehouse. Hot smoking requires the use of a smoker which generates heat either from a charcoal base, heated element within the smoker or from a stove-top or oven, food is hot smoked by cooking and flavoured with wood smoke simultaneously. Like cold smoking, the item may be hung first to develop a pellicle, it is then smoked from 1 hour to as long as 24 hr. Although foods that have been hot smoked are often reheated or further cooked, they are typically safe to eat without further cooking. Hams and ham hocks are fully cooked once they are properly smoked, and they can be eaten as is without any further preparation.

Hot smoking usually occurs within the range of 52 to 80°C (126 to 176°F). When food is smoked within this temperature range, foods are fully cooked, moist, and flavourful. If the smoker is allowed to get hotter than 85°C (185°F), the foods will shrink excessively, buckle, or even split. Smoking at high temperatures also reduces yield, as both moisture and fat are cooked away.

Liquid Smoke

Liquid smoke, a product derived from smoke compounds in water, is applied to foods through spraying or dipping.

Smoke Roasting

Smoke-roasting refers to any process that has the attributes of both roasting and smoking. This smoking method is sometimes referred to as barbecuing or pit-roasting. It may be done in a smoke-roaster, a closed wood-fired oven, or a barbecue pit, any smoker that can reach above 121°C (250°F), or in a conventional oven (one that a person does not mind having smoky all the time) by placing a pan filled with hardwood chips on the floor of the oven so that the chips can smolder and produce a smoke-bath. In North America, this smoking method is commonly referred to as 'barbecuing,' 'pit baking,' or 'pit roasting'.

WOOD SMOKE

Hardwoods are made up mostly of three materials: Cellulose, hemicellulose, and lignin. Cellulose and hemicellulose are the basic structural material of the wood cells, lignin acts as a kind of cell-bonding glue. Some softwoods, especially pines and firs, hold significant quantities of resin, which produces a harsh-tasting soot when burned, these woods are not often used for smoking.

Cellulose and hemicellulose are aggregate sugar molecules, when burnt, they effectively caramelise, producing carbonyls, which provide most of the colour components and sweet, flowery, and fruity aromas. Lignin, a highly complex arrangement of interlocked phenolic molecules, also produces a number of distinctive aromatic elements when burnt, including smoky, spicy, and pungent compounds such as guaiacol, phenol, and syringol, and sweeter scents such as the vanilla-scented vanillin and clove-like isoeugenol. Guaiacol is the phenolic compound most responsible for the 'smoky' taste, while syringol is the primary contributor to smoky aroma. Wood also contains small quantities of proteins, which contribute roasted flavours. Many of the odour compounds in wood smoke, especially the phenolic compounds, are unstable, dissipating after a few weeks or months.

A number of wood smoke compounds act as preservatives. Phenol and other phenolic compounds in wood smoke are both antioxidants, which slow rancidification of animal fats, and antimicrobials, which slow bacterial growth. Other antimicrobials in wood smoke include formaldehyde, acetic acid, and other organic acids, which give wood smoke a low pH—about 2.5. Some of these compounds are toxic to people as well, and may have health effects in the quantities found in cooking applications.

Since different species of trees have different ratios of components, various types of wood do impart a different flavour to food. Another important factor is the temperature at which the wood burns. High-temperature fires see the flavour molecules broken down further into unpleasant or flavourless compounds. The optimal conditions for smoke flavour are low, smoldering temperatures between 300 and 400°C (570 and 750°F). This is the temperature of the burning wood itself, not of the smoking environment, which uses much lower temperatures. Woods that are high in lignin content tend to burn hot, to keep them smoldering requires restricted oxygen supplies or a high moisture content. When smoking using wood chips or chunks, the combustion temperature is often raised by soaking the pieces in water before placing them on a fire. Various smoking methods are given in Tables 19.1.

Table 19.1: Smoking methods.

Cold smoking	***Hot smoking***
Temperature of smokehouse	*Temperature of smokehouse*
70°F and 100°F	160°F for all sausage (casings)
(80°F) is average temperature	185°F for all solid meats
Result of cold Smoking	*Result of hot smoking*
Product does not cook	Product cooks during the smoking process
Slight dehydration of overall texture	
	Final internal temperature of cured hot smoked products
	All poultry 165°F internal
	All meats 155°F internal
	Final internal temperature of uncured hot smoked items
	Beef (suitable cuts) 130–135°F for rare
Uses	*Uses*
Sausage in the uncooked smoked category	To produce a fully cooked, smoked item
Smoked salmon	Sausage in the smoked cooked category
Addition of smoke to an item that will be finished by some other cooking method	

Preparation and smoking process (hot or cold) are given in Table 19.2.

Table 19.2: Preparation and smoking process (hot or cold).

Cold smoke	*Hot smoke*
Preparation before smoking	*Preparation before smoking*
Trim item, truss, net or tie as necessary	Trim item, truss, net or tie as necessary
Cure item by desired method	Cure item by desired method (optional)
When cure is done, rinse item	If item is cured, rinse when done
Form pellicle	Form pellicle
Smokehouse preparation	*Smokehouse preparation*
Place items on racks or hang from sticks	Place items on racks or hang from sticks
Smoke process	*Smoke process*
Smoke foods until desired color/flavor is achieved	Solid meat (185°F) smoke until proper internal temperature
Product can be air-dried further if drier product is desired	Sausage (160°F) smoke until 140°F internal finish by poaching in 170°F water until proper internal temperature
Refrigerate	Refrigerate

Note: It is recommended to cure all items that are to be cold-smoked because of possibility of botulism. Items that are hot-smoked can be left uncured if desired.

Other Items used for Smoking

- Dry herbs and spices can be used.
- Jasmine and other teas, also peanut shells are used by the Chinese.

Working of Smokehouse

Figure 19.1 shows smokehouse works. Many of the larger smokehouses are computer programmed as to time and temperature.

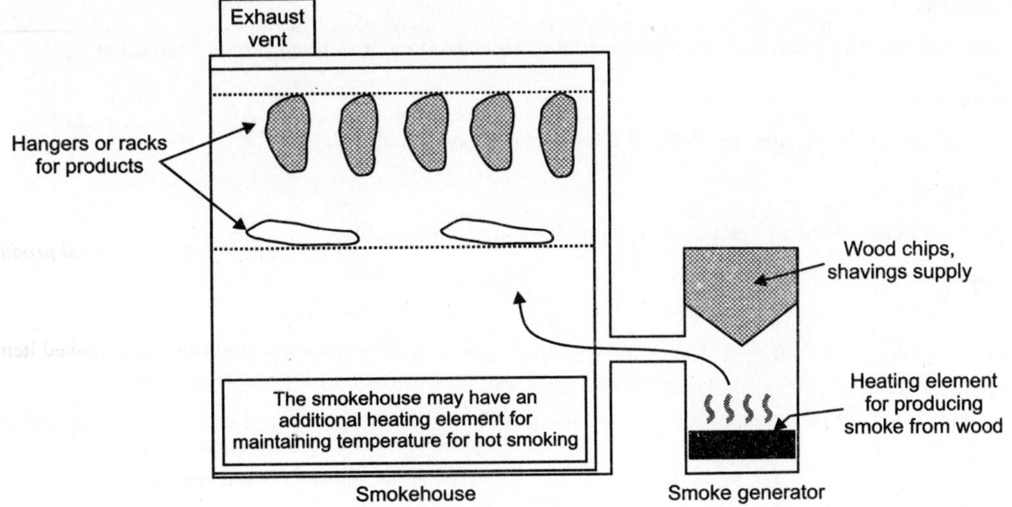

Fig. 19.1: Smokehouse works.

Smoke Roasting (Foil Pan Method)

Smoke roasting (foil pan method) are shown in Fig. 19.2.

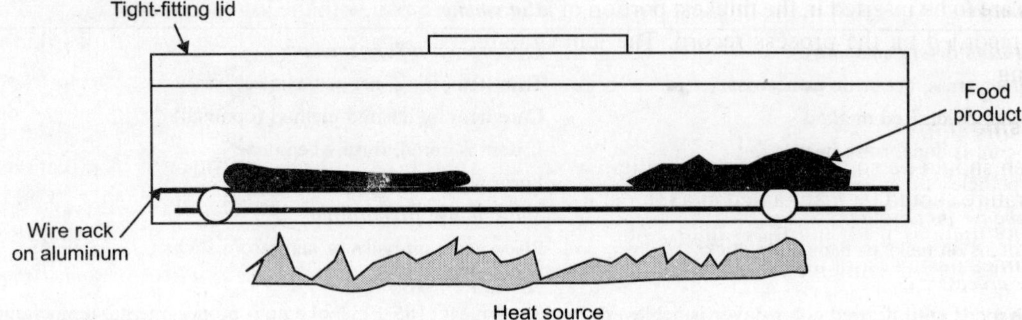

Fig. 19.2: Setup for smoke roasting

Methods

1. Use an aluminum foil disposable hotel pan for top and bottom
2. Place ¼ inch of hickory chips on the bottom of the pan.
3. Make four 1-inch balls out of aluminum foil and place one in each corner of the pan.
4. Place a wire rack on top of the foil, arrange your product to be smoked on the rack.
5. Cover the pan with the second foil pan and secure with a weight.
6. Place the pan on the stove and smoke the desired amount of time with high heat, when done, allow the pan to cool slightly before opening.

Process Schedule for Hot and Cold Smoked Fish

Fish (Salmon)

Raw material must be fresh with no signs of detectable spoilage and must be maintained at 33°F or less.

Thawing

Thawing of frozen food must be done at a temperature no greater than 45°F.

Evisceration

Fish must be eviscerated in a separate area and washed thoroughly.

Brining

Mixing of fish species in brine is not allowed. Brining or dry salting, in excess of 4 hr, must take place at a temperature of 38°F or less. Salt concentration and period of time must be adequate to ensure salt penetration to give a water phase salt (WPS) of 2.5%.

The determination of water phase salt must be done on the thickest piece of fish, sufficient times to meet requirements.

Hot smoking

The fish should be so arranged as to facilitate complete smoking of all product surfaces. Fish temperature in the smoker must reach a minimum of 145°F and be held for at least thirty minutes. Temperature probes are to be inserted in the thickest portion of at least three fish with the lowest temperature reading being recorded on the process record. The temperature will be recorded at least three times during smoking.

Cold smoking

The fish should be so arranged as to facilitate complete smoking of all product surfaces. Smokehouse temperature should be maintained at a temperature not to exceed 50°F for a time not to exceed 24 hr, or not more than 90°F for not more than 20 hr. The smokehouse temperature should be recorded at least three times during smoking.

Cooling

Fish shall be cooled to 50°F within five hours and to 33°F within 12 hr and maintained at that temperature until sold.

Packaging

This fish can only be sold air-packaged and must be labeled in bold print 'Keep Refrigerated at 38°F or below'.

Three Smoking Methods

Conventional

- More smoke flavour, air does not circulate as much.
- Product must be dry.

Convection

- Less smoke flavour because the air is being circulated.
- Product does not have to be dry because of the air circulation.

Pan smoking

- Pan smoking gives a lot of flavour in short period of time.
- Can be done with no special equipment.

Suggestions for use of Wood Chips in Smoking

Alder: This has quite a mild taste, ideal to use with vegetables and fish.

Apple: This has a unique fruity flavour, ideal to use with fresh ham, frog legs, pork chops, sweet sausages, Cornish hens and salmon.

Cherry: This is similar to the characteristics of apple, but with a slight tart aftertaste, ideal to use with lamb, pheasant, duck, venison and steak.

Maple: This has a universal subtle hint of sweet flavour, ideal to use with turkey, ham Canadian bacon, tenderloin of beef and pork, poultry, most kinds of game and vegetables.

Hickory: This has a strong heavy bacon flavour, ideal for use with ribs, barbecue items, steaks, chops, and spicy food, broiled chicken.

Oak: This is a mellow version of mesquite, ideal to use with steaks, duck, and hamburgers.

Mesquite: This has authentic Southwest twang, leaving a little bit of a hot burning sensation as an aftertaste, ideal to use with pork, spare ribs, steaks, and most red meats. If used with great care it can also be used across the whole ingredient spectrum.

Sweet birch: This leaves a sweet delicate taste on the palate, ideal to use with chicken, swordfish, tuna, salmon, lamb, barbecued pork items, all vegetables especially members of the lily family.

Pecan: This has quite a mellow flavour to it similar to hickory, cool burning is one of its major characteristics, ideal to use with chicken and duck and most game that is of the winged variety.

Types of Smokers

Offset

The main characteristics of the offset smoker are that the cooking chamber is usually cylindrical in shape, with a shorter, smaller diameter cylinder attached to the bottom of one end for a firebox. To cook the meat, a small fire is lit in the firebox, where airflow is tightly controlled. The heat and smoke from the fire are drawn through a connecting pipe or opening into the cooking chamber. The heat and smoke cook and flavour the meat before escaping through an exhaust vent at the opposite end of the cooking chamber. Most manufacturers models are based on this simple but effective design, and this is what most people picture when they think of a 'BBQ smoker'. Even large capacity commercial units use this same basic design of a separate, smaller fire box and a larger cooking chamber.

Upright drum

The upright drum smoker (also referred to as an ugly drum smoker or UDS) is exactly what its name suggests, an upright steel drum that has been modified for the purpose of pseudo-indirect hot smoking. There are many ways to accomplish this, but the basics include the use of a complete steel drum, a basket to hold charcoal near the bottom, and cooking rack (or racks) near the top, all covered by a vented lid of some sort. This design is similar to smoking with indirect heat due to the distance from the coals and the racks, which is typically 24 inches (61 cm). The temperatures used for smoking are controlled by limiting the amount of air intake at the bottom of the drum, and allowing a similar amount of exhaust out of vents in the lid.

Vertical water

A vertical water smoker (also referred to as a bullet smoker because of its shape) is a variation of the upright drum smoker. It uses charcoal or wood to generate smoke and heat, and contains a water bowl between the fire and the cooking grates. The water bowl serves to maintain optimal smoking temperatures and also adds humidity to the smoke chamber. It also creates an effect in which the water vapor and smoke condense together, which adds flavour to smoked foods. In addition, the bowl catches any drippings from the meat that may cause a flare-up. Vertical water smokers are extremely temperature stable and require very little adjustment once the desired temperature has been reached. Because of their relatively low cost and stable temperature, they are sometimes used in barbecue competitions where propane and electric smokers are not allowed.

Propane

A propane smoker is designed to allow the smoking of meat in a somewhat more temperature controlled environment. The primary differences are the sources of heat and of the smoke. In a propane smoker, the heat is generated by a gas burner directly under a steel or iron box containing the wood or charcoal that provides the smoke. The steel box has few vent holes, on the top of the box only. By starving the heated wood of oxygen, it smokes instead of burning. Any combination of woods and charcoal may used. This method uses much less wood but does require propane fuel.

Smoke box

This more traditional method uses a two-box system: a fire box and a food box. The fire box is typically adjacent or under the cooking box, and can be controlled to a finer degree. The heat and smoke from the fire box exhausts into the food box, where it is used to cook and smoke the meat. These may be as simple as an electric heating element with a pan of wood chips placed on it, although more advanced models have finer temperature controls.

Electric smokers

The most convenient of the various types of smokers are the insulated electric smokers. These devices house a heating element that can maintain temperatures ranging from that required for a cold smoke all the way up to 135°C (275°F) with little to no intervention from the user. Although wood chunks, pellets, and even in some cases automatically-fed wood pucks are used to generate smoke, the amount of flavour obtained is less than traditional wood or charcoal smokers.

Trench

In this method the firebox is a narrow trench cut down a slope pointing into the prevailing wind. The middle part of the trench is covered over to make it into a tunnel. At the upper end of the trench is a vertical framework covered to form a chimney within which is placed the rack of foodstuff. At the lower upwind end of the trench is lit a small smokey fire, and sustained day and night until the foodstuff is cured.

Commercial smokehouse

Commercial smokehouses, mostly made from stainless steel, have independent systems for smoke generation and cooking. Smoke generators use friction, an electric coil or a small flame to ignite sawdust on demand. Heat from steam coils or gas flames is balanced with live steam or water sprays to control the temperature and humidity. Elaborate air handling systems reduce hot or cold spots, to reduce variation in the finished product. Racks on wheels or rails are used to hold the product and facilitate movement.

Pellet smokers

A pellet smoker is a temperature controlled smoker that burns wood pellets made of dried out sawdust, about an inch long and ¼ inch wide. The wood pellets are stored in a gravity-fed hopper that feeds into a motor controlled by the temperature regulator. This motor pushes the pellets into an auger that sits underneath the heat box. An ignition rod within the auger ignites the pellets where a combustion fan keeps them smouldering. The motor and the combustion fan regulate the temperature of the smoker by feeding it more pellets and increasing airflow in the auger. Above the auger is a heat shield to disperse the direct heat before it reaches the heat box to allow the wood smoke to keep the heat box at an even temperature throughout. The heat sensor inside the heat box relays the current temperature inside the box back to the temperature regulator which then controls the fan speed and pellet hopper motor which will either increase or decrease the amount of pellets in the auger or the amount of air available to the fire to maintain the desired temperature for the cook.

Preservation

Smoke is both an antimicrobial and antioxidant, however it is insufficient alone for preserving food as smoke does not penetrate far into meat or fish, it is thus typically combined with salt-curing or drying.

Smoking is especially useful for oily fish, as its antioxidant properties inhibit surface fat rancidification and delay interior fat exposure to degrading oxygen. Some heavily-salted, long-smoked fish can keep without refrigeration for weeks or months. Artificial smoke flavouring (such as liquid smoke) can be purchased to mimic smokings flavour, but not its preservative qualities.

List of Smoked Foods and Beverages

Some of the more common smoked foods and beverages include.

Beverages

1. Lapsang souchong tea leaves are smoked and dried over pine or cedar fires
2. Malt beverages
   - The malt used to make whisky.
   - Rauchbier (smoked beer).

Fruit and vegetables

1. Capsicums: Chipotles (smoked, ripe jalapeños), paprika.
2. Prunes (dried plums) can be smoked while drying.
3. Wumei are smoked plum fruits.
4. Iburi-gakko are a smoked daikon pickle from Akita Prefecture, Japan.

Meat, fish, and cheese

1. Beef:
   - Pastrami (pickled, spiced and smoked beef brisket)
2. Pork:
   - Bacon
   - Ham
   - Bakkwa
3. Turkey

4. Sausage:
   - Salami
5. Jerky
6. Fish:
   - Eel popular in eastern/northern Europe
   - Traditional Grimsby smoked fish (cod and haddock)
   - Haddock and Arbroath Smokies (haddock)
   - Buckling, kippers and bloater (herring)
   - Salmon
   - Mackerel
7. Egg (eggs and fish eggs).
8. Cheese:
   - Gouda
   - Gruyère

Other proteins

1. Nuts
2. Tofu

Spices

1. Paprika
2. Salt

CURING AND SMOKING POULTRY MEAT

Cured and smoked poultry meats have become popular. Curing and smoking imparts a unique, delicate flavour and pink colour to poultry meat and increases the refrigerator storage life. When preparing smoked poultry products most people use mild cures (relatively low salt) to maintain the poultry flavour. Smoked poultry, like ham, can be served hot or cold for sandwiches, salads or party snacks. You can use the bones to replace ham bones for flavouring soups or bean dishes.

Preparations

First step in the curing and smoking process is to obtain the following materials and ingredients:

1. Poultry meat.
2. Non-iodised salt.
3. Sugar and/or brown sugar.
4. Cure (containing 6.25 per cent sodium nitrite).
5. Other seasonings according to your recipe.
6. Food grade plastic or stainless steel tub.
7. Smoker*.

8. Wood chips or liquid smoke if you choose not to use natural smoke.
9. Cheesecloth or stockinette for hanging in the smokehouse.
10. Airtight packaging for storage.

*You can make or buy several types of smokehouses and smokers. An old refrigerator with a vent cut in the top and an electric hot plate with variable heat settings in the bottom works very well. Keep the vent covered except when reducing the temperature in the smoker. Remove all plastic shelf support, line the refrigerator with boards and secure shelving to the boards. Drill a hole for the hot plate's electric cord. Put an iron container filled with hardwood twigs, shavings or sawdust on the hot plate. Put poultry on the racks or hang from overhead racks.

Place a metal or aluminum foil baffle over the wood chips to protect them from meat drippings. This will prevent wood chips from catching fire and prevent smoke produced by drippings. Safety precaution: For the safety of small children, remove the door's locking device and install a simple latch that must be manually locked. You can also use portable electric smokers. These smokers usually come complete with a pan for wood chips or sawdust and an electric heating unit.

Selecting poultry meat

Cured and smoked poultry meat is quite susceptible to rancidity. Therefore, it is very important to select poultry that is as clean and fresh as possible. Farm dressed poultry works well if proper dressing procedures are followed. Chill the birds immediately and cure and smoke within 1–2 days (the sooner the better). Many commercially frozen birds also work very well. Birds with the neck skin removed can be smoked, but it is preferable to fold the flaps of neck skin over the back to reduce drying during smoking.

Curing

Preparing brine

Many different curing formulations are available. The following recipe can be used: (This recipe is based on an 11.8 per cent total pickup of brine. After injecting brine and soaking in the brine, birds should weigh 11.8 per cent more than before injection and soaking.)

5 gals	Water
5 lbs	Non-iodised salt
3 lbs	Sugar (brown sugar can be substituted for all or part of this amount)
1.25 lbs	Cure (containing 6.25 per cent sodium nitrite)

Optional ingredients*

4 Tbsps. (1 oz. or 28 g)	Black pepper
1 cup (1 oz. or 28 g)	Crumpled bay leaves
1.3 lbs. (1 lb. 5 ozs.)	Sodium tripolyphosphate**
0.21 lb. (3 1/3 ozs. or 95 g)	Sodium erythorbate or sodium ascorbate@

*Other flavourings often are added to turkey, including monosodium glutamate, spices or spice extractives. Commonly used spices include cloves, cinnamon, oil of celery, and oil of black pepper. Add these ingredients according to personal preference.

**Phosphate will help hold moisture in the meat and slow development of rancidity. Phosphate can sometimes be obtained from a local locker plant.

Follow these procedures when making the brine:

1. Use cold water (36–40°F).
2. If you use phosphate, dissolve it in 3 gallons of the water. Stir it vigorously until it is all dissolved. (Some types of phosphate go into solution slowly.)
3. Dissolve the sodium erythorbate (if used) in the water.
4. Add salt, cure, sugar, and remaining water and stir until all ingredients are dissolved and the pickle solution is clear.
5. Add additional flavourings and mix well.

Cover brine curing procedure

Soaking time depends on the size of the bird. For example, keep a 2-pound broiler in the brine for 2 to 3 days. Cure larger birds—one day per pound of carcass:

1. Put birds in the curing vat and hold them under the brine with a clean board, stone or container of water. Be sure the brine fills the body cavity.
2. Keep the brine temperature between 32 and 40°F during the curing process.
3. At least once per week, remove birds from the vat, remix the brine and repack the birds to allow uniform contact of the brine with all parts of each carcass.

When the curing time is complete, remove excess salt by washing birds inside and out with fresh, cold tap water and soak them overnight in cold tap water. Remove birds from the water and allow them to drip dry in a cool place for about ½ hr before smoking.

Stitch curing procedure

For more rapid curing of large birds, you can inject the brine using a large syringe with a 12-gauge needle. Inject small amounts of brine into numerous locations to insure uniform distribution into all parts of the carcass. Try to inject into several locations through each hole you make in the skin. Numerous holes in the skin will detract from the appearance of your finished bird. Inject the bird with the pickle solution described above until the carcass weighs 11.8 per cent more than it did before injection. Then place the bird in the remainder of the pickle solution for 2 to 3 days. To remove excess salt, rinse the bird in cold tap water for 1 hr and allow to drip dry (about ½ hr).

Smoking and Cooking

Liquid smoke procedure

You can brush birds with liquid smoke, put into an oven at 300 to 325°F and cook to an internal temperature of 165°F. However, many people prefer the natural smoking procedure described below.

Natural smoking

The natural smoking procedure yields a product that is fully cooked and ready-to-eat. During the smoking process, maintain 80–90 per cent humidity in the smokehouse by dampening the sawdust or wood chips used for the smoke or by placing a pan of water near the heat source and adding water as it evaporates. This will help prevent weight loss and drying of the product. Put birds in stockinettes or cheesecloth, and hang in the smokehouse with the tail end up with no birds touching each other. You can use various types of hardwood, including apple, hickory, alder, and maple. Keep the sawdust or chips moist to prevent flare-ups and to provide humidity. Use a smokehouse temperature of 170°F for 6–10 hr (depending on amount of smoke desired) until the skin turns the desired light brown colour. Then raise the temperature of the smokehouse to 185–200°F and cook the meat until it reaches an internal temperature of 165°F. Insert a meat thermometer into the thickest part of the breast to determine the internal temperature. This entire smoking and cooking process will take from 16–24 hr for turkeys. During the final cooking phase, some people wrap the birds in foil to prevent excessive drying. The meat can be eaten immediately or it can be stored and eaten cold or properly reheated.

Storage

You should have an excellent product when you remove your smoked poultry from the smokehouse or oven. However, improper storage can ruin both the flavour and safety of your masterpiece. Put cured and smoked poultry, like all cured meats, in a container that will minimise exposure to air. Cured meats, especially cured poultry meats, are very susceptible to rancidity. Cured and smoked poultry requires refrigeration at 40°F or below and will keep for 2 to 3 weeks at those temperatures. If longer storage is necessary, properly packaged cured and smoked poultry can be frozen at 0°F for up to one year. Use a plastic bag for refrigerator storage. For long-term frozen storage, use a moisture-vapour-proof bag.

Chapter 20

Food Frying

INTRODUCTION

Frying is a popular method used in food preparation and manufacturing. During frying, several physical and chemical changes occur in foods that impart desirable characteristics. For example, a popular fried food, French Fries, is noted for its crunchy exterior and soft, moist interior. While oil is an excellent heating medium, a number of physical and chemical changes occurring in oil during heating are detrimental to the properties of oil.

These changes, due to oxidation, hydrolysis, and polymerisation, require that used oil be discarded at frequent intervals. The design of batch and continuous fryers is influenced by such changes in cooking oil. Oil migration into foods is another critical issue in frying. Recent developments in mathematical models provide quantitative descriptions of heat and mass transfer to help minimise oil uptake by foods during frying.

Frying is an old and widely used method of cooking and processing food. Typically, a food is immersed in heated oil for a short duration in a process known as immersion-oil frying. Numerous types of edible oils of plant and animal origin are used in frying, depending on regional availability. Palm oil is often used in Southeast Asia, coconut and groundnut oil in the Indian subcontinent, and olive oil in the Mediterranean region. During the last five decades, the Western food industry has become increasingly dependent on the frying process to manufacture a variety of snack foods. Fried foods such as potato chips, French fries, and fried fish and chicken have gained worldwide popularity. In this article, the term frying is used to describe a process in which a food is cooked by immersion in heated oil. Alternatively, this process is also referred to as immersion-oil frying and deep fat frying.

A wide variety of products are fried on an industrial scale. Among the most popular are potato chips (also called potato crisps), expanded snacks, roasted nuts, French fries (also called potato chips), extruded noodles, doughnuts, and frozen foods covered with batter, such as fish and chicken.

Deep frying is a most useful method of cooking food for four main reasons:

1. It is a fast.
2. Because of the short cooking period, it is possible to prepare food as it is required thereby keeping waste is kept to a minimum.

3. In deep frying, the food is immersed in a very hot material which sears and seals the food, keeping in more flavour then by many other methods of cooking.
4. The layer of fat or oil deposited on the food during frying improves the eating quality of the food. Frying also imparts a characteristic flavour which is different to that obtained by other methods of cooking.

Oils and fats are expensive and they are worth looking after carefully if they are to give a long and economic frying life. These guidelines set out the basic rules and principles of the process.

GENERAL RULES OF FRYING

1. Never heat the oil above 205°C (400°F) or it will spoil more rapidly. Use a thermostat or thermometer and regularly check them for accuracy, regulate the temperature of the oil as carefully as possible, avoiding hot spots and high flames. Frying at too low temperatures will result in greasy products and an excessive absorption of fat by the food.
2. Fry the food in the correct amount of oil. The general rule for batch fryers is to fry one part of food in six parts of oil. If too much food is immersed, the temperature of the oil will drop and the food will be greasy. If too little food is immersed, the amount of fat needed to top up the fryer becomes small and the main bulk of the oil will spoil more rapidly.
3. Choose the right medium for the job and use it properly. Solid fats should be treated more carefully during melting down and during topping up. Temperatures should not exceed 132°C (270°F) during the melting down of solid fats. Once melted, the fat can be heated to normal frying temperature.
4. Prepare the food carefully, ensuring that it is as dry as possible before frying. Wet foods – particularly potatoes – tend to make the oil froth and break down and this is unsafe and wasteful. Fragile foods must be handled carefully to avoid break-up during frying. If a potato whitener is used, the manufacturer's instructions should be followed.
5. Clean the oil regularly by filtering at the end of each day to remove the small pieces of charred food which might accumulate. Clean the equipment by scrubbing with soap and water once a week.

Rinse away any soap or detergent used in cleaning. Do not use iron, or copper utensils as these metals can accelerate the breakdown of oil.

PHYSICO-CHEMICAL CHANGES IN FOODS DURING FRYING

The immense popularity of fried foods is due to the unique flavour and texture imparted to food as it is fried. Many fried foods typically have a porous, crispy outer crust layer with unique flavour but are also soft and moist internally. With starchy foods, it is generally agreed that the crust layer develops as starches in the food gelatinise and the outer layer rapidly dries. However, the kinetics and mechanisms involved in crust formation and related structural changes have yet to be well understood. These mechanisms are dependent on the physical and chemical properties of the food material and the oil used in frying. The complexity of the frying process can be seen in many aspects. For instance, the structure and thickness of the porous crust layer is dependent on the product composition, the processing time, temperature, and composition of the frying oil and material being fried. Heat transfer between the oil and food surface is largely due to the convection mode, whereas heat flux across the crust layer is characterised by the conduction mode of heat transfer. Inter- and intra-sample irregularities pose a significant problem when trying to understand the basic driving forces involved in the movement of oil in a food during frying. This heterogeneity has led to the development of product-specific, empirical models that yield little in the way of fundamental knowledge. As a result, only limited progress has been made in developing a mechanistic understanding of the frying process. Frying is often the preferred method of cooking for several reasons. The relatively high temperature of the oil used as a heating medium in the process sharply reduces the cooking time, resulting in desirable sensory characteristics like crispy texture and pleasant aroma. In fried foods, such as potato chips and noodles, a product is fried until most of the moisture is removed and a porous structure is created throughout the product. With French fried potatoes, among other foods, the potato strips are fried for a sufficient duration until the outer region becomes porous and stiff, giving it a crispy texture, while the inner region is cooked and moisture is retained. Chemical changes create desirable aromas. The amount of oil absorbed during frying increases the total fat content and caloric value of a food, of concern when a low fat diet is desired.

EDIBLE OILS USED IN FRYING FOODS

The oil content of selected fried foods is shown in Table 20.1. In most cases, these foods have little or no native fat prior to frying. Most of the oil absorbed by a food takes place either during immersion in oil or immediately upon the removal from oil. With nuts and other foods having high oil content, the exchange of oil between the food and that used during frying alters the sensory and nutritional characteristics of the fried product.

Table 20.1: Typical oil content of fried foods.

Product	*Oil content*
Potato chips (also known as crisps)	33–38%
Precooked potato French fries	10–15%
Doughnuts	20–25%

Some of the commonly used oils in industrial applications involving food frying are listed in Table 20.2. In addition to the oils mentioned, many modified, fractionated, or hydrogenated oils are used in frying that provide required performance in terms of process, cost, and quality characteristics.

Table 20.2: Different types of oils used in food frying.

Coconut oil
Corn oil
Palm oil
Palm oleine
Rapeseed oil (low euricic acid)
Soybean oil
Sunflower seed oil

Physico-chemical Changes in Oil during Frying

Oil is an excellent heating medium, because it allows high rates of heat transfer into foods being cooked. However, the frying process also causes a number of chemical and physical changes in the oil. These changes not only influence the heating characteristics, but also bring about changes in the sensory and nutritional characteristics of foods.

Physico-chemical changes in the oil are due to three factors:

- Oxidative changes due to atmospheric oxygen entering the oil from the exposed surface of the oil to the surrounding atmosphere.
- Hydrolytic changes due to water vapours from the product undergoing frying.
- Thermal changes due to oil being maintained at high temperatures.

Hydrolytic reactions cause cleavage of the ester bond of a lipid, resulting in the formation of fatty acids, glycerol, and mono- and diglycerides. Because oxidative reactions and thermal changes alter the unsaturated constituents of triglycerides, at least one of the acyl radicals of the triglyceride molecule is altered. The three causative agents namely, moisture, oxygen, and temperature—have a synergistic effect on the compounds produced during frying. Volatile compounds produced during frying influence the organoleptic quality of the food. Non-volatile compounds in the oil are important, because they migrate into the food undergoing frying and are subsequently ingested. These non-volatile compounds are also the basis of several analytical procedures used to measure alterations in the oil due to frying.

The preceding mechanisms occur simultaneously. They depend on different types of foods and on interaction with food components. The reactions taking place in the oil are highly complex and are responsible for variation in the results of analytical methods. Several changes are observed in oils when used in repeated frying. These changes include:

- Development of unique sensory characteristics of oil and food being fried.
- Change in density and viscosity.
- Change in colour, such as darkening due to formation of polar compounds.
- Formation of foam due to polymer formation.
- Specific extinction of 232 and 270 nm of conjugated double bonds.
- Change in fatty acid composition, with increase in saturated acids.
- Increase in acid value due mostly to hydrolytic reactions.
- Decrease in iodine value due to elimination of double bonds resulting from polymerisation and other reactions.

Numerous factors are used to assess the quality of edible oils used in frying: oil colour, odour and taste, percentage of free fatty acids, peroxide value, iodine, and smoke point. These factors also play an important role in determining the final quality of fried foods.

TEMPERATURE CONTROL

Accurate control of temperature is essential and is best achieved by the use of a thermostat or by the regular use of a thermometer. It is also important to check the accuracy of the thermostat and thermometers themselves from time to time and to ensure that any instrument used is kept clean. In purchasing a thermometer, remember that the temperature to be measured will be high and probably at least 205°C (400°F) at times. Ensure that the instrument purchased is rated for use at these high temperatures. An automatic cut out which comes into operation at a temperature above normal frying temperature and well below the flash point of the frying medium, is useful as a safety precaution.

Heating a fat or oil to the normal frying temperature of 191°C (375°F) greatly increases its tendency to spoil and is one of the most important factors governing the life of oil. The higher the temperature, the quicker the oil will deteriorate. On frying equipment where gas flames are used, the flame must be adjusted so that it does not flare up round the sides of the frying vessel and never to a height above the surface of the oil, because of the danger of fire. Hotspots are also dangerous and should be corrected. As well as speeding up the breakdown of the frying medium, frying at too high a temperature will result in food which is darkly coloured – or charred on the outside before the inside is properly cooked. If the frying temperature is too low, the resulting product will be greasy because the surface of the food is not sealed rapidly enough on entering the frying medium. Low temperature frying will also result in excessive absorption of fat by the food.

An important factor when considering the frying temperature is the relative amount of frying medium to the food being fried. When too small a quantity of oil is used, the sudden introduction of an excessive amount of food – at room temperature or below – will result in a large drop in temperature and the appearance of faults associated with low temperature frying. This is even more important in the case of frozen foods; for example, falls of temperatures of 18–28°C (30–35°F) can occur when frozen fish pieces are immersed in hot oil. On the other hand, when too large a quantity of oil is used, only a small proportion of it will be lost by absorption. Only a low rate of 'topping up' is then required and because regular topping up with fresh oil tends to damp down the rate of spoilage, the bulk of the oil in the fryer can deteriorate more rapidly. As a general rule, one part of food should be fried in six parts of oil or fat.

PREPARATION OF FOOD

All food to be deep dried should be as dry as possible before immersion in hot oil. If foods – particularly potatoes – are fried too wet, there will be a tendency for the oil to froth and break down. As a result the oil will have a shorter life and frothing oil is dangerous. Fragile foods and foods with loose coatings must be handled carefully to avoid break-up during frying and the accumulation of charred material at the bottom of the kettle. The accumulation of material can accelerate fat spoilage.

Chips and other potato products are often prepared in advance of requirements. It is well known that potatoes discolour under these circumstances. There are several preparations on the market which stop this discolouration. Care should be taken not to use solutions which are too strong. Soaking for too long or neglecting to drain carefully after treatment also tends to discolour frying oil more rapidly. Do not add salt to the food before frying. If salt accumulates within the fryer, the oil will deteriorate prematurely.

FAT ABSORPTION AND TOPPING UP

Most operators top up the fryer from time to time. As a general guide the fat absorption of potato chips is usually 5–6%. That is, 10 kg of potato chips will pick up about 500–600 g of fat during frying. More porous foods such as doughnuts will absorb more fat than this and figures of up to 30% have been recorded. Fat absorption depends upon the time of frying (the longer the frying period, the greater the absorption), the total surface area of the food (the greater the area, the more absorption), the type of food surface (rough or porous surfaces absorb more fat), the frying temperature (the lower the temperature, the greater the absorption), the nature of the food and the nature and condition of the fat.

The general procedure in frying is to top up the fat as required. To some extent, the natural spoilage of the fat by heat is controlled or damped down by this process of continually adding fresh fat to the fryer. It is important to use the optimum amount of fat for the weight of the food being fried as this results in the best rate of topping up.

For this reason, it is wise to reduce the number of fryers in use when trade is less brisk. It has been said that if at least 20% of the fat is replaced daily, the frying medium is much less likely to require changing. Now-a-days with the use of blanched chips being more popular, top up rates are lowered and frying life extended due to the incorporation of blanching oil into the frying medium.

CHOICE OF FRYING MEDIUM

Due to the nature of their composition, some oils and fats tend to be more sensitive to heat and spoil more rapidly, than others. It is therefore safer to use the fats and oils which have been specifically designed and processed for the purpose of frying.

There is a wide range of frying media on the market, and the ones which are available can be divided into three groups, depending on their appearance at room temperature:

1. Solid – palm oil, lard, dripping, proprietary brands.
2. Liquid – groundnut oil, soyabean oil, rapeseed oil, corn oil etc. and blends of liquid oil and proprietary brands.
3. Fluid – proprietary brands.

Solid frying fats are generally very stable if they have been refined and stored properly. An exception is unrefined dripping which is more sensitive to heat and which is generally used at frying temperatures which are lower than normal.

Solid frying fats have to be dug out of the carton and the correct procedure is to melt them out gently (at temperatures not exceeding 132°C (270°F) before heating to frying temperature. Otherwise, they might burn before they melt. Many operators ignore this precaution, and frying life can be reduced as a result, despite the intrinsic stability of the material.

Liquid oils are easier to handle and use because they can be poured. The most stable liquid oils – groundnut and corn oils, for example – are generally the most expensive. Other oils and blends of oils are more economical, but rather less stable chemically.

Fluid frying media can offer the best of both worlds. They are pourable and do not need special melting before heating to frying temperature. They are generally more stable than normal vegetable oil blends. This improved stability, and the longer frying life which this entails, is brought about by additional processing during the production of the frying medium.

Price, stability and flavour (lack of off-flavour) are other considerations when choosing oil. Frying media often contain other materials, the most important being antioxidants and antifoaming agents or silicones. Antioxidants improve the storage life by suppressing spoilage by oxidation, and antifoaming agents extend frying life in batch fryers by controlling foaming.

It is useful to choose the frying medium to fit the food being fried and the busy-ness of the frying cycle. It has already been mentioned that regular topping up can damp down the rate of spoilage. If the food has a very low rate of fat absorption, or if the frying process is not busy, it is a definite advantage to choose from the most stable media. If the food has a high rate of absorption, fat spoilage is more likely to be controlled by continuous topping up with fresh fat or oil. In this case there may be less need to use a long-life frying medium.

SPOILAGE OF FATS AND OILS

As a fat or oil is used for frying, certain changes take place which are mainly caused by the effect of high temperature in the presence of air and water. The oil becomes darker in colour and more viscous. It will tend to froth particularly when wet foods are fried in it, smoke is more readily formed. Surfaces of the frying vessel become coated with a brown resinous material which is difficult to remove. Fried food becomes more discoloured and patchy in colour, and it begins to possess a poorer flavour and a greasier texture. Off odours will begin to be noticeable.

These are all caused by the natural deterioration of the oil. By the time a frying medium is discarded, probably about one fifth of it will have been altered by these breakdown processes. The frying life of oil will depend on the nature of the oil being used and on the way in which it has been treated.

The rate of breakdown of oil will depend upon its exposure to the oxygen in the air. It is, therefore, dependent on the surface area of the oil exposed to air and to a certain extent the steam which is given off from the food during frying tends to blanket the oil from oxygen. This suggests that it is better to keep the oil busily frying food for as long as possible. Oil held at frying temperature but standing idle is more likely to deteriorate. Many metals, notoriously copper, (and its alloys such as brass) and iron tend to accelerate the breakdown of fat. Some types of thermometer are made of brass, and often drainage taps and 'home-made' pieces of equipment including strainers, ladles and containers, are made from the wrong metal. These should all be avoided.

CLEANING

Once oil begins to deteriorate as a result of heating, the products which are formed tend to promote further deterioration and a sort of chain reaction is set up. A good system of cleaning should be in operation to help control this, and this implies the regular cleaning of both oil and equipment. The oil itself should be cleaned at the end of each day's run by passing it through a fine mesh strainer to remove particles of food. If left in the fryer, these particles will char; accelerating decomposition and producing smoke and off flavours. A stainless steel mesh is preferable to one made of copper or iron, as mentioned earlier. If a very fine mesh or filter paper or filter cloth is used to strain the frying medium it must be remembered that a fat which is solid at room temperature will tend to set up and block the strainer as it cools. The equipment must be emptied and cleaned at least once a week, to avoid the build-up of brown resinous material which is a natural breakdown product of oil. Cleaning should be effected by scrubbing with hot water and soap or detergent. Care must be taken where electric elements are located inside a fryer, partly to ensure they are thoroughly clean, and partly to avoid corrosion. Whatever soap or detergent is used it must be thoroughly rinsed away because soap and alkaline materials greatly promote the breakdown of oil. Also, if a fryer is not properly rinsed after cleaning, the fresh oil will already form a thin layer of fine foam on melting or initial heating. If the equipment is fitted with a fat trap, ensure that it is regularly cleaned to avoid odours and fire hazards. For the same reasons, regular attention should be paid to extractor hoods and ducts.

FRYING SPECIFIC FOODS

Doughnuts - it has already been mentioned that doughnuts absorb up to 30% of fat during frying and therefore the fat used for frying doughnuts discolours and smokes more readily than fat used for frying potato chips. However, because of the higher rate of absorption, the frying medium is 'turned over' at a greater rate. It is necessary to be particularly careful when frying doughnuts. For example, it is preferable to rest or prove the doughnuts on greased, rather than floured, surfaces because the flour will tend to fall off into the frying fat and char. In chemically raised doughnuts, it appears that increased fat and increased sugar in the recipe both result in more fat being absorbed during frying. The greater the surface area, the greater the absorption; cracks and rough surfaces increase the area, and finger shapes and rings have more surface area than spheres. There is also evidence that fat absorption is decreased by warmer ingredients, longer mixing times and stronger flours, although each of these may also result in poorer eating qualities. It is also advisable to experiment before adopting a new method.

Unless automatic equipment is being used, it is not easy to handle fully proved pieces of dough without damaging the structure. The dough can be transferred to the fryer by means of an oiled palette knife and the finger tips. Yeast raised doughnuts should be placed in the frying medium upside-down; this avoids the instability of the doughnuts during the second half of the frying process, after they have been turned over.

Many types of doughnuts are sugared after frying. For this reason, it is preferable to use a solid fat, because sugar adhesion is better and the sugar does not discolour so readily. The flavour of the doughnuts can be improved by adding a small quantity of cinnamon or mixed spice to the sugar. The doughnuts should be allowed to cool before sugaring, to prevent the formation of a wet, sodden coating caused by the steam escaping from the doughnut during cooling. The sugar in which doughnuts are rolled will pick up a quantity of fat; in bakeries, this sugar should be kept separate because some confectionary products, notably meringues, will suffer if fatty sugar is used.

Frozen fish - when frying frozen fish, the main point to bear in mind is that the sudden immersion of very cold material into frying oil is likely to reduce the temperature considerably. The effect of this will depend on the type of frying equipment used. In automatically controlled fast recovery kettles, the temperature of the oils will return quickly to the correct point while the food is being fried. In slower kettles and ones which are controlled by hand, the frying temperatures may not recover in time and allowances must therefore be made when setting the temperature of the oil before the food is introduced.

Above 191°C (375°F) the oil will spoil rapidly and if fish is fried at too high a temperature, the batter will cook too quickly and too hard, while the fish at the centre may remain relatively uncooked. If the temperature is too low (because of the effect of the frozen fish), fat absorption will be greater and the food will be soft and greasy.

Frozen food generally - the points made in the section on frozen fish are true of frozen foods in general. As well as these, it must be remembered that free ice is often present in foodstuffs which have been frozen. This ice becomes water and produces steam during frying and there is therefore the danger of introducing excess moisture into the frying kettle with the food. Also, thick pieces of frozen food are difficult to cook right through, and they considerably reduce the temperature of the frying medium. As long as the food is small or in thin sections, this may not be a problem, but larger pieces benefit from thawing before frying. In this case, it is preferable to drain the defrosted food to remove excess moisture produced by the melting ice. Defrosted foods should be handled carefully, because they are often fragile.

Potatoes - potatoes should be stored in a cool, 7–10°C (45–50°F) dark, dry, airy place and not in close proximity to strong smelling produce or products. Medium to large tubers tend to give a higher yield of long chips and many buyers therefore purchase supplies graded over a 45mm or 50mm square riddle. Potatoes with low dry matter content tend to produce soggy chips. Processors test samples with a potato hydrometer and will not usually use samples with dry matters below 19%. If the tubers have been stored at below 7–10°C (45–50°F) or are immature, the reducing sugar content may be too high (over 0.25%). Such samples produce dark brown chips. Samples can be test fried before purchase to eliminate those samples with excess sugar or which produce chips that turn black after cooking.

After peeling and chipping, the pieces should be kept soaking in water until required, to remove surface starch and to retard the development of discolouration or browning. Several proprietary potato 'whiteners' are available and these prevent discolouration; when used, the manufacturer's directions should be carefully followed. Too strong a solution, too long an immersion period or insufficient draining can result in a discolouration of the frying medium. In some cases, excess free starch on the potato is transferred to the frying medium where it will carbonise and cause the medium to deteriorate more rapidly. Deep fried potatoes can be cooked by straight through methods or by blanching and browning in two stages. In the 'straight through' method, raw potato chips are deep fried at 188–191°C (370–375°F) until brown and cooked, (4–5 minutes). These can be stored for short periods in a warm dry place.

In the blanching and browning method, the potato chips are first blanched by frying at 168–177°C (330–350°F) until cooked but not brown (4-6 minutes). After draining, these can be stored, but should be refrigerated if kept for more than two hours. When required, blanched chips are browned by frying at 191°C (375°F) for 2–3 minutes. The advantage of this two-stage method is that much of the cooking process can be completed during slack periods.

Vegetables and Fruit - firm vegetables (cauliflower, carrot, onion) can be cut and separated into uniform pieces and fried at 177–191°C (350–375°F). Before frying the pieces are dusted with flour and dipped in batter, or soaked in milk or beaten egg and dipped in breadcrumbs or seasoned flour. Frying times will vary according to size but is generally between 2–4 minutes. Softer vegetables (corn etc.) can be mixed with a batter and spooned into the frying medium.

Fruit is generally dipped in fritter (that is, sweetened) batter and fried at 177–188°C (350–370°F) for 2–4 minutes depending on size and type. Pineapple, bananas, peach, apple slices etc. can be treated in this manner. Foods containing fat - precautions should be taken against contaminating the frying medium with other fats. Sausages, chicken, beefburgers and other meat products all contain various amounts of fat which is still in its natural unrefined state. Obviously these will tend to melt during the frying process and their presence will lessen the life of the frying medium. Enclosing such food in batter before frying will tend to reduce this danger.

RECOMMENDED FRYING TEMPERATURES

The actual temperatures and times used for frying will depend on the type of equipment used, the throughput and oil recovery rate, the size of the pieces being fried, the nature and condition of the frying fat or oil and upon local taste. However, the following temperatures and times are offered as a guide. Frozen foods may take up to a minute longer than the times indicated.

Items	*Suggested temperatures*		*Approximate time*
	°C	*°F*	*(minutes)*
Potato chips, straight through	188	370	4–5
Potato chips, blanching	166	330	4–6
Potato chips, browning	191	375	2–3
Potato chips, frozen, blanched	180	355	4–5
Fish (battered pieces)	188	370	3–5
Prawns and Scampi (battered)	177	350	3–5
Meat cutlets	177	350	3–6
Chicken pieces	171	340	6–12
Sausages	177	350	1–2
Fruit fritters	177	350	2–4
Vegetables	177	350	2–4
Onion rings	177	350	2–4
Doughnuts	188	370	1–2
Choux paste	182	360	1–2

BASIC CHEMISTRY OF FATS AND OILS

Fats and oils are obtained from a wide variety of sources and each one has its own individual properties. They are, however, all of the same chemical type. Each of the 'arms' of this shape can combine with another substance known as a fatty acid, to build up a molecule. Because of the way in which its composition is built up, the chemical substance having this form is known as a triglyceride, and all fats and oils are made up of a mixture of these triglycerides. A number of different fatty acids exist and to a large extent the character of a particular oil or fat (and its frying properties) is dictated by the actual fatty acids which are present in the individual triglyceride molecules. Some of these component fatty acids are longer or shorter than others and they can all combine with a glycerol 'arm'.

There's another complication. Some of these fatty acids possess what could be called a point of weakness (a chemist would call it a double or triple bond) in the molecule. The reason for this is bound up with the chemistry of the molecule and its presence tends to make that particular material more sensitive and more unstable. To make matters worse, some fatty acids can have two of these points of weakness and some have three. The more there are, the more unstable the material is likely to be.

Finally, it is possible to have these points of weakness in different places. In the case of a fatty acid with two points of weakness, they can be sited to each other or far from each other. The closer they are together, the more unstable the resulting molecule will be.

From these descriptions, it can be seen that there can be hundreds of ways in which a triglyceride molecule may be built up. A particular fat is a mixture of many of these different triglycerides. The properties of lard are dictated to a large extent by the types of fatty acid which are present. Groundnut oil is also a mixture but the basic substances, though belonging to the same family, are slightly different and are present in different proportions.

CHEMISTRY OF FAT SPOILAGE

With a basic idea of the simple chemistry of fats and oils, it is possible to explain how they can spoil. Fats and oils are natural products obtained from plants and animals, and no matter how well they have been selected and refined, they will begin to spoil as time goes by. In frying, oil is forced to break down at a greater rate than normal because of the high temperatures which are involved.

Stages of Spoilage

During frying, it is possible to define three different stages over which spoilage and breakdown can occur:

1. The storage period, which starts as soon as the fat is produced and ends when it is placed in the fryer. During this time, the fat is exposed to air at room temperature.
2. The standby period, when the fat is heated in the fryer, including the time taken to bring the fat up to frying temperature, and the time taken for it to cool when frying is finished. During this period, the fat is exposed to air at high temperature.
3. The frying period, when the fat is actually being used for frying. During this time, the fat is exposed to air, steam and the food being fried, at temperatures varying between 177–191°C (350–375°F).

Reactions involved

There are a number of things which can break a fat down, and the type of reaction which takes place depends upon the particular period under consideration. The main reactions which can occur are summarised in the Table 20.3.

Table 20.3: Period and speed of reaction.

Period	*Reaction*	*Speed of reaction*
Storage	Oxidation	Slow
Standby	Oxidation	Fast
	Isomerisation	Fast
	Polymerisation	Slow
	Pyrolysis	Slow
Frying	Oxidation	Fast
	Isomerisation	Fast
	Polymerisation	Slow
	Pyrolysis	Slow
	Hydrolysis	Fast

Oxidation

During the storage period, the only chemical spoilage reaction which normally takes place is known as oxidation, attack by oxygen in the air, In fact, it is a special type of oxidation in which the products that are formed tend to promote the reaction, making it take place at an ever increasing rate. The oxygen in the air attacks the points of weakness in the fat.

Obviously, the more points of weakness there are in a particular fat, the more the effect will be. In the storage period, it is some time before the effect becomes really noticeable.

During the standby and frying periods, the fat is heated to about 191°C (375°F). Once a fat is heated, the process of oxidation, which was going on during storage, becomes much faster. As a result, the weak links in the fat are broken and new substances begin to be formed in the fryer. Unfortunately, most of these substances are evil smelling and are responsible in part, for the characteristic odour in a well-used fat and for off-tastes in the fried food.

Certain metals such as iron and copper accelerate oxidation of fats and should be avoided. For this reason it is also advisable not to add salt before frying, because the salt's sodium ions act as an oxidation catalyst. Salt also contains other impurities such as copper and iron ions. These impurities cause increased oxidation of the frying medium.

Isomerisation

In the process of isomerisation, the molecule shuffles itself around and the points of weakness often end up closer together as a result. Isomerisation can therefore make the fat more unstable and more sensitive to oxidation.

Polymerisation

This means, simply, that two or more molecules of the same material have joined together to make a larger one. For example, polystyrene ceiling tiles and coving are made from a colourless liquid called styrene. The molecule of this liquid are made to join together – polymerise – to such an extent that they produce a solid. In frying, there is a tendency, more marked with some oils than others, for a yellowish-brown resin-like substance to be formed on the surfaces of the fryer and baskets. This substance is formed by the process of polymerisation.

Pyrolysis

This also occurs during the standby and frying period, although it proceeds at a slow rate. Pyrolysis is a sort of burning, where the fat simply breaks up into smaller compounds.

Hydrolysis

When food is fried in hot oil, this further reaction is introduced. The water which is present in the form of steam (from the chips for example) attacks the oil. This is the reverse reaction to the way in which the triglyceride molecule was built up, and the parts broken off are fatty acids. They are called 'free' fatty acids. The smoke point of oil is related to the amount of free fatty acids present and their breakdown products have objectionable smells. Eventually, they cause the oil and fried food to develop off-flavours. Caustic Soda and other alkalis used for cleaning tend to promote hydrolysis and should be well rinsed away after they have been used.

VISIBLE EFFECTS OF CHEMICAL SPOILAGE

It is interesting at this stage to study the frying process in the light of these reactions. When oil is heated and used for frying, a number of changes become apparent.

Distinctive Odours and Flavours Develop

This is caused by the appearance of new compounds as the fat breaks down. Most of these new compounds have an objectionable smell and flavour but because they are relatively light weight, they tend to be driven off by the steams as they are formed. They can be smelt in the atmosphere or tasted in the first pieces of food that are fried but eventually they can become more pronounced. They are mainly caused by the oxidation and hydrolysis of the fat.

Colour darkens

Most properly refined oils are pale in colour but as they are heated, they become darker until eventually they approach the colour of strong black coffee. This is mainly the result of the oxidation process which yields substances by mechanisms which are still not fully understood. There are also colour changes taking place in the frying food, the surfaces taking on colour by caramelisation as it is cooked. These colours can dissolve in oil and will tend to darken the frying medium. Indeed, some of the dark colour is due to the presence of carbon in very fine form; so fine that filtration will not remove it.

Oil tends to smoke

The larger the quantity of fatty acids present in the heated oil, the more it tends to smoke. As the oil begins to deteriorate under the effect of heat, more of these breakdown products appear. Consequently smoke is formed at lower and lower temperatures as frying proceeds. As long as the frying areas is well ventilated, this may not be a serious performance fault in itself, but the smoke is acrid and objectionable and it serves as an indication of the condition of the oil. Moreover, all the associated properties are affected, and the flash points and fire points are reduced, increasing the risk of fire.

Oil becomes thicker

As oil is heated, it becomes thicker and more viscous. This is mainly due to polymerisation, by which molecules join together to make larger ones. It is a serious performance fault as it causes a number of problems. As the oil becomes more viscous, fat absorption increases because the oil does not drain from the food so readily. Also, the bubbles which are formed at the surface are more stable, longer lasting. The amount of oil in contact with air at the surface is increased, and increased oxidation results.

Oil tends to foam

Some of the compounds which are formed when oil is heated are chemically related to those which are actually made commercially for their foaming properties. They are formed by oxidation and hydrolysis. At the same time, impurities can accelerate these reactions, particularly the presence of alkaline materials which might have been used to clean the kettles. These reactions, as well as making the oil foam, also tend to increase the penetration of the oil into the fried food, which results in higher fat absorption. There are various important effects of chemical spoilage which become visible in frying oil. They are summarised in the Table 20.4.

Table 20.4: Effects of chemical spoilage and their causes.

Fault	*Causes*
Odours and flavours develop	Oxidation, Hydrolysis
Smoke forms	Oxidation, Hydrolysis, Pyrolysis
Oil foams	Oxidation, Hydrolysis
Colour darkens	Oxidation, Caramelisation
Oil thickens	Polymerisation, Oxidation
Oil forms resins	Hydrolysis, Isomerisation

ROLE OF THE OIL REFINER

The oil refiner can do a number of things to help damp down the chemical spoilage of a frying oil or fat. Oils have different stabilities towards heat and frying, and these differences are due to their basic chemistry. In particular these differences are related to the number of points of weakness in the molecule. Some oils and fats are stable enough for many food applications, but are too sensitive to heat to merit consideration for use as a frying medium. The refiner will know from experience which oils, and which blend of oils are likely to give better performance than others. Those which find commonest use include palm, soyabean and rapeseed oils, lard and tallow or dripping, also available are corn, groundnut and cottonseed oils, but these are generally more expensive.

It is more important to properly refine a frying fat or oil than any other. If all the impurities naturally present in the crude oil are not removed in the refining process, they can cause all these spoilage reactions to go on at a faster rate. Naturally occurring emulsifiers such as lecithin, which is found in most crude oils, will cause a frying medium to smoke or discolour sooner. Small quantities of metal elements such as copper and iron are fatal because they will provoke the reaction known as oxidation. Special efforts are made by the refiner to remove these metals and in normal circumstances; one would expect to find less than one part of them in about one million parts of refined oil. This care can be completely cancelled out by the fryer by using equipment containing, say copper or brass.

The refiner can use additives to improve the stability of his oil. Antioxidants, for example are permitted additives which slow down the rate of oxidation. This effect is most marked in the storage period, when it delays the onset of spoilage by oxidation. Once the oil is heated to frying temperature, this effect tends to be lost because the antioxidant is eventually boiled off.

The refiner can also add substances known as antifoaming agents. These tend to reduce the amount of frothing or foaming which takes place at the surface of the fat and by doing this, they cut down the rate of deterioration, particularly that caused by oxidation. Because antifoaming agents are extremely effective, the average rate of addition is as low as two parts per million. It is also possible to improve the stability of an oil or fat by chemical modification. It is possible to use a chemical process to reduce the number of points of weakness in a fat or oil. This process is called hydrogenation and it is achieved by bubbling gas called hydrogen through the heated oil under very carefully controlled conditions. It results in the gradual disappearance of these points of weakness and because of this, the oil becomes more stable. The melting point of the oil is increase at the same time, and because of this, the process is often called 'hardening'.

Physical modification of oils is also possible, and it can take several forms. For example, it is possible to take fat which is normally solid at room temperature, melt it and allow it to cool slowly in a tank so that it begins to crystalise. After allowing this to occur, it can be filtered to give a liquid portion and solid portion. Palm oil can be subjected to this process and the liquid part which is obtained can be used as frying oil.

To summarise, an oil refiner can use a number of techniques in order to produce a frying medium, of good performance: Choice of oil – Proper refining – Use of additives – Chemical modification – Physical modification.

ROLE OF THE FRYER

It doesn't matter how carefully the frying process is conducted, all these spoilage reactions will be going on in the fryer to some extent. However, if good fats and good frying practices are used, some of the effects can be minimised. This is why the food should be as dry as possible, why cleaning both the oil and the equipment should be carried our regularly, and why the oil should not be overheated. The hotter the oil, the faster will be the rate of all these reactions. However, frying must be carried out at a certain minimum temperature, or the fried food will be greasy and the fat usage (by absorption) will go up. Therefore, a watchful eye should be kept on the temperature, and thermostats should be checked regularly to make sure they are working correctly.

In a more optimistic vein, there is a tendency for the heat and steam generated during frying to drive off some of the breakdown products that are formed. Also, if the fryer is regularly topped up with fresh fat, the effect of these spoilage reactions may be damped down so that they might not get out of hand. Because of this last point, it is advisable to fry the correct proportion of food to fat. In general, the best ration appears to be to fry one part of food in six parts of fat.

It is not necessarily wise to economise by only filling the fryer, say, and half full of oil or fat. The specific surface area of the frying medium is the surface area of the medium divided by its volume. The specific surface area of a half full fryer is twice that of a full fryer. That is to say, twice the proportion of frying medium is on the surface if the fryer is half full. Oxidation is a result of the oxygen of the air attacking the frying medium, and common sense will indicate that oxidation occurs at the surface of the fat or oil. It can therefore be argued that, the shallower the oil in the fryer, the bigger proportion of it will be at the surface, and the more important oxidation becomes. Remember, that as soon as oil is heated, it will begin to break down, however good it is. It is best to keep the oil as busy as possible. Never heat three fryers when two will do.

FIRE HAZARDS

Fire properties of oils and fats. Oil is a fire hazard. In general, there is little difference in the fire properties of refined oils and fats of various types. Most refined oils have flash points of between 310–330°C

(590–625°F), the flash point being the temperature at which the oil is capable of being ignited but not of supporting combustion. Most refined oils have fire points in the range of 365–375°C (690–710°F), the fire point being the temperature at which the oil will support continued combustion. In the case of unrefined oils and fats (some drippings, for example), or fats which have already deteriorated by heating, these figures are correspondingly lower.

Preventing fires

In commercial frying processes, it appears that most fires occur because a thermostat has failed after a kettle has been left unattended. They can also be caused by the frying medium frothing over (because of the continued frying of wet food for example), particularly when a naked flame is nearby or is used as the source of heat. Once started, a fire can quickly spread to the ducting of an exhaust system, particularly if this is not regularly cleaned or fitted with a fat filter.

Putting out a fire

If noticed early, many fires can be extinguished by cutting of the source of heat and closing the lid of the equipment (if there is one), and/or covering the burning oil with a fire blanket. The blanket should be left in position for at least 20 minutes to ensure that the temperature has dropped below the fire point. Foam can be used, but this should be allowed to fall gently onto the burning oil, otherwise the fire may spread. Warn the occupants of the building and alert the Fire Brigade.

Never overheat oil. Always dry the food as much as possible before frying to minimise frothing. Never leave the kettle unattended while the oil is heating. Fit a thermostat. An overriding thermal cut out is also useful. Regularly clean ducting and exhaust system. Keep fire-fighting equipment handy. Have a word with the local Fire Officer. If a fire starts, switch of the heat and close the lid of the kettle. Cover the fire with a fire blanket and leave in position for at least 20 minutes. Warn the occupants of the building and alert the local Fire Brigade.

Chapter 21

Microwave, Ohmic and Radio Frequency Heating

INTRODUCTION

This chapter discusses latest methods of food processing, i.e. microwave heating, ohmic heating and radio frequency heating in food processing industries.

Microwave heating: Microwave ovens have become an indispensable appliance in the 21st century household in countries like the United States and Canada, as well as many European countries. The increasing urbanisation in developing countries and accessibility to power has also led to an increase in the usage of microwave ovens at the household level worldwide. Even today, microwave ovens are mainly used for heating and reheating of foods, however, trends show that they are used increasingly also for cooking and defrosting.

The industrial applications using microwaves have seen an expansion in recent years and industrial scale microwave processing units have been developed for drying, precooking of meat, pasteurisation of ready meals, and tempering of meat and fish. Modern food consumers are demanding high quality, minimally processed products, which has led to the development of novel microwave processing technologies for thawing, blanching, baking, pasteurisation, and microwave-assisted extraction of bioactive compounds.

Ohmic heating: Ohmic heating the innovative method of food processing technology, which supersede retort, and aseptic packaging. Electrical heating involves the application of alternating voltage to food. Compared with retort heating, which uses a heat transfer medium, ohmic heating allows for high heating efficiency and rapid heating.

Radio frequency heating: Radio frequency (RF) heating is an advanced and emerging technology for food application because of its higher penetration depth, heat distribution and low energy consumption. Due to this reason, RF has entered the food industry to sterilise, pasteurise, disinfect food and agricultural commodity like fruits and dry nuts, post baking and in many other applications. The demand for safe, hygienic, tastier, no fat and preservative free food has widened up RF application in the modern industries.

MICROWAVE HEATING

This section discussing microwave heating as one method of thermal food processing. The higher standard of living and soaring income of consumers have lead for the demand for the modern food processing application. The technological revolution and nutritional awareness have increased the popularity of the microwave heating. Microwave heating is known for its operational safety and nutrient retention capacity with minimal loss of heat-labile nutrients such as vitamins B and C, dietary antioxidants, phenols and carotenoids. This review aims to provide a brief update of microwave heating and its application for food processing applications, with special emphasis on its impact on food quality in terms of microbial and nutritional value changes.

The microwave technology was principally used for communication, with the development of radar during the Second World War. It was during 1946, a self taught engineer Dr. Percy Spencer was testing a new vacuum tube called a magnetron, to his surprise the candy bar in his pocket melted. This incident lead to the introduction of microwave energy into the food industry. In recent years, microwave oven has become one of the most popular home appliances for food processing applications. The consumers have widely accepted the microwave technology due to its wide range of advantages, which has helped them to overcome from the fear and taboos that existed in the beginning. Microwave heating is a volumetric heating process, where heat is generated evenly throughout the entire volume of the food material. This is due to the complete interaction between microwave, polar water molecules and charged ions in food. Microwave energy is selectively absorbed by areas of greater moisture, with more uniform temperature and moisture profiles. The microwave technology has emerged as one of the most promising food processing technology. It has gained popularity due to its considerable advantages over conventional heating methods. It has been applied in various food processing industries such as cooking, pasteurisation, sterilisation, thawing, baking, blanching and drying of food materials. The reimbursements include high heating rates, lower processing time, more uniform heating, safe handling, easy operation, low maintenance and energy efficiency.

Electromagnetic Spectrum

Microwaves are form of electromagnetic energy. Microwave energy is a non ionising radiation that causes molecular motion by migration of ions and rotation of dipoles but does not cause change in molecular structure. Microwave energy occupies a part of electromagnetic spectrum, and is characterised by being situated in the wavelength interval between 1mm to 1m and frequency interval between 300 MHz and 300 GHz. These are normally used for the industrial processing of foods being between 915 and 2450 MHz and, for domestic use, of 2450 MHz

How Micro Oven Works

The most prominent characteristic of microwave heating is volumetric heating, which is quite different from conventional heating. In volumetric heating the materials can absorb microwave energy directly and internally and convert it to heat. It is this characteristic that leads to advantages using microwaves to process materials. Microwave oven uses electromagnetic waves called microwaves to heat food. The micro-waves oscillate at a very high speed, normally 2450 times per second. When food is placed in a microwave oven, various food ingredients behave differently. The main ingredient that enables food to be heated by micro-waves is water. The higher the water content of food, the faster is the heating rate. Water in molecular level behaves exactly like a magnet. Water has two oppositely charged ends due to presence of positively charged 2 Hydrogen atoms and a negatively charged Oxygen molecule. Therefore, water in food behaves like a magnet. If a bar magnet is held above another bar magnet, and you rotate the held magnet, the other one also rotates. Similarly, due to two different poles in water, when micro-waves oscillate the water molecules rotate. This is because the negatively charged end of water is attracted to positively charged end of micro-wave, while the positive end of water is attracted to the negative charged end of micro-waves. The micro- waves rotate at extremely high speed of 2450 time per second. This means for every second a micro-wave rotates, the water molecule also rotates 2450 times. This extremely high rotation rate causes water molecules to collide with each other at very fast rate. This creates friction between water molecules. This friction generates heat. The heat flows through the food by conduction, convection or radiation. Therefore food warms up.

Dielectric Properties

The feasibility of using microwave energy for the heating or drying of any material is dependent on dielectric properties of the food sample (dielectric constant and dielectric loss factor), which determine microwave power absorption as well as microwave energy penetration. The heating pattern of a sample, heated with microwave energy will depend upon the dissipation factor (tan δ) of the sample. The dissipation factor is the ratio of samples dielectric loss or loss factor (ε'') to its dielectric constant (ε'). The dielectric constant is the measure of the samples ability to obstruct the microwave energy as it passes through it, and the loss factor measures the sample ability to dissipate the energy, i.e. the amount of input microwave energy being converted into heat. The dissipation factor is finite for absorptive material. The dissipation factor is different for different materials. The greater the dissipation factor of a sample less is the penetration of the microwave energy at a given frequency. Therefore more amount of microwave energy is dissipated as heat. Microwave energy is dissipated as heat in the sample by two mechanisms: ionic conduction and dipolar rotation.

Ionic conduction: Ionic conduction is the conductive migration of the dissolved ions in the applied electromagnetic field. The ionic migration is a flow of current that results in I^2R losses (heat production) due to resistance to ion flow. The ionic conduction is affected by ion concentration, ion mobility and solution concentration. All ions in the solution contribute to ionic conduction process. Every ionic solution consist of at least two ionic species (e.g. Na^+ and Cl^- ions) and each species will conduct current according to its concentration and mobility, (the net movement of ions in the electric field generates heat, which increases the temperature of the sample). The increase in concentration increases ionic conduction.

Dipolar rotation: Dipolar rotation refers to the alignment of molecules in the sample that have dipole moments, when exposed to the electric field. As the electric field of the microwave energy increases, it aligns the polarised molecules. As the field decreases, thermally induced disorder is restored. The applied micro field causes the molecules temporarily to align in one same direction, when the field is removed, the molecules return to disorder causing agitation and release of thermal energy. At 2450 MHz, the alignment of the molecules followed by their return to disorder occurs 4.9×10^9 times per second and results in very rapid heating.

Industrial application of microwave heating

Pasteurisation and sterilisation: Microwave assisted pasteurisation and sterilisation have been motivated by the fast and effective microwave heating of many foods containing water or salts and better quality of product. Pasteurisation is a process applied generally to liquid foods mainly to kill key pathogens and inactivate vegetative bacteria and enzymes to make food safe for consumption. The experiments have showed that microwave pasteurisation of milk for 2.5 min resulted in 97.7% reduction of bacteria Villamiel and others. Microwave heat treatment of milk for 3, 8 and 10 min completely inactivated *C. jejuni, Y. enterocolitica and L. monocytogenes,* respectively. The effect of microwave heating of milk was studied on the parameters such as denaturation of α-lactoglobulin and the inactivation of alkaline phosphatase and lactoperoxidase. The results obtained were compared with the conventional heating in a plate heat exchanger, and found that the degree of inactivation in both cases was similar. Nikdel and others described a continuous-flow microwave system to pasteurise orange juice using PME (pectin methyl esterase (PME) and microbial count as an index of the adequacy of pasteurisation. The inactivation of PME and *Lactobacillus plantarum* was found to be more pronounced using microwaves as compared to conventional heating. Microbial destruction thus was much more temperature sensitive under microwave heating than under thermal heating.

Sterilisation is a more severe thermal treatment of foods. The sterilisation is recognised as a thermal process sufficient to eliminate toxin-producing *C. botulinum* from the food, make the food commercially sterile if adequately packed and stored at room temperature. Microwave sterilisation has been studied for potential commercial applications. However, the commercialisation has faced several problems with some limited success. A 915-MHz, single-mode, MW sterilisation system for processing packaged foods was developed at Washington State University (WSU) to provide the concept of MW technology in pasteurisation and sterilisation applications. This system has been used for studying the influence of MW sterilisation on quality of various foods, Sun and others studies demonstrated that asparagus sterilised by microwave-circulated water combination shoed greater antioxidant activity and greener colour than did asparagus processed by conventional method.

Guan and others study suggest that macaroni and cheese products processed by MCWC showed a reduced microbial count and matched the calculated degree of sterilisation (F_0 value). However, microwave sterilisation has some problems such as unpredictable and non-uniform energy distribution. Therefore, progress of microwave sterilisation at the industrial level has been relatively slow. But continuous studies and researches have overcome this problem.

Thawing and tempering: Thawing is the process of taking a frozen product from frozen state to an unfrozen state (at temperature usually above 0°C) where there is no residual ice, i.e. 'defrosting'. Thawing is often considered as simply the reversal of the freezing process. The frozen foods are thawed before cooking, to ensure that during cooking the food is heated sufficiently to kill harmful bacteria. If large frozen foods are not thawed prior to cooking, it will remain uncooked in the centre whilst being burnt or overcooked on the surface. The major problem of conventional thawing are large space requirements and long time which may result in chemical and bacteriological deterioration. When frozen foods are thawed, the surface area of the food is the first to rise in temperature and bacterial multiplication can recommence which were restricted in frozen foods. The use of Microwave energy can overcome this problem, as heat is generated with the food from the center to the surface, hence making microwave thawing a faster process than other methods. The major disadvantage of microwave thawing is that it does not occur uniformly and this phenomenon is known as runaway heating. Non uniformity in heating arises due to uneven power distributions and the increasing power absorption in liquid regions.

Therefore, it is necessary to control the heat generated by the microwaves. Tong and others designed a microwave oven with variable continuous power and a feedback temperature controller to maintain a desired temperature gradient within a model food system. Using this apparatus, thawing time was reduced by a factor of seven compared to convective thawing. In commercial practice the thawing is applied for relatively few products such as frozen meat, fish, vegetables, fruit, butter and juice concentrate. The thawing allowed the seafood product to be easily separated. The microwave thawing of frozen, raw, headless shrimp was noted as advantageous for many reasons, production control was improved, water usage was substantially reduced, ice requirements were reduced, since there was no temperature overshoot, bacteriological quality control was improved and costs were lower than for air or water thawing.

Tempering is the process of taking a product to a temperature where a substantial amount of the water in the product is in the form of ice but not all the water has turned to ice. This temperature must be below the freezing point and is usually between –5 to –2°C. At this state the product is rigid, but not hard and thus easier to cut. The product can either be cooled to this state from a temperature above the freezing point or warmed from a frozen temperature. The idea of microwave tempering as opposed to microwave thawing was studied by many scientists. Early work predicted that complete thawing with microwave was not practical, however, microwave tempering showed great potential. Microwave tempering can be used as an alternative to thawing because in most cases complete thawing is not necessary, and is a waste of energy, affects quality, and increases processing time. Microwave tempering has several advantages over most thawing processes. The microwave tempering process can handle large amounts of frozen product at small cost, has a high yield, and is accomplished in small spaces with no bacterial growth. In meat processing industry, the meat used is usually obtained in thick frozen blocks below –18°C. The primary operation of meat processing is to separate individual sections into smaller pieces. The mechanical operation requires the blocks be tempered from their solid frozen state to a point where cutting or separation can be carried out easily without damage to the product. Conventional tempering techniques either with water or air, subject the outer surfaces of the product bulk to warmer temperatures for long periods. This results in large temperature gradients. In addition, the conventional tempering process takes a long time (several days) with considerable drip loss especially resulting in loss of protein, which represents an economic loss. Microwaves can easily penetrate the whole frozen product, thus effectively reaching the inner regions within a short time. The process has been successfully used by meat, fish, and poultry industries for further processing while the dairy industry has exploited the technology for tempering of butter and frozen foods and to reduce the chances of rancidity during bulk freezing of butter. It has been the most successful applications of microwave in the dairy industry.

Precooking and cooking: The objective of pre-cooking operations is to reduce preparation time for the consumer. Precooking is recommended for many foods such a cereal flours, parboiling of rice, bacon and dried meats such as beef jerky which is precooked to a safe internal temperature before drying. The combined benefits of convenience, health and variety have increased the market of precooked products. However a second heat treatment is required for cooking of the precooked products. Microwave heating is found to be an ideal system for cooking bacon compared to conventional grilling. It is reported that most of the bacon usage in food services is precooked in microwave ovens. Microwave heating of bacon produces better structure with less shrinkage. Microwave heating has also found a possible application in precooking of various cereal products which helps in treating the starch, basically to reduce its gelatinisation time during final preparation of the food product. Velupillai and others developed a process for parboiling rough rice using microwave technology. Kaasova and others found that during parboiling process the gelatinisation of rice starch is progressively faster during microwave treatment than conventional treatment.

Cooking is one of the most familiar application of microwave oven. Microwave heating is so rapid that it takes the product to the desired temperature in a short time, hence it is possible to do selective and quick cooking. The microwave oven is well suited for cooking the food in small quantities, especially for households, though not convenient for mass cooking. If the sizes of foods are small and the shape of foods is flat, the uniform heating through overall volume is possible. Microwave cooking has advantage of less loss of moisture contents and the greatest energy savings, and the nutrition of foods will be preserved very well. Various studies have been conducted to study the effect of microwave cooking on the food components. The controlled microwave cooking of unsoaked rice and presoaked rice compared with conventional cooking showed a reduction in energy consumption. The microwave cooking of chickpea flour have shown to retain higher percentage of major minerals (such as K, Ca, Na, and Mg) and minor elements (Cu, Fe and Zn) contrasting to fried cooking and traditional cooking methods. Various studies were conducted to study the effect of microwave cooking on vitamin content of foods. Alajaji and El-Adawy 2006 studies reported that higher concentration of riboflavin, thiamin, and pyridoxine were retained in microwave cooked chickpea seeds than compared with boiling and autoclave cooking. A significant reduction in cooking time was observed with microwave cooking. Marconi and others reported that microwave cooking with sealed vessels enabled a drastic reduction in cooking time, for chickpeas and beans compared with conventional cooking. The cooking time is effected by a few components of food (such as water fat, etc.). Das and Rajkumar 2011 investigated the effect of various fat levels on microwave cooked goat meat patties. Microwave cooking time was found to reduce with an increase in fat level, as the dielectric constant and loss factor decreases with fat. The nutritious characteristics of the food are quite well retained in microwave cooking, but it does not reach the typical flavour of the cooked dish and cooking of multiple foods containing particles of any shape and size together cannot be achieved. Therefore, new combination techniques, of microwave treatment with conventional technologies would be feasible.

Baking: Bakery industry has an important place in food industry. Bakery products have now become essential food items of vast majority of population. Baking is an important step in manufacturing of all bakery products, where the dough is subjected to heat in a baking oven. Baking process includes expansion of dough, moisture loss, rise in product height and at last rate of moisture loss decreases because the structure of the air cells within the dough medium collapses as a result of increased vapour pressure. The microwave baking of bread has found hopeful, despite of lack of commercial application. It is surprising that microwave heating has not met with greater success in the field of baking. This is due to internal heating mechanism of microwave energy which would seem ideal for ever expanding heat insulating foam in dough. Many researchers have addressed various problems related to the microwave baking. These problems include texture, low volume, lack of colour, and crust formation, more dehydration and rapid staling. Megahey and others observed the influences of different baking conditions on quality in terms of texture of cake using microwave oven at 250 W and conventional oven at 200°C. Microwave baked cake was found to possess high springiness, moisture content and the low firmness as texture attributes compared with the cake that baked in convection method. Fox and Dungan 1969 and Chamberlain 1973 have noted the importance of the pans used for microwave baking. Baking pans have always posed a problem of non uniform heating. The problem was solved by the use of metal pans.

The metal pans have always proved to be good heat conductors and high heat transfer coefficient can be achieved with air impingement heating technology. The air impingement heating reduces the time lag between crumb baking and crust formation. The metal pans have also posed a problem of uneven baking, due to poor microwave permeability. Hence an ideal microwave baking pan must have excellent microwave permeability and thermal conductivity. Ovadia, found that modification of existing metal pan could provide solution. He used metal pans with holes on the sides and the bottom, through which microwaves pass through. The amount that will pass depends on diameter of holes. At 2450 MHz the holes need to be more than 3 mm in diameter hence increasing the penetration of microwave into dough.

To avoid the flow of dough through holes the pan was lined with common baking paper (0.08 mm thick). Results obtained were significantly improved over pan with no holes. Another problem related to microwave baking is the formation of a pale, weak and soggy crust.

The solution was to bake the loaf by conventional method in metal pan, then remove it from the pan and complete the baking with microwaves. Lefeuver 1981 suggested an innovative method, where baking was initiated by a combined infrared and microwaves applied simultaneously for one minute followed by infrared baking for 10 minutes thereby reducing the conventional baking time by more than half. Hence to overcome these problems researchers found that combination of infrared-microwave system is best alternative. The combination of microwave with other heating systems has been an interesting area, to reduce processing time and increase the quality of products. The combined heating technique has solved many issues such as low moisture content, the bread formation with firm inside and tougher outside, weak crust formation, etc.

Blanching: Blanching is a unit operation practiced in food industry. Blanching serves a variety of functions, one of the main being to destroy enzymatic activity in vegetables and some fruits, prior to further processing. Blanching is not solely a preservation method but acts as a pre-treatment which is normally carried out between the preparation of the raw material and later operations particularly heat sterilisation, dehydration and freezing. The two most widely used commercial blanching methods are hot water and steam blanching treatment. However, the conventional blanching method is closely associated with the serious issues like loss of weight, leaching and degradation of nutritive components such as sugar, vitamins and minerals. To retain nutritional quality of food products, several researchers suggested the use of microwave heating as an alternative to conventional blanching method for food products. Microwave blanching requires little or no water for efficient heat transfer in food, and hence reduces the leaching of nutrients compared with hot water immersion. The advantage of microwave blanching over conventional method include speed of operation, no additional water required, energy savings, precise process controls and faster start up and shut down times. The study on microwave blanching was reported by many scientists, Osinboyejo and others. Studied the effect of microwave blanching (MWB) versus boiling water blanching (BWB) on retention of selected water soluble vitamins in turnip greens and found that BWB lost 16% ascorbic acid, and 100% folic acid, thiamin and riboflavin while MWB lost 28.8% ascorbic acid, 25.7% folic acid 16.9% thiamin and 7.2% riboflavin. In another recent study comparing traditional hot-water and microwave blanching on quality of green beans, the microwave treatment of pods, showed a reduced processing time with better retention of ascorbic acid in addition to an effective peroxidase enzyme inactivation. Schirack and coworkers studied the microwave blanching of peanuts and found that microwave blanching was better than traditional blanching techniques in terms of energy and time savings. The studies comparing microwave blanching versus hot water blanching on three vegetables namely spinach, carrot and bell peppers revealed that there was reduced loss of valuable nutrients and the kinetics of peroxidase inactivation indicated that microwave blanching was comparable to water blanching with higher reaction rate in the case of water blanching.

Drying: Drying is one of the thermal processes, intended to reduce the moisture content of food materials, and it's one of the time-and energy-consuming processes in the food industry. Consequently, new methods are aimed to decrease drying time and energy consumption with preservation of quality. Microwave drying is a newer addition to the family of dehydration methods. The mechanism for drying with microwave energy is quite different from that of ordinary drying. In conventional drying, moisture is initially flashed off from the surface and the remaining water diffuses slowly to the surface. Whereas, in microwave drying, heat is generated directly in the interior of material creating a higher heat transfer and thus a much faster temperature rise than in conventional heating. In microwave system, mass transfer is primarily due to the total pressure gradient established because of the rapid vapour generation within the material. Most of the moisture is vaporised before leaving the sample. If the sample is initially very wet and the pressure inside the sample rises very rapidly, liquid may be removed from the sample under the influence of a total pressure gradient. The higher the initial moisture, the greater is the influence of the pressure gradient on the total mass removal. Thus, there is, a sort of 'pumping' action, forcing liquid to the surface, often as a vapour. This leads to very rapid drying without the need to overheat the atmosphere and perhaps cause case hardening or other surface overheating phenomena. The major disadvantage of microwave drying is difficulty in control of final product temperature. This causes excessive temperature along the corner or edges of food products results in scorching and production of off-flavors especially during final stages of drying. This could be overcome by combination of microwave drying with conventional drying which has various advantages and widespread application in food industry. The combined microwave drying methods include Microwave-Assisted Freezing Drying (MFD), Microwave-Assisted Vacuum Drying (MVD), Microwave-Assisted Hot Air Drying (MHD) and Microwave-Enhanced Spouted Bed Drying (MSD).

Microwave assisted drying as final stage for air drying reduces the drying time and increases the thermal efficiency. Maskan, 2000 reported that hot air drying combined with microwave finish drying reduced the drying time by 64% as compared to convective air drying. Microwaves can be combined with vacuum drying which improves the thermal efficiency. Vacuum microwave drying of banana slices was examined at a microwave power supply of 150 W and under a vacuum of less than 2500 Pa. It was determined that the drying was achieved in less than 30 minutes without exceeding 70°C and the quality of the product was found to be good and was comparable to that of freeze dried product. Freeze drying can maintain the quality of heat sensitive dried products compared with other conventional techniques but it is a long time processing and brings high energy consumption issue. The microwave assisted freeze drying could be a one of alternatives to be able to avoid these weaknesses. It can produce the same quality as that of conventional freeze drying and can reduce the drying time effectively. In microwave freeze drying of cabbage, the drying rate of microwave freeze drying was twice greater than that of vacuum freeze drying. Fluidised bed dryers are of the most efficient equipments and are suitable for a variety of drying applications. However major disadvantage of fluidised bed dryers is, long drying time during the falling rate period and low energy efficiency. Assisting conventional fluidised bed dryers by microwave heating provides an effective means of overcoming this limitation. Most of the microwave assisted drying of fruits and vegetables were performed in lab scale and hence more industrial scale applications with optimisations need to be conducted.

Thus, microwave ovens are common place in households and are established there as devices of everyday use. Knowledge of dielectric properties is very helpful for designing microwave oven. Microwave heating technology has been successfully applied for processing of various foods in various industries. The microwave pasteurisation and sterilisation of foods have claimed to effectively destroy pathogenic micro-organisms and significantly reduce processing time without serious damage to overall quality of product compared to traditional methods. The microwave heating applied for food processes such as blanching, cooking and baking have the advantages of retaining more taste, colour, quality and nutritional value and has a great effect on preservation compared to the conventional methods. The microwave heating has drastically reduced the energy consumption during drying of foods compared to conventional method. The greater advantages have been observed with the combined microwave heating method supplemented with conventional methods. The benefits include uniform heating of particulate foods, increased thermal efficiency, reduction in drying time, higher rehydration capacity and retain heat sensitive components of food material in case of microwave assisted freeze drying. The main obstacle for development of microwave heating applications is the high cost of the process. Electrical power, which is more expensive than combustion energy, is used with low yield. Therefore, the investigation of parameters which can influence the workability of microwave heating such as dielectric, physical, and chemical properties of food products should be carried out.

OHMIC HEATING

Ohmic heating is a thermal process in which heat is internally generated by the passage of alternating electrical current (AC) through a body such as a food system that serves as an electrical resistance. Ohmic heating is alternatively called resistance heating or direct resistance heating. During ohmic heating, AC voltage is applied to the electrodes at both ends of the product body. The rate of heating is directly proportional to the square of the electric field strength, the electrical conductivity, and the type of food being heated. The electric field strength can be controlled by adjusting the electrode gap or the applied voltage, while the electrical conductivities of foods vary greatly, but can be adjusted by the addition of electrolytes.

Sufficient heat is generated to pasteurise or sterilise foods. Generally, pasteurisation involves heating high-acid ($pH < 4.5$) foods to 90–95°C for 30–90 seconds to inactivate spoilage enzymes and micro-organisms (vegetative bacteria, yeasts, molds, and *lactobacillus* organisms). Low-acid ($pH > 4.5$) foods can support *Clostridum botulinum* growth, and depending on the actual pH and other properties of the food, require heating to 121°C for a minimum of 3 minutes. The particular interest in this technology stems from the food industry ongoing interest in aseptic processing of low-acid liquid-particulate foods. In the case of particulates suspended in viscous liquids, conventional heating transfers heat from the carrier medium to the particulates, and the time required to heat sufficiently the center of the largest particulate (the designated 'cold-spot') results in over processing. In contrast, ohmic heating is volumetric and heats both phases simultaneously. Ohmic heating is a high-temperature short-time method (HTST) that can heat an 80% solids food product from room temperature to 129°C in about 90 seconds, allowing the possibility to decrease the extent of high temperature over processing. A stark contrast between ohmic heating and conventional heating is that ohmic can heat particulates faster than the carrier liquid, called the heating inversion, which is not possible by traditional, conductive heating.

Ohmic Heating as an Alternative Food Processing Technology

Ohmic heating for the food industry consists of using electrical energy to heat foods as a method of preservation, which can in turn be used for microbial inactivation or several other processes such as pasteurisation, extraction, dehydration, blanching or thawing. Few studies have been conducted on the usefulness of this environmentally friendly processing technique.

An ohmic heating system may be particularly useful in this important process of food manufacturing, particularly the dairy industry, where fermentation by *Lactobacillus acidophilus* is necessary for the production of cheese and yogurt. Cho and others showed that ohmic heating of a fermentation vessel containing *L. acidophilus* reduced the lag period of the bacteria in the early stages of growth. With this knowledge, a dairy manufacturer utilising the ohmic heating process in the early stages of fermentation may shorten the total processing time of a dairy product. This speedier process would save untold amounts of time in overhead and labour costs.

The demand for alternative food processing techniques has increased at a rapid rate as manufacturing moves further into the 21st century. As technology advances, more efficient equipment can be retrofitted to replace antiquated machinery and processing methods for the food industry. With growing concerns on the safety of food for consumption by animals and humans, a processing technique that is more easily controlled, more efficient, and just as effective as current techniques could revolutionise the food industry in the coming years. Ohmic heating is one of the newest alternative processing techniques to emerge in the last 15 years. Using electric current, food can be pasteurised, fermented, or sterilised in a manner that is equally comparable, if not better, than the current methods of processing. Ohmic heating is referred to as Joule heating, electrical resistance heating or electro conductive heating.

Advantages of Ohmic Heating

The advantages of ohmic heating are as follows:

- The food is heated rapidly at the same rate throughout and the absence of temperature gradients results in even heating of solids and liquids if their resistances are the same.
- Heat transfer coefficients do not limit the rate of heating.
- Temperatures sufficient for UHT processing can be achieved.
- There are no hot surfaces for heat transfer, as in conventional heating, and therefore no risk of surface fouling or burning of the product which results in reduced frequency of cleaning.
- Heat sensitive foods or food components are not damaged by localised over-heating.
- Liquids containing particles can be processed and are not subject to shearing forces that are found in, for example, scraped surface heat exchangers.
- It is suitable for viscous liquids because heating is uniform and does not have the problems associated with poor convection in these materials.
- Energy conversion efficiencies are very high (>90%).
- Lower capital cost than microwave heating.
- Suitable for continuous processing.

The most important feature of ohmic heating is the rate of heat generation, which in addition to the electrical resistance of the product, depends on the specific heat capacities of each component, the way that food flows through the equipment and its residence time in the heater. If the two components have similar resistances, the lower moisture (solid portion) heats faster than the carrier liquid. The resistance in an ohmic heater depends on the specific resistance of the product, and the geometry of the heater:

Equipment and Applications

The ohmic heaters must include the electrical properties of the specific product to be heated, because the product itself is an electrical component. This concept is only found elsewhere in radio frequency heating and requires more specific design considerations than those needed when choosing other types of heat exchangers. Ohmic heaters should therefore be tailored to a specific application and the following factors taken into account:

- The type of product (electrical resistance and change in resistance over the expected temperature rise).
- Flowrate.
- Temperature rise (determines the power requirement).

- Heating rate required.
- Holding time required.

To be commercially successful, ohmic heaters must:

- Have effective control of heating and flow rates.
- Be cost effective.
- Allow aseptic processing and packaging.
- Have an electrical design that avoids electrolysis or product scorching.

Pre-treatments of solid components include:

- Pre-heating in the carrier liquid to equilibrate resistances.
- Blanching pasta for moisture absorption.
- Heating the carrier liquid to pre-gelatinise starch.
- Heating to melt and expel fats.
- Stabilisation of sauces by homogenisation, especially dairy sauces or others that contain fats and heat sensitive proteins.
- Blanching vegetables to expel air and/or to denature enzymes.
- Enzymic marinades to soften texture and enhance flavour of meats.
- Soaking in acids or salts to alter the electrical resistance of particles.
- Sauteing to improve appearance of meat particles.

Ohmic heating has been used to process various combinations of meats, vegetables, pasta and fruits when accompanied by a suitable carrier liquid. A variety of shapes, including cubes, discs, spheres, rods and twists have been processed. In operation, the bulk of the carrier liquid is sterilised by conventional plate or tubular heat exchangers and then injected into the particle stream as it leaves the holding tube. This has the advantage of reducing the capital and operating costs for a given throughput and allows a small amount of carrier liquid to be used to suspend the particles, thus improving process efficiency. Ohmic heating costs were found by Allen and others to be comparable to those for freezing and retort processing of low acid products.

Food is pumped up through a vertical tube containing a series of electrodes where it is heated to process temperature. The stainless steel cantilever electrodes (supported from one side) are contained in a PTFE housing and fit across the tube. An alternating current from a 3-phase supply flows between the electrodes and through the food as it moves along the tube. The tube sections are made from stainless steel, lined with an insulating plastic such as polyvinyidene fluoride (PVDF), polyether ether ketone (PEEK) or glass. The system is designed to maintain the same impedance in each section between the electrodes, and the tubes therefore increase in length between inlet and outlet because the electrical conductivity of the food increases as it is heated. Typically, an overall tube dimension of 0.3 cm internal diameter and 30 cm length could heat several hundred litres per hour, whereas a tube of 2.5 cm diameter and 2 m length could heat several thousand litres per hour. Commercial equipment is available with power outputs of 75 and 300 kW, which correspond to throughputs of approximately 750 and 3000 kg h^{-1} respectively. The process is automatically controlled via a feed-forward system, which monitors inlet temperature, product flow rate and specific heat capacity and continuously adjusts the power required to heat the product. The almost complete absence of fouling in ohmic heaters means that after one product has been processed, the plant is flushed through with a base sauce and the next product is introduced. At the end of processing, the plant is flushed with a cleaning solution. The process is suitable for particulate foods that contain up to about 60% solids. In contrast to conventional UHT processing of particulate foods, where the liquid component is an important medium for heat transfer into the particles, in ohmic heating a high solids content is desirable for two reasons: faster heating of low-conductivity particles than the carrier liquid and plug flow in the heater tubes. High solids concentrations can be processed if the particles are pliable and small, or their geometry is varied to reduce the void spaces between particles. Lower concentrations require a higher viscosity carrier liquid to keep the particles in suspension. The density of the particles should also be matched to the carrier liquid: if particles are too dense or the liquid is not sufficiently viscous, the particles will sink in the system and be over-processed.

Conversely, if the particles are too light they will float and this leads to variable product composition and the risk of under-processing. It is almost impossible to determine the residence time or heating profiles of particles that float or sink. The viscosity of the fluid (sauce or gravy) should therefore be carefully controlled and for example, pre-gelatinised starches should be used to prevent viscosity changes during processing.

In order for ohmic UHT processing of particulate foods to be accepted by the regulatory authorities, it is necessary to ensure that the coldest part of the slowest heating particle in the food has received sufficient heat to ensure sterility. It is not easy to measure heat penetration into particles, whereas it is relatively easy to measure the temperature of the carrier liquid. The process must therefore demonstrate that solid particles are heated to an equal or greater extent than the liquid when they enter the holding tube. By adjustment of the electrical properties of each component (e.g. by control of salt content in the formulation) it is possible to ensure that this takes place for homogenous particles, but data is not yet available for non-homogenous particles (e.g. fatty meat pieces) which have variable electrical resistance. The situation is made more complex when a batch of food is held before processing and, for example, salt leaches out of the particles into the surrounding sauce. This results in changes to the electrical resistance of both components and hence their rate of heating. Furthermore, the presence of fats and other poorly conductive materials means that particles will heat mostly by conduction and a cold spot will be created within the particle. It is important that there is no accidental inclusion of either highly conducting materials, or more likely insulating materials such as pieces of bone, fat, nuts or ice in a food, because neither will be heated. If this happens, the surrounding food may also be under-processed.

Other factors that need to be defined include:

- Size and shape of particle pieces.
- Moisture content of solids.
- Solids/liquid ratio.
- Viscosity of liquid component.
- Amount and type of electrolytes.
- pH.
- Specific heat.
- Thermal conductivity.

Additionally, the effect of processing on the above factors needs to be determined to detect whether they change and hence alter the heating characteristics of the product. Any changes to ingredients that are made to take account of changing consumer tastes or cost/availability should be tested to determine the effects on heating characteristics.

Effect of Ohmic Heating on Nutrient Loss

Since systematic research on ohmic heating has a much shorter history than has conventional heating, food scientists and technologists might look to microwave heating for information on nutrient changes. In general, many improvements in nutritional quality were found using microwaves (cooking in a minimum of water retained more K, vitamin B_{12}, and vitamin C, and the absence of surface browning retained more amino acid availability, especially lysine), and microwave heating induces no significant effects different to those induced by conventional heating.

The benefit of attaining food safety with less nutrient degradation using HTST processes such as ohmic heating or microwave heating is based on differences in the kinetics parameters (k, z, Ea) for bacterial spores compared to those for biochemical reactions. First, rate constants for microbial destruction are usually much larger than those for the chemical reactions responsible for nutrient degradation, and second, rate constants for microbial destruction are usually more sensitive to temperature increases [z (thiamin) = 48, z (peroxidase) = 36.1, and z (*C.botulinum*) = 10°C]. Methods for rapidly reaching the target temperatures therefore tend to destroy micro-organisms while giving less time to compromise the nutrient content and other quality attributes. In fact, the slow heating rate associated with conventional retorting can activate protease to degrade myofibrillar proteins before the protease is eventually heat-inactivated. Tests for conventional heating showed that heating large (25 mm) particulates in a liquid medium at 135°C to achieve $F_o = 5$ at the particulate center required extensive over processing of the liquid phase ($F_o = 150$ for the liquid). For this reason, the common process conditions for scraped surface heat exchangers are maximum particulate sizes of 15 mm and sterilisation temperatures of 125–130°C (producing liquid $F_o = 25$) while limiting particulates to 30–40% so that there is enough hot liquid available to heat particulates. For ohmic heating, direct heating sterilisation temperatures can reach 140°C (the temperature limit of plastics in the machinery) without grossly overheating the liquid phase and can support greater particulate loading suspended in highly viscous carrier liquids.

Vitamin losses in foods are determined by the temperature and the moisture of the applied heating method. Vitamin C is particularly temperature sensitive and destroyed at relatively low temperatures, so heating foods must be for as short a time as possible to retain the vitamin C. Thiamin and riboflavin are unstable at higher temperatures such as those used in rapid grilling. Vitamin C is also water soluble and can be lost when cooking with moist heat or by autooxidation with dissolved oxygen in the food or cooking water. This reaction is catalysed by adventitious iron and copper ions. Ohmic heating is an effective method to pasteurise milk and has been used successfully to produce quality viscous products and to foods containing various combinations of particulates such as meat, vegetables, pastas, or fruits in a viscous medium, including a wide variety of high acid (ratatouille, pasta sauce and vegetables, vegetables Provençale, fruit compote, strawberries, apple sauce, sliced kiwi fruit) and low acid (tomato sauce) There are several reports on relationships between ohmic heating and changes in properties of carbohydrates and fats. These studies did not directly address the nutrition issues of ohmically heated foods, although the physical changes that occur during ohmic heating affect the heating characteristics of the solids and liquids, which may have impact on thermal destruction of nutrients. Halden and others suggested that changes in starch transition, melting of fats and cell structure changes of the food material were responsible for changes in electrical conductivity that influenced the heating rate in foods such as potato during ohmic heating. In conventional thermal processes, starch gelatinisation was found to cause rheological and structural changes, and similar changes were observed for ohmic heating. Wang and Sastry indicated that ohmic heating caused significant changes in physical properties including viscosity, heat capacity, thermal and electrical conductivity. They found that conductivity decreased with degree of gelatinisation. When we design ohmic heating processes, we must take changes in electrical conductivity caused by physical property changes of major compounds such as starch, fats and proteins into account so that no significant under cooking of solids or over-cooking occurs.

Major Challenges and Needs for Future Research and Development

Three major challenges hindering the commercialisation of ohmic heating processing are:

1. Lack of a complete model that takes into account differences in electrical conductivity between the liquid and solid phases and the responses of the two phases to temperature changes, which affect relative heating rates and distribution.
2. Lack of data concerning critical factors affecting heating, including residence time, orientations, loading levels, etc.
3. Lack of applicable temperature validating techniques for locating cold/hot spots.

Develop reliable, predictive models of ohmic heating patterns

Modelling ohmic heating is difficult owing to the unique character of this mode of heating, which requires much understanding of the critical factors. The ohmic heating rate is critically dependent on the electrical conductivity of the foods being processed for which only limited information is available. If the electrical conductivities of the liquid and particulate phases are the same, the mixture can be heated rapidly and uniformly to a high temperature irrespective of particle size. If the conductivity of the particulate is higher than the liquid, then it heats faster and transfers heat to the liquid, which has advantages for ensuring process adequacy. Nevertheless, possible heat channelling, which could cause coupling between temperature and electrical field distributions as well as sensitivity to process parameters, e.g. particle shape and orientation, could contribute to the complexity of the process. To ensure sterilisation, the heating behaviour of the food must be understood, so process reliability and safety could be demonstrated. Kim and others showed that monitoring the temperature at the entrance and exit of the holding tube could provide such assurances.

Develop product specifications and process parameters for specific products

Particulates are the centerpiece around which an ohmic heating formulation is built. Contrary to conventional heating, in which we expect little difference in heat transfer due to changes in particle orientation, the heating pattern of an ohmically-heated food system would be influenced by particle orientation. De Alwis and others showed the heating of identically-shaped potato particles differed depending on whether the particles were aligned parallel or perpendicular to the electric field. De Alwis and others explained that this difference is due to changes in the electric field, but it also reflects a change in the equivalent resistance of the overall circuit. When both the heating and cooling stages are considered, a practical limitation on particle size and shape might be expected. Cooling of particulates will always be thermal conduction controlled. The center of large particles may cool too slowly and thus become over processed during prolonged cooling. Consequently, particulate size is limited to 1 in. Various combinations of particulates can be successfully processed when accompanied by suitable product and process control. Optimising the combination will results in excellent particulate texture through uniform heating.

The liquid phase must also be optimised. Viscosity should be determined at various temperatures to assure adequate suspension of particulates and to facilitate liquid/particle interface heat transfer. Overall product specification is important in determining how much lethal treatment is delivered during the process. Critical factors include particle size, shape, and orientation, viscosity, pH, specific heat, thermal conductivity, solid liquid ration, and electrical conductivity.

Develop real-time temperature monitoring techniques for locating slowest heating regions

Pioneers of ohmic heating research have documented that a particle does not heat uniformly during an ohmic heating process because of the non-uniform nature of the electric field and the differences in the physical properties of the food materials. As with any other thermal process, it is important to have information on the temperature-time history of the coldest point within the liquid-particulate system undergoing ohmic heating. Conventional tools such as thermocouples and fibre optic probes are invasive when used to measure ohmic-heated food systems. A non-destructive and noninvasive technique that can be used to monitor the spatial distribution of temperature is important for understanding and controlling ohmic heating.

RADIO FREQUENCY HEATING

Conventional thermal treatment in food processing relies on the transfer of heat by conduction and convection. One alternative to this conventional thermal treatment is radio-frequency (RF) heating in which electromagnetic energy is transferred directly to the heated product. The longer wavelengths of RF compared with microwaves are able to penetrate further into the food products resulting in more even heating. A review of RF heating for the food processing industry is presented here with an emphasis on scientific principles and the advantages and applications of RF. Applications of RF heating include blanching, thawing, drying, and processing of foods. RF heating represents considerable potential for additional research and the transfer of technology to the food processing industry. Computer simulation can be used to improve RF heating uniformity. Moreover, the heating uniformity in the rotated eggs is greater than in the static eggs. RF has also been used to blanch vegetables to increase ascorbic acid content to achieve the highest vitamin C levels. The use of the thawing technology has resulted in better quality of treated food. There has been increased interest in the RF-drying method due to the homogeneity of heating, greater penetration depth, and more stable control of the product temperature. RF-treated meat had improved quality and coagulation with acceptable taste and appearance. In addition, RF heating is used in pasteurisation of yogurt and destruction of micro-organisms in liquid and solid foods.

Thermal treatment is a very common method in food processing industries to eliminate micro-organisms and inhibit the activity of harmful enzymes in order to ensure the safety of food products and extend product shelf life. Thermal treatment involves the transfer of heat through conduction and convection, which can prolong the time required for heating depending on the food matrix. These restrictions can lead to significant physico-chemical changes within thermally treated food products which can result in alterations in sensory and textile properties and can also lead to a decrease in nutritional value.

Researchers have been searching for alternative technologies to traditional thermal treatment. Recently new technologies and method have been developing in food processing industries. The use of radio frequency (RF, between 10 and 50 MHz) is one of the most important and promising modern heating techniques. RF as a heat source was first described in the middle of the 20th century and was used to melt frozen foods and to process and preserve meat products. Electromagnetic heating is characterised by its ability to generate heat inside the food material by polarising the guidance of polar diodes such as water or forced movement of ions. In this way, limits imposed by conventional heating are overcome. The electromagnetic heating process is relatively quick and takes place through the transmission of electromagnetic energy directly to the product. The heat is generated within the product without the need for heat transference, in contrast to conventional heating.

Microwave heating has also been used in the manufacture of food products. This heating method improves the sensory, chemical, and physical properties of food material exposed to electromagnetic waves compared with conventional heating. However, researchers have found that frequencies used in microwave technology at about 2.45 kHz have a limited ability to penetrate larger food volume. For example, the penetration depth was measured at 1 cm for microwaves at 2.35 kHz in milk or yogurt products, whereas Felke and others showed that the penetration depth was about 20 cm when using RFs at 27.12 MHz which resulted in the heating being more consistent for the food material, and the affected diameter was greater. Previous studies have shown that longer wavelengths used in radio frequency heating (RF-H) do not result in any interference or negative effects inside the food, whereas the use of microwaves has led to patterns of cold and hot spots inside the food items.

Scientific Principle of RF-H

RF is electromagnetic waves in the range of 10 to 300 GHz, but the range of frequencies used for industrial heating lies between 10 and 50 MHz . In addition, the permitted frequencies for medical, scientific, and industrial applications are 13.56, 27.12, and 40.68 MHz, respectively. RF is also referred to as dielectric loss heating and dielectric heating. RF-H is classified as a novel thermal processing method in the field of food engineering. Since the electrical insulators of food materials are limited, the electrical energy is dissipated and stored by food when placed in an electromagnetic field. Maxwell wave equations are used to describe the absorption of this energy. The bound water in food plays an important role in dielectric heating in the frequency range between 20 and 30000 MHz.

When foods (having polar molecules such as water) are exposed to an alternating electric field, dielectric heating occurs. The polar molecules have electric dipole moments, and the negative and positive charge centres do not align when food is placed in an electric field and polar molecules align to the electric field. Polarisation occurs due to the migration of positive and negative charges to the different ends of the molecules. Polar molecules also rotate continuously to align with the changing field within an alternating electric field. This process is called dipole rotation. During this process, the friction among molecules converts electromagnetic energy into heat, so the temperature of treated materials rises. However, the motion of dissociative ions in foods corresponding to an applied alternating electric field is in the same direction. Consequently, the oscillating motion of ions (forward and backward) in the material generates heat due to friction. This mechanism is known as ionic conduction. Dipole rotation and ionic conduction are the primary dominant techniques in RF-H. Temperature and frequency play an important role in both of these mechanisms due to an increase in the movement of molecules by increasing frequency and temperature. A RF-H system consists of an alternating voltage source, capacitor, and two electrodes, all of which are connected to form an electric circuit for a dielectric heating system.

Advantages of RF-H

RF-H presents multiple characteristics compared with conventional heat transfer and heat diffusion units. It is very important that the electrodes do not contact the food directly when using RF-H units to avoid the formation of Joule heating (Ohmic heating). This technique can be applied to both liquid and solid foods. In addition, it has been shown that the wavelength of RF (11 m at 27.12 MHz) is greater than those of microwave frequencies. Moreover, because of the capacity of RF power to penetrate deeper into foods than conventional microwaves, the heat is generated inside the food and distributed evenly. It is well-documented that construction of a large-scale RF-H is easier and improves the quality of the final product. Another advantage of this eco-friendly technology is its higher energy use efficiency.

Disadvantages of RF-H

Like the most current technologies, RF-H presented some disadvantages that are limited essentially to the reduction in power density as reported by Jones and Rowley. In addition, because of its high efficiency and output quality, RF-H equipment is more expensive compared with equipment used in traditional heating systems.

Improvement of RF-H uniformity using computer simulation

Volumetric and rapid heating occurs when RF-H is used. The RF commercial applications are limited because of non-uniformity heating (uneven temperature distribution) in the product by using RF-H. There are many other factors that have an important effect on the RF-H uniformity such as physical properties, dielectric properties, thermal properties, the distance between the treated product and electrodes, chemical properties of the medium, and engineering design of RF-H devices. Non-uniformity RF-H may cause damage to the product and package. To solve this problem, there are many methods used to improve RF-H uniformity such as placing the product into hot air, hot water, or saline water. Birla and others have used rotation for improving RF-H uniformity. Wang and others and Ling and others have used agitation and mixing of product containers between electrodes. There is another method used for improving RF-H uniformity which is called pulse mode. Computer simulation can be used to enhance RF-H uniformity via development of several models for studying different factors and methods for various foods like wheat flour, wheat kernel, soyabeans, meat, and dry food. Computer simulation is used to understand the new test strategy, the mechanism, parameters optimisation, and determination of the best conditions of RF-H treatments for specific food products.

Dev and others have used the simulation of RF-H in eggshell at 27.12 MHz to study the uniformity of heating within the treated eggs and determination of locations of hot and cold spots generated due to non-uniform heating.

The heating is non-uniform due to the generation of hot and cold spots within the eggshell, because the egg closest to electrodes heats faster than the egg farther away from electrodes. The non-uniformity of RF-H increased as the air gap between eggs and parallel electrodes decreased from 5 to 0.5 mm. On the other hand, the uniformity heating in the rotated eggs is greater than the static eggs.

Applications of RF-H in Food Processing

Heating of bread

One of the earliest explorations into the RF pasteurisation process was reported more than 70 years ago using two kinds of bread. A portion of sliced white bread and Boston brown bread were exposed to 14 and 17 MHz in an RF unit. Forty-seven seconds were enough to raise the temperature of the sliced bread to 60°C. This sterilisation had a positive impact on the preservation of both the sliced white bread and the Boston brown bread. A quality check demonstrated an absence of mould after 10 days' storage at 24°C and 29°C. More importantly, the new technology had a positive impact on bread texture. The previously dry, leathery texture of the bread was reported to be absent after RF-H, with no change in thiamine content. A year after this discovery, another study reported the ability of RF to control both *Aspegillus* and *Penicillium* in sliced bread when treated at 26 MHz.

Blanching

RF has also been used to blanch vegetables and to limit the loss of their nutritive value. By using an RF self-excited oscillator at 15 MHz, vegetable temperature reached 77°C. RF-H was shown to have a negative impact on the catalase activity of the treated vegetables after a few days of storage at '23°C. Additionally, vegetables blanched at 88°C had an increase in ascorbic acid content at the highest vitamin C levels. Vitamin C is essential for the maintenance of healthy connective tissue and may also act as an antioxidant. However, it was reported that RF blanching negatively affected both vegetable flavour and colour when compared with the conventional blanching method using water and steam.

Thawing

After using RF for food heating and blanching in 1947, attempts were made to use RF energy for thawing frozen products. RF at 14–17 MHz was sufficient to thaw 450 g–13.6 kg of frozen eggs, fruits, vegetables, and fish within 2 to 15 min. The use of this technology resulted in better quality due to minimal discoloration and loss of flavour when compared with traditional thawing. Fifteen years later, Jason and Sanders used RF frequencies ranging from 36 to 40 MHz to thaw white fish frozen at '29°C. RF successfully decreased the thawing time of 3 and 16 hr, when using air and water, respectively, to 12 min with RF. Using the same protocol, Sanders was able to decrease the thawing time of different food sausages, meat, pies, and bacon to 10–50 min after several passes through the RF unite. Thawing time depends on multiple factors including the uniformity of the blocks used as well as size and dielectric properties. In general, the study demonstrated that thawing time using RF was much shorter than conventional methods.

Drying

Drying based on RF-H offers multiple advantages over conventional drying and microwave drying. For example, the MacrowaveTM 7000 Series post-baking (i.e. cookies and crackers) dryer was developed by Radio Frequency, Inc. (Millis, MA) and presented multiple benefits including the following: the possibility to increase oven line speed, heat uniformity, precise power control, no temperature differential, space savings, development of desired crumb structure, and capacity to equilibrate and control moisture content resulting in a completely uniform moisture profile. RF-H was also used to sterilise packaged flour and dry food with poor thermal characteristics, such as coffee, nuts, beans, cocoa, corn, grains, and beans. A vertical RF unit at 60 MHz frequency was capable of increasing the temperature of roasting cocoa beans to 130°C, which reduced the moisture content from 6 to 1 per cent. Because of its greater potential for penetrating to the center of the food by the emitted energy, RF-H can dry foods evenly.

RF has been classified as a fourth generation drying technology. There has been increased interest in the RF-drying method due to the homogeneity of heating, greater penetration depth, and more stable control of the product temperature. The RF-drying method is also known as dielectric heating. Heating food by using RF and microwaves is faster and volumetrically efficient due to the internal heat generation in the treated food, which occurs due to ionic conductance and the dipole rotation of molecules. Food drying by RF requires less drying time and has a more uniform drying rate, and the dried food has acceptable quality. RF is considered a potential advanced drying method, and many researchers have used RF for drying foods such as macadamia nuts and peanut kernels. Zhou and others studied the effects of three drying methods (RF, vacuum, and hot air drying) on walnut-drying characteristics. The time required to dry walnuts using RF was shorter than that of vacuum or hot air drying. In RF drying, the temperature increased rapidly when compared with vacuum or hot air drying because the moisture content plays an important role in the rise of treated food temperature by RF-H (9.8% dry basis). The RF-drying rate was faster than that of vacuum or hot air drying. In addition, three drying rate stages were observed (increasing, constant, and falling rate stages) with RF drying, whereas with vacuum and hot air drying, only the constant rate stage was observed. Combined RF drying includes tandem and parallel drying. Tandem drying (hybrid drying) includes different drying methods at different stages in order to increase energy efficiency, thermal performance, drying uniformity, and quality enhancement.

Meat processing

The first RF meat pasteurisation studies date back to 1953. An RF unit operating at 9 MHz was able to sterilise 2.7 kg of boned ham by reaching the desired temperature of 80°C in approximately 10 min. Seventeen years later, Bengtsson and Green developed continuous RF pasteurisation of cured hams packaged in Cryovac casings, which was shifted from 35 to 60 MHz, reaching a temperature of 80°C at the centre of the ham. Compared with traditional hot water processing, the processing time, quality of meat, and juice losses improved significantly by using the RF unit. In addition, the RF unit required only one-third of the time for processing 0.91 kg of lean ham heated in a condenser tunnel at 60 MHz. The results showed that juice losses were reduced and quality tended to improve when compared with traditional processing with hot water. In 1991, a linear relationship was observed between temperature and electrode voltage used to pasteurise sausage emulsion. Two minutes were sufficient to treat sausage emulsion at a mass flow rate of 120 kg/hr. When exposed to 27 MHz, the temperature increased from 15°C to 80°C. Although a conventional heating process had a heating rate of 1°C/min, an RF unit was able to treat the centre (about 50 mm diameter) of a sausage with a 40°C/min heating rate. RF heat treatments have exhibited a lethal effect on tested organisms at the same pasteurisation values as conventional heat treatments, whereas RF-treated meat had better quality and coagulated better with acceptable taste and appearance.

Dairy products

In a recent study, it has been demonstrated that the electrical conductivity of yogurt was directly proportional to its temperature. The reported conductivity was higher than that of milk, which could be due to the lactic acid conductivity in yogurt. When using RF-H (yogurt starting at 40°C), 60, 90, and 120 s were necessary in order to reach 58°C, 65°C, and 72°C, respectively, with a heating rate of $0.28 \pm 0.02\ K \cdot s^{-1}$. Temperatures of 58°C and 65°C were consistently applied to stir yogurt in an RF water bath. However, heating yogurt jars at very high temperatures such as 72°C could cause significant overheating followed by a strong contraction of the yogurt curd and whey separation.

When the same temperatures (58°C, 65°C, and 72°C) were applied to stirred yogurt in a convection oven, heat transfer limitations were observed, unlike RF-H. The convection oven heating rate was 0.30, 0.41, and $0.55\ K \cdot min^{-1}$, which was comparatively lower when compared with the heating rate of RF-H ($0.28 \pm 0.02\ K \cdot s^{-1}$). Although heating was successfully applied at most temperatures, some problems were reported for the dielectric heating of yogurt gels at 72°C. To date, most ongoing studies aim to extend yogurt shelf life while maintaining high-product quality including texture and sensorial properties.

Effects of RF-H on inactivating micro-organisms

RF-H can be used to control pathogen in foods because of fast and volumetric heating, as well as reducing loss in food quality. Using RF-H leads to the reduction of pathogen in agriculture materials by

4 log. Some studies mentioned that RF-H possessed the ability to inactivate *Bacillus cereus* and *Clostridium perfringens* in pork luncheon meat, *Escherichia coli*, and *Listeria innocua* in milk, and *Clostridium sporogenes* in scrambled eggs.

Future aspects of RF-H

RF technology has considerable potential to replace traditional (water and steam) and microwave heating for food processing. RF offers major advantages including the possibility to immediately penetrate up to 20 cm or more into food for more uniform and efficient heating and limited negative side effects such as reduced food quality or objectionable sensory perception. Food scientists and engineers can anticipate determining optimum RF frequencies, exposure time, and configuration for heating a single food or group of similar foods. At the same time, the relative impact of RF on food quality and sensory perception can be studied with the goal of designing the optimum RF unit for a particular food or group of foods. This heating of foods could be for pasteurisation, processing of prepared foods, or consumer reheating, with each situation having different requirements. Since RF units do not have magnetrons, RF units are typically less expensive than microwaves with regard to scaling up from a laboratory to a processing plant application and would thus incur lower maintenance costs.

A potential limitation to optimum RF selection is RF-band designations within the country of operation. For example, current frequencies allocated for industrial, scientific, and medical (ISM) applications typically include those centred at 6.78, 13.56, 27.12, and 40.68 MHz. Any telecommunication devices using these frequencies must be able to withstand RF interference from other devices. Consequently, the use of other frequencies dedicated to telecommunication equipment would require shielding of RF to prevent interference. Fortunately, RF with its longer wavelengths is easier to shield than microwaves.

In the future, consumer microwaves may also be replaced by RF units that are much more efficient at cooking or warming foods. Current microwaves have single button controls for different foods that control the cycling of microwaves over time. However, imagine an RF oven with similar single button controls that can vary the frequency, duration, and cycling of RF in order to maximise the quality and health benefits of a particular food. The research results with RF-H over the past few decades have clearly shown that in the near future, RF-H will be a very attractive processing technology to provide safe and high quality of food products because of its ability to penetrate deeply with rapid uniform heating.

Chapter 22

Chilling

INTRODUCTION

Chilling is the unit operation in which the temperature of a food is reduced to between 1 and 8°C. It is used to reduce the rate of biochemical and microbiological changes, and hence to extend the shelf life of fresh and processed foods. It causes minimal changes to sensory characteristics and nutritional properties of foods and, as a result, chilled foods are perceived by consumers as being convenient, easy to prepare, high quality and 'healthy', 'natural' and 'fresh'.

Chilling is often used in combination with other unit operations (for example fermentation or pasteurisation) to extend the shelf life of mildly processed foods. There is a greater preservative effect when chilling is combined with control of the composition of the storage atmosphere than that found using either unit operation alone.

However, not all foods can be chilled and tropical, subtropical and some temperate fruits, for example, suffer from chilling injury at 3–10°C above their freezing point. Chilled foods are grouped into three categories according to their storage temperature range as follows:

1. 1 to +1°C (fresh fish, meats, sausages and ground meats, smoked meats and breaded fish).
2. 0 to +5°C (pasteurised canned meat, milk, cream, yoghurt, prepared salads, sandwiches, baked goods, fresh pasta, fresh soups and sauces, pizzas, pastries and unbaked dough).
3. 0 to +8°C (fully cooked meats and fish pies, cooked or uncooked cured meats, butter, margarine, hard cheese, cooked rice, fruit juices and soft fruits).

Details of the range of available chilled foods and future trends are discussed below:

The successful supply of chilled foods to the consumer is heavily dependent on sophisticated and relatively expensive distribution systems which involve chill stores, refrigerated transport and retail chill display cabinets, together with widespread ownership of domestic refrigerators. Precise temperature control is essential at all stages to avoid the risk of food spoilage or food poisoning. In particular, low-acid chilled foods, which are susceptible to contamination by pathogenic bacteria (for example fresh and pre-cooked meats, pizzas and unbaked dough) must be prepared, packaged and stored under strict conditions of hygiene and temperature control.

FRESH FOODS

The rate of biochemical changes caused by either micro-organisms or naturally occurring enzymes increases logarithmically with temperature. Chilling therefore reduces the rate of enzymic and microbiological change and retards respiration of fresh foods. The factors that control the shelf life of fresh crops in chill storage include:

- The type of food and variety or cultivar.
- The part of the crop selected (the fastest growing parts have the highest metabolic rates and the shortest storage lives (Table 22.1).
- The condition of the food at harvest (for example the presence of mechanical damage or microbial contamination, and the degree of maturity).
- The temperature of harvest, storage, distribution and retail display.
- The relative humidity of the storage atmosphere, which influences dehydration losses.

The rate of respiration of fresh fruits is not necessarily constant at a constant storage temperature. Fruits which undergo 'climacteric' ripening show a short but abrupt increase in the rate of respiration which occurs near to the point of optimum ripeness.

Climacteric fruits include apple, apricot, avocado, banana, mango, peach, pear, plum and tomato. Non-climacteric fruits include cherry, cucumber, fig, grape, grapefruit, lemon, pineapple and strawberry. Vegetables respire in a similar way to non-climacteric fruits. Differences in respiratory activity of selected fruits and vegetables are shown in Tables 22.1 and 22.2.

Table 22.1: Botanical function related to respiration rate and storage life for selected products.

Product	*Relative respiration rate*	*Botanical function*	*Typical storage life (weeks at 2°C)*
Asparagus	40	Actively growing shoots	0.2–0.5
Mushrooms	21		
Artichokes	17		
Spinach	13	Aerial parts of plants	1–2
Lettuce	11		
Cabbage	6		
Carrots	5	Storage roots	5–20
Turnips	4		
Beetroots	3		
Potatoes	2	Specialised storage organs	25–50
Garlic	2		
Onions	1		

Undesirable changes to some fruits and vegetables occur when the temperature is reduced below a specific optimum for the individual fruit. This is termed *chilling injury* and results in various physiological changes (for example internal or external browning, failure to ripen and skin blemishes). The reasons for this are not fully understood but may include an imbalance in metabolic activity which results in the over production of metabolites that then become toxic to the tissues. It is found for example in apples (less than 2–3°C), avocados (less than 13°C), bananas (less than 12–13°C), lemons (less than 14°C), mangoes (less than 10–13°C) and melons, pineapples and tomatoes (each less than 7–10°C).

Table 22.2: Heat produced by respiration in selected foods.

Food	*Heat ($W t^{-1}$) of respiration for the following storage temperatures*		
	0ºC	*10ºC*	*15.5ºC*
Apples	10–12	41–61	58–87
Bananas	–	65–116	–
Beans	73–82	–	440–580
Carrots	46	93	–
Celery	21	58–81	–
Oranges	9–12	35–40	68
Lettuce	150	–	620
Pears	8–20	23–63	–
Potatoes	–	20–30	–
Strawberries	36–52	145–280	510
Tomatoes	57–75	–	78

The optimum storage temperature and relative humidity, and expected storage times are shown in Table 22.3 for a variety of fresh fruits and vegetables. Undesirable changes due to incorrect relative humidity are described by van den Berg and Lentz.

Table 22.3: Optimum storage conditions for some fruits and vegetables.

Food	*Temperature (ºC)*	*Relative humidity (%)*	*Storage life (days)*
Apricot	–0.5–0	90	7–14
Banana	11–15.5	85–95	7–10
Bean (snap)	7	90–95	7–10
Broccoli	0	95	10–14
Carrot	0	98–100	28–42
Celery	0	95	30–60
Cherry	1	90–95	14–20
Cucumber	10–15	90–95	10–14
Eggplant	7–10	90–95	7–10
Lemon	10–14	85–90	30–180
Lime	9–10	85–90	40–140
Lettuce	0–1	95–100	14–20
Mushroom	0	90	3–4
Peach	0.5–0	90	14–30
Plum	1–0	90–95	14–30
Potato	3–10	90–95	150–240
Spinach	0	95	10–14
Strawberry	0.5–0	90–95	5–7
Tomato	4–10	85–90	4–7
Watermelon	4–10	80–90	14–20

In animal tissues, aerobic respiration rapidly declines when the supply of oxygenated blood is stopped at slaughter. Anaerobic respiration of glycogen to lactic acid then causes the pH of the meat to fall, and the onset of *rigor mortis*, in which the muscle tissue becomes firm and inextensible. Cooling during anaerobic respiration is necessary to produce the required texture and colour of meat and to reduce bacterial contamination. Undesirable changes, caused by cooling meat before rigor mortis has occurred, are termed cold shortening. Details of these and other post-mortem changes to meat are described by Laurie. To chill fresh foods it is necessary to remove both sensible heat (also known as field heat) and heat generated by respiratory activity. The production of respiratory heat at 20°C and atmospheric pressure is given by Eq. 22.1.

$$C_6H_{12}O_6 + 6O_2 \rightarrow 6CO_2 + 6H_2O + 2835 \times 10^6 \text{ J kmol}^{-1}\ C_6H_{12}O_6 \qquad \ldots(22.1)$$

The size of refrigeration plant and the processing time required to chill a crop are calculated using unsteady-state heat transfer methods. The calculations are simpler when processed foods are chilled as respiratory activity does not occur. A number of assumptions are made to simplify calculations further, for example the initial temperature of a food is constant and uniform throughout the food, and the temperature of the cooling medium, respiratory activity and all thermal properties of the food are constant during cooling.

Processed Foods

A reduction in temperature below the minimum necessary for microbial growth extends the generation time of micro-organisms and in effect prevents or retards reproduction. There are four broad categories of micro-organism, based on the temperature range for growth:

1. Thermophilic (minimum: 30–40°C, optimum: 55–65°C).
2. Mesophilic (minimum: 5–10°C, optimum: 30–40°C).
3. Psychrotrophic (minimum: <0–5°C, optimum: 20–30°C).
4. Psychrophilic (minimum: <0–5°C, optimum: 12–18°C).

Chilling prevents the growth of thermophilic and many mesophilic micro-organisms. The main microbiological concerns with chilled foods are a number of pathogens that can grow during extended refrigerated storage below 5°C, or as a result of any increase in temperature (temperature abuse) and thus cause food poisoning. Previously it was considered that refrigeration temperatures would prevent the growth of pathogenic bacteria, but it is now known that some species can either grow to large numbers at these temperatures, or are sufficiently virulent to cause poisoning after ingestion of only a few cells. Examples of these pathogens are *Aeromonas hydrophilia*, *Listeria* spp, *Yersinia enterocolitica*, some strains of *Bacillus cereus*, *Vibrio parahaemolyticus* and enteropathogenic *Escherichia coli*. An example of the last (*E. coli* 0157:H7) may cause hemorrhagic colitis after ingestion of as little as ten cells. It is therefore essential that good manufacturing practice (GMP) is enforced during the production of chilled foods. The shelf life of chilled processed foods is determined by:

- The type of food.
- The degree of microbial destruction or enzyme inactivation achieved by the process.
- Control of hygiene during processing and packaging.
- The barrier properties of the package.
- Temperatures during processing, distribution and storage.

Each of the factors that contribute to the shelf life of chilled foods can be thought of as 'hurdles' to microbial growth.

Cook–chill Systems

Individual foods (for example sliced roast meats) or complete meals are produced by cook–chill or cook–pasteurise–chill processes. An example is sous-vide products, which is the term commonly used to refer to foods that are vacuum packed prior to pasteurisation (although it strictly refers only to vacuum packing). These products, which include complete meals or components such as sauces, were developed for institutional catering to replace warm-holding, which reduces losses in nutritional and eating quality and is less expensive.

The range of chilled foods can be characterised by the class of microbial risk that they pose to consumers as follows:

Class 1 foods containing raw or uncooked ingredients, such as salad or cheese as ready-to-eat (RTE) foods (also includes chill-stable raw foods, such as meat, fish, etc.).

Class 2 products made from a mixture of cooked and low risk raw ingredients.

Class 3 cooked products that are then packaged.

Class 4 products that are cooked after packaging, including ready-to-eat-products for- extended-durability (REPFEDs) having a shelf life of 40+ days (the acronym is also used to mean refrigerated-pasteurised-foods-for-extended durability).

In the above classification, 'cooking' refers to a heat process that results in a minimum 6*D* reduction in target pathogens. Some Class 1 products require cooking by the consumer, whereas other cooked–chilled products may be ready to eat or eaten after a short period of reheating. Gorris and Betts describe other methods of mild processing to improve the safety of ready-to-eat foods. The manufacturer is only able to control the safety of these products by minimising the levels of pathogens on the incoming ingredients and by ensuring that processing and storage procedures do not introduce pathogens or allow their numbers to increase.

Therefore, in addition to normal hygienic manufacturing areas, the products in Classes 1, 2 and 4 require a special 'hygienic area', designed to be easily cleaned to prevent bacteria, such as *Listeria* spp. becoming established in it. Products in Classes 2 and 3 also require an additional 'high-care area', which is physically separated from other areas and is carefully designed to isolate cooked foods during preparation, assembly of meals, chilling and packaging. Such areas have specified hygiene requirements including:

- Positive pressure ventilation with micro-filtered air supplied at the correct temperature and humidity.
- Entry and exit of staff only through changing rooms.
- No-touch washing facilities.
- Construction standards and materials for easy cleaning.
- Only fully processed foods and packaging materials admitted through hatches or airlocks.
- Special hygiene training for operators and fully protective clothing (including boots, hairnets, coats, etc.).
- Operational procedures to limit the risk of contamination.
- Production stopped for cleaning and disinfection every 2 hr.

After preparation, cooked–chilled foods are portioned and chilled within 30 min of cooking. Chilling to 3ºC should be completed within 90 min and the food should be stored at 0–3°C. In the cook–pasteurise–

chill system, hot food is filled into a flexible container, a partial vacuum is formed to remove oxygen and the pack is heat sealed. It is then pasteurised to a minimum temperature of 80°C for 10 min at the thermal centre, followed by immediate cooling to 3°C. These foods have a shelf life of 2–3 weeks.

EQUIPMENT FOR CHILLING FOOD

Chilling equipment is classified by the method used to remove heat, into:

- Mechanical refrigerators.
- Cryogenic systems.

Batch or continuous operation is possible with both types of equipment, but all should lower the temperature of the product as quickly as possible through the critical warm zone (50–10°C) where maximum growth of micro-organisms occurs.

Mechanical refrigerators

Mechanical refrigerators have four basic elements: an evaporator, a compressor, a condenser and an expansion valve. Components of refrigerators are frequently constructed from copper as the low thermal conductivity allows high rates of heat transfer and high thermal efficiencies.

A refrigerant circulates between the four elements of the refrigerator, changing state from liquid to gas, and back to liquid as follows:

- In the evaporator the liquid refrigerant evaporates under reduced pressure, and in doing so absorbs latent heat of vaporisation and cools the freezing medium. This is the most important part of the refrigerator, the remaining equipment is used to recycle the refrigerant.
- Refrigerant vapour passes from the evaporator to the compressor where the pressure is increased.
- The vapour then passes to the condenser where the high pressure is maintained and the vapour is condensed.
- The liquid passes through the expansion valve where the pressure is reduced to restart the refrigeration cycle.

The important properties of refrigerants are as follows:

- A low boiling point and high latent heat of vaporisation.
- A dense vapour to reduce the size of the compressor.
- Low toxicity and non-flammable.
- Low miscibility with oil in the compressor.
- Low cost.

Ammonia has excellent heat transfer properties and is not miscible with oil, but it is toxic and flammable, and causes corrosion of copper pipes. Carbon dioxide is nonflammable and non-toxic, making it safer for use for example on refrigerated ships, but it requires considerably higher operating pressures compared to ammonia. Halogen refrigerants (chlorofluoro-carbons or CFCs) are all non-toxic and non-flammable and have good heat transfer properties and lower costs than other refrigerants. However, their interaction with ozone in the earth's atmosphere, and consequent contribution to global warming as 'greenhouse gases', has resulted in an international ban on their use as refrigerants under the Montreal Protocol. Partially halogenated CFCs (or HCFCs) are less environmentally harmful and existing HCFCs are being temporarily substituted for CFCs, but these too are to be phased out before the first decades of the new century. Newer, ozone-friendly HCFCs are being developed and are likely to become important refrigerants. These developments are described in more detail by Heap. The main refrigerants that are now used are Freon-22 and ammonia, with the possibility of future use of propane. However, the latter two in particular are more expensive and could cause localised hazards, thus requiring additional safety precautions and training for equipment users.

The chilling medium in mechanically cooled chillers may be air, water or metal surfaces. Air chillers (for example *blast chillers*) use forced convection to circulate air at around 4°C at high speed (4 ms^{-1}), and thus reduce the thickness of boundary films to increase the rate of heat transfer. Air-blast chillers are also used in refrigerated vehicles, but food should be adequately chilled when loaded onto the vehicle, as the refrigeration plant is only designed to hold food at the required temperature and cannot provide additional cooling of incompletely chilled food. *Eutectic plate systems* are another type of cooling that is used in refrigerated vehicles, especially for local distribution. Salt solutions (e.g. potassium chloride, sodium chloride or ammonium chloride) are frozen to their eutectic temperature (from 3 to 21°C) and air is circulated across the plates, to absorb heat from the vehicle trailer. The plates are regenerated by re-freezing in an external freezer.

Retail chill cabinets use chilled air which circulates by natural convection. The cost of chill storage is high and to reduce costs, large stores may have a centralised plant to circulate refrigerant to all cabinets. The heat generated by the condenser can also be used for in-store heating. Computer control of multiple cabinets detects excessive rises in temperature and warns of any requirement for emergency repairs or planned maintenance. Other energy-saving devices include night blinds or glass doors on the front of cabinets to trap cold air. Details of the design and operation of refrigerated retail display cabinets, chilled distribution vehicles and cold stores are given by Heap.

Other methods of cooling

Foods with a large surface area (for example lettuce) are washed and *vacuum cooled*. The food is placed in a large vacuum chamber and the pressure is reduced to approximately 0.5 kPa. Cooling takes place as moisture evaporates from the surface (a reduction of approximately 5ºC for each reduction of 1% in moisture content). Direct immersion in chilled water (*hydrocooling*) is used to remove field heat from fruit and vegetables, and cheese is often cooled by direct immersion in refrigerated brine. Recirculated chilled water is also used in *plate heat exchangers* to cool liquid foods after pasteurisation. Liquid and semi-solid foods (for example butter and margarine are cooled by contact with refrigerated, or water-chilled metal surfaces in *scraped-surface heat exchangers*.

Cryogenic Chilling

A cryogen is a refrigerant that changes phase by absorbing latent heat to cool the food. Cryogenic chillers use solid carbon dioxide, liquid carbon dioxide or liquid nitrogen. Solid carbon dioxide removes latent heat of sublimation (352 kJ^{-1} kg at 78°C), and liquid cryogens remove latent heat of vaporisation (358 kJ kg^{-1} at 196°C for liquid nitrogen, liquid carbon dioxide has a similar latent heat to the solid). The gas also absorbs sensible heat as it warms from 78°C (CO_2) or from 196°C (liquid nitrogen) to give a total refrigerant effect of 565 kJ kg^{-1} and 690 kJ kg^{-1} respectively.

The advantages of carbon dioxide include:

- A higher boiling and sublimation point than nitrogen, and therefore a less severe effect on the food.
- Most of enthalpy (heat capacity) arises from the conversion of solid or liquid to gas.

Only 13% of the enthalpy from liquid carbon dioxide and 15% from the solid is contained in the gas itself. This compares with 52% in nitrogen gas (that is, approximately half of the refrigerant effect of liquid nitrogen arises from sensible heat absorbed by the gas). Carbon dioxide does not therefore require gas handling equipment to extract most of the heat capacity, whereas liquid nitrogen does. The main limitation of carbon dioxide, and to a lesser extent nitrogen, is its ability to cause asphyxia. There is therefore a maximum safe limit for operators of 0.5% CO_2 by volume and excess carbon dioxide is removed from the processing area by an exhaust system to ensure operator safety, which incurs additional setup costs. Other hazards associated with liquefied gases include cold burns, frostbite and hypothermia after exposure to intense cold. Solid carbon dioxide can be used in the form of 'dry-ice' pellets, or liquid carbon dioxide can be injected into air to produce fine particles of solid carbon dioxide 'snow', which rapidly sublime to gas. Both types are deposited onto, or mixed with, food in combo bins, trays, cartons or on conveyors. A small excess of snow or pellets continues the cooling during transportation or storage prior to further processing. If products are despatched immediately in insulated containers or vehicles, this type of chilling is able to replace onsite cold stores and thus saves space and labour costs. Snow is replacing dry-ice pellets because it is cheaper and does not have the problems of handling, storage and operator safety associated with dry ice. For example, in older meat processing operations, dry-ice pellets were layered with minced meat as it was filled into containers. However, lack of uniformity in distribution of pellets resulted in some meat becoming frozen and some remaining above 5°C, which permitted bacterial growth and resulted in variable product temperatures for subsequent processing. More recently the use of snow horns to distribute a fine layer of snow over minced meat as it is loaded into combo bins has eliminated these problems and resulted in rapid uniform cooling to 3–4°C. A recent advance in the use of carbon dioxide snow for chilled and frozen distribution of foods.

Liquid nitrogen is used in both freezing and chilling operations. For batch chilling, typically 90–200 kg of food is loaded into an insulated stainless steel cabinet, containing centrifugal fans and a liquid nitrogen injector. The liquid nitrogen vaporises immediately and the fans distribute the cold gas around the cabinet to achieve a uniform reduction in product temperature. The chiller has a number of pre-programmed time/temperature cycles which are microprocessor controlled. A food probe monitors the temperature of the product and the control system changes the temperature inside the cabinet as the food cools, thus allowing the same pre-programmed cycle to be used irrespective of the temperature of the incoming food. As with other types of batch equipment, it is highly flexible in operation and it is therefore suitable for low production volumes or where a large number of speciality products are produced.

For continuous chilling, food is passed on a variable speed conveyor to an inclined, insulated, cylindrical barrel having a diameter of 80–120 cm and length 4–10 m depending on the capacity. The barrel rotates slowly and internal flights lift the food and tumble it through the cold nitrogen gas. The temperature and gas flow rate are controlled by a microprocessor and the tumbling action prevents food pieces sticking together, to produce a free-flowing product. It is used to chill diced meat or vegetables at up to 3 t h^{-1}. Controlled temperature liquid nitrogen tumblers are used to improve the texture and binding capacity of mechanically formed meat products. The gentle tumbling action in a partial vacuum, cooled by nitrogen gas to 2°C, solubilises proteins in poultry meat, which increases their binding capacity and water holding capacity, thus improving later forming and coating operations.

An alternative design is a screw conveyor inside a 2.5 m long stainless steel housing, fitted with liquid carbon dioxide injection nozzles. Foods such as minced beef, sauce mixes, mashed potato and diced vegetables are chilled rapidly as they are conveyed through the chiller at up to 1 t h^{-1}. It is used to firm foods before portioning or forming operations or to remove heat from previous processing stages.

Other applications of cryogenic cooling include sausage manufacture, where carbon dioxide snow removes the heat generated during size reduction and mixing and *cryogenic grinding* where the cryogen reduces dust levels, prevents dust explosions and improves the throughput of mills. In spice milling, cryogens also prevent the loss of aromatic compounds. In the production of multi-layer chilled foods (for example trifles and other desserts) the first layer of product is filled and the surface is hardened with carbon dioxide. The next layer can then be added immediately, without waiting for the first layer to set, and thus permit continuous and more rapid processing. Other applications include cooling and case-hardening of hot bakery products and chilling flour to obtain accurate and consistent flour temperatures for dough preparation.

Chill Storage

Once a product has been chilled, the temperature must be maintained by refrigerated storage. Chill stores are normally cooled by circulation of cold air produced by mechanical refrigeration units, and foods may be stored on pallets, racks, or in the case of carcass meats, hung from hooks. Transport of foods into and out of stores may be done manually using pallet trucks, by forklift truck or by computer-controlled robotic trucks. Materials that are used for the construction of refrigerated storerooms are described by Brennan and others.

Control of storage conditions

The importance of maintaining temperatures below 5°C to meet safety, quality and legal requirements for high-risk products. Fresh products may also require control of the relative humidity in a storeroom, and in some cases control over the composition of the storage atmosphere. In all stores it is important to maintain an adequate circulation of air using fans, to control the temperature, relative humidity or atmospheric composition. Foods are therefore stacked in ways that enable air to circulate freely around all sides. This is particularly important for respiring foods, to remove heat generated by respiration or for foods, such as cheese, in which flavour development takes place during storage. Adequate air circulation is also important when high storage humidities are used for fresh fruits and vegetables as there is an increased risk of spoilage by mould growth if 'deadspots' permit localised increases in humidity. In some situations, a lower relative humidity may be used, with some product wilting accepted as a compromise for reduced microbial spoilage.

Temperature monitoring

Temperature monitoring is an integral part of quality management and product safety management throughout the production and distribution chain. Improvements to microelectronics over the last ten years has enabled the development of monitoring devices that can both store large amounts of data and integrate this into computerised management systems. Woolfe lists the specifications of commonly used data loggers. These are connected to temperature sensors which measure either air temperatures or product temperatures to give a representative picture of the way in which the refrigeration system is functioning.

There are three main types of sensor that are used commercially: thermocouples, platinum resistance thermometers and semiconductor (thermistors). Thermocouples are a pair of dissimilar metals joined together at one end. The most widely used are Type K (nickel-chromium and nickel-aluminium), or Type T (copper and copper-nickel). The advantages over other sensors are lower cost, rapid response time and very wide range of temperature measurement (184–1600°C). Thermistors change resistance with temperature and have a higher accuracy than thermocouples, but they have a much narrower range

(40–140°C). Platinum resistance thermometers are accurate and have a temperature range from 270–850°C, but their response time is slower and they are more expensive than other sensors. Sensors are usually connected to either a chart recorder or an electronic digital display, which may also be able to store data and sound an alarm if the temperature exceeds a pre-set limit.

Monitoring air temperatures is more straightforward than product temperature monitoring and does not involve damage to the product or package. It is widely used to monitor chill stores, refrigerated vehicles and display cabinets, and Woolfe describes in detail the positioning of temperature sensors in these types of equipment. However, it is necessary to establish the relationship between air temperature and product temperature in a particular installation. Air is continuously recirculated through the refrigeration unit and storeroom. Cold air is warmed by the product, by lights in a store, by vehicles or by doors opening or operators entering. The temperature of the returning air is therefore likely to be the same as the product temperature or slightly higher. By comparing this to the temperature of the air leaving the evaporator in the refrigeration unit to find the temperature differential, it is possible to measure the performance of the refrigeration system and its effectiveness in keeping the food cold. To relate air temperature to product temperature it is necessary to conduct a 'load test', which involves examining the differential in air temperatures over a length of time and comparing it with the product temperature under normal working conditions.

Where a store, cabinet or vehicle is not opened for long periods, the only changes in temperature come from defrost cycles and intermittent door opening, and the relationship between product and air temperature is relatively simple. However, the operation of open retail display cabinets is more sensitive to variations in room temperature or humidity, the actions of customers and staff in handling foods, and lighting to display products. The temperature distribution in the cabinet can therefore change and load testing becomes more difficult. In such situations there is likely to be substantial variations in air temperature, but the mass of the food remains at a more constant temperature, and air temperature measurement has little meaning. To overcome this problem the food temperature can be measured or the air temperature sensor can be electronically 'damped' to respond more slowly and eliminate short-term fluctuations.

In addition to temperature sensors, the temperature of chilled foods can be monitored by temperature- or time-temperature indicators, which use physico-chemical changes to display · the current temperature

- Crossing of a threshold temperature.
- Integration of the temperature and the time that a food has been exposed to a particular temperature.

These devices are based on either melting point temperature, enzyme reaction, polymerisation, electro-chemical corrosion or liquid crystals.

Effect on Foods

The process of chilling foods to their correct storage temperature causes little or no reduction in the eating quality or nutritional properties of food. The most significant effect of chilling on the sensory characteristics of processed foods is hardening due to solidification of fats and oils. Chemical, biochemical and physical changes during refrigerated storage may lead to loss of quality, and in many instances it is these changes rather than micro-biological growth that limit the shelf life of chilled foods. These changes include enzymic browning, lipolysis, colour and flavour deterioration in some products and retrogradation of starch to cause staling of baked products (which occurs more rapidly at refrigeration temperatures than at room temperature). Lipid oxidation is one of the main causes of quality loss in cook–chilled products, and cooked meats in particular rapidly develop an oxidised flavour termed 'warmed-over flavour' (WOF), described in detail by Brown. Physico-chemical changes including migration of oils from mayonnaise to cabbage in chilled coleslaw, syneresis in sauces and gravies due to changes in starch thickeners, evaporation of moisture from unpackaged chilled meats and cheeses, more rapid staling of sandwich bread at reduced temperatures and moisture migration from sandwich fillings may each result in quality deterioration. Vitamin losses during chill storage of selected fresh and processed foods.

In cook–chill systems, nutritional losses are reported by Bognar as insignificant for thiamine, riboflavin and retinol, but vitamin C losses are 3.3–16% day at 2°C. The large variation is due to differences in the chilling time, storage temperature, oxidation (the amount of food surface exposed to air) and reheating conditions. Vitamin C losses in cook–pasteurise–chill procedures are lower than cooked–chilled foods (for example spinach lost 66% within 3 days at 2–3°C after cook–chilling compared with 26% loss within 7 days at 24°C after cook–pasteurising–chilling.

Chapter 23

Freezing

INTRODUCTION

The spectacular growth of the frozen food industry has been largely due to favourable economics of process, convenience of preparation, and the high quality of processed products. The range of frozen products includes fruits, vegetables, juices, meats, dairy products, and bakery goods. Modern freezing systems cause minimal changes in the quality attributes of products during processing. The ice crystallisation process is carefully controlled to obtain desired quality characteristics. During frozen storage, the environmental conditions are maintained at subfreezing levels with minimum fluctuations in temperature to minimise undesirable alterations in quality. Designing a freezing process involves calculations of the total heat being removed to accomplish freezing, and the time needed to lower the temperature to the required frozen storage conditions. A variety of different systems are used in commercial freezing, including air blast freezing, fluidised bed freezing, cryogenic freezing, and plate freezing. These systems are selected based on the requirements of the product being frozen. New developments in the freezing industry are expected, with improved knowledge of food properties and other changes in foods associated with the freezing process.

Frozen foods are valued for their superior sensory and nutritional quality when compared with foods preserved by other methods. The quality attributes of a frozen food can be maintained with a properly designed freezing process, and a carefully monitored handling and storage practice. Furthermore, frozen foods are convenient to cook in the home (or institutional kitchen) prior to consumption. Consumer demand for foods easy and quick to prepare has increased over the last several decades in a number of industrialised countries. Freezing is a technique in which the temperature of any food product is reduced below its freezing point and water content undergoes a change in state into ice. Implementing freezing technique for storing food product after harvest has been presented in this paper. Degree of cell wall rupture is related to freezing produced. Small sized ice crystals are responsible for less cell wall rupture than large ice crystals. If freezing is rapid a large number of small ice crystals are produced while slow freezing produces a few large ice crystals. Effect of freezing rate on quality and texture has also been presented. It was observed that freshness, texture, colour, flavour and nutrient values of food product remain preserve during freezing.

Freezing of foods is one of the best available methods for preservation of the food products. It maintains the quality of the food products quite close to that of the fresh ones. Freezing is a phase transformation process, in which a liquid is converted into solid when its temperature is lowered below its freezing point. Hence, in order to achieve freezing, the food product should be exposed to low temperature. Micro-organisms (such as bacteria, yeast and moulds) cause spoilage of food products like meats, poultry, fish, dairy products, etc. At normal room temperature, micro-organisms are active and cause spoilage of food products. If the temperature of food products is lowered significantly, the action of these micro-organisms is retarded to a greater extent, making it possible to store the food products for longer duration of time.

In early freezer designs, freeze food products were found to be laced with crystals of ice. However, in modern designs, the temperature is plunged quickly through the freezing zone. Generally, liquids freeze by crystallisation which consists of- nucleation and crystal growth. Nucleation is the process in which the molecules start to gather into clusters (on the nanometer scale), arranging in a defined pattern that defines the structure of crystal. It takes place in a gas, liquid or solid phase. For example, ice formation from water. The crystal growth is the subsequent growth of the nuclei that succeed in achieving the critical cluster size. Nucleation can take place at nucleation sites on surfaces contacting the liquid or vapour. Suspended particles or minute bubbles can also act as a site for nucleation. This is known as heterogeneous nucleation. Nucleation that takes place without preferential nucleation sites is known as homogeneous nucleation. Homogeneous nucleation takes place spontaneously and in random manner, but it needs super-cooling of the medium.

FOOD QUALITY AND THE FREEZING PROCESS

Handling Prior to Freezing

Prior to freezing, the time elapsed in initial preparation of a food commodity is a critical factor influencing the quality of the frozen product. Once a fruit or vegetable is harvested or an animal slaughtered, the intrinsic biochemical reactions do not cease. Instead, varieties of reactions continue to alter the food's quality, often in a deteriorative mode. Therefore, the handling of foods prior to freezing, and environmental conditions such as temperature and humidity, require careful control. With vegetables, intrinsic enzymes must be inactivated prior to freezing. Otherwise, enzymatic reactions occurring at frozen storage temperatures may degrade such attributes as colour, flavour, texture, and nutritional value.

Vegetables are blanched prior to freezing to inactivate their inherent enzymes. Typically, the activity of three enzymes—peroxidase, catalase, and lipoxygenase—is monitored to determine the effectiveness of a blanching treatment. In an industrial blanching process, vegetables are either submerged in hot water or exposed to steam.

The blanching process is designed with the following criteria in mind:

- All food particulates should be uniformly exposed to the heating medium.
- Blanching time for all food particulates should be uniform.
- Food particulates should not be physically damaged during blanching.
- Any leaching of product components should be minimised.
- The blanching process should conserve energy and water.

Developments in the design of blanching equipment have addressed some of these criteria. Hot water blanchers sometimes have tubular systems, where water heated with steam injection is used to heat and convey food particulates. In a rotary, screw blancher system, hot water and food particulates are brought into contact in a static drum with a central screw that turns and improves the contact between the food and hot water. An integrated blancher and cooler design involves heating and cooling sections within the same unit. The product enters the blancher on a conveyor belt and is preheated, followed by blanching in a steam environment, and the cooling zones. Some researchers believe this system has improved energy efficiency and reduced water consumption. Although there has been considerable interest in the use of microwaves for blanching, problems exist in achieving uniform heating when water distribution within a particulate is non-uniform. Moreover, the operational costs of a microwave system for industrial scale blanching are significantly higher than with conventional units using water or steam. Typical blanching conditions are shown in Table 23.1. After blanching, the product is cooled by immersion in chilled water. Blanched vegetables are either packaged in retailsise packages or frozen without packaging. For meats and poultry products, pretreatment processes such as ageing, chilling, trimming, cutting, cleaning, sorting, and grading influence the final frozen quality.

Table 23.1: Typical blanching conditions for vegetables.

Product	*Blanching time (s)*	*Heating medium*
Asparagus	210–300	Steam
Broccoli	210	Steam
Carrots	120–180	Water at 99°C
Cauliflower	240–300	Steam
Corn on the cob	360–660	Steam
Corn	180	Steam
Peas	48–60	Water at 99°C
Spinach	120–180	Steam

Freezing Conditions

In modern freezers, the time of exposure and temperature of the freezing medium are carefully controlled. Ice crystallisation during freezing, where water present in a food crystallises into ice, is the most fundamental step in the freezing process. The crystallisation process is comprised of the nucleation stage and the crystal growth stage. In the first stage, nucleation establishes sites in a food where ice crystals may later grow. Nucleation sites are typically the non-aqueous entities. In heterogeneous nucleation, the type common in the freezing of foods, water molecules aggregate around the nucleate. Other factors, such as supercooling, physical disturbance, and change in viscosity with temperature, also affect the rate of nucleation. After the nuclei are formed, crystals begin to grow, often at a rapid rate. Among the factors affecting crystal growth are the rate of heat removal, temperature of the cooling medium, diffusion, and change in viscosity with temperature.

The number of nuclei formed during the nucleation stage and the ultimate size of the crystal formed during crystal growth may affect the final quality of some frozen foods, such as ice cream and berry fruits. In a slow freezing process, ice crystals grow into large sizes in the extra-cellular spaces, causing damage to the plant or animal tissue being frozen. The deleterious effects of freezing on product quality are partially due to ice crystal growth at the expense of water extracted from the interior of the cells. When small ice crystals form in the intra- and extra-cellular spaces, damage to quality is minimised. For example, in the formation of small ice crystals, the drip loss during thawing associated with the expulsion of juices from frozen products such as meats is minimised.

During Frozen Storage

Physical and chemical changes continue to occur in frozen foods during storage. They include lipid oxidation, insolubilisation (or gelation of proteins), loss of vitamins, and degradation of chlorophyll. These changes can profoundly affect the sensory characteristics of foods. In frozen storage, microbial growth is arrested, and even psychrophilic microbes generally cease to grow below –10°C.

Localised surface dehydration, also called 'freezer burn', is a serious physical change that leads to localised surface dehydration and discolouration. This phenomenon is most common in meats, fish, and poultry products, and is caused by small changes in local vapour pressure occurring due to fluctuations in storage temperature. Proper packaging and the use of low and uniform storage temperatures can help alleviate this problem. Three colour changes can be observed in frozen foods during storage: (i) fading of natural colour constituents due to changes in chlorophylls (e.g. green vegetables), (ii) loss of colour from product to surrounding medium (e.g. diffusion of pigments from red cherries stored in sugar syrups), and (iii) change in colour (e.g. darkening of bone in frozen chicken upon cooking, and browning of sliced peaches due to polyphenoloxidase reacting with air in headspace). These types of changes in colour are indicative of quality deterioration during frozen storage. Future research is necessary to minimise these adverse changes.

Flavour changes due to rancidity in frozen meats, poultry, and fish cause major deterioration. For example, fatty fish is prone to oxidative rancidity and must be stored at temperatures below –25°C to avoid undesirable changes. Similarly, blanching of vegetables is necessary to avoid off-flavour problems during frozen storage. Other textural defects that may occur during improper storage conditions include loss of juiciness in meats, dryness of fish muscle that makes it crumbly, loss of fluidity in egg yolk, and aggregation of starches in sauces.

Although freezing is one of the best preservation methods for maintaining the nutrient content of foods during storage, the pre-freezing steps of washing and blanching may be responsible for loss of water-soluble nutrients. Loss of nutrients during thawing is slight, except when associated with drip loss in improperly frozen fruits, meats, fish, and poultry products. Damage to the frozen food frequently occurs when a product is thawed prior to consumption. The consumer often conducts the thawing process, unaware of its implications on product quality. During thawing, physical and chemical changes and microbial growth may significantly alter a products quality attributes.

RATE OF FREEZING

Freezing produced controls the degree of cell wall rupture of food products. In fast freezing, a large number of small ice crystals are produced. These small sized ice crystals leads to less cell wall rupture than slow freezing which produces only a few large ice crystals. Therefore, freezer manuals suggest that the temperature of the freezer be set at the coldest setting several hours before food products are placed inside it. Some manuals recommend the location of the coldest place inside the freezer and suggest placing unfrozen products at that site. The maximum number of cubic feet of unfrozen food product, which can be frozen at a given time, is also specified. Overloading the freezer with unfrozen food products can lead to long and slow freezing rate. Thus, overloading of freezer should be avoided.

FREEZING EQUIPMENTS

The industrial equipment for freezing can be categorised as follows:

1. Air-blast freezing equipments, where refrigerated air at certain velocity is blown over food products.

2. Contact freezing equipments, where the food products are placed in contact with metal surfaces.
3. Immersion freezing equipments, where the food product is placed in a low-temperature brine.
4. Fluidised-bed freezing equipments, where the individual food products are moved along a conveyor belt and kept in suspension by an upward-directed stream of sufficiently cold air.
5. Equipments utilising a cryogenic substance (such as nitrogen or carbon dioxide).

EFFECT OF FREEZING RATES ON QUALITY AND TEXTURE

In order to obtain frozen food products of high quality and maximum nutritional value, one should have sufficient knowledge of:

1. The chemical and physical reactions that take place during the freezing process.
2. Scientific knowledge of the effect of freezing on the tissues of food products.
3. Food microbiology.

The function of freezing process is to preserve food products at the same time its quality is maintained. This is achieved by lowering down the temperature of food product, hence slowing the quality deterioration processes, the oxidation of fat, the retarding action of micro-organisms, enzymatic reactions and the loss of moisture from the surface of food products. Fresh fruits and vegetables, after being harvested, continue to undergo chemical changes, which deteriorate quality of the food product. Therefore such products should be stored in freezer soon after being harvest and at their peak degree of ripeness. Fresh food products contain chemical compounds known as enzymes, which cause the loss of texture, loss of nutrients, flavour changes in frozen products. These enzymes should therefore be inactivated to prevent such reactions. The blanching process is employed for inactivation of enzymes in vegetables. In blanching process, vegetable is the exposure to boiling water, steam or micro-oven for a short duration of time. This process is followed by rapid cooling of the vegetable in ice water.

The formation of small ice crystals during freezing is required. Rapid freezing is the practical way to form large number of small ice crystals. Large ice crystals produced as a result of on slow freezing leads to damage of cell, causing unnecessary change in. Most of fruits and vegetables contain about 90% of water by weight held within the cell walls and provides structural support and texture to them. Freezing fruits and vegetables mainly results in freezing of this water. When the water freezes, it expands and the ice crystals cause damage to the cell walls. Consequently, the texture of the defrosted food product will be much softer than it was when raw. This textural change is discernable in products, which are consumed raw. For example, a frozen tomato when defrosted becomes mushy and watery. Therefore, tomatoes are not generally frozen. Textural changes due to freezing are not noticeable in products which are cooked before eating because cooking also softens cell walls. Also, these changes are not observed in vegetables having high starch content such as peas, corn, etc.

TYPES OF FREEZERS

Important types of freezer are described below:

Blast Freezer

The simplest technique of freezing is to place the food product in insulated cold storage room maintained at sub-freezing condition. In such case, heat transfer is by natural convection will occur. This result to slow freezing rat and produces large ice crystals in the food products and gives sufficient time for missing of flavours of different food products. Thus, deteriorate the quality of the food products. In air-blast freezers, refrigerated air at certain velocity is blown over the food product and convective heat transfer takes place. Figure 23.1 shows working of a simple blast freezer. It can be seen from that figure that blast freezers is provided with blowers to pass on refrigerated air over the surface of the food products in order to freeze them at a rapid rate. Modern blast freezers are equipped with movable trays for customizing location of food products for freezing. A blast freezer quickly lowers the temperature of foods product. In such freezers, an extremely cold temperature promotes very quick freezing, which produces small ice crystals. At normal temperature, bacterial growth in food products takes place at a rapid rate. Thus, food product becomes unsafe for consumption. The micro-organism can't survive in the extremely cold condition of blast freezer. These freezers are used in food industry to preserve meat, fish, dairy products, etc. Blast freezer preserves texture, colour, flavour and nutritional value of the food products.

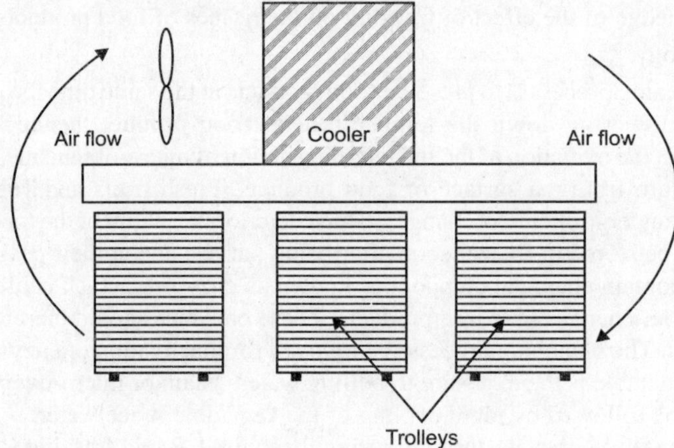

Fig 23.1: Blast freezer.

Contact Plate Freezer

In contact plate freezer, food products are frozen by placing them in contact with metal surfaces cooled by refrigerants (such as refrigerant-12, 22 or ammonia). The food products can rest on, slide against or be pressed between metal plates. In all cases, cooling is achieved by heat conduction. Contact plate freezers consist of a series of flat hollow refrigerated metallic plates. The plates are arranged parallel to each other and may be either horizontal or vertical. The spaces between the plates can be varied, the plates can be opened out for loading and closed so that the surface of the metallic plates is in direct contact with the food products. A slight pressure is applied between the plates and the food product during freezing process in order to achieve good face to face contact. Contact plate freezers are quick and efficient, however, their use is limited to flat foods with thickness not more than 8 cm. For example meat, fish, ice creams, chopped leafy vegetables, etc.

Individual Quick Freezing

Individual Quick Freezing (IQF) is the modern freezing technique and it enables preservation and storage of raw fruit and vegetables in the farm-fresh condition for more than a year. This technique is very effective in preserving colour, flavour and texture of food product. IQF is the only process in which all the properties of most of the parent food products are preserved. The important characteristic of this type of freezing is ultra-quick freezing to very low temperatures (–30 to –40°C) designed to inactive the activities of the micro-organisms that cause deterioration of food products. In this type of freezing process, each piece is frozen individually using fluidisation technique (i.e. product is suspended on high velocity air) which leads to freezing of food products in 10 to 12 minutes which otherwise takes at least 3 to 4 hr or even more in the blast freezer. Air directed up through perforated belt. Product flows in one end and overflows out other end. It gives high heat transfer rates. IQF is applicable to food products such as fruits, vegetables, meat, pasta, rice, etc.

Cryogenic Freezer

In cryogenic freezer, the food product is brought into direct contact with the refrigerant. The food products placed on the conveyor belt come into contact with the counter current flow of nitrogen gas (at a temperature of about –50°C). As the product passes to the pre-cooling stage of the freezer, the gaseous nitrogen partially freezes it and up to 50% of the product heat is extracted. The food product then passes below the spray of liquid nitrogen where freezing process is completed. The end stage in the freezer provides some time for the product temperature to reach equilibrium. The main advantage of this system is that freezing is very rapid and size of the freezer is comparatively small. Also, compressor and condenser are not the integral part of this freezer. Liquid nitrogen must be retained in a vacuum insulated pressure vessel with continuous venting to keep the contents cool and the internal pressure down. The limitation of cryogenic freezer is cost of nitrogen and regular supply of nitrogen gas.

GROWTH OF SPOILAGE ORGANISMS

Freezing does not destroy spoilage organisms, it merely stops their growth temporarily. During the freezing process, microbial growth can occur under the following circumstances:

- When freezing does not take place rapidly.
- When freezer temperature is above 0°F.

Keep the freezer temperature at or below 0°F to prevent the growth of spoilage organisms and to minimise changes in flavour, texture and nutritive value of food. To prevent contamination of all foods by spoilage organisms, always keep your equipment, work surfaces and hands clean. Washing produce thoroughly before freezing removes garden soil, a source of spoilage organisms.

Freezing does not destroy *Clostridium botulinum*, the spoilage organism that causes the greatest problem in canning low acid foods like vegetables and animal products. However, *Clostridium botulinum* will not grow and produce toxin (poison) at correct freezer temperatures (0°F or below). Therefore, freezing is a safe and easy alternative to pressure canning low acid foods.

When thawing food, remember that freezing did not destroy any spoilage organisms that might have been present in the food. As the temperature of food rises during thawing, growth of spoilage organisms begins. The faster the food warms up, especially on the surface, the faster the growth of spoilage organisms occurs. If you store raw or precooked frozen foods long enough at a high enough temperature after thawing, spores of *Clostridium botulinum* can grow and produce toxin. For this reasons it is recommend that food be thawed in the refrigerator where spoilage organisms will not grow as quickly.

Chemical Changes during Freezing

Enzymes are proteins present in plants and animals. While the plant or animal lives, enzymes help speed up the ripening and maturing processes. Even after we harvest plants or slaughter animals, enzyme reactions can continue and result in undesirable colour, flavour and texture changes in the food. Freezing slows down, but does not destroy, enzymes in fruits and vegetables. That is why it is important to stop enzyme activity before freezing. The two methods you can use are blanching and adding chemical compounds such as ascorbic acid.

Enzymes in vegetables

Enzymes in vegetables are inactivated by blanching. To blanch vegetables, place them in boiling water or steam for a brief period of time. Next, cool the vegetables rapidly in ice water (this prevents further cooking). Although some publications state that blanching is unnecessary, it is essential for top quality, frozen vegetables. Blanching also helps to destroy micro-organisms on the surface of the vegetables. It makes vegetables like broccoli and spinach more compact, and as a result, they take up less room in the freezer. Follow the recommended time for blanching each vegetable carefully. Over-blanching results in a cooked product and a loss of flavour, colour and nutrients. Under-blanching speeds up enzyme activity and is worse than no blanching at all.

Enzymes in fruits

Enzymes in fruits can cause browning and loss of vitamin C. People generally serve fruits raw, so instead of blanching fruits to control enzyme activity, they are treated with a chemical compound. The most common additive is ascorbic acid (vitamin C). Ascorbic acid may be used in its pure form or in commercial mixtures of ascorbic acid and other ingredients such as sugar. Some publications suggest using an acid solution (citric acid or lemon juice) to control browning for a short time. These publications instruct you to place fruit in the acid solution while preparing it for the freezer. Then place the fruit in freezer containers and either freeze it dry or cover the fruit with unsweetened fruit juice. Acid solutions work well as holding treatments for fruit but do not prevent browning as effectively as treatment with ascorbic acid. An alternative to holding fruit in an acid solution is to prepare a syrup (light, medium or heavy) that has ascorbic acid added to it. After preparing fruit for the freezer, it is then added to the syrup and packaged for freezer storage.

Rancidity in foods

Fats in meat, fish and poultry become rancid during freezer storage. This is caused by contact with air left in the package or air that enters the package because proper storage materials were not used. However, even with proper packaging materials, rancidity will occur over time. Off flavours are the result of this chemical change. Control rancidity by trimming excess fat from meat before freezing, using a wrapping material that prevents air from reaching the product, and by storing foods for the recommended length of time.

Changes in Food Texture during Freezing

Freezing involves the change of water contained in the food from a liquid to a solid (ice). When water freezes it expands, and the ice crystals formed cause cell walls of food to rupture. As a result, the texture of the product will be much softer when it thaws.

These textural changes are most noticeable in fruits and vegetables that have a high water content. For example, when frozen lettuce thaws, it turns limp and wilted. This is the reason vegetables with a high water content, such as celery and salad greens, are not usually frozen (Table 23.2). It is also the reason why many frozen fruits are best served while they still contain a few ice crystals. The effect of freezing on fruit tissue is less noticeable when fruit is still partially frozen.

Table 23.2: Foods that do not freeze well.

Foods	*Usual use*	*Condition after thawing*
Cabbage[1], celery, cress, cucumbers[1], endive, lettuce, parsley, radishes	As raw salad	Limp, water-logged, quickly develop off-color, odour and flavor
Irish potatoes, baked or boiled	In soups, salads, sauces or with butter	Soft, crumbly, water-logged, mealy
Cooked macaroni, spaghetti or rice	As a side dish or in casseroles	When frozen alone for later use, mushy and has warmed-over flavor
Egg whites, cooked sandwiches, sauces, gravy or desserts	In salads, creamed foods	Tough, rubbery, spongy
Meringue	In desserts	Toughens
Icings made from egg whites	Cakes, cookies	Frothy, weepy
Cream or custard fillings	Pies, baked goods	Separates, watery, lumpy
Milk sauces	For casseroles or gravies	May curdle or separate
Sour cream	As topping, in salads	Separates, watery
Cheese or crumb toppings	On casseroles	Soggy
Mayonnaise or salad dressing	On sandwiches (not in salads)	Separates
Gelatin	In salads or desserts	Weeps
Fruit jelly	Sandwiches	May soak bread
Fried foods potatoes and onion rings	All except French fried	Lose crispness, become soggy

[1]Cucumbers and cabbage can be frozen as marinated products such as 'freezer slaw' or 'freezer pickles.' These do not have the same texture as regular slaw or pickles

Textural changes due to freezing are not as apparent in products that are cooked before eating because cooking also softens cell walls. Textural changes are also less noticeable in high-starch vegetables, such as peas, corn and lima beans.

Rate of Freezing

The amount of damage to cell walls can be controlled by freezing products as quickly as possible. In rapid freezing, a large number of small ice crystals are formed. These small ice crystals cause less damage to cell walls than slow freezing, which produces larger ice crystals. For best results, freeze foods at 0°F or lower as soon as they are packaged and sealed. Set the temperature control at –10°F or lower about 24 hr in advance to help food freeze rapidly. Do not overload your freezer with unfrozen food. Add only the amount that will freeze within 24 hr, which is usually two to three pounds of food per cubic foot of freezer space. Overloading results in a long, slow freeze and a poor quality product. Place packages in contact with refrigerated surfaces in the coldest part of the freezer. Leave a little space between packages so that air can circulate freely. When the food is frozen, packages can be restacked close together.

To maintain top quality, store frozen foods at 0°F or lower. This temperature can be maintained in separate freezer units and in some combination refrigerator-freezers. A freezer thermometer can help determine the actual temperature of your freezer. Spoilage occurs more quickly and shelf life is shorter when you store frozen foods at a temperature higher than 0°F. For example, the same loss of quality in frozen beans stored at 0°F for one year will occur in three months at 10°F, in three weeks at 20°F and in five days at 30°F. Do not attempt to save energy in your home by raising the temperature of frozen food storage above 0°F.

Temperatures that fluctuate up and down cause the ice in foods to thaw slightly and then refreeze. Each time this happens, smaller ice crystals become larger, further damaging cells and creating a mushier product. Frequent changes in temperature also cause water to move out of the product resulting in a less juicy product that is generally lower in quality and nutritive value. For highest quality and nutritive value, use home frozen foods within the recommended storage times given in Table 23.3. Food will still be safe to eat after the recommended time period is past if the freezer has been kept at 0°F or lower. However, the quality and nutritive value will be lower.

Table 23.3: Storage times for home-frozen foods.

Food	*Storage period at 0°F*
Butter	6 to 9 months
Margarine	12 months
Cheese	
Natural	6 to 8 weeks
Processed	4 months
Cream (all kinds)	2 months
Whipped	1 month
Eggs (whole, white, yolks)	9 to 12 months
Fish	
Fatty (perch, salmon, mackerel)	2 to 3 months
Lean (cod, flounder, haddock, sole)	3 to 6 months
Fruit and fruit juice (except citrus)	8 to 12 months
Citrus fruit and juice	4 to 6 months
Ice cream or sherbet	2 months
Meat	
Bacon	1 month
Frankfurters and luncheon meat	Not recommended
Ham	1 month
Ground beef, lamb, veal	2 to 3 months
Ground pork	1 to 2 months
Meat, roasts	
Beef 6 to 12 months	
Lamb, veal 6 to 9 months	
Pork 3 to 6 months	
Meat, steaks, chops	
Beef	6 to 12 months
Lamb, veal	1 to 2 months
Pork	3 to 6 months
Milk, fresh fluid	1 month
Poultry (chicken, turkey, duck)	
Whole — chicken or turkey	12 months
— duck or goose	6 months

(Cont'd...)

Food	*Storage period at 0°F*
Cut up — chicken	9 months
— turkey	6 months
Giblets	3 months
Home prepared foods	
Bread	3 months
Cake	3 months
Casseroles (meat, fish, poultry)	3 months
Cookies (baked and unbaked)	3 months
Pies (unbaked fruit)	8 months
Vegetables	
Home frozen	10 months
Purchased	8 months
Yogurt	
Plain	1 month
Flavored	5 months

Moisture Loss (Freezer Burn)

Moisture loss, or ice crystals evaporating from the surface area of a product, produces freezer burn. Freezer burn appears as a fuzzy, grayish white spot on the food surface. Freezer burn is not harmful, but it causes off-flavour and dries out and toughens food. Packaging food in moisture/vapour-proof containers or wrapping and storing food for the recommended length of time will help prevent freezer burn. Covering fruit with syrup and cooked meat with gravy or sauce helps prevent freezer burn in these products.

Containers for Freezing

Proper packaging material protects the flavour, colour, moisture content and nutritive value of frozen foods from the dry climate of the freezer. Selection of containers depends on the type of food to be frozen, personal preference and types that are readily available. Foods in larger containers freeze too slowly to result in a satisfactory product. For example, do not freeze fruits and vegetables in containers larger than a halfgallon. In general, packaging materials for the freezer must have the following characteristics:

- Moisture- and vapour-proof.
- Odourless, tasteless and greaseproof.
- Foodgrade.
- Durable and leak-proof.
- Not become brittle and crack at freezer temperatures.
- Protect foods from absorption of odours.
- Easy to use, seal and label.
- Designed for compact stacking and economical use of freezer space.
- Reasonable cost.

There are two types of packaging materials for use in home freezing: rigid containers and flexible bags or wrap made for freezer use. If labels of packaging material do not state that the material is for freezer use, it probably is not.

Rigid Containers

Rigid containers made of plastic or glass are suitable for all packs and are especially good for liquid packs as well as fragile or easily broken food. The straight sides on rigid containers make the frozen food much easier to get out and make it easier to stack foods in the freezer. Most rigid containers can be reused. Regular glass jars, including jars made specifically for canning, break easily at freezer temperatures. If using glass jars, choose wide mouth, dual purpose jars made for freezing and canning. These jars have been made to withstand extremes in temperatures. The wide mouth and straight sides allow easy removal of partially thawed foods. Covers for rigid containers should fit tightly. If they do not, reinforce the seal with freezer tape. Freezer tape is especially designed to stick at freezing temperatures. Do not use masking tape because it will not stick at low temperatures.

Flexible Bags or Wraps

Bags and sheets of moisture/vapour-proof materials (labelled freezer bags or freezer wrap) and heavy-duty aluminium foil are suitable for dry-packed vegetables and fruits, meats, fish or poultry. Protective cardboard cartons may be used to protect bags and sheets against tearing and to make stacking easier.

Packaging and labelling foods:

- Cool all foods and syrup before packing. This speeds up freezing and helps retain the natural colour, flavour and texture of food.
- Pack foods in quantities that will be used for a single meal.
- Follow directions for each individual food to determine which can be packed dry and which need added liquid. Some loose foods such as blueberries may be tray-packed (quick-frozen first on a tray before packaging).
- Pack foods tightly leaving as little air as possible in the package.
- Most foods require headspace between the packed food and closure to allow for expansion of the food as it freezes. (See directions for individual foods included in other home economics guides in the freezer series.) Foods that do not need headspace include loose-pack vegetables such as asparagus and broccoli, bony pieces of meat, traypacked foods and baked products.
- When food is packed in bags, press air from the bag. Press firmly, begin at the bottom of the bag and move toward the unfilled top part of the bag to prevent air from reentering. Seal by twisting and folding back the top of the bag (gooseneck) and securing with a string, good quality rubber band or covered-wire twist tie. Some bags are made specifically for heat sealing. These should be used only with a heating element specifically made to seal storage containers. Never use an iron to heat seal these storage containers.
- Seal rigid containers carefully. Use a tight lid and keep the sealing edge free from moisture or food to ensure a good closure. Secure loose-fitting covers with freezer tape. Meats may be packaged using either the drugstore wrap or the butcher wrap.
- Label each package with the name of the product, any added ingredients, packaging date, number of servings or amount and the form of the food, such as whole, sliced, etc. Use freezer tape or self-adhesive labels and marking pens or crayons to label packages. Also label commercially frozen foods with the storage date.

Effect of Freezing on Spices and Seasonings

When preparing food for freezing, especially dishes that contain several ingredients, it is more convenient to add all ingredients before placing the food in the freezer. However, some spices and seasonings change during freezer storage. To avoid undesirable changes in the food product during freezer storage, note the following:

- Pepper, cloves, garlic and synthetic vanilla tend to become strong and bitter.
- Onions change flavour during freezing.
- Celery seasoning becomes strong.
- Curry may develop a musty off-flavour.
- Salt loses flavour and has a tendency to increase rancidity of any item containing fat.

Freezer Plan

You get maximum convenience and economy through carefully planning the use of your freezer. The secret lies in an easy management plan. Plan the freezer contents. Freeze foods you need and use often. Freeze only the foods your family likes and in amounts you will use within the recommended storage period. Budget freezer space first for basic foods such as meats, vegetables and fruits. Then, if there is room, plan to freeze baked goods, main dishes, snacks or desserts. Keep contents organised. An orderly freezer holds many more packages than a disorderly one. Stack similar foods together. Packages you will use first should be the easiest to get to.

Use baskets, shelves, or dividers that are furnished with the freezer to help organise the contents. Keep an inventory. You will always know what is on hand if you keep an inventory of the foods that are in the freezer. A current inventory can help you plan meals and remind you to use old packages of food within their recommended storage times.

Keep the inventory in a handy place so food can be added and subtracted without much trouble. Remember, the simpler it is to use, the more you will use it. You might want to use an index card system with a separate card for each food item. This makes it easy to add items to the inventory and to determine the total amount of a specific food on hand. A sample freezer inventory is shown in Table 23.4.

Table 23.4: Sample freezer inventory.

Food	*Number of packages*	*Date frozen*	*Number of packages removed*
Green beans	Pints: 10	8/85	~~IIII~~
Carrots	Quarts: 5	7/85	III
Corn	Pints: 20	7/85	~~IIII~~ I

FREEZING METHODS FOR VARIOUS FRUITS

In this section, details of the processing procedures for selected fruits are given.

Apple

Not all varieties of apple result in an acceptable product when frozen, whether the end use is for the bakery trade or for other purposes, however, some cultivars of apple are suitable for freezing. These are sorted, washed, peeled, cored and sliced. The sliced fruit is treated to minimise enzymatic browning.

This can be achieved by application of antioxidant solutions, including some proprietary treatments. One common treatment is salt brining, soaking slices in a 1 per cent salt solution in order to remove intercellular air. Ascorbic acid solutions can also be used, but these tend to be expensive. A surface blanch, using steam or boiling water, can also be employed, though it results in a softened slice that may not be suited for some uses. The treated slices in a ratio of five parts fruit to one part dry sugar are frozen in large 30- to 50 lb containers in a blast freezer below –10°F. Some apples may be frozen using a dehydrofreezing process where about 50 per cent of the water is removed from the apple slices by standard drying equipment prior to freezing the slices.

Apricot

Though some apricots are frozen whole for later processing, the major proportion of apricots are usually frozen as peeled apricot halves. This enhances the tendency for browning and therefore, requires steps to be taken to minimise browning. The apricots are peeled, halved and pitted and dipped in ascorbic acid solution to minimise browning or blanched fora short time to inactivate the enzymes. The halves are packed in sugar or sugar syrup prior to freezing at a 3:1 or 4:1 ratio of fruit to sugar. Air blast freezers are adequate. It is best to freeze the apricots on trays or on a belt prior to packing into barrels or 30 lb containers. This helps minimise discolouration. Storage should be below 0°F. For good retention of ascorbic acid, storage should be at –20°F.

Avocado

Aocados present a challenge to the commercial freezer due to their high oil content that readily becomes rancid and also because of a very active oxidative browning system. Pureed avocado is a successful product. Preservation life is enhanced by lowering the pH of the puree to below 4.5 through the addition of lemon juice, lime juice and salt. Packaging under nitrogen also enhances shelf life. Vacuum packaging has also been employed. Any reasonably rapid freezing method can be employed. Storage should be around 0°F for a reasonable shelf life.

Berries

Many varieties of berries are frozen. Berries can be frozen in syrup or as individual berries. As individual berries, they may be tray frozen or IQF frozen on a belt in an air blast or cryogenic freezer.

Red raspberries for retail are packed in an approximately 50 per cent syrup, in the proportion of six parts berry to four parts syrup and 10- and 16-oz containers are used. Any reasonably rapid freezing method may be employed.

Black raspberries are used for further processing and are packed in 30 lb containers or larger. In order to successfully freeze berries in a large container, the following procedures have been shown to be necessary:

1. The temperature of the fruit should not exceed 60°F at the time of filling.
2. The containers should be moved to the freezer as quickly as possible.
3. The temperature on entering the freezer should be below 70°F.
4. Freezer conditions (air temperature <–15°F and airflow velocity high) should allow for the center of the container to reach a temperature of 32°F or less within 48 hr.
5. Freezing should be continued until the center temperature is 0°F. This should take no more than 4 to 5 days.

6. Storage should be below 0°F.

Blackberries, boysenberries, loganberries and others are frozen utilising the same procedures as have been described for raspberries. Blueberries are frozen in 20 lb containers, with steps being takers to minimise or eliminate air in the package.

Cherry

The major portion of cherries frozen are tart cherries, though some sweet cherries are also frozen. The procedures for freezing are essentially the same. Tart cherries are harvested when bright red, sweet cherries when mature. The cherries are held and transported in ice-cold water, which reduces losses due to crushing and bruising and makes the fruit firmer for pitting. Fruits are size graded, pitted, packed with sugar in large cans and frozen in a blast freezer.

Coconut

Shredded coconut can be frozen without any particular preparation. The rate of freezing is not critical so long as cooling is sufficiently rapid to minimise microbiological contamination. Storage, in large containers is at 0°F.

Cranberry

Cranberries are frozen at 0°F using conventional techniques. The majority of the frozen crop is used for processing.

Dates

Fresh dates may be frozen. The use of a good moisture-proof and vapour-proof wrapping is recommended to prevent moisture loss during freezing or storage.

Figs

Figs can be frozen as whole fruit in heavy syrup or as sliced fruit as four parts fruit to one part water. Standard freezing methods are employed. Storage temperatures should be below 0°F.

Mango

Mango is frozen as slices in syrup. The syrup contains ascorbic acid to inhibit polyphenol oxidase-induced browning. In addition, mango puree is a significant frozen product. Purees can be single or double strength. Storage should be at or below 0°F. Browning can be a significant problem at higher storage temperatures due to non-enzymic browning.

Melon

Melon is frozen when the texture is firm enough to allow for cutting of cubes or balls that retain their integrity. If too ripe, a very mushy product will result because fully thawed melon loses considerable texture. Melon is usually frozen in syrup.

Papaya

Papaya puree is prepared from ripe papaya. Steamed fruit can be sliced and crushed and the pulp can be separated from the skin. The acidified pulp is passed through a heat exchanger to inactivate enzymes before cooling and freezing to –10°F.

Peach

In general, freestone peaches are used for freezing. Yellow fleshed varieties are preferred for better texture and lower susceptibility to oxidative browning. Fruit for freezing is usually harvested while still firm and then ripened under control. The peaches are pitted, peeled and sliced prior to freezing. The usual pack is in syrup (one part syrup to five parts peach) containing around 250 ppm ascorbic acid to help protect against browning.

Freezing is usually in packages, 32- to 40 lb packs are common. Larger barrels are also available. Freezing methods are, in general, as described for other bulk frozen fruit products. Some IQF slices are frozen for special markets. Storage should be at temperatures below 0°F if extended shelf life is required. The limiting change is the browning.

Pineapple

Pineapple for freezing is prepared in the same way as pineapple for canning. Rectangular chunks are filled in syrup into cans or bulk containers and frozen. The cans are frozen in a blast tunnel, the bulk containers in a blast freezer. The Smooth Cayenne variety should be frozen. The Red Spanish variety has a tendency to develop off-flavours on freezing.

Plum

A small volume of purple plums and prunes are frozen for institutional markets and for further processing. The fruit is halved, pitted and packed in syrup in barrels. Freezing is by standard methods. Storage is at or below 0°F.

Rhubarb

Rhubarb freezes easily and requires no special treatment, though a short blanch can extend the storage life significantly. Rhubarb can be frozen with or without sugar. Stalks are trimmed to fit the package. Storage life at 0°F is at least 6 months.

Strawberry

Not all varieties of strawberry freeze well. The selection of varieties for freezing should be made in conjunction with agricultural advisors familiar with the production state. Strawberries are frozen in several forms, depending on the final end use. Most strawberries are frozen as a raw material for use in further processing. Depending on the final product, different freezing procedures might be appropriate. For use in jam manufacture or ice cream, strawberries are packed in syrup and frozen. This can be in 30 lb tins or 50 gal barrels.

The strawberries may be sliced and sugared for this process. The procedures described under berries are appropriate. Because strawberries are even more fragile than many other berries, it is recommended that the critical times be shorter. For example, a core temperature of 15°F should be reached in no more than 24 to 36 hr. Storage should be at 0°F or below for a reasonable shelf life. Flavour and colour are lost rapidly if the storage temperature is too high.

Prefreezing treatments may be applied to strawberries to stabilise the integrity of the tissues. Suutarinen studied the effects of various calcium chloride or sucrose prefreezing treatments on the textural integrity and drip loss in frozen strawberries. Smith examined $CaCl_2$ concentration of the dipping solution (1, 5.5 or 10 g/l), dipping time (0.25, 7.625 or 15 minute and solution temperature (25, 37.5 or 50°C) and found the greatest firmness resulted from the combination of 5.5 g/l $CaCl_2$ applied for 7.625 minute at 37.5°C. Crystallised sucrose was compared to dips in water–sucrose solutions (350 and 700 g sucrose/l) and dipping times of 1 and 15 minute were utilised. Sucrose prefreezing treatments also resulted in greater cellular integrity, with those strawberries sprinkled with crystalline sucrose having the highest firmness.

IQF methods are used to produce frozen whole strawberries for both institutional and retail trade. Freezing utilises air blast, liquid nitrogen or carbon dioxide belt freezers. Storage of IQF fruit should be at a stable, low temperature to prevent clumping of the berries (due to moisture migration) and loss of the IQF character.

Tomato

Whole tomatoes are not an item of frozen commerce. They lose turgor and hence, texture on freezing and are no longer suited to the uses common for fresh tomatoes. Chopped or pureed whole tomatoes can be frozen and stored for 6 to 9 months at 0°F for use in further processing. Other tomato products such as purees, sauces and pastes can readily be frozen. They are commonly employed as ingredients in other frozen products. Freezing provides an advantage of colour stability compared to other storage methods.

Effects of Freezing on Nutritional Components

Consumers are becoming increasingly aware of the importance of nutritional components in their diets and the potential for fruit and vegetables in particular, to provide beneficial health effects. Fruits are a relatively significant source of various antioxidant compounds, including the polyphenolics, carotenoids and vitamins. Preservation of fruit by freezing and the effect of this process on various antioxidant components, have been the subject of many recent investigations.

Asami evaluated the effects of storage at refrigeration and frozen temperatures on the concentration of total phenolics in clingstone peaches. Maturity stage III peaches of the Ross variety were peeled, pitted, sliced and frozen at –12°C for a period of 3 months. There appeared to be a statistically significant increase ($P < 0.05$) in total phenolic content following freezing and this higher content was retained after 2 and 3 months of frozen storage. It was postulated that the freezing process may have resulted in cellular disruption and more facilitated extraction of phenolics.

In the early-season cultivars, freezing resulted in increased anthocyanin content, while in the late-season cultivars, which initially had higher concentrations of anthocyanins, freezing caused an overall reduction. Ancos and others suggested that the preservation of anthocyanins during freezing depends on the pH of the fruit, organic acid content, sugar concentration, initial anthocyanin concentration and initial cyaniding-3-glucoside content. They did not find a relationship between polyphenol oxidase activity and anthocyanin content.

Smith and others also found that freezing had a slight effect on ellagic acid, vitamin C and total phenolics, depending on the raspberry cultivar. Free radical scavenging capacity was decreased as a result of the freezing process, anywhere from 4 to 26 per cent, again related to cultivar. Frozen storage of raspberries at –20°C for a 1 year period did not appear to affect total phenolics or free radical scavenging capacity, but did cause a decline in ellagic acid vitamin E.

In another study of the effects of freezing on raspberry phenolics, ellagitannins, flavonoids and antioxidant capacity, these authors found that the antioxidant capacity of the fruit and vitamin C levels were not affected by freezing. The raspberry cultivar used in this study differed from those evaluated by Ancos, however and this may have affected the results.

Freezing preservation of fruit and vegetables is less destructive toward some antioxidant compounds, in particular total phenolics and ascorbic acid, than other means of preservation. Marionberries, strawberries and corn were preserved using freezing, freeze-drying and air-drying methods. The highest levels of both total phenolics and ascorbic acid (reduced form) were consistently found in the extractions of frozen samples, followed by those of freeze-dried and then air-dried samples.

Freezing may cause some damage to cell structure and application of a drying procedure following freezing, even though this is under vacuum at reduced temperatures, may result in even greater losses of beneficial nutrients. Air-drying at temperatures above 60°C may result in oxidative condensation or decomposition of thermolabile compounds, such as (+)catechin and ascorbic acid. Therefore, the presence of total phenolics and ascorbic acid in the air-dried products was lower than that in either frozen or freeze-dried products.

SECTION IV

Processing and Preservation of Fruits, Vegetables and Meat Products

Chapter 24

Apples and Apple Processing

INTRODUCTION

The apple species *Malus pumila*, from which the modern apple developed, had its origin in southwestern Asia in the area from the Caspian to the Black seas. The stone age lake dwellers of central Europe used apples extensively. Remains found in their habitations show that they stored apples fresh and also preserved them by cutting and drying in the sun. The apple was brought to America by early colonists from Europe. In these early times, most of the apple crop was home processed into cider. The common seedling trees were satisfactory for this cider production. Not many of the cultivars brought across the Atlantic by our ancestors adapted well to the North American climate. There was a need to develop American cultivars from the seedlings to improve the apple production and storage characteristics.

The original red delicious apple was discovered as a chance seedling in 1881 by Jesse Hiatt near Peru, Iowa. Red delicious is a sweet, mild apple for eating, not cooking. The trees are productive and adaptable to different growing conditions.

Golden delicious originated around 1900 in West Virginia have a sweet, delicate flavour and store well. The Golden Delicious is the parent of several modern varieties such as Jonagold, Spigold, Gala and Mutsu. McIntosh is the dominant commercial apple in New England and eastern Canada is a parent of Spartan, Empire and other hardy modern cultivars. Granny Smith, the third most popular apple in the world, originated in the 1960s. It was a chance seedling in Marie Smith's back yard near Sydney, Australia, thus, the name Granny Smith. The Granny Smith needs a long growing season and is grown commercially in the US, mainly on the West coast. It is a very firm, green, juicy, tart apple ideal for apple pie and contributes acidity when used in juice production.

HANDLING OF APPLES FOR PROCESSING

All of the apple varieties grown commercially are used to some extent in processed products. Processing quality can be affected by decay, damage, maturity, firmness, colour, soluble solids, acids and other chemical compounds, such as tannins, contained in the fruit. Apples for processing should be harvested at optimum maturity for good fresh market storage and handling. Only in a few instances are apples harvested with the processed product in mind. To date the majority of the apple crop is still harvested by hand. Processing of apples is mainly regarded as a salvage operation. The majority of the processing apples are sort-outs from the fresh market packing line. The volume available depends on fresh market demand and the quality of the current apple crop. As a result those apples to be processed are picked and stored in the same manner as fruit destined for the fresh market. Few if any processors can utilise all of the fruit as it is delivered to the plant during the harvest season. Early in the season some fruit to be processed will be stored directly in the bins in regular atmosphere storage without the benefit of refrigeration. This type of storage is short term and limited to the plant's immediate processing capacity. Refrigerated storage temperatures range from 1 to 4°C, depending on the cultivar in question.

Controlled atmosphere apples are generally stored four to six months before removal from storage and distribution to market. Apples from controlled atmosphere storage are generally in very good condition. However, the apples should be allowed to 'normalise' several days prior to being processed. There is some loss of apple flavour and acid during Controlled Atmosphere (CA) storage but not significant enough to make the apples undesirable for processing. These apples are capable of producing good quality processed apple products. Due to higher cost of controlled atmosphere storage, the maximum volumes of apples are marketed fresh and the desired quantities of apples for processing are not always available.

Apples from both refrigerated and controlled atmosphere storage are capable of producing quality products. The product produced and the grade desired must be taken into consideration by the manufacturer when considering apples from not only the different types of storage but directly from the field as well. The processor may choose to hold the fruit at elevated temperature to allow for further maturation development (softening, colour change, etc.). Some cultivars such as Delicious require additional press aid and filtration as they advance in maturity and become softer. Different grades of applesauce can be manufactured from the same cultivar depending on the type of storage, time of storage and maturity when processed.

APPLE JUICE PROCESSING

Apple juice is processed and sold in many forms. Fresh apple juice or sweet cider is considered to be the product of sound, ripe fruit that has been pressed and bottled or packaged with no form of preservation being used, other than refrigeration. Worldwide, naturally fermented applejuice is called apple cider and is usually fermented to a specific gravity of 1 or less. In the US, apple cider refers to 'sweet cider' that is made from the unfermented applejuice pressed from early-season, tart apples.

Shelf-stable apple juice is sweet cider that has been treated by some method for preservation. This processed apple juice can be in several styles: clarified juice, crushed apple juice, 'natural' unfiltered juice or apple juice concentrate, either frozen or high brix. Apple juice that has been clarified with some form of depectinisation and filtration before pasteurisation and bottling is the most popular apple juice product produced in the US. 'Natural' juice is juice as it comes from the press with often about 2 per cent ascorbic or erythorbic acid added to preserve colour. It is then pasteurised and bottled. Some forms of natural apple juice are produced with the use of heat treatment only. This process results in a darker apple juice. Crushed apple juice is a product with a high pulp content. The crushed apple juice is produced, without the aid of a cider press, by passing coarsely ground apples through a pulper and desecrator before pasteurisation. Frozen apple juice concentrate can be either natural or clarified juice concentrated to 42° Brix, packaged and quick frozen. Commercial apple juice concentrate is normally the clarified apple juice that has been concentrated to 70° Brix or higher, evaporating much of the water.

Figure 24.1 illustrates the process typically used for making apple juice and concentrate. Apples for juice are dumped, either by the bulk truck load or pallet bins, into a water filled receiving tank. In this

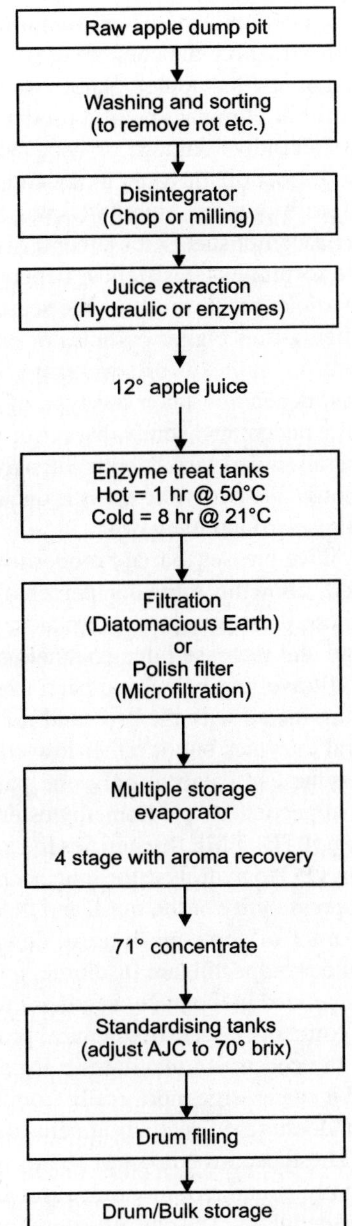

Fig. 24.1: Apple juice concentrate flowchart.

tank the apples are soaked to remove soil and other foreign material. The raw fruit is then conveyed from the water to be inspected and any damaged or decayed fruit removed or trimmed. In recent years there has been concern for the presence of over 50 ppb of patulin in the finished juice. Patulin is a micotoxin produced by the mold *Penicillium expansium*, found in 'bulls eye' rot of apples. Although this micotoxin is easily destroyed by oxidation, the concern of patulin is an indicator to determine if the juice was produced from mistreated or spoiled apples. Some manufacturers rely on brush scrubbers to remove any decayed areas on the fruit to eliminate patulin producing mold spots from the apples.

Sorting and trimming of apples to remove damage or decayed fruit is mandatory. If not removed, damaged or decayed fruit may also impart off-flavours to the finished product and increase the risk of microbiological contamination. Before pressing, whole apples are ground into a mash or pulp for extraction. This mashing process is accomplished with either a disintegrator, hammer or grating mills. These mills crush or cut the apple to proper consistency, depending on the maturity of fruit. When milling firm fruit for juice, small particles are desired. As the season progresses and the apples become softer, pressing becomes more difficult, thus bigger particles of pulp are preferred for pressing.

Equipment used to extract juice from apples is of several types and many variations. The pressing process can be batch or continuous, depending upon the type of press used. More common types of presses apply pressure via hydraulic, pneumatic, screw, basket or travelling belt methods. The vertical hydraulic press is a batch type operation and very labour intensive but requires no press aid and the juice has a low level of solids. Although the hydraulic press is one of the older types of juice extraction, it is still in widespread commercial use around the world.

There are several other types of juice presses that are modern versions of the basic hydraulic press. These newer presses are automated, allowing a greater percentage of juice extraction from a given volume of apple pulp. However, these presses require press aids, as added 1 to 2 per cent paper pulp and/or rice hulls, to reduce slippage and increase juice channels in the mash. Predrainers of different types, including rotating basket and travelling belt, have been used to extract free-run juice from the mash. This reduces the volume being mixed with the press aid for final pressing.

The apple mash has many natural enzymes but at rather low concentrations. Enzymes are substrate specific, which means a given enzyme can catalyse only one particular reaction. Pectolytic enzyme products contain the primary types of pectinases: pectinmethylesterase (PME), polygalacturonase (PG), pectinlyase and pectin transeliminase (PTE). PME deesterifies the galacturonic acid, liberating methanol from the side chain, which then allows PG to hydrolyse the long pectin chains. Enzymatic mash treatment has been developed to improve the pressability of the mash and therefore the throughput and yield. The enzymes added at about 80 to 120 ml/T of apple mash break down the cell structure. High molecular weight constituents of cell walls, like protopectin, are insoluble, inhibit the extraction of the juice from the fruit and keep solid particles suspended in the juice. Pectinase used in the apple process is extracted from the mold *Aspergillus niger,* a commonly occurring natural product. Pectinase developed for apple mash pretreatment acts mainly on the cell wall breaking the structure and freeing the juice. Also the viscosity of the juice is lowered and it can emerge more easily from the mash. The high content of pectin esterase (PE) causes the formation of deesterified pectin fragments that have a low water-binding capacity and which reduce the slipperiness. These pectins consist of chains of galacturonic acid joined by alpha-glycoside linkage. Xylose is covalently bound as a monomer and galactose and arabinose as polymers. These polymers form a link with the cellulose. The entire system forms a gel that retains the juice in the mash. Even if the pectins are partially broken down by the pectinase enzyme, more juice is released from the mash and pressing or extraction becomes easier. When used with mash predraining, the pomace acts like a pressing aid. By inexpensive pretreatment of mash with enzymes and heating to 50°C, the press throughput can be increased about 30 to 40 per cent and juice recovery increased over 20 per cent. Mash pretreatment will also increase the flux rate of ultrafiltered apple juice up to 50 per cent.

When using enzymes for mash treatment, particularly in Europe, care must be taken to avoid over treatment, thus rendering the pressed apple pomace undesirable for commercial pectin extraction processing. Residual pectic enzymes in apple concentrate can cause set-up problems when the concentrate is used in making apple jelly.

In recent years there has been development of juice extraction by 'liquefaction' of the raw fruit by using enzymes. Apple mash contains pectins, starch, arabinose, hemicelluloses and cellulose. The liquefaction procedure is facilitated by heating the mash and treating with an enzyme 'system' to completely break down and free the juice from the mash. The commercial enzyme systems available contain up to 120 substrate specific enzyme components. The liquefied juice is extracted from the residual solids by the use of decanter centrifuges and rotary vacuum filters. Some processors have added additional cellulase enzyme to the mash to further break down the cellulose to soluable solids, increasing the juice brix nearly 5 per cent.

Mention should be made of the counter-current extraction method or diffusion extraction first developed in South Africa and refined in Europe. Europeans report a recovery of 75 to 80 per cent, but this depends on water temperature, enzymes and apple variety. The counter-current system recovery is best with hard apples and does not work well with soft dessert apples. In this system the mash is heated, predrained and counter-washed with water and recycled hot juice. Capacity of the system is about 5 T/hr. A 90 to 95 per cent recovery is obtained when the throughput is reduced to 3 T/hr. Due to dilution, the final juice brix drops from 11° Brix to between 6° and 8° Brix. Some industry regulators consider the extracted juice not true apple juice.

Juice yields from the different types of extraction processes vary greatly from about 70 to 95 per cent. Juice yield depends on many factors, including the variety and maturity of the fruit, type of extraction, equipment and press aids, time, temperature, and the addition and concentration of commercial enzymes to the apple mash.

After juice extraction, raw apple juice for clarified juice is enzyme-treated to remove suspended solid material The soluable pectin in the juice has colloidal properties and inhibits the separation of the undissolved cloud particles from the clear juice. Pectinase enzyme hydrolyses the pectin molecule so it can no longer hold juice. Treatment dosage of pectinase depends on the enzyme strength and varies from one manufacturer to another. A typical '3×' enzyme dosage would be about 100 ml/1000 gal of raw juice. Depectinisation is important for a viscosity reduction and the formation of galacturonic acid groups that help flocculating the suspended matter. This material, if not removed, blinds filters, reduces production and can result in a haze in the final juice product.

Two methods of enzyme treatment are commonly used: (i) hot treatment where the enzymes are added to 54°C juice, mixed and held for 1 to 2 hr, or (ii) cold treatment where the enzymes are added to room temperature (20°C) juice and held for 6 to 8 hr. The complete breakdown of the pectin is monitored by means of an acidified alcohol test, 5 ml of juice is added to 15 ml of HCl acidified ethyl alcohol. Pectin is present if a gel develops in 3 to 5 minute after mixing the juice with the ethanol solution. When no gel formation is observed, the juice depectinisation is complete.

Other polymers such as starch and arabans may cause post-process clouding in a clear juice and can be treated with amylase and arabinase enzymes. The purpose of using enzymes is to bring about a partial or complete breakdown of these substances in the process. The fractured pectin chains and tannins are scavenged from apple juice by addition of about 1 to 1.5 lb of 200 bloom, type A or B gelatine per 1000 gal of juice. Best results are obtained when hydrating 1 per cent gelatine in 60°C water. Gelatine can be added in combination with the enzyme treatment or bentonite or by adding midway through the enzyme treatment period. The positively charged gelatine will facilitate removal of the negatively charged suspended colloidal material from the juice. Bentonite, a clay fining agent has been successfully used in the wine industry. The legal limits for use are 8 lb/1000 gal of product. Common usage is about 3 to 5 lb of rehydrated bentonite per 1000 gal of juice to be fined. Bentonite can be added to increase efficiency of settling, for protein removal and to prevent cloudiness caused by metal ions. Enzymes are usually not used when producing cloudy or natural apple juice.

After the enzyme treatment and the fining and settling process, the apple juice is pumped from the settled material (lees) and further clarified by filtration. Many types of juice filters are available and their capacity can accommodate any scale of production. These include pressure leaf, rotary vacuum, frame, belt and millipore filters. To obtain the desired product colour and clarity, most juice manufacturers use a filter medium or filter aid in the filtration process. The filter mediums include diatomaceous earth, paper pulp pads, cloth pads or socks and ceramic membranes, to name a few. The filter aid helps prevent blinding of the filters and increases throughput. As the fruit matures, more filter aid will be required. Several types of filter aids are available, the most commonly used is diatomaceous earth or cellulose type materials. Additional juice can be recovered from the tank bottoms ('lees') by centrifugation or filtration. This recovered juice can then be added back to the raw juice prior to filtration).

Diatomacious earth (kieselguhr) is a form of hydrated silica. It has also been called *fossil silica* or infusorial earth. Diatomacious earth is made up of the skeletal remains of prehistoric diatoms that were single-cell plant life related to the algae that grow in lakes and oceans. Diatomacious earth nitration is a three-step operation. First a firm, thin, protective precoat layer of filter aid, usually a cellulose, is built up on the filter septum (which is usually a fine-wire screen, synthetic cloth or felt) by recalculation. Second, the use of the correct amount of a diatomite body feed or admix (about 10 lb/1000 ft^2 of filter screen). Third is the separation of the spent filter cake from the septum prior to the next filter cycle.

Before filtration, centrifugation may be used to remove a high molecular weight suspended solids. In some juice plants, high speed centrifugation is used instead of filtration. This centrifugation process produces a product not as clear as filtered juice, however, it allows more or less continuous production. Centrifugation used with filtration reduces the solids about 50 per cent, thus reducing the amount of filter aid required.

Pressure, vacuum and membrane filter equipment are available and all can produce an acceptable product. The type of filter used must match the capacity to maintain plant production. The filtration process is critical not only from production consideration, but quality of the end product. Both pressure and vacuum filters have been used with success in juice production. Membrane (ultrafiltration) filtration is a recent development. Ultrafiltration based on membrane separation has been used with good results to separate, clarify and concentrate various food products. Ultrafiltration of apple juice cannot only clarify the product but, depending on the size of the membrane, can remove the yeast and mold micro-organisms common in apple juice.

Preservation of apple juice can be by refrigeration, pasteurisation, concentration, chemical treatment, membrane nitration or irradiation. By far the most common method is heat pasteurisation based on temperature and time of exposure. The juice is heated to over 83°C, held for 3 minute, filled hot into the container (cans or bottles) and hermetically sealed. The apple juice is held 1 minute, then cooled to less than 37°C. When containers are closed when they are hot and then cooled, a vacuum develops, reducing the available oxygen that also aids in the prevention of microbial growth. After the heat treatment the juice product may also be stored in bulk containers, but aseptic conditions must be maintained to prevent microbial spoilage. Aseptic packaging is another common process where, after pasteurisation, the juice is cooled and packaged in a closed, commercially sterile system under aseptic conditions. This process provides the shelf-stable juice in laminated, softsided consumer cartons, bag-in-box cartons or aseptic bags in 55 gal drums.

Apple juice concentration is another common method of preservation. The single-strength apple juice is concentrated by evaporation or freeze concentration, preferably 70 to 71° Brix. By an alternate method, the single-strength juice is preconcentrated by reverse osmosis to about 40° Brix, then further conventionally concentrated. This method of final concentration is energy-saving. The reduced water activity and natural acid make the final concentrated apple juice relatively shelf stable at room temperature. There are several evaporation systems used for apple juice, including rising film evaporators, falling film evaporators, multiple effect tubular and plate evaporators. Due to the heat sensitivity of the apple juice, the multiple effect evaporator with aroma recovery is most commonly used.

The general method in a multiple effect evaporator is heating the juice in the second stage to about 90°C and evaporate-capturing the volatile (aroma) by distillation. This is followed by reheating the 20 to 25° Brix juice concentrate in the first stage to about 100°C and evaporating it to about 40 to 45° Brix, heating it again to about 45°C and evaporating it in the third stage to about 50 to 60° Brix, then, final heating in the fourth stage to 45°C and evaporating it to 71° Brix. The warm concentrate is chilled to 4 to 5°C prior to standardising to 70° Brix prior to barreling or bulk storage.

Preservation by use of chemicals such as benzoic or sorbic acid and sulphur dioxide is not commonly practiced. If chemicals are used, it is only to reduce spoilage of unpasteurised juice either in bulk storage or as an aid in helping to preserve refrigerated products. There are several other methods of apple juice preservation that have not been adopted commercially but may be used in the future. These include, but are not limited to, irradiation and ultrasonics.

Apple essence is recovered during the concentration of apple juice. The identification of volatile apple constituents, commonly known as essence or aroma, has been the subject of considerable research. Early progress was very slow due to two problems: first, the difficulty of recovering representative quantities of the volatiles and, second, the analytical techniques that were laboured and unsusceptible to trace components. The essence recovery problems were resolved by Milleville, with the development of the essence recovery system during apple juice concentration. This system was the forerunner of the commercial concentration systems used throughout the world today.

The analytical problems were solved by the application of a combination of mass spectrometry and gas chromatographic instrumentation. These compounds were further refined by organoleptic identification, using a trained panel of sensory specialists. These laboratory evaluations revealed 18 threshold compounds, identified as Delicious apple components consisting of alcohols, aldehydes and esters. Three of the 18 compounds had 'apple like aromas,' according to the taste panel. These were 1 hexanal, trans-2-hexenal and ethyl 2-methyl butyrate.

PROCESSED APPLE PRODUCTS

Apples for Processing

Most all apple cultivars can be used for processing applesauce but only a few are considered ideal. Desirable characteristics in apples for applesauce include high sugar solids, high acid, aromatic, bright golden or white flesh, variable grain or texture and sufficient water-holding capacity. In the Appalachian region the most important sauce-type apples are York Imperial, Golden Delicious, Jonathan, Stayman, Rome and Winesap. New York uses primarily Rhode Island Greening, Northern Spy, Twenty Ounce,

Cortland and to a lesser extent, Mutsu and Monroe. In some states, Gravenstein and Yellow Newtown are used, along with Granny and Golden Delicious. McIntosh, though not considered an ideal sauce apple, is used because it is so plentiful. McIntosh is generally blended with three or four other cultivars, a common technique used by processors to maintain a uniform product in taste and texture.

A typical apple blend for applesauce might be primarily York (more than 50 per cent) with Golden Delicious and Rome, each contributing a lesser percentage. Rome is a popular cultivar in a number of regions because the tree yields a heavy crop and because the apple's shape is well suited to mechanical peeling. However, for applesauce, Rome is less desirable than most cultivars because of poor flesh colour. Sauce made with a high percentage of Rome apples will have an off-colour and weak, runny texture. Processors in the Appalachian region consider York the ideal processing apple. York has a very firm creamy yellow flesh producing a high quality sauce with grainy texture and good colour. The fruit resists bruising and stores exceptionally well, characters favoured by processors. York apples have a small core and thus yield a high percentage of processed product when peeled, cored and trimmed.

Golden delicious, a popular fresh-market apple, is also processed in large quantities. Its high soluble solids and resistance to oxidative browning of the flesh make it attractive for sauce and slicing. Applesauce produced from Goldens in the Pacific Northwest exhibits a runny consistency due to the higher moisture content of the apples grown with extensive irrigation programmes. It is often necessary to sweeten this applesauce with dry sugar rather than syrup to improve the consistency.

Apples for applesauce, slices and other canned products are received and handled by the processor similarly. When a load of fruit is received, a representative sample is taken for grading and testing. The standard tests include flesh firmness, soluble solids (brix), acid, defects and decay. Processing apples are graded after peeling into categories based on the percentage trim waste and presence of major defect. Some processors also downgrade for bruises. Fresh bruises are generally not considered serious because they do not interfere with the finished product, however, if the fruit is stored, bruised tissue becomes corky and may appear as a defect in the finished product. Tests to predict the quality of finished product from raw-product indices have not been too successful.

Apples for processing are dumped in water, blended at dumping, washed, size graded, peeled, cored, inspected for defects and trimmed before delivery to the designated processing line. Automatic peeling and coring machines have replaced the once common labour intensive hand-fed. Automatic peelers require more uniform sized, firm fruit because soft fruit tends to spin off these peelers. Some processors use sodium hydroxide (NaOH) or potassium hydroxide (KOH), chemical peelers that produce a reduced trim waste. Another method used by some processors relies on high-pressure steam for peeling. Labour shortages and higher production costs have encouraged apple processing plants to become highly automated. Electronics has enabled a number of hand labour tasks to be automated including defect elimination.

Apple Sauce

Apples previously selected and prepared for sauce are diced or chopped and fed to a stainless steel screw type cooker, either live steam injected or steam jacketed. Sugar, either liquid blend or dry and other desired ingredients are added into the sauce just before cooking. Liquid sugar is preferred because it imparts a desirable 'sheen' to the finished applesauce appearance. Cooking to a temperature of between 93 and 98°C for about 4 to 5 minute softens the fruit tissue and inactivates the polyphenoloxidase that is responsible for enzymatic browning. Time, temperature and raw product input must be controlled to produce sauce of good texture, colour and consistency.

After cooking, applesauce is passed through a pulper with a 0.065 to 0.125 inch 'finishing' screen that removes defects and defines texture as smooth or grainy. Large screens produce a more grainy sauce. Baby food sauce is 'finished' with fine, 0.033 inch screens to a very smooth texture. The hot applesauce is poured over a flat plastic sheet with back lighting and inspected for defects. Any defects such as specks, peel, blossoms or stems are removed by hand, using a flexible vacuum tube.

The inspected applesauce is preheated to 90°C and piston-filled into glass jars or metal cans immediately. Applesauce must be closed at a temperature of 88°C in the seamer or capper. To insure a vacuum in the container, a jet of steam may be passed over the top of the container just prior to sealing. As the steam condenses, a vacuum is created in the container. This step is important in cans to prevent headspace detinning. The containers are held for 1 to 2 minute prior to cooling to insure sterilisation of the lids or caps. Water is cooled in draper belt, walking beam or reel coolers to an average of 35 to 40°C to prevent 'stack cooking' in the warehouse.

The finished product may be conveyed to the labeler and/or caser prior to palletising. Alternately, the containers may be conveyed to a palletising machine where they are 'bright stacked,' unlabelled for completing future private label orders. Some processors pack aseptic individual molded plastic single-serving size containers. In addition to regular applesauce, many processors produce specialty products such as natural, no sugar added, 'chunky,' cinnamon or a mixture of applesauce and other fruit such as apricot, peach or cherry.

Sliced Apples

The dumping, washing, grading, peeling and coring steps for processing apple slices are similar to those used for sauce production with a few notable exceptions. Slice packs generally consist of a single cultivar, thus eliminating the need for blending. Apple slice texture is very important. Therefore, apples with firm flesh and high quality are desired. Consistency of slice size can be controlled by using fruit from within a preselected size range. The slicing operation is usually an integral part of the peeling and coring process where the apples are sliced into 12 to 16 pieces in the coring section. After slicing, the apples are inspected for defects such as blossom or calyx, carpel tissue, skin and bruises and are conveyed over a shaker screen to remove small chips. The slices must be handled quickly at this point to avoid enzymatic browning.

Apple slices contain about 25 per cent occluded oxygen that is removed by vacuum treatment. The apple slices are placed in a vessel that is sealed and a 27 to 29 inch Hg vacuum drawn. The vacuum is broken by the injection of water, salt, ascorbic acid and/or sugar. The apple slices are then steam blanched to soften and to allow specified container fill. From the blanched, the slices are filled hot, 77 to 82°C, into cans (sizes 303, 2½ or no. 10). The slices are normally over-filled into cans from premeasuring pockets. An automatic plunger gently pushes the over-fill volume into the can.

The cans are closed with a steam-vacuum process after adding hot water or syrup to insure there is no entrapped air. Some processors use the steam flow closing method. A jet of live steam is passed over the top of the can immediately prior to applying the lid to insure a vacuum will be developed. The canned apples must be processed immediately after closing to a can center temperature of 82.2°C, there are several types of sterilisers available. Batch retort vessels and continuous rotary cookers operate either at atmospheric or pressurised conditions. Immediately after sterilising, the cans should be cooled at 37 to 40°C to prevent 'stack burn' or loss of product colour in storage.

Refrigerated, frozen or dehydrofrozen apple slices, representing only about 15 per cent of the apples processed, are prepared much like canned apple slices except they are not heat processed. To prevent enzymatic browning, sliced raw product is subjected to one of several available antibrowning treatments. Apple slices to be bulk frozen are vacuum treated and blanched in the same manner as canned apple slices. From the blancher, the apples are filled into 30 lb tins or poly-lined boxes by an automatic particulate net weight filler. The tins or boxes are then sealed, frozen and stored frozen at –17°C or lower.

Individually quick frozen (IQF) apple slices are usually treated with a sodium bisulphate bath after inspection. The slices are then filled into vacuum tanks where the vacuum is pulled and broken with a brine or ascorbic acid solution. From the vacuum tank, the apples pass through an IQF unit where the slices are individually frozen. Various freezing mediums can be used: the apple slices are subjected to nitrogen (N_2) or carbon dioxide (CO_2) on a metal draper type belt. The freezing air is forced upward through a perforated tray that fluidises the product, plus acts as a freezing medium. From the freezing unit, the slices are filled into tins or poly-lined boxes and stored frozen at –17°C or below.

Dehydrofrozen apple slices are dehydrated and frozen to less than 50 per cent of their original weight and volume. The dehydrofrozen slices are packed in cardboard containers or large metal cans with polyethylene liners and rapidly frozen in forced-air freezers before storing. Frozen slices are thawed then soaked in a combined solution of sugar, $CaCl_2$ and ascorbic acid or SO_2.

Fresh and refrigerated sliced apples are desired by many bakeries in the manufacture of their products. From the slicing and inspection operations, the apple slices are normally treated with 0.2 to 0.4 per cent SO_2 alone or in combination with 0.1 to 0.2 per cent $CaCl_2$. Ascorbic acid has been substituted for SO_2 with good results. Calcium-treated apples appear to resist enzymatic browning and microbial spoilage better than non-Ca treated slices. Fresh slices, if blanched, will resist browning up to 48 hour, however, blanching does result in loss of sugar, acid and flavour that can produce a blander product. The treated slices are passed over a shaker screen and packed into 30 lb poly-lined boxes for shipment. This type of product is usually shipped and used in a very short period of time.

Apple-pie filling is another preparation of apple slices. Varieties preferred in Michigan for good quality pie filling are Ida Red, Jonathon, Empire, Spy and York of medium-firmness, with 12 to 16 pressure test. As given previously in this section, the apples are selected, peeled, cored and sliced into 12 or 16 segments. The slices are vacuum treated in a brine solution to inhibit polyphenoloxidase enzyme activity that causes browning. The treated slices are filled into containers by volume. A precooked slurry mixture of water, corn syrup or sugar, starch and spice is poured into the cans and rapidly occupies any air spaces in the container. Precooking of the slurry activates the starch, causing it to gel or set slightly as it cools. The container is closed and is conveyed to the retort cooker where it is cooked to render it commercially sterile, to tenderise the apples and to set the starch slurry. The containers are cooled to about 37°C to allow evaporation of the water from the container and to avoid any continued cooking. The cooled containers are either labelled and cased or 'bright' stacked on pallets to be labeled later.

DRIED APPLE PRODUCTS

Drying has been used for centuries to preserve food products. Dried apples are convenient to handle, store and use. Under proper storage conditions they are almost immune to spoilage. Dried apple products are prepared from sound, properly ripened fruit that has been peeled, sorted, trimmed and cut into the desired piece size prior to drying. Most good processing cultivars are acceptable for drying. A desirable characteristic in apples for drying is a high sugar-water ratio. Delicious apples, either Golden or Red, are generally recognised by industry as superior for drying. Sulphur dioxide (SO_2) is the primary agent used to control enzyme activity and preserve the colour of dried apple tissue. A number of factors affect drying including size and geometry of pieces, temperature, humidity, air velocity and pressure within the drier and wet-bulb depression. Evaporated apples, also called *regular moisture* and dried, are cut to desired size and dried to average not more than 24 per cent moisture by weight. Evaporated apples are either cut to rings, pie pieces or dices prior to drying, 'fresh cut', or sliced to rings then dried to 24 per cent moisture prior to cutting to the desired 'dry cut' dimensions. Unsulphured evaporated apples should average not more than 20 per cent moisture. Packaging is usually in fiber board boxes of 40 lb net weight Evaporated apples can be stored for short periods of time, less than three months, at ambient, room temperatures in a dry atmosphere. For prolonged storage, 7°C or less is required. Unsulphured evaporated apples require 4 to 5°C cold storage. The end usage, process, size and style of cut will dictate the correct reconstitution ratio. Evaporated apples will generally fully reconstitute with one part apple in five parts water by weight

Dehydrated apples, also called low moisture apples, are cut to desired sizes, pie pieces, dices, flakes or granules prior to drying to not more than 3½ per cent moisture by weight. A variation of this is a flake powder prepared from pureed, sieved applesauce then dried to 3½ per cent moisture on a rotary drum drier. Only 300 ppm maximum SO_2 is necessary to prevent colour deterioration in apple-flake powders. To prevent caking, 0.5 per cent maximum calcium stearate may be added. Packaging is generally in fiber board boxes with a net weight from 15 to 40 lb, depending upon the product density. Dehydrated apples should be stored in a cool, less than room temperature, dry atmosphere. The end usage, process, size and style of cut will dictate the correct reconstitution ratio. Dehydrated apples will generally fully reconstitute with one part apple in six parts water by weight.

Maximum allowable SO_2 level in dried apple products in the US is 1000 ppm, maximum 500 ppm is allowed in the European Community (EC). A unique method for producing dehydrated apples is 'explosion puffing,'. In this process, partially dehydrated apple pieces are heated in a closed rotating cylindrical container called a 'gun' until the internal pressure has reached a predetermined value. At this point the gun is discharged instantly to atmospheric pressure producing a highly porous piece of apple tissue. Evaporated and dehydrated apples are used in many baking, cereal and snack applications. Low moisture apples also make an excellent substitute for other fruit and berries in dry products. The neutral flavoured low moisture apple is colour dyed then impregnated with the desired fruit or berry flavour. This apple product has gained wide acceptance in the breakfast cereal industry around the world.

SPECIALTY APPLE PRODUCTS

Specialty apple products usually require more time and hand labour than applesauce or apple slice products. Less than 1 per cent of the processed apple volume is in this specialty category. Examples of specialty apple products are whole baked or glazed apples, spiced apple rings, spiced crabapples, apple butter and apple jelly.

Baked and glazed apples require large, 2¾ to 3 inch firm, symmetrical fruit such as Rhode Island Greening, Rome or Stayman. These apples are cored, partially peeled and baked at 176.6°C either by the short method in the can or by the long method before canning. A 40 to 50° Brix syrup is used as a cooking or filling media. The canned, sealed product should be processed to a center temperature of 87.7 to 90.5°C, then cooled to about 37°C.

Spiced apple rings are used as a garnishment. The apples are cored and sliced on the apple peeler to about ⅜ inch thick and then smaller rings and end pieces are sorted out, prior to blanching, to remove the air. The apple slices are filled into jars and covered with a hot 40 to 42° Brix seasoned syrup and processed at 87.7°C for 20 to 30 minute, then cooled. A typical syrup formula for apple rings: to 80 gal of hot water in a steam kettle, add 7 to 8 oz of colouring (either FD and C 90 per cent Lime Green Shade or FD and C Red 40), mix the colour well and add 400 lb of sugar, add additional water to a volume of 100 gal and heat to 87.7°C, and finally add either peppermint or cinnamon flavouring. The flavouring mix can be obtained from any of the spice or flavour manufacturers.

Apple butter is processed much like applesauce except a slower batch cooking in swept-surface, steam-jacketed kettles is used to produce a thicker, carmelised, more stable product. Fresh, whole, small apples are usually used but 'tailings' (peel waste) and lower quality fruit may also be used in making pulp for apple butter. More sugar is used in this process than in applesauce. A typical apple butter formula: to 100 gal of apple pulp, add 30 gal of 44° Brix apple concentrate, 150 lb of sugar and spice with 8 oz of ground cinnamon, 4 oz of ground cloves and 4 oz of ground allspice. The final cooked down product should be about 45 per cent solids. Fill into containers as with applesauce.

Apple jelly is made from apple juice concentrate. EPA regulations dictate the amount of fruit solids required. When concentrate is used, it is necessary to use sufficient concentrate to provide the amount of apple solids normally obtained from single strength juice. Example: for 165 lb of a 65 per cent soluable solids '45 to 55' apple jelly, the basic formula would be 15.6 lb of 70° Brix apple juice concentrate, about 8 gal or 65 lb of water, 12 oz of 150 grade citrus pectin (slow set) and 100 lb of sugar. Adjust the pH to between 3.0 and 3.2 with a citric acid solution. The pectin should be dispersed in water. The water may be adjusted so very little cooking is needed to reach the desired jelly soluable solids.

QUALITY CONTROL OF APPLE PROCESSING

Good process quality programmes are essential to provide assurance that a safe, sound, wholesome product is shipped to the consumer. These programmes can provide both financial and other intangible benefit, such as improving operating efficiencies and reducing waste. Quality control is maintained throughout processing, beginning with information on growers pesticide programmes and maturity of fruit, then blending as it relates to finished product specifications, on-line measurements such as trim and coring efficiency, filling volumes and processing and cooling temperatures.

Finally, there is the container condition for consideration, including closing, head space and labelling quality. Finished products are examined and tested to insure commercial sterility and buyers specifications, plus maintenance of various national and international standards for grades of canned apple products, when applicable. The microbiology of apple products is generally restricted to yeasts, molds and aciduric bacteria capable of growth at the low pH of apple products. The previously mentioned micotoxin, patulin, can be avoided by using only whole, clean, sound fruit that has been carefully handled. The micro-organisms found in apples are heat sensitive and usually destroyed when recommended processing times and temperatures are attained. Viability is further restricted by the reduced water activity of apple juice concentration and apple dehydration.

To conform to FDA standards, products should be filled to not less than 90 per cent of the overflow capacity of the container. One exception is glass containers with an over-flow capacity of 6½ fluid ounces or less, where the fill is not less than 85 per cent. There are several approaches to quality management available today. Statistical Quality Control (SQC). Total Quality Management (TQM), Hazard Analysis and Critical Control Points (HACCP) and in international trade, International Organisation for Standardisation (ISO or ISO 9000).

NUTRITIONAL VALUE OF APPLES

Almost everyone has heard the expression 'An apple a day keeps the doctor away,' reflecting the notion that apples and apple products are nutritious. Fresh apples are considered moderate in energy value and low in protein, lipid and vitamin content. Carbohydrates are the principal nutrient of apples and apples are a good source of dietary fiber, while low in fat and sodium. Fructose, sucrose and glucose are the most abundant sugars. The nutritive value of most processed apple products is similar to the fresh raw product. Dried or dehydrated apples have a higher energy value per gram tissue due to the concentration of sugars. Apples contain about 84.5 per cent water, 1 per cent fibre, 14.5 per cent carbohydrates, 0.6 per cent fat and 0.2 per cent protein.

In recent years there has been growing interest in the presence of polyphenolic antioxidants in various fruit and vegetable crops. Apples are a rich source of these beneficial phytonutrients that epidemiological studies have found to be associated with protection against ageing diseases and cancers. Four apple cultivars (Jonagold, Golden Delicious, Cox's Orange and Elstar) that can be utilised either fresh or as processed products were compared with regard to flavonol, catechins, phloridzin and chlorogenic acid concentrations and antioxidant activity. Jonagold apples had both the highest polyphenolic concentration and antioxidant activity. There were no differences related to season in the 3 year study nor did long term storage under refrigerated air or controlled atmospheres affect either polyphenolic concentration or antioxidant activity.

Juice produced from Jonagold apples by either pulping or straight pressing had a significantly lower level of both polyphenolics and antioxidant activity. Polyphenolic levels were reduced to between 50 per cent (chlorogenic acid) and 3 per cent (catechins) of the concentrations in fresh apples. Antioxidant activity was reduced to only 10 to 13 per cent of that in fresh apples by the juice-making process.

It was determined that most of the polyphenolic antioxidants were retained in the pomace or press cake and were not extracted into the juice. These results have ramifications for apple juice processors interested in producing juice with higher nutritional value. It may be of interest to either market cloudy apple juice as a superior product or at least to utilise the pomace as a source of polyphenolic antioxidants.

Chapter 25

Cherry, Strawberries, Raspberries and Grape Juice Processing

INTRODUCTION

This chapter discusses various fruits such as cherry, strawberries, raspberries and grape juice processing. The sweet cherry (*Prunus avium* L.) is believed to have come from the region between the Caspian and Black Seas. Wild cherry trees, however, do inhabit all of continental Europe where it is likely that birds were responsible for significant spread of the seeds. Cherries were among the earliest fruit brought to and cultivated in the New World by settlers when they arrived from Europe.

Sweet cherries are mainly used for the fresh market although they are also processed into canned, frozen, brined, candied and dried forms, juice, wine, jams and jellies. Increased interest in cherry products has been motivated by new studies that highlight the health benefits associated with consumption of cherries and other fruits. Cherries are good sources of antioxidants, anthocyanins, phenolic compounds and melatonin, which may help to relieve the pain of arthritis, gout and possibly fibromyalgia. Antioxidants in cherries can help fight cancer and heart disease. To obtain high-quality processed products, one must start with high-quality fruit. Although cherries are almost 90 per cent water by weight, cherry trees require less water for good production than do apple or pear trees. Any substantial reduction in sunlight intensity may be accompanied by a lower level of photosynthesis that will adversely affect fruit set and growth. Cherry growth in an environment of high temperature and low humidity will lead to excess transpiration and subsequent reduction in fruit size.

Cracking of fruit on the tree is due to osmotic absorption of water through the skin of the fruit. Cracking occurs when the fruit becomes wet with rain or fog, or upon immersion in water. This absorption of water may increase the cherry volume by as much as 10 per cent before the skin fractures and cracks. Cherries that are likely to crack tend to have a higher proportion of pectic substances than those that do not crack. Cracking is more likely in fruit harvested late in the season. An increase in the temperature of the water on the fruit leads to increased incidence of cracking.

Fresh cherries should be stored cold for maximum storage life. Optimum conditions are –1 to 0°C at 90 to 95 per cent relative humidity. Montmorency cherries have been shown to freeze at or below 28°F

(–2°C). Under optimum refrigeration storage, Montmorency fruit can be expected to keep well for at least 2 weeks. The greatest, weight loss during storage is due to transpiration. Storage conditions must include maintenance of high humidity in order to forestall weight loss. Extended storage of fresh sweet cherries under controlled atmosphere (CA) conditions has been shown to be possible. Better flavour, reduced decay and acid retention were listed as the main benefits when the fruit was stored at 0 to 2°C for up to 3 weeks. Other work on CA storage of cherries showed mixed results. Relatively high levels of CO_2 have proved to be effective. Smith showed that 10.5 per cent CO_2 and 2.5 per cent O_2 at 1°C was an effective storage environment for cherries.

Significant studies on radiation of cherries in order to extend storage life have been concluded. Overall assessments appear to indicate that excessive softening occurs even at levels of 50 krad, with an initial reduction of micro-organisms, followed by increased microbial spoilage. In other work, gamma radiation was found to increase darkness, redness and soluble solids content of the cherries. At the highest dosage, yellowness was increased and in one cultivar, firmness was decreased. In some cultivars, certain dosages increased darkness and caused a shift in colour from red towards green. Considerable fruit injury was caused by all dosages from 126 to 1000 krad.

MODIFIED ATMOSPHERE PACKAGING (MAP) OF SWEET CHERRIES

Proper handling and cooling practices such as hydrocooling are essential to maintaining the quality of sweet cherries after harvest. Temperature and humidity management are still the most important factors that limit water loss and prolong the shelf life of cherries. The success of MAP depends on the physical properties of the film that determine permeability to oxygen and carbon dioxide and on the respiration rate of the product, which is partially dependent on harvest date, maturity, variety and other factors.

Canned Sweet and Sour Cherries

A traditional approach to preserving cherries is canning. Although the market for canned cherries has been flat or declining somewhat, it is still a significant market segment for the current cherry harvest.

Soaking

Canning cherries requires that the fruit be prepared and washed prior to pitting. The cherries must be firmed by soaking them in chilled or iced water to prepare for the pitting process, room temperature water is not effective. When soaking cherries for pitting, drain weights generally decrease as soak time increases. Increasing soak time also causes a 5 to 10 per cent decrease in total acidity and soluble solids. Lowering the temperature of the soak will produce fewer losses and a better, firmer cherry. Soaking, in general, will also increase the gross weight of the cherry prior to pitting.

Soaking cools the fruit, firms it, removes residues and provides an opportunity to separate trash and rotted fruit from the good fruit as well as facilitates the easy distribution of fruit into process. It also allows for temporary storage of the fruit. Once the fruit has been soaked and prepared for pitting, it is sized and colour-graded, depending on the quality conditions of the pack desired. Some canneries prefer to refrigerate the cherries overnight or for over 3 hr instead of soaking.

Pitting

Most sweet cherries are not pitted prior to canning. Incomplete pitting, resulting in pits that remain in the product, is a continuing problem. A low-temperature blanch (at 60°F for 5 to 20 minutes) has been reported to cause a significant increase in firmness of the pitted cherries prior to canning.

Filling

Once the cherries are pitted, they are ready to be filled into cans or jars. Some packs require slicing of the cherries, a process that has been accomplished mechanically and can be added to a process line. The filling operation is typically done either by hand or by using a shaker filler. After filling, the product is ready for syruping. Syruping levels used in the canning operation vary, depending on the quality and type of product, from simple water to fruit juice of up to 45° Brix solution.

Exhausting and process

The syrup is applied at 65 to 77°C and poured over the fruit in the can. The can is then routed to an exhausting tunnel where environmental temperatures are maintained at 88°C either by water or steam. Duration in the tunnel is timed to deliver an internal fruit temperature of 77°C at the time of exit. The purpose of exhausting is to remove air from the product, which enhances the stability and quality of the pack. Once exhausting is complete, the can is routed to a closing machine and loaded for processing. Actual process conditions of temperature and time depend on the size of the can, the pack weight and the internal temperature upon process initiation. A can center temperature of 80 to 82°C is usually recommended. Cooling the product after canning is very important in product quality preservation. Typical cooling level is a temperature no greater than 38°C upon exiting the exhaust tunnel.

Preservation by Freezing

If blanching is not utilised, then chemical treatment must be used to neutralise the oxidising enzymes of the cherry, offsetting browning. A possible chemical combination would be citric and ascorbic acid, with typical levels in the range of 350 mg/15 oz for citric acid and 200 mg/15 oz for ascorbic acid. The cherries are then ready for initial freezing. They are IQF for easy handling and movement into consumer retail packs of 16 oz, 32 oz and so on or into large-scale commercial tins for use by bakeries. The typical size of a bakery tin is 30 lb (14 kg).

Dehydrofreezing is another alternative for the economical preservation of cherries. This process involves slowly drying the fruit at a low temperature and gradually replacing water with a fructose invert sugar syrup. The advantage of dehydrofreezing is related to the product's lack of water—there is no seepage and the product will not freeze solid.

Brined Cherries

Brining is primarily done with sweet cherries. The process involves the use of sulphur dioxide, which causes bleaching of the cherry to a yellowish white colour and a stabilisation and inactivation of the enzyme systems. Further, it prevents microbial growth. Generally, fruit targeted for the brining operation is harvested slightly below full maturity. This delivers fruit that is firmer and less coloured, which facilitates the bleaching process and also strengthens the fruit to withstand the brining process. Individual steps in the brining process begin with a sort of the fruit for bruised, scarred or cracked tissue. The damaged fruits are removed and the healthy cherries are then moved on to the brining solution, usually held in large tanks. Sometimes, in the Midwest, cellophane or polyethylene lined pits dug into the ground are used.

Once the fruit is adequately brined, it can be moved on to various processes, including maraschino or glace cherries. During the first several days of brining, the texture of the cherries deteriorates and then gradually becomes firm again. At the same time, pH changes can be significant, typically, a sharp increase is followed by a slow decrease until equilibrium is reached. A brining period of 4 to 6 weeks usually is adequate to ensure pH equilibrium and for fruit to reach a uniform straw colour with modest levels of firmness. At that point, the fruit is ready for remanufacture in other products.

Problems can arise during brining, a lack of firming in the calcium bisulphite solution, losses due to cracked skin and solution pockets have been reported. Solution pockets are gaseous pockets formed in the brined cherries where the fruit appears to completely degrade. These solution pockets occur more frequently later in the season and as maturity increases. A sodium chloride and calcium chloride prebrine soak treatment may be effective in reducing the occurrence of solution pockets. It is further likely that softening of brined cherry fruit is due to some types of pectinolytic enzymes. After brining, cherries destined for maraschino production may be placed in a sodium chloride solution to further remove skin discolouration.

Cherry Juice Processing

Cherry juice processing can lead to exceptional, high-quality, fully coloured products without resorting to unusual varietal blends or specialised process techniques. As with any juice operation, quality of the product is highly dependent upon incoming raw material and quality of the process. Current trends in cherry juice processing favour the use of cold cherries that have been dumped into large bins, frozen bulk, defrosted at a later time and then utilised for juice extraction. As one might expect, the quality of this product is quite poor.

There are two general approaches to cherry juice production: One is a hot extraction process and the other is a cold extraction process. Both yield reasonable quality products, however, the hot extraction process (heating to 70°C) results in a somewhat higher colour extraction and greater amounts of insoluble solids that must be removed in the final filtration operation. The cold extraction process involves taking fresh cherries and either pitting them or running them through a hammer mill that has been adjusted for minimum breakage of pits. Pit breakage leads to excessively strong maraschino-type or almond-type flavour and pit fragments could tear filtration cloth segments in an automated or manual press system. Control of pit breakage also tends to leave larger chunks of fruit for juice extraction.

Cherry juice is generally clarified and filtered, but other related products may be produced starting with the raw juice. A high-solids nectar can be produced using fine mash for pressing. Use of homogenisation could possibly assist in leading to a stable nectar. A full-solids cherry puree is sometimes produced for use in toppings and ice cream addition. A partial concentration of cherry puree will produce a paste with a typical solids level of 30 per cent.

Dehydrated Cherries

Dehydration reduces the moisture content of cherries, making them ideal for shipping, baking and other uses. Dried cherries have a characteristic flavour, chewy texture and moisture content of 25 per cent. Dehydrated fruit pieces are widely used in foods such as pastry, confectionery products, ice cream, frozen desserts, sweets, fruit salad, cheese and yogurt. The compatibility of the fruit pieces with the food is dependent on equilibrium vapour pressures or the water activity of the components, it is necessary to avoid diffusion of moisture between the fruit and the food. Dehydration is beneficial in that it may conceal imperfections such as split, cracked, bird-pecked or rain-damaged skin in otherwise useable cherries. Both sweet and sour cherries are used for dehydration.

The process involved in drying cherries is similar to that used in canning, however, fully ripened cherries are used in the dehydration process. Successful drying of cherries aims to accelerate the rate of drying, preserve colour and flavour, inactivate enzymes and improve the fruit's ability to reconstitute.

After the pre-dehydration methods have been employed, the drying may begin through the use of a dehydrator. The cherries are normally placed on flats before being introduced into the dehydration chamber. Temperature (60 to 71°C, dry bulb, 32 to 38°C, wet bulb) and humidity (10 to 25 per cent) are controlled in the chamber and fans circulate the hot air to evenly dehydrate the fruit.

Once the fruit has been dehydrated, the cherries may be prepared for packaging or storage. Cherries that have been placed in a vacuum for 3 to 5 minutes with 2000 to 3000 ppm of sulphur dioxide retain a brighter colour in storage than those cherries that do not receive such treatment. Packaging should protect against insects and increased moisture absorption. In past work, cellophane and thermoplastic wax containers offered the best protection, however, it is likely that many modern package films would offer good, if not better, protection.

Cherries may be rehydrated by being placed in a 107°C chamber for 5 minutes or by a slow simmer for 30 minutes in water. However, Alderman and Newcombe found an improved method in which the cherries are simmered for 30 minutes in water at 79 to 82°C. Three parts sugar is then added to four parts cherry and boiled for 3 minutes. Colour is not diminished as readily and the mixture is ready for the next steps in preparing pie filling.

Waste Management

With ever-increasing pressure to minimise fluid and solid waste from food processing plants, every unit operation must be looked at for potential recycle opportunities, by-product potential and waste stream pre-treatment. A study of cherry processing plants concluded that, by eliminating the waste-water discharge from the depitting operation and by recycling the water, total waste-water treatment costs can be reduced by about 50 per cent. Other studies confirm the need to address waste-water usage in soak tanks and pit flumes, the impact on the cost of operations can be significant.

The brining operation offers particular challenges to waste management. Alternative procedures for the disposal of waste-cherry-processing brine have been investigated. SO_2 concentration in waste brine can be reduced to several hundred parts per million by neutralisation with lime and filtration or sedimentation to separate precipitated $CaSO_3$. Lower SO_2 concentration can be achieved by oxidation with H_2O_2. Anaerobic storage of sludge and supernatant from neutralised brine may produce objectional odours. Brine to be disposed of in deep wells should be pre-treated by neutralisation and sedimentation.

STRAWBERRIES AND RASPBERRIES

Strawberries, red raspberries and black raspberries are known and cultivated throughout the world and are prized for their fresh, fruity flavour and bright red colour. To a botanist, strawberries and raspberries are not true berries. True berries, such as blueberries, cranberries, grapes and citrus are simple fruits that develop from a single, entire ovary. An ovary is the part of the flower that contains or will become the seed or seeds of the plant. Strawberries and raspberries are really aggregate fruits or multiple fruits.

Strawberries

Strawberries belong to the family Rosaceae and the genus *Fragaria*. Most domesticated cultivars are crosses between *Fragaria chiloensis* and *Fragaria virginiana* and also typed as *Fragaria ananassa*. Plantings of strawberries are made in the fall or spring, depending on the location. In California and warmer climates, fall plantings are preferred. Varieties may be of the spring-bearing type or the ever-bearing type. In colder regions, plants are usually put into the ground in the spring unless the roots in a fall planting can be established prior to a cold winter.

Red Raspberries

Red raspberries are called 'cane berries' because they grow on 3 to 6-ft erect stalks with many short thorns. Known as bramble fruits, they are members of the Rosaceae family, genus *Rubus*. Most cultivars originated from *Rubus idaeus*. A raspberry is an aggregate fruit composed of bright red drupelets that are fleshy and contain seeds. Raspberries grow best in climates with cool summers and moderate winters. The plant yields fruit in its second year after planting. The canes are biennial, producing for 2 years. Pruning and training are important to the continuous production of a raspberry plant.

Processed Strawberry and Raspberry Products

Frozen purees and puree concentrates

Frozen purees: Frozen berry purees are used in jams and preserves and also in beverages such as nectars. Many industrial ingredients such as bakery fillings or formulated fruit pieces contain puree as the source of fruit solids. Puree is processed from fresh berries that are transported directly from the grower or packer to the processor or from frozen sortouts or sieved berry pieces that do not meet standards for IQF, straight pack or fresh fruit. The berries should be clean and free of rot or significant mould and possess typical colour and flavour. Strawberries may still have berry caps attached because the berry will be screened prior to packing as a puree. Some small levels of extraneous material such as leaves may also be present in the stock material to be used for strawberry, red, or black raspberry puree. The berries are pregraded for Howard mould count, Brix, pH, titratable acidity and visual colour and appearance. Based on industry standards, the berries are graded as 'puree stock'.

The berries are dumped from the plastic crates or flats into a cleaning chamber. Using high air volume exhaust, a McLaughlan or similar air blower pulls extraneous materials from the berries as they are conveyed through the chamber. After washing with chlorinated water, the berries are sorted and inspected. The inspectors remove rot and major defects. The empty crates are washed thoroughly and returned to the field for the next picking cycle. After inspection, the berries are either frozen in drums or totes for further processing or conveyed to a chopper or disintegrator. After chopping, the berry pulp is sieved or screened in a pulper or finisher to remove extraneous material (leaves, caps) and a homogeneous puree is produced. For a seedless strawberry puree, a screen with openings of 0.027 inch or 0.033 inch is used. Sieves of 0.045 inch or 0.60 inch are used to produce strawberry puree with seeds. Seedless raspberry puree is produced using a screen of 0.045 inch, screens of 0.060 inch or 0.125 inch are used for a raspberry puree with seeds.

The berry purees may be pasteurised at 190°F (88°C) for 1½ to 2 minutes prior to cooling to 60 to 70°F (15 to 21°C). Some purees may be packed without pasteurisation to maintain fresh strawberry flavour. Enzymatic browning may occur with some varieties during thawing of non-pasteurised purees. Packing types are high-density polyethylene pails, polyethylene-lined kraft card-board cases or food grade steel drums lined with low-density polyethylene liners.

The containers are placed immediately into a blast freezer at –5 to –10°F (–20 to –23°C) and then transferred into cold storage rooms at 0°F (–18°C).

Puree concentrates: Puree concentrate has the advantage of increased soluble solids content. Often, the concentration is referred to as -fold (×). A twofold (2×) raspberry puree concentrate would be approximately 20° Brix or twice the soluble solids of single-strength puree. A typical strawberry puree concentrate is 4× or 28° Brix. Sometimes, sucrose may be added to the puree prior to concentration to achieve higher soluble solids in the finished product and a sweeter puree. The sugar also helps to stabilise the anthocyanin pigments. The advantage of puree concentrates is a reduction in total weight and, thus, decreasing storage and shipping costs. The jam, preserve, filling and confection industry requires higher fruit solids to reduce process time, maintain fruit flavour and achieve a low water activity level (0.5 to 0.7 a_w) to minimise microbiological growth and migration of moisture in a finished bakery product. Typically, the viscosity of puree concentrate is higher due to pectin levels. Some manufacturers add pectinase enzymes to reduce pectin levels in purees prior to concentration. The depectinised purees are pasteurised and then concentrated in multieffect vacuum evaporators designed to handle pulpy products. Purees are thawed for 40 to 48 hr in refrigerated storage prior to use. Care must be taken to use the berry purees while they are still in the semithawed state to avoid microbiological growth.

Frozen whole and sliced fruit

Individually quick frozen (IQF): Strawberries must be firm, ripe, fully coloured and flavourful to be selected for the IQF process. The berries are picked at optimum ripeness and transported to the processing plant. If mechanical freezing is used, berries are forced-air cooled at 35°F (2°C) to remove field heat. It takes 15 to 30 hours to lower the product temperature to 35°F (2°C), resulting in 4 to 5 per cent loss in product weight due to dehydration. After being transferred from flats or crates, the berries are gently washed and cleaned prior to inspection. Unripe, soft or unacceptable berries are sorted on the inspection belt. Inspection lines and equipment are rinsed clean sanitised on a regular basis (every 2 to 4 hr). Individual fruits are quick frozen in a blast air freeze tunnel (–40°F), liquid carbon dioxide or nitrogen freezer or on trays in a blast freezer (–5 to –10°F, –20 to –23°C). Quick freezing reduces ice crystal size and thus minimises drip loss upon thawing. The original shape of each berry is maintained and the berries are free-flowing, allowing ease of use. Glassy state is a term often used to describe a product at a temperature where molecules are slowed to the point where they are no longer reacting with each other. Some processors are implementing this technology into their freezing operations and storage facilities. Each fruit has a different minimal critical temperature that results in longer shelf life, better colour and flavour and reduced drip loss in the final product. Different methods of freezing are chosen, depending on availability of the refrigerant or cryogenic gas and also the developing regulations governing the environmental policies. Mechanical systems depend on refrigerants such as chlorofluorocarbons (CFC), hydrochlorofluorocarbons (HCFCs), ammonia, or liquid carbon dioxide in a closed loop. Ammonia is being chosen as the replacement for HCFC and CFC in spite of safety hazards in the event of leakages. The capital costs are high for mechanical systems, but operational costs are less than those of cryogenic freezing. Mechanical freezers operate at –40°F and freeze the berries to 10°F (–13°C) in 10 to 15 minutes. A dehydration loss of 1 to 2 per cent occurs in this process. Some of the disadvantages of mechanical freezing are product dehydration, product breakage, evaporator coil frosting in mechanical chillers reducing performance and lower quality than a cryogenically frozen product.

Berries are also frozen individually by spreading them in thin layers on trays in a blast freezer and then packing them in cartons once they are frozen. The freezing time is longer than the above processes, resulting in increased ice crystal damage. The capital costs are lower with this method, but the labour inputs are higher. Because drip loss is a concern for many applications such as yogurt fruit preparations, the processors will need to consider their customer's needs as they choose freezing systems.

Canned and aseptic berry products

Canned products: Raspberries and strawberries for canning are picked as firm as possible and transported to the plant where they are graded. After cooling for several hour at 35°F (2°C) to firm the berries, they are washed and sorted. Inspectors remove mushy, mouldy, green and damaged berries from the inspection belt. Raspberries are handled as little as possible, so they are not screened prior to packing. Strawberries are graded over screens to remove oversized or undersized berries. The canning berries are filled into cans and the cans are weighed. Weights are adjusted for each can to assure the proper level of berries in each can. Hot corn syrup or sucrose syrup is then added to each can. A steam jet exhausts each can as it is conveyed to the seamer. The lids are then seamed on the cans. Production codes are affixed to each can. The cans are transported to a cooker that oscillates the can to bring the internal temperature to at least 190°F (88°C). An oscillating cooler is then used to cool the cans to approximately 95°F (35°C). The cans are dried and palleted until labelling. The labels are glued onto each can. The cans are placed in trays of eight cans and then wrapped with plastic shrink-wrap film. The trays are stacked onto pallets and stored in a cool, dry warehouse until shipping.

Aseptic products: Juice is prepared by extracting fresh fruit or reconstituting juice concentrates to single-strength juice. Juice is introduced into the deaerator, which removes entrained oxygen. Loss of colour and vitamin C results in the heating and subsequent storage if oxygen is not removed. Deaeration should not remove fruit volatiles. The juice is typically heated using a plate heat exchanger system to 200°F (93°C) and held at that temperature for several minutes to destroy spoilage organisms. The juice is then cooled to 75°F (24°C) and filled into aseptic packages using aseptic fillers. The process is controlled to avoid product recirculation due to insufficient heating or filler stoppages. A new process called ohmic heating was found to significantly improve the quality of chunky fruit in aseptic processes such as fruit for yogurt. The product is heated using direct electrical resistance heating. The particulates and liquid phase are heated simultaneously by the passage of electric current through the product. Due to even heating, the overall process time is reduced and the product quality is improved.

Juice concentrate

Raw material receiving: Diagrams showing unit operations for berry juice and juice concentrate processing. Berries are delivered to the plant as fresh berries and are graded prior to processing. Precooling and cool storage may be necessary if plant capacity does not allow immediate processing. The berries may also be inspected and frozen in bulk drums for later processing. Frozen fruit is then thawed prior to processing in a tempering room or for several days at room temperature. Proper thawing times are important to avoid fermentation of the frozen berries. The berries are mechanically cleaned in a machine with air blowers to remove leaves or other debris.

Berry preparation: The berries are washed minimally with low-pressure water sprays to remove dirt and are then inspected for excessive mould, rot, green and other defective berries. The berries are chopped to a mash or pulp in a distintegrator or roller-type mill.

Heat treatment: Blanching has been indicated as a method to improve the colour in strawberry juice concentrate due to deactivation of polyphenoloxidase and glycosidase. The process must be controlled to minimise degradative processes that are accelerated by heat. Heat treatment also acts to deactivate anthocyanases that will break down the anthocyanin pigments present in strawberries and raspberries and also polyphenoloxidases that can contribute to browning of macerated pulps. The cell wall membranes are denatured, allowing the cell contents to pass through the membranes. The pulp is heated in a continuous heat exchanger, typically of the tubular, spiral or augur type. A preheating treatment is necessary for the pectolytic enzymes to optimally break down the cell structure and allow the juice to be extracted from the fruit. The optimal temperature for enzyme treatment is around 120°F (50°C).

Enzyme treatment: The pulp is treated with enzymes prior to pressing to allow maximum juice yield. The enzyme is metered into the digestion tanks or added just after the heat treatment. Traditional methods consist of treatment with pectolytic enzymes such as pectin methyl esterase, polygalacturonase and pectinylase. Maceration enzyme preparations also contain hemicellulase, cellulase and amylase. Recently, it has been noted that side chain activity of these enzyme preparations may adversely affect the anthocyanin contents in the finished juice. The enzyme manufacturers each have a blend of enzymes that are suited to berry juice manufacture. The pH and temperature of the pulp is critical to its efficiency. The pH of raspberry and strawberry pulp will not typically adversely affect the enzyme activity. However, temperature is critical for maximising the capacity of the process. The fruit pulp is treated with the enzymes until a negative pectin result occurs. Generally, treatment time in stainless steel tanks at 120 to 125°F (49 to 52°C) consists of 1 to 2 hr.

Pressing and centrifugation: Selection of the proper press for a juice operation is dependent on capital funds available, desired product yields and availability of press aids. The types of presses that have been used to extract berry juice are horizontal hydraulic, mechanical horizontal basket, horizontal pneumatic, horizontal and vertical screw type and belt.

Centrifugation is finding several applications in juice processing. Some plants have converted from press systems to self-cleaning centrifuges. Press aids have been eliminated. Yields are higher and waste is decreased. One plant reports a processing rate using four centrifuges of 1000 tonnes/days. Decanter centrifuges separate fiber solids and clear juice.

Filtration: Traditionally, plate filters operated under pressure have been used to clarify juices. The plates are coated with a layer of diatomaceous earth, which filters colloids, particles, high-molecular-weight carbohydrates and protein complexes from the juice. The clarity of a single-strength juice is measured in nephelometric turbidity units (NTU) in a Hach Turbidimeter. A visual examination under strong light will also reveal particles that were not completely filtered from the juice or were reintroduced into the juice in the latter stages of the process.

Another process that has been tested and used commercially on strawberry and raspberry juice is ultrafiltration. One study used hollow fiber membranes with a cut-off of 10000 molecular weight. The result is a greater loss of anthocyanin pigments using the ultrafiltration process. Ultrafiltration also removes a significant level of polymerised pigments. Melanoidin pigments, however, smaller than the molecular-weight cut-off, are not removed to a significant degree. Browning also increases in storage due to non-enzymatic changes rather than enzymatic. Earlier studies with molecular-weight cut-offs of 10000 to 50000 found that polyphenoloxidase was removed, therefore, ultrafiltered juice would not be susceptible to postfiltration or concentration enzymatic browning. Heating of the enzyme in the concentration process would also deactivate it.

Concentration and essence recovery: The following types of evaporators are available for juice or puree concentration processes: batch pan and plate-type evaporators such as rising-falling film, falling film, Paravap and Paraflash systems. Batch pan systems are used in some jam processes. Soluble solids are increased to 65 per cent or above in a jacketed vacuum kettle.

The rising-falling film plate package consists of a single pass rising and falling film principle. The liquid is vapourised as it contacts steam-heated plates and is discharged to the vapour-liquid separator. This separator condenses flavour volatiles from the vapour using differential temperatures of vapour condensation. Several effects are typically used in tandem to concentrate to high-soluble solids of 65° Brix. The falling film plate evaporator's advantages over the rising-falling film evaporator are decreased residence times and higher evaporation capacity. A double pass is possible with this system. The Paravap system is used to concentrate both juices and purees. A corrugated plate pattern in the plate heat exchanger allows fluids to vapourise at high velocities, resulting in greater liquid surface area for mass transfer. Products that are highly viscous can be evaporated because only moisture is transported in the vapour. Two or three effects are typically used.

Essence is condensed from the evaporated vapours by controlling condenser liquid temperatures. Essence recovery is important to the quality of the juice and puree concentrate. It may be added back as essence returned or sold separately as essence separate. Storage of the essence should be in refrigerated conditions (35 to 40°F) (2 to 4°C). Essence should not be frozen because the volatiles will separate from the water phase, resulting in loss in the freezer or upon thawing.

Dehydrated berries

Berry flavour and colour degrades with exposure to prolonged elevated temperatures. Also, the juices of both strawberries and raspberries tend to drip with heating and progression of ripening. Therefore, conventional air-drying techniques, such as continuous belt dryer with counterflow air movement, are not used in dry berries. Tray dryers are used to produce batches of whole dried strawberries. The flavour tends to have cooked notes and the colour is typically browner than fresh due to degradation of the anthocyanins. Freeze-drying has been the typical method for drying strawberry and raspberry pieces. The berries are individually quick frozen to minimise cell damage and then spread onto drying trays. The freeze-dry chamber is filled with the trays and the shelf temperatures during a cycle are varied to maintain an optimal product temperature. Studies have shown that the most important processing variable is temperature. The packaging selected must be a high-moisture barrier film such as foil-paper laminate or foil polyethylene laminate. With exposure to air, freeze-dried berries absorb moisture very quickly and the physical structure changes, therefore, the water activity of the final product is critical to maintenance of crisp texture in the freeze-dried berries. Cereal and confection products often contain freeze-dried berry products.

Spray-drying of strawberry and raspberry juices is done at high temperatures for a short time. Typically, a carrier must be added such as maltodextrin, starch or corn syrup solids to prevent dumping during drying and in storage. A fine powder is produced by this process, which is suitable for instant drinks.

Composition and Chemistry of Colour

Strawberry colour is based on the presence of two major anthocyanin pigments: pelargonidin-3-glucoside and cyanidin-3-glucoside. A total of eight pelargonidin and three cyanidin-based anthocyanins were found in 39 strawberry cultivars. Pelargonidin-3-glucoside was the most prevalent pigment, ranging from 100 per cent to 82 per cent. Cyanidin-3-glucoside was present in all but three of the 39 cultivars analysed. Strawberry pigments are very unstable due to the following chemical changes: hydrolysis of unstable aglycones, degradation of intermediaries, formation of copigment complexes with flavonoids and degradation due to polyphenoloxidase. High temperatures, ascorbic acid, pH, lack of sucrose, heavy metals, oxygen, light and nonenzymatic and enzymatic browning have all been shown to degrade or cause bathochromic in anthocyanin colour. Even with blanching and the inactivation of polyphenol-oxidase, intermediate oxidation polymers or quinones that were formed in earlier enzymatic browning reactions will initiate reactions that lead to loss of anthocyanins. However, in juices, strawberry colour can be stabilised through addition of sucrose or other sugar.

Cyanidin-3-sophoroside is the major pigment in most red raspberries. Other significant pigments are cyanidin-3-glucosylrutinoside, cyanidin-3-rutinoside and cyanidin-3-glucoside, as well as pelargonidin-3-sophoroside. A content of higher cyanidin-3-glucoside, low monomeric anthocyanin content and high polymeric colour in raspberry juice is an indication of pigment degradation due to poor processing techniques and storage. In frozen raspberries, the pigment degradation varied with the cultivars, each having a different anthocyanin profile. Juice pH, organic acid concentration, sugar and initial anthocyanins are all factors that affect anthocyanin stability. Additionally, cyanidin-3-glucoside was reported to be the most unstable anthocyanin during processing. Black raspberries can be distinguished from red raspberries by the presence of cyanidin-3-sambubioside and cyanidin-3-xylosylrutinoside.

Flavour

Like with many fruits, strawberry aroma varies with cultivars and changes during the course of ripening. Although there is no one character impact compound associated with strawberry aroma, furaneol (2,5-dimethyl-4-hydroxy-3(2H)-furanone) and mesifurane (2.5-dimethyl-4-methoxy-3(2H)-furanone) are considered as the most important contributors to strawberry odour. Also, g-dodecalactone has a specific strawberry odour when described by gas chromatography-olfactometry (GCO), it is used by the food industry as an additive in the manufacture of strawberry jams. Additionally, some esters contribute to the floral and fruity notes and alcohols and aldehydes are responsible for the green and pungent impressions. Furaneol, (Z)-3-hexenal, methyl butanoate, ethyl butanoate and ethyl-2-methylpropanoate were found to be the most important contributors of aroma in freshly juiced strawberries, as determined by a combination of three methods: GCO, odour activity values and comparison of model mixtures with the juice. Other esters contributing to the fruity aroma are ethyl-2-methylbutanoate, methyl 3-methyl-butanoate, methyl hexanoate, ethyl hexanoate and hexyl acetate. *n*-Hexanal, (Z)-3-hexenal, non-2-en-l-ol and nona-2(E),4(E)dienal have green, leaf like and tissue odours. Freezing and storage of strawberry fruits does not affect the content of furaneol and mesifurane, while esters, on the other hand, decrease.

Raspberry aroma is due to one character impact compound, the raspberry ketone, 4-*p*-hydroxyphenyl-2-butanone. Other significant contributors are a and b-ionones, linalool, geraniol and (Z)-3-hexenol. β-Damascenone, diacetyl, sotolon, 1-hexen-3-one, 1-nonen-3-one, 1-octen-3-one and (Z)-3-hexenal were the most important flavour compounds analysed by GCO.

Berries contain high amounts of antioxidants, providing protection against harmful free radicals known to be involved in degenerative diseases such as cancer and cardiovascular diseases.

PROCESSING OF GRAPE JUICE

The composition of grape juice is similar to that of whole grapes except that crude fiber and oils, which are primarily present in the seed, are removed. Sugars, acids, methyl anthranilate (in *Vitis labruscana* Bailey), volatile esters, alcohols and aldehydes are major flavour constituents. Glucose and fructose are the major sugars present in grape juice. The only sugars found in Concord grapes are glucose, fructose and sucrose and the major nonvolatile acid found were tartaric and malic. It was also found that, in addition to the mineral elements of sodium, potassium, calcium, phosphorus, iron, copper and manganese, grapes contain the organic substances biotin, niacin, inositol, pantothenic acid, pyridoxine hydrochloride, thiamine, folic acid, ascorbic acid, choline and trace amounts of riboflavin and vitamin B_{12}. According to Robinson, the quality of grape juice largely depends upon sugar level, acid content and flavour constituents such as methyl anthranilate and other volatiles, tannins and colour substances. Changes that occur in grapes during growth and maturation determine the quality of the juice.

Natural acidity, colour and aroma of fresh grape berries provide quality in single-strength concord grape juice. Acidity above 0.85 per cent results in juice that is too tart. Sugar may be added for sweetening, but the words 'sugar added' must be placed on the label. According to Pederson, the principal acids of grape juice are tartaric, malic and citric, but small quantities of other acids are also present. The tartaric acid may be in the form of free tartaric acid or its salts.

Flavour and aroma develop during the ripening process. The aroma of grapes consists of many volatile organic compounds. Methyl anthranilate, which produces an aroma similar to that of concord grapes, was one of the first compounds associated with odour character of a particular grape species. Other species of American grapes also contain anthranilic esters but at levels much lower than those in Concord grapes. 'Foxy' aromas, in addition to methyl anthranilate, in lubruscana and rotundifolia include *o*-aminoacetophenone.

Colour in grape juice is largely the result of anthocyanin pigments located in and near the skin.

The specific composition of juice from any grape species can never be assumed because composition varies from year to year and changes continually during ripening. Likewise, the composition of a given species and cultivar will vary from area to area depending upon soil, location and climatic conditions. In general, as fruit matures, the sugar and colour increase and the titratable acidity decreases.

In recent years, some processors have been interested in considering the parameters of flavour, colour acids and pH to determine optimum maturity, however, the Concord juice industry usually uses 15 per cent soluble solids as the lower level of acceptable quality and pays a premium for grapes based on each increase in percentage soluble solids up to 18 per cent.

Because of the industry emphasis on the importance of percentage soluble solids to quality, most of the literature dealing with the effects of preharvest variables on fruit and juice quality has used percentage soluble solids as the major index for quality. However, this is not the only method of predicting quality. It is important to consider all major quality attributes such as flavour, pH, acidity, colour and percentage of soluble solids to properly evaluate juice quality.

Juice Production

Hot press

Methods for commercial preparation of grape juice have undergone continuous change. In most commercial operations, the continuous pressing method is used. Hot-press juice production involves the addition of a pectolytic enzyme to break down naturally occurring pectins and it uses paper pulp or rice hulls to facilitate extraction of juice. A hot-press method yields more juice that contains higher total solids, more nonsugar solids, tannins, pigments and other substances than a cold-press juice operation. When hot-pressing, the temperature and time in processing can be varied within a range to produce juice with uniform colour from grapes harvested throughout the season. Excessive extraction temperatures (exceeding 65°C or 150°F) must be avoided to preserve juice quality.

Harvested grapes are dumped into a hopper and transported by augers or pumps to a rotary stemmer-crusher that separates the fruit from the stem. The crushed berries are pumped through a steam-jacketed, vacuum preheater in which the pulp is heated to 60–63°C (140–145°F) and passed into holding tanks.

At this point, slow-moving agitators mix pectolytic enzyme and 6.8 kg of purified paper pulp into each tonne of grapes. It takes between 30 and 60 minute for the enzyme to break down the pectin to make the grape pulp ready for pressing. This part of the process helps to extract colour from the skins into the juice.

Next, a dejuicer removes 30–35 per cent of the free-run juice through a 40 mesh screen. The remaining pulp empties into a continuous screw press. The free-run juice may have as much as 20–40 per cent suspended solids and the pressed juice may have only 5–6 per cent. After juice extraction, the argols (tartar in crude form) and tartrates must be precipitated. To accomplish this, the filtered juice is flash-heated to 80–85°C (176–185°F) in a tubular or plate type heat exchanger, cooled in another heat exchanger to 2.2°C (36°F) and placed in tanks for rapid settling of argols. The final processing into a single-strength juice or concentrate can occur once the argols have settled and the juice is racked off. The sediment can be filtered, resterilised and stored to allow the argols to settle again for optimal recovery of juice.

The juice is now passed through a heat exchanger (heating it to 77°C or 170.6°F) into an automatic filler and then into preheated bottles. The bottles are capped, pasteurised at 85°C (185°F) for 3 minute, cooled and labelled. Grape concentrate of depectinised juice can be concentrated to 72° Brix, but most juice is concentrated to 55, 65 or 68° Brix. Grape juice concentrate is diluted into single-strength grape juice, multifruit juice and sparkling juice. It is also used to sweeten jams, jellies, yogurt, frozen fruit desserts, cereals, cookies and other bakery products. Fruit concentrates are replacing table sugar and corn syrup as many consumers perceive fruit concentrate as a healthier sweetener.

Cold press

The only difference between this method of juice production and the hot-press methods are the that allow for heating of the crushed berries to 60–63°C (140–145°F) and holding in tanks with pectolytic enzymes. Without these steps, the dark colour from the dark-skinned grapes is not extracted and the juice is a light colour. Enzymes are added to the cold-press juice to facilitate the clarification and filtration process following cold stabilisation.

Processing Factors that Influence Quality

Colour is one of the most important qualities of grape products. A typical purple-red is associated with high-quality concord grape juice, but changes in colour during processing and storage from purple-red to brown cause a drastic decline in quality. This is true of all cultivars and species of grapes. It has already been pointed out that the red colour of muscadine grapes is extremely unstable under conventional warehouse storage temperatures.

The increase in soluble solids of concord grapes from 14 to 18 per cent during maturity usually corresponds to an increase in colour. The development of the typical purple-red colour in concord grapes begins at veraison and continues through maturation. However, as the pH of concord grapes gets to 3.7–3.8 or higher, a change in the pigment occurs, which results in a colour change from purplered to blue therefore it is important to harvest at a low pH (3.3–3.4) to maintain stable colour in processed juice. Extraction temperature influences juice colour by affecting the activity of polyphenoloxidase (PPO), which accelerates the rate of degradation of anthocyanins (colour ingredients) in crushed grapes. Inactivation of PPO by heat prior to depectination prevents loss of anthocyanins during extraction and subsequent storage. Storage temperature and time are primary factors for stability of colour in long-term storage. Previous studies showed that maturity, total acidity and juice storage time affect the percentage of tartrates or argol level in grape juice. The percentage of total phenols was increased in less mature grapes and at high extraction temperatures. Sorted grapes are heated in lots to either 60°C (140°F), 85°C (185°F) or 99°C (210°F) in steam kettles and cooled to 60°C (140°F) in 20–1 polypropylene containers submerged in cold water. Pectic enzyme (Ergazyme 1000â) was added to all lots at 60°C (140°F) and the mixture was stirred frequently for 1 hr to hydrolyse the pectins. The pulp can pressed through a press cloth to remove skins and seeds. Juice can be stored at 24°C (75°F) or 35°C (95°F), which represented ambient temperature and elevated storage temperature, respectively. Quadruplicate samples of each lot were analysed the day after pressing and after 1, 5, 10 and 18 months of storage.

Extraction of juice at 60°C (140°F) resulted in lower pH, soluble solids and less precipitated argols but higher acidity compared to juice extracted at 85°C (185°F) and 99°C (210°F). Juice extracted at 99°C (210°F) was rated higher in colour and flavour than juice extracted at 60°C (140°F) (the conventional processing temperature). The total anthocyanins (TAcy), browning index and CDM a/b values were higher at 99°C (210°F) extraction than at 60°C.

Grape Juice Concentrate

Grape juice is concentrated to 55, 65 or 68° Brix and used in making grape and multifruit juices and as a sweetener in other food products and fruit spreads. Grape concentrate competes with apple and other fruit juice concentrates, as well as sugar. There are several options for grape growers to capture a large share of the juice concentrate market. These options include development of new cultivars and viticultural practices suited to juice concentrate production, development of uniform standards for concentrates and development of educational resources to broaden industry understanding of how concentrates may be used. Juice may be concentrated by evaporation or freeze concentration. Historically, evaporation has been the most important concentration process for grape juice. Many types of evaporators are available, but all have essentially the same components. Evaporators generally include a heat transfer surface, a feed distribution device, a liquid-vapour separator and a condenser. With grape juice, it is desirable to heat the juice for as short a time as possible and to rapidly cool the product. This minimises the effect on flavour, aroma and sugar components. The following systems are used by juice processors and are often coupled with essence recovery systems. The recovery systems are often activated carbon columns that adsorb flavour and aroma compounds. Steam stripping can then be used to selectively remove these compounds for later addition to the concentrate or for other uses.

Rising film evaporator

A rising film evaporator or long-tube vertical is sometimes used for juice processing. This evaporator has the advantage of short evaporation times due to high heat transfer rates through thin films at high temperature differentials. The evaporator consists of a steam chest with bundled tubes inside. The feed stream is heated and introduced into the bottom of the tubes where it vapourises. The fluid rises in a thin film along the tubes under vacuum. The fluid enters a vapour/liquid separator and the vapour enters a condenser to be liquefied or is passed through a carbon column.

Falling film evaporator

A falling film is almost identical to a rising film evaporator, except that fluid is pumped over the top of the tube bundle. This is the most popular type of evaporator because it can handle more viscous fluids than the rising film type and can be operated at lower temperature differentials.

Plate evaporators

Plate evaporators operate similarly to plate heat exchangers. The fluid to be evaporated passes on one side of a plate and steam flows on the other side. The fluid is superheated and passes into a flash chamber. The vapour flashes off and the product and vapour are separated. High-viscosity fluids can be efficiently concentrated in these evaporators, with possible concentration above 60° Brix.

Centrifugal or conical evaporators

These evaporators are relatively new. A thin film is produced by centrifugal force in single or nested cones. The cones have steam on the alternate side to provide a heat transfer surface. The system operates under vacuum. This allows the total time on the juice transfer surface to be as little as 0.5 sec, with only a small increase in product temperature. They are good for extremely heat-sensitive and/or high-viscosity products. Their major drawback is low capacity and high capital cost. These evaporators not only concentrate, but also distill, degas and deodourise liquids that have a high sensitivity to heat.

Freeze concentration

This process is based on the physical phenomenon of freezing point depression. Pure water freezes at a temperature of 0°C (32°F) and in the case that dry solid is dissolved, this temperature is lower. In freeze concentration, three fundamental elements are employed: (i) a freezer or crystalliser that produces a slurry of ice crystals, (ii) a device for separating the ice crystals from the slurry (a centrifuge, wash column or filter press), and (iii) a refrigeration unit to reduce the heat from fusion and the heat generated by friction from hydraulic flow, wall scraping and agitation of the slurry.

Freeze concentration avoids the difficulties associated with evaporation methods that depend upon heat. It is capable of concentrating most fruit juices to 50° Brix without appreciable loss of taste, aroma, colour or nutritive value. Even with these favourable results, freeze concentration has not been used commercially due to its relatively high capital cost.

Grape Spreads

Making grape jelly, jam, preserves, butter or marmalade consists mainly of cooking the grapes and/or their juice in combination with sweeteners and pectins to the proper solids level. There are various standards that dictate the ingredients, their proportions and the final concentration of soluble solids. Jam, preserves and grape butter are made from whole or crushed grapes. Preserves differ from jam only in that the fruit pieces are usually larger. Grape butter is made from screened grapes and differs from jam in its ratio of fruit to sweetener and in the final solids concentration.

Chapter 26

Miscellaneous Fruits

INTRODUCTION

This chapter discusses various important fruits such as oranges, tangerines, plums, prunes, cranberry, blueberry, currant, gooseberry, grapefruits, lemons, limes, bananas, guava, lychee, mango, papaya and Avocados, etc.

ORANGES AND TANGERINES

It is believed that citrus originated somewhere on the slopes of the Himalayas in northeastern India. The citron, lemon, lime and some mandarins spread south into India and then eastward into Southeast Asia. Juices and fruit products play a major role in human nutrition and in the food industry around the world. Citrus fruit comprise the major portion of the worldwide fruit product market as every continent except Antarctica is endowed with citrus-growing regions. Within the citrus juice industry, orange and tangerine products dominate.

Citrus Fruit Classification

The commonly accepted Swingle and Reece classification of citrus fruits describes two main species of commercial oranges: *Citrus sinensis* L. Osbeck or sweet orange and (*Citrus aurantium* L.) Seville or sour orange. It also describes five main tangerine species. Tangerines are often referred to as exotics in the citrus industry due to the great diversity in characteristics exhibited by the fruit. The main five Swingle and Reece species are *Citrus reticulata* Blanco (common tangerines), *Citrus unshiu* Marc. (Satsuma tangerines), *Citrus deliciosa* Tenore (Mediterranean tangerines), *Citrus nobilis* Lourerio (King tangerines) and *Citrus madurensis* Lourerio (calamondin tangerines).

The sweet oranges can be further divided into four main varietal groups: common, Navel, blood and acidless or sugar oranges. The common oranges comprise the largest group of commercial citrus fruits and processed products. The dominant sweet orange variety is the Valencia orange. It is believed to have originated in the Azore Islands or Portugal and not in Valencia, Spain, a well-known citrus-growing area. There are several reasons why this variety is the main world citrus variety. It is a hardy tree that adapts to a wide variety of climates and horticultural conditions. It also possesses an excellent flavour, both as a fresh fruit and as a juice. Citrus juice is the principal citrus product in the world and the Valencia orange is believed to provide the best orange juice. The orange is very juicy and has a high juice yield when processed. In Florida, over 95 per cent of the Valencia oranges are grown specifically for juice processing. It has a better or deeper colour than many varieties and it contains few seeds.

Another important variety of the sweet orange is the Navel orange. A rudimentary secondary fruit in the apex of the primary fruit, which resembles a human navel, characterises Navel oranges. Navel oranges are considered the best fresh-fruit orange because they are less juicy than the Valencia, have excellent flavour and mature early in the season. Some Navel varieties have been bred to mature especially early in order to maximise the benefits of the Christmas markets. The main variety in this group is the Washington Navel, which is the second most popular citrus variety behind the Valencia orange. The Washington Navel originated in Riverside, California and has since spread around the world. The main attraction of the Washington Navel orange, as with other fresh market citrus varieties, is that it generates greater profits when sold as fresh fruit than processed oranges. A common practice is to harvest Navel or common oranges for available fresh fruit markets and then send culls or extraneous fruit to a juice plant. This maximises grower returns on their fruit. The disadvantage of Navel oranges is that they develop a delayed bitterness after juicing that degrades their value as juice products. This disadvantage has been largely overcome by the advent of commercial debittering that renders Navel and other bitter citrus varieties, less bitter or nonbitter.

Blood oranges are a delicious citrus fruit found primarily in the Mediterranean area. The main disadvantage of this fruit is that the anthocyanins that provide the deep red colour have a tendency to fade during processing and storage. This undesirable muddy colour can be removed with treatment of activated charcoal but significant losses of ascorbic acid also occur. High and stable ascorbic acid levels have always been associated with citrus juices and are considered a major source of appeal. Replenishing of lost ascorbic acid is not allowed in most markets, rendering blood orange juice inferior to other major juice varieties.

'Acidless' oranges produce juice very low in acid. Citrus juices generally possess a low enough pH or high enough acid level to prevent the growth of pathogenic micro-organisms although bacterial pathogens may survive in acidic chilled citrus juices for weeks. In acidless orange juice, the low acid level will allow growth of bacterial pathogens.

Processing of Citrus Fruits

Even though fresh-fruit packing is common and more financially lucrative, processing is still the major treatment for citrus fruit. The main reason for this is that fruit supply exceeds the fresh market demand, thus requiring juice production. Additionally, there is an established market for good quality citrus juices. Citrus fruit is processed in a number of ways.

Fruit arrives at the juice plant from either the citrus grove or a packinghouse. The source of the fruit is important to the processor. Fruit from the field usually contains many leaves and stems that can affect conveying equipment. Such fruit can be passed over a trash or leaf eliminator, such as a slanted tilted belt that allows round fruit to roll down the tilt while conveying nonround trash perpendicularly up the slant into a trash container. Another popular trash eliminator is the spread roller conveyer that consists of roll bars with sufficient separations between them to allow trash to fall between but retain the larger diameter fruit. Fruit destined for fresh fruit markets is generally harvested into 4 × 4 × 3 ft bins to protect the fruit, however, open trailers, which may contain 45000 lb of fruit, usually convey fruit destined for juice. Fruit can be unloaded using bin dumpers if it comes to the plant in bins. If the fruit comes in trucks, the truck usually mounts a tilted ramp and is unloaded from the side or rear of the trailer. Instead of a ramp, hydraulic lifts can elevate the trailer.

Fruit can be directly unloaded into the plant for immediate processing, or it can be stored in large fruit storage bins. The use of bins provides a surge supply that enables the plant to run more efficiently because the rate of unloading inbound fruit rarely matches the rate of processing. Inbound fruit surges are common because fruit can be harvested only during daylight hours and is generally packed only in the daytime at packinghouses. The fruit to be processed builds up during the day and must be stored until it can be processed.

Fruit washing and grading

The fruit source affects the preparation prior to juice extraction. Fruit coming directly from the field must have extraneous leaves and twigs removed from the fruit during unloading. Fruit from the field is more likely to be a source of soil and trash than cull fruit coming from a packinghouse. Although fruit from a packinghouse may appear clean, it can actually have a large microbial population on the fruit surface and requires a wash step prior to juice extraction. Also, the waxes put on the fruit at the packinghouse cause the fruit to stick to conveyers. Washing removes some of this wax and allows the fruit to be conveyed more efficiently.

The use of rotating brushes under a water spray with an added cleaner is a common practice for washing fruit just prior to processing. This is followed with a potable water rinse that may include a sanitiser. Fruit washers also often eliminate much of the trash and damaged fruit that had not been previously removed. The best fruit-washing system consists of slanted, expanded metal under the washer that funnels solid trash into a screw conveyer running under the washer but allows water from the washing to penetrate the expanded metal to a parallel solid metal sheet behind the expanded metal, which funnels the water to a waste-water sump. It is important to separate the solid and liquid debris that falls through a brush roller fruit-washing system. Fruit washing is best done outside the plant due to the fact that the debris has a tendency to attract insects. Washed fruit enters the plant clean and free from extraneous trash, insects and excessive levels of micro-organisms.

Fruit-washing in the production of unpasteurised citrus juice must be thorough and scrupulous. It is common for fruit to undergo several washing or sanitising steps prior to juice extraction. Some companies provide a heat treatment of the clean fruit surface (hot water or steam) just prior to the juice extraction step. This heat treatment provides the required 5-log reduction needed to comply with the FDA Juice HACCP Rule.

Washed fruit then enters the plant and should be immediately graded by hand. Graders are the final check on the quality of the fruit entering the processing area. They look for broken and decayed fruit. In plants that thermally treat the juice, the USDA allows 10 per cent or less of the fruit leaving the grading table to be broken and 2 per cent or less of the fruit to have evidence of decay. Discarded fruit is joined with peel wastes and conveyed out of the plant. In fresh juice plants, only good quality oranges, free of defects that would compromise peel integrity, should enter the juice extractor.

Juice and oil extraction

The extraction of juice from the orange or tangerine is generally done in one of two ways. Even though there are juice extractors that differ somewhat, the FMC cup extractors and the Brown reamers set the standard in juice extraction equipment. Both extractors are widely used and are known to produce high-quality citrus juices.

The FMC juice extractor consists of three to eight upper and lower cups. When a fruit is placed in the cup, the upper cup descends and squeezes the fruit down into the lower cup. A five-headed FMC extractor can theoretically process 500 fruit/min at the design rate of 100 strokes/min. The upper and lower cups have holes in the center of the cup, with a sharp edge that cuts about a 1 inch diameter hole through the fruit and all of the inside portion of the fruit and the two peel plugs are forced down into a perforated pipe. This orifice tube creates backpressure on the incoming fruit material by a restricted opening in the bottom where the solid part of the inside portion of the fruit is ejected. This material is discarded from the bottom of the extractor with the peel going into a screw conveyor for transport to the feed mill. The juice is squeezed through the openings in the orifice tube and flows to the finishers for pulp reduction and further processing.

In order for the FMC extractor to function properly, the fruit must be sized prior to entering the extractor in order to match the cup size of the machine. If the fruit is too large for the cup, the upper cup will chop, rather than squeeze, the fruit. If the fruit is too small for the cup, the upper cup will smash, rather than squeeze, the fruit. A typical array of FMC extractors will consist of machines containing various size cups fed by previously sized fruit. Generally, three to six-cup sizes are adequate for most processing plants. Improper sizing will have a significant effect on juice yield and quality.

Oil levels in freshly extracted juice can be greatly reduced by using low oil components of the FMC extractor. It has been found that most of the oil in the juice comes from the flavedo of the peel plug or the portion of the peel cut out by the sharp edges of the 1 inch diameter holes in the fruit in the upper and lower cups. If using a smaller diameter cutter reduced the amount of flavedo cut out, the amount of oil found in the juice can be greatly reduced. This is of greater significance to not-from-concentrate (NFC) juice and fresh-squeezed juice processors who would normally produce single-strength juices with excessive oil levels. Excess oil in juice destined for evaporation is removed during evaporation and is not affected by excessive oil levels.

The hole cut in the fruit by the upper cup enables the peel to exit the cup through the small ring opening around the cutter. The restricted ring diameter forces the peel to be compressed and scraped as it exits the cup. The expressed peel liquid is rich in essential oils originating from the peel and is washed with a water spray down the back manifold of the extractor. This oil slurry is sent to a finisher that removes excess solid material. The resulting slurry is then processed using a desludging centrifuge that separates the slurry into an aqueous phase and a concentrated oil emulsion. The aqueous phase may be treated and recycled to the extractor. This way, any trace amount of citrus oil that may remain in the aqueous phase will be recycled and recovered. The concentrated emulsion is centrifuged in a high-speed polishing centrifuge that separates the emulsion into a viscous opaque material and clear, pure citrus oil. Oil can also be dewaxed (winterised) after production, refiltered or decanted and packaged into 55-gal polymerlined drums (lemon oil is stored in tin-lined drums).

Pulp and core washing

Both extracting systems require primary and secondary finishing prior to entering evaporators. The reason for this is that the solid pulpy material has a tendency to hang up in restricted spaces and adhere to heated surfaces. The FMC uses its orifice tube as a primary finisher followed by an external secondary finisher. The Brown extractor usually employs two external finishers. Both FMC and Brown finishers commonly use a screw to force the juice and pulp against the finisher screen, but certain applications use paddle finishers. The unit operations of the Brown process require the first finisher to have openings of generally 0.040 inch and the secondary finisher 0.020 inch diameter.

Discarded finisher pulp can be heat-treated to deactivate pectinase enzymes, frozen and added to citrus juice products. The discarded pulp can also be washed with water, mixed in a screw conveyer and refinished to produce pulp wash or water-extracted soluble solids. The pulp discarded in so doing can be washed and refinished again to produce additional pulp wash. This can continue several times until 85 per cent of the available soluble solids have been extracted from the pulp. Generally, three to five stages with a water/pulp ratio of 1:2 are the most effective and efficient. A portion of this pulp wash juice can be added directly to the extracted juice in-line without violating US Standards of Identity for most citrus concentrates. Core wash is the water-extracted soluble solids from the core material or peel plugs ejected by the FMC extractor. Core wash is generally of lower quality than pulp wash. Enzymes are used sometimes to reduce viscosity of pulp and core wash solutions. The higher viscosities result from increased soluble pectin and suspended solids and often limit the Brix level to which they can be concentrated as separate products. Pulp wash that has been processed separately (not in-line) cannot be added to orange juice products without violating standards of identity.

Evaporating, NFC and aseptic processing

Evaporation for production of citrus concentrates affords several advantages to the citrus processor. It reduces storage space, pasteurises the juice, deactivates pectinesterase enzymes that affect juice cloudiness, inhibits microbial growth due to lower water activity of the concentrate and saves transportation costs. The disadvantage is that the heat and vacuum treatment reduces the shelf life of the product due to thermal degradation and loss of sensitive volatile flavour components. Proper refrigeration during storage can negate some degradative product reactions. For concentrates kept in storage longer than 6 to 12 months, storage temperatures between 15 and 20°F are common. Flavours lost during evaporation can be largely restored by the addition of aqueous aromas recovered from evaporator condensates and oil-based essences extracted from citrus peel. These natural flavours are often folded or concentrated by oil manufacturers and sold to citrus processors for use in their products.

Evaporation of citrus juice may involve several types of evaporators. The most common and one of the most efficient is the thermally accelerated short time evaporator or the 'Taste evaporator'. A common Taste evaporator consists of seven effects. Each effect consists of a tubular heat exchanger using condensate from another effect as the heat source. The first effect uses steam from a boiler as the heat source. It transfers its heat to the juice via the heat exchanger. The juice, under a vacuum, evaporates some of its water, which turns to steam and is used to transfer its heat to the juice in the next effect. The condensate from the last effect is processed in the aroma and *d*-limonene recovery system accompanying most Taste evaporators.

Plate heat exchangers are also used in smaller evaporators and employ up to four effects. Even though aroma and essence recovery units are available for these smaller plate heat exchanger evaporators, they do not come as standard equipment as they do with the Taste evaporators. Brazil is presently making use of the thermal vapour recompression or TVR evaporator. This evaporator employs the same juice residence time as the Taste, but due to the use of vapour recompression instead of direct vapour heat, it removes the same amount of water using only five effects. This translates into a better quality of concentrate due to less heat treatment.

Growth of not-from-concentrate (NFC) juices have seen the most rapid growth of all citrus juice products in the last decade. The fresh-like flavour of NFC is largely dependent on the processing and blending steps, requiring judicious attention to the flavour package added by the processor. Pasteurisation conditions commonly used to produce NFC juices stabilise the juice cloud by deactivating the pectinesterase enzymes and inactivate virtually all micro-organisms in the juice. This allows the product to be stored aseptically in large tank farms, with each tank containing a million gallons of juice held near freezing temperatures. During NFC manufacturing, a de-oiling, de-aeration step is required, which may amount to a centrifugation (hermetically sealed) step and vacuum flashing to lower the peel oil content to near 0.020 per cent. The juice may have sensitive aromas added at the time of blending and packaging to enhance the flavour. It is possible to capture the volatiles removed during the de-oiling step for reuse as a flavour product. Some juices may be processed into aseptic products. Aseptic juices are heat-treated and packaged in an ultraclean environment. Due to the limiting effect that heat treatment has on the oxidative shelf life of all juices, it should be kept to a minimum.

Also, because aseptic citrus juices undergo the severest heat treatment and because the main advantage of aseptic juices is to provide for room temperature storage, care should still be taken to minimise storage time and temperature in regard to oxidative shelf life. Citrus juices are very susceptible to shelf-life degradation and most aseptic 100 per cent juices are inferior in quality by the time the consumer purchases the product. However, aseptically packaged citrus concentrates have found a home in the food service markets for institutional use. Aseptic concentrates require less storage space than single-strength juices and do not need to be frozen. Under normal 30–35°F storage, they have a shelf life more than adequate for most food service uses.

Quality Control in Citrus Processing

Quality control is a critical aspect of food production and may take many forms depending upon the type of food produced, corporate culture and customer demands. One management style employed by some companies to address quality control is known as Total Quality Management (TQM). TQM is a management tool to enhance long-term success through customer satisfaction. TQM basically consists of involving all company personnel in quality assurance by the use of such strategies as quality circles where groups of employees are organised to regularly meet and develop ways to improve an operation. Including all of the management/employee team in quality assurance and improvement of operations not only improves morale, but also boosts productivity and profits. Proper and fair employee relations are essential for the success of a TQM programme.

Another important component of TQM is customer-based activities. Specifications and operations should all be customer-based, as well as marketing strategies and activities. International standards have been set for TQM and those companies adhering to these standards are well on their way to maximising their potential. A good rule of thumb is that what is really best for a company is what is best for customers, employees, management, productivity and profits. Short-change any link in the chain and you short-change the whole operation. All employees should be inspired to become involved in quality control activities. However, quality control personnel have unique and specific duties. Quality control activities can be divided into five basic areas: plant and product sanitation, raw material inspection, product preparation, in-process monitoring and final product characterisation. Additionally, quality control personnel often take a lead role in the development and implementation of HACCP activities in juice plants to comply with 21 CFR 120.

Sanitation

Plant and product sanitation fall generally under the direction of the quality control department. A plant should be clean enough to pass the random Food and Drug Administration (FDA) inspections that occur anywhere from every few years to much less frequently.

HACCP requirements in juice plants specifically identify eight key sanitation requirements that must be addressed in the facility's sanitation standard operating procedures (SSOPs). These include:

1. Safety of water.
2. Condition and cleanliness of food contact surfaces.
3. Prevention of cross-contamination.
4. Toilet facilities and facilities for hand washing/sanitising.
5. Protection of juice, packages and food-contact surfaces from contamination.
6. Labelling, storage and proper use of toxic compounds.
7. Employee health.
8. Pest control.

Companies must show appropriate documentation to indicate that these critical SSOPs are monitored regularly and corrective actions are taken when needed.

Microbiological Aspects in Citrus Processing

Microbiological testing is one of the more important sanitation activities in citrus processing. Common human pathogens are incapable of growing in the low pH environment characteristic of citrus juices, with the exception of acid less oranges. However, citrus juices have been associated with disease outbreaks and *salmonellae* have been shown to survive from days to weeks in chilled orange juice.

Proper QC testing to determine the presence of spoilage-related micro-organisms can control microbiological spoilage. Testing can be conducted on incoming raw materials, at various points during processing and on the end-product. Microbiological testing in the citrus processing industry historically involves total aciduric counts on orange serum agar and yeast and mold counts on an appropriate agar such as acidified potato dextrose agar.

Fermentative yeasts are the most common spoilage agents of packaged, chilled, pasteurised and single-strength orange juice. Typical genera include *Saccharomyces*, *Candida*, *Hanseniaspora*, *Mrakia*, *Pichia*, *Schizosaccharomyces* and *Zygosaccharomyces* among others. This spoilage is characterised by production of copious amounts of CO_2, ethanol and higher alcohols. If packaged in gable-top cartons, chilled, single-strength orange juice may occasionally experience mold spoilage near the end of shelf-life. Research has indicated that mold propagules are capable of growing from the paper fibers in the packaging material into the juice during refrigerated storage. Bacterial spoilage of finished product is less common but possible. Species of *Lactobacillus*, *Leuconostoc* and *Weisella* are capable of producing lactic acid fermentation in orange juice, producing a buttery off-flavour due to diacetyl production.

Most of the safety and spoilage-related micro-organisms of concern in citrus juices can be controlled by pasteurisation conditions typically used by citrus processors. Spoilage of the finished product is usually related to poor sanitation although improper pasteurisation can also result in microbiological spoilage. Citrus concentrates typically have a low microbial population in the range of 10 to 1000 per gram, although higher counts occasionally occur. Bacterial spores are heat resistant and may survive the evaporation process. In addition to *Bacillus* and *Alicyclobacillus* spores that survive evaporation, the concentrate may also contain heat sensitive bacteria and fermentative yeasts that contaminate the concentrate during pumping, blending, bulk transport and other handling procedures that occur after evaporation.

In addition to thermal pasteurisation, another way to reduce microbial flora in concentrate is to store it in freezers for several months. While this may eliminate some cold sensitive micro-organisms, freezing should not be thought of as a kill step. Freezing will not eliminate micro-organisms from concentrates or single-strength juices. Interestingly, research indicates that very low freezing temperatures may act to preserve microbial viability and that death rates of some micro-organisms are higher at temperatures just below the freezing point of single-strength juice.

Microbiological testing is not common by citrus packers who market fresh fruit rather than juice. Typically, packers have been concerned about postharvest pathogens such as certain molds and bacteria. It would be appropriate for packers of fresh market citrus to consider implementing programmes to address the potential for contamination of fruit by human pathogens.

Raw material inspection

Once a sanitary environment has been established in a citrus processing plant, the next step is raw material inspection. Inbound juice is generally first quantified by count or weight. Product samples should be drawn and inspected by quality control personnel prior to storage and checked for concentration, acid, essential oils, pulp, colour, flavour, texture and extraneous matter. It would be appropriate to have adulteration screening procedures using either in-house methods or outside laboratories, Most adulteration screening procedures are determined by cost and resources, however, if an adulterated product is purchased and incorporated into a company's products, that company is equally liable for the adulteration, regardless of the cost and resources of a screening procedure. The use of a simple isocitric acid test kit can be economic, easy to use and quite effective in detecting most types of adulteration. Periodic use of commercial laboratories with extensive experience in the detection of juice adulteration is recommended

Product from concentrate

With raw materials on board and adequately inspected, preparations can begin to make a reconstituted citrus juice product. Formulations and blend calculations can generally predict the final quality of a product prior to batching or blending. This minimises costly errors and minimises or eliminates rework material. Carefully tested and prepared formulations or blend instructions form the foundation of product preparation. With the blend instructions, product specifications and procedures clearly spelled out, raw material data can be entered into a computer and the final product quality and quantity can be calculated. Two main parameters are used in blend calculations: the Brix or percent soluble solids (sugar equivalent) and the Brix/(w/w per cent acid as citric acid) ratio. The sweetness of the sugars and the sourness of the acids combine to provide much of the sensory characteristics of citrus juices. Thus, the ratio of the two provides an excellent indicator of general juice quality.

Final batch quality control

Once a batch of the product is ready for packaging, a final analysis is generally performed that can be used to identify or be associated with the batch in the future. The batch may be used as a future blend component, as a final retail product, or in the manufacture of another product on-site or at another plant. The final analysis can be used in these future activities, Some of the parameters that define a juice product include Brix, acids, Brix/acid ratio, oils, pulp, cloud stability, colour, flavour, bitterness, nutritional profile, rheology and microbiological profile.

PLUMS AND PRUNES

The plum is a fleshy fruit (*drupaceous*) of the family Rosaceae and genus *Prunus*. In this family, the flesh of the fruit surrounds a hard pit or stone in which there is one seed. *Prunus* also includes several familiar stone fruits—apricot, cherry and peach. There are more than 2000 varieties of plums, among which relatively few are of commercial importance. In recent years, however, as prunes and prune products are used increasingly as food ingredients by the food processors, the question of what defines a prune became an important marketing issue because marketers believe that the term dried plum has a more positive image to customers than dried prune.

Canned Plums

The plum at one time was a favourite canned fruit, but it has been supplanted today by the peach, apricot and pear.

Frozen plums

Preparation for freezing of plums and dried plums is similar to that for peaches and other stone fruits, except that the fruit need not be peeled.

Dried Plums (Prunes)

As noted above, a large percentage of plums (prunes) are dried. By definition, a prune is a dried plum with moisture content reduced to between 19 and 35 per cent. Dried plums have been considered a delicacy in their native France for centuries. The process of drying fresh fruits to produce dried plums on a large scale was practiced in Europe, primarily in France, Italy and Austria, before the prune industry commenced in the US.

The soluble solids content of the juice must reach at least 22 per cent prior to harvest for high-quality dried plums. Scott found linear regressions between the eating quality of rehydrated dried plums (determined by sensory test) and the total soluble solids content and soluble solids to titrable acidity ratio of the fruit measured at harvest time.

Processing fresh plums

In the dehydration plant, the fruits are prepared for drying by cleaning with air blast and water sprays, followed by dipping in water. The fruits are then spread in a single layer on large wood trays and dehydrated—under carefully controlled conditions—to about 18 per cent moisture. Mostly, forced-draft tunnel dehydrators are used, where the drying process usually requires from 24 to 36 hours depending on the size and solids content of the dried plums. The tunnel is operated under 74°C (165°F) dry bulb temperature, with wet bulb temperature 9°C (15°F) lower than the dry bulb at the cool end. In this process, 3 kg fresh fruit will yield 1 kg dried plums.

Packing and storing

From the dehydrator, the dried plums are moved to the packaging unit, where they are first graded for size (measured as number of fruits per pound) and then inspected once more. The largest size grade has 20 to 30 fruits per lb and smallest grade has 90 to 100 fruits per lb. Dried plums store best when their moisture content is reduced to about 21 per cent. This is generally referred to as a 'natural condition' prune. Then the fruits remain in cool storage facilities until they are sold or utilised in further processing.

Automated high-speed sorting systems to substitute for the traditional visual inspection are under investigation. Delwiche tested a multicamera processor system capable of sorting dried plums for surface defects. Three line-scan cameras were used to view the dried plums.

Each camera was connected to a sub-system computer to analyse and classify the images and remove defective dried plums by a pneumatic system.

Dried plums with pits

If dried plums are marketed as 'dried plums with pits', then the fruits are taken from the warehouse and rehydrated to between 24 and 30 per cent moisture, sterilised, inspected again and packaged. The package sizes are usually 11.2 or 13.5 kg (25 or 30 lb) bulk cases for the institutional users or 450 gram or 900 gram (1 or 2-lb) containers for the retail trade.

Use of preservatives and other food additives

The high sugar content of California French dried plums allows long shelf life for most products. Chemical preservative is required only for those fruits with moisture content higher than 25 per cent. Bolin determined that dried plums should be pasteurised or treated with potassium sorbate if they are marketed at a water activity (a_w) above 0.7. Almost exclusively, potassium sorbate applied by dip or spray is used as a preservative for dried plums. It is suggested that trials be done with solutions containing from 2 to 7 per cent potassium sorbate, to achieve a deposit of the preservative on the fruit from 0.02 to 0.05 per cent by weight. As for the use of other chemical additives, some industrial applications of dried plums require coatings to ensure easy handling of fruit pieces in high-speed processing operations (e.g. to improve free-flowing properties). Such coatings are applied as required by the customer's specification and may include vegetable oils, monoglycerides and diglycerides, dextrose, cornstarch, rice powder and so on. Calcium stearate is usually added, at concentrations between 0.1 and 0.05 per cent, to low-moisture prune products (<4 per cent moisture content) as a processing aid and free-flowing agent.

Further processing of dried plums

From dried prunes, the industry processes several products including:

1. Prune juice from unpitted whole dried fruits.
2. Prune juice concentrates from unpitted whole dried fruits.
3. Fresh plum juice concentrate prepared from fresh plum juice.
4. USDA dried plum puree composed of prune juice concentrate, pitted and disintegrated dried plums and water.

Various forms of dry and low-moisture products are:

1. Prune paste.
2. Prune fillings and toppings.
3. Low-moisture diced prune.
4. Low-moisture prune bits.
5. Low-moisture prune granules.
6. Low-moisture prune powder.
7. Prune fibre.

Prune Juice

Prune juice differs from other fruit beverages in that it is a water extract of dried fruit, rather than squeezed fresh produce. The concentration of single-strength commercial juice ranges from 18.5° to 21° Brix. EPA Standards of Identity require that prune juice contain not less than 18.5 per cent (by weight) soluble solids extracted from dried plums.

Two methods are used commercially for making prune juice from dried plums. One of these, the diffusion method, is rarely used now in modern processing operations. Briefly, it involves extracting the soluble components from the dried fruit by three successive leachings with hot water. Each extraction step requires 2 to 4 hr. The process begins with thoroughly washing the dried plums and dumping them into tanks. About 92 liter (25 gal) of water is added to each 45 kg (100 lb) of prune and the mixture is heated to 85°C (185°F) by steam coils. After the leachate is drained, the process is repeated twice with fresh water, less water is used in the second and third extraction steps. About 56 liter (15 gal) water is added to each 45 kg (100 lb) of prune for the second extraction and about 37.5 liter (10 gal) of water to 45 kg (100 lb) of fruit for the third extraction. At the completion of the third extraction, the three batches are combined and the liquid evaporated until its concentration reaches 19 to 21° Brix.

The second prune juice processing technology, known as the disintegration method, is the current choice for processing because of the higher yields achieved and because the flavour of the juice is superior to that made by the diffusion process.

The process consists of breaking up the washed dried plums by cooking in water for a minimum of 8 hr with vigorous agitation. Pressure cookers may be used so that the cooking time can be reduced to as little as 10 minutes. Industry sources indicated that, by maintaining moderate temperature during cooking, following a short initial boiling (2 to 5 minutes), certain quality attributes of the finished product improve. Such milder heat treatment results in lighter colour and greater viscosity of the finished juice. From the disintegrated fruit, the juice is separated, either by squeezing the pulp in a hydraulic press or by high-speed centrifugation (at approximately 4000 rpm). The extract is then clarified, by allowing the solids to settle and siphoning off the clear juice, or by filtering through a filter press using 1 per cent infusorial earth, rice hulls, or other filter aid, or by a second centrifugation (at 5000 rpm). The resulting extract, a clear liquid, is collected in surge tanks and concentrated by heating in open vats or under vacuum to the desired 19 to 21° Brix concentration.

When the extract reaches the desired concentration, it is heated in a heat exchanger to 88°C (190°F) prior to filling into the containers. Occasionally, citric acid is added to make the juice more tartaric. The addition of 900 g (2 lb) of citric acid per 378 liter (100 gal) juice is recommended. Preheated juice is filled into cans or bottles, seamed or capped. Large cans (46 oz) and bottles (32 oz) are then conveyed through a cooling tunnel. Cooled containers of juice pass through an air curtain at the end of the cooling tunnel to remove pools of water and to dry the exterior of the container. Small cans (5½ or 6 oz) are not cooled, but the seamed cans of juice pass through a washer to remove traces of juice on the can exterior.

Pitted Dried Plums

Dried plums are size-graded, sorted for defects, washed, steamed and the pits removed by specially designed equipment. The same type of equipment is utilised in pitting prunes as for pitting cherries and olives. But unlike these fruits, dried plums are not freestone fruits and therefore dried plums must be thoroughly preheated by steam treatment to ensure proper pit removal by the pitter equipment.

Canned Dried Plums

Three types of canned, pitted dried plums are produced:

1. Regular—packed in sugar syrup.
2. Nectarised—water-packed with a smaller amount of topping liquid and about a third more dried plums per can than the regular canned prune pack.

3. Moist-pack—regular pitted dried plums, at higher moisture content (35 to 42 per cent moisture) than dried bulk plums—packed without addition of liquid.

Low-Moisture Plums

Conventional dried plums may be dehydrated to low moisture in vacuum shelf dryers. The finished low-moisture dried plums contain less than 4 per cent moisture. Because of the high sugar content of dried plums, dehydration to such a low moisture level can be achieved only under subatmospheric conditions. Moreover, drying under vacuum reduces oxidation during drying and because the process is carried out at lower temperatures than with air drying, heat damage to the fruit (such as caramelisation of sugars, destruction of carotene, etc.) is minimised.

The process is initiated with perforation treatment of the whole, pitted and dried plums to achieve better dehydration and reconstitution character, followed by dehydration under vacuum. Low moisture diced plums, granules (8 mesh particle size) and dried plum powder (20 mesh) are also commercially available. One kilogram of low-moisture plums is equivalent to 1.5 kg of dried plums.

Because they are free-flowing and highly hygroscopic, dehydrated plums require very careful handling and packaging that provides a good moisture barrier. To avoid severe caking of low-moisture prune products, final product inspection and filling are usually done in a dehumidified, air-conditioned room.

Low-moisture diced plums and plum granules are recommended for bakery fillings and spreads. Low-moisture prune powder can be utilised as a sweetening and flavouring agent for whole wheat, rye or pumpernickel breads or the preparation of instant prune spread.

Low-moisture plum powder may be produced with the drum drying process. However, the highly sugary, sticky product would require sophisticated handling and the use of advanced anticaking food additives.

Nutrition and Health Benefits

Dried plums are a good source of dietary fiber, sorbitol, potassium, copper, boron and phenolic compounds, which are active in a web of interrelated physiological and health-promoting functions. Together, these constituents are involved in bone metabolism and may help regulate glucose metabolism, promote cardiovascular health, protect against cancer and contribute to laxation.

Phenolic compounds, particularly hydroxicinnamates, have shown strong antioxidant properties and are believed to be very important for human health because some chronic diseases begin with oxidation damage of free radicals. Daily consumption of either dried plums or prune juice would increase daily intake of these phytochemicals.

Dried plums are long known for their supportive role in normal digestive functioning. Currently, the precise substances in dried plums that help promote bowel movement remain unidentified. It is common to think of fiber as responsible for the laxative effect. Generally, it is believed that the laxative effect of dried plums is most likely due to a combined action of fiber, sorbitol and phenolic compounds, which might affect electrolyte and water balance in the intestinal tract.

Potential of plums as a functional food ingredient

Dried plums might be utilised as a functional food ingredient. Recent academic studies suggested that they may function as a natural antioxidant, fight pathogens and serve as an antimicrobial agent in processed food. One of the study showed that dried plum ingredients were as effective in reducing oxidative rancidity in precooked sausage products as some traditional synthetic antioxidants compounds.

PROCESSING OF CRANBERRY, BLUEBERRY, CURRANT AND GOOSEBERRY

The utilisation of cranberry, blueberry, currant and gooseberry has occurred for many centuries and began with eating of the fresh fruit from wild species. These fruits have many characteristics in common. One essential characteristic is that these fruits have a soft consistency, except the cranberry, which is very firm. These fruits are small and have a characteristic colour from anthocyanin pigments (except gooseberry). Most of these fruits have a characteristic flavour and aroma that distinguishes them as value-added foods for preparing fruit products. They have lately become of importance due to their potential nutraceutical properties in human health.

Fresh Fruit Cultivation

Cranberry

The cultivated cranberry (*Vaccinium macrocarpon Ait.*) is native to peat bogs of many northern states from Maine to Minnesota, as far south as Virginia and Tennessee and in some Canadian provinces, but is not native to the Pacific coast. The common wild cranberry (*Vaccinium oxycoccus*), also called the small cranberry or European cranberry, is native to the coastal peat bogs and open Cascade mountain meadows on the Pacific coast as well as Europe and North Asia. The fruit is often round and speckled and does not hybridise with *V. macrocarpon*. This wild cranberry is not grown commercially, primarily due to smaller berries than those of the cultivated cranberry.

Blueberry

The blueberry belongs to the *Ericaceae* family, subfamily *Vacciniaceae*. Blueberries are found in many areas of the world but have gained greatest acceptance in the US and Canada. The true blueberries belong to the ancient genus *Vaccinium*, subgenus *Cyanococcus*.

Fruits for Processing

Cranberry

The crop is processed into mainly juice or juice drink products and this trend of juice usage continues to increase as consumer demands grow for cranberry juice related products. Ocean spray® introduced a new line of white cranberry juice drinks that has gathered much attention in the beverage market. This juice is made from early harvest fruit that lacks the finished pigment structure of fully ripened fruit.

Marketability of the cranberry is based on the extent of colour development for both fresh and processed fruits. The trend is to leave the berries on the vines as long as possible in order to gain maximum red colour development. The outer tissue structure of the berry contains all the red pigment while the inner structure is void of red pigment. Many cultivars continue to develop colour when stored above 10°C (50°F) and this colour development may diffuse into the flesh, as the fruit becomes overripe. When fresh cranberries are being sorted, the use of an UV light source can be used to detect internal rot in otherwise perfect-looking fruit.

Blueberry

The most significant change in the blueberry production within the last few years is the increase of blueberries in processed products. In general, depending on the cultivar and the cultural and environmental conditions, the soluble solids content of the blueberry will range from 7 per cent in green lit to about

15 per cent in ripe fruit. Within cultivars, earlier ripening fruit tend to have a greater soluble solids content than those that ripen later. Berries will continue to ripen after harvest, however, a berry ripened off the bush will never achieve the soluble solids content of one that ripens on the bush. Where practical, allow berries to ripen fully on the bush, delaying harvest several days after they turn blue.

Blueberries contain more mucilaginous material than most berries that can cause difficulty in juice preparation. Clarified blueberry juice posses relatively little flavour due to the processing it encounters. The colour of blueberries is greatly influenced by the state of their epicuticular wax, i.e. the presence of a rodlet wax structure that produces the glaucous effect responsible for the typical light blue colour of blueberries.

Currants

Currants are utilised for fresh market production, mainly and the processed market must rely on imports to supply their needs. Growing and usage of currants is greater in Europe. Black currants yield 2 T/acre in the UK and Poland while red currants yield 5 to 7 T/acre. Currants have shown they can tolerate relatively high CO_2 concentrations with 20 per cent as the optimum storage condition. Higher concentrations of CO_2 caused a faster decline in vitamin C content. Controlled atmosphere (CA) storage did not bring obvious advantages in comparison to CO_2, but did cause higher ethanol accumulation.

Gooseberry

Oregon produces the majority of gooseberries with yields of 4 to 5 T/acre. A simple method for estimation of maturity of the gooseberry is evaluation of the seed colour that changes from yellow to brown during ripening. It has been found that early harvest gave rise to fruit with the strongest gooseberry flavour. Gooseberries harvested at commercial maturity apparently contain more anthocyanins and fewer tannins than fruit harvested when fully ripe. Most fruits reach the maximum anthocyanin content at the fully ripe stage of maturity.

Cranberries have received considerable attention lately for their antioxidant abilities. Ten cranberry cultivars were evaluated for oxygen radical absorbance capacity (ORAC), anthocyanins and total phenolics content after 3 months of storage at 0, 5, 10, 15 and 20°C. Cultivars and storage temperatures affected the antioxidant capacity of cranberry.

Wang and Hongjun showed that cranberry antioxidant activities against H_2O_2 were the lowest among the berry crops he investigated. In a study by Zheng and Shetty, cranberry, pomace was shown to contain large amounts of phenolic gylcosides. After 50 days of cultivation, the of total free phenolics reached a maximum of 0.5 mg/g of pomace. The study suggests that cranberry pomace is a potential substrate for producing food-grade phenolics.

Oxygen and ascorbic acid affect the colour stability in cranberry juice cocktail in that an increase in either factor causes a proportional increase in the disappearance of the anthocyanin in the juice. Blanching of whole cranberries inactivates the oxidising enzymes and this leads to a higher anthocyanin concentration in juices made from blanched berries. Cranberry juice yield and anthocyanin recovery have been studied by Sapers and found that freeze-thawing of the berries is particularly effective because it increases juice yield by as much as 50 per cent and juice anthocyanin content by up to 15 fold.

Blueberry

The nutritional composition of the blueberry shows high levels of vitamin C and potassium as was seen also in cranberry. According to Francis blueberry anthocyanins are the most complex mixture occurring in a single plant. Anthocyanin content (mg/cm^2 of berry surface) was found to be significantly correlated with sugar-acid ratio and soluble solids-acid ratio. The typical aroma compounds in highbush blueberry were found to be the following: hydroxycitronellol, farnesyl acetate, farsenol and myristicin.

Currants

Red and black currants have significant nutritional quantities of vitamin C, potassium, phosphorus, calcium and fiber. There are reports of pharmacological properties by black currants involving night vision and capillary resistance. Black currants have shown to contain between 14 and 142 mg/kg of the flavonol myricetin. The total contents of the flavonols quercetin, myricetin and kaempferol have been reported to be 157 mg/kg in black currants.

Major Processed Products

Cranberry juice processing

Fresh or frozen fruit is washed and then size reduced by a mill. The degree of size reduction varies depending upon the use of the fruit. If the fruit is for pressed juice, the size reduction will be less since the spent presscake can be used for sauce products or dried and infused with sweetener to make a raisin-like product that 'Ocean Spray Cranberries' has developed. If the fruit is for juice concentrate, the size reduction can be greater and the fruit mash can be extracted by pressing, decanting or counter current methods. The fruit is depectinised to increase juice yield and fruit solids recovery.

Juice extraction by pressing can be done with batch or continuous presses. Press aids may or may not be used, depending upon the processor. The use of press aids such as rice hulls or cellulose wood fiber will increase yield recoveries but may not allow reuse of the presscake for other food production. This presscake with press aids has been used as a supplement to animal feed. Juice extraction by decanters is very popular in the US and parts of Europe. Some processing facilities have only decanters installed and thus they have developed the techniques to extract juice from fruits successfully with good yields and high quality products.

Juice extraction by counter-current method involves the transport of milled fruit by a screw conveyor with a slight incline while hot water is added at the opposite end of the conveyor and allowed to extract the fruit solids from the fruit.

Filtration of cranberry juice is done by use of plate and frame, pressure leaf or rotary vacuum filters using diatomaceous earth as a filter aid or a similar product. Recent development in membrane filtration has allowed the use of such filters to clarify the juice while not causing substantial loss of the pigments.

The filtered Juice is concentrated to 50° Brix using any of several commercial evaporators. There are single-effect and multiple-effect evaporators in use and most have an essence recovery system for collection of the aromatic volatiles. The use of reverse osmosis as a preconcentration step before evaporation has been used by industry processors.

Cranberry drinks are made from blending cranberry juice and concentrate with other fruit juices and concentrates, sugars and water. Vitamin C may be added up to the recommended daily allowance. Once the drink formula is confirmed to be correct, the product is then filtered and thermally processed and packaged by one of the methods.

Blueberry, Currant and Gooseberry Juice Processing

The description for juice processing of these three fruits is so similar that they will be dealt with as one product. The equipment used for juice extraction is the same for each fruit and only the processing techniques usually vary depending on the fruit or the processors and how they believe they get the best quality and yield.

The fruit is received at the plant in either a fresh state or can be in a frozen state. If the fruit is in a fresh state and if the fruit has extraneous materials, they are removed, usually with air cleaning equipment and grated trash removal screens vibrating to move the fruit in a forward motion. After the cleaning process, the fruit is washed by means of water spray or water immersion and is put then onto an inspection belt for removal of defective fruit according to the processor guidelines. If the fruit is received in a frozen state it is allowed to partially thaw and then is dumped into a mill that reduces the frozen fruit into frozen slurry like mash, it is then heated for further processing. The freezing of fruits can aid in the breakdown of cell walls and help in the extraction of sugars, anthocyanins and other soluble solids.

The fruit then is milled or disintegrated for size reduction to aid in yield recovery and efficient extraction of the pigments and other soluble components. These fruits only require a soft crushing as compared to cranberries and the type of equipment is usually a set of rollers or blades that basically crush the fruit. The use of heat at this stage helps in cell rupture and aids in the ability of pectolytic enzymes to increase their reaction rates for juice yields. Other purposes of heating at this stage are to help inactivate enzymes that can cause stability problems in clear juices at later stages of production. The heating also helps stabilise the anthocyanin pigments and helps extract more of the pigment from the skin and flesh of the fruit.

Enzyme-catalysed anthocyanin pigment degradation is a recognised adverse effect of enzymes used in fruit juice processing. This degradation may be caused by polyphenol oxidase activity that induces coupled oxidative browning reactions or it may be attributable to the presence of galactosidase or α-L-arabinosidase side activities in multicomponent pectolytic enzyme preparations that cause hydrolysis of the native glycosylated anthocyanins to produce unstable aglycons and in turn cause colour loss.

Anthocyanins as well as other polyphenolics are readily oxidised because of their antioxidant properties and thus, are susceptible to degradative reactions during various processing unit operations. Because of their possible beneficial roles as micronutrients, it is critical that changes in polyphenolics during processing be measured to better assess the dietary value of the processed products. Kalt reported that native polyphenol oxidase in highbush blueberries accelerated anthocyanin pigment destruction in crushed blueberries. Skrede showed that substantial losses of anthocyanins and polyphenolics occurred when blueberries were processed into juice and concentrate and that different classes of compounds had varying susceptibility to degradation with different unit operations.

Heavy losses of anthocyanins and chlorogenic acid occurred with milling and depectinisation, which is believed to have been aggravated by native PPO. Polyphenolic and anthocyanin losses were relatively low when pasteurised single-strength juice was concentrated, except for the procyanidins, which showed marked reduction. Considerable anthocyanins remained in the press cake, which may be a potential colourant source.

Extraction techniques used may be batch presses, continuous presses, decanters and counter current. The most common method is the use of presses with some companies using decanters. Many of the soft fruits have a considerable volume of free-run juice that must be taken into consideration when determining what type of press to use for extraction. In some cases, this freerun juice is taken away from the mash by means of a vibrating screen or rotary screen separator to reduce hydraulic loading on presses. The use of press aids such as rice hulls or cellulose wood fibers are employed with presses to facilitate maximum yields. In many processing facilities, the presscake or pomace is treated with hot water and pressed again (sometimes 2 to 3 times) to achieve greater yields of total soluble solids.

After the juice is extracted, it needs to be clarified if it is going to be used to make a clear juice or juice concentrate. Clarification can be accomplished by many different means. The use of centrifuges, plate and frame filters, pressure leaf filters, rotary vacuum filters, membrane filters, clarifying agents (such as gelatine, bentonite, silica sol, polyvinylpolypyroidine and tannin), decanting and air flotation and flocculation have been employed. Centrifuges help in removing many of the clouding components in juices but do not allow for complete removal of all suspended panicles for a clear juice. A centrifuge allows continuous flow of product and an economical means for preliminary solids removal to aid in further clarification steps. Some companies will allow for the suspended particles to settle out into a conical bottom tank and then draw the clear juice off by means of valving on the tank side. This is known as decantation and the remaining solids are then processed through a centrifuge, decanter, plate and frame, membrane or pressure leaf filter.

In some instances, the uses of enzymes and clarifying methods are employed a second time to help produce clear juices. This is company dependent and can be product dependent. This also can depend upon unusual circumstances that occur sometimes during a processing season where the usual methods of clarification do not work and other means must be used.

Concentration of fruit juices can be considered a final processing step for many fruits. The use of concentrates for many food products has grown rapidly over the last decade and appears to continue this upward trend. In some instances, the concentration step is not the final step for the fruit juice but gives a semi finished product in which the concentrate will be blended back in with other ingredients by the processor to achieve a final finished product. The use of concentration has allowed processors to store concentrated juices in bulk form and continues year-round processing of other finished products.

The soft fruits such as blueberry, currants and gooseberry require selection of the proper 'concentration equipment due to the thermal sensitivity of the pigments and volatile flavour compounds. There are many manufacturers of concentration equipment and with the proper criteria, most manufacturers can design an evaporator that will give high quality juice concentrates and that recovers the volatile aroma compounds known as essence. The use of single pass and multiple effect evaporators is favoured in the industry due to the short time-cycle and thermal properties of these juices.

There are other methods of concentration such as freeze concentration and reverse osmosis. The use of freeze concentration with these soft fruits is currently not being done due to the capital costs of equipment and the requirement of large-scale production. The use of reverse osmosis should be considered for preconcentration before evaporation. This can allow for smaller evaporators to accomplish the same goal of concentration or allow a company to increase existing capacity without requiring additional evaporator capacity.

Other processed fruit products

Cranberry products such as sauce have been around for many decades now. Modern canning methods allowed for the increased production of sauce and changed cranberries from a seasonal fruit to a year-around commodity.

Blending a mixture of cranberries, sugar and water so that the mixture will form a gel produces cranberry sauces. The gel-forming property of the sauce is dependent on the pectic substances, soluble solids and acids in the fruit and the amount of sweetener added. The gel-forming property of cranberries may vary not only by cultivar but also with maturity, season, horticultural practices and conditions of storage. Cranberries have been and still are being investigated as a possible source of natural red pigments. At the moment, the one major drawback is the sensitivity to processing conditions these red pigments have shown. Cranberries are combined with oranges to make a cranberry-orange relish used in making candied and spiced cranberries and processed into liqueurs.

The fermentation of cranberries into wines and ciders is done on a very limited basis. At present, these products do not appear to be gaining any widespread acceptance.

Utilisation of by-products from cranberry production has always been of interest. The use of pressed cranberries as an animal feed supplement or as an ingredient in plant and animal waste composting operations is being investigated. The extraction of wax and oils are also being investigated. Zheng and Shetty have shown that cranberry pomace may be a potential substrate for producing food-grade phenolics.

The use of blueberries in other processed fruit products would include pie fillings, wines and syrups that are done on limited basis and are more regional than widespread commercial products.

The use of currants and gooseberries in other fruit products is very limited and would be considered in the home use instead of commercial processing category. Landbo and Meyer showed that black currant pomace extracts exerted a pronounced antioxidant activity against human LDL oxidation *in vitro* when tested at equimolar phenol concentrations of 7.5 to 10 μM. Further studies of phenolic compounds may also reveal additional benefits for by-products of these fruits.

However the supply of cranberries, blueberries, currants and gooseberries does fluctuate from year to year. This fluctuation causes problems for the processor in the supply of a raw material for his products and has caused some products that were developed to be discontinued from production.

GRAPEFRUITS, LEMONS AND LIMES

This chapter will provide unique information pertaining to these citrus fruits. Grapefruits are known for their large size and for their tendency to grow in clusters like grapes. They have higher acid levels than oranges as well as a distinctive flavour and bitter taste. Lemons and limes have characteristic flavours, small size and high acid content that imparts a sour taste, they may produce multiple crops in a season.

Although grapefruit, lemons, and limes have higher acid and lower sugar contents than sweeter citrus species, they possess other important characteristics that perpetuate their production.

The second varietal grapefruit group is the pink or pigmented grapefruit. This group differs from the former, in that the internal fruit flesh contains variable concentrations of the red pigment lycopene. Although deeper coloured grapefruits are considered more attractive than the less coloured or white grapefruit, there is no scientific evidence that coloured grapefruit possess better flavour. Seediness is a deterrent to the quality of grapefruit as a fresh fruit. Also, the lycopene has a tendency to fade during processing, as do the anthocyanins in blood oranges. Even though the bright colours are attractive in the fresh fruit, the juice from pigmented grapefruit has a tendency to brown with time.

A close relative of the grapefruit that is also produced commercially is the pummelo. It is believed that the grapefruit is perhaps a hybrid of the pummelo, rather than its own species.

Lemons are contained in the single species *Citrus limon* (L.) Burm. f. and contain the widest divergence of all citrus species. One of the oldest commercial varieties is the 'Eureka' lemon, which is being replaced by the 'Lisbon' lemon. The two fruits are almost impossible to distinguish, especially at the juice plant. The 'Mesero' lemon of Italy is considered to be the best processing lemon in the world.

Limes are greener in colour than lemons, both on the exterior and interior of the fruit. Limes are considered a tropical fruit and are generally preferred to lemons because of their distinctive flavour. Mexico is considered the major producer of limes. Florida also produces a significant amount of limes. The three lime species include the small-fruited *Citrus aurantifolia* Swing., the large fruited *Citrus latifolia* Tan., and the sweet lime *Cirrus limettoides* Tan.

Processing of Grapefruits, Lemons and Limes

Similar to oranges and tangerines, the fresh grapefruit, lemon, and lime industries yield a higher percentage of profit to the grower than the processed fruit. However, fruit grown with insufficient exterior quality to sell as fresh fruit has found a commercial home in the processing industry. Even though the fruit is less palatable than sweeter citrus species, the unique characteristics of yellow citrus lend themselves to unique processed products.

Juice extraction

Both FMC and Brown extractors are used for juice extraction. However, the large size of grapefruit and the small size of the lemons and limes require different machine components. The operating principles of the FMC and Brown citrus juice extractors may be obtained from the companies websites (www.fmcfoodtech.com or www.brown-intl.com). Extractors equipped with large reamers or cups are primarily used for grapefruit and smaller reamers or cups are used for lemons or limes. However, such processing is slow and if a large amount of yellow citrus is to be run, the machine components should be changed to maximise yield and speed. Many plants have separate lines of extractors for yellow citrus and can run both types of fruit by merely switching lines.

Pulp removal

Pulp removal is generally performed using at least two stages of screening or finishing, as mentioned in the chapter on oranges and tangerines. This is done in order to prevent pulp from sticking to the interior surface of evaporators and burning. Burnt pulp can be a source of unsightly black flakes occasionally found in citrus concentrates and pasteurised juices. However, further pulp removal is sometimes desirable in order to reduce grapefruit juice bitterness and to reduce concentrate viscosity. Reduced viscosities allow for greater concentration and a reduction in storage and transportation costs. A third reason for depulping is to meet customer specifications. Some products require depulped or even clarified juices. Ultrafiltration used in conjunction with juice debittering provides a clarified product that may be of interest to a customer. A more common approach is to use centrifuges to reduce juice pulp levels to 3 per cent or less. Pulp removal must take into account the changing nature of the pulp as it is processed. Pulp content from freshly extracted juice is generally in the neighbourhood of 20 per cent by volume, using methods common in the industry. As the juice proceeds through the evaporator, the pulp level will diminish due to heat-accelerated breakdown of the pulp and mechanical shredding.

Oil extraction

Oils extracted from the flavedo of grapefruit, lemons, and limes are more valuable than orange oils. The lemon oil market is especially lucrative and surpasses orange and tangerine oil in value and price. The reasons for this are the high aldehyde content in lemon oil and the smaller worldwide production of lemons, compared with oranges (supply and demand for the oil). Aldehydes provide the greatest contribution to flavour in citrus oils. The prominent aldehyde found in lemon oil is citral, a mixture of neral and geranial. Lemon oil has 2–4 per cent aldehydes, compared to 1–2 per cent found in orange oil. Grapefruit oil contains terpene thiols and nootkatone that give the oil its characteristic grapefruit flavour and aroma.

The Scott method is the primary quality control method used to determine the amount of oil in grapefruit, lemon and lime juices. The Scott estimate of grapefruit juice oil is accurate, similar to orange and tangerine, because the oil is near 95 per cent limonene. However, for lemon juice, a factor is included in the calculation, as the oil is only 80 per cent limonene and contains 4 per cent citral that consumes bromine at half the rate of limonene.

Evaporation and pasteurisation

The same methods of pasteurisation and evaporation are used with yellow citrus as with orange citrus. Due to the high acid nature of lemon and lime juices, greater care must be taken in heat treatment. If too much heat is applied to deactivate pectinases, acid hydrolysis of pectin and sugars can occur. This results in cloud loss and gelation, the same as with pectinase activity. The excessive acid content also accelerates Maillard browning. Couple these facts with the phenomenon of heat sensitivity of the lycopene in pigmented grapefruit, and one can conclude that yellow citrus juices have a greater heat sensitivity in processing than orange and tangerine juices. In spite of this, high-quality grapefruit and lemon concentrates can be commercially produced. However, lemon processors prefer evaporators to operate at medium temperatures instead of at high temperatures in order to minimise the negative heating effects mentioned above.

Grapefruit concentrates can be evaporated to high Brix levels (60–65° Brix), the same as with orange and tangerine juices, although 55° Brix grapefruit concentrate is also commonly produced. However, lemon and lime concentrates do not use Brix or percent sucrose equivalents as the measure of concentration. Because the major soluble solid is citric acid, lemon and lime concentrations are described as grams of equivalent citric acid per liter of solution (GPL). The most common concentration of lemon concentrate is 400 ± 5 GPL, which is about 57° Brix. This is less than the orange juice range of commercial concentrates of 60–65° Brix.

Quality Control

Grapefruit juice is similar to orange juice in basic composition with a few notable exceptions such as the higher acid content. Commercial single-strength orange juices generally have acid levels of less than 1 per cent (w/w as citric acid). Single-strength grapefruit juices generally have 1–1.5 per cent acid. This results in the Brix/acid ratios ranging from 7 to about 10 for grapefruit juice, compared to commercial orange juice ranging from 13 to about 18. Because bitterness plays a large role in grapefruit juice processing, the monitoring of bitterness levels is important. The Davis test for flavonoids has historically been an effective, simple and rapid method to monitor the naringin levels in grapefruit juices. It can also be used to monitor hesperidin in orange and tangerine juices should the need arise.

Raw material inspection

Grapefruit sampling and analysis is identical to Oranges and Tangerines, however, lemon and lime fruit sampling and analysis is very different. Because lemon and lime juices contain more acid than carbohydrates, their soluble solids are in citric acid equivalents instead of sugar equivalents.

Citrus Drinks

Juices from yellow citrus fruit may be less attractive in flavour and colour than those from orange varieties. Thus, drinks and beverages that are less than 100 per cent juice have become popular for grapefruit, lemons and limes. Drink formulations offer competitive advantages over 100 per cent pure juices. For example, the colour of pink grapefruit juice may fade or turn brown with time whereas the colour of pink grapefruit juice cocktail remains attractive over time due to the addition of food-grade colours. Pure lemon juice is used as a flavour enhancer for cooked fish and other products, however, to make a thirst-quenching drink, the excessive acidity has traditionally been countered by adding sugar and water to form lemonade. Pink lemonade has been well received despite the fact that there are no pigmented or pink lemon fruit. Even though orange drinks are widely consumed, lemonade, as a drink, holds a significant role in the citrus drink industry.

With the freedom to add noncitrus ingredients, we see that citrus drinks take on a wide variety of forms. Industrially, drink bases or drinks minus the major portion of water and sugar, are commonly produced. Drink bases are called squashes in the UK and cordials in Australia. Whatever the type of drink or drink base, citrus drinks consist of at least some of the following components: juices, sweeteners, acids, colourants, flavours, texturisers, clouding agents, nutrients and preservatives.

Juices

All citrus juice drinks (beverages) must contain some citrus juice by definition. Grapefruit juice cocktail and lemonade contain grapefruit and lemon juices, respectively, however, because there are no standards of identity for grapefruit cocktail, other juices can be added. In the absence of standards of identity, any ingredients can be used as long as they correctly appear on the label.

Sweeteners

The use of low-cost sweeteners renders citrus drinks an economic alternative to pure citrus juices. Among the sweeteners permitted in the US are sucrose, invert sugar, fructose, corn syrup, glucose syrup, sorbitol or any combination. The use of artificial sweeteners provides a low-calorie alternative for many drinks.

Acids

When orange citrus juices are diluted in making a drink, the sugar and acids must be replenished, however, in yellow citrus drinks, the excessive acid makes acid addition largely unnecessary. In many combined citrus drinks, lemon juice is used as the supplier of the needed acid. In making lemonades, sugar and water are added to match the acid levels, making an acceptable palatable drink.

Flavours

Natural lemon and grapefruit oils and aromas are common flavour enhancers in yellow citrus drinks. Flavours that are recovered from fruit (cold-pressed oils) or removed from juice during evaporation (essences) can be added back to the juice prior to packaging. The common scenario is for the citrus processor to sell the oils to a flavour company, where they are formulated for specific products, then purchased by the juice or drink manufacturers.

Texturisers

It is often important to duplicate the mouthfeel of 100 per cent natural juices by adding texturisers. Some commonly used texturisers are glycerol, guar gum, hydroxylated lecithin, lecithin, methyl cellulose, mono and diglycerides of fat-forming fatty acids, polyglycerol esters of fatty acids, propylene glycol alginate, sodium metaphosphate, gum acacia, gum arabic, xanthan gum, vegetable gums and brominated oils, gum tragacanth, carob bean gum, carrageenan, ester gum, sodium carboxymethylcellulose, cotton-seed oil or pectin. The best texturiser is determined by texturising effect, cost and availability. It should be emphasised that texturisers cannot be legally added to 100 per cent citrus juices, and are used in juice drinks that do not contain 100 per cent juice.

Preservatives

Benzoate (0.10 per cent or more) and sorbate (0.05 per cent or more) preservatives are commonly used to minimise microbial activity in citrus drinks but cannot be added to 100 per cent juices. Modern pasteurisation practices have made aseptic products a common occurrence and have diminished the need for preservatives. Refrigerated concentrated drink bases are sometimes preserved only by low temperatures and osmotic effects, although addition of benzoate or sorbate may be necessary in instances where temperature abuse is likely.

The high acidity of drink bases inhibits growth of most bacteria, but fermentative yeasts may cause spoilage. Additionally, certain osmophilic yeasts such as *Zygosaccharomyces bailii* and *Z. rouxii* have demonstrated resistance to sorbate and benzoate and are capable of spoiling drink bases and concentrates upon thermal abuse.

Citrus Fruit Sections

Citrus fruit sections are a popular method of processing citrus fruit. Grapefruits are prepared for sectionising by a series of fruit softening and scalding steps to facilitate peeling. Once peeled, the fruit is treated with hot caustic sprays and water chilling, prior to sectionising by hand or by mechanical sectionisers. The sections are hand graded and filled in cans, along with syrups consisting of various combinations of grapefruit juice and sweeteners. Sections are either cold-filled with sodium benzoate added as a preservative or hot-filled into cans.

The main quality control parameter of grapefruit sections is the drain weight. USDA grade A grapefruit sections must have at least 53 per cent drain weight, with 65 per cent of the fruit being in whole sections along with subjective organoleptic minimum score.

Pectin Production

Citrus pectin is generally manufactured from lemon peel. The essential oils are extracted from the peel prior to pectin processing. The peel is then shredded and washed with water to remove carbohydrates and then is extracted several times with dilute hot acid to dissolve the protopectin in the peel into a water-soluble form. The extractant is filtered and concentrated to about 3–4 per cent pectin. Alcohol is then added to precipitate the pectin as a gelatinous mass before separation using a hydraulic press. After several alcohol and water washings, the pectin is warm-air dried. The dried pectin is pulverised and packaged as a yellowish white powder. Rinsing the pectin with dilute acid prior to drying produces rapid-set pectin. Because inorganic acids are used in the manufacture of pectin, heavy metal contaminants in the acids become quality control issues in the food-grade pectin product. Even though atomic absorption and HPLC are recommended for heavy metal analysis, the Food Chemicals Codex (FCC) uses the ash content to estimate heavy metal levels along with a heavy metal test procedure. The maximum level of heavy metals as Pb is 40 ppm.

Another important quality control parameter is the degree of esterification. The number of methoxy groups of the pectin determines its gelling ability. Related to this parameter is the jelly grade. As 75 per cent of the pectin manufactured is used to make jams and jellies, the jelly grade becomes a major factor in pectin quality. The jelly grade is measured using a Ridgelimeter. The procedure consists of preparing a gel from the pectin in a container and measuring the ridged nature of the gel produced using a needle-like probe. Lemon peel produces pectin with a jelly grade of 300–350, 250–300 from grapefruit and 150–250 from orange peel. Most commercial pectins are standardised to have a jelly grade of about 150.

Animal Feed By-products

The main by-product of the citrus juice industry is the citrus peel, which is dried and manufactured into cattle feed. Unless it is dehydrated to approximately 10 per cent moisture, the sugar in citrus peel ferment readily, limiting bulk storage time to hours. Also, the cost of transporting wet peel (80 per cent moisture) is prohibitive. Dried citrus peel has been found to be a competitive feed for ruminants. Its value as an animal feed is generally based on the nitrogen-free extract (primarily carbohydrates), protein, crude fiber, and fat. Dried citrus peel generally contains about 6 per cent protein, 5 per cent fat, 12 per cent crude fiber, 7 per cent ash and about 60 per cent nitrogen-free extract.

Citrus Molasses

Citrus molasses is the concentrated version of the liquid pressed from the peel (press liquor) during dried pulp manufacture, and is used sometimes directly as an animal feed supplement. Its primary use is as a bonding agent in the manufacture of citrus pellets or as a drying aid in the drying of peel. The addition of molasses to peel entering the dryer helps withdraw the moisture from the peel. Citrus molasses is also used to make beverage and fuel alcohol.

Citrus Wastes

Citrus processing generates many wastes that are typical of a food processing plant. Generally, air pollution consists of particulate emissions and volatile organic compounds from the feed mill drying operation. Solid and liquid wastes are handled in typical waste treatment operations, similar to sewage and sludge. Care must be taken to avoid allowing large amounts of peel oil or limonene to enter the waste treatment process, as this material may poison the microbes active in the digestion of wastes. Packaging debris is a common solid waste and is dealt with largely by recycling or solid disposal in a landfill.

BANANAS

Bananas are considered the fourth most important food crop in the world, after the three main cereals rice, wheat and corn. In the-tropical countries of all continents, bananas have been a staple food for centuries, with high per capita consumptions. The seedless bananas consumed today in the industrialised countries are the result of long painstaking selection and breeding, some done by our primitive ancestors. Until a few years ago banana seeds from seminal varieties were used in breeding. Tissue culture is widely used at present to improve the varieties.

Although fresh bananas are widely consumed in developed countries, the consumption of processed banana products is less than that of other processed fruits. Several attempts to launch consumer products such as canned sliced bananas in syrup have failed. This is partially because fresh ripe bananas are readily available year-round. On the other hand, seasonal crops such as apples produce an abundant crop in a short time. In the not too distant past, the only way to use so many apples in the short crop period was to process them into products such as juice and applesauce. There is no such pressure with bananas, they are produced any time of the year with little volume variation. Therefore, the volume of processed banana products has developed slowly. Processed bananas are still produced mostly from rejects of the fresh banana trade. Therefore, the varieties used are the same as for fresh fruit, but there has been a decline in the number of varieties being grown, resulting in only a few selected varieties and sub-varieties of the Cavendish type being used for processing.

The banana plant is a perennial that yields a bunch every 3 months. The plant grows new pseudostems from new rhizomes in the roots. Excess new sprouts are removed so that a 'mother', a 'daughter' and a 'grand daughter' are always growing. Colour coding with plastic ribbons marks the generation of the bunch and allows for easy identification at harvest time. Once a stem, yielding one bunch of bananas is harvested, it is chopped and left in the field as mulch. At the packing stations, green banana rejects, not suitable for export as fresh fruit, are accumulated and picked up by a truck or cart to be transported to the processed bananas plant. Most plants receive the green fruit in bulk and rarely in crates. Sometimes, full containers of export quality bananas will start to turn colour, signalling premature ripening and are not shipped. This fruit is then available to the processed bananas plant also. Some packers receive the bananas from truckers or other intermediaries who do the ripening for them, usually by primitive means such as using calcium carbide to generate acetylene gas under a tarpaulin. The intermediaries pick up green rejects from several farms and sometimes even from different banana companies and they take over the job of ripening and delivering the bananas to the processed bananas plant. Finally, some packers buy the fruit on the open market or contract with intermediaries who do so. This is more likely to happen in countries such as India and Brazil, where there are no large-scale fresh banana export operations providing reject bananas.

Bananas for Processing

Fresh-fruit operations, though continuing year-round, are still affected by seasonality and by supply and demand situations. Seasonality is not primarily due to the growth habits of bananas. It is caused indirectly, by the seasonality of other fruits indigenous to the Northern Hemisphere. When apples, pears, peaches and so on, are abundant and are sold at low prices at harvest time, the demand for bananas declines and vice versa. Production-area restrictions in supply are usually due to severe weather conditions. Most commonly, a storm with strong winds blows down a good part or all of a producing region. The rebuilding of a plantation takes from 2 to 3 months and with 9 months required for growing, almost a year passes before the first bunches can be harvested again. Sometimes the big multinational companies use such storms as an excuse to cut down production in areas where the business climate has become unattractive to their operations. Other factors that may affect supply are strikes by the relatively powerful unions in some of the producing countries, sometimes, an oversupply situation is due to plain human miscalculation.

Ideally, the processed banana plant will be centrally located within a growing area. In such cases, it is possible to move the bananas to the plant using tractor-drawn dump carts. For gathering bananas from farther distances, trucks, railroads and even barges may be used for transportation.

Ripening

The ripening of green bananas for processing is somewhat different, as the fruit is greener by up to 2 weeks. Generally in the tropics the ripening cycles are run at higher temperatures than at the developed countries markets. Also, in the tropics there is no need to either control the humidity or heating as done in, northern countries.

One of the most widely used systems to estimate the degree of ripeness of the fruit is the peel colour index (PCI). Colour charts are readily available from large banana companies. The modem charts show seven degrees rather than the eight degrees in the ripening process used earlier. However, the additional degree of ripeness is useful for the processed banana packer.

Good temperature control and air circulation are indispensable for good ripening. Overloading of the rooms results in poor air circulation, which causes erratic ripening. Water leaks, such as those caused by improperly maintained drip pans under elevated cookers, may also result in uneven ripening. If this happens and the greener fruit is not separated from the properly ripened fruit, there can be nasty surprises with the consistency of the banana puree. In some cases, the puree may even jell at the markets during the winter, resulting in complaints and claims from customers.

Major Processed Banana Products Solid as Ingredients

This section covers the main processed banana products and their modes of processing.

Banana puree

This is probably the most important processed banana product. The ripe bananas are peeled mostly by hand but also by means of mechanical peelers. The most successful systems for mechanical peeling are those using adaptations of fish and meat deboning machines. Although cost advantages are realised, mechanical peeling requires careful supervision and continuity of operation to reduce the discolouration of the resulting puree. Because most producers have abundant low cost hand labour, hand peeling is still widely used.

Once the peels are separated, the mashed bananas are passed through screens that vary in size and type, depending on whether or not a deseeded puree is desired. The puree is then homogenised. Commercial varieties of bananas have no seeds as such. The black specks one sees are atrophied seed bags, however, they are commonly referred to as 'seeds'. The next process step, deareation, is one of the most important in determining the colour of the finished puree. During de-aeration under vacuum, the air present in the puree is removed to a large extent. The volatile components of the banana aroma are also removed and are condensed to produce banana essence.

The volatile aroma components and water are recovered in the working fluid (water) of a liquid ring vacuum pump. Some of the fluid is drawn off as banana essence once the desired concentration is reached. The working fluid is kept cold by circulating it through a heat exchanger operated to maintain it at a temperature just above freezing. Due to the interruptions in the operation, one ends up with essences of different strengths, which must be blended to meet the desired specification.

After de-aeration, the puree is held under vacuum in a surge tank, from where it is metered into the aseptic process. For concentrated puree, a vacuum evaporation step is done at this point. Because the tank is under vacuum, there are normally two pumps. The first one is a sanitary positive displacement pump, which feeds the second pump, usually a triplex metering pump. For low acid banana puree, the metering pump determines the flow rate, which is a critical parameter of the process.

In the aseptic process, scraped-surface heat exchangers (SSHEs) are normally used, both for heating to the holding temperature and for cooling to the filling temperature. Another critical parameter for low acid banana puree production is the residence time in the holding tube at the required processing temperature.

Finally, the filling is done aseptically in presterilised containers, mostly bag in box or drum. The filling temperature should be a happy medium—below 40 to 45°C, to prevent the growth of heat-resistant thermophilic bacteria, but higher than room temperature (30 to 35°C), to prevent condensation of ambient air moisture on the boxes, drums or cans. Bag in box, drum or bin are used for large containers over 21 kg (5 gal).

Dehydrated Banana Products

Banana flakes

These are made by drum drying in large chrome-plated drums dryers heated internally with steam. The puree, extracted in a similar way to banana puree, is fed directly to the drum dryers. The water evaporates as the drum turns, forming a film of dried material on the drum surface. Carefully adjusted knives remove the dry film as a more or less continuous sheet, which passes to an air-conditioned room where it is broken into flakes, sifted for classification and packaged in bag-in box containers.

The fine solids resulting as a by-product of this operation are sold separately as dehydrated banana powder. Drum-dried mixtures of bananas with cereals are made similarly to pure banana flakes and are also important in the ingredients market.

Banana figs

Banana figs are produced in the tropics in dehydrators with hot air circulation. Originally, the drying was done in the sun, but more and more, it is being done by dehydration with tunnel or cabinet dryers. Indirect heating of the air with steam coils to generate hot air for drying is preferred. Some plants use combustion of a fuel directly in the air stream to heat the air up.

Banana powder

This section deals with: (i) by-product fines from banana flakes production, and (ii) spray-dried banana powder.

As with flakes, the production of the powder by-product starts with the feeding of banana puree to the steam-heated drum dryers. When the dry sheet passes through the screw conveyors, it starts to break down. This continues in the grinding and screening operations. Almost half the weight of the flakes goes through a 100-mesh screen. Therefore, depending on requirements, the manufacturer can adjust grinding fineness to produce more or less powder. The dry powder is packed in the same bag-in-box packaging as the flakes. The better bags are made from laminated material with a good moisture barrier layer. Of late, cost pressure in the industry has made the use of lower cost polyethylene bags more common even though the shelf life is reduced with this packaging.

Other Processed Banana Products

Banana chips

Banana chips in the Philippines are normally made from green Saba cooking bananas. They are peeled and sliced thin, deep-fried to an intermediate moisture content, dipped in or coated with cane sugar solution and briefly fried a second time in hot oil to the final moisture. The Saba cooking banana presents less of a problem with enzyme-catalysed browning than the Cavendish varieties and the resulting chips have a light colour. So-called natural banana chips are made in a single fry, without the sugar solution dipping step.

Normally, coconut oil is used for frying. However, other vegetable oils may be used as well. Commercial banana chips in the supermarkets often have a taste of artificial banana flavour, which is not always declared. The chips are normally packed in bulk with two separate plastic bags per carton, with a combined net weight of around 8 kg. Most chips are repacked at the markets in moisture resistant plastic pouches made from laminated material.

Sliced bananas in syrup (shelf stable)

It is used by packers who need banana piece identity for the product. Calcium carbonate is normally used as a firming agent and tartaric or citric acids may be used to lower the pH and allow a milder thermal process.

Banana starch

The building consists of an open structure similar to those used in the production of starch from yuca, manioc or cassava. There are four levels besides the ground level. The open structure prevents the accumulation of fine starch powder laden air, which is explosive at certain concentration and moisture levels. Typically, in such a plant, the heavy equipment used for disintegration of the starch-bearing material is installed on the ground floor, where the peels, bagasse or other trash are separated. The pulp is passed through successive vibrating screens to end with a milky suspension containing the starch.

This suspension is pumped up to the top floor of the building and then flows down from floor to floor in the separation steps of the process. The starch is separated by means of centrifuges, first to concentrate it and then, in basket centrifuges, to obtain a cake that is scraped off with a doctor's knife. The basket centrifuge operates in a programmed cycle, first building up and rinsing the cake and then drying it and scraping it off. Earlier methods of separating and washing starch included settling in long, shallow troughs from which the starch cake was eventually removed. The cake was then ground to a coarse powder. The starch had a slight blue hue to it, probably from iron contamination and a purity of around 95 per cent. Regardless of the extraction method, the coarse powder is dried with hot air prior to grinding, sieving and bagging. The banana starch is not an item of significant international trade at present.

GUAVA, LYCHEE, MANGO AND PAPAYA

Guava

Guava (*Psidium guajava* L.), an important member of the Myrtaceae family, is believed to have originated in Central America and the southern part of Mexico. The Spanish explorers took the guava to the Philippines and the Portuguese disseminated it from the Philippines to India. It now grows throughout the tropics and sub-tropics in the world in almost all habitats as one of the most widely utilised fruits. The leading country in the world in fresh guava production is India. The producers of guava products include India, Brazil, South Africa, Hawaii, Columbia, Puerto Rico, Dominican Republic, Jamaica, Israel, Philippines, Taiwan, Fuji, Sudan, Kenya, Egypt, Mexico, Malaysia, Pakistan, Thailand, Australia, Nicaragua and Guadeloupe.

The guava fruit can be consumed fresh, processed into a semiproduct in the form of puree, clarified juice or concentrate and frozen or aseptically stored, or processed continuously all the way to the final products, which include guava nectar, guava syrup, guava jam, guava jelly, guava bar, guava cheese, guava chutney and guava powder, as well as canned guavas. Among them, guava nectar is far more important than the others in the quantity of production and the popularity among consumers.

Nutritionally, guavas are an excellent source of ascorbic acid. The ascorbic acid contents in guavas from many cultivars are well above 100 mg/100 gram and may even reach 1 g/100 g in some cases, which are considerably higher than the contents in other common fruits. Guavas are also a good source of niacin, thiamine, riboflavin, calcium, iron, phosphorus and dietary fiber. Roughly 15 per cent of the fresh weight of guava fruit comes from carbohydrates that are the principal nonaqueous components.

Approximately 40 per cent of the total carbohydrates are sugars, which include fructose as the predominant one, followed by glucose and sucrose. Guava fruit from most cultivars contain more citric acid than ascorbic acid. Malic acid and glycolic acid are the other two major organic acids.

Fresh-cut guava wedges

The shelf life of fresh-cut guava fruit is limited by the occurrence of softening, discolouration and microbial growth. However, fresh-cut guava wedges can be washed with ozone-injected water to reduce the microbial load and stored at 5°C (41°F) for 5 days with acceptable quality.

Guava puree

The harvested fruit is usually ripened at room temperature for 2–7 days. Slightly over-ripened guava fruit, which is characterised by a fully yellow skin with brown spots and soft watery flesh with intense distinctive musky odour, is the preferred raw material.

Guavas are dumped onto an inspection belt. The seriously spoiled pieces are discarded and the under-ripened ones are set aside for further ripening. Those fruit that have passed inspection are conveyed toward a washing system that is normally made up of a soaking section, a brushing section and a rinsing section in series. In the soaking section, mechanical agitation and the addition of detergent help to loosen dirt, debris and other contaminants from the surface of fruit. In the brushing section, the residual contaminants on the surface of fruit are detached by the action of a mechanical brush. Clean water is sprayed onto the fruit in the rinsing section to remove the detergent. Cleaned guavas leave the washing system on a belt for the final inspection before maceration. In the inspection, fruit having major defects are discarded, while those having minor defects are hand-trimmed.

The guava fruit are then macerated and finished by a rotor crusher, a paddle pulper and a paddle finisher, all lined up in sequence or by some other equipment with similar functions. The pulper and the finisher are fitted with 0.6-1-mm and 0.3 mm screens, respectively. The screen on the pulper removes the seeds and the fibrous fragments of skin tissue. The finisher removes large aggregates of stone cells. The residual stone cells may be ground by passing the finished pulp through a mill. The milling operation improves the mouthfeel but downgrades the colour quality, thus, it is not very popular in the industry. Centrifugation is usually performed to adjust the serum to insoluble solids ratio in the finished puree and to serve as an effective way for removing the residual stone cells to improve the mouthfeel and to reduce the precipitability of the product. The type of centrifuge and the operation condition being used vary among factories. An example is the use of a 12 inch solid bowl spinning at 2100 rpm. Vacuum deaeration may be practiced during or after centrifugation to improve the heat-transfer efficiency and the storage quality of guava puree.

The puree that is prepared by following the described procedure can be processed further into nectar, syrup, jam or concentrate in the production line or it can be pasteurised in a tubular or scraped-surface heat exchanger at 93–96°C (199–205°F) for 36 seconds or at 88–90°C (190–194°F) for 60 seconds, cooled in two stages to 4°C (39°F), filled into flexible containers such as plastic bags in 20 kg carton boxes or rigid containers such as 5-gal rectangular parallelepipedon-shaped metal cans, and then frozen and stored at 18°C (0°F) as a semiproduct for later use. In a storage period up to 1 year, the quality of the frozen guava puree remains acceptable.

Guava puree may also be packed aseptically. After flash-heating and cooling in a scraped surface heat exchanger system, the puree can be filled into a presterilised, low-oxygen-permeability, laminated bag under aseptic conditions. The bag is then placed in a fiberboard carton for storage and transportation at ambient temperature. The major disadvantage of the aseptic ambient storage, as compared with frozen storage, is the much faster deterioration in sensory quality. Chemical reactions in guava puree simply proceed at a much higher rate at room temperature than in subzero environment.

Clarified guava juice

Clarified guava juice can be used in the manufacture of clear guava nectar, clear guava juice blend, clear guava jelly or guava powder. It is basically transparent and slightly coloured pink, yellow or white, depending on the cultivar.

A typical procedure for the manufacture of clarified guava juice is described as follows: The fruit are macerated and treated with a commercial pectic enzyme preparation. The pulp is then passed through a hydraulic-plate-pack press to obtain the cloudy juice, normally over 80 per cent in the yield. The cloudy juice is quickly heated in a plate heat exchanger for enzyme inactivation and then clarified by flowing through a plate or membrane microfilter. Finally, the clarified juice is packed and stored, following procedures similar to those for guava puree or concentrated. For facilitating the filtration process, a filter aid such as bentonite can be added.

Carbonated guava beverage

The clarified guava juice can be converted to a sugar syrup base containing 40 per cent guava juice at 40° Brix and 1 per cent acidity. After dosing 50 ml of this syrup into a glass bottle (200 ml capacity) filled with chilled, 4–6°C (39–43°F), carbonated water at 80 psi (5.6 kg/cm^2) pressure of carbon dioxide gas, the bottle is sealed and pasteurised at 60°C (140°F). The carbonated guava beverage can be stored for 3 months at room temperature maintaining acceptable colour, flavour and overall quality.

Lychee

Lychee (*Litchi chinensis* Sonn.), also known as litchi, is a fruit with a cultivation history of more than 2000 years. It originated in southern China and was introduced to many tropical and subtropical countries later. The lychee is found in most countries of Latin America, the Caribbean, India, Mauritius, Africa, Australia, Israel, the Canary Islands, the Madeira Islands and many other countries. It is also grown in Florida and Hawaii.

Lychee is a nonclimacteric fruit. The harvest season in the Northern Hemisphere is between late May and early August. In the Southern Hemisphere, lychees are harvested between November and February. The ripe fruit is spherical, about 2.5–4 cm in diameter and composed of a reddish, prickly, leather-like pericarp (shell or peel), a white juicy aril (flesh) and a shiny brown seed in the center. The flesh has a pleasant floral flavour and delicious sweet taste.

Studies on fresh lychee handling and preservation have been reviewed by Nip. Fruit rotting and pericarp browning have been the major problems confronted. Many chemicals were tested for the prevention of these problems. Scott dipped lychee in hot 0.05 per cent benomyl solution at 52°C (126°F) for 2 minutes, packed the fruit in punnets, over-wrapped with a PVC film and found that the shelf life at room temperature was extended for one extra week. Sulphur dioxide can also be used to prevent the browning of lychee pericarp and to provide some disease control. Application of chitosan coating may delay pericarp browning through the reduction in the desiccation rate.

Refrigeration also extends the shelf life. However, too low a temperature may accelerate pericarp browning instead. Lee recommended 5°C (41°F) as the best temperature for fresh lychee storage. Jiang and Fu found that lychee fruit stored at 1°C (34°F) and 90 per cent relative humidity and in controlled atmosphere (3–5 per cent oxygen and 3–5 per cent carbon dioxide) maintained good quality for more than 30 days. Lichter sprayed lychee fruit with hot water at 55°C (131°F) for 20 seconds dipped in 4 per cent hydrochloric acid, drained and packed. The shelf life at 18°C (64°F) and 88–92 per cent relative humidity was found to be longer than 35 days.

Canned lychee

Most lychees are consumed as fresh fruit. Some are processed into canned fruit, juice and dehydrated products, especially at the peak production season.

Canned lychee is the most important processed product of lychee. The fruits are washed, peeled (shelled), pitted and filled into No. 2 (307 × 409) enameled cans with a 1-lb tin coating per base box. Then, 30° Brix sucrose syrup and 0.1–0.2 per cent citric acid solution are added as a packing medium to improve the flavour and to lower the product pH to approximately 3.8. The lychee cans are usually exhausted at 80°C (176°F), vacuum-sealed, processed in boiling water for 12 minutes, followed by rapid cooling. An alternative is to process the cans in a high-speed spin cooker at 90.6°C (195°F) for 2–3 minutes, which results in a better quality. Peeling (shelling) and pitting were labour-intensive steps in lychee processing.

Similar to many other fruits and vegetables, pink discolouration occurs in canned lychee. Wu found that sterilisation temperature and pH have strong effects on the colour development. Hwang and Cheng reported that cultivar and maturity also have an influence on the discolouration. The Haak Yip cultivar and unripe fruits are relatively less prone to discolour. Wu successfully isolated flavanone-3-hydroxylase and dihydroquercetin-4-reductase from lychee flesh and concluded that these two enzymes play a key role in the biosynthesis of leucoanthocyanin. He proposed a pathway for the pink discolouration during canning as follows.

After peeling and pitting, the flavonones in mature lychee flesh first get converted into eriodictyol-containing compounds, then are hydrolysed by flavanone-3-hydroxylase to dihydroquercetin-containing compounds and are further reduced to leucocyanidin-containing compounds by dihydroquercetin-4-reductase, when the lychee is heated, the leucocyanidin-containing compounds are converted into cyanidin-containing coloured compounds finally. In the storage of canned lychee, leucocyanidin-containing compounds may develop into pink pigments via some other pathways in addition to the above-described one that prevails in the heating step of canning. Prevention of canned lychee pink discolouration has been studied in several laboratories.

Smith suggested preventing discolouration by packing the lychee in 30° Brix sucrose syrup containing 0.1–0.15 per cent citric acid and restricting the processing time in boiling water to within 10 minutes. Hwang and Cheng reported that shortening the lapse of time between peeling and heating and immersing the lychee flesh in sodium bisulphite solution prior to thermal processing are good measures for reducing the extent of discolouration. Wu and Fang suggested packing the lychee in 20° Brix syrup that contains 0.1–0.2 per cent citric acid. Wu and Chen recommended packing the lychee with syrup at the same Brix and ratio of sugar types as in the lychee flesh.

Lychee juice

Taiwan, South Africa and China are the major lychee juice producers in the world. In Taiwan, Haak Yip is the major cultivar for juice making, simply due to its high availability. The fruits are usually delivered to the factory shortly after harvesting, without much postharvest treatment.

The peeling is a necessary step prior to juice extraction. Pressing of unpeeled lychees obtains a juice with a very bitter taste. The peeling of lychees used to be done by hand. Hand-peeling takes a great deal of labour, delays production and downgrades the quality of juice because it allows time for the formation of precursors of pink pigments and for microbial growth. Therefore, mechanical peeling has become a favourite. Pitting is no longer a stand-alone step in current processing of lychee juice. The peeled lychee fruit with pits inside are directly conveyed to a two-stage, paddle-type pulper-finisher for juice extraction. By proper control of the clearance between paddle and screen on the pulper-finisher, the percentage of broken seeds can be reduced to less than 2 per cent. The seed fragments, if any, can be removed from the juice by the finishing screen.

The pH of lychee juice is adjusted to approximately 4 by the addition of citric acid prior to pasteurisation at 95°C (203°F) for 30 seconds. The pasteurised juice may either be hot-packed in 20–1 tin cans or frozen in 20–1 plastic drums. Lychee juice can also be vacuum concentrated twofold, frozen and shipped overseas in containers at temperature no higher than –18°C (0°F).

Single-strength lychee juice is usually sold as a semiproduct. The juice is often mixed with other juices to make juice blends or diluted into 10–30 per cent lychee juice drinks.

The lychee juice drinks are popular among consumers in Taiwan, China, Japan, South Africa and many southeastern Asian countries.

Mango

The mango (*Mangifera indica* L., family Anacardiaceae) is native to South and Southeast Asia. It is one of the most important tropical and subtropical fruits in terms of production, acreage and popularity. Other major mango-producing countries are China, Mexico, Thailand, Indonesia, Pakistan, Philippines, Nigeria and Brazil.

There are hundreds of mango cultivars grown all over the world. Mangoes can tolerate a wide spectrum of soil and climate conditions, as long as there is no frosting problem. Mangoes are climacteric fruit. They are usually harvested in a mature, but unripe, stage and allowed to ripen in a few days for fresh consumption or for processing into various products, except green mango slices and their derivatives that use unripened fruit as the starting material.

Minimally processed mango slices

Alzamora recommended minimum processes for the making of shelf-stable, high moisture, tropical fruit products. The processes include a mild heat treatment, a slight reduction in water activity and in pH in some cases and the addition of antimicrobial chemicals.

The hurdles in the processing for mango slices that have a shelf life of more than 6 months at room temperature included the reduction of water activity to 0.93 and pH value to 3.3 by immersing in acidified sugar syrup and the addition of potassium benzoate at 1400 ppm and sodium bisulphite at 150 ppm.

Mango puree

Mango puree is the most common semiproduct of this fruit. It can be used in the preparation of jams, jellies, beverages, including nectar, and various dairy and bakery products that contain mango as an ingredient.

Mango fruit that is good for puree processing has flesh with a good taste and colour and is without any objectionable terpeney odour. The consistency of the puree obtained needs to be appealing to the consumer, too. Some cultivars, e.g. 'Totapuri', develop a disagreeable flavour after processing and are not preferred. Some other cultivars, though fibrous, soft and inadequate for fresh consumption, possess high-quality juice and can be processed. Two cultivars that differ widely in sensory quality attributes may be blended together to compensate each other. For example, 'Langra' and 'Chausa' cultivars lack intense colour and are not suitable for processing unless blended with cultivars having more colour, such as 'Dasheri' or 'Bombai Green'.

Peeling

Mango peel constitutes a significant portion of the fruit. The peel weighed 6.5–24.4 per cent of the fresh fruit, while the edible pulp or flesh weighed 32.7–85 per cent. Some reports indicated that complete peeling of mangoes before pulping may not be necessary. However, this statement is true only for certain cultivars of which the peel is thin and yellow to yellowish-orange in colour. With most cultivars, the peel is greenish-yellow, thick and abundant in polyphenols, contamination by peel constituents often results in unacceptable off-taste and discolouration in the puree and accelerated detinning in the canned products.

Mangoes should be thoroughly washed to remove dirt, adhering latex and other foreign matters before peeling. It is preferable to wash them in a soaker-washer fitted with brushes using a detergent and chlorine wash at 20–60 ppm of active chlorine, followed by rinse in a rotary washer.

The applicable methods for peeling mangoes include hand peeling, lye peeling, freeze peeling, hot water peeling and steam peeling. Among these methods, hot water peeling and steam peeling are most often used. Hot water or steam peeling is the most practical method for peeling mangoes. The traditional way is to submerge the fruit in hot water, which needs to be changed intermittently to avoid cross-contamination, at approximately 90°C for 5 minutes in a batch type operation. An improved way is to steam the fruit on a conveyor belt at atmospheric pressure for 2–3 minutes. The heated fruit is cooled in a water bath. A small slit is cut in the peel. The peel is then stripped off by hand.

Pulping

A paddle pulper is used for disintegrating the flesh of the peeled mango, leaving the seed intact. The seeds, the residual peels and a large part of the fibers can be separated from the semiliquid pulp by centrifugation or by pressing through a series of screens, usually at 0.8, 0.6 and/or 0.5 mm pore diameters. The use of an additional finishing screen with a pore diameter smaller than 0.5 mm removes virtually all the fibers and makes the puree smoother and easier to be heat-treated.

Puree yield varies with the thickness of the peel and the size of the seed. Generally speaking, it is about 70 per cent of the weight of fruit.

Depending on the cultivar, cultivation practice, climate condition, ripeness at harvest and postharvest storage and treatment of the fruit, the composition of mango flesh for making puree varies considerably. Normally, the total soluble solids content is in the range between 15° Brix and 20° Brix, but various values between 4° Brix and 27° Brix have been reported. The reported values of titratable acidity vary in the range between 0.1 per cent and 1.1 per cent and the pH values between 2.6 and 5.8. For safety and quality preservation purposes, it is advisable to lower the pH of puree prepared from fruit with low acidity to below 4 by adding citric acid before heat treatment.

Preservation

Mango puree is often preserved by a heat treatment, followed by cool or frozen storage. Sometimes it may also be preserved by freezing without a heating pre-treatment or by aseptic processing and packaging followed by ambient storage.

Prior to the heat treatment, mango puree is usually vacuumed to drive out air. There are a number of heat treatment procedures available for the industry. A popular one that preserves good quality is to heat the fresh puree at 95°C (203°F) for 2 minutes in a heat exchanger, cool immediately, pack in 50–100 kg drums with polyethylene liners and then rapidly freeze and store at –18°C (0°F) or below. Collin showed that minimum safe thermal processes based on pectinesterase inactivation ensure microbiologically safe and organoleptically acceptable mango products. Argaiz recommended a heat treatment at 98.5°C (209.3°F) for 1 minute or its equivalent for the inactivation of pectinesterase in mango puree. The z value of this enzyme was found to be 10.5°C (18.9°F). However, Labib reported the z value at 18.5°C (33.3°F) in a previous research work.

Freezing preservation of unpasteurised mango puree is not good for long-term storage due to the activity of residual enzymes. Acidification may help to maintain the quality to some extent. Mango puree can also be aseptically packaged in bag-in-box and stored at ambient temperature, low-temperature storage preserves better quality though.

Mango puree can be concentrated to reduce the cost in storage and transportation. However, common commercial vacuum evaporators are not able to concentrate the puree beyond 30–32° Brix without severe loss of flavour. For producing good quality mango puree concentrates of higher °Brix, the treatment of serum-pulp separation or enzymatic liquefaction is usually practiced prior to the concentration process.

Mango jams

The procedures for the making of jams are basically similar among common fruits, including the mango. The pH value of jelled mixture is maintained in a range between 2.8 and 3.4. The sucrose content is formulated to 65° Brix or higher. The total pectin content is adjusted to approximately 0.4 per cent for attaining a desirable gel strength.

Collin described the making of mango jam as follows:

Pectin is mixed with a small amount of sugar, mango puree and the balance of the sugar are mixed thoroughly and heated to 103°C (218°F), citric acid solution and the pectin-sugar mixture are added to the mango-sugar mixture and heated to 106°C (222°F), the jam is poured hot into jars, the jars are sealed, inverted for the residual heat to sterilise the lids and then returned to their upright position before the jam sets.

Papaya

The papaya (*Carica papaya* L.) is native to eastern Central America and now distributed throughout the tropical areas in the world. The leading production country is Brazil, followed by Nigeria, Mexico, India and Indonesia, etc.

Papaya puree

Papaya puree is the major semiproduct of papaya as a food. Many papaya products, such as juice, nectar, jams, jellies, fruit roll and leather, can be made from papaya puree.

The processing of papaya puree was difficult in the past. Two problems, product gelation and off-flavour development, often encountered and limited the production. Stafford found that gelation, which is a result of pectinesterase activity, can be prevented by heat treatment in advance. Adding sucrose to the puree to bring up the total solids content to 26° Brix or acidifying the puree to pH 3.4 inhibits gelation, too. Heat inactivation also stops enzymatic off-flavour reactions. However, the off-flavour in papaya puree basically results from the contamination by peel, seed, seed sac and latex materials. Sorting out these materials quickly and completely during processing prevents the occurrence of unpleasant flavour and bitter taste in the product. Brekke developed a process to produce high-quality papaya puree devoid of gelation and off-flavour. The procedure is described as follows:

Ripe, whole papayas are steamed for 2 minutes to inactivate enzymes in the peel, to coagulate peel latex and to soften the fruit, then they are cooled by spraying with water, the cooled fruit are sliced by rotary blades at 2.5 cm clearance, the slices are fed into a crusher-scraper to loosen the pulp and seeds from the peel, the whole mass is fed to a centrifugal separator with 4-mm perforations on the centrifugal basket, to separate the peel and most of the seeds from the pulp, the blend of pulp and those seeds that pass through the centrifugal basket is fed into a pulper equipped with rubber paddles (which are aligned at a 25° angle to the line of product flow and are rotated at a moderate speed to prevent breakage of the seeds) and a 0.8 mm screen to obtain the seed-free puree, citric acid is added to the puree to reduce the pH to about 3.4, which inhibits gelation, flavour deterioration and microbial growth, the acidified puree is finished by a paddle finisher equipped with a 0.5-mm screen, pasteurised at 96°C (205°F) for 2 minutes by a plate heat exchanger, cooled to 29°C (84°F), packed and then stored at –23°C (–9°F) or below.

Canned papaya products

Canned papaya chunks or slices are popular ingredients in fruit salad preparation. Fully ripened, soft papaya fruit are ideal for fresh consumption but not suitable for canning. The fruit to be canned are in a green, mature or semi-ripe stage.

Papaya chutney

Ripe papayas are washed, peeled and deseeded. The flesh is chopped finely, added with vinegar, lemon juice, vegetable oil, honey and spices and then heated to boil. Reduce the temperature slightly to allow simmer for 40 minutes with occasional stirring. After cooling, the product is obtained.

AVOCADOS

The avocado is a subtropical evergreen tree. They grow best on well-drained soil, free from extreme temperatures—temperatures over 30°C and lower temperatures below 5°C (40°F). Avocado trees can grow on a great variety of soils, ranging from light to heavy. The roots are particularly sensitive to poor aeration. In general, the trees are sensitive to the salinity of irrigation water, 120–150 ppm chlorides will cause leaf burn. The tree root system is superficial.

The quality of the fruit on the tree depends upon many factors, including grove maintenance, i.e. pest control programme, regular and sufficient irrigation and proper fertilisation. Damage to the tree and the fruit could also be caused by frosts or freezes. The fruit looks normal, but after cutting the fruit near the stem end, brown dots are clearly visible. This indicates vascular bundle discolouration due to freezing temperatures. Temperatures above 30°C (86°F) will cause scorching of the fruit in the form of dark scars on the fruit surface.

Avocados that turn brown rapidly are not suitable for processing. Rapid discolouration may occur due to unknown reasons like physiological stress conditions in the grove—either an excess or deficiency of some trace element in the soil. Fruit should be free of open cracks, deep insect damage (under the skin), fresh unhealed mechanical damage, sun scorch, fungi and mould damage, rodent or bird scarring, desiccation stem out or soft spots.

Ripening

The avocado is a climacteric fruit, meaning its respiration pattern of CO_2 production rises after harvesting from 40 mg/kg/hr. to a peak of 170 mg/kg/hr. at 21°C (70°F). This was associated with fruit softening by Biale. Plant researchers also pointed out that the length in days of the lag period (time until the onset of the climacteric rise) depends on the state of maturity.

Ripening does not take place on the tree: it starts after the fruit is harvested. The rate depends on the physiological maturity of the avocados, the temperature, the levels of oxygen, carbon dioxide and humidity in the room atmosphere. There is some confusion regarding the word ripe. Most fruits are considered ripe when they are mature enough to be consumed, however, avocados and bananas, to be palatable, must go through an additional process that is called ripening (softening and flavour change).

Another change during ripening, which is typical of Hass avocados, is the colour change of the peel. The peel changes from green to black. Another phenomenon in this variety of avocados is that early fruit has a small peel colour change and remains green after ripening. As the fruit becomes more mature, it turns brown and approximately two months from the start of the season, all fruit peel turns black.

This ripening process is especially important for the manufacture of processed products. By having controlled ripening, the plant will be able to have better yield, a more uniform final product, and a more desirable viscosity. The following are the main steps in ripening:

1. The fruit is cooled to 5°C (40°F).
2. The fruit is heated to 22°C ± 2°C (71°F).
3. Ethylene gas is applied to the room.
4. After 2 to 5 days, when the fruit is soft, it is again cooled to 5°C (40°F).

A good ripening room should have a good distribution of air—either cold or hot. Uniform temperature in every part of the room is important to achieve a uniformly ripened fruit. Other important factors are good ventilation and high humidity (80–90 per cent).

It is also a common practice by the California avocado packers to pre-condition the fruit before shipping to the fresh market. This 1 to 2 days treatment of avocados with ethylene triggers a faster and more uniform ripening at the supermarket level, as well as the restaurant level.

Avocado Browning

One of the major problems in processing avocados is the rapid discolouration of the product. The industry has tried many ways to overcome this problem. The first step was variety selection based on the rate of discolouration. Varieties that discolour rapidly are not used in processing. For example, Zutano, which is an early variety in California, discolours within minutes after it is cut open.

This rapid rusty red discolouration also happens in some years with Fuerte, another green skin variety. Hass's slow rate of discolouration is one of many reasons why it became the preferred variety for processing. The chemical reactions involved in the oxidation process are outlined below:

Oxidation process

1. Monophenol + O_2 + AH_2 → *O*-Dihydroxyphenol + H_2O + A (AH is a reducing agent).
2. *O*-dihydroxyphenol + ½ O_2 → *O*-Quinone + H_2O.
3. *O*-quinone + O_2 + amino acids → dark polymers (melanin).

The enzyme catalysing the first and second reactions is polyphenol oxidase, commonly called PPO. The third reaction is an oxidative polymerisation reaction. Other known factors that affect the browning rate are: location of the avocado grove, dry matter and oil content, levels of calcium, zinc, iron and copper.

Frozen Avocado Products

Avocado sauce process flow

Avocado sauce processing is the same as guacamole up to pulp extraction, the next step is high shear blending of pulp with water, gums, thickeners, and spices. A thick sauce should have 8000–12000 centipoise viscosity as measured by a Brookfield viscometer spindle number 4. The sauce is pumped to a filler and filled into either polyethylene ½-gal jugs or ½-gal milk cartons, the product is then blast frozen, cased in, sealed, and stored at –18°C (–0°F).

Avocado halves and slices

Avocado halves are produced from selected Hass avocados, which are ripened to a firm stage. The avocados are hand-cut, the seed and peel removed, sprayed or dipped in an antioxidant solution and then rapidly frozen. After freezing, they are packed in high-barrier multilayer co-extruded bags with nitrogen atmosphere. The bags are cased in cases sealed and stored at –18°C (0°F) in a warehouse.

High-pressure Processed

High-pressure processing enables the product to stay fresh with minimum flavour deterioration. This product is very well accepted in the food service market as well as the retail market. The shelf life of the product is 30 days at refrigeration temperature. The high-pressure treatment kills *Listeria monocytogenes*, *Escherichia coli* and yeast and mould. The Gram-positive population is more tolerant to high-pressure treatment, except for *L. monocytogenes*. The drastic reduction of bacterial flora present including spoilage bacteria, yeast and mould enables the product to have 30 days shelf life. However, high pressure processing also has some limitations. Although the taste is fresher than the frozen guacamole during the normal season, the quality of the Mexican avocado deteriorates during the summer months and therefore the high-pressure product will be inferior in appearance, colour and flavour. This new technology does not inactivate the polyphenoloxidase enzyme that causes the avocado to turn brown. Once the vacuum package is opened, the product will discolour within 24 hr.

Dehydrated Avocado Products

The process of dehydrating avocado is done either with a spray dryer—like milk powder—or by drum drying. These products do not have a big market. The main drawbacks of this product are a lack of colour (pale green) and a chalky off-flavour. The off-flavour can be masked with proper spices. A ready mix of guacamole may be produced, but it will have inferior flavour and colour. Another use of dehydrated avocados is in dog food as an ingredient rich in oil.

Avocado Oil

Avocado belongs to Lauraceae family. It is cultivated widely in all tropical and sub-tropical regions. More than 200 varieties have been identified. The pulp (60–75 per cent of the fruit) has a remarkably high oil content. Depending on the varieties, it varies between 5 and 30 per cent. The avocado kernel, on the other hand, has very little oil (≤ 2 per cent). This oil can be used in seasoning, but considering its high cost, it is usually not used for such purposes in Europe. Part of this oil is used in the soap industry but most of it is used by the pharmaceutical and cosmetic industries.

Extraction of avocado oil is difficult because the oil is found in a very fine emulsion in the fruit cells. Two processes exit: either processing fresh fruit or dried fruit. Treatment of fresh fruit is not economically advantageous and produces an oil loaded with water, making the storage of the oil difficult. For these reasons, the process on dried fruit is preferred: the fruits are cut into slices and dried (80°C, 24–48 hr), after dehydration (residual humidity: 5–9 per cent) the pulp is pressed and/or solvent extracted. Crude oil which is viscous, strongly coloured, 'winterised' at 5°C has to be refined (giving a yellow or yellowish green coloured oil) for its main applications.

The residue obtained after oil extraction (deoiled pulp) has very little nutritive value. A product with strong antibiotic properties has been obtained from the avocado's kernel. Since, avocado oil has a particularly high unsaponifiable content, many industrial processes have been developed to extract this fraction (concentration by molecular distillation, then purification by saponification and counter-current solvent extraction). The unsaponifaible matter of avocado is used in many cosmetic formulations.

The oil is extracted by various methods:

1. Solvent extraction from a dehydrated avocado: This method extracts almost all the oil present. It also enables one to extract various fractions that are used in the pharmaceutical industry. One known fraction is the unsaponifiables. Extracting this way may be difficult due to EPA rules that prohibit release of solvent fumes into the atmosphere.
2. Hydraulically: Expressing the oil from the dried avocado flakes. This is also a natural way, but the yields are very low.
3. Centrifugation or mechanical way of oil extraction: This method requires soft fruit. The recovery is only about 50 per cent of oil content. Oil expressed by centrifugation is more desirable because it is free from solvent residues or flavour deterioration due to ultra-high temperatures.

The oil extracted by these methods is in its crude stage. In order to increase its value either for cosmetics use or for food consumption, the avocado oil must be refined. By refining, we mean the removal of off-flavours, free fatty acids, and most of the chlorophyll, phosphatides and waxes. The refining process will include alkali treatment, clay bleaching, deodourisation, and winterisation.

Food consumption

Avocados contain large amounts of oleic acid (69–74 per cent), which is considered a desirable mono-unsaturated fatty acid. The oil is also quite stable. Avocado oil has a high smoke point 255°C (490°F), which makes it possible to use the oil for frying and baking in addition to using it on fresh salads. It is also consumed (in Japan) in gelatine capsules by swallowing.

Chapter 27

Vegetables

INTRODUCTION

All living creatures, including humans, depend on nature for their food. Humans are not only hunters and gatherers, but also farmers. We live from hunting and fishing, agriculture and animal husbandry. Most of our food consists of agricultural products, which are usually seasonal and spoil quickly. To make food available throughout the year, humans have developed methods to prolong the storage life of products to preserve them. The rotting process can be postponed by adding preservatives, optimising storage conditions or applying modern techniques.

Fruits and vegetables provide an abundant and inexpensive source of energy, body-building nutrients, vitamins and minerals. Their nutritional value is highest when they are fresh, but it is not always possible to consume them immediately. During the harvest season, fresh produce is available in abundance, but at other times it is scarce. Moreover, most fruits and vegetables are only edible for a very short time, unless they are promptly and properly preserved.

Vegetables are parts of plants, which can be consumed either, raw or processed in some way. Vegetables such as tomatoes, cucumbers, peppers, eggplant, lady's finger and sweet corn are in fact seed bearing fruits. Based on consumer acceptance and usage, vegetables are those plants parts consumed with the main course of a meal while fruits are commonly consumed as dessert.

Vegetables, apart from providing nutrition, contribute to the appetising colour, texture and flavour to the food. Vegetables are classified into groups based on their growing season or based on the parts of plants consumed and shape or appearance, but none of the classifications is either complete or satisfactory.

Root vegetables include carrot, radish, beetroot, parsnip and turnip. Carrot is rich in carotene a precursor for Vitamin A. Beetroot (garden beet) is similar to sugar beet with a high content of sugar. Radish (mooli) in white or red colour has a pungent flavour. These vegetables are consumed as raw vegetables as salad, cooked or pickled in vinegar. Fruit vegetables include tomato, bell pepper (capsicum), okra (lady's finger), egg plant (brinjal) and chow-chow. Cole crops grow best in cool moist conditions. These vegetables are rich in calcium and Vitamin C. This group includes cabbage, knol-khol, cauliflower and Brussels sprouts. Cabbage (ghobi) consists of thick overlapping leaves attached to a short thick stem to form a spherical or oval shaped head. It is consumed as raw shredded cabbage, in the form of salad, as cooked curry or pickled (Sauerkraut). Cauliflower (phul ghobi) has a single stem bearing a large rounded flower head of creamy white flower buds. It is used in soup, curry and in mixed vegetable pickles. Tubers are rich in carbohydrates and can be stored for long periods. Potato, sweet potato, tapioca (cassava), yarn and arrowroot belong to this group. Bulbs are underground buds having fleshy leaves and include onion, garlic and leek which have a characteristic pungent flavour. Curcurbits include cucumber, pumpkin, gourds such as bitter gourd, ribbed or ridged gourd, sponge gourd, snake gourd, bottle gourd and white or ash gourd. Cucumber is consumed as raw vegetable, in salads and in pickled form. Gourds and pumpkin are usually consumed mostly as cooked curries. Leafy vegetables or greens from many plants are part of Indian diet. These include agathi, amaranth spinach, spinach beet, celery, curry leaves, fenugreek, lettuce, parsley and purslane. Other vegetables widely consumed in India include drumstick, leguminous vegetables such as peas and beans and mushroom.

Most vegetables are high in water (>80 per cent) and low in protein (3–3.5 per cent) and fat contents. Legumes such as peas and beans have relatively higher protein content and sweet corn has a higher fat content. The dry matter content of most vegetables vary between 10 and 20 per cent. Carbohydrates (3–20 per cent), nitrogenous compounds (1–5 per cent), minerals (1 per cent), crude fibre (1 per cent) and fats (0.1–0.3 per cent) constitute the dry matter. They also contain vitamins and flavour substances. Glucose and fructose (0.3–4 per cent) and sucrose (0.1–12 per cent) are main carbohydrate constituents. Starch occurs as a storage polysaccharide particularly in tuber vegetables. Other polysaccharides such as cellulose, hemicellulose and pectins contribute to the firmness of the tissues.

The major constituent of nitrogenous substances include proteins, particularly enzymes such as oxidoreductases (lipoxygenases, phenoloxidases, peroxidases), hydrolases (proteases, glycosidases, esterases), transferases (transaminases), lyases (glutamic acid decarboxylase) and ligases (glutamine synthetase). Besides, free amino acids, peptides and enzyme inhibitors are also present. Malic and citric acids occur in most vegetables while oxalic acid is present in relatively large amounts in green beans, rhubarb, Brussels sprouts and red beet. Most of the vegetables contain ascorbic acid, riboflavin and thiamine. The main minerals include potassium followed by calcium, iron, sodium and magnesium with anions such as phosphate, chloride and carbonate. Phenolic compounds, hydroxy acids, flavones and flavonols also occur in vegetables. Aroma of vegetables is due to a single character impact compound as in the case of potato (2-isopropyl-3-methoxypyrazine), cabbage (dimethyl sulphide), onion (thriopropanal-S-oxide), garlic (di-2propenyldisulphide), red beet (geosmin) or mixtures of flavour compounds. Pigments include chlorophyll, betalains and carotenoids.

HARVEST OF VEGETABLES

Vegetables during their growth and maturation on the plants undergo changes in their colour, texture and flavour day by day. Harvesting is timed so as to capture the peak qualities in vegetables. Freshly harvested vegetables have the desired plumpness, succulence, crispness attributed to a high degree of turgor. Cell turgor in vegetables and fruits is due to osmotic force, which influences the texture. The cell walls in the living or freshly harvested vegetables and fruits have varying degrees of elasticity and selective permeability to water and small molecules due to osmotic pressure within the cell.

The selective permeability and elasticity are responsible for the desirable textural characteristics. After harvest, the vegetables lose their peak quality quickly depending on post harvest practice of storing and further processing. For example, sweet corn loses its sweetness by about 25 per cent in one day after harvest, partly due to conversion of sugars into starch and partly due to continued respiration wherein sugars are utilised for energy.

A similar loss of sweetness is observed in peas and lima beans. Some vegetables liberate heat, even after harvest, affecting their flavour and texture characteristics as well as facilitating the growth of micro-organisms. Harvested vegetables lose water due to transpiration, respiration and physical drying resulting in loss of weight, wilting of leafy vegetables, loss of plumpness of fleshy vegetables. Therefore, cooling of vegetables by cold water spray soon after their harvest slows down the degradative changes in vegetables.

PRE-PROCESSING OPERATIONS

Vegetables can be processed in different ways including canning, freezing, freeze-drying, pickling and dehydration. The operations involved in the processing depend on the type of vegetable and the method to be used. After harvest, the processing steps involved in canning are washing, sorting and grading, peeling, cutting and sizing, blanching, filling and brining (brining is very important for filling weight and heat transfer), exhausting (helps maintain high vacuum, exhaust temperature in the center of the can should be about 71°C), sealing, processing (heating cycle), cooling, labelling and storage.

Every change in food that causes it to lose its desired quality and eventually become inedible is called food spoilage or rotting. As noted earlier, this chapter focuses specifically on fruits and vegetables. As long as they are not harvested, their quality remains relatively stable—if they are not damaged by disease or eaten by insects or other animals. However, the harvest cannot be postponed indefinitely: when the time is right, it is time to act. As soon as the fruits and vegetables are cut off from their natural nutrient supply, their quality begins to diminish. This is due to a natural process that starts as soon as the biological cycle is broken by harvesting. Once it is harvested, the agricultural product is edible for only a limited time, which can vary from a few days to weeks. The product then begins to spoil or 'rot'. We distinguish between various types of spoilage:

1. Physical spoilage.
2. Physiological ageing.
3. Spoilage due to insects or rodents.
4. Mechanical damage.
5. Chemical and enzyme spoilage.
6. Microbial spoilage.

Physical spoilage is caused for example by dehydration. Physiological ageing occurs as soon as the biological cycle is broken through harvesting. Neither process can be prevented, but they can be delayed by storing the agricultural products in a dry and draft-free area at as low a temperature as possible.

Insects and rodents can cause a lot of damage. Not only by eating the products, but also by passing on micro-organisms through their hair and droppings. The affected parts of the plants are then especially susceptible to diseases.

Chemical and enzyme spoilage occurs especially when vegetables and fruit are damaged by falling or breaking. Such damage can release enzymes that trigger chemical reactions. Tomatoes become soft, for example, and apples and other types of fruit turn brown. The fruit can also become rancid. The same processes can also be triggered by insects: the fruit becomes damaged, which causes enzymes to be released. Enzymes can be deactivated by heating the fruit or vegetables. The same effect can be achieved by making the fruit or vegetables sour or by drying them, but the enzymes become active again as soon as the acidity is reduced or water is added. The peel of a fruit or vegetable provides natural protection against micro-organisms. As soon as this shield is damaged by falling, crushing, cutting, peeling or cooking, the chance of spoilage increases considerably. Crushing occurs most often when fruits or vegetables are piled up too high. To prevent harvested products from spoiling, they can be preserved: physiological ageing and enzyme changes are then stopped and micro-organisms are prevented from multiplying on the product. To retain the desired quality of a product longer than if it were simply stored after harvesting, it must be preserved. To preserve food it must first be treated, with the goal of stopping physiological ageing and enzyme changes and preventing the growth of micro-organisms. Before discussing the specific treatment methods, we will first focus on the subject of micro-organisms. What are micro-organisms? Why are they dangerous? How can you prevent them from making you sick? The answers to these questions will help you understand the steps required to safely preserve food.

Micro-organisms and Factors Affecting their Growth

Micro-organisms are very small, one-celled animals. There are three types: bacteria, molds and yeasts. Bacteria and yeasts cannot be seen with the naked eye, but molds are often visible because they form visible thin threads (filaments) or a solid cluster. Just like humans, micro-organisms require certain minimum living conditions. They cannot survive without:

1. Sufficient water.
2. Oxygen.
3. The right degree of acidity.
4. Nutrients.
5. The right temperature.

Water is necessary for maintaining many physical processes. Where there is a shortage or lack of water micro-organisms cannot grow, such as in dried legumes. Drying is therefore one way to prevent spoilage. Meat and fish do not have to be 100 per cent dry in order to preserve them. By adding salt, the remaining water becomes unsuitable for micro-organisms. The same effect can be achieved by adding sugar to fruit. Enzymatic spoilage is also inhibited by drying.

Most micro-organisms need oxygen. If there is a shortage of oxygen, it is difficult for bacteria to survive, let alone multiply. But there are always a few that manage to survive. As soon as the oxygen supply is increased, these remaining bacteria will again grow and multiply. Some types of micro-organisms even thrive in an oxygen-poor environment.

Bacteria grow best in an environment that is not too acidic. Less acidic products are therefore especially susceptible to bacterial spoilage. Examples of such products are meat, eggs, milk and various types of vegetables. Beer, yoghurt, wine, vinegar and fruit are less sensitive because they are more acidic. Adding acidity to products slows down the process of microbial spoilage. The degree of acidity is measured as a pH level. A neutral product like milk has a pH of 7, meat has a pH of about 6, carrots have a pH of 5 and oranges about 4. The more acidic a product is, the lower the pH value will be.

Just like humans, micro-organisms also need nutrients: sugars, proteins, fats, minerals and vitamins. These are rarely in short supply, because they can be found in all food products. To thrive, micro-organisms need a temperature of between 5° and 65°C. At temperatures above 65°C it becomes very difficult for them to survive, and they definitely die if boiled, as long as they are boiled for a certain length of time, such as 10 minutes.

When heated, the micro-organisms slowly die off, but not all at the same time. Heating at temperatures lower than 100°C thus has to be sustained for a longer period. The growth of micro-organisms is also slowed down significantly at temperatures between 0 and 5°C (as in a refrigerator), which makes it possible to store the food products for a few additional days. At temperatures below 0°C microbial growth is stopped completely, but the micro-organisms themselves remain alive. They will become active again as soon as the temperature rises above 0°C. To preserve food, it is sometimes necessary to make drastic changes to the micro-organisms' living conditions. We can remove water (drying), increase the acidity, or first heat the products (to kill the bacteria) and then store them in air-tight containers to prevent oxygen from entering (preserving/canning).

Micro-organisms Grow Differently on Vegetables and Fruit

Vegetables and fruit have a lot in common. But there are also important differences, which determine the type of spoilage they are most susceptible to. Damaged fruits, which are usually somewhat acidic, are very susceptible to the growth of yeasts and molds. Vegetables are generally less acidic, and their spoilage is usually caused by bacteria. Though not visible to the naked eye, bacteria can still be present in large numbers.

Types of Micro-organisms Grow on What Products

1. Molds can be found on almost all food products. They are often very visible and can significantly alter the taste of the products. They grow the best in low temperatures in an acidic environment and on dry products such as grains and bread. Some molds produce poisonous substances, especially in moist seeds such as peanuts, corn and soyabeans.
2. Yeasts can also cause food to spoil. They prefer low temperatures and acidic products.
3. Bacteria can grow on almost all types of fresh food that is not too acidic: meat, fish, milk and vegetables. One type of bacteria carries a kind of seed, called a spore. Spores can survive at a temperature of 100°C, even though the bacteria themselves die. Once the temperature drops, new bacteria can grow out of the spores. To kill the spores, they must be exposed to a temperature of 121°C. This is called sterilisation.

EFFECTS OF MICRO-ORGANISMS ON FRUITS AND VEGETABLES

Micro-organisms take from food products the various substances they need to survive and multiply. Their secreted waste products can have either a negative or positive effect on the affected food and the humans who eat it.

Positive Effects of Micro-organisms in Food

The waste products secreted by some micro-organisms can have a positive effect on food. Lactic acid bacteria, for example, are used to make cheese and yoghurt from milk, and sauerkraut from white cabbage. Molds are used to make tempeh from soyabeans, and yeasts are used to make beer and bread. These substances influence the taste and structure of the food products and generally increase their shelf-life. The products can be kept longer because the desired micro-organisms decrease the food's pH level or because they are present in such huge numbers that other micro-organisms have no chance to grow. This use of micro-organisms for the preparation of food is called fermentation.

Negative Effects of Micro-organisms in Food

Sometimes the negative effects of bacteria are clearly apparent, such as when milk has turned sour and curdled, when meat is covered in slime, when molds and gasses have formed, and when food has a distinctly putrid smell. However, food spoilage is not always this obvious. There are bacteria whose presence in food does not always cause a change in its taste or appearance. In any case, it is important to avoid eating rotten food, because it can make a person seriously ill. Eating rotten food can cause contamination or poisoning. A food contamination occurs when a person consumes a large number of living micro-organisms in a meal. These can multiply rapidly in the person's gastrointestinal tract and severely disturb the digestive system. The result is often diarrhoea and sometimes also bleeding. The symptoms appear between 3 and 24 hr after eating the rotten food. A food contamination can be prevented by frying or boiling the food thoroughly, since sufficient heating will kill the micro-organisms.

Food poisoning occurs when a person consumes food containing the poisonous waste products secreted by the bacteria. Heating the food does not help in this case: the bacteria will be killed, but the poisonous waste will remain unharmed. Both food poisoning and food contaminations can be *lethal,* but usually they only make a person sick.

Micro-organisms Come in Contact with Fruits and Vegetables

Spoilage caused by yeasts, molds and bacteria develops slowly and is not always noticeable. The most important sources of microbial contaminations are sand, water, air, and pests such as insects and rodents. Food products can also be infected by people. Micro-organisms are everywhere around us. To prevent them from reaching our food in great numbers, it is important to work as hygienically as possible when handling fruits and vegetables, for example.

The following practices are therefore recommended:

1. Wash your hands thoroughly with hot water and soap before beginning to prepare food.
2. Make sure that kitchen utensils and appliances are well cleaned and disinfected.
3. Always store food in a clean place.
4. Use herbs and spices as little as possible, because they are an important source of contamination.
5. Use clean and pure salt only—if the salt is not pure, heat it on a dry, metal sheet above the fire.
6. Allow only clean drinking water to come in contact with fruits and vegetables.
7. Never allow anyone who is sick or has open wounds to come in contact with food that is to be preserved.

Sorting and Grading

This operation is done using a roller grader, air blower or any mechanical device, followed by sorting on conveyor bells. Electronic sorting is commonly used recently to remove vegetables affected by diseases and insects.

Washing

Vegetables are washed to remove not only field soil end surface micro-organisms, but also fungicides, insecticides and other pesticides. There are laws specifying the maximum allowed level of contaminant. In order to remove dirt, insects and small debris, vegetables are rinsed with water or with detergent in some cases. Mechanically harvested tomatoes, potatoes, red beets and leafy vegetables are washed with fruit grade detergents. The choice of washing equipment depends on the size, shape and fragility of the particular type of vegetable. Flotation cleaners can he used for peas and other small vegetables, whereas fragile vegetables such as asparagus may be washed by gentle spraying while being transported on conveyer belts.

Peeling

Several methods are used to remove skins from vegetables including lye, steam and direct name. Lye peeling of mechanically harvested tomatoes and potatoes is a common practice. Vegetables with loosened skins are jel washed with water to remove skins and residual sodium hydroxide. Steam is used to peel vegetables with thick skins such as red beets and sweet potatoes, whereas for onions and peppers direct flame or hot gases in rotary tube flame peelers are used.

Cutting and Trimming

Cutting, stemming, pitting or coring depends on the type of vegetable. Asparagus spears are cut to precise lengths. The most fibrous part is used for soup and other healed products where heat tenderises them. Green beans are cut by machine into several different shapes along the length of the vegetable. Brussels sprouts are trimmed by hand by pressing the base against a rapidly rotating knife. Olives are pined by aligning them in small cups and mechanically pushing plungers through the olives.

Blanching

The purpose of blanching is to inactivate the enzymes present in the vegetables. Since many vegetables don't receive a high temperature heat treatment, heating to a minimal temperature before processing or storing inactivates the activity of enzymes responsible for changes in the texture, colour, flavour and nutritional quality of the produce. Several enzymes are responsible for the loss of quality in vegetables.

The blanching process also reduces the microbial load of vegetables and renders packaging into containers easier. To evaluate the effectiveness of blanching, indicator enzymes such as catalase and peroxidase are traditionally used. The reason for using indicators is that blanching is not a process of indiscriminate heating: too little heating is ineffective, whereas heating too much negatively impacts the freshness of certain vegetables. The choice of an indicator depends on the vegetable being processed. For example lipoxygenase may be an ideal indicator for peas and beans. The problem with using peroxidase as a universal indicator is that it sometimes overestimates heat requirements, which may vary from one product to another.

Blanching or precooking is done by immersing fruits or vegetables in water at a temperature of 90°–95°C. Exposing them to steam is also possible. The result is that fruits and vegetables become somewhat soft and the enzymes are inactivated. Leafy vegetables shrink in this process and some of the micro-organisms die. Blanching is done before a product is dried in order to prevent unwanted colour and odour changes and an excessive loss of vitamins. Fruit that does not change colour generally does not need to be blanched. Onions and leek are not at all suited for blanching.

Blanching is quite simple. The only thing you need is a large pan with a lid and a metal, or in any case heat-resistant, colander. Place the fruit or vegetable in the colander (a linen cloth with a cord will also do) and immerse this in a pan with sufficient nearly boiling water to cover the food completely. Leave the colander in the pan for a few minutes and turn the food occasionally to make sure that it is heated evenly. Immediately after the colander is removed from the pan the food has to be rinsed with cold, clean running water. Make sure that the extra water can run off. If no faucet is available, a container with drinking-water can also be used, as long as the water is cold and clean. During the blanching process, it is important to monitor the time and the water temperature.

The disadvantage of this blanching method is that many vitamins are lost in the hot water. Steaming is therefore a better alternative. Only a small amount of water has to be added to the pan and brought to the boil. Make sure that the fruit or vegetable in the colander is touched by the steam but not by the water.

Drying Potatoes and Tomatoes

Drying potatoes

Choose potatoes that are firm and undamaged. Peel the potatoes, wash them under the faucet or in a container with clean water, and cut them in slices about 3 mm thick. Immerse the slices in boiling water, let them cook for 3–5 minutes, rinse them off with clean water, dry them with a clean cloth and place them on a piece of black plastic or on trays to dry for 2 to 3 days in the sun. Turn them regularly, about 2 to 3 times per day. The drying process is finished when the potatoes are hard and crumble easily when squeezed in your hand. The dried potatoes have to be soaked in water before they can be consumed.

Drying tomatoes

Use firm, not too ripe, undamaged tomatoes. Wash and then cut them in half or in quarters (or in smaller pieces), and remove the seeds. Blanch the tomato pieces for one minute at 90°C and then allow them to cool off quickly under cold, running water. Once cooled, they have to be immersed for 10 minutes in water to which lemon juice has been added. Strain and then dry them with a clean cloth. Place the tomatoes on a piece of black plastic and let them dry in the sun. To make sure that they dry evenly, turn them 2 to 3 times per day. Place them under a shelter in the evenings. After 2 to 3 days they will feel brittle, and the drying process will have been completed.

PRESERVING VEGETABLES WITH SALT AND/OR VINEGAR

Adding salt is one of the oldest ways to preserve food, except fruit, especially in areas that have easy access to inexpensive salt. Since salt absorbs much of the water in food, it makes it difficult for micro-organisms to survive. There are two salting methods. One uses a lot of salt, and the other only a small amount. The disadvantage of using a lot of salt is that it has a very negative impact on the taste of the food. To overcome this problem, the food can be rinsed or soaked in water before it is eaten, but this also decreases the nutritional value of the food. It is, therefore, advisable to use a lot of salt only when there is a surplus of fresh vegetables and no other preservation method is possible. The use of a small amount of salt is in itself not enough to prevent the growth of bacteria, but it does result in the development of a certain kind of acid-producing bacteria that limits the growth of other bacteria. One example of a product made in this way is sauerkraut, which has a high nutritional value. Another way to preserve vegetables is by adding vinegar.

Preserving with Salt

This section describes the two salting methods and the equipment that is needed. In both cases, the vegetables have to be hygienically prepared. Detailed information lists the methods recommended and the amounts of salt needed per type of vegetable.

Preserving with a large amount of salt

Heavy salting means that approximately 1 part salt is used for 5 parts of vegetables. This gives the vegetables a very salty taste, which makes it necessary for the vegetables to be soaked in water a few times before they can be eaten. The salt can be added as dried granules or as brine (a salt-water solution in various concentrations).

Sometimes a little bit of vinegar also has to be added. Heavy salting is a simple preservation method, and much less labour intensive than preserving with a small amount of salt.

Heavy salting (20–25 per cent): Mix the vegetables and the salt well, using 250 g of salt per kg of vegetables. Fill crocks with the mixture of vegetables and salt, cover with muslin cloth, a pressure plate and a weight. Add brine (250 g of salt per litre of water) until the pressure plate is just submerged. After about two weeks the salted product must be repacked into smaller jars. These jars should only be big enough to contain enough for one meal, as contamination can occur quickly in an opened jar. Pour the remaining liquid from the crocks over the salted product in the smaller jars, until the vegetables are completely covered. Seal the jars tightly and then store them at as cool a temperature as possible. Before using, the vegetables normally have to be soaked in freshwater for half a day. However, the vegetables lose nutrients during soaking, and this should therefore be avoided where possible, for example, when the vegetables are to be used in soup. Always cook the vegetables before use.

Heavy brine (20 per cent): Fill the crocks or jars with the prepared vegetables (to which no salt has yet been added). Pour the brine (in this case 200 g salt + 65 ml vinegar per litre water) over the vegetables until the pressure plate is just submerged. The required quantity of brine is about half of the volume of the vegetables. To maintain the proper salt concentration sprinkle 200 g of salt per kg of vegetables over the pressure plate. Store the crocks at 21°–25°C and make sure that the vegetables remain under the brine. Add fresh brine (200 g salt + 65 ml vinegar per litre water) when necessary. The vegetables have to be packed into smaller jars after about two weeks. Shell peas and brown beans if this has not been done yet. After repacking the vegetables add the old brine plus fresh brine where necessary so that the vegetables are submerged. Close the jars tightly. Before use, soak the vegetables as described above.

Use of small amounts of salt

Enough salt is added to the vegetables to create appropriate conditions for the growth of micro-organisms that form acids, which will in turn preserve the vegetables. The acid gives the product a special taste that is often appreciated. Add 1 part salt to 20 parts of vegetables as dry salt or as light brine. When vinegar is also added to this light brine less salt is needed. The brine method is easier than the dry salt method, as brine gives an even distribution of salt and vegetables. This even distribution is a necessary condition for success. With the dry salt method, the product will shrink as liquid leaves the product. However, the colour, odour and taste are better when preserved with salt than with brine. The preparation for salted or pickled vegetables is the same as for fresh vegetables, although longer cooking times are sometimes necessary. A description of the equipment needed for salting and the special product data, followed by exact instructions, are given in this section.

Light salting (2.5–5 per cent): One product made according to this method is sauerkraut. Mix the prepared vegetables with salt (25 g salt per kg vegetables, for green beans 50 g salt + 50 ml vinegar per kg). Fill the crocks with the vegetables and salt mixture, packing tightly. Cover the vegetables with several layers of muslin cloth, the pressure plate and the weight. The salt draws the liquid from the vegetables, which should gradually become covered with brine. If this does not happen within a few hours, add light brine (25 g salt per litre of water). Brine for green beans should be made from 50 g salt plus 50 ml vinegar per litre of water. Store the crocks at 20–25°C. The vegetables will undergo an acid fermentation lasting 2–3 weeks. Skim the froth regularly from the surface of the vegetables, using the following method. A white layer of froth will appear on the vegetables after a few days when fermenting with the light brine and light salting methods (sometimes with other methods as well). This is caused by the growth of undesirable micro-organisms. If this froth is left undisturbed it will use up the acid from the fermentation process and can cause an unpleasant smell and taste in the vegetables.

The froth is best removed by first removing the weight and pressure plate and carefully lifting the muslin cloth, keeping the froth on the cloth. Rinse this, together with the pressure plate and weight. This treatment should be carried out every other day, especially when the froth is produced in large quantities.

If the vegetables are to be kept longer than 2–3 weeks, they have to be repacked into smaller containers after fermentation. Vegetables fermented in small jars do not need repacking. The fermented product is packed tightly into glass jars of 0.5–1 litre with a screw cap. Pour brine over the product until it is covered, using the old brine plus, where necessary, fresh brine made from 25 g salt plus 50 ml vinegar per litre of water. Close the jars, but make sure that air can escape by twisting the lid closed and then giving it a quarter turn (back the turn back should be less than one quarter). Heat the jars in a boiling water bath for 25 minutes (for 0.5 litre jars) or 30 minutes (for 1 litre jars). The jars should be tightly closed immediately after heating. This process will pasteurise the contents and stop fermentation.

Light brine (5 per cent): Fill jars or crocks with the prepared vegetables and cover with the muslin cloth, the pressure plate and the weight. Add brine (50 g salt + 50 ml vinegar per litre of water) until the pressure plate is just submerged. You will need about half of the volume of the vegetables in brine. Keep the jars or crocks in a cool place (±15°C). An acid fermentation will take place during the next 2–3 weeks. Remove the froth regularly (as described above). After the fermentation, it is best to repack the vegetables from the crocks into smaller jars with twist lids. Pack the glass jars tightly and add brine until the vegetables are submerged. Where necessary fresh brine can be made using 50 g salt + 50 ml vinegar per litre of water. Close the jars so that air can escape by closing the twist lid and giving it a quarter turn back. Pasteurise the contents by heating the jars in a boiling water bath (25 minutes for 0.5 l jars and 30 minutes for 1 litre jars). Close the jars tightly immediately after heating. The vegetables need only be drained and rinsed before use.

Requirements for Salting

1. Salt: This should be finely granulated and without a drying agent. Disinfect salt that is not pre-packed or that is locally extracted by sprinkling the salt on a metal sheet and heating this over a hot fire.
2. Vinegar: Use white or cider vinegar with a 4–5 per cent concentration.
3. Jars and crocks or other vessels: These can be made of wood, plastic, ceramic, glass or stainless steel. Barrels made from pinewood should be avoided as they can change the taste of the vegetables. The jars must be very clean. Wash them in hot soda water and rinse with clean hot water.
4. Muslin cloth: This is laid over the vegetables and under the pressure plate. The cloth is used to remove the froth from the surface of the vegetables.
5. Pressure plate: This is a plate or grid of wood, ceramic, glass, stainless steel or plastic. A weight is put on top of this to keep the vegetables under the surface of the liquid. The pressure plate should be slightly smaller than the diameter of the vessel. A pressure plate that catches under the neck can be used with certain jars, in which case a weight is not needed.
6. Weight: This is put on the pressure plate to keep the vegetables under the level of the liquid. The weight can be a clean stone or a waterfilled glass jar.
7. Scales and/or measuring cup: These are needed to weigh or measure correct amounts of vegetables, salt and vinegar.
8. Knives: Stainless steel knives are needed to cut the vegetables.

Warning

Peas, beans, sweet corn and greens preserved with salt always have to be cooked for at least 10 minutes before use. Do not eat (even for tasting) preserved vegetables that have not yet been cooked. It is important that the vegetables are always kept submerged below the level of the liquid.

Preserving in Vinegar

Pickling in vinegar or acetic acid can also preserve food. This method of preserving can be done with vegetables (cabbage, beets, onions, cucumber) and fruits (lemons, olives). To obtain a product that can be stored, the food first has to be salted and heated before being put into vinegar. An example of a vinegar preserved food is Atjar Tjampoer.

When ordinary vinegar is used (5 per cent acetic acid in water), it has to be heated in a closed pan. The utensils should be made of enamel or stainless steel, because the high acid concentration of the vinegar corrodes other materials. The vinegar should have a minimum concentration of 4 per cent. (The pH has to be lower than 3.5, this can be checked with pH papers.) The following vinegars can be used: white or cider vinegar (5 per cent acetic acid) or pickling vinegar (concentrations vary up to 100 per cent acetic acid). Vinegar can be homemade by fermenting fruit juice with water and sugar. A kind of wine is produced first, which subsequently turns into vinegar when it comes in contact with the oxygen in the air. Experiment to find the best way to make wine and vinegar using local ingredients.

The following method is generally used: The prepared fruits or vegetables are put into cold heavy brine (200 g of salt per litre of water) for several hours, depending upon the size and shape of the product. Next they are put into a boiling salt solution, boiled, and cooled to 70°–80°C. At this temperature the product (with herbs and spices if necessary, but without the brine) is transferred to jars. The jars are filled to 1.5 cm under the rim and the product is covered with warm vinegar so that all pieces are covered by at least 1 cm of the liquid. The jars are thus filled to 0.5 cm under the rim. The vinegar used must have a final concentration of about 5 per cent after dilution. Always use clean glass jars. Close the jars as quickly as possible and cool quickly in a cool, airy place. Store the products at as cool a temperature as possible. Gherkins are sometimes fermented first (lactic acid fermentation) by storing them for some time in a salt-vinegar solution in crocks, after which they are packed into jars. If you have no previous experience with this process, caution is advised.

PASTEURISATION OF FRUITS AND VEGETABLES

Table 27.1 shows pasteurisation of fruits and vegetables.

Table 27.1: Preparation methods and packing liquid.

Product	*Preparation*	*Add to product when packing into jar, bottle or tin*
Apricots	Peel, split and remove pits	Cold 75% sugar solution
Apple sauce	Make apple sauce, reduce liquid, do not add any sugar	–
Broad beans	Shell, wash, boil in lightly salted water for 5 minutes	Boiling water
Carrots	Clean, wash, boil in lightly salted water for 5 minutes	Boiling water, plus salt to taste
Cauliflower	Cut, wash, boil 1–2 minutes	Boiling water

(Cont'd...)

Product	Preparation	Add to product when packing into jar, bottle or tin
Cherries	Wash, remove stems	Cold water, sugar (sweet cherries need 25% sugar solution, sour cherries need 75% sugar)
Currant juice	Wash currents, remove stems, boil shortly, simmer 1 hr, strain if cloudy	–
Endive	Cut, wash, boil 10 minutes in 1% salt, pack tightly	Boiling water
Green beans	Wash, break, boil 10 minutes in lightly salted water	Boiling water
Mango	Steam 2 minutes, peel, slice, remove pit, pack into flat jars or tins	Boiling water, 40% sugar + 0.25% vinegar
Pears	Hard: peel, cook for ½ hr Soft: peel and cut	Cold water, 40% sugar
Peaches	Peel, halve and remove pits	Cold water, 40% sugar
Peas	Shell, wash, do not boil	Boiling water
Plums	Wash, peel if desired, halve, remove pits	Cold water, 40% sugar
Raspberries	Wash, sprinkle with ¼ weight in sugar, let stand 2 hr before packing	–
Rhubarb	Clean, cut into pieces, sprinkle with ¼ of the product weight in sugar. Pack with juices after 2 hr.	–
Snow peas	Remove ends, wash, boil in lightly salted water for 10 minutes	Boiling water
Spinach	Use fresh leaves only, wash, boil without water for 5 minutes with some salt, pack tightly	Boiling water
Strawberries	Wash, sprinkle with ¼ of product weight in sugar, let stand 2 hr before packing	–
Tomatoes	Wash	Warm salted water (1% salt solution)
Tomato puree	Wash tomatoes, boil for short time, strain, reduce juice	–
Turnip tops	Wash, boil for 5 minutes	Boiling water

Table 27.2 shows pasteurisation times and temperatures.

Table 27.2: Pasteurisation times and temperatures.

Product	Pasteurisation time (jars of 1–2 litre)	Temperature
Apricots	30 min.	80°C
Apple sauce	30 min.	80°C
Broad beans	1½ hr	100°C
Carrots	1½ hr	100°C
Cauliflower	1½ hr, wash, boil 1–2 minutes	100°C
Cherries	30 min.	80°C

(Cont'd...)

Product	Pasteurisation time (jars of 1–2 litre)	Temperature
Currant juice	20 min.	75°C
Endive	1½ hr	100°C
Green beans	1 hr	100°C
Mango	10 min.	91°C
Pears	30 min.	80°C
Peaches	30 min.	80°C
Peas	1½ hr—repeat after 24 hr	100°C
Plums	30 min.	80°C
Raspberries	20 min.	75°C
Rhubarb	30 min.	80°C
Snow peas	1 hr	100°C
Spinach	1½ hr	100°C
Strawberries	30 min.	80°C
Tomato puree	30 min.	80°C
Tomatoes	20 min.	80°C
Turnip tops	1½ hr	100°C

Table 27.3 shows sterilisation times and sealing temperatures.

Table 27.3: Sterilisation times and sealing temperatures.

Product	Sealing temp. °C	Sterilisation times in boiling water bath (minutes)				
		Glass jars		Tins		
		½ l	1 l	0.58 l	0.85 l	3.1 l
Apples	60	20	20	15	15	20
Applesauce	82	5	5	5	5	10
Apricots	60	25	25	15	20	30
Banana	71	15	15	10	12	20
Berries	70	25	25	15	20	30
Cherries	70	25	25	15	20	30
Figs	95	15	15	15	20	30
Fruit puree	71	20	20	15	15	25
Grapefruit	60	10	10	15	18	20
Grapes	77	20	20	12	15	20
Lychee	77	15	15	10	12	20
Oranges	77	10	10	15	18	20
Papaya	77	20	20	15	20	30
Peaches	71	20	20	20	25	40
Pears	71	35	35	30	30	30
Pineapple	75	20	20	20	30	40

(Cont'd...)

Product	*Sealing temp. °C*	*Sterilisation times in boiling water bath (minutes)*				
		Glass jars		*Tins*		
		½ l	*1 l*	*0.58 l*	*0.85 l*	*3.1 l*
Plums	82	20	20	15	22	35
Sauerkraut	71	10	10	15	18	20
Strawberries	77	10	10	15	18	20
Sweet pepper	60	20	20	20	25	–
Tomatoes	60	45	45	45	55	90

Table 27.4 shows preparation and packing aspects of various vegetables.

Table 27.4: Preparation and packing liquid.

Product	*Preparation*	*Add to product when packing into jar, bottle or tin*
Beet root	Wash, blanch 20 minutes, peel (slice if desired)	Boiling salted (1%) water, sugar to taste
Broad beans	Shell, wash, blanch 3 minutes	Boiling salted (2%) water
Green beans	Wash, cut tips, break or cut, for young beans blanch 1½ minutes, for old beans blanch 3 minutes, fill, shaking tin to pack tightly	–
Cabbage	Use only solid cabbages, cut, wash, blanch until soft (±10 minutes)	Boiling salted (1.5%) water
Carrots	Remove tops and tips, blanch 5 minutes, peel and scrape, cut if desired	Boiling salted (2%) water
Celery (roots)	Cut, blanch 4 minutes in 2% citric acid	Boiling salted (1.5%) water
Cauliflower	Cut into small rosettes (soak a few hours in 1% salt), wash, blanch 4 minutes in 0.5% citric acid	Boiling salted (1.5%) water + 0.1 citric acid
Sweet corn	Remove kernels from cob, wash	Boiling salted (0.5%) water
Eggplant	Wash, cut into pieces ±2 cm long	Boiling salted (1%) water
Greens	Sort, wash well, blanch 3 minutes, add boiling liquid to the jars or cans first, then lower greens into the liquid	Boiling salted (3%) water
Mushrooms	Use fresh mushrooms, scrape caps, cut off base, soak in lemon juice 10 minutes, rinse with cold water, blanch 8 minutes	Boiling salted (2%) water + 0.1% citric acid
Okra (fermented)	Remove stems, soak in 2% salt for 18 hr, blanch 3 minutes, cut	Boiling salted (2%) water
Okra (fresh)	Blanch 2 minutes, rinse in cold water immediately	Boiling salted (2%) water

(Cont'd...)

Product	Preparation	Add to product when packing into jar, bottle or tin
Olives	Soak in 1% sodium lye for 6–8 hr, oxidise in the open air, soak again in 1% lye for 6 hr, soak in water 4–6 days until all lye has been removed, then soak 1 day in 1% salt, 1 day in 2% salt and 1 day in 3% salt	Boiling salted (2%) water
Onions	Remove outer skins, blanch 5 minutes	Boiling salted (1.5%) water
Peas	Shell, wash, blanch 2 minutes, rinse with cold water immediately	Boiling salted (2.5%) water
Potatoes	Peel, wash, blanch 5 minutes	Boiling salted (1.5%) water
Pumpkin	Remove dirt, brush, halve, remove seeds, steam for 45 minutes	–
Salsify	Wash, scrape, blanch 5 minutes	Boiling salted (3%) water
Summer squash	Wash, halve, remove seeds, cut into pieces	–
Swedes	Wash, scrape, blanch 10 minutes, pack immediately	Boiling salted (2%) water
Sweet potato	Wash, cook, remove skin while hot, pack while hot	Boiling salted water or boiling sugar water to taste
Yams	Wash, cook, peel, pack while still hot	Boiling water
White beans (soya, kidney)	Peel, wash, blanch 3 minutes, big, dry beans need to be soaked overnight	Boiling salted (2%) water

Table 27.5 shows vegetables preparation and drying conditions.

Table 27.5: Vegetables preparation and drying conditions.

Product	Preparation	Blanching time (min.)	Remarks
Beans	Remove tops and strings, wash, break by hand	5–8 min.	Dried products should not be packed directly in tins or bags
Cabbage	Wash, cut (5 mm thick), blanch immediately	3–4 min.	Moderately long storage
Carrots	Use fresh, young roots, wash, remove tops and tips	None	Cut with stainless steel knife
Chillies capsicum	Select, remove stems, do not cut little chillies, cut big ones into 5–10 mm pieces	None	Sometimes blanched
Eggplant	Remove stem and flower parts, wash and cut in slices 3 mm thick	2–6 min.	–
Garlic	Peel (not necessary when making powder), cut slices 3 mm thick	None	Can be ground to powder
Greens	Select, cut, wash	2 min.	–
Okra	Select, wash, remove stems, slice 6 mm thick	4 min.	Rinse after blanching

(Cont'd...)

Product	*Preparation*	*Blanching time (min.)*	*Remarks*
Onions	Peel, cut slices 3 mm thick	None	Can be ground to powder
(Sweet) potatoes	Wash, peel, remove eyes, slice 2–3 mm thick, dip in lemon juice to prevent brown discolouration	4–6 min.	Irish potatoes can be ground to a powder to be used as a thickener
Pumpkin	Remove stem and flower parts, cut, remove seeds, peel, slice 3 mm thick	3–6 min.	Need to peel when making powder
Tomatoes	Wash, dip in boiling water, peel, cut in slices 7–10 mm thick	1½ min.	Rub paraffin oil on the rack to prevent sticking

VEGETABLE SALADS

The term includes uncooked, raw or green vegetables sometimes seasoned with salad dressing. Salad is prepared by mixing sliced or diced carrots, onions, cabbage, cauliflower, lettuce, spinach, parsley, celery, cucumber, beetroot and served as appetiser or first course or as a separate course of meal.

VEGETABLE PRODUCTS

These include dehydrated vegetables, canned vegetables, pickled vegetables and vegetable pastes and juices produced to preserve the vegetables and also to provide new instant or convenience products.

Dehydrated Vegetables

Dehydration reduces the moisture content of vegetables below the required level for the growth of micro-organisms and at the same time preserves the flavour, aroma and appearance. The dehydrated vegetable on the addition of water regains the original shape or appearance. Significant changes in the composition of nutrients occur due to dehydration. Concentration of proteins, carbohydrates and minerals occur along with some chemical changes. Fats are oxidatively degraded, accompanied with decrease of odour or flavour. Maillard reaction is facilitated resulting in darker colour and development of new aroma substances. Vitamin levels decrease and original volatile flavour and aroma compounds are lost to a major extent.

Vegetables for dehydration are washed, peeled, cleaned and may be sliced or diced. Blanching for 2–7 minutes using hot water or steam or sulphur dioxide inactivates the native enzymes. The blanched vegetables are then dehydrated in a conveyor or tube drier maintained at 55–60°C to a final moisture content of 4–8 per cent. Liquid or paste forms such as tomato or potato mash are dried in a spray or drum drier. Dehydration may be carried out by freeze-drying to yield high quality products as in the case of peas and cauliflower used for the production of soup powders. Dehydrated vegetables are light, air and moisture sensitive and hence require careful packaging under nitrogen or vacuum in wax-impregnated paper or cardboard, multilayer foils, metal cans or glass jars.

Pickled Vegetables

Spontaneous lactic acid fermentation of vegetables such as cabbage, cucumber and beans yields pickled vegetables. Fermentation lowers the pH, inhibits the growth of spoilage micro-organisms and simultaneously brings about enzymatic softening of cells and tissues improving the digestibility and wholesomeness of the vegetables. Salt is used as a preservative and also to facilitate fermentation. Cucumbers (unripe ones) after addition of dill herb or other flavouring spices are placed in salt solution (4–6 per cent) and glucose may be added and then allowed to ferment at 18–20°C. Initially, fermentation is primarily due to heterofermentative (*Leuconostoc* sp) bacteria followed by homofermentative *Lactobacillus plantarum* and yeasts. Lactic acid, ethanol, volatile acids, carbon dioxide and small amounts of aroma substances are formed. Lactic acid (0.5–1 per cent) is metabolised by film yeasts partially.

Sauerkraut is pickled white cabbage heads obtained by lactic acid fermentation in the presence of salt (1.5–2.5 per cent) at 18–24°C for 3–6 weeks. Lactic acid content in the final product is not less 6 g/l with a final pH of 3.6. The sauerkraut may be canned by filling the cans at 70°C, followed by exhausting, sealing and sterilising at 95–100°C.

Vinegar pickled vegetables are prepared by pouring preboiled and still hot vinegar (2.5 per cent) onto unblemished vegetables such as cucumbers, red table beets, onions, pepper or mixed vegetables including carrots, cauliflower, onions, peas and mushrooms. Salt, spices, herb extracts, sugar and chemical preservatives are usually added.

Vegetables Pastes, Juices and Powders

Vegetable puree or paste is a finely dispersed slurry of the vegetable such as tomato. After removing the skin and seeds the vegetable is passed through a pulping machine. Vegetable juices of tomatoes, cucumbers, carrots, radishes, red beet and cabbage are obtained by disintegrating the cleaned and blanched vegetables. The juice is filtered or centrifuged and salt (0.25–1 per cent) is added. The juice is pasteurised for improving storage. Vegetable powders are produced by spray drying, vacuum drum drying or freeze drying the vegetable juice with or without the addition of a drying enhancer such as starch to a residual moisture content of 3 per cent. Tomato powder is the most important product. Spinach and red beet powders are used for food colouring.

Chapter 28

Meat, Fish and Egg Products

INTRODUCTION

Meat is the most valuable livestock product and for many people serves as their first-choice source of animal protein. Meat is either consumed as a component of kitchen-style food preparations or as processed meat products. Processed meat products, although in some regions still in their infancy, are globally gaining ground in popularity and consumption volume. The rising demand for meat in developing countries is mainly a consequence of the fast progression of urbanisation and the tendency among city dwellers to spend more on food than the lower income earning rural population. Given this fact, it is interesting that urban diets are, on average, still lower in calories than diets in rural areas. Quantitatively and qualitatively, meat and other animal foods are better sources of protein than plant foods (except soyabean products). In meat, the essential amino acids – the organic acids that are integral components of proteins and which cannot be synthesised in the human organism – are made available in well balanced proportions and concentrations. As well, plant food has no Vitamin B_{12}, thus animal food is indispensable for children to establish B_{12} deposits. Animal food, in particular meat, is rich in iron, which is of utmost importance to prevent anemia, especially in children and pregnant women. The advantage of meat processing is the integration of certain animal tissues (muscle trimmings, bone scraps, skin parts or certain internal organs which are usually not sold in fresh meat marketing) into the food chain as valuable protein-rich ingredients. Animal blood, for instance, is unfortunately often wasted in developing countries largely due to the absence of hygienic collection and processing methods and also because of sociocultural restrictions that do not allow consumption of products made of blood. While half of the blood volume of a slaughtered animal remains in the carcass tissues and is eaten with the meat and internal organs, the other half recovered from bleeding represents 5–8 per cent of the protein yield of a slaughter animal. In the future, we cannot afford to waste such large amounts of animal protein. Meat processing offers a suitable way to integrate whole blood or separated blood fractions (known as blood plasma) into human diets. Thus, there are economic, dietary and sensory aspects that make meat processing one of the most valuable mechanisms for adequately supplying animal protein to human populations, as the following explains:

- Lean meat is one of the most valuable but also most costly foods and may not regularly be affordable to certain population segments. The blending of meat with cheaper plant products through manufacturing can create low-cost products that allow more consumers access to animal protein products. In particular, the most needy, children and young women from low-income groups, can benefit from products with reduced but still valuable animal protein content that supply essential amino acids and also provide vitamins and minerals, in particular iron.

- All edible livestock parts that are suitable for processing into meat products are optimally used. In addition to muscle trimmings, connective tissue, organs and blood, this includes casings of animal origin that are used as sausage containers.
- Unlike fresh meat, many processed meat products can be made shelf-stable, which means that they can be kept without refrigeration either as (i) canned heat sterilised products, (ii) fermented and slightly dried products and (iii) products where the low level of product moisture and other preserving effects inhibit bacterial growth. Such shelf-stable meat products can conveniently be stored and transported without refrigeration and can serve as the animal protein supply in areas that have no cold chain provision.
- Meat processing 'adds value' to products. Value-added meat products display specific flavour, taste, colour or texture components, which are different from fresh meat. Such treatments do not make products necessarily cheaper, on the contrary in many cases they become even more expensive than lean meat. But they offer diversity to the meat food sector, providing the combined effect of nutritious food and food with excellent taste.

The term meat refers mainly to skeletal muscle and adhering fat obtained from warm-blooded animals, though other parts including internal organs which are fit for human consumption are also considered as meat. Apart from skeletal muscle, meat includes heart muscles and smooth muscles of spleen, lymphatic glands, epidermis, intestinal tract and mucous linings. The muscle tissue contains moisture (75 per cent), nitrogenous substances (22 per cent), fat (1.5–2 per cent), minerals (1 per cent) and small amounts of carbohydrates (0.05–0.2 per cent). The nitrogenous substances are mainly proteins which belong to three groups, proteins of the contractile apparatus which are extractable with salt solution, water soluble proteins and water insoluble proteins. The contractile apparatus proteins constitute the major amount of proteins and include myosin, actin, tropomyosin and troponin. The soluble proteins include myoglobin, haemoglobin and enzymes. The insoluble proteins are the proteins (mainly collagen and elastin) of the connective tissue and lipoproteins of membranes. Other nitrogenous substances include free amino acids, peptides, amines, guanidine compounds, purines, pyrimidines and quaternary ammonium compounds. The glycogen content of muscle varies depending on the age and condition of the animal prior to slaughter. Sugars constitute only to the extent of 0.1 per cent. Lactic acid, glycolic acid and succinic acid are also present in the muscle. Muscle tissues are rich in vitamins such as thiamine, riboflavine, nicotinamide, pyridoxine, pantothenic acid, folic acid, biotin, cyanocobalamin and minerals such as potassium, sodium, magnesium, calcium, iron, zinc, phosphorus and chloride. The red colour of meat is due to myoglobin and meat cured with nitrates remain pink for a long time.

POST MORTEM, AGEING OR RIPENING

As soon as the animal is slaughtered blood circulation stops and anaerobic conditions set in and energy rich phosphates such as creatine phosphate, ATP and ADP undergo degradation. Glycogen remains the sole energy source and glycolytic reactions continue for some time till the pH of the muscle decreases to about 5.5 due to the formation of lactic acid, or till glycogen reserve is available. As glycolysis comes to a stop, ATP generation also comes to an end and the muscle tissue becomes stiff and rigid or the state of rigor mortis sets in. The onset of rigor mortis occurs at different times in different species and also depends on the age, state of activity of the animal before its slaughter and feeding practices. In general, rigor mortis sets in within 10–20 hr in beef, 4–18 hr in pork and 2–4 hr in chicken. The rate of decrease in pH and the final pH of the muscle influence the water holding capacity of meat and are of significance in determining the quality of meat. Rapid decrease in pH and ATP level causes pork muscle to become pale, soft and undergo extensive drip loss because of lower water holding capacity. Such a PSE (pale, soft and exudative) meat has a low tensile strength, loses substantial amount of weight on hanging and on thawing, drip losses continue. Similarly, the occurrence of DFD (dark, firm and dry) meat is characteristic of a stress impaired hog. DFD meat has high pH due to low level of lactic acid.

The PSE effect is not significant in beef muscle as fat oxidation slows down glycogen breakdown during post mortem. Rapid and intense cooling of the muscle tissue leaves the meat with a greater water holding capacity and makes it of better quality compared to muscle tissue cooled slowly.

Rigor mortis in beef muscle resolves in about 2–3 days. The meat again becomes soft and tender due to ageing. The connective tissue proteins breakdown due to the action of native proteolytic enzymes during ageing. Tenderness in meat is a desired quality. Ageing improves tenderness and allows time for the development of aroma depending on the temperature of storage. Beef requires ageing for 14 days at 0°C, 6 days at 8–10°C or 4 days at 16–18°C. A slight increase in pH and increase in water holding capacity occur during ageing.

Muscle tissue contains about 20–25 per cent protein and about 75 per cent water, i.e. about 350–360 gram of water per 100 gram of protein. About 95 per cent of this water is held by capillary forces between the thick and thin filaments and only 5 per cent is bound directly to the hydrophilic groups on the proteins. The extent of water holding by the protein gel network depends on the abundance of cross-linking between the peptide chains. A decrease in the number of cross-linkages results in swelling of the muscle while increase in the cross-linkages shrinks the protein gel causing syneresis. The muscle is swollen, soft and juicy when it holds a large amount of water. As rigor mortis sets in and ATP level decreases, the water holding capacity also decreases. Addition of salt and increase in pH generally improves the water holding capacity of meat. Meat swelling and water holding capacity are low at pH 5.0–5.5. Ageing is adopted only in the case of beef and occasionally in the case of lamb and mutton. Pork is never aged because of its high fat content.

Tenderising Meat

Tenderness in meat depends on the extent of cross-linkages between muscle fibres and collagen, and decreases with increasing age of the animal. The meat of aged animals is tough and difficult to chew. In addition, during cooking, collagen is solubilised and tenderness of meat decreases. Ageing improves tenderness of meat. Meat is tenderised by mechanical methods such as cutting, pounding, grinding or needling, use of ultrasonic vibrations to break the meat fibres or by enzymes. Papain (proteolytic enzyme from papaya) or bromelain (from pineapple) is rubbed into the fresh meat or sprinkled in the form of a powder or solution. The enzyme is also injected into the veins of living animals just before their slaughter. The protein fibres are hydrolysed by the enzyme thereby improving tenderness of the meat.

Types and Grades of Meat

Beef

Beef is bright cherry red or dark red lean meat or meat marbled with fat obtained from the muscle fibres and associated connective tissue of cows and bulls, the best quality being obtained from young bulls and 4–6 year old oxen. The meat of old cows and discarded dairy cattle of more than 12 years old is of lower quality. Beef from the carcasses are hung for about a week before being cut up for soup meat and for about two weeks for roasts and steaks. *Veal* is white to pale red meat with tender, limp and sticky muscle fibres of 6–14 weeks old young calves. The meat is hung for about a week before use.

Mutton

Mutton is meat with associated fat from sheep older than an year, the best quality being obtained from 2–4 year old sheep slaughtered in autumn. *Lamb* is meat from younger sheep with mild flavour and taste. Goat meat is lighter in colour than mutton. Ram meat (from male goat) is also used.

Pork

Pork is meat from pigs with fine muscle fibres, soft and tender, interspersed with as much as 20–40 per cent fat and is grey-white to pale pink in colour. The meat is hung for about 4 days before butchering. Young horse meat is bright red compared to dark red colour of older animals consisting of firm muscle fibres and a characteristic sweet taste and flavour due to high glycogen content. The linolenic acid content of horse meat is relatively greater compared to that in beef or pork. The small quantity of white fat which melts at about 30°C during cooking, appears as drops on the surface.

Poultry meat

Poultry meat includes meat from chicken, ducks, geese, pigeons, turkeys and peacocks. The quality and colour of the meat vary with the breed, age and feeding habits as well as the body parts. The meat of wild game such as wild boar and rabbit, birds or fowl such as pheasant and partridge have distinct characteristics depending on the breed.

Organ meat or variety meat

Organ meat or variety meat includes organs of various animals such as tongue, heart, liver, kidney, brain, spleen, bladder, stomach and intestines. These may be consumed as such (as in the case of liver, kidney, or heart) or minced and then filled into sausages (spleen, tongue, cow's udder, beef stomach, etc.). Blood, which drains from the slaughtered animal, is used for making sausages. Glands of animals such as adrenal, pancreas, mammary, ovary, pituitary and thyroid are used for extracts or pharmaceutical products.

Meat sold in the market must be from healthy living animals, slaughtered hygienically and certified as fit for human consumption by a competent authority. Meat after proper inspection is graded based on maturity and marbling which influence the quality and palatability of meat. The maturity of the animal affects the texture, firmness and colour of the meat. Fine structural lean meat is tender compared to a meat with a coarse texture. The tenderness of the meat of a young animal increases as it matures to an optimum age. Marbling refers to the amount and distribution of fat in the meat which appears as white flecks within the lean meat and is considered as an index of quality. In addition to these, high juice content and bright reel or pink colour also indicate the freshness of meat.

Preservation

Meat may be preserved by cold storage, drying, pickling or smoking.

Refrigeration and freezing

The slaughtered animal carcasses are skinned and the fresh meat is preserved in the form of sides or quarters by refrigeration or freezing. Cooling process for preservation of meat is carried out in a step wise manner with a blast of air (3.5 m/s) at –10°C for about 3 hr, with a blast of air (1.2 m/s) at 2°C for about 18–19 hr and over 18 days with air at 4°C. The shelf life of meat at 0°C is about 3–6 weeks. Freezing and storing at –18 to –20°C prolong the shelf life substantially to about 12–15 months. Freezing may be carried out in a single step of direct freezing or two steps of initial cooling and freezing using an air blast at –40°C. During cold storage, water holding capacity of meat increases. Lipid oxidation is very slow in large cuts. Freezing meat immediately after slaughter while the carcass is still warm results in meat which after thawing loses a large amount of fluid (called thaw rigor) due to a sudden high rate of ATP breakdown. The thaw rigor can be avoided if the warm meat is disintegrated in the presence of sodium chloride before freezing it.

Drying

Drying is yet another method of meat preservation. Drying in a stream of hot air at 40–60°C, drying in vacuum or freez-drying may be used. The moisture content of the dried meat is about 3–10 per cent. The shelf life is limited due to oxidative degradation and discolouration due to Maillard reaction. Dried beef and chicken are used for making soup powders. Meatballs and minced meat pieces are also dried.

Salt curing and pickling

Salting meat with sodium chloride or curing and pickling by the addition of sodium nitrite and or sodium nitrate is common practice. Sodium chloride in high concentrations inhibits microbial spoilage of meat, causes swelling (at >5 per cent) and induces shrinkage (10–20 per cent) in meat. Salted meat retains its natural dark red colour and on cooking, becomes grayish brown. Salt curing is done either by dry curing, i.e. rubbing salt on the meat surface or by wet pickle curing by submerging meat in 15–20 per cent brine or by rapid pickling involving injection of salt solution into blood vessels. Curing with sodium nitrite and nitrate produces meat of highly stable colour. Additives, such as sugar or spices may be added to pickling salts to improve colour, flavour and formation of meat aroma. Aroma formation and stabilisation of the red colour of pickled meat are also enhanced by *Micrococcus* and *Achromabacter* species in the pickling brine.

Smoking

Smoking of meat is usually associated with salting. Volatile compounds in sawdust smoke or wood-smoke have bactericidal and antioxidative properties and they deposit on the surface and also penetrate into the meat.

Heating

This is an important finishing process and is also used for the production of canned meat. Heat treatment results in protein coagulation, release of juices, increase in pH, development of cooked or roasted meat aroma, softening and shrinking and also partial conversion of collagen of the connective tissue into gelatine.

Cooking of Meat and Meat Products

Cooking brings about changes in the meat texture by melting the fat, thermal breakdown of gelatine into soft gelatine and its solubilisation, tissue softening and muscle fibre separation. Overheating causes extensive contraction, shrinking and toughening of meat. Generally, cooking at lower temperatures for a longer time yields cooked meat with minimum drip loss and shrinkage and increased juiciness and uniform colour than cooking at higher temperatures for short time. Meat may be cooked by moist heating or dry heating methods. Moist heating methods of cooking include braising, stewing and pressure cooking.

Meat may be cooked to rare, medium or well-done stages depending on temperature. Braising involves cooking the broiled or fried meat cuts with small amounts of water in a closed vessel. Stewing is adopted to cook large pieces of tough cuts of meat in simmering water. Less tender meat cuts are usually cooked by moist heating to convert the collagen into gelatine and increase the tenderness of meat. Dry heating methods such as roasting, broiling or frying are used for tender meat cuts. Roasting usually in an open pan at 160–170°C yields a cooked meat with adequate surface browning with a good flavour and appearance as heat is transferred from the outer surface to the interior. Roasting produces juicy and tender meats compared to other dry heating methods. Broiling involves cooking meat by direct radiant heat such as open fire of gas flame, live coals or electric oven. Broiling is used to cook tender meat cuts which are at least 3 cm thick, as thinner cuts will become too dry on broiling. Broiling is carried out by placing the meat in a rack and heating to about 175°C till the heated surface becomes brown. The broiled surface is salted and turned and broiled on the other side. Frying is carried out either by pan frying with small amount of fat added or deep fat frying where the melted fat is deep enough to cover the meat.

A number of changes occur during cooking of meat which include changes in colour, texture and flavour of meat due to denaturation of proteins and conversion of collagen into gelatine. Nutritional value of cooked meat remains high, though loss of B-vitamins occurs. Moot aroma of raw meat is weak. Heat treatment intensifies the aroma of meat and the character of the aroma depends on the type of meat and also on the method of heat treatment such as cooking, pressure cooking, roasting, stewing, broiling or barbecuing. The differences in the nature of lipid degradation products in different types of meat at different temperatures and concentrations of degradation products are primarily responsible for the characteristic aroma variations. Meat aroma consists of volatile aroma compounds, non-volatile flavour compounds and flavour enhancers. The volatile aroma compounds are formed by Maillard and Strecker degradation reactions and include alcohols, aldehydes, ketones, carboxylic acids, benzene derivatives, furans, lactones, pyrans, pyrroles, pyrimidines, pyrazines, thiols, sulphides, thiophenes, thiazoles and trithiolanes. Sulphur compounds play a significant role in the meat aroma. Meat like aroma can be generated by heating cystine, cysteine, methionine or thiamine with reducing sugars or by reaction of hydrogen sulphide with alkenals and hydroxydihydrofurans or by other reactions. The nonvolatile flavour compounds include amino acids, peptides and lactic acid. Flavour enhancers in meat are glutamic acid and inosine-5'-monophosphate (IMP).

Meat Products

Commercially available important meat products include canned meat, ham, bacon, sausages and pastes. Canned beef, pork, corned beef, cooked sausages, jellied meat, pickled ham are canned under sterile conditions after appropriate heat treatment. Ham is salt-cured and pickled, smoked hind leg of pig. The hind leg section extending from the knee to the hip is cut either long or short. The long cut includes the whole hip and a long part of the shank, i.e. part of the leg above the knee. The short cut ham consists of a part of the hip and a short section of the shank. Fresh or green ham is unprocessed ham used for preparing dry country ham with ethnic flavour. The prime cuts or halves of ham include butt (part of the hip), center (bone-in) and shank (bone-out). Boneless ham and bone-in ham are either dry or wet cured, matured for 3 weeks and smoked or cooked. Bacon is either dry cured or pickled pork belly. The belly portions are then matured for about 2 weeks and smoked or cooked. Sausage making consists of grinding, mincing or chopping the muscle tissue and other organs and blending them with fat, salts, seasonings (herbs and spices) and binders or extenders. The sausage mix or dough is stuffed into cylindrical natural casings such as hog or sheep intestine or hog's bun (for liver sausage) or synthetic casings made of cellulose and sold as raw or cooked or smoked sausages. Depending on the type of processing, sausages are classified as: raw or coarsely ground or fermented and emulsified pork or beef, water cooked luncheon and breakfast sausage, heat treated frankfurters (hot dogs) and wieners or mortadella. Meat pastes are spreadable pastes containing delicately cooked high quality meat products (free from slaughter scrapings) made from meat and fat of calves, hogs, poultry or wild animal meat. Beef extract is a concentrate of water soluble beef ingredients without fat and proteins. Finely comminuted beef is extracted with water at 90°C by countercurrent extraction. Fat is removed by separators and the filtered extract containing about 5 per cent solids is concentrated to about 60–65 per cent solids content by multiple stage vacuum evaporation with decreasing gradient from 92 to 46°C. The final evaporation to 80–85 per cent solids is carried out under atmospheric pressure and 65°C or higher. Chicken extract is obtained by evaporation of chicken broth or by extraction of chicken halves with water at 80°C followed by concentration in vacuum to get a finished product containing 75–80 per cent solids content. Yeast extract is made from yeast cells of *Saccharomyces* and *Torula* species. The cells are forced to undergo plasmolysis by the addition of salts or autolysis by exposing to steam and then extracted with water. The extract is concentrated to a brown paste which is rich in B group vitamins.

POULTRY

The term poultry refers to domestic fowls such as chicken, ducks, turkey, pigeons, geese and guineas of which chicken and turkey are commonly used for their meat. Poultry is usually classified on the basis of age, since age influences the tenderness of the meat and fat content and determines the cooking method. Broiler or fryer chicken is about 8–10 weeks of age with tender meat, a soft, smooth textured skin and flexible breastbone cartilage. A rooster chicken is 12–20 weeks of age with similar characteristics as the broiler but less flexible breastbone cartilage. A stag is a male chicken of less than 10 months of age with a coarse skin, toughened and darkened flesh and a hard breastbone cartilage. A cock is a mature male chicken over 10 months of age with similar characteristics of a stag but more hardened breastbone.

Poultry Processing

Generally, birds meant for slaughter are not fed for about 12 hours prior to ensure their crops are empty to facilitate cleaner operation. The live bird is stunned and made unconscious and jugular vein is cut to bleed the bird completely in about 3–4 minutes. The bird is then scalded by dipping in hot water to facilitate defeathering. After removal of feathers the bird is eviscerated, i.e. the entrails (stomach, intestine, lungs, kidney, head, feet and oil gland) are removed. The eviscerated bird is washed and chilled rapidly to about 2°C. The chilled chicken is graded and packed in films or bags which have high resistance to transmission of moisture and air. The packed poultry may be stored in a refrigerator for a few days or stored up to a few months in a deep freezer (–22 to –18°C). Poultry goes into rigor mortis and relaxes rapidly compared to meat. Hence poultry is ready for cooking only about 5 hours after slaughter. The dressed chicken may be cooked by broiling, frying, or roasting. Birds with tough meat may be braised or stewed. Chicken meat has a high protein to fat ratio with a protein content of 20–25 per cent and very low fat content. The fat contains relatively more of unsaturated fatty acids. The flesh is also rich in B group vitamins and minerals.

SEAFOODS

Fish, whales, crustaceans and molluscs are a rich source of biologically valuable proteins, fats and fat-soluble vitamins. Out of 25000 species of fish, only about 250 species are considered as edible ones.

Edible fish may be classified into finfish and shellfish on the basis of their anatomy. Finfish are the type of fish with vertebrae and fin-appendages and are covered with protective scales. Finfish are found in salt water (shark, salmon, mackerel, tuna, herring, cod, ribbon fish, etc.) as well as in fresh water (sardine, mullet, catfish, carp, trout, etc.). Finfish such as salmon and eels can live in both salt and fresh waters. Saltwater fish have a more distinctive flavour than freshwater fish. Shellfish are without a skeleton but covered with a hard shell and may be sub-classified into molluscs and crustaceans. Molluscs have a soft unsegmented body enclosed partially or wholly in a hard shell. Molluscs include oysters, clams, scallops and mussels. Crustaceans have a segmented body covered with crustlike shells, e.g. crabs, lobsters, shrimps and crayfish. Edible shell-fishes are mainly salt water fishes.

Fishes are also classified on the basis of their fat content as lean fish with less than 2 per cent fat (e.g. cod, haddock, sole, etc.) medium with 2–5 per cent fat (e.g. sardine, halibut, etc.) and fat fish with more than 5 per cent fat (e.g. salmon—14 per cent, eel—26 per cent, mackerel—12 per cent, tuna—16 per cent, herring—18 per cent, etc.). Fat fish taste better than other types.

Fish protein content varies between 13 and 22 per cent. Other main constituents include lipids, Vitamins A, D, E and K and minerals particularly calcium, magnesium, iron, copper and phosphorus.

Storage and Processing of Fish and Fish Products

Fish undergo decomposition and spoilage readily and rapidly even at temperatures close to 0°C. Hence they are cooled or frozen, or dried, salted and smoked followed by pickling in vinegar or in gelatine with vinegar added.

Refrigeration or freezing of fish preserves freshness, wholesomeness and the nutritive value. Fish are packed in ice on the ship itself almost immediately after the catch. Fish such as tuna, mackerel, cod, haddock, red fish, etc. may also be frozen on ships or on land either as whole fish, or gutted, with or without head. Quick freezing to about –30 to –40°C is adopted to quickly pass over the critical temperature range of –0.5 to –5°C. Liquid nitrogen or dichlorodifluoromethane is used as coolant. The whole fish are sprinkled with water so as to form a glaze of ice to protect from oxidation. Alternatively, fish may be frozen in an alginate jelly or coated with latex film. Glass jars, plastic films or wax impregnated cartons are used for packaging fillets. Fillet sides are strips of flesh cut parallel to the central bone, from which main bones, fins, belly flap and skin removed. The fillets may be sprinkled with egg or bread crumbs. The residues from hygienically cut fillets are processed into fish balls.

Refrigerated and frozen fish must be consumed soon after thawing, otherwise juices drip out and meat decays rapidly. Since fish muscle enzymes retain some activity even at –10°C prolonged storage or insufficient cooling leads to rapid deterioration.

Drying using solar radiation or driers is adopted for non-fatty fish such as cod, haddock, ling, tuck or saithe. The head is removed and the fish is split, gutted and dried. Alternatively, machine-cut, headless belly clipped fish are salted and dried.

Salting is one of the oldest methods of preservation. Salting is carried out by rubbing, sprinkling or steeping in brine the whole fresh or frozen fish or parts of fish. The salt content may be about 12–20 per cent of the tissue. Salting provides a finished or semi-finished product amenable for further processing.

Smoking is carried out with fresh or frozen fish by exposing the same to freshly generated sawdust smoke. Cold smoking at 20–25°C over 2–4 days of salted fish or hot smoking at 100–120°C for 2–4 hr of whole, gutted or descaled fish with limited shelf life of about 3–4 days is quite common.

Marinated fish of limited shelf life are marketed in cans or jars and is carried out by soaking or steeping spiced and salted fish in marinade which consists of vinegar, wine or a mixture of both. Fried and cooked fish and fish products are also marketed in cans. Fish with extended shelf life up to one year without cold storage, are made by steam retorting of fresh or frozen fish or fish portions followed by packaging in vacuum sealed air-tight containers. Lacquer coated tin cans or inert aluminium cans are used when fish is canned with tomato or mustard sauce, vinegar or lemon juice.

Whales and crustaceans

Whale (a sea mammal) meat is similar to that of game meat or beef with long coarse muscle fibres. The fresh meat has a gray-reddish colour and a pleasant flavour but deteriorates rapidly due to fat oxidation. Frozen whale meat is dark blackish brown in colour with a rough, firm texture. Whale meat has a very short shelf life.

Crustaceans have no backbone but the body which is divided into sections is protected by a hard shell. Crustaceans include shrimp, cray or crab fish, crabs and lobster. Shrimps are marketed live with shell or fresh with or without head and shell. Canned shrimps are pasteurised at 80–90°C and have a short shelf life. Crabs and lobsters are usually marketed live or frozen fresh and canned. Crab meat, crab paste, lobster meat or paste are other processed products.

Molluscs

These include clams, oysters, mussels and scallops. The best meat is obtained from a 3–5 year old oyster. Mussel is consumed as cooked meat, fried or marinated. The meat is rich is protein (17 per cent) and in Vitamins A and B.

Turtles and frogdrums

Turtle or tortoise is consumed mostly as a soup or stew. Frogdrums (thigh portion of frogs) have a soft texture and white colour, are eaten as cooked, roasted or stewed.

EGG PRODUCTS PROCESS AND PLANT FAMILIARISATION

Hen's egg consists of three main parts, the shell, the egg white and the egg yolk. The shell consists of calcite crystals embedded in a matrix of proteins and polysaccharide complex. Inside the shell the viscous colourless liquid called the egg white accounts for about 60 per cent of the total egg weight. Ovalbumin is readily denatured by shaking or whipping its aqueous solution but is resistant to thermal denaturation. Other constituents of egg white include carbohydrates (1 per cent), minerals (0.6 per cent mainly sulphur, sodium, potassium, phosphorus and calcium) and minor quantities of lipids and vitamins. The third component of egg is the egg yolk with a solid content of 50 per cent. It is a fat-in-water emulsion containing lipids (about two-thirds of dry matter content) and proteins (about one-third). Egg yolk separates into granules and a clear supernatant plasma on high speed centrifugation. The granules contain egg yolk proteins, lipovitellins (high density lipoproteins), phosvitin (a phosphoprotein), livetin and low density lipoproteins. The egg yolk lipids include triacylglycerols, phospholipids, cholesterol and cholesterol esters. Carbohydrate content in egg yolk is about 1 per cent.

Eggs have high nutritional value. Moreover, eggs may be used as thickening agents, binding and coagulating agents, coatings, foaming agents, emulsifiers, shortening agents, flavouring agent and colourant in a variety of food products.

Eggs stored at room temperature lose their prime quality in about a week. Refrigerated storage enhances the storage stability to about two weeks. Eggs may be stored for about 6 months in cold storage at –1°C and relative humidity of 80 per cent. Eggs may also be stored by spraying cleaned eggs with mineral oil to close the pores in the shell, thereby retarding the loss of moisture and rise in pH due to loss of carbon dioxide. Egg products include dried eggs, frozen egg products and liquid egg products. Dried egg powder is used in the preparation of egg based products. The whole liquid content of the eggs or the separated egg white and egg yolk is homogenised by mixing or churning and then pasteurised.

Sugars present in the liquid egg are removed by microbial fermentation (*Streptococcus* sp, *Aerobacter* or yeasts) or by glucoseoxidase/catalase enzymes (to oxidise glucose to gluconic acid) to prevent reaction with amino components resulting in undesirable brown discolouration and faulty aroma. The liquid egg is then spray dried with jet or centrifugal spray drier and rapidly cooled. The shelf life of dried egg white is unlimited while whole egg powder devoid of sugar is stable up to one year at room temperature. Sugarless yolk powder has a shelf life of 8 months at room temperature. Frozen egg powder is prepared by homogenising, pasteurising whole liquid or separated egg white and egg yolk and then frozen to –23 to –25°C. It has a shelf life of about 8 months at storage temperature of –18°C. Liquid egg product is obtained by homogenising the, liquid and pasteurisation at 65°C for about 3 minutes. Pasteurisation alone however, cannot protect the product from microbial attack, particularly from *Salmonella* sp. Hence preservatives such as sorbic acid or benzoic acid are added.

As egg products regulators, we must have a general understanding of the processes that the industry uses to produce egg products. Understanding the processes and equipment involved in handling egg products will help inspectors to perform verification procedures. This chapter discusses the term "egg products" refers to eggs that are removed from their shells for processing. Egg products processing includes breaking eggs, filtering, mixing, stabilising, blending, pasteurising, cooling, freezing or drying, and packaging. Egg products include whole eggs, whites, yolks, and various processed and pasteurised blends, with or without non-egg ingredients. These egg products may be available in liquid, frozen, and dried forms. The design of the production facilities must provide flexibility and efficiency to accommodate the specific processes required for producing different egg products. Some plants also have shell egg grading facilities and dual jurisdiction activities such as cooking and hard-boiled operations in the egg products facility.

Egg Products Processing

The processing of egg products includes:

- Receiving shell eggs.
- Washing/sanitising/handling eggs.
- Breaking eggs.
- Handling liquid egg product – filtering.
  - o Blending
  - o Mixing
- Cooling
- Pasteurisation
- Freezing or drying
- Packaging
- Storage
- Shipping

Receiving Eggs

Eggs are transported to the plant directly from either laying hens or contract flocks, or both. When eggs come directly from the egg-laying farm to the egg breaking or processing plant, they are called in-line operations. There is a very short time between when the eggs are laid and when they reach the egg processing plant. Most new complexes are in-line systems designed to move eggs directly on conveyors from laying houses to the processing area. The eggs presented for breaking in these operations are called 'nest run'. The nest run are eggs that have never been sized, washed, or graded. A high percentage of the eggs gathered by this method are first-rate quality, if good flock-management practices are in place.

Another way of delivering eggs is in filler-flats (off-line systems) that come from contract flocks. Contract flocks are chicken houses that the company contracts to furnish eggs. The eggs from off-line systems can come from multiple chicken farms and there may be a lot of variability (hours to days to weeks) in the age of the eggs. Eggs are packed in plastic filler-flats, palletised, and transported to the processing facility. These plastic flats are to be thoroughly cleaned, sanitised, and dried after each use to avoid cross-contamination and the creation of insanitary conditions. The proper handling of eggs is important, as it helps to prevent egg damage, minimises any quality loss, and avoids compromising the safety of the egg. In egg-breaking plants, the production starts with the loading of eggs as either in-line operations or off-line systems. In off-line systems, once the egg filler-flats or nest-run eggs arrive in the transfer room, flats of eggs are loaded to the off-line conveyors and moved to conveyor spools going through the egg washers.

Washing Eggs and Sanitising

Shell eggs, when presented for breaking, must be clean. Modern egg washers use pressure sprays, rotating brushes, and an egg-spinning device that increases contact between the egg and the brush and minimises damage to the eggs.

Pasteurisation

The Egg Product Inspection Act requires that all egg products distributed into commerce be pasteurised. Pasteurisation involves rapidly heating the product and holding the product at a minimum required temperature for a specific time. The reason for pasteurisation is to destroy *Salmonella* without affecting the characteristics of the final egg product. Two common types of pasteurisation are high temperature-short time (HTST) pasteurisation and batch pasteurisation. In this training, we will focus on HTST pasteurisation. Batch pasteurisation is no longer used.

After pasteurisation, it is essential to handle the pasteurised egg product in a sanitary manner to prevent cross-contamination. The pasteurised liquid product may be handled as follows:

- Packed in containers (plastic buckets, bag-in-box, packages, milk containers, etc.) to be marketed.
- Further processed (add ingredients post pasteurisation, freeze or dry).
- Shipped in tankers to another egg products plant or distributor.

Freezing

Frozen egg products include separated whites and yolks, whole eggs, blends of whole eggs and yolks, and whole eggs with added ingredients. They are produced from pasteurised liquid egg products by using a blast freezer at temperatures of –10°F to – 40°F. Frozen egg products have a long shelf life when kept at less than 10°F.

Drying

Industry has developed a variety of dried egg products, including dried egg white, dried plain whole egg and yolk, and specialty dried egg products.

Egg products fall under two basic categories when considering their drying characteristics:

- Egg white products.
- Whole egg and yolk products.

Before the liquid egg products go through the drying process, industry uses processing techniques to achieve the desired finished product. These techniques alter the composition of egg components by changing the lipid or sugar composition, concentrating solids, or separating egg components (e.g. lysozyme and avidin). The two common methods that industry uses to produce dried egg products are:

- Spray drying – atomised liquid egg product is sprayed into a stream of hot air, collected and packaged. This is the predominant method used by the dried egg product industry. Spray drying does not kill micro-organisms. However, it does extend product shelf life.
- Pan drying or albumen flake process – unpasteurised egg whites are dried on pans to produce a flake-type or granular material. This method is used for the confectionary industry.

Another method of drying is the Refractance Window® drying system. This operation is a low temperature drying technique, which removes moisture from high moisture products that generally vary in solid content between 3% and 70%. Briefly, the operation consists of:

- Slurry of liquid is evenly applied to the top surface of a continuous sheet of transparent plastic.
- This continuous plastic film slowly moves across a hot water reservoir (210°F) which provides an infrared energy source (i.e. infrared energy and conducted heat) permitting the rapid drying at atmospheric pressure rather than under vacuum.
- Results in dry flakes on the opposite end and the process provides retention of the egg product's functional properties and nutritional value.

This type of drying is very uncommon. Currently, only one egg products plant in the US uses this type of drying process. Industry uses chemical additives to improve and keep the functional properties (whipping, coagulation, emulsification, flavour, nutrition, and colour) of the final dried egg products. Examples of chemical additives include carbohydrates, whipping aids, emulsifiers, and anti-caking agents (colloidal silicon dioxide). The dried egg product must be handled aseptically during packaging. The advantages of dried egg products compared to their liquid frozen counterparts are shelf life, storage, and low transportation costs.

References

Alford, G., *Food Chemistry*, John Wiley & Sons, New York.

Alouf, D., *Biotechnological Innovations in Food Processing*, Butterworths, London.

Anke, J.T., *Food Engineering Operations*, Marcel Dekker Inc., New York.

Berg, V.T., *Dairy Microbiology*, Applied Science Publishers, London.

Batterman, S.A., *Sampling and Analysis of Food Products*, McGraw-Hill, Tokyo.

Benaim Pinto, C., *Sampling and Analysis of Airborne Micro-organisms*, Prentice Hall, London.

Brown, N.K., *Environmental Microbiology*, Cambridge University Press, Cambridge.

Bradley, S.M., *Food Microbiology*, Academic Press, London.

Budyko, N.P., *Food Processing Waste,* Progress Publishers, Moscow.

Chang, G.D., *Introduction to Environmental Microbiology*, John Wiley & Sons, New York.

Commoner, R.M, *Food Enzymes*, John Wiley & Sons, New York.

Coolingwood, S.A., *Food Flavours,* John Wiley & Sons, New York.

Cox, C.V., *Food Science*, S.P. Medical and Scientific Books, New York.

Daniel, G.L., *Canned Foods and Their Microbiology*, Pergamon Press, Oxford.

Dennis, R.H., *Principles of Food Processing*, Springer, US.

Downe, S.A., *Dairy Microbiology*, John Wiley & Sons, New York.

Dugan, P.R., *Fermentation of Beer*, Plenum Publishing Corporation, London.

Earle, R.L., *Unit Operation in Food Processing*, Butterworth-Heinemann, Ltd., London.

Goldman, M.B., *Treatment of Food Waste*, Gordon and Breach, Science Publishers, New York.

Gould, G.W., *Food Biochemistry*, D. Van Nostrand, New York.

Harding, G.E., *Transport Processes and Unit Operations*, Prentice-Hall, London.

Jatinder, K.S., *Advanced Food Process Engineering*, CRC Press, London.

Krieg, G.M., *Food Engineering and Process Applications,* Heinemann, London.

Lewis, B.B., *Applied Environmental Microbiology*, Elsevier Scientific Publishing Co., Amsterdam.

Lodish, H.K., *Food Processing Technology*, W. H. Freeman and Company, New York.

Miller, M.S., *Food Microbiology*, Prentice-Hall, London.

Park, S.H., *Fundamentals of Food Processing*, Wiley-Blackwell, New York.

Pilar, M.C., *Novel Food Processing Technology*, CRC Press, London.

Riemann, D.L., *Food Processing Technology*, Academic Press, London.

Robert, B.L. and Evison, L.W., *Principles of Food Science*, John Wiley & Sons, New York.

Sengner, J., *Micro-organisms in Food*, John Wiley & Sons, New York.

Smith, P.A., *Encyclopedia of Environmental Microbiology*, John Wiley & Sons, New York.

Tanaka, S.K., *Flavonoids: Dietary Occurrence and Biochemical Activity*, Marcel Dekker, New York.

Wilson, A.L., *Encyclopedia of Food Science*, Academic Press, London.

Index

E

N

O

P

V

W

Z

Volume II

Food Processing and Preservation

DS Warris

CBS Publishers & Distributors Pvt Ltd

New Delhi • Bengaluru • Chennai • Kochi • Kolkata • Mumbai
Bhopal • Bhubaneswar • Hyderabad • Jharkhand • Nagpur • Patna • Pune
Uttarakhand • Dhaka (Bangladesh) • Kathmandu (Nepal)

Disclaimer

Science and technology are constantly changing fields. New research and experience broaden the scope of information and knowledge. The author has tried his best in giving information available to him while preparing the material for this book. Although, all efforts have been made to ensure optimum accuracy of the material, yet it is quite possible some errors might have been left uncorrected. The publisher, printer and the author will not be held responsible for any inadvertent errors, omissions or inaccuracies.

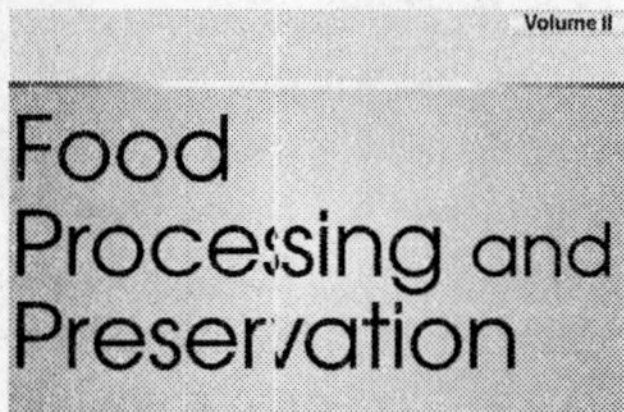

ISBN: 978-93-8988-59-7

First Edition: 202

Published by Scish Kumar Jain and produced by Varun Jain for

CBS Publisher & Distributors Pvt Ltd

4819/XI PrahladStreet, 24 Ansari Road, Daryaganj, New Delhi 110 002, India.

Ph: 23289259, 2266861, 23266867 Website: www.cbspd.com

Fax: 011-2324304 e-mail: delhi@cbspd.com; cbspubs@airtelmail.in.

Corporate Office: 204 FIE, Industrial Area, Patparganj, Delhi 110 092

Ph: 4934 4934 Fax: 4934 4935 e-mail: publishing@cbspd.com; publicity@cbspd.com

Branches

- **Bengaluru:** Seema House 2975, 17th Cross, K.R. Road, Banasankari 2nd Stage, Bengaluru 560 070, Karnataka
  Ph: +91-80-26771678/79 Fax: +91-80-26771680 e-mail: bangalore@cbspd.com
- **Chennai:** 7, Subbaraya Street, Shenoy Nagar, Chennai 600 030, Tamil Nadu
  Ph: +91-44-26680620, 26681266 Fax: +91-44-42032115 e-mail: chennai@cbspd.com
- **Kochi:** 68/1534, 35, 36, Power House Road, Opp. KSEB, Kochi 682018, Kerala
  Ph: +91-484-4059061-65 Fax: +91-484-4059065 e-mail: kochi@cbspd.com
- **Kolkata:** 6/B, Ground Floor, Rameswar Shaw Road, Kolkata-700 014, West Bengal
  Ph: +91-33-2289116, 22891127, 22891128 e-mail: kolkata@cbspd.com
- **Mumbai:** 83-C, Dr E Moses Road, Worli, Mumbai-400018, Maharashtra
  Ph: +91-22-24902340/41 Fax: +91-22-24902342 e-mail: mumbai@cbspd.com

Representative

- **Bhopal** 0-8319310552 • **Bhubaneswar** 0-9911037372 • **Hyderabad** 0-9885175004 • **Jharkhand** 0-9811541605
- **Nagpur** 0-9421945513 • **Patna** 0-9334159340 • **Pune** 0-9623451994 • **Uttarakhand** 0-9716462459
- **Dhaka (Bangladesh)** 01912-003485 • **Kathmandu (Nepal)** 977-9818742655

Printed at Mudrak, Noida, UP, India

Preface

The increasing global demand for processed foods has led to a greater prominence of the food industry, its specific needs and processing challenges. Consequently, in recent times the role of the engineer in the food industry has gained considerable prominence. In contrast to other more traditional processing industries, the raw materials or ingredients that are used tend to be of greater complexty in nature. While processing conditions are also more moderate in that temperatures even in hottest ovens may not exceed 200°C and pressures rarely exceed one or two bar, the materials themselves are highly complex in composition, textural and flavour characteristics. During their handling and processing, many changes to their properties occur. The extent of these changes is often a strong function of their process history. In the food industry, one plant is frequently required to perform one purpose. To produce a product which is constituent and desirable to the consumer's expectations in terms of appearance, texture and taste all year round from raw materials which may be derived from different sources or suppliers together with seasonal variability, requires a sound understanding of the physical and chemical properties of the food materials being processed and the detailed understanding of the function of various unis operations. In all of this, food safety is paramount. Understanding the nature and sources of contamination is essential, and its control critical to ensure that the processed foods are safe to eat. Product safety isas critical as process safety. Over the past couple of decades, the role of the engineer in the food industy has gained considerable prominence. The food processing industry is extremely complex, diverse and evolved. With the consumer market becoming ever more sophisticated and demanding, there is a continual need for process innovation. Even allowing for the demands of the consumer for product consistency and quality, the consumer expects excitement, novelty, value for money and a product that is safe in tamper-proof packaging. For the food process engineer, the challenge is to use process plant and associated equipment which is sufficiently flexible to respond to any changes in demand.

The complexity and challenges of food processing engineering is best illustrated by considering the mixing criteria used in the food industry. Process engineers will be more familiar with the handling and mixing of robust components with the aim of achieving homogeneity in which liquids have low viscosity or exhibit straightforward Newtonian behaviour and where scale-up is based on simple power-to-volume ratios. In contrast, the criteria for food mixing involve ingredients which have complex components with each exhibiting very different chemical and physical properties. They often have high viscosities and exhibit non-Newtonian behaviour. Consumers are increasingly demanding foods which are nutritious and healthy such as fortified organic and minimally processed foods. There is also a considerable demand for foods which are highly processed such as sausages, burgers, baked beans and dehydrated foods, and foods which have long shelf-life and total sterility such as canned and bottled foods with packaging that is tamper-proof yet can be easily opened. Production runs are becoming ever shorter as tastes and fads change. While food processing may be classified into either chemical, physical or biological operations, there are many major issues affecting food process engineering including molecular genetics with the use of GMOs, the use of animal cloning, new regulatory procedures, ethical issues, public concerns, planetary considerations and a number of major socioeconomic considerations. The underlying requirements for technological progress in food processing are a minimum of risks acceptable for the benefits gains, as well as a full public understanding. The role of the food process engineer is critical in all of this.

This reference textbook on *Food Processing and Preservation* is divided in two volumes. This volume is divided into nine sections and comprises 1 to 33 chapters.

Section I discusses pollution control in food processing industry. Chapter 1 is devoted to pollution control in food processing industry: A review. The key environmental issues for the food industry include wastewater, solid wastes, etc. Chapter 2 deals with food pollution – basic concepts. This chapter deals with some major characteristics of food pollution. Chapter 3 concentrates on pollution control in wheat, pulse and rice mills. Environmental issues related to this industry are dust emissions, air pollution, water pollution and noise pollution. Chapter 4 focuses on pollution control in vegetable and palm oil industry. The key environmental issues related to this industry are solid wastes and by-products, greenhouse gas emissions, etc. Chapter 5 explains pollution control in dairy industry which is a major sources of water pollution, the special characteristics of dairy waste being a high percentage of dissolved organic matter responsible for the high BOD of dairy effluents. Various methods of recovery and reuse of milk by-products and prevention of dairy wastes are also discussed. Chapter 6 is devoted to pollution control in bakery industry. Even though bakery industry is a low polluting industry but for the ovens, boilers, hot water generators, DG sets they all come under the air pollution act due to emission of flue gases through stack. Chapter 7 deals with pollution control in poultry industry and discusses technical options to mitigate environmental impacts, such as improvements to farm management, animal waste management and nutrition management, along with options to reduce the impacts of intensive feed production. Chapter 8 focuses on pollution control in meat industry which has the potential for generating large quantities of solid wastes and wastewater with a BOD of 600. Chapter 9 concentrates on pollution control in seafood food industry. Environmental issues in fish processing industries primarily include– water consumption and wastewater generation, solid waste generation and by-products production, emission to air and energy consumption. Chapter 10 discusses potato wastewater treatment. Potato processing and sources of waste-water treatment and potato wastes as substrate for organic material production are also discussed. Chapter 11 explains residual management in fruit processing plants.

Section II discusses solar energy and water conservation in food processing. Chapter 12 is devoted to solar energy potential in food industry. Chapter 13 deals with water conservation in food processing industry. Water has been used in the food processing industry as a medium of great convenience for transportation, heat transfer and sanitation. Developing a water conservation/waste minimisation programme for a food processing plant is a very simple and economical way to increase overall plant efficiency.

Section III discusses emission of greenhouse gases sustainability and carbon footprint. Chapter 14 focuses on food production and emission of greenhouse gases. Food chains around the world are responsible for a large share of total emissions of greenhouse gases (GHG). There are no studies presenting the share for the global food production system, but as an indication, Steinfeldt and others reported that 18% of global GHG emissions could be attributed to animal products alone. Chapter 15 concentrates on impact of food processing on the sustainability of the food supply chain. Environmental sustainability cannot be considered in isolation because economic and social sustainability are essential to the industry. To ensure that the food processing industry is economically and environmentally sustainable, it is important to take an integrated approach of the whole food supply chain including farm and post operations. Chapter 16 explains carbon and water footprint in food industry. The carbon footprint is a measure of the amount of greenhouse gases (GHG) produced by our activities in relation to carbon dioxide (CO_2) or carbon. The water footprint of a good or a service is the total amount of water, external and internal, that is required to produce it. The concept can be used to calculate and compare the strain on water resources resulting from different options. It can also be extended to provide water budgets for whole nations or continents.

Section IV discusses nanotechnology, hydrocolloides and enzymes. Chapter 17 is devoted to nanotechnology in agriculture and food industry. Nanotechnology has the potential to revolutionise the agricultural and food industry with new tools for the molecular treatment of diseases, rapid disease detection, enhancing the ability of plants to absorb nutrients, etc. Chapter 18 deals with hydrocolloids in food industry. Hydrocolloids or gums are a diverse group of long chain polymers characterised by their property of forming viscous dispersions and/or gels when dispersed in water. They also produce a dispersion, which is intermediate between a true solution and a suspension, and exhibits the properties of a colloid. Chapter 19 concentrates on enzymes in food processing industry. Food processing enzymes are used in starch processing, meat processing, dairy industry, wine industry and in manufacture of pre-digested foods.

Section V discusses spices, sweetners and vitamins. Chapter 20 focuses on spices and allied products. Various species such as—ajowan, amchur, anardana, hing, lalmirch, etc. are discussed in detail. Chapter 21 discusses sweeteners in foods. Chapter 22 explains vitamins. Vitamins are a group of organic nutrients of various nature required in small quantities for multiple biochemical reactions for the growth, survival and reproduction of the organism, and which, generally, cannot be synthesised by the body and must therefore be supplied by the diet. The most prominent function of the vitamins is to serve as co-enzymes (or prosthetic group) for enzymatic reactions.

Section VI discusses food flavours and food additives. Chapter 23 is devoted to food flavours. Classification of flavours and their applications in fruit, beverages, species, meat, etc. are briefly discussed. The reality of good food production is in learning how to control flavours during manufacturing. Process conditions can be maximised for flavour constituents and the resulting isolates which can be utilised to control the flavour of foods. But in order to control flavour, one must be able to analyse the flavour components both qualitatively and quantitatively. Chapter 24 deals with food additives. Function of food additives and their applications in particular processing is discussed.

Section VII discusses cleaning and disinfection, food poisoning, toxicity and HACCP. Chapter 25 concentrates on disinfection and sanitation. The chapter describes the principles of sanitation, the chemicals and equipment involved, and the programme of events to be followed. Chapter 26 explains food poisoning. Food poisoning syndrome results from ingestion of water and wide variety of food contaminated with pathogenic micro-organisms (bacteria, viruses, protozoa, fungi), their toxins and chemicals. Chapter 27 discusses food toxicity and safety. Sources of food toxicity are diverse, both biological and environmental in nature. Major biological sources of food toxicity are viral, bacterial and fungal contamination which cause different gastrointestinal disorders, predominantly diarrhoea, cholera, typhoid fever and hepatic viral diseases while environmental sources include fertilisers and pesticide application and diverse chemical wastes emitting form industries which make their way to food through several means, ranging from direct pathogenic infestations to pre-harvest irrigation with contaminated water, application of fertilisers and pesticides to chemical wastes. Chapter 28 focuses on hazard analysis critical control point. Hazard Analysis Critical Control Point (HACCP) is a food safety system designed to identify and control hazards that may occur in the food production process. The HACCP approach focuses on preventing potential problems that are critical to food safety known as 'critical control points' (CCP) through monitoring and controlling each step of the process.

Section VIII discusses packaging of food and allied products. Chapter 29 is devoted to modified atmosphere packaging. Modified atmosphere packaging (MAP) is defined as 'the packaging of a perishable product in an atmosphere that has been modified so that its composition is other than that of air'. Whereas controlled atmosphere storage (CAS) involves maintaining a fixed concentration of gases surrounding the product by careful monitoring and addition of gases, the gaseous composition of fresh MAP foods is constantly changing due to chemical reactions and microbial activity. Chapter 30 deals with biodegradable polymers in food packaging. The principal function of packaging is protection and preservation of food from external contamination. This function involves retardation of deterioration, extension of shelf life, and maintenance of quality and safety of packaged food. Biodegradable polymers are the one which fulfill all these functions without causing any threat to the environment. Chapter 31 focuses on recent developments in food packaging based on nanomaterials. This chapter summarises the recent developments of nanomaterials in food packaging. Two categories of nanomaterials (i.e. inorganic and organic) are included. This chapter also highlights the possible mechanisms of antimicrobial activity against bacteria of certain active nanomaterials and their health concerns. It concludes with an outlook of the nanomaterials functionalised in food packaging.

Section IX discusses food laws and food ethics. Chapter 32 concentrates on food laws and regulations. Food law is based on scientific studies. The principles or general provisions to be included in food law are primarily: basic purposes and scope, definitions of basic concepts, inspection, enforcement, biological and chemical contaminants, packaging and labelling, and procedures for the preparation and amendment of the regulations for implementation of the law. Chapter 33 explains food ethics. Food ethics refers to the moral consequences of food choices, both those made by humans for themselves and those made for food animals. Common concerns are damage to the environment, exploitive labour practices, food shortages for others, inhumane treatment of food for animals, and the unintended effects of food policy. Ethical eating is a type of ethical consumerism.

Diagrams, figures, tables and index supplement the text. All topics have been covered in a cogent and lucid style to help the reader grasp the information quickly and easily.

It may not be wrong to hold that the present reference textbook of *Food Processing and Preservation* is a complete treatise on this subject. It is essential reading for BTech. (environmental biotechnology/ microbiology/food biotechnology/microbiology/biomedical and biochemical engineering) and students pursuing BSc/MSc course in biotechnology and microbiology. Besides students, this book will prove useful to industrialists and consultants in the respective fields.

The reference textbook also caters to the requirement of the syllabus prescribed by various universities for undergraduate and postgraduate courses in the above subjects. It has been prepared with meticulous care, aiming at making the book error-free. Constructive suggestions are always welcome from users of this book.

DS Warris

Contents

SECTION I

Pollution Control in Food Processing Industry

Chapter 1

Pollution Control in Food Processing Industry: A Review

INTRODUCTION

The food processing industry has special concerns about the health and safety of the consumer. Key resources used by the food processing industry include the water, raw materials and energy. Traditionally, the food processing industry has been a large water user. Water is used as an ingredient, an initial and intermediate cleaning source, an efficient transportation conveyor of raw materials and the principal agent used in sanitising plant machinery and areas. Although water use will always be a part of the food processing industry, it has become the principal target for pollution prevention, source reduction practices.

The key environmental issues for the food industry include the following:

Wastewater: Primary issues of concern are Biochemical Oxygen Demand (BOD), Total Suspended Solids (TSS), excessive nutrient loading, namely nitrogen and phosphorus compounds, pathogenic organisms, which are a result of animal processing, and residual chlorine and pesticide levels.

Solid waste: Primary issues of concern include both organic and packaging waste. Organic waste, that is, the rinds, seeds, skin and bones from raw materials, results from processing operations. Inorganic wastes typically include excessive packaging items that are, plastic, glass and metal. Organic wastes are finding ever-increasing markets for resale and companies are slowly switching to more biodegradable and recyclable products for packaging. Excessive packaging has been reduced and recyclable products such as aluminium, glass and High-Density Polyethylene (HDPE) are being used where applicable. The food processing factories should follow the major technological innovations in the industry, including those in clean technologies and processes. Clean technologies include:

1. Advanced wastewater treatment practices: Use of wastewater technologies beyond conventional secondary treatment.
2. Improved packaging: Use of less excessive and more environmentally friendly packaging products.
3. Improved sensors and process control: Use of advanced techniques to control specific portions of the manufacturing process to reduce wastes and increase productivity.

4. Food irradiation: Use of radiation to kill pathogenic micro-organisms.
5. Water and wastewater reduction (closed loop/zero emission systems): Reduction or total elimination of effluent from the manufacturing process

POLLUTION FROM FOOD PROCESSING

Food processing can be divided into four major sectors including fruit and vegetables, meat, poultry and seafood, beverage and bottling and dairy operations. All of these sectors consume huge amount of water for processing food. A considerable part of these waters are potential wastewaters to be treated for safe disposal to the environment. Table 1.1 shows typical rates of water use for various food processing sectors. An abundant and inexpensive source of water is a requirement for success in the food processing industry. This coincides with the same need for water resources in agricultural farm land activities.

Table 1.1: Typical rates for water use for various industries.

Industry	*Range of flow gal/T product*
Fruits and vegetables	
Green beans	12000–17000
Peaches and pears	3600–4800
Other fruits and vegetables	960–8400
Food and beverage	
Beer	2400–3840
Bread	480–960
Meat packing	3600–4800
Milk products	2400–4800
Whiskey	14400–19200

Fruit and Vegetable Food Processing Sector

The primary steps in processing fruits and vegetables include:

1. General cleaning and dirt removal.
2. Removal of leaves, skin and seeds.
3. Blanching.
4. Washing and cooling.
5. Packaging.
6. Cleanup.

Wastewater and solid wastes are the primary area of pollution control within the fruit and vegetable food processing industry. Their wastewater is high in suspended solids and organic sugars and starches and may contain residual pesticides. Solid wastes include organic materials from mechanical preparation processes that is, rinds, seeds and skins from raw materials. For the most part, solid waste that is not resold as animal feed is handled by conventional biological treatment or composting. The total amount of material generated is a function of the amount of raw material moved through a facility, for example, for a given weight of apples processed comes a set amount of peel and seed waste.

Attempts to decrease solid waste streams have not been an area of great development for pollution prevention opportunities and clean technologies. Pre-treatment opportunities intended to reduce the amount of raw materials lost to the waste stream have been an area of clean technology development. For the most part, the majority of clean technology advances and research have been in reducing the volume of wastewater generated in food processing operations. Most fruit and vegetable processors use traditional biological means to treat their wastewater. Advancements in the degradation chemistries of pesticides have aided in reducing their quantities and toxicity in process wastewater.

Washing fresh produce (also known as surface treatment) can reduce the overall potential for microbial food safety hazards. This is an important step since most microbial contamination is on the surface of fruits and vegetables. If pathogens are not removed, inactivated, or otherwise controlled, they can spread to surrounding produce, potentially contaminating a significant proportion of the produce.

Sanitizers or anti-microbials in wash water and other processing water may be useful in reducing pathogens on the surface of produce and/or reducing pathogen build-up in water.

The effectiveness of a sanitiser depends on its chemical and physical nature, treatment conditions (such as water temperature, pH and contact time), resistance of pathogens and the nature of the fruit or vegetable surface. Chlorine is a commonly used anti-microbial.

Chlorine dioxide, trisodium phosphate, organic acids and ozone have also been studied for use as anti-microbials in produce wash water. All chemical substances that contact food must be used in accordance with FDA and EPA regulations.

Meat, Poultry and Seafood Sector

The primary steps in processing livestock include:

1. Rendering and bleeding.
2. Scalding and/or skin removal.
3. Internal organ evisceration.
4. Washing, chilling and cooling.
5. Packaging.
6. Cleanup.

Meat, poultry and seafood facilities offer a more difficult waste stream to treat. The killing and rendering processes create blood by-products and waste streams, which are extremely high in BOD. These facilities are very prone to disease spread by pathogenic organisms carried and transmitted by livestock, poultry and seafood. This segment of the food processing industry is by far the most regulated and monitored.

Waste streams vary per facility, but they can be generalised into the following: process wastewaters, carcasses and skeleton waste, rejected or unsatisfactory animals, fats, oils and greases (FOG), animal feces, blood and eviscerated organs. The primary avenue for removal of solid waste has been its use in animal feed, cosmetics and fertilisers. These solid wastes are high in protein and nitrogen content. They are excellent sources for recycled fish feed and pet food. Skeleton remains from meat processing are converted into bonemeal, which is an excellent source of phosphorus for fertilisers. FOG waste (typically from industrial fisheries) is used as a base raw material in the cosmetics industry.

Beverage and Fermentation Sector

The primary steps in processing beverages are:

1. Raw material handling and processing.
2. Mixing, fermentation, and/or cooking.

3. Cooling.
4. Bottling and packaging.
5. Cleanup.

Wastewater and solid waste are the primary waste streams for the beverage and fermentation sector. Solid wastes result from spent grains and materials used in the fermentation process. Wastewater volume of 'soft drink processes' is lower than in other food processing sectors, but fermentation processes are higher in BOD and overall wastewater volume compared to other food processing sectors. Ozone technology has proven very useful in the beverage market since the earliest 20th century. In bottled water plants, ozone can be used to disinfect product water without leaving any residual taste or odour. At beverage plants, ozone can reduce or eliminate the need for chemical or high temperature disinfections during clean-in-place (CIP) cycles, reducing downtime and chemical costs.

Dairy Sector

A majority of the waste milk in dairy wastewaters comes from start-up and shutdown operations performed in the High-Temperature Short Time (HTST) pasteurisation process. This waste is pure milk raw material mixed with water. Another waste stream of the dairy sector is from equipment and tank-cleaning wastewaters. These waste streams contain waste milk and sanitary cleaners and are one of the principal waste constituents of dairy wastewater. Over time, milk waste degrades to form corrosive lactic and formic acids. Approximately 90% of a dairy's wastewater load is milk.

Can Cooker Products

Water plays a role in most of the problems associated with metal food containers after processing. Whether steam, hot water or cold water, each can serve as the vehicle to transport undesirable substances. It is important to understand, when designing an effective, comprehensive water treatment programme, how these mechanisms chemically interact.

Wastewater from Food Processing Industries

Food processing wastewater can be characterised as nontoxic, because it contains few hazardous and persistent compounds. With the exception of some toxic cleaning products, wastewater from food processing facilities is organic and can be treated by conventional biological technologies. Part of the problem with the food processing industry's use and discharge of large amounts of water is that it is located in rural areas in which the water treatment systems (i.e. potable and wastewater systems) are designed to serve small populations. As a result, one medium-sized plant can have a major effect on local water supply and surface water quality. Large food processing plants will typically use more than 1000000 gallons of potable water per day.

Another contaminant of food processing wastewaters, particularly from meat-, poultry- and seafood processing facilities, is pathogenic organisms. Wastewaters with high pathogenic levels must be disinfected prior to discharge. Typically, chlorine (free or combined) is used to disinfect these wastewaters. Ozone, ultraviolet (UV) radiation and other nontraditional disinfection processes are gaining acceptance due to stricter regulations on the amount of residual chlorine levels in discharged wastewaters.

The pH of a wastewater is of paramount importance to a receiving stream and POTW. Biological micro organisms, used in wastewater treatment, are sensitive to extreme fluctuations in pH. Companies that are found to be the responsible polluter are fined and/or ordered to shut down operations until their pH level meets acceptable values. Wastewater discharge values that range from 5 to 9 on the pH logarithmic scale are usually acceptable. Low pH values are more damaging to a receiving stream and POTW biological treatment process. The food processing industry utilises water to meet its individual day-to-day needs. Fifty per cent of the water used in the fruit and vegetable sector is for washing and rinsing. Water is the primary ingredient in products for the beverage and fermentation sector and dairies utilise water as the standard cleaning agent for process machinery.

Defining Load using BOD_5 and COD

Chemical Oxygen Demand (COD) and biochemical oxygen demand (BOD_5) are common measurements used to determine water quality. They measure the strength of the waste stream by measuring the oxygen required to stabilise the wastes. The five-day biochemical oxygen demand (BOD_5) value is used as a gauge to measure the level of treatment needed to discharge a wastewater safely to a receiving water treatment center. The BOD for all food processing wastewater is relatively high compared to other industries. A high BOD level indicates that a wastewater contains elevated amounts of organic material, dissolved and/or suspended solids, minerals, nitrogen and phosphorus.

COD and BOD_5 are important to the food processing industry because they can be used to indicate lost product and wasteful practices. High BOD_5 and COD levels indicate increased amounts of product lost to the waste stream. Measurements at various process locations can help locate sources of waste.

Relating COD to BOD_5

At any point in a particular food processing operation, the relationship between BOD_5 and COD is fairly consistent. However, the ratio's of these two measures varies widely with the type of product (Table 1.2).

Table 1.2: Typical values of BOD_5 and COD for different food plant wastewater.

Type of processor	*BOD_5 (mg/L)*	*COD (mg/L)*	*BOD_5/COD*
Bakery products	3200	7000	0.46
Dairy processing	2700	4700	0.57
Jams and jellies	2400	4000	0.60
Meat packing	1433	2746	0.52
Meat specialties	530	900	0.59
Poultry processor	1306	1581	0.83

ENVIRONMENTAL PROTECTION

Source Reduction

The most effective method of environmental protection and reducing your disposal costs is to decrease the volume of waste material and by-products generated in the production process. If less waste is generated, then less material needs to be disposed of. Source reduction should be the most logical starting point for reducing disposal costs since your company is in business to produce a saleable product, not waste materials or by-products.

Examples of source reduction include:

1. Use brooms and scrapers to clean floors and equipment while they are dry before washing them down with water.
2. Use high-pressure spray washes during cleanup to conserve water.

3. Dedicate mixing lines to certain products to reduce changeover cleanups.
4. Minimise spills and leaks on the production line to prevent raw materials from becoming wastes.

Management Alternatives

If source reduction is not a viable solution, management alternatives exist, including:

1. Using the food by-product as an animal feed.
2. Composting or land spreading the food by-product.

Animal feed

Feeding food by-products directly to livestock allows for former wastes to be useful again. In addition, the quantity of liquid and solid waste is reduced when by-products are fed to livestock rather than being disposed of in landfills or wastewater treatment plants.

Composting and land spreading

When it is impractical to feed by-products to livestock, both composting and land spreading the food waste are viable alternatives. Both methods degrade food by-products into a useful soil additive called 'humus.' Composting degrades by-products above ground in a concentrated area, while land spreading degrades by-products beneath the soil in a cultivated field.

Composting: With proper management, food by-products can be kept out of the landfill and instead be composted and added to the soil at appropriate rates. Composting has the following benefits:

1. Low transportation costs: The by-products can be composted on site and the resulting humus can have a volume and weight reduction of up to 40%.
2. Low capital investment: Composting is a batch process that can be done by using either a mound or a windrow system. In both systems all the by-products are managed to accelerate biological breakdown.
3. Good for seasonal processors: For a company (such as a cannery) that only processes food for several months a year, composting may be a suitable alternative to animal feeding or land filling. Livestock producers may be unwilling to switch to a livestock feed that is only available for a short period.
4. Long shelf life: Humus can be stored without spoiling and applied to enrich the soil as needed.

Land spreading: If your company has sufficient land, it is possible to incorporate food by-products directly into the soil on site . A farmer can be paid to take the by-products to a suitable field. Again, with proper management, food is kept out of the landfill and is used to enhance the soil. Land spreading has the following benefits:

1. A separate compost facility is not necessary.
2. The finished product does not have to be stored.
3. The finished product does not have to be transported. It is left in the soil as a plant nutrient.

Clean Technology Developments

Because wastewater generation is the industry's biggest area of concern, the following clean technologies focus on source reduction, recycling, reuse and treatment of wastewater. Clean technologies are defined as 'manufacturing processes or product technologies that reduce pollution or waste, energy use, or material use in comparison to the technologies that they replace.' The food processing industry has special concerns about the health and safety of the consumer. It should be noted that some of the technologies outlined in the report target both human health and environmental pollution issues.

Common source reduction methods employed at most plants include improving good housekeeping practices, making process modifications, substituting more environmentally friendly raw materials and segregating waste streams. Some simple cost-effective means of achieving source reduction include installing automatic shut-off valves, using low-flow or air injected faucets/spray cleaners, switching from chemical caustic peeling processes to mechanical peeling and converting from water to mechanical conveyance of raw materials through a production line.

Advanced Wastewater Treatment Practices

Advanced wastewater treatment is defined as any treatment beyond secondary (or biological) treatment. These treatment practices are employed to target specific discharge constituents that are of concern. Typically, pathogens, suspended solids, dissolved solids, nitrogen and phosphorus are removed in advanced wastewater treatment. The following is a listing of some technologies being used in advanced wastewater treatment.

1. Membrane applications.
2. Disinfection.
3. Charge separation.
4. Other separation practices.

Membrane applications

Membrane applications focus on separating water from contaminants, using semi permeable membranes and applied pressure differentials. In generic terms, they work like window screens that let air but not insects and other larger objects pass through. The smaller the screen holes, the smaller the objects need to be to pass through. Pressure is applied to reverse the natural equilibrium between the clean water and wastewater. The basic principle of natural equilibrium is that the clean water tends to migrate to the wastewater side to equalise the concentrations across the membrane. Mechanical pressure is used to force water molecules from the wastewater side to the clean water side and, thus, a 'high-tech' filtration of the wastewater occurs.

In the past, the energy needed to apply the pressure and the fragility of the membrane surface made use of these alternatives economically unjustifiable. There are varying degrees of membrane filtration. Microfiltration, Ultrafiltration (UF) and Reverse Osmosis (RO) are the current membrane systems used commercially.

The filtering capabilities of each (i.e. ability to filter based on contaminant particle size) decrease respectively. Microfiltration is only recommended for removing particles from 0.05 to 2 microns in size, UF is used for particles and suspended solids from 0.005–0.1 microns and RO is used for particles, suspended solids and dissolved solids in the Angstrom range (e.g. molecular weight above 200).

Problems with membrane applications include befouling of the membrane and fragility of the membrane surface. Toxic synthetic compounds can oxidise the surface of the membrane, thus, destroying it. New innovations in membrane technology have advanced the 'cleanability' and reuse of membranes. The use of stainless steel and ceramic materials for membranes has greatly improved their use in advanced wastewater treatment.

Sanitary conditions have always been a concern for food products created in the manufacturing process. In recent years, they have also become a requirement of wastewater effluent. As for water treatment practices, disinfection through chlorination has been the quickest means of disinfecting wastewater. Disinfection has come under criticism due to chlorination by-products and toxicity concerns that residual chlorine pose to aquatic life. The two principal means of disinfecting wastewater without using chlorination are ozone disinfection or UV disinfection. Ozonation works on the same principle as chlorination but leaves no residual in the treated wastewater and does not produce the magnitude of disinfection by-products that chlorination produces. UV disinfection is even more environmentally friendly than ozone but requires more space and cleaner wastewater to be effective. Both technologies require high capital and operating costs.

Charge separation

Charge separation involves separating uncharged water molecules and charged contaminants, such as nitrogen compounds and phosphates (i.e. NH_4^+, NO_2^-, NO_3^- and PO_4^{-3}). Electro-coagulation is starting to be an economical way of removing charged particles from wastewater, utilising charge separation. Ion exchange is widely used to filter wastewater through cationic and anionic resins to remove the wastewater's charged ions of concern. Ion exchange replaces the waste particles with a donor ion from the resin. The resins eventually reach a capacity at which all the ions have been replaced or exchanged. The resin manufacturer typically recycles spent resin. Problems with using ion exchange are that it requires monitoring for breakthrough contamination and pH fluctuations can greatly affect the removal rates of specific ions (e.g. a pH greater than 9.3 makes ammonium removal inefficient). Also, resins remove ions selectively, meaning the greater the charge differential from neutrality, the greater the exchange attraction between the resin and the charged contaminant (e.g. Ca^{+2} will be removed before NH_4^+).

Other separation practices

Other separation practices include using centrifugal and gravity mechanisms to separate and remove contaminants from a wastewater. Air flotation systems use diffused pumped air to lift suspended solids and FOG wastes to the surface of a wastewater for removal. Skimmers and mechanical devices are then employed to separate waste from the surface. Problems with using either of these methods include capital costs to modify current treatment processes and increased operational energy costs. With the exception of centrifugal and gravity separation, all these advanced treatments require a wastewater influent that is low in turbidity.

Benefits

Studies have shown that membrane applications can be less energy intensive than evaporation and distillation operations and take up less space. The technology gives better control of the process effluent. Unlike chemical precipitation, membrane technology does not produce a sludge disposal problem, but it does produce a concentrated brine solution. The main benefit of disinfecting wastewater is that it improves and protects water quality of and aquatic life in the receiving water. Similar to membrane applications, ion exchange does not produce a chemical sludge and, like disinfection, it protects the water quality of receiving water and decreases the nutrient-loading problems that cause eutrophication in receiving waters. Electro-coagulation is beginning to receive attention as a treatment option and is expected to increase in use in the food processing industry.

Centrifugal and gravity separation processes are placed before any of the preceding advanced operations. This ensures that a cleaner, less turbid wastewater reaches these advanced operations. As stated earlier, the recovered FOG is a resalable by-product. Use of any of these advanced processes improves the final wastewater effluent quality and also increases the likelihood of recycling renovated process water.

Water and Wastewater Reduction (Closed Loop/Zero Emission Systems)

An increasingly viable option for companies is the 'zero-discharge' system. Many food processing facilities are looking to pre-treatment options that can help reduce the amount of lost product. Once a part of the food product is lost to a waste stream, it represents a decrease in product utilisation and an increase in treatment costs. A large capital expenditure and a customised treatment solution are required to handle a zero-discharge option. Furthermore, the uniqueness of the various food processing operations makes it impossible to find 'off-the-shelf' treatment designs to fit a user's needs. A more plausible approach is that of achieving zero emissions.

As noted earlier, the 'zero emissions' strategy relies on a network of companies utilising each other's waste streams. The strategy is a more economically efficient system than a 'closed loop' because the waste products do not have to be fully treated. Although facilities are moving toward decreased effluent quantities, material mass balances still dictate that process residuals such as sludge will require management and possibly off-site disposal. Both zero discharge and zero emission systems achieve better effluent water quality and have fewer negative impacts on the environment.

FUTURE TRENDS

Regulations and Standards

International standards developed by the Geneva based International Organisation of Standardisation, called ISO 14000, represent the latest attempts to provide a global environmental management system. ISO 14000 was intended to help organisations manage and evaluate the environmental aspects of their operations without being prescriptive.

The International Organisation of Standardisation intends to provide companies with a framework to comply with both domestic and foreign environmental regulations. ISO 14000 contains sections calling for implementation of pollution prevention programmes and many US, companies are evaluating the pros and cons of becoming fully certified in ISO 14001. Furthermore, EPA is talking about easing reporting requirements for US, companies that earn ISO 14001 certification.

Industry Trends

There are several ongoing trends and research and development activities apparent within the food processing community in the areas of pollution prevention and clean technology implementation.

Solid waste reduction

Companies will continue to look at ways to reduce solid waste generation, use less or reusable packaging and use biodegradable packing products. Excessive packaging has been reduced and recyclable products such as aluminium, glass and HDPE are expected to continue being used to a wider degree in packaging situations.

Mechanical versus chemical processing

Companies will show increased consideration for using mechanical methods for food processing (e.g. the fruit and vegetable sector). Mechanical processing can be used to perform many of the same functions as chemical processing. The costs and benefits of using mechanical versus chemical processing will be further quantified to aid in decision making.

Pre-treatment Options, Water Conservation and Wastewater Reduction

Pre-treatment opportunities and water conservation will continue to be principal targets for pollution prevention source reduction practices in the food processing industry. Pre-treatment options look to minimise the loss of raw materials to the food processing waste streams. Water used in conveying materials, facility cleanup, or other non-ingredient uses will be reduced, which in turn will reduce the wastewater volume from food processing facilities. Wastewater treatment will continue to be the pollution prevention treatment focus for food processing companies. The industry will continue to implement advanced innovative techniques to lessen the environmental impact of food processing discharge wastewaters.

Chapter 2

Food Pollution – Basic Concepts

INTRODUCTION

There are many well-known forms of environmental pollution such as air or water pollution, but there is one pollution even more insidious than these and yet it has been neglected almost completely. It is the pollution of our food. This chapter deals with some major characteristics of food pollution.

Environment has been defined as 'the sum total of all conditions and influences that affect the development and life of organisms'. This is a very comprehensive definition since it stresses the totality of the environment and includes not only human beings but also every living organism. It is obvious that environmental pollution will have adverse effects on the life and well-being of all living things and, if not checked in time, it may threaten the very existence of life on our planet.

Food is more than just physical fuel. Its quality can affect individual and public health in a fundamental manner. The choice of food depends on culture, social class and status, income levels, the place we live in and so on. Food is also a vehicle for social relationships. That is why there is an urgent need to address the issue of food pollution.

This chapter will deal with more specific aspects of food pollution such as additives, pesticide residues, fertilisers, food irradiation and food poisoning.

Food pollution may be defined as all accidental or nonaccidental preventable changes in foods or food processes which reduce the quality of foods and/or create avoidable risks. Food pollution, as defined above, may be classified under three broad categories as follows:

1. Addition: Use of various food additives such as colours, flavours, texture modifiers, etc. to make food products more attractive or to make food processing mechanically easier and faster.
2. Contamination: Unintentional infection or tainting of foods, meaning undesirable residues, inappropriate particles or micro-organisms getting into foods.
3. Adulteration: Intentional debasement or counterfeiting of foods, dressing up or manufacturing foods so they can be passed off as something that they are not.
4. Food pollution can be intentional as well as accidental, and often it is perfectly legal (e.g. the use of approved colours and flavours).

FOOD POLLUTION AND PUBLIC HEALTH

Health concerns about food (and its pollution) are in plenty. Some of these are: Saturated fats and coronary heart disease, debate on salt and sugar, food additives, irradiation of foods, pesticide residues, nitrates in food and water, hormones and antibiotics, and the impact of poverty on food intake and health. The concern about health hazards of contaminated and adulterated food has emerged from a varied coalition of interests, which include those of consumers, environmentalists, epidemiologists, nutritionists and researchers into worker health and safety. The explosion of public interest in food and health in the last two decades is not confined to a few developed countries alone, almost every country, regardless of its state of development, shares it to some extent.

In the real world, however, food manufacturers (and also governments) have considerations other than public health. Some of these considerations are: What are the competitors doing? How profitable will the new products or processes be? How can the new products be sold? Will there be consumer reaction? These considerations can easily take precedence over ensuring that a product or process is safe. There is an urgent need, therefore, to have a more developed and critical food science which can cry 'foul' on the behalf of public if necessary. Certainly there should be more awareness about how foods are produced and processed since the quality of food depends on the manner of its production and processing.

Fighting Food Pollution

All people have the right to unpolluted food. What is needed is a food policy which ensures that all people have affordable, good quality, safe, nutritious and enjoyable food. Since food is human fuel, it should also be a pleasure, but not at the cost of health or welfare. Open information and education about food is essential to achieve these objectives. Some suggestions to fight food pollution and make foods safe for the public are given below:

1. Public protection should be given the highest priority by the governments when any decisions are made by them about food. Industry must not be allowed to adulterate food, at the expense of public health, merely for commercial advantage.
2. Access to information is essential if consumers are to participate fully in the matters concerning food, so there should be a Freedom of Information Act. Full labelling of processed foods should be mandatory and manufacturers should be obliged to disclose full information on food ingredients and additives used by them.
3. Addition of non-nutritional substances to food should be minimised. Food industry's requests to use additives and potential contaminants should be strictly assessed by government agencies so that the public is not exposed to substances that may have long-term adverse effects on health or food quality.
4. Existing legal controls should be improved to protect the public. Standards are, in many cases, either absent or too low. New standards should be created to give the public highest degree of protection and boost export of foods.
5. More resources, statutory powers and duties should be given to local authorities to empower them to protect the public interest in matters of food.
6. A starting point for fighting food pollution is a well-informed, vigilant and assertive alliance of consumers, trade unions, environmentalists and health groups. Since such alliances play a vital role in creating public debate and educating the public on food matters, they should be encouraged as a matter of policy.

FOOD POLLUTION: PESTICIDE RESIDUES IN FOOD

Environmental pollution is among the major problems facing the developing countries like India today. Pollution of food though not as familiar as air or water pollution, is even more insidious and widespread than these. This section presents a detailed discussion on an important aspect of food pollution, viz., pesticide residues in food, with special reference of India. The injudicious use of agrochemicals, drugs, cosmetics, food additives, etc. coupled with the simultaneous pollution of the environment, is not only disturbing the ecological balance, but also nullifying the benefits of scientific and technological advances. It is hardly necessary, therefore, to stress an urgent need to safeguard men and animals from the hazards of toxic chemicals and environmental pollution.

Pesticides and the Environment

Pesticides

Pesticides are not a recent invention. Dried chrysanthemum flowers, still used to prepare natural pyrethroid pesticides, have been used for at least a century to kill insect pests on food crops. The development of chemical methods of pest control, however, only started in the middle of the nineteenth century, initially for insect pests, but later on for the control of weeds, fungal infections and for other competitive organisms.

Most pesticides can be classified as insecticides, herbicides or fungicides. On the other hand, some pesticides (known generally as fumigants) can perform simultaneously the functions of all the three types of pesticides mentioned above. Pesticides have a wide variety of modes of action against intended pests but, in simple terms, they may be categorised as systemic or contact pesticides. Systemic pesticides are those which actually enter the plant. These pesticides are, therefore, able to attack pests at other parts of the plant away from the areas of application. On the other hand, contact pesticides are those which act upon the intended pest or weed at the point of contact.

Environmental hazards

Pesticides came into extensive use in the early forties of the twentieth century and led to enhanced farm productivity and inexpensive control of vector-borne diseases. Chlorinated pesticides such as DDT, dieldrin and mirex were hailed with great enthusiasm as the harbingers of a new era of freedom from hunger and pestilence. Inspite of all these benefits, however, the indiscriminate use of pesticides may be considered as one of the most hazardous operations posing potential threat to our living environment. When carelessly applied, chemical pesticides can result in many acute and long-term side-effects such as sickness and death of human beings, useful animals, fish and birds and destruction of crops. Even when properly used, chemical pesticides have many unavoidable and adverse side-effects. Their long persistence in the environment, combined with a tendency of some pesticides to concentrate in organisms as they move up the food chain, may increase their toxicity to fish, birds and other forms of life including man. The harmful pesticide residues that remain on crop (especially the edible portion) have been a cause of great concern to everyone. In addition to the contamination of food, the pesticides (particularly the persistent ones) get translocated into the air, water and soil system from the point of initial application and endanger the life of non-target organisms inhabiting the soil and aquatic system. There is ample evidence to show that animals in higher levels of food chain accumulate more pesticide than lower organisms. This results in a large bioaccumulation and biomagnification of persistent pesticides like DDT and BHC in the bodies of fish-eating birds, predatory birds, animals and human beings. Thus the pesticide residues present in animal tissues, food products and human bodies are a cause of great concern about their long-term toxic effects.

Health Hazards of Pesticide Residues

Possible hazards

Most foods probably contain pesticide residues. In connection with food, pesticide toxicity may be classified as acute or chronic. Acute toxicity is the type of poisoning which leads to almost immediate symptoms of poisoning. Although the route of poisoning may be through inhalation, through the skin or through ingestion, it is the latter route which is of most relevance in studying the effects of pesticide residues in foods. Chronic toxicity, on the other hand, is the type of ill health where long-term intake of lower doses produces symptoms which may be hard to attribute to a specific source.

It is well known that entire groups of pesticides are poisonous—often because the very mechanism by which they are effective against pests is equally effective against human beings. Thus all the major groups of insecticides used (organochlorides, organophosphates, carbamates and pyrethroids) are thought to be effective by immobilising the nervous system in Insects. Given sufficient doses, most of these insecticides have similar effects on people, although their toxicity varies widely. Quite apart from severe acute insecticide poisoning, which requires emergency treatment in a hospital, many other illnesses caused by malfunctions of the nervous system may be attributed to pesticide residues in food. Chronic poisoning effects such as cancer and birth defects have been linked with many pesticides.

Chemical ecologists believe that pesticide residues in foods induce a whole range of debilitating effects such as migraine, abdominal pain, behaviour disorder, fits, asthma and eczema. It is very difficult, however, to identify and establish precise links between these ill health effects and individual chemicals. The reason is that the range of harmful chemicals in the environment is so large and the treatment method usually involves removing the patient from all possible chemical stimuli.

Overall toxicity

The Environmental Protection Agency of the USA had commissioned a report from an independent organisation the National Research Council (NRC)—on how to minimise the cancer risks of pesticides. By comparing data on toxicology and the levels of pesticides use, the NRC estimated that 30 per cent of insecticides, 60 per cent of herbicides and 90 per cent of fungicides could cause tumours. On the other hand, the types of pesticides products used on particular crops differ very little from one country to another since the pesticide market is now international.

By comparing the likelihood of different pesticides causing tumours with their usage on different crops in the USA, the NRC compiled a list of 15 foods most likely to contain the highest levels of tumour-causing pesticide residues. These 15 most risky foods listed in order of decreasing toxicity were: (i) tomatoes, (ii) beef, (iii) potatoes, (iv) oranges, (v) lettuce, (vi) apples, (vii) peaches, (viii) pork, (ix) wheat, (x) soyabeans, (xi) beans, (xii) carrots, (xiii) chicken, (xiv) corn, and (xv) grapes. On the basis of epidemiological studies, it has been estimated that one in about 200 cancer cases in the USA may be attributed to pesticides. Such figures, however, underestimate the true incidence of pesticide-induced diseases. The reason is that chronic effects like cancer may take many years to become evident. Pesticide usage, on the other hand, has risen rapidly since the Second World War, so the current mortality reflect old risk levels—not the present ones.

Controlling pesticides use

One of the reasons why it is important for governments to protect public health from pesticides is that it is very difficult for individuals to fully protect themselves. Washing fresh fruit and vegetables before use, for example, will certainly remove some pesticide residues from surface, but systemic pesticides are designed to enter into the target crop and in addition to the surface, they will also be present inside the fruit and vegetables. Such difficulties are often compounded by the conflict between avoiding pesticides and pursuing healthy eating habits. Nutritionists, for example, recommend eating more fresh fruits and vegetables to get the needed vitamins and minerals. On the other hand, the fresher a food item, the greater may be its pesticide content. Similarly, the advantages of breast feeding are well-known, yet the levels of pesticide residues in some breast-milk are a cause of great concern.

It may be noted that reducing the use of pesticides is likely to benefit both users and consumers. Chemical pest control will only be effective for as long as the target organisms do not develop resistance. Widespread and indiscriminate use of pesticides speeds the rates at which pesticides resistance grows in pests. In recognition of this, many national and local governments in developed countries have often introduced Integrated Pest Management (IPM) schemes to reduce pesticide usage to the benefit of both users and consumers.

Food from animal sources

The analysis of samples of meat, milk and eggs collected from the organised farm at the Central Veterinary Research Institute, Izatnagar, revealed the presence of DDT. There was a high level of DDT (0.528 ppm) in milk. Fat contained the highest level of DDT (1.2 ppm) as compared to other tissues. Almost all the samples of meat, fish and eggs collected from Uttar Pradesh, Delhi, Andhra Pradesh and Punjab have shown the presence of DDT and BHC residues, but they were usually found to be below the recommended upper limit.

The highest concentration of DDT in meat samples was 1.6 ppm. It was less than 1.0 ppm in most other samples of meat. The egg samples from Delhi, Punjab and Uttar Pradesh contained less than 1.0 ppm pesticide residues. Egg samples from Hyderabad, however, contained as high as 8.01 ppm of DDT and 2.5 ppm of BHC. Analysis of even some popular brands of baby foods showed DDT residues at levels higher than the recommended upper limit of 1.25 ppm.

Food commodities

The studies conducted in Punjab, Haryana, Delhi and Mumbai have revealed widespread contamination of wheat grain with DDT and BHC residues. Residues of other chlorinated insecticides have also been reported in rice from Mumbai. Like cereals, pulse samples collected from market have also shown the presence of excessive amounts of both DDT and BHC. A high level of DDT and BHC residues found in some of the wheat, rice and pulse samples might be the result of direct mixing of these insecticides during storage. Pesticide residues have also been reported in many spices (such as black pepper, celery seed, turmeric, ginger, etc.) exported from India, but the level of contamination was within the prescribed limit. Analysis of oil and oil seeds has shown the presence of excessive amounts of DDT and BHC. Samples of cotton seed from Punjab showed 0.85 to 1.28 ppm of DDT and 0.56 to 0.87 ppm of BHC. It is evident, therefore, that the limited surveys conducted in India clearly indicate the presence of pesticide residues (often in excessive amounts) in animal tissues and food commodities.

FOOD POLLUTION: THE MENACE OF FOOD ADDITIVES

Air, water and food are the three major components constituting the human environment. Food safety, therefore, is an essential element of environmental protection. In addition to main nutrients such as protein, fat, vitamins, etc. food products usually contain food additives, generally in small quantities, to improve the appearance, flavour, texture or storage properties of food. In this section, we discuss various aspects of food additives in detail and analyse the hazards they pose to human health. Food additives are also discussed, such as cosmetic additives, preservatives and processing aids.

Food Additives

In addition to the main nutrients such as protein, carbohydrates and fat, processed food products usually contain additives. Governments in most countries issue lists of permitted food additives, stating the highest acceptable concentration in food products, defining food products in which various additives may be used and sometimes even recommending their maximum daily consumption. Such legislation is revised periodically in the light of new findings on the safety or health hazards of various additives. Products may be added to or deleted from the permitted lists of additives because of additional scientific knowledge and experience in their use.

Food additives can be divided into three main categories:

1. Cosmetic additives.
2. Preservatives.
3. Processing aids.

Cosmetic additives

Cosmetic additives make food products look more attractive by modifying their colour, taste, smell or texture. They also allow manufacturers to add excess water to processed foods. Cosmetic additives may be sub-divided into colours, flavours, flavour enhancers, sweeteners and texture modifiers.
Flavours are the largest group of cosmetic food additives—about 3500 or more substances. Flavouring materials are added to basic foodstuffs to provide a characteristic food flavour or to supplement or modify the original flavour.

Most flavouring materials are still of natural origin, but progress in organic chemistry has made it possible to analyse flavouring materials and then to synthesise products identical with those found in nature. Flavours can also be influenced by the addition of a flavour enhancer such as mono-sodium glutamate, which intensifies the perception of flavour. Additives that affect the texture of foods are mainly emulsifiers and stabilisers. Emulsifiers bind fat to water, while stabilisers prevent the two from separating. Phosphates of various types, for example, bind water into meat and fish products to firm their texture and increase their weight.

Preservatives

Some food preservatives extend the shelf life of food products by slowing down the growth of micro-organisms, other preservatives (called antioxidants) slow down the deterioration of fats, colourings and flavourings in food. There are micro-organisms and rancid fats which are harmful, so preservatives and antioxidants serve a useful purpose. However, the presence of a preservative in a food item does not guarantee total freedom from bacterial contamination. Excessive amounts of added water held into bread, meat and fish products by emulsifiers actually promotes the growth of micro-organisms.

The food industries generally rely on such physical factors as heat, cold and low moisture for product preservation, but the use of antimicrobial chemical preservatives is growing. Most countries control their use by legislation by recommending the maximum permissible concentration for each preservative for specified foods.

Processing aids

Processing aids are food additives that help during production. They may, for example, stop products sticking to machinery, or may help speed up the manufacturing of specific food items. Processing aids include release agents (such as powders and greases to stop food sticking), acids (to produce gassy raising agents), bases (to alter acidity of food), anti-caking agents (to stop powders like salt forming lumps), glazing agents (to give surface shine) and bleaching agents (to bleach flour).

Inappropriate nutrition

Colouring and flavouring additives are generally used in foods of inappropriate or poor nutritional value. The additives may make foods high in fat, sugar and starch more palatable and attractive than they otherwise would be. Cosmetic additives encourage the consumer to eat more of these types of foods and therefore, they contribute to the problem of inappropriate nutrition and consequent diet-related diseases such as coronary heart diseases, stroke, several types of cancer, diabetes and dental caries. While some food additives, e.g. vitamins and minerals, enhance the nutritional value of foods and antioxidants preserve some vitamins in foods, most of the additives have no nutritional value at all. On the other hand, some additives, such as sulphites, can even destroy existing vitamins in foods, cosmetic additives can often mislead consumers about the nature of foods.

Excessive use of additives

Clearly some additives do have a useful role. For example, there are food preservatives that help prevent food poisoning. Similarly emulsifiers are useful since they make low-fat spreads possible. It cannot be denied, however, that most additives have been used in excess. In the past, the food industry had claimed that all additives are necessary, but this argument is not true since in recent years manufacturers of processed foods have removed, reduced or replaced many colours and additives previously claimed to be essential.

Health Hazards of Additives

Safety considerations

When approving a particular food additive, the most important consideration should be its safety to the consumer. However, many additives (especially natural colours and flavours) have not been thoroughly tested. Moreover, even in the case of additives that have been tested, there is much scientific controversy over their health hazards. In addition to these, there are also difficulties in conducting and interpreting animal tests for food additives. Problems arise in interpretation and application of test results since animal tests are mostly conducted singly (i.e. using one additive at a time) and not in the combination in which additives are consumed through various food items. There is a good possibility that some additives (especially flavourings and preservatives) may react with the food and/or other additives to produce untested combinations.

In recent years, much public attention has been drawn to the problem of intolerant reactions to food in the case of some people, especially children. Even the governments now acknowledge that some people are allergic to (or intolerant of) certain food. Allergies can, of course, be caused by certain foods such as milk or eggs, but these can be more easily identified and avoided than food additives. Not enough research has been conducted to tell how many people show intolerant reactions to food additives, but it has been estimated that 0.03 to 0.15 per cent of the population may be allergic to common food additives.

A single meal may contain a cocktail of 12 to 60 different additives, which may react with each other and with foods to produce new chemical substances. These new products should be tested for their safety to human beings, but they are not. In fact, it would be very time consuming and costly to test all possible combinations of thousands of additives and foods. Far more logical and inexpensive would be to reduce considerably the number and amount of food additives already in use.

Double exposure of food workers

Food additives pose extra health hazards to workers of food processing plants since they receive a double exposure to additives—as workers and also as consumers. In addition to eating them, the food workers are also exposed to dusts, fumes and splashes of additives. Like consumers, food workers are exposed to untested combinations of food additives. The actual levels of exposure may vary over a very wide range, but they tend to be highest in plants dealing with soft drinks, snacks, baked goods, confectionery and meat products. Almost half of the food workers are women and they are particularly at risk because women tend to do the relatively 'dirtier' jobs in food industry.

FOOD POLLUTION: NITRATES IN FOOD

In this section, we will discuss in detail various aspects of the pollution of food by nitrates, which results mainly from indiscriminate and often excessive application of chemical fertilisers to food and vegetable crops. This section gives a detailed discussion of the pollution of environment by nitrogen fertilisers. It includes a discussion of the nitrogen cycle and the pollution of ground, surface and marine waters by nitrates.

There are numerous national and international organisations devoted to the assessment of food quality. In recent years, organisations responsible for environmental protection have rightly focused their attention on the chemical, radiological and microbiological quality of food and established upper limits for food contaminants in many cases.

Although in some parts of the world the limits for radio-active contaminants are exceeded, these occurrences are rare and their potential impact is relatively small. Moreover, because radio-activity is easily detected and measured at trace levels, corrective steps can be taken before the radio-active contamination reaches the consumer. In contrast to this, the contamination of food with harmful chemicals is more prevalent, especially in developing countries like India, where pesticides and other chemicals are often used carelessly and find their way into food. The situation is significantly different for microbiological contamination of food. Even in highly developed countries like the USA, there are repeated occurrences of microbiological contamination of food.

Nitrate Fertilisers and Environment

Fertilisers and the nitrogen cycle

Nitrogen is a vital element in the biosphere, making its way through many plant and animal pathways, soil, water and air. A critical question, therefore, is: does the quantity of inorganic nitrogen, derived from the atmospheric nitrogen and used in agriculture as fertilisers, constitute a significant distance of the nitrogen cycle and hence the environment. Extremely large amounts of nitrate nitrogen are being added to the soil, which would otherwise remain as atmospheric nitrogen. A large proportion of this nitrogen in the fertilisers is not taken up by the agricultural crop, but eventually goes to surface and groundwaters and air (via denitrification, volatilisation and stubble burning), depending on local conditions. Thus large amounts of nitrogen fertilisers added to the soil lead to increase nitrate leaching in the long run.

Pollution of groundwater

The upper 20 cm of cultivated soil contains about 3–8 T of nitrogen per hectare. Only 2–7 per cent of this is in the form of inorganic nitrate or ammonium nitrogen, which is directly available to the growing food crop. Since the inorganic nitrogen is highly soluble in water, the water draining from the soil will leach variable amounts of nitrates. Water which runs off the surface will have less contact time with the soil nitrate, so it tends to have a fairly low concentration of nitrates. On the other hand, leached water (which has drained through the soil) will generally have a higher nitrate level, depending on the nitrate available in the soil.

Pollution of surface water

The problem of increasing nitrate concentrations in rivers, lakes and other surface water bodies has been recognised for some time. The increased levels of nitrates in surface waters can be attributed to five major factors:

1. The discharge of treated (or even untreated) sewage effluents.
2. The ploughing up of grassland.
3. Improved land drainage.
4. The release of silage effluents and slurry from livestock units.
5. The use of large amounts of nitrogen fertilisers.

The best-known effect of fertiliser run-off is eutrophication (the extreme enrichment of surface waters causing a devastating damage to the ecological balance in affected areas), which can seriously affect the quality of drinking water.

Pollution of marine waters

While nitrate itself is non-toxic, its presence may cause serious disturbance to the ecology of coastal waters. Its presence stimulates growth of phytoplanktons. The death of these micro-organisms can lead to the release of fish toxins and deoxygenation of the water.

There is good evidence that rising nitrate level is altering the marine environment since the occurrence of plankton blooms is increasing in many parts of the world, though other pollutants and climatic factors may also be responsible for this. In Western Europe, for example, reports of increasing frequency of algal blooms have come from countries with shallow coastal waters and areas where effluent discharges are not rapidly diluted, especially Denmark, Norway and Germany.

Nitrates in Our Food

Nitrate occurs in food products for the following three reasons:

1. Naturally: as a component of plant tissue, at fairly low levels.
2. Excess nitrate residues, derived from the use of excessive amounts of nitrate fertilisers in agriculture.
3. Preservative nitrate and nitrite added to cured meats, meat products and some cheeses during manufacture.

Naturally occurring nitrate

It is well-known that plants synthesise organic compounds of nitrogen, such as proteins, from inorganic nitrate and to a lesser extent, ammonia derived from the soil. Legumes such as peas and beans also have the ability to fix the atmospheric nitrogen through the action of symbiotic bacteria in root nodules of these crops. Inorganic nitrate is generally utilised by the plant in its leaves. As a result, the green leafy part of the plant is most likely to accumulate the highest level of nitrate. For example, leafy vegetable such as spinach, lettuce, cabbage and celery contain 60–1200 ppm of nitrates by wet weight.

Several crops have been found to contain a very low or even zero nitrate level (i.e. below the detection limit of 50 ppm of nitrate by dry weight). Legumes (e.g. broad beans, French beans and peas), cereals (e.g. wheat and rice), storage roots (e.g. carrot and sugar beet) and onions do not accumulate nitrate even when high-nitrogen fertilisers are used.

Excess nitrate levels

Nitrate levels in some commercially grown vegetable crops may be as high as 10000 ppm or about 8 per cent of dry matter. The nitrate content of vegetables and salad crops generally increases in direct proportion to the amount of applied nitrogen fertilisers. Research conducted in Switzerland and Germany shows that using compost rather than chemical fertilisers produces lettuce with a far lower nitrate concentration and that too without a large reduction in yield. Similar studies with corn salad have shown not only that nitrate levels are much lower when compost is used, but that vitamin C and dry matter levels are higher. Vitamin C is considered to be a major protective factor for stomach cancer. Since both nitrate and nitrite are water soluble ions, it is not surprising that cooking reduces their concentration in vegetables. Boiling cabbage for five minutes, for example, reduces the nitrate level by about 20 per cent. Longer cooking reduces the nitrate level further, but significant nitrate levels still remain even after overcooking.

Preservative nitrate and nitrite

The maximum permitted level for nitrates is 500 mg/kg and that for nitrites is 200 mg/kg. Nitrates and nitrites are banned from infant foods. The main argument for the continued use of these preservatives is that they prevent the growth of the bacterium *clostridium botulinum*, which causes botulism (the often lethal food poison). However, because of the potential cancer hazard of these additives, sincere effort has to be made to eliminate the use of nitrates and to reduce nitrite levels in food as soon as practicable.

Nitrate in the diet

The main source of nitrates in the diet is generally thought to be the drinking water, but food usually supplies more than half of the nitrate intake. The main food sources of nitrates are leafy vegetables. Cabbage and lettuce contribute roughly 75 per cent of vegetable nitrates. Meat products contribute only a small amount of nitrate in diet. Greenwood and Hunt have estimated that if organically grown vegetables are eaten, the nitrate intake via vegetables is only about 100 mg per week. This level increases as the amount of nitrogen fertilisers used to grow vegetables is increased, going up to about 500 mg per week if excess fertilisers are used.

Nitrates and Human Health

Health hazards of nitrates

The effects of nitrate consumption on human health have been the subject of a great deal of public discussion since the 1970s. High concentration of nitrates in drinking water poses a small but well-recognised risk to bottle-fed babies. Nitrate has also been linked with human cancer (particularly stomach, gullet and bladder cancers). It may be noted here that health concern about nitrates is not focused on the direct effect of nitrate (since it is not toxic by itself unless swallowed in large amounts), but because of the possible adverse effects of nitrite produced from it. The reduction of nitrate to nitrite is caused by the bacteria normally found in the mouth and occasionally (during infection, for example) in the stomach and bladder. This is the major source of nitrite for most people, although it also comes from several food items (such as vegetables and meats cured with additive nitrite). Nitrite may also be produced when the food is poorly stored.

Nitrosamines and cancer

N-nitroso compounds are considered to be among the most powerful chemical carcinogens. These compounds are produced in the body by the reaction of nitrite with several protein substrates such as amines, amides and ureas. Direct nitrosamine exposure also occurs via tobacco, smoke, some rubber products (e.g. contaminated baby bottle teats), cured meats, bacon, some fish and cheeses and beer.

Several hypotheses link nitrate and nitrite to stomach, bladder, gullet and intestinal cancer. All these hypotheses are based on the formation of *N*-nitroso compounds (nitrosation) under varying conditions. The key factors for their formation in the stomach are decreased acidity (due to illness, for example), the concentration of reactants and the presence of modifiers. It is known that vitamins C and E inhibit nitrosation, while phenols accelerate it, so vegetables contain both types of modifiers. Nitrosamines have shown carcinogenic effects in 39 animal species, including primates.

Methaemoglobinaemia

Nitrate-reducing bacteria are often found in the stomach of infants before the stomach has reached its normal level of acidity. Thus the nitrite derived from the high-nitrate water used to make up bottled milk passes into the bloodstream to combine with haemoglobin. The methaemoglobin produced in this way has a much lower capacity for oxygen binding and, at high levels, it causes the 'blue baby syndrome' or methaemoglobinaemia.

It may be noted here that the risk of methaemoglobinaemia is not serious in the case of vegetables. Since the susceptible sectors of the population are bottle-fed babies and young babies who are unwell, they are unlikely to eat large quantities of vegetables, although they may eat some vegetables (in the form of prepared baby foods). That is why nitrate content of baby foods is regulated in several advanced countries such as Austria and Switzerland.

FOOD POLLUTION: IRRADIATION OF FOODS

Techniques for preserving food from deterioration date back to pre-historic times. Among the oldest methods of food preservation are drying, refrigeration and fermentation, while more recent techniques include the addition of chemical preservatives and food irradiation. This section deals with both the positive and negative aspects of food irradiation as a technique for extending the shelf-life of food. The technical aspects of food irradiation such as the irradiation technology and radiation doses are also discussed.

In recent years, the organisations responsible for environmental protection have rightly concentrated their efforts on the chemical, radiological and microbiological purity of food and have established safety limits for various contaminants of food. Techniques for preserving food from natural deterioration, following harvest or slaughter, date back to prehistoric times. Among the oldest methods of food preservation are drying, refrigeration and fermentation. More recent techniques for preserving foods include the addition of chemical preservatives and food irradiation. There is a widespread concern, however, about the possible adverse effects of chemical preservatives such as nitrates and nitrites that are so much a part of modern preservation techniques. Increasingly, the consumers are seeking out additive free foods. In this context, the alternative way of extending the shelf-life of food, i.e. food irradiation, naturally appears to be very attractive. In fact, food irradiation is doubly attractive since, in addition to extending the shelf-life of foods, it also seems to provide a solution to the growing problem of food poisoning.

Technical Aspects of Food Irradiation

Food irradiation is basically the use of very large doses of ionising radiations (usually X-rays or gamma rays) to produce physical, chemical or biological changes in food. These changes can have the effect of extending the shelf-life of food.

The use of large doses of ionising radiations can have the following effects:

1. Delaying the ripening of fruits.
2. Killing (or at least rendering sterile) insect pests infesting the food.
3. Killing micro-organisms (and thus reducing the level of bacterial contamination of food).

In addition to these food preservation techniques, irradiation can also be used for the following applications:

1. To improve the baking and cooking characteristics of wheat. It has been found that irradiation enables bread manufacturers to add upto 15 per cent soya flour to wheat flour without loss of baking quality. Moreover, the elasticity and volume of dough are also improved and yeast is stimulated (thus leading to faster bread-making).
2. To increase the yield of barley during melting in brewing. Irradiation can also be used to age spirits and obtain more juice from grapes in wine-making and distilling.
3. To reduce the time needed to reconstitute and cook dehydrated vegetables, enhance the flavour of carrots and tenderise meats.
4. To modify starches for the paper and textile industries, improve the insulation qualities of plastic-coated electrical cable and sterilise gelation for the photo film industry.

It may be noted here that irradiation techniques are already used extensively in industrially advanced countries to sterilise medical supplies and equipment.

Irradiation technology

The technology of food irradiation is fairly simple. The food to be irradiated is exposed to a source of ionising radiations (either high-energy electrons, X-rays or gamma rays) until it has received a sufficient dose to achieve the desired effect. This is done inside a shielded irradiation cell. The food to be irradiated is loaded on a conveyor that carries it into the irradiation cell. The time the foodstuff remains there, its distance from the radiation source and the aspect to the source will determine the radiation dose received and its distribution. In general, the outside of a food package will receive higher levels of radiation than the middle part of it.

Radiation doses

In connection with food irradiation, the dose of ionising radiations is measured in 'Gray' (abbreviated to Gy). The Gray is quite a large unit of radiation dose. For example, one KGy (= 1000 Gy) is roughly equivalent to the radiation received in about 10 million chest X-rays or about a million times the dose we receive from natural sources in one year. The radiation doses required to achieve various desired effects in connection with food irradiation are shown in Table 2.1.

Table 2.1: Recommended dose ranges for various food irradiation effects.

Desired effect	*Dose range (KGy)*
Inhibition of sprouting	0.05–0.15
Delaying ripening of fruits	0.2–0.5
Insect disinfestation	0.2–1.0
Elimination of parasites	0.03–6.0
Shelf-life extension	0.5–5.0
Elimination of pathogens	3.0–10.0
Bacterial sterilisation	Up to 50.0

It may be noted here that these recommended doses are considerably higher than dose levels considered lethal and much higher than those where significant risks of cancer or genetic damage in exposed population are likely. It may be said, therefore, that food irradiation has to be considered as a very hazardous technology.

Hazards of Irradiated Foods

Safety considerations

There are four areas where the safety and wholesomeness of irradiated food must be considered, viz.,

1. Possible radio-activity of the irradiated food.
2. Possible creation of toxic chemicals in the food by irradiation.
3. Hazardous microbiological changes in the food that may result from irradiation.
4. Any unacceptable changes in nutritional quality of the irradiated food that might have adverse health effects.

Possible radio-activity: It is generally agreed that irradiation should not make the irradiated food radio-active if the process is properly controlled. Since the energy level of the source is limited, the amount of radio-activity created in the food is negligible.

Possibility of toxic chemicals: Bombarding food with ionising radiations can alter its chemical structure. In the first stage of this process are created the free radicals, which rapidly combine with other radicals or initiate changes in other chemical components of food. In most cases, this leads to familiar chemical changes (similar to those that occur in cooking, for example), but completely new chemical substances may be created in some cases. Since the chemical reactions resulting from irradiation are highly complex, it is very difficult to identify all of the radiolytic products and to test them for toxicity in the usually accepted way. Moreover, even small quantities of hazardous chemicals created by irradiation may be sufficient to produce long-term adverse effects.

Possible microbiological hazards: Irradiation is used to kill yeasts, molds and bacteria that cause the food to spoil. It also renders sterile any insects that infest the food. There is a possibility, therefore, of the irradiation causing mutations in viruses, bacteria and insects in food leading to more resistant strains of these. There are numerous examples of insects developing resistance to pesticides. They could also become resistant (or genetically altered) by radiation. Some strains of resistant salmonellae have been developed by repeated irradiation under laboratory conditions. Irradiation may, therefore, provide only a short-term solution to the problem of food poisoning (due to contamination of food with salmonellae). Radiation-resistant bacteria have also been found in environments with high natural (or even artificial) radiation levels. Sublethal doses of ionising radiations can produce chemical changes in the genetic material of micro-organisms (i.e. mutations) leading to altered characteristics, which will be propagated in subsequent generations. Such mutant micro-organisms could be more pathogenic than native forms.

In addition to possible mutations of micro-organisms, there is another aspect of food irradiation that is of even greater concern. Though irradiation can kill bacteria in food, it will not remove the toxins that have already been created by the bacteria at the earlier stages of contamination, and it is these toxins that are of real public health hazard. Aflatoxins, for example, are powerful chemical agents for causing liver cancer. Increased production of aflatoxins following irradiation was confirmed by subsequent studies on wheat, corn, sorgum, millet, potatoes and onions.

Possible nutritional effects: The effects of irradiation on major food components are generally small. Protein chemistry, for example, is only slightly affected and, moreover, most of the changes are in the same direction as the breakdown of proteins that occur during their digestion in the body. Sugars and starches are also little affected by irradiation. Fats, however, develop quite rancid flavours and odours as a result of irradiation. This has been identified as the source of most of the undesirable changes in irradiated foods that lead, for example, to oils tasting 'burnt'. So severe is this problem that most milk products and oily or fatty foods are not even being considered for irradiation. Another problem in connection with fats is that of polyunsaturated fats, which are regarded as vital components for health. There is no doubt that these polyunsaturated fatty acids are changed by radiation, but there is little research so far on the effect this might have on dietary health.

Radiation Health and Safety

The other aspect of food irradiation that should concern the public and governments is the standards for the protection of workers who work in food irradiation plants and those people who live near such facilities. Supporters of food irradiation strongly emphasise the fact that such facilities will operate under internationally agreed standards for radiation protection, but the simple fact is that there is no safe level of nuclear radiations. Any exposure can be the one that does the damage which, years later, may show up as cancer or genetic defects in future generations. Protection standards, in general, are a compromise between these risks and assumed benefits. Even here, the protection agencies have been shown to have the balance of risks and benefits very wrong. The risk estimates recommended by the International Commission on Radiological Protection have been shown to be at least three times (and often five to ten times) too low and, therefore, the permitted dose limits for irradiation plant workers and the public too high by the same factors. As indicated earlier, food irradiation is an extremely hazardous process. Exposure to unshielded sources may deliver radiation doses likely to be lethal. Even routine exposure to much lower levels could lead to long-term adverse effects. The radio-active materials, moreover, have to be transported into the irradiation plant, the spent sources (which are still radio-active) have to be removed and any contaminated materials have to be disposed of.

Further Work Needed

In previous sections, we have discussed many positive and negative aspects of food irradiation. As the things stand at present, we cannot conclude that irradiated food is definitely unsafe or harmful. The testing programme undertaken so far does i· dicate, however, that at least some possibly harmful effects of irradiated food could occur and that these effects do need proper investigation. There are, moreover, some areas where the results of testing done so far are inconclusive and where possible problems have not been considered. Even experts in the field of radiation chemistry from within the food industry have drawn attention to areas where hardly any work has been done into potential harms, e.g. the effect of irradiation on pesticide residues in food. The following are some of the areas in the field of food irradiation where further work is needed:

1. The possibility of chromosome aberrations resulting from reactive radiolytic chemicals in freshly irradiated foods.
2. The potential stimulation of harmful aflatoxins and other undesirable changes resulting from destruction of the natural balance of microbiological activity in food.
3. The potential for creation of unique radiolytic chemicals that may be analogues of carcinogens and mutagens and, therefore, capable of having long-term adverse effects even at very small doses.
4. The possibility that the irradiated food may lead to lower immune response due to either chemical, bacterial or nutritional changes in the food.

Unless these investigations are undertaken, the public must be provided objective information on the possible harmful effects of food irradiation and the uncertainties in the available evidence and not merely vague reassurances by food processing industries and governments.

FOOD POLLUTION: MICROBIAL CONTAMINATION AND FOOD POISONING

Foods are often contaminated by various micro-organisms and thus rendered unfit for human consumption. Food poisoning is a disturbance of the gastrointestinal tract with abdominal pain and diarrhoea with or without vomiting and with or without fever. Inspite of many improvements and advances in hygiene during the twentieth century foodborne infection is still a major cause of illness even in industrially advanced countries. In this section we discuss various aspects of the problem of food poisoning in detail. The areas covered in the present section are the incidence and distribution of food poisoning, role of food industry, sources of infection (such as the livestock farm, contaminated animal feed and the use of antibiotics), food processing, the catering industry and control of food poisoning.

The food micro-organisms include molds, yeasts and bacteria. Some micro-organisms exist in spore as well as vegetative form. Spores are more difficult to destroy by heat or other means than the vegetative forms. Growth of molds on foods make such foods unfit for consumption. Molds are most likely to grow in warm, damp and dark places and they are inhibited by sunlight. Some molds can produce mycotoxins (especially on groundnut and wheat, if these are not dried properly after harvest).

Yeasts generally grow in foods which contain sugar and water, e.g. fruits. They grow better in acidic media and convert the sugar in the food into alcohol and carbon dioxide. Honey, jams and jellies usually become contaminated by yeast. On the other hand, bacteria usually grow on and spoil foods which are neutral in reaction (e.g. milk, eggs, meats and vegetables). Aerobic bacteria grow only in the presence of oxygen, while anaerobic bacteria can grow even in the absence of oxygen. For the growth of micro-organisms on foods, therefore, the favourable conditions are: (i) Presence of moisture, (ii) Presence of warmth, and (iii) Presence of oxygen (i.e. air). So the growth of micro-organisms on foods can be prevented and foods can be preserved for a longer period by the following methods:

1. Airtight or vacuum packing (to eliminate air or oxygen).
2. Dehydration of foods (to remove the moisture).

3. Refrigeration (to eliminate warmth).
4. Sterilisation (to kill bacteria, molds, etc.).
5. Addition of chemical preservatives (to retard the growth of micro-organisms).

Micro-organisms of many types such as molds, yeasts, fungi and bacteria find their way into foods and grow under favourable conditions, as discussed above. Although some micro-organisms are not harmful, many of them have been clearly established as causative agents of human and animal diseases. Food poisoning is an acute health effect of the contamination of foods by certain micro-organisms.

Food Poisoning

Food poisoning, in brief, is a disturbance of the gastrointestinal tract with abdominal pain and diarrhoea with or without vomiting and with or without fever. The time onset of the symptoms of food poisoning may range from less than one hour to more than 48 hr after eating the contaminated food. In general, a large number of micro-organisms actively growing in food is required to initiate the symptoms of food poisoning. Outbreaks of food poisoning attract considerable publicity from the news media for a brief period, but behind the headlines is a serious health problem which has not received sustained attention so far. The incidence of food poisoning has been rising in India in recent years if the reports of its occurrence in newspapers are taken as an evidence. In spite of many improvements and advances in hygiene during the last one hundred years, foodborne infection is still a major cause of illness even in advanced countries such as the USA and UK and the situation is worse in developing countries like India. *Salmonella*, the micro-organism most commonly associated with food poisoning, has become so widely distributed that it will be very difficult to eradicate it.

Unfortunately, there are no simple solutions for the problem of food poisoning. This problem cannot be traced to a single cause, nor it is confined to any particular sector of the food chain. Consequently, investigator trying to control this problem have to look at the inter-relationship of a number of contributory factors from many different sources. According to the World Health Organisation, microbiological hazards cause more ill-health than the hazards of pesticide residues, food additives, natural poisons and toxic substances combined.

In spite of this, the problem of food poisoning has not yet attracted the same kind of attention from the public and scientific community as have food additives or pesticide residues, even though the impact of food poisoning on human health is more immediate and dramatic. Nevertheless, food poisoning is a major cause of ill health throughout all advanced and highly industrialised countries, who have to pay a price for a highly centralised and convenient food processing system.

Incidence and Distribution

Although *salmonella* is the most common cause of food poisoning as mentioned earlier, there are many different organisms which can cause food poisoning. *Salmonella* is still the largest and most important group among them. Salmonellosis (the illness caused by *salmonella*) has been largely responsible for the increased incidence of food poisoning and accounts for roughly 90 per cent of all reported incidents.

Although salmonellosis is by far the most common type of food poisoning, other micro-organisms can be important too. Incidents of food poisoning due to *Clostridium perfringens*, for example, are also significant and are increasing. Infection due to these bacteria is linked to poor temperature control and particularly associated with large catering establishment. Another commonly identified group of micro-organisms associated with food poisoning is *Staphylococcus aureus*, which is carried on the skin and in the nose of many people and is usually associated with poor personal hygiene in food handlers. Finally,

Bacillus cereus is most often associated with the cases of food poisoning involving reheated rice dishes. Beef and other meat products, on the other hand, have most often been linked to *Clostridium perfringens*.

Apart from causing ill-health, food poisoning imposes other costs on the community, especially in financial terms. The studies done so far suggest that the economic impact of the outbreaks of food poisoning could be considerable. One such study looked at the costs of salmonellosis due to the drinking of unpasturised milk in Scotland. It involved a detailed cost analysis of a major outbreak (affecting 654 individuals and-causing two deaths) of milkborne *salmonella* in and around the town of Keith in Scotland during 1998. A wide range of direct and indirect costs (including the use of medical services, loss of productivity, etc.) were taken into account in this study.

Role of Food Industry

The response of the food industry to the problem of food poisoning has been a mixed one so far. For larger and more respectable companies, the potentially adverse effects of an outbreak of food poisoning on the corporate image are enough of an incentive to improve hygiene in the food processing plant. For the smaller food companies, however, there are few effective inducements to adhere to the 'best practice' standards. After all, the food industry itself does not have to foot the bill for the cost of foodborne infection in the community and the legal requirements to comply with minimal hygiene standards are not often enforced with the strictness they deserve.

Instead of inducing the food industries to 'clean up their act', however, more effort is directed to promote good kitchen hygiene and thus to expect individuals to shoulder the entire responsibility to guard themselves against foodborne infection. Adequate cooking, proper temperature control and measures to avoid cross-contamination are the main safeguards against infection in the kitchen. Greater public awareness of these simple rules would, of course, help to make food safer to eat, but good hygiene in the kitchen is not the complete solution. If the war against food poisoning is to be waged in every kitchen, the question has to be asked as to why the enemy has been allowed to advance so far.

Ever since the official records began to be maintained, the incidence of the outbreaks of food poisoning has steadily increased. The problem is not simply that promotion of good hygiene has been neglected, but that the kitchen has somehow become the only line of defence. Too little attention has been paid to reducing microbial contamination throughout the food chain. It is officially recognised that a high proportion of raw foods reaching the kitchen are contaminated, but reducing contamination at source, further up the chain of food production, has never been a high priority. Even on the grounds of public health, preventing food contamination in the first place should be a top priority. The original source of infection can be traced right back to the farm and to the livestock reared for food.

Sources of Infection

Livestock farm

It would be hard to devise a better system of spreading *salmonella* than modern livestock farming in industrially advanced countries. Its methods appear tailor-made to spread *salmonella* infection amongst the livestock raised for human consumption. The aim of modern livestock farming is to ensure a rapid and high yield. Unfortunately, many of the new animal feeds are themselves contaminated with salmonella. The effect of feeding *salmonella* contaminated feeds directly to animals confined in cramped and overcrowded conditions has contributed significantly to the spread of *salmonella* infection in the rest of the food chain. Modern livestocks are more susceptible to infection than traditional breeds since they have been primarily selected for their growth potential rather than disease resistance.

Once *salmonella* takes hold, it is difficult to keep it from spreading to the rest of the herd or flock. An infected animal literally excretes *salmonella* and will cross-infect any other healthy animal with which it comes into contact. The pertinent questions to ask in this connection are: Why are farmers allowed to use contaminated feeds for animals destined for human consumption? Why are the suppliers permitted to sell *salmonella* contaminated feeds? And how do they become contaminated in the first place?

Contaminated animal feed

The link between contaminated feed and animal salmonellosis is well recognised. Animal feed is contaminated because its raw materials are themselves contaminated. High-protein animal feed is made from a variety of ingredients, many of them such as blood, bone and even manure originating from animal sources. This ensures that *salmonella* is continually recycled to successive generations of livestock. This cycle of infection, however, is not inevitable. Feed manufacturers can break this cycle.

For the most part, the lapses in the animal feed plant are due to inadequate heat treatment and cross-contamination. In these plants, raw protein material is turned into compounded feed, often in the form of heat-treated pellets. Any bacteria surviving in the protein material should be destroyed by the heat treatment or diluted when mixed with other less contaminated materials. However, heat treatment can fail to achieve this because of insufficiently high temperatures. Unless sufficient care is taken to ensure effective pasteurisation and to prevent cross-contamination, even small amounts of infected material can contaminate the entire contents of a factory. Moreover, it only needs a relatively small dose of *salmonella* in the feed to rapidly infect a whole herd or flock of farm animals.

Use of antibiotics

The use of antibiotics in animal husbandry has a controversial history. Antibiotics are used in livestock farming to treat clinically sick animals or to prevent the disease spreading to the rest of the herd or flock. In addition, antibiotics are added routinely to animal feeds in order to promote growth. The widespread use of antibiotics in animal husbandry means that the threat of virulent, drug-resistant strains is an over-present possibility. Moreover, the potential for those particular strains to transfer their resistance to more ubiquitous micro-organisms like *Escherichia coli* is even more worrying. For the time being, however, the prevalence of resistant salmonellas is only a problem in the calf industry and that is why the problem has not attracted so much attention.

Food Processing

It has always been assumed that food processing is generally the least problematic sector in the chain of foodborne infection. The number of food poisoning outbreaks caused by faulty processing has been much lower than those caused by poor food handling within other sectors such as catering industry. This good safety record has been attributed to high standards of hygiene within the food processing sector as a whole. This comforting assumption, however, is now being questioned as a result of some serious food poisoning outbreaks associated with large food processors.

Detailed investigations of such outbreaks have made it increasingly clear that perfecting food processing techniques will not by itself guarantee *salmonella*-free food products. Any food processing factory that admits contaminated raw materials must also prevent it from cross-contaminating the uncontaminated finished products. Once any part of the plant becomes contaminated, the bacteria can survive fat very long period and be very difficult to eradicate. Cross-contamination, therefore, can occur in the most modern, high-tech factory, even with high standards of hygiene and quality assurance.

Poorly designed processing equipment can make effective cleaning almost impossible, thus leaving food processing plants vulnerable to undetected contamination.

Catering Industry

The incidence of food poisoning caused by the catering industry is greater than by any other sector of the food industry. Catering, however, is a very diverse industry and some sectors of it bear a larger responsibility than others. As the top of the food poisoning league are restaurants and buffet receptions, followed by hospitals, institutions, schools and canteens.

What makes the catering industry so dangerous from the point of view of food poisoning? The simple answer is poor hygiene. In reality, however, the problems of the catering industry are much more complex. A combination of poor food handling, inadequately trained staff and insufficient legal controls create an environment in the catering industry highly conducive to outbreaks of food poisoning. The conditions under which some caterers have to operate make good-hygiene almost impossible. Badly designed kitchens, insufficient (or non-existent) cold storage facilities and poorly maintained equipment produce a working environment highly conducive to cross-contamination.

The reasons why food preparation on a large scale creates problems are well known. The most commonly identified factors leading to food poisoning are: (i) advanced preparation, (ii) storage at ambient temperature, (iii) inadequate cooling, (iv) inadequate reheating, (v) use of contaminated processed food, (vi) undercooking, and (vii) cross-contamination.

Given that so much is known about how food poisoning occurs in catering establishments, why are the customers still exposed to these risks? According to the Institution of Environmental Health Officers (IEHO), much of the illness of food poisoning could be prevented by proper legislation which ensures observance of strict rules with regard to preventing food contamination, strict temperature control and effective staff training.

Controlling Food Poisoning

Throughout the last century, successive foodborne illnesses, were identified, controlled and eventually eliminated. Food poisoning, however, is a notable exception and its incidence has significantly increased in recent years. The main factors contributing to the problem of food poisoning have already been clearly identified, so its persistence reflects not so much a lack of knowledge, but the lack of determination to apply the necessary counter measures.

Food poisoning is as much a political issue as a public health problem. The chain of bacterial infection linking diseased livestock to sick people is an increasingly long and complex one. The effect of feeding *salmonella* contaminated feed to animals inevitably work its way through the system to contaminate a large proportion of processed food.

The initial microbial load can be increased or reduced by what subsequently happens during processing, distribution and cooking. Poor hygiene throughout the food system ensures that infection is spread widely. More often than not, contamination levels are unacceptably high by the time food reaches the final link in the food chain (the kitchen). As a result, caterers and householders alike are unnecessarily exposed to high levels of risk. Food poisoning clearly illustrates one of the major issues of food pollution, viz., that the individual alone is limited to what he or she can do to ensure that food is safe to eat. Several partial solutions to the problem of food poisoning are already available, but the necessary political will to apply them is lacking. Removing various obstacles to effective political action will require concerted public pressure.

FOOD POLLUTION: MICROBIAL CONTAMINATION AND HUMAN MYCOTOXICOSES

Food poisoning and mycotoxicoses are two of the main health hazards of the contamination of foodstuffs by micro-organisms. In this section, we will discuss in detail various types of human mycotoxicoses. Mycotoxius resulting from mold growth on foods are dealt with another section, followed by a discussion of various types of mycotoxicoses found in India (i.e. ergotism, Indian childhood cirrhosis, cardiac beri-beri, aflatoxicosis and polyuria) in the next section. Mycotoxicoses found in other parts of the world (i.e. alimentary toxic alukeia, yellow rice syndrome, Reye's syndrome and Balkan nephropathy) are also described. Finally this section deals with some aspects of the prevention human mycotoxicoses.

Organisations responsible for environmental protection have rightly concentrated their efforts on the chemical, radiological and microbiological purity of food and have established standards (i.e. upper limits) for these contaminants of food. Although in some parts of the world the limits for radio-active contaminants are occasionally exceeded, these occurrences are quite rare.

Moreover, radio-activity is fairly easily detected and measured at trace levels, so counter measures can be taken before radio-active contamination reaches the consumer. The contamination of food with chemical agents is somewhat more prevalent, because in many regions of the world (especially in developing countries), chemicals are often not used carefully and find their way into food. However, the limits established for chemical contaminants in food have a large safety factor. So even when these limits are exceeded, their human health implications are relatively small. The situation is quite different for the microbiological contamination of food. Even in highly advanced countries such as the USA, UK and Germany, there are repeated occurrences of microbial contamination of food. In such cases, national or international standards are exceeded, sometimes by several orders of magnitude. Moreover, the consequences of exceeding limits for these three classes of contaminants are significantly different as discussed below. Radio-active contaminants often have short half lives, so their concentration is reduced significantly with time. The situation is somewhat similar with chemical contaminants.

Natural biodegradation reduces the concentration of organic chemicals, so a large number of chemical contaminants are naturally reduced to an acceptable level. In sharp contrast to these, microbial contaminants increase their concentration in food, unless stringent hygienic requirements are met. Micro-organisms are widely distributed and pathogenic micro-organisms are present wherever human beings and animals live. Microbial contaminants therefore, have to be destroyed by heat, chemical disinfectants or ionising radiations to make the food safe to eat. Food poisoning and mycotoxicoses are two of the major health hazards of the contamination of foods by micro-organisms.

Mycotoxins in Food

Microbiological contaminants of many types find their way into the food. Although many of these are not hazardous to health, some microbial contaminants have been clearly established as causative agents of human and animal diseases. Since the discovery of aflatoxins in 1960, there has been increasing concern about the health hazards resulting from toxic chemical compounds introduced into foods by toxigenic molds.

These compounds are generally known as 'mycotoxins', which comprise a group of chemically unrelated metabolites having the ability to induce a variety of toxic responses in human beings and/or animals when foods containing them are consumed. A wide variety of foods are subject to contamination by molds and their metabolites during the production, harvesting, transportation, storage and processing of foods. The diseases that are caused by the ingestion of toxins produced by molds growing on foods and feeds are collectively known as mycotoxicoses.

The probability of mold growth on foods depends on many factors—the most important among them being the moisture content of the food concerned, relative humidity and the ambient temperature. Grains, oilseeds and other agricultural commodities are relatively more likely to be damaged by mold growth than other food items. Mold growth on food grains can only be controlled by a careful regulation of moisture content, temperature and other environmental factors during the post-harvest period. Mycotoxicoses in human beings have not received as much attention from researchers as they deserve. The first known mycotoxicosis (i.e. an illness caused by mycotoxins) was related to ergot infestation of cereal grains. It is described in the following section.

FOOD POLLUTION: MICROBIAL CONTAMINATION AND ANIMAL MYCOTOXICOSES

The toxins produced in cereals and animal feeds due to their contamination with fungi constitute a serious health hazard to human beings and animals. In addition to causing various types of mycotoxicoses and associated production losses, some of the mycotoxins are even capable of inducing teratogenic and carcinogenic conditions in man and animals. This section is a brief review of animal mycotoxicoses caused by fungal contamination of feedstuffs.

Of the mycotoxins (toxic substances produced by fungi) known to occur in feedstuffs, the most prevalent and highly toxic ones are ochratoxins, aflatoxins and trichothecenes. In addition to causing various types of mycotoxicoses and associated production losses, some of the mycotoxins are even capable of inducing teratogenic and carcinogenic conditions in animals and human beings. In recent years, considerable attention has been attracted to mycotoxins because of their involvement in immuno-suppression (due to impairment of immunogenesis), thus predisposing the host to secondary infections or diseases.

In the early 1980s, mycotoxins hit the headlines in international print and electronic media due to their alleged use as a chemical warfare agent in certain parts of the world such as South-East Asia, Afghanisthan and Iran. Mycotoxins are usually not eliminated from foods and feedstuffs by cooking or food processing practices and, therefore, pose a serious threat to human and animal health.

The problem of the contamination of cereals and feedstuffs due to toxigenic fungi, although distributed world-wide, is of particular significance for countries like India where climatic conditions and unsatisfactory post-harvest and storage practices favour mold growth. Of still more concern is the contamination of animal feeds by fungi since moldy grains, found unfit for human consumption, are utilised for the production of animal feeds.

Mycotoxins

Mycotoxins are chemical compounds produced by molds as secondary metabolites, which are toxic to man and animals. Foods and feeds get contaminated with toxigenic species or fungi during various agricultural operations, storage, handling and processing. Mold growth occurs under appropriate climatic conditions (mainly temperature and humidity) and proper nutrients of substrate feeds. Human being and their livestocks have been the victims of mycotoxins throughout history. Perhaps the oldest known example of mycotoxicosis (a disease caused by mycotoxins) is ergotism, which afflicted thousands of people of the rural community in Europe. However, it was only during the last four decades that toxigenic species of fungi producing toxic metabolites and causing mycotoxicoses have been identified, their toxic metabolites isolated, characterised, toxicologically investigated and their toxicoses recognised.

Mycotoxins began to receive much attention only after 1960, when an outbreak of the 'Turkey X-Disease' took toll of more than 100000 birds in the United Kingdom. The cause of this outbreak was found to be a toxic substance produced by the organism *Aspergillus flavus* in the groundnut-based feed. The toxic compound concerned was subsequently named as aflatoxin. The identification of this toxin stimulated more research in this field, leading to the discovery of many other mycotoxins whose natural occurrence, synthesis and toxic properties have been fully documented.

Toxigenic Molds

The mycotoxins most frequently found in cereals and animal feeds are produced by the *Fusaria Aspergilli* and *Pencillia* fungi. The natural occurrence of some common toxigenic fungi, their mycotoxins and substrate feed commodities. Among the three types of fungi mentioned above, *Fusaria* occasionally grow on stored cereals having a high moisture content. On the other hand, *Aspergilli* and *Pencillia* are primarily responsible for the post-harvest deterioration of cereals since they are able to grow at lower water activity than *Fusaria*.

Several other toxigenic fungi are responsible for the production of toxic metabolites and may be associated to several diseases, e.g. sweet clover poisoning, infertility problems due to lucerne (*Medicago sativa*), 'Degnala' disease and other diseases.

The *Fusaria* produce two classes of mycotoxins, viz., zearalenone (together with its derivatives) and the trichothecenes. The *Aspergilli* and the *Penicilla* produce a variety of mycotoxins including aflatoxin, ochratoxin A, citrinin and patulin. Among these, ochratoxin and citrinin are nephrotoxic in pigs and are responsible for ochratoxicosis, bovine abortion and other syndromes in swine, birds and cattle. Patulin has been associated with the outbreaks of bovine hyperkeratosis in the USA. The biological effects of mycotoxins vary considerably from species to species, so they are not always predictable on the basis of our present knowledge derived from animal models or from structural activity relationship. In higher animals, the actions of mycotoxins are affected by sex, strains, environmental factors, nutritional status and interactions with other chemicals.

Mycotoxicoses in Animals

Many incidences of mycotoxicoses are recorded every year in farm animals the world over and as a result, the animal industry suffers enormous production and reproduction losses as well as animal mortality. The occurrence of mycotoxicoses under natural conditions in animals may be either by feeding them on moldy grains, corn and legumes, moldy hay or the standing pastures containing mycotoxins.

Outbreaks of mycotoxicoses must have occurred in India in the past, but due to lack of proper records and poor follow-up system, they have gone undetected. However, some isolated reports on the outbreaks of aflatoxicosis are available, e.g. the incidence in duckling at Hosur farm in 1974 and at a poultry farm in Kerala, 1982. In an incidence of aflatoxicosis involving man and domestic dogs, more than 100 tribals were reported dead in Banswada district of Rajasthan and Panchmahal district of Gujarat.

The disease (hepatitis) was identified as resulting from the consumption of maize containing 6.5 to 15.6 ppm aflatoxin. Similarly, some other reports are also available on the aflatoxicoses in cattle, buffaloes, poultry and ducklings. Prior to 1960 in India, outbreaks of mycotoxicoses in animals did not receive much attention. In spite of the worldwide awareness of the harmful effects of mycotoxins, reports on the occurrence of mycotoxins in animal feeds and the diseases caused by them in animals in India are very few, as mentioned earlier. It is a common knowledge, however, that damaged and moldy food grains, once rejected as unfit for human consumption, find their way into animal feeds, so the problem of mycotoxicoses must be significant in India. Some well-known incidences of the animal mycotoxicoses in India are described in the following section.

Indian Scenario

Aflatoxicosis in dairy cattle

One of the earliest outbreaks of aflatoxicosis in cattle was reported by Sastry and co-workers. The disease was characterised by loss of appetite, dullness, diarrhoea, emaciation and anaemia. This outbreak affected 24 murrah buffaloes.

Based on the clinical course of the disease, autopsy findings and histopathological studies of the livers of the animals that had died, it was speculated that the toxin was present in some consignments of the groundnut cakes fed to these animals. More recently Manickam and his associates reported an incident of aflatoxicosis, where nine buffaloes were affected and one of them died. The affected animals were fed sorghum stalks for about 4 months as the only source of feed. The affected animals showed dyspnoea, in-coordination in movements, falling suddenly and not being able to get up without help and a loss of sensory perception in the hind quarters. The mycotoxins detected in the contaminated sorghum stalks were aflatoxin B_1, citrinin and penicillic acid.

Aflatoxicosis in poultry and rabbits

India has a considerable poultry population. Aflatoxicosis in poultry occurs quite often as a result of consuming feed contaminated with aflatoxin, but most of these outbreaks are never investigated and rarely is the analysis of feeds for aflatoxins carried out. One such outbreak occurred in Karnataka, which resulted in the death of 2219 chicks. The symptoms were sudden anorexia, loss of weight, stagering gait and convulsive movements.

An outbreak of aflatoxicosis in a private farm in Kulu Valley, resulted in the death of over 4000 rabbits. In the 15 autopsies conducted on animals that had died of chronic toxicity, the characteristic changes in the liver were found to be marked proliferation of the connective tissue and hyperplasia of the bile duct.

Other Types of Mycotoxicosis

Reports of mycotoxicosis in animals caused by mycotoxins other than aflatoxin are very few in India. Shirlaw reported the occurrence of 'Degnala' disease in buffaloes in Punjab of undivided India. The disease was characterised by fever, pain in the abdomen, painful gait and anorexia. More recently a peculiar disease similar to the 'Degnala' disease affecting more than 1400 buffaloes in Punjab. The disease was characterised by necrosis of the tips of the ears, tail and tongue and swelling of the extremities (with subsequent peeling of the skin, leaving open wounds).

Singh and Prasad reported a similar disease in buffaloes and cattle in Patna and Nalanda district of Bihar. The affected animals showed lesions of tail gangrene, necrosis of lower parts of limbs and extremities and the swelling of feet and hooves. (The samples of straw fed to animals in affected areas showed their contamination with fungi such as *Aspergillus flavus*, *A fumigatus*, *A niger*, *Fusarium* spp., *Alternaria* spp. and *Rhizopus* spp.)

Thus, it is evident from the discussion that animal mycotoxicoses can cause significant economic losses resulting from decreased production, reduced growth and increased mortality in farm animals and birds. From the number of outbreaks of mycotoxicoses reported in India and other parts of the world, it is easy to see that the magnitude of this problem is quite considerable.

There may be subclinical forms of the disease and also other types of mycotoxicosis we are still unaware of. These situations need to be followed up by intensive research efforts and systematic reporting to create awareness of the health hazards of fungal contamination of foods and feedstuffs. The best way to control the contamination by mycotoxins is to prevent their production in the first place. This can be achieved by proper application of food and feed technology to prevent the proliferation of potentially hazardous fungi.

This involves maintaining the product quality during the growth, harvest transportation, processing and storage of foods and feeds. Probably the most important factors in controlling mold growth are the prevention of damage to crops during harvest and rapid post-harvest reduction in the moisture content to levels below those required for the growth of hazardous fungi. It is also desirable to carry out intensive monitoring for mycotoxins in feeds and to fix national standards for them commodity-wise in order to safeguard livestock and human health.

Chapter 3

Pollution Control in Wheat, Pulse and Rice Mills

INTRODUCTION

Pulses occupy important place in the world food and nutrition economy. Pulses are an important constituent in the diet and are primary sources of protein. They also provide substantial quantity of minerals and vitamins to the diet. Wheat is commonly used all over the country. Numerous type of qualities of wheat products and by-products of wheat like wheat flour, suji, maida and dalia, etc. are produced by the wheat flour and processing mills. The wheat flour is used in domestic purposes for making chapatti. Wheat in combination of maida is used for making bread, biscuit, etc.

Rice is also a staple food in India. It is processed from paddy both at household level and industrial level. It is either used in raw or parboiled form. There are many varieties of paddy cultivated in different parts of the country. Primary milling of rice, wheat and pulses is the most important activity in food grains. These grains are grown in almost all parts of world. Today, due to industrialisation and global competitive market trend, it has emerged as a major industrial activity in small medium scale sector to cater to the needs of increasing population.

ENVIRONMENTAL POLLUTION ASPECTS IN PULSE/WHEAT/RICE MILLS

The raw material received by the mills commonly contain much fine dust in addition to long fibre shaped dust particles. In the conveying equipments, the rubbing friction of the raw-material creates fine dust particles. Dust is generated at the transfer points of the enclosed conveying equipment, carried through bucket elevators and emitted at the discharge of the conveyed materials.

The main pollutant of concern in pulse, wheat and rice milling facilities is particulate matter emission generated from material handling, cleaning, milling or packing operations. These operations are typically located inside the mill buildings. Dust released from these operations spread inside the shop floor environment of the factory. Dust extraction systems are generally used to collect the dust and to improve the shop floor environment. Dust emitted inside the mill may settle on the floor and wall surfaces, or may be emitted to the environment through doors and windows. The environmental aspects associated with the pulse, wheat and rice mills from the view point of air pollution, water pollution and noise, etc. are discussed below.

AIR POLLUTION

Pulse Making Mills

During the process of the pulse making, dust is generated/emitted from various points, which spreads into the surrounding areas and pollute the shop floor environment.

Sources of dust emissions

1. Cleaning section: In the cleaning section, fine dust is generated at various points: (i) while unloading the pulses, (ii) at different stages of lifting and discharging of pulses through bucket elevator and pipes, (iii) during rotary screening, (iv) during scratching of pulses for breaking of tips in roller type m/c, (v) at discharge points of the rotary screens, (vi) de-stoner machines, and (vii) blown away dust/bhussi.
2. Milling section: In this section, the dust generated is lesser compared to the cleaning section, as most of the dust has already been cleaned in the cleaning section. The dust emanating from this section is mainly due to breaking of chana and its movement. The points of generation are: (i) the bucket elevator discharge points, (ii) chakki discharge (milling/grinding), (iii) chillka collection/ storage room, (iv) the reel machines, (v) the grinding chakki/machines, and (vi) the rotary screen classifiers.

The dust and powder emitted from the cleaning and milling sections need to be separately extracted and captured in separate air pollution control systems. The dust collected from the cleaning section primarily contains impurities like soil, silica, stones, etc. which needs to be disposed, whereas, the powder collected from the milling section is a by-product which can be sold as animal feed.

Pulse Grinding Mills

In the pulse grinding mills, since the raw material is clean dal, there is hardly any dust emission at the sections like bucket elevator discharge point or classifying screen. After grinding, the besan is pneumatically transported and separated in the centrifugal/cyclone type equipment and the fine besan escaping the centrifuge is collected in filter bags. No fine besan is allowed to escape from leakages, etc. as it would be loss of product. There are no fugitive emission sources observed in these mills.

Sources of dust emissions

In the pulse grinding mills, the source of emissions could be leakages in the system if any. No stack is provided discharging emissions to environment.

WHEAT FLOUR MILL

Sources of Dust Emissions

Cleaning section

1. While unloading the wheat.
2. At different stages of lifting and discharging of wheat through bucket elevator and screw conveyor.

3. At reel machine.
4. During vibrating screening.
5. At de-stoner machines.
6. At scourer machine.
7. At aspirator machine.
8. At magnetic separator.
9. At toggle cylinder.

Milling section

1. At bucket elevator discharge points.
2. At grinding mill discharge.
3. At purifier machine.
4. At plansifter machine.

Wheat Processing (Roasting) Mill

In the wheat roasting mill, the dust emission occur primarily from the cleaning section and fumes/ combustion gases are emitted from the roaster. The points of dust/fume emissions are as given below:

Sources of dust emissions

1. Raw wheat unloading point.
2. Wheat conveying bucket elevator discharge points.
3. Rotary screen.
4. Roaster feeding end and discharge end.
5. Points of free fall of wheat through pipes.

Sources of fumes/gas emissions

1. Oily fumes from the material discharge end of the roaster.
2. Combustion gas emission through leakages in the roaster walls and roofs.

The dust/fume generated from above mentioned sources need to be extracted/sucked from various point as close to the source of generation as possible and it should be directed through efficient control equipment.

RICE MILL

Sources of dust emissions

Cleaning section

1. While unloading the paddy.
2. At different stages of lifting and discharging of paddy rice through bucket elevator.
3. During pre-cleaning.
4. During paddy cleaning in paddy cleaner/vibrating screen.

5. At destoner machine.
6. At magnetic separator.

Milling section

1. At different stages of lifting and discharging of paddy/rice through bucket elevator.
2. During dehusking in rubber roll.
3. At Aspirator used for husk removal.
4. During polishing of rice.
5. During grading of rice in rice grader.

Boiler house: Flue gas through boiler stack.

WATER POLLUTION

Pulse Making Mills

In the pulse making mills, there is no wastewater generation from process, since whatever little quantity of water if used for conditioning the pulses gets consumed/evaporated completely. However, the storm (rain) water from the rooftops may carry the organic residual material comprising of pulses/shells, etc. lying on the roof terrace during Sun drying. This storm water is generally let out to the public sewer directly.

Rice Mills

In rice mill, the wastewater is usually generated in the parboiled rice mills from the soaking operation. In addition, in few older mills where mechanical cleaning facilities are not available, the cleaning is done by washing of paddy prior to further processing and this leads to generation of wastewater. In the parboiled type of rice mills, wastewater is also generated from the boiler section in the form of boiler blow down, backwash of DM plant/softener and from discharge of wet scrubber type air pollution control equipments installed for the controlling of boiler stack emission. In the dry rice grinding mills, there is no use of water in the process and therefore there is no generation of wastewater.

NOISE POLLUTION

Noise is generated from various material handling and process equipments, which are highlighted in Table 3.1.

EMISSION CONTROL PRACTICES IN US

Techniques Used to Reduce Emissions

1. Controls are often used at unloading and loading areas.
2. Control systems include cyclones, fabric filters, baffles in unloading pits, choke unloading, dust covers, or belt wipers, oil suppression and use of dead-boxes or specially designed spouts for grain loading.
3. Deepening the trough of the open-belt conveyors.
4. Slowing the conveyor speed.

Table 3.1: Typical noise pollution sources in pulse/wheat/rice mills.

Types of mill	*Section*	*Points of noise emission*
Pulse	Cleaning	Vibrating screen Reel machine Destoner Bucket elevator
	Milling	Bucket elevator Chakki
Wheat	Cleaning	Separator Scourer Vibratory screen Reel machine Destoner
	Milling	Packing machine Roller mill Purifier Planshifter Blower Bran finisher Milling fan ID Fan
Rice	Cleaning	Destoner Vibratory screen Bucker elevator Dryer
	Milling	De-stoner Polisher Colour sorter Length grader Blower Dehusker Paddy separator Thickness grader Whitener Packing section Paddy cleaner
	Boiler house	ID fans, soot blowing

Apart from the above sections, noise is also generated from the diesel generating sets.

5. Increasing the size of leg belt buckets.
6. Slowing leg velocity.
7. In addition, for modern elevators, process vents are tied to ventilation systems and exhausted to air pollution control systems.

General Types of Measures to Reduce Emissions

Process modifications for emission prevention/reduction

1. Enclosing the receiving area to the degree practicable.
2. Specifying dust-tight cleaning and processing equipment.
3. Providing lip-type shaft seals at bearings on conveyor and other equipment housings.
4. Providing flanged inlets and outlets on all spouting, transitions and miscellaneous hoppers.
5. Full enclosure and sealing of all areas in contact with products handled.
6. By reducing grain free fall distances and grain velocities.
7. Extraction of the entrained air and dust liberated at the point of grain free falls to a dust collector.

EMISSION CONTROL PRACTICES IN GERMANY

1. All equipment handling materials and machinery should be enclosed and fitted with appropriate aspiration connections.
2. Mass separators or filter separators may be used.
3. Dust from aspiration and cleaning systems to be collected and bagged.
4. Dust waste and granular cleaning waste is treated and added to mill after products (bran).
5. The live pests from cleaning waste to be destroyed immediately.

Noise Control Requirement in Germany

1. Precautions must be taken to protect employees and local residents.
2. Structural measures, such as the lining of ceilings and walls with sound-proofing materials, must be taken.
3. Vibration isolation materials must be used for machine foundations.

SUITABLE TREATMENT TECHNOLOGY

Primary Treatment

Screen

The wastewater generated after washing of wheat carry floating waste agricultural material (like stem, husk, etc.). These materials clog the drain and obstruct during pumping of wastewater from one treatment unit into other. It may lead to frequent breakdown of pump. Therefore, to avoid these difficulties, it is recommend to install a two stages screening system consisting of coarse and fine screens.

To facilitate manual cleaning of the screens, a screen chamber should be constructed based on the peak flow. The location of screen chamber should be below the level of the main drain. The suspended/ floating solids retained on the screen would be manually removed as and when required and would be disposed off as solid waste in a safe manner.

The screened wastewater should either flow by gravity or pumped to the settling tank/primary clarifier. In case of pumping, a pump sump should be constructed to collect and transfer wastewater coming from screen to the settling tank/primary clarifier.

Oil and grease trap

The oil and grease concentration in the wastewater is in the range of 5~10 mg/L. It is meeting the normal discharge limit and it won't affect the biological treatment. Therefore, there may not be a need to install oil and grease trap.

Chemical treatment

The pH of the wastewater generated from washing operation of wheat flour mill is in the range of 6.4~7.5. There is no possibility of the presence of heavy metals. Therefore, there is no need for going in for chemical treatment.

Settling tank/primary clarifier

The suspended solid concentration varies between 215~325 mg/L. The desirable suspended solid concentration should be less than 600 or 200 or 100 mg/L for discharge into public sewer or land for irrigation or inland surface water respectively. Therefore, a settling tank/primary clarifier is required to be installed for the settlement of suspended solids for discharging either on land or surface water.

Secondary Biological System

The BOD concentration of the wastewater varies in the range of 450~600 mg/L. The desirable BOD concentration should be 350 or 100 or 30 mg/L for discharge into Public Sewer or land for irrigation or inland surface water respectively. Therefore desirable BOD efficiency varies between 42 to 95%. This could be achieved by means of different modes of activated Sludge Process (ASP) such as high rate, conventional, extended aeration process, etc. A sedimentation tank/secondary clarifier should be installed close to the aeration tank for solid liquid separation and sludge recirculation, so as to maintain the desired range of MLSS concentration

Tertiary Treatment System

There is no need to go for tertiary treatment of the wastewater. The proposed limit of discharge could be achieved through primary and secondary treatments, discussed above.

Chapter 4

Pollution Control in Vegetable and Palm Oil Industry

INTRODUCTION

The production process of vegetable oil involves the removal of oil from plant components, typically seeds. This can be done via mechanical extraction using an oil mill or chemical extraction using a solvent. The extracted oil can then be purified and, if required, refined or chemically altered.

Mechanical extraction: Oils can be removed via mechanical extraction, termed 'crushing' or 'pressing.' This method is typically used to produce the more traditional oils (e.g. olive, coconut, etc.), and it is preferred by most 'health-food' customers in the United States and in Europe.

Solvent extraction: The processing of vegetable oil in commercial applications is commonly done by chemical extraction, using solvent extracts, which produces higher yields and is quicker and less expensive. The most common solvent is petroleum-derived hexane. This technique is used for most of the 'newer' industrial oils such as soyabean and corn oils. Supercritical carbon dioxide can be used as a non-toxic alternative to other solvents.

Hydrogenation: Oils may be partially hydrogenated to produce various ingredient oils. Hardening of vegetable oil is done by raising a blend of vegetable oil and a catalyst in near-vacuum to very high temperatures and introducing hydrogen.

This causes the carbon atoms of the oil to break double-bonds with other carbons, each carbon forming a new single-bond with a hydrogen atom. Adding these hydrogen atoms to the oil makes it more solid, raises the smoke point and makes the oil more stable.

Deodorisation: In the processing of edible oils, the oil is heated under vacuum to near the smoke point and water is introduced at the bottom of the oil. The water immediately is converted to steam, which bubbles through the oil, carrying with it any chemicals which are water-soluble. The steam sparging removes impurities that can impart unwanted flavours and odours to the oil. Deodorisation is key to the manufacture of vegetable oils. Nearly all soyabean, corn and canola oils found on supermarket shelves go through a deodorisation stage that removes trace amounts of odours and flavours and lightens the colour of the oil.

ENVIRONMENTAL ISSUES RELATED TO VEGETABLE OILS

Environmental issues associated with the operational phase of vegetable oil production and processing primarily include the following:

1. Solid waste and by-products.
2. Water consumption and management.
3. Energy consumption and management.
4. Atmospheric emissions.
5. Greenhouse gas emissions.
6. Hazardous materials.

Solid Waste and By-products

Vegetable oil processing activities generate significant quantities of organic solid waste, residues and by-products, such as Empty Fruit Bunches (EFBs) and waste palm kernels from palm oil processing or olive oil cake and pulp from olive processing. The amount of waste generated depends on the quality of the raw materials and on process efficiency. Wastes, residues and by-products may be used for producing commercially viable by-products or for energy generation.

Other solid wastes from the vegetable oil manufacturing process include soap stock and spent acids from chemical refining of crude oil, spent bleaching earth containing gums, metals and pigments, deodoriser distillate from the steam distillation of refined edible oils, mucilage from degumming, and spent catalysts and filtering aid from the hardening process.

Recommended techniques for minimising the volume of solid waste and by-products for disposal include the following:

1. Reduce product losses through better production/storage control (e.g. monitor and adjust air humidity to prevent product losses caused by the formation of molds on edible materials).
2. Collect residues from the raw material preparation phase for conditioning (drying) and reprocessing (grinding) to yield by-products (e.g. animal feed).
3. Return waste and residues to fields to assist in soil nutrient management, for example, EFBs from oil palm plantations with tree trimmings are a valuable soil amendment and/or can be composted with vegetable oil wastewater effluent.
4. Use waste and residues for energy generation in the project plant's boiler(s). Note, however, that relatively high atmospheric emissions [such as particulate emissions (PM)] are possible when burning crop residues and potential fire risks (e.g. from combustible dust) may arise from handling, storing and processing crop residues, as such, expert advice on fuel characteristics and boiler design should be solicited when planning to use biofuels in this manner.
5. Investigate the following options for the responsible disposal of spent bleaching earth:
   - Use as fertiliser, if not contaminated with heavy metals such as nickel, pesticide residues, or other contaminants.
   - Recover non-food-grade oils from spent bleaching earth that could be used in other applications (feedstock for conversion to biodiesel or in bio-lubricants).
   - Avoid direct recycling on agricultural land. Add spent earth to other organic waste and compost to avoid contact with air and risk of spontaneous combustion of spent bleaching earth.
   - Consider use as a feedstock for brick, block and cement manufacturing.

6. Investigate the following options for the use of distillates [e.g. free fatty acids and volatile organic compounds (VOCs)], depending on the level of contaminants (pesticides and/or residues):
   - Use free fatty acid as animal feed if uncontaminated.
   - Apply as a feedstock for chemical industry processes (e.g. antioxidants).
   - Use as fuel for energy production.
7. The nickel catalyst from hydrogenation should be either:
   - Recycled and recovered for reuse as a nickel catalyst or as nickel metal, salt, or other application.
   - Stored and disposed of according to the hazardous waste management guidelines.
8. Manage filtering aid mixed with nickel in accordance with the recommendations for nickel catalyst.
9. Use uncontaminated sludge and effluent from on-site wastewater treatment as fertiliser in agricultural applications or as a supplemental boiler fuel. Dispose of contaminated sludge from wastewater treatment at a sanitary landfill or by incineration. Incineration should only be conducted in permitted facilities operating under internationally recognised standards for pollution prevention and control.

Water Consumption and Management

Vegetable oil facilities require significant amounts of water for crude oil production (cooling water), chemical neutralisation processes and subsequent washing and deodorisation. Sector-specific recommendations to reduce water consumption, optimise water use efficiency and reduce subsequent wastewater volumes include the following:

1. When economically viable, consider the use of physical refining instead of chemical refining to reduce water consumption.
2. Replace water-based conveyor systems by mechanical systems (augers or conveyors).
3. Apply cleaning-in-place (CIP) procedures to help reduce chemical, water and energy consumption in cleaning operations.
4. Recover and reuse condensate from heating processes.
5. Upgrade equipment water sprays (e.g. to include jets or nozzles).
6. Use dry cleanup techniques before rinsing floors.
7. Manually clean vessels before rinsing to remove solids for recovery or disposal.
8. Use high-pressure, low-volume washing systems and auto shut-off valves.
9. Vegetable oil processing wastewater generated during oil washing and neutralisation may have a high content of organic material and, subsequently, a high biochemical oxygen demand (BOD) and chemical oxygen demand (COD). Wastewater may also have a high content of suspended solids, organic nitrogen and oil and fat and may contain pesticide residues from the treatment of the raw materials. Recommended measures to reduce contaminant loading includes the following:
   - Install spill collection trays to collect solids at appropriate places in the production line.
   - Use emulsion breaking techniques, [e.g. dissolved air flotation (DAF)], to segregate high BOD and COD oils from wastewater.
10. Use grids to cover drains in the production area to prevent solid wastes and concentrated liquids from entering the wastewater stream.
11. Select disinfection chemicals to match the cleaning operation being applied on the process equipment to the type of problem. Caustics (e.g. lye) are typically used for polymerised fat and acids are used for lime deposit acids.

12. Apply cleaning chemicals using the correct dose and application method.
13. Properly treat and discharge cleaning solutions (e.g. through a soap-splitting process) to separate oil and fatty acids from the water phase and then pass through a fat trap.
14. When appropriate and feasible, reduce phosphoric acid in degumming operations through the use of improved neutralisation processes or alternative methods, such as enzymatic degumming (this reduces the phosphorus load in the wastewater and also brings about a slight reduction in sludge quantities).

Process wastewater treatment

Techniques for treating industrial process wastewater in this sector include: grease traps, skimmers or oil water separators for the removal of floatable solids, flow and load equalisation, sedimentation for suspended solids reduction using clarifiers, biological treatment—typically anaerobic, followed by aerobic treatment—for the reduction of soluble organic matter BOD, biological nutrient removal for reduction in nitrogen and phosphorus, chlorination of effluent when disinfection is required and dewatering and disposal of residuals. In some instances, composting or land application of wastewater treatment residuals of acceptable quality may be possible. Additional engineering controls may be required to contain and neutralise nuisance odours.

Energy Consumption and Management

Vegetable oil processing facilities use energy to heat water and produce steam both for process applications (especially for soap splitting and deodorisation) and cleaning processes. Other common energy consumption systems include refrigeration and compressed air. In addition to the energy conservation sector-specific recommendations include the following:

1. Improve uniformity of feed to stabilise and reduce energy requirements.
2. Increase efficiency of air removal in sterilisation vessels to improve heat transfer.
3. Identify and implement opportunities for process heat exchange, e.g. optimised oil-oil heat exchangers in continuous deodorisation.
4. Reduce stripping steam consumption by improving process efficiency, e.g. improve stripping tray design. Where possible, consider technologies such as dry ice condensing systems that may lower energy consumption.
5. Consider co-generation (combined heat and power (CHP)) to improve energy efficiency.
6. Consider more advanced approaches such as the use of enzymes for processes such as degumming and oil recovery.
7. Where feasible, use anaerobic digestion for wastewater treatment and capture methane for heat and/or power production.

Atmospheric Emissions

Process emissions

Particulate matter (dust) and VOCs are the principal emissions from vegetable oil production and processing. Dust results from the processing, including cleaning, screening and crushing, of raw materials, whereas VOC emissions are caused by the use of oil-extraction solvents, normally hexane. Several sources within vegetable oil processing plants generate solvent emissions, including the solvent-recovery unit, the meal dryer and cooler, leaks in piping and vents and product storage. Additional emissions will result from the refining process if a fractionation method is used. Small quantities of solvent may be present in the crude vegetable oil if the oil has been extracted by a solvent and will volatilise during the oil refining process, particularly during deodorisation. Odour emissions are produced by multiple sources (e.g. cookers, soap splitting and vacuum generation).

Recommended management techniques to prevent and control VOCs include the following:

1. Process improvements, for example:
   - Optimise recovery of solvents by distilling the oil from the extractor.
   - Back-vent to the solvent delivery tanks during bulk storage tank filling.
   - Improve exhaust air collection systems.
   - Implement leak prevention systems.
2. Adoption of abatement technologies:
   - Recover solvent vapours where feasible, primarily through the use of counter current flow desolventiser – toaster in vegetable oil extraction.
   - Use a condenser, a reboiler and a gravity separator to treat condensates with high solvent content, to reduce both solvent emissions and the risk of explosions in the sewer.
   - Treat hexane-laden air from the condenser/reboiler process with a mineral oil scrubber.
   - Consider cryogenic condensation in the solvent fractionation process. Best practice approaches use a closed loop process in which 99.9% of the solvent input is reused.

The recommended management techniques to prevent and control dust and odours include the following:

1. Ensure proper maintenance of cleaning, screening and crushing equipment—including in any ventilation and air handling systems—to reduce emissions of fugitive dust and avoid the use of compressed air or steam for cleaning.
2. Install cyclones and/or fabric filters or electrostatic precipitators on selected vents including meal dryers, coolers and grinders—to remove odour emissions.
3. Reduce odour emissions (e.g. from soap splitting, cookers in the extraction process, vacuum systems and pressurised systems) with a caustic, alkaline, or ozone scrubber system, or incinerate the gas in a boiler plant or in separate incinerator systems.

Combustion products

Vegetable oil processing plants are large energy consumers, making use of auxiliary boilers for the generation of steam energy. Emissions related to the operation of these steam energy sources typically consist of combustion by-products, such as NO_x, SO_x, PM, VOCs and greenhouse gases (CO_2). Recommended management strategies include adoption of a combined strategy, which involves a reduction in energy demand, use of cleaner fuels and the application of emissions controls, where required.

Greenhouse Gas Emissions (GHG)

Vegetable oil processing produces GHG emissions through the use of fossil energy.

1. The high nutrient loading of wastewater can be a source of methane (CH_4) when treated or disposed of anaerobically. It can also be a source of nitrous oxide (N_2O) emissions associated with the degradation of nitrogen components in the wastewater (e.g. urea, nitrate and protein).

Recommended measures to prevent and control non-fossil-fuel-related GHG emissions include:

- Avoid open anaerobic conditions for wastewater treatment by ensuring a regular programme of operational maintenance in the wastewater treatment system.
- Consider biological methods of wastewater treatment, such as anaerobic digestion and methane capture, use of waste effluent for irrigation, co-composting of by-products, where appropriate (e.g. oil palm empty fruit bunches with palm oil mill effluent nutrient waste or olive mill waste residue with wastewater) and detoxification by nitrogen fixation.

Hazardous Materials

Vegetable oil processing involves the transport, storage and use of bulk quantities of acids, alkalis, solvents and hydrogen during extraction and refining. Their transport, storage and handling provide opportunities for spills or other types of releases with potentially negative impacts on soil and water resources. Their flammability and other potentially hazardous characteristics also present a risk of fire and explosions.

Chemical hazards

Operators in vegetable oil facilities may be exposed to hazardous substances via, inhalation of hexane or other solvents used for extraction, inhalation of toxic chemicals (e.g. sodium methylate can cause burns on the skin and lung tissue if inhaled), eye or skin exposure to acids or bases, inhalation of dust from the transportation of raw materials (e.g. seeds and beans to the crushing plant), inhalation of dust from meal treatment and shipment, inhalation of dust from bleaching earth, filter aid and nickel catalyst and inhalation of aflatoxins present in raw materials.

Additional industry-related recommendations include the following:

1. In oil extraction areas, ensure that there is adequate air circulation to reduce the concentration of solvents.
2. Provide ventilation, especially at workstations devoted to raw-material handling, milling, handling of bleaching earth and use of solvents.
3. Maintain air concentrations of VOCs below 10% of lower explosive limits. For hexane, the lower explosive limit is 1.1% volume per volume (v/v) and the upper explosive limit is 7.5% v/v.
4. Ensure proper distillation of oil after extraction for effective solvent removal.
5. Prevent leaks and spills of oils in the extraction plant.
6. Control the flash-point temperature of the incoming extracted oils and use temperature control for all facilities receiving solvent-extracted oils.
7. When feasible, use hot water, rather than solvents, to facilitate cleaning.

Physical hazards

Physical hazards in vegetable oil production and processing facilities are similar to those present in other industry sectors and include the potential for falls caused by slippery floors and stairs, injuries caused by unprotected machinery or moving parts, hazards associated with potential collisions with internal transport, such as trucks, and accidental contact with conveyor systems, such as those used in crushing plants and in the removal of spent earth.

Electrical hazards: Electrical systems are a source of danger for workers that can lead to injuries or fatalities.

Risk of fire and explosion

Risks of fire and explosion occur at different stages of vegetable oil production and processing and can lead to loss of property, as well as possible injury or fatalities among project workers. Sector-specific risks are related to the combustibility of vegetable oil and the high volumes of combustible dust present both in grain and oil-seeds handling and in storage facilities. The control and removal of this dust and the control or removal of potential ignition sources are key to eliminating the explosion hazard. The storage of grains and seeds represents a combustion risk, owing to the potential for self-heating and ignition. Silo safety for these products, as well as for oil storage, is critical. Vegetable oil facilities also present the risk of explosions resulting from the volatilisation of solvent dissolved in the oil (e.g. hexane), along with the risk of fire from spent bleaching earth with a high iodine-value oil, high ambient temperature and high circulation-draft of air.

ENVIRONMENTAL ISSUES RELATED TO PALM OIL MILLS

Palm oil is one of the two most important vegetable oils in the world's oil and fats market following soyabeans. Oil palm (*Elaeis guineensis*) is the most productive oil producing plant in the world. Crude palm oil contains fatty acid ester of glycerol commonly referred to as triglycerides, therefore, contributing to the worlds need of edible oil and fats. It is composed of approximately 50% saturated fats (primarily palmitic acid) and 40% unsaturated fats (principally linolenic and oleic acid), a unique composition if compared with other major fats. The distinctive colour of the oil is due to the fat soluble carotenoids (pigment) which are also responsible for its vitamins E (tocopherols and tocotrienols) content. There are several stages of processing the extraction of palm oil from fresh fruit bunches. These include sterilisation, bunch stripping, digestion, oil extraction and finally clarification and purifications, each process with its own various unit operations. Palm oil production process is shown in Fig. 4.1. These extraction and purification processes generate different kinds of wastes.

Oil Palm Waste Products

The oil palm mills generate many by-products and wastes beside the liquid wastes that have been mentioned, that may have a significant impact on the environment if they are not properly dealt with. The most common among these by-products is the empty fruit bunch. The empty bunch is a solid waste product of the oil palm milling process and has a high moisture content of approximately 55–65% and high silica content, from 25% of the total palm fruit bunch. The treated empty bunches are mechanically crushed (de-watered and de-oiled) in the process, but are rich in major nutrients and contained reasonable amounts of trace elements. They have a value when returned to the field to be applied as mulch for the enrichment of soil. However, it was noted that over application of the effluent must be avoided as it may result in anaerobic conditions in the soil by formation of an impervious coat of organic matter on the soil surface. Air emission from the oil palm mills are from the boilers and incinerators and are mainly gases with particulates such as tar and soot droplets of 20–100 microns and a dust load of about 3000 to 4000 mg/nm. Incomplete combustion of the boiler and incinerator produce dark smoke resulting from burning a mixture of solid waste fuels such as shell, fibre and some times empty bunches. These boiler fly ashes are also a waste in them and also pose problems of disposal. In the bid to achieve a zero discharge of the palm oil mill, boiler fly ash have been used to reduce the BOD, TSS, colour and other contaminants from POME before discharge. Boiler fly ash has also been used in the removal of heavy metals from other industrial effluents.

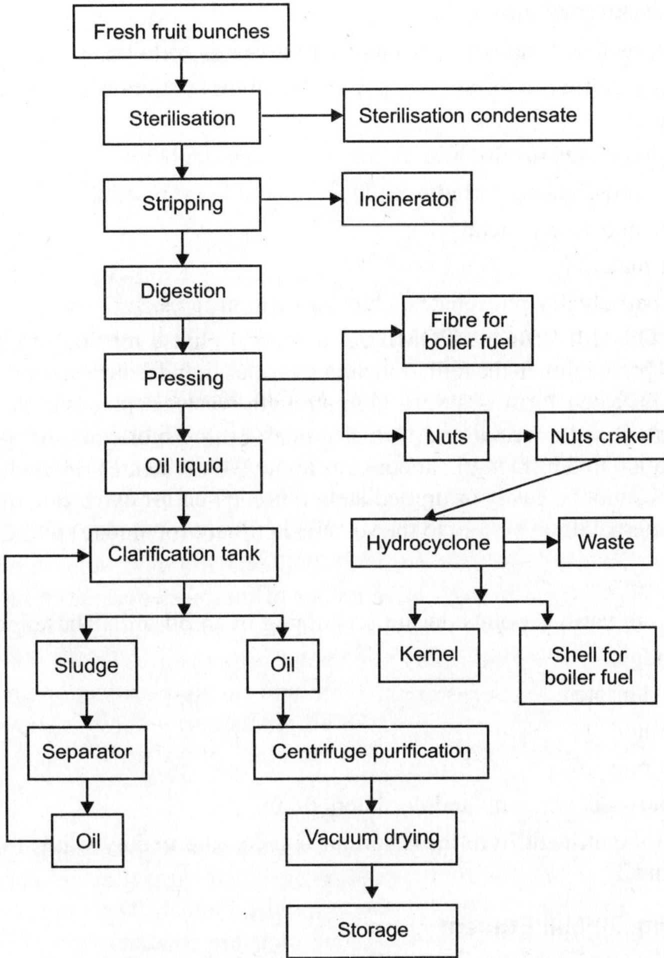

Fig. 4.1: Flow diagram of the palm oil mill process.

Palm Oil Mill Effluent (POME)

Effluent water is defined as water discharged from industry, which contains soluble materials that are injurious to the environment. Such soluble materials may be gases such as CH_4, SO_2, NH_3, halogens or soluble liquids or solids which contain ions of either organic or inorganic origin and with their concentration above the threshold value. Since these compounds are harmful to the environment, it becomes necessary that effluents water should be treated or purified before discharged into the environment. Thus, the major objective of industrial effluents treatment is to reduce the amount of these potentially toxic compounds to their acceptable threshold limit value (TLV), according to some standards of the Federal Environmental Protection Agency (FEPA), World Health Organisation (WHO), Department of Petroleum Resources (DPR), etc.

Characteristics of industrial effluents

Generally, the characteristics of industrial effluents are given as follows:

1. Soluble organics resulting in dissolved oxygen depletion in streams and estuaries and/or causing taste and odour.
2. Organic suspended solids resulting in dissolved oxygen depletion.
3. Inert suspended solids causing turbidity and resulting in bottom sediments.
4. Toxic substances and heavy metals.
5. Oil and floating materials.
6. Dissolved salts particularly phosphates, chlorides and nitrates.

Specifically, Palm Oil Mill Effluent (POME), is a general phrase referring to the effluent from the final stages of palm oil production in the mill. It includes various liquids, dirties, residual oil and suspended solids. POME in its untreated form is a very high strength waste, depending on the operation of the process, that is, informal, semi-formal and formal processes, the biological oxygen demand of these wastes ranges from 25000 to 35000 mg/L. It contains about 94% water. POME actually is the sum total of liquid waste which cannot be easily or immediately reprocessed for extraction of useful products and is run down the mill internal drain system to the so called effluent (or sludge) pit.

Sources of wastes

POME is generated from various points during processing in an oil mill. These include:

1. Clarification sludge.
2. Sterilisation condensates.
3. Fruit washing water.
4. Hydro cyclone drain-off.
5. Various boiler blows down, tank and decanters drain.

The composition of the effluent from these various sources, are mainly water, oil, solids (suspended and dissolved) and sand.

Management of Palm Oil Mill Effluent

Effluent management involves the typical handling of liquid waste. The mechanical technique often involves sedimentation, filtration and decolorisation of effluent. Mechanical technique is normally at the first stage of purification process to remove suspended solid particles. This is called primary treatment. The commonly used devices include sieve, sedimentation bed and filter. Physicochemical technique involves coagulation of finely dispersed and suspended solid particles, adsorption of the dissolved impurities such as heavy metals, selective crystallisation, reverse osmosis and ion-exchange processes. Reverse osmosis is most often used at the final stage of effluent treatment. Secondary treatment is biological process following primary treatment. The forms of secondary biological process include activated sludge, tricking filters, contact stabilisation, etc. There are widely known methods of effluent treatment in palm oil mill industries. These include the following:

Tank digestion and facultative ponds

In this system, raw effluent after oil trapping is pumped to a closed tank which has a retention time of about twenty days. The liquid is mixed by means of horizontal stirrers. The methane gas (CH_4) generated is flared off into the atmosphere, but the flaring of the CH_4 is unacceptable and calls for improvement on this method. Digested liquid is discharged into a holding pond before it is disposed on land.

Tank digestion and mechanical aeration

This group consists of cooling/acidification ponds, an anaerobic digestions tank and an aeration pond. Raw effluent after oil trapping is pumped to the acidification pond through a cooling tower and retained for one to two days. It is then mixed with an equal volume of liquid from the anaerobic digester before it is fed back to the digester and the achievement recorded indicates that the effluent water has been treated. The hydraulic retention time of the digester is about twenty days. The digested liquid is discharged to an aeration pond with two floating aerators. The liquid is aerated for twenty days before it is discharged.

Decanter and facultative ponds

In a few mills, decanters are used to separate the fruits juice after pressing into liquid and solid phase, the liquid which is mainly oil is fed to the conventional clarification process. The water resulting from the clarification station is recycled. The solid is either disposed off on land or is dried in a rotary drier to about 10% moisture and then used as fuel. Thus, the effluent which consists of only the steriliser condensate and waste from the hydro cyclone is greatly reduced in volume and is treated in a series of ponds.

Anaerobic and facultative ponds

This system consists of a series of ponds connected in series for different purposes. The effluent after oil trapping is retained in an acidification buffering pond for about two or three pond with a hydraulic retention time of thirty to eighty days depending on the mills. This digested liquid is further treated in a series of facultative ponds before it is discharged. In some cases, part of the digested liquid is recycled to the acidification and buffering pond. The total hydraulic retention time of the system ranges from 75 to 120 days.

Antra system

The treatment consists of a combination of mechanical chemical process and ponds. The raw effluent after oil trapping is separated into water and solid phases using a three- phase decanter. The oil is returned to the main line while the solid is dried in a rotary drier after the filter press. The water containing dissolved and suspended solids is treated with coagulants and flocculants to remove as much solids as possible before it is fed to an anaerobic digester which has a hydraulic retention time of about ten days. The digested liquid is further treated in an aeration tower and then oxidised.

Process treatment of the effluent water

Figure 4.2 shows the flow chart for the treatment of the effluent water showing the different stages. This is divided into the acidic, methanogenic and aerobic phases.

Acidic phase: This is the first phase of the anaerobic digestion process. It is a very rapid process whereby acid bacteria converts the organic components of the waste into volatile fatty acids (VFA) which in turn acts as substrate for the next phase of the anaerobic process. The pH of the system is depressed during VFA formation. The phase is not susceptible to environmental influence in that changes in environmental conditions like temperature do not affect its required performance, so open ponds are suitable and cost effective. At the start, anaerobic liquid is run down to the pond and then mixed with

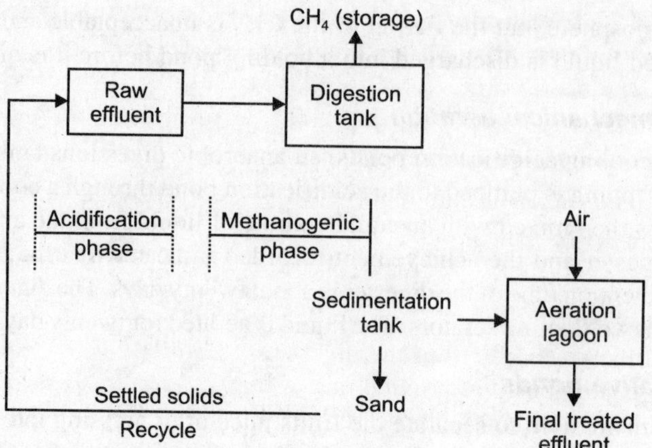

Fig. 4.2: Flow chart for process treatment of the effluent water.

clarification waste and then pumped over cooling tower in the ratio of 1:1 to 1.5:1. The mixture is left overnight to react. Recycling of anaerobic liquid helps to supply seed bacteria for continuous acidification, cools hot effluent and improves the pH.

Methanogenic phase: Methanogenic phase is susceptible to the environment in that changes in environmental conditions like temperature would affect its required performance. Thus, it is best carried out in a tank with so many advantages which are found using a tank digester and this includes:

1. The tank can be dislodged easily and efficiently – uncontrolled build up of organic sludge's would lead to loss of retention volume and eventual system failure.
2. Rainwater dilution is reduced as volume/surface area ratio is high. Rain water is acidic and harmful on anaerobic process.
3. There can be no subsurface inflows or outflows into the system hence the process can be monitored very easily. In lagoons, the same uniformity is not possible.
4. High gas production rates over a low surface area results in the break-up of scum formation which, if allowed to build-up will lead to loss of retention time. Disadvantages can come in the corrosion of tank, which can be controlled by better protective paint work.

The digestion tank is completely closed and the biogas ratio (methane/CO_2) produced is higher in the two phase mode of operation than in the single phase indicating higher digesters rate and this gas is trapped and stored in a floating roof storage tank and may be used as energy source. The liquid discharged from the methanogenic phase is transferred to a sedimentation tank and offer over night settlement. The settled solids are recycled to the acidification ponds and the supernatant is discharged to the aerobic lagoon. To give room for maintenance, three tanks with a combined full load retention time of 20 days can be used.

The efficiency of an anaerobic system cannot be calculated by considering only the input and output BOD. The build-up of organic matter in the system has to be considered. The digester tanks have to be dislodged periodically to minimise sand accumulations, such sludge have a high nitrogen content which are good replacement for fertiliser and withdrawal of 0.1 T of sludge/T of feed is allowed.

Aerobic phase: For a 20 T fresh fruit Bunch per hour (FFB/hr) oil mill, an aerobic lagoon with 20 days retention at 0.1 kg BOD: kg Mixed Liquid Suspended Solid (MLSS), a minimum of two 11 KW mechanical aerators can be used.

An extended aeration process is advantageous in the following ways:

1. Operation is simple and the problem of solid generation and handling are reduced.
2. Nitrogen destruction efficiencies are high.
3. Power requirement is not critical.
4. Construction costs are low.
5. Land usage is reasonable.

After sedimentation the discharge from the digester is dumped in the aeration lagoon at the start. Twin aerators, operate continuously to provide mixing and oxygen transfers. The lagoon discharge is passed through a sedimentation tank and the settled suspended sludge is at present recycled to the acidification pond but can be used as fertiliser because of its high nitrogen content.

It is essential that the lagoon content are well mixed as failure will result to a build up of facultative condition in unstirred parts of the system. The process streams are shown in Fig. 4.3.

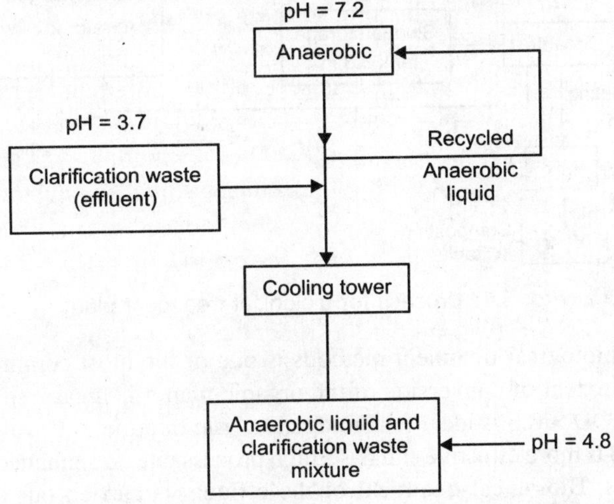

Fig. 4.3: Flow diagram of the process showing stream.

Process flow of the biological treatment plant

The liquid discharged from the tank is transferred to a sedimentation tank. The supernatant liquid from this tank overflows to the aeration lagoon. The concentrated digested liquid is recirculated into the digestion tank, to maintain a constant level of suspended solids in the digestion tank. When solids level exceeds the desired concentration, some of it is taken off into the sludge storage tank and sent to the decanter for dewatering. The sludge cake produced is mixed with fibre until a moisture content of about 60% is obtained. This mixture is then placed in the composting tank. This process biological treatment plant is shown in Fig. 4.4.

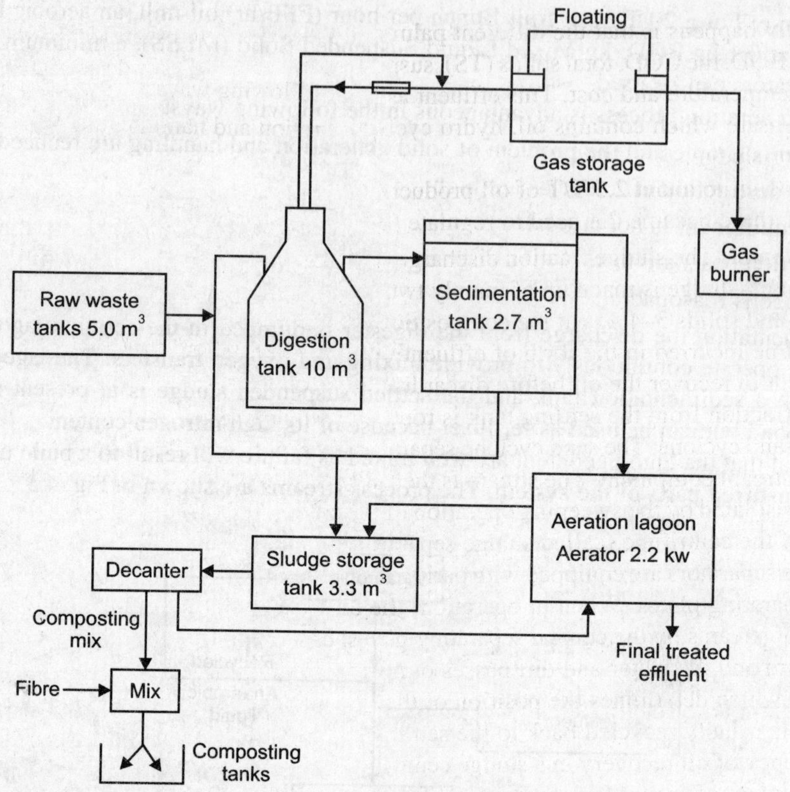

Fig. 4.4: Process for biological treatment plant.

Smith, suggests that biological treatment methods is one of the most common ways of treating the effluent water. Also, the extent of conversion of the organic matter is measured by the ratio of BOD to COD. The ratio BOD: COD > 0.6 is ideal for biological waste treatment. It was also found out that the aerobic treatment method is more effective and has a high process rate and enhances maximum destruction of carcinogenic products. Biological treatment of the effluent is carried out in filter bed, biological pond, bio-filter and aeration are commonly used. Bio-filters are concrete wall reservoirs with perforated bottom, filled with packing of various sizes and inhabited by micro-organisms. The microbes form a thin layer on packing surface.

This effluent water is evenly distributed on the filter bed-layer to ensure contact with the microbes. In all these effluent types, it is evident that anaerobic digestion is the most attractive biological process as it requires minimum power input. Unfortunately, it operates within a relatively narrow range of physical conditions. However, the process is more stable with wider range if the acidic and methanogenic phases of digestion are separated.

After anaerobic digestion, the waste is normally still too strong for discharge to waterway and extended aeration and sedimentation provides a supernatant of low BOD. The settled solids from the anaerobic and aerobic digestion process are higher in nitrogen content than raw waste and are eminently suitable for use as fertiliser.

What actually happens is that the different palm oil mill effluent management methods are selected to optimise the BOD, the COD, total solids (TS), suspended solids (SS), oil and grease (O&G), ammonical nitrogen, pH, temperature and cost. This effluent as stated earlier comes from three major streams, i.e. steriliser condensate which contains oil, hydro cyclone waste which comes from kernel operation and finally separator sludge.

All these amount to about 2.5 T/T of oil product and are highly polluting. Realising the seriousness of the problem, there became the need to regulate the effluent.

Sludge treatment: The sludge fraction discharge from the tanks usually contains oil >15%. The palm oil mill effluent ex-sludge is made up of mainly two other components in addition to the oil, which are water 93–94% and solids 3–4%, but the composition may very widely. If the oil is not recovered some what loses will be incurred in the form of effluent waste. The sludge fraction is therefore subjected to further treatment to recover the oil before discarding to the effluent pit.

The sludge fraction from the settling tank is routed to a holding tank (sludge tank), from where it is pumped to the sand cyclone. The sand cyclone separates the sand from the stream which will cause severe wear on down stream equipment. The stream is then routed to a rotating brush strainer where fibres and other solids are isolated by the sweeping operation of the rotating brush strainer. This is to avoid choking and blocking of the centrifuge (called sludge separator) which is responsible for this work.

These sludge separators are equipped with paring discs, sprawt wear resistant tungsten carbide nozzles and conical separating plates. When in operation, the centrifugal force exerted by splitting of the feed into a number of streams by the conical separating plates, causes the separation achieved eventually. The oil passes inward and the water and dirt passes outwards, part of water and dirt escapes over a gravity ring the size of which determines the position of the interface between the aqueous and oily zones.

Oil fraction is usually recycled back to the settling tank while the water and dirt is discarded to the effluent. Efficiency of oil recovery in a sludge centrifuge is dependent on oil content of recycled stream over total oil content of feed. More especially, efficiency of sludge separator is gauged by the residual oil content of the centrifuge waste which includes dirties, H_2O, heavy sludge, sand, etc. The variables affecting centrifuge efficiency are feed rate, nozzle diameter, feed temperature, dilution (viscosity) of feed oil and particles.

Chapter 5

Pollution Control in Dairy Industry

INTRODUCTION

Dairy products include milk and any of the foods made from milk, including butter, cheese, ice cream, yogurt and condensed and dried milk. Milk has been used by humans since the beginning of recorded time to provide both fresh and storable nutritious foods. In few countries almost half the milk produced is consumed as fresh pasteurised whole, low-fat or skim milk.

PROCESSING

Pasteurisation

Pasteurisation is most important in all dairy processing. It is the biological safeguard which ensures that all potential pathogens are destroyed. Extensive studies have determined that heating milk to 63°C (145°F) for 30 minutes or 72°C (161°F) for 15 seconds kills the most resistant harmful bacteria. In actual practice these temperatures and times are exceeded, thereby not only ensuring safety but also extending shelf life.

Most milk today is pasteurised by the continuous High Temperature Short Time (HTST) method (72°C or 161°F for 15 seconds or above). The HTST method is conducted in a series of stainless steel plates and tubes, with the hot pasteurised milk on one side of the plate being cooled by the incoming raw milk on the other side. This 'regeneration' can be more than 90% efficient and greatly reduces the cost of heating and cooling.

There are many fail-safe controls on an approved pasteuriser system to ensure that all milk is completely heated for the full time and temperature requirement. If the monitoring instruments detect that something is wrong, an automatic flow diversion valve will prevent the milk from moving on to the next processing stage. Higher temperatures and sometimes longer holding times are required for the pasteurisation of milk or cream with a high fat or sugar content. Pasteurised milk is not sterile and is expected to contain small numbers of harmless bacteria. Therefore, the milk must be immediately cooled to below 4.4°C (40°F) and protected from any outside contamination. The shelf life for high-quality pasteurised milk is about 14 days when properly refrigerated.

Extended shelf life can be achieved through ultra pasteurisation. In this case, milk is heated to 138°C (280°F) for two seconds and aseptically placed in sterile conventional milk containers. Ultra pasteurised milk and cream must be refrigerated and will last at least 45 days. This process does minimal damage to the flavour and extends the shelf life of slow-selling products such as cream, eggnog and lactose-reduced milks. Ultrahigh Temperature (UHT) pasteurisation is the same heating process as ultra pasteurisation (138°C or 280°F for two seconds), but the milk then goes into a more substantial container—either a sterile five-layer laminated 'box' or a metal can. This milk can be stored without refrigeration and has a shelf life of six months to a year. Products handled in this manner do not taste as fresh, but they are useful as an emergency supply or when refrigeration is not available.

ENVIRONMENTAL ASPECTS

Pre-treatment of effluents: Pre-treatment of effluents consists of screening, flow equalisation, neutralisation and air flotation (to remove fats and solids), it is normally followed by biological treatment. If space is available, land treatment or pond systems are potential treatment methods. Other possible biological treatment systems include trickling filters, rotating biological contactors and activated sludge treatment.

Air emissions: Odour controls (such as absorbents/biofilters on exhaust systems) should be implemented where necessary to achieve acceptable odour quality for nearby residents. Fabric filters should be used to control dust from milk powder production to below 50 milligrams per normal cubic meter (mg/Nm^3). Odour control by ventilation and scrubbing may be required where cheese is stored or melted. Dust control at milk powder plants is provided by fabric filters.

Ambient noise: Noise abatement measures should achieve either the levels given below or a maximum increase in background levels of 3 decibels (measured on the A scale) [dB(A)]. Measurements are to be taken at noise receptors located outside the project property boundary.

	Maximum allowable log equivalent (hourly measurements), in dB(A)	
Receptor	***Day (07:00–22:00)***	***Night (22:00–07:00)***
Residential, Institutional, Educational	55	45
Industrial, Commercial	70	70

WASTEWATER TREATMENT IN DAIRY INDUSTRY

The dairy industry involves processing raw milk into products such as consumer milk, butter, cheese, yogurt, condensed milk, dried milk (milk powder) and ice cream, using processes such as chilling, pasteurisation and homogenisation. The typical by-products of milk are buttermilk, whey and their derivatives. The effluents are generated from milk processing through milk spillage, drippings, washing of cans, tankers bottles, utensil and equipment's and floors. The dairy industry generate on an average 2.5–3.0 litres of wastewater per litre of milk processed. Generally this wastewater contains large quantities of fat, casein, lactose and inorganic salts, besides detergents, sanitizers, etc. used for washing. These all contribute largely towards their high biological oxygen demand (BOD), chemical oxygen demand (COD) and oil and grease much higher than the permissible limits. Among the biological treatments trickling filter and activated sludge process involve more economy high power requirement, more chemical consumption and large area requirement. Use of a dairy wastewater for irrigation after primary treatment in an aerated lagoon may also be good for the disposal of dairy wastes.

The food industry have one of the highest consumptions of water and is one of the biggest producers of effluents per unit of production, in addition they generate a large volume of sludge during biological treatment. The dairy industry is one of those sector, in which the cleaning silos, tanks, homogenisers, pipe sand, heat exchangers other equipment, engenders a large amount of effluents with a high organic load. This organic load is basically constituted of milk (raw material and dairy products), reflecting an effluent with high levels of chemical oxygen demand (COD), biochemical oxygen demand (BOD), oils and grease, nitrogen and phosphorus. The automatic cleaning system – CIP (cleaning in place) – discard rinse waters with pH varying between 1.0 and 13.0, further complicating the question of treatment. BOD is directly related to milk wastes (90% to 94% of the effluent BOD) and in some cases losses can reach 2% of the volume processed by the industry.

In order to reduce the effects of industrial sector pollutants, the end-of-pipe treatment techniques have been improved at the same time prevention measures are being implemented in order to minimise the production of residues. End-of-pipe control captures wastewater after its generation, enabling its discharge into environment. These are peripheral solutions that focus primarily on the chemical, biological and physical treatment of terminal streams. However, they address the symptoms and not the true causes of the environmental problems and therefore they are not cost effective or sustainable. The essential feature of the pollution prevention programme is the concept of reduction at sources, based on the idea that the generation of pollutant can be reduced or eliminated by increasing efficiency in the use of raw materials, energy, water and some other resources. Cleaner production intends to integrate the production aims in order to reduce the quantity and toxicity of residues and discharges. Pollution prevention or source generation reduction refers to any processor technology that seeks the reduction or elimination of the volume, concentration or toxicity of generating source residues.

The concept of cleaner production involves the reduction of negative environmental impacts throughout the products life cycle, from extraction of raw material to its final use.

The dairy is a multiproduct factory and its wastewater treatment process is based on five steps: (i) screening, (ii) sand trap/oil and grease separation in a tank, (iii) flow equalisation in a tank, (iv) an activated sludge process, and (v) tertiary treatment in three facultative lagoons.

However, the process is almost overloaded and requires a more complete diagnosis. On the other hand, minimisation of the pollution index indicator must be evaluated, not only in terms of final treatment, but also as an opportunity to reduce production costs, by optimising them and increasing process efficiency and profit.

SOURCES OF WASTES

The liquid waste from a large dairy originate from the following sections of plants- receiving station, bottling plant, cheese plant, butter plant , casein plant, condensed milk plant, dried milk plant and ice cream plant. Waste also comes from water softening plant and from bottle and can washing plants. At the receiving station the milk is received from the farms and after inspection the same is emptied into large containers for transport to bottling or other processing's. The empty cans are rinsed, washed sterilised and are returned to the farmers. At the bottling point, the raw milk delivered by the receiving station is stored. The processing includes cooling, clarification, filtration, pasteurisation and bottling. In the above two sections, the liquid wastes originate out of rinse and washings of bottles, cans and equipment's and thus contain milk drippings and chemicals used for cleaning containers and equipment's.

The skimmed milk may now be sent for bottling for human consumptions or for further processing in the dairy for other products like non-fat milk powders. Milk powders are produced by evaporation followed by drying by either roller process or spray process. The dry milk plant wastes consist chiefly of wash waters used to clean containers and equipment's. The soured or spoiled milk and sometimes the skimmed milks are processed to produce caseins used for preparation of some plastics, the process involves the coagulation and precipitation of the caseins by the addition of some minerals acids. The waste from the section includes whey, washings and the chemicals used for precipitation. Very large dairies also produce condensed milk and ice creams. In addition to the wastes from all the above milk processing's units, some amount uncontaminated cooling water comes as wastes, these are very often recirculated. The dairy wastes are very often discharge intermittently, the nature and composition of waste also depends on the types of products produced and the size of the plants.

WASTE CHARACTERISTICS

Dairy effluents contain dissolved sugars proteins and fats and possibly residues of additives. The key parameters are biochemical oxygen demand (BOD), with an average ranging from 0.8 to 2.5 kilograms per metric ton (kg/MT) of milk in the untreated effluent, chemical oxygen demand (COD), which is normally about 1.5 times the BOD level, total suspended solids, at 100–1000 milligrams per litre (mg/L), total dissolved solids: phosphorus (10–100 mg/L) and nitrogen (about 6% of the BOD level). Cream, butter, cheese and whey production are major sources of BOD in wastewater. The waste load equivalents of specific milk constituents are: 1 kg of milk fat = 3 kg COD, 1 kg of lactose = 1.13 kg COD and 1 kg protein = 1.36 kg COD. The wastewater may contain pathogens from contaminated materials or production processes. A dairy often generates odours and, in some cases, dust, which need to be controlled. Most of the solid wastes can be processed into other products and by-products.

Effects of Wastes on the Receiving Streams/Sewers

Composition of the wastewater of typical dairy industries is shown in Table 5.1.

Table 5.1: Composition of the wastewater of typical dairy industries.

Item	*Value (influent)*
pH	7.2
Alkalinity	600 mg/L as caco3
Total dissolved solids	1060 mg/L
Suspended solids	760 mg/L
BOD	1240 mg/L
COD	84 mg/L
Total nitrogen	84 mg/L
Phosphorus	11.7 mg/L
Oil and grease	290 mg/L
Chloride	105 mg/L

This is also slightly alkaline when fresh. Dairy effluents decompose rapidly and deplete the dissolved oxygen level of the receiving streams immediately resulting in anaerobic conditions and release of strong foul odour due to nuisance conditions. The casein precipitation from dairy waste decomposes further into a highly odorous black sludge. At certain dilutions the dairy waste is found to be toxic for fish and other aquatic living being and becomes breeding place for flies and mosquitoes. Dairy effluent contains soluble organics and suspended solids, they degrade to promote release of gases, odour, imparts colour or turbidity and promotes eutrophication.

TREATMENT OF THE DAIRY WASTES

Dairy wastewater have low COD and BOD ratio and it can be treated efficiently by biological processes. These wastes contain sufficient nutrients for bacterial growth and this can be prevented by:

1. The prevention of spills, leakages and dropping of milks from cans.
2. The requirement of water can be minimised during washes.
3. By segregating the uncontaminated cooling water and recycling the same.
4. Utilisation of butter milk and whey for the production of dairy by-products.

Both high rates tricking filters and activated sludge plants can be operated very effectively for complete treatment of dairy waste. But these conventional methods involve much skilled persons and special type of equipment's. On the other hand the low cost treatment method like oxidation ditches is also used commonly. Use of dairy waste for irrigation after primary treatment in an aeration lagoon may also be good answer for disposal of dairy waste.

DAIRY EFFLUENT

pH: It is a term used to express the intensity of the acid or alkaline condition of a solution. It is a way of expressing the hydrogen-ion concentration or the hydrogen-ion activity. Pure water is said to be neutral, with a pH close to 7.0 at 25°C (77°F). Solutions with a pH less than 7 are said to be acidic and solutions with a pH greater than 7 are said to be basic or alkaline.

Chemical oxygen demand (COD): The COD test is widely used as a means of measuring the organic strength of effluents. This test allows measurement of waste of a waste in terms of the total quantity of oxygen required for oxidation to CO_2 and H_2O. During the determination of COD, organic matter is converted to carbon dioxide and water regardless of the biological assimilability. The dichromate reflux method is preferred over procedures using other oxidants (e.g. potassium permanganate) because of its superior oxidising ability, applicability to a wide variety of samples and ease of manipulation.

Biochemical oxygen demand (BOD): It is defined as the amount of oxygen required by bacteria while stabilising decomposable organic matter under aerobic conditions. The BOD test is widely used to determine the pollution strength of domestic and industrial wastes in terms of oxygen that they will require if discharged into natural water courses in which aerobic condition exist. It is not a precise quantitative test, although it is widely used as an indication of the organic quality of water. It is most commonly expressed in milligrams of oxygen consumed per litre of sample during 5 days of incubation at 20°C. The BOD is used for measuring the oxygen consumed by living organisms (mainly bacteria) while utilising the organic matter present in wastewater.

Total dissolved solids (TDS): It is a measure of the combined content of all organic and inorganic substances present in a liquid in molecular, ionised or micro-granular (colloidal solution) suspended form. Generally the operational definition is that the solids must be small enough to survive filtration through a sieve the size mm of two micrometer. The principal application of TDS is in the study of water quality for streams, rivers and lakes, although TDS is not generally considered a primary pollutant. It is used as an indication of aesthetic characteristics of drinking water and as an aggregate indicator of the presence of a broad array of chemical contaminants.

Suspended solids (SS): It refers to small solid particles which remain in suspension form in water as a colloid. It is used as one of the indicator of water quality. It is sometimes abbreviated SS, but is not to be confused with settleable solids, which contribute to the blocking of sewer pipes.

Oil and grease: Dissolved or emulsified oil and grease is extracted from water by intimate contact with an extracting solvent. Some extractable, especially unsaturated fats and fatty acids oxidise readily, hence special precautions regarding temperature and solvent vapour displacement are included to minimise this effect. Organic solvents shaken with some samples may form an emulsion that is very difficult to break. This method includes a means for handling such emulsions.

Sulphate: In inorganic chemistry, a sulphate is a salt of sulphuric acid. The sulphate ion is a polyatomic anion with the empirical formula SO^{2-4} and a molecular mass of 96.06 daltons (96.06 g/mol), it consists of a central sulphur atom surrounded by four equivalent oxygen atoms in a tetrahedral arrangement. Many examples of ionic sulphates are known and many of these are highly soluble in water. Exceptions include calcium sulphate, strontium sulphate, lead (II) sulphate and barium sulphate, which are poorly soluble.

Chloride: The chloride ion is formed when the element chlorine picks up one electron to form an anion (negatively-charged ion) Cl^-. The salts of hydrochloric acid (HCL) contain chloride ions and can also be called chlorides. The word chloride can also refer to a chemical compound in which one or more chlorine atoms are covalently bonded in the molecule. This means that chlorides can be either inorganic or organic compounds. The simplest example of an inorganic covalently-bonded chloride is hydrogen chloride, (HCL). A simple example of an organic covalently-bonded (an organochloride) chloride is chloromethane (CH_3Cl), often called methyl chloride.

PREVENTION OF WASTES

Cleaning by means of the clean in place (CIP) system and the reuse and the recycling of water are examples of processes which reduce the volumetric coefficient. It minimised water consumption, in most of the processes, however, there were some exceptions, such as a few trucks that were not adapted with a 'spray bowl' for washing by the CIP system. In addition, the spray dryer was operated manually rather than automatically, which consumed large amounts of water. The action proposed in two ways:

1. A reduction in water consumption.
2. Minimisation of the organic load.

Water reuse and recycling is a reality in the dairy industry. Many processes, such as centrifugal separation with cooling water in a closed circuit recycled water. The filling machines (for milk packaging) can be cooled with recovered water and the evaporated water (from the milk evaporator for the production of powdered milk) can be used for cleaning trucks and outside floors. The retentate from the reverse osmosis system (used for desalination of boiler feed water) can be mixed into the water supply reservoir. The effluent considered water consumption while the water evaporated in the boiler and cooling towers are not computed in the material balance. The sum of these preventive actions account for a 10% decrease in total effluents generated. The industry can take action to reduce of effluents loads, which is reflected by the low BOD, nitrogen, phosphorus and oil and grease coęfficients. The actions taken should be for separation of discharged milk by automatic ejection of sludge in the centrifugal separators, segregation of whey from butter for use in animal feed and recirculation of the first rinse water from the evaporators at the beginning of the process, reducing the organic load of fluids and dry products In spite of the great concern of the industry to minimise waste, there are still opportunities for the reduction of previous coefficients. The recovery of solids in the first rinse could be a pollution prevention action. There are examples of milk solids recovered by the use of membrane separation processes (reverse osmosis) used for production ice-cream and milk desserts. Three direct results were obtained: minimisation of impact of the effluent generated, the production of casein and reuse of the permeated stream, which is of a high quality enough to be used for drinking water. A central system for treatment of these rinse waters could be installed, recovering the milk solids, mainly from the reception and the fluid products sector. This is the direct result of the production of pasteurised butter and cream, which generates effluents with high values for this parameter. In this case, the simple separation of the first rinse water and its use for animal feed would be beneficial in the reduction of organic load. Thus, the membrane separation process is a promising alternative to the recovery of nutrients found in the effluents.

In the light of above mentioned facts the industry should have comprehensive treatment system consisting of primary or secondary and/or tertiary treatment as is warranted with reference to influent quality and operate and maintained the same continuously so as to achieve the quality of the treated effluent.

Quality of raw milk: The collected raw milk contains bacteria. Bacteria release enzymes which is harmful for human being. Acid forming bacteria consumes sugar in the milk and forms acid and gases. In short they decompose the milk within very few time, so total quality of milk depends upon the number of initial bacterial count.

Method for Counting Bacterial Growth

Method for counting bacterial growth can be done by chemical and electrical methods.

Chemical method

1. Standard plate count method.
2. Litmus paper test.
3. MBRT test (methyl blue reduction time).

Electrical method

1. Milk barometer.
2. Online system.

LAND TREATMENT AND IRRIGATION

Land Treatment

Dairy wastewater, along with a wide variety of other food processing wastewaters, has been successfully applied to land in the past. Interest in the land application of wastes is also increasing as a direct result of the general move of regulatory authorities to restrict waste disposal into rivers, lakes and the ocean, but also because of the high costs of incineration and landfilling. Nutrients such as N and P that are contained in biodegradable processing wastewaters make these wastes attractive as organic fertilisers, especially since research has shown that inorganic fertilisers might not be enough to stem soil degradation and erosion in certain parts of the world.

Land application of these effluents may, however, be limited by the presence of toxic substances, high salt concentrations or extreme pH values. It might be, according to Wendorff, the most economical option for dairy industries located in rural areas.

Irrigation

The distribution of dairy wastewaters by irrigation can be achieved through spray nozzles over flat terrain or through a ridge and furrow system. The nature of the soil, topography of the land and the waste characteristics influence the specific choice of irrigation method. Wastewater would typically percolate through the soil, during which time organic substances are degraded by the heterotrophic microbial population naturally present in the soil. An application period followed by a rest period (in a 1:4 ratio) is generally recommended.

Specific wastewater characteristics can have an adverse effect on a spray irrigation system that should also be considered. Suspended solids, for instance, may clog spray nozzles and render the soil surface impermeable, while wastewater with an extreme pH or high salinity might be detrimental to crop cover. Highly saline wastewater might further cause soil dispersion and a subsequent decrease in drainage and aeration, as a result of ion exchange with sodium replacing magnesium and calcium in the soil. Generally, it was found that hydraulic conductivity, microbial content and *N*-cycling processes all increased substantially in long-term irrigated soils. Since increases in infiltration as well as biochemical processing were noted in all the irrigated soils, most of the changes in soil properties were considered to be beneficial.

SLUDGE DISPOSAL

Different types of sludge arise from the treatment of dairy wastewaters. These include: (i) sludge produced during primary sedimentation of raw effluents (the amounts of which are usually low), (ii) sludge produced during the precipitation of suspended solids after chemical treatment of raw wastewaters, (iii) stabilised sludge resulting from the biological treatment processes, which can be either aerobic or anaerobic and (iv) sludge generated during tertiary treatment of wastewater for final suspended solid or nutrient removal after biological treatment.

Primary sedimentation of dairy wastewater for BOD reduction is not usually an efficient process, so in most cases the settleable solids reach the next stage in the treatment process directly. An important advantage of anaerobic processes is that the sludge generated is considerably less than the amount produced by aerobic processes and it is easier to dewater. Final wastewater polishing after biological treatment usually involves chemical treatment of the wastewater with calcium, iron or aluminium salts to remove dissolved nutrients such as nitrogen and phosphorus. The removal of dissolved phosphorus can have a considerable impact on the amount of sludge produced during this stage of treatment.

The application of dairy sludge as fertiliser has certain advantages when compared to municipal sludge. It is a valuable source of nitrogen and phosphorous, although some addition of potassium might be required to provide a good balance of nutrients. Sludge from different factories will also contain different levels of nutrients depending on the specific products manufactured. Dairy sludge seldom contains the same pathogenic bacterial load as domestic sludge and also has considerably lower heavy metal concentrations. The recognition of dairy sludge as a fertiliser does, however, depend on local regulations. Some countries have limited the amount of sludge that can be applied as fertiliser to prevent nitrates from leaching into groundwater sources. It is generally agreed that disposal of sludge by land spraying or as fertiliser is the least expensive method. If the transport and disposal of liquid sludge cannot be done within reasonable costs, other treatment options such as sludge thickening, dewatering, drying or incineration must be considered. Gravity thickeners are most commonly used for sludge thickening, while the types of dewatering machines most commonly applied are rotary drum vacuum filters, filter presses, belt presses and decanter centrifuges.

POLLUTION PREVENTION

Reduction of wastewater pollution levels may be achieved by more efficiently controlling water and product wastage in dairy processing plants. Comparisons of daily water consumption records vs. the amount of milk processed will give an early indication of hidden water losses that could result from defective subfloor and underground piping. An important principle is to prevent wastage of product rather than flush it away afterwards. Spilled solid material such as curd from the cheese production area and spilled dry product from the milk powder production areas should be collected and treated as solid waste rather than flushing them down the drain.

Small changes could also be made to dairy manufacturing processes to reduce wastewater pollution loads. In the cheese production area, milk spillage can be restricted by not filling open cheese vats all the way to the rim. Whey could also be collected sparingly and used in commercial applications instead of discharging it as waste. Manual scraping of all accessible areas after a butter production run and before cleaning starts would greatly reduce the amount of residual cream and butter that would enter the wastewater stream. In the milk powder production area, the condensate formed could be reused as cooling water (after circulation through the cooling tower) or as feed water to the boiler. Returned product could be emptied into containers and used as animal feed. Milk and product spillage can further be restricted by regular maintenance of fittings, valves and seals and by equipping fillers with drip and spill savers. Pollution levels could also be limited by allowing pipes, tanks and transport tankers adequate time to drain before being rinsed with water.

The management of dairy wastes becomes an ever-increasing concern, treatment strategies will need to be based on state and local regulations. Because the dairy industry is a major water user and wastewater generator, it is a potential candidate for wastewater reuse. Purified wastewater can be utilised in boilers and cooling systems as well as for washing plants and so on. Even if the purified wastewater is initially not reused, the dairy industry will still benefit directly from in-house wastewater treatment, since levies charged for wastewater reception will be significantly reduced. Before selecting any treatment method, a complete process evaluation should be undertaken along with economic analysis. This should include the wastewater composition, concentrations, volumes generated and treatment susceptibility, as well as the environmental impact of the solution to be adopted. All options are expensive, but an economic analysis may indicate that slightly higher maintenance costs may be less than increased operating costs. What is appropriate for one site may be unsuitable for another.

The most useful processes are those that can be operated with a minimum of supervision and are inexpensive to construct or even mobile enough to be moved from site to site. The changing quantity and quality of dairy wastewater must also be included in the design and operational procedures. Since no single process for treatment of dairy wastewater is by itself capable of complying with the minimum effluent discharge requirements, it is necessary to choose a combined process especially designed to treat a specific dairy wastewater.

Chapter 6

Pollution Control in Bakery Industry

INTRODUCTION

Food industry plays a significant role in country's economic development. Processed agricultural products account for about 30% of the processing industry's, out of which 90% is produced by the food industry. The food industry is a complex and global collective of diverse businesses that supply most of the food consumed by the world population. Agriculture is the process of producing food, feeding products, fibre and other desired products by the cultivation of certain plants and the raising of domesticated animals (livestock).

Food processing includes the methods and techniques used to transform raw ingredients into food for human consumption. Food processing takes clean, harvested or slaughtered and butchered components and use them to produce marketable food products. There are several different ways in which food can be produced. Modern food production is defined by sophisticated technologies. These include many areas. Agricultural machinery, originally led by the tractor, has practically eliminated human labour in many areas of production. Biotechnology is driving much change, in areas as diverse as agrochemicals, plant breeding and food processing.

BAKERY INDUSTRY

The bakery industry comprises mainly of bread, biscuits, cakes and pastries manufacturing units. Bread is the product of baking a mixture of flour, water, salt, yeast and other ingredients. The basic process involves mixing of ingredients until the flour is converted into a stiff paste or dough, followed by baking the dough into a loaf. Mixing has two functions: (i) to evenly distribute the various ingredients and (ii) allow the development of a protein (gluten) network to give the best bread possible. Each dough has an optimum mixing time, depending on the flour and mixing method used. Process flow diagram of bakery industry is shown in Fig. 6.1.

Rising (fermentation): Once the bread is mixed, it is then left to rise (ferment). As fermentation takes place, the dough slowly changes from a rough dense mass lacking extensibility and with poor gas holding properties into a smooth, extensible dough with good gas holding properties. The yeast cells grow, the gluten protein pieces stick together to form networks and alcohol and carbon dioxide are

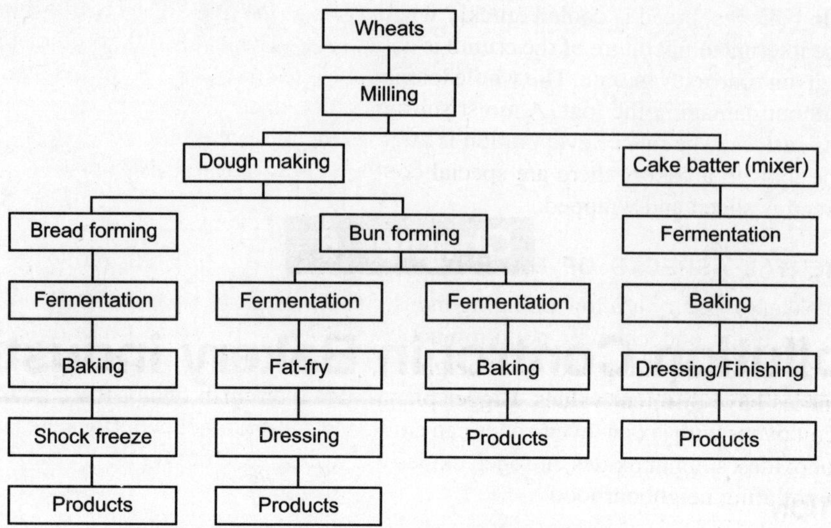

Fig. 6.1: Process flow diagram of bakery industry.

formed from the breakdown of carbohydrates (starch, sugars) that are found naturally in the flour. The yeast uses sugars in much the same way as we do, i.e. it breaks sugar down into carbon dioxide and water. Enzymes present in yeast and flour also help to speed up this reaction. The energy which is released is used by the yeast for growth and activity. In a bread dough where the oxygen supply is limited, the yeast can only partially breakdown the sugar. Alcohol and carbon dioxide are produced in this process known as alcoholic fermentation. The carbon dioxide produced in these reactions causes the dough to rise and the alcohol produced mostly evaporates from the dough during the baking process. During fermentation, each yeast cell forms a centre around which carbon dioxide bubbles are formed. Thousands of tiny bubbles, each surrounded by a thin film of gluten, form cells inside the dough piece.

Kneading: Any large gas holes that may have formed during rising are released by kneading. A more even distribution of both gas bubbles and temperature also results. The dough is then allowed to rise again and is kneaded, if required by the particular production process being used.

Second rising: During the final rising, the dough again fills with more bubbles of gas and once this has proceeded far enough, the doughs are transferred to the oven for baking.

Baking: The baking process transforms an unpalatable dough into a light, readily digestible, porous flavourful product. During baking the yeast dies at 46°C and so does not use the extra sugars produced between 46–75°C for food. These sugars are then available to sweeten the bread crumb and produce the attractive brown crust colour. As baking continues, the internal loaf temperature increases to reach approximately 98°C. The loaf is not completely baked until this internal temperature is reached. Weight is lost by evaporation of moisture and alcohol from the crust and interior of the loaf. Steam is produced because the loaf surface reaches 100°C. As the moisture is driven off, the crust heats up and eventually reaches the same temperature as the oven. Sugars and other products, some formed by breakdown of some of the proteins present, blend to form the attractive colour of the crust. These are known as 'browning' reactions and occur at a very fast rate above 160°C. They are the principal causes of the crust colour formation.

Cooling: In bakeries, bread is cooled quickly when it leaves the oven. The crust temperature is over 200°C and the internal temperature of the crumb is about 98°C. The loaf is full of saturated steam which also must be given time to evaporate. The whole loaf is cooled to about 35°C before slicing and wrapping can occur without damaging the loaf. A moist substance like bread loses heat through evaporation of water from its surface. The rate of evaporation is affected by air temperature and the movement of cool air around the loaf. In a bakery there are special cooling areas to ensure efficient cooling takes place before the bread is sliced and wrapped.

ENVIRONMENTAL ASPECTS OF BAKERY INDUSTRY

Even though bakery industry is a low polluting industry but for the ovens, boilers, hot water generators, DG sets they all come under the air pollution act due to emission of flue gases through stack. Acts prescribes limits on the emission and stack height and in addition to it covers noise pollution with it. Various countries have different values. Bigger plants with more than two or three production line of bread or biscuit ovens with six or seven zones can emit considerable amount of flue gases which consists of carbon monoxides, sulphur oxides, nitrogen oxides which are dangerous for health and if not monitored can result in polluting neighbourhood.

Air Pollution

Air pollution can be minimised with following steps:

1. Use flue gas analyser for stack monitoring in regular intervals.
2. Do regular burner maintenance.
3. Substitute if possible diesel oil to LPG or natural gas.
4. Use high pressure monoblock burners.
5. Get low sulphur diesel oil.

Dust

Flour production workers are usually harmed by dust pollution. Lengthy exposure time at a high exposure level can cause serious skin and respiration diseases. The control approaches include prevention of the leakage of flour power, provision of labour protection instruments and post-treatment. Filters and scrubbers are commonly used.

Refrigerant

In the chilling, freezing storage or transport of bakery products, a large amount of refrigerant is used. Chlorofluorocarbons (CFCs) and Hydrochlorofluoro-carbons (HCFCs) are the common refrigerants and can damage the ozone layer. They can be retained in the air for approximately 100 years. Owing to the significantly negative environmental effects, replacement chemicals such as Hydrofluorocarbons (HFC) have been developed and used. Another measure is the prevention of the refrigerant leakage.

VOC Emissions

The primary emission source at a bakery is the oven, which produces VOCs and carbon dioxide from the release of compounds formed in the yeast fermentation process. The main VOC emitted from bakery operations is ethanol. In yeast leavened products, the yeast metabolises sugar and produces carbon dioxide gas bubbles in the dough which causes the product to rise. The ethanol produced by yeast metabolism is generally a liquid at temperatures below 77°C (170°F) and is not emitted in large amounts until the dough is exposed to high temperatures in the oven around 240°C (464°F). Therefore, the bakery oven is the main source of ethanol. Ethanol and other VOCs combine in the atmosphere to form smog and therefore ethanol is regulated as an ozone precursor under EPA's criteria pollutant programme. The primary source of VOC emissions at a bakery is the oven. Screening measurements taken at mixers, fermentation vessels, comfort hoods, proof boxes, oven exhausts, cooling area exhausts and packaging areas suggests that greater than 90% of VOC emissions are from the oven.

Noise Pollution

Noise pollution can be controlled by following steps. Safe limit prescribed in Act is 70 db in night time and 75 db in day time as CPCB standards:

1. Monitor noise through decibel meter.
2. DG set room to be to be lined with acoustic lining.
3. Maintain equipment with maintenance schedules.
4. Use equipments with enclosure.
5. Use screw compressors instead of reciprocating compressor.
6. Silencers in stack for DG sets.
7. Put anti-vibration pad where ever possible for machinery.

Ear plugs can help to effectively reduce the suffering. Other noise control measures include the reduction of source noise, use of noise enclosures, reduction of reverberation and reduction of exposure time.

Wastewater

The ratio of water consumed to products is about 10 in common food industry, much higher than that of 5 in the chemical industry and 2 in the paper and textiles industry. Normally, half of the water is used in the process, while the remainder is used for washing purposes (e.g. of equipment, floor and containers).

Different products can lead to different amounts of wastewater produced. The wastewater from cake plants has higher strength than that from bread plants. The pH is in acidic to neutral ranges, while the 5-day biochemical oxygen demand (BOD_5) is from a few hundred to a few thousand mg/L, which is much higher than that from the domestic wastewater. The suspended solids (SS) from cake plants is very high. Grease from the bakery industry is generally high, which results from the production operations. The waste strength and flow rate are very much dependent on the operations, the size of the plants and the number of workers. Generally speaking, in the plants with products of bread, bun and roll, which are termed as dry baking, production equipment (e.g. mixing vats and baking pans) are cleaned dry and floors are swept before washing down.

The wastewater from cleanup has low strength and mainly contains flour and grease. On the other hand, cake production generates higher strength waste, which contains grease, sugar, flour, filling ingredients and detergents.

Due to the nature of the operation, the wastewater strength changes at different operational times. Bakery wastewater lacks nutrients, the low nutrient value gives BOD_5:N:P of 284:1:2. This indicates that to obtain better biological treatment results, extra nutrients must be added to the system. The existence of oil and grease also retards the mass transfer of oxygen. The toxicity of excess detergent used in cleaning operations can decrease the biological treatment efficiency. Therefore, the pre-treatment of wastewater is always needed.

Solid Wastes

Solid wastes generated from bakery industries are principally waste dough and out-of-specified products and package waste. Solid waste is the loss of raw materials, which may be recovered by cooking waste dough to produce bread crumbs and by passing cooked product onto pig farmers for fodder.

TREATMENT OF BAKERY WASTES

Generally, bakery industry waste is nontoxic. It can be divided into liquid waste, solid waste and gaseous waste. In the liquid phase, there are high contents of organic pollutants including chemical oxygen demand (COD), BOD_5, as well as fats, oils and greases (FOG) and SS. Wastewater is normally treated by physical, chemical and biological processes.

Pre-treatment Systems

Pre-treatment or primary treatment is a series of physical and chemical operations, which precondition the wastewater as well as remove some of the wastes. The treatment is normally arranged in the following order: screening, flow equalisation and neutralisation, optional FOG separation, optional acidification, coagulation-sedimentation and dissolved air flotation.

In the bakery industry, pre-treatment is always required because the waste contains high SS and floatable FOG. Pre-treatment can reduce the pollutant loading in the subsequent biological and/or chemical treatment processes, it can also protect process equipment. In addition, pre-treatment is economically preferable in the total process view as compared to biological and chemical treatment. It is usually economical to use a flow equalisation tank to meet the peak discharge demand. However, too long a retention time may result in an anaerobic environment.

Screening

Screening is used to remove coarse particles in the influent. Coarse screen, fine screen. Smaller opening can have a better removal efficiency, however, operational problems such as clogging and higher head lost are always observed.

FOG separation

As wastewater may contain high amount of FOG. The FOG can be separated and recovered for possible reuse, as well as reduce difficulties in the subsequent biological treatment.

Acidification

Acidification is optional, depending on the characteristics of the waste. Owing to the presence of FOG, acid (e.g. concentrated H_2SO_4) is added into the acidification tank, hydrolysis of organics can occur, which enhances the biotreatability. Grove designed a treatment system using nitric acid to break the grease emulsions followed by an activated sludge process. A BOD_5 reduction of 99% and an effluent BOD_5 of less than 12 mg/L can be obtained at a loading of 40 lb BOD_5/1000 ft^3 and detention time of 87 hour. The nitric acid also furnished nitrogen for proper nutrient balance for the biodegradation.

Coagulation-flocculation

Coagulation is used to destabilise the stable fine SS, while flocculation is used to grow the destabilised SS, so that the SS become heavier and larger enough to settle down. The coagulation-flocculation process can be used to remove fine SS from bakery wastewater. It normally acts as a preconditioning process for sedimentation and/or dissolved air flotation. The wastewater is preconditioned by coagulants such as alum. The pH and coagulant dosage are important in the treatment results.

Sedimentation

Sedimentation, also called clarification, has a working mechanism based on the density difference between SS and the water, allowing SS with larger particle sizes to more easily settle down. Rectangular tanks, circular tanks, combination flocculator-clarifiers and stacked multilevel clarifiers can be used.

Dissolved air flotation (DAF)

Dissolved Air Flotation (DAF) is usually implemented by pumping compressed air bubbles to remove fine SS and FOG in the bakery wastewater. The wastewater is first stored in an air pressured, closed tank. Through the pressure-reduction valves, it enters the flotation tank. Due to the sudden reduction in pressure, air bubbles form and rise to the surface in the tank. The SS and FOG adhere to the fine air bubbles and are carried upwards. Dosages of coagulant and control of pH are important in the removal of BOD_5, COD, FOG and SS. Other influential factors include the solids content and air/solids ratio. With the DAF treatment, 48.6% of COD and 69.8% of SS can be removed in 10 minutes at a pressure of 4 kg/cm^2 and pH 6.0. Mulligan used DAF as a pre-treatment approach for bakery waste. At operating pressures of 40–60 psi, grease reductions of 90–97% were achieved. The BOD_5 and SS removal efficiencies were 33–62% and 59–90%, respectively.

Biological treatment

The biological treatment removes the dissolved and particulate biodegradable components in the wastewater. It is a core part of the secondary biological treatment system. Micro-organisms are used to decompose the organic wastes. With regard to different growth types, biological systems can be classified as suspended growth or attached growth systems. Biological treatment can also be classified by oxygen utilisation: aerobic, anaerobic and facultative. In an aerobic system, the organic matter is decomposed to carbon dioxide, water and a series of simple compounds. If the system is anaerobic, the final products are carbon dioxide and methane. Compared to anaerobic treatment, the aerobic biological process has better quality effluent, easier operation, shorter solid retention time, but higher cost for aeration and more excess sludge. When treating high-load influent (COD > 4000 mg/L), the aerobic biological treatment becomes less economic than the anaerobic system. To maintain good system performance, the anaerobic biological system requires more complex operations. In most cases, the anaerobic system is used as a pre-treatment process. Suspended growth systems (e.g. activated sludge process) and attached growth systems (e.g. trickling filter) are two of the main biological wastewater treatment processes. The activated sludge process is most commonly used in treatment of wastewater. The trickling filter is easy to control and has less excess sludge. It has higher resistance loading and low energy cost. However, high operational cost is its major disadvantage. In addition, it is more sensitive to temperature and has odour problems. Comprehensive considerations must be taken into account when selecting a suitable system.

AEROBIC TREATMENT

Activated Sludge Process

In the activated sludge process, suspended growth micro-organisms are employed. A typical activated sludge process consists of a pre-treatment process (mainly screening and clarification), aeration tank (bioreactor), final sedimentation and excess sludge treatment (anaerobic treatment and dewatering process). The final sedimentation separates micro-organisms from the water solution. In order to enhance the performance result, most of the sludge from the sedimentation is recycled back to the aeration tanks, while the remaining is sent to anaerobic sludge treatment.

The performance of activated sludge processes is affected by influent characteristics, bioreactor configuration and operational parameters. The influent characteristics are wastewater flow rate, organic concentration (BOD_5 and COD), nutrient compositions (nitrogen and phosphorus), FOG, alkalinity, heavy metals, toxins, pH and temperature. Configurations of the bioreactor include PFR, CSTR, SBR, membrane bioreactor (MBR) and so on. Operational parameters in the treatment are biomass concentration [mixed liquor volatile suspended solids concentration (MLVSS) and volatile suspended solids (VSS)], organic load, food to micro-organisms (F/M), dissolved oxygen (DO), sludge retention time (SRT), hydraulic retention time (HRT), sludge return ratio and surface hydraulic flow load. Among them, SRT and DO are the most important control parameters and can significantly affect the treatment results. A suitable SRT can be achieved by judicious sludge wasting from the final clarifier. The DO in the aeration tank should be maintained at a level slightly above 2 mg/L. Owing to the high organic content, it is not recommended that bakery wastewater be directly treated by aerobic treatment processes.

Trickling Filter Process

Aerobic attached-growth processes include trickling filters (biotower) and Rotating Biological Contactors (RBC). In these processes, micro-organisms are attached onto solid media and form a layer of biofilm. The organic pollutants are first adsorbed to the biofilm surface, oxidation reactions then occur, which break the complex organics into a group of simple compounds, such as water, carbon dioxide and nitrate. In addition, the energy released from the oxidation together with the organics in the waste is used for maintenance of micro-organisms as well as synthesis of new micro-organisms. The trickling filter can be used to treat bakery wastewater. Solid media such as crushed rock and stone, wood and chemical-resistant plastic media are randomly packed in the reactor. In trickling filter surface area and porosity are two important parameters of filter media. A large surface area can cause accumulation of a large amount of biomass and result in high treatment efficiency, large porosity would lead to higher oxygen transfer rate and less blockage. A common problem in trickling filter systems is the excess growth of micro-organisms, which can cause serious blockage in the medium and reduce the porosity.

ANAEROBIC BIOLOGICAL TREATMENT

In addition to accommodating organic waste treatment, anaerobic treatment can produce methane, which can be used for production of electricity. The disadvantages, however, include complexity in operation, sensitivity to temperature and toxicity, time-consuming in startup and susceptibility to process upset. Anaerobic processes are suitable for a variety of bakery wastewater. For example, an anaerobic contactor was successfully used to treat wastewater from a production facility of snack cake items. Alternatively, a subsequent aerobic treatment can be used to further reduce the waste strength and the effluent can then be discharged to a watercourse.

Solid Waste Management

Bakery solid waste includes stale bakery products, dropped raw materials (e.g. dough) and packages. The most simple and common way is to directly transport these to landfill or incineration. Landfill can cause the waste to decompose, which eventually leads to production of methane (a greenhouse gas) and groundwater pollution (organic compounds and heavy metals). Incineration of bakery waste can also release nitrogen oxide gases. Reclamation of the bakery waste can play an important role in its management. The waste consists primarily of stale bread, bread rolls and cookies—all of which contain high energy and can be fed directly to animals, such as swine and cattle. Another application is to use the waste for production of valuable products.

Cleaner Production in the Bakery Industry

The production of bakery products involves many operation units that may cause a variety of wastes. Most bakery industries are of small or medium size and are often located in densely populated areas, which makes environmental problems more critical. Nevertheless, the conventional 'end-of-pipe' treatment philosophy has its restrictions in dealing with these problems. It only addresses the result of inefficient and wasteful production processes and should be considered only as a final option. Manufacturing will always cause direct or indirect pollution of the environment. It is hard to realise 'zero discharge' and waste treatment is always expensive. Cleaner Production (CP) has two key components: maximisation of waste reduction and minimisation of raw material usage and energy consumption.

Cleaner production results from one or a combination of conserving raw materials, water and energy, eliminating toxic and dangerous raw materials, and reducing the quantity and toxicity of all emissions and wastes at source during the production process. It aims to reduce the environmental, health and safety impacts of products over their entire life-cycles, from raw materials extraction, through manufacturing and use, to the 'ultimate' disposal of the product. It implies the incorporation of environmental concerns into designing and delivering services.

In the CP process, raw materials, water and energy should be conserved, their emission or wastage should be reduced and application of toxic raw materials must be avoided. It is also important to reduce the negative impacts during the whole production life-cycle, from the design of the production to the final waste disposal.

Chapter 7

Pollution Control in Poultry Industry

INTRODUCTION

This chapter analyses the environmental impacts arising from intensive poultry production, evaluating such impacts across the food chain. The chapter also discusses technical options to mitigate environmental impacts, such as improvements to farm management, animal waste management and nutrition management, along with options to reduce the impacts of intensive feed production. The use of large facilities associated with higher concentrations of poultry, has given rise to environmental concerns that are not only limited to the local production settings, but extend to environmental problems at regional and global scales. The obvious and often limited, impacts observed at production-site level, thus, tend to obscure much larger impacts on the regional and global environment.

PRODUCTION AND PROCESSING UNITS IN POULTRY

This section provides an overview of environmental concerns at the local level, arising from two point sources: the animal production site and the abattoir. At this level, impacts are usually directly observed by farmers, neighbours and policy-makers.

Animal Production Units

Local disturbances (e.g. odour, flies and rodents) and landscape degradation are typical local negative amenities in the surroundings of poultry farms. Pollution of soil and water with nutrients, pathogens and heavy metals is generally caused by poor manure-management and occurs where manure is stored. Water and soil pollution related to poultry litter is, however, generally not an issue at the production site, as poultry manure is only directly discharged into the environment in exceptional conditions. Indeed, the high nutrient content and low water content of poultry litter make it a valuable input to agriculture. Manure is either recycled on cropland belonging to the animal farm or marketed. In the usual setup, an intermediary or a processor collects manure from poultry farms. Manure is either resold rough or processed into compost or pellets. Manure products are used as fertiliser, or as animal feed especially for fish and cattle. Poultry facilities are a source of odour and attract flies, rodents and other pests that create local nuisances and carry disease. Odour emissions from poultry farms adversely affect the life of people living in the vicinity. Odour associated with poultry operations comes from fresh and decomposing waste products such as manure, carcasses, feathers and bedding/litter. On-farm odour is mainly emitted from poultry buildings and manure and storage facilities. Odour from animal feeding operations is not caused by a single compound, but is rather the result of a large number of contributing compounds including ammonia (NH_3), Volatile Organic Compounds (VOCs) and hydrogen sulphide (H_2S). Of the several manure-based compounds which produce odour, the most commonly reported is ammonia. Ammonia gas has a sharp and pungent odour and can act as an irritant when present in elevated concentrations.

Odour is a local issue, which is hardly quantifiable, the impact greatly depends on the subjective perception of populations neighbouring the farm. It is, therefore, difficult to evaluate the maximum distance over which odorous gas travels, however, odour problems are generally concentrated within 500 metres of the farm. Although generally not causing any public-health concern, odours can represent a strong local problem that is frequently reported by farms' neighbours as the most disturbing environmental impact.

The emission of odours mostly depends on the frequency of animal-house cleaning, on the temperature and humidity of the manure, on the type of manure storage and on air movements. For these reasons it is generally higher in waterfowl farms than in chicken farms. Flies are an additional concern for residents living near poultry facilities. In addition to the nuisance they cause, flies and mosquitoes can transmit diseases, such as cholera, dysentery, typhoid, malaria, filaria and dengue fever. Although less often reported than flies and mosquitoes, rats and similar pests are also a local nuisance associated with poultry production. As with flies and mosquitoes, they can be a vector for disease transmission. Their presence is mainly related to animal-feed management and especially to storage and losses from feeding systems.

Pesticides used to control pests (e.g. parasites and disease vectors) and predators have been reported to cause pollution when they enter groundwater and surface water. Active molecules or their degradation products enter ecosystems in solution, in emulsion or bound to soil particles and may, in some instances, impair the uses of surface waters and groundwater.

The trend to larger production units and their regional concentration, certainly has the potential to adversely affect surrounding land use and the appearance of the landscape. Massive industrial poultry installations can create an adverse aesthetic impact. Impact on land use in highly concentrated areas is manifested through conflict with development needs and in some areas with rural tourism.

Improper disposal of poultry carcasses can contribute to water-quality problems especially in areas prone to flooding or where there is a shallow water table. Methods for the disposal of poultry carcasses include burial, incineration, composting and rendering. In the case of recent Highly Pathogenic Avian Influenza (HPAI) outbreaks, the disposal of large numbers of infected birds has presented new and complex problems associated with environmental contamination. Large volumes of carcasses can generate excessive amounts of leachate and other pollutants, increasing the potential for environmental contamination.

SLAUGHTERHOUSE

The most significant environmental issue resulting from slaughterhouse operations is the discharge of wastewater into the environment. Like many other food-processing activities, the necessity for hygiene and quality control in meat processing results in high water usage and consequently high levels of wastewater generation. Poultry processing activities require large amounts of high-quality water for process cleaning and cooling. Typical water usage in poultry slaughterhouses ranges between 6 and 30 cubic metres/T of product. Large quantities of water are consumed in poultry slaughterhouses for evisceration, cleaning and washing operations. Process wastewater generated during these activities typically has high biochemical and chemical oxygen demand (BOD and COD_3) due to the presence of organic materials such as blood, fat, flesh and excreta. In addition, process wastewater may contain high levels of nitrogen, phosphorus and residues of chemicals such as chlorine used for washing and disinfection, as well as various pathogens including *Salmonella* and *Campylobacter*.

Poultry by-products and waste may contain up to 100 different species of micro-organisms, including pathogens, in contaminated feathers, feet and intestinal contents. Typical values for wastewater produced from poultry processing are 6.8 kg BOD/T Live Weight Killed (LWK) and 3.5 kg suspended solids per tonne of LWK.

Poultry slaughterhouses release large amounts of waste into the environment, polluting land and surface waters as well as posing a serious human-health risk. The discharge of biodegradable organic compounds may cause a strong reduction of the amount of dissolved oxygen in surface waters, which in turn may lead to reduced levels of activity or even death of aquatic life.

Macronutrients (nitrogen, phosphorus) may cause eutrophication of the affected water bodies. Excessive algal growth and subsequent dying off and mineralisation of these algae may lead to the death of aquatic life because of oxygen depletion. Slaughterhouses are usually located in urban or peri-urban locations, where transport costs to markets are minimised and where there is abundant labour supply. This situation increases the risk of environmental impacts: first, because slaughterhouses often lack the land required to set up waste-management facilities, second, because the pollutants that are emitted add to those emitted by other human activities, and third, because neighbouring communities are directly affected by surface-water and groundwater contamination.

WATERSHED-LEVEL POLLUTION ASSOCIATED WITH WASTE MANAGEMENT

Intensification of production and the geographical concentration of production units often results in environmental concerns. The decoupling of crop and livestock production through the migration of livestock production away from crop activities into areas with little or no agricultural land leads to high levels of environmental impact – mainly related to manure mismanagement and nutrient overloads.

Poultry Manure

Poultry manure contains considerable amounts of nutrients such as nitrogen, phosphorus and other excreted substances such as hormones, antibiotics, pathogens and heavy metals which are introduced through feed. Leaching and runoff of these substances has the potential to result in contamination of surface water and groundwater resources.

Nutrients

Animals reared in intensive production systems consume a considerable amount of protein and other nitrogen-containing substances in their diets. The conversion of dietary nitrogen to animal products is relatively inefficient, 50 to 80% of the nitrogen is excreted. Nitrogen is excreted in both organic and inorganic compounds. Nitrogen emissions from manure take four main forms: ammonia (NH_3), dinitrogen (N_2), nitrous oxide (N_2O) and nitrate (NO_3^-). Phosphorus is an essential element for animal growth. Unlike nitrogen, phosphorus is relatively stable once attached to soil particles and does not leach through the soil into groundwater. It does not pose any environmental risks except as a nutrient, it limits biological activity in water resources and builds up in soil when applied in excess. Phosphorus emissions from manure occur in one main form: phosphate.

Heavy metals

Manure contains appreciable quantities of potentially toxic metals such as arsenic, copper and zinc. In excess, these elements can become toxic to plants, can adversely affect organisms that feed on these plants and can enter water systems through surface run-off and leaching. Trace elements are introduced into poultry diets either involuntarily through contaminated feedstuffs or voluntarily, as feed additives used to supply animals requirements or – in much greater proportions – as veterinary medicines or growth promoters.

Pathogens

Manure also contains pathogens which may potentially affect soil and water resources, particularly if poorly managed. Parasites such as *Cryptosporidium* and *Giardia* spp., can easily spread from manure to water supplies and can remain viable in the environment for long periods of time.

POULTRY WASTES

Poultry processing is a speciality segment of the meat industry. Although poultry plants bear a resemblance in general production sequences to meat processing plants, they have specific distinctions and problems, including the characteristics and treatment of wastewaters.

Processing Plants

The poultry processing plant should be highly mechanised having high production facilities. Conveyor speeds of 35–50 turkeys per minute or 100 broilers per minute are common. The sequence of processing operations is: live bird receiving, killing, bleeding, plucking and eviscerating, chilling and packing in ice or freezing for shipment. Inventories of live birds are kept low by scheduling incoming truck shipments in a manner to reduce holding time and inventory level. It is good practice to receive and process poultry on the same day, without hold-over of live birds. Storage of dressed ice-packed or frozen poultry is minimal also, with a significant reduction of holding inventory. The egg processing plant cannot be typified because any or all egg processing operations may be found in any location. The fresh shell egg is a complete food and package in itself. Processing consists of candling for blood spots and other inside defects, examination of the shell for defects, washing, grading and cartoning. Hand methods are in general use, however, where quantity and quality permit, bulk candlers, sizers and automatic car toners are being installed. Egg breaking operations consist of separating the yolks from the whites, which are then either frozen separately or blended to a customer's specifications and frozen. The breaking of eggs is, in part, a salvage operation of the shell egg business where cracked shells or otherwise substandard conditions are encountered. Further processing of eggs or yolks and whites through spray drying is common. These dried egg products are used by bakeries, home cake or bake mixes and similar applications.

Blood wastes

The major source of pollution in poultry processing is generally the waste blood, which contains feathers, dirt and some manure. The majority of poultry processors attempt to recover free-draining blood. For good blood recovery, an area must be restricted to the collection of the blood, allowing for 2 minutes drainage time from the kill station. Even with the best of recovery practices, some blood is introduced into the plant sewer system. In addition, cleanup operations in the kill and bleed area send congealed blood and other matter to the plant sewers.

Approximately 6% of the poultry body weight is blood, 4% drainable in the bleeding area, leaving about 2% by weight in the bird. Tests have shown that chickens contain sufficient blood to equal a 5-day BOD of about 17.5 lb per 1000 chickens processed. In a good poultry plant operation, where blood wastes are carefully salvaged in the killing area, approximately 3–5 lb BOD per 1000 chickens may be sent to the plant wastes collectively from all operations.

Defeathering wastes

In the customary processing progression, the next wastes result from defeathering operations. These wastewaters consist mainly of the continuous scalder overflow, continuous water spray flow from the defeathering machines and final cleanup operations from dumping of scalder water and wash down of floors and equipment. Where the sudden release of water from a tank or vat might cause sewer overflow, it is good practice to provide a restricted drain opening.

Prior to entry into the defeathering machine, the bird is immersed in a scalder to relax feather follicles for easier feather removal. The scalder, operating on a continuous feed of approximately 1 quart of water per bird, therefore provides a steady flow to the plant sewer system. This waste is high in pollutional strength and contains feathers, some blood and dirt. Defeathering machines are equipped with beaters (rubber fingers) that force the feathers from the skin. Simultaneously with the beating, warm water is applied to lubricate the rubber fingers, to prevent epidermis removal and to carry or 'flow away' the feathers from the machine area. The continuous flow of water used in the defeathering machines is high in volume but relatively low in pollutional strength.

Solid wastes

Following defeathering, the eviscerating and cutting operations produce solid wastes consisting of feet, heads, inedible viscera, crops and windpipes, lungs, grit, sand, gravel, trimmings, grease and blood. Lungs are generally removed by suction to a storage tank and then released to a flow-away system. In a hand removal operation, the lungs are discarded at the viscera trough with the remainder of the wastes.

Environmental Issues

Gerber and others summarise some of the major potential impacts of intensive livestock production on land and water resources:

1. Eutrophication of surface waters, caused by the input of organic substances and nutrients either through wastewater from production, runoff or leakages from storage and handling facilities – affecting aquatic ecosystems and drinking water quality.
2. Leaching of nitrate and possible pathogen transfers to groundwater – affecting the quality of drinking water.
3. Accumulation of nutrients and other elements in soil due to continuous application of excess quantities of manure.
4. Impacts of pollution on nutrient-sensitive ecosystems resulting in biodiversity losses.

In most cases, structural changes in the production system have a rather negative impact on manure management practices. In particular, growth in the scale of production and geographical concentration in the vicinity of urban areas, cause dramatic land – livestock imbalances, hampering manure recycling options. Indeed, in such conditions, transport costs associated with carrying manure back to the field are prohibitive.

Waste Disposal

The location of the poultry processing plant dictates the extent and method of waste treatment. In the search for a new plant site, the economics of waste disposal are an important factor. In locations where a municipal treatment plant is available, the plant pre-treatment provisions depend on the municipal plant's available extra capacity and efficiency.

Pre-treatment

Regardless of the treatment system, pre-treatment at the plant is necessary. The first pre-treatment stage is the use of screens to remove the larger materials from the defeathering and eviscerating flow-away systems. The reuse of water of defeathering and eviscerating flow-away water for the removal of feathers, but flow-away water from either system may not be reused for eviscerating flow-away. Therefore, these two wastes are pre-treated separately. The feather flow-away wastes, which are high in water content, are passed over a screen of 20–50 mesh.

This is generally a rotary or a vibrating screen from which the feathers are discharged directly to a container or into a conveyor. Water from this screening is collected in a sump, some is recirculated by pump and reintroduced into the flow-away flumes of the defeathering operations. The offal flow-away wastes from the eviscerating area are discharged into a collection tank and are pumped over a rotary or vibrating screen of 20–50 mesh. The screened water is discharged into the feather water collection sump. Screened offal material is discharged to a bin or container for further disposal.

Primary material disposal: Feathers and offal, in plants not processing these materials further, are commonly removed by a truck trailer, in which the feathers and eviscerating wastes are separately compartmented. Where permitted, these materials may then be buried or incinerated. More often, poultry plants not further processing these primary waste materials sell the separated materials to rendering companies for further processing to feather meal, cracklings for animal feeds and other by-products. Innovations and improvements in rendering have resulted in a market for primary waste materials in many locations.

Grease removal: In addition to the screening of feathers and offal, the treatment of wastes should include grease removal. Wastes from all poultry plants contain grease that may be removed by skimming in a primary settling basin, by a grease trap or by air flotation. Egg processing plants have no special or unusual wastes because whole eggs, whites or yolks introduced to sewers would be a loss of revenue. The only waste produced is egg shells, which are handled as common trash. Shells are accumulated in drums or directly in trucks and hauled to dumps.

Complete treatment of poultry process wastes

Methods available to the poultry processor for the complete treatment of the wastes are trickling filter, activated sludge, extended aeration, lagooning, land irrigation, sand filtration and chemical treatment.

Settling tanks: In all treatment systems, the floatable and sinkable materials must be separated in sedimentation tanks. The sludge requires additional handling by drying, lagooning, digestion or burial. For each plant design, settling rates and sludge volumes are determined by laboratory tests.

Trickling filters: Trickling filter systems in general, because of the high construction cost and operational requirements, are not often used where the processing plant is treating its own sewage. Trickling filter plant design for poultry wastes should not materially differ from standard practices for other biological wastes.

Activated sludge: The conditions outlined in regard to the trickling filter plant apply also to the activated sludge process. The construction costs of an activated sludge plant to obtain the same results as a trickling filter process are generally higher. The extended aeration process is a modification of activated sludge and utilises a 24 hr aeration or longer in the presence of activated sludge, followed by settling of the mixture. Part of the liquids discharged from the settled sludge tank are returned to the aerator. Lagooning may be required for additional purification of effluent before discharge into the natural waterway. The stream pollution regulations govern this action.

Lagoons: Lagoons or ponds are the most common type of waste treatment for poultry wastes. The lagoons generally require large areas of land and should be isolated from populated regions. Five-day BOD loadings vary from 20 to 150 lb per acre per day, depending upon pollution control regulations. Although lagooning is common, there is much still to be learned about it. Many states are running tests on mechanical agitation, heating of the aerobic ponds and other experimental practices, and some industries, in connection with state authorities, are testing other types of modified lagooning designs to provide design data for future installations.

ENVIRONMENTAL IMPACTS RELATED TO FEED PRODUCTION

Intensive Agriculture

Intensification of feed production affects land and water resources through pollution caused by the intensive use of mineral fertiliser, pesticides and herbicides to maintain high crop yields. Intensive feed production also contributes to air pollution. The application of nitrogen fertiliser to cropland is a major source of air pollution through the volatilisation of ammonia.

Intrusion into Natural Habitats

Increases in feed production, have to some extent been related to the expansion of cropland dedicated to feed. Feed production to satisfy the feed demand of intensive systems indirectly affects the global land base through changes in land use.

Erosion of Biodiversity

Feed production is also driving biodiversity erosion through the conversion of natural habitats and the over exploitation of non-renewable resources for feed production. Intensive feed production contributes to biodiversity loss through land use and land-use change and modification of natural ecosystems and habitats.

Over Exploitation of Natural Resources

The production of fishmeal for the poultry sector is an important factor contributing to the over exploitation of fisheries. The expansion of the aquaculture sector and its demand for fishmeal as a feed ingredient has led to a reduction in the use of fishmeal by the poultry sector.

Climate Change

The relatively high energy input in intensive livestock systems has given rise to concerns regarding greenhouse gas emissions and climate change. The energy consumption of industrially produced poultry is relevant because of the production of carbon dioxide (CO_2) along the production chain. Carbon dioxide emissions are produced by the burning of fossil fuels during animal production and slaughter and transport of processed and refrigerated products, but importantly also through land use and land-use change and the use of inputs for the production of feed.

On-farm energy consumption

On-farm energy consumption includes direct and indirect energy input – direct energy refers to fossil energy used for the production process (e.g. energy input for poultry housing systems) and indirect energy to that used as an integral part of the production process (e.g. feed processing). Due to a lack of information on energy use for processing, this estimation of on-farm fossil fuel consumption is limited to quantifying energy use associated with poultry housing.

The energy used for heating, ventilation and air conditioning systems typically accounts for the largest quantity of energy used in intensive poultry operations. Animal housing facilities are therefore potential sources of carbon dioxide emissions from intensive poultry farms. Other sources of carbon dioxide emissions include energy used for feed preparation, on-farm transport and burning of waste.

Generally, on layer farms, artificial heating of housing is not commonly applied, due to the low temperature needs of birds and the high stocking density. The activities that require energy are ventilation, feed distribution, lighting and egg collection, sorting and preservation. On broiler farms, the main energy consumption is related to local heating, feed distribution and housing ventilation. Quantification of the energy consumption of intensive poultry farms is a complex undertaking because systems are not homogeneous. The amount of energy consumed varies with the technologies applied, the production characteristics of the farms and climatic conditions.

Carbon dioxide emissions from slaughtering

Poultry processing facilities use energy to heat water and produce steam for process applications and cleaning and for the operation of mechanical and electrical equipment, refrigeration and air compressors. In poultry abattoirs, fossil fuel is mainly used for process heat, while electricity is used for the operation of machinery and for refrigeration, ventilation, lighting and the production of compressed air.

Greenhouse Gases Emissions from Feed Production

Emissions of greenhouse gases such as carbon dioxide and nitrous oxide are influenced in an indirect way by intensification of feed production, which requires energy input for the production of mineral fertiliser and the subsequent use of this fertiliser in the feed production process.

Carbon dioxide (CO_2)

This greenhouse gas is produced by the burning of fossil fuels during the manufacture of fertiliser.

Nitrous oxide (N_2O)

Poultry production is indirectly associated with the greenhouse gas nitrous oxide because of the sector's high concentrate-feed requirements and the related emissions from arable land due to the use of nitrogen fertiliser.

Overall, intensive poultry production (indirectly and directly) contributes an estimated 3% of the total anthropogenic greenhouse gas and is responsible for about 2% of the total greenhouse gas emissions from the livestock sector. This estimate however does not include emissions from land use and land-use change associated with feed production or emissions related to transport of feed.

Odour Emissions

Odour emissions can be controlled by:

1. Minimising the surface of manure in contact with air – frequent collection of litter (once a week in dry seasons and twice a week in rainy seasons), closed storage (bags or closed sheds).
2. Cooling animal manure, achieved as a positive side effect of cooling the animal houses – cooling systems can be equipped with biofilters and air scrubbers that trap odours from the ventilation airflow.
3. Lowering litter's water content – achieved by the incorporation of hydro-philic products such as hashes, rice husk, peanut husk, dust or sawdust.
4. Applying deodorant products to feed or directly to animal houses.
5. Building wind protection structures.

Flies and mosquitoes

The proliferation of flies and mosquitoes can be controlled by:

1. Minimising the surface of manure in contact with air – frequent collection of litter (once a week in dry seasons and twice in rainy seasons, i.e. at shorter intervals than the length of the larvae development cycle), closed storage (bags or closed sheds).
2. Lowering litter's water content – achieved by the incorporation of hydro-philic products such as hashes, rice husks, peanut husks, dust, sawdust or available dry crop residues.
3. Applying insecticides (this practice may however have significant public health-related side effects).
4. Building wind protection structures.
5. Positioning nets around the farm.

Rat proliferation can be controlled by:

1. Minimising feed losses during storage and feeding.
2. Raising cats or keeping snakes in cages close to the poultry barn to scare rats.
3. Use of poison or traps.

Visual impact and landscaping can be improved by:

1. Use of screening trees around the farm facility to reduce the visual impact of farm infrastructure and of noise, dust, light and odour.
2. Use of the natural topography and terrain of the site and the existing vegetative cover to maximise visual screening.
3. Use of construction materials that minimise visual impact.

ANIMAL WASTE MANAGEMENT

Soil and water pollution is controlled through the implementation of good fertilisation practices. In brief: environmental risks are reduced when manure is applied in amounts and at times that correspond to crop or fishpond uptake. Water pollution is often an acute problem in waterfowl production, especially when the flock is concentrated on relatively small ponds. There is currently a lack of information with regard to the effects of waterfowl production on surface water and groundwater resources.

Water- and food-borne disease propagation can be prevented by:

1. Storing manure in closed buildings or bags – a storage system allows producers to hold manure until a convenient and optimum time for use, storing poultry manure in closed buildings reduces the emissions of gaseous compounds to the air and the risk of environmental contamination as compared to the risk associated with leaving manure exposed.
2. Storing the manure for one to two months before its application on land or fish ponds.
3. Composting manure – potentially reduces or even eliminates certain pathogens and fly larvae and improves the handling characteristics of manure and other residues by reducing their volume, weight and moisture content (most manure and other organic residues usually contain high nitrogen content and are, therefore, subject to nitrogen loss during composting).
4. Drying (with machine or by spreading out) – minimises the moisture content of manure, inhibits chemical reactions and thus reduces emissions (the best way to prevent ammonia emissions from poultry litter and manure is to reduce microbial decomposition, which can be accomplished by drying the freshly produced manure as soon as possible and keeping it dry).
5. Timing and rate of manure application – this is a critical management factor, manure must be applied at the correct time of year to prevent losses to surface water, groundwater and the atmosphere and to optimise the utilisation of manure nutrients by growing plants, proper timing is a function of several variables, including weather, soil conditions and stage of crop growth.
6. Dead-bird management and disposal, which must comply with legally accepted practices including rendering, composing, incineration and burial, a contingency plan should be in place for disposal of large numbers of dead birds in the event of disease outbreaks, in addition, consideration should be given to impacts on the physical environment, e.g. burial pits should be at least 3 metres above the maximum groundwater table.

Chapter 8

Pollution Control in Meat Industry

INTRODUCTION

Meat is animal flesh that is eaten as food. Meat is mainly composed of water, protein and fat and is usually eaten together with other food. It is edible raw, but is normally eaten after it has been cooked and seasoned or processed in a variety of ways. Unprocessed meat will spoil or rot within hours or days as a result of infection with and decomposition by bacteria and fungi. Most often, meat refers to skeletal muscle and associated fat and other tissues, but it may also describe other edible tissues such as offal.

The meat processing and rendering industry includes the slaughter of animals and fowl, processing of the carcasses into cured, canned and other meat products and the rendering of inedible and discarded remains into useful by-products such as lards and oils. Processed meat products are those in which the properties of fresh meat have been modified by the use of one or more procedures, such as grinding, adding of seasoning, alteration of colour or heat treatment.

It includes curing by smoking and any treatment or process resulting in a substantial change in the natural state of the meat but does not include boning, cutting, cleaning or trimming.

There is a concept of inevitable association between processing and preservation of meat. This is because some processing method result in products which have long shelf life, for example salted and smoke meat is processed for flavour and it is also preserved by the presence of sale, smoke and heat treatment. On the contrary raw, seasoned beef sausage is processed but it is not preserved. A wide range of processes are used. Table 8.1 provides information on water usage in the industry.

Table 8.1: Typical water usage in the meat industry.

Process	*(Cubic meters per metric tonne of product)* *Water use*
Slaughterhouse	
Pigs	1.5–10
Cattle	2.5–40
Poultry	6–30
Meat processing	2–60

FERMENTED MEAT

Fermented meat is a type of dried meat that has been prepared and dehydrated according to specific techniques that alter some of the chemical make-up of normally perishable foods. Fermentation typically involves the introduction of bacteria or yeast that convert certain meat nutrients into mixtures of carbon dioxide and alcohol. This process of making fermented meat can both increase the flavour intensity and prevent the end product from spoiling for relatively long periods of time. Successful fermentation of meat can only be accomplished under specific environmental conditions in order for the end product to be completely safe to eat. Various culinary traditions often have their own unique types of fermented meat such as salami or chorizo sausage.

Meat must be fermented in an environment without oxygen, which is frequently called an anaerobic condition. Removing the oxygen is essential for the meat to correctly dehydrate without the possibility of harmful bacterial invasion. The fermentation catalyst bacteria is usually introduced in controlled amounts. This type of bacteria is usually one of several varieties derived from lactic acid. Cooks with experience in fermenting frequently use a strain of lactic acid bacteria called pediococus cerevisiae. This important step is normally accomplished by sealing the cuts of meat to be dried in an airtight container.

Various flavours of salami are normally made through this basic fermentation process. This kind of dehydrated sausage is often made with a combination of catalyst bacteria and other additives called nitrates. The inclusion of nitrates can often lessen the chances of contamination by allowing the beneficial lactic acid bacteria to grow and spread through the meat at a faster rate. Once the technique of fermenting meat has been perfected, the process is normally not limited to meats such as beef or pork. Some types of seafood can also be successfully fermented, although health professionals sometimes advise that this practice should be approached carefully. Fermented fish can often have high rates of bacterial contamination that can lead to serious food-borne illnesses such as botulism.

Some of the benefits of fermented meat include economic practicality and environmental necessity. People who live in remote geographic areas with harsh winters often ferment large stores of meat due to limited access to other food sources during the worst weather conditions. Fermented meats are generally able to stand up to extreme temperatures at a better rate than other foods.

WASTE CHARACTERISTICS

The meat industry has the potential for generating large quantities of solid wastes and wastewater with a Biochemical Oxygen Demand (BOD) of 600 milligrams per litre (mg/L). BOD can be as high as 8000 mg/L or 10–20 kilograms per metric tonne (kg/L) of slaughtered animal, and suspended solids levels can be 800 mg/L and higher. In some cases, offensive odours may occur. The amounts of wastewater generated and the pollutant load depend on the kind of meat being processed. For example, the processing of gut has a significant impact on the quantity and quality (as measured by levels of BOD and of Chemical Oxygen Demand (COD), of wastewater generated. The wastewater from a slaughterhouse can contain blood, manure, hair, fat, feathers and bones. The wastewater may be at a high temperature and may contain organic material and nitrogen, as well as such pathogens as salmonella and shigella bacteria, parasite eggs and amoebic cysts. Pesticide residues may be present from treatment of animals or their feed. Chloride levels from curing and pickling may be very high—up to 77000 mg/L. Smoking operations can release toxic organics into air. Rendering is an evaporative process that produces a condensate stream with a foul odour.

All slaughtering wastes (generally, 35% of the animal weight) can be used as by-products or for rendering. The only significant solid waste going for disposal is the manure from animal transport and handling areas.

Pollution Prevention and Control

Separation of product from wastes at each stage is essential for maximising product recovery and reducing waste loads. The materials being handled are all putrescible, hence, cleanliness is essential. Water management should achieve the necessary cleanliness without waste. The amounts and strength of wastes can be reduced by good practices such as dry removal of solid wastes and installation of screens on wastewater collection channels.

In-plant measures that can be used to reduce the odour nuisance and the generation of solid and liquid wastes from the production processes include the following:

1. Recover and process blood into useful by-products. Allow enough time for blood draining (at least seven minutes).
2. Process paunches and intestines and utilise fat and slime.
3. Minimise water consumed in production by, for example, using taps with automatic shut-off, using high water pressure and improving the process layout.
4. Eliminate wet transport (pumping) of wastes (for example, intestines and feathers) to minimise water consumption.
5. Reduce the liquid waste load by preventing any solid wastes or concentrated liquids from entering the wastewater stream.
6. Cover collection channels in the production area with grids to reduce the amount of solids entering the wastewater.
7. Separate cooling water from process water and wastewaters and recirculate cooling water.
8. Implement dry precleaning of equipment and production areas prior to wet cleaning.
9. Equip the outlets of wastewater channels with screens and fat traps to recover and reduce the concentration of coarse material and fat in the combined wastewater stream.
10. Optimise the use of detergents and disinfectants in washing water.
11. Remove manure (from the stockyard and from intestine processing) in solid form.
12. Dispose of hair and bones to the rendering plants.
13. Reduce air emissions from ham processing through some degree of air recirculation, after filtering.
14. Isolate and ventilate all sources of odorous emissions. Oxidants such as nitrates can be added to wastes to reduce odour.

In rendering plants, odour is the most important air pollution issue. To reduce odour:

1. Minimise the stock of raw material and store it in a cold, closed, well-ventilated place.
2. Pasteurise the raw material before processing it in order to halt biological processes that generate odour.
3. Install all equipment in closed spaces and operate under partial or total vacuum.
4. Keep all working and storage areas clean.

Treatment Technologies

Wastewaters from meat processing are suitable for biological treatment and (except for the very odorous rendering wastewater) could be discharged to a municipal sewer system after flow equalisation, if the capacity exists. Sewer authorities usually require pre-treatment of the wastewater before it is discharged into the sewer. Screens and fat traps are the minimum means of pre-treatment in any system. Flotation, in some cases aided by chemical addition, may also be carried out to remove suspended solids and emulsified fats, which can be returned to the rendering plant. The choice of an appropriate biological treatment system will be influenced by a number of factors, including wastewater load and the need to minimise odours. Rendering wastewater typically has a very high organic and nitrogen load.

Extended aeration is an effective form of treatment, but care must be taken to minimise odours. Disinfection of the final effluent may be required if high levels of bacteria are detected. Ponding is a simple solution but requires considerable space. Chemical methods, usually based on chlorine compounds, are an alternative. Biofilters, carbon filters and scrubbers are used to control odours and air emissions from several processes, including ham processing and rendering. Recycling exhaust gases from smoking may be feasible in cases where operations are not carried out manually and smoke inhalation by workers is not of concern.

Air Emissions

Odour controls should be implemented, where necessary, to minimise odour impacts on nearby residents. Particulate matter emissions of smokehouses should be kept below 150 milligrams per normal cubic meter (mg/Nm^3), with a carbon content of less than 50 mg/Nm^3.

Liquid Effluents

The liquid effluent levels presented in Table 8.2 should be achieved.

Table 8.2: Effluents from meat processing and rendering industry.

Parameter	*(Milligrams per litre, except for pH and bacteria)* *Maximum value*
pH	6–9
BOD	50
COD	250
TSS	50
Oil and grease	10
Nitrogen (total)	10
Total phosphorus	5
Coliform bacteria	400 MPN/100 mL

Note: Effluent requirements are for direct discharge to surface waters. MPN, most probable number.

PROCESSING FACILITIES AND WASTES GENERATED

As a direct result of its operation, a slaughterhouse generates waste comprised of the animal parts that have no perceived value to the slaughterhouse operator. It also generates wastewater as a result of washing carcasses, processing offal and from cleaning equipment and the fabric of the building. Additionally, wastes and wastewaters are also generated from the stockyards, any rendering process, cooling facilities for refrigeration, compressors and pumps, vehicle wash facilities, wash rooms, canteen and possibly laundry facilities.

Waste Characteristics and Quantities Generated

In general the characteristics of the solid wastes generated reflect the type of animal being killed, but the composition within a particular type of operation is similar regardless of the size of the plant. Once on the slaughter line, the quantity of waste generated depends on the number of animals slaughtered and the type of animal.

Wastewater flow

Water is used in the slaughterhouse for carcass washing after hide removal from cattle, calves and sheep and after hair removal from hogs. It is also used to clean the inside of the carcass after evisceration and for cleaning and sanitising equipment and facilities both during and after the killing operation.

Wastewater characteristics

Effluents from slaughterhouses and packing houses are usually heavily loaded with solids, floatable matter (fat), blood, manure and a variety of organic compounds originating from proteins. As already stated the composition of effluents depends very much on the type of production and facilities. The main sources of water contamination are from lairage, slaughtering, hide or hair removal, paunch handling, carcass washing, rendering, trimming and cleanup operations.

These contain a variety of readily biodegradable organic compounds, primarily fats and proteins, present in both particulate and dissolved forms. The wastewater has a high strength, in terms of biochemical oxygen demand (BOD), chemical oxygen demand (COD), suspended solids (SS), nitrogen and phosphorus, compared to domestic wastewaters. The actual concentration will depend on in-plant control of water use, by-products recovery, waste separation source and plant management. In general, blood and intestinal contents arising from the killing floor and the gut room, together with manure from stockyard and holding pens, are separated, as best as possible, from the aqueous stream and treated as solid wastes. This can never be 100% successful, however and these components are the major contributors to the organic load in the wastewater, together with solubilised fat and meat trimmings.

Wastewater characteristics

Effluents from slaughterhouses and packing houses are usually heavily loaded with solids, floatable matter (fat), blood, manure and a variety of organic compounds originating from proteins. As already stated the composition of effluents depends very much on the type of production and facilities. The main sources of water contamination are from lairage, slaughtering, hide or hair removal, paunch handling, carcass washing, rendering, trimming and cleanup operations.

These contain a variety of readily biodegradable organic compounds, primarily fats and proteins, present in both particulate and dissolved forms. The wastewater has a high strength, in terms of biochemical oxygen demand (BOD), chemical oxygen demand (COD), suspended solids (SS), nitrogen and phosphorus, compared to domestic wastewaters. The actual concentration will depend on in-plant control of water use, by-products recovery, waste separation source and plant management. In general, blood and intestinal contents arising from the killing floor and the gut room, together with manure from stockyard and holding pens, are separated, as best as possible, from the aqueous stream and treated as solid wastes. This can never be 100 per cent successful, however and these components are the major contributors to the organic load in the wastewater, together with solubilised fat and meat trimmings. The aqueous pollution load of a slaughterhouse can be expressed in a number of ways. Within the literature reports can be found giving the concentration in wastewater of parameters such as BOD, COD and SS. These, however, are only useful if the corresponding wastewater flow rates are also given. Even then it is often difficult to relate these to a meaningful figure for general design, as the unit of productivity is often omitted or unclear. These reports do, however, give some indication as to the strength of wastewaters typically encountered and some of their particular characteristics, which can be useful in making a preliminary assessment of the type of treatment process most applicable. These values could be averaged, but the value of such an exercise would be limited as the variability between the wastewaters, for the reasons previously mentioned, is considerable. At best it can be concluded that slaughterhouse wastewaters have a pH around neutral, an intermediate strength in terms of COD and BOD, are heavily loaded with solids and are nutrient-rich.

It is, therefore, clear that for the purposes of design of a treatment facility a much better method of assessing the pollution load is required. For this purpose the typical pollution load resulting from the slaughter of a particular animal could be used, but as animals vary in weight depending upon their age and condition at the time of slaughter, it is better to use the live weight at slaughter as the unit of productivity rather than just animal numbers.

Very little information is available on where this pollution load arises within the slaughterhouse, as waste audits on individual process streams are not commonly reported. Nemerow and Agardy describe the content of individual process wastes from a slaughterhouse. It can be seen that the two most contaminated process streams are related to blood and paunch contents. Blood and meat proteins are the most significant sources of nitrogen in the wastewater and rapidly give rise to ammonical nitrogen as breakdown occurs.

The wastewater contains a high density of total coliform, fecal coliform and fecal streptococcus groups of bacteria due to the presence of manure material and gut contents. Numbers are usually in the range of several million colony forming units (CFU) per 100 ml. It is also likely that the wastewater will contain bacterial pathogens of enteric origin such as *Salmonella* sp., and *Campylobacter jejuni*, gastrointestinal parasites including *Ascaris* sp., *Giardia lamblia* and *Cryptosporidium parvum* and enteric viruses. It is, therefore, essential that slaughterhouse design ensures the complete segregation of process washwater and strict hygiene procedures to prevent cross-contamination. The mineral chemistry of the wastewater is influenced by the chemical composition of the slaughterhouse's treated water supply, waste additions such as blood and manure, which can contribute to the heavy metal load in the form of copper, iron, manganese, arsenic and zinc and process plant and pipework, which can contribute to the load of copper, chromium, molybdenum, nickel, titanium and vanadium.

Wastewater Minimisation

The overall waste load arising from a slaughterhouse is determined principally by the type and number of animals slaughtered. The partitioning of this load between the solid and aqueous phases will depend very much upon the operational practices adopted, however and there are measures that can be taken to minimise wastewater generation and the aqueous pollution load.

One of the major contributors to organic load is blood, which has a COD of about 400000 mg/L and washing down of dispersed blood can be a major cause of high effluent strength. Minimisation can be achieved by having efficient blood collection troughs allowing collection from the carcass over several minutes. Likewise the trough should be designed to allow separate drainage to a collection tank of the blood and the first flush of washwater. Only residual blood should enter a second drain for collection of the main portion of the washwater.

An efficient blood recovery system could reduce the aqueous pollution load by as much as 40% compared to a plant of similar size that allows the blood to flow to waste. The second area where high organic loads into the wastewater system can arise is in the gut room. Most cattle and sheep abattoirs clean the paunch (rumen), manyplies (omasum) and reed (abomasum) for tripe production. A common method of preparation is to flush out the gut manure from the punctured organs over a mechanical screen and allow water to transport the gut manure to the effluent treatment system.

Within the slaughtering area and cutting rooms, measures should be adopted to minimise meat scraps and fatty tissue entering the floor drains. Once in the drains these break down due to turbulence, pumping or other mechanical actions (e.g. on screens), leading to an increase in effluent COD. These measures include using fine mesh covers to drains, encouraging operators to use collection receptacles for trimmings and using well-designed equipment with catch trays. Importantly, a 'dry' cleaning of the area to remove solid material, for example using cyclonic vacuum cleaners, should take place before any washdown.

Other methods can also be employed to minimise water usage. These will not in themselves reduce the organic load entering the wastewater treatment system, but will reduce the volume requiring treatment and possibly influence the choice of treatment system to be employed.

Water use minimisation methods include:

1. The use of directional spray nozzles in carcass washing, which can reduce water consumption by as much as 20%.
2. Use of steam condensation systems in place of scald tanks for hair and nail removal.
3. Fitting washdown hoses with trigger grips.
4. Appropriate choice of cleaning agents.
5. Reuse of clear water (e.g. chiller water) for the primary washdown of holding pens.

WASTEWATER TREATMENT PROCESSES

The degree of wastewater treatment required will depend on the proposed type of discharge. Wastewaters received into the sewer system are likely to need less treatment than those having direct discharge into a watercourse. In European countries, direct discharges have to comply with the Urban Wastewater Treatment Directive and other water quality directives. In the United States the EPA has proposed Effluent Limitations Guidelines (ELGs) and standards for the Meat and Poultry Products industries with direct discharge. These proposed ELGs will apply to existing and new Meat and Poultry Products (MPP) facilities and are based on the well-tested concepts of 'Best Practicable Control technology currently available' (BPT), the 'Best Conventional Pollutant control technology' (BCT), the 'Best Available Technology economically achievable' (BAT) and the 'best available demonstrated control technology for New Source Performance Standards' (NSPS). In summary, the technologies proposed to meet these requirements use, in the main, a system based on a treatment series comprising flow equalisation, dissolved air flotation and secondary biological treatment for all slaughterhouses, and require nitrification for small installations and additional denitrification for complex slaughterhouses.

There is some potential, however, for segregation of wastewaters allowing specific individual pre-treatments to be undertaken or, in some cases, bypass of less contaminated streams. Depending on local conditions and regulations, water from boiler houses and refrigerating systems may be segregated and discharged directly or used for outside cleaning operations.

Primary Treatment

In primary treatment grease removal is a common first stage in slaughterhouse wastewater treatment, with grease traps in some situations being an integral part of the drainage system from the processing areas. Where the option is taken to have a single point of removal, this can be accomplished in one of two ways: by using a baffled tank or by Dissolved Air Flotation (DAF).

The flotation process is dependent upon the release of sufficient air from the pressurised fluid when the pressure is reduced to atmospheric. The nature of the release is also important, in that the bubbles must be of reasonably constant dimensions (not greater than 130 microns) and in sufficient numbers to provide blanket coverage of the retaining vessel. In practice, the bubble size and uniform coverage give the appearance of white water. The efficiency of the process depends upon bubble size, the concentration of fats and grease to be separated, their specific gravity, the quantity of the pressurised gas and the geometry of the reaction vessel. Dissolved air flotation has become a well-established unit operation in the treatment of abattoir wastes, primarily as it is effective at removing fats from the aqueous stream within a short retention time (20–30 minutes), thus preventing the development of acidity.

Chemical treatment can improve the pollution removal efficiency of a DAF unit and typically ferric chloride is used to precipitate proteins and polymers used to aid coagulation.

Secondary Treatment

Secondary treatment aims to reduce the BOD of the wastewater by removing the organic matter that remains after primary treatment. This is primarily in a soluble form. Secondary treatment can utilise physical and chemical unit processes, but for the treatment of meat wastes biological treatment is usually favoured.

Physico-chemical secondary treatment

Chemical treatment of meat-plant wastes is not a common practice due to the high chemical costs involved and difficulties in disposing of the large volumes of sludge produced. There are, however, instances where it has been used successfully. Nemerow and Agardy reported a treatment facility that used $FeCl_3$ to reduce the BOD from 1448 to 188 mg/l (87 per cent reduction) and the suspended solids from 2975 to 167 mg/l (94 per cent reduction). Using chlorine and alum in sufficient quantities could also significantly reduce the BOD and colour of the wastes, but once again the chemical costs are high. With this approach the BOD of raw wastewaters ranging from 1500 to 3800 mg/l can be reduced to between 400 and 600 mg/l. Dart reported a 64 per cent reduction in BOD using alumina-ferric as a coagulant with a dosing rate equivalent to 17 mg/l of aluminium. Chemical treatment has also been used to remove phosphates from slaughterhouse wastewater. Aguilar used $Fe_2(SO_4)_3$, $Al_2(SO_4)_3$ and poly-aluminium chloride (PAC) as coagulants with some inorganic products and synthetic polyelectrolyte to remove approximately 100 per cent ortho-phosphate and between 98.93 and 99.90 per cent total phosphorus. Ammonia nitrogen removal was very low, however, despite an appreciable removal of albuminoidal nitrogen (73.9–88.77 per cent).

Biological Secondary Treatment

Using biological treatment, more than 90% efficiency can be achieved in pollutant removal from slaughterhouse wastes. Commonly used systems include lagoons (aerobic and anaerobic), conventional activated sludge, extended aeration, oxidation ditches, sequencing batch reactors and anaerobic digestion. A series of anaerobic biological processes followed by aerobic biological processes is often useful for sequential reduction of the BOD load in the most economic manner, although either process can be used separately. As noted above, slaughterhouse wastewaters vary in strength considerably depending on a number of factors. For a given type of animal, however, this variation is primarily due to the quantity of water used within the abattoir, as the pollution load (as expressed as BOD) is relatively constant on the basis of live weight slaughtered. Hence, the more economical an abattoir is in its use of water, the stronger the effluent will be and *vice versa*.

Anaerobic treatment

Anaerobic digestion is a popular method for treating meat industry wastes. Anaerobic processes operate in the absence of oxygen and the final products are mixed gases of methane and carbon dioxide and a stabilised sludge. Anaerobic digestion of organic materials to methane and carbon dioxide is a complicated biological and chemical process that involves three stages: hydrolysis, acetogenesis and finally methanogenesis. During the first stage, complex compounds are hydrolysed to smaller chain intermediates. In the second stage acetogenic bacteria convert these intermediates to organic acids and then ultimately to methane and carbon dioxide via the methanogenesis phase.

In the United States, anaerobic systems using simple lagoons are by far the most common method of treating abattoir wastewater. These are not particularly suitable for use in the heavily populated regions of western Europe due to the land area required and also because of the difficulties of controlling odours in the urban areas where abattoirs are usually located.

The extensive use of anaerobic lagoons demonstrates the amenability of abattoir wastewaters to anaerobic stabilisation, however, with significant reductions in the BOD at a minimal cost.

The anaerobic lagoon consists of an excavation in the ground, giving a water depth of between 10 and 17 ft. (3–5 meters), with a retention time of 5–15 days. Common practice is to provide two ponds in series or parallel and sometimes linking these to a third aerobic pond. The pond has no mechanical equipment installed and is unmixed except for some natural mixing brought about by internal gas generation and surface agitation, the latter is minimised where possible to prevent odour formation and re-aeration. Influent wastewater enters near the bottom of the pond and exits near the surface to minimise the chance of short-circuiting. Anaerobic ponds can provide an economic alternative for purification. The BOD reductions vary widely, although excellent performance has been reported in some cases, with reductions of up to 97 per cent in BOD, up to 95 per cent in SS and up to 96 per cent in COD from the influent values.

Anaerobic lagoons are not without potential problems, relating to both their gaseous and aqueous emissions. As a result of breakdown of the wastewater, methane and carbon dioxide are both produced. These escape to the atmosphere, thus contributing to greenhouse gas emissions, with methane being 25 times more potent than carbon dioxide in this respect. Gaseous emissions also include the odouriferous gases, hydrogen sulphide and ammonia. The lagoons generally operate with a layer of grease and scum on the top, which restricts the transfer of oxygen through the liquid surface, retains some of the heat and helps prevent the emission of odour. Reliance on this should be avoided wherever possible, however, since it is far from a secure means of preventing problems as the oil and grease cap can readily be broken up, for example, under storm water flow conditions. Odour problems due to anaerobic ponds have a long history: even in the 1960s when environmental awareness was lower and public threshold tolerances to pollution were higher, as many as nine out of ten anaerobic lagoons in the United States were reported as giving rise to odour nuisance. A more satisfactory and environmentally sound solution is the use of membrane covers that prevent odour release, while at the same time allowing collection of the biogas that can be used as fuel source within the slaughterhouse. This sort of innovation moves the lagoon one step closer to something that can be recognised as a purpose-built treatment system and provides the opportunity to reduce plant size and improve performance.

The use of fabricated anaerobic reactors for abattoir wastewater treatment is also well established. To work efficiently these are designed to operate either at mesophilic (around 95°F or 35°C) or thermophilic (around 130°F or 55°C) temperatures. Black reported that the practicality of using anaerobic digestion for abattoir wastewater treatment was established in the 1930s. Their own work concerned the commissioning and monitoring of an anaerobic contact process installed at the Leeds abattoir in the UK. The plant operated with a 24 hr retention time at a loading of 29.3 lb BOD/10^3 gal (3.5 kg BOD/m^3) and showed an 88–93 per cent reduction in BOD, giving a final effluent concentration of around 220 mg/l. Bohm conducted trials using a 106 ft^3 (3 m^3) anaerobic contact process at a loading of 21.7 lb BOD/10^3 gal day (2.6 kg BOD/m^3 day), with a removal efficiency of 80 per cent. An economic evaluation of the process showed savings on effluent disposal charges. The review by Cillie refers to work by Hemens and Shurben showing a 95 per cent BOD reduction from an influent BOD of 2000 mg/l. Gas production was only just sufficient to maintain the digester temperature of 91°F (33°C), however, Kostyshyn and others used both mesophilic and thermophilic anaerobic contact processes as an alternative to physico-chemical treatment over an 8-month trial period. At a loading rate of 22.9 lb COD/10^3 gal day (2.75 kg COD/m^3 day) and a retention time of 2.5 days they achieved an average of 93.1 per cent BOD removal and 74.9 per cent COD removal. The process appears to be able to operate successfully at loadings of up 20.9 lb COD/10^3 gal day (2.5 kg COD/m^3 day). This is possible because the anaerobic contact process maintains a high biomass density and long solids retention time (SRT) in the reactor by recirculation of sludge from a separation stage, which usually involves sedimentation. The high biomass density, long SRT and elevated temperature enable a short hydraulic retention time. As with most anaerobic reactor systems, however, they are expensive to install and require close technical supervision.

Anaerobic filters have also been applied to the treatment of slaughterhouse wastewaters. These maintain a long SRT by providing the micro-organisms with a medium that they can colonise as a biofilm. Unlike conventional aerobic filters, the anaerobic filter is operated with the support medium submerged in an upflow mode of operation. Because anaerobic filters contain a support medium, there is potential for the interstitial spaces within the medium to become blocked and effective pre-treatment is essential to remove suspended solids as well as solidifiable oils, fats and grease.

Andersen and Schmid used an anaerobic filter for treating slaughterhouse wastewater and encountered problems with grease in the startup period. The problem was solved by introducing dissolved air flotation as a pre-treatment for the removal of grease. The filter showed between 62 and 93 per cent removal of COD over a trial period of 22 weeks, but the authors concluded that the process required close supervision and emphasised the need for good pre-treatment. Routh also used an anaerobic filter with a 24 hr retention time and loads of up to 58.4 lb COD/10^3 gal day (7.0 kg COD/m^3 day). Treatment efficiency was up to 90 per cent at loadings up to 45.9 lb COD/10^3 gal day (5.5 kg COD/m^3 day). Festino and Aubart used an anaerobic filter for wastewaters containing less than 1 per cent solids, but the main focus of their work was on the high solids fraction of abattoir wastes in complete mix reactors. Generally speaking, a safe operational loading range for a mesophilic anaerobic filter appears to be between 16.7 and 25.0 lb COD/10^3 gal day (2–3 kg COD/m^3 day) and at this loading a COD reduction of between 80 and 85 per cent might conservatively be expected.

The third type of high-rate anaerobic system that can be applied to slaughterhouse wastewaters is the upflow anaerobic sludge blanket reactor (UASB). This is basically an expanded bed reactor in which the bed comprises anaerobic micro-organisms, including methanogens, which have formed dense granules. The mechanisms by which these granules form are still poorly understood, but they are intrinsic to the proper operation of the process. The influent wastewater flows upward through a sludge blanket of these granules, which remain within the reactor as their settling velocity is greater than the up flow velocity of the wastewater. The reactor therefore exhibits a long sludge retention time, high biomass density per unit reactor and can operate at a short HRT.

UASB reactors overcome the limitations of anaerobic contact plant and anaerobic filters, yet their application to slaughterhouse wastewater appears limited to laboratory and pilot-scale reactors. The reason for this is the difficulties in trying to form stable granules when dealing with slaughterhouse wastewater and this may be due to the high fat concentrations.

Although anaerobic processes have generally shown good results in the treatment of abattoir wastewaters, some problems have also been reported. Nell and Krige comment on aerobic composting systems that in the anaerobic process the high organic content leads to a resistance to fermentation and there is a tendency towards scum formation. Grease was also shown to be a problem in the digester operated by Andersen. Cooper on abattoir waste treatment in New Zealand, state that the use of anaerobic contact and anaerobic filter is not economic as the energy content in the fat is adsorbed and not really broken down in the anaerobic process. This demonstrates the need for proper pre-treatment and for an energy balance as part of the design work.

There is a substantial amount of evidence at laboratory, pilot and full scale that anaerobic systems are suitable for the treatment of abattoir wastewaters. There is also evidence that with the weaker abattoir wastewaters with BODs around 2000 mg/l, gas production is only just sufficient to maintain reactor temperature as might be predicted from thermodynamics.

Aerobic treatment

Aerobic processes can roughly be divided into two basic types: those that maintain the biomass in suspension (activated sludge and its variants) and those that retain the biomass on a support medium (biological filters and its variants). There is no doubt that either basic type is suitable for the treatment of slaughterhouse wastewater and their use is well documented in research done by Broils and Broughton, where aerobic processes are compared with anaerobic ones. In selecting an aerobic process a number of factors need to be taken into account.

The most common aerobic biological processes used for the treatment of meat industry wastes are biological filtration, activated sludge plants, waste stabilisation ponds and aerated lagoons.

Waste stabilisation ponds: A waste stabilisation pond (WSP) is the simplest method of aerobic biological treatment and can be regarded as bringing about the natural purification processes occurring in a river in a more restricted time and space. They are often used in countries where plenty of land is available and weather conditions are favourable.

Biological filters: Biological filters can also be used for treating meat industry wastes. In this process the aerobic micro-organisms grow as a slime or film that is supported on the surface of the filter medium. The wastewater is applied to the surface and trickles down while air percolates upwards through the medium and supplies the oxygen required for purification. The treated water along with any microbial film that breaks away from the support medium collects in an under-drain and passes to a secondary sedimentation tank where the biological solids are separated. Trickling filters require primary treatment for removal of settleable solids and oil and grease to reduce the organic load and prevent the system blocking. Because of the relatively high strength of slaughterhouse wastewater, biological filters are more suited to operation with effluent recirculation, which effectively increases surface hydraulic loading without increasing the organic loading. This gives greater control over microbial film thickness.

In the United States, high-rate single-stage percolating filters with high recirculation ratios have been used. An overall BOD removal of 92–98 per cent was reported using a high-rate filter with a BOD loading of 2.6–3.8 lb BOD/10^3 gal media day (0.31–0.45 kg BOD/m^3 media day) and a recirculation ratio of about 5:1 for treating preliminary treated slaughterhouse wastes. Dart reported that a high-quality effluent with 11 mg/l of BOD and 25 mg/l SS could be obtained using alternating double filtration (ADF) at a loading rate of 2.8 lb/10^3 gal day (0.34 kg BOD/m^3 day) for treating screened and settled abattoir waste, the influent was diluted 1:1 with recirculated effluent. Higher loadings with a BOD of between 17 and 33 lb/10^3 gal (2–4 kg BOD/m^3) and a surface hydraulic loading of 884 gal/ft^2 day (1.5 m^3/m^2 hr) and recirculation ratios of 3–4 are given as a typical French design guideline aimed at providing a roughing treatment in reactors 13.1 ft (4 m) high. Such a design is likely to give a BOD removal of less than 75 per cent and not to provide any nitrification.

Biological filters have not been widely adopted for the treatment of slaughterhouse wastewaters despite the lower operating costs compared with activated sludge systems. Obtaining an effluent with a low BOD and ammonia in a single-reactor system can provide conditions suitable for the proliferation of secondary grazing macro-invertebrate species such as fly larvae and this may be unacceptable in the vicinity of a slaughterhouse. There is also the need for very good fat removal from the influent wastewater flow, as this will otherwise tend to coat the surface of the biofilm support medium.

Rotating biological contactors

Rotating biological contactors (RBCs) are also fixed biofilm reactors, which consist of a series of closely spaced circular discs mounted on a longitudinal shaft. The discs are rotated, exposing the attached microbial mass alternately to air and to the wastewater being treated and allowing the adsorption of organic matter, nutrients and oxygen. Typical design values for hydraulic and organic loading rates for secondary treatment are 2–4 gal/ft^2 day (0.08–0.16 m^3/m^2 day) and 2.0–3.5 lb total BOD/10^3 ft^2 day (0.01–0.017 kg BOD/m^2 day) respectively, with effluent BOD concentrations ranging from 15 to 30 mg/l. For secondary treatment combined with nitrification, typical hydraulic and organic loading rate design values are 0.75–2 gal/ft^2 day and 1.5–3.0 lb total BOD/10^3 ft^2 day, respectively (0.03–0.08 m^3/m^2 day and 0.007–0.014 kg BOD/m^2 day), producing effluent BOD concentrations between 7 and 15 mg/l and NH_3 concentrations of less than 2 mg/l. The above performance are typical of this type of unit, but are not necessarily accurate when applied to the treatment of slaughterhouse wastewaters. Bull and Blanc reported that the performance of RBCs appeared inadequate when compared to activated sludge or high-rate biological filtration.

Aerated filters

These comprise an open tank containing a submerged biofilm support medium, which can be either static or moving. The tank is supplied with air to satisfy the requirements of the bio-oxidation process. There are a number of proprietary designs on the market, but each works on the principle of retaining a high concentration of immobilised biomass within the aerobic reaction tank, thus minimising the need for secondary sedimentation and sludge recycle. The major differences between the processes are the type of biomass support medium, the mechanism of biofilm control and whether or not the support medium is fixed or acts as an expanded or moving bed. As an example of the use of such a process, a Wisconsin slaughterhouse installed a moving-bed biofilm reactor (MBBR) to treat a wastewater flow of 168000

USgal/day, with surge capabilities to 280000 gal/day (636 and 1060 m^3/day). Average influent soluble BOD and soluble COD concentrations were 1367 mg/l and 1989 mg/l, respectively. The Waterlink, Inc., process selected used a small polyethylene support element that occupied 50 per cent of the 9357 ft^3 (265 m^3) volume provided by two reactors in series to give 10 hr hydraulic retention time at average flows and 6 hr at peak hydraulic flow. Effluent from the second MBBR was sent to a dissolved air flotation unit, which removed 70–90 per cent of the solids generated. The average effluent soluble BOD and COD were 59 mg/l and 226 mg/l, respectively.

Activated sludge: The activated sludge process has been successfully used for the treatment of wastewaters from the meat industry for many decades. It generally has a lower capital cost than standard-rate percolating filters and occupies substantially less space than lagoon or pond systems. In the activated sludge process the wastewaters are mixed with a suspension of aerobic micro-organisms (activated sludge) and aerated. After aeration, the mixed liquor passes to a settlement tank where the activated sludge settles and is returned to the plant inlet to treat the incoming waste. The supernatant liquid in the settlement tank is discharged as plant effluent. Air can be supplied to the plant by a variety of means, including blowing air into the mixed liquor through diffusers, mechanical surface aeration, and floor-mounted sparge pipes. All the methods are satisfactory provided that they are properly designed to meet the required concentration of dissolved oxygen in the mixed liquor (greater than 0.5 mg/L) and to maintain the sludge in suspension, for nitrification to occur it may be necessary to maintain dissolved oxygen concentrations above 2.0 mg/L.

The activated sludge process can be designed to meet a number of different requirements, including the available land area, the technical expertise of the operator, the availability of sludge disposal routes and capital available for construction. The first step in the design of an activated sludge system is to select the loading rate, which is usually defined as the mass ratio of substrate inflow to the mass of activated sludge (on a dry weight basis), this is commonly referred to as the food to micro-organism (F:M) ratio and is usually reported as lb BOD/lb MLSS day (kg BOD/kg MLSS day). For conventional operation the range is 0.2–0.6, the use of higher values tends to produce a dispersed or nonflocculent sludge and lower values require additional oxygen input due to high endogenous respiration rates. Systems with F:M ratios above 0.6 are sometimes referred to as high rate, while those below 0.2 are known as extended aeration systems. The latter, despite their higher capital and operating costs are commonly chosen for small installations because of their stability, low sludge production and reliable nitrification. Because of the stoichiometric relationship between F:M ratio and mean cell residence time (MCRT), high-rate plants will have an MCRT of less than 4 days and extended aeration plants of greater than 13 days. Because of the low growth rates of the nitrifying bacteria, which are also influenced markedly by temperature, the oxidation of ammonia to nitrates (nitrification) will only occur at F:M ratios less than 0.1. It is also sometimes useful to consider the nitrogen loading rate, which for effective nitrification should be in the range 0.03–0.08 lb N/lb MLSS-day (kg N/kg MLSS day).

Conventional plants can be used where nitrification is not critical, for example, as a pre-treatment before sewer discharge. One of the main drawbacks of the conventional activated sludge process, however, is its poor buffering capability when dealing with shock loads. This problem can be overcome by the installation of an equalisation tank upstream of the process, or by using an extended aeration activated sludge system. In the extended aeration process, the aeration basin provides a 24–30 hr (or even longer) retention time with complete mixing of tank contents by mechanical or diffused aeration. The large volume combined with a high air input results in a stable process that can accept intermittent loadings.

A further disadvantage of using a conventional activated sludge process is the generation of a considerable amount of surplus sludge, which usually requires further treatment before disposal. Some early work suggested the possible recovery of the biomass as a source of protein, but concerns over the possible transmission of exotic animal diseases would make this unacceptable in Europe. The use of extended aeration activated sludge or aerated lagoons minimises biosolids production because of the endogenous nature of the reactions. The size of the plant and the additional aeration required for sludge stabilisation does, however, lead to increased capital and operating costs. Considering the high concentrations of nitrogen present in slaughterhouse wastewater, ammonia removal is often regarded as essential from a regulatory standpoint for direct discharge and increasingly there is a requirement for nutrient removal. It is, therefore, not surprising that most modern day designs are of an extended aeration type so as to promote reliable nitrification as well as to minimise sludge production. Efficient designs will also attempt to recover the chemically bound oxygen in nitrate through the process of denitrification, thus reducing treatment costs and lowering nitrate concentrations in the effluent.

Design criteria and loadings for activated sludge treatment have been widely reported and reliable data can be found in a number of reports.

In recent years, a great deal of interest has been shown in the use of sequencing batch reactors (SBRs) for food-processing wastewaters, as these provide a minimum guaranteed retention time and produce a high-quality effluent. A batch process also often fits well with the intermittent discharge of an industrial process working on one or two shifts. Advantages are an ideal plug flow that maximises reaction rates, ideal quiescent sedimentation and flow equalisation inherent in the design. Decanting can be achieved using floating outlets and adjustable weirs, floating aerators are commonly employed and an anoxic fill overcomes problems of effluent turbidity as well as providing ideal conditions for denitrification reactions.

Hadjinicolaou described using a pilot-scale SBR activated sludge system for the treatment of cattle slaughterhouse wastewaters. The system was operated on a 24 hr cycle and 97.8 per cent of COD removal was achieved with an influent COD concentration of 3512 mg/l. A case study showing the use of an SBR in conjunction with an anaerobic lagoon has shown the potential of the system for both organic load reduction and nutrient removal. The main effluent stream from the slaughterhouse containing some blood, fat and protein enters a save-all for separation of fat and settleable solids. The flow is then equally split, one portion going to the anaerobic lagoon, which also receives clarified effluent from settling pits that are used to collect manure and paunch material and the other to the SBR, the effluent from the lagoon subsequently also enters the SBR. The average ratio of BOD:total N entering the SBR is 3:1, which provides sufficient carbon to achieve complete nitrification and denitrification. The SBR has a cycle during which filling takes place over an 11 hr period corresponding to the daily operation and cleaning cycle of the slaughterhouse. The aeration period is 12 hr, settlement 1 hour and decanting to a storage lagoon over 3 hr. The total volume of the plant is 0.33 Mgal (1250 m^3), with a daily inflow of 66000 gal (250 m^3) at a BOD of 600–800 mg/l, total N of 200 mg/l and total P of 40 mg/l. The plant is reported to achieve a final effluent with values less than 2 mg/l NH_3-N, 10 mg/l NO_3-N, total P 20 mg/l, BOD 20 mg/l and SS 20 mg/l. Additionally, all surplus activated sludge from the SBR is returned to the anaerobic lagoon.

SOLID WASTES

If good operational practice is followed in the slaughterhouse, the solids and organic loading entering the aqueous phase can be minimised. The separated solids still require treatment prior to disposal, however and traditional rendering of some of these fractions is uneconomic because of the high water and low fat content. These fractions are the gut manures, the manure and bedding material from holding pens, material from the wastewater screens and traps on surface drains, sedimentation or DAF sludge and possibly hair where no market exists for this material. Other high-protein and fat-containing residues such as trimmings, non-edible offal and skeletal material can be rendered to extract tallow and then dried to produce meat and bone meal.

Composting

Composting can be defined as the biological degradation of organic materials under aerobic conditions into relatively stable products, brought about by the action of a variety of micro-organisms such as fungi, bacteria and protozoa. The process of composting may be divided into two main stages: stabilisation and maturation. During stabilisation, three phases may be distinguished: first a phase of rising temperature, secondly the thermophilic phase where high temperature is maintained and thirdly, the mesophilic phase where the temperature gradually decreases to ambient.

During the first phase, a vigorous multiplication of mesophilic bacteria is observed and a transformation of easily oxidised carbon compounds, rich in energy, to compounds of lower molecular structure takes place. Excess energy results in a rapid rise in temperature and leads to the thermophilic phase when less easily degraded organic compounds are attacked. When the energy source is depleted the temperature decreases gradually to ambient. Actinomycetes and fungi become active in the mesophilic phase, during which biological degradation of the remaining organic compounds is slowly continued. At this stage the composting material is stabilised but not yet matured. During maturation, mineralisation of organic matter continues at a relatively slow rate until a carbon:nitrogen (C:N) ratio of 10:1 is reached and the volatile matter content falls below 50%. Only then is the compost completely matured.

Composting of dewatered sedimentation tank solids from a slaughterhouse in mechanically turned open windrows was described by Supapong. The material was kept in windrows for 40 days and the temperature fluctuated between 149 and 158°F (65–70°C) for up to 3 weeks. The resulting product was a friable, odourless and microbiologically satisfactory material whose bulk was only one-fifth of the original volume. It contained 0.5 and 3% by weight of phosphorus and nitrogen, respectively and was an acceptable soil conditioner.

Anaerobic digestion

Anaerobic digestion of abattoir solid wastes is not common in the United States, UK or elsewhere, despite the potential for stabilisation of the solid residues with the added bonus of fuel gas production. Cooper and Allen looked at the potential in New Zealand for production of methane from both the solid and liquid fraction of abattoir wastes. Based on tests carried out by Buswell and Hatfield, they concluded that paunch content and fecal matter would not give an economic return. In these very early tests it was reported that a retention time of 38–40 days might be required and that the expected gas yield would be 2500 ft^3/lb solids added (156 m^3/kg). In the UK the first of a new generation of well-mixed digestion plants to treat slaughterhouse wastes was installed in 1984 to treat all the paunch wastes, blood and settlement tank solids produced by a small abattoir in Shropshire. The operation and performance of a 3531 ft^3 (100 m^3) demonstration-scale anaerobic digester treating cattle and lamb paunch contents, blood and process wastewaters from a slaughterhouse was described by Banks. Anaerobic digestion of the solid fraction of abattoir wastes suffers from low methane production and solid reduction as well as requires a longer retention time compared to sewage and food processing wastes. Steiner reported the failure of a digester when treating a mixture of abattoir wastes. The mixture contained 13 per cent of rumen and intestine contents, 25 per cent of manure from animal buildings, 44 per cent of surplus sludge from an aerobic sewage treatment plant and 19 per cent fat derived from the fat separator and exhibited a COD of 165 g/l, a BOD of 112 g/l, a dry weight of 120 g/l and a volatile solids concentration of 105 g/l consisting of 25 per cent fat and 23 per cent protein. The experiment was carried out in a cylindrical completely mixed reactor with a capacity of 0.07 ft^3 (2 liter). When the organic loading rate was raised to more than 73 lb VS/10^3 gal day (8.75 g VS/l day), digestion failure occurred and was caused by enrichment of volatile acids in the digester. Banks also mentioned serious problems associated with the accumulation of ammonia concentration in the process. Several other authors also indicate that where blood and fat form a significant proportion of the feedstock it is found to be digestible in only limited quantities due to an inhibitory effect on methanogenesis, thought to be caused by accumulation of toxic intermediates produced by the hydrolysis/acidification stages.

Using a two-stage anaerobic process, Banks and Wang successfully overcame the toxicity problems associated with the accumulation of ammonia and volatile fatty acids when treating a mixture of cattle paunch contents and cattle blood. The first-stage reactor was operated in a hydraulic flush mode to maintain a significantly shorter liquid retention time than the solids retention time of the fibrous components in the feedstock. The first-stage reactor was run in this mode using solids retention times of 5, 10, 15, 20 and 30 days with liquid retention of between 2 and 5 days. Up to 87 per cent solid reductions were achieved compared to a maximum of 50 per cent when the control reactor was operated in single-pass mode with solids and liquid retentions of equal duration.

The liquid effluent from the first stage hydrolysis reactor was treated by a second-stage completely mixed immobilised-cell digester. Operated at a retention time of between 2 and 10 days with loading rates in the range of 36–437 lb/10^3 ft^3 day (0.58–7.0 kg COD/m^3 day), the second stage reactor achieved a COD removal of 65–78 per cent with a methane conversion efficiency between 2 and 4 ft^3 CH_4/lb COD removed (0.12–0.25 m^3 CH_4/kg COD removed).

Other than these few reports there has been little research on the anaerobic digestion of the solid waste fraction and it is clear that certain conditions and waste types lead to operational instability. Early work questions the economic viability of the digestion process when used only for the treatment of paunch content and intestinal fecal material and it may be necessary to look at the codigestion of slaughterhouse waste fractions with other waste materials. One successful operation is the Kristianstad biogas plant in Sweden, which coprocesses organic household waste, animal manure, gastrointestinal waste from two slaughterhouses, biosludge from a distillery and some vegetable processing waste. The slaughterhouse waste fraction is 24600 T per annum of a total throughput of 71200 T which is treated in the 1.2 Mgal (4500 m^3) digester. The plant biogas production was equivalent to 20000 MWh and the digester residue is returned to the land as a fertiliser. The plant represents an environmentally friendly method of waste treatment and appears to have overcome the problems of trying to digest slaughterhouse solid wastes in isolation.

MEAT INDUSTRY – PART OF THE FOOD MASS PRODUCTION CHAIN

Meat industry is an important link in the food production chain. Together with intensification of the production process and with production of the even larger quantities of meats, problems with dead animals and accumulation of slaughterhouse wastes also emerge. Solution of the problem of harmless removal of waste products of animal origin, are of exceptional economic importance, today, it is irreplaceable veterinary-sanitary and preventive usage in the suppression of catlle infections and zoonoses and special attention is paid to environmental protection and rehabilitation. Quantity of animal waste which appear in circulation of goods (raw meat, intestines, cured products, sausages, fat) as well as quantity of animal corpses which can be collected, should be added to this quantity. If the production of livestock and meat industry is not going to change drastically, there are 125.000 T of animal by-products annualy, or cca 496 T daily, which should be harmlessly removed.

Importance of Safe Disposal of Animal by Products

Necessity of solution of safe disposal of animal by-products by their utilisation with processing into animal feed and bioenergents, grows with the intensification of animal growing and the increasing of capacities of industrial slaughterhouses, construction of new small slaughterhouses, building of plants for meat processing and increasing of the volume of international trade of commercial animal products. Correct solution of safe disposal of animal by-products can be seen from three key aspects that should fulfill the technological solutions for solving of disposal of such materials by their processing, namely: from the epidemiologic-epizoothiologic aspect, with the aspect of environment protection, and the economic aspect.

According to Risti and others, with out any doubt, the newest and the best method of safe disposal of animal wastes is their technical processing in separate categories into products for chemical industry, bio-fuels and feed for specific animals. Prerequisite for safe disposal of animal wastes, using one of the described methods is organised collection and delivery of raw materials. Modern disposal of waste materials demands orderly constructed plants with adequate capacities, which should assure permanent and continuous supply of raw materials.

This confirms the importance of recognising the raw materials fundamentals for each object, i.e. organising of epizoothiologically and economically acceptable region, which should enable obtaining adequate quantities of animal wastes leading to designing and construction of modern object for their safe disposal.

In such collecting circle, organising of collection of animal wastes represents a very delicate problem, from whose solution to a large extent depends the successful operation of the plant that is going to process such raw materials. This problem, in any case, has to take into consideration both, plant that processes raw materials of animal origin or cattle-growing farms, and slaughterhouses that generate such raw materials. Also, important role in solving of the problem have local municipal communities. They are, according to the existing legislative rules on suppression of contageous diseases, obliged to organise safe disposal of animal wastes in their region. In other words, organising the collection of mentioned raw materials should be based on contractual linking of plants for safe disposal and processing of animal wastes and local municipal communities or their corresponding organisations (slaughterhouses, animal farms etc.) The emphasis on the necessity of transferring of animal wastes from the place where they were generated to the storaging place as fast as possible, is of grate importance, as well as the necessity of rapid performing procedure of their processing.

This is very significant, not only from the epidemiologicepizoothiologic aspect, or from environmental protection aspects, but also from the aspect of their technical processing. Namely, fresh raw materials are processed more easily with generation of lower quantities of waste gases and obtaining of better quality products.

Safe disposal of the described animal waste (material Category 1) by combustion on high temperatures (over 850°C) enables obtaining of warm water or steam, as anenergent for processing plant that use warm water or steam and ash as construction material for roads.

We shall mention only that, with the respecting procedures of blood collection and its technological processing, various articles for human use can be obtained, primarily products which are used as functional additives in manufacture of meat products. Special processing procedures enable their use as raw materials in pharmaceutical industry or for production of functional foods.

On the other hand, industrial waste blood can be collected and processed using corresponding technological procedure in a plant for processing of other animal by-products, using special processing unit. Such a one procedure enables obtaining of feed with high protein content, which contains, mostly, high quantities of essential amino acids, vitamins and mineral substances, and, particularly, iron.

Articles (meat- and bone meal and fat) obtained by processing of Category 1 of materials are suitable for use as fuel, i.e. as fuel for direct combustion in architecturally separated objects, respecting the corresponding legislative rules.

Chapter 9

Pollution Control in Seafood Food Industry

INTRODUCTION

Seafood is any form of sea life regarded as food by humans. Seafood prominently includes fish and shellfish. Shellfish include various species of molluscs, crustaceans and echinoderms. Historically, sea mammals such as whales and dolphins have been consumed as food, though that happens to a lesser extent in modern times. Edible sea plants, such as some seaweeds and microalgae, are widely eaten as seafood around the world, especially in Asia. In North America, although not generally in the United Kingdom, the term 'seafood' is extended to fresh water organisms eaten by humans, so all edible aquatic life may be referred to as seafood.

The seafood industry consists primarily of many small processing plants, with a number of larger plants located near industry and population centers. Numerous types of seafood are processed, such as mollusks (oysters, clams, scallops), crustaceans (crabs and lobsters), saltwater fishes and freshwater fishes. As in most processing industries, seafood-processing operations produce wastewater containing substantial contaminants in soluble, colloidal and particulate forms. The degree of the contamination depends on the particular operation, it may be small (e.g.washing operations), mild (e.g.fish filleting) or heavy (e.g.blood water drained from fish storage tanks).

The world seafood industry plays a significant role in the economic and social wellbeing of nations, as well as in the feeding of a significant part of the world's population. Fishing and fish farming has emerged as one of the major food processing occupations of mankind. In ancient times, economically and socially backward people were employed in this profession. The advent of modern mechanised fishing vessels has brought vast changes in the attitude of the public fishing and seafood processing. From low income and socially backward communities the profession has shifted to the hands of industrialists and technologists. Today fishing and processing activities provide employment to millions of people around the world.

Fresh fish cannot be kept for a long time without refrigerating, so we have to process the fish for preservation. There are several different ways of processing fish, mainly according to the kinds of fish.

Sun-dried fish: Sun drying is a popular way of processing small fish, such as Utaka, Usipa, Mathemba and small size of Mcheni. To dry the fish, you have to put the fish on the reads-made drying rack and turn the fish once or twice a day to dry evenly. It takes 3–4 days to finish the process and the fish should be taken away from the rack at night or in the rain.

Boil-dried fish: This type of processing is only used to process Usipa. The fish is first boiled in water and then put on the rack to be dried under the Sun. This process takes less time than the Sun drying (for 2–3 days) and the taste is also distinctive.

Roast-dried fish: This type of processing is especially for the flat fish like Utaka, Mayani and Chendamwamba. First the fish is dried for a few hours and then roasted on a steel pan to cook both sides. The fish are put back to the rack to dry again for rest of the day. This process can be completed for 1–2 days and also produces a different taste.

Smoked fish: Smoking is the only way to process the bigger fishes such as Chambo, ampango, Mlamba and bigger size of Mcheni. Small fishes are also smoked because of its fairly distinctive taste and of the shorter time for processing.

Fish are first dried for about half a day and then put on the wired oven overnight. Big fish like Kampango, Chambo or Mlamba are opened and gutted before drying. Smoking is especially favoured in rainy season, for the process is not affected from the rain.

Fish smoking and forest management: Compared to other types of fish processing, smoking requires fairly large amount of firewood. To keep the fire for smoking fish for one night, you may need almost the same amount of firewood that you use for cooking for one week.

FERMENTED FISH

Fermentation is one method of fish curing in which the development of a distinctive flavour in the final product is the principal objective. Therefore, this product is mainly used as a condiment in the preparation of traditional sauces. Fermentation alone as a curing process does not preserve fish because it results in the breakdown of fish muscle. For this reason, fermentation is often combined with salting and/or drying in order to reduce water activity and retard or eliminate the growth of proteolytical and putrefying bacteria. In Southeast Asia the fermentation process often lasts for several months and the final product is usually a paste, sauce or liquid. In Africa, however, fish fermentation lasts from a few hours to about two weeks. Under such conditions, fermentation is usually partial and the muscle structure is not broken down completely. Consequently, the fish retains its original form of whole or cut pieces after fermentation and can be eaten as food fish or used as a condiment.

Fish fermentation is generally accompanied by the development of a mild or strong odour which becomes associated with the final product. Fermented fishery products in Africa may either be soft with a high moisture content, semi-dry or very dry. Some products are also heavily salted and dried whilst others are dried without any salting. Some types of fermented products have a rancid taste. The fermented fish includes salted and/or Sun-dried fishery products in which some degree of desirable enzymatic or microbiological change has taken place in the fish muscle. Fermented fish is, therefore, any fishery product which has undergone degradative changes through enzymatic or microbiological activity either in the presence or absence of salt.

ENVIRONMENTAL ISSUES RELATED TO SEAFOOD PROCESSING

Environmental issues in fish processing industries primarily include the following: Water consumption and wastewater generation, solid waste generation and by-products production, emission to air and energy consumption.

Water Consumption

Most seafood processors have a high baseline water use for cleaning plant and equipment. Therefore, water use per unit product decreases rapidly as production volume increases. Major sources of water consumption include: fish storage and transport, cleaning, freezing and thawing, preparation of brines, equipment sprays, offal transport, cooling water, steam generation, and equipment and floor cleaning. Water consumption in fish processing operations has traditionally been high to achieve effective sanitation. Several factors affect water use, including: the type of product processed, the scale of the operation, the process used and the level of water minimisation practices in place. General cleaning contributes significantly to total water demand so smaller-scale sites tend to have significantly higher water use per unit of production.

Energy Consumption

Seafood processing industries consumes large quantities of electrical energy. Most of the power is used for magnetic induction equipment, such as electric motors (compressors for freezers, cold stores, ice-making machines, water pumps, etc.) and lighting that requires magnetic ballasts, air-conditioning. For fish and fish meal processing energy is required for cooling, cooking, sterilizing, drying, evaporation, can cleaning, fork-lifting. For wastewater treatment energy is applied for pumping and aerating. Energy consumption depends on various factors like age and scale of plant, the level of automation and the range of products. Processes which involve heating, such as canning and fish meal production need more energy than other processes.

Effluent Discharge

Sources of effluent from fish processing include the handling and storage of raw fish prior to processing, fluming of fish and product around the plant, defrosting, gutting, scaling, portioning and filleting of fish and the washing of fish products. Effluent streams generated from seafood processing contain high loads of organic matter due to the presence of oils, proteins and suspended solids. They can also contain high levels of phosphates and nitrates. In canning operations, effluent is also discharged from the draining of cans after pre-cooking, from the spillage of sauces, brines and oil in the can filling process and from the condensate generated during pre-cooking. Effluent quality highly depends on the type of fish being processed and type of processing undertaken. Pollution loads generated from the processing of oily fish species are much higher than from white fish species, due to the high oil content and the fact that these species are usually not gutted or cleaned on the fishing vessel.

If the effluent streams described above are discharged without treatment into water bodies, the pollutants they contain can cause eutrophication and oxygen depletion. In addition, fish processing industries have been known to pollute nearby beaches and shores by releasing wastewater containing oils. Since oil floats on water, it can end up on the surrounding coastline.

SEAFOOD-PROCESSING WASTEWATER CHARACTERISATION

Seafood-processing wastewater characteristics that raise concern include pollutant parameters, sources of process waste and types of wastes. In general, the wastewater of seafood-processing wastewater can be characterised by its physico-chemical parameters, organics, nitrogen and phosphorus contents. Important pollutant parameters of the wastewater are five-day biochemical oxygen demand (BOD_5), chemical oxygen demand (COD), total suspended solids (TSS), fats, oil and grease (FOG) and water usage. As in most industrial wastewaters, the contaminants present in seafood-processing wastewaters are an undefined mixture of substances, mostly organic in nature. It is useless or practically impossible to have a detailed analysis for each component present, therefore, an overall measurement of the degree of contamination is satisfactory.

Physico-chemical Parameters

pH

pH serves as one of the important parameters because it may reveal contamination of a wastewater or indicate the need for pH adjustment for biological treatment of the wastewater. Effluent pH from seafood processing plants is usually close to neutral. For example, a study found that the average pH of effluents from blue crab processing industries was 7.63, with a standard deviation of 0.54, for non-Alaska bottom fish, it was about 6.89 with a standard deviation of 0.69. The pH levels generally reflect the decomposition of proteinaceous matter and emission of ammonia compounds.

Solids content

Solids content in a wastewater can be divided into dissolved solids and suspended solids. However, suspended solids are the primary concern since they are objectionable on several grounds. Settleable solids may cause reduction of the wastewater duct capacity, when the solids settle in the receiving water body, they may affect the bottom-dwelling flora and the food chain. When they float, they may affect the aquatic life by reducing the amount of light that enters the water.

Soluble solids are generally not inspected even though they are significant in effluents with a low degree of contamination. They depend not only on the degree of contamination but also on the quality of the supply water used for the treatment. In one analysis of fish filleting wastewater, it was found that 65 per cent of the total solids present in the effluent were already in the supply water.

Odour

In seafood-processing industries, odour is caused by the decomposition of the organic matter, which emits volatile amines, diamines and sometimes ammonia. In wastewater that has become septic, the characteristic odour of hydrogen sulphide may also develop. Odour is a very important issue in relation to public perception and acceptance of any wastewater treatment plant. Although relatively harmless, it may affect general public life by inducing stress and sickness.

Temperature

To avoid affecting the quality of aquatic life, the temperature of the receiving water body must be controlled. The ambient temperature of the receiving water body must not be increased by more than 2 or 3°C or else it may reduce the dissolved oxygen level. Except for wastewaters from cooking and sterilisation processes in canning factories, fisheries do not discharge wastewaters above ambient temperatures. Therefore, wastewaters from canning operations should be cooled if the receiving water body is not large enough to restrict the change in temperature to 3°C.

Organic Content

The major types of wastes found in seafood-processing wastewaters are blood, offal products, viscera, fins, fish heads, shells, skins and meat 'fines'. These wastes contribute significantly to the suspended solids concentration of the waste stream. However, most of the solids can be removed from the wastewater and collected for animal food applications.

Wastewaters from the production of fish meal, solubles and oil from herring, menhaden and alewives can be divided into two categories: high-volume, low-strength wastes and low-volume, high-strength wastes. High-volume, low-strength wastes consist of the water used for unloading, fluming, transporting and handling the fish plus the washdown water.

The degree of pollution of a wastewater depends on several parameters. The most important factors are the types of operation being carried out and the type of seafood being processed. Several methods are used to estimate the organic content of the wastewater. The two most common methods are biochemical oxygen demand (BOD) and chemical oxygen demand (COD).

Biochemical oxygen demand

Biochemical oxygen demand (BOD) estimates the degree of contamination by measuring the oxygen required for oxidation of organic matter by aerobic metabolism of the microbial flora. In seafood-processing wastewaters, this oxygen demand originates mainly from two sources. One is the carbonaceous compounds that are used as substrate by the aerobic micro-organisms, the other source is the nitrogen-containing compounds that are normally present in seafood-processing wastewaters, such as proteins, peptides and volatile amines. Standard BOD tests are conducted at 5-day incubation for determination of BOD_5 concentrations.

Wastewaters from seafood-processing operations can be very high in BOD_5. Literature data for seafood processing operations show a BOD_5 production of one to 72.5 kg of BOD_5 per tonne of product. White fish filleting processes typically produce 12.5–37.5 kg BOD_5 for every tonne of product. The BOD is generated primarily from the butchering process and from general cleaning, while nitrogen originates predominantly from blood in the wastewater stream.

Chemical oxygen demand

Another alternative for measuring the organic content of wastewater is the chemical oxygen demand (COD), an important pollutant parameter for the seafood industry. This method is more convenient than BOD_5 since it needs only about 3 hours for determination compared with 5 days for BOD_5 determination. The COD analysis, by the dichromate method, is more commonly used to control and continuously monitor wastewater treatment systems. Because the number of compounds that can be chemically oxidised is greater than those that can be degraded biologically, the COD of an effluent is usually higher than the BOD_5. Hence, it is common practice to correlate BOD_5 vs. COD and then use the analysis of COD as a rapid means of estimating the BOD_5 of a wastewater.

Depending on the types of seafood processing, the COD of the wastewater can range from 150 to about 42000 mg/l. One study examined a tuna-canning and by-product rendering plant for five days and observed that the average daily COD ranged from 1300–3250 mg/l.

Total organic carbon

Another alternative for estimating the organic content is the total organic carbon (TOC) method, which is based on the combustion of organic matter to carbon dioxide and water in a TOC analyser. After separation of water, the combustion gases are passed through an infrared analyser and the response is recorded. The TOC analyser is gaining acceptance in some specific applications as the test can be completed within a few minutes, provided that a correlation with the BOD_5 or COD contents has been established. An added advantage of the TOC test is that the analyser can be mounted in the plant for online process control. Owing to the relatively high cost of the apparatus, this method is not widely used.

Fats, oil and grease

Fats, oil and grease (FOG) is another important parameter of seafood-processing wastewater. The presence of FOG in an effluent is mainly due to the processing operations such as canning and the seafood being processed. The FOG should be removed from wastewater because it usually floats on the water surface and affects the oxygen transfer to the water, it is also objectionable from an aesthetic point of view. The FOG may also cling to wastewater ducts and reduce their capacity in the long term. The FOG of a seafood-processing wastewater varies from zero to about 17000 mg/l, depending on the seafood being processed and the operation being carried out.

Nitrogen and Phosphorus

Nitrogen and phosphorus are nutrients that are of environmental concern. They may cause proliferation of algae and affect the aquatic life in a water body if they are present in excess. However, their concentration in the seafood-processing wastewater is minimal in most cases. It is recommended that a ratio of N to P of 5 : 1 be achieved for proper growth of the biomass in the biological treatment. Sometime the concentration of nitrogen may also be high in seafood-processing wastewaters. One study shows that high nitrogen levels are likely due to the high protein content (15–20 per cent of wet weight) of fish and marine invertebrates. Phosphorus also partly originates from the seafood, but can also be introduced with processing and cleaning agents.

Emission to Air

Point-source emission

These emissions are exhausted into a vent or stack and emitted through a single point source to the atmosphere. The major air pollution sources in a typical seafood industry are from combustion sources like boiler and generators for electric power. Boiler is used for steam supply during pre-cooking and sterilisation process. The examples of fuels used in the boilers are electricity, fuel oil, coal and LPG.

Odour

Odour is often the most significant form of air pollution in fish processing. Major sources include storage sites for processing waste, cooking by-products during fish meal production, fish drying processes and odour emitted during filling and emptying of bulk tanks and silos. Fish quality may deteriorate under the anaerobic conditions found in onboard storage on fishing processing facilities. This deterioration causes the formation of odorous compounds such as ammonia, mercaptans and hydrogen sulphide gas.

Noise Pollution

Noise is not a significant problem in seafood industries. Noise may be generated during cutting, pre-cooking, filing and weighing the can, can seaming and sterilisation. The noise measurements at any sources in the process do not exceed the standard of maximum sound level (140 dB), but they have more value than equivalent continuous sound level 24 hr. Sources of noise pollution are given in Table 9.1

Solid Waste Generation

Solid waste is mainly in the form of organic wastes generated in the production processes. It consists of fish shells and heads from the seafood processing. The majority of captured species are ground fish and it is estimated that only 25–50% of the raw material is utilised for primary products. The remaining 50–75% of the raw material is considered processing waste and is utilised for low-valued products or disposed.

Table 9.1: Sources of noise pollution

Source	*Causes of noise*	*Emission, dB*
Pre-cooking	Steam blow out from vent	80–85
Filling and weighing the can	Collision of cans	92–93
Can seaming	Seamer operating to seam the can	86–87
Sterilisation	Venting process, steam is continuously blowing out through the hole	90–95

Seafood processing activities generate potentially large quantities of organic waste and by-products from inedible fish parts and endoskeleton shell parts from the crustacean peeling process. The waste generation depends on the species and the process. If coal is used as a fuel in the boiler, ash will be generated depends on the ash content of the coal. Generally, 80% of the ash becomes fly ash and the remaining 20% will be bottom ash. Source and quantities of solid waste are given in Table 9.2.

Table 9.2: Source and quantities of solid waste.

Process	*Waste generation (kg/T)*
Eviscerating	240
Cleaning	400
Seaming	50
Total	
Organic	640
Inorganic	50

WASTE TREATMENT PRACTICES

Wastewater from seafood processing operations can be very high in biochemical oxygen demand (BOD), fat, oil and grease (FOG) and nitrogen content. White fish filleting processes typically produce 12.5–37.5 kg of BOD for every tonne of product. BOD is derived mainly from the butchering process and general cleaning and nitrogen originates predominantly from blood in the wastewater stream. It is difficult to generalise the magnitude of the problem created by these wastewater streams, as the impact depends on the strength of the effluent, the rate of discharge and the assimilatory capacity of the receiving water body.

In general, the wastewater of seafood processing waste water can be characterised by its physico-chemical parameters, organics, nitrogen and phosphorus contents. Important pollutant parameters of the wastewater are five-day biochemical oxygen demand (BOD_5), chemical oxygen demand (COD), total suspended solids (TSS), fats, oil and grease and water usage.

WASTEWATER TREATMENT METHODS

Seafood processing facilities typically employ a combination of primary and secondary wastewater treatments, depending on the degree to which organic materials are collected separately or mixed into the effluent stream. Wastewater from seafood processing facilities typically has a very high organic and nitrogen load which can be effectively treated in aerobic or anaerobic systems, including lagoons. However, care should be taken to reduce odours including those from extended biological and/or chemical phosphorus removal. Effluent standard for wastewater of different countries are given Table 9.3.

Table 9.3: Effluent standard for wastewater of different countries.

Parameters	*Units*	*Germany**	*Thailand*	*Sri Lanka*	*Bangladesh*
pH	pH	5.5–9	5.5–9	6–8.5	6–9
BOD_5	mg/L	25	20	100	50
COD	mg/L	110	120	250	250
Nitrogen	mg/L	25 (NH_4 – N) and 25 (TKN)	100	50 (NH_4 – N)	10 (TN)
Total phosphorous	mg/L	2	–	–	5
Oil, fats and grease	mg/L	–	5	20	10
Total suspended solids	mg/L	–	50	150	50
Total dissolved solids	mg/L	–	3000–5000	–	05
Temperature	°C	–	<40	<45	–

*Specially for seafood industry

Primary Treatment

This wastewater contains considerable amounts of insoluble suspended matter, which can be removed from the waste stream by chemical and physical means. For optimum waste removal, primary treatment is recommended prior to a biological treatment process or land application. For seafood-processing wastewater, the primary treatment processes are screening, sedimentation, flow equalisation and dissolved air flotation. These unit operations will generally remove up to 85% of the total suspended solids and 65% of the BOD_5 and COD per cent in the wastewater.

Screening

The removal of relatively large solids (0.7 mm or larger) can be achieved by screening. This is one of the most popular treatment systems used by food-processing plants, because it can reduce the amount of solids being discharged quickly. Usually, the simplest configuration is that of flow-through static screens, which have openings of about 1 mm. Sometimes a scrapping mechanism may be required to minimise the clogging problem in this process.

Fish solids dissolve in water with time, therefore, immediate screening of the waste streams is highly recommended. Likewise, high-intensity agitation of waste streams should be minimised before screening or even settling, because they may cause breakdown of solids rendering them more difficult to separate. In small-scale fish-processing plants, screening is often used with simple settling tanks.

Sedimentation

Sedimentation separates solids from water using gravity settling of the heavier solid particles. In the simplest form of sedimentation, particles that are heavier than water settle to the bottom of a tank or basin. This operation is conducted not only as part of the primary treatment, but also in the secondary treatment for separation of solids generated in biological treatments, such as activated sludge or trickling filters. For flocculent suspension, the formation of larger particles due to coalescence depends on several factors, such as the nature of the particles and the rate of coalescence. A theoretical analysis is not feasible due to the interaction of particles, which depends, among other factors, on the overflow rate, the concentration of particles and the depth of the tank.

The primary advantages of using sedimentation basins to remove suspended solids from effluents from seafood-processing plants are: the relative low cost of designing, constructing and operating sedimentation basins, the low technology requirements for the operators, and the demonstrated effectiveness of their use in treating similar effluents. Therefore, proper design, construction and operation of the sedimentation basin are essential for the efficient removal of solids. Solids must be removed at proper intervals to ensure the designed removal efficiencies of the sedimentation basin.

Rectangular settling tanks are generally used when several tanks are required and there is space constraint, because they occupy less space than several circular tanks. Usually there is a series of chain-driven scrapers used for removal of solids. The sludge is collected in a hopper at the end of the tank, where it may be removed by screw conveyors or pumped out.

Circular tanks are reported to be more effective than rectangular ones. The effluent in a circular tank circulates radially, with the water introduced at the periphery or from the center. Solids are generally removed from near the center and the sludge is forced to the outlet by two or four arms provided with scrapers, which span the radius of the tank. For both types of flows, a means of distributing the flow in all directions is provided. An even distribution of inlet and outlet flows is important to avoid short-circuiting in the tank, which would reduce the separation efficiency.

Flow equalisation

A flow equalisation step follows the screening and sedimentation processes and precedes the dissolved air flotation (DAF) unit. Flow equalisation is important in reducing hydraulic loading in the waste stream.

Separation of oil and grease

Seafood processing wastewaters contain variable amounts of oil and grease, which depend on the process used, the species processed and the operational procedure. Gravitational separation may be used to remove oil and grease, provided that the oil particles are large enough to float towards the surface and are not emulsified otherwise, the emulsion must be first broken by pH adjustment. Heat may also be used for breaking the emulsion but it may not be economical unless there is excess steam available. The configurations of gravity separators of oil-water are similar to the inclined tubes separators discussed in the previous section.

Flotation

Flotation is one of the most effective removal systems for suspensions that contain oil and grease. The most common procedure is that of dissolved air flotation (DAF), which is a waste treatment process in which oil, grease and other suspended matter are removed from a waste stream. This treatment process has been in use for many years and has been most successful in removing oil from waste streams.

This treatment process has been in use for many years and has been most successful in removing oil from waste streams. Essentially, DAF is a process that uses minute air bubbles to remove the suspended matter from the wastewater stream. The air bubbles attach themselves to a discrete particle, thus effecting a reduction in the specific gravity of the aggregate particle to less than that of water. Reduction of the specific gravity for the aggregate particle causes separation from the carrying liquid in an upward direction. Attachment of the air bubble to the particle induces a vertical rate of rise. The mechanism of operation involves a clarification vessel where the particles are floated to the surface and removed by a skimming device to a collection trough for removal from the system. The raw wastewater is brought in contact with a recycled, clarified effluent that has been pressurised through air injection in a pressure tank. The combined flow stream enters the clarification vessel and the release of pressure causes tiny air bubbles to form and ascend to the surface of the water, carrying the suspended particles with their vertical rise. Key factors in the successful operation of DAF units are the maintenance of proper pH (usually between 4.5 and 6, with 5 being most common to minimise protein solubility and break up emulsions), proper flow rates and the continuous presence of trained operators.

In one case, oil removal was reported to be 90 per cent. In tuna processing wastewaters, the DAF removed 80 per cent of oil and grease and 74.8 per cent of suspended solids in one case and a second case showed removal efficiencies of 64.3 per cent for oil and grease and 48.2 per cent of suspended solids. The main difference between these last two effluents was the usually lower solids content of the second. However, although DAF systems are considered very effective, they are probably not suitable for small-scale, seafood-processing facilities due to the relatively high cost.

Biological Treatment

To complete the treatment of the seafood-processing wastewaters, the waste stream must be further processed by biological treatment. Biological treatment involves the use of micro-organisms to remove dissolved nutrients from a discharge. Organic and nitrogenous compounds in the discharge can serve as nutrients for rapid microbial growth under aerobic, anaerobic or facultative conditions. The three conditions differ in the way they use oxygen. Aerobic micro-organisms require oxygen for their metabolism, whereas anaerobic micro-organisms grow in absence of oxygen, the facultative micro-organism can proliferate either in absence or presence of oxygen although using different metabolic processes.

Most of the micro-organisms present in wastewater treatment systems use the organic content of the wastewater as an energy source to grow and are thus classified as heterotrophes from a nutritional point of view. The population active in a biological wastewater treatment is mixed, complex and interrelated. In a single aerobic system, members of the genera *Pseudomonas*, *Nocardia*, *Flavobacterium*, *Achromobacter* and *Zooglea* may be present, together with filamentous organisms. In a well-functioning system, protozoas and rotifers are usually present and are useful in consuming dispersed bacteria or nonsettling particles.

Biological treatment systems can convert approximately one-third of the colloidal and dissolved organic matter into stable end products and convert the remaining two-thirds into microbial cells that can be removed through gravity separation.

The organic load present is incorporated in part as biomass by the microbial populations and almost all the rest is liberated gas. Carbon dioxide (CO_2) is produced in aerobic treatments, whereas anaerobic treatments produce both carbon dioxide and methane (CH_4). In seafood-processing wastewaters, the non-biodegradable portion is very low.

The biological treatment processes used for wastewater treatment are broadly classified as aerobic and anaerobic treatments. Aerobic and facultative micro-organisms predominate in aerobic treatments, while only anaerobic micro-organisms are used for the anaerobic treatments.

If micro-organisms are suspended in the wastewater during biological operation, this is known as a 'suspended growth process', whereas the micro-organisms that are attached to a surface over which they grow are said to undergo an 'attached growth process'.

Biological treatment systems are most effective when operating continuously 24 hr/day and 365 days/year. Systems that are not operated continuously have reduced efficiency because of changes in nutrient loads to the microbial biomass. Biological treatment systems also generate a consolidated waste stream consisting of excess microbial biomass, which must be properly disposed. Operation and maintenance costs vary with the process used.

Aerobic process

In seafood processing wastewaters, the need for adding nutrients (the most common being nitrogen and phosphorus) seldom occurs, but an adequate provision of oxygen is essential for successful operation. The most common aerobic processes are activated sludge systems, lagoons, trickling filters and rotating disc contactors. Apart from economic considerations, several factors influence the choice of a particular aerobic treatment system. The major considerations are: the area availability, the ability to operate intermittently is critical for several seafood industries that do not operate in a continuous fashion or work only seasonally, the skill needed for operation of a particular treatment cannot be neglected, and finally the operating and The considerations for rotating biological contactors (RBC) systems are similar to those of trickling filters.capital costs are also sometimes decisive.

Activated sludge systems: In an activated sludge treatment system, an acclimatised, mixed, biological growth of micro-organisms (sludge) interacts with organic materials in the wastewater in the presence of excess dissolved oxygen and nutrients (nitrogen and phosphorus). The micro-organisms convert the soluble organic compounds to carbon dioxide and cellular materials. Oxygen is obtained from applied air, which also maintains adequate mixing. The effluent is settled to separate biological solids and a portion of the sludge is recycled, the excess is wasted for further treatment such as dewatering.

Most of the activated sludge systems utilised in the seafood processing industry are of the extended aeration types: that is, they combine long aeration times with low applied organic loadings. The detention times are 1 to 2 days. The suspended solids concentrations are maintained at moderate levels to facilitate treatment of the low-strength wastes, which usually have a BOD_5 of less than 800 mg/L.

It is usually necessary to provide primary treatment and flow equalisation prior to the activated sludge process, to ensure optimum operation.

The most common types of activated sludge process are the conventional and the continuous flow stiffed tanks, in which the contents are fully mixed. In the conventional process, the wastewater is circulated along the aeration tank, with the flow being arranged by baffles in plug flow mode. This arrangement demands a maximum amount of oxygen and organic load concentration at the inlet. Unlike the conventional activated sludge process, the inflow streams in the completely mixed process are usually introduced at several points to facilitate the homogeneity of the mixing such that the properties are constant throughout the reactor if the mixing is completed. This configuration is inherently more stable in terms of perturbations because mixing causes dilution of the incoming stream into the tank. In seafood-processing wastewaters the perturbations that may appear are peaks of concentration of organic load or flow peaks. Flow peaks can be damped in the primary treatment tanks.

The conventional configurations would require less reactor volume if smooth plug flow could be assured, which usually does not occur. To ensure the optimum operation of the activated sludge process, it is generally necessary to provide primary treatment and flow equalisation prior to the activated sludge process. Pilot or laboratory-scale studies are required to determine organic loadings, oxygen requirements, sludge yields and sludge settling rates for these high-strength wastes. There are several pieces of information required to design an activated sludge system through the bench-scale or pilot-scale studies:

1. BOD_5 removal rate.
2. Oxygen requirements for the degradation of organic material and the degradation of dead cellular material (endogenous respiration).
3. Sludge yield, determined from the conservation of soluble organics to cellular material and the influx of inorganic solids in the raw waste.

4. Solid/liquid separation rate, the final clarifier would be designed to achieve rapid sedimentation of solids, which could be recycled or further treated. A maximum surface settling rate of 16.5 m^3/m^2 day has been suggested for seafood-processing wastes.

Typically, 85–95 per cent of organic load removals can be achieved in activated sludge systems. Although used by some large seafood-processing industries that operate on a year-round basis, activated sludge may not be economically justified for small, seasonal seafood processors because of the requirement of a fairly constant supply of wastewater to maintain the micro-organisms.

Aerated lagoons: Aerated lagoons are used where sufficient land is not available for seasonal retention or land application and economics do not justify an activated sludge system. Efficient biological treatment can be achieved by the use of the aerated lagoon system. The major difference with respect to activated sludge systems is that the aerated lagoons are basins, normally excavated in earth and operated without solids recycling into the system.

Two types of aerated lagoons are commonly used in seafood-processing wastewater treatment: completely mixed lagoons and facultative lagoons. In the completely mixed lagoon, the concentrations of solids and dissolved oxygen are uniformly maintained and neither the incoming solids nor the biomass of micro-organisms settle, whereas in the facultative lagoons, the power input is reduced, causing accumulation of solids in the bottom that undergo anaerobic decomposition, while the upper portions are maintained in an aerobic state.

In the aerated lagoon a stabilisation/polishing ponds system is commonly used to improve the effluent treated in the aerated lagoon. This system depends on the action of aerobic bacteria on the soluble organics contained in the waste stream. The organic carbon is converted to carbon dioxide and bacterial cells. If excavated basins are used for settling, care should be taken to provide a residence time long enough for the solids to settle and provision should also be made for the accumulation of sludge. There is a very high possibility of offensive odour development due to the decomposition of the settled sludge and algae might develop in the upper layers causing an increased content of suspended solids in the effluent. Odours can be minimised by using minimum depths of up to 2 m, whereas algae production can be reduced with a hydraulic retention time of fewer than 2 days.

Solids will also accumulate all along the aeration basins in the facultative lagoons and even at corners or between aeration units in the completely mixed lagoon. These accumulated solids will, on the whole, decompose at the bottom, but since there is always a non-biodegradable fraction, a permanent deposit will build up. Therefore, periodic removal of these accumulated solids is necessary.

Stabilisation/polishing ponds

A stabilisation/polishing ponds system is commonly used to improve the effluent treated in the aerated lagoon. This system depends on the action of aerobic bacteria on the soluble organics contained in the waste stream. The organic carbon is converted to carbon dioxide and bacterial cells. Algal growth is stimulated by incident sunlight that penetrates to a depth of 1–1.5 m. Photosynthesis produces excess oxygen, which is available for aerobic bacteria, additional oxygen is provided by mass transfer at the air-water interface.

Aerobic stabilisation ponds are 0.18–0.9 m deep to optimise algal activity and are usually saturated with dissolved oxygen throughout the depth during daylight hours. The ponds are designed to provide a detention time of 2–20 days, with surface loadings of 5.5–22 gram BOD_5/day/m^2. To eliminate the possibility of shortcircuiting and to permit sedimentation of dead algal and bacterial cells, the ponds usually consist of multiple cell units operated in series. The ponds are constructed with inlet and outlet structures located in positions to minimise shortcircuiting due to wind-induced currents, the dimensions and geometry are designed to maximise mixing. These systems have been reported achieving 80–95 per cent removal of BOD_5 and approximately 80 per cent removal of suspended solids, with most of the effluent solids discharged as algal cells.

During winter, the degree of treatment decreases markedly as the temperature decreases and ice cover eliminates algal growth. In regions where ice cover occurs, the lagoons may be equipped with variable depth overflow structures so that processing wastewater flows can be stored during the winter. An alternative method is to provide long retention storage ponds, the wastes can then be treated aerobically during the summer prior to discharge. Aerobic stabilisation ponds are utilised where land is readily available. In regions where soils are permeable, it is often necessary to use plastic, asphaltic or clay liners to prevent contamination of adjacent groundwater.

Trickling filters

The trickling filter is one of the most common attached cell (biofilm) processes. Unlike the activated sludge and aerated lagoons processes, which have biomass in suspension, most of the biomass in trickling filters are attached to certain support media over which they grow.

Typical micro-organisms present in trickling filters are *Zoogloea*, *Pseudomonas*, *Alcaligenes*, *Flavobacterium*, *Streptomyces*, *Nocardia,* fungi and protozoa. The crux of the process is that the organic contents of the effluents are degraded by these attached growth populations, which absorb the organic contents from the surrounding water film. Oxygen from the air diffuses through this liquid film and enters the biomass. As the organic matter grows, the biomass layer thickens and some of its inner portions become deprived of oxygen or nutrients and separate from the support media, over which a new layer will start to grow. The separation of biomass occurs in relatively large flocs that settle relatively quickly in the supporting material. Media that can be used are rocks (low-rate filter) or plastic structures (high-rate filter). Denitrification can occur in low-rate filters, while nitrification occurs under high-rate filtration conditions, therefore, effluent recycle may be necessary in high-rate filters.

In order to achieve optimum operation, several design criteria for trickling filters must be followed:

1. Roughing filters may be loaded at a rate of 4.8 kg BOD_5/day/m^3 filter media and achieve BOD_5 reductions of 40–50 per cent.
2. High-rate filters achieve BOD_5 reductions of 40–70 per cent at organic loadings of 0.4–4.8 kg/BOD_5/day/m^3.
3. Standard rate filters are loaded at 0.08–0.4 kg/BOD_5/day/m^3 and achieve BOD_5 removals greater than 70 per cent.

The trickling filter consists of a circular tank filled with the packing media in depths varying from 1–2.5 m or 10 m if synthetic packing is used. The bottom of the tank must be constructed rigidly enough to support the packing and designed to collect the treated wastewater, which is either sprayed by regularly spaced nozzles or by rotating distribution arms. The liquid percolates through the packing and the organic load is absorbed and degraded by the biomass while the liquid drains to the bottom to be collected.

With regard to the packing over which the biomass grows, the void fraction and the specific surface area are important features, the first is necessary to ensure a good circulation of air and the second is to accommodate as much biomass as possible to degrade the organic load of the wastewaters. Although more costly initially, synthetic packings have a larger void space, larger specific area and are lighter than other packing media. Usually, the air circulates naturally, but forced ventilation is used with some high-strength wastewaters. The latter may be used with or without recirculation of the liquid after the settling tank. The need for recirculation is dictated by the strength of the wastewater and the rate of oxygen transfer to the biomass. Typically, recirculation is used when the BOD_5 of the seafood-processing wastewater to be treated exceeds 500 mg/l. The BOD_5 removal efficiency varies with the organic load imposed but usually fluctuates between 45 and 70 per cent for a single-stage filter. Removal efficiencies of up to 90 per cent can be achieved in two stages.

Rotating biological contactors (RBC)

Increasingly stringent requirements for the removal of organic and inorganic substances from wastewater have necessitated the development of innovative, cost-effective wastewater treatment alternatives in recent years. The aerobic rotating biological contactor (RBC) is one of the biological processes for the treatment of organic wastewater. It is another type of attached growth process that combines advantages of biological fixed-film (short hydraulic retention time, high biomass concentration, low energy cost, easy operation and insensitivity to toxic substance shock loads) and partial stir. Therefore, the aerobic RBC reactor is widely employed to treat both domestic and industrial wastewater. Aeration of the culture is accomplished by two mechanisms. First, when a point on the discs rises above the liquid surface, a thin film of liquid remains attached to it and oxygen is transferred to the film as it passes through air, some amount of air is entrained by the bulk of liquid due to turbulence caused by rotation of discs. Rotation speeds of more than 3 rpm are seldom used because this increases electric power consumption while not sufficiently increasing oxygen transfer. The ratio of surface area of discs to liquid volume is typically 5 l/m^2. For high-strength wastewaters, more than one unit in series (staging) is used.

Anaerobic Treatment

Anaerobic biological treatment has been applied to high BOD or COD waste solutions in a variety of ways. Treatment proceeds with degradation of the organic matter, in suspension or in a solution of continuous flow of gaseous products, mainly methane and carbon dioxide, which constitute most of the reaction products and biomass. Anaerobic treatment is the result of several reactions: the organic load present in the wastewater is first converted to soluble organic material, which in turn is consumed by acid-producing bacteria to produce volatile fatty acids, plus carbon dioxide and hydrogen. The methane-producing bacteria consume these products to produce methane and carbon dioxide.

Digestion systems

Anaerobic digestion facilities have been used for the management of animal slurries for many years, they can treat most easily biodegradable waste products, including everything of organic or vegetable origin. Recent developments in anaerobic digestion technology have allowed the expansion of feedstocks to include municipal solid wastes, biosolids and organic industrial waste (e.g.seafood-processing wastes). Lawn and garden or 'green' residues, may also be included, but care should be taken to avoid woody materials with high lignin content that requires a much longer decomposition time. The digestion system seems to work best with a feedstock mixture of 15–25 per cent solids. This may necessitate the addition of some liquid, providing an opportunity for the treatment of wastewater with high concentrations of organic contaminants. A typical anaerobic system diagram is shown in Fig. 9.1.

The flow of anaerobic digestion resembles that of an activated sludge process except that it occurs in the absence of oxygen. Therefore, it is essential to have a good sealing of the digestion tanks since oxygen kills some of the anaerobic bacteria present and presence of air may easily disrupt the process. From the anaerobic digester the effluent proceeds to a degasifier and to a settler from which the wastewater

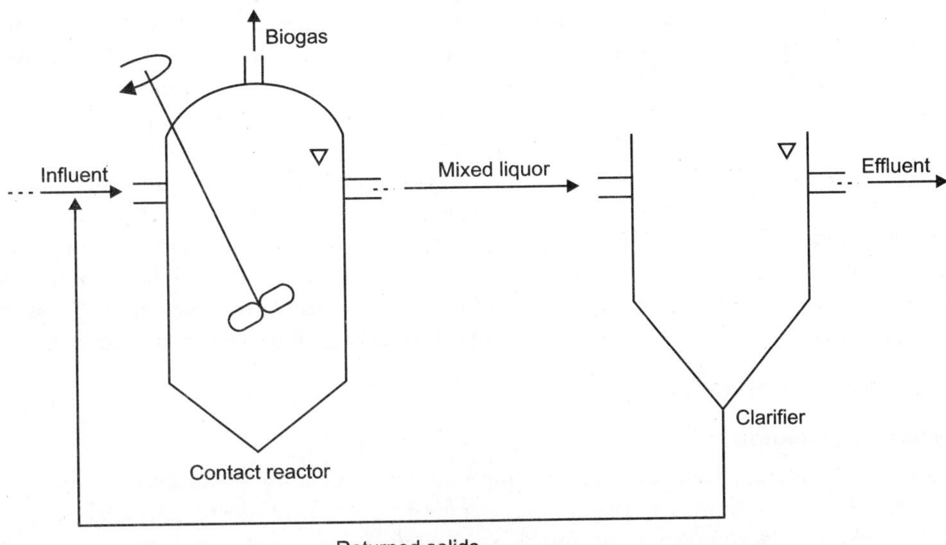

Fig. 9.1: Diagram of an anaerobic digestion process.

is discharged and the solids are recycled. The need for recycling is attributed to the fact that anaerobic digestion proceeds at a much slower rate than aerobic processes, thereby requiring more time and more biomass to achieve high removal efficiencies. The amount of time required for anaerobic digestion depends upon its composition and the temperature maintained in the digester, because anaerobic processes are also sensitive to temperature. Mesophilic digestion occurs at approximately 35°C and requires 12–30 days for processing. Thermophilic processes make use of higher temperatures (55°C) to speed up the reaction time to 6–14 days. Mixing the contents is not always necessary, but is generally preferred, as it leads to more efficient digestion by providing uniform conditions in the vessel and speeds up the biological reactions.

Anaerobic processes have been applied in seafood-processing wastewaters, obtaining high removal efficiencies (75–80 per cent) with loads of 3 or 4 kg of COD/m^3 day.

In total, 60–70 per cent of the gas produced by a balanced and well-functioning system consists of methane, with the rest being mostly carbon dioxide and minor amounts of nitrogen and hydrogen. This biogas is an ideal source of fuel, resulting in low-cost electricity and providing steam for use in the stirring and heating of digestion tanks.

Imhoff tank

The Imhoff tank is a relatively simple anaerobic system that was used to treat wastewater before heated digesters were developed. It is still used for plants of small capacity. The system consists of a two-chamber rectangular tank, usually built partially underground.

Wastewater enters into the upper compartment, which acts as a settling basin while the settled solids are stabilised anaerobically at the lower part. Shortcircuiting of the wastewater can be prevented by using a baffle at the entrance with more than one port for discharge. The lower compartment is generally unheated. The stabilised sludge is removed from the bottom, generally twice a year, to provide ample time for the sludge to stabilise, although the removal frequency is sometimes dictated by the convenience of sludge disposal. In some cases, these tanks are designed with inlets and outlets at both ends and the wastewater flow is reversed periodically so that the sludge at the bottom accumulates evenly. Although they are simple installations, Imhoff tanks are not without inconveniences, foaming, odour and scum can form. These typically result when the temperature falls below 15°C and causes a process imbalance in which the bacteria that produce volatile acids predominate and methane production is reduced. This is why in some cases immersed heaters are used during cold weather. Scum forms because the gases that originate during anaerobic digestion are entrapped by the solids, causing the latter to float. This is usually overcome by increasing the depth in the lower chamber. At lower depths, bubbles form at a higher pressure, expand more when rising and are more likely to escape from the solids. Odour problem is minimal when the two stages of the process of acid formation and gas formation are balanced.

Physico-chemical Treatments

Coagulation/flocculation

Coagulation or flocculation tanks are used to improve the treatability of wastewater and to remove grease and scum from wastewater. In coagulation operations, a chemical substance is added to an organic colloidal suspension to destabilise it by reducing forces that keep them apart, that is, to reduce the surface charges responsible for particle repulsions. This reduction in charges is essential for flocculation, which has the purpose of clustering fine matter to facilitate its removal. Particles of larger size are then settled and clarified effluent is obtained.

In seafood processing wastewaters, the colloids present are of an organic nature and are stabilised by layers of ions that result in particles with the same surface charge, thereby increasing their mutual repulsion and stabilisation of the colloidal suspension. This kind of wastewater may contain appreciable amounts of proteins and micro-organisms, which become charged due to the ionisation of carboxyl and amino groups or their constituent amino acids. The oil and grease particles, normally neutral in charge, become charged due to preferential absorption of anions, which are mainly hydroxyl ions.

Several steps are involved in the coagulation process. First, coagulant is added to the effluent and mixing proceeds rapidly and with high intensity. The purpose is to obtain intimate mixing of the coagulant with the wastewater, thereby increasing the effectiveness of destabilisation of particles and initiating coagulation. A second stage follows in which flocculation occurs for a period of up to 30 minutes. In the latter case, the suspension is stirred slowly to increase the possibility of contact between coagulating particles and to facilitate the development of large flocs. These flocs are then transferred to a clarification basin in which they settle and are removed from the bottom while the clarified effluent overflows.

Several substances may be used as coagulants. The pH of several wastewaters of the proteinaceous nature can be adjusted by adding acid or alkali. The addition of acid is more common, resulting in coagulation of the proteins by denaturing them, changing their structural conformation due to the change in their surface charge distribution. Thermal denaturation of proteins can also be used, but due to its high energy demand, it is only advisable if excess steam is available. In fact, the 'cooking' of the blood-water in fishmeal plants is basically a thermal coagulation process. Another commonly used coagulant is polyelectrolyte, which may be further categorised as cationic and anionic coagulants. Cationic polyelectrolytes act as a coagulant by lowering the charge of the wastewater particles, because wastewater particles are negatively charged. Anionic or neutral polyelectrolyte are used as bridges between the already formed particles that interact during the flocculation process, resulting in an increase of floc size. Since the recovered sludges from coagulation/flocculation processes may sometimes be added to animal feeds, it is advisable to ensure that the coagulant or flocculant used is not toxic. In seafood-processing wastewaters there are several reports on the use (at both pilot plant and working scale) of inorganic coagulants such as aluminum sulphate, ferric chloride, ferric sulphate or organic coagulants. On the other hand, fish scales are reported to be used effectively as an organic wastewater coagulant. These are dried and ground before being added as coagulant in powder form. Another marine by-product that can be used as coagulant is a natural polymer derived from chitin, a main constituent of the exoskeletons of crustaceans, which is also known as chitosan.

Electrocoagulation

It reduces organic levels in various food- and fish-processing waste streams. During testing, an electric charge was passed through a spent solution in order to destabilise and coagulate contaminants for easy separation. Initial test results were quickly clarified with a small EC test cell-contaminants coagulated and floated to the top. Analytical test results showed some reduction in BODs, but not as much as originally anticipated when the pilot test was conducted. Additional testing was carried out on site on a series of grab samples, however, these runs did not appear to be as effective as originally anticipated. The pH was varied in an attempt to optimise the process, but BOD_5 reductions of only 21–33 per cent were observed. Also, since metal electrodes (aluminum) were used in the process, the presence of metal in the spent solution and separated solids posed a concern for by-product recovery. But satisfactory BOD_5 reductions could not be achieved easily. It was determined that long retention times would be needed in order to make EC work effectively.

Disinfection

Disinfection of seafood processing wastewater is a process by which disease-causing organisms are destroyed or rendered inactive. Most disinfection systems work in one of the following four ways: (i) damage to the cell wall, (ii) alteration of cell permeability, (iii) alteration of the colloidal nature of protoplasm and (iv) inhibition of enzyme activity.

Chlorination: Chlorination is a process commonly used in both industrial and domestic wastewaters for various reasons. In fisheries effluents, however, its primary purpose is to destroy bacteria or algae or to inhibit their growth. A problem that may occur during chlorination of fisheries effluents is the formation of chloramines. These wastewaters may contain appreciable amounts of ammonia and volatile amines, which react with chlorine to give chloramines, resulting in an increased demand for chlorine to achieve a desired degree of disinfection.

Ozonation: Ozone (O_3) is a strong oxidising agent that has been used for disinfection due to its bactericidal properties and its potential for removal of viruses. It is produced by discharging air or oxygen across a narrow gap with application of a high voltage.

Ozonation has been used to treat a variety of wastewater streams and appears to be most effective when treating more dilute types of wastes. It is a desirable application as a polishing step for some seafood-processing wastewaters, such as from squid-processing operations, which is fairly concentrated.

Ozone reverts to oxygen when it has been added and reacted, thus increasing somewhat the dissolved oxygen level of the effluent to be discharged, which is beneficial to the receiving water stream. Contact tanks are usually closed to recirculate the oxygen-enriched air to the ozonation unit. Advantages of ozonation over chlorination are that it does not produce dissolved solids and is affected neither by ammonia compounds present nor by the pH value of the effluent. On the other hand, ozonation has been used to oxidise ammonia and nitrites presented in fish culture facilities.

Ozonation also has limitations. Because ozone's volatility does not allow it to be transported, this system requires ozone to be generated onsite, which requires expensive equipment. Although much less used than chlorination in fisheries wastewaters, ozonation systems have been installed in particular in discharges to sensitive water bodies.

Ultraviolet (UV) radiation: Disinfection can also be accomplished by using ultraviolet (UV) radiation as a disinfection agent. UV radiation disinfects by penetrating the cell wall of pathogens with UV light and completely destroying the cell and/or rendering it unable to reproduce. However, a UV radiation system might have only limited value to seafood processing wastewater without adequate TSS removal, because the effectiveness decreases when solids in the discharge block the light.

LAND DISPOSAL OF WASTEWATER

Generally, several methods are used for land application, including irrigation, surface ponding, groundwater recharge by injection wells and subsurface percolation. Although each of these methods may be used in particular circumstances for specific seafood processing waste streams, the irrigation method is most frequently used. Irrigation processes may be further divided into four subcategories according to the rates of application and ultimate disposal of liquid. These are overland flow, normal irrigation, high-rate irrigation and infiltration percolation.

The treatability of seafood processing wastewater by land application has been shown to be excellent for both infiltration and overland flow systems. With respect to organic carbon removal, both systems have achieved pollutant removal efficiencies of approximately 98 and 84%, respectively. The advantage of higher efficiency obtained with the infiltration system is offset somewhat by the more expensive and complicated distribution system involved. Moreover, the overland flow system is less likely to pollute potable water supplies. Nitrogen removal is found to be slightly more effective with infiltration land application when compared to overland flow application. However, the infiltration type of application has been shown to be quite effective for phosphorus and grease removal and thus offers a definite advantage over the overland flow if phosphorus and grease removal are the prime factors. One factor that may negate this advantage is that soil conditions are not favourable for phosphorus and grease removal and chemical treatment is required.

Irrigation is a treatment process that consists of a number of segments:

1. Aerobic bacterial degradation of the deposited suspended materials and evaporation of water and concentration of soluble salts.
2. Filtration of small particles through the soil cover and biological degradation of entrapped organics in the soil by aerobic and anaerobic bacteria.
3. Adsorption of organics on soil particles and uptake of nitrogen and phosphorus by plants and soil micro-organisms.
4. Uptake of liquid wastes and transpiration by plants.
5. Percolation of water to groundwater.

The importance of these processes depends on the rate of application of waste, the characteristics of the waste, the characteristics of soil and substrata and the type of cover crop grown on the land.

Potential Problems in Land Application with Seafood Processing Wastewater

Two potential problems may be encountered with land application of seafood processing wastewaters the presence of disease-producing bacteria and unfavourable sodium absorption ratios of the soil. A key to minimising the risk of spreading disease-producing bacteria can be accomplished by using low-pressure wastewater distribution systems to reduce the aerosol drift of the water spray. With respect to unfavourable sodium absorption ratios associated with the soil type, the seafood processor should be aware that clay-containing soils will cause the most serious sodium absorption problem.

Sandy soils do not appear to be affected by unfavourable sodium absorption ratios and seem to be the best suited for accepting the high sodium chloride content found in most meat packing plant wastewaters. As seafood-processing plant wastewaters are applied to land, certain types of grasses have been found to be compatible with these wastewaters. In some cases, the use of land application systems by today's seafood processors is feasible. However, in many cases, land disposal of seafood-processing wastes must be ruled out as a treatment alternative. Coastal topographic and soil characteristics, along with high costs of coastal property are the two major factors limiting the use of land application systems for treating seafood-processing wastes.

GENERAL SEAFOOD-PROCESSING PLANT SCHEMES

Seafood processing involves the capture and preparation of fish, shellfish, marine plants and animals, as well as by-products such as fish meal and fish oil. The processes used in the seafood industry generally include harvesting, storing, receiving, eviscerating, precooking, picking or cleaning, preserving and packaging. It is a summary of the major processes common to most seafood processing operations, however, the actual process will vary depending on the product and the species being processed.

There are several sources that produce wastewater, including:

1. Fish storage and transport.
2. Fish cleaning.
3. Fish freezing and thawing.
4. Preparation of brines.
5. Equipment sprays.
6. Offal transport.
7. Cooling water.
8. Steam generation.
9. Equipment and floor cleaning.

Organic material in the wastewater is produced in the majority of these processes. However, most of it originates from the butchering process, which generally produces organic material such as blood and gut materials. The volume and quality of wastewater in each area is highly dependent on the products or species being processed and the production processes used.

Most seafood processors have a high baseline water use for cleaning plant and equipment. Therefore, water use per unit product decreases rapidly as production volume increases. Reducing wastewater volumes tends to have a significant impact on reducing organic loads as these strategies are typically associated with reduced product contact and better segregation of high-strength streams.

Water consumption in seafood processing operations has traditionally been high to achieve effective sanitation. Industry literature indicates that water use varies widely throughout the sector, from 5–30 l/kg of product. Several factors affect water use, including the type of product processed, the scale of the operation, the process used and the level of water minimisation in place. General cleaning contributes significantly to total water demand so smaller scale sites tend to have significantly higher water use per unit of production. Thawing operations can also account for up to 50 per cent of the wastewater generated. A figure for water use of around 5–10 l/kg is typical of large operations with dedicated, automated or semi-automated equipment that have implemented water minimisation practises.

ECONOMIC CONSIDERATIONS OF SEAFOOD PROCESSING WASTEWATER TREATMENT

Economic considerations are always the most important parameters that influence the final decision as to which process should be chosen for wastewater treatment. In order to estimate cost, data from the wastewater characterisation should be available together with the design parameters for alternative processes and the associated costs. Costs related to these alternative processes and information on the quality of effluent should also be obtained prior to cost estimation in compliance with local regulations.

During the design phase of a wastewater treatment plant, different process alternatives and operating strategies could be evaluated by several methods. This cost evaluation can be achieved by calculating a cost index using commercially available software packages. Nevertheless, actual cost indices are often restrictive, since only investment or specific operating costs are considered. Moreover, time-varying wastewater characteristics are not directly taken into account but rather through the application of large safety factors. Finally, the implementation of adequate control strategies such as a real-time control is rarely investigated despite the potential benefits. In order to avoid these problems, a concept of MoSS-CC (Modelbased Simulation System for Cost Calculation) was introduced by Gillot, which is a modeling and simulation tool aimed at integrating the calculation of investment and fixed and variable operating costs of a wastewater treatment plant. This tool helps produce a holistic economic evaluation of a wastewater treatment plant over its life cycles.

Preliminary Costs of a Wastewater Treatment Plant

Several methods may be used to assess the preliminary costs of a wastewater treatment plant to facilitate a choice between different alternatives in the early phase of a process design. One method is cost functions.

Cost of Operation and Maintenance

Several main factors influence the costs of operation and maintenance, including energy costs, labour costs, material costs, chemical costs and cost of transportation of sludges for final disposal and discharge of treated wastewater. The relative importance of these items varies significantly depending on the location, the quality of the effluent discharged and on the specific characteristics of the wastewater being treated. The total operating cost of a wastewater treatment plant may be related to global plant parameters (e.g.average flow rate, population equivalent), generally through power laws. However, such relationships apply to the average performance of plants and often suffer from a high uncertainty, unless very similar plant configurations are considered.

Capital costs

These comprise mainly the unit construction costs, the land costs, the cost of the treatment units and the cost of engineering, administration and contingencies. The location should be carefully evaluated in each case because it affects the capital costs more than the operating costs. When comparing different alternatives, special attention should be paid to the time and space scales chosen, since it may influence the choice of the implemented cost functions. At best, an overall plant evaluation over the life span of the plant should be conducted.

USE OF FISH AND SHELLFISH WASTES AS FERTILISERS AND FEEDSTUFFS

The practicality and economic attractiveness of recovering seafood wastes as fertilisers and feedstuffs is directly dependent on the waste composition, including protein, fat, mineral and moisture content. The characteristics of seafoods and seafood wastes are summarised below.

Product yields in fish and shellfish processing range from nearly 100% for whole rendered fish to a low of 15% for some crabs. The portions not incorporated as final products or by-products become waste. This waste is removed from seafood processing plants as either wastewater or solid waste. Wastewater (fresh or sea water) solutions contain dissolved materials (proteins and breakdown products) and suspended solids consisting of bone, shell, or flesh and foreign material. Solid wastes consist of flesh, shell, bone, cartilage and viscera. Many of these waste materials have sufficient nutrients to be valuable as fertilisers and feedstuffs.

The recovery of seafood wastes as fertilisers and feedstuffs is generally directed at the solid waste fraction, since most wastewater solutions (washwaters, etc.), are too dilute for recovery. Increasingly, however, wastewater streams are being treated to meet effluent requirements for discharges. Typically, screening, settling or dissolved air flotation methods are utilised and this results in the production of additional quantities of solid waste.

Seafood Processing and Solid Waste Generation

The nature and quantities of solid wastes generated from seafood processing are discussed with the descriptions of the processes typically used for major fish and shellfish species.

Bottom fish

Bottom fish are most commonly filleted and frozen for shipment. Most plants processing fillets use mechanised equipment, although some small plants use hand filleting. Solid wastes from filleting and skinning are usually rendered for pet food or animal meal. These wastes constitute 35 to 75 per cent of the total processed weight, with the higher percentages more typical of filleting operations.

Catfish

Catfish are harvested primarily in the southern and south-central states. Presently, over 60 per cent of the catfish harvest is from farm ponds or raceways. Solid wastes are processed into pet food, fish feed or fish meal where processing facilities are available and into landfills where such facilities are not. Wastewater treatment is usually not practiced.

Halibut

The halibut is a large fish, and commercially landed sizes vary from 10 to over 30 kg. Halibut are generally gutted at sea, therefore, solid waste quantities generated in processing are relatively small. Also, the edible cheeks are removed from the heads, bagged and frozen.

Menhaden and anchovies

Menhaden and anchovies are the major species of small, oily fishes which are harvested primarily for fish meal production. Menhaden is harvested on both the Atlantic and Gulf coasts and anchovies only on the west coast.

Ninety-nine per cent of the menhaden landed in the United States and most of the anchovies are rendered for fish meal, oil, and fish solubles.

Essentially all of the fish is processed into fish meal or by-products, leaving no solid waste. The fish meal is primarily utilised as a protein supplement in animal feeds. The fish oil has a variety of commercial and industrial uses. Stickwater from the rendering process is evaporated at larger plants from a consistency of 5 to 8 per cent solids to a fish solubles concentrate containing 50 per cent solids. Fish solubles are combined with the fish meal for use as animal feed or marketed as a liquid fertiliser.

Salmon

Five species of Pacific salmon are presently harvested in Alaska, Oregon and Washington. Most salmon is canned, however, fresh freezing is increasing in popularity. Either hand or mechanical butchering is employed to remove the heads, tails, fins, and viscera. Product yield is slightly greater with hand butchering. Most salmon are mechanically packed.

Tuna

Tuna are harvested by line or net and frozen on board the fishing vessel. After thawing at the processing plant, the tuna are butchered, pre-cooked, and cleaned before being packed in cans. Dark (red) meat, amounting to about 6 to 10 per cent of the tuna, is processed for pet food and white meat is used for human consumption. Due to the large size of most tuna processing plants, extensive by-product recovery is normally practiced. Viscera and other solid wastes are further processed to fish meal. Concentrated solubles are marketed as an animal feed additive or used to produce tuna oil or other by-products. Generally, only about 1 per cent of the tuna is wasted.

FISHERIES WASTE BIOMASS: BIOCONVERSION ALTERNATIVES

When compared with the rest of the food industry, it has been generally regarded that the fish processing industry has been late in introducing new technologies to its production operations, including the treatment and/or recovery of wastes. Recently, interest has been focused on the applications of new technological methods to operations related to the seafood industry, with the objective of increasing its general efficiency. To this end, the effects of technology on the nutritional value of seafoods has been presented by Pigott and Tucker. In this context, it has been evident that the application of biotechnology to the utilisation of biomass from by-products or wastes of the seafood industry could bring about improvements in its overall economy.

Marine biomass constitutes an abundant and relatively inexpensive source of feed and food and of potential raw materials for several industries. Although fishing for food is the main activity relating to the exploitation of marine resources, biopolymers, enzymes and pharmaceuticals are among the other valuable products that can be extracted from marine organisms. For example, enzymes extracted from fisheries biomass, specifically proteases, have several potential uses, including uses in the seafood industry itself and in other valuable products that can be extracted from marine organisms. For example, enzymes extracted from fisheries biomass, specifically proteases, have several potential uses, including uses in the seafood industry itself and in other food industries.

Increased coastal and sea pollution had led to the need for better ways to dispose of fisheries wastes among others. The exhaustion of many fishing areas and the need for increased economy in processing operations also contributes to the requirement for better and more extensive utilisation of the fisheries biomass harvested. Given the potential value of many of their components, such as high-quality protein and oils, enzymes and complex polysaccharides, the recovery of much of the presently discharged fisheries wastes and by-products and their conversion to value-added products is a solution to such problems that should not be difficult to achieve. Biotechnological processes offer many possibilities for their incorporation into the processing of fisheries biomass.

Borrensen noted that the application of biotechnology to the seafood industry is mostly related to the utilisation of enzymes and micro-organisms. The use of micro-organisms in the seafood processing industry has been developed less than has the application of enzymes to some specific fisheries processes. Indeed, the use of enzymes and specifically the use of microbial enzymes, has a great potential in the seafood industry. In addition to the protein fraction of the fisheries biomass, the bio-processing of fish oils and chitin may yield important new sources of raw materials. As indicated above, fisheries, including aquaculture processes, presently constitute the main form of exploitation of marine resources, therefore, they are also the main source of marine wastes. Wastewater treatments for fisheries applications can also involve biological operations, in the so-called secondary treatments.

Hydrolytic Processes for the Recovery of Fish Protein

The hydrolysis of fisheries biomass for the recovery of fish protein can be catalysed by acids, alkalis or by biochemical agents. Among the last, the use of proteases and of proteolytic micro-organisms present good potential for the production of an acceptable fish protein hydrolysate product.

In the past few decades, better knowledge about enzyme biochemistry has resulted in the increased utilisation of enzymes in industry and other activities. Simultaneously, applications of enzymes in the seafood industry have been developed and the use of enzymes extracted from fisheries biomass has emerged. Most of the enzymes used in industry, specifically the food industry, are hydrolases and an important percentage of them are proteases.

Fisheries biomass contains a number of proteolytic enzymes, mostly from the digestive organs, such as chymotrypsin, pepsin and trypsin. Fish muscle tissue also contains enzymes such as peptidases, cathepsins, transminases, amidases, amino-acid decarboxylases and glutamic dehydrogenases. Exogenous enzymes also participate in the degradation of fisheries wastes, most of these being from microbial sources. In non-traditional methods for the production of fish sauce, the process could be quickened by adding enzymes. Microbial enzymes such as those from *Aspergillus oryzae* and *Monascus purpureus* have been used as accelerators in the production of fish sauce.

Endogenous proteases are also responsible for the liquefaction of fisheries wastes in the process resulting in the product known as fish silage, which is generally employed as animal feed or fertiliser. *Mowbray* produced solubles from dogfish (*Squalus acanthias*) by digestion and concentration of ground dogfish processing wastes under acidic and heated conditions.

Acid is generally added to accelerate the process of protein hydrolysis by creating appropriate conditions for the enzymes to work and to limit the growth of spoilage micro-organisms. Oil should be removed after liquefaction to enhance the product's acceptability. The resulting product is regarded as a good animal feed with a long storage life.

Several acids have been used for the fish ensiling process. The reduction of pH could be also achieved by inducing a lactic acid fermentation in the ensiling process, requiring the addition of fermentable carbohydrates to it. *Fagbenro* and *Jauncey* reported on the chemical and nutritional attributes of raw, cooked and salted fish silages of tilapia (*Oreochromis niloticus*) fermented with *Lactobacillus plantarum*. *Levin* studied lactic acid-aided fish silage processes. The effect of different concentrations of molasses, used as the carbohydrate source and salt on a fermented fish ensiling process was presented by *Martin*. *Martin* used fish viscera from tropical freshwater fish and also studied the changes in microbial population during the process.

It is to be expected that the composition of fish silage will be similar to that of the material from which it is made, containing approximately 80 per cent water, the rest being protein, liquid and ash from the bones. The lipid composition will depend upon the characteristics of the raw material and whether the oil had been removed during the process. Fish silage with an appropriate pH value could be kept at room temperature for at least 2 years without putrefaction.

An indication of the great number of possibilities existing for the design of silage processes is given by the studies of Samuels. It has been found that fermentation of fish and crab processing wastes combined with low-quality roughages such as corn stover or peanut hulls. Experiments also included the addition of molasses and of wilted Johnsongrass (*Sorghum halepense* L).

Enzymatic methods

The use of enzymes for the processing of wastes in the food industry has been discussed by Reed. Hydrolases such as amylases, pectinases, mannanases, cellulases, hemicellulases and lactases find applications in the fruit, vegetable, grain, coffee and dairy industries. In the fisheries, chitinases and proteases are the enzymes with the most potential for application.

Proteases extracted from fish biomass can be used in the same fisheries industry for the production of silage, fish sauce and fish solubles. New technologies employ fish enzymes for skin, membrane and scale removal in fish preparation, roe production and extraction and recovery of flavourings and pigments.

There is a growing need for new sources of protein with appropriate functional properties to be incorporated into foods. Concentrates of fish proteins have a potential role in satisfying this need, depending on their functional and organoleptic properties. There remains a need for the development of new technologies for the production of good-quality fish protein concentrates. However, in general those concentrates have not been used for human consumption, primarily due to their poor functional properties. The same problem has limited the use of fish meal. Therefore, those products have been mostly utilised for animal feed. The production of fish protein concentrates was attempted with the main objectives of obtaining a new food source and solving some of the chronic problems of the seafood industry, such as incomplete utilisation of the catch and perishability of the product, among others. Initial works were based on solvent extraction. However, there was practically no commercial acceptance of these products because of their already mentioned deficient functional properties. For the food industry, it is important to produce fish protein concentrates with acceptable functional properties. The final product, after concentration and drying, should be soluble to be successfully incorporated into foods. The use of proteases has also been reported in the protein hydrolysis of stickwater, an aqueous by-product of fish meal production. In this application, energy savings resulting from the reduction in viscosity of the stickwater contribute to the overall economy of the process.

Emulsification capacity and solubility are among the functional properties of protein concentrates needed for the food processing industry. Solubilisation of proteins can be accomplished by breaking them down into smaller-sized peptides by hydrolysis. The product resulting from this process is known as fish protein hydrolysates. Adler-Nissen discussed the production of fish protein hydrolysates by biological methods.

Protease enzymes with broad specificity are preferred for commercial processes, as they are capable of splitting the protein at random independently of the given patterns of amino acids in the proteins. The optimum pH values of proteolytic enzymes can vary from those of pepsin and some fungal enzymes (acidic) to those of bacterial proteases (alkaline or neutral). A potential market for fish protein concentrates and hydrolysates is in the production of animal feed, including pet food.

Another category of products which can be obtained by enzymatic hydrolysis of fish biomass is seafood flavourings. One commercial operation has been reported in France. The final product is in the form of a paste or powder for incorporation into food products such as sauces, seasonings and seafood analogues. This kind of product can be used to bolster the flavour of expensive fish products such as crab, lobster and salmon, whose original flavours are reduced during storage. *Pan* studied the recovery of the volatile components of shrimp, responsible for its taste, after an enzymatic digestion process.

Methods employing micro-organisms

It has been reported that microbial proteases have been found to be superior to proteolytic enzymes from other sources for the solubilisation of proteins, owing to their broader specificities. Sources of proteolytic enzymes, including microbial proteases and their applications in the food industry have been presented by Löffler. Martin immobilised cells of *Bacillus megaterium, Aeromonas hydrophila* and *Pseudomonas marinoglutinosa* and applied them to the protein hydrolysis of a low-cost fish (*Johnius dissumeri*) meat suspension in water. The cells secreted protease, which solubilised the fish meat. *B. megaterium* was found to be the most efficient hydrolysis agent, producing the solubilisation of 30 per cent of the fish protein.

Biomass recovered from fisheries sources contains lipids which are a significant component of fishery wastewater. For many seafood processing operations, the removal and possible recovery of lipids from fish wastes cannot be justified economically. Even in fisheries processing plants having wastewater treatment facilities, the disposal of fish oils is frequently a problem.

Stickwater is usually evaporated to a product known as 'fish solubles', which can in turn be processed and incorporated into animal feed. However, Green indicated that the lipid content in fish solubles (approximately 11 per cent) limits the use of stickwater in feeds. As is well- known, lipids can develop oxidative rancidity. Potential markets exist for fish oils of good quality. However, the technology for their recovery and processing could be expensive. Biological methods could assist in economically reducing the oil content of fish biomass. Lipolytic fish fermentations have been reported successful in decreasing the lipid contents of fish and fish wastes. Martin indicated that the biologial removal of fish oils using micro-organisms, by contributing microbial biomass protein, could improve the nutritional value of the recovered fish protein.

The studies of Burkholder found that the yeasts *Candida lipolytica* and *Geotrichum candidum* produced a reduction of the lipid content of young menhaden (*Brevortia tyrannus*) by 30–50 per cent. Studies on the fermentation of fish lipid *in situ*, of stickwater and of fish oils have been conducted with those yeasts. In all cases, it was reported that the lipid content was reduced and microbial cells growth was obtained. However, no commercial applications have been developed, as yet, for this technology.

Biological Methods for the Recovery of Chitin and Chitosan

The presence of relatively insoluble crustacean shells in shellfish processing wastes presents an environmental problem, which requires appropriate technological solutions. In these shells, chitin is associated with such components as lipids, pigments and protein. It is estimated that chitin is the most widely distributed polymer on earth and is one of the most abundant. Chitin is a polymer of *N*-acetyl-glucosamine and glucosamine residues. Chitin and its deacetylated derivative, chitosan, are polysaccharides with interesting characteristics. Chitin is insoluble in many solvents and resists most chemical reactions, however, it is deacetylated to chitosan by hot concentrated NaOH. Chitosan is soluble in organic acid solutions and carries amine groups with positive charges. In general, it has a variety of potential applications.

Biotechnological methods for the recovery and processing of chitin have been studied as a waste treatment alternative to the disposal of shellfish waste. Cosio studied the conditions for crustacean chitin waste pretreatment (size reduction, deproteination and demineralisation) and the production of chitinase by *Serratia marcescens*. Gagne reported on the use of bacterial protease, chymotrypsin and papain to deproteinise crustacean shells and found that the deproteinisation achieved with chymotrypsin was similar to that produced by using NaOH, making it the most effective enzyme. Because traditional methods of processing chitin and chitosan can produce depolymerisation and deacetylation of the original compounds, it has been expected that biotechnology could become the choice for their recovery, minimising the loss of their characteristics. Simpson studied the biological based technologies for chitin and chitosan processing and presented their processing and biotechnologically characteristics.

Biotechnological procedures can be also employed for the deacetylation of chitin to produce chitosan. The following micro-organisms have been found to produce enzymes for the deacetylation of chitin: *Mucor rouxii, Colletotrichum lindemuthianum* and *Phycomyces blakesleeanus*. Chitosan can be hydrolysed by chitosanases and some micro-organisms are able to produce them. These include bacteria, Tominaga, fungi and actinomycetes.

Other Products from Fisheries Waste Biomass

Fermentation substrates

The utilisation of nutrient-rich fisheries wastes as substrates sources for fermentation processes could create a new incentive for their recovery.

Lipids such as fish oils can be employed as energy and carbon sources for the growth of microbial populations and the production of microbial products. Martin discussed the aspects of fish oil that could make it an attractive alternative to carbohydrates as a fermentation substrate. An example of the many existing possibilities in this regard is the production of microbial biomass protein employing fisheries wastes as substrate in submerged fermentation processes. Microbial biomass protein, also known as single cell protein (SCP), is potentially useful as a protein and vitamin supplement for animal feeds and human foods. Using a concentration of up to 5 per cent fish oil in the culture media, Smith reported an average crude protein content of 40 per cent for both species of micro-organisms. Hottinger reported that alewife (*Alosa pseudoharingus*) oil in a basal medium was as effective a nutrient supplement as yeast extract or corn steep liquor for the above mentioned yeasts. The increase in cell yield stopped at the 5 per cent oil level. The operating conditions for this process were optimised. Those studies suggested the possibility of obtaining 800 gram of dry yeast biomass with a crude protein yield of 320 gram from 1 kg of fish oil using both batch fermentation and continuous fermentation processes.

The use of fish lipids for fermentation processes, owing to the specific properties of this substrate, requires further study. For example, Smith observed that growth in a fish lipid fermentation in shake flasks stopped before the expected level of consumption of the substrate was reached.

Fish oil contains a high concentration of polyunsaturated fatty acids which, in the presence of oxygen in aerobic fermentations, produce high concentrations of peroxides. These are oxidative deterioration products which could inhibit the growth of micro-organisms. Higgs tested various micro-organisms for their ability to metabolise fish oil. The addition of food-grade antioxidants to the fish oil prior to fermentation, at concentrations of approximately 0.5–1.0 per cent eliminated the growth inhibition produced by high peroxide concentrations. Zajie discussed the additional advantages that reduced oxidative deterioration could provide during fish oil fermentation, such as better emulsification of the oil during the process and the prevention of the formation of polymers and soaps, which decrease the fermentation yields, in the fermentation equipment. Other seafood processing wastes, beside fish lipids, can be employed in fermentation processes. As mentioned above, Carroad and Tom proposed chitin bioconversion to yeast SCP as a waste treatment alternative to the disposal of shellfish waste. *Pichia kudriavzevii* grew well on chitin hydrolysates and yielded a microbial protein with acceptable animo-acid composition. Cosio presented process design information and economic analysis for an integrated process for the conversion of shrimp shell chitin waste to microbial biomass. Revah studied the use of *N*-acetylglucosamine, released by the chitinase reaction, as a substrate to grow yeast for use in the production of SCP. Salt brines are used as contact refrigerants aboard fishing ships. In the process, they generally become contaminated with organic matter from the fish. Those brines should be treated before being discarded and biological process could make it possible to recycle them while yielding some useful product. To that end, a method was presented by Welsh for growing *C. utilis* yeasts on spent food processing brines to produce SCP.

The growth of microfungi and yeast in mussel processing wastes has also been studied, with the aim of developing a biological waste treatment process by means of their use as fermentation substrate.

Enzymes from fish biomass

Fisheries waste biomass is an important potential source for a variety of enzymes, some of them with unique attributes. The recovery of enzymes from fish wastes was suggested by Green.

Fish are known to adapt to quite low temperatures, which could affect such enzyme properties as binding affinity, cold stability, molecular activity, specificity and thermodynamic properties in general. Haard discussed the features of some enzymes from marine organisms. Regarding their proteases, it was been reported that they differ from those present in terrestrial animals and in plants. Enzymes from marine organisms may be exploited in certain food processing operations. Haard and Simpson discussed the proteases from aquatic organisms and their uses in the seafood industry. Other potential applications include the detergent and leather industries and the food industry in general. For example, *Brewer* reported that it is possible to prepare satisfactory cheddar cheese using proteases from marine organisms.

Chapter 10

Potato Wastewater Treatment

INTRODUCTION

The potato industry is well-known for the vast quantities of organic wastes it generates. Treatment of industrial effluents to remove organic materials, however, often changes many other harmful waste characteristics. Proper treatment of potato processing wastewaters is necessary to minimise their undesirable impact on the environment.

Currently, there is an increasing demand for quality improvement of water resources in parallel with the demand for better finished products.

These requirements have obliged the potato industry to develop methods for providing effective removal of settleable and dissolved solids from potato processing wastewater, in order to meet national water quality limits. In addition, improvement and research have been devoted to the reduction of wastes and utilisation of recovered wastes as by-products.

This chapter discusses: (i) the various potato processing types and steps including their sources of wastewaters, (ii) characteristics of these wastewaters, (iii) treatment methods in detail, and (iv) by-product usage.

POTATO PROCESSING AND SOURCES OF WASTEWATER

High-quality raw potatoes are important to potato processing. Potato quality affects the final product and the amount of waste produced. Generally, potatoes with high solid content, low reducing sugar content, thin peel and of uniform shape and size are desirable for processing. Potatoes contain approximately 18 per cent starch, 1 per cent cellulose and 81 per cent water, which contains dissolved organic compounds such as protein and carbohydrate. Harvesting is an important operation for maintaining a low level of injury to the tubers. Improved harvesting machinery reduces losses and waste load.

The type of processing unit depends upon the product selection, for example, potato chips, frozen French fries and other frozen food, dehydrated mashed potatoes, dehydrated diced potatoes, potato flake, potato starch, potato flour, canned white potatoes, prepeeled potatoes and so on. The major processes in all products are storage, washing, peeling, trimming, slicing, blanching, cooking, drying, etc.

Major Processing Steps

Storage

Storage is needed to provide a constant supply of tubers to the processing lines during the operating season. Potato quality may deteriorate in storage, unless adequate conditions are maintained. The major problems associated with storage are sprout growth, reducing sugar accumulation and rotting. Reduction in starch content, specific gravity and weight may also occur. Handling and storage of the raw potatoes prior to processing are major factors in maintaining high-quality potatoes and reducing losses and waste loads during processing.

Washing

Raw potatoes must he washed thoroughly to remove sand and dirt prior to processing. Sand and dirt carried over into the peeling operation can damage or greatly reduce the service life of the peeling equipment. Water consumption for fluming and washing varies considerably from plant to plant. Flow rates vary from 1300 to 2100 gal/T of potatoes. Depending upon the amount of dirt on the incoming potatoes, wastewater may contain 100–400 lb of solids per tonne of potatoes. For the most part, organic degradable substances are in dissolved or finely dispersed form and amount to 2–6 lb of BOD_5/T of potatoes.

Peeling

Peeling of potatoes contributes the major portion of the organic load in potato processing waste. Three different peeling methods are used: abrasion peeling, steam peeling and lye peeling. Small plants generally favour batch-type operation due to its greater flexibility. Large plants use continuous peelers, which are more efficient than batch-type peelers, but have high capital costs. Abrasion peeling is used in particular in potato chip plants where complete removal of the skin is not essential. High peeling losses, possibly as high as 25–30 per cent may be necessary to produce a satisfactory product. Steam peeling yields thoroughly clean potatoes. The entire surface of the tuber is treated and size and shape are not important factors as in abrasion peeling. The potatoes are subjected to high-pressure steam for a short period of time in a pressure vessel. Pressure generally varies from 3 to 8 atmospheres and the exposure time is between 30 and 90 second. While the potatoes are under pressure, the surface tissue is hydrated and cooked so that the peel is softened and loosened from the underlying tissue. After the tubers are discharged from the pressure vessel, the softened tissue is removed by brushers and water sprays. Screens usually remove the peelings and solids before the wastewater is treated. Lye peeling appears to be the most popular peeling method used today. The combined effect of chemical attack and thermal shock softens and loosens the skin, blemishes and eyes so that they can be removed by brushes and water sprays. Lye peeling wastewater, however, is the most troublesome potato waste. Because of the lye, the wastewater pH is very high, usually between 11 and 12. Most of the solids are colloidal and the organic content is generally higher than for the other methods. The temperature, usually from 50 to 55°C, results in a high dissolved starch content and the wastewater has a tendency to foam.

Types of Processed Potatoes

Potato chips

The processing of potatoes to potato chips essentially involves the slicing of peeled potatoes, washing the slices in cool water, rinsing, partially drying and frying them in fat or oil. Whiteskinned potatoes with high specific gravity and low reducing sugar content are desirable for high-quality chips.

Frozen french fries

For frozen French fries and other frozen potato production, large potatoes of high specific gravity and low reducing sugar content are most desirable. After washing, the potatoes are peeled by the steam or lye method. Peeling and trimming losses vary with potato quality and are in the range 15–40 per cent. After cutting and sorting, the strips are usually water blanched. Because the blanching water is relatively warm, its leaching effect may result in high dissolved starch content in the wastewater. Surface moisture from the blanching step is removed by hot air prior to frying. After frying, the free fat is removed on a shaker screen and by hot air stream. The fries are then frozen and packed.

Dehydrated diced potato

Potatoes with white flesh colour and low reducing sugar content are desirable for dice production. After washing and preliminary sorting, the potatoes are peeled by the steam or lye method. Minimum losses amount to 10 per cent. One important factor during trimming is minimising the exposure time. The tubers are cut into different sized pieces. After cutting and washing, the dice are blanched with water or steamed at 200–212°F. Following blanching, a carefully applied rinsing spray removes surface gelatinised starch to prevent sticking during dehydration. Sulphite is usually applied at this point as a spray solution of sodium sulphite, sodium bisulphite or sodium metabisulphite. Calcium chloride is often added concurrently with sodium bisulphite or sodium metabisulphite. Following drying, the diced potatoes are screened to remove small pieces and bring the product within size specification limits. Finally, the potatoes are packed in cans or bags.

Potato starch

Potato starch is a superior product for most of the applications for which starch is used. After fluming and washing, the potatoes are fed to a grinder or hammer mill and disintegrated to slurry, which is passed over a screen to separate the freed starch from the pulp. The pulp is passed to a second grinder and screened for further recovery of starch. The starch slurry, which is passed through the screen, is fed to a continuous centrifuge to remove protein water, which contains soluble parts extracted from the potato. Process water is added to the starch and the slurry is passed over another screen for further removal of pulp. Settling vats in series are used to remove remaining fine fibers. The pure starch settles to the bottom while a layer of impurities (brown starch) forms at the top. The latter is removed to the starch table consisting of a number of settling troughs for final removal of white starch. The white starch from the settling tanks and the starch table is dried by filtration or centrifugation to a moisture content of about 40 per cent. Drying is completed in a series of cyclone driers using hot air.

Potato flour

Potato flour is the oldest commercial processed potato product. Although widely used in the baking industry, production growth rates have not kept pace with most other potato products. After the prewashing, the potatoes are peeled, usually with steam. Trimming requirements are not as high as for most potato products. The flaking operation requires well-cooked potatoes, the tubers are conveyed directly from the cooker to the dryer, where 4–5 applicator rolls along one side of the drum contribute a thin layer of potato mesh. The mesh is rapidly dried and scraped off the drum at the opposite side by a doctor knife. The dried sheets are passed to the milling system where they are crushed by a beater or hammer mill and then screened to separate granular and fine flour.

CHARACTERISTICS OF POTATO PROCESSING WASTEWATER

Because potato processing wastewater contains high concentrations of biodegradable components such as starch and proteins, in addition to high concentrations of chemical oxygen demand (COD), total suspended solids (TSS) and total kjeldahl nitrogen (TKN), the potato processing industry presents potentially serious water pollution problems. An average sized potato processing plant producing French fries and dehydrated potatoes can create a waste load equivalent to that of a city of 200000 people. About 230 million liters of water are required to process 13600 T of potatoes. This equals about 17 liter of waste for every kilogram of potatoes produced. Raw potato processing wastewaters can contain up to 10000 mg/l COD.

Total suspended solids and volatile suspended solids can also reach 9700 and 9500 mg/l, respectively. Wastewater composition from potato processing plant depends on the processing method, to a large extent. In general, the following steps are applied in potato processing: washing the raw potatoes, peeling, which includes washing to remove softened tissue, trimming to remove defective portions, shaping, washing and separation, heat treatment (optional), final processing or preservation, and packaging.

The potato composition used in potato processing operations determines the components of the resultant waste stream. Foreign components that may accompany the potato include dirt, caustic, fat, cleaning and preserving chemicals. Generally, the various waste streams are discharged from the potato plant after being combined as effluent. It is difficult to generalise the quantities of wastewater produced by specific operations, due to the variation in process methods. Many references and studies in this respect show wide variations in water usage, peeling losses and methods of reporting the waste flow.

Processing involving several heat treatment steps such as blanching, cooking, caustic and steam peeling, produces an effluent containing gelatinised starch and coagulated proteins. In contrast, potato chip processing and starch processing produce effluents that have unheated components. It is evident that if the pulp is kept and not wasted, the organic load is significantly reduced. Potato pulp has been proven to be a valuable feed for livestock when mixed with other ingredients and thus represents a valuable by-product. Protein water is difficult to treat because of the high content of soluble organic water.

TREATMENT METHODS

Wastewater from fruit and vegetable processing plants contains mainly carbohydrates such as starches, sugars, pectin, as well as vitamins and other components of the cell wall. About 75 per cent of the total organic matter is soluble, therefore, it cannot be removed by mechanical or physical means. Thus, biological and chemical oxidations are the preferred means for wastewater treatment.

Waste Treatment Processes

An integrated waste treatment system usually consists of three phases: primary treatment, secondary treatment and advanced treatment. Primary treatment involves the removal of suspended and settleable solids by screening, flotation and sedimentation. Secondary treatment involves the biological decomposition of the organic matter, largely dissolved, that remains in the flow stream after treatment by primary processes. Biological treatment can be accomplished by mechanical processes or by natural processes.

The flow from the biological units is then passed through secondary sedimentation units so that the biological solids formed in the oxidation unit may be removed prior to the final discharge of the treated effluent to a stream. When irrigation is used as the secondary treatment system, bacteria in the topsoil stabilise the organic compounds. In addition, the soil may accomplish removal of some ions by adsorption or ion exchange, although ion exchange in some soils may fail. In all cases, great importance should be given to the steps that contribute to reducing the waste load in the plant itself. As for the industrial wastewaters, most of them require equalisation (buffering) and neutralisation prior to biological treatment, according to the characteristics of the resultant effluents.

Currently the most commonly used treatment methods, depend on screening, primary treatment and settling of silt water in earthen ponds before discharging to municipal sewers or separate secondary treatment systems. Many countries that have potato processing industries have determined current national minimum discharge limits following secondary treatment or in-land disposal.

To meet national effluent limits or standards, advanced waste treatment is needed in many cases to remove pollutants that are not removed by conventional secondary treatment. Advanced treatment can include removal of nutrients, suspended solids and organic and inorganic materials.

In-plant treatment

Minimising waste disposal problems requires reduction of solids discharged into the waste stream and reduction of water used in processing and clean-up. To reduce the solids carried to waste streams, the following steps should be undertaken:

1. Improvement of peeling operation to produce cleaner potatoes with less solids loss.
2. Reduction of floor spillage.
3. Collection of floor waste in receptacles instead of washing them down the drains.
4. Removal of potato solids in wastewater to prevent solubilisation of solids.

Waste volume can be reduced by reusing process water, with several advantages. First, the size of wastewater treatment facilities can be decreased accordingly. Secondly, with improvement of peeling operation to produce cleaner potatoes with less solids loss, reduction of floor spillage, concentration of the waste, the efficiency of a primary settling tank is increased. In the final processing stages, chlorinated water should be utilised to prevent bacterial contamination of the product. Other steps to reduce wastewater volume include alternate conveying methods of transporting potatoes other than water fluming, improved cleaning facilities for equipment and floors (high-pressure nozzles, shut-off nozzles for hoses), collecting clean waste streams and discharge to natural drainage or storm water systems.

Primary treatment

Sedimentation: Sedimentation is employed for the removal of suspended solids from wastewater. After screening, wastewater still carries light organic suspended solids, some of which can be removed from the wastewater by gravity in sedimentation tanks called clarifiers. These tanks/clarifiers can be round or rectangular, are usually about 3.5 m deep and hold the wastewater for periods of 2 to 3 hr. The required geometry, inlet conditions and outlet conditions for successful operation of such units are already known. The mass of settled solids is called raw sludge, which is removed from the clarifiers by mechanical scrapers and pumps. Floating materials such as oil and grease rise to the surface of the clarifier, where they are collected by a surface skimming system and removed from the tank for further processing.

Flotation: Flotation is another method used for the removal of suspended solids and oil and grease from wastewater. The pre-treated waste flow is pressurised to 50–70 lb/in^2 (345–483 kPa or 3.4–4.8 atm) in the presence of sufficient air to approach saturation. When this pressurised air-liquid mixture is released to atmospheric pressure in the flotation unit, minute air bubbles are released from the solution. The suspended solids or oil globules are floated by these minute air bubbles, which become enmeshed in the floc particles. The air-solids mixture rises to the surface, where it is skimmed off by mechanical collectors. The clarified liquid is removed from the bottom of the flotation unit. A portion of the effluent may be recycled back to the pressure chamber.

The performance of a flotation system depends upon having sufficient air bubbles present to float substantially all of the suspended solids. This performance in terms of effluent quality and solids concentration in the float, is related to an air/solids ratio that is usually defined as mass of air released per mass of solids in the influent waste. Pressure, recycle ratio, feed solid concentration and retention period are the basic variables for flotation design. The effluent's suspended solids decrease and the concentration of solids in the float increase with increasing retention period. When the flotation process is used for primary clarification, a detention period of 20–30 minute is adequate for separation and concentration. Rise velocity rates of 1.5–4.0 gal/(min/ft^2) [0.061–0.163 m^3/(min/m^2)] are commonly applied.

Major components of a flotation system include a pressurising pump, air-injection facilities, a retention tank, a backpressure regulating device and a flotation unit. The pressurising pump creates an elevated pressure to increase the solubility of air. Air is usually added through an injector on the suction side of the pump or directly to the retention tank. The air and liquid are mixed under pressure in a retention tank with a detention time of 1 to 3 minute. A backpressure regulating device maintains a constant head on the pressurising pump.

Equalisation

Equalisation is aimed at minimising or controlling fluctuations in wastewater characteristics for the purpose of providing optimum conditions for subsequent treatment processes. The size and type of the equalisation basin/tank used varies with the quantity of waste and the variability of the wastewater stream. In the case of potato processing wastewater, the mechanically pre-treated or preclarified wastewater flows into a balancing tank (buffer tank). Equalisation serves two purposes: physical homogenisation (flow, temperature) and chemical homogenisation (pH, nutrients, organic matter, toxicant dilution). For proper homogenisation and insurance of adequate equalisation of the tank content, mixing is usually provided, such as turbine mixing, mechanical aeration and diffused air aeration. The most common method is to use submerged mixers.

Neutralisation

Industrial wastewaters that contain acidic or alkaline materials should be subjected to neutralisation prior to biological treatment or prior to discharge to receiving wastes. For biological treatment, a pH in the biological system should be maintained between 6.5 and 8.5 to ensure optimum biological activity. The biological process itself provides neutralization and a buffer capacity as a result of the production of CO_2, which reacts with caustic and acidic materials. Therefore, the degree of the required preneutralisation depends on the ratio of BOD removed and the causticity or acidity present in the waste.

As for potato processing wastewater in general, the water from the balancing tank (buffer tank) is pumped into a conditioning tank where the pH and temperature of the wastewater are controlled or corrected. Continuous monitoring of the pH of the influent is required by dosing a caustic or acidic reagent, according to the nature of resulting wastewater. The required caustic or acidic reagent for dosing in the neutralisation process is strongly related to the different peeling methods used in the potato processing plant, since peeling of potatoes forms the major portion of the organic load in potato processing waste. Three different peeling methods are used extensively today: abrasion peeling, steam peeling and lye peeling. Between lye and steam peeling wastes, the biggest difference is the pH of the two wastes. While steam peeling wastes are usually almost neutral (pH values vary between 5.3 and 7.1), lye peeling wastes have pH values from 11 to 12 and higher.

Secondary treatment

Secondary treatment is the biological degradation of soluble organic compounds from input levels of 50–1000 mg/l BOD or more to effluent levels typically under 15–20 mg/l. In all cases, the secondary treatment units must provide an environment suitable for the growth of biological organisms that carry out waste treatment. This is usually done aerobically, in an open aerated tank or lagoon. Also, wastewaters may be pre-treated anaerobically, in a pond or a closed tank. After biotreatment, the micro-organisms and other carried-over solids are allowed to settle. A fraction of this sludge is recycled in certain processes. However, the excess sludge, along with the sedimented solids, must be disposed of after treatment. As for potato waste, among the different known aerobic processes for secondary treatment of wastewater, we concentrate here on the most common treatment processes for potato processing wastewater.

Chapter 11

Residual Management in Fruit Processing Plants

INTRODUCTION

Residuals are a necessary consequence of processing agricultural raw materials. These residuals, dumped at local landfills and discharged to natural streams, have now become a major environmental concern. Environmental protection standards are becoming more stringent, causing disposal costs to escalate. Meeting these challenges of environmental protection and economic competitiveness requires a fresh look at the management of fruit processing residuals. Fruit processing waste is extremely diverse due to the wide variety of fruits, the broad range of processes and the multiplicity of products that characterise the industry. Residual management in the fruit processing industry reflects this diversity, however, basic principles involved in assessment, characterisation and categorisation of residuals and in management strategies can be applied across the industry.

Fruits are processed for marketing as fresh produce, in refrigerated, frozen, dehydrated, canned and pureed forms, as juices, jams and jellies and more. The unit operations involved in these processes include washing, sorting, trimming, stemming, peeling, coring, pitting, halving, slicing, dicing, pressing, cooking, blending, blanching, canning, sterilising, retorting, cooling, refrigerating, freezing, thawing, pulping, finishing, concentrating, bleaching, curing, brining, drying and so on.

ENVIRONMENTAL IMPACT

Fruit processing plants are major water users and residue generators. Water use and residual generation in fruit processing are extremely variable because they are affected by numerous factors. These factors include raw commodity and processed products, plant size and age, processing rate and plant capacity utilisation, raw material quality and preparation equipment, water reuse frequency and housekeeping practices. The wastewater parameters that are of major pollutional significance are biochemical oxygen demand (BOD), total suspended solids (TSS), oils and grease (O&G) and pH. Other parameters that are of occasional importance are temperature, nitrogen, phosphorus, chemical oxygen demand (COD) and total dissolved solids (TOS).

Some of these parameters are defined below:

1. Biochemical oxygen demand (BOD): The quantity of oxygen used in the biochemical oxidation of organic matter in a specified time under specified conditions, usually specified as milligrams of oxygen used per liter of effluent at 20°C in a 5-day period.
2. Chemical oxygen demand (COD): The quantity of oxygen used in the chemical oxidation of organic and inorganic matter, invariably higher than BOD.
3. Total suspended solids (TSS): Organic and inorganic particles that exist in suspension in the effluent, can be partially separated by gravity settling and completely separated by filtration.
4. Total dissolved solids (TDS): Organic and inorganic matter that is dissolved in the effluent, cannot be separated by filtration.

A major portion of fruit processing plant residuals can be used for different purposes because of their nontoxic nature. The residual hierarchy concept is an excellent approach that emphasises the uses of food processing residuals.

Reduction of both material losses and waste generation is the most effective residual management strategy and is at the top of the residual hierarchy. Product recovery for human uses, by product recovery for animal feed, land application as fertiliser, landfill disposal and disposal at hazardous waste facilities are the levels that follow down the hierarchy. Higher levels in this hierarchy result in greater benefits. At lower levels, costs and liabilities of residual management are higher, therefore, greater emphasis should be laid on employing management strategies at higher levels of the hierarchy.

REDUCTION OF WASTE AT SOURCE

Reduction of waste at the source is the most effective form of residual management because it results in a reduction in raw materials input or an increase in product output: however, source reduction and water conservation require a thorough knowledge of product, residue and water flow in the plant, in contrast to 'end of the pipe' waste management.

The first step in this direction is to conduct an overview of the plant flow that identifies the major systems in the plant where residuals are generated. This is followed by a more detailed survey, during which residuals and water flows are measured and sampled in the identified systems.

The next step is to quantify the solid residues and process water flows. Solid residues are relatively easy to quantify. Weighing and counting residue containers is the most frequently used method. Sometimes, volumetric measurements are more convenient. The determination of density and moisture content of solid materials is important to convert all measurements to a common basis such as 'weight of dry matter per day'.

Water flows are somewhat more difficult to measure. Most food plants have flowmeters permanently installed on the main inlet. Some plants have flow meters on several major distribution lines. Propeller-type flowmeters with counters have been the most common type. Magnetic flowmeters are finding increasing use in remote readout and automatic flow control situations. Frequently, the main outlet from the plant is a drain. Flumes and weirs are permanent features of outlet drains.

Evaluation of water conservation strategy requires placing more emphasis on process water flows in individual unit operations. Installation of permanent water flowmeters is not practical in these situations. Simpler methods such as container and timer for flows out of open-ended spouts and float and timer for open drains are the most widely used under these conditions. The portable ultrasonic flowmeter is a versatile method for measurement of flow in pipes. This nonintrusive technique is fast and reasonably accurate. Characterisation of process water requires adequate sampling and numerous analytical tests. Grab samples taken several times a day and composite samples consisting of measured portions collected at regular intervals are the most common sampling methods. Representative sampling is extremely important irrespective of the sampling method used. Sample analysis is done to obtain characteristics required to evaluate water conservation strategies. When reuse of water in another operation is the objective, some characteristics of interest are: temperature, pH, acidity, alkalinity, residual chlorine, dissolved solids and suspended solids. When product or by-product recovery is the objective, it is important to conduct compositional analysis of the process water streams.

WATER CONSERVATION

Water is the most convenient transfer medium in a food processing plant. It functions as a momentum transport medium in cleaning and in hydraulic conveying applications. In blanching, retorting and cooling operations, water acts as a heat transfer medium. In sanitising and brining operations, it is used as a mass transfer medium. In some operations such as cooking and peeling, it serves as a momentum, heat and mass transfer medium. The nature and degree of contamination and regulatory constraints on reuse of water in food contact applications govern the water conservation prospects in these operations.

The general principles that govern water use in food contact applications are that it be free of micro-organisms, toxic chemicals, discolouration and off-flavours that make it harmful to public health or adversely affect the quality of the processed food. Good Manufacturing Practice guidelines state, 'Water used for washing, rinsing or conveying of food products shall be safe and of adequate sanitary quality. Water may be reused for washing, rinsing, or conveying of food if it does not increase the level of contamination of food'. The industrywide practice is to use potable water for the final rinse, while reusing water after some degree of treatment in the upstream washing operations.

Water Quality Preservation

Water conservation frequently involves the reuse of process water in either the same or another operation. Process water accumulates solids during use. Reuse of water involves treatments to remove accumulated solids. Gravity settling is used to remove particles that are significantly heavier than water. Screening is used to separate large particles. Both these methods remove solids that are suspended in water.

Buildup of dissolved solids in process water is more difficult to control. Dissolved solids can be inorganic matter such as salts, acids and alkali or organic matter such as sugars and organic acids. Inorganic matter buildup affects mass transfer, hindering cleaning and washing operations. Organic matter buildup in process water leads to microbial growth, in addition to affecting mass transfer.

Batch recirculation with periodic renewal is the simplest method of achieving dissolved solids control. Batch renewal intervals as low as 2 hr have been observed in raisin washing, where dirt accumulation is very high. When the operation involves relatively little contamination, as in hydraulic transport of frozen cranberries using hot water, a batch time of 24 hr has been observed.

Semicontinuous systems that allow for overflow of recirculating water balanced by the introduction of fresh water is another approach used to control dissolved solids buildup. When the buildup is through ordinary diffusion driven by a concentration difference, the buildup itself serves as a self-limiting mechanism, however, overflow/makeup systems also need complete renewal at intervals due to other quality concerns. The microbial buildup is kept under control through the use of sanitising agents. Gaseous chlorine is the most commonly used sanitiser due to its ease of application and low cost, however, its use requires evacuation plans to be in place for emergencies. Chlorine derivatives, such as sodium hypochlorite and calcium hypochlorite, overcome the need for evacuation plans but are costlier than gaseous chlorine. Chlorine dioxide is another sanitiser that is increasingly used in food processing plants. It is a greenish-orange-coloured gas, generated at the site using sodium chlorate as the raw material. Chlorine dioxide has a stronger residual action and is effective in lower concentrations and over a wider pH range than chlorine, however, it has been approved only for use with uncut produce at present. Cut and peeled potatoes are exempted from this limitation.

Safety concerns arising due to by-products of chlorination have created a need for alternative methods of microbial control. Ozonation is one avenue that is being actively evaluated. Ozone is an extremely powerful oxidiser and has been used in drinking water treatment since the turn of the century in Europe and Africa. More recently, it has been introduced for sanitation of noncontact cooling water in cooling tower systems.

Inorganic matter and organic matter in process water act as initiators, promoters and inhibitors of ozonation reactions in water, therefore, the effectiveness of ozone in process water treatment is significantly lower compared to drinking water treatment. Ozonation of water in hydrocooling systems in cherry packing houses, which has been reported recently, is a direct food contact application. This development could lead to a wider application of this technology subject to regulatory concurrence.

Membrane Technology

Dissolved solids comprised of organic and inorganic matter of low molecular weight cannot be removed by simple methods such as gravity settling or screening. High-pressure membrane filtration is an alternative method that can remove dissolved solids from water under most conditions. This technology has found several applications in industrial water conservation. Cross flow membrane filtration is used to separate particles ranging in size from about 5 μm down to about 5 Å. The membrane filtration spectrum is divided into four narrower ranges based on the particle size.

Microfiltration separates large suspended particles that are typically over 0.1 μm in diameter. The permeate recovered from microfiltration is clear and sterile under most conditions. Recovery of spent caustic from evaporator cleaning operations at a orange juice plant has been reported by Smith. Microfiltration can be used to maintain sanitary conditions in recirculating water streams, but this is found to be uneconomical under present conditions.

Reverse osmosis separates small dissolved molecules such as salts, sugar and organic acids. It can be used to produce soft water for boiler feed and for other cleaning applications in food processing plants. Polishing of evaporator condensate by reverse osmosis has been reported recently. Reverse osmosis can be used to separate salts from brining, curing and grading operations, when disposal of salts is a concern. These applications are rarely economical from a water and salt recovery perspective under present conditions. Nanofiltration is a recently introduced term to identify the filtration range that separates sugars from water. These membranes operate at a lower pressure and produce higher permeate fluxes than does reverse osmosis and hence, are more cost-effective. Therefore, nanofiltration systems can separate dissolved sugars from process water streams and enable reuse of water and recovery or alternative disposal of sugar concentrates.

Other Separation Technologies

Electrodialysis is a well-established membrane process where a series of anion and cation exchange membranes are placed between two electrodes to selectively transport ions in an aqueous salt solution. A salt concentrate and salt-free water are the final products. This process is widely used in seawater desalination and desalting of whey. Conceptually, it is more advantageous to move the solute than the solvent through a membrane in the case of dilute solutions. This technology has the potential for water conservation and salt recovery applications in brining and curing and for grading process waters that contain salts. Bipolar electrodialysis uses two selectively bipolar membranes to separate a salt solution into a concentrated acid, a concentrated base and water. This process, presently being tested on bench scale, is an attractive means of recovering process water and chemicals from caustic peeling, caustic cleaning and acid cleaning applications.

Capacitive deionisation of water by a stack of carbon electrodes, where ions are electrostatically separated and held in electric double layers at the electrodes, has been demonstrated. This process is somewhat similar to ion exchange but has the advantage that regeneration is done electrically and not chemically. This technology also has application potential in salty process water.

Pervapouration is a membrane process where a solute is separated from a solution by permeation through a selectively permeable membrane and evaporation into an inert gas. It is used for separation of water from azeotropic mixtures of ethanol-water, isopropanol-water, etc., on a commercial scale. Recovery of low-molecular-weight organic aroma compounds from evaporator condensates in tomato, orange and other juice concentrators is possible and some have been tested,

Hydraulic Transport

Direct contact between food and water results in the transfer of food solids to water, which gradually increases the level of solids in recirculating water until equilibrium conditions are reached. Gravity settling and screening are commonly used to separate heavy and large particles, while makeup/overflow maintains dissolved solids at acceptable levels. Prolonged use of recirculating water gives rise to microbial growth and development of off-flavours. Sanitising chemicals such as chlorine and chlorine dioxide are used to control these effects.

Heating Operations

When water is used as a heat transfer medium, it gets thermally contaminated. In heating operations such as blanching and pasteurisation, hot water gets cooled. Spent water is heated by passing it through heat exchangers and recirculating it back, forming a closed circuit. In the case of blanching, water has to be periodically renewed or continuously diluted to maintain the quality of recirculating water.

Pasteuriders in fruit juice processing use hot water for pasteuriding the juice. This water can be reused indefinitely by recirculation through heat exchangers. Pasteuriders also use cooling water to cool already pasteurided juice when use of the downstream equipment is interrupted. Water use in this situation can be reduced by countercurrent juice-to-juice heat exchangers.

Direct Contact Cooling Operations

Freezing plants use chilled water to cool fruits prior to freezing them. This is done in belt coolers where a large flow of chilled water trickles on the moving product, or in a flume that transports as well as cools the fruit. The temperature of water increases due to heat removed from the product during the cooling process. Water is recirculated through the chiller to remove this heat and is reused repeatedly. Prolonged recirculation results in buildup of product solids and microbes in the water, which is kept under acceptable limits by limited makeup/overflow and by the use of sanitising chemicals. Public health and environmental concerns, as well as the rising cost of chemicals dictate a fresh look at these systems. The short contact time limits the temperature rise of water in the belt coolers. Reusing the cooling water after rechilling is economical under these conditions. A countercurrent cooler—where chilled water is reused several times is a better alternative from an overall water, energy and chemical management perspective. Cooling water leaves the countercurrent cooler well above room temperature, making it more economical to use fresh water in the chiller while the warm water is reused in washing processes upstream. Figure 11.1 illustrates the conventional cooling water system and the countercurrent system.

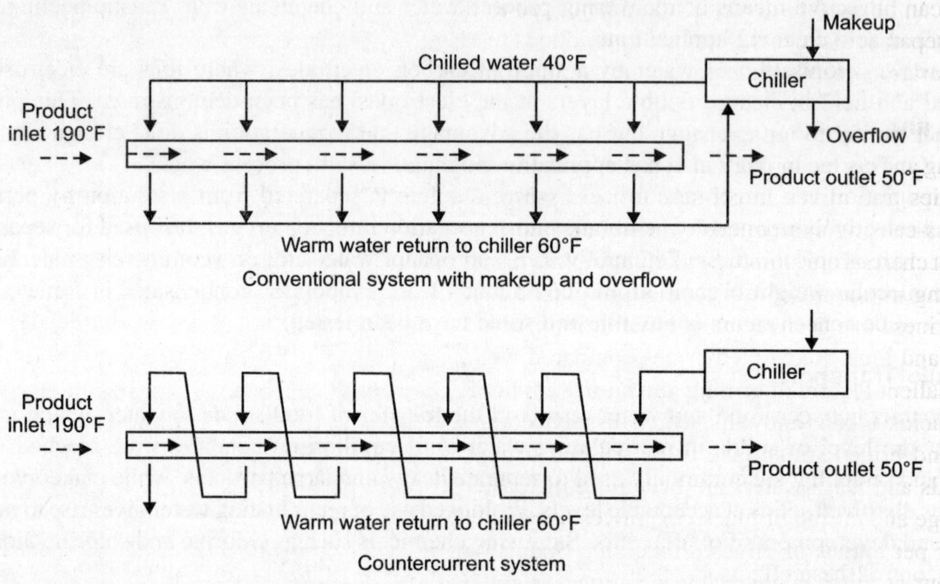

Fig. 11.1: Direct contact cooling systems: conventional and countercurrent.

Multiple use of water in one pass allows shorter residence time for the water in the system, which limits solids buildup and microbial growth, thus reducing or eliminating chemical use. The only disadvantage of the countercurrent cooler is that it requires a larger heat transfer area due to reduction in the effective temperature available for heat transfer. This is more than compensated for by optimising the design process and by other savings.

Indirect Contact Cooling Operations

Cooling of cans and bottles after retorting or aseptic filling requires large quantities of water. This water is relatively uncontaminated. The practice in many plants is to discharge the spent cooling water to natural waters under a noncontact cooling water discharge permit. Temperature is the only permit limit of concern in this situation. In locations where water is in plentiful supply, use of excess water easily overcomes this difficulty. When fresh water is in short supply, this practice is not possible. When the quality of water is poor, the addition of chemicals is required to improve its quality, which may preclude discharge of spent cooling water to natural streams. Cooling towers that enable reuse of cooling water is a solution under these conditions.

Evaporator Condensate

Fruit juice is concentrated in multiple effect evaporators. Steam from the last effect is condensed in a barometric leg rising from a wet well. This water absorbs the heat of the steam and the trace organic matter accompanying it. The temperature of water is maintained by the introduction of fresh makeup water. Overflow from the system is used for cleaning and for other applications that require moderate-quality water.

Evaporator condensate is not used in many plants due to the risk of contamination with the product through occasional tube failures or due to the presence of volatile organic compounds. Detection-rejection circuits can be used to divert contaminants due to tube failures, while reverse osmosis systems can be used to separate most of the volatile compounds to enable reuse of the condensate. Reverse osmosis and pervapouration enable the recovery of useful aroma compounds from the condensate.

Brining and Curing

In brining and curing of fruits, water serves as the mass transfer medium. Brining is used for preservation of cherries and olives in off-season processing. Curing of olives involves lye treatment to remove bitterness-causing compounds, while cherry curing involves removal of colour-causing chemicals.

Sweet cherries are stored in calcium sulphite brines to bleach, firm and preserve the fruit for subsequent processing into maraschino, candied, or glazed cherries. Disposal of spent brines is an acute problem. These brines have been reclaimed by filtration, activated carbon treatment and by the addition of sulphur dioxide and lime. Reclaimed brines compared well with fresh brines in brining trials.

The salient feature of brining and curing applications is the use of large amounts of chemicals. These include acids, alkalis and salts, which dissolve completely in water and have very low molecular weights. Cured and brined fruits have to be washed to remove chemicals. Disposal of storage brines, curing chemicals and wash waters are becoming increasingly troublesome due to environmental concerns.

Storage and curing of black ripe olives use about 200 lb of chemicals (dry basis) and about 5000 gal of water per tonnes of olives. Processing Spanish olives requires a smaller quantity of chemicals and water, but at much higher concentrations. Black ripe olive storage brine and curing lye have been successfully treated by activated carbon treatment and reused on a pilot scale. Spent Spanish olive storage brines are clarified by microfiltration and used for packing cured olives at a commercial level but on a small scale.

Peeling Operations

Peeling of fruits is done by the use of hot caustic (for peaches, apricots, pears and apples) or by mechanical means (for pears, pineapples, apples and oranges). Caustic peeling is a leading source of wastewater in peach canning operations. Dry caustic peeling was introduced for peaches following its success with potatoes. The process involved hot caustic application, followed by removal of loosened peel by the mechanical rubbing action of rubber rollers.

Dry caustic peeling of peaches was done successfully on a commercial scale. The peeling effectiveness and peeling losses were similar to those for wet caustic peeling, while water use was drastically reduced, however, this method has become obsolete due to problems in disposal of dry peels and the benefits of caustic peeling wash water in balancing acidity of fruit processing effluents.

BY-PRODUCT RECOVERY FOR HUMAN CONSUMPTION

By-products recovered for human consumption yield a high return to the producer, therefore they are placed at a high level in the residual management hierarchy. Investigation of alternative residual recovery strategies should begin at this level, however, it should be recognised that this category faces the highest regulatory scrutiny due to health and safety concerns.

Handling and preservation of residues need special care when recovery for human consumption is intended. Often, it becomes necessary to separate the residuals and process water streams at the point source. Cleaning chemicals and low-grade residuals are common sources of contamination. Blending of a product containing a substance in excess of an action level with another product is not permitted, regardless of the level of the contaminant in the final mix. The action levels are revised by the FDA at intervals. Pesticide residues are a common source of most of the action level substances. Peels may contain a high concentration of pesticide residues, hence, peel recovery schemes should pay special attention to this concern.

Dietary Fiber and Pectins From Pomace

Dietary fiber extracted from apple and pear pomace is marketed by several producers. The extraction process involves mechanical filtration, dehydration of filtered solids and screening. The marketed apple product contains 56 per cent fiber and the pear product contains 77 per cent fiber. The products have the consistency of wheat flour and a bland taste. They are used in breads, baked foods, cereals, granola products, laxatives, pharmaceuticals and pet foods.

Fiber extraction from apple pomace by solvents has been done on a laboratory scale. This process involved drying, grinding, sieving and extraction with sodium hydroxide or other aqueous solvents.

Pectin can be extracted from apple pomace, citrus peel and several other pulpy fruit wastes. It is used as a gelling agent in jams and fruit preserves. Apple pectin has superior gelling properties compared to citrus pectin. The process involves shredding the raw material, extraction with hot water, concentration by evaporation, precipitation by organic solvents (ethanol or hexane) and drying.

Grape Sugar From Grape and Raisin Residues

Manufacture of brandy and alcohol for wine fortification must be done with grape sugars because of regulatory requirements. This makes the recovery of sugars from grape and raisin processing waste a profitable exercise. Rejects from grape processing plants are routinely used as raw material in the manufacture of alcoholic beverages.

Wash water from raisin packaging plants also contain grape sugars. Recovery of sugar from this water by clarification and concentration through membrane systems for fermentation. This can be done by installing a tubular reverse osmosis system to process about 70000 gal/day of raisin washwater and the plant can reduce its sewer bill and create a new source of income.

Fruit Juice and Syrup Recovery from Fruit Process Water

Peels and cores from apple and pear processing plants are used in fruit juice manufacture. Pectinase enzymes are used to facilitate juice recovery by depectinisation. This juice is frequently used as a filler in cans in place of syrup. Pomace left after extraction of cranberry juice is used in the manufacture of cranberry sauce. It is possible to recover fruit juice from peach pitter water by clarification and concentration using membrane systems. The recovered juice can be used as a filler in peach cans.

Orange peels are sliced and blanched in the marmalade process. Blanching water contains sugar and other orange solids including bitterness-causing compounds. Recovery of orange juice from this water requires debittering. The process involves concentration and clarification using membranes and debittering using ion exchange process. Dyeing of maraschino cherries is done using a solution of dye and sugar. The water used to wash the dyed cherries contains residual dye and from about 2 to 3 per cent sugar. This water is concentrated using reverse osmosis and both sugar and dye are recovered. The payback on this membrane system was reported to be only 4 months.

Candid Fruit Peels and Reformed Fruit Pieces

Candied citrus fruit (orange, lemon, grapefruit) peels can be used in baked goods or as snack food. The candying process involves slicing the peels, boiling them in 20 per cent sugar syrup, gradually increasing the sugar concentration lip to between 65 and 70 per cent over 4 to 5 days, then rinsing and drying. The marmalade process for orange peels is similar to candying with the omission of drying.

Pulp extracted from sound fruit processing residue can be reformed into artificial fruit pieces. The process involves concentrating the pulp, adding sugar and the gelling agent sodium alginate and mixing with calcium chloride to solidify the structure.

Oils From Seeds and Stones

Seeds of some fruits have significant quantities of oils that may have specialised markets. These include grape, papaya, passion fruit, mango, apricot and peach. The process involves drying, grinding and pressing or solvent extraction. Mango oil is considered to have a fatty acid profile very similar to cocoa butter. Grape seed oil has been proposed as an alternative to olive oil.

Functional Food Compounds

Fruit processing residuals are a promising source of functional food compounds that have favourable nutritional properties. The beneficial compounds include carotenoids, polyphenolics, tocopherols and ascorbic acid. Dietary supplements and food fortification are possible ways to incorporate these compounds into diets.

Apple and grape pomace are good sources of polyphenolics that are localised mostly in the peels and extracted partially into juice. Grape seeds are also a rich source of polyphenols. Drying pomace at high temperatures reduces the extractable polyphenols and also affects the antioxidant activity. Extraction by organic solvents has been reported. Enzyme treatment enhances release of phenolic compounds. Peels and seeds of citrus and mangos also have high antioxidant activity.

BY-PRODUCT RECOVERY FOR ANIMAL FEED

Solid waste from fruit processing plants is a valuable feed source for the animal farms in the area. Some of these by-products have good nutritional value, while others are only of limited value. By-product feeds are classified as concentrates and roughages based on energy and fiber contents, while concentrates are subdivided further into energy feeds and protein feeds. The nutrient content of some fruit processing by-products used in animal feeds. The composition is based on a dry matter basis while the dry matter content on an 'as fed' basis is also listed.

Ruminant animals are capable of fermenting fibrous materials such as cellulose to metabolic compounds. This ability makes it possible for a ruminant to utilise fibrous by-products that are of little value to humans. The ruminant converts this waste material into milk and meat, which are valuable human foods. The most important by-product of the fruit industry is the presscake left over in fruit juice plants by apple, citrus, pineapple, grape and cranberry juice processes, for example. Peels, cores and process rejects also contribute to animal feed. Cull fruits and surplus from the fields are also used in animal feed.

Pomace is the presscake left after the extraction of juice from apples, grapes, cranberries and so forth. It is used as animal feed: fresh, dried or ensiled. Most juice extraction processes use rice hulls—as an aid in a squeezing operation—that end up in the pomace as a contaminant. Rice hulls have very little nutritional value and hence reduce the feeding value of the pomace. Pesticide contamination has been a concern when feeding the pomace to animals. More stringent control of pesticide application has helped alleviate this concern. Apple pomace is a medium-energy, low-protein, very palatable feed. It has been used—with proper supplementation—up to about 33 per cent in dairy cattle concentrates and from 15 to 20 per cent in complete feed lot rations. Grape pomace consists mainly of seeds, stems and skins. It is very low in energy and protein. In concentrates, it serves only as a filler.

Citrus pulp has both energy and digestible fiber and, hence, is of value as a concentrate and as roughage. It has to be introduced gradually into a ration to get cattle accustomed to its distinct taste and smell. Once cattle get accustomed, up to 40 per cent in concentrate and from 15 to 20 per cent in the total ration are acceptable. Citrus pulp is usually fed in the dried form but can also be used in fresh or ensiled form. Feeding level of fresh pulp is about 25 to 30 lb per cow per day. Transportation costs make it uneconomical for use in farms far from processing plants. Sludge from activated sludge treatment of concentrated citrus waste has been further processed and successfully used as an ingredient in poultry feed. The sludge can be thickened by gravity settling, dewatered by centrifuging and dried in a kiln. The dried sludge contained 38.6 per cent crude protein and high levels of crude fiber, calcium and phosphorus. The dried sludge was incorporated up to a 7.5 per cent level in poultry feed without any detrimental effects on meat or egg quality.

Pineapple bran consists of the outer shell of the fruit and other waste from the pineapple canning operation. It has a high fiber level, but the digestibility of the fiber is relatively low. It is fed up to 15 lb per cow per day in Hawaii during the season. Pineapple juice presscake is the high moisture residue from the juice pressing process. It has been fed fresh up to 30 lb per cow per day in Hawaii. Pineapple presscake is a high-acid product, hence, animals should become accustomed to it gradually. Due to its high acidity, it does not undergo a normal fermentation process during ensiling, however, it keeps well, for up to 2 weeks when held in stacks. Addition of non-protein nitrogen increases the value of low-quality roughages. Urea is the most widely used nitrogen source, while ammonia is the most economical. Ammoniation of citrus pulp increases the protein level, prevents spoilage, inhibits energy losses due to respiration and increases digestibility.

RECOVERY OF ENERGY

The extent and methods of energy recovery from food residuals depend on its moisture content. Solid residuals such as peach pits and olive pits are burned directly in boiler furnaces or converted to charcoal briquettes. Wet residues and process water containing fruit sugars are potential raw materials for ethanol fermentation and methane production.

Ethanol From Wet Residues

Fruit processing residues, including sorting rejects and liquid waste, contain sugars that can be converted to ethanol through fermentation. Ethanol is a very versatile source of energy because it can be used as a transportation fuel, however, its production is an expensive process involving fermentation and distillation. The economics of ethanol production can compete with other waste handling alternatives only in a few situations. In many instances, residuals with high potential are already being used in ethanol production or have been evaluated and found uneconomical. Apple pomace fermentation was found to be uneconomical due to the high cost of the enzyme. Another study concluded that grape pomace fermentation for ethanol production was not economical even when cellulose was converted. Apple, cantaloupe, grape, honeydew, orange, peach, pear and plum culls were fermented and the resulting beers were distilled on a laboratory scale to obtain alcohol yields ranging from 12.5 to 82.4 l/T. The resulting stillages were then digested anaerobically to produce methane. In most cases, the heat content of the methane (estimated at 22.5 MJ/m^3) was adequate to provide the energy for distillation (estimated at 10 MJ/l). Ethanol has a heating value of 22.3 MJ/l. Based on these values, the combined process has a net energy surplus.

Alcohol is sold for blending with gasoline in the production of unleaded high octane gasoline. Other by-products include dry brewers yeast for pet foods and liquid protein supplement for animal feed.

Liquid waste from fruit processing plants contains significant quantities of sugars but in a very dilute form. Using membrane systems to concentrate the process waters in recovering reusable permeate and as a concentrate in ethanol fermentation has added benefits. These include savings in water supply costs, wastewater disposal costs and BOD disposal costs, however, the volume of concentrate available at individual plants is not adequate to justify fermentation/distillation operations. The feasibility of collecting the concentrate at a centrally located plant for ethanol production is presently being evaluated.

Methane Gas from Solid Residues

Wet fruit processing residues can be digested anaerobically to produce methane gas, which can be used as a boiler fuel. A laboratory-scale study to digest tomato, peach and honeydew solids was reported by Hills and Roberts. Carbon:Nitrogen:Phosphorus ratio was satisfactory for tomato and honeydew residues, but peach residue was deficient in nitrogen. Under standard conditions, about 0.31 m^3 of methane gas with a heating value of 7.0 MJ was obtained per kg of COD digested.

Anaerobic digestion is more often used with the primary objective of wastewater treatment, energy extraction being a secondary benefit. Different digester designs used for anaerobic treatment include anaerobic lagoons, anaerobic contact reactors, anaerobic filters, upflow anaerobic sludge blankets, anaerobic fluidised beds and hybrids. Anaerobic fermentation of liquid waste is more efficient at high-organic-matter concentrations. Therefore, it could be used to digest the concentrate stream from a membrane system recovering process water for reuse.

Catalytic Gasification of Wet Residues

Food processing liquid waste has been gasified using a nickel metal as a catalyst. The process, carried out on a laboratory scale at 360°C and 3000 psi, converts 99 per cent of the COD in a 10 per cent lactose solution during a residence time of less than 5 minutes. The product of the process is a fuel gas containing methane, carbon monoxide and hydrogen, which can be burned in a furnace. Like anaerobic fermentation, this process is also better suited for high-strength waste, hence, it will fit in well with process water recovery systems using membranes. This process is presently being tested on a pilot scale.

Olive and Peach Pits as a Boiler Fuel

Olive pits were burned in fluidised bed burners to produce steam at Lindsay Olive Growers. Olive pits contained 50 per cent moisture and provided 25 per cent of the steam energy requirements of the plant. Crushed peach pits are fired with 20 per cent supplementary conventional fuel in a boiler. Scrubbers and other air pollution control equipment are used to maintain air quality standard. Several biomass-fueled cogeneration plants were begun as a result of the Public Utilities Regulatory Policies Act, which required public utilities to purchase power from qualifying facilities at the avoided cost. Changing economic conditions have forced many of these facilities out of operation in recent years.

Charcoal Briquettes from Peach, Apricot and Olive Pits

Peach, apricot and olive pits are converted to charcoal briquettes by using fruit pits and nut shells to generate high-quality charcoal briquettes.

The process involves controlled burning under low oxygen conditions in a series of four hearths. The charred product is quenched by water as it is discharged, ground, screened, mixed with 5 per cent starch binder and formed into briquettes. Flue gasses are preheated with natural gas and burned completely.

LAND APPLICATION AS FERTILISERS AND SOIL CONDITIONS

Fertilisers supply growing plants with essential nutrients, while soil conditioners produce physical and chemical changes that enhance plant growth. Food process residues can serve as fertilisers and soil conditioners when used in well-designed and properly managed land application systems.

The BOD loading rates vary among soil types from about 30 to about 100 lb/acre/d. When BOD loading is too high, the soil becomes anaerobic and odours arise. Calcium carbonate equivalent is a measure of the liming characteristics of soil conditioners. Carbon-nitrogen ratio is an indicator of inorganic nitrogen availability from organic matter. Nitrogen, phosphorus and potassium are essential nutrients for plant growth. Soluble salts primarily include calcium, magnesium, sodium, potassium, chlorides, sulphates, bicarbonates and nitrates.

Electrical conductivity (EC) of process water is a good indicator of the total amount of soluble salts. TDS in mg/l is estimated by multiplying the EC reading in milliSiemens by 700. Excessive salt content increases the osmotic pressure, which makes it difficult for roots to extract water and reduces plant growth. High levels of sodium ions compared to calcium and magnesium ions alter the soil structure and reduce soil permeability.

In addition to these effects, certain specific ions can have toxic effects on plants. Land application of food processing residuals in solid or liquid form requires a nutrient management programme designed to suit the fields. This programme should consider the field fertility, nutrient requirements of the planted crop and nutrient application history to sustain the quality of the soil.

WASTEWATER TREATMENT

Natural water streams possess the ability to purify themselves. Water becomes aerated as it flows and dissolved oxygen enables it to sustain a variety of micro-organisms. These micro-organisms are primarily responsible for the stream's self-purification ability. Food process effluent is harmless compared to effluents from other major industries, but it is rich in organic matter. This organic matter creates an additional demand for dissolved oxygen that can far exceed the aeration capacity of the stream.

The suspended matter in food process effluent, if discharged to natural streams, increases the turbidity of water, which reduces sunlight's ability to penetrate into water. Light suspended matter forms scum on the water surface and heavy suspended matter settles to the bottom as sludge. Creation of foul odours, colour and attraction of insects are secondary effects of suspended matter. For these reasons, food process wastewater treatment involves removal of dissolved and suspended solids.

Pretreatment and Primary Treatment

Pretreatment and primary treatment are intended for physical separation of solids from water, usually through size and density difference. They also remove BOD associated with the separated solids. The bulk of the BOD in fruit processing plants is associated with dissolved organic matter, which is not removed in primary treatment.

Grit chambers with grids and coarse screens are used to separate twigs, bottle caps and other large objects. This is followed by separators with finer screens. Static tangential screens without moving parts are fast, trouble-free devices that work well with fibrous waste. Vibratory and rotary screens are used where separation of finer solids is desired. These devices typically have openings down to about 100 μm. Wedge wire filters and centrifugal screens are also used in this particle range. These devices are capable of accommodating screens down to a few microns in opening size, but in this range, the throughput becomes low and frequent plugging becomes a problem.

Density separation is effective in removing heavier and lighter particles from water. The gravity sedimentation tank is the most elementary density separator and also the most widely used one. The settling rate of particles in water depends mainly on their diameter and density. More effective density separation requires an increase in particle size, a change in density, or an increase in gravity.

Decanter centrifuges and basket centrifuges generate separation effects equivalent to up to 30000 gram (acceleration due to gravitational force). These are used frequently in sludge thickening but rarely in pretreatment. Hydrocyclones operate at a much lower range, typically about 1000 gram but are more popular in pretreatment applications. Hydrocyclones have a definite advantage over centrifuges in not having high-speed moving parts. Both centrifuges and hydrocyclones are used as classifiers, where both denser and lighter fractions are separated from water.

Coagulation and flocculation are used to remove colloidal particles that are larger than dissolved molecules but smaller than settleable particles. Colloidal particles are held in emulsion by electrostatic forces. Flocculation and coagulation involve destabilising the emulsion by the introduction of coagulating agents. A variety of multivalent inorganic compounds, polyelectrolytes and natural materials are used for this purpose. In electrocoagulation, polyvalent metallic ions are introduced directly into water by gradual decomposition of a metallic electrode through electrolysis.

Flotation is density separation in which contaminants lighter than water are allowed to rise to the surface and are removed as a scum layer. Unaided flotation is strongly rate-limited. Increasing gravity through centrifugation and cycloning is one method of aiding flotation action. Increasing buoyancy by introduction of fine air bubbles is another approach.

Dissolved air flotation (DAF) involves attachment of fine air bubbles to suspended matter to increase buoyancy. Air bubbles are provided by dissolving air in a smaller volume of water at high pressure and releasing the pressurised water in a larger tank. The sudden lowering of pressure forces the dissolved air to come out of solution as fine bubbles. This technology finds applications in water with suspended oily waste such as olive waste.

Coagulation and flocculation are used frequently to further aid dissolved air flotation. A disadvantage of the use of coagulants in food plant wastewater is that several chemicals used for this purpose prevent the separated solids from being used as animal feed. Electroflotation is a related technology where air bubbles are produced by electrolysis of water, it has not found much applicability.

Stabilisation is an essential pretreatment when some effluent characteristics such as temperature and pH vary widely over time. Wastewater is allowed to accumulate in large stabilisation tanks, which evens out the temporal fluctuations. Sometimes, this is not adequate to rectify the situation. Adjustment of pH by addition of acids or alkali is required under these conditions.

Secondary Treatment

Secondary treatment of food process wastewater involves biochemical reactions to decompose dissolved organic matter. This is done by aerobic treatment in the presence of oxygen or by anaerobic treatment in the absence of oxygen.

Aerobic treatment systems vary in sophistication from simple lagoons to high-rate activated sludge plants. Shallow ponds are the simplest aerobic treatment systems, but their BOD removal capacity is limited. A typical loading rate is 20 to 40 lb of BOD per acre per day. Addition of supplementary aeration enables ponds to be more efficient in BOD removal. Aerated lagoons are about 12 ft deep with typical loading rates of 600 to 800 lb of BOD per acre per day. Aeration and mixing require about 1.2 kWh/lb of BOD removal.

The activated sludge process involves returning a portion of the clarified sludge to be mixed with the effluent-entering system and activating biodegradation, thus giving the process its name. The activated sludge process originated as a plug flow system, effluent and sludge enter at one end and move along the system, while aeration is supplied through its full length.

Step aeration and complete mix systems were developed to overcome the problems due to high local oxygen demand in handling high-strength waste. A complete mix system is preferred for high-strength food processing waste. Instead of air, a high-purity oxygen system uses nearly pure oxygen generated at the site, thus accelerating the process. This system is used successfully in several food processing plants.

The activated sludge process is the most common treatment system used with food processing wastewater. A typical design for 1 million gal/d containing 1000 mg/l of BOD requires about 600 hp of installed electric motors and consumes about 1.4 kWh/lb of BOD removed.

Oxidation ditch is a process developed in Europe for small municipalities. It is a compact, efficient activated sludge process designed as a closed-loop channel with brush-type aerators in the channel. This relatively trouble-free system has found several applications in the food industry.

A rotating biological contactor (RBC) has several large-diameter disks mounted on a horizontal shaft in a semicircular tank. The disks are rotated slowly with the lower half submerged in water. Microorganisms grow on the disk surfaces. The rotating action introduces oxygen into the water and helps shear excess cell mass from the disks. This system has not found many applications in food plants.

A trickling filter is one of the oldest biological treatment systems, but it is not really a filter. A typical trickling filter is a 6-ft deep bed of 2.5 to 4-inch rocks arranged in a 25-ft diameter circle. Effluent is trickled over the bed, while atmospheric air moves within the voids in the rock bed, creating contact between water and air. The loading rates are about 5 to 20 lb of BOD per day per 1000 ft^3 of filter volume for standard filters. Plastic or wooden media and effluent recirculation are used in super-rate filter towers, where loading rates are about ten times those for the standard filters.

Tertiary Treatment

Tertiary treatment processes, also known as advanced water treatments (AWT), are used increasingly for reuse of water or to meet NPDES permit requirements for discharge to natural streams. Tertiary treatments include polishing lagoons, sand filters, activated carbon filters, ion exchangers, chlorinators, ozonators, electrodialysis and cross-flow membrane filtration.

Advanced water treatments are sometimes used as pretreatments with food process wastewater. Lagoons and filters fall into this category. Tertiary treatments are also used in the food industry to remove colour, odour, salt and taste compounds that are not removed by biological treatment. Activated carbon, reverse osmosis and chlorination fall into this category.

Filters are used as tertiary treatment to remove suspended solids. Microstrainers, sand filters and multimedia filters are used for this purpose. Microstrainers come with screen openings down to 1 μm. However, the practical range is about 20 to 100 μm. Sand filters and multimedia filters are equivalent to about 20 to 30 μm screens in rejection characteristics.

Slow sand filters require periodic manual cleaning and the filtration fluxes are about 60 to 90 gfd (gallons per square foot per day). Rapid sand filters employ graded sand and periodic backwashing. They are easier to maintain and the filtration fluxes are about 3000 to 10000 gfd. Multimedia filters use graded media of different densities so that the optimum layered structure is self-maintained during backwashes.

Activated carbon is an excellent adsorption medium (due to its large surface area) for removing dissolved organic matter that is leftover from biological treatments. Once limited to chemical industries, it is now finding increased use in other industries due to improved equipment and cost reductions.

Anaerobic Treatment

In comparison to aerobic treatment, anaerobic technology requires a lower energy input. It can deliver a net energy surplus under most conditions. Methane gas produced in anaerobic treatment can itself be used to provide the heating energy required for the process, while the excess can be used to fuel boilers or internal combustion engines. Advances made in recent years in the development of this technology have reduced the retention times from weeks to hours. New applications have broadened the range of wastewater amenable to anaerobic treatment.

Anaerobic treatment is better suited to high concentration waste, while aerobic treatment is better suited to low-concentration wastewater. Concentration of process waters by reverse osmosis would enable the reuse of permeate in the process, while the concentrate can be treated by anaerobic digestion. This would result in more compact, more cost-effective water management systems.

A major problem in anaerobic treatment of food process wastewater is competition from sulphate-reducing bacteria. These anaerobes convert sulphates into a series of sulphur compounds from thiosulphate to hydrogen sulfide. These compounds are responsible for the odours and corrosion frequently associated with anaerobic digestion. Several methods can remove hydrogen sulphide and the products of its combustion.

FOOD PROCESS RESIDUAL MANAGEMENT IN THE FUTURE

Planning and design of food plants in the past were based on the availability of good-quality fresh water at low cost and easy disposal of solid waste and process waters. As these conditions change, it becomes necessary to reduce water use and residue generation, however, plant design limits the success of these efforts. Often, it appears that major changes in plant design are necessary to achieve substantial improvements. Water conservation and residue reduction should be important aspects of the design of food processing plants in the future.

When plant modifications, new equipment additions and process changes are planned, water use, chemical use and residue generation should be considered as important evaluation criteria. Integrated evaluation procedures encompassing all aspects of the process change are necessary to prevent unpleasant surprises. The planned deregulation of electric utilities could make operation of biomass cogeneration plants uneconomical. Several million tonnes of fruit processing residue is burned in these plants annually. This convenient and beneficial means of disposal would be lost to the fruit processing plants if cogeneration plants cease to function. Air quality standards are restricting incineration which is another avenue for disposal of solid waste. The Clean Air Act, amended in 1990, calls for reducing carbon monoxide emissions and ozone-forming compounds through changes in fuel formulation. Blending with ethanol is one means of achieving this objective. Use of food process residues in ethanol production may become attractive under these conditions.

Anaerobic treatment is a very attractive alternative to the more popular aerobic treatment for treating high-strength organic waste from food processing plants. It involves lower capital investment, energy consumption and chemical use. Recent advances in membrane technology can supplement anaerobic technology through preconcentration of effluent while recovering clean water for reuse. One factor preventing wider use of anaerobic treatment is restrictive air emission standards.

Food processing residues finally have to end up in one or more of the three disposal media: air, water and land. All three are being subjected to increased scrutiny by environmental regulations, often with valid reasons. Decision making in residue disposal has become a sophisticated exercise requiring in-depth knowledge of a wide range of subjects. Source reduction is undoubtedly the best path to follow in directing future policy.

SECTION II

Solar Energy and Water Conservation in Food Processing

Chapter 12

Solar Energy Potential in Food Industry

INTRODUCTION

There is a vast potential for use of solar energy devices/systems in industries for process heat and other thermal applications. Presently, energy for these applications is being met mainly through fuel oil which is not only import dependent but is also creating huge GHG emissions in atmosphere resulting threat to our planet. India is consuming over 100 million tons of oil every year for various uses. Out of this, almost 40% is being consumed in the industrial sector alone. Further, 40–50% of this consumption is in thermal form alone with temperature range below 250°C which comes to around 15 million tons of fuel oil per annum. The applications include mercerising, drying and finishing in textile industry, drying, dissolving, thickening, leaching and distillation in chemical industry, cooking, drying and canning in food industry, craft pulping, bleaching and drying in pulp and paper industry, drying and cleaning in leather industry and various such applications in many more industries. The working fluid required for these applications is either pressurised hot water, steam or hot air in temperature range of 60–250°C.

This industry can be identified as a prospective area for the application of solar thermal energy systems because the relatively lower temperature at which the processes are carried out here can be achieved easily through solar heating. Again, since solar radiation is available in abundance in the country, this is a quite feasible solution. Considered from the point of view of cleanliness, which is a vital requirement in the food processing industry, the application of solar energy could be a big advantage for this industry. The food processing industry plays an important role in the country's economic development as a result of the vital linkages and synergies that it promotes between the industrial and the agricultural sector, the two most important sectors in the economy.

There are number of solar energy technologies which can be used for such applications and reduce consumption of fuel oil mainly during day time. The technologies include solar water heating systems, steam generating systems and air heating systems based on flat plate or evacuated tube collectors and automatically tracked solar concentrating collectors.

Solar water heating: Solar water heating is a well established technology and is in promotion world wide. It can be used in industries for boiler feed applications in raising water temperature from 25 to 80°C and thereby saving a substantial amount of fuel oil being used in boilers.

Solar concentrated technology: It can provide steam up to a temperature of say 300°C which is the direct need of industries.

SUN AND SOLAR DRYING, TECHNIQUES AND EQUIPMENT

Sun Drying

Food drying is a very simple, ancient skill. It is one of the most accessible and hence the most widespread processing technology. Sun drying of fruits and vegetables is still practised largely unchanged from ancient times. Traditional Sun drying takes place by storing the product under direct sunlight.

Sun drying is only possible in areas where, in an average year, the weather allows foods to be dried immediately after harvest. The main advantages of Sun drying are low capital and operating costs and the fact that little expertise is required. The main disadvantages of this method are as follows: contamination, theft or damage by birds, rats or insects, slow or intermittent drying and no protection from rain or dew that wets the product, encourages mold growth and may result in a relatively high final moisture content, low and variable quality of products due to over- or under-drying, large areas of land needed for the shallow layers of food, laborious since the crop must be turned, moved if it rains, direct exposure to sunlight reduces the quality (colour and vitamin content) of some fruits and vegetables. Moreover, since Sun drying depends on uncontrolled factors, production of uniform and standard products is not expected. The quality of Sun dried foods can be improved by reducing the size of pieces to achieve faster drying and by drying on raised platforms, covered with cloth or netting to protect against insects and animals.

Solar Drying

Due to the current trends towards higher cost of fossil fuels and uncertainty regarding future cost and availability, use of solar energy in food processing will probably increase and become more economically feasible in the near future. Solar dryers have some advantages over Sun drying when correctly designed. They give faster drying rates by heating the air to 10–30°C above ambient, which causes the air to move faster through the dryer, reduces its humidity and deters insects. The faster drying reduces the risk of spoilage, improves quality of the product and gives a higher throughput, so reducing the drying area that is needed. However care is needed when drying fruits to prevent too rapid drying, which will prevent complete drying and would result in case hardening and subsequent mold growth. Solar dryers also protect foods form dust, insects, birds and animals. They can be constructed from locally available materials at a relatively low capital cost and there are no fuel costs. Thus, they can be useful in areas where fuel or electricity are expensive, land for Sun drying is in short supply or expensive, sunshine is plentiful but the air humidity is high. Moreover, they may be useful as a means of heating air for artificial dryers to reduce fuel costs.

Solar food drying can be used in most areas but how quickly the food dries is affected by many variables, especially the amount of sunlight and relative humidity. Typical drying times in solar dryers range from 1 to 3 days depending on Sun, air movement, humidity and the type of food to be dried.

The principle that lies behind the design of solar dryers is as follows: in drying relative and absolute humidity are of great importance. Air can take up moisture, but only up to a limit. This limit is the absolute (maximum) humidity and it is temperature dependent. When air passes over a moist food it will take up moisture until it is virtually fully saturated, that is until absolute humidity has been reached. But, the capacity of the air for taking up this moisture is dependent on its temperature. The higher the temperature, the higher the absolute humidity and the larger the uptake of moisture. If air is warmed, the amount of moisture in it remains the same, but the relative humidity falls and the air is therefore enabled to take up more moisture from it's surrounding.

To produce a high-quality product economically, it must be dried fast, but without using excessive heat, which could cause product degradation. Drying time can be shortened by two main procedures: one is to raise the product temperature so that the moisture can be readily vapourised, while at the same time the humid air is constantly being removed. The second is to treat the product to be dried so that the moisture barriers, such as dense hydrophobic skin layers or long water migration paths, will be minimised.

Parabolic Concentrator System

By using parabolic concentrators, the aperture required to attain the working temperature of a heat-transfer fluid can be computed and the required heat flow can also be determined, which together would determine the overall size of the concentrator. Industrial process heat using this parabolic concentrator has already been developed earlier in many countries.

In order to deliver the required temperature with good efficiency, a high performance solar collector is required. Systems with light structures and low cost technology for process heat applications up to 2500°C could complete the variety of solar thermal collectors. Parabolic trough collectors (PTC) can effectively produce heat at temperatures between 500°C and 4000°C. The biggest application of this type of system is in the Southern California power plants, known as Solar Electric Generating Systems (SEGS), which have a total installed capacity of 354 MWe.

Types of Solar Dryers

There are mainly three types of solar dryers:

1. The absorption or hot box type dryers in which the product is directly heated by Sun.
2. The indirect or convection dryers in which the product is exposed to warm air which is heated by means of a solar absorber, or heat exchanger.
3. Dryers combining the principles of the above two, where the product is exposed to the Sun and a stream of pre-heated air simultaneously.

Direct Absorption Dryers

Direct drying consists of using incident radiation only, or incident radiation plus reflected radiation. Most solar drying techniques that use only direct solar energy also use some means to reflect additional radiation onto the product to further increase its temperature. The aim of this type of a dryer is mainly to improve product quality by reducing contamination by dust, insect infestation and animal or human interference. It consists of a hot box with a transparent top and blackened interior surfaces. Ventilation holes in the base and upper parts of slide walls maintained a natural air circulation.

SOLAR ENERGY FOR QUALITY IMPROVEMENT IN FOOD PROCESSING INDUSTRY

For promoting solar energy application on a large scale in the food processing industry, it is very important to integrate knowledge of food processing with capabilities of different solar gadgets. Application of existing solar gadgets and developing new designs of solar gadgets based on case-to-case basis are key for adoption of this beautiful technology by the food processing industry. Great quality improvement in solar processed food was observed in terms of retention of colour, aroma and taste. Solar processed products could fetch much higher prices in the market because of better quality of the product.

Application of solar energy in food processing industry is mainly limited to drying operations. Solar vegetable-fruit dryers, operating below 55°C, are used for the purpose. In recent years many solar gadgets have been developed for variety of applications. Different solar concentrators can provide excellent boiling, steaming, blanching and roasting capabilities while solar air dryers/heaters can effectively remove moisture. Efforts are required to integrate knowledge of food processing with capabilities of available solar thermal gadgets. Field trials on a variety of solar gadgets like 'parabolic concentrators', box ovens and solar dehydrators show not only huge fuel savings but also great value addition because of better quality of produce in terms of colour, aroma and taste. Because of excellent consistent quality, materials processed on these units can enjoy great market potential, in-house and for exports as well. Extremely low capital investment in this technology makes it financially viable. Open Sun drying is traditionally practiced for many vegetables, fruits and fishes. Dehydrated foodstuff has a higher shelf life, making it available throughout the year. The dehydrated fruits and vegetables have much smaller weight and hence are easy to transport. They cater to the needs of defence establishments, adventure expeditions, mountaineering, etc. These dehydrated products can be used in various preparations even in off-season.

Drying vegetables, fruits and fishes by traditional open air Sun drying is time consuming and less hygienic. In industrialised regions and sectors, mechanised dryers, with fans have now largely replaced open air-drying. Mechanised drying is faster than open-air drying and it uses much less land. But the equipment is expensive and requires higher energy cost with fuel or electricity to operate. Higher capital investment and lack of confidence in the technology are the main hurdles in popularising this beautiful gadget. Applications of solar dryers are known to many. In recent years many solar gadgets have been developed for a variety of applications.

Different solar concentrators and box ovens can provide excellent boiling, steaming, blanching and roasting capabilities while solar air dryers/heaters do the work of moisture removal. Combinations of such solar gadgets can take care of major energy needs in food processing industry. In spite of such developments, application of solar energy in food-processing industries has not picked up. There exists a big communication gap between solar researchers and food technologists. Food technologists are not aware of capabilities of new breeds of solar gadgets like solar concentrators, ovens and dryers, while solar technologists are unaware of technical requirements of different processes followed in food processing. These gadgets have capabilities of bringing in revolutionary change in food processing technology.

Solar Concentrator for Baking and Roasting Applications

A new industrial concentrator is capable of delivering hot air up to 200°C. This concentrator is suited for oven-like applications for baking and roasting in high temperature ovens.

Solar Dryers

Solar dryers are normally designed for use below 55°C, assisted with airflow. The following features are used in the new dryer to reduce the cost and improve the performance of the unit.

1. Arrangement is proposed to install the cabinet for loading the material on a rooftop, while collector panels were laid on the south side towards the ground. This saved cost of a fabricated support structure. As the cabinet is placed at higher elevation than the collector panels, with uniform slope, natural draught assists the induced draught created by fan. Because of combined draught overall auxiliary power consumption for the fan is reduced.

2. In case of power cuts natural draught maintains airflow and overall temperatures are maintained slightly above the set temperatures. This provision avoids overheating and spoilage of the material in the cabinet.
3. Solar collectors are constructed in powder-coated mild steel sheets instead of aluminium sheets. This can reduce the cost of solar collector panels by around 50%. The outer shell of the panel is constructed from a single sheet without any joints, which takes care of the possibility of hot air leakages.
4. A cabinet for loading material is constructed with glass on three sides and a plywood door on the rear side. Cost of the cabinet contributes a lot in conventional solar or other mechanised dryers as it is to be constructed in stainless steel and needs to be properly insulated. Replacing this envelop by glass saves 80% of the cabinet cost. No insulation is required in this case.
5. Use of glass for the cabinet permits trapping additional solar energy. In the current design glass cabinet contributes approximately 25% of the aperture area of the unit.
6. Use of glass for the cabinet also permits better control on the process as the operator can see the material being processed, without opening the cabinet. Over drying can be avoided.
7. Design of the cabinet permits even distribution of hot air throughout the cross section, which permits uniform drying rates. Control on maintaining moisture at the desired level is easily possible. Even an unskilled worker can operate the unit.
8. Simple design permits manufacturing at the local level through local fabricators.

SOLAR DRYING OF FRUITS AND VEGETABLES

Tomatoes

Due to the increasing demand to dried tomatoes from the industry, especially from the soup manufacturers, interest in producing high quality dried tomatoes has been increasing. Therefore, it is important to establish a drying method, which yields products with higher sensory and sanitary quality in a shorter drying time compared to the conventional Sun-drying method. Both 2% $Na_2S_2O_5$ and 2% citric acid pre-treatments can be used to protect the bright, red colour of tomatoes. However, citric acid did not prevent the growth of molds and yeasts effectively. Therefore, dipping into sodium metabisulphite solution for 3 min is the best type of pretreatment. Tomatoes can be dried at 55°C in solar tunnel dryer without a darkening in colour. At this temperature the drying takes 4–5 days to a final moisture content of 111%.

Red Pepper

Red peppers are deseeded, cut into small pieces and washed before loading into the tunnel solar dryer. Pretreatment with 2% $Na_2S_2O_5$ for 1 second gives the best colour. Moreover, the drying temperature and piece size of red peppers affects the final product quality. Temperatures higher than 60°C results in dark brown colour formation in red peppers. Red peppers that are cut into bigger pieces needs a longer time period to dry and therefore the colour of the final product is darker. Drying at low temperatures (45–50°C) for about 1 day gives good results. To increase the capacity of the solar dryer, a double layer system can be constructed, but with this system, drying needs a more careful control. Final moisture content of dried red peppers which are pre-treated with 2 $Na_2S_2O_5$ for 1 second is 3.5%. The yield is 9% for both pre-treated and naturally dried peppers.

Green Pepper

Green peppers are used especially in the soup manufacturing. Therefore, establishing an efficient and economic method for peppers is important for the food industry. Green peppers are washed, deseeded and cut into small pieces before loading into the dryer. Green peppers are very sensitive to high temperatures and light. Therefore, green peppers should be dried under dark and at 45–50°C to preserve the natural green colour. 2% $Na_2S_2O_5$ dipping for 1 sec can be applied to obtain a microbiologically safe product. Drying at 45–50°C under dark conditions takes about 1 day. Green peppers dried under these conditions have a final moisture content of 6% and a yield of 10%.

Onion

A large part of the dehydrated onion production is used as seasoning in production of catsup, chilli sauce and meat casseroles, as well as cold cuts, sausages, potato chips, crackers and other snack items. Food service outlets also use dehydrated onions because of its convenience in storage, preparation and use. Before drying, onions are peeled and sliced into desired shapes. Onions can be dried at 45–50°C for 2–3 days to a final moisture content of 15% in tunnel solar dryers. Sodium metabisulphite dipping can be used to preserve colour. Drying temperatures of onions should not exceed 50°C in order to prevent browning of the product. The yield in onion drying is 8%.

Carrot

Before loading into the dryer, carrots are peeled, washed, cut into small cubes and treated with 2% sodium metabisulphite solution for 1s and 10s or dried as natural. Carrots can be dried at 50–55°C for 1–1.5 days to a final moisture content of 7.5 %. Naturally dried carrots loss their bright orange colour. The sodium metabisulphite treated ones preserve their colour to the largest extent.

Prunes

It is known that certain treatments used to modify the waxy cuticle of the surface of various fruits (prunes, grapes, cherries, etc.), accelerate the drying as a result of an increase in the skin permeability. Dipping in olive oil emulsions is a traditional practice in direct solar drying of pieces and it is recorded that this increases the drying rate of grapes approximately 30%. Different olive oil concentrations combined with sodium or potassium carbonate or ethyl esters of fatty acids are used for this purpose.

Researches have found that the most effective compounds are the ethyl esters of fatty acids in the C_{10}–C_{18} range with ethyl oblate being the easiest to handle. Prunes can be dried at 55–60°C in solar tunnel driers. At this temperature, prunes pre-treated with 2% ethyl oleate or 2% olive oil + 4% potassium carbonate dried in 3–4 days.

Peach

Peaches are washed, destoned and sliced 1–2 cm thick. The thickness of the slices is very important since very thin slices causes hardening and brownish colour in the final product. Different concentrations of $Na_2S_2O_5$ and citric acid can be used as pretreatment agent: 2% citric acid for 30s, 1 $Na_2S_2O_5$ for 1s and 1% citric acid + 0.5% $Na_2S_2O_5$ for 1s. Peaches which are consumed directly or used in recipes can be dried at 45–50°C in 2 days. The yield of the final product is 11% and final moisture content is about 8.5%.

Okra

Okra is one of the most popular vegetables consumed in tropical and subtropical countries, because of its adaptability and resistance to hot and humid weather. Before loading into solar dryer, okra is washed and its head is removed. One of the following treatments can be applied to okra prior to solar drying: dipping in 0.2% $Na_2S_2O_5$ for 20 min, 0.1% Na_2SO_3 for 30 min, 0.3% $Na_2S_2O_5$ 10 min, 2% $Na_2S_2O_5$ for 1s and 3 min of blanching followed by dipping in 0.2% Na_2SO_3 for 15 min and finally blanching and dipping in 0.2% Na_2SO_3 for 15 min.

On the basis of colour, flavour and microbiology of the final product, it was observed that high quality dried okra was obtained using 2% $Na_2S_2O_5$ dipping as a pretreatment and drying of okra at 50–55°C in the solar dryer under dark conditions. Drying time was about 1 day. Blanching of okra before drying needs ice-bath dipping. Therefore it is not considered as a practical method.

Apple

Golden apples are cleaned, cored and sliced to 3–5 mm thick. To prevent browning, the apples can be immersed for 1s in 2% citric acid or 2% $Na_2S_2O_5$ solutions immediately after slicing. The apples dried under light conditions becomes a little brown but the ones that are dried without exposure to light are kept their natural, light colour. The choice of drying conditions depends on the consumer's demand. Dried apples have a water activity of 0.38 and a yield of 15%.

Solar Box Ovens

Solar box ovens were tried for roasting and baking applications successfully. Some of these developments include:

1. Roasting of 'soyabean' for baby food.
2. Roasting of 'cashew nut'.
3. Roasting of ground-nut.
4. Baking breads and cakes.

Following are the results and lessons learned during the trials on different solar gadgets used for food processing applications.

1. Prior to use of solar gadgets, 'Amla Candy', Amla used to be boiled using conventional fossil fuels and then final produce dried in open Sun. Colour of 'Amla Candy' used to be brown-black and maintaining moisture level of around 20% was difficult. Hence quality of the produce was not consistent. Same product on solar dryer gave excellent green-yellow colour with much natural and fresh looks. Moisture retention is more uniform and quality is consistent. Value addition is great. No fossil fuels are required in this case. Boiling of Amla is carried out on solar concentrators, while drying of final product is done on solar dryers.
2. Trials on green chilly, moringa leaves, asparagus, Aloe Vera, ladies finger and gourd showed excellent colour retention. The dehydrated produce meet higher quality norms in terms of colour, aroma and taste.
3. Powders of green chilly, moringa leaves, wheat grass, tomato, etc. were prepared after drying. These powders have approval from food product manufacturers.

4. In cashew processing the shelled kernel is covered with the testa and, to facilitate removal, i.e. to peel in order to produce the blanched kernel, the shelled kernel is dried. The moisture content is approximately 6% before drying and 3% after. The same unit was used for drying shelled kernel successfully.
5. In cashew nut processing, roasting of the nut in box ovens gives excellent quality nuts. Breakage of nuts was reduced by 50% and roasting was uniform. Nuts roasted in box ovens followed by drying kernels in solar dryers, not only save energy cost but also fetch more price than the nuts produced by electrical boilers and dryers.
6. Drying of juices takes more time. It was observed that instead of preparing juices, it is better to dry the stuff in sliced form. Dehydration rate was 2 to 4 times faster when material is placed in sliced form than drying juices.
7. Powdery material is more difficult to dry, than granular or sliced material.
8. The solar dryer design, with natural draught assisted by induced draught created by fan saves auxiliary power. Specific energy consumption in forced draught solar dryer is in the range of 3 kWh for removal of 100 kg of water, while natural draught assisted with the induced draught dryer was consuming 2 kWh for the same moisture removal.
9. Roasting with a solar concentrator requires great skill and there were incidences of food burning, especially with cashew nuts, soyabean and groundnut. It is observed that solar ovens are better suited for baking and roasting applications than concentrators. Uniform baking and roasting are observed in solar ovens. Even an unskilled worker can work well with ovens, but not with the concentrators.
10. The moisture removal rate was observed at around 3 kg per sq. mtr. area of panel in dry climate. Apart from fossil fuel savings, quality improvement of the food product and better process control are the main advantages.

Thus, solar energy is available abundantly in the country and can be used to good benefit in sweetmeat production. Ordinarily, insolation of around 600 W/m^2 is not considered to be sufficient for attaining the required temperatures. With the help of concentrators, higher temperatures can be achieved and solar heating systems with concentrators can be effectively used in this particular industry. This basic principle is very simple but the development of such systems in India for this particular area of application have so far been overlooked by the solar energy technologists.

There are undoubtedly many problems in the utilisation of solar heating principally because of the hygienic conditions required to be maintained in the food processing industries. In this typical application, low temperature processing heat exchangers are considered to be the most critical component of the solar thermal system because the heat exchanger responsible for the easy transfer of heat is to be a very special one allowing efficient heat transfer and also allowing the use of traditional containers used in this industry. Post heat cleaning and easy removal of the container after the heating cycles are important requirements of the heating system. As a result the heat exchanger should preferably allow heating from the bottom and there should not be any direct contact of the heat exchanger with the liquid under process, which has been taken as milk in this case, to avoid contamination. However, such heat exchangers will be of lower efficiency. The temperature differential also being low, the amount of heat finally transferred to the milk will be at a very slow rate. Temperatures attained at the RTDs are very satisfactory and the system will definitely attract the attention of the planners and it is expected that it will be used in a good number of areas in the near future.

SOLAR HEATING IN FOOD PROCESSING

Conventional Drying Process

Traditionally, in India people have been using solar energy for centuries mainly for agricultural purpose such as drying of grains and species, drying of fish, preservation of food products. The drying process removes moisture and helps in the preservation of the product. Open drying (or direct solar heating) of food products is done under Sun by spreading it on open ground or a base plate is a common practice a various places. This method is cheap but has several disadvantages:

1. Possibility of contamination of the food product dirt, insects, rodents, birds which makes it unhygienic.
2. Exposure of food product to the elements such as rain and wind which causes spoilage and losses.
3. Loss of nutrition values and natural appearance like colour, texture, etc.
4. The process is slow and long time period is required.
5. Uneven heating or drying can be done.

In indirect heating (drying) is done by using a solar heater of a type which furnishes hot air to a separate drying unit. This can be advantageously used for big industries which require hot air. The system consists of air heater, drying chamber and thermal storage device. Solar collector collects radiation which heats the air which is blown to drying chamber for drying process. Air, thermal liquids or water can be used as heating medium.

Thermal liquid is limited in quantity whereas water has uncertainty and low thermal efficiency. Air is ideal medium as it is free, easily available in bulk quantity and no extra auxiliary equipment is required. Parabolic dish collectors, flat plate collectors and shuffler system can be used for collecting solar radiations. Figure 12.1 shows the block diagram of indirect heating. It consists of some basic components which are: (a) solar collectors, (b) solar heating chamber, (c) drying chamber and (d) inlet fan.

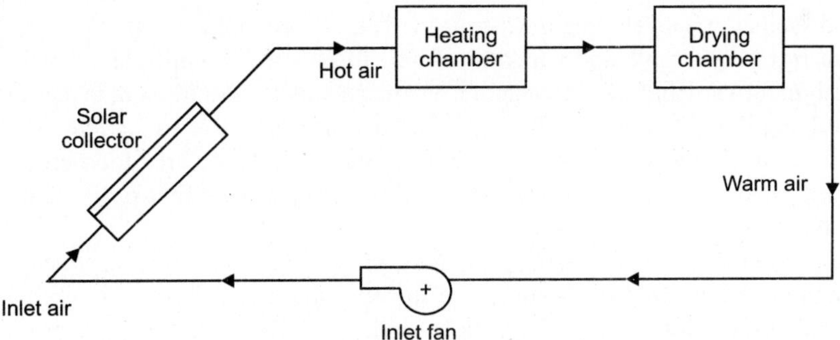

Fig. 12.1: Solar indirect heating.

Chapter 13

Water Conservation in Food Processing Industry

INTRODUCTION

All industrial and commercial organisations use water. However, organisations often do not know how much they are using or that by using water more efficiently they could reduce what they pay for water supply and effluent disposal. The food and drink industry is no exception. This chapter describes how businesses in all sectors of the industry can take steps to minimise their water use without compromising their processes or hygiene standards. The information can be used to help build an environmental action plan, which helps a business to assess environmental performance, prioritise actions and set targets. Water has been used in the food processing industry as a medium of great convenience for transportation, heat transfer and sanitation. Developing a water conservation/waste minimisation programme for a food processing plant is a very simple and economical way to increase overall plant efficiency. The steps involved are straight forward, but require planning and management commitment to make the programme work. The underlying thought is: If you don't put product into the waste stream, you don't have to pay to take it out. Just as the body is made up of many parts that work together, a food processing plant has many contributing factors to total water use and waste discharge. So the first step is to know your plant, inside and out, backwards and forwards.

Learning the layout of a food processing plant may be more involved than most people would think. Over time most plants have had modification and upgrades that have altered the original piping of the plant. Starting with a set of blue prints, if available, determine where incoming water lines are located, if water meters are present, pressure regulators and back flow prevention. Follow water lines through the plant identifying main truck lines and what processes feed off from them. Once the incoming water flow patterns have been established, identify outgoing water flow patterns from the plant. Most plants will have more than one incoming and outgoing water sources, so make sure all have been identified. At this point it should be possible to develop a water balance for the plant, water in should equal water out plus estimated losses. It is a good idea to look at water data over a 10 to 14 day period to make sure all aspects of plant operations and down time are represented.

The next is stage is to evaluate the water use of individual pieces of equipment in the plant. It can take some time to accurately quantify everything in the plant, however as this task is performed take note of variations in water use of similar equipment or where water is being used inefficiently. Another aspect will be to determine water use patterns for the plant on an hourly, daily and weekly basis. This is important when evaluating employees effectiveness in conserving water. If water usage stays at production level during breaks, this is a good indication that equipment is being left on when no product is being processed. These pieces of data will be very valuable when it comes time to implement water conservation practices in the plant and in determining overall water savings.

Now that all water usage has been explored, it's time to evaluate sources of waste generation inside the plant. In food processing, wasted product usually cost the company twice. One, it is product that wasn't sold or rendered for profit and second, it effects the wastewater treatment cost and may contribute to surcharges or fines. Therefore it is important to be very meticulous in looking at waste generation, especially waste from ineffective equipment, plant personnel and sanitation procedures.

Once all these pieces of information have been gathered, it is time to perform a 24 hr waste water characterisation. This should include final plant effluent and all previous identified sources of waste generation. To perform a wastewater characterisation, four types of information will be needed: location of wastewater sample, time sample was taken, volume of wastewater discharged and concentration of contaminants in the sample. With this data it will be possible to develop a wastewater profile and quantify what is happening in the plant. Water conservation and waste reduction in the food processing industry is a cost effective means to increase plant efficiency. This efficiency can be measured by the economic and environmental impact it has on the plant and in the community. As water cost continue to rise and regulations become more stringent, this type of plant management will play a key role in helping the food processing industry stay competitive in a global market.

WATER CONSERVATION IN FOOD INDUSTRY

Reducing the amount of water you use will save you money in water supply charges. In most cases, it will also have the effect of reducing the volume of effluent your organisation discharges, which will cut your trade effluent charges. You will be reducing your company's impact on the environment as well as saving money. Think also about the hidden costs associated with water use, the energy you could be saving, for example, by reduced pumping requirements or having to heat less water.

There may be other benefits too. Some of the water saving measures described in this chapter will also enable you to recover some of the raw material or product from your process or cleaning chemicals, which previously may have been lost in the effluent stream. This will have the added benefit of lowering effluent strength, which will reduce your trade effluent charges further. Reducing the amount of water you use can also demonstrate continual environmental improvement, one of the key pillars when implementing an environmental management systems (EMS), particularly in relation to a formal EMS.

Managing Water Use

This section looks at how to manage water use in your company, from initial investigations and commitment from senior management, through to imple-mentation and continuous improvement. It is vital to have effective procedures in place to manage a water reduction programme, otherwise any improvement may become a one-off initiative with no follow-up, employees will not be motivated to continue good practices and the programme will lose momentum and fail. Ensure your employees are aware of the total cost of water to your site – water is often an undervalued resource and some sites still believe it is 'free'. Potential cost savings associated with water efficiency improvements are often the driver that motivates management to support a water use reduction programme. Successful management involves identifying and initiating water saving projects, continual monitoring of water use and company/staff practices and a timely, appropriate response to the information gathered.

MEASURING WATER USE AND FLOW

This section looks at how you can measure and account for the water that you use on your site. Knowing how much water you are using and where it goes are the first steps towards being able to control and reduce the amount you need. Suggested actions in this section include carrying out a water survey to create a water balance and considering the different options available for devices that measure quantity and flow. Regular surveys will keep water and effluent systems in order. Checks should be carried out on a monthly basis, at least until full control of water use has been established, when an annual survey may be sufficient. Surveys typically reveal leaks, incorrectly set, poorly maintained or broken equipment, unidentified connections, redundant lines, unknown or unauthorised use or discharge and clean water discharges to effluent streams. Once identified, these are all things that can be rectified quickly.

If adopted, many of these actions can be included in your management programme/action plan. This will provide documented evidence of your commitment to drive forward your company's EMS, while demonstrating continual environmental improvement.

Carry Out a Water Survey and use the Information to Create a Water Balance

A water balance is a numerical account of where water enters and leaves your site and where it is used in the business. It lists the amounts of water used by each main process. It can be kept quite simple or be made very detailed, depending on your situation and needs. It is also possible to use modelling software to establish a water balance. Models can be proprietary packages that require a licence fee to be paid or can be developed at a more basic level using standard spread sheet packages. These models can also be used as production tools to establish supply and demand of water for processing.

PROCESS WATER USE IN FOOD INDUSTRY

This section deals with the way you use water as part of your production system. Following the preparation of a water balance and identifying key effluent streams, an assessment of them – as individual or combined streams – can be made, reviewing water usage, effluent flow and load generation and identifying any actions that can be taken to minimise either. Methods to eliminate water use or individual effluents should be considered first. These may also recover product and eliminate treatment costs and could include:

1. Spillage and leak prevention.
2. Storage of product residues to be added to the next production batch.
3. Sale of one or more effluent streams as a by-product.
4. Process change to eliminate water use or generation of effluent.
5. Substituting a wet process with a dry one.

Basic measures, such as not leaving taps or hoses running and fixing leaks, can bring substantial savings in water use. There are also many simple and easy-to-install devices that will make it easier to save water. For example, consider interlocking water use with production breaks to minimise process water use during downtime. This can be achieved through the use of solenoid valves to shut off water supply to equipment (such as spray bars).

Making staff aware of how much water costs and how much is used in different processes is also key to controlling use. If adopted, many of these actions can be placed on your management programme/ action plan. This will provide documented evidence of your commitment to drive forward your company's EMS, while demonstrating continual environmental improvement.

PROCESS CONTROL

This section describes how you can use process control to optimise water use. Effective process control enables water to be used more efficiently. It can:

1. Reduce the amount of water used in your processes.
2. Better control the use of water and optimise process performance.
3. Reduce the volume of effluent generated.

This can help you make substantial savings on your water supply and effluent bills. Process control methods range from individual, simple-to-install devices (e.g. orifice plates to restrict flow) to fully automatic process control systems managing all the processes on a site. You do not need to automate everything to realise savings, a few simple manual or automatic devices linked to your key water-using processes can make a great deal of difference.

Most process control systems are made up of three distinct elements: sensors, transmitters and control devices. Process control involves manipulating process variables (e.g. valve positions, flow rates, motor speeds on pumps) based on the values of one or more measured process parameters (e.g. temperatures, flow, concentration). This can be done manually, such as when an operator visually inspects the level in a tank and decides to add more water, or automatically by a mechanical or electronic device. In the latter case, signals from sensors mounted in the tank are transmitted to an electronic device. This calculates the required control action and transmits signals to actuators that adjust valve positions, etc. and eventually shuts off the water flow to the tank when the right level is reached.

The process controls can also be written into a formalised procedure to ensure that all relevant employees are aware of the new controls installed. If implementing an EMS, this will provide documented evidence that one of your key environmental aspects (water) is controlled. In all cases, remember to check hygiene requirements before fitting intrusive devices into process equipment.

PRODUCT AND WATER RECOVERY TECHNIQUES

Once process changes and/or process control have been reviewed to see whether water use can be reduced, it may be worthwhile considering product and water recovery techniques.

This section discusses the techniques for recovering product and/or water, which will reduce water use and effluent volume and strength. Separating out and collecting different solids and liquids that enter the effluent stream can have many benefits.

Firstly, it can provide the opportunity to reuse or recycle water. This will not only reduce the amount of water you need to pay for, but will also reduce the volume of effluent you will have to pay to discharge. Secondly, if you can separate raw materials or product from the water for reuse, you will be reducing the concentration of your effluent. This will lower your trade effluent bills.

You may also have the benefit of recovering saleable product, which would otherwise be discharged to drain. There are many treatment options available to accomplish this – from the very simple (e.g. screening water before recirculating for reuse) through to more complex approaches that may involve a multi-stage treatment process. If adopted, many of these actions can be placed on your management programme/action plan. This will provide documented evidence of your commitment to drive forward your company's EMS, while demonstrating continual environmental improvement.

Consider using a Pigging System to Reduce Water Usage

Product recovery can be achieved by using a pig, which is typically an engineered plug or ball that fits inside the pipe and is pushed through by the product itself or by some other propellant (such as water, nitrogen or compressed air). More recently, pigs made from ice or ice slurry have been used to clean pipework. The pig empties the pipe and removes deposits adhering to the walls (Fig. 13.1). In most cases, the material the pig pushes through the pipe can be reused. In summary, the benefits of product recovery include:

1. Valuable product/raw materials can be reused.
2. Reduced water and chemical use required for pipe cleaning.
3. Reduced effluent load (COD and SS) of washwater.
4. Reduced effluent costs.
5. Reduced production downtime.

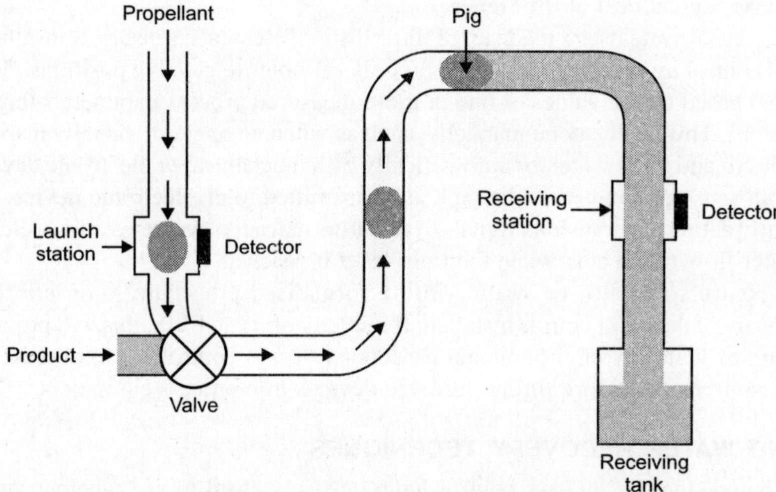

Fig. 13.1: Schematic of product recovery.

This technology can also be used to remove water after sterilisation, cleaning-in-place (CIP) or manual rinsing. The removal of water often ensures that the next batch of product can be processed without the need to purge the line first with product, thus minimising raw material use. Whereas the traditional pigs can become inflexible when navigating some of the complicated internal workings of pipes, the ice pig forms a soft plug and can adapt its shape to fill may complex pipework runs.

Consider using Membrane Separation to Recover Product and/or Water

Membrane separation selectively removes contaminants from a solution. There are various different forms of membrane technology, as outlined in Table 13.1. The method used will depend on the level of filtration required. A membrane is a thin physical barrier through which materials can either pass (the permeate) or be rejected and retained (the retentate). The structure and character of the membrane determine the nature of the separation. Membranes have many uses in the food and drink industry. Apart from recovering water, they can be used to concentrate or purify product and recover raw materials and product from waste streams.

Table 13.1: Membrane separation options.

Option	*Application*
Microfiltration	Microfiltration (MF), pore size range 0.1–5 µm, can be used to remove bacteria from skim milk or for fractionation of skim milk into a casein-rich retentate and a milk serum devoid of casein
Nanofiltration	Nanofiltration (NF), pore size range 1–10 nm, with selective permeability for minerals, is used predominantly for concentration and pre-demineralisation in the dairy industry
Ultrafiltration	Ultrafiltration (UF), pore size range 10–100 nm, is applied to skim milk and whey with the objective of concentrating the respective protein components. Other applications include removal of animal fat from the effluent of UK meat processing
Reverse osmosis	This process is best known for its use in desalination (removing the salt from sea water to produce fresh water), but it can also be used to purify fresh water for medical, industrial and domestic applications

CLEANING ACTIVITIES TO MINIMISE WATER USE

This section looks at optimising cleaning activities to minimise water use. Cleaning can account for as much as 70% of a site's water use. Changing cleaning routines to optimise water use will not only cut your water supply bills, but can have the added benefits of reducing the volume and concentration of effluent. Remember, that excessive use of water for cleaning brings many additional costs, such as labour, downtime, lost materials, cleaning chemicals and energy for heating and pumping.

Where possible, try to use dry clean-up – eliminating the use of water entirely. Dry clean-up is simple – don't use water and keep waste materials out of the drains. It is often the most practicable and effective way of reducing water consumption and COD levels in effluent and most of it is common sense. If there is waste material on the floor or in a machine, pick it up, brush it into a waste container, vacuum it out or remove it in some other way before cleaning with water.

When water is required, using a hose to clean floors and surfaces can consume a large volume of water, especially if the hose is left unattended or forgotten. Use brushes, squeegees and scrapers to remove solids from areas before they start to dry out, thus minimising or often eliminating the need for water. Caked-on dirt can take longer to remove and lead to corrosion if the slurry has a high acid, alkali or salt content (e.g. acidic fruit juices).

Used extensively throughout the food and drink industry, CIP systems are used to clean tanks, vessels, pipework or complex processing equipment. Non-foaming detergents and disinfectants are circulated through the pipework and process equipment in the assembled state.

Tanks, exceptionally large diameter pipes and large containers may be thoroughly cleaned using spray balls or rotating jet devices. This avoids the unnecessary and uneconomical filling of vessels with solution. It also removes the need for operators to climb into vessels to carry out manual scrubbing. Because CIP is an automated process with no human contact, strong detergents can be used for circulation. The combination of longer contact time, mechanical energy, temperature and chemical strength, make this method more effective than manual, soak or foam cleaning. CIP systems offer fast, efficient, reliable and repeatable cleaning of many types of process plant.

Cleaning is vital to ensure food safety, but overuse of water for cleaning tasks is common. It is also the case that where there are concerns over hygiene, staff would rather be 'safe than sorry'. If adopted, many of these actions can be placed on your management programme/action plan. This will provide documented evidence of your commitment to drive forward your company's EMS, while demonstrating continual environmental improvement.

EFFLUENT TREATMENT IN FOOD INDUSTRY

This section looks at the important points to consider for a business that treats its own effluent and the options available to reduce trade effluent charges. Many companies in the food and drink sector operate an effluent treatment plant to reduce the potential of pollution entering receiving waters and to comply with increasingly stringent discharge consent conditions. Furthermore, the rise in effluent discharge costs levied by utility companies has resulted in on-site effluent treatment facilities offering reduced payback periods and a significant cost benefit.

Industries using aqueous processes will inevitably produce an aqueous effluent that can be:

1. Discharged to sewer untreated.
2. Treated and discharged to sewer.
3. Discharged to controlled water with permission from the relevant regulatory body.
4. Treated and recycled.

A key element of an EMS is to ensure compliance with environmental legislation. If your organisation is seeking ISO 14001 certification or EU Eco-Management and Audit Scheme (EMAS) registration, your application may be unsuccessful if you have breached the terms of your trade effluent consent.

To ensure that this does not occur, an EMS often requires documented evidence, in the form of an operational control procedure, that covers effluent treatment on site. The EMS will also require documented evidence outlining robust effluent monitoring techniques used on site to ensure the strength of effluent does not exceed the limits stipulated in the trade effluent consent. It should be noted that further operational control procedures will need to be developed (e.g. dry clean work instructions) to help your business comply with the conditions set out in the trade effluent consent.

Effluent treatment processes can be categorised into three main areas:

1. Primary treatment may comprise balancing, pH control or the removal of insoluble material from the process effluent stream prior to downstream biological treatment and/or final discharge. Primary effluent treatment is designed to:
   - Balance flows and loads.
   - Reduce the load on downstream processes.
   - Protect pumps, etc.
   - Give the last chance for product/raw material recovery.
2. Secondary treatment typically uses natural biological processes and intensifies them in a controlled manner. By using naturally occurring bacteria, the biochemical oxygen demand (BOD) and chemical oxygen demand (COD) are reduced and removed as biological sludges from an effluent treatment system. Secondary biological treatment can be one of two main types:
   - Aerobic (in the presence of oxygen).
   - Anaerobic (in the absence of oxygen).

3. Tertiary treatment is used to describe the 'polishing' of the effluent following primary and secondary treatment. Some tertiary treatment techniques include equipment that may be eligible for 100% first year capital allowances under the ECA Water Technology List. Whether or not tertiary treatment is undertaken depends on whether a company wants to recycle final effluent for use in on-site process, the quality requirements of the final effluent as determined by the consent conditions imposed by the water companies. Tertiary treatment techniques are the same techniques that can be used for effluent recycling: (i) macro filtration, (ii) membrane techniques, and (iii) sterilisation and disinfection.

ANCILLARY WATER USE

This section looks at practices and devices to reduce water consumption in areas of your site not directly related to production. These areas include kitchens, laundries, washbasins, showers and toilets. Applying some basic and often low cost, water saving measures can result in a 30% to 50% reduction in water use in ancillary areas.

BEST AVAILABLE TECHNIQUES

The most effective and advanced stage in the development of activities and their methods of operation which indicate the practical suitability of particular techniques for providing in principle the basis for emission limit valves designed to prevent and, where that is not practicable, generally to reduce emissions and the impact on the environment as a whole. Operators should, where appropriate, identify and evaluate opportunities for recycling or reusing water, taking into consideration hygiene issues and practical constraints. An optimal scheme is likely to include a combination of:

1. Sequential reuse where the water stream is used for two or more processes or operations before disposal.
2. Countercurrent flow where the water flows in the opposite direction to the product so that the final product comes into contact with clean water.
3. Recycling in a unit process or group of processes without treatment. Recirculating systems should be used to recycle water. Once-through cooling systems should not be used.
4. Recycling condensate as boiler feedwater (where it is of suitable quality). Contaminated condensate should be used for lower grade cleaning activities (e.g. yard washing).
5. Recycling following treatment – this may include tertiary treatment such as membrane technology. Best available technique (BAT) for operators are shown in Table 13.2.

Table 13.2: Indicative BAT – considerations for operators.

Indicative BAT	*Operator consideration*
Process control	Level measurement on storage or processing tanks –prevent overflow and avoid need to clean up spills Flow measurement – control and optimise water use and minimise effluent generation on cleaning systems Flow control – control flow rate to water ring vacuum pumps. Control process water flow rates for specific processes Assess product loss against benchmarks

(Cont'd...)

Indicative BAT	*Operator consideration*
	Set up effluent monitoring to provide baseline information. You should set improvement targets this could be a reduction in daily COD
	Continue monitoring and reviewing your performance regularly
Raw material preparation	When choosing a peeling technique or when replacing peeling plant, demonstrate that the selection takes into account water efficiency, energy efficiency and product loss
Heat processing using steam and water	Install a condensate reuse system
	Consider reusing blanching water in other processes
	If evaporation is used to pre-concentrate food, the hot water resulting from this process can be used as boiler feed make-up and potential reuse within the factory (e.g. CIP make-up)
Cooling, chilling, freezing and freeze drying	Recirculating systems should be used to recycle water, once-through cooling systems should not be used
Cleaning and	Wherever possible, raw materials and product should be kept out of sanitation the wastewater system
Equipment design	Consider ease of cleaning when ordering new equipment
	Wherever practicable, process lines and operations that cause excessive spillage of material onto the floor should be modified to eliminate or reduce the problem
	Dry clean-up procedures should remove as much residual material as possible from vessels and equipment before they are washed
	Drains should be equipped with catchpots
	Catchpots should be in place during cleaning (e.g. by installing lockable catchpots)
	Optimise water pressure at jets, nozzles and orifices
	Trigger-operated spray guns or hoses should have an automatic water supply shut off
Good housekeeping	Install trays to collect waste to prevent it falling to the floor
	Spilt material should be swept, shovelled or vacuumed rather than hosed down the drain
	Ensure that suitable dry clean-up equipment always readily available
	Optimise cleaning schedules
	Cleaning cycle durations should be matched to the vessel size
	Use smart scheduling to minimise numbers of product changes and subsequent cleaning between products
Manual cleaning	Develop procedures so that hoses are only used after dry clean-up
	Use automatic shut off on hand-held hoses and water lances to minimise the use of washdown water
	High-pressure/low-volume systems should be used wherever practicable
CIP	Dry product should be removed before the start of the wash cycle by gravity draining, pigging or air blowdown
	Pre-rinsing should be used to enable remaining product to be recovered for reuse or disposal
	Use of turbidity detector to maximise product recovery
	Optimal CIP programme for the size of plant/vessel and type of soiling
	Optimising frequency and duration of rinses to reduce water use
	Automatic dosing of chemicals at correct concentrations
	Internal recycling of water and chemicals
	Recycle control on conductivity rather than time
	Continuous cleaning of recirculated solutions
	Water efficient spray devices

SECTION III

Emission of Greenhouse Gases Sustainability and Carbon Footprint

Chapter 14

Food Production and Emission of Greenhouse Gases

INTRODUCTION

Food chains around the world are responsible for a large share of total emissions of greenhouse gases (GHG's). There are no studies presenting the share for the global food production system, but as an indication, Steinfeldt and others reported that 18% of global GHG emissions could be attributed to animal products alone. For the EU, a figure of 29% of all consumption derived GHG emissions are food related. The latter study analysed the whole life cycle for all goods consumed within EU, i.e. including all imports and excluding goods produced within the EU and exported.

FOOD'S CLIMATE IMPACT IN BRIEF

Food production systems as a group are very heterogeneous, the range of products is huge and production systems vary within product groups as well. However, there are some common traits. To start with, emissions of fossil carbon dioxide (CO_2) are less important than for most other products, instead emissions of biogenic GHG's are more important. For vegetable products, nitrous oxide (N_2O) are often the most important emission, as well as for production of monogastric animals (pork, poultry), whereas for ruminants methane (CH_4) is often the dominating gas emitted. Methane and nitrous oxide are very potent GHG's, methane having a weighting factor of 25 times CO_2 and nitrous oxide 298. For seafood products, correlation between energy use and climate impact is higher, especially for wild-caught fish. The climate impact of products from capture fisheries is dominated by fossil CO_2 emissions from fuel use on fishing boats.

Products of animal origin, such as meat and dairy, have on average higher emissions per kilogram than vegetable products, but there are many exceptions. Transports play a role, but often smaller than anticipated. However, if less efficient transport modes are used, as air freight or inefficient distribution to grocery stores, transports can be of significance also in a life cycle perspective. An important share of food's life cycle impact is caused by the consumers, in developed countries the transport from the grocers' by car is very inefficient, and globally cooking can play an important role. Food waste ending up in landfills are also an important contribution to GHG emissions, methane is formed when food is degraded under anaerobic conditions in landfills. Packaging can be of significance, but it is a trade-off between functionality of the packaging as protecting the food and emissions of the packaging material.

Food production demands land, and fertile land is a scarce resource. Hence a high land use per unit food produced, i.e. low yield, is negative even if the direct emissions for the product are low. This is a result of the fact that if the yield were higher the land could have been used for alternative production such as biofuels or forest. It must also be kept in mind that how the land is used has significant impact on other environmental impacts, as eutrophication and biodiversity. Land use is also crucial for important aspects as valuable ecosystem services, provision of drinking water and clean air. How land is managed is also important for the GHG budget of food products. By employing farming methods that conserve soil carbon, farmland can become a carbon sink while still producing food.

A severe impact of food production is deforestation. In the report from Steinfeldt and others around one third of the 18% of GHG's allocated to animal production is due to emissions caused by deforestation, especially in developing countries. A large share of global deforestation is driven by need for more arable land, especially in South America where soya cultivation and beef production is expanding.

Food chains are often complex with many interdependent actors, and increasingly also spans geographically large areas. Moreover, the products are often perishable which increase the complexity in maintaining environmentally efficient food chains. As a result of the above, losses in food chains can be significant. Wasted food means that all emissions caused and resources used are in vain, wastage contributes to the problems but not to food supply. In the industrialised world there is an ongoing debate about organic versus conventional production about what production system is most 'climate friendly'. To describe it simplistically, the proponents of conventional farming use arguments of production efficiency per hectare whereas advocates of organic farming highlights the more resilient way of farming as an important aspect in the larger context. Important activities are similar between the two production systems, although absolute levels of impact differ, but since there is no general trend with organic production always being more efficient than conventional, we do not distinguish between them is this report. In short, there are differences in absolute numbers, but the key issues are similar. Basic knowledge about food production's climate impact can guide improvements in both production systems.

Methodological basis for the Report

The basis for this description of food productions climate impact is mainly based on research within Life Cycle Assessment (LCA). LCA is an ISO standardised method for environmental assessment of products or services. In short LCA can be said to include all environmental impact caused by a product, from 'cradle-to-grave' which means that all flows necessary to produce, process and deliver the product is included in the analysis. Within LCA, methods for transforming emissions of single substances into environmental impact categories are used. Examples of impact categories are climate change, eutrophication, acidification and toxicity. For resource use the methodology is less developed but resources as energy, land, water and minerals are included in LCA results. Production systems generally are complex with a lot of interdependencies with other technical and natural systems. Methods for defining systems boundaries and allocation of environmental burdens between products are slightly open, so results from LCA studies of similar systems can vary. This is not a result of one of them being wrong, but that different methodological choices have been made. Consequently results from LCA's must be interpreted as having uncertainties, but still very useful for identification of the most important parts of the system and also for identification and evaluation of improvement potentials.

In food chains, the earlier parts (primary production and processing) of the chain differ significantly between product groups, whereas latter parts are more similar. Hence the first part of the report covers primary production of different product groups, and the second part covers post-farm activities of all product groups together.

Delimitations

This section describes food production's emissions of greenhouse gases. Food production affects our environment in many ways, eutrophication of waterways, acidification, spreading of toxic chemicals in pesticides, biodiversity and emissions of GHG's. Moreover, the cultural landscape in many parts of the world is depending on food production. We are certainly aware of this and strongly recommend that a broader spectrum is used when discussing sustainability of food systems.

Greenhouse gas emissions from land use change (LUC), most importantly due to deforestation, are not covered in this report, data availability is limited and methodological issues on how to allocate deforestation emissions to products needs to be resolved. A final important notion is that the mix of products we choose to consume, our diet, is a very important parameter for the total climate impact of food consumption. By changing diets on a large scale long term improvements can be gained, but with large consequences for all actors in the chain. To discuss and implement diet changes a good understanding of how production systems work is essential, it is not either or but both.

GREENHOUSE GAS IMPACT FROM DIFFERENT PRODUCT GROUPS

Meat and Dairy Products

To discuss emissions of GHG's from animal products, we need to divide them in two groups, monogastric animals and ruminants. For monogastric animals as pigs and poultry the feed provision is the most important activity, followed by manure management. The emissions are dominated by nitrous oxide (N_2O) from soil turnover of nitrogen and emissions from production of mineral fertilisers. Energy use can be of significance for some animals as chicken in cold climates where houses have to be heated during winter, and in warm climates where houses have to be cooled. For ruminants, as cattle, sheep and goats, emissions of methane (CH_4) are often the most important. Most methane originates from the enteric fermentation, i.e. when feed is digested in the rumen, a minor share comes from manure management. The second most important emission is nitrous oxides from nitrogen turnover in feed production and manure management. Generally emissions from manure management are more important in warmer climates, since the processes generating GHG emissions are stimulated by higher temperatures. For all animal products later steps in the chain as transport, processing and packaging are less important, in a relative sense.

Beef

Beef are produced in extremely different production systems globally, but also within countries and regions. Beef is either produced in 'dedicated' beef herds, where beef is the only main product, or as a co-product from dairy production, i.e. bull calves from dairy herds are raised for beef and culled cows are used for meat. The common picture from all these varied systems is that methane from enteric fermentation (feed digestion) is important for the life cycle GHG emissions. When ruminants consume feed, micro-organisms in their rumen degrade the cellulose and hemicelluloses into substances the cattle can utilise. In this process, which is anaerobic, methane is formed by the micro-organisms and emitted. The ability to utilise roughage feeds is not only negative, from a resource point of view ruminants can make use of lands where only grass can be grown, hence can be said to valorise non-edible feeds to high quality food.

In systems where a large share of the feed is concentrated, as grain and soya, the emissions for feed provisions increases, both nitrous oxide and CO_2. At the same time, the methane emissions are lower if concentrate feed is used, but the balance is not clear. Since emissions from biological processes in the rumen are important, it is vital that the growth of cattle is high in order to have low emissions per kg of meat. If animals grow very slow, a lot of methane is produced from the digestion of feed needed to maintain the animals' life, without producing any meat. Along the same line of reasoning an important explanation to the high GHG emissions for beef is the slow regeneration rate. Cows give birth to at best one calf per year, which means that all emissions during one cow-year have to be carried more or less by the meat produced by the calf. In combined dairy-meat production systems the cow produces both milk and a calf every year which makes beef from such systems less emission intense.

It should be noted that the studies presented can not be compared directly. There are differences in methodology, as allocation between hides, meat and milk and sometimes the system boundaries differ slightly. Moreover, the weighting factors for methane and nitrous oxide was changed by the IPCC in 2007, which make results from older studies slightly lower than results from newer studies. Moreover, some studies are based on one or a few farms, others on farm modelling and still others on national averages. The latter have a tendency to show higher results, partly since more flows are covered than in the other two types but mainly due to changed weighting factors for methane introduced in 2007.

Dairy

The GHG emissions from dairy production are similar to that of beef production, enteric fermentation and manure dominates with a contribution of 50–60% and nitrous oxides from feed production and manure management contributes with around 30%. There are however differences, dairy farming in developed countries are generally more intense with a larger use of concentrate feeds as grain and soya. As a consequence feed provision is slightly more important.

The milk yield per cow is a determining factor. Using a slightly technical perspective it is important to have as large share as possible of total feed intake (and methane emissions) being used for producing milk as opposed to the animal using a large share for maintenance. It is important to include also the feed and time needed to raise the calf. Conclusively, the yield must be balanced with the risk of having shorter productive life for the average cow. Milk is one of the products being most extensively analysed by LCA. There are a number of studies from Europe and New Zealand, very few (if any) from developing countries. The results are rather similar, and varies between 0.8–1.4 kg CO_2-equiv./kg milk at farmgate. In addition around 0.1 for processing and transports up to retail is presented. Since milk has high water content (around 88%) it is reasonable to consider that in comparisons with other animal products. Normalising milk to 70% water means the emissions of GHG's is between 3.1 and 3.8 kg CO_2-equiv./kg, on a similar dry matter basis as meat (still other properties differ).

Pork

Pigs are monogastric animals and only produce very small amount of methane in their feed digestion. But pigs can not utilise cellulose and hemicellulose in feeds, but need to be fed grains and alike, feed that could be used directly as food by humans. The life cycle emissions are normally dominated by agriculture and inputs to it, the later steps in the chain are less important, besides unnecessary wastage.

The emissions of GHG's from pork are lower than for beef, and production is dominated by nitrous oxide. Since no methane is formed in the feed digestion, the feed provision is the most important parameter, and accounts for between 60–70% of total emissions up to farm gate. Feed provision includes emissions caused by production of fertilisers, soil emissions of nitrous oxides and energy used in arable farming. The remainder of emissions is mainly manure management, energy use for animal husbandry being a minor part. In warmer climates manure emissions is probably more important, since more methane are formed at higher storage temperatures. Besides the differences in feed digestion, pork cause lower GHG emissions than beef due to a higher feed conversion and also the fact that one sow can produce up to 25 offsprings yearly, hence the sows environmental impact is shared by many producing animals, i.e. the slaughter pigs.

Poultry

The only LCA studies of poultry concern chicken, no studies of duck, geese or turkey is presented. Since chicken is the absolutely dominating type of poultry globally as well as within the EU this is still relevant. Chickens are, as pigs, monogastric animals, and have a high feed efficiency. At the same time chicken have high demands on feed composition, e.g. high demand on protein, both quality and quantity, which in turn puts high demands on feed production. The high feed efficiency is the explanation to the relatively low emissions of GHG's, the proportion of feed consumed by the chicken used for growing versus maintenance is high. In temperate and cold climates barns have to be heated, and depending on what energy source is being used the emissions vary. For example, in Sweden biofuels as straw or wood chips is the most common fuel used, whereas in most other parts of the EU fossil fuel is dominating. In a sensitivity analysis presented in Tynelius, the total emission of GHG's is increased with around one third if biofuels were replaced with fossil oil. In warmer climates cooling of barns can be an important contributor, but no studies including this have been found.

Seafood

Since the 1950s, fishing has seen considerable technological development on all levels and has progressed from an industry making small-scale use of certain wild fish stocks to become a large scale industrial operation that is highly efficient in localising and utilising wild stocks. The seafood market is one of the most globalised markets, in part due to the seasonality in supply, the huge variety in products and qualities and the described general lack of raw material experienced by the seafood processing industry driving it to new sourcing strategies and markets. Fresh and frozen seafood is therefore flown, shipped and trucked all around the globe. The demand for seafood is projected to continue to increase over the coming decades both due to growth of the world population and economic growth in new regions. In this perspective, achieving more sustainable production systems for seafood products is urgent.

Fisheries

The climate impact of fisheries is dominated by carbon dioxide emissions from onboard diesel combustion, which is directly related to the amount of fuel used. The second major factor is the leakage of refrigerants from onboard cooling equipment if the refrigerants used have a high climate impact. Analysing the entire production chain from fisheries to fish consumption, it is the fishing phase that accounts for the greatest share of total energy utilisation and climate impact through onboard fuel combustion during fishing in modern, industrialised fisheries. A number of factors affect the climate impact per kilo of fish landed, perhaps the most significant are fishing gear and species biology. The stock situation is another key factor that affects fuel efficiency. Low-density fish stocks mean that more time is required to accumulate the same catch compared with the same fish stock at a higher density, using the same gear. It is difficult, if not impossible, to fish an overexploited stock in an energy-efficient manner. In other words, in addition to the fishing method, the stock situation is a key factor in determining the energy efficiency of fisheries.

Aquaculture

The climate impact of seafood products from aquaculture is often dominated by production of fish farm inputs, most importantly the feed. Filtrating mussels that are farmed require no feed input, as opposed to farmed fish. Some fish (such as carp, tilapia, and pangasius) are omnivores and can survive without animal-based feed ingredients, which means they can normally be fed using agricultural products or residues. Other species, including those that have become very popular recently, salmon, trout, and cod, are predators that require some input of marine-based feed, i.e. in industrialised production systems a combination of fishmeal and fish oil.

What about the role of the supply chain after landing? Seafood is one of the most traded food commodities globally, so transports can play a role. The demand for fresh fish means that some fish is air freighted which has severe consequences for total emissions of GHG's, this is discussed in more detail in following sections. Since seafood is perishable, cooling or freezing is needed which add to GHG emissions. Otherwise, the proportion of frozen seafood products total emissions of GHG's represented by transport is typically under 20%, which is showed in several studies.

Vegetable Products

Grains

The climate impact of grains is fairly well investigated. Even though there are some differences in the impact between different grain and energy crops, mostly depending on the yield level, there is a common pattern of what the most important aspects are when it comes to emissions of GHG's. First, the production and application of nitrogen fertiliser is a very important contributor to the overall climate impact of these products. Production of nitrogen fertiliser generates fossil CO_2, but also, and more importantly, nitrous oxide. Moreover, when the fertiliser is applied, nitrous oxide is emitted both directly when applying the fertiliser and indirectly as a consequence of ammonia release and leakage of nitrate. Secondly, the use of diesel for agricultural operations (ploughing, harvesting, etc.) and for drying the produce results in CO_2 emissions. It is quite evident that nitrogen fertiliser is the dominant source of GHG's, a result of the emissions of CO_2 and N_2O from production of the fertiliser and the direct and indirect emissions of nitrous oxide when applying it. One of the most important foods globally is rice. There are two main production methods, dry (upland) and wet (paddy) rice. Production of upland rice is similar to other grain crops from a climate impact perspective, so this section focuses on paddy rice which is also the most important production form globally. The specific issue with paddy rice is that methane is formed under the anaerobic conditions in the flooded fields. There are few LCA studies on rice, but on a global level it is reported that rice accounts for 10–13% of global methane emissions. Blengini and Busto presents an LCA of Italian paddy rice, and although Italy is not a large rice producer globally, some of the findings have general bearing on paddy rice production. The total emissions of GHG's are 2.9 kg CO_2 equiv./kg of white milled rice, which is in the order of six times higher than the wheat flour. The main difference is the field emissions, mainly methane, amounting to around 70% of total emissions. But also a high use of fossil energy for processing contributed to the difference.

Grain legumes

Grain legumes, such as peas, fava beans and soyabeans, are efficient sources of protein compared to animal protein, i.e. they do not require the same amount of inputs per kg protein as compared to the inputs required to produce 1 kg of animal protein. Grain legumes' ability to fixate nitrogen from air means that only small, if any, nitrogen fertiliser is applied in the cultivation, which of course benefits the climate profile of these products. There are a few studies assessing the impact of grain legumes, e.g. Lagerberg-Fogelberg and Carlsson-Kanyama which compared beans and peas with different origin as well as different types of processing (drying, canning). The study showed that the cultivation, i.e. use of diesel, is an important contributor to the total GHG emissions of the product, and that for canned products the packaging also plays an important role. Another study, by Davis and others, which compared meals with varying protein sources (similar content of protein, fat and energy), showed that a meal with a pea burger is associated with significantly less GHG's compared to a pork chop meal. However, this study highlighted the need for efficient processing of products with vegetable protein such as veggie burgers, since these products are often sold frozen due to small stock units, which can result in high energy costs for freezing and frozen storage.

Fruits and vegetables

In general, the production of fruits and vegetables are associated with fairly low emissions of climate gases. As for grains, the most significant aspects of GHG's sources are use of diesel and nitrogen fertilisers, as well as yield level. Potatoes and other root vegetables are particularly efficient in the cultivation, since the yield level is so high per ha, resulting in low emissions of GHG's per kg product. However, depending on soil type the emissions can vary, cultivation on peat soils results in quite significant losses of CO_2 and nitrous oxide from the soil. Nevertheless, because the cultivation typically is efficient, i.e. low inputs and emissions per produced unit, the importance of downstream processes is higher in relative terms. This means that production and waste handling of the packaging, as well as processing and transport, are often important contributors to the overall carbon footprint for these types of products. For products grown in heated greenhouses, the type of heat production is the most important parameter for the product's carbon footprint, where of course use of fossil fuels result in high emissions of GHG's. A switch to renewable fuels alters the picture, even though this does not eliminate the need for more efficient heating in the greenhouse, to save energy. The choice of heating affects the carbon footprint of tomatoes, where a fossil based heating system results in more than three times higher emissions of GHG's than from tomatoes grown in a greenhouse heated with biofuel. Cultivation in Spain does not require any heating, the contribution from the example in the figure predominantly comes from soil emissions of N_2O. Thus, the scale of difference between cultivation on mineral and peat soil, giving an example of cultivation of carrots where growing on peat soil gives considerable emissions of CO_2 from the soil. Another important environmental aspect when it comes to fresh fruits and vegetables is that these types of products are often sensitive to handling and have limited storage time, which can result in significant quantities of wastage. The wastage means that unnecessary environmental impact has occurred when producing the food item if it is just thrown away, and moreover, further environmental impact might follow when treating the generated waste. This is discussed more in the following sections.

TRANSPORTS, PACKAGING, RETAIL AND CONSUMPTION

As mentioned earlier post farm activities are of less significance for animal products but more for vegetable products. The absolute impact for e.g. a certain transport per kg of product is similar regardless of product group, but since there are so large differences in emissions of GHG's from primary production the relative importance of transports, packaging and consumption for product groups differ.

Transports

The food sector is transport-intense, a lot of inputs to food production as well as food products themselves are transported in large volumes and sometimes long distances. This can sometimes be of great significance for the total life cycle GHG emission of a product, but often transports contribute relatively little in a life cycle perspective. There are some important aspects when discussing transports. One thing is the transport mode, what type of vehicle is used. For some high value, perishable foods airfreight is used, but for most foods truck, rail or sea transport is the most common. These transport modes differ significantly in energy intensity and hence GHG emissions. Finally, distribution of foods from warehouses to retail stores are often less efficient, slow driving with a lot of stops combined with low load factor. The last link in the transport chain, between retail stores to households are probably the least efficient, at least for industrialised countries were a significant percentage of these transports are performed by car.

A simplified summary of food transports are that they become less efficient the longer down the supply chain you get. So, transports of feed and other agricultural impacts are often very efficient, high density, often by ship, train or large lorries and rarely refrigerated. Transports from farms to industry are often slightly less efficient since some products are perishable. The next step, from industry to warehouses or retail entails high volume and low weight goods and to some extent less efficient distribution. The last step, consumers' home transports is the least efficient, if cars are used, small loads (typically 10–20 kg per trip) using a vehicle weighing more than 800 kg indicates a very low efficiency. It can be argued that food shopping is done in conjunction with other errands, hence the food shouldn't carry all responsibility for the emissions, which make sense. There are few studies on consumer behaviour in relation to food shopping, but Sonesson and others found that in Sweden, more than 60% of shopping trips were made using car, around 50% of these trips were made with the sole purpose of food shopping, so food shopping are an important driver for car use in Sweden at least.

Food Wastage

Food is wasted in all nodes in the food chain. Data on what percentages of food being wasted in different parts of the world are scarce, no overview is found. According to Stuart, who summarised a vast volume of data from literature combined with own investigations, the possible savings amounts to 33% of global food supply, meaning that 33% of food produced is avoidable waste, globally. Reasons for wastage differ, but many foods are perishable by nature. Other reasons are lack of co-ordination along the supply chain, inadequate packaging and storage conditions and finally consumer's lack of meal- and purchase planning. In agriculture most wastage is due to harvest and storage. In industry food is wasted due to cleaning but also production planning, which in turn depends on lacking coordination along the supply chain. Since some food products carry a heavy 'climate backpack' when entering the industry (notably products of animal origin), reduced wastage is often the most efficient improvement potential for food industries. This has been demonstrated in several studies of the dairy industry. As an example, the GHG emission caused by raw material production of milk being wasted at the dairy was 33% of the dairy' total emissions. For food of animal origin the wastage might not be as important as primary production on a per kg base, but vegetable products, especially vegetables and fruit show large losses, and the waste management might cause considerable emissions. If food waste is being put into landfill large quantities of methane is formed. In industrialised countries it is a well known fact that large volumes of food are being wasted by households. This is based on waste statistics, what products are being wasted is less clear. From a study performed in the UK wastage of different product groups were presented. The results showed that there were large differences between product groups, with 'salad greens' at the top with 45% of purchased products being wasted, followed by bread with 31% and fruits with 26%. At the other end of the scale we find dairy products (3%) and meat- and seafood (13%). The figures represent 'avoidable waste', i.e. excluding peels, kernels, etc. There are few other studies on household waste, but Sonesson and others presents figures for some products being in the same range as the ones mentioned above.

Retail

The retail sector's direct impact on total life cycle GHG emissions is often limited. In retail, energy use, mainly for freezers and refrigerators, and refrigerant leakage are the most important sources for direct emissions, but probably more important are the emission caused by wastage in the sector. The retail sector also has an important role in the coordination of activities in the food chain, being placed between the consumers and producers.

Packaging

Food packaging is often thought of as a bad thing for the environment, with excessive use of plastics and paper. However, packaging has important roles to play in the food chain, it protects the food thus keeping it safe and healthy. But packaging also reduces wastage, which is very important from a climate point of view, and packaging can be used to transform information along the supply chain which facilitates efficiency improvements. What type of packaging being used influences the transport efficiency since it has its own weight but also affect the weight/volume ratio of the product. So, the climate impact of packaging is a trade-off between the positive function (reduce wastage, facilitate communication) and the negative impacts (increased volumes and weight to transport, emissions caused by production and waste management of packaging materials).

Consumption

The most important impact from the consumer stage in the chain is already covered, wastage and home transports. But cooking can also be an important contributor to total life cycle GHG emissions, especially for vegetable products (with low emissions in earlier stages) that require long boiling times.

IMPROVEMENT OPTIONS AND POTENTIALS

This section gives a brief overview of improvement potentials. It is not possible to present in-depth descriptions of improvements for the large and varying product group foods.

Primary Production

A key issue in decreasing climate impact of foods from agriculture is nitrogen turnover. To produce nitrogen as mineral fertiliser cause GHG emissions, soil turnover of nitrogen and manure management as well. So, if less nitrogen is wasted, less needs to be produced and fewer emissions will occur from nitrogen 'at the wrong place'. Nitrogen use can be optimised in arable farming by more accurate application, in animal husbandry by reduced emissions from manure storage and spreading but also through optimised feeding. By using land management that increases the content of organic content in soils, a globally important carbon sink can be created. Good land management, i.e. maintaining soil fertility is a second key issue since it facilitates high yields which in turn are important for a climate- and economic efficient agriculture.

In fishery one of the most efficient improvements are maintaining or rebuilding fish stocks. By this more fish can be caught with less effort, hence less fuel is used per ton of fish. Deploying more energy efficient fishing methods, or avoid the most energy intense, is also important. Generally passive gears (set nets, traps) are more energy efficient than active gears such as trawls. To phase out synthetic refrigerants is also an efficient measure. In aquaculture improvements can be made by optimising feed use, both by less wastage and higher biological utilisation and by using less resource demanding feed ingredients, e.g. avoiding use of feed fish that are caught in energy demanding fisheries.

In the Food Chain as a Whole

In the post farm food chain, raw material utilisation is a key issue. By minimising waste, fewer raw materials is needed to provide the same amount of products, thus reducing the need for arable land which can be used for other purposes. Wastage can be reduced by technical means as better storage conditions, but a lot can be done within food industry by working with 'lean production' concepts. Improved shelf life with maintained or better product quality by novel processing technologies is another means to reduce wastage, both at retail and households. Packaging is an area where there are trade-offs between function and environmental impact, and specific considerations are needed for specific products. Generally, it is possible to reduce 'over-packed' products or to avoid heavy and voluminous packaging. For some products, as yoghurt, around 8% of the product might still be left in the container when the consumer judges it as empty. By good packaging design the possibility to empty the package is increased, hence wastage is reduced. Introduction of efficient recycling of packaging material is also positive.

There are several possibilities to improve the 'climate efficiency' by working in a food chain perspective. By increased transparency in the supply chain, i.e. information flows with useful information between nodes, wastage can be significantly reduced by better match between consumer demand and production. In this field the retail sector has an important role.

CLIMATE LABELLING – PRINCIPLES AND POSSIBILITIES

In recent years climate labelling has been proposed as a means of reducing food's climate impact, by empowering consumers to make informed choices and hence put pressure on producers. There are two different principles in climate labelling, 'declarations' and 'criteria based'. Climate declarations, often referred to as 'Carbon Footprinting', build on quantitative data which is presented on the package, sometimes combined with information about whether the figure is high or low in comparison with other products. The climate labelling introduced by Tesco in the UK is a declaration labelling. Criteria based labelling use the same principle as eco-labelling, a set of criteria is described for each product or product group, and if the producers fulfil these criteria they are entitled to label their product. There are strengths and weaknesses with both principles. Declarations make it possible to compare products from different product groups, as meat and beans. At the same time declarations demands high quality analyses of the products, and this is costly. More important, declarations build on life cycle assessments (LCA), and the methodology and standards for performing LCA is open to different choices, and detailed knowledge about biogenic emissions is lacking, and hence results can differ for that reason. Moreover, the variations between farms and years pose another complicating factor. A second weakness is that quantification requires detailed data from actors in the food chain, and since they are stakeholders as well, third party verification becomes necessary. Even if the present work on standardisation is successful and the problem of verification can be resolved, there will still be large uncertainties about data quality etc. since the analysed systems are large, complex and varying over time.

In summary, climate declarations are efficient since they directly show the emissions and also since they leave open for the producers to improve their production in the most efficient way, not delimited by production based criteria as in criteria based labelling. But there are severe practical and methodological constraints. Criteria based declarations are easier to implement and check, there is no need for calculations. To identify and describe criteria is difficult and demands high level competence on systems level about food systems. The major drawback is that criteria labelling doesn't inform consumers about differences between product groups, it can in general only inform about what product in the category is better than other within the same category. Moreover, criteria might hamper innovation, since the producer is obliged to follow the rules set on how to produce, and little room is left for 'thinking out of the box'.

To sum up, the main source of knowledge is LCA studies of different products, which gives hard numbers and are easy to understand. However, when using LCA some important assumptions are often made that needs to be considered. One of the most important is that the results represent a static picture of reality. The feedback loops from consumption to production are rarely covered, so structural changes in the food system are not accounted for. Moreover, the data quality might differ significantly between studies. So, LCA results should be interpreted bearing this in mind. For a better and more complete picture, scenario studies of different food systems covering more than just climate impact should be performed but such studies presented hitherto are on a high systems level and doesn't inform on details within product groups. Scenario studies needs to be large, and this is very resource demanding and also have inherent limitations, as, e.g. how to define scenarios to study which also will be strongly value laden. Conclusively LCA studies presently provide the best basis to understand food systems climate impact, but figures should be interpreted with care when comparing similar products.

As mentioned in the introduction, this report focuses on the climate impact of foods. Food production and consumption contributes largely to other important sustainability aspects which must be taken into account in broader discussions and work on sustainable food systems.

There are obvious knowledge gaps in the quantification of climate impact from products. One is the fact that present data does not include land use and land use change, which is a potentially important parameter for food products. This point is not only about deforestation, which is a 'land use change' but also management of soils in general, 'land use'.

More research is needed, both in order to develop methods to incorporate these issues in LCA, and also to build knowledge about how carbon flows to and from soils are affected by farm practices. A second area of research concerns the emissions of biogenic GHG's, methane and nitrous oxide. This is a complex area since the substances are formed in biological systems, hence vary with e.g. climate, soil type and management.

One aspect that potentially is one of the most powerful in combating food's impact on climate change is the choice of products, i.e. our diets. Since the differences in life cycle GHG emissions are so very large between products fulfilling similar nutritional functions, the scope for improvement is large. In order to efficiently work with 'climate smart diets' more knowledge is needed about life cycle impact of single products (not only agricultural data) and connections between diets and how the food chain is affected by changed diets.

Chapter 15

Impact of Food Processing on the Sustainability of the Food Supply Chain

INTRODUCTION

The demand for high quality, safe, nutritious processed foods will continue to increase as the global population and affluence increases. This imposes an enormous burden on the environment and the food processing industry has responded by making progress in reducing the carbon and water footprints of products and the amount of waste generated. However, environmental sustainability cannot be considered in isolation because economic and social sustainability are essential to the industry. To ensure that the food processing industry is economically and environmentally sustainable, it is important to take an integrated approach of the whole food supply chain including farm and post operations. Life Cycle Assessment (LCA) is a tool that facilitates this approach and will enable meaningful environmental messages to be communicated to consumers who are becoming increasingly aware of the environmental impact of the products that they purchase. As the food processing industry becomes more globalised it is importance that analyses standardise social and economic factors in environmental assessment so that meaningful comparisons can be made for monitoring environmental performance, regulatory compliance and consumer communication. As well as technological advances to enable the reduction of the environmental footprints of processed foods, it is necessary to change consumer behaviour to reduce consumption to ensure that the global food processing system is sustainable.

Sustainable development from a business perspective is defined as 'meeting the needs of the business without compromising the ability of future generations to meet their own needs' Brundtland. Issues relating to sustainable living and production systems are important topics that are driven mainly by economic, social, environmental and political factors. As the global food consumption continues to increase because of the rapid growth in the global population and increasing affluence in emerging economies such as China and India, global resources such as energy and water are being consumed quickly and arable land utilised at an alarming rate. If this trend continues, our society will not be sustainable and future generations will not be able to enjoy the standard of living that we enjoy today. From a simplistic point of view, businesses could be sustainable by reducing the ecological footprint by reducing the amount of resources that are used, the waste that is generated and the amount of emissions produced. However, the business systems are complex and in order for the whole food supply chain to sustainable, it is important to understand the impact of food processing on the input side (raw material production, storage and distribution) and the output side (finished product storage, distribution, retailing and the consumer).

The food manufacturing industry is highly competitive and multi nationals as well as small to medium sized enterprises strive to grow and remain profitable while complying with regulatory requirements, government policy (such as reducing carbon emissions to comply with environmental regulations and the further development of the Kyoto protocol), operating in an ethical and an environmentally responsible manner and satisfying the requirements of the consumers and retailers. While consumers are continuing to demand fresh and processed foods that are safe to eat, convenient to consume, contribute to the health and well being, are of high sensory quality and are affordable, another consumer demand that is becoming increasingly important is that the products have been manufactured in an environmentally sustainable manner.

Retailers, who are becoming very influential in specifying the requirements of the foods that consumer purchase, are also addressing the environmental issue and are exerting pressure on the food manufacturers to adopt sustainable manufacturing processes. This is evident from developments in the UK where some supermarkets have introduced a number of products with the carbon footprint of the product on the product label. This trend is spreading globally and products with the carbon footprint on the labels will be launched in Australia later in 2010. Companies all over the world are adopting environmentally friendly practices into their business models and are conserving their natural resources, reducing waste, improving recycling practices and using sustainable packaging and supply chain systems. Sustainable processing is becoming increasingly important in food ingredients as well as finished products and in the case of dairy ingredients, Berry points out that social responsibility (how a business impacts employees, customers and communities in which it operates), ecological integrity (how a company's operations impact the world and its resources) and economic stability (how a company makes, spends and saves money) become important messages that marketers are using to communicate to consumers on product packaging and web sites.

MATERIALS AND METHODS

In order to set goals and monitor sustainable performance in the food processing industry, it is necessary to define matrices to measure sustainable processing. Typically these matrices include the amount of Green House Gas (GHG) emissions, water usage and waste generation associated with products. As GHG emissions take place in different parts of a product's life cycle, it is necessary to calculate the total GHG emissions by carrying out a life cycle assessment (LCA). In LCA studies, the GHG emissions during the production, storage and distribution of raw materials, product manufacture, distribution and storage of the product, consumption and disposal and recycling of packaging are taken into account and the GHG emissions for the whole life cycle of the product is expressed as grams CO_2 equivalent per unit mass of product. This value is referred to as the carbon footprint of the product. The green house gases include methane and nitrous oxide emitted in farming operations, the energy used in the manufacture of fertilisers and the energy used in post farm operations including product manufacture.

The method of calculating the carbon footprint (using a LCA approach) is documented by a Publicly Available Specification (PAS 2050) by the British Standard Institute and the associated Carbon Label system (LCA-like) developed by the UK's Carbon Trust. There are now widely used globally as a standard method for calculating the carbon footprint of goods and services. A draft ISO standard (ISO 14067) for calculating carbon footprints for products using a similar approach to PAS 2050 has been product and the full standard is expected to be published in 2012. The use of LCA in the food industry in Australia and Europe is described through case studies by Simons and Sanguansri, Zufia and Arana and Andersson and others.

Another metric that is often quoted when referring to the sustainability of a product is 'food miles'. Quite simply, food miles are defined as the distance the food travels from farm to plate. According to this definition, locally grown and locally manufactured foods are more environmentally sustainable than products that have to be shipped from long distances. However, this is not the case because it can be more energy efficient for a British household to buy tomatoes or lettuce from Spain than from heated greenhouses in the UK. The invalidity of using food miles as an indicator of sustainability is further confirmed from a study carried out in New Zealand by Saunders and others who showed that the carbon footprint of lamb from New Zealand is less than the carbon footprint of lamb produced in the UK and a recent study in Australia which showed that transport emissions are only 3% of the total GHG emissions for lamb exported from Australia to the USA. These observations are consistent with a study carried out in the USA by Webber and Matthews who found that transportation of food accounts for only 11% of the GHGs generated by the food consumed by an average US household annually.

The main flaw of food miles is that it takes into account only the GHG emissions during storage and transport of the product and ignores the GHG emissions during the growing of the raw materials and processing. The product's carbon footprint on the other hand, includes GHG emissions during every stage of the product's life cycle and is therefore a much better indicator of the product's impact on the environment. As it is necessary to calculate the GHG emissions for each stage of the product's life cycle in order to calculate the carbon footprint, manufacturers can use the carbon footprint to make important management decisions on the sourcing of the raw materials, location of manufacturing, sources of energy used and the type of packaging used so that the environmental impact of the product is minimised. It is not possible to make such management decisions from food miles alone.

Although the methodology for calculating the carbon footprint for a product is well defined and documented, this is not the case with water footprints. The term 'virtual' water usually means 'embedded' water in commodities such as grain and is used in the context of international trade when 'virtual water' moves from one country to another when commodities are exported. The water footprint on the other hand, like the carbon footprint, is calculated using a life cycle assessment for the product. However, the conventional method of calculating the water footprint is flawed because it only refers to the total volume of the water used in the product life cycle and does not take into account the type of water used, for example 'green' (rain water) or 'blue' (water from rivers and reservoirs), nor whether or not the water comes from a water stressed or water sufficient areas.

Thus, the impact on the environment when rain water is used in an area where there is an abundance of water is very different to the scenario where irrigated water is used in a water stressed area. Ridoutt and Pfister have suggested a revised method of calculating the water footprint of a product by taking into account the type of water used, the Water Stress Indicator of the area where the water is used and the volume of the water used. This correction gives a much better result on the environmental impact of making that product compared to using the volume of water alone. This methodology was effectively used in a study carried out in Australia by CSIRO (Commonwealth Industrial and Scientific Research Organisation) with Mars Australia on four commercial products and opportunities to reduce the environmental impact of these products (for water and carbon) were readily identified.

The amount of food waste generated is another important metric in measuring sustainable food processing and it is important to quantify the amount of waste generated at every stage of a product's life cycle. The amount of waste generated is simply reported as the weight of waste per unit mass of the finished product. These figures could then be used for comparative purposes and benchmarking and to identify opportunities to develop waste minimisation strategies. Identifying opportunities for the use of ungraded produce, out of date products or packaging compromised products will be a significant area of future innovation in the food processing sector. This is because there are growing markets for fine chemical (e.g. Plant antioxidants) and bioethanol (raw sugar and starch) feedstocks.

Discussion

For a business enterprise to be sustainable from an economic and an environmental point of view it has to use its resources efficiently and minimise waste generation. In a study carried out with 13 companies in East Anglia, UK, it was found that annual savings of ≤1.1m could be realised by reducing the use of raw materials, energy, water and waste generation. Food waste occurs in every part of the supply chain and the magnitude of the problem is well documented by Stuart. Food waste has an adverse effect on the environment because it contributes to the problem of landfill and when food is wasted, it also contributes to GHG emissions and water usage because energy and water are used in growing the raw materials, processing the product and in storage and distribution. In a recent life cycle assessment carried out with fresh Australian mangoes, it was shown that waste contributed to 53% of the overall GHG emissions during production, distribution and consumption phases. As well as minimising food waste, consideration should be given to value adding to waste by recovering valuable by products from waste and using food waste as a substrate to generate energy, thus closing the loop and having a 'zero waste' system. However, this is not always possible or economically feasible.

Large amounts of packaging are used in the manufacture of consumer foods and consideration should be given to minimising the amount of packaging used without compromising the quality or shelf life of the product within a sustainable food processing system. A range of biodegradable plastics are becoming readily available now and although they have certain limitations in terms of barrier properties and strength, and may not be suitable for all the food packaging requirements, developments in biodegradable packaging are likely to overcome these limitations. As a result, biodegradable packaging will be used in more applications and they will have market appeal for environmentally conscious consumers.

As the cost of energy has been steadily rising, the food industry has made advances in reducing its energy consumption through process optimisation and control, energy recovery and recycling systems and good manufacturing practices. As a result, GHG emissions have been reduced. This trend is likely to continue because of the enforcement of legislation in carbon trading systems and escalating energy prices. In parallel, advances of technology will make food factories more energy efficient as shown by a recent study of the Australian prune drying industry, which demonstrated that up to 60% energy could be saved by optimisation and control of the process and utilising solar energy. However, in order to reduce the carbon footprint significantly, it is necessary to use renewable sources of energy and technological advances will continue to make renewable energy sources such as solar and wind energy and lignocellulose technically and economically feasible.

Although steady progress has been made in energy and waste minimisation in the food industry, water minimisation has been not as effective. This is mainly because of legislation against the use of recycled water in processed foods, consumer perception and the fact that in most countries, water is still relatively cheap. As a result, recycled water is not used in processed foods. Therefore, even though it is possible to purify waste water to high standards of quality and safety through filtration and membrane technologies such as reverse osmosis, recycled water is not used because very often it is cheaper to pay for fresh water than investing capital in water purification plants. This observation appears to be relevant even in a dry continent like Australia as shown in a recent study. However, it is likely that recycled water will be used in food processing plants in the future as the cost of water increases and become more scarce (especially in countries such as Australia). Furthermore, changes in legislation will allow recycled water to be used as technologies will be developed to ensure that the required safety and quality standards will be met and consumer perceptions towards the use of recycled water in processed foods will change.

A sustainable diet has the least amount of impact to the environment. Therefore, a high protein, meat based diet is not so good for the environment because meat products have a high carbon footprint compared to a vegetarian diet. For example, based on the annual consumption per person, a vegetarian diet produces only about half the amount of GHG emissions of a typical meat based Australian diet. Therefore, environmentally conscious consumers may want to switch from a meat based diet to a vegetarian diet. However, it is important to consider the nutritional as well as the environmental implications of consuming a vegetarian diet. The importance of environmentally friendly (so called 'green' or 'eco') products to consumers is demonstrated from a recent study by Manget and others of the Boston Consulting Group, where a global consumer survey was carried out to assess green attitudes and shopping behaviours across nine countries. This study found that the green market share is growing and that consumers want to buy green products even during the economic downturn. What is interesting in this study is that it appears that consumers are willing to pay a little more (5–10%) for green products. This is not always the case however and generally, except for a niche market of environmentally conscious consumers, most consumers will not pay more for green products. This was confirmed in a recent focus group carried out in Australia, where the participants pointed out that although the consumer awareness and demand for green products are increasing, the cost of the product is still one of the most important factors in consumer choice.

Consumer communication with respect to environmentally friendly products is also important. As with nutritional labelling, consumers become confused with too much information on the product labels and it is important to communicate the environmental friendliness of a product simply, so that an informed decision could be made at the time of purchase of a product. One of the difficulties in communicating the environmental impact of a product to the consumer is not knowing what an environmentally friendly product really mean because currently there is no clear definition or standard for such products. Generally a environmentally friendly product will have a positive impact on the environment in terms of low carbon and water footprints and minimum waste generation. As the food processing industry is a global industry with many imported products on supermarket shelves, it is necessary to standardise the methodology used for quantifying the environmental impact of products. The carbon reduction label is one such example. In order to minimise consumer confusion with respect to product labelling, it is important that retailers and manufacturers improve consumer awareness of environmentally friendly products and communicate the environmental messages to consumers clearly and succinctly.

Although environmentally friendly products are important to consumers, from a business perspective, environmental friendliness on its own is not sufficient for the sustainability of a company. Ultimately, a company's sustainability is dependent on its economic viability. Therefore, a business has to consider sustainability from a holistic viewpoint and integrate all activities in the food processing system and the supply chain, including the production and sourcing of raw materials, storage and distribution of raw materials and products, manufacturing processes, product formulation, packaging and waste minimisation and management as well as efficient business practices. With such an approach, as well as improving its environmental credentials, it will also be possible for a company to reduce its operating costs and thus produce and sell environmentally friendly products without charging a premium from the consumer.

Although considerable advances are being made towards a sustainable food system in food processing and integrating farm and post farm operations, real sustainability will only be possible by reducing consumption. This will not be easy because of increasing global affluence and will only be possible by adopting behavioural changes by consumers so that good quality, nutritious food could be eaten in adequate quantities without imposing a burden on the environment, thus conserving our finite resources towards a sustainable future.

Chapter 16

Carbon and Water Footprint in Food Industry

INTRODUCTION

The carbon footprint is a measure of the amount of greenhouse gases (GHG) produced by our activities in relation to carbon dioxide (CO_2) or carbon. All activities caused by mankind from building our homes, using our cars to flying on holiday can be the subject of carbon footprinting.

The carbon footprint on food is an estimate of all the emissions caused by the production (e.g. farming), manufacture and delivery to the consumer and the disposal of packaging.

Thus, the carbon footprint is a measure of the exclusive total amount of carbon dioxide emissions that is directly and indirectly caused by an activity or is accumulated over the life stages of a product. This includes activities of individuals, populations, governments, companies, organisations, processes, industry sectors, etc.

Products include goods and services. In any case, all direct (on-site, internal) and indirect emissions (off-site, external, embodied, upstream, downstream) need to be taken into account.

After air and water, food is the most essential resource people require to sustain themselves. These resources are provided by the layer of inter-connected life that covers our planet: the biosphere. Yet the way the food system provides food often severely damages the health of the biosphere through soil and aquifer depletion, deforestation, aggressive use of agro-chemicals, fishery collapses and the loss of biodiversity in crops, livestock and wild species.

The global food system has become such a dominant force shaping the surface of this planet and its ecosystems that we can no longer achieve sustainability without revamping the food system.

At the same time sustainable food systems provide great hope for building a sustainable future—a future in which all can lead satisfying lives within the means of the biosphere.

In order to create a sustainable food system, we must break down the food footprint into its primary components: the cropland footprint, dairy farm footprint the pasture footprint, the fisheries footprint and the energy footprint. By understanding consumption patterns by sector, it becomes easier to target specific areas of consumption.

CARBON FOOTPRINT FROM VARIOUS SOURCES IN FOOD INDUSTRY

Cropland Footprint

The world's cropland produces human food, animal feed, fibre and other non-food crops and makes up 53% of the global food footprint. Footprint accounts analyse the consumption of 75 primary crop products and 15 secondary products.

The cropland footprint has steadily increased with global population. The intensification of farming, using agrochemicals, irrigation and monoculture cropping, has slowed the expansion of cropland: the cropland footprint grew by less than 10% over the last 60 years, while the world population doubled. But these gains have ecological costs: a swollen energy footprint and increased demands on neighbouring ecosystems to cope with nutrient loading, soil erosion, toxicity and water shortages.

Agribusiness consolidation and large-scale, monoculture cash-cropping also leads to the loss of crop and livestock diversity. Wheat, rice and corn are now the three most abundant plants on earth, providing 60% of human food.

At the same time, industrial agriculture threatens crop diversity through the replacement of native varieties with hybrid strains and the contamination of crop and wild species from the introduction of genetically modified organisms. As the global food supply relies on a diminishing variety of crops, it becomes vulnerable to pest outbreaks, the breeding of superbugs and climate disruptions, all of which could further expand the human footprint even as it must shrink.

Carbon Footprint in Dairy Farm

Carbon footprinting helps to quantify the farms greenhouse gas emissions. Acting on this information not only helps minimise emissions, in addition it can provide significant efficiency and economic benefits at farm level. Improving on-farm efficiencies through better use of inputs strongly correlates with reduced production costs per litre of milk leading to improved profitability for the farm business.

Emissions in dairy farm

Emissions from livestock farming include carbon dioxide (CO_2) produced by burning fossil fuels, methane (CH_4) as a natural by-product of animal digestion and nitrous oxide (N_2O) from soils, manure and nutrient management. Changes in land use and vegetation can also have an impact on greenhouse gas emissions from the farm.

Calculation of carbon footpint in dairy farm

To establish a starting point, baseline information on available land area and type, breeding cow numbers, stock and milk sales is recorded along with feed, fertiliser and fuel use. The carbon footprint is expressed on a 'per net unit of food product leaving the farm' basis. For a dairy unit, this would be in kg of greenhouse gas (normally a measure of all greenhouse gases but expressed as a carbon dioxide equivalent CO_2e) per litre of milk sold.

The carbon footprint shows how much greenhouse gas is being produced through routine activities on your farm. It highlights areas of the business where greenhouse gas emissions seem high and allows you to compare your farm performance against other similar enterprise types (benchmarking like for like).

High farm emissions reflect poor utilisation of costly inputs, highlighting scope to implement efficiency savings – benefiting both the farm business and the wider environment. Some supermarkets already ask suppliers to provide this information.

Improving efficiency in dairy farm

The key measures of a dairy farms performance with regard to greenhouse gas minimisation are broadly similar to already familiar technical efficiency easures used by the industry today. Improvement in productive efficiency is the most important factor that farmers have within their control to reduce emissions and positively steer profit. The following three example measures are based on actual farm data and indicative of what could be expected in specific scenarios. It also broadly illustrates that greenhouse gas emission reductions are achievable and compatible with maximising farm profits.

The following efficiency measures are adopted for the dairy farm.

1. Forage quality.
2. Fertiliser requirements.
3. Electricity consumption.
4. Milk sales per cow.
5. Feed conversion efficiency.
6. Disease level/challenge.
7. Stocking rate/forage yield per hectare.
8. Age to first calving.
9. Replacement rate.
10. Calving index.
11. Calf mortality.
12. Diesel use.

Example of efficiency measure 1: Improve forage quality

Unimpaired field drainage, modern grass varieties and timely field operations present opportunities to increase forage quality without necessarily compromising yield. Improved forage quality will encourage intakes, promoting milk yield or off-set purchased feed use. Improving grass silage energy content by 1 MJ/kg DM is equivalent to near 1 kg barley per cow in a ration or an additional two litres of milk from the full winter ration. Increasing milk production from forage improves how effectively you are turning livestock feed into milk. Based on this scenario, where better quality forage is used to promote milk yield giving an additional 7% in milk sales, dairy herd greenhouse gas emissions were also expected to reduce by 10% for each litre of milk sold.

Example efficiency measure 2: Improve nutrient use

Targeting and applying manure and fertiliser in line with crop requirements is an effective method of reducing purchased fertiliser cost and increasing nutrient utilisation (minimising the risk of nutrients lost to the environment) without compromising crop yield. A 10% reduction in fertiliser purchase will be a financial saving to the business, require better use of inputs and could reduce the carbon footprint by around 2% per litre of milk sold.

Example efficiency measure 3: Improve energy use

Relative to other livestock enterprises, dairy unit power requirements are high. This is mainly due to high demand in the milking parlour, especially for hot water washing. Since electricity production emits carbon dioxide (CO_2) as opposed to the more potent climate change gases such as methane (CH_4)

or nitrous oxide (N_2O), the impact on the dairy unit carbon footprint is less. However, there does remain some opportunity to reduce emissions from the dairy unit and potentially significant cost savings.

Lowering emissions and saving on the electricity bill: More effective milk cooling, reusing hot water from the plate cooler, matching equipment size to demand, checking insulation and thermostat settings and only heating the amount of water needed will all reduce power requirement. A 10% reduction in electricity demand could translate into significant financial savings on the annual electricity spend and approximately a 0.5% reduction in the dairy unit's carbon footprint per litre of milk sold.

Undertaking a farm carbon footprint will help establish an action plan to improve business resource efficiencies and assess year on year change. Regular assessment can help quantify progress and positively direct efforts to make the most of inputs whilst reducing farm greenhouse gas losses. An action plan based on technical performance targets should aim to take one step at a time towards a more efficient, lower cost system with a reduced carbon footprint.

Pasture Footprint

The world's grazing lands provide us with meat, milk, wool and hides and represent 13% of the global food footprint. Footprint accounts analyse eight pasture dependent categories and show a growing pasture footprint as the world consumes more animal products. While the pasture and grassland footprint has not grown as rapidly as the consumption of animal products, this is due to the increased use of fertilised pastures for grazing, breeding and managing livestock to boost production efficiency and feeding livestock from cropland production. In many countries, livestock are at least partially, sometimes exclusively, fed from corn, soyabeans, other crops and crop residues and fishmeal.

Fisheries Footprint

Industrial scale fisheries are rapidly changing the ecology of ocean eco-systems, while an increasing number of studies document the damaging effects of aquaculture and farmed fish. Footprint accounts analyse 22 fish and aquaculture categories, incorporating 40 species groups. The global fisheries footprint has risen more dramatically than other food categories, as the world craves more and bigger fish—that is, fish higher on the food chain. Overall, the world's fisheries are losing productivity. There are fewer and smaller fish. While the catch tonnage remains constant, the quality of fish is declining, as measured by their average trophic level—their status on the food chain. If trends continue and fish populations from higher trophic levels continue to be overfished or collapse, we may be moving toward oceans of jellyfish or other sea life low on the food chain and with little economic value.

Energy Footprint

The global food system is responsible for a sizeable portion of the world's fossil fuel consumption and corresponding carbon dioxide emissions. Estimates vary depending on how the food system is defined or bounded—we use 10% as a conservative place holder for calculating the global food energy. This 10% includes the energy used in food production, for inputs like fertilisers, pesticides and irrigation and in post-production. Post-production, which accounts for 80–90% of the food system's fossil fuel use, includes processing, packaging, transportation, storage and retail. An increasingly globalised food supply means a hefty transport footprint. The food system's thirst for fossil fuel energy leads to stunning imbalances: the energy required to produce, process, package and distribute a can of corn is six times the food energy contained in that corn. The packaging alone uses more than twice the energy of production, driving the corn home from the store and preparing it also uses more energy than production.

Other Food System Impacts—beyond the Ecological Footprint

As we have seen, the global food footprint represents a significant portion of the earth's total biomass production, yet even this is a conservative underestimate of the true area required for food production. Several other factors could be included, as described below.

Unsustainable yields: Footprint accounts currently do not reflect the environmental damage associated with industrial yields, such as soil degradation from intensive agricultural practices, water eutrophication, salinisation from irrigation, or pesticide toxicity.

Climate change: Besides the CO_2 from its fossil fuel use, agricultural production adds to the atmospheric carbon stock through forest clearing and the release of soil carbon through cultivation. Food production also contributes to global warming through the release of methane from livestock, rice cultivation and the burning of agricultural residues. Yet agriculture has the potential to act beneficially as a carbon sink, through farming practices like conservation tillage that build up organic carbon in soil rather than release it to the atmosphere.

Fresh water: The shortage of fresh water is one of the most immediate and potentially devastating environmental challenges facing humanity. Agriculture depletes water stocks and compromises water quality through increasing loads of organic and inorganic pollutants. Despite its significance, current ecological footprint accounts leave out the consumption of water due to a lack of adequate data documenting the impact of a given unit of water, which varies widely depending on soil composition, watershed hydrology, seasonal availability, withdrawal methods and water quality. Footprint accounts also do not incorporate human activities that cause irreversible damage to the environment, such as aquifer depletion or the bio-accumulation of persistent toxins from pesticides.

EATING LESS BEEF WILL REDUCE CARBON FOOTPRINT

Beef's environmental impact dwarfs that of other meat including chicken and pork. New research reveals that eating less red meat would be a better way for people to cut carbon emissions than giving up their cars. The heavy impact on the environment of meat production was known but the research shows a new scale and scope of damage, particularly for beef. The popular red meat requires 28 times more land to produce than pork or chicken, 11 times more water and results in five times more climate-warming emissions. When compared to staples like potatoes, wheat and rice, the impact of beef per calorie is even more extreme, requiring 160 times more land and producing 11 times more greenhouse gases.

Agriculture is a significant driver of global warming and causes 15% of all emissions, half of which are from livestock. Furthermore, the huge amounts of grain and water needed to raise cattle is a concern to experts worried about feeding an extra 2 billion people by 2050. But previous calls for people to eat less meat in order to help the environment, or preserve grain stocks, have been highly controversial.

Researchers analysed how much land, water and nitrogen fertiliser was needed to raise beef and compared this with poultry, pork, eggs and dairy produce. Beef had a far greater impact than all the others because as ruminants, cattle make far less efficient use of their feed. 'Only a minute fraction of the food consumed by cattle goes into the bloodstream, so the bulk of the energy is lost.' Feeding cattle on grain rather than grass exacerbates this inefficiency, although Eshel noted that even grass-fed cattle still have greater environmental footprints than other animal produce. 'The biggest intervention people could make towards reducing their carbon footprints would not be to abandon cars, but to eat significantly less red meat,' 'Another recent study implies the single biggest intervention to free up calories that could be used to feed people would be not to use grains for beef production.'

SHRINK YOUR FOOD FOOTPRINT

A person's food footprint (foodprint) is all the emissions that result from the production, transportation and storage of the food supplied to meet their consumption needs. We chose to focus on food supply, rather than only food consumption, because a large proportion of food is lost at retail and consumer level. Although emissions also occur when people transport, store and cook food, these emissions are omitted from our calculations as they are captured in travel and housing footprints.

The biggest sources of emissions are from the beef (0.8 T), dairy (0.5 T) and chicken (0.3 T) food groups. This isn't because these food groups dominate intake in the US diet, but rather that they are relatively carbon intensive to produce, in particular beef and dairy. The remaining food footprint is reasonably well distributed across other groups like cereals, vegetables, fruit, oils, sugars and drinks. In terms of shares, the footprint breaks down like this.

Food Waste

The simplest and most cost-effective way to reduce your food footprint is to minimise food waste. Although not all food waste is within your control, your purchasing and cooking habits can play a large part in reducing food losses. For each of our food groups we divide total food supply into three groups: retail losses, consumer losses and consumption. Each are expressed as a share of total food supplied.

Retail losses: Retail losses are food that is supplied to stores but never sold, due to spoilage and processing. Consumer losses are food purchased but not eaten due to a combination of spoilage, the non-edible share of food, cooking waste and plate waste. Consumption is the portion of total food supplied that is actually eaten. Even though not all food supplied can be eaten (e.g. bones, cores, skins), the scale of food loss is still surprising. While small amount of fresh food can be lost during repackaging within stores, the vast majority of retail losses occur because shops are unable to sell food before it goes out of date. In fruit, vegetables, chicken and beef this is more than a quarter of all food supplied.

Consumer losses: Consumer losses are between 10% and 25% of total food supplied for each group, meaning that as a share of purchased food they are actually much higher. Take the beef example, 23% of total supply is consumer loss, which corresponds to a loss of 33% of purchased food. Consumer losses are made up of food that is non-edible, allowed to go out of date, wasted during cooking or wasted from the plate.

Consumption: With the exception of the non-edible share of food you can generally make large reductions in your food footprint by simply ensuring that you eat everything you buy. Doing so just takes some common sense and is action we would naturally take if food was more expensive or scarce. By being careful about the portions you cook, eating what you cook or storing leftovers, you can easily reduce plate waste. By being careful about what you buy, eating perishable things on time and being less squeamish about used by dates where sensible, you can also minimise food spoilage in your home. A large proportion of retail losses is food that is perfectly fine to eat but is discarded due to supermarket caution and food aesthetics. Although retail losses are largely out of our hands we can still affect them to a degree. Buying food which is close to its 'best before' date often avoids such waste.

This makes sense if you know you are going to eat it soon after purchase and such food will often be subject to discounts. By reducing food waste you may be able to shrink your food footprint by as much as a quarter. Although it can be hard to quantify this improvement in your calculations, limiting food waste should result both in a reduction in your kitchen waste volume and food costs. As such reducing food waste is the natural place to start shrinking your food footprint.

Carbon Intensity of Food

The great variation in how foods are produced processed and transported means their footprints are very different. The vast majority of emissions, typically around 80%, occur during food production. This means how your food is produced is the most important factor in your food footprint.

Unlike in other sectors of your personal footprint, which are typically dominated by carbon dioxide emissions, both nitrous oxide and methane play an important role in food production. Nitrous oxide emissions are significant in most food groups due to the widespread use of nitrogen based fertilisers in agriculture. In the US nitrous oxide emissions makes up around a third of total food emissions. Methane emissions occur mostly due to enteric fermentation in animals like cows, sheep and goats so they are largely limited to the beef and dairy food groups. Despite this, methane emissions account for around a quarter of total food emissions in the US.

By using weighted averages for the production of foods within each group we can calculate an average carbon intensity for each. Although such averages aren't accurate for specific foods, they are very good for assessing complete diets. Having converted our intensities to food energy we also want to account for the emissions from retail and consumer losses. By dividing our intensities by one minus the percentage loss for both consumer and retail losses, we produce intensities in terms of grams of carbon dioxide equivalents per kilocalorie (g CO_2e/kcal) of food eaten. This captures all the emissions from the food the food typically supplied for each kilocalorie consumed.

After being adjusted for energy content and losses, our results look similar but there are subtle changes. Because of their high energy content snacks, oils and cereals are the least carbon intensive ways to supply food energy. Beef at 14 g CO_2e/kcal remains the most intensive while fruit, dairy and chicken are also relatively high. Again, these are weighted averages so within each group there may be wide variation depending on production methods, food losses and energy content. Using food energy rather than food weight to assess footprints is very useful, because it gives us an idea of the most and least carbon intensive ways we can supply our energy needs. Although daily kilocalorie intake is not the only important factor in diet, it is a simple and clear way to think about different diets while ensuring estimated consumption is in a reasonable range. And the better you understand the carbon intensity of the food you eat, the more effectively you will be able to reduce your footprint.

Different Diets

Because the majority of food supply emissions occur during production, changing our diet is the most effective way to shrink our footprint. Reducing our consumption of beef, lamb and dairy products will have the largest effect, due to their high carbon intensity. Additional reductions may also be found by limiting consumption of other meats and certain types of fruits. Choosing to switch food consumption from high carbon intensity foods (e.g. beef, cheese) to low-carbon intensity foods (bread, potatoes, grains) can reduce emissions by as much as 90% for that food consumption.

Food Miles

Despite often being highlighted in the media the significant distance that much of our food travels is not the major source of food emissions. This is confirmed by bottom up studies of individual foods and well as top down studies of entire food supply markets. Although this varies from country to country, a rough guide of food supply emissions is something like 80% production, 10% transport and 10% storage at wholesale and retail level. Transport emissions are in fact dominated by the upstream emissions of moving food stuffs to production facilities, with the remainder of transport emissions being from delivering final products to wholesalers and retailers. Reducing these transport emissions can help reduce total emissions, but only if it makes sense in the context of the foods entire footprint. Foods for which transport is a significant factor are often those which are shipped by air due to their perishing quickly and having high value per unit weight.

Cooking and Storage

After its sale, food is generally transported home, stored and often cooked before being eaten. Because emissions from these processes are accounted for in our travel and housing footprints, we do not calculate them as part of our food footprint. This is not to say they are unimportant, it merely avoids double counting. Because fridges and freezers are on all day every day they are often a major use of electricity. In the US refrigeration accounts for 12% of domestic electricity use, which has a footprint of around 400 kg CO_2e a year per person. To a limited degree you reduce the electricity your fridge and freezer consume by not setting them too cold, insuring they have proper seals, are well defrosted and located in the coolest area possible. Much more important however is the choice you make when replacing an old fridge and freezer.

Land use Emissions

Emissions from land use, land-use change and forestry (LULUCF) are a major part of global emissions. Although these emissions are generally not calculated as part of the food supply footprint, the expansion of agriculture is a major driver of deforestation, which dominates LULUCF emissions. More than 60% of these land use emissions occurred in Brazil and Indonesia, largely as the result of deforestation. By helping to drive deforestation the production of beef, soya and palm oil, along with other crops in tropical regions, has a very large indirect footprint. Though these emissions are generally not quantified as part of the food supply footprint, they are hugely important and an additional reason to consider switching away from particular foods.

FOOD TRANSPORTATION ISSUES AND REDUCING CARBON FOOTPRINT

Transportation is the largest end-use contributor toward global warming in the United States and many other developed countries. Transportation has a significant impact within the food and beverage sector because food is often shipped long distances and not infrequently via air. Although the impact of transportation is important, full life cycle analyses indicate that for most foods transportation does not have the largest environmental impact.

Some analysts, such as Weber and Matthews, estimate that given the typical household food basket, aggregate transportation accounts for just 11% of total carbon emissions associated with food production. Therefore, it is still worth while to consider improving the food distribution system. There are often many options for delivering food to consumers and these supply chain configurations can result in vastly differing energy and emissions profiles.

Supply Chain Basics

Before we can further investigate transportation impacts, we must first introduce the concept of the supply chain: the sequenced network of facilities and activities that support the production and delivery of a good or service. A supply chain starts with basic suppliers and extends all the way to consumers via stages. These stages may include such facilities as suppliers, factories, warehouses and other storage facilities, distribution centers and retail outlets.

Weber and Matthews estimate that food transportation may account for 50% of total carbon emissions for many fruits and vegetables, but less than 10% for red meat products. Although inbound logistics can require substantial energy use, it is considered part of the production process.

Although the interrelationships between supply chain stages may be quite complex, all supply chains have one aspect in common—they end with a consumer. Supply chains for different products may be interlinked, one supply chain's end consumer may represent an intermediate node for another supply chain. Examples include a firm that buys components and assembles them into consumer items and a soft drink producer that buys cylinders of compressed CO_2 to carbonate its products. Much supply chain complexity results from the fact that few supply chains are completely controlled by one firm or vertically integrated. For example, producers and retailers are not typically owned by the same firm.

Transport Modes

Within the developed world there are four basic transport modes for shipping large quantities of packaged products: water, rail, truck and air. Trucking dominates, comprising more than 75% of the total U.S. freight transit bill. Trucking variables include truck type, ownership model (such as 3PL or company-owned fleet) and loading option (less-than-truckload or full-truckload). The dominant transport mode has shifted over time. Short sea shipping, using ocean-going vessels for delivering cargo domestically, is popular in Europe and also holds promise for replacing many truck deliveries in the United States. The water and rail transport modes are contingent upon the availability of navigable water and established railroad tracks. An additional consideration is the potential need for supply chain responsiveness: air freight may be the only viable option for long-distance transport when customer orders require immediate fulfillment.

To sum up, the transportation-related carbon footprint varies from a few per cent to more than half of the total carbon footprint associated with food production, distribution and storage. Supply chains are complex and varied and food supply chains are especially challenging because of seasonality, freshness, spoilage and sanitary considerations. Measuring transportation-related carbon footprint involves careful choice of the scope of the analysis and there is much uncertainty in the results. Caution is warranted regarding the absolute numbers from carbon assessments, so it may be best to focus primarily on relative comparisons.

Supply chain planners must carefully consider the trade-off between transportation-related energy cost and carbon footprint and storage-related energy cost and carbon footprint. Also, the frequent small deliveries called for by lean manufacturing practices, although optimising efficiency within a facility can increase overall carbon footprint. Packaging is another important consideration and the use of plastics rather than glass tends to lower carbon footprint. Benefits for the environment and health are further accrued by plastic recycling. To reduce carbon footprint, suppliers are consolidating their operations, increasing their use of rail and water transit and increasing transport efficiency by filling trucks and considering backhaul opportunities. Food waste is another potentially significant contributor to carbon emissions, which could potentially be reduced via alternative packaging options.

CARBON FOOTPRINT RANKING OF FOOD

Table 16.1 shows the greenhouse gas emissions produced by one kilo of each food. It includes all the emissions produced on the farm, in the factory, on the road, in the shop and in our home. It also shows how many miles we need to drive to produce that many greenhouse gases. For example, we need to drive 63 miles to produce the same emissions as eating one kilogram of beef.

Table 16.1: Greenhouse gas emission produce by 1 kg of each food.

Rank	*Food*	*CO_2 Kilos equivalent*	*Car miles equivalent*
1	Lamb	39.2	91
2	Beef	27.0	63
3	Cheese	13.5	31
4	Pork	12.1	28
5	Turkey	10.9	25
6	Chicken	6.9	16
7	Tuna	6.1	14
8	Eggs	4.8	11
9	Potatoes	2.9	7
10	Rice	2.7	6
11	Nuts	2.3	5
12	Beans/tofu	2.0	4.5
13	Vegetables	2.0	4.5
14	Milk	1.9	4
15	Fruit	1.1	2.5
16	Lentils	0.9	2

Meat, cheese and eggs have the highest carbon footprint. Fruit, vegetables, beans and nuts have much lower carbon footprints. If we move towards a mainly vegetarian diet, we can have a large impact on our personal carbon footprint.

WATER FOOTPRINT OF FOOD

The water footprint of a good or a service is the total amount of water, external and internal, that is required to produce it. The concept can be used to calculate and compare the strain on water resources resulting from different options. It can also be extended to provide water budgets for whole nations or continents.

Water management is no longer an issue restricted to individual countries or river basins. Even a continental approach is not sufficient. The water footprint of Europe – the total volume of water used for producing all commodities consumed by European citizens – has been significantly externalised to other parts of the world. Europe is for example a large importer of sugar and cotton, two of the most thirsty crops. Coffee is imported from countries such as Colombia, soyabean from Brazil and rice from Thailand. European consumption strongly relies on water resources available outside Europe. How is Europe going to secureits future water supply? China and India are still largely water self-sufficient, but with rising food demand and growing water scarcity within these two major developing countries, one will have to expect a larger demand for food imports and thus external water demand. Water is increasingly becoming a global resource.

Although in many countries most of the food still originates from the country itself, substantial volumes of food and feed are internationally traded. As a result, all countries import and export water in virtual form, i.e. in the form of agricultural commodities. Within Europe, France is the only country with a net export of virtual water. All other European countries have net virtual water import, i.e. they use some water for making export products but more water is used elsewhere to produce the commodities that are imported. Europe as a whole is a net importer of virtual water. Europe's water security thus strongly depends on external water resources. Related to this, a substantial proportion of existing problems of water depletion and pollution in the world relates to export to Europe. The 'water footprint' has been developed as an analytical tool to address policy issues of water security and sustainable water use. The water footprint shows the extent and locations of water use in relation to consumption by people.

The water footprint of a community is defined as the volume of water used for the production of the goods and services consumed by the members of the community. The water footprint of a nation is an indicator of the effects of national consumption on both internal and external water resources. The ratio of internal to external water footprint is relevant, because externalising the water footprint means increasing the dependency on foreign water resources. It also results in externalising the environmental impacts. European countries such as Italy, Germany, the UK and the Netherlands have external water footprints contributing 50–80% to the total water footprint

The global water demand for production of food, feed, fibre and energy crops is rapidly increasing. A key question for regions that already now depend on external water resources is whether they can keep up their position as net virtual water importers. Another key question is which role businesses in the food sector can play in delivering products in a water sustainable way.

New Concepts: Virtual Water Trade and Water Footprints

The water footprint concept is an analogue to the ecological footprint, but indicates water use instead of land use. The water footprint is an indicator of water use that looks at both the direct and indirect water use of a consumer or producer. The water footprint of an individual, community or business is defined as the total volume of freshwater that is used to produce the goods and services consumed by the individual or community or produced by the business. Water use is measured in terms of water volumes consumed (evaporated) and/or polluted per unit of time. The water footprint is a geographically explicit indicator that not only shows volumes of water use and pollution, but also the locations.

The total water footprint of an individual or community breaks down into three components: the blue, green and grey water footprint. The blue water footprint is the volume of freshwater that is evaporated from the global blue water resources (surface and ground water) to produce the goods and services consumed by the individual or community. The green water footprint is the volume of water evaporated from the global green water resources (rainwater stored in the soil). The grey water footprint is the volume of polluted water, which can be quantified as the volume of water that is required to dilute pollutants to such an extent that the quality of the ambient water remains above agreed water quality standards.

A water footprint can be calculated for any well-defined group of consumers (e.g. an individual, family, village, city, province, state or nation) or producers (e.g. a public organisation, private enterprise or economic sector). One can also calculate the water footprint of a particular product. The water footprint of a product (a commodity, good or service) is the volume of freshwater used to produce the product, measured at the place where the product was actually produced. It refers to the sum of the water used in the various steps of the production chain. The 'water footprint' of a product is the same as what at other times is called its 'virtual water content'. Table 16.2 shows the water footprint for a number of common food items. Consider the water footprint of beef. In an industrial beef production system, it takes on average three years before the animal is slaughtered to produce about 200 kg of boneless beef. The animal consumes nearly 1300 kg of grains (wheat, oats, barley, corn, dry peas, soyabean meal and other small grains), 7200 kg of roughages (pasture, dry hay, silage and other roughages), 24 cubic metres of water for drinking and 7 cubic metres of water for servicing.

Table 16.2: The water footprint of different food items.

Food item	*Unit*	*Global average water footprint (litres)*
Apple or pear	1 kg	700
Banana	1 kg	860
Beef	1 kg	15500
Beer (from barley)	1 glass of 250 ml	75
Bread (from wheat)	1 kg	1300
Cabbage	1 kg	200
Cheese	1 kg	5000
Chicken	1 kg	3900
Chocolate	1 kg	24000
Coffee	1 cup of 125 ml	140
Cucumber or pumpkin	1 kg	240
Dates	1 kg	3000
Groundnuts (in shell)	1 kg	3100
Lettuce	1 kg	130
Maize	1 kg	900
Mango	1 kg	1600
Milk	1 glass of 250 ml	250
Olives	1 kg	4400
Orange	1 kg	460
Peach or nectarine	1 kg	1200
Pork	1 kg	4800
Potato	1 kg	250
Rice	1 kg	3400
Sugar (from sugar cane)	1 kg	1500
Tea	1 cup of 250 ml	30
Tomato	1 kg	180
Wine	1 glass of 125 ml	120

This means that to produce one kilogram of boneless beef, we use about 6.5 kg of grain, 36 kg of roughages and 155 litres of water (only for drinking and servicing). Producing the volume of feed requires about 15300 litres of water on average. The water footprint of 1 kg of beef thus adds up to 15500 litres of water. This still excludes the volume of polluted water that may result from leaching of fertilisers in the feed crop field or from surplus manure reaching the water system.

The numbers provided are estimated global averages, the water footprint of beef will strongly vary depending on the production region, feed composition and origin of the feed ingredients.

New Accounting Framework

Traditional national water use accounts only refer to the water use within a country. In order to support a broader sort of analysis, the accounts need to be extended. This has resulted in an accounting framework as shown in Fig. 16.1. As can be seen in the Fig. 16.1, the water footprint of a nation has two components. The internal water footprint is defined as the water used within the country in so far as it is used to

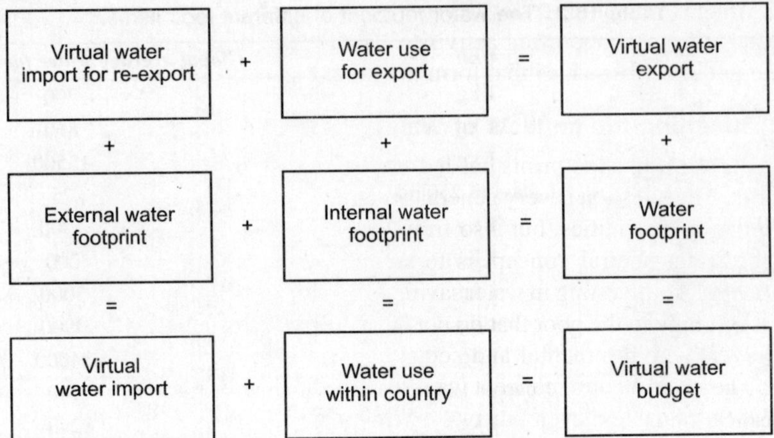

Fig. 16.1: The new national water accounting framework.

produce goods and services consumed by the national population. The external water footprint of a country is defined as the annual volume of water resources used in other countries to produce goods and services imported into and consumed in the country considered. It is equal to the virtual-water import into the country minus the volume of virtual-water exported to other countries as a result of re-export of imported products.

The virtual-water export consists of exported water of domestic origin and re-exported water of foreign origin. The virtual water import will partly be consumed, thus constituting the external water footprint of the country and partly re-exported. The sum of virtual water import and water use within a country is equal to the sum of the virtual water export and the country's water footprint. This sum is called the virtual-water budget of a country.

Not only national water use accounts need to be adjusted. Also business water accounts need to be extended in order to address issues of sustainability. Figure 16.2 shows the so-called virtual-water chain', which is the chain of production and consumption of water-intensive goods. A typical virtual-water chain consists of a farmer at the primary production end, a consumer at the consumption end and depending on the commodity at stake, some inter-mediaries such as a food processor and a retailer.

The water footprint of a business is defined as the total volume of freshwater that is used, directly and indirectly, to produce the products and services of that business. The water footprint of a business consists of two parts: the operational water footprint and the supply-chain water footprint.

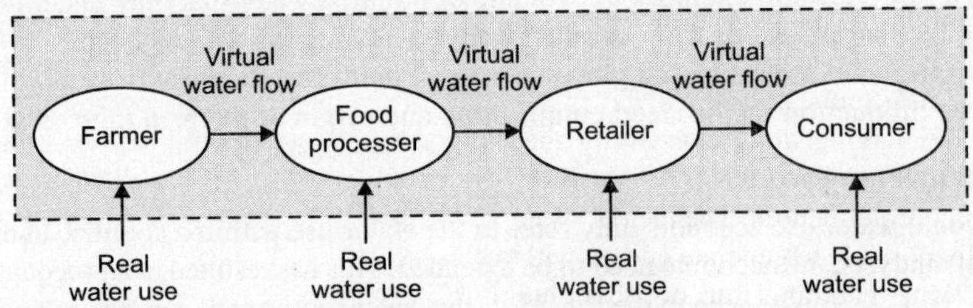

Fig. 16.2: The virtual-water chain.

The first refers to the amount of freshwater used within the business, i.e. the direct freshwater use for producing, manufacturing or supporting activities. The second refers to the amount of freshwater used to produce all the goods and services that form the input of the business, i.e. the indirect water use.

Reducing and Offsetting the Impacts of Water Footprints

The increasing focus on water footprints has led to the question of how humans can neutralise or offset their water footprint. The question is very general and interesting from the point of view of both individual consumers and larger communities, but also from the perspective of governments and companies.

The idea of the water-neutral concept is to stimulate individuals and corporations to make their activities 'water neutral' by investing in water saving technology, water conservation measures, wastewater treatment and water supply to the poor that do not have proper water supply. In other words, water neutral means that the adverse environmental and social consequences of a water footprint are reduced and compensated for. The water-neutral concept was conceived by Pancho Ndebele at the 2002 Johannesburg World Summit for Sustainable Development.

The idea at the time of the Summit was to quantify the water consumed during the conference by delegates and translate this into real money. Delegates, corporations and civil society groups were encouraged to make the summit water neutral by purchasing water-neutral certificates to offset their water consumption during the ten-day summit, with the offset investment being earmarked for improving water supply to the poor in South Africa and for water conservation initiatives. The water-neutral concept is currently being discussed within various communities, including academia, NGOs and businesses, as a potential tool to translate water footprints into modes of action.

Now that the water-neutral concept has been discussed in a bit wider audience it has become clear that the concept of water neutrality can be applied in a variety of contexts. Individual consumers or communities can try to become water neutral by reducing their water footprint and offsetting their residual water footprint. Rich travellers who visit a water-scarce country where many people do not even have basic water supply facilities can try to 'neutralise' their water use during their stay by investing in projects to enhance sustainable and equitable water use. Large events like the Johannesburg Conference or the Olympic Games, that generally have a significant additional impact on local water systems, can be organised in a water-neutral way by minimising water use and pollution by all possible means and by investing in local water projects aimed at improved management of the water system as a whole and for the benefits of society at large. Finally, businesses may like to become water neutral, be it from the perspective of minimising business risks (the risk of running out of water) or from the idea that it offers an attractive way of presenting the business to the consumer.

Water neutrality can be an instrument to raise awareness, stimulate measures that reduce water footprints and generate funds for the sustainable and fair use of freshwater resources. In a strict sense, however, the term 'water neutral' can be misleading. It is often possible to reduce a water footprint, but it is generally impossible to bring it down to zero. Water pollution can be largely prevented and much of the water used in various processes can be reused. However, some processes like growing crops and washing inherently need water. After having done everything that was technically possible and economically feasible, individuals, communities and businesses will always have a residual water footprint. In that sense, they can never become water neutral. The idea of 'water neutral' is different here from 'carbon neutral', because it is theoretically possible to generate energy without emitting carbon, but it is not possible to produce food without water. Water neutral is thus not about nullifying water use, but about water saving where possible and offsetting the negative environmental and social effects of water use.

In order to become 'water neutral' there are at least two requirements:

1. All that is 'reasonably possible' should have been done to reduce the existing water footprint.
2. The residual water footprint is offset by making a 'reasonable investment' in establishing or supporting projects that aim at the sustainable and equitable use of water.

The investment can be made in the form of own effort, but it can also be in terms of providing funds to support projects run by others. The size of the investment (the offset or 'pay off ' price) should probably be a function of the vulnerability of the region where the (residual) water footprint is located. A water footprint in a water-scarce area or period is worse and thus requires a larger offset effort than the same size water footprint in a water-abundant region or period. Besides, compensation is to be made in the same river basin as where the water footprint is located, which differs from the case of carbon offsetting, where the location of the offset does not make a difference from the viewpoint of its effect.

Educating Community to Reduce Water Footprints

For the last 10 years there has been increasing interest in water footprint accounting, primarily from the international NGO and business community. Governments respond more slowly, but several governments at different levels have started to respond as well. Water footprint accounting is about extending the knowledge base in order to improve the base for decisions. Ideas about water neutrality are expected to receive more debate. The water-neutral concept includes a normative aspect in that consensus needs to be reached about what effort to reduce an existing water footprint can reasonably be expected and what effort (investment) is required to sufficiently offset the residual water footprint.

The remaining key questions are:

1. How much reduction of a water footprint can reasonably be expected? Is this performance achieved by applying so called better management practices in agriculture, or best available technologies in manufacturing? How does one deal with totally new products or activities?
2. What is an appropriate water-offset price? What type of efforts count as an offset?
3. Over what time span should mitigation activities be spread and how long should they last? If the footprint is measured at one period of time, when should the offset become effective?
4. What are the spatial constraints? When a water footprint has impacts in one place, should the offset activity take place in the same place or may it take place within a certain reasonable distance from there?

Finally, accounting systems need to be developed that prevent double offsetting. For example, a business can offset its supply chain water footprint while the business in the supply chain offsets its own operational water footprint. How to share offsets? And where offsets are achieved in projects that are joint efforts, how much of any calculated water benefits can an individual entity claim?

Despite the possible pitfalls and yet unanswered questions, it seems that the water-neutral concept offers a useful tool to bring stake holders in water management together in order to discuss water footprint reduction targets and mechanisms to offset the environmental and social impacts of residual water footprints. The concept will be most beneficial in actually contributing to wise management of the globe's water resources when clear definitions and guidelines will be developed.

There will be a need for scientific rigour in accounting methods and for clear (negotiated) guidelines on the conditions that have to be met before one can talk about water neutrality.

Ways to Reduce Carbon Footprint

1. Eat local, vegetarian, or organic foods. For non-vegetarians, replace some beef consumption with chicken.
2. Walk, bike, carpool, use mass transit, or drive a best-in-class vehicle.
3. Replacing 80% of conditioned roof area on commercial buildings in the US with solar reflective material would offset 125 mmt CO_2 over the structures' lifetime, equivalent to turning off 36 coal power plants for one year.
4. Using a low-flow shower head can save 350 pounds of CO_2e per year. Setting the temperature to 120°F can help improve a hot water heater's efficiency.
5. Turn off your TV, computer and other electronics when not in use to reduce your carbon footprint by thousands of pounds of CO_2e each year. Unplug unused electronics to further reduce your footprint.
6. Choose energy-efficient lighting. If every home in the US replaced their 5 most used light bulbs with Energy Star bulbs, the reduction in carbon emissions would be equivalent to removing 10 million cars from the road.
7. Recycling half a household's waste can save 2400 pounds of CO_2 per year. Buying products with minimal packaging also helps reduce waste. For every 10% of waste reduction, 1200 pounds of CO_2e are avoided.
8. Shop smart and purchase items with a comparatively low carbon footprint when possible. Some manufacturers have begun assessing and publishing their products' carbon footprints.

To sum up, carbon footprinting is a method used to determine the amount of GHG emitted by a food processor as a result of manufacturing. Carbon footprint information can be used to help make decisions on how to manage and reduce GHG emissions.

Carbon footprinting also may be used to calculate the GHG produced by activities that are upstream and downstream of the manufacturing process (farming, distribution, retail, consumer use and disposal). Knowledge of GHG sources beyond the manufacturing scope can be useful to help identify opportunities to reduce GHG emissions in the overall lifecycle of a product.

SECTION IV

Nanotechnology, Hydrocolloides and Enzymes

Chapter 17

Nanotechnology in Agriculture and Food Industry

INTRODUCTION

Nanoscience and nanotechnology are concerned with the understanding and rational manipulation of materials at the atomic and molecular levels, generally with structures of less than 100 nm in size. Scientifically, nanoscience is defined as the study of phenomena and the manipulation of materials at the atomic, molecular, and macromolecular scales, where the properties differ from those at a larger scale and have unique novel functional applications.

Nanotechnology has the potential to revolutionise the agricultural and food industry with new tools for the molecular treatment of diseases, rapid disease detection, enhancing the ability of plants to absorb nutrients, etc. Smart sensors and smart delivery systems will help the agricultural industry combat viruses and other crop pathogens. Nanostructured catalysts will increase the efficiency of pesticides and herbicides, allowing lower doses to be used. Nanotechnology will also protect the environment indirectly through the use of alternative (renewable) energy supplies, and filters or catalysts to reduce pollution and clean-up existing pollutants. Agriculture is the backbone of most developing countries, with more than 60% of the population reliant on it for their livelihood. As well as developing improved systems for monitoring environmental conditions and delivering nutrients or pesticides as appropriate, nanotechnology can improve our understanding of the biology of different crops and thus potentially enhance yields or nutritional values. In addition, it can offer routes to added value crops or environmental remediation.

APPLICATIONS OF NANOTECHNOLOGY IN AGRICULTURE

Nanotechnology in Seed Science

Seed is most important input determining productivity of any crop. Conventionally, seeds are tested for germination and distributed to farmers for sowing. Inspite of the fact that seed testing is done in well equipped laboratories, it is hardly reproduced in the field due to the inadequate moisture under rainfed conditions. A group of research workers are currently working on metal oxide nano-particles and carbon nanotube to improve the germination of rainfed crops. Khodakovskaya and others have reported the use of carbon nanotube for improving the germination of tomato seeds through better permeation of moisture. Their data show that carbon nanotubes (CNTs) serve as new pores for water permeation by penetration of seed coat and act as a passage to channelise the water from the substrate into the seeds. These processes facilitate germination which can be exploited in rainfed agricultural system.

Nano-fertilisers for Balanced Crop Nutrition

Nano-fertiliser technology is very innovative however, some of the reports and patents strongly suggest that there is a vast scope for the formulation of nano-fertilisers. Significant increase in yields have been observed due to foliar application of nano particles as fertiliser. It was shown that 640 mg ha^{-1} foliar application (40 ppm concentration) of nanophosphorus gave 80 kg ha^{-1} P equivalent yield of clusterbean and pearl millet under arid environment.

Nano-herbicide for Effective Weed Control

Weeds are menace in agriculture. Herbicides are designed to control or kill the above ground part of the weed plants. None of the herbicides inhibits activity of viable below ground plant parts like rhizomes or tubers, which act as a source for new weeds in the ensuing season. Soils infested with weeds and weed seeds are likely to produce lower yields than soils where weeds are controlled. Improvements in the efficacy of herbicides through the use of nanotechnology could result in greater production of crops. The encapsulated nano-herbicides are relevant, keeping in view the need to design and produce a nano-herbicide that is protected under natural environment and acts only when there is a spell of rainfall, which truly mimics the rainfed system.

Nano-pesticide

In order to protect the active ingredient from the adverse environmental conditions and to promote persistence, a nanotechnology approach, namely 'nano-encapsulation' can be used to improve the insecticidal value. Nano-encapsulation comprises nano-sized particles of the active ingredients being sealed by a thin-walled sac or shell (protective coating). Nano-encapsulation of insecticides, fungicides or nematicides will help in producing a formulation which offers effective control of pests while preventing accumulation of residues in soil. In order to protect the active ingredient from degradation and to increase persistence, a nanotechnology approach of 'controlled release of the active ingredient' may be used to improve effectiveness of the formulation that may greatly decrease amount of pesticide input and associated environmental hazards. Nano-pesticides will reduce the rate of application because the quantity of product actually being effective is at least 10–15 times smaller than that applied with classical formulations.

Nanotechnology in Water Management

Nanotechology, offers the potential of novel nanomaterials for the treatment of surface water, groundwater and waste-water contaminated by toxic metal ions, organic and inorganic solutes and micro-organisms. Due to their unique activity towards recalcitrant contaminants many nanomaterials are under research and development for use for water purification. To maintain public health, pathogens in water need to be identified rapidly and reliably. Unfortunately, traditional laboratory tests are time consuming. Faster methods involving enzymes, immunological or genetic tests are under development. Water filtration may be improved with the use of nanofiber membranes and the use of nanobiocides, which appear promisingly effective. Biofilms contaminating potable water are mats of bacteria wrapped in natural polymers which are difficult to treat with antimicrobials or other chemicals. They can be cleaned up only mechanically, which cost substantial down-time and labour. Work is in progress to develop enzyme treatments that may be able to break down such biofilms.

Nano-scale Carriers

Nano-scale carriers can be utilised for the efficient delivery of fertilisers, pesticides, herbicides, plant growth regulators, etc. The mechanisms involved in the efficient delivery, better storage and controlled release include: encapsulation and entrapment, polymers and dendrimers, surface ionic and weak bond attachments among others. These help to improve stability against degradation in the environment and ultimately reduce the amount to be applied, which reduces chemical runoff and alleviates environmental problems. These carriers can be designed in such a way that they can anchor plant roots to the surrounding soil constituents and organic matter. This can only be possible if we unrevel the molecular and conformational mechanisms between the nanoscale delivery and targeted structures, and soil fractions. Such advances as and when they happen will help in slowing the uptake of active ingredients, thereby reducing the amount of inputs to be used and also the waste produced.

BIOSENSORS TO DETECT NUTRIENTS AND CONTAMINANTS

Protection of the soil health and the environment requires the rapid, sensitive detection of pollutants and pathogens with molecular precision. Soil fertility evaluation is being carried out for the past sixty years with the same set of protocols which may be obsolete for the current production systems and in the context of precision farming approaches.

Biosensors provide high performance capabilities for use in detecting contaminants in food or environmental media. They offer high specificity and sensitivity, rapid response, user-friendly operation, and compact size at a low cost. While the direct enzyme inhibition sensors currently lack the analytical ability to discriminate between multiple toxic substances in a sample (such as simultaneous presence of heavy metal and pesticide), they may prove useful as a screening tool to determine when a sample contains one or more contaminants. These methods are amenable to deployment in single-use test strips (making them useful to those in the field). According to Cambell and others, detection of multiple residues of organo-phosphorus pesticides has been accomplished using a nanomagnetic particle in an enzymelinked immunosorbent assay (ELISA) test.

Agricultural Engineering Issues

Nanotechnology has many applications in the field of agricultural machinery. These cover: application in machine structure and agricultural tools to increase their resistance against wear and corrosion and ultraviolet rays; producing strong mechanical components with use of Nano-coating and use of bio-sensors in smart machines for mechanical-chemical weed control; production of Nano-cover for bearings to reduce friction. The use of Nanotechnology in production of alternative fuels and reduction of environmental pollution are also worth mentioning.

Application of Nanotechnoiogy in Animal Sciences

Nanotechnology has the ability to provide appropriate solutions for addressing the issues of food items, veterinary care and prescription medicines as well as vaccines for domesticated animals. Taking certain medications such as antibiotics, vaccines, and probiotics, would be effective in treating the infections, nutrition and metabolic disorders, when used at the nano level. Medicines used at the nano level have multilateral properties to remove biological barriers for increased efficiency of the applied medicine. Appropriate timing for the release of drug and self-regulatory capabilities are the main advantages of the use of nanotechnology in the application of drugs.

The C-60 carbon particle (bucky ball) is spherical molecule having nearly 1 nm diameter. It is non-toxic to the live cells and biocompatible in nature. It can be used as a carrier to deliver the water soluble peptides and drugs. The nanotechnology can help to understand certain drug behaviour in an animal body. The nano particles can penetrate the skin through minor abrasions; these are reported to be used as sensor to detect the altered cell behaviour. The dendrimers are synthetic three dimensional macromolecules having a core particle surrounded by branches like a tree. They can be conjugated with the target molecule like drug as they are biocompatible and are easily cleared from blood through the kidney. It was observed that *in vivo* delivery of dendrimer-methotrexate reduce the tumour size ten times more than the free methotrexate.

The nano-magnets can be used as drug delivery system specially to treat the cancerous growth without any harm to the surrounding tissues. Different types of proteins like albumin, gelatin, gliadin and legumin can be used to prepare nanoparticle-based drug delivery system. Inert nanobeads were used to neutralise the antigen causing osteoarthritis in racing horses. Use of nano based antibiotics in treatment of animal diseases requires less amounts of antibiotics leaving less antibiotic residues.

Nanoparticle based chromium supplementation has beneficial effects on growth performance and body composition and it increases tissue chromium concentration in the muscles. Iron deficiency is a common problem in animals, especially during the early stage of life, gestation and parasitic infestation due to less bioavailability.

The bioavailability can be increased with the supplementation of ferric phospholic nano-particles.

Nanotechnology is used to produce the chicken/goat meat in the laboratory in large quantities maintaining the same nutritive value, taste, texture without any hazard (*vegetarian meat*). Use of nanotechnology in *designer egg* production is well-known. It can produce the eggs with low cholesterol, less yolk content, more nutrients, and desired antibodies. In addition, nano-based sensors can help in early detection of egg-borne pathogens.

Nano Technology Application in Fisheries and Aquaculture

Nanotechnology has tremendous potential to revolutionise fisheries and aquaculture sector. Nanotechnology tools like nano-materials, nano-sensor, DNA nano-vaccines, gene delivery and smart drug delivery have the potential of solving many puzzles related to fisheries nutrition and health production, reproduction, prevention and treatment of disease. Nanotechnology will help fish processing industry for producing quality products by detecting bacteria in packaging, producing strong flavour, colour quality and safety.

SMART DELIVERY SYSTEMS

Nanoscale devices are envisioned that would have the capability to detect and treat diseases, nutrient deficiencies or any other maladies in crops long before symptoms were visually exhibited. 'Smart Delivery Systems' for agriculture can possess timely controlled, spatially targeted, self-regulated, remotely regulated, pre-programmed, or multi-functional characteristics to avoid biological barriers to successful targeting. Smart delivery systems can monitor the effects of delivery of nutrients or bioactive molecules or any pesticide molecules. This is widely used in health sciences wherein nanoparticles are exploited to deliver required quantities of medicine to the place of need in human system. In the smart delivery system, a small sealed package carries the drug which opens up only when the desirable location or infection site of the human or animal system is reached. This would allow judicious use of antibiotics than otherwise would be possible.

Nanodevices for Identity Preservation (IP) and Tracking

One of the major constraints in Indian agriculture is the quality maintenance of agricultural produce. Proper monitoring of production system through nanotechnology will be appropriate to promote quality and make a clear distinction with organic products. Identity Preservation (IP) is a system that creates increased value by providing customers with information about practices and activities used to produce a particular crop or other agricultural products. Certifying inspectors can take advantage of IP as a better way of recording, verifying, and certifying agricultural practices. Through IP, it is possible to provide stakeholders and consumers with access to information, records and supplier protocols. Quality assurance of agricultural products safety and security could be significantly improved through IP at the nano-scale. Nano-scale IP holds the possibility of continuous tracking and recording of the history which a particular agricultural product experiences. The nano-scale monitors may be linked to the recording and the tracking devices to improve identity preservation of food and agricultural products. The IP system is highly useful to discriminate organic versus conventional agricultural products.

Nanolignocellulosic Materials

Recently, nanosized lignocellulosic materials have been obtained from crops and trees which had opened up a new market for innovative and value-added nanosized materials and products, e.g. nano-sized cellulosic crystals have been used as lightweight reinforcement in polymeric matrix. These can be applied in food and other packaging, construction, and transportation vehicle body structures. Cellulosic nano-whisker production technology from wheat straw has been developed by the Michigan Biotechnology Incorporate (MBI) International, and is expected to make biocomposites that could substitute for fiberglass and plastics in many applications, including automative parts.

Photocatalysis

One of the processes using nanoparticles is photocatalysis. The mechanism of this reaction is that when nanoparticles of specific compounds are subjected to UV light, the electrons in the outermost shell (valence electrons) are excited resulting in the formation of electron hole pairs, i.e. negative electrons and positive holes. Analogy with *n*- and *p*-type semiconductors, i.e. the Group IV elements, e.g. Germenium of the Periodic Table, dopted with, respectively, minute quantities of the Group V and Group III impurities, is worth noting. Due to their large surface-to-volume ratio, these have very efficient rates of degradation and disinfection. As the size of the particles decrease, surface atoms are increased, which results in tremendous increase in chemical reactivity and other physico-chemical properties related to some specific conditions such as photocatalysis, photoluminescence, etc. So this process can be used for the decomposition of many toxic compounds such as pesticides, which take a long time to degrade under normal conditions. Nanoparticles can be used for the bioremediation of resistant or slowly degradable compounds like pesticides.

The removal of toxins from wastewater is an emerging issue due to its effects on living organisms. Many strategies have been applied for wastewater treatment with little success. Photocatalysis can be used for purification, decontamination and deodorisation of air. It has been found that semiconductor sensitised photosynthetic and photocatalytic processes can be used for the removal of organics, destruction of cancer cells, bacteria and viruses. Application of photocatalytic degradation has gained popularity in the area of wastewater treatment.

Nanobarcode Technology

In our daily life, identification tags have been applied in wholesale agriculture and livestock products. Due to their small size, nanoparticles have been applied in many fields ranging from advanced biotechnology to agricultural encoding. Nanobarcodes (>1 million) have been applied in multiplexed bioassays and general encoding because of their possibility of formation of a large number of combinations that render them attractive for this purpose. The UV lamp and optical microscope are used for the identification of micrometer-sized glass barcodes which are formed by doping with rare earth containing a specific type of pattern of different fluorescent materials. The particles to be utilised in nanobarcodes should be easily encodeable, machinereadable, durable, sub-micronsized taggant particles. For the manufacture of these nanobarcode particles, the process is semi-automated and highly scalable, involving the electroplating of inert metals (gold, silver, etc.) into templates defining particle diameter, and then the resulting striped nanorods from the templates are released.

Nanobarcodes have been used as ID tags for multiplexed analysis of gene expression and intracellular histopathology. In the near future, more effective identification and utilisation of plant gene trait resources is expected to introduce rapid and cost effective capability through advances in nanotechnology based gene sequencing. Nanobarcodes serve as uniquely identifiable nanoscale tags and have been applied for non-biological applications such as for authentication or tracking in agricultural food and husbandry products. Such nanobarcode technology will enable one to develop new auto-ID technologies for the tagging of items previously not practical to tag with conventional barcodes. With the enhanced importance of traceability in food trade, such technologies will be helpful in promoting biosafe international food trade.

Quantum Dots (QDs) for Staining Bacteria

Bacteria, the most primitive life forms present almost everywhere, are useful as well as harmful for life. There are numerous bacteria which are responsible for many diseases in human like tetanus, typhoid fever, diptheria, syphilis, cholera, food-borne illness, leprosy and tuberculosis caused by different species. As a remedial process, we need to detect bacteria and for this, dye staining method is used. To stain bacteria, the most commonly used biolabels are organic dyes, but these are expensive and their fluorescence degrades with time. Fluorescent labelling by quantum dots (QDs) with bio-recognition molecules has been discovered through the recent developments in the field of luminescent nanocrystals. QDs are better than conventional organic fluorophores (dyes) due to their more efficient luminescence compared to the organic dyes, narrow emission spectra, excellent photostability, symmetry and tunability according to the particles sizes and material composition.

By a single excitation light source, they can be excited to all colours of the QDs due to their broad absorption spectra. Bio-labelled *Bacillus* bacteria with nanoparticle consisting of ZnS and Mn^{2+} capped with bio compatible 'chitosan' gave an organ glow when viewed under a fluorescence microscope. For the detection of *E. coli* O157 : H7, QDs were used as a fluorescence marker coupled with immune magnetic separation. For this purpose, magnetic beads were coated with anti-*E. coli* O157 antibodies to selectively attach target bacteria, and biotin-conjugated anti-*E. coli* antibodies to form sandwich immune complexes. QDs were labelled with the immune complexes via biotin-streptavidin conjugation after magnetic separation.

Nanobiotechnology

Nanobiotechnology has the potential to increase the efficiency and quality of agricultural production and food storage, to enhance the safety of food supplies for the protection of consumers and producers and to introduce new functionality (value-added products) for food, fiber and agricultural commodities. Nano-biotechnology will pave the ways for new researchable areas and applications such as DNA chip, protein identification and manipulation, novel nucleic acid engineering based films, smart delivery of DNA using gold nanoparticles. Biological tests measuring the presence or activity of selected substances become quicker, more sensitive and more flexible when nano-particles are put to work as tags or labels. Magnetic nanoparticles, bound to suitable antibody, are used to label specific molecules, structures or micro-organisms.

Nano-food Industry

Nanostructures in food

Understanding the nature of nanostructures in foods allows for better selection of raw materials and enhanced food quality through processing. Techniques such as electronmicroscopy and the newer probe microscopies, such as atomic force microscopy (AFM), have begun to reveal the nature of these structures, allowing rational selection, modification and processing of raw materials. For example, the creation of foams (e.g. the head on a glass of beer) or emulsions (e.g. sauces, creams, yoghurts, butter, margarine) involves generating gas bubbles, or droplets of fat or oil, in a liquid medium. This requires the production of an air-water or oil-water interface and the molecules present at this interface determine its stability.

Nanoparticles in foods

Nanotechnology has applications in food safety (e.g. detecting pesticides and micro-organisms), in environmental protection (e.g. water purification), and in delivery of nutrients.

Food contact materials

Various additives or ingredients are approved for use in food contact materials. The types of materials approved and the regulations on their use will vary for different countries. If the materials do not partition into foods, then there should be little concern over the safety of their use in food contact applications. Should some degree of partitioning occur, then the limitations on their use are based on an acceptable daily uptake (ADI) for these additives or ingredients. The inclusion of nanoparticles in food contact materials can be used to generate novel types of packaging materials and containers. Nanoparticles of pigments such as TiO_2 become transparent but retain their ultraviolet (UV) absorption characteristics. This suggests applications in transparent wraps, films, or plastic containers where absorption of UV radiation needs to be avoided.

Foods

Worldwide commercial foods and food supplements containing added nano-particles are becoming available. A major growth area appears to be the development of 'nanoceuticals' and food supplements. The general approach is to develop nanosized carriers or nanosized materials, in order to improve the absorption and, hence, potentially the bioavailability of added materials such as vitamins, phytochemicals, nutrients, or minerals. The materials can be incorporated into solid foods, delivered as liquids in drinks, or even sprayed directly on to mucosal surfaces.

Food packaging

Novel food packaging technology is by far the most promising benefit of nanotechnology in the food industry in the near future. Companies are already producing packaging materials based on nanotechnology that are extending the life of food and drinks and improving food safety.

While the nanofood industry struggles with public concerns over safety, the food packaging industry is moving full-speed ahead with nanotechnology products. Leading the way is active or 'smart' packaging that promises to improve food safety and quality and optimises product shelf life. Numerous companies and universities are developing packaging that would be able to alert if the packaged food becomes contaminated, respond to a change in environmental conditions, and self-repair holes and tears.

Some examples of the use of nanotechnology in food products are cooking oils that contain nutraceuticals within nanocapsules, nanoencapsulated flavour enhancers, and nanoparticles that have the ability to selectively bind and remove chemicals from food. The main reasons for the late incorporation of food into the nanotechnology sector are issues associated with the possible labelling of the food products and consumer-health aspects.

Smart packaging and active packaging: One of the most promising innovations in smart packaging is the use of nanotechnology to develop antimicrobial packaging. Packaging that incorporates nanomaterials can be 'smart,' which means that it can respond to environmental conditions or repair itself or alert a consumer to contamination and/or the presence of pathogens. These smart packages, will also detect public health pathogens such as *Salmonella* and *E. coli*.

Scientists in The Netherlands are taking smart packaging a step further with nanopackaging that will not only be able to sense when food is beginning to spoil, but will release a preservative to extend the life of that food. Because of their ability to improve safety and extend the life of food, these nanopackaging solutions are some of the most exciting innovations in the food industry today.

Clay nanoparticles to improve plastic packaging for food products: The nanoclay also makes the plastic lighter, stronger, and more heat-resistant. Clay nanocomposites are being used in plastic bottles to extend the shelf life of beer and make plastic bottles nearly shatter proof. Embedded nanocrystals in plastic create a molecular barrier that helps prevent the escape of oxygen. The technology currently keeps beer fresh for 6 months, but developers at several companies are already working on a bottle that will extend shelf life to 18 months. Several large beer makers, including South Korea's Hite Brewery and Miller Brewing Company, are already using the technology.

Nanoparticles for Filtration

The NRC report on emerging technologies that will benefit farmers in Africa and Asia lists several nanomaterials that are believed to be economical and effective for water purification. Nano-enabled water treatment techniques rely on membranes and filters made of carbon nanotubes, nanoporous ceramics, and magnetic nanoparticles rather than the use of chemicals and ultraviolet light used in conventional water treatment. Carbon nanotube filters can be used to remove impurities from drinking water. A fused carbon nanotube mesh that can filter out water-borne pathogens, lead, uranium, and arsenic has been suggested as a useful nanotechnology. The application of the NanoCeram filter, which uses a positively charged filter to trap negatively charged bacteria and viruses. This filtering device removes endotoxins, DNA, viruses, and micron-sized particles. A simple handheld magnet can be used to remove the nanocrystals and the arsenic from water. Such a treatment could be used as a point-of-use water filtration process. However, the problem remains as how to dispose of the enriched product generated during the filtration process in an eco-friendly manner.

Wireless Nanosensors for Precision Agriculture

Crop growth and field conditions like moisture level, soil fertility, temperature, crop nutrient status, insects, plant diseases, weeds, etc. can be monitored through advancement in nanotechnology. Such real-time monitoring is done by employing networks of wireless nano-sensors across the cultivated fields, providing essential data for agronomic processes like optimal time of planting and harvesting of the crops. It is also helpful for monitoring the time and amount of water application, fertilisers, pesticides, herbicides and other treatments. This has moved precision agriculture to a much higher level of control, for instance, in water usage, leading eventually to conservation of water. More precise water delivery systems are likely to be developed in the near future. The factors critical for such development include water storage, *in situ* water holding capacity, water distribution near roots, water absorption efficiency of plants, encapsulated water released on demand, and interaction with field intelligence through nano-sensor systems.

Future for Nanofood

Nanotechnology can confer unique advantages on processed foods in many ways. Programmable foods, considered the ultimate dream of the consumer, will have designer food features built into it and a consumer can make a product of desired colour, flavour, and nutrition using specially programmed microwave ovens. The trick is to formulate the food at the manufacturer's end with millions of nanoparticles of different colours, flavours, and nutrients and under the program in the oven set by the consumer based on his preferences, only selective particles are activated while others stay inert, giving the desired product profile. Nano-based polymers with silica-based nanoparticles sandwiched can enhance the properties of pressure-sensitive adhesive labels and create biodegradable properties in them. Enhanced solubility, improved bioavailability, facilitating controlled release and protecting the stability of micronutrients in food products, are other virtues of nanotechnology.

The impact of nanotechnology is huge, ranging from basic food to food processing, from nutrition delivery to intelligent packaging.

Nanotechnology is becoming increasingly important for the food sector. Promising results and applications are already being developed in the areas of food packaging and food safety. Nanotechnology has begun to find potential applications in the area of functional food by engineering biological molecules toward functions very different from those they have in nature, opening up a whole new area of research and development. Of course, there seems to be no limit to what food technologists are prepared to do to our food and nano-technology will give them a whole new set of tools to go to new extremes. Many have taken critical view of food nanotechnology in the past. Today, though, we look at the potentially beneficial effects nanotechnology enabled innovations could have on our foods and, subsequently, on our health.

Nanotechnology also has the potential to improve food processes that use enzymes to confer nutrition and health benefits. For example, enzymes are often added to food to hydrolyse antinutritive components and hence increase the bioavailability of essential nutrients such as minerals and vitamins. To make these enzymes highly active, long-lived, and cost-effective, nanomaterials can be used to provide superior enzyme-support systems due to their large surface-to-volume ratios compared to traditional macroscale support materials.

The incorporation of nanomaterials into food packaging is expected to improve the barrier properties of packaging materials and should thereby help to reduce the use of valuable raw materials and the generation of waste. Edible nanolaminates could find applications in fresh fruits and vegetables, bakery products, and confectionery, where they might protect the food from moisture, lipids, gases, off-flavours, and odours. Natural biopolymers of nanosize scale, such as polysaccharides, can be used for the encapsulation of vitamins, prebiotics, and probiotics and for delivery systems of drugs or nutraceuticals. In the food sector, one of the most important problems is the time-consuming and laborious process of food quality-control analysis. Innovative devices and techniques are being developed that can facilitate the preparation of food samples and their precise and inexpensive analysis. From this point of view, the development of nanosensors to detect microorganisms and contaminants is a particularly promising application of food nanotechnology. Table 17.1 summaries the application of nanotechnology in agriculture and food industry.

To sum up as developments in nanotechnology continue to emerge, its applicability to the food industry is sure to increase. Most aspects of incremental nanotechnology are likely to enhance product quality and choice and will be perceived as progressive changes in standard and accepted technology. There are a few issues, particularly regarding the accidental or deliberate use of nanoparticles in food, or food-contact materials, which may provoke consumer concern. It is particularly important to ensure that consumers are able to exercise choice in the use of the products of nanotechnology and that they have the information to assess the benefits and risks of such products. The success of these advancements will be dependent on consumer acceptance and the exploration of regulatory issues.

Food producers and manufacturers could make great strides in food safety by using nanotechnology, and consumers would reap benefits as well. Many companies are conducting research in nanotechnology and its application to food products and as more of its functionalities become evident, the level of interest is certain to increase. Nanotechnology has already made inroads into the food industry and it is claimed that more than 300 foods have already been developed with this technology. To maintain leadership in food and food-processing industry, one must work with nanotechnology and nanobio-info in the future. The future belongs to new products and new processes with the goal to customise and personalise the products. Improving the safety and quality of food will be the first step. Designing and producing food by shaping molecules and atoms is the future of the food industry worldwide.

RISK ASSESSMENT OF NANOPARTICLES AND NANOSTRUCTURES

A risk assessment report has been published about Magic Nano, which was a spray-on ceramic sealant to repel dirt. Over 110 European consumers showed respiratory symptoms after using this product, therefore the product was pulled out in March 2006. A preliminary framework has been developed to inform the risk analysis and risk management of nanomaterials. So, a list of factors potentially affecting human health and ecological risks of nanoparticles has been studied. A forum series of seven articles on research strategies for safety evaluation of nanomaterials was presented in toxicological science in 2005–2006. Some of the techniques were explained for basic nanoparticles characterisation through the body to asses how they will interact with biological systems.

Determination of solubility of nanoparticles and their biological fate and effects on the health are very important. There are a lot of factors that affect dissolution including concentration, surface area, surface energy, surface morphology, aggregation, dissolution layer properties, and adsorbing species. The risk assessment of nanoparticles and nanostructures showed that the potential routes of human exposure to nanoparticles are skin, lungs, and the gastrointestinal tract. By the addition of nanostructured materials to food, water, and drugs, nanoparticles can be absorbed from the intestine and enter the circulatory system but there is not much research focused on this potential route of entry. In recent years, there is a great focus on the skin as a potential route of absorption of nanoparticles due to increased

Table 17.1: Nanotechnology applications in agriculture and food.

Agriculture	*Food processing*	*Food packaging*	*Supplements*
Single molecule detection to determine enzyme substrate interactions	Nunocapsules to improve bioavailability of neutraceuticals in standard ingredents such as cooking oils	Antibodies attached to fluerescent nanoparticles to detect chemicals or foodborne pathogens	Nanosize powders to increase absorption of nutrients
Nanocapsules for delivery of pesticides, fertilizer and other agrichemicals more efficiently	Nanoencapsulated flavor enhancers	Biodegradable nanosensors for temperature, moisture and time monitoring	Cellulose nanocrystal composite as drug carrier
Delivery of growth hormones in a controlled fashion	Nanotubes and nanoparticles as gelation and viscosifying agents	Nanoclays and nanofilms as barrier materials to prevent spoilage and prevent oxygen absorption	Nanoencapsulation of neutraceuticals for better absorption, better stability of targeted delivery
Nanosensors for monitoring soil conditions and crop growth	Nanocapsule infusion of plant based steroids to replaces meat's cholesterol	Electrochemical nanosensors to detect ethylene	Nanocochleates (coiled nanoparticles) to deliver nutrients more efficiently to cells without affeccting colour or taste of food
Nanochips for identity preservation and tracking	Nanoparticles to selectively bind and remove chemicals or pathogens from food	Antimicrobial and antifungal surface coatings with nanoparticles (silver, magnesium, zinc)	Vitamin sprays dispersing active molecules into nano-droplets for belter absorption
Nanosensors for detection of animal and plant pathogens	Nanoemulsions and particles for better availability and dispersion of nutrients	Lighter, stronger and more heat-resistant films with silicate nanoparticles	
Nanocapsules to deliver vaccines		Modified permeation behavior of foils	
Nanoparticles to deliver DNA to plants (targeted genetic engineering)			

consumption of cosmetics and sunscreens. Nanoparticles are able to penetrate through the outer layers of the skin and there is little information on the hazard which they might present. Inhalation of airborne material is an important potential exposure route as well. Nanoliposomes with several applications in several scientific and technological fields, for example, gene delivery and medicine, can provide controlled release of various bioactive agents, including food ingredients and nutraceuticals, at the right place and the right time. Therefore, they increase the effectiveness and cellular uptake of the encapsulated material. Reactive, sensitive, or volatile additives (vitamins, enzymes, antioxidants, slimming agents, etc.) can be turned into stable ingredients using nanoliposomes. Mozafari and others have recently reviewed various aspects of nanoliposomes including currently available preparation methods, and their application in food technology.

REGULATIONS OF USING NANOTECHNOLOGY IN FOOD PRODUCTION

Now-a-days, there are no special regulations for using nanotechnology in foods. The Food and Drug Adminstration (FDA) regulates on a product-by-product basis and and points out many products which are currently regulated produce of nanoparticles. FDA has traditionally regulated many products with particulate material in nano-size range but has not focused on applied technology for their preparation. It is clear that there are other government agencies that have different missions with regard to nanotechnology including to solve environmental problems and to improve technology to treat disease, etc. The Institute of Food Science and Technology (IFST) suggested that when nanoparticles are used as food additives, the conventional E-numbering system for labeling should be used along with the subscript 'n'. The British government agreed to this suggestion that nanoparticles ingredients be subjected to a full safety assessment before using them in food products.

The Codex Alimentarius which was created in 1963 contains a set of standards about practices, recommendations, and characteristics of food products and its handling. To the recommendation of the World Health Organisation (WHO) and the United Nations Food and Agriculture Organisation (FAO), the Codex Alimentarius updates through the use of nanotechnology in food and agriculture. FAO and WHO have recently started preparations to hold an expert consultation in 2008 that identify the applications of nanotechnology in the food sector at present or in the future and the potential food safety issues, as well as exploring areas for future research and international guidance. Recently, the Institute of Food Science Technologists (ISFT) has presented important documents and member experts for addressing each of these issues. Supporting research and development in food nanoscience is a priority for ISFT. The European Commission intends to apply current food laws for nanofoods but these lawswill require modifications and plans to use case-by-case analysing methods for risk assessment. It is anticipated that nanotechnology standards are being developed by organisations such as the International Standards for Organisation (ISO) and ASTM International on terminology, nomenclature, measurement and characterisation, and environment, safety, and health.

Thus, the nanotechnology may develop devices for rapid identification deficiencies of nutrients (such as AFM) and the presence of pathogens in food (including Nanosensors). Numerous applications of nanotechnology in food systems and processing have been developed in many countries, some of which include nano based-food additives, Nanosensors, nancapsules, nanobased smart delivery systems, nano-packaging, and health care and medicine. Now-a-days people fairly identified and accepted the effects of using nanotechnology in their life. The potential of nanotechnology make it suitable for developing countries because these countries could potentially engage some of the new markets for new nanomaterials and production processes. Nanotechnology can improve public awareness. Many government departments paid more money towards research and development of functional food, nutrient delivery systems, colour, flavour and consistency, food packaging, and detection of nano based nutrients and metabolites structure. Base on the above descriptions, nanofoods would be produced by the use of nanotechnology techniques and devices for cultivation, processing, packaging, production, suitable detection of fine food molecule structure, or molecular interactions on nanoscale and food quality. Finally, nanotechnology enables to change the existing food systems and processing to ensure products safety, creating a healthy food culture, and enhancing the nutritional quality of food.

WAY FORWARD: POLICY OPTIONS AND ACTIONS

Nanotechnology has emerged as a cutting edge technology with profound realised and potential outcomes and impacts. It is a powerful tool for food and nutritional security, management of abiotic and biotic stresses, enhanced input use efficiency, elevated yield potential and superior quality traits. However, the process and products if not handled properly, may pose human health and environmental risks. Hence, strategic research and policy options and actions, as informed by rigorous science, are needed to judiciously develop this new emerging technology to be used in agriculture and food industry for congruent enhanced productivity, profitability, social equity, biosafety and environmental sustainability.

Chapter 18

Hydrocolloids in Food Industry

INTRODUCTION

Hydrocolloids or gums are a diverse group of long chain polymers characterised by their property of forming viscous dispersions and/or gels when dispersed in water. These materials were first found in exudates from trees or bushes, extracts from plants or seaweeds, flours from seeds or grains, gummy slimes from fermentation processes, and many other natural products. Occurrence of a large number of hydroxyl groups noticeably increases their affinity for binding water molecules rendering them hydrophilic compounds.

Further, they produce a dispersion, which is intermediate between a true solution and a suspension, and exhibits the properties of a colloid. Considering these two properties, they are appropriately termed as 'hydrophilic colloids' or 'hydrocolloids'.

Hydrocolloids have a wide array of functional properties in foods including, thickening, gelling, emulsifying, stabilisation, coating and, etc. Hydrocolloids have a profound impact on food properties when used at levels ranging from a few parts per million for carrageenan in heat-treated dairy products to high levels of acacia gum, starch or gelatin in jelly confectionery.

The primary reason behind the ample use of hydrocolloids in foods is their ability to modify the rheology of food systems. This includes two basic properties of food systems that is, flow behaviour (viscosity) and mechanical solid property (texture). The modification of texture and/or viscosity of food systems helps modify its sensory properties, therefore hydrocolloids are used as significant food additives to perform specific purposes. It is evident that several hydrocolloids belong to the category of permitted food additive in many countries throughout the world.

Various food formulations such as soups, gravies, salad dressings, sauces and toppings use hydrocolloids as additives to achieve the preferred viscosity and mouth feel. They are also used in many food products like icecreams, jams, jellies, gelled desserts, cakes and candies, to create the desired texture. In addition to the functional attributes, future acceptance and, possibly, positive endorsement may derive from the recognition that fibres contribute many physiological benefits to the natural function and well-being of the body.

The aim of this chapter is to highlight the importance of the hydrocolloids in food industry.

FUNCTIONAL PROPERTIES OF HYDROCOLLOIDS

Viscosity Enhancing or Thickening Properties

The foremost reason behind the ample use of hydrocolloids in foods is their ability to modify the rheology of food system. The modification of texture and/or viscosity of food system helps to modify its sensory properties, and hence, hydrocolloids are used as important food additives to perform specific purposes. The process of thickening involves nonspecific entanglement of conformationally disordered polymer chains, it is essentially polymer-solvent interaction. Hydrocolloids that have been used as thickening agents. The thickening effect of produced by the hydrocolloids depends on the type of hydrocolloid used, its concentration, the food system in which it is used and also the pH of the food system and temperature. Ketchup is one of the most common food items where the hydrocolloid thickeners are used to influence its viscosity.

The question that arises is how hydrocolloids thicken solution. In dilute dispersion, the individual molecules of hydrocolloids can move freely and do not exhibit thickening. In concentrated system, these molecules begin to come into contact with one another, thus, the movement of molecules becomes restricted. The transition from free moving molecules to an entangled network is the process of thickening.

The viscosity of polymer solutions is influenced significantly by the polymer molecular mass. In addition to molecular mass effects, the hydrodynamic size of polymer molecules in solution is significantly influenced by molecular structure. Linear, stiff molecules have a larger hydrodynamic size than highly branched, highly flexible polymers of the same molecular mass and hence give rise to a much higher viscosity.

Gelling Properties of Hydrocolloids

Swollen particulate forms of gelled hydrocolloids are particularly useful as they combine macroscopic structure formation with an ability to flow and often have an attractive soft solid texture, which is especially sought in food applications, all at high water contents (>95%). There is a potential opportunity for particulate hydrocolloid systems to replace chemically cross-linked starches based on appropriate structuring, processing, and molecular release properties without the need for chemical treatment.

The characteristics of gel particles, and the application for which they are used, will depend on the type of hydrocolloid, the network formation mechanism and the processing method used for particle formation. Hydrocolloid gel networks form through entwining and cross-linking of polymer chains to form a three-dimensional network. The mechanism by which this interchain linking occurs can vary.

Hydrocolloid gelation can involve a hierarchy of structures, the most common of which is the aggregation of primary interchain linkages into 'junction zones' which form the basis for the three-dimensional network characteristic of a gel. Various parameters such as temperature, the presence of ions, and the inherent structure of the hydrocolloid can affect the physical arrangement of junction zones within the network.

Surface Activity and Emulsifying Properties

The functionality of hydrocolloids as emulsifiers and/or emulsion stabilisers correlates to phenomena such as: retardation of precipitation of dispersed solid particles, decreased creaming rates of oil droplets and foams, prevention of aggregation of dispersed particles, prevention of syneresis of gelled systems containing oils and retardation of coalescence of oil droplets. It is believed that gums will adsorb (onto solid or liquid surfaces) very slowly, weakly and with very limited surface load if at all. The hydrocolloids were classified according to their activity at the interface. Gum Arabic is probably the most studied hydrocolloid that proved significant surface activity. Gum arabic is the only gum adsorbing onto oil-water interfaces and imparting steric stabilisation. Other gums such as galactomannans, xanthan, pectin, etc. have been known to reduce surface and interfacial tensions, to adsorb onto solid surfaces and to improve stability of oil-in-water emulsions. Micro crystalline cellulose (MCC) is an example of a hydrocolloid with no solubility in water that adsorbs mechanically at the interface.

It is well documented that gum arabic, a natural polysaccharide, has excellent emulsification properties for oil-in-water emulsions. An excellent example of its use is in cloudy emulsions, as opacity builders for citrus beverages. Related the significance of protein components presenting in gum arabic to its emulsifying properties. It seems that the protein-hybrid in gum arabic meets all the necessary requirements in a capacity similar to emulsifying proteins (such as casein, or soy protein) via its numerous adsorption sites, flexibility, conformational change at the interface and the entropy gain (solvent depletion). Gum arabic works by reducing the oil-water interfacial tension, thereby facilitating the disruption of emulsion droplets during homogenisation. The peptides are hydrophobic and strongly adsorb on to the surface of oil droplets, whilst the polysaccharide chains are hydrophilic and extend out into the solution, preventing droplet flocculation and coalescence through electrostatic and steric repulsion forces.

Microcrystalline cellulose is also able to stabilise the oil-in-water emulsions. Its strong affinity for both the oil and the water results in precipitation and some orientation of the solid particles at the oil-in-water interface. It was proposed that the colloidal network of the free MCC thickens the water phase between the oil globules preventing their close approach and subsequent coalescence. Therefore, the MCC provides long term stability.

As the galactomannans structure gives no suggestion of the presence of any significant proportion of hydrophobic groups, it is generally assumed that this type of hydrocolloid functions by modifying the rheological properties of the aqueous phase between the dispersed particles or droplets. It has been suggested that these gums stabilise emulsions by forming liquid crystalline layers around the droplets. It should be noted that this putative adsorption of the gum to the oil-water interface is reportedly rather weak and reversible. That is, the associated emulsion stability is lost on diluting the aqueous phase of the emulsion with water. Pectin is another class of hydrocolloid whose emulsifying character has attracted attention in recent years. While citrus and apple pectin is normally used as low-pH gelling or thickening agents (are not effective as emulsifying agents), sugar beet pectin does not form gels with calcium ions or at high sugar concentrations. Due to its higher protein content, sugar beet pectin is considerably more surface-active than gum arabic, and it is very effective in stabilising fine emulsions based on orange oil or triglyceride oil at a pectin/oil ratio of 1:10.

Hydrocolloids as Edible Films and Coatings

An edible film is defined as a thin layer, which can be consumed, coated on a food or placed as barrier between the food and the surrounding environment. The most familiar example of edible packaging is sausage meat in casing that is not removed for cooking and eating. Hydrocolloids are used to produce edible films on food surfaces and between food components. Such films serve as inhibitors of moisture, gas, aroma and lipid migration. Many gums and derivatives have been used for coating proposes. They include alginate, carrageenan, cellulose and its derivatives, pectin, starch and its derivatives, among others. Since these hydrocolloids are hydrophilic, the coatings they produce have nature limited moisture barrier properties. However, if they are used in a gel form, they can retard moisture loss during short term storage when the gel acts as sacrificing agent rather than a barrier to moisture transmission. In addition, since in some cases an inverse relationship between water vapour and oxygen permeability has been observed, such films can provide effective protection against the oxidation of lipid and other susceptible food ingredient. The hydrocolloid edible films are classified into two categories taking into account the nature of their components: proteins, polysaccharides or alginates. Hydrocolloidal materials, i.e. proteins and polysaccharides, used extensively for the formation of edible films and coatings.

Hydrocolloids as Fat Replacers

The changes in modern lifestyle, the growing awareness of the link between diet and health and new processing technologies have led to a rapid rise in the consumption of ready-made meals, novelty foods and the development of high fibre and low-fat food products. Caloriedense materials such as fats and oils may be replaced with 'structured water' to give healthy, reduced-calorie foods with excellent eating quality. In particular, numerous hydrocolloid products have been developed specifically for use as fat replacers in food. This has consequently led to an increased demand for hydrocolloids. As an example, the Italian dressing includes xanthan gum as a thickener and the 'Light' mayonnaise contains guar gum and xanthan gum as fat replacers to enhance viscosity.

The traditional approach is the partial replacement of fat using starches which, when dissolved in water, create stable thermo-reversible gels. Soft, fat-like gels can be created by conversion modifications to the degree necessary to produce thermo-reversible, spreadable gels. Typically, 25–30% solids, i.e. starch in water, form an optimal stable structure for fat replacement. New generation fat replacers are tailored to mimic more closely the many and complex properties of fats or oils in a particular application. These are referred to as fat mimetics. Maximising the synergies of functional ingredients such as hydrocolloids generally in combination with specific starch fat mimetics can mean that 100% fat reduction is achievable.

Based on the particle gel characteristics of inulin, it can be concluded that inulin functions as a fat replacer but only in water-based systems. When concentrations exceed 15%, insulin has the ability to form a gel or cream, showing an excellent fat-like texture. This inulin gel is a perfect fat replacer offering various opportunities in a wide range of foods. Each inulin particle dispersed in the water phase of any food system will contribute to the creaminess of the finished food. Inulin is also destined to be used as a fat replacer in frozen desserts, as it processes easily to provide a fatty mouth-feel, excellent melting properties, as well as freeze–thaw stability, without any unwanted off-flavour.

ORIGINS AND STRUCTURES OF HYDROCOLLOIDS

Plant hydrocolloids

Cellulose and derivatives

Cellulose is the most abundant naturally occurring polysaccharide on earth. It is the major structural polysaccharide in the cell walls of higher plants. It is also the major component of cotton boll (100%), flax (80%), jute (60 to 70%), and wood (40 to 50%). Cellulose can be found in the cell walls of green algae and membranes of fungi. *Acetobacter xylinum* and related species can synthesise cellulose. Cellulose can also be obtained from many agricultural by-products such as rye, barley, wheat, oat straw, corn stalks, and sugarcane. Cellulose is a high molecular weight polymer of (1→4)-linked β-D-glucopyranose residues. The β-(1→4) linkages give this polymer an extended ribbon-like conformation. The tertiary structure of cellulose, stabilised by numerous intermolecular H-bonds and van der Waals forces, produces three-dimensional fibrous crystalline bundles. Cellulose is highly insoluble and impermeable to water. Only physically and chemically modified cellulose finds applications in various foodstuffs.

Microcrystalline cellulose: Microcrystalline cellulose (MCC) is purified cellulose, produced by converting fibrous cellulose to a redispersible gel or aggregate of crystalline cellulose using acid hydrolysis. Microcrystalline cellulose is prepared by treating natural cellulose with hydrochloric acid to partially dissolve and remove the less organised amorphous regions of this polysaccharide. The end product consists primarily of crystallite aggregates. MCC is available in powder form after drying the acid hydrolysates. Dispersible MCC is produced by mixing a hydrophilic carrier (e.g. guar or xanthan gum) with microcrystals obtained through wet mechanical disintegration of the crystallite aggregates. These colloidal dispersions are unique when compared to other soluble food hydrocolloids. They exhibit a variety of desirable characteristics including suspension of solids, heat stability, ice crystal control, emulsion stabilisation, foam stability, texture modification and fat replacement.

Carboxymethylcellulose: Carboxymethylcellulose (CMC) is an anionic, water-soluble polymer capable of forming very viscous solutions. CMC is prepared by first treating cellulose with alkali (alkali cellulose), and then by reacting with monochloroacetic acid. The degree of substitution (DS) with the carboxyl groups is generally between 0.6 to 0.95 per monomeric unit (maximum DS is 3), and occurs at *O*-2 and *O*-6, and occasionally at *O*-3 positions.

Methylcellulose and its derivatives: Methylcellulose (MC) has thickening, surface activity (due to hydrophobic groups), and film forming properties. MC is prepared by treating alkali cellulose with methyl chloride. Other MC derivatives are also available, of which hydroxypropylmethylcellulose (HPMC) has been widely used. The reagent for HPMC is mixture of methyl chloride and propylene oxide. These two cellulose derivatives are non-ionic.

Hemicelluloses

Hemicelluloses are a heterogeneous group of polysaccharides constituting the cell walls of higher plants, these polysaccharides are often physically entangled, covalently and/or noncavalently bonded to cellulose and lignins. The structure of hemicelluloses may vary depending on their origin, but they can be divided into four groups based on composition of their main backbone chain:D-xylans with (1→4)-linked β-D-xylose, D-mannans, with (1→4)- linked β-D mannose, D-xyloglucans with D-xylopyranose residues attached to the cellulose chain, and D-galactans with (1→3)-linked β-D-galactose. The first three groups are very similar to cellulose in having the main chain backbone linked via (1→4) diequatorial linkages and capable of adopting extended ribbon conformations. Most of the hemicelluloses, however, are substituted with various other carbohydrate and noncarbohydrate residues, and unlike cellulose, they are heteropolysaccharides. This departure from uniformity because of various side branches renders them at least partially soluble in water.

Mannans and galactomannans: The cell walls of seeds are especially rich in mannans and galactomannans. D-Mannans, found in tagua palm seeds, have a backbone composed of linear (1→4)-linked β-D-mannose chains. The best known D-galactomannans, locust bean, guar, and tara gums have the same linear mannan backbone but they are substituted with α-D-Gal*p* side units linked to O-6. The degree of substitution in galactomannans, which profoundly affects their solution properties, differs in galactomannans extracted from various plants. Widely used galactomannans are from the carob tree (*Ceratonia siliqua*), named as locust bean gum (LBG) or carob bean gum (CBG), and the guar plant (*Cyamopsis tetragonoloba*), namely guar gum. The ratio of D-mannosyl to D-galactosyl units is about 1.8:1 in guar gum and 3.9:1 in LBG. Guar gum containing galactose content of 33–40% (w/w) is soluble in water of 25°C. The rate of dissolution of guar gum increases with decreasing particle size and with increasing temperature. In the case of LBG, with the larger part containing galactose contents of about

17–21% (w/w), it needs a heat treatment during 10 min at 86–89°C under stirring to dissolve in water. Like most hydrocolloids, both guar gum and LBG shows pseudoplastic, or shear-thinning, behaviour in solution. The degree of pseudoplasticity increases with both concentration and molecules weight.

Xyloglucans: Xyloglucans, like cellulose, have linear backbones of (1→4)-linked β-D glucopyranoses. Numerous xylopyranosyl units are attached along the main backbone. In many plant xyloglucans, the repeating unit is a heptasaccharide, consisting of a cellotetraose with three subtending xylose residues. Some xylose residues may carry additional galactosyl and fucosyl units. A few plants may have arabino- instead of fucogalactosylgroups attached to the xylose residues. One of the best characterised is the xyloglucan from the cotyledons of the tamarind seed (*Tamarindus indica*).

Glucomannans: Glucomannans are linear polymers of both (1→4)-linked -D-mannose and (1→4)-linked β-D-glucose residues. Glucomannans are obtained from dried and pulverised root of the perennial herb *Amorphophallus konjac*. Acetyl groups scattered randomly along the glucomannan backbone promote water solubility. Konjac glucomannan is a high molecular weight polymer (>300 kDa) which can form viscous pseudoplastic solutions. It can form a gel in the presence of alkali.

Arabinoxylans: D-Xylans are composed of (1→4)-linked β-D-xylopyranoses with various kinds of side branches, the most common being 4-*O*-methyl-D-glucopyranosyl uronic acid linked mostly to *O*-2 of β-Xyl*p* units and α-L-Araf linked to *O*-3 of β-Xyl*p* units. The amount of arabinose and glucuronic acid in glucuronoarabinoxylans may vary substantially, ranging from substitution at almost all Xyl*p* to polymers having more than 90% of unsubstituted β-Xyl*p* units. Many cereal (wheat, barley, rye, oats) arabinoxylans do not carry glucuronic acid units.

β-D-Glucans: β-D-Glucans are high molecular weight, viscous polysaccharides. Mixed linkage (1→3), (1→4) β-D-glucans are present in the grass species, cereals, and in some lichens (e.g. *Cetraria islandica*). Cereal β-D-glucans contain predominantly (1→4) linked β-D-Glc*p* units (~70%) interrupted by single (1→3)-linked β-D-Glc*p* units (~30%). The distribution of β-(1→4) and β-(1→3) linkages is not random, this leads to a structure of predominantly β-(1→3)-linked cellotriosyl and cellotetraosyl units. There are also longer fragments of contiguously β-(1→4)-linked glucose units (cellulose fragments) in the polymer chain. The main source of food β-D-glucans are the kernels of oats, barley, wheat, and rye. β-D- glucans have been ascribed cholesterol and blood glucose lowering properties.

Arabinogalactan: Arabinogalactan is a major D-galactan obtained from soft-woods such as pine, larch, cedar, and spruce. This polymer has a main backbone of (1→3)-linked β-D-galactopyranosyl residues with α-(1→6)-linked disaccharides of β-D-Gal*p*-(1→6)-β-D-Gal*p* and α-(1→6)- linked disaccharides of β-L-Ara*f*-(1→3)-α-L-Ara*f*. Arabinogalactan is generally a highly branched polymer with arabinose and galactose ratio of 1:6. Commercially available arabinogalactan, obtained from the butt wood of Western larch, has a relatively low molecular weight of 15000 to 25000, little impact on viscosity, colour, and taste. It is used as a low-calorie additive in beverages to increase the fibre content.

Pectins

Pectins are polysaccharide and are the major components of most higher plant cell walls, they are particularly prevalent in fruits and vegetables. Commercial pectins are prepared mostly from some by-products of the food industry, such as apple pulp, citrus peels, and sugarbeet pulp. Pectins are the most complex class of plant cell wall polysaccharides. They comprise of two families of covalently linked polymers, galacturonans and rhamnogalacturonans. Galacturonans are segments of pectins with (1→4)-linked α-D-galactosyluronic acid residues in the backbone, such as those in the linear homogalacturonans, in the substituted xylogalacturonans and in rhamnogalacturonans type II (RG II). The carboxylic acid groups in galacturonans may be methyl esterified, the degree of esterification has an important effect on the conformation and solution properties of these polymers. Based on the degree of esterification, pectins are divided into two categories: low methyl (LM) pectin that contains less than 50% methyl esters, and high methyl (HM) pectin with more that 50% methyl esters. Xylogalacturonans are relatively recently discovered subunits of pectic polysaccharides, present in storage tissue of reproductive organs of peas, soyabeans, apple fruit, pear fruit, onions, cotton seeds, and watermelon. The rhamnogalacturonans type II have been found in the cell walls of many tissues of edible plants, such as apple (juice), kiwi, grape (wine), carrot, tomato, onion, pea, and radish. Rhamnogalacturonans type I (RG I) have a backbone composed of alternating (1→2)-linked α-L rhamnosyl and (1→4)-linked β-D-galacturonic acid residues. Depending on the source of pectins, 20 to 80% of rhamnose residues may be branched at *O*-4 with side chains which vary in length and composition. The side branches may be composed of arabinans, galactans and type I arabinogalactans. Pectins with type I arabinogalactans have been found in potato, soyabean, onion, kiwi, tomato, and cabbage.

Exudate gums

Exudate gums are polysaccharides produced by plants as a result of stress, including physical injury and/or fungal attack. Gum arabic, gum tragacanth, gum karaya, and gum ghatti have been used by humans for many thousands of years in various food and pharmaceutical applications. Generally, these gums are structurally related to arabinogalactans, galacturonans, or glucuronomannans. They all contain a high proportion of glucuronic or galacturonic acid residues (up to 40%).

Gum arabic: Acacia gum, also known as gum arabic, is a natural, vegetable exudate from acacia trees (primarily in Africa) known since antiquity and used for thousands of years in foods as an additive and ingredient, in the pharmaceutical industry and for technical purposes. The thorny trees grow to a height of 7 to 8 meters, and the gum is obtained by cutting sections of the bark from the tree. The structure of gum arabic is relatively complex. The main chain of this polysaccharide is built from (1→3) and (1→6)-linked β-D-galactopyranosyl units along with (1→6)-linked β-D-glucopyranosyl uronic acid units. Side branches may contain α-L-rhamnopyranose, β-D-glucuronic acid, β-D-galactopyranose, and α-L-arabinofuranosyl units with (1→3), (1→4), and (1→6) glycosidic linkages. Gum arabic has a high water solubility (up to 50% w/v) and relatively low viscosity compared to other exudate gums. The highly branched molecular structure and relatively low molecular weight of this polymer are responsible for these properties. Another unique feature of gum arabic is its covalent association with a protein moiety. It is thought that the protein moiety rich in hydroxyproline (Hyp), serine (Ser), and proline (Pro) constitutes a core to which polysaccharide subunits are attached via Ara-Hyp linkages (the wattle blossom model). The protein moiety of gum arabic is responsible for the surface activity, foaming, and emulsifying properties of this polymer.

Tragacanth gum: In the *European Pharmacopoeia, gum tragacanth* is defined as 'the airhardened gummy exudates, flowing naturally or obtained by incision from the trunk and branches of *Astragalus gummifer* Labillardiere and certain other species of *Astragalus* from western Asia (mostly in Iran, some in Turkey)'. Tragacanth gum contains a water-soluble fraction and a water-insoluble fraction and the water-soluble fraction is accounted for 30 to 40% of the total gum. The water soluble fraction (tragacanthin) is a highly branched neutral polysaccharide composed of 1→6-linked D-galactosyl backbones with L-arabinose side chains joined by 1→2-, 1→3- and/or 1→5-linkages. The water-insoluble fraction (~60 to 70%), is tragacanthic acid (bassorin) which is a water-swellable polymer and is consisted of

D-galacturonic acid, D-galactose, L-fucose, D-xylose, L-arabinose and L-rhamnose. It has a (1→4)-linked α-D-galacturonopyranosyl backbone chain with randomly substituted xylosyl branches linked at the 3 position of the galacturonic acid residues. In spite of the availability of alternative materials, the continued use of the gum is the result of its unique functional properties combined with a high degree of stability in a range of conditions.

Gum karaya: Gum karaya, also known as sterculia gum, is a branched acidic polysaccharide obtained from the exudates of the *Sterculia urens* tree of the *Sterculiaceae* family grown in India. The backbone chain is a rhamnogalacturonan consisting of α-(1→4)-linked D-galacturonic acid and α-(1→2)-linked-L-rhamnosyl residues. The side chain is made of (1→3)-linked -D-glucuronic acid, or (1→2)-linked β-D-galactose on the galacturonic acid unit where one half of the rhamnose is substituted by (1→4) linked β-D-galactose.

Gum ghatti: Gum ghatti is an amorphous translucent exudate of the *Anogeissus latifolia* tree of the Combretaceae family grown in India. The monosaccharide constituents of gum ghatti are Larabinose, D-galactose, D-mannose, D-xylose, and D-glucuronic acid in the ratio of 10:6:2:1:2, with traces of 6-deoxyhexose.

Mucilage Gums

Mucilage gums are very viscous polysaccharides extracted from seeds or soft stems of plants, examples are psyllium (from *Plantago* species), yellow mustard (from *Sinapis alba*), and flax mucilage (from *Linum usitatissimum*). All of them are acidic polysaccharides with structures somewhat related to some of the exudate gums. Their utilisation in certain food products is increasing due to their functional properties (viscosity, gelation, water binding) as well as to their bio-active role in prevention and/or treatment of certain diseases.

Psyllium gum: Psyllium gum can be extracted from seeds of the *Plantago* species. The gum is deposited in the seed coat, it is, therefore, advantageous to mechanically separate the outer layers from the rest of the seed before extraction. Psyllium gum can be extracted with hot water or mild alkaline solutions. The molecular structure of the gum is a highly branched acidic arabinoxylan. D-Glucuronic acid residues have also been found in this gum. Psyllium gum has a very high molecular weight (~1500 kDa) and does not completely dissolve in water. When dispersed in water, it swells and forms a mucilageous dispersion with gel-like properties. It is used primarily as a laxative and dietary fibre supplement in pharmaceutical and food industries.

Yellow mustard mucilage: Yellow mustard mucilage can be extracted from whole mustard seeds or from the bran. The mucilage contains a mixture of a neutral polysaccharide, composed mainly of glucose, and an acidic polysaccharide, containing galacturonic and glucuronic acids, galactose, and rhamnose residues. Detailed analysis of the neutral fraction of yellow mustard mucilage showed that it contains mainly (1→4)-linked β-D-glucose residues. The *O*-2, *O*-3, and *O*-6 atoms of the (1→4)-β-D-glucan backbone may carry ether groups (ethyl or propyl). Depending on the polymer concentration, yellow mustard mucilage can form either viscous solution of weak gels. When it is mixed with locust bean gum, however, the gel rigidity can be increased substantially. It has been shown that the neutral (1→4)-β-D-glucan fraction of yellow mustard mucilage synergistically interacts with galactomannans. Yellow mustard is used in processed meat formulations and salad dressing as a stabiliser and bulking agent.

Flaxseed mucilage: Flaxseed mucilage can be easily extracted from the seeds by soaking them in warm water. The mucilage constitutes the secondary wall material in the outermost layer of the seed.

Upon hydration of the seeds, it expands, breaks the mucilage cells, and exudes on the surface of the seeds. Flaxseed mucilage contains 50 to 80% carbohydrates and 4 to 20% proteins and ash. Flaxseed mucilage contains a mixture of neutral polysaccharides, composed mainly of xylose, arabinose and galactose residues, and acidic polysaccharides, containing galactose, rhamnose, and galacturonic acid residues. The neutral fraction of flaxseed mucilage has a backbone of (1→4)-linked β-D-xylopyranosyl residues, to which arabinose and galactose containing side chains are linked at *O*-2 and/or *O*-3.

The acidic fraction of flaxseed mucilage has a rhamnogalacturonan backbone with (1→4)-linked α-D-galacturonopyranosyl and (1→2)-linked α-L-rhamnopyranosyl residues. The ratio of neutral to acidic polysaccharides in flaxseed may vary substantially with their origin. Unfractionated flaxseed mucilage forms a viscous solution, but it is the neutral fraction that mainly contributes to the high viscosity and weak gel-like properties of this gum. Flaxseed mucilage has not yet been widely utilised mostly because of limited information about the structure and functional properties of this gum. Similar to other gums, flaxseed mucilage can be used as a thickener, stabiliser, and water-holding agent.

Fructans

Fructans are reserve polysaccharides in certain plants, either complementing or replacing starch. They can also be produced by certain species of bacteria. A main kind of fructans is inulin. Inulins are found in roots or tubers of the family of plants known as Compositae, including dandelions, chicory, lettuce, and Jerusalem artichoke. They can also be extracted from the Liliacae family, including lily bulbs, onion, tulips, and hyacinth. Inulin is a low molecular weight polysaccharide containing (2→1) linked β-D-Fru*p* residues.

Seaweed Hydrocolloids

Alginates

Alginates constitute the primary structural polysaccharides of brown seaweeds (*Phaeophyceae*). The alginate molecules provide both flexibility and strength to the plants and these properties are adapted as necessary for growth conditions in the sea. The major species of seaweeds that produce alginates are *Macrocystis pyrifera,* grown primarily along the California coast of the USA, south- and north-western coasts of South America, and coasts of Australia and New Zealand. Other good sources of alginates are *Laminaria hyperborea*, *Laminaria digitata*, and *Laminaria japonica*, grown along the north Atlantic coast of the USA, Canada, France, and Norway. Alginates can also be synthesised by bacteria, *Pseudomonas aeruginosa* and *Azobacter vinelandii*. Alginates are unbranched copolymers of (1→4)-linked β-D-mannuronic acid (M) and -L-guluronic acid (G) residues. If the uronic acid groups are in the acid form (–COOH), the polysaccharide, called alginic acid, is water insoluble. The sodium salts of alginic acid (–COONa), sodium alginates, are water soluble. The sequence of mannuronic and guluronic residues significantly affects the physicochemical properties of alginates. The ratio of β-D-mannuronic acid to α-L-guluronic acid residues is usually 2:1, although it may vary with the algal species, the age of the plant as well as the type of tissue the alginates are extracted from. The main advantage of alginate as a gel former is its ability to form heat-stable gels which can set at room temperatures. In food applications, it is primarily gel formation with calcium ions which is of interest.

Carrageenans

Carrageenans are structural polysaccharides of marine red algae of the Rhodophyceae class. They are extracted mainly from *Chondrus crispus*, *Euchema cottoni*, *Euchema spinosum*, *Gigartina skottsbergi*, and *Iradaea laminarioides*. These red seaweeds grow mostly along the Atlantic coasts of North America, Europe, and the western Pacific coasts of Korea and Japan. Carrageenan extracted from seaweed is not assimilated by the human body, providing only fibre with no nutritional value, but it does provide unique functional characteristics that can be used to gel, thicken and stabilise food products and food systems. κ-carrageenans, τ- carrageenans, and furcellarans are linear polysaccharides whose backbone structure is based on a repeating disaccharide sequence of sulphate esters of (1→3) linked β-D-galactose and (1→4) linked 3,6-anhydro-α-D-galactose.

They differ from each other in the number and position of sulphate groups. κ-carrageenans have one sulphate group per repeating disaccharide unit, positioned at C-4 of the β-D-galactopyranosyl residue, whereas - carrageenans have two sulphate groups, positioned at C-4 of the β-D-galactopyranosyl residue and C-2 of the 3,6-anhydro-α-D-galactopyranosyl residue. Furcellaran has a similar structure to κ-carrageenan, but it is less sulphated, only 40% of the β-D-galactopyranosyl residues carry the sulphate group at C-4. These two types of monosaccharide conformations, along with the presence of axial and equatorial glycosidic linkages, allow κ- and τ- carrageenans to assume a helical conformation. In solution, in the presence of some cations (K^+, Rb^+, Ca^{++}), the double helices of furcellaran, κ- and τ-carrageenans can aggregate and form gel. τ-carrageenan and κ-carrageenan form thermally reversible gels, which range in texture from firm and brittle to soft and elastic.

The functional properties of carrageenan gels, such as rigidity, turbidity, and tendency to syneresis (separation of water from gel upon aging), generally decrease with the increasing degree of sulphation in these polymers. λ-carrageenans constitute another group of the red seaweed polysaccharides. The repeating disacharide unit in -carrageenans consists of β-D-galactopyranosyl residue sulphated at C-2 (instead of C-4 as in τ- and κ-carrageenans) and 2, 6-di-*O*-sulfato-α-D-galactopyranosyl units (instead of 3, 6-anhydro-α-D-galactopyranosyl residue). λ-carrageenans are nongelling polysaccharides used as cold soluble thickeners in syrups, fruit drinks, pizza sauces, and salad dressings.

Agar

Agar constitutes another group of polysaccharides from red-purple algae of the *Rhodophyceae* class. The agar-yielding species of *Gracilaria* and *Gelidium* grow in the waters along the coast of Japan, New Zealand, South Africa, Southern California, Mexico, Chile, Morocco, and Portugal. Agar is a linear polysaccharide built up of the repeating disaccharide unit of (1→3)-linked β-D-galactose and (1→4)-linked 3,6-anhydro-α-Lgalactose residues.

In contrast to carrageenans, agar is only lightly sulphated and may contain methyl groups. Methyl groups, when present, occur at C-6 of the (1→3)-linked β-D-galactose or C-2 of (1→4)-linked 3,6-anhydro-β-L-galactose residues. Agar, containing 3,6-anhydro-α-L-galactose residues, forms three-fold left-handed helices. These left handed threefold helices are stabilised by the presence of water molecules bound inside the double helical cavity and exterior hydroxyl groups allow aggregation of up to 10000 of these helices to form microdomains of spherical microgels.

The agar helix is more compact due to the smaller amount of sulphate groups. Agar is a well known thermo-reversible gelling polysaccharide, which sets at 30 to 40°C. Being less sulphated than furcellaran, and - and -carrageenans, agar can form strong gels, which are, subject to pronounced syneresis, attributed to strong aggregation of double helices (not weakened by the sulphate groups). The ability to form reversible gels by simply cooling hot, aqueous solutions is the most important property of agar. Gelation depends exclusively on the formation of hydrogen bonds, where the random coils associate to form single helices and double helices.

Microbial Hydrocolloids

Xanthan gum

Xanthan gum is an extracellular polysaccharide produced by the bacterium *Xanthomonas campestris*. The primary structure of xanthan gum consists of a cellulosic backbone of β-(1→4) linked D-glucose units substituted on alternate glucose residues with a trisaccharide side chain. The trisaccharide side chain is composed of two mannose units separated by a glucuronic acid. Approximately half the terminal mannose units are linked to a pyruvate group and the non-terminal residue usually carries an acetyl group. The carboxyl groups on the side chains render the gum molecules anionic. The pyruvic acid content of xanthan can vary substantially depending on the strain of *X. campestris*, resulting in different viscosities of xanthan solutions.

Molecular modelling studies suggest that xanthan gum can assume a helical structure, with the side branches positioned almost parallel to the helix axis and stabilising the structure. Xanthan gum forms very viscous solutions, and, at sufficiently high polymer concentration, it exhibits weak gel-like properties. It can form thermo-reversible gels when mixed with certain galactomannans (e.g. locust bean gum) or konjac glucomannan. Xanthan is widely used in foods because of its good solubility in either hot or cold solutions, high viscosity even at very low concentrations, and excellent thermal stability.

Pullulan

Pullulan is an extracellular homopolysaccharide of glucose produced by many species of the fungus *Aureobasidium*, specifically *A. pullulans*. Pullulan contains (1→4) and (1→6)-linked α-D-glucopyranosyl residues. The ratio of (1→4) to (1→6) linkages is 2:1. Pullulan is generally built up of maltotriose units linked by (1→6) with much smaller amount of maltotetraose units. The presence of (1→6) glycosidic linkages increases flexibility of pullulan chains and resulted in their good solubility in water compared with other linear polysaccharides (e.g. amylose). Pullulan easily dissolves in cold or hot water to form a stable, viscous solution that does not gel. A pullulan solution is stable over a wide range of pH and is also relatively stable to heat.

Gellan gum

Gellan gum is a fermentation polysaccharide produced by the microorganism *Sphingomonas elodea* (previously identified as *Pseudomonas elodea,* but later reclassified). Gellan gum is now approved for food use in many countries including Australia, Canada, United States, Mexico, Chile, Japan, South Korea, and Philippines.

The molecular structure of gellan gum is a straight chain based on repeating glucose, rhamnose and glucuronic acid units. In its native or high-acyl form, two acyl substituents – acetate and glycerate – are present. Both substituents are located on the same glucose residue and, on average, there is one glycerate per repeat and one acetate per every two repeating unit. In low-acyl gellan gum, the acyl groups are absent. Upon cooling of gellan solutions, the polysaccharide chains can assume double helices, which aggregate into weak gel structures (supported by van der Waals attractions). In the presence of appropriate cations (Na^+ or Ca^{++}), the double helices form cation-mediated aggregates, which leads to formation of strong gel networks.

Acyl substituents present in native gellan interfere with the aggregation process, giving much weaker gels. In the branched variants of gellan, the side chains also interfere with the cation-induced aggregation, allowing only 'weak gel' formation.

Animal Hydrocolloids

Chitin and chitosan

Chitin is a structural polysaccharide that replaces cellulose in many species of lower plants, e.g. fungi, yeast, green, brown, and red algae. It is also the main component of the exoskeleton of insects and shells of crustaceans (shrimp, lobster, and crab). The molecular structure of chitin is similar to that of cellulose, except that the hydroxyl groups at *O*-2 of the -D-Glc*p* residues are substituted with *N*-acetylamino groups. Chitin forms a highly ordered, crystalline structure, stabilised by numerous intermolecular H-bonds. It is insoluble in water. However, when chitin is treated with strong alkali, the *N*-acetyl groups are removed and replaced by amino groups. This new water-soluble polysaccharide, called chitosan, contains, therefore, (1→4)-linked 2-amino-2-deoxy-β-D-glucopyranosyl residues. Chitosan is the only polysaccharide carrying a positive charge. It is not digested by humans and can be used as a dietary fibre.

Gelatin

Gelatin is a proteinaceous material obtained from animal connective tissue (collagen) using hydrolysis in acidic (type A) or basic (type B) solution followed by hot water extraction. Commercially, skins or bones of different animal species, such as beef, pork, fish and poultry, form the main raw material for gelatin production. The extracted gelatin is a group of molecules of different molecular weight. The molecular weight profile depends on the process. The amino acid profile determines hydrogen bond formation and reactivity via side groups such as amine, imidazole, alcohol, amide and carboxylic acid. It hydrates readily in warm or hot water to give low-viscosity solutions that have good whipping and foaming properties. After cooling, the network of polypeptide chains associates slowly to form clear, elastic gels that are syneresis free.

Chemically Modified Hydrocolloids

Although all natural gums have inherently useful and uniquely functional properties, they also have inherent limitations and deficiencies which restrict their overall utilisation. In many cases, these limitations can be removed by selective chemical modification and derivatisation of the gum. In other cases, the overall functional properties can be improved by the chemical modification of the natural hydrocolloid.

Thus, while sodium alginate is quite soluble, it does not have good stability at low pHs. By treating alginates with propylene oxide to form propylene glycol alginate ester, a modified soluble alginate is formed that has exceptional stability under acidic conditions. In a similar fashion, while normal guar gum is quite soluble in cold water, solubility can be greatly increased by forming the hydroxypropyl guar derivative, while simultaneously giving a greatly increased viscosity. Pure cellulose is completely in soluble in water as well as being poorly absorptive in its native form. By chemical treatment to form cellulose ether compounds, such as methyl cellulose and hydroxypropyl cellulose, water solubility can be imparted, thus making a useful series of water soluble functional hydrocolloid polymers.

HYDROCOLLOIDS IN THE PRODUCTION OF SPECIAL PRODUCTS

Soft Gelatin Capsules

Liquid foods, as well as instant (soluble) coffee and other food powders, can be conveniently contained in a gelatin capsule. The interior of the capsule contains a suitable instant food which dissolves or disperses promptly upon addition of water. The capsule is maintained in a dry form in a suitable enclosure, such as a hermetically sealed bottle, blisterpack packaging or the like, until use. Soft gelatin capsules are commonly used in food supplements. Gelatin is the basic capsule shell component and it is formulated with suitable ingredients to encapsulate a wide variety of materials. Gelatin's special properties are of particular interest in foods since it acts as a barrier and protects liquid capsule contents from the outside environment. On the one hand, gelatin acts as a physical barrier to bacteria, yeasts and molds. On the other, it provides a low-permeability membrane to gases. The gelatin shell is transparent, can be formed in a wide range of sizes and shapes and dissolves quickly in hot water, releasing its encapsulated liquid. The advantages of encapsulation are: portion control, easy use and storage, extended shelf-life, improved aesthetic appeal, the variety of sizes available, disposability and edibility, improved product aromatics versus time, and biodegradability. A wide range of filler materials can be encapsulated within these capsules, such as most vegetable oils, essential oils and fish oils, as well as suspensions of crystalline materials milled with oils. A few food applications are: real chicken broth capsules which retain and deliver flavour more effectively than the powder system, encapsulated lemon oil for meringue pie mix, mint essence capsules for the tinned goods market.

Liquid-core capsules

Liquid-core hydrocolloid capsules are liquids encapsulated in a spherical polymer membrane. Production of these capsules included suspending cells in a sodium alginate solution, forming small spherical calcium alginate beads by cross-linking with calcium salt, and reacting with polylysine to create a polylysine alginate membrane around the bead. In the final stage, the bead's core, composed of calcium alginate gel, was solubilised, thus forming a liquid-core micro-capsule containing cells. With this procedure, cells could also be found in the membrane matrix, leading to the proposal of an approach to eliminate this possibility. In the latter approach, cells were entrapped in alginate-gel micro-spheres, which in turn were contained within larger beads, resulting in a greater distance between the cells and the surface of the larger alginate bead. Similar to procedure, the surface of the largermicro-sphere was reacted with poly-L-lysine and then with alginate to form a coating membrane. The contents of the micro-capsule were then liquefied with sodium citrate to remove the calcium from the array. The cells in the smaller entrapped gel micro-sphere were released and allowed to float freely in the liquid core of the resultant beads.

The contents of the capsule were either distilled water or sucrose solutions (2.5 and 30%, w/w), although other viscous liquids can be used. Beads with 0, 2 and 5% sucrose were produced by diffusion of sucrose out of liquid-core capsules containing 30% sucrose. The spherical shape of the capsule was retained after diffusion. Capsules with a higher hydrocolloid concentration within their membrane displayed more stress at failure (strength) and less brittleness than those with lesser solid membrane content. Following diffusion, capsules with 2 and 5% sucrose were weak compared to those with 30% sucrose, however, no membrane rupture was observed after incubation.

Jelly-like Foods

Natural gums are used in the confectionary industry. At one time, guar was used for production of jellies (candies) and marshmallows, and gum arabic was used gum drops. The gum within the formulation served to form *jelly*, but an additional function was to prevent sugar crystallisation and to emulsify fat, keeping it evenly distributed within the product. The gum powder swells and gels when added to water and heated. Its gels are thermally irreversible and unaffected by further addition of water and can be produced over a pH range of 2.0–9.5 in the presence of many food additives. The gels may be used to make novel food products consisting of a jelly-like skin with a liquid core, and canned jellies. The concentration of the polysaccharide in water must be greater than 1.5% for gel stability and less than 0.6% for taste acceptability. The gels are freeze-thaw stable and may be used to make an ice confection contained in an elastic gel skin.

Fruit Products

A combination of compression and shearing forces is used to extract juice from fruits or vegetables. For pulp production, and in the case of grapes, tomatoes or other soft fruits, are heated, if necessary, to soften their tissues and pulp is forced through the perforations of the pulping equipment's screen, the size of which determines the consistency of the resultant product. Unique uses of such fruit products (i.e. juice, pulp or puree) for production of soft viscous, fruit-based, membrane-coated items by a membrane were described decades ago. For example fruit juice, pulp or puree containing soluble Ca salt is extruded to form drops which are coated with a thin skin of alginate or pectate sol. The coated drops are exposed to an aqueous setting bath containing a soluble Ca salt. Drops of aqueous fruit material are coated with an aqueous alginate or pectate solution and applied in a solution containing Ca or Al ions to gel the surface.

Frozen Product

Frozen desserts are mixtures of ice crystals in flavoured liquid syrup. The most common frozen dessert is ice cream. During the last 50 years, a huge change in the texture of icecream products has occurred. Gum karaya can be used as a stabiliser in ice cream, ice milk, mellorine and related products. In ice pops and sherbets, formation of large ice crystals and syneresis can be prevented by including 0.2-0.4% gum karaya. Combinations of 0.15% gum karaya and 0.15% LBG can be used successfully for ice pop stabilisation. Karaya, as well as carrageenan, can be used as a binder and emulsifying agent in quantities of less than ~1%. The binders are used to absorb the water resulting from the ice during chopping. LBG is used in the food industry for its ability to bind and immobilise large amounts of water. This property helps inhibit ice crystal formation in frozen products, produce viscosity, modify texture and stabilise product consistency in the face of temperature changes. Sodium CMC in its highest purified form is used in many food applications. In frozen desserts (such as ice cream), cellulose gum inhibits the formation of ice crystals. Gum arabic, because of its water-absorbing properties, gum inclusion inhibits the formation and growth of ice crystals. Other stabilisers, such as carrageenan and LBG, can be used for the same purposes. Guar gum is used in the food industry for its ability to bond and immobilise large amounts of water. This property contributes to inhibition of ice crystal formation, product texture, stabilisation of product consistency to changes in temperature, and viscosity.

Freezing often causes undesirable changes in foods, and hydrocolloids are used to improve their quality. To produce a high-quality ice cream, a blend of guar gum or CMC with a smaller amount of carrageenan may be used. If xanthan and guar gum are used instead, viscosity is lower and faster processing is obtained. Karaya gum has been used in the past as a stabiliser for frozen desserts, but has been replaced almost completely by other gums. Carrageenan, guar gum and CMC have also been used as stabilisers in other frozen products. In foods containing starch as the main ingredient, there is a tendency for water to exude from the gel. Thus starch-based products curdle and undergo syneresis (loss of water) after freezing and thawing. Modified starches have been developed to deal with the problem.

Frozen doughs are widely used in industrial bakeries to make baking more profitable. However, loaf volumes are usually smaller and quality poorer for breads baked from frozen doughs, especially in those with low fat content . Addition of hydrocolloids such as CMC, alginate, and different blends in quantities of up to 1.5% yielded higher total dough water content without changing baking properties. There were no obvious differences between analysed samples or added hydrocolloid levels.

Candies

Candies are popular products among children and adults and their versatility is visually alluring as well as pleasing to the consumer. The confectionery industry uses gum arabic to a great extent, for crystallisation prevention, as an emulsification agent of fat and as a glaze in candies, chewing gum. Gum arabic serves to coat the center of sugar-coated tablets. It is the main ingredient in gumdrops (regular and dietetic) and other chewy-type gums, where pectin or modified starches can also play a major role. The incorporation of sorbitol, mannitol and gum arabic can produce dietetic candies. The higher the gum arabic content, the softer and chewier the candy.

Fabricated Foods

Using fish, meat, fruit or vegetables as main ingredients within a matrix, which is usually produced from a gum, can create fabricated foods. Gums were incorporated into meat products to achieve better control of their texture, improve sliceability and increase yield. In some meat products, hydrocolloids are responsible for the undesirable broad dark striations (called tiger stripping), running parallel to the meat fibres. The swelling ability of the type of carrageenan used influences its activity within the product.

Semi-refined carrageenan (less swelling) improved performance in injected poultry by reducing the incidence of tiger stripping without reducing purge controls.

Fabricated fruit is easily manufactured with alginates. A gel is readily formed when a soluble calcium salt is added to a sodium alginate solution. This gel is stable over a wide range of temperatures, has excellent syneresis control, and is irreversible to heat. Possible uses for this fabrication concept include imitation cocktail cherries, imitation glazed fruit pieces for cakes, breads, cookies, ice cream and candy products, icing, and gelled products containing pureed fruit. Other hydrocolloids - carrageenan, gelatin (and recently gellan), and combinations of gums such as carrageenan and locust bean gum (LBG) - have been used to fabricate food products. Examples include reconstituted pimento strips (based on alginate and gum arabic), the aforementioned imitation caviar, and restructured fish and shellfish.

Use of sodium carboxymethyl cellulose (CMC) in food applications is on the rise, especially in developed countries where the popularity and convenience of fabricated foods has grown rapidly since the early 1950s. Hydroxypropylcellulose can also be used in fabricated foods to a large extent. Its useful properties are its ability to form solvent-soluble films and its surface-active stabilisation.

HEALTH BENEFITS OF HYDROCOLLOIDS

Hydrocolloid and the Risk of Cardiovascular Disease (CVD)

Dietary fibre was briefly mentioned in the WHO report to reduce total and LDL cholesterol, and probably also to decrease the risk for cardiovascular diseases. Several studies have dealt with the association between dietary fibre intake and risk for cardiovascular disease. The main interest has been focused on effects of soluble fibres, such as different hydrocolloids, and thus on foods rich in soluble fibres. Both mixture of hydrocolloids and only one hydrocolloid were investigated. In one study, subjects with increased plasma cholesterol values were given a daily supplement of 15 g of psyllium, pectin, guar gum, and locust bean gum during 6 months. The fibres were mixed in water and consumed with each of three major daily meals. In comparison with the control group given acacia gum, the total and LDL cholesterol values were significantly lower in the test group. After 8 weeks, the reductions in comparison with baseline were 6.4 and 10.5%, respectively, and about the same reductions were found at weeks 16 and 24. In another study, a combination of soluble fibres from psyllium, oats, and barley was given to men with hypercholesterolemia. They consumed the fibres as a breakfast cereal (50 g containing 12 g of soluble fibre) for 6 weeks. In comparison with a control group given a breakfast cereal based on wheat, the total cholesterol and LDL cholesterol levels fell significantly in the test group, with 3.2 and 4.4%, respectively.

Psyllium has been extensively investigated in relation to its effects on CVD. As in the study of Anderson and others, the fibre preparations were mixed in water and taken before regular meals three times per day. A dose–response study was made by Davidson and others using psyllium seed husk given in daily doses of 0, 3.4, 6.8, or 10.2 g for 24 weeks. The fibres were included in different foods like ready-to-eat cereals, bread, pasta, and snack bars. A change in LDL cholesterol (–5.3% in comparison to control) after 24 weeks consumption was only shown for the group that took the highest dose of psyllium husk-10.2 g/day. The reduction in LDL cholesterol was more pronounced in the beginning of the intervention (week 4) for all groups. Davidson and others also investigated the lipid-lowering effect of psyllium in hypercholesterolemic children (6 to 18 years). They were given psyllium for 6 weeks and, after a 6-week washout period, a control cereal. Consumption of psyllium gave a 7% reduction in LDL cholesterol compared with the control cereal.

Many human studies on guar effect on lipid metabolism have been conducted. The dose of guar gum was 10 g and it was taken three times a day for 6 weeks. In comparison with a placebo, the guar gum decreased the blood cholesterol and triglyceride levels and blood pressure significantly. The effect of guar gum on LDL metabolism seemed to be related to an increased LDL a polipoprotein B fractional catabolism. Modified guar gum has also been studied, and in one study partially depolymerised guar gum decreased the total cholesterol levels by 10%, which is a reduction similar to that found earlier for high molecular weight guar gum. The effects of solid or liquid guar gum and preparations with high or medium viscosity on lipid metabolism were followed in hypercholesterolemic subjects. Both solid and liquid guar gum preparations lowered the total and LDL cholesterol, but the high-viscosity preparation gave a larger reduction in blood lipid levels than the medium-viscosity preparation.

Pectin can be included in the diet as a supplement, but also as fruits, which often contain much pectin. In a study, subjects with hypertension were given guava fruits before meals during 12 weeks, and the effect on the blood lipids and blood pressure was followed. In comparison with a group that was not given guava, the total cholesterol, HDL cholesterol, triglycerides, and blood pressure decreased significantly. Several studies have also been done with different kinds of pectins. Dongowski and Lorentz gave diets containing pectin with different degrees of methylation (34.5, 70.8, and 92.6%) to rats for 3 weeks. The concentration of bile acids in the plasma decreased when pectin was given, and with increasing degree of methylation more bile acids were excreted with the feces.

Hydrocolloids and Type 2 Diabetes

It has been reported that dietary soluble fibre such as -glucan, psyllium, and guar gum decreases glucose and insulin responses to carbohydrates if taken in sufficient amounts. A study comparing the effects over 6 months of barley bread, high in-glucan, to white bread found that barley bread improved glycemic control compared with white wheat bread in 11 men with type 2 diabetes. Insulin responses were increased, which hypothetically could reflect recovered -cell function. In men with diabetes and hypercholesterolemia participating in a crossover trial, 8 weeks of psyllium (15 g/day) decreased haemoglobin A1c 6.1% (absolute change, 0.8%), with similar 6% decreases in fasting postprandial glucose. Improved fasting and postprandial glycemic control was found in 11 type 2 diabetic patients taking 21 g/day of guar gum or placebo in a randomised doubleblinded crossover trial. Small improvements in overall glycemic control and sizable improvements in postprandial glycemia after 4 weeks of treatment in a randomised controlled crossover trial were reported by Fuessl and others Guar gum decreased fasting blood glucose from 11.4 to 9.5 mmol/l in 19 obese patients with type 2 diabetes who were enrolled in a randomised double-blind crossover trial. Guar gum (15 g/day) has also improved long-term glycemic control and postprandial glucose tolerance in 15 type 2 diabetic patients treated with guar gum over an 8-week period. Viscosity is an important determinant of soluble hydrocolloid in retarding glycemic responses.

Hydrocolloids as Laxative and Antidiarrhea

The laxative activity of bulk forming substances has been known since the time of Hippocrates. Hydrocolloid fractions of psyllium and ispaghula are common bulk forming laxative. The fibre from foods, such as carrots, cabbage, apple, and bran compared to guar, produces very different responses in colon function 104. Fecal weight is increased more by a bran supplement than by guar supplement. The results from a study of digestion of hemicelluloses in humans suggest that arabinoxylan is not digested and perhaps may be the active component in laxation. One hypothesis for judging the value of a bulk former as a laxative concerns its ability to hold water. However, some new evidence appears to contradict this. Since the greater the water holding capacity of a fibre source, the less the effect on fecal bulk.

HYDROCOLLOIDS – HOW TO CHOOSE?

A colloid is a substance microscopically dispersed evenly throughout another substance. A colloidal system consists of two separate phases: a dispersed phase and a continuous phase. A hydrocolloid is defined as a colloidal system, in which the colloid particles are dispersed in water. A hydrocolloid has colloid particles spread throughout the water and depending on the quantity of water available, that system can be a gel or a sol (liquid). Some hydrocolloids can exist in both a gel and a sol state, and can alternate between the states with the addition or elimination of heat. Hydrocolloids used in food are polysaccharides of high molecular weight, extracted from plants and seaweeds or produced by microbial synthesis. The plant raw materials are then partly processed further, e.g. by the addition of functional sidegroups, by hydrolysis, by purification and by standardisation. Hydrocolloids are used for a wide range of different functions within food: thickening, gelling, generating mouth-feel, film-forming, foaming, improving bake-stability, improving freeze-thaw stability, preventing crystal growth, stabilising suspensions or emulsions, and encapsulation. It can therefore be a challenge to select the right hydrocolloid for a specific food end-product, which is why many users ask whether this choice can be simplified by the creation of practical 'Guidance Notes'.

Chapter 19

Enzymes in Food Processing Industry

INTRODUCTION

Enzymes are protein molecules functioning as specialised catalysts for chemical reactions. Enzymes have always been important to food technology because of their ability to act as catalysts, transforming raw materials into improved food products. Food processing enzymes are used as food additives to modify food properties. Food processing enzymes are used in starch processing, meat processing, dairy industry, wine industry and in manufacture of pre-digested foods. This chapter discusses the enzyme biotechnology towards food processing applications and discusses the important characteristics of various enzymes and its sources, used in food industries. Various methods of enzyme immobilisation for food processing applications have also been discussed in detail.

The term enzyme is derived from the Latin word meaning in yeast. Enzymes are proteins, produced by living organisms to increase the rate of an immense and diverse set of chemical reactions required for life. In other words, they are highly specific biological catalyst. They are involved in all processes essential for life such as, DNA replication and transcription, protein synthesis, metabolism, cell regulation and signal transduction often via kinases and phosphatases. They also generate movement, with myosin hydrolysing adenosine triphosphate (ATP) to generate muscle contraction and also moving cargo around the cell as part of the cytoskeleton. Enzymes are usually named according to the reaction they carry out. Typically, the 'suffix ase' is added to the name of the substrate (e.g. glucoseoxidase, an enzyme which oxidises glucose) or the type of reaction (e.g. a polymerase or isomerasefor a polymearisation or isomerisation reaction). The exceptions to this rule are some of the enzymes studies originally, such as pepsin, rennin and trypsin. The International Union Biochemistry (IUB) initiated standards of enzyme nomenclature which recommend that enzymes names indicate both substrates acted upon and the type of reaction catalysed. The ability to perform very specific chemical transformations has made them increasingly useful in industrial processes.

Enzymes have been exploited by human for thousands of years. Food processing through the use of biological agents is historically a well-established approach. The earliest applications go back to 6000 BC or earlier, with the brewing of beer, bread baking, and cheese and wine making whereas the first purposeful microbial oxidation dates from 2000 BC, with vinegar production. The epoch of classical biotechnology was marked by landmark discoveries of microbes by Leeuwenhook of fermentation as biological processes by Pasteur, of enzymes as protein by Buchner and of the first enzyme crystal structures by summer. In the middle of the nineteenth century, Northrop and Stanley developed a complex procedure for isolating pepsin. Their precipitation technique has since been used to crystallise many enzymes. Pectinases were used for juice clarification in the 1930s, and for a short period during World War II, invertases were also used for the production of invert sugar syrup in a process that pioneered the use of immobilised enzymes in the sugar industry. A few years later, for the first time, an enzyme (a protease) was produced by fermentation of *Bacillus licheniformis*. In this, way, large-scale production of enzymes became possible, thus facilitating the industrial application of enzymes. Still, the large-scale application of enzymes only became really established in the 1960s, when the traditional acid hydrolysis of starch was replaced by an approach based in the use of amylases and amyloglucosidaes (glucoamylases), a cocktail that some years later would include glucose (xylose) isomearse. Enzymes are currently among the well-established products in biotechnology from US $4.5 billion to US $4.8 billion in 2013, it is expected to have reached around US $7.1 billion by 2018, a compound annual growth rate (CAGR) of 8.2% from 2013 to 2018. Part of this market is ascribed to enzymes used in large-scale applications, among them are those used in food and feed applications. These include enzymes used in baking, beverages and brewing, dairy, dairy supplements, as well as fats and oils, and they have typically been dominating one, only bested by the segment assigned to technical enzymes.

ENZYMES IN FOOD PROCESSING

In the twentieth century, enzymes began to be isolated from living cells, leading to a large-scale commercial production and with wider application in the food industry. Micro-organisms are being the most important source of commercial enzymes today. Although they do not contain the same enzymes as plants or animals, a micro-organism can usually be found to produce a related enzyme that will catalyse the desired reaction. Enzyme manufacturers have optimised micro-organisms for the production of enzymes through natural selection and classical breeding techniques. Food Biotechnology has grown to include cloning of plants and animals, as well as more development in genetically modified foods in more recent years.

Enzymes have always been important to food technology because of their ability to act as catalysts, transforming raw materials into improved food products. The main values of enzymes are their substrate specificity, catalytic effectiveness and a rate enhancement of 10^{10} or more over chemical reactions when working under mild conditions of ion concentration, temperature and pH. Enzymes can modify and improve the functional, nutritional and sensory properties of ingredients and products, and therefore enzymes have found widespread applications in processing and production of all kinds of food products. Food technologist selects those enzymes which can improve one particular unit operation of food production. These improvements involve substituting fish protein hydrolysates for milk in calf feed, saving energy and money in production proceses and modifying the functional properties of proteins. More and more enzymes for food technology are now derived from specially selected or genetically modified micro-organisms grown in industrial scale fermenters and Table 19.1 enlist the range of examples and applications. About 158 enzymes were used in food industry, 64 enzymes in technical application and 57 enzymes in feedstuff, of which 24 enzymes are used in three industrial sectors. Almost 75% of all industrial enzymes are hydrolytic enzymes. Carbohydrases, proteases and lipases dominate the enzyme market, accounting for more than 70% of all enzyme sales. Table 19.2 gives the representative examples of enzyme applications based on different industrial sectors, and discusses the technical benefits in various fields.

Table 19.1: Enzymes derived from micro-organisms and used in food technology.

Enzyme	*Source*	*Action*	*Application*
α-Amylase	*Aspergillus* spp., *Bacillus* spp.*, *Microbacterium irnperiale*	Wheat starch hydrolysis	Dough softening, increased bread volume, aid production of sugars for yeast fermentation
Lipase and Esterase	*Aspergillus* spp.*, *Candida* spp., *Rhizomucor miehei*, *Penicillium roqueforti*, *Rhizopus* spp., *Bacillus subtilis**	Hydrolyses triglycerides to fatty acids and glycerol, hydrolyses alkyl esters to fatty acids and alcohol	Flavour enhancement in cheese products, fat function modification by interesterification, synthesis of flavour esters
Pectinase (polygalacturonase)	*Aspergillus* spp., *Penicillium funiculosum*	Hydrolyses pectin	Clarification of fruit juices by depectinisation
Pectinesterase	*Aspergillus* spp.*	Removes methyl groups from galacose units in pectin	With pectinase in depectinisation technology
Hemicellulase and xylanase	*Aspergillus* spp.*, *Bacillus subtilis**, *Trichoderma reesei**	Hydrolyses hemicelluloses (insoluble nonstarch polysaccharides in flour)	Bread improvement through improved crumb structure
Glucose oxidase	*Aspergillus niger**, *Penicillium chrysogenum*	Oxidises glucose to gluconic acid	Oxygen removal from food packaging, removal of glucose from egg white to prevent browning
Glucose isomerase	*Actinplanes missouriensis*, *Bacillus coagulans*, *Streptomyces lividans*,* *Streptomyces rubiginosus*	Converts glucose to fructose	Production of high fructose corn syrup (beverage sweetener)
β-glucanase	*Aspergillus* spp., *Bacillus suhtilis**	Hydrolyses betaglucans in beer mashes	Filtration aids, haze prevention in beer production
β-galactosidase (lactase)	*Aspergillus* spp., *Kluyvennnvces* spp.	Hydrolyses milk lactose to glucose and galactose	Sweetening milk and whey, products for lactoseintolerant individuals, reduction of crystallisation in ice cream containing whey, improving functionality of whey protein concentration, manufacture of lactulose
Cyclodextrin glucanotransferase	*Bacillus* spp.*	Synthesise cyclodextrins from liquefied starch	Cyclodextrins are food-grade microencapsulants for colours, flavours and vitamins
Chymosin	*Aspergillus awamori** *Kluyvemmyces lactis**	Hydrolyses kappacasein	Coagulation of milk for cheese making

(Cont'd...)

Enzyme	*Source*	*Action*	*Application*
α- Acetoluctute decarboxylase	*Bacillus subtilis**	Converts acetolactate to acetoin	Reduction of wine maturation time by circumventing need for secondary fermentation of diacetyl to acetoin
Cellulase	*Aspergillus niger, Trichoderma* spp.	Hydrolyses cellulose	Fruit liquifaction in juice production
Catalase	*Aspergillus niger* Micrococcus luteus*	Breaks down hydrogen peroxide to water and oxygen	Oxygen removal technology, combined with glucose oxidase
Aminopeptidase	*Lactococcus lactis, Aspergillus* spp., *Rhizopus oryzae*	Releases free amino acids from *N*-terminus of proteins and peptides	De-bittering protein hydrolysates accelerating cheese maturation
Amyloglucosidase	*Aspergillus niger, Rhizopus* spp.	Hydrolyses starch dextrins to glucose (saccharitication)	One stage of high fructose corn syrup production, production of Mite' beers
Pentosanase	*Humicola insolens, Trichoderma reesei*	Hydrolyses pentosans (soluble non-starch polysaccharides in wheat flours)	Part of bread dough improvement technology
Pullulanase	*Bacillus* spp.*, *Klebsiella* spp.*	Hydrolyses 1-6 bonds that form 'branches' in starch structure	Starch saccharification (improves efficiency)
Protease (proteinase)	*Aspergillus* spp.*, Rhizomucor miehei, *Cryphonectria parasitica, Penicillium citrinum, Rhizopus niveus, Bacillus* spp.*	Hydrolysis of kappa-casein, hydrolysis of animal and vegetable food proteins, hydrolysis of wheat glutens	Milk coagulation fᴦr cheese making, hydrolysate production for soups and savoury foods, bread dough improvement

*These enzymes are commercially available from GMO versions of the source microorganism.

Table 19.2: Enzyme application in food processing.

Application fields of food processing	*Enzymes*	*Technical benefits*
Dairy industry	Chymosin, lipases, lysozymes	Cheese manufacturing.
	β-galactosidase, lactases	Breaking down lactose to glucose and galactose in milk processing to avoid lactose intolerance
	Lactoperoxidase	Cold sterilisation of milk: milk replacers for calves
	Acid proteinases	Milk coagulation
	Neutral proteinases and peptidases	Accelerated cheese ripening, de-bittering, enzyme modified cheese, production of hypoallergenic milk-based foods
Baking Industry	α-amylases	Degrading starch in flours and controlling the volume and crumb structure of bread
	β-xylanases	Improving dough handling and dough stability
	Oxidoreductase	Giving increased gluten strength
	Lipases	Improving stability of the gas cells in dough

(Cont'd...)

Application fields of food processing	*Enzymes*	*Technical benefits*
	Proteases	Reducing the protein in flour
	Maltogenic α-amylases	Improves self-life of bread and cack
	Glucose oxidase	Oxidative reaction with gluten to make weak doughs stronger, drive and more elastic
	Asparginase	Reduces the amount of acrylamide formed during baking
	Lipoxygenase	Bleaching and strengthening dough
Juice industry	Amylases, glucoamylases	Breaking down starch into glucose. Clarifying cloudy juice, especially for apple juice
	Pectinases	Degrading pectins which are structural polysaccharides present in cell wall. Increase the overall juice production.
	Cellulases, hemicellulose	Acting on soluble pectin hydrolysis and on cell wall components with pectinases. Lowering viscosity and maintenance of texture
	Laccase	Increasing the susceptibility of browning during storage
	Naringinase and limoninase	Acting on compounds that cause bitterness in citrus juices
Starch processing	α-amylases	Cleaving α-1, 4-glycosidic bonds in the inner region of the starch Causing a rapid decrease in substrate molecular weight and viscosity
	Pullulanases	Attacking α-1,6-linkage, liberating straight-chain oligo-saccharides of glucose residues linked by α-1,4-bonds
	Neopullulanases	Acting on both α-1,6-and α-1,4-linkages
	Amylopullulanases	Cleaving α-1,4-linkages from nonreducing ends of amylose, amylopectin and glycogen molecules
	β-amylases	Producing low-molecular weight carbohydraetes, such as maltose and β-limit dextrin
	Glucoamylases	Attacking α-1,4-linkages and α-1,6-linkages from the non-reducing ends to release β-d-glucose
	Isoamylases	Hydrolysing α-1,6-linkages in glycogen and amylopectin.
	Glucose isomerases	Catalysing isomerisation of glucose to fructose Transferring a segment of a 1,4- α-Dglucan chain to a primary hydroxyl group in a similar glucan chain to create 1,6-linkages
	Glycosyltransferases	Increasing the number of branched point to obtain modified starch with improved functional properties such as higher solubility, lower viscosity and reduced retrogradation
Brewing industry	α-amylases	Hydrolysing starch to reduced viscosity, Liquefying adjunct, Increasing maltose and glucose content
	β-glucanases	Hydrolysing glucans into oligomers and leading to lower viscosity and better filterability, Improving wort separation
	Pullulanases	Hydrolysing α-1,6 branch points of starch. Securing maximum fermentability of the wort
	Amyloglucosidases	Increasing glucose content. Increasing 1% fermentable sugar in light beer

(Cont'd...)

Application fields of food processing	*Enzymes*	*Technical benefits*
	Proteases	Increasing soluble protein and free aminonitrogen (FAN). Malt improvement Improving yeast growth
	Pentosanases, xylanases	Hydrolysing pentosans of malt, barley and wheat Improving extraction and beer filteration
	α-acetolactatedecarboxylases (ALDC)	Converting α-acetolactate to acetoin directly Decreasing fermentation time by avoiding formation of diacetyl Making beer taste right
Meat processing	Acid proteases	Improve flavouring, nutritional and functional properties of proteins. Converts animal carcasses into flavourous compounds under mild condition without by-product formation
	Tyrosinase	Cross-link meat protein, enhances functional properties of enzymes
	Glutaminase	Enhances flavour of the meat protein due to L-glutamic acid.
	Elastase	Tenderise meat, improve the commercial value of the low value meat
	Papain/ficin/bromelain	Meat tenderisation Hydrolyse both animal and plant proteins Increases protein dispersability, palpability, solubility and digestibility
	Transglutaminase	Improves the structural properties of the processed or cooked meat
	Lipase	Hydrolyse triglycerides, Improves flavour in sausages
	Actidin	Improve tenderness in processed meat

Enzymes in Dairy Industry

India being the highest producer of milk in the world, and consequently the surplus availability of milk in our country has triggered the food and dairy industry to convert the liquid milk into value-added products using biochemical and enzymatic processes. The use of rennet in cheese manufacturing was among the earliest applications of exogenous enzymes in food processing. In recent years, proteinases have found additional applications in dairy technology, for example in acceleration of cheese ripening, modification of functional properties and preparation of dietic products. Animal rennet (bovine chymosin) is conventionally used as a milk-clotting agent in dairy industry for the manufacture of quality cheeses with good flavour and texture. Rennin acts on the milk protein in two stages, by enzymatic and by non-enzymatic action, resulting in coagulation of milk.

Lactose, the sugar found in milk and whey, and its corresponding hydrolase, lactase or β-galactosidase, have been extensively researched during the past decade. Lactose can be obtained from various sources like plants, animal organs, bacteria, yeasts (intracellular enzyme), or molds. Aminopeptidases are important for the development of flavour in fermented milk products, since they are capable of releasing single amino acid residues from oligopeptides formed by extracellular proteinase activity. Proteases and lipases have significant role in dairy food industry. The other minor enzymes having limited applications in dairy processing include glucose oxidase, catalase, superoxide dismutase, sulphydryl oxidase, lactoperoxidase, and lysozymes. Glucose oxidase and catalase are often used together in selected foods for preservation.

Enzymes in Brewing

Beer and wine are both alcoholic beverages, produced by yeast fermentation of sugars. Beer is the World's most widely consumed alcoholic beverage, it is the third most popular drink after water and tea. Wine is based on grapes, and beer is traditionally based on barley. The matured grapes already contain the sugars needed for the fermentation, while barley contain starch that has to be broken down to fermentable sugars before the yeast can make alcohol. In the brewing process enzymes have an important role especially starch from leaven that promotes some transformations during the saccharification process. Some enzymes are already present in the barley, e.g. β-amylases, but the majority of enzymes are produced during the germination, e.g. α-amylases and proteases, and in the final malt all the enzymes needed for the conversion of 'grains' into a fermentable liquid (wort) is present. The enzymes used in brewing are needed for saccharification of starch (bacterial and fungal β-amylases), breakdown of barley β-1,4- and β-1,3- linked glucan (β-glucanase) and hydrolysis of protein (neutral protease) to increase the (later) fermentation rate, particularly in the production of high-gravity beer, where extra protein is added. Cellulases are also occasionally used, particularly where wheat is used as adjunct but also to help breakdown the barley β-glucans. Due to the extreme heat stability of the *B. amyloliquefaciens* β-amylase, where this is used the wort must be boiled for a much longer period (e.g. 30 min) to inactivate it prior to fermentation. Papain is used in the later post-fermentation stages of beer-making to prevent the occurrence of protein- and tannin-containing 'chill-haze' otherwise formed on cooling the beer.

Enzymes in Potable Alcohol and Wine Production

Wine is the result of the fermentation of grape juice. Enzymes play a pivotal role in the winemaking process. Many of these enzymes originate from the grape itself, the indigenous microflora on the grape and the micro-organisms present during winemaking (Table 19.3). The most widely used enzymes available for commercial use in winemaking are: pectinases, glucanases, xylanases and proteases-to improve the clarification and processing of wine, glycosidase-the release of varietal aromas from precursor compounds, urease-the reduction of ethyl carbamate formation, glucose oxidase-the reduction in alcohol levels. The main activities currently used in winemaking preparations are derived from the pectinase family. They include pectin lyase (PL), pectin methyl-esterase (PME) and polygalacturonase (PG). Food grade industrial enzymes offer significant processing improvements. These result in overall economic benefits. Industrial enzymes offer quantitative benefits as increased free run and press juice yields. The qualitative benefits as improved colour extraction in red grape varieties, colour stability and phenolic extraction of red wines, and improvements in the aging process of wines, i.e. flavour enhancement. Processing benefits resulted in shorten the time of maceration, settling, and filtration.

The pectic enzymes play an important role in breaking down grape pulp and skin cells and are able to split those chains and saccharide bonds between the chains. The first commercial enzyme preparations used in wine industry consisted of pectinase. Today, pectic enzymes alone account for about one-quarter of the world's food enzyme production. Most commercial preparations of pectic enzymes are obtained from fungal sources. In red wine, tannins and anthocyanins are the most important phenolic classes. Tannins contribute to the mouthfeel of wines but they also form pigmented polymers in association with the anthocyanins to provide the stable pigments required to give red wine its long term colour

Table 19.3: Enzymes derived from grapes and wine associated microbes involved in winemaking.

Source	*Enzyme*	*Remark*
Grape (*Vitis vinifera*)	Glycosidases	Hydrolyse sugar conjugates of tertiary alcohols, inhibited by glucose, optimum pH 5–6
	Protopectinases	Produce water-soluble, highly polymerised pectin substances from protopectins
	Pectin methylesterases	Saponifying enzymes that split metyl ester groups of polygalacturonic acids thereby releasing methanol and converting pectin into pectate, thermostable, optimum pH 7–8
	Polygalacturonases	Hydrolyse α-D-1,4-glycosidic linkages adjacent to a free carboxyl group in low methylated pectins and pectate, optimum pH 4–5
	Pectin lyases	Depolymerise highly esterified pectins
	Proteases	Hydrolyse the peptide linkages between the amino acid residues of proteins, inhibited by ethanol, thermostable, optimum pH2
	Peroxidases	Play an important role in the oxidation metabolism of phenolic compounds during grape maturation, activity is limited by peroxide deficiency and sulphur dioxide in must
	Tyrosinases (oxidoreductases)	Oxidise phenols into quinones resulting in undesirable browning
Fungi (*Botrytis cinerea*)	Glycosidases	Degrades all aromatic potential of fungal infected grapes
	Laccases	Broad specificity towards phenolic compounds and cause serious oxidation and browning problems.
	Pectinases	Saponifying and depolymerising enzymes causing the degradation of plant cell walls and grape rotting
	Cellulases	Multicomponent complexes comprising endoglucanases, exoglucanases (cellobiohydrolases) and cellobiases (a member of β-glucosidases) that act synergistically in a stepwise process to degrade plant cell walls thereby causing grape rotting
	Phospholipase	Degrades phospholipids in cell membranes
	Esterases	Involved in ester formation
	Proteases	Aspartic proteases are produced at the early stage of fungal infection of grapes and determine the subsequent rate and extent of rotting caused by pectinases, soluble, thermostable
Yeast (*Saccharomyces cerevisiae*)	β-Glucosidases	Some yeasts produce β-glucosidases which are not repressed by glucose
	β-Glucanases	Consist of extracellular, cell wall bound and intracellular, sporulation specific glucanases, accelerate autolysis process and release mannoproteins
	Proteases	Acidic endoprotease, Accelerates autolysis process
	Pectinases	Some yeasts degrade pectic substances to a limited extent, inhibited glucose levels higher than 2%
Bacterial (Lactic acid bacteria)	Malolactic enzymes	Convert malic acid to lactic acid
	Esterases	Involved in ester formation
	Lipolytic enzymes	Degrade lipids

stability. Grape anthocyanins are red pigments, located in the first external layers of the hypodermal tissue and mainly in the vacuoles, as well as in special structures called anthocyanoplasts.

Enzymes in Bakery Technology

The development of bread process was an important event in mankind. After the 19th century, with the agricultural mechanisation, bread's quality was increased while its price was reduced, thereby white- and rye-bread became a commodity within almost everyone's reach. An important aspect that contributed to evolution of the baking market was the introduction of industrial enzymes in the baking process, where bakery enzymes represent a relevant segment of the industry. The world bakery and enzyme demand between 2000 and 2020, segmented according to products. It is possible to observe that the enzymes market for baked goods is expected to increase from 420 million dollars in 2010 to 900 million dollars in 2020, although maintaining its representativeness in this segment, varying from 34.4 in 2010 to 35.7% in 2020.

Baking comprises the use of enzymes from three sources: the endogenous enzymes in flour, enzymes associated with the metabolic activity of the dominant micro-organisms and exogenous enzymes which are added in the dough. The supplementation of flour and dough with enzyme improvers (technical enzymes) is a usual practice for flour standardisation and also as baking aids. Enzymes are usually added to modify dough rheology, gas retention and crumb softness in bread manufacture, to modify dough rheology in the manufacture of pastry and biscuits, to change product softness in cake making and to reduce acrylamide formation in bakery products. The enzymes can be added individually or in complex mixtures, which may act in a synergistic way in the production of baked goods, and their levels are usually very low.

Enzymes as technological aids are usually added to flour, during the mixing step of the breadmaking process. The enzymes most frequently used in breadmaking are the α-amylases from different origins. Amylases can degrade starch and produce small dextrins for the yeast to act upon. Enzymes such as hemicellulases, xylanases, lipases and oxidases can directly or indirectly improve the strength of the gluten network and so improve the quality of the finished bread.

The addition of certain types of pentosanases or xylanases at the correct dosage can improve dough machinability yielding more flexible, easier-to-handle dough. The addition of functional lipases modifies the natural flour lipids so they become better at stabilising the dough. The addition of lipases has been claimed to retard the rate of staling in baked products. Lipoxygenases are also employed to improve mixing tolerance and dough handling properties. The action of lipoxygenase can lead to undesirable flavours in bread. Glucose oxidase can be used as alternative oxidising agent instead of potassium bromate in breadmaking. Addition of increasing glucose oxidase concentrations to wheat flour dough produced significant changes on dough rheology and bread quality, and the extent of the effect was highly dependent on the amount of enzyme and the original wheat flour quality. Furthermore, glucose oxidase was able to recover the breadmaking ability of damaged gluten. Asparaginase is claimed to have a high potential of reducing formation of acrylamide during baking.

Enzymes in Fruit and Vegetable

Processing and Juice Extraction India is the second largest producer of fruits and vegetables after china. Total production of fruits during 2012–13 was 81.2 million tonnes while that of vegetables was 162 million tonnes whereas the second advance estimates put the production at 84.4 million tonnes and 170.2 million tonnes respectively for 2013–14. The expansion of the global fruit and vegetable juice industry is forecast to reach 3.7% p.a. in the coming years. Between 2007 and 2013 the market increased with an average annual growth of 3.5%. China, France, Germany, the United Kingdom and the United

States represent the largest fruit and vegetable juice markets while the strongest annual growth is forecast to occur in Morocco (30.5%), India (18.0%), Rwanda (17.0%), Egypt (13.8%) and Moldova (12.0%).

Enzymes are processing aids used worldwide for fruit processing, particularly for the production of clear fruit juice and concentrate. Enzymes can increase the yield of solid recovery during pulp washing, facilitate the production of highly concentrated citrus bases, improve essential oil recovery from peel, debitter juice, clarify lemon juice or increase the worth of waste products. Pectinases are one of the important upcoming enzymes of the commercial sector especially for fruit juice industry as prerequisites for obtaining well clarified and stable juices with higher yields. Other enzymes used in the juice industry are amylases, glucoamylases, cellulases, hemicellulose, laccase, naringinase and limoninase. Amylases are added together with pectinases at the start of the processing season when apples contain starch. Vegetable juice processing therefore requires more cellulases in addition to pectinases to reduce viscosity sufficiently for juice extraction using a decanter. Peclyve LI (Lyven) or Rapidase Vegetable Juice (DSM) is recommended for vegetable juice extraction: they contain pectinases and cellulases.

Enzymes in Meat Processing

Tenderness of meat is considered as the most important quality distinguishing feature of meat in consumer evaluation. Tenderness in meat results from a combination of breakdown within muscle fibres, primarily because of the activity of enzymes, and loosening of connective tissue, in particular collagen. Various pre-slaughter and post-slaughter factors and their mutual effect influence tenderness of meat. In meat industry and catering predominantly protein-degrading enzymes have been used. Of the protein cross-linking enzymes, transglutaminases (TGase) have been used as texture improvers already for several years. Structure engineering by oxidative enzymes and flavour design by lipases, glutaminases, proteases and peptidases are examples of emerging enzyme technologies in the food sector. One of the potential areas in meat processing is meat tenderising using enzymes such as papain and bromelain derived from plant sources such as papaya and pine apple plant, respectively. Toughness of meat is generally due to the presence of collagen, elastin and actomycin. Meat cuts that are considered as lower quality due to toughness are as nutritious as prime quality meat, which can be tenderised using enzymes to convert it to prime quality meat. Even the flavour of the meat depends on the peptides and the amino acids present in meat. Enzymes such as proteases are utilised for tenderisation and marination. Proteases can be applied for production of protein hydrolyzates from different meat by-products such as bones, sheep visceral mass, chicken by-products or bovine by-products.

Enzymes in Starch Processing

Starch is a widely used renewable resource. It is present as a storage compound in the leaves, tubers, seeds and roots of many plants. The starch is usually modified chemically or enzymatically to a wide variety of derivatives. The industrial degradation of starch is usually initiated by α-amylases (α-1,4-glucanohydrolases) a very common enzymes in micro-organisms. Together with other starch-degrading enzymes (e.g. Pullulanases), α-amylases are included in family 13 of glycosyl hydrolases. Pullulanases specifically attack α-1, 6- linkages, liberating linear oligosaccharides of glucose residues linked by α-1,4-bonds. Pullulanases are divided into type I that exclusively hydrolyse α-1, 6 linkages and produce branched dextrins, and type II that hydrolyse both α-1,4 and α-1,6 linkages and produce mainly maltose and maltotriose. These enzymes specifically hydrolyse the α-1, 6 glycosidic linkages in amylopectin or glycogen but they do not show any activity towards pullulan.

There are three basic steps in the enzymatic conversion of starch: gelatinisation, liquefaction and saccharification. Two types of exo-acting hydrolases are commonly used for starch saccharification: β-amylases and glucoamylases. β-amylases are unable to cleave α-1,6-linkages and the final product consists of maltose and β-limit dextrin. Thus degradation of amylopectin is incomplete. Glucoamylases cleave preferentially α-1,4-linkages and can also cleave α-1,6-glycosidic linkages at a much lower rate. As a consequence, glucoamylases have the ability to carry out almost complete degradation of starch into glucose. The isomerisation of starch-derived glucose leads to greater sweetness of the obtained syrup which is commonly used in many food and beverage products. Fructose syrups are usually made in a continuous process catalysed by immobilised glucose (xylose) isomerase. In order to produce the syrup containing the standard concentration (55%) of fructose, cation-exchange fractionation of carbohydrate is used. Maltose can be converted into isomaltooligosaccharides (IMO) using specific β-glucosidases. These are exo-acting enzymes that hydrolyse amylose, amylopectin and oligosaccharides including maltose from the non-reducing end producing glucose.

Immobilised Enzyme Technology for Food Application

There are very few examples of commercial food processing operations that use immobilised enzymes currently, despite their introduction in the 1970s. Immobilisation generally reduces the enzyme's activity and the enzymes are subject to mass transfer limitations. The cost of the matrix and support and regenerative capability of the biocatalyst also contribute to the cost of the immobilised enzyme process. Immobilisation can be performed by several methods, namely, entrapment/ microencapsulation, binding to a solid carrier, and cross-linking of enzyme aggregates, resulting in carrier-free macromolecules. Immobilised enzymes are of great value in the processing of food samples and its analysis. The extent of lactose hydrolysis whey processing, skimmed milk production, etc. has been greatly enhanced by using respective enzymes as immobilised forms.

The production of high fructose corn syrup has been greatly facilitated by the use of immobilised glucose isomerase. A relatively new concept is the use of a single matrix for immobilising more than one enzyme to enhance food processing. Two of the most successful examples of immobilised enzymes are the production of high-fructose corn syrup and the enzymatic modification of oils. Immobilised lipases are used as alternatives to hydrogenation and non-specific chemical esterification of oils to produce transfat free margarines and shortening, cocoa butter equivalents, medium chain triacylglycerols, diacylglycerols, fatty acid esters, and tailored fat products. The use of lipases in the immobilised form, versus sodium methylate, allows for oil modifications in solvent free systems, specificity in the modification and the products need minimal post treatment purification. Previous commercial processes that used immobilised enzymes include β-galactosidase for production of lactose hydrolysed whey syrups and immobilised amylase for production of L-aspartic acid. Pilot scale processes have been developed including the production of 5′-ribonucleotides using immobilised 5′-phosphodisterase, production of isomaltulose using immobilised isomaltulose synthase, sucrose hydrolysis using immobilised invertase and aspartame synthesis using immobilised thermolysin.

Immobilised multi-enzyme system offer many attractive advantages however, such a process also raises some interesting questions about kinetics. Compared to the free enzyme, the higher activity of the immobilised enzyme at the higher temperature and the ability to hydrolyse raw starch such as that of potato would help overcome problems related to gelatinisation of starch during hydrolysis. Table 19.4 summarise the processing of various food substrates using respective immobilised enzymes.

Table 19.4: Immobilised enzymes used in food industry.

Enzyme	*Immobilisation support*	*Food substrate*
β-galactosidase and amyloglucosidase	Bone powder	Lactose, whey, wheypermeates, skimmed milk
Pectinase	Anion exchange resin	Pectin
Laccase	Silica gel	Wine, fruit juice and beer processing
Trypsin	Cellulose	β-lactoglobulin
Cardosin-A (protease)	Agarose glutarldehyde	α-lactalbumin
Pectin lyase	Alginate beads	Esterified pectin
Tyrosinase	Polyacrylic-acid carbon nanotubes	Phenolic in red wine
β-galactosidase	Organic and inorganic support	Removal of lactose from milk
Lipase	Calcium-alginate beads	Oil and grease
Pectinase	Anion-exchange resin	Pectin solution
β-galactosidase	Duolite A-568	Muscat wine
Glucoamylase	Chitin	Starch and hydrolysed mannose starch

To sum up, the enzymes in the food industry is a well-established approach, in particular due to the specificity of enzyme action and their green, environmentally friendly nature. As mentioned above, enzymes are currently used in several different food products and processes and new areas of application are constantly being added. The introduction of enzymes as effective biocatalysts working under mild conditions results in significant saving in resources such as energy and the environment. Evidence clearly shows that dedicated research efforts are consistently being made as to make this application of biological agents more effective and diversified. These endeavours have been anchoring in innovative approaches for the design of new/improved biocatalysts, more stable, less dependent on metal ions and less susceptible to inhibitory agents and to aggressive environmental conditions, while maintaining the targeted activity or evolving novel activities. This is a particular relevance for application in the food sector, for it allows enhanced performance under operational conditions that minimise the risk of microbial contamination. Immobilisation of enzymes has been a key supporting tool for rendering these proteins fit for food application, while simultaneously enabling the improvement of their catalytic features. Again, and despite the developments made in this particular field, there is still the lack of a set of unanimously applicable rules for the selection of carrier and method of enzyme immobilisation. In a world with a rapidly increasing population and approaching exhaustion of many natural resources, enzyme technology offer a great potential for many food industries to help meet the challenges they will face in years to come.

SECTION V

Spices, Sweetners and Vitamins

Chapter 20

Spices and Allied Products

INTRODUCTION

A spice is a seed, fruit, root, bark, or other plant substance primarily used for flavouring, colouring or preserving food. Spices are distinguished from herbs, which are the leaves, flowers, or stems from plants used for flavouring or as a garnish. Sometimes, spices may be ground into a powder for convenience. Right from the kitchen and medicinal uses in homes spices have an important role to play in different places. As India is blessed with a varied climate each of its state produces some spice or the other. No wonder why spices are used so extensively for cooking in India. Not only in India but also in some other countries spices are considered to be of great use.

Spices are expensive additives to processed foods and form an important class of agricultural food commodities of international commerce It imparts appealing aroma, flavour, colour and texture to food. Apart from their use as flavouring agents in food and beverages industry, their antimicrobial, antioxidant, anti-inflammatory, antitoxic and hypolipidermic properties extend their use in medicines and cosmetics.

India is one of the largest producers, consumers and exporters of spices and spice products in the world. Spices are traded in different forms as whole fresh spice, whole dried spice and their value-added products such as crushed or powdered forms (black pepper powder, chilli powder, turmeric powder, cumin powder, mustard powder, cinnamon powder, curry powder, curry masala, etc.) pastes (garlic paste, chilli paste, curry paste, ginger paste, etc.) dehydrated forms (dehy green pepper, dehy garlic flakes, dehy garlic powder, etc.) spice oils, spice oleoresin and spice extractives. Spice powders are presently gaining much importance in the market because of their high process friendly nature Black pepper, chilli and turmeric are the three major spices exported from India in powder form.

QUALITY EVALUATION OF SPICES

Quality of spices is assessed by its intrinsic as well as extrinsic characters. The former consists of chemical quality, i.e. the retention of chemical principles like volatile oil, alkaloids and oleoresins while the latter emphasizes physical quality. This include appearance, texture, shape, presence or absence of unwanted things, colour, etc. In addition certain health requirements are also implemented as export quality standard viz., pesticide residue, aflatoxin, heavy metals, sulphur dioxide, solvent residues, and microbiological quality. However, physico-chemical quality remains the ultimate attribute, while considering export requirement of spices as these properties delineate its grade in the market. These qualities vary unpredictably. According to Menon the physicochemical characteristics vary widely depending on the variety, agro-climatic conditions existing in the area of production, harvest, and post-harvest operations.

Drying as a post-harvest method: Considering each and every step under post-harvest technology of spices, drying remains the most important operation. At the time of harvesting, spices like all other agricultural commodities invariably contain high moisture that must be brought down into the desired level at which attack of micro-organisms would be minimum. At the same time retention of quality attributes should also be at the maximum. However the percentage moisture content of spices varies considerably at the time of harvest. Pruthi had the opinion that spices contain high moisture (55–85%) at the time of harvest, which must be reduced into 8–12%. Exceptionally, some spices like garcinia contains more than 90% of moisture content at harvest. The period between initial moisture level and final moisture level, however, is more crucial while adopting postharvest technologies.

The removal of moisture is attained either naturally or artificially by heat or pressure. Thermal mode of drying is more prevalent and most studied. Adiabatic drying is the drying of a product simply by circulating relatively dry air around it. Factors influencing the rate of evaporation are the ambient temperature, relative humidity, pressure and velocity of air, size and shape of the wet material, and direction of air movement.

An important phenomenon to be considered during drying is 'critical moisture content'. The mean moisture content of the body at the time when constant rate drying ends is called the 'critical moisture content'. This will vary according to different spices. But it has colossal importance in drying, because if dried beyond critical moisture level the spice may become over dried or deteriorated. Almost all spices are hygroscopic in nature Thus during drying, water evaporates at a rate which, in the falling rate phase, becomes smaller as the mean moisture content diminishes. Thus the drying rate falls towards zero as the moisture remaining in the body approaches vapour pressure equilibrium with the surrounding air. During drying, various other processes also takes place, such as cooling effect, shrinkage effect, case hardening, loss of rehydration ability, browning, scorching or heat damage, loss of flavour, and migration of soluble constituents. Different methods of drying are in vogue for various spices.

HERBS

Most herbs can be grown successfully with a minimum of effort. Several are drought-tolerant, some are perennials, and many are resistant to insects and diseases. They are versatile plants, providing flavours for seasoning food and fragrances for room-freshening potpourri.

Herbs can be planted with vegetables or mixed in garden beds with annuals, perennials, shrubs, and trees. And with their enticing scents, diverse textures, attractive shapes, and countless shades of green and gray, herbs are often used to make a landscape that appeals to the senses of touch and smell, as well as sight.

Annual herbs are best started from seed. When starting small seeds indoors, the easiest method is to sow them directly into individual pots filled with seed-starting mix at about six weeks before the last frost date. Cover the seed with a thin layer of moist seed-starting mix or milled sphagnum moss. Later, thin the seedlings to four or five per pot. Larger seeds may also be started by this method, then thinned to one plant per pot. Keep the soil surface moist by misting until the plants are established.

It is best to harvest your herbs in the morning, just after the dew has dried, but before the sun gets hot. The concentration of essential oils is highest at this point. Harvest your herbs for fresh use all season, but for drying, cut just before the plants bloom. This will ensure the maximum concentration of essential oils. When harvesting, cut just above the first joint of tender growth — it takes the plant longer to send out new shoots from woody growth.

The best dried herbs are those that have been dried rapidly, without excessive heat or exposure to sunlight. When harvesting to dry, it is often necessary to spray the plants with a garden hose the day before cutting to clean dirt and dust off the leaves. The next morning, after the leaves have dried, make your harvest. Remove dead or damaged leaves and make small bunches of the herbs. Tie the stems together and hang them in a temperate, well-ventilated, darkened room that has little dust. Label each bunch, because several of the herbs look similar when dried.

CONDIMENTS

Condiments are edible food items which are additions to a dish or meal. These items are not strictly necessary in themselves to the dish or meal, but add to the enjoyment by enhancing or contrasting with the main food.

Condiments is an umbrella term which takes in such items as sauces, spreads, vinegars, flavoured and unflavoured oils, relishes and pickled items: some people broaden the term to include spice mixes, pepper and finishing salts.

Some definitions include simple slices of vegetables such as tomato, cucumber, etc.

Condiments are generally prepared and ready to use as a final addition to a prepared dish by the diner at the table. A jar of taco seasoning mixed dried spice would not usually be classed as a condiment, as it is meant to be used in cooking, whereas a jar of taco sauce would be, because even though it can be used in cooking, it can also be applied right at the table.

Many food items serve a dual purpose as both condiment and ingredient. Ketchup and mustard, for instance, are often called upon to be ingredients in baked bean recipes. Sauces such as Mayonnaise and pesto can be used as a condiment (for instance, on French Fries or sandwiches), even though their prime purpose in theory is to be an ingredient in something, hummous and guacamole, which are used as dips, being food items in themselves, can be used as a condiment on sandwiches or burgers.

Some condiments are healthier than others: some may add amounts of calories, fat, or sodium to a meal that can be hard to justify. Condiments that are generally low in calories, fat and sodium include the millenia-old classics of mustard and vinegar (note though that some types of mustard, such as Dijon, can be higher in sodium than other mustards are).

Almost every cuisine has its own range of unique condiments, though mustard and vinegar tend to be universal for the most part. Condiments can be sweet, or savoury. Examples of sweet condiments include carmelised onion relishes, cranberry sauce, and mint sauce (depending on the recipe).

Some of important spices and allied products are discussed below:

AJOWAN OR BISHOP'S WEED (*AJOWAN*)

Ajowan is an annual herbaceous plant bearing the greyish-brown fruits (seeds) which constitute the spice. Ajowan seeds, like other spices, are not viewed nutritionally. They are more known as adjuncts used in small quantities for flavouring numerous foods, as antioxidants, as preservatives, or in medicine or for the manufacture of essential oils for ultimate use in perfumery, essences and medicine, etc.

Uses

Steam distillation of crushed seeds yields 2.0 to 4.0 per cent essential oil which is valued considerably in medicine on account of the presence of thymol therein. Ajowan seeds also contain fatty oil to the extent of 16.5 to 23.5 per cent. The oil is reported to be a rich source of a unique fatty acid—petroselenic acid which is a base for the manufacture of many chemicals. Oil of ajowan is almost colourless to brownish liquid, possessing a characteristic odour and a sharp burning taste. On standing, a part of the thymol may separate from the oil in the form of crystals, which is sold in Indian market under the name of *ajowan ka phool* or '*sat ajowan*' and is much valued in medicine, as it has nearly all the properties ascribed to the ajowan seeds. Ajowan seeds are reported to be useful in preparing various medicines.

AMCHUR, KACHCHA AM (*KERI*)

Amchur is the dried or dehydrated product prepared from unripe mango flesh in the form of peeled slices or powder used for acidification of curries etc. Mango is the most important fruit of India and is grown in many states of India. The unripe fruits are peeled and the flesh cut into thin slices. The slices are then dried in the sun and packed in gunny bags for sale.

Uses

Amchur is used as an 'acidulant' or a 'souring agent' for curries, like similar to the use of tamarind pulp extracts in the South Indian curries *sambar* and *rasam*. It is also used in chutneys, soups and certain specific vegetable curries. The main purpose of its addition is to lower the pH of gravy whereby, the destruction of spoilage organisms in the vegetable curry, etc. is made much easier at boiling point. It is further reported that unripe mango is useful in opthalmia and eruptions. The rind is astringent, stimulating, tonic in debility of stomach. The kernel, too, is astringent, used in haemorrhage and diarrhoea and is anthelmintic, its juice, if snuffed, can stop nasal bleeding.

ANARDANA

'Anardana' comprises the dried seeds (dried along with the natural flesh) of pomegranate fruit. Pomegranate is a shrub or a small tree, 5–8 meter high, considered to be a native of Iran, Afghanistan and Baluchistan.

Uses

Anardana is mostly used as a condiment for acidification of chutneys and certain curries, as in the case of tamarind or amchur. The seeds are reported to be stomachic while the pulp is both cardiac and stomachic. The rind of the fruit combined with cloves, etc. is useful in diarrhoea and dysentery. Seeds are also reported to have estrogenic activity as they contain steroidal estrogens. Stem bark and root bark are astringent, anthelmintic and specific in tape-worms. They contain alkaloids.

ANGELICA

The fruit, young stem and roots of angelica plant are used for flavouring foods. Angelica is a stout and aromatic perennial herb, 1.5 to 3 meter high with small, pale yellowish-brown fruits, found in Kashmir. It has an agreeable perfumed odour similar to that of juniper berries.

Uses

The stems, roots and fruits of the plant are used for flavouring wines, liquors and confectionery. The dry root, root-stalk and the fruits possess stimulant, expectorant and diaphoretic properties. The fresh stems and leaf stalks serve as a garnish and are also used for confectioneries. The flavour and perfume industries employ chiefly the root and seed or their respective volatile oils, which can be recovered by steam distillation. It is also used in medicine.

ANISEED (VALAITI SAUNF OR SAWONF, BADAIN)

Aniseed is an annual herbaceous plant belonging to the ajowan family and a native of the East Mediterranean region. Aniseed bears fruits which contain volatile oil similar to that of-star-anise. Therefore, they have almost similar odour and flavour. Of course, anise oil is finer and has a more delicate flavour than that of star-anise oil. Aniseed is ground-grey to greyish-brown in colour, 3.2 to 4.8 mm in length, oval in shape and with a short stalk (pedicel) attached. Five longitudinal ridges are visible on each pericarp.

Uses

Aniseed possesses a sweet, aromatic taste and emits, when crushed, a characteristic agreeable odour and is used for flavouring food, confectionery, bakery products, beverages, 'anisette' and other liquors. It is also used in medicine and perfumery. Its residues is utilised as cattle feed.

ASAFOETIDA (HING)

Asafoetida or Asafoetida is the dried latex or oleogum oleoresin exuded from the living rhizome or rootstock or taproot of several species of Ferula, three of which grow in India, mainly in Kashmir. These are the perennial herbs belonging to the genus Ferula which are the sources of the oleogum resins used as condiment as well as in medicine. Asafoetida is acrid and bitter in taste and emits a strong, disagreeable, pungent, alliaceous odour due to the presence of sulphur compounds therein. Hence its common name abroad, 'Devil's dung'. The oil of asafoetida is obtained by steam distillation of the gumresin.

Uses

Asafoetida is extensively used in India for flavouring curries, sauces and pickles in conjuction with onion and garlic. In Iran (Persia), the natives rub asafoetida on warmed plates prior to placing meat on them. Besides, the large cabbage like tops of the plants are relished raw by the natives. It is also used in medicines.

CAPSICUMS OR CHILLIES (LAL MIRCH)

Chillies are the dried ripe fruits of the species of genus *capsicum*. They are also called red peppers or capsicums and they constitute an important, well-known commercial crop used both as a condiment or culinary supplement and as a vegetable. It is virtually an indispensable item in the kitchen. Commercially, chillies may be classified on the basis of their colour, size, pungency and the end-use to which they are put. The varieties of chillies are broadly divided into two groups as follows: (i) the long pungent type, including the pickling type, used as a spice, and (ii) the bell-shaped, non-pungent or mild and thick-fleshed type, popularly known as '*Simla Mirch*' which is commonly used as curried vegetable.

Paprika (*C. Annum*)

Paprika of Hungarian Paprika, also called 'sweet pepper' or *Spanish pimento*, is the mild or non-pungent variety of chilli or capsicum. The dried ripe red paprikas are valued chiefly for their brilliant red colour and mild flavour. Paprika is used for its colouring and flavouring properties. In homes and public eating places, paprika is used largely as a garnish for light coloured foods, such as eggs (poultry), fish, potatoes, pasta, salads and salad dressings. In food manufacturing, as flavour is important, this spice becomes a vital ingredient of sausages, soups, salad dressings and many ready prepared foods.

Bird Chillies and Tabasco Chillies (*C. Frutescens Linn.*)

Bird chilli is a shrubby perennial plant, 0.9 to 1.2 meters high, bearing small conical fruits, 12–25 mm long which are extremely pungent. It occurs wild or semi-wild in the tropics. The ripe fruits of these species are dried in the sun or in a mechanical drier. They are then powdered to the desired mesh as in chillies or peppers. They are sold whole or ground.

Uses

Dry chilli is extensively used as a spice in all types of curried dishes in India and abroad. Curry powder is made by grinding roasted dry chilli with other condiments such as coriander, cumin, turmeric and farinaceous matter, etc. It is also used for seasoning of egg, fish and meat preparations, sauces, chutneys, pickles, frankfurters, sausages, etc. Bird chilli is used in making hot sauces such as chilli sauce and tabasco sauce. '*Mandram*' is a West Indies stomachic preparation made by adding cucumber, shallot, lime juice and Madeira wine to mashed fruits of bird chilli. It is sometimes added to tannin or rose gargles for pharyngitis and sore throat. It is administered in the form of powder, tincture, linament, plaster, ointment, medicated wool, etc.

CARAWAY (SHIA JIRA)

Caraway or 'Caraway seed' of commerce, is the fruit of a biennial herb known botanically as *Carum carvi*, Linn.

Uses

Caraway is widely used as a spice for culinary purposes and for flavouring bread, biscuits, cakes and cheese. It is also used in the manufacture of Kummel and as an ingredient of sausage seasoning and pickling spice. It also used in medicines and soaps.

CASSIA (JANGLI DALCHINI)

Cassia (*Jangli Dalchini*) and Cinnamon (*Dalchini* or *Darchini*) are very popular spices commonly used in the Indian diet. The name *Darchini* which has come to stay in Indian parlance, is actually a derivation from the Arabian term *Dar-al-chini*, meaning the wood (or bark) of China, one of the oldest and largest producers of China Cassia so well-known in commerce.

Uses

It is extensively used as a spice in the form of small pieces of powder for flavouring confectionery, liquors and soaps. The bark contains 0.5 per cent volatile oil with the odour of cloves and musk. Its wood is light brown, fairly hard, shining. It machines well, takes on a good finish and hence can be used for the manufacture of light furniture.

CELERY SEED (SHALARI, AJMUD)

Celery seed is the dried ripe fruit of the umbelliferous herb, usually 60 to 180 cm high, erect, with conspicuously jointed stems bearing well-developed leaves on long expanded petiodes.

Celery seed is available both as whole and ground. It is subject to adulteration by addition of exhausted or spent seeds (from which oleoresin or oil has been extracted), excess stems, chaff, earth, etc. The ground celery is sometimes adulterated with farinaceous products, linseed meal, worthless vegetable seeds or weed seeds, etc. The celery fruits yield 2–3 per cent of a pale yellow volatile oil with a persistent odour, characteristic of the plant.

Uses

The dried ripe fruits (celery seeds) are used as spice. Leaves and stalks are used as salads in soups and as a pre-dinner appetiser. It is also used in medicine and perfumery.

CHERVIL (BAZ-ALTRILA)

'Chervil' or 'Salad chervil' is an annual herb. Its leaves are used both for flavouring salad and as a condiment for garnishing some foods. Its flavour is similar to that of mild parsley and aniseed.

Uses

Chervil leaves are mainly used for garnishing and flavouring food, their flavour being similar to that of aniseed and parsley. It is chopped fine and sprinkled over fish before removing from the boiler. It is also used in soups, salads, sauces (tartar sauces), egg dishes and in medicine.

CHIVES OR CIVES

Chive or Cive, a perennial herb belonging to the onion family, is a native of Europe and adjoining part of Asia. In India, it is grown as a garden crop. Chive is raised in many parts of the world as a vegetable or herb in the home garden, where its small size and great adaptability make it more useful than the common onion. Like onions, chives contain volatile oil which is rich in sulphur compounds like 'allicin' (which contains amino acid with a strong natural antibiotic action).

Uses

Leaves constitute the main part of the plant and are used principally for flavouring soups, stews, omelettes, cottage cheese, cream cheese and for seasoning salads. Chives are practically always used fresh.

CINNAMON (DARCHINI)

Cinnamon is one of the most important tree spices of India. Like its cousin cassia, cinnamon consists of layers of dried pieces of the inner bark of branches and young shoots from the evergreen tree *Cinnamomum zeylanicum* which is obtained when the cork and the cortical parenchyma are removed from the 'whole bark'. The thickness of the bark ranges from 0.2 to 1.0 mm. Pure cinnamon is free from any admixture with cassia which is considered inferior to the former in appearance, flavour and odour.

Uses

Cinnamon is a very useful tree. Every part of the tree-bark, wood, leaves, buds, flowers, fruits and roots—finds some use or the other as indicated below:

Cinnamon bark primarily is one of the most popular spices in use in every home. It has a delicate fragrance and a warm agreeable taste. It is extensively used as a spice or condiment in the form of small pieces or powder. It is aromatic, astringent, stimulant and carminative and also possesses the property of checking nausea and vomiting.

Cinnamon is used for flavouring confectionery, liquors, pharmaceuticals, soaps and dental preparations. Powdered cinnamon is a constituent of chocolate preparations made in Spain. Cinnamon is also used in candy, gum, incense and perfumes Bark oil is extensively used for flavouring confectionery, liquors, pharmaceuticals, soaps and dental preparation.

CLOVE (LAUNG)

The clove of commerce is the air-dried, unopened flower-bud obtained from a handsome, medium-sized, evergreen, straight-trunked three that grows in Kerala and Tamil Nadu. Clove is one of the most ancient and valuable spices of the Orient, known as far back as the first century before Christ.

Uses

Clove is very aromatic, has a fine flavour and imparts warming qualities. Clove is used for flavouring curries, gravies, pickles, ketchup and sauces, spice mixtures, and pickling spice. It is highly valued in medicine as carminative, aromatic and stimulant. It is also used in flatulence and dyspepsia. Clove has stimulating properties and is one of the ingredients of betlelnut chew. In Java, clove is used in the preparation of a special brand of cigarette for smoking.

CORIANDER (DHANIA OR DHANYA)

Coriander seed and fresh coriander (*dhania*) leaves are too well known to need any introduction or description in India, particularly to the housewife, as coriander is used almost daily in scores of curries, etc.

Uses

The fresh stem, leaves and fruits of coriander have a pleasant aromatic odour. The entire plant, when young, is used in preparing chutneys and sauces and the leaves are used for flavouring curries and soups. The fruits (seeds) are extensively employed as condiment in the preparation of curry powder, pickling spices, sausages and seasonings. They are used for flavouring pastry, cookies, buns, cakes and tobacco products. It is also used in medicine and perfumery.

CUMIN SEED (JIRU OR JEERU)

Cumin of *Safaid Zeera* comprises the dried yellowish to light greyish brown seeds of a small slender annual herb of the coriander family, believed to be native of Egypt and Syria, Turkestan and Eastern Mediterranean region.

Uses

Cumin seeds have an aromatic odour and a spicy and somewhat bitter taste. They are largely used as condiment and form an essential ingredient in all mixed spices and curry powder for flavouring soups, pickles and for seasoning breads and cakes. It is also used in medicines.

CUMIN BLACK (KALUNJI, KALA JIRA)

Black cumin is the dried seed-like fruit of a small herb about 45 cm in height and a native of the Levant (eastern Mediterranean region). It is said to be cultivated or occasionally found as a weed of cultivation in Punjab, Himachal Pradesh, Bihar and Assam.

Uses

It is can be used as a stabilising agent for edible fats. Seeds are scattered between folds of linen or woollen clothes to preserve them against insect attack. It is also used in medicine.

CURRY LEAF (KATHNIM, MITHA NEEM, KURRY PATTA, GANDHELA, BARSANGA)

Curry leaves (*Murraya koenigii* Linn) or '*Curry Patte*' are derived from a handsome, aromatic, more or less deciduous shrub (0.9 m) or a small tree, upto 6 m in height (in the Himalayan region) and 15–40 cm in diameter, found almost throughout India and the Andaman Islands upto an altitude of 1500 m.

Uses

The leaves of this plant have been used for centuries in South India as a natural flavouring agent in various curries and chutneys. It is also used in medicines.

DILL AND INDIAN DILL (SOWA, SOYA)

The genus *Anethum* comprises three specie, two of which yield dill oil used in medicine. These two species are:

1. *Anethum graveolens* (European Dill).
2. *Anethum sowa* (Indian Dill).

A. sowa is a herbaceous umbelliferous annual with pinnately divided leaves, found practically throughout India. It is also cultivated as a cold weather crop in many parts of India. The ripe, light brown seeds emit an aromatic odour faintly resembling that of caraway, and possess a warm, aromatic and slightly sharp taste almost akin to that of caraway seeds.

Uses

Dill seeds are used, both whole and ground, as a condiment in soups, salads, processed meats, sausages, spicy table sauces, salads, sauerkraut and particularly in dill pickling. The dried residue left after the distillation of the essential oil from the seeds of *A. graveolens* contains fat: 16.8 per cent, protein: 15.1 per cent. It may be used as cattle feed. It is also used in medicine.

FENNEL (SAUNF, SONP)

The dried, ripe fruit (seed) of cultivated varieties of *Foeniculum vulgare* Mill., fam. *Umbelliferae*, which is a biennial or parennial, aromatic, stout, glabrous herb, 1.5–1.8 meter high, cultivated in Mediterranean countries, in Romania and in India.

Uses

The plant is pleasantly aromatic and is used as a pot-herb. The leaves are used in fish sauce and for garnishing, leaf stalks are used in salad. Thickened leaf stalks of Florence fennel are blanched and used as vegetable. Dried fruits of fennel have a fragrant odour and a pleasant aromatic taste. It is also used in medicines.

FENUGREEK (METHI)

Fenugreek is the dried ripe fruit of an annual herb, native of south-eastern Europe and West Asia and now cultivated in India, Argentina, Egypt and Mediterranean countries (southern France, Morocco and

Lebanon). The seed is small and yellowish brown in colour. It has a pleasantly bitter taste and a peculiar odour and flavour of its own. The seed is produced as a spice, as a vegetable for human consumption, as forage for cattle and to some extent, for medicinal purposes. This robust herb has light green leaves, is 30 to 60 cm tall and produces slender beaked pods 10 to 15 cm long.

Uses

Fenugreek has been used both as a food or food additive as well as in medicine. Fresh tender pods, leaves and shoots which are rich in iron, calcium, protein, vitamin A and vitamin C, are eaten as curried vegetable since ancient times in India, Egypt, etc.

Ground fine and mixed with cotton seed, it is fed to cows to increase the flow of milk. Mildewed or sour hay is made palatable to cattle when fenugreek herbage is mixed with it. It is also used in veterinary medicinal preparations. It is used as a conditioning powder to produce a glossy coat on horses. It is also used in medicine and cosmetics.

GARLIC (LASUM, LASSAN)

Garlic of *Lassan* needs no introduction since it has long been recognised all over the world as a valuable condiment for foods and a popular remedy or medicine for various ailments and physiological disorders. Garlic has since long been cultivated practically throughout India as an important minor spice or condiment crop.

Uses

According to the Unani and Ayurvedic systems as practised in India, garlic is carminative and is a gastric stimulant and thus aids in digestion and absorption of food. It is also given in flatulence. In modern allopathy, it is being used in a number of patented medicines and other preparations. Besides, garlic is also anthelmintic and antiseptic. The active principle in garlic is an antibiotic—allicin, which is an enymatic clevage product from its precursor, 'allin', naturally present in garlic. Garlic is used practically all over the world for flavouring various dishes. It is also used in medicine.

GINGER (ADRAK)

Ginger of commerce or '*Adrak*' is the dried underground stem or rhizome of the Zingiberous herbaceous plant, *Z. officinale*, which consititutes one of the five most important major spices of India, standing third or fourth, competing with chillies, depending upon fluctuations in world market prices and world demand and supply position.

Ginger, like cinnamon, clove and pepper, is one of the most important and oldest spices. It consists of the prepared and sundried rhizomes known in trade as 'hands' or 'races' which are either with the outer brownish cortical layers intact ('coated' or 'unscraped') or with outer peel or coating partially or completely removed (i.e. 'uncoated' or 'scraped' or 'decorticated' ginger.) To improve their appearance, some grades of ginger are bleached by various means, e.g. by liming, etc.

Uses

The aroma of ginger is pleasant and spicy and its flavour penetrating, slightly biting due to antiseptic or pungent compounds present in it, which make it indispensable in the manufacture of a number of food products like ginger bread, confectionery, ginger ale, curry powders, certain curried meats, table sauces, in pickling and the manufacture of certain soft drinks like cordials, ginger cocktail, carbonated drinks, bitters, etc. Ginger is also used for the manufacture of ginger oil, oleoresin, essences, tinctures, etc. A number of alcoholic beverages are prepared from ginger in foreign countries, such as ginger brandy, ginger wine, ginger beer and ginger ales, etc. It is also used in medicines and perfumery.

JUNIPER (AARAAR, HAUBERA, ABHAL)

Juniper, which is found in the Himalayas from Kumaon west-wards at altitudes of 1520 to 4270 meter, is an evergreen shrub, sometimes attaining the height of a small tree with erect trunk and spreading branches, covered with a shreddy bark.

Uses

These are employed for flavouring gin and food products. Large quantities of the fruit are used in Europe for preparation of alcoholic beverages of the gin type. For this purpose, the fruits are crushed, immersed in warm water and fermented, the fermented mass is then distilled and rectified, 1000 kg of fruit yields 16–18 liter of beverage (containing 40–50 per cent alcohol) and 5–6 kg of volatile oil. It is also used in medicines.

MINT OR JAPANESE MINT (PUDINA)

Mint or '*Pudina*' is known to one and all, as used in 'chutney' and as an old popular household remedy for relieving cold and cough. It belongs to the genus Mentha which consists of about 40 species of aromatic perennial herbs distributed mostly in Europe, America, Japan, China, Brazil and Formosa. In India, about eight species of Mentha are reported to occur or grow.

Uses

Mint of '*Pudina*' is very popular for use in the common 'Pudina'/Dhania' chutney. Mint is also used for flavouring meat, fish, sauces, soups, stews, vinegar, teas, tobacco and cordials. The fresh leaf tops of all mints are used in beverages, fruit cups, apple sauces, ice cream, jellies, salads, sauces for fish and meats, also to flavour vegetables, chutneys, etc. Roast lamb and ming jelly have become inseparable companions. Japanese mint oil is used as a substitute for true peppermint oil (from *M. piperita*) which resembles it in physico-chemical properties. It possesses a somewhat bitter flavour and is considered inferior to *M. piperita* oil in aroma and quality. *Arvensis* oil with low menthol content is finding some use in cheap perfumery. The main use of mint is the extraction of volatile oil which contains menthol and is used in medicine for stomach disorders, in ointments for headaches, rheumatism an other pains, in cough drops, inhalation, mouthwashes, toothpastes, etc. and also for flavouring in cigarettes.

MUSTARD (RAI, BANARSI RAI, SAFED RAI, KALEE SARSON)

The genus *Brassica* consists of over 150 species of annual or biennial herbs several of which are cultivated as oilseed crops (as rape, sarson, toria, etc.) or a vegetable or fodder crops.

The 'mustard flour' of commerce is a mixture of the flours of two types of mustard seeds, brown or black mustard (*Brassica nigra*) and white mustard (*Sinapis alba*). Its condimental properties are largely due to the essential principles of these two seeds. The essential principle or volatile oil, of brown mustard is allyl isothiocyanate, while that of white or yellow mustard is acrinyl isothiocyanate. The essential principles are not present as such in the seeds of brown and white mustards but are produced as a result of hydrolysis of their respective glycosides, '*sinigrin*' (potassium myronate) and '*sinalbin*', by the action of the enzyme myrosin, in the presence of moisture under suitable conditions.

White Mustard (*Sinapis alba* or *B. hirta*)

White mustard (also commonly called 'yellow mustard') or 'sufed rai' is a self-sterile species, easily recognised by its hairy stem devoid of any bloom.

Uses

The seeds of *B. alba* are rarely used alone, but they are mixed with black mustard in the preparation of mustard. They are not much used for the extraction of oil. In Europe, the oil cake is used for fattening sheep. Young leaves and tender shoots are used as potherb. The species is sometimes cultivated for green manure.

Black Mustard or True Mustard (*B. Nigra* Koch)

Black mustard or 'banarsi rai' is highly self-sterile and is quite distinct from other brassicas. The fruits at maturity are closely appressed to the inflorescence axis. The seed coat shows fine reticulations under a lens and is mucilaginous.

Uses

Black mustard is ground with white mustard for preparing table mustard and also various medicinal mustard preparations, such as bath mustard, mustard bran and mustard flour. The expressed oil has mild rubefacient properties and is used as a liniment. The technical oil obtained during the preparation of mustard also contains the oil from white mustard seeds. In Europe, it is used for making soap, for burning and as lubricant. In India seeds of black mustard are used in pickles and curries.

Indian Mustard (*B. juncea*)

Indian Mustard or Rai is a self-fertile species and is a very variable annual. Its narrow-based leaves are not stem-clasping like those of atoria and sarson. Rai matures later than either. The seeds are rugose, reddish-brown and generally smaller. There are two races of rai: a tall, *late* and a short, *early*.

Uses

Rai is an efficient substitute for black mustard. The USP recognises this species also as mustard. 'Brown mustard' and the expressed oil of mustard prepared from the seeds of *B. juncea* are included in the Indian Pharmaceutical Codex (IPC). The former should contain not less than 0.6 per cent of allyl isothiocyanate.

NUTMEG (JAIPHAL)

Nutmeg is the dried seed (kernel) of the peach-like ripe fruit of *Myristica fragrans*—the evergreen tree, native of Moluccas and cultivated in Indonesia, West Indies, etc. Indonesia is one of the largest world suppliers of nutmeg. In India, nutmeg is grown on a small scale in Tamil Nadu (Nilgiris, etc.) Kerala, Karnataka, Assam and other states, but it is not enough to meet the country's own requirements.

Uses

Both nutmeg and mace are used as condiment and in medicine. In eastern countries, they are used more as a drug than as condiment. Nutmeg is stimulant, carminative, astringent and aphrodisiac. It is used in tonics and electuaries and forms a constituent of preparations prescribed for dysentery, stomachache, flatulence, nausea, vomiting, malaria, rheumatism, sciatica and early stages of leprosy.

Oil of nutmeg or mace is employed for flavouring food products and liquor. It is used for scenting soaps, tobacco and dental creams and also in perfumery. It is mildly counter-irritant and used in liniments and hair lotions. It has been recommended for the treatment of inflammations of bladder and urinary tract. The oil is somewhat toxic owing to the presence of myristicin and should be used with caution.

Nutmeg butter is used as a mild external stimulant in ointments, hair lotions and plasters and forms a useful application in cases of rheumatism, paralysis and sprains. It is used in perfumes for imparting a spicy odour and in the manufacture of soaps and candles. Alcoholic extracts of nutmeg show antibacterial activity against *Micrococcus var, aureus*. Aqueous decoctions are toxic to cockroaches.

ONION (PIYAZ)

Onion is too well known to need any description. It is used both for cooking and as a condiment for flavouring or for pickling. Mild onions are used for cooking or a salad. Pungent varieties are used as condiment for flavouring a number of foods. Pearl onions or small onions are used in pickles, including vinegar pickles. For dehydration purposes and for manufacture of onion powder, white onions of desired quality are preferred.

Uses

Because of the presence of several sulphur compounds, onion has antiseptic properties. Onion is said to possess stimulant, diuretic and expectorant properties and is considered useful in flatulence and dysentery. Freshly expressed onion juice has moderate bactericidal properties. Onions are used as salad, cooked in several ways in all types of curries, they are baked, boiled, fried and used in fresh or dehydrated or powder form in soups, pickles, sauces, etc. They are also eaten raw as a salad.

PEPPER—BLACK, WHITE AND GREEN (KALI MIRCH)

Black Pepper or Kali Mirch is known to one and all due to its day-to-day use as one of the most popular spices. Black pepper is rightly considered the 'King of Spices' as judged from the volume of international trade, being the highest among all the spices known. Black pepper is the dried, mature but unripe berries (fruit) of *P. nigrum*, a branching vine or a perennial climbing shrub mostly found in hog and moist parts of southern India notably Kerala and Karnataka (3.5 per cent) and the rest in Tamil Nadu and Pondicherry. There are nearly 24 varieties/types of black pepper grown in India and their identification is rather difficult, since some of them go by different names in different regions.

Uses

Pepper is a valuable adjunct in the flavouring of sausages, canned meats, soups, table sauces and certain beverages and liquors. It is used in perfumery, particularly in bouquets of the oriental type of to which it imparts spicy notes difficult to identify. It is also used in soaps and medicines.

PEPPER, LONG (PIPLI, PIPLAMUL)

Long pepper is the dried fruit of *Piper longum* L, which is a slender aromatic climber with perennial woody roots occurring in the hotter parts of India.

Uses

The fruits are used as spice and also in pickles and as preservatives. They have a pungent pepper-like taste and produce salivation and numbness of the mouth. It also finds uses in medicines.

PEPPERMINT (GAMATHI PUDINA, PAPARAMINTA)

Peppermint is a perennial, glabrous, strongly scented herb grown or cultivated in temperate regions of Europe, Asian, etc.

Uses

Peppermint oil is one of the most popular and widely used essential oils. It is employed for flavouring pharmaceuticals, dental preparation, mouth washes, cough, drops, soaps, chewing gums, candies, confectionery and alcoholic liquors. It is valued in medicine both for internal and external uses, for internal use, it is preferred to menthol because of its more pleasant taste. It is widely employed in flatulence, nausea and gastralgia. It may be administered with sugar or in the form of tablets and lozenges. The oil has mild antiseptic and local anaesthetic properties. It is used as an external applications in rheumatism, neuralgia, congestive headache and toothache. The green plant, left after the extraction of oil, may be dried into hay or silaged for use as cattle feed.

POPPY SEED (KASKASH)

Poppy is cultivated either for manufacture of opium or for seeds. In India, var. *album* of poppy with white seeds has been cultivated for many years for the production of seeds under license in Dehradun and Tehri Garhwal districts of UP, Jullundur, Kapurthala, Hoshiarpur and Patiala districts of Punjab.

Uses

The poppy seeds are utilised as food and as a source of fatty oil. They are considered nutritive and are used in breads, curries, sweets and confectionery.

Seeds are demulcent and are used in the form of emulsion as an emollient and specifically for obstinate constipation and in catarrh of the bladder. The white seeds are used in pharmaceuticals. Poppy seeds or seed meal also find use in the production of lecithin. It also find uses in medicines and soaps.

ROSEMARY (RUSMARY)

Rosemary is a unique leafy spice of great value. Rosemary of commerce comprises dried leaves derived from an exotic, leafy, evergreen shrub of *R. officinalis*.

The colour of the dried herb is brownish green. Rosemary leaves have a tea-like fragrance. Crushed rosemary, however, has an agreeable and fragrant, spicy aroma with a camphoraceous note. The taste has fragrant, spicy, pungent, bitter and camphoraceous notes.

Uses

Fresh tender tops are used for garnishing and for flavouring cold drinks, pickles, soups and other foods. The leaves are employed as a condiment, dried and powdered, they are added to cooked meats, fish, poultry, soups, stews, sauces, dressing, preserves and jams. They are mixed with sage in pork and veal stuffings and sometimes are added to biscuits. It also finds uses in medicne and perfumery.

SAFFRON (ZAFFRAN, KESAR)

Saffron consists of the dried stigmas of *Crocus sativus* which is a bulbous perennial. It is a low growing plant with an underground globular corm. It is cultivated for its large, scented, blue or lavender flowers. The flowers have trifid, orange-coloured stigmas which along with the style-tops yield the saffron of commerce.

Uses

Saffron is famous for its extraordinary medicinal, flavouring and colouring properties. It is used abroad in exotic dishes particulary in Spanish rice specialities and French fish preparations. It is also used in fine bread in many countries, viz. in Scandinavia as well as in the Balkans. The principal colouring agent of saffron is the glycoside *crocin*, the bitter substance is the glucoside *picrocrocin*.

TAMARIND (IMLI)

The ripe fruit of the tree (*Tamarindus indica*) is used as condiment or more precisely, as an 'acidulant', like *amchur* (dried slices of raw green mango or its powder) or *anardana* (the dried sour pomegranate seeds) or kokam fruit (*Garcinia indica*). Tamarind fruit or tamarind pulp is quite popular all over India, particularly in southern India where tamarind constitutes an essential ingredient of sambars, rasams, chutneys and curries.

Uses

Practically all the parts of tamarind three have one use or the other. Ripe fruit or tamarind pulp has an important role numerous culinary preparations in the country, notably Sambar, Rasam, curries, chutneys, etc. which are quite popular in the southern parts of India. It also finds uses in medicines.

THYME (BANAJWAIN)

The dried leaves and flowering tops of *T. vulgaris* are called 'thyme' and those of *T. serpyllum* 'wild thyme' which is found in Himalayas and Kashmir of Kumaon.

Uses

It is used in tomato soups, 'clam chowder' and juice, fish and meat dishes (particularly poultry dressing). It is also used in liver sausage, pork sausage, head cheese, collage and cream cheese and bockwurst. It also finds uses in medicines.

TURMERIC (HALDI)

The spice, turmeric or *haldi*, consists of the dried, boiled, cleaned and polished rhizomes (the underground swollen stem of the plant) of *Curcuma longa*. It is used extensively daily by all classes of people in the preparation of tasty curried dishes. Turmeric not only adds its typical flavour but its colour also, thereby helping to bring out the best in curried dishes. Besides, it is also used as dye in certain cotton textiles, in medicine and in cosmetics. Further, it is also regarded by the Hindus as something 'sacred' for use in ceremonial and religious functions.

Uses

Turmeric is largely consumed as spice while only limited quantities are utilised for other purposes. By far the largest quantity of turmeric is utilised in most of the Asiatic countries as a food adjunct in many vegetable, meat and fish preparations. It is used to flavour and at the same time to colour butter, cheese, margarine, pickles, mustard and other foodstuffs. It is also used to colour liquor, fruit drinks, cakes and table jellies. It is one of the principal ingredients of curry powder which is a blend of many spices, common salt and farinaceous matter. Turmeric, by dint of its aromatic oil content, flavours food-stuffs, acts as an appetiser and aids digestion. A pinch of turmeric powder is often added to most of our savouries to impart simultaneously an agreeable flavour and colour and to improve the keeping quality.

VANILLA (VANILLA)

Venilla is a tropical orchid cultivated for its delicate pleasant flavour, usually added to sweet dishes, etc. The vanilla pods or sticks of commerce are the cured fruits or beans of the climbing orchid *V. fragrans* or *V. planifolia*. It is a native of the Atlantic coast from Medico to Brazil.

Uses

Vanilla, today, constitutes the world's most popular flavouring for numerous sweetened foods. 'Vanilla sugar' is used in the manufacture of chocolates. Vanilla flavouring is used in countless commercial food products, in liquor, in cheap brandy and in whisky. It also finds uses in medicines.

SALT

Salt occupies a special position as an ingredient to enhance the taste, palatability and flavour of foods. It is also a preservative of a variety of food products when used in large amounts. The need for maintaining a constant level of sodium and chloride ions in plasma and extracellular fluids is an important factor in the human diet. The daily requirement of common salt is about 5 gram and excessive intake is also detrimental to health. Cooking salt is almost entirely sodium chloride with other salts such as magnesium and calcium chlorides and magnesium, calcium and sodium sulphates constituting about 2–2.5 per cent. Other trace elements are also found to be present in the cooking salt. The moisture content is about 3 per cent. Salt occurs naturally as rock salt, in seawater (3–3.7 per cent) or salt springs. Salt production depends on the source. Rock salt is mined, crushed and finely ground. Brine (4 per cent) from salt springs is evaporated directly or pre-concentrated to about 20 per cent sodium chloride in cascade solar evaporation units and then under vacuum. During crystallisation, additives such as calcium or magnesium carbonate (0.25–2.0 per cent) prevent lumping of the salt. The addition of potassium ferrocyanide (20 ppm) modifies the crystallisation pattern of sodium chloride during evaporation to dendrite form. The dendrite crystals have low density, smaller volume and low tendency to agglomerate. In tropical places, sea water is concentrated in shallow flat basins by sun, heat and wind until it crystallises.

Iodised salt containing 5 mg of sodium or potassium or calcium iodide per kg of cooking salt is used to cater to the need of iodine in our diet to prevent goitre, a disease of the thyroid gland. Nitrite salt containing 0.5 per cent of sodium nitrite in common salt is used for pickling or dry curing of meat. Low sodium diet required by some patients to avoid excess sodium intake involves the use of substitutes for common salt in the form of flavouring agents. The substitutes marketed as diet salts include potassium, calcium and magnesium salts of adipic, succinic, glutamic, carbonic, lactic, tartaric and citric acids or monopotassium phosphate, adipic and glutamic acids and potassium sulphate.

Chapter 21

Sweeteners in Foods

INTRODUCTION

Our quality of life is highly dependent on our taste sensory system. Taste is the final check used to evaluate the quality of a food, and we select foods guided primarily by the emotions of pleasure or displeasure experienced upon tasting them. Research on taste indicates that 'sweet' is an innately preferred sensation—infants favour sweetness when presented with the other basic tastes (salty, bitter, sour) or even umami, the so-called fifth basic taste, characterised as 'savory.' This recognition of the importance of sweetness confirms why sweet foods are by far the most popular treats.

Sugars are forms of monosaccharide. Examples of monosaccharides are glucose (also called dextrose), fructose, and galactose. When two monosaccharides combine, a disaccharide is formed. For example, when glucose and fructose join together, the disaccharide sucrose, or table sugar, results. Maltose is composed of two glucose molecules, while lactose (milk sugar) is formed by one molecule of glucose and one molecule of galactose. All sugars are carbohydrates and contain four calories per gram.

To most people, 'sweet' is synonymous with table sugar (sucrose), which is derived from sugarcane or sugar beets and contains 16 calories per teaspoon. Fructose is commonly referred to as 'fruit sugar' because of its presence in fruits. Fructose as a product is available in crystalline form (from cornstarch), as liquid honey, or as liquid high-fructose corn syrup (HFCS) when combined with glucose. HFCS is used in the preparation of many beverages. Sugars are widespread in nature and are the building blocks of carbohydrates. Sugar is naturally found in many foods, including milk, grains, fruit, and vegetables. The sugar found in these foods provides an important fuel source. Certain tissues in the body, such as the brain and red blood cells, exclusively use sugar for energy. Furthermore, these carbohydrate-rich foods provide a variety of other nutrients, such as fiber, vitamins, and minerals.

Sugar is also added to many foods, such as breads and other baked goods, cereals, flavored yogurt, sweetened beverages, and sauces. Many foods with added sugar provide energy (calories) but contain few other nutrients. They may replace other foods that are high in vitamins, minerals and other important nutrients in the diet. Therefore, it is important to moderate the consumption of these foods.

The World Health Organisation recommends consuming no more than 10% of daily calories from added sugar and 'free sugars,' such as honey, syrup, or juices. High consumption of added sugars has been linked to certain illnesses such as obesity, diabetes, and heart disease. Therefore, it is important to consume them in moderation.

METABOLISM AND DIGESTION

Although carbohydrate digestion starts in the mouth, the small intestine is the major area of digestion and absorption. Here, carbohydrates are broken into individual sugar molecules, or monosaccharides, such as glucose, fructose, galactose, and glucose- the most common sugar found in naturally occurring foods. Once broken down to monosaccharide form, the molecules are absorbed into the blood for transport throughout the body. Energy needs of the body determine if the glucose will be shipped out to the brain, muscles, kidneys or heart for immediate use, or stored for later energy needs. In the liver or skeletal muscles, glucose can be stored as branched chains called glycogen. Glucose that exceeds immediate energy needs and glycogen storage capacity is converted to fat and stored in adipose tissue.

Regardless of its food source, glucose is always digested in the same manner. However, simple carbohydrates are digested more quickly than complex carbohydrates, which can lead to a more dramatic increase in blood sugar levels.

When metabolised for energy, all sugars contribute four calories per gram. Some foods contain more concentrated sources of calories than others. For example, a teaspoon of table sugar contains 16 calories. Honey is a denser calorie source - a teaspoon contains 22 calories. However, a teaspoon of orange juice or applesauce has just four calories, and also contains vitamins, minerals, and fiber.

It is important to note that fructose and glucose are metabolised differently. Fructose is metabolised primarily in the liver, and so it does not lead to a significant increase in blood sugar levels. As a result of this fact, products high in fructose, such as agave, were proposed as a good sugar alternative for individuals looking to manage blood glucose levels. However, recent research has suggested that consumption of high levels of fructose may be detrimental, because the liver is unable to regulate its metabolism in the same way it can regulate glucose metabolism. Excessive fructose consumption may be associated with non-alcoholic fatty liver disease. It may also lead to increased risk for obesity and visceral fat, as well as increased dysregulation of lipids in the body and decreased insulin sensitivity. These factors have been linked to an increased risk for cardiovascular disease and type 2 diabetes.

Sweeteners

Sweeteners are prolific in the American food system, found in everything from candy to crackers to soups and salad dressings. The sugars and sweeteners listed below come from naturally occurring sources. However, in some circumstances a great deal of refinement may occur to form the final product.

Table Sugar

Table sugar is made of a type of sugar called sucrose, and is regularly produced from beets or sugar cane. Sucrose is composed of the two simple sugars, glucose and fructose. Itis the most abundant sugar in nature, important for its palatability, availability, low cost, and simplicity of production. Additional products resulting from the refinement process of sucrose are molasses, brown sugar, and confectioners' sugar. Table sugar is highly processed and refined.

Molasses

Molasses is formed during the production of table sugar. It is the heavy dark liquid portion remaining after sugar is extracted from beet or sugar cane through crystallisation. Molasses can vary in grade, depending on which extraction it is harvested from. Molasses obtained after only one extraction is sweeter and lighter in color because more sugar remains in the solution. Blackstrap molasses is formed during the third extraction of cane sugar. It is comprised of 55% sucrose, and is significantly less sweet. Therefore, it is commonly used in industrial production or as an ingredient in animal feed.

Honey

Honey is produced by honeybees, formed from nectar, and is composed primarily of sucrose. It has antimicrobial properties and can be a good source of antioxidants. However, the composition of honey can vary significantly from region to region, due to the variation of plants present. Processing can also greatly affect the quality of honey. Some manufacturers produce artificial honey, made from beet or cane sugar. These products are more uniform in flavor and color, but lack the antimicrobial and antioxidant properties of pure honey. It is important to note that honey may harbor spores of the bacteria that causes Infant *Botulism, Clostridium botulinum*. Therefore, honey should never be given to any child under the age of one.

REDUCED-CALORIE AND LOW-CALORIE SWEETENERS

Polyols

Also called 'sugar alcohols' or sugar replacers, polyols may be classified as monosaccharide-derived (sorbitol, erythritol, xylitol, mannitol), disaccharide-derived (maltitol, isomalt, lactitol), and polysaccharide derived (hydrogenated starch hydrolysates). They are carbohydrates imparting a sweet sensation but are neither sugars nor alcohols. Polyols are mostly reduced-calorie sweeteners and may be used in the same amount as table sugar but are frequently used in conjunction with other sweeteners to achieve the desired sweetness level and taste. With fewer calories than sucrose, they provide sweetness to sugarfree cookies, candies, chewing gum, baked goods, ice cream, toothpastes, mouthwashes, breath mints, and pharmaceuticals. The US Food and Drug Administration allows the use of the following caloric values for polyol sugar replacers:

Polyol	*(cal/g)*	*Sweetness relative to sucrose (%)*
Hydrogenated starch hydrolysates	3.0	25–50
Sorbitol	2.6	50–70
Xylitol	2.4	100
Maltitol	2.1	75
Isomalt	2.0	45–65
Lactitol	2.0	30–40
Mannitol	1.6	0–70
Erythritol	0.2	60–80

Polyols also add bulk and texture to foods, provide a cooling effect or 'cool' taste, help retain moisture in foods, do not lose sweetness, and do not cause browning when heated. Because molds do not grow well on polyols, they may contribute to longer shelf life of foods. They are naturally occurring in many fruits and beverages, but for commercial uses they are made from other carbohydrates, such as starch, sucrose, and glucose. The FDA considers the sugar alcohols listed above as either generally recognised as safe (GRAS) or approved food additives.

Polyols are incompletely absorbed from the small intestine into the bloodstream, producing a lower glycemic response (i.e. a lesser effect on blood glucose) than sucrose or glucose. When absorbed, they are metabolised to energy with little or no production of insulin. In theory, polyols may be useful to diabetics, but it is advised that diabetics first consult with their physician, dietitian, or other health professional before using polyols in meal plans. Physicians and other health professionals should also be consulted before the use of polyols in weight management. To date, there is no conclusive evidence that glycemic index is related to weight control.

Unabsorbed polyols continue to the large intestine, where they are fermented by bacteria. Some individuals who consume excessive amounts of polyols may experience gastrointestinal symptoms, such as gas and laxative effects, similar to reactions to high-fibre foods and beans. The American Dietetic Association advises that consuming more than 50 grams per day of sorbitol or 20 grams per day of mannitol may cause diarrhea. In such cases, the amount consumed on a single occasion should be reduced. Consequently, labels of polyol-containing products must bear the statement, 'Excess consumption may have a laxative effect.'

Polyols are also non-cariogenic—they do not promote tooth decay because bacteria in the mouth do not metabolise and convert the sweetener into plaque or harmful acids that cause tooth decay. The US Food and Drug Administration (FDA) authorises the use of this claim on labels of products containing sugar alcohols. Xylitol is found even to inhibit oral bacteria. This is the reason for the use of polyols in many sugarless mints and chewing gums.

The name of the polyol used in a product is listed in the ingredient statement. The term 'sugar alcohol' must be used if more than one polyol is used. Polyols are also included in the total carbohydrate content in the Nutrition Facts panel of the product label. If the terms 'sugarfree' or 'no added sugar' are used, the sugar alcohol content must be declared separately under carbohydrates in the Nutrition Facts panel. Some food manufacturers are using the new descriptions 'net carb,' 'low carb,' or 'impact carb,' where net carbohydrate is calculated by subtracting carbohydrates from fibre and sugar alcohols from the total carbohydrate. FDA has not defined these new terms, and this calculation is still being debated in the scientific community.

Tagatose

Tagatose is a low-carbohydrate sweetener contributing 1.5 calories per gram, and it is especially suitable as a flavour enhancer at low doses. Technically known as Dtagatose, it is a white, crystalline powder that is prepared from lactose. It was first launched in the United States in May 2003 with FDA notification as a GRAS ingredient. It was approved for use as a general-purpose sweetener in Korea in 2003 and in Australia and New Zealand in April 2004. Its safety was confirmed by the Joint FAO/WHO Committee on Food Additives (JECFA) in June 2004 with no limited acceptable daily intake (ADI), JECFA's safest category for a food ingredient. Other regulatory approvals are currently under way in major markets worldwide. Tagatose is ideal for use in diet soft drinks because of its synergistic flavour-enhancing effect when used in combination with other high-intensity sweeteners such as acesulfame-K, sucralose, and aspartame. Sweetness onset occurs rapidly, and bitterness is reduced. Tagatose is found to enhance mint and lemon flavours in chewing gums and mints, toffee flavour, and creaminess in some dairy product applications. It is pH-stable in acidic products, such as carbonated beverages and yogurts. It performs well in frostings because of its easy crystallisation properties. Tagatose may be used in small amounts in baking applications to increase moistness and flavour while maintaining sweetness, but it caramelises or browns more readily than sucrose.

Tagatose behaves like fructose in the body, but only 15–20 per cent of tagatose is absorbed in the small intestine. Due to this incomplete absorption, tagatose has minimal effect on blood glucose and insulin levels. The rest of the ingested tagatose proceeds to the large intestine where it acts as a *prebiotic*, promoting the production of butyrate and lactic acid bacteria (considered "good" bacteria), which are essential in maintaining a healthy digestive system. Like other low-digestibility carbohydrates and dietary fibres, tagatose is fermented in the colon to short-chain fatty acids that decrease acidity and may contribute to a healthy epithelium in the large intestine. These short-chain fatty acids are then almost completely absorbed and metabolised. This fermentation, however, may result in mild gastrointestinal discomfort (e.g. flatulence and laxation) in some sensitive individuals, just as high-fibre carbohydrates do.

Tagatose is also non-cariogenic. The FDA has approved the use of dental claims on products containing tagatose provided that the products satisfy all the requirements for a tooth-friendly product. The approved claims may state 'Tagatose sugar does not promote tooth decay' and 'Tagatose sugar may reduce the risk of tooth decay.' Products containing up to 0.5 gram per serving of tagatose may be labelled 'sugar free,' while products with less than 3.33 grams per serving may be labelled 'zero calorie.'

Trehalose

Trehalose is a disaccharide consisting of two glucose molecules. It is found in common foods such as honey, mushrooms, and shrimp and is naturally produced by the body. It is half as sweet as sucrose, provides sustained energy, and elicits a very low insulin response. Trehalose may be used in foods and beverages such as fruit juices, white chocolate chips, nutrition bars, and dehydrated fruits and vegetables.

It is heat stable, and in addition to being a sugar, it also stabilises proteins, or prevents protein aggregation, making it useful as a biological preservative. Trehalose protects and preserves cell structure in foods and may be useful in freezing and thawing processes by maintaining a desired texture.

The FDA has given trehalose a GRAS designation. It is approved for use in Japan, Taiwan, and Korea, and it may be used in the preservation of freeze-dried products in the United Kingdom. Trehalose is commercially prepared from starch and is available as Ascend™.

Acesulfame Potassium

Also known as acesulfame-K or 'Ace-K,' acesulfame potassium is a high-intensity, non-nutritive sweetener that is 200 times sweeter than sucrose. It imparts a clean, sweet taste with no lingering aftertaste. It is non-cariogenic, is stable under high temperatures, and has an excellent shelf life. It is used as a sweetener in many foods, including chewing gums, baked goods, dessert and dairy products, alcoholic beverages, canned foods, and candies—all told, in more than 4000 products in about 90 countries including Australia, the UK, Canada, and Germany. Acesulfame potassium is often used as a blend with other sweeteners to achieve a more sugarlike taste with the finished product containing about 40 per cent less total sweetener added. It is not metabolised or stored in the body, being quickly absorbed and then excreted unchanged.

The FDA first granted the use of acesulfame potassium in soft drinks in July 1988 and has since reaffirmed its safety on several occasions until granting its general-use approval in December 2003 with no restrictions for any segment of the population, including pregnant women and diabetics. Use of acesulfame potassium does not require a warning label or information statement. It has been used in Europe since 1983, and the European Union's Scientific Committee for Food (SCF) has accepted its use in foods and beverages. JECFA has also found it safe. Like the FDA, JECFA set an acceptable daily intake (ADI) of 15 mg/kg body weight as the amount of this ingredient a person can safely consume each day for an entire lifetime. This means that a 70-kg (154-lb) person would have to consume about 1.05 grams of acesulfame potassium per day, or about 210 grams sugar, or the equivalent of about two gallons beverage per day. Because acesulfame potassium is a high-intensity sweetener that is used in very small amounts, even if it were the only low-calorie sweetener used today, the daily intake by a heavy food and beverage consumer would be only 3.8 mg/kg body weight, which is much lower than the ADI of 15 mg/kg body weight.

The results of several long-term animal studies using much higher amounts of acesulfame potassium than are normally consumed by humans indicated no evidence of cancers or tumours. There is also no evidence of potential health concern from the 10 mg of potassium in a packet of acesulfame potassium table-top sweetener. For comparison, a banana may contain 400 mg potassium and a sweet potato 390 mg. In addition, there have been no documented cases of allergic reactions to acesulfame potassium. Acesulfame potassium is sold under the brand name Sunett™.

Aspartame

Aspartame is a nutritive sweetener containing 4 calories per gram. Because it is 200 times sweeter than sucrose, however, very little aspartame is needed to impart the same sweetness as sugar, resulting in minimal calories added to foods. Aspartame completely breaks down upon digestion into small amounts of methanol and the amino acids aspartic acid and phenylalanine. These components are then absorbed into the blood and used by the body in exactly the same ways as when they come from other foods and beverages. No accumulation of aspartame or its components occurs in the body over time.

Aspartame has a clean, sugar-like taste, enhances fruit and citrus flavours, can be safely used under heat with some loss of sweetness at higher temperatures, and is non-cariogenic. It is primarily responsible for the growth of the low-calorie and reduced-calorie product market in the past two decades and is today an important component of thousands of foods and beverages. Because aspartame helps impart a good, sweet-tasting flavour to low-calorie and reduced-calorie foods and beverages, it is helpful to diabetics and beneficial in weight control by managing caloric intake while still maintaining a healthful diet.

The FDA approved aspartame first in 1981 for use in table-top low-calorie sweeteners and powdered mixes and later in 1983 for carbonated beverages. It was given approval for use in all foods and beverages in 1996. Aspartame is considered one of the most thoroughly researched food additives in the world. The FDA continues to confirm its safe use by the general public, including diabetics, pregnant and nursing women, and children. People with a rare hereditary disease known as phenylketonuria (PKU) must control their phenylalanine intake from all sources, including aspartame. Products sweetened with aspartame must carry a statement on the label that they contain phenylalanine.

Aspartame is used in more than 100 countries including Canada, Japan, the UK, and Germany. It is found in more than 6000 products and is estimated to be consumed by more than 200 million people worldwide. JEFCA and the EU's SCF have also found aspartame safe for food use. In the United States, health organisations such as the American Medical Association, the American Dietetic Association, and the American Diabetes Association have reviewed research on aspartame and also concluded that it is safe. The FDA has established an ADI for aspartame of 50 mg/kg body weight. This ADI is equivalent to a daily dietary intake for a 150-lb adult of about 20 cans of soft drink, 42 servings of sugar-free gelatin, or 97 packets of low-calorie tabletop sweetener—all much higher than normal levels of consumption. For a 50-lb child, the ADI is equivalent to a daily consumption of 6 cans of soft drink, 11 servings of sugar-free gelatin, and 32 packets of low-calorie tabletop sweetener over a lifetime. Occasional consumption of aspartame greater than the ADI has been shown to have no adverse health effects. Results of extensive market research studies indicate that 9 out of 10 people consume less than 10 percent of the ADI. It must also be remembered, however, that children, especially those under 2 years of age, need adequate calories for growth and development.

Aspartame is available under the brand names Nutrasweet®, Equal®, Spoonful®, and Equal-Measure®. Aspartame has had its share of allegations and unfounded claims, including being linked to tumours, cancer, epilepsy, headaches, multiple sclerosis, and weight increase.

Neotame

This is a non caloric sweetener consisting of two amino acids, aspartic acid and phenylalanine. It has a clean, sugar-like taste and is non-cariogenic. It is 30–40 times sweeter than aspartame, or about 8000 times sweeter than sucrose. Through normal biological processes, neotame is quickly metabolised, fully eliminated, and does not accumulate in the body. No special labelling for PKU is required. Neotame is used in many cooking and baking applications. It is found in chewing gums, carbonated soft drinks, frozen desserts and novelties, yogurt-type products, refrigerated and non-refrigerated ready-to-drink beverages, and puddings and fillings.

Neotame also has unique flavour-enhancement properties. It prolongs flavour and sweetness in chewing gum and masks flavours unique to soya-based, nutritionallyfortified products, vitamins, and minerals, even at nonsweetening levels. Possible benefits of these properties are cost reduction and better sensory acceptance qualities. In July 2002 the FDA allowed its use as a general purpose sweetener for the general population, including pregnant and nursing women, diabetics, and children. Neotame is also approved for use in Australia and New Zealand.

Saccharin

Saccharin has been in use for over a century to sweeten foods and beverages without adding calories or carbohydrates. It was especially useful in Europe during the two world wars, when sugar was in short supply. It has been an integral component of the lifestyle of many people for weight control and caloric or carbohydrate intake restriction. Like most other low-caloric sweeteners, saccharin helps prevent the formation of dental cavities, compared to sugar.

In 1977, FDA proposed a ban on saccharin based on studies that linked its use to bladder cancer. Research methodologies involved the use of a sensitive strain of laboratory rats fed with extremely high doses of saccharin. Although the United States Congress overrode the ban because of the need at that time for a low-calorie alternative to sucrose, a warning label was required on products containing saccharin. In May 2000, due to a preponderance of scientific results obtained from nearly 20 years of studies, the government removed saccharin from its list of substances reasonably anticipated to be human carcinogens. The federal requirement for a warning label on products containing saccharin has also been removed. Saccharin is not metabolised by the body and does not react with DNA, lacking two of the major characteristics of a classical carcinogen.

Saccharin continues to be used in a wide range of low-calorie and sugar-free foods and beverages. It is found in soft drinks, baked goods, chewing gum, canned fruit, salad dressings, and also in cosmetic products and pharmaceuticals. It is approved for use in more than 100 countries. Its safety has been affirmed by JEFCA and EU-SCF. Its use is also supported by many health organisations including the American Diabetes Association, the American Medical Association, and the American Cancer Society.

Sucralose

The only non-caloric sweetener prepared from sucrose, sucralose is manufactured through a patented multi-step process that replaces three hydroxyl groups of the sucrose molecule with three chloride groups. These tightly bound chloride groups make sucralose exceptionally stable and indigestible, which makes sucralose free of dietary calories. Sucralose is a sweetener that is 600 times sweeter than sugar with a clean, sugar-like taste and no lingering objectionable aftertaste. It can be used anywhere sugar is used without losing its sugar-taste properties even when heated and stored for a long time. Thus it is now used as a spoonful-for-spoonful replacement for sugar in eating, baking, cooking, and other sugar applications.

In 1998, sucralose was given the broadest initial approval by the FDA for a food ingredient for use in 15 foods and beverages. The FDA expanded its use in 1999 as a general-purpose sweetener without excluding any population subgroup, such as pregnant or breast feeding women, children, and diabetics. It is now used in more than 3500 products in over 60 countries, including Canada, Australia, and Mexico.

Like the other low-calorie sweeteners, sucralose passes quickly through the body relatively unchanged and is not converted to energy. It is not recognised by the body as either a sugar or a carbohydrate. Sucralose is also non-cariogenic because it is an inert ingredient that cannot be acted upon by bacteria in the mouth. It is also stable over a wide range of temperatures over time, and it is used in many applications such as canned fruit, low-calorie beverages, apple sauce, baked goods, nutritional supplements, and medical foods.

Sucralose joins the other food ingredients that have been extensively studied. More than 100 scientific studies over a 20-year period were conducted to assess its safety regarding cancer, reproduction and fertility, genetic effects, birth defects, immunology, the central nervous system, and metabolism. Scrutiny using the highest scientific standards has indicated that sucralose does not cause cancer, genetic defects, birth defects, or tooth decay. In addition, sucralose has no effect on the immune system, female or male reproduction, blood glucose levels, insulin production, and carbohydrate metabolism. The added chloride is a natural component of many everyday foods and beverages, such as natural waters, lettuce, and tomatoes, and is safe. The safety of sucralose is confirmed by JECFA, EU-SCF, Food Standards Australia/New Zealand, the Health Protection Branch of Health and Welfare Canada, and other regulatory bodies in Asia and South America. Sucralose may be consumed safely every day without concern of exceeding a maximum safety level. Products containing sucralose are not required to carry a warning label. Sucralose is currently marketed under the name Splenda®.

OTHER LOW-CALORIE SWEETENERS OF THE FUTURE

Alitame

Sold under the name Aclame™, alitame is a sweetener formed from the amino acids L-aspartic acid and D-alanine and a new amine. It is 2000 times sweeter than sucrose, with a clean, sweet taste, and has synergistic sweetening properties when combined with other low calorie sweeteners. Because it is a high intensity sweetener, its caloric contribution to the diet is insignificant. The aspartic acid component of alitame is completely metabolised in the body. The alanine amide component passes through the body with minimal metabolic changes. Alitame is highly soluble in water and is also pH and heat-stable. It has an excellent shelf life but may produce off-flavours under prolonged storage in some standard acidic conditions. It may be used in products where sweeteners are currently used, such as baked goods, hot and cold beverages, fruit preparations, chewing gum, and pharmaceuticals.

Pfizer, Inc., the company that discovered alitame, has completed extensive animal and human studies to support its claim of alitame's safety for human consumption and has petitioned the FDA for approval for its use in a broad range of foods and beverages. Alitame is approved for use in a variety of foods and beverages in Australia, New Zealand, Mexico, and the People's Republic of China. Approval for its use is being sought from regulatory bodies of major countries worldwide.

Cyclamate

Cyclamate is a non-caloric sweetener that is 30 times sweeter than sucrose and is widely used in foods and beverages. It is the least intense of all the commercially acceptable high-intensity sweeteners. It is stable under a wide range of temperatures and has a long shelf life. Because of its solubility in liquids, it is attractive for use in beverages and a variety of other foods including some baked goods. When used with other low-calorie sweeteners, particularly saccharin, a product sweeter than the combination of the individual sweeteners results. Most people do not metabolise cyclamate.

Cyclamate is approved for use in Canada and in more than 50 countries in Asia, South America, Europe, and Africa. Because of a study suggesting cyclamate may be related to the development of tumours in rats, cyclamate was banned for use in the United States in 1970. In 1984, the FDA's Cancer Assessment Committee reviewed scientific evidence and concluded that cyclamate is not a carcinogen. The National Academy of Sciences reaffirmed this conclusion in 1985. There is currently a petition to the FDA to have cyclamate approved again for use in the United States.

Dihydrochalcones

Also known as DHCs, dihydrochalcones are non-caloric sweeteners derived from the bioflavonoids of citrus fruits that are 300 to 2000 times sweeter than sucrose. DHCs give a delayed sweet taste with a licorice aftertaste. Neo-DHC from Seville oranges is 1500 times sweeter than sucrose and currently has the greatest potential for use in foods such as chewing gum and candies and other applications such as toothpaste, mouthwash, and some pharmaceuticals. DHCs are approved for use in the United States as a flavouring in baked goods, beverages, chewing gum, frozen dairy products, candies, and sauces. These sweeteners are approved for use in the European Union and Zimbabwe.

Stevioside

Stevioside is a low-calorie sweetener derived from *Stevia rebaudiana*, a South American plant, and is 300 times sweeter than sucrose. The plant leaves have been used for centuries in Paraguay to sweeten bitter beverages and to make tea. Stevioside is highly soluble in water, very sweet in taste, and synergistic with other sweeteners. It exhibits a menthol-like, bitter aftertaste that diminishes with increasing purity of the extract. The metabolism of stevioside in humans has not yet been investigated, but results from limited studies in laboratory rats indicate that some is excreted unchanged. Most ingested stevioside is degraded by intestinal bacteria.

Since the 1970s, stevioside has been used as a sweetener in Japan, by itself or with other sweeteners in beverages, pickles, dried seafoods, flavourings, confections, chewing gum, and table-top sweeteners. It is also approved for use as a sweetener in South Korea and Brazil. In 1999, JECFA and EU-SCF reviewed available studies and concluded that current scientific information is not acceptable to support its use as a sweetener. A subsequent review by JECFA in 2004 resulted in the granting of a temporary designation for stevioside of an acceptable daily intake of 2 mg/kg body weight. To remove its temporary designation, JECFA is requiring, by 2007, additional information on the pharmacological effects of stevioside on humans, as well as analytical data. Citing insufficient testing, the FDA has not allowed the use of stevioside in the United States as a sweetener food additive, but it may be sold as a dietary supplement without any reference to sweetness.

Glycyrrhizin

Glycyrrhizin is a non-caloric sweetener that is extracted from licorice root and is 50 to 100 times sweeter than sucrose. Because of its pronounced licorice flavour, its uses are limited. It is used as a flavouring in tobacco, pharmaceuticals, and some confectionary products. It is also used as a foaming agent in some non-alcoholic beverages. Glycyrrhizin is approved for use in the United States as a flavour and flavour enhancer.

Thaumatim

Thaumatin is a mixture of intensely sweet proteins extracted with water from the katemfe fruit (*Thaumatococcus daniellii*) of West Africa. The fruit contains from one to three black seeds surrounded by a gel and capped by a membranous sac containing the sweet material. Thaumatin is 2000 times sweeter than sucrose, with a slow-onset but lingering sweet taste and a licorice-like aftertaste. It has synergistic sweetening effects with saccharin, acesulfame-K, and stevioside. Although it cannot be used in baked or boiled goods, it may be used as a flavour extender for some cosmetic and pharmaceutical products. Thaumatin is approved for use in foods and beverages in Israel, Japan, and the European Union. It is approved for use in the United States as a flavour enhancer in beverages, jams and jellies, condiments, milk products, yogurt, cheese, instant coffee and tea, and chewing gum. Thaumatin is available under the brand name Thalin™ .

Be Prudent

More than 180 million adult Americans now consume low-calorie or sugar-free foods and beverages. This number has doubled within the past decade. Calorie-consciousness is part of today's lifestyle, and reduced-calorie, low-calorie, and non-caloric sweeteners are a major component of this lifestyle. The growing consumer demand challenges food manufacturers to provide a wider selection of good tasting, more stable, more economically available, and safe foods and beverages.

Health professionals continue to assert that excessive caloric intake leads to weight gain. People should avoid over-consumption of any food, including those with reduced or low-calorie sweeteners. As a helpful step in achieving a lower caloric intake, one recommendation from to the US government's Dietary Guidelines for Americans is to 'choose the foods and beverages to moderate your intake of sugars.' Thus, reduced-calorie and low-calorie sweeteners are part of a healthy lifestyle that includes a variety of nutritious foods in moderate portions combined with a program of appropriate physical activity.

CONTAMINATION

Sucrose

The raw juice expressed from sugarcane may become high in microbial content unless processing is prompt. The relevant micro-organisms are those from the sugarcane and the soil contaminating it and therefore comprise slime producers, such as species of *Leuconostoc* and *Bacillus*, representatives of the genera *Micrococcus*, *Flavobacterium*, *Alcaligenes*, *Xanthomonas*, *Pseudomonas*, *Erwinia* and *Enterobacter*, a variety of yeasts, chiefly in the genera *Saccharomyces*, *Candida* and *Pichia*, and a few moulds (Table 21.1).

Table 21.1: Microbiological profile of sugarcane, cane juice, raw sugar and sucrose.

Product	*Micro-organisms present*	*Approximate quantitative range*
Sugarcane	Bacteria	10^2–10^8/g
	Enterobacter	
	Leuconostoc	
	Flavobacterium	
	Xanthomonas	
	Bacillus	
	Erwinia	
	Pseudomonas	
	Moulds	10^2–10^4/g
	Yeast	10^2–10^4/g
Raw cane juice	Bacteria	10^4–10^8/ml
	As above plus *Micrococcus*	
	Lactobacillus	
	Actinomyces	
	Moulds	
	Aspergillus	
	Cladosporium	
	Monilia	
	Penicillium	
	Yeast	
	Saccharomyces	
	Candida	
	Pichia	
	Torulopsis	
Raw sugar	Bacteria	10^2–10^4/g
	Bacillus	
	Clostridium	
	Desulphotomaculum	
	Osmophilic yeast	
	Aspergillus	
	Penicillium	
	Osmophilic moulds	
	Hansenula	
	Pichia	
	Saccharomyces	
Sucrose	Bacteria	10^1–10^2/g
	Mostly sporeformers, if any, and minimal yeast and moulds	

Much contamination may come from debris or fine particles on the sides or joints of troughs at the plant. If organisms grow to any extent, inversion of sucrose or even destruction of sugar may take place. Activity of the organisms continues from cutting of the cane through extraction to clarification of the juice, a process which kills yeasts and vegetative cells of bacteria. Bacterial spores are present from then on, through sedimentation, filtration, evaporation, crystallisation and centrifugation, but may be reduced in numbers by these processes, although spores of thermophiles may be added from equipment. Bagging of the raw sugar also may add some micro-organisms. During the refining of the raw sugar, contamination may come from equipment and organisms are added during bagging.

In the manufacture or beet sugar, cleaned beets are sliced into thin slices and the sugar is removed by a diffusion process at 60° to 85°C. Sources of contamination are flume waters and diffusion-battery waters. Thermophiles may grow in the latter up to 70°C. Contamination also may take place during refining and bagging of the sugar. Granulated sugar now on the market is very low in microbial content for the most part, containing from a few to several hundred organisms per gram, mostly bacterial spores.

Maple Syrup

Sap of the sugar maple in the vascular bundles is sterile or practically so but becomes contaminated from outside sources in the tapholes and by the spout, plastic tubing and buckets of other collection vessels. If a period of unusual warmth occurs before the sap is collected, considerable growth of yeasts and bacteria may take place in the sap.

Micro-organisms entering sap between its flow from the tree and being boiled and concentrated are mostly psychrotrophic, gram-negative rods of *Pseudomonas*, *Alcaligenes* and *Flavobacterium*, plus yeasts and moulds. Paraformaldehyde taphole pellets are inserted into the drilled hole to prevent microbial growth from blocking the flow. In sugar-bush locations that are exposed to unusual dust and air contamination, collection of sap by a series of plastic tubes results in lower bacterial contamination. However, in a well-controlled sugar bush the microbial content of sap collected by tubing is not significantly different from that obtained by using individual pails. Sap-gathering tanks, usually mobile, must be sanitised regularly to prevent development of high numbers of bacteria in the sap when it reaches the evaporator. Bacterial counts in sap are usually less than 10,000 per millilitre, but higher numbers can develop as a result of warmer temperatures near the end of the season and poor sanitation.

Honey

The chief sources of micro-organisms in honey are the nectar of flowers and the honeybee. Yeasts have been shown to come from the nectar and from the intestinal content of the bee, bacteria also come from the latter source. Honey rarely contains staphylococci or enteric bacteria. Common isolates are usually acidophilic and glycolytic yeasts, which can damage the product. Honey has been found to contain lysozyme, an enzyme with a bacteriostatic as well as a lytic effect on most gram-positive bacteria. The use of antibiotics such as neomycin and streptomycin is widespread in beekeeping, and these antibiotics have been found in the honey obtained from treated larvae and bees. Traces of these antibiotics in the honey would, of course, have an effect on its microbial flora. Honey is one of the suspected food vehicles for the source of *C. botulinum* spores in cases of infant botulism. About 10 per cent of the suspected honey samples contained viable spores.

A study by Ruiz-Argueso and Rodriguez-Navarro suggested that *Gluconobacter* and *Lactobacillus* are the two main groups of bacteria present during maturation of nectar to honey.

Candy

Candies from retail markets contain from 0 to 2 million bacteria per piece, but most pieces harbour no more than a few hundred. Few coliform bacteria are found. The candies receive most of their contamination from their ingredients, although some contamination may be added to unwrapped pieces by air, dust and handling. The several thousand types of candies and confections can be divided into two categories for microbiological consideration: (i) cold-processed, and (ii) hot-processed confections. Moulded chocolate and chocolate coatings for creamed centres fall into the first category. Temperatures during processing may only approach pasteurisation temperature. Examples of the second category include hard candy, jellies, caramels and fudges. Processing temperatures for these items vary, but they all are exposed to a more severe heat treatment than are items in the first category.

Candies are infrequently associated with food-poisoning outbreaks, but chocolate candies have been incriminated in cases of salmonellosis. The problem appears to be one of cross contamination in the plant between raw and roasted cocoa beans, with the raw beans or environmental isolates serving as the source of contamination. Although temperatures of 60°C for 10 hours. are not uncommon during processing and blending of milk chocolate, the low moisture content or the dryness of the chocolate apparently protects the salmonellae from heat.

PRESERVATION

Like cereals, sugars normally have a_w's so low that micro-organisms cannot grow. Only when moisture has been absorbed is there any chance for microbial spoilage. Storage conditions should be such that vermin are kept out and the sugar remains dry. The recommended storage temperature is similar to that for cereals. Cane or sugar beets may be stored in a controlled atmosphere. Fungal growth is inhibited by 6 per cent carbon dioxide and 5 per cent oxygen.

During the manufacture of raw sugar and the subsequent refining process the numbers of micro-organisms present, which may have been large during extraction from cane or sugar beet, are reduced by most subsequent processes, e.g. clarification, evaporation, crystallisation, centrifugation and filtration. Chemical preservatives are effective in reducing microbial numbers during sugar refining. Special treatments to reduce numbers and kinds of organisms may be given during refining when the sugar is to be used for a special purpose, e.g. for soft drinks or canning. Care is taken to avoid buildup of organisms and their spores during processing, and numbers may be reduced by irradiation with ultraviolet rays or combined action of heat and hydrogen peroxide.

Because of their high sugar concentration and low a_w, most candies are not subject to microbial spoilage, although soft fillings of chocolate-covered candies may support the growth of micro-organisms. The bursting of chocolates is prevented by a uniform and fairly heavy chocolate coating and use of a fondant or other filling that will not permit the growth of gas formers.

Sirups and molasses usually have undergone enough heating to destroy most micro-organisms but should be stored at cool temperatures to prevent or slow chemical changes and microbial growth. Some molasses may contain enough sulphur dioxide to inhibit micro-organisms, but most sirups and molasses contain no added preservatives and prevent microbial growth because of the high osmotic pressure of the sugar solution. The osmotic pressure increases with the extent of inversion (hydrolysis) of the sucrose. Mould growth on the surface is prevented by a complete fill of the container and is reduced by periodic mixing of the sirup or molasses.

The boiling process during evaporation of maple sap to maple sirup kills the important spoilage organisms. Such sirup, bottled hot and in a completely filled container, usually keeps well.

Honey distributed locally on a small scale usually is not pasteurised and therefore may be subject to crystallisation and to possible spoilage in time by osmophilic yeasts. Commercially distributed honey usually is pasteurised at 71° to 77°C for a few minutes. A recommended treatment is to heat fairly rapidly to at least 71°C, hold there for 5 minutes, and cool promptly to 32.2° to 38°C.

SPOILAGE

The spoilage of sugars or concentrated solutions of sugars is limited to that caused by osmophilic or xerotolerant micro-organisms. Certain yeasts, especially those of the genus *Saccharomyces* and certain moulds would be the principal spoilage flora. Some species of bacteria have also been suggested as possible spoilage problems, including species of *Bacillus* and *Leuconostoc*. As the sugar concentrations decrease, increasing numbers of kinds of organisms can grow, so that sap from a maple tree would show types of spoilage that maple sirup could not.

Sucrose

During the manufacture of sugar, the original cane or beet juice becomes more and more purified toward sucrose and the concentration of sugar in solution becomes greater and greater until finally crystalline sugar is attained plus molasses that is high in sugar. The purer the product, the poorer it becomes as a culture medium for micro-organisms, the more concentrated it gets, the fewer kinds of organisms can grow in it.

Raw juice

The raw cane or beet juice is not high in sugar and contains a good supply of accessory foods for micro-organisms, it therefore is readily deteriorated by the numerous organisms present if sufficient time is allowed. Until clarification, gum and slime may be formed, e.g. dextran by *Leuconostoc mesenteroides* or *L. dextranicum* and levan by *Bacillus* spp. or, less commonly, by yeasts or moulds.

Sugar in storage

Liquid sugar with sugar content as high as 67° to 72°brix will support the growth of yeasts (*Candida, Saccharomyces*, *Rhodotorula*) and moulds which may enter from the air. Dilution by absorption of moisture at the surface may result in growth of micro-organisms and hence deterioration of the product. This can be prevented by circulation of filtered sterile air across the top of the storage tank or exposure to ultraviolet lamps.

Molasses and syrups

Microbial spoilage of molasses is not common, although it is difficult to sterilise by heat because of the protective effect of the sugar. Canned molasses or syrup may be subject to spoilage by osmophilic yeasts that survive the heat process. Molasses or syrup exposed to air will mould, in time, on the surface, and this also may occur at the surface of a bottled or canned syrup if air is left there and contamination has taken place prior to sealing. Some kinds of molasses are acid enough to cause hydrogen swells upon long storage.

Maple Sap and Syrup

As previously stated, sap from the sugar maple becomes contaminated when drawn. Although a moderate amount of growth may improve flavour and colour, the sap often stands under conditions that favour excessive growth of micro-organisms and hence spoilage.

Five chief types of spoilage are recognised: (i) ropy or stringy sap, usually caused by *Enterobacter aerogenes*, although *Leuconostoc* spp. may be responsible, (ii) cloudy, sometimes greenish sap resulting from the growth of *Pseudomonas fluorescens*, with species of *Alcaligenes* and *Flavobacterium* sometimes contributing to cloudiness, (iii) red sap, coloured by pigments of red bacteria, e.g. *Micrococcus roseus* or of yeasts or yeast like fungi, (iv) sour sap, a catchall grouping for types of spoilage not showing a marked change in colour but having a sour odour and caused by any of a variety of kinds of bacteria or yeasts, and (v) mouldy sap, spoiled by moulds.

Maple syrup can be ropy because of *Enterobacter aerogenes*, yeasty as the result of growth of species of *Saccharomyces* yeasts, pink from the pigment of *Micrococcus roseus* or mouldy at the surface, where species of *Aspergillus*, *Penicillium* or other genera may grow. The sirup may become dark because of alkalinity produced by bacteria growing in the sap and inversion of sucrose. Maple sugar keeps well unless moistened, at which time moulds may grow.

Honey

Honey is variable in composition but must contain no more than 25 per cent moisture. Because of its high sugar content, 70 to 80 per cent, mostly glucose and levulose and its acidity, pH 3.2 to 4.2, the chief cause of its spoilage is osmophilic yeasts: species of *Zygosaccharomyces*, such as *Z. mellis*, *richteri* or *nussbaumeri* or *Torula* (*Cryptococcus*) *mellis*. Most moulds do not grow well on honey, although species of *Penicillium* and *Mucor* have developed slowly.

Most honey yeasts do not grow in the laboratory in sugar concentrations as high as those usually found in honey. Therefore, special theories for the initiation of growth of yeasts in honey have been advanced: (i) honey, being hygroscopic, becomes diluted at the surface, where yeasts begin to multiply and soon become adapted to the high sugar concentrations, (ii) crystallisation of glucose hydrate from honey leaves a lowered concentration of sugars in solution, and (iii) on long-standing, yeasts gradually become adapted to the high sugar concentrations. The critical moisture content for the initiation of yeast growth has been placed at 21 per cent. The degree of inversion of sucrose to glucose and levulose by the bees and the content of available nitrogen also are listed as factors determining the likelihood of growth. The fermentation process usually is slow, lasting for months, and the chief products are carbon dioxide, alcohol, and nonvolatile acids which give an off-flavour to the honey. Darkening and crystallisation usually accompany the fermentation.

Candy

Most candies are not subject to microbial spoilage because of the comparatively high sugar and low moisture content. Exceptions are chocolates with soft centres of fondant or of inverted sugar, which, under certain conditions, burst or explode. Yeasts growing in these candies develop a gas pressure which may disrupt the entire candy or more often will push out some of the syrup or fondant through a weak spot in the chocolate coating. Often this weak spot is on the poorly covered bottom of the chocolate, where a cylinder of fondant squeezes out.

The defect is prevented by using a filling that will not support growth of the gas formers and by coating the candy with a uniformly thick and strong layer of chocolate. The microbial spoilage flora of many confectionery products is summarised in Fig. 21.1.

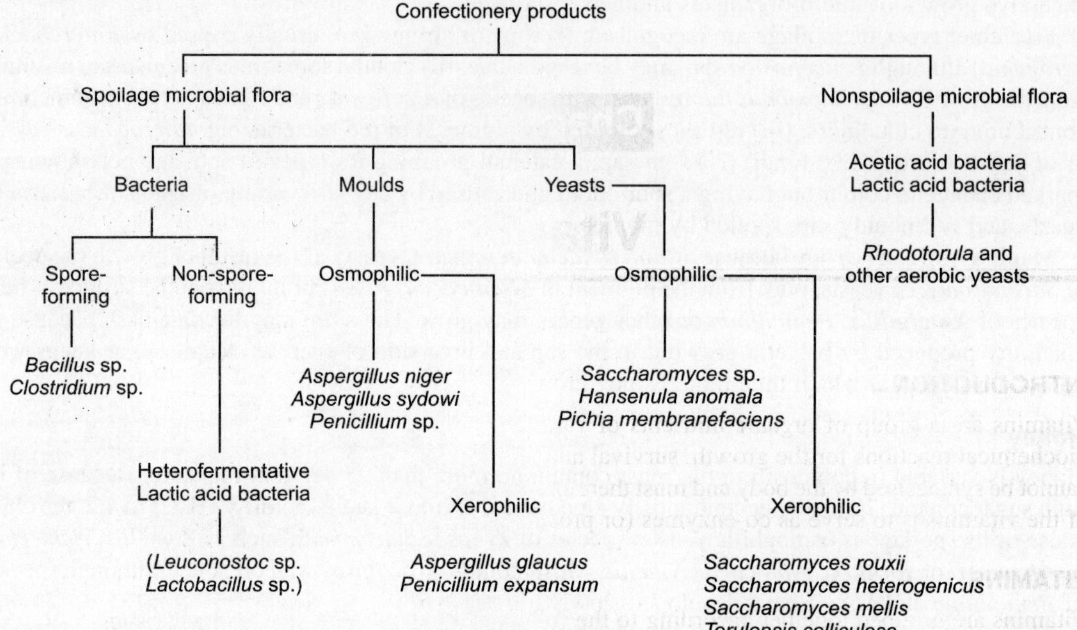

Fig. 21.1: Spoilage flora of confectionery products.

Chapter 22

Vitamins

INTRODUCTION

Vitamins are a group of organic nutrients of various nature required in small quantities for multiple biochemical reactions for the growth, survival and reproduction of the organism, and which, generally, cannot be synthesised by the body and must therefore be supplied by the diet. The most prominent function of the vitamins is to serve as co-enzymes (or prosthetic group) for enzymatic reactions.

VITAMINS

Vitamins are grouped together according to the following general biological characteristics:

1. Vitamins are not synthesised by the body and must come from food. An exception are vitamin B_3 (PP), which active form NADH (NADPH) can be synthesised from tryptophan and vitamin D_3 (cholecalciferol), synthesised from 7-dehydrocholesterol in the skin. Amount of those ones and vitamins partially synthesised by intestinal microflora (B_1, B_2, B_3, B_5, B_6, K and others) is normally not sufficient to cover the body's need them.
2. Vitamins are not plastic material. Exception is vitamin F.
3. Vitamins are not an energy source. Exception is vitamin F.
4. Vitamins are essential for all vital processes and biologically active already in small quantities.
5. They influence biochemical processes in all tissues and organs, i.e. they are not specific to organs.
6. They can be used for medicinal purposes as a non-specific tools in high doses for: diabetes mellitus - B_1, B_2, B_6, colds and infectious diseases - vitamin C, bronchial asthma - vitamin PP, gastrointestinal ulcers - vitamin-like substance U and nicotinic acid, in hypercholesterolemia - nicotinic acid.

Since only a few vitamins can be stored (A, D, E, B_{12}), a lack of vitamins quickly leads to deficiency diseases (hypovitaminosis or avitaminosis). These often affect the skin, blood cells, and nervous system. The causes of vitamin deficiencies can be treated by improving nutrition and by administration vitamins in tablet form. An overdose of vitamins leads to hypervitaminosis state only, with toxic symptoms, in the case of vitamins A and D. Normally, excess vitamins are rapidly excreted with the urine. Lack of vitamins leads to the development of pathological processes in the form of specific hypo- and avitaminosis.

Widespread hidden forms of vitamin deficiency have not severe external manifestations and symptoms, but have a negative impact on performance, the overall tone of the body and its resistance to various adverse factors. Avitaminosis is a disease that develops in the absence of a particular vitamin. Currently avitaminosis are not commonly found, but hypovitaminoses are observed with vitamin deficiency in the body.

External Causes for Hypovitaminosis

1. Lack of the vitamin in the diet or presence of food factors hindering the absorption of vitamin. For example, use of large amounts of raw eggs (they contain protein avidin binds vitamin H (biotin)) as a result may develop a state of hypovitaminosis H.
2. Do not take into account the need for a particular vitamin. For example, in protein-free diet is increasing demand for vitamin PP (with normal diet it may be partially synthesised from tryptophan). If a person consumes much protein, it can increase the need for vitamin B_6 and reduce the need for vitamin PP.
3. Social reasons: urbanisation, power and extremely high purity of canned food, antivitamin presence in food. People are not enough exposed to sunlight in large cities - so it can be hypovitaminosis D. In such cases, the medicine uses ultraviolet radiation in the form of different physical treatments, which activate the synthesis of vitamin D_3 from 7-dehydrocholesterol in the skin cells.

Internal Causes of Hypovitaminosis

1. Physiological increased need for vitamins, for example, during pregnancy, with heavy physical labour.
2. Long-term severe infectious diseases, as well as during the recovery period.
3. Disturbance of vitamin absorption in some diseases of the digestive tract, for example impaired absorption of fat-soluble vitamins is observed at cholelithiasis, vitamin B_{12} is done with atrophy of the gastric mucosa and a deficiency of Castle intrinsic factor. Another case if a person who hadn't been consuming fats but had been getting enough carbohydrates and proteins for long time revealed dermatitis, poor wound healing, vision impairment. Lack of vitamins A, D, E, K, F (linoleic, linolenic, arachidonic acids) is probable cause of the metabolic disorder.
4. Intestinal dysbacteriosis. It has the meaning as some vitamins are synthesised by the intestinal microflora (these vitamins are B_3, B_6, B_7 (H), B_9, B_{12}, and K).
5. Cirrhosis. The liver is the major depot of many vitamins, particularly fat-soluble (especially high hepatic reserves of fat soluble vitamins A, D), but also certain water-soluble, such as B_9, B_{12}, etc. In case of vitamin consumption increase and reducing their dietary intake, which is usually the case, for example, in alcoholism, megaloblastic anemia is developed in a short time as a characteristic sign of hypovitaminosis B_9. Patients with cirrhosis may experience blurred vision in the twilight due to malabsorption of vitamin A in the intestine and its reduced deposit in the liver.
6. Genetic defects of some enzymatic systems. For example, vitamin D-resistant rickets occurs in children lack the enzymes involved in the formation of the active form of vitamin D - calcitriol (1,25-dihydroxycholecalciferol).

CLASSIFICATION AND NOMENCLATURE OF THE VITAMINS

In addition to systematic chemical nomenclature, the vitamins have an apparently illogical system of accepted trivial names arising from the history of their discovery. For several vitamins, a number of chemically related compounds show the same biological activity, because they are either converted to the same final active metabolite or have sufficient structural similarity to have the same activity. Different chemical compounds that show the same biological activity are collectively known as vitamers. Where one or more compounds have biological activity, in addition to individual names there is also an approved generic descriptor to be used for all related compounds that show the same biological activity.

When it was realised that milk contained more than one accessory food factor, they were named A (which was lipid-soluble and found in the cream) and B (which was water-soluble and found in the whey). This division into fat- and water-soluble vitamins is still used, although there is little chemical or nutritional reason for this, apart from some similarities in dietary sources of fat-soluble or water-soluble vitamins. Water-soluble derivatives of vitamins A and K and fat-soluble derivatives of several of the B vitamins and vitamin C have been developed for therapeutic use and as food additives. As the discovery of the vitamins progressed, it was realised that 'Factor B' consisted of a number of chemically and physiologically distinct compounds. Before they were identified chemically, they were given a logical series of alphanumeric names: B_1, B_2, and so forth. And such vitamins or vitamin similar compounds as:

Vitamin C - ascorbic acid.

Vitamin P - bioflavonoids: quercetin, rutin, myricetin, apigenin, hesperin, hesperidin, luteolin, catechin, eriodictyol, cyaniding and others.

Vitamin N - lipoic acid.

Vitamin U (ulcus - ulcer) - a derivative of methionine-methionine-methyl sulfonium (pharmacology known as 'metiosulfoniya chloride'). As can be seen from Table 22.1, a number of compounds were assigned vitamin status, and were later shown either not to be vitamins, or to be compounds that had already been identified and given other names.

Table 22.1: Classification of vitamins. Group B.

Alphanumeric name of vitamin	*Chemical and other names of vitamin*
Vitamin B_1	Thiamine
Vitamin B_2	Riboflavin
Vitamin B_3	Niacin, niacinamide, niacin, niacinamide, RR
Vitamin B_4	Choline
Vitamin B_5	Pantothenic acid
Vitamin B_6	Pyridoxine, pyridoxal
Vitamin B_7	Biotin, vitamin H
Vitamin B_8	Inositol, myo-inositol, vitamin U
Vitamin B_9	Folic acid, foliatsin, vitamin BC, M
Vitamin B_{10}	Para-aminobenzoic acid, PABA, vitamin H_1
Vitamin B_{11}	L-carnitine, vitamin T, vitamin D
Vitamin B_{12}	Cyanocobalamin, cobalamin
Vitamin B_{13}	Orotic acid
Vitamin B_{14}	Pyrrolo-quinoline quinone, metoksantin, coenzyme of PQQ (Pyrroloquinoline Quinone)
Vitamin B_{15}	Pangamic acid, sometimes referred to as vitamin B_{16}
Vitamin B_{16}	Sometimes pangamic acid - B_{15}, and sometimes cyanocobalamin - B_{12}
Vitamin B_{17} (misnomer)	L-citral, letral, letril, amygdalin (The structure - a 2glucose + mandelonitrile)

For a compound to be considered a vitamin, it must be shown to be a dietary essential. Its elimination from the diet must result in a more-or-less clearly defined deficiency disease, and restoration must cure or prevent that deficiency disease. Demonstrating that a compound has pharmacological actions, and possibly cures a disease, does not classify that compound as a vitamin, even if it is a naturally occurring compound that is found in foods. Equally, demonstrating that a compound has a physiological function as a coenzyme or hormone does not classify that compound as a vitamin. It is necessary to demonstrate that endogenous synthesis of the compound is inadequate to meet physiological requirements in the absence of a dietary source of the compound. There is some evidence that premature infants and patients maintained on long-term total parenteral nutrition may be unable to meet their requirements for carnitine, choline, and taurine unless they are provided in the diet, and these are sometimes regarded as 'marginal compounds,' for which there is no evidence to estimate requirements.

The rigorous criteria outlined here would exclude niacin and vitamin D from the list of vitamins, because under normal conditions endogenous synthesis does indeed meet requirements. Nevertheless, they are considered to be vitamins, even if only on the grounds that each was discovered as the result of investigations into once common deficiency diseases, pellagra and rickets.

In addition to the marginal compounds like carnitine choline, there are a number of compounds present in foods of plant origin that are considered to be beneficial, in that they have actions that may prevent the development of atherosclerosis and some cancers, although there is no evidence that they are dietary essentials, and they are not generally considered as nutrients.

GROUP I: FAT-SOLUBLE VITAMINS

Group I is Fat-soluble vitamins: A (retinol), D (calciferol), E (tocopherol), K (naphthoquinone), F (polyunsaturated fatty acid: linoleic, linolenic, arachidonic).

Vitamin A

Vitamin A includes two vitamers: retinol and dehydroretinol but group of vitamin A consists and their biologically active molecules retinal (retinaldehyde) and retinoic acid. Each of these compounds are derived from the plant produced molecule carotene (a member of a family of molecules known as carotenoids). Beta-carotene, which consists of two molecules of retinal linked at their aldehyde ends, is also referred to as the provitamin form of vitamin A.

Ingested β-carotene is cleaved in the lumen of the intestine by beta-carotene dioxygenase to yield retinal. Retinal is right here reduced to retinol by retinaldehyde reductase, an NADPH requiring enzyme within the intestines. Retinol is esterified to palmitic or stearic acids and delivered to the blood via chylomicrons. The uptake of chylomicron remnants by the liver results in delivery of retinol to this organ for storage as a lipid esters. Transport of retinol from the liver to extrahepatic tissues occurs by binding of retinol to retinol binding protein (RBP) the retinol-RBP complex is then transported to the cell surface within the Golgi and secreted. Within extrahepatic tissues retinol is bound to cellular retinol binding protein (CRBP). Plasma transport of retinoic acid is accomplished by binding to albumin. One protein else is capable to transport of vitamin A: it is transthyretin. Transthyretin (TTR) is a serum and cerebrospinal fluid carrier of the thyroid hormone thyroxine (T4) and retinol-binding protein bound to retinol. This is how transthyretin gained its name, transports thyroxine and retinol. The liver secretes transthyretin into the blood, and the choroid plexus secretes TTR into the cerebrospinal fluid.

TTR was originally called *prealbumin* (or thyroxine-binding prealbumin) because it ran faster than albumin on electrophoresis gels.

Gene control exerted by retinol and retinoic acid

Within cells both retinol and retinoic acid bind to specific receptor proteins. Following binding, the receptor-vitamin complex interacts with specific sequences in several genes involved in growth and differentiation and affects expression of these genes. In this capacity retinol and retinoic acid are considered hormones of the steroid/thyroid hormone superfamily of proteins. Vitamin D also acts in a similar capacity. Several genes whose patterns of expression are altered by retinoic acid are involved in the earliest processes of embryogenesis including the differentiation of the three germ layers, organogenesis and limb development.

Vision and the role of vitamin A

Photoreception in the eye is the function of two specialised cell types located in the retina, the rod and cone cells. Both rod and cone cells contain a photoreceptor pigment in their membranes. The photosensitive compound of most mammalian eyes is a protein called opsin to which is covalently coupled an aldehyde of vitamin A. The opsin of rod cells is called scotopsin. The photoreceptor of rod cells is specifically called rhodopsin or visual purple. This compound is a complex between scotopsin and the 11-*cis*-retinal (also called 11-*cis*-retinene) form of vitamin A. Rhodopsin is a serpentine receptor imbedded in the membrane of the rod cell. Coupling of 11-*cis*-retinal occurs at three of the transmembrane domains of rhodopsin. Intracellularly, rhodopsin is coupled to a specific G-protein called transducin.

When the rhodopsin is exposed to light it is bleached releasing the 11-*cis*-retinal from opsin. Absorption of photons by 11-*cis*-retinal triggers a series of conformational changes on the way to conversion all-*trans*-retinal. One important conformational intermediate is metarhodopsin II. The release of opsin results in a conformational change in the photoreceptor. This conformational change activates transducin, leading to an increased GTP-binding by the α-subunit of transducin. Binding of GTP releases the α-subunit from the inhibitory β- and γ-subunits. The GTP-activated α-subunit in turn activates an associated phosphodiesterase, an enzyme that hydrolyses cGMP to GMP. cGMP is required to maintain the Na^+ channels of the rod cell in the open conformation. The drop in cGMP concentration results in complete closure of the Na^+ channels. Metarhodopsin II appears to be responsible for initiating the closure of the channels. The closing of the channels leads to hyperpolarisation of the rod cell with concomitant propagation of nerve impulses to the brain.

Additional role of retinol

Retinol also functions in the synthesis of certain glycoproteins and mucopolysaccharides necessary for mucous production and normal growth regulation. This is accomplished by phosphorylation of retinol to retinyl phosphate which then functions similarly to dolichol phosphate.

Clinical significances of vitamin A deficiency

Vitamin A is stored in the liver and deficiency of the vitamin occurs only after prolonged lack of dietary intake. The earliest symptoms of vitamin A deficiency are night blindness. Additional early symptoms include follicular hyperkeratinosis, increased susceptibility to infection and cancer and anemia equivalent to iron deficient anemia. Prolonged lack of vitamin A leads to deterioration of the eye tissue through progressive keratinisation of the cornea, a condition known as xerophthalmia.

The increased risk of cancer in vitamin deficiency is thought to be the result of a depletion in beta-carotene. β-carotene is a very effective antioxidant and is suspected to reduce the risk of cancers known to be initiated by the production of free radicals. Of particular interest is the potential benefit of increased beta-carotene intake to reduce the risk of lung cancer in smokers. However, caution needs to be taken when increasing the intake of any of the lipid soluble vitamins. Excess accumulation of vitamin A in the liver can lead to toxicity which manifests as bone pain, hepatosplenomegaly, nausea and diarrhea.

Vitamin D

Vitamin D is a steroid hormone that functions to regulate specific gene expression following interaction with its intracellular receptor. The biologically active form of the hormone is 1,25-dihydroxy vitamin D_3 (1,25-$(OH)_2D_3$, also termed calcitriol). Calcitriol functions primarily to regulate calcium and phosphorous homeostasis. Active calcitriol is derived from ergosterol (produced in plants) and from 7-dehydrocholesterol (produced in the skin). Ergocalciferol (vitamin D_2) is formed by UV (ultraviolet) irradiation of ergosterol. In the skin 7-dehydrocholesterol is converted to cholecalciferol (vitamin D_3) following UV irradiation.

Vitamin D_2 and D_3 are processed to D_2-calcitriol and D3-calcitriol, respectively, by the same enzymatic pathways in the body. Cholecalciferol (or ergocalciferol) are absorbed from the intestine and transported to the liver bound to a specific vitamin D-binding protein. In the liver cholecalciferol is hydroxylated at the 25 position by a specific D_3-25-hydroxylase generating 25-hydroxy-D_3 [25-$(OH)D_3$] which is the major circulating form of vitamin D. Conversion of 25-$(OH)D_3$ to its biologically active form, calcitriol, occurs through the activity of a specific D_3-1-hydroxylase present in the proximal convoluted tubules of the kidneys, and in bone and placenta. 25-$(OH)D_3$ can also be hydroxylated at the 24 position by a specific D_3-24-hydroxylase in the kidneys, intestine, placenta and cartilage. Calcitriol functions in concert with parathyroid hormone (PTH) and calcitonin to regulate serum calcium and phosphorous levels. PTH is released in response to low serum calcium and induces the production of calcitriol. In contrast, reduced levels of PTH stimulate synthesis of the inactive 24,25-$(OH)_2D_3$. In the intestinal epithelium, calcitriol functions as a steroid hormone in inducing the expression of calbindinD_{28K}, a protein involved in intestinal calcium absorption. The increased absorption of calcium ions requires concomitant absorption of a negatively charged counter ion to maintain electrical neutrality. The predominant counter ion is Pi. When plasma calcium levels fall the major sites of action of calcitriol and PTH are bone where they stimulate bone resorption and the kidneys where they inhibit calcium excretion by stimulating reabsorption by the distal tubules. The role of calcitonin in calcium homeostasis is to decrease elevated serum calcium levels by inhibiting bone resorption.

Clinical significance of vitamin D deficiency

As a result of the addition of vitamin D to milk, deficiencies in this vitamin are rare in this country. The main symptom of vitamin D deficiency in children is rickets and in adults is osteomalacia. Rickets is characterised improper mineralisation during the development of the bones resulting in soft bones. Osteomalacia is characterised by demineralisation of previously formed bone leading to increased softness and susceptibility to fracture.

Vitamin E

Vitamin E is a mixture of several related compounds known as tocopherols. The α-tocopherol molecule is the most potent of the tocopherols. α-Tocopherol is the main source found in supplements and in the European diet, where the main dietary sources are olive and sunflower oils, while α-tocopherol is the most common form in the American diet due to a higher intake of soyabean and corn oil. Tocotrienols, which are related compounds, also have vitamin E activity. All of these various derivatives with vitamin activity may correctly be referred to as 'vitamin E'.

Tocopherols and tocotrienols are fat-soluble antioxidants but also seem to have many other functions in the body. Vitamin E is absorbed from the intestines packaged in chylomicrons. It is delivered to the tissues via chylomicron transport and then to the liver through chylomicron remnant uptake. The liver can export vitamin E in VLDLs. Due to its lipophilic nature, vitamin E accumulates in cellular membranes, fat deposits and other circulating lipoproteins. The major site of vitamin E storage is in adipose tissue.

The major function of vitamin E is to act as a natural antioxidant by scavenging free radicals and molecular oxygen. In particular vitamin E is important for preventing peroxidation of polyunsaturated membrane fatty acids. The vitamins E and C are interrelated in their antioxidant capabilities. Active α-tocopherol can be regenerated by interaction with vitamin C following scavenge of a peroxy free radical. Alternatively, α-tocopherol can scavenge two peroxy free radicals and then be conjugated to glucuronate for excretion in the bile.

Clinical significances of vitamin E deficiency

No major disease states have been found to be associated with vitamin E deficiency due to adequate levels in the average American diet. The major symptom of vitamin E deficiency in humans is an increase in red blood cell fragility. Since vitamin E is absorbed from the intestines in chylomicrons, any fat malabsorption diseases can lead to deficiencies in vitamin E intake. Neurological disorders have been associated with vitamin E deficiencies associated with fat malabsorptive disorders. Increased intake of vitamin E is recommended in premature infants fed formulas that are low in the vitamin as well as in persons consuming a diet high in polyunsaturated fatty acids. Polyunsaturated fatty acids tend to form free radicals upon exposure to oxygen and this may lead to an increased risk of certain cancers.

Vitamin K

The K vitamins exist naturally as K_1 (phylloquinone) in green vegetables and K_2 (menaquinone) produced by intestinal bacteria and K_3 is synthetic menadione (vicasol). When administered, vitamin K_3 is alkylated to one of the vitamin K_2 forms of menaquinone.

The major function of the K vitamins is in the maintenance of normal levels of the blood clotting proteins, factors II, VII, IX, X and protein C and protein S, which are synthesised in the liver as inactive precursor proteins. Conversion from inactive to active clotting factor requires a posttranslational modification of specific glutamate residues. This modification is a carboxylation and the enzyme responsible requires vitamin K as a cofactor. The resultant modified protein residues are λ-carboxyglutamate. This process is most clearly understood for factor II, also called preprothrombin. Prothrombin is modified preprothrombin. The λ-carboxyglutamate residues are effective calcium ion chelators. Upon chelation of calcium, prothrombin interacts with phospholipids in membranes and is proteolysed to thrombin through the action of activated factor X (Xa). During the carboxylation reaction reduced hydroquinone form of vitamin K is converted to a 2,3-epoxide form. The regeneration of the hydroquinone form requires an uncharacterised reductase. This latter reaction is the site of action of the dicoumarol based anticoagulants such as warfarin.

The isoprene-derived molecule whose structure is shown here is known alternately as Coumarinand warfarin. By the former name, it is a widely prescribed anticoagulant. By the latter name, it is a component of rodent poisons. How can the same chemical species be used for such disparate purposes? The key to both uses lies in its ability to act as an antagonist of vitamin K in the body. Vitamin K stimulates the carboxylation of glutamate residues on certain proteins, including some proteins in the bloodclotting cascade. Carboxylation of these coagulation factors is catalysed by a carboxylase that requires the reduced form of vitamin K (vitamin KH2), molecular oxygen, and carbon dioxide. KH2 is oxidised to vitamin K epoxide, which is recycled to KH2 by the enzymes vitamin K epoxide reductase and vitamin K reductase. Coumarin/warfarin exerts its anticoagulant effect by inhibiting vitamin K epoxide reductase and possibly also vitamin K reductase.

This inhibition depletes vitamin KH2 and reduces the activity of the carboxylase. Coumarin/warfarin, given at a typical dosage of 4 to 5 mg/day, prevents the deleterious formation in the bloodstream of small blood clots and thus reduces the risk of heart attacks and strokes for individuals whose arteries contain sclerotic plaques. Taken in much larger doses, as for example in rodent poisons, Coumarin/warfarin can cause massive hemorrhages and death.

Clinical significance of vitamin K deficiency

Naturally occurring vitamin K is absorbed from the intestines only in the presence of bile salts and other lipids through interaction with chylomicrons. Therefore, fat malabsorptive diseases can result in vitamin K deficiency. The synthetic vitamin K3 is water soluble and absorbed irrespective of the presence of intestinal lipids and bile. Since the vitamin K2 form is synthesised by intestinal bacteria, deficiency of the vitamin in adults is rare. However, long term antibiotic treatment can lead to deficiency in adults. The intestine of newborn infants is sterile, therefore, vitamin K deficiency in infants is possible if lacking from the early diet. The primary symptom of a deficiency in infants is a hemorrhagic syndrome.

GROUP II: WATER-SOLUBLE VITAMINS

Group II is water-soluble vitamins:

- Group B: B_1 (thiamine), B_2 (riboflavin), B_3 or PP (nicotinamide, niacin), B_5 (pantothenic acid), B_6 (pyridoxine), B_7 or H (biotin), B_9 or Bc (folic acid), B_{12} (cyanocobalamin).
- Vitamin C (ascorbic acid).
- Vitamin P (rutin and other bioflavonoids). Water-soluble vitamins are usually functioning as precursors of coenzymes and prosthetic groups of enzymes. For example, coenzyme form of.
- Vitamin B_1 is TPP (thiamine pyrophosphate) (trade name - cocarboxylase).
- Vitamin B_2 is FMN (flavin mononucleotide) and FAD (flavin adenine dinucleotide).
- Vitamin B_3 is NAD^+ (nicotinamide adenine dinucleotide) or $NADP^+$ (nicotinamide adenine dinucleotide phosphate).
- Vitamin B_5 is Coenzyme A (coenzyme of acylation).
- Vitamin B_6 is PLP (pyridoxal phosphate).
- Vitamin B_9 is THFA (tetrahydrofolic acid).
- Vitamin B_{12} is adenosylcobalamin and methylcobalamin.

Holoenzymes containing coenzymes (as its non-protein part) which are often vitamin derivatives perform multiple functions. For example, the first enzyme in gluconeogenesis pyruvate carboxylase uses biotin for carboxylation of pyruvate, but the transformation of the pyruvate to acetyl-CoA by pyruvate dehydrogenase complex requires five coenzymes: TPP, lipoic acid, CoA, FAD, NAD^+. Since TPP is involved in this conversion first, pyruvate accumulation in cells of the nervous system (primarily) and then increase in pyruvate content in the blood and urine of patients in the case of vitamin B_1 deficiencies becomes obvious.

Vitamin B_1

Vitamin B1 is also known as thiamine. Thiamine is derived from a substituted pyrimidine and a thiazole which are coupled by a methylene bridge. Thiamine is rapidly converted to its active form, Thiamine Pyrophosphate (TPP), in the brain and liver by a specific enzymes, thiamine diphosphotransferase. TPP is necessary as a cofactor for the pyruvate and α-ketoglutarate dehydrogenase catalysed reactions as well as the transketolase catalysed reactions of the pentose phosphate pathway. A deficiency in thiamine intake leads to a severely reduced capacity of cells to generate energy as a result of its role in these reactions. The dietary requirement for thiamine is proportional to the caloric intake of the diet and ranges from 1.0–1.5 mg/day for normal adults. If the carbohydrate content of the diet is excessive then an in thiamin intake will be required.

Clinical significances of thiamine deficiency

The earliest symptoms of thiamine deficiency include constipation, appetite suppression, nausea as well as mental depression, peripheral neuropathy and fatigue. Chronic thiamine deficiency leads to more severe neurological symptoms including ataxia, mental confusion and loss of eye coordination. Other clinical symptoms of prolonged thiamine deficiency are related to cardiovascular and musculature defects.

The severe thiamine deficiency disease known as Beriberi, is the result of a diet that is carbohydrate rich and thiamine deficient. An additional thiamine deficiency related disease is known as Wernicke-Korsakoff syndrome. This disease is most commonly found in chronic alcoholics due to their poor dietetic lifestyles.

Vitamin B_2

Vitamin B_2 is also known as riboflavin. Riboflavin is the precursor for the coenzymes, flavin mononucleotide (FMN) and flavin adenine dinucleotide (FAD). The enzymes that require FMN or FAD as cofactors are termed flavoproteins. Several flavoproteins also contain metal ions and are termed metalloflavoproteins. Both classes of enzymes are involved in a wide range of redox reactions, e.g. succinate dehydrogenase and xanthine oxidase. During the course of the enzymatic reactions involving the flavoproteins the reduced forms of FMN and FAD are formed, $FMNH_2$ and $FADH_2$, respectively. The normal daily requirement for riboflavin is 1.2–1.7 mg/day for normal adults.

Clinical significances of riboflavin deficiency

Riboflavin deficiencies are rare due to the presence of adequate amounts of the vitamin in eggs, milk, meat and cereals. Riboflavin deficiency is often seen in chronic alcoholics due to their poor dietetic habits. Symptoms associated with riboflavin deficiency include, glossitis, seborrhea, angular stomatitis, cheilosis and photophobia. Riboflavin decomposes when exposed to visible light. This characteristic can lead to riboflavin deficiencies in newborns treated for hyperbilirubinemia by phototherapy.

VITAMIN B_3

Vitamin B_3 is also known as niacin (nicotinic acid and nicotinamide). Both nicotinic acid and nicotinamide can serve as the dietary source of vitamin B_3. Niacin is required for the synthesis of the active forms of vitamin B_3, nicotinamide adenine dinucleotide (NAD^+) and nicotinamide adenine dinucleotide phosphate ($NADP^+$). Both NAD^+ and $NADP^+$ function as cofactors for numerous dehydrogenase, e.g. lactate and malate dehydrogenases.

Niacin is not a true vitamin in the strictest definition since it can be derived from the amino acid tryptophan. However, the ability to utilise tryptophan for niacin synthesis is inefficient (60 mg of tryptophan are required to synthesise 1 mg of niacin). Also, synthesis of niacin from tryptophan requires vitamins B1, B2 and B6 which would be limiting in themselves on a marginal diet.

Examination of the structures of NADH and NADPH reveals that the 4-position of the nicotinamide ring is pro-chiral, meaning that while this carbon is not chiral, it would be if either of its hydrogens were replaced by something else. The hydrogen 'projecting' out of the page toward you is the 'pro-R' hydrogen because, if a deuterium is substituted at this position, the molecule would have the R-configuration. Substitution of the other hydrogen would yield an S-configuration.

An interesting aspect of the enzymes that require nicotinamide coenzymes is that they are stereospecific and with draw hydrogen from either the pro-Ror the pro-Sposition selectively. This stereospecificity arises from the fact that enzymes (and the active sites of enzymes) are inherently asymmetric structures. These same enzymes are stereospecific with respect to the substrates as well.

The NAD- and NADP-dependent dehydrogenases catalyse at least six different types of reactions: simple hydride transfer, deamination of an amino acid to form an α-keto acid, oxidation of α-hydroxy acids followed by decarboxylation of the α-keto acid intermediate, oxidation of aldehydes, reduction of isolated double bonds, and the oxidation of carbon–nitrogen bonds (as with dihydrofolate reductase).

The recommended daily requirement for niacin is 13–19 niacin equivalents (NE) per day for a normal adult. One NE is equivalent to 1 mg of free niacin).

Clinical significances of niacin and nicotinic acid

A diet deficient in niacin (as well as tryptophan) leads to glossitis of the tongue, dermatitis, weight loss, diarrhea, depression and dementia. The severe symptoms, depression, dermatitis and diarrhea, are associated with the condition known as pellagra.

Pellagra is a disease characterised by dermatitis, diarrhea, and dementia, has been known for centuries. It was once prevalent in the southern part of the United States and is still a common problem in some parts of Spain, Italy, and Romania. Pellagra was once thought to be an infectious disease, but Joseph Goldberger showed early in this century that it could be cured by dietary actions. Soon thereafter, it was found that brewer's yeast would prevent pellagra in humans. Studies of a similar disease in dogs, called black tongue, eventually led to the identification of nicotinic acid as the relevant dietary factor. Elvehjem and his colleagues at the University of Wisconsin in 1937 isolated nicotinamide from liver, and showed that it and nicotinic acid could prevent and cure black tongue in dogs. That same year, nicotinamide and nicotinic acid were both shown to be able to cure pellagra in humans. Interestingly, plants and many animals can synthesise nicotinic acid from tryptophan and other precursors, and nicotinic acid is thus not a true vitamin for these species. However, if dietary intake of tryptophan is low, nicotinic acid is required for optimal health. Nicotinic acid, which is beneficial to humans and animals, is structurally related to nicotine, a highly toxic tobacco alkaloid. In order to avoid confusion of nicotinic acid and nicotinamide with nicotine itself, niacin was adopted as a common name for nicotinic acid. Cowgill, at Yale University, suggested the name from the letters of three words—nicotinic, acid, and vitamin.

Several physiological conditions (e.g. Hartnup disease and malignant carcinoid syndrome) as well as certain drug therapies (e.g. isoniazid) can lead to niacin deficiency. In Hartnup disease tryptophan absorption is impaired and in malignant carcinoid syndrome tryptophan metabolism is altered resulting in excess serotonin synthesis. Isoniazid (the hydrazide derivative of isonicotinic acid) is the primary drug for chemotherapy of tuberculosis.

Nicotinic acid (but not nicotinamide) when administered in pharmacological doses of 2–4 g/day lowers plasma cholesterol levels and has been shown to be a useful therapeutic for hypercholesterolemia. The major action of nicotinic acid in this capacity is a reduction in fatty acid mobilisation from adipose tissue. Although nicotinic acid therapy lowers blood cholesterol it also causes a depletion of glycogen stores and fat reserves in skeletal and cardiac muscle. Additionally, there is an elevation in blood glucose and uric acid production. For these reasons nicotinic acid therapy is not recommended for diabetics or persons who suffer from gout.

Vitamin B_5

Vitamin B_5 is also known as pantothenic acid. Pantothenic acid is formed from β-alanine and pantoic acid. Pantothenate is required for synthesis of coenzyme A, CoA and is a component of the acyl carrier protein (ACP) domain of fatty acid synthase. Pantothenate is, therefore, required for the metabolism of carbohydrate via the TCA cycle and all fats and proteins. At least 70 enzymes have been identified as requiring CoA or ACP derivatives for their function.

Deficiency of pantothenic acid is extremely rare due to its widespread distribution in whole grain cereals, legumes and meat. Symptoms of pantothenate deficiency are difficult to assess since they are subtle and resemble those of other B vitamin deficiencies.

Vitamin B_6

Vitamin B_6. are collectively known as pyridoxal, pyridoxamine and pyridoxine. All three compounds are efficiently converted to the biologically active form of vitamin B_6, pyridoxal phosphate. This conversion is catalysed by the ATP requiring enzyme, pyridoxal kinase.

Pyridoxal phosphate functions as a cofactor in enzymes involved in transamination reactions required for the synthesis and catabolism of the amino acids as well as in glycogenolysis as a cofactor for glycogen phosphorylase.

A specific example would be glutamate : aspartate aminotransferase. It is a pyridoxal phosphate – dependent enzyme. Glutamate : aspartate aminotransferase isan enzyme conforming to a double-displacement bisubstrate mechanism. The pyridoxal serves as the -NH_2 acceptor from glutamate to form pyridoxamine. Pyridoxamine is then the amino donor to oxaloacetate to form asparate and regenerate the pyridoxal coenzyme form.

The requirement for vitamin B_6 in the diet is proportional to the level of protein consumption ranging from 1.4–2.0 mg/day for a normal adult. During pregnancy and lactation the requirement for vitamin B6 increases approximately 0.6 mg/day. Deficiencies of vitamin B_6 are rare and usually are related to an overall deficiency of all the B-complex vitamins. Isoniazid and penicillamine (used to treat rheumatoid arthritis and cystinurias) are two drugs that complex with pyridoxal and pyridoxal phosphate resulting in a deficiency in this vitamin.

Vitamin B_7

Vitamin B_7 is known as biotin. Biotin is the cofactor required of enzymes that are involved in carboxylation reactions, e.g. acetyl-CoA carboxylase and pyruvate carboxylase. Biotin is found in numerous foods and also is synthesised by intestinal bacteria and as such deficiencies of the vitamin are rare. Deficiencies are generally seen only after long antibiotic therapies which deplete the intestinal fauna or following excessive consumption of raw eggs. The latter is due to the affinity of the egg white protein, avidin, for biotin preventing intestinal absorption of the biotin.

Vitamin B_9

Vitamin B_9 is known as folic acid. Folic acid is a conjugated molecule consisting of a pteridine ring structure linked to para-aminobenzoic acid (PABA) that forms pteroic acid. Folic acid itself is then generated through the conjugation of glutamic acid residues to pteroic acid. Folic acid is obtained primarily from yeasts and leafy vegetables as well as animal liver. Animal cannot synthesise PABA nor attach glutamate residues to pteroic acid, thus, requiring folate intake in the diet.

When stored in the liver or ingested folic acid exists in a polyglutamate form. Intestinal mucosal cells remove some of the glutamate residues through the action of the lysosomal enzyme, conjugase. The removal of glutamate residues makes folate less negatively charged (from the polyglutamic acids) and therefore more capable of passing through the basal lamenal membrane of the epithelial cells of the intestine and into the bloodstream. Folic acid is reduced within cells (principally the liver where it is stored) to tetrahydrofolate (THF also H4folate) through the action of dihydrofolate reductase (DHFR), an NADPH-requiring enzyme.

The function of THF derivatives is to carry and transfer various forms of one carbon units during biosynthetic reactions. The one carbon units are either methyl, methylene, methenyl, formyl or formimino groups. These one carbon transfer reactions are required in the biosynthesis of serine, methionine, glycine, choline and the purine nucleotides and dTMP.

The ability to acquire choline and amino acids from the diet and to salvage the purine nucleotides makes the role of N^5,N^{10}-methylene-THF in dTMP synthesis the most metabolically significant function for this vitamin. The role of vitamin B_{12} and N^5-methyl-THF in the conversion of homocysteine to methionine also can have a significant impact on the ability of cells to regenerate needed THF.

Clinical significance of folate deficiency

Folate deficiency results in complications nearly identical to those described for vitamin B_{12} deficiency. The most pronounced effect of folate deficiency on cellular processes is upon DNA synthesis. This is due to an impairment in dTMP synthesis which leads to cell cycle arrest in S-phase of rapidly proliferating cells, in particular hematopoietic cells. The result is megaloblastic anemia as for vitamin B_{12} deficiency. The inability to synthesise DNA during erythrocyte maturation leads to abnormally large erythrocytes termed macrocytic anemia.

Folate deficiencies are rare due to the adequate presence of folate in food. Poor dietary habits as those of chronic alcoholics can lead to folate deficiency. The predominant causes of folate deficiency in non-alcoholics are impaired absorption or metabolism or an increased demand for the vitamin. The predominant condition requiring an increase in the daily intake of folate is pregnancy. This is due to an increased number of rapidly proliferating cells present in the blood. The need for folate will nearly double by the third trimester of pregnancy. Certain drugs such as anticonvulsants and oral contraceptives can impair the absorption of folate. Anticonvulsants also increase the rate of folate metabolism.

Vitamin B_{12}

Vitamin B_{12} is known as cobalamin. Cobalamin is more commonly known as vitamin B_{12}. Vitamin B_{12} is composed of a complex tetrapyrrol ring structure (corrin ring) and a cobalt ion in the center. Vitamin B_{12} is synthesised exclusively by micro-organisms and is found in the liver of animals bound to protein as methycobalamin or 5′-deoxyadenosylcobalamin. The vitamin must be hydrolysed from protein in order to be active. Hydrolysis occurs in the stomach by gastric acids or the intestines by trypsin digestion following consumption of animal meat. The vitamin is then bound by intrinsic factor, a protein secreted by parietal cells of the stomach, and carried to the ileum where it is absorbed. Following absorption the vitamin is transported to the liver in the blood bound to transcobalamin II.

There are only two clinically significant reactions in the body that require vitamin B_{12} as a cofactor. During the catabolism of fatty acids with an odd number of carbon atoms and the amino acids valine, isoleucine and threonine the resultant propionyl-CoA is converted to succinyl-CoA for oxidation in the TCA cycle. One of the enzymes in this pathway, methylmalonyl-CoA mutase, requires vitamin B_{12} as a cofactor in the conversion of methylmalonyl-CoA to succinyl-CoA. The 5′-deoxyadenosine derivative of cobalamin is required for this reaction.

The second reaction requiring vitamin B_{12} catalyses the conversion of homocysteine to methionine and is catalysed by methionine synthase. This reaction results in the transfer of the methyl group from N^5-methyltetrahydrofolate to hydroxycobalamin generating tetrahydrofolate (THF) and methylcobalamin during the process of the conversion.

Clinical significances of B_{12} deficiency

The liver can store up to six years worth of vitamin B_{12}, hence deficiencies in this vitamin are rare. Pernicious anemia is a megaloblastic anemia resulting from vitamin B_{12} deficiency that develops as a result a lack of intrinsic factor in the stomach leading to malabsorption of the vitamin. The anemia results from impaired DNA synthesis due to a block in purine and thymidine biosynthesis. The block in nucleotide biosynthesis is a consequence of the effect of vitamin B_{12} on folate metabolism. When vitamin B_{12} is deficient essentially all of the folate becomes trapped as the N^5-methylTHF derivative as a result of the loss of functional methionine synthase. This trapping prevents the synthesis of other THF derivatives required for the purine and thymidine nucleotide biosynthesis pathways.

Neurological complications also are associated with vitamin B_{12} deficiency and result from a progressive demyelination of nerve cells. The demyelination is thought to result from the increase in methylmalonyl-CoA that result from vitamin B_{12} deficiency. Methylmalonyl-CoA is a competitive inhibitor of malonyl-CoA in fatty acid biosynthesis as well as being able to substitute for malonyl-CoA in any fatty acid biosynthesis that may occur. Since the myelin sheath is in continual flux the methylmalonyl-CoA-induced inhibition of fatty acid synthesis results in the eventual destruction of the sheath. The incorporation methylmalonyl-CoA into fatty acid biosynthesis results in branched-chain fatty acids being produced that may severely alter the architecture of the normal membrane structure of nerve cells.

Vitamin C

Vitamin C is more commonly known as ascorbic acid. Ascorbic acid is derived from glucose via the uronic acid pathway. The enzyme L-gulonolactone oxidase responsible for the conversion of gulonolactone to ascorbic acid is absent in primates making ascorbic acid required in the diet.

The active form of vitamin C is ascorbate acid itself. The main function of ascorbate is as a reducing agent in a number of different reactions. Vitamin C has the potential to reduce cytochromes a and c of the respiratory chain as well as molecular oxygen. The most important reaction requiring ascorbate as a cofactor is the hydroxylation of proline residues in collagen. Vitamin C is, therefore, required for the maintenance of normal connective tissue as well as for wound healing since synthesis of connective tissue is the first event in wound tissue remodeling. Vitamin C also is necessary for bone remodeling due to the presence of collagen in the organic matrix of bones. Scurvy results from a dietary vitamin C deficiency and involves the inability to form collagen fibrils properly. This is the result of reduced activity of prolyl hydroxylase, which is vitamin C–dependent. Scurvy leads to lesions in the skin and blood vessels, and, in its advanced stages, it can lead to grotesque disfiguration and eventual death. Although rare in the modern world, it was a disease well known to sea-faring explorers in earlier times who did not appreciate the importance of fresh fruits and vegetables in the diet. Hydroxylation of proline residues is catalysed by prolyl hydroxylase. The reaction requires α-ketoglutarate and ascorbic acid.

Several other metabolic reactions require vitamin C as a cofactor. These include the catabolism of tyrosine and the synthesis of epinephrine from tyrosine and the synthesis of the bile acids. It is also believed that vitamin C is involved in the process of steroidogenesis since the adrenal cortex contains high levels of vitamin C which are depleted upon adrenocorticotropic hormone (ACTH) stimulation of the gland. Deficiency in vitamin C leads to the disease scurvy due to the role of the vitamin in the post-translational modification of collagens. Scurvy is characterised by easily bruised skin, muscle fatigue, soft swollen gums, decreased wound healing and hemorrhaging, osteoporosis, and anemia. Vitamin C is readily absorbed and so the primary cause of vitamin C deficiency is poor diet and/or an increased requirement. The primary physiological state leading to an increased requirement for vitamin C is severe stress (or trauma). This is due to a rapid depletion in the adrenal stores of the vitamin. The reason for the decrease in adrenal vitamin C levels is unclear but may be due either to redistribution of the vitamin to areas that need it or an overall increased utilisation.

GROUP III: VITAMIN-LIKE SUBSTANCES

Group III is vitamin-like substances. They are separated:

- Fat-soluble: Coenzyme Q (ubiquinone).
- Water-soluble vitamins: B_4 (choline), B_8 (inositol), B_T or B_{11} (carnitine), B_{13} (orotic acid), B_{15} (pangamic acid), U (S-methylmethionine), N (lipoic acid).

Most water-soluble vitamins must be supplied regularly with food, as they are quickly removed or destroyed in the body. Fat-soluble vitamins can be deposited in the body. Furthermore, they are poorly excreted, therefore, hypervitaminosis as diseases associated with high doses of fat-soluble vitamin intoxication of organism are observed. Such diseases are described for vitamins A and D.

Choline

Choline appears to be an essential nutrient for a number of animals and micro-organisms that cannot synthesise adequate quantities to satisfy their requirements. Choline is a constituent of an important class of lipids called phospholipids, which form structural elements of cell membranes, it is a component of the acetylcholine molecule, which is important in nerve function. Choline also serves as a source of methyl groups ($-CH_3$ groups) that are required in various metabolic processes. The effects of a dietary deficiency of choline itself can be alleviated by other dietary compounds that can be changed into choline. Choline also functions in the transport of fats from the liver, for this reason, it may be called a lipotropic factor. A deficiency of choline in the rat results in an accumulation of fat in the liver. Choline-deficiency symptoms vary among species, it is not known if choline is an essential nutrient for humans since a dietary deficiency has not been demonstrated.

Myo-inositol

The biological significance of *myo*-inositol has not yet been established with certainty. It is present in large amounts—principally as a constituent of phospholipids—in humans. Inositol is a carbohydrate that closely resembles glucose in structure, inositol can be converted to phytic acid, which is found in grains and forms an insoluble (and thus unabsorbable) calcium salt in the intestines of mammals. Inositol has not been established as an essential nutrient for humans, however, it is a required factor for the growth of some yeasts and fungi.

Para-aminobenzoic acid

Para-aminobenzoic acid (PABA) is required for the growth of several types of micro-organisms, however, a dietary requirement by vertebrates has not been shown. The antimicrobial sulfa drugs (sulfanilamide and related compounds) inhibit the growth of bacteria by competing with PABA for a position in a coenzyme that is necessary for bacterial reproduction. Although a structural unit of folic acid, PABA is not considered a vitamin.

Carnitine

Carnitine is essential for the growth of mealworms. The role of carnitine in all organisms is associated with the transfer of fatty acids from the bloodstream to active sites of fatty acid oxidation within muscle cells. Carnitine, therefore, regulates the rate of oxidation of these acids, this function may afford means by which a cell can rapidly shift its metabolic patterns (e.g. from fat synthesis to fat breakdown). Synthesis of carnitine occurs in insects and in higher animals, therefore, it is not considered a true vitamin.

Lipoic acid

Lipoic acid has a coenzyme function similar to that of thiamin. Although it is apparently an essential nutrient for some micro-organisms, no deficiency in mammals has been observed, therefore, lipoic acid is not considered a true vitamin.

Bioflavinoids

The bioflavinoids once were thought to prevent scurvy and were designated as vitamin Pc, but additional evidence refuted this claim.

HEALTH EFFECTS OF VITAMINS AND ANTIVITAMINS

Currently, vitamins and antivitamins widely used to prevent and treat a variety of disorders of metabolism. For example:

- Vitamin K or menadione, or vicasol (both are synthetic water-soluble analogue of vitamin K) are prescribed to stimulate the synthesis (specifically post-translational γ-carboxylation of glutamic acid residues) such enzymes of coagulation system as factors II (prothrombin), VII, IX and X in the liver. They are usually used after long-term antibiotic treatment (if there is increased bleeding with small injuries, increase in blood clotting time) and in the preoperative period.
- Vitamin K antagonist (antivitamin K) dicumarol reduces the efficiency of the blood coagulation promoting blood thinning thereby it use for the treatment of blood clotting diseases, in particular, thrombosis, thrombophlebitis.
- Vitamin A and its derivatives like retinol acetate are used for treating of vitamin A deficiency. For example, they can be administered a patient in order to restore his vision if the patient suffers from vision impairment hemeralopia (night blindness, twilight vision impairment), age-related glaucoma, cataracts, etc. Vitamin A drug is also used for skin conditions including acne, eczema, psoriasis, cold sores, wounds, burns, sunburn. It is also used for gastrointestinal ulcers, gum disease, urinary tract infections, diseases of the nervous system.

- Drug isoniazid which is antivitamin nicotinic acid and pyridoxine is used In the treatment of patients with pulmonary tuberculosis.
- The structural analogue of vitamin B_2 acrichine is formerly widely used as an antimalarial drug but superseded by chloroquine in recent years. It has also been used as an anthelmintic (in enterobiasis) and in the treatment of giardiasis and malignant effusions. The mechanism action of the drug is based on preventing of micro-organism FAD(FMN)-dependent dehydrogenases.
- Ascorutinum is recommended to use as a more effective drug in comparison with ascorbic acid for patients with reduced immunity and frequent colds. Vitamin C (Ascorbic acid) is involved in the hydroxylation of prolyl- and lysyl residues by prolyl 3(4)-hydroxylase and lysyl 5-hydroxylase during collagen synthesis. Effect of the vitamin C is enhanced by vitamin P, which stabilises the ground substance of fibrous connective tissue in way of hyaluronidase inhibition. Ascorutinum can be recommended in case of bleeding gums, petechial hemorrhages.
- Sulfonamide drugs are folic acid antivitamin. They are structurally resemble paraaminobenzoic acid and due to this similarity it is displaced from its complex with the enzyme synthesising folic acid. This leads to the inhibition of bacterial growth. This mechanism of action of sulfonamides allows their use as antibacterial agents.
- Pregnant women with a history of several miscarriages is assigned the therapy including α-tocopherol (vitamin E) vitamin supplements using, It contributes to the childbearing. Furthermore, tocopherol acetate, vitamin preparation is usually given in the course of radiation therapy, since this substance has a distinct radioprotective membrane stabilising action due to its antioxidant activity.
- Derivatives of pyridoxine (vitamin B_6) are used as neurotrophic agents for the correction of mental retardation in childre, in cases of mental disorders in adults, as neuroprotective agents in rehabilitation of patients with stroke and other pathological conditions. The positive effects of pyridoxine is explained by its use as a precursor of PLP that is prosthetic group of the enzyme glutamate decarboxylase in neurons. The enzyme carries out inhibitory neurotransmitter GABA formation.
- Cabbage and potato juices rich in vitamin U are recommended to drink for patient with duodenal ulcer after the therapy course. Whether taken as a supplement or from foods, vitamin U has been shown to be able to treat a variety of gastrointestinal conditions, including ulcerative colitis, acid reflux, and peptic ulcers. It may also be able to treat skin lesions, improve the symptoms of diabetes, and strengthen the immune system. Some studies show that it can also help prevent liver damage by protecting the organ from the effects of high doses of acetaminophen. Additionally, it may be able to reduce allergies and sensitivities to cigarette smoke and improve cholesterol levels.

The aforecited examples are only a small part of the use of vitamins and their derivatives in medicine. Therefore, knowledge of the biochemical basis of vitaminology is of great importance for future doctors.

METHODS USED IN VITAMIN RESEARCH

Determination of Vitamin Requirements

If a specific factor in food is suspected of being essential for the growth of an organism (either by growth failure or some other clinical symptoms that are alleviated by adding a specific food to the diet) a systematic series of procedures is used to characterise the factor.

The active factor is isolated from specific foods and purified, then its chemical structure is determined, and it is synthesised in the laboratory. Structural determination and synthesis, which may be achieved only after long and intensive research, must be completed before the function and the quantitative requirements of the factor can be established accurately. Established organic and analytical chemical procedures are used to determine the structure of the factor and to synthesise it.

Biological studies may be performed to determine functions, effects of deprivation, and quantitative requirements of the factor in various organisms. The development in an organism of a deficiency either by dietary deprivation of the vitamin or by administration of a specific antagonist or compound that prevents the normal function of the vitamin (antivitamin) often is the method used. The obvious effects (e.g. night blindness, anemia, dermatitis) of the deficiency are noted. Less obvious effects may be discovered after microscopic examination of tissue and bone structures. Changes in concentrations of metabolites or in enzymatic activity in tissues, blood, or excretory products are examined by numerous biochemical techniques. The response of an animal to a specific vitamin of which it has been deprived usually confirms the deficiency symptoms for that vitamin. Effects of deprivation of a vitamin sometimes indicate its general physiological function, as well as its function at the cellular level. Biochemical function often is studied by observing the response of tissue enzymes (removed from a deficient host animal) after a purified vitamin preparation is added. The functions of most of the known vitamins have been reasonably well defined, however, the mechanism of action has not yet been established for some.

The procedure for determining the amount of a vitamin required by an organism is less difficult for micro-organisms than for higher forms, in micro-organisms, the aim is to establish the smallest amount of a vitamin that produces maximal rate of multiplication of the organisms when it is added to the culture medium. Among vertebrates, particularly humans, a number of procedures are used together to provide estimates of the vitamin requirement. These procedures include determinations of: the amount of a vitamin required to cure a deficiency that has been developed under controlled, standard conditions, the smallest amount required to prevent the appearance of clinical or biochemical symptoms of the deficiency, the amount required to saturate body tissues (i.e. to cause 'spillover' of the vitamin in the urine, valid only with the water-soluble vitamins), the amount necessary to produce maximum blood levels of the vitamin plus some tissue storage (applicable only to the fat-soluble vitamins, particularly vitamin A), the amount required to produce maximum activity of an enzyme system if the vitamin has a coenzyme function, the actual rate of utilisation, and hence the requirement, in healthy individuals (as indicated by measuring the excreted breakdown products of radioisotope-labeled vitamins).

The above procedures are practical only with small groups of animals or human subjects and thus are not entirely representative of larger populations of a particular species. A less precise, but more representative, method used among human populations involves comparing levels of dietary intake of a vitamin in a population that shows no deficiency symptoms with levels of intake of the vitamin in a population that reveals clinical or biochemical symptoms. The data for dietary intakes and incidence of deficiency symptoms are obtained by surveys of representative segments of a population.

Determination of vitamin sources

A quantitative analysis of the vitamin content of foodstuffs is important in order to identify dietary sources of specific vitamins (and other nutrients as well). Three methods commonly used to determine vitamin content are described below.

Physicochemical methods: The amount of vitamin in a foodstuff can be established by studying the physical or chemical characteristics of the vitamin, e.g. a chemically reactive group on the vitamin molecule, fluorescence, absorption of light at a wavelength characteristic of the vitamin, or radioisotope dilution techniques. These methods are accurate and can detect very small amounts of the vitamin. Biologically inactive derivatives of several vitamins have been found, however, and may interfere with such determinations, in addition, these procedures also may not distinguish between bound (i.e. unavailable) and available forms of a vitamin in a food.

Microbiological assay: Microbiological assay is applicable only to the B vitamins. The rate of growth of a species of micro-organism that requires a vitamin is measured in growth media that contain various known quantities of a foodstuff preparation containing unknown amounts of the vitamin. The response (measured as rate of growth) to the unknown amounts of vitamin is compared with that obtained from a known quantity of the pure vitamin. Depending on the way in which the food sample was prepared, the procedure may indicate the availability of the vitamin in the food sample to the micro-organism.

Animal assay: All of the vitamins, with the exception of vitamin B_{12}, can be estimated by the animal-assay technique. One advantage of this method is that animals respond only to the biologically active forms of the vitamins. On the other hand, many other interfering and complicating factors may arise, therefore, experiments must be rigidly standardised and controlled. Simultaneous estimates usually are made using a pure standard vitamin preparation as a reference and the unknown food whose vitamin content is being sought, each test is repeated using two or more different amounts of both standard and unknown in the assays listed below.

In a growth assay, the rat, chick, dog (used specifically for niacin), and guinea pig (used specifically for vitamin C) usually are used. One criterion used in a vitamin assay is increase in body weight in response to different amounts of a specific vitamin in the diet. There are two types of growth assay. In a prophylactic growth assay, the increase in weight of young animals given different amounts of the vitamin is measured. In a curative growth assay, weight increase is measured in animals first deprived of a vitamin and then given various quantities of it. The curative growth assay tends to provide more consistent results than the prophylactic technique.

In a reaction time assay, an animal is first deprived of a vitamin until a specific deficiency symptom appears, then the animal is given a known amount of a food extract containing the vitamin, and the deficiency symptom disappears within a day or two. The time required for the reappearance of the specific symptoms when the animal again is deprived of the vitamin provides a measure of the amount of vitamin given originally. The graded response assay, which may be prophylactic or curative, depends on a characteristic response that varies in degree with the vitamin dosage. An example of this technique is an assay for vitamin D in which the measured ash content of a leg bone of a rat or chick is used to reflect the amount of bone calcification that occurred as a result of administration of a specific amount of vitamin D. In an all-or-none assay, the degree of response cannot be measured, an arbitrary level is selected to separate positive responses from negative ones. The percent of positively reacting animals provides a measure of response, i.e. vitamin E can be measured by obtaining the percent of fertility in successfully mated female rats.

SECTION VI

Food Flavours and Food Additives

Chapter 23

Food Flavours

INTRODUCTION

Flavour is the sensory impression of food or other substances, and is determined primarily by the chemical senses of taste and smell. The 'trigeminal senses', which detect chemical irritants in the mouth and throat, as well as temperature and texture, are also important to the overall gestalt of flavour perception. The flavour of the food, as such, can be altered with natural or artificial flavourants which affect these senses. A 'flavourant' is defined as a substance that gives another substance flavour, altering the characteristics of the solute, causing it to become sweet, sour, tangy, etc. A flavour is a quality of something that affects the sense of taste.

Of the three chemical senses, smell is the main determinant of a food items flavour. Five basic tastes – sweet, sour, bitter, salty and umami (savory) are universally recognised, although some cultures also include pungency and oleogustus ('fattiness'). The number of food smells is unbounded, a foods flavour, therefore, can be easily altered by changing its smell while keeping its taste similar. This is exemplified in artificially flavoured jellies, soft drinks and candies, which, while made of bases with a similar taste, have dramatically different flavours due to the use of different scents or fragrances. The flavourings of commercially produced food products are typically created by flavourists.

Although the terms flavouring and flavourant in common language denote the combined chemical sensations of taste and smell, the same terms are used in the fragrance and flavours industry to refer to edible chemicals and extracts that alter the flavour of food and food products through the sense of smell. Due to the high cost or unavailability of natural flavour extracts, most commercial flavourants are 'nature-identical', which means that they are the chemical equivalent of natural flavours, but chemically synthesised rather than being extracted from source materials. Identification of components of natural foods, for example a raspberry, may be done using technology such as headspace techniques, so the flavourist can imitate the flavour by using a few of the same chemicals present.

Flavourings are focused on altering the flavours of natural food product such as meats and vegetables, or creating flavour for food products that do not have the desired flavours such as candies and other snacks. Most types of flavourings are focused on scent and taste. Few commercial products exist to stimulate the trigeminal senses, since these are sharp, astringent, and typically unpleasant flavours.

Most artificial flavours are specific and often complex mixtures of singular naturally occurring flavour compounds combined together to either imitate or enhance a natural flavour. These mixtures are formulated by flavourists to give a food product a unique flavour and to maintain flavour consistency between different product batches or after recipe changes. The list of known flavouring agents includes thousands of molecular compounds, and the flavour chemist (flavourist) can often mix these together to produce many of the common flavours. Many flavourants consist of esters, which are often described as being 'sweet' or 'fruity'.

FLAVOUR CHEMISTRY

There are many problems facing the flavourist trying to relate chemical compounds to flavours. Flavour compounds can be found in any class of chemical compounds: neutral compounds, acids, nitrogen and sulphur compounds, with high volatility, compounds with low volatility, etc. These compounds are susceptible to chemical changes of various kinds. For example, aldehydes are easily oxidised to acids, amines may complex with metal ions, in the presence of acids, terpenes rearrange and isomerise, exposure to light may cause photo-oxidation or rearrangements, and polymerisations of unsaturated compounds do occur. These transformations are a real concern during the collection and concentration of foods for flavour determinations, particularly because there is such a low quantity of flavour compounds in foods. The instability of many compounds generates artefacts during the isolation of flavours, e.g. when flavours are isolated by bubbling air through oils, the triglycerides are oxidised and so new flavours are formed. Flavours also change with time and processing conditions, e.g. freshly squeezed orange juice is easily distinguished from juice reconstituted from frozen concentrate, juice that is bottled or canned and even from freshly squeezed orange juice that has been allowed to stand at room temperature open to the air for an hour or two.

It has been estimated that as few as eight molecules are required to trigger one human olfactory neuron and that as few as 40 molecules can produce an identifiable sensation. Such levels are below the sensitivity limits of present-day analytical techniques, thus, the human nose is a better detector than the best instruments of today! To give an idea of how small an amount we can smell, consider the powerful odourant, 1-*p*-menthene-8-thiol, which gives a grapefruit aroma at 10^{-4} ppb. This concentration corresponds to 10^{-4} mg/MT of water.

Human flavour receptors are stimulated by various compounds with different sensitivities. The flavour chemist cannot just determine the concentration of each flavour compound in foods to decide how important it is to the resulting flavour, each threshold value must also be determined. For example, the flavour thresholds of the pyrazines vary in concentration by as much as eight orders of magnitude. The lowest level at which a compound can be detected is its detection threshold. A recognition threshold is the lowest concentration at which the flavour of the detected compound is recognised.

Since odour quality may change with concentration, a chemical such as *trans*-non-2-enal has more than one recognition threshold: just above its detection threshold of 0.1 ppb, *trans*-non-2-enal possesses a woody character. Above 8 ppb, it smells fatty, becoming unpleasant at 30 ppb and in an aqueous solution at 1000 ppb, it has a strong flavour of cucumber. This change in flavour with increasing concentration of an individual compound can perplex the flavour chemist. Another example is 2-pentylfuran which smells beany when diluted at 1–10 ppm in oil, but when concentrated as an eluant from the gas chromatogram (GC), it elicits the distinct aroma of liquorice.

Another problem that can occur is interaction when compounds are mixed together. When they interfere with flavour detection, this is called antagonism. When they enhance the ability to detect the flavour, it is called synergism. An example of flavour antagonism can be seen with *cis*-hex-3-enal, which has a distinct green bean aroma at 1.0 ppm in paraffin oil, when *trans*, *trans*-deca-2, 4-dienal (12.5 ppm) is mixed into *cis*-hex-3-enal (13.2 ppm), there is almost no odour or taste. Thus, the antagonist decadienal interferes with the detection of hexenal. To demonstrate flavour synergism, one can look at ketones at concentrations where each, individually, has no aroma in water (butan-2-one, 5 ppm, pentan-2-one, 5 ppm, hexan-2-one, 1 ppm, heptan-2-one, 0.5 ppm, octan-2-one, 0.2 ppm), but a solution containing all of them together at these specific concentrations has a definite aroma.

Lastly, the types of compounds surrounding the flavour chemical can affect how much of that flavourant reaches the nose, tongue or walls of the mouth. For example, how well a flavourant can evaporate from the food determines its detection threshold. The more lipophilic (non-polar) a molecule, the less it will hydrogen bond to water. Therefore, it has lower solubility and higher vapour pressure in water and thus can be more easily inhaled when dispersed in water. The opposite is also true: the more lipophilic (non-polar) a molecule, the lower the vapour pressure it has in lipids and the harder it is to smell when dissolved in fats or oils. The different ketones placed in either water or corn oil at 200 ppm will equilibrate at different headspace concentrations above the liquid. As the hydrocarbon chain is lengthened, the ketone becomes more lipophilic, less is in the air above the oil and more is in the air above the water.

IMPORTANCE OF FLAVOUR CHEMISTRY

If the chemical composition of flavours is understood, then better control of these flavours is possible. If we can understand the mechanisms of their formation, then we can suppress unwanted flavours and enhance the desired ones.

During the growing and processing of foods, off-flavours occasionally develop. It is important to the quality of these foods to try to prevent or at least retard this process. Sometimes fresh flavours need to be restored to processed foods, so research is required to determine what gave the unprocessed food its original fresh flavour and what happened to this under the conditions of processing. Other times, processing creates flavours, so a thorough understanding of the reactions that produce flavour compounds can help the food processor to improve the flavour of his foods by accelerating these reactions. Occasionally, added flavour compounds not naturally found in certain foods will improve their flavours. In this way, new food items are created.

There are many different flavour-related jobs in the food industry, which include work in creation, analysis, applications and general flavour science. The creative role is very specialised. The primary focus of the creative 'flavourist' is to create flavours by combining pure chemicals or any of thousands of plant, microbial and/or animal extracts together, much like a painter mixes colours on a palette. The flavourist continuously builds on previous knowledge, as an artist, to blend flavouring materials in new ways. It is the flavour applications expert who takes that blend and applies it to a variety of different canvases. The applications expert is concerned with the flavour quality of the overall product. He or she must have a strong food science background, understanding both food chemistry and processing and their effects on foods.

The analytical flavour chemist uses instrumentation in either a quality control or a research setting. In quality control the analytical chemist may determine specifications for raw materials coming into the plant or test the flavours throughout the process to control the quality of out-going food products. In the research setting, an analytical flavour chemist might break down competitors flavours to understand or duplicate them. He or she may even assist geneticists to breed better raw materials for food by monitoring target flavour compounds or flavour precursors.

The flavour scientist, on the other hand, broadly researches the unknown. Many flavour scientists are trying to understand how flavours interact with each other, within the food product or with the package. Outside the food industry, there are some flavour scientists who work with biologists and medical personnel to apply their methodologies to develop a more thorough understanding of the biological functions of taste and smell. For example, they might research how the variations in taste and olfactory perception influence our diet.

CLASSIFICATION OF FOOD FLAVOURS

Flavours can be classified by the general sensations that one feels when eating different foods. Flavour comes from three different sensations: taste, trigeminal and aroma (odour). It is generally agreed that taste sensations are divided into four major categories: saltiness, sweetness, sourness and bitterness. However, some Japanese scientists also include a fifth category called *umami* (savoury) that can be represented by the flavour of glutamate. Trigeminal sensations give us the descriptors of astringency, pungency and cooling. Both taste and trigeminal sensations occur upon contact with food in the mouth, as most substances which produce these flavours are non-volatile, polar and water-soluble. For aroma sensations to occur, an aromatic compound must be sufficiently volatile to allow detection at a distance. The physical interaction between the volatile compound and the receptor site occurs in the nasal passages. Those molecules that reach the olfactory receptors, either via the nasal passage or oral passageway, trigger the odourous sensations. However, food flavourants are usually classified by the food sources in which they are normally detected because more than one flavour sensation is usually triggered by a food flavourant. Given a specific flavourant, the food industry wants to know what type of image the average consumer will envision when he or she encounters it. For example, celery flavourant (from an extract of celery seed) used in a soup is bitter with a floral aroma, but to an average consumer this flavourant just elicits the thought of celery soup. The problem with using food sources to classify flavours is that flavours may vary with the history of the food source. For example, fresh cabbage has a quite different aroma than cooked cabbage and sauerkraut is a vastly different olfactory and gustatory experience. Thus classifying flavours by food source is somewhat arbitrary, with the processing method frequently denoted in the descriptive name of the flavour.

Fruit Flavours

The *tastes* of fruit are a blend of the sweetness due to sugars (such as glucose, fructose and sucrose) and the sourness of organic acids (such as citric and malic). However, it is the *aromas* of the different volatile components of fruits that allow us to distinguish among them. When one's sense of smell is eliminated (temporarily having a stuffy nose from a cold), it is extremely difficult to distinguish between onions and apples. A typical fruit may have well over a hundred different volatile components, but in total, these compose only a few parts per million of the entire fruit. Fruit aromas vary widely. Citrus, such as grapefruit, orange, lemon and lime, are rich in terpenoids whereas most non-citrus fruits, such as apple, raspberry, cranberry and banana, are characterised by esters and aldehydes.

Vegetable Flavours

Most cultivated vegetables have a milder flavour than the corresponding wild species. Over the years of plant cultivation, the milder varieties, that were high yielding and disease resistant, were chosen for propagation unless the plant was also used to 'spice' up other foods. Many vegetable flavours are only released from the raw vegetable when they are chopped or cooked, because the aroma compounds are tied up as glycosides (celery, lettuce) or glucosinolates (cabbage, radish), which makes them non-volatile. When the glycoside or glucosinolate linkage is broken via either enzymatic cleavage or heat, then the aroma compounds are released.

The 'green' flavour of many vegetables (peas, pepper, beans, asparagus, carrot, lettuce) comes from alkylalkoxypyrazines. Other alkylalkoxypyrazines are responsible for earthy aromas (potato). Phthalides give the bitter flavour to celery. When vegetables (or fruits) are dried, many of the original flavour volatiles are removed with the water. Heat is usually used to speed the drying process (unless freeze-dried) and many of the flavour compounds change with elevated temperatures and air oxidation. New flavours can be developed from non-volatile precursors.

Spice Flavours

Some vegetables, such as onion and garlic, can also be considered spices. The onion is classified as *lachrymatory* as the initial flavour compound released upon enzymatic cleavage will bring tears to the eyes. Luckily it is short-lived and reacts to form other more appreciated flavour compounds. This lachrymatory compound is not formed in garlic.

Aromatic spices are the dried fruits and *aromatic* herbs are the dried leaves of plants. Volatile compounds give the characteristic aromas to the spices: eugenol (cloves), cinnamaldehyde (cinnamon) and menthol (mint). Some of these volatile substances, such as eugenol and cinnamaldehyde, also produce a slight pungent sensation via the trigeminal nerves.

The hot spices include chilli or red pepper, black pepper and ginger. All have aromatic characters, but the pungent sensation in the mouth is overwhelming. Garlic, nutmeg and cinnamon are also sometimes considered hot spices, however, here the trigeminal sensation occurs mainly in the nose.

In food processing, spices are often used in the form of essential oils or oleoresins. Essential oils are prepared by steam distillation of the dried ground spices and contain the volatile flavour compounds. Oleoresins are the solvent extracts of the spices and contain both the volatile essential oil as well as non-volatile resinous material and are more characteristic of the original ground spice.

Beverage Flavours

Beverage flavours can be divided into three types: unfermented, fermented and compounded. Unfermented beverages include milk and fruit and vegetable juices. Coffee might fall under this classification as it is not fermented, but because the beans are roasted to develop the flavour, it also can be considered an empyreumatic flavour. Tea is usually classified as a fermented flavour. However, this is a misnomer. Fermentation refers to microbial growth (e.g. yeast), but the formation of flavour (and colour as well) during 'fermentation' in tea manufacturing is related predominantly to the oxidation of the phenolic compounds by enzymes found in the fresh tea leaves.

Alcoholic beverages use microbes to process the beverage and the chemical transformations that occur during fermentation generate flavours. However, the primary distinguishing flavours between beer and wine develop via non-fermentative processes. The bitter flavour of beer comes from hops that are transformed during the boiling of the wort before fermentation begins. Many wine flavours develop from interactions among fermentation products, flavonoid and the wooden containers during the long ageing process after fermentation has stopped.

Compounded beverage flavours can be found in the soft drinks and cordials of today that have been completely blended by flavourists. Here, the flavourist has been creative in the combination of natural and/or artificial flavours to make beverages that excite the palate.

Meat Flavours

Meats are cooked, dried or even smoked to develop their flavours. The application of heat produces complex reactions between amino acids (often sulphur containing) and sugars (containing a carbonyl), that are given a singular name of Maillard reaction and are discussed in detail later. How long the meat is cooked, whether a dry method (broiling) or wet method (stewing) is used and the temperatures obtained during cooking can alter the compounds formed and change the flavours dramatically. Besides the cooking methods giving different flavour reactions, each animal contains a unique ratio of amino acids, fatty acids and sugars and thus generates its own flavours. In beef, lamb and pork, the lipids contain mostly saturated fatty acids that do not break down as quickly as do unsaturated fatty acids. However, in fish and fowl, there are many unsaturated lipids that generate flavours and small reactive molecules which interact with the amino acid/ sugar reaction products to produce even more complex flavours. Also, because of these unsaturated lipids, rancid flavours develop more quickly in fish and fowl than in beef.

Fat Flavours

As suggested above, unsaturation in fats leads to oxidative cleavage and the formation of both desirable and undesirable flavours. The development of rancidity in oils is greater when oxygen and metals are present. The more refined an oil is, the quicker it develops rancidity because natural antioxidants, such as vitamin E, are removed during processing. When frying, the combination of heat, fat and food leads to the development of many different flavours.

Cooked Flavours

During heating in the presence of water, many flavours change and new flavours can be developed from non-volatile precursors, thus these altered flavours are in a different category after they are cooked. Examples of cooked flavours can be found in soups and broths, vegetables and fruits.

Empyreumatic Flavours

Empyreal refers to being in a fire that is usually smoky and hotter than the boiling point of water. Thus, empyreumatic flavours emphasise the difference between water cooking and non-water cooking and are usually divided into three major categories: (i) smoked, (ii) broiled or fried, and (iii) roasted, toasted or baked.

When foods such as ham are smoked, the phenolic compounds in wood transform and vapourise to infiltrate the meat and preserve it. Broiled and fried flavours are developed at extremely high temperatures with high heat being transferred via radiation (broiling) or via conduction (through oil in frying). Examples are processed meat products and fried foods.

The roasted, toasted or baked category denotes flavours that are developed from the caramelisation of sugars and deamination of amino acids. Note that in this category, the sugar caramelisation products and amino acid deamination products do not always react with each other to form Maillard reaction products, as they normally do in the development of meaty flavours. Examples here are roasted coffee beans, snack foods, processed cereals and some bakery products.

Stench Flavours

Strong aromas can be produced during microbial growth, such as during the fermentation of cheeses or the spoilage of foods. Also, air oxidation can give a rancid or putrid note to foods containing unsaturated lipids, such as fish or soyabeans.

Chemical Compounds Responsible for Flavour

The many different possible flavours are due to interactions of chemical compounds with taste, trigeminal or aroma receptors. The characteristic taste (including trigeminal stimulations) of a food is normally related to a single class of compounds. But, an odour is usually elicited by a combination of volatile compounds each of which imparts its own smells. Differences in characteristics of certain aromas can be equated to the varying proportions of these volatiles. However, some substances contain trace amounts of a few volatile compounds that possess the characteristic essence of the odour. These are called character-impact compounds.

FLAVOUR COMPOUNDS

A single class of chemical compounds can elicit many different flavours, but normally evoke one type of response from one type of receptor. That is to say, a compound class, such as terpenes, is usually volatile and elicits an aroma. However, the functional groups that are on the terpene as well as the overall size and shape of the molecule determine its unique flavour. Most sugars are sweet (or bitter) and most esters are fruity. The reality of good food production is in learning how to control flavours during manufacturing. Processing conditions can be maximised for flavour constituents the resulting isolates which can be utilised to control the flavour of foods. But in order to control flavour, one must be able to analyse the flavour components both qualitatively and quantitatively.

Classification of Flavour Compounds

The first major classification of flavour chemicals is by volatility or how easily the compound evaporates into the air. This is a good working classification because the volatile compounds travel through air into the nose or the oesophageal passageway to arrive at the nasal receptors and elicit a response. The non-volatile compounds must be carried to the taste buds of the tongue or the inner lining of the mouth via food or saliva to elicit a response.

Volatile flavour compounds

It has been estimated that humans are responsive to 5000 to 10000 aromatic compounds. So far, over 2600 chemicals have been recognised as volatile components of aromas. They are partially lipid-soluble organic chemicals of low molecular weight (below 300 m.u.). Many of these have been identified since the invention of gas chromatography (GC). However, an analytical flavour chemist cannot simply identify and quantify the volatile compounds in foods, as the GC analysis does not establish the contribution of individual volatile compounds to flavour. It is now well established that many of the larger peaks on gas chromatograms of foods do not correlate to flavour. For example, limonene is the major component by weight of citrus oils, but it has a weak aroma. It is the oxygenated terpenes present in small amounts in these oils that have the major impact on the flavour. Although hydrocarbons like limonene may not have much aroma, they do act as a solvent for the powerful odourants. A volatile solvent might allow odourants to evaporate more efficiently (perhaps as an azeotrope) and help to carry them through the air to the nose, such as steam does when that tempting soup is simmering.

What follows are examples of the range of aroma characteristics provided by individual chemical groups. It must be remembered that a single fruit, vegetable or food contains a variety of aroma chemicals and that some chemicals can contain more than one of these functional groups. Thus, the flavour characteristics of each functional group are, by necessity, a generalisation and may not apply to every member of that group.

Aldehydes

Aldehydes play an important role in providing flavour characteristics of a wide range of foods. The unsaturated aliphatic aldehydes tend to produce stronger aromas than their saturated analogues.

In vegetables, for example, the 'green' flavour note is produced by *trans*-hex-3-enal and in leaves it is mainly *trans*-hex-2-enal. The overall flavour of dehydrated potato products is believed to be determined by a number of alk-2-enals found together with their corresponding saturated analogues. Short-chain saturated aliphatic aldehydes constitute an essential part of the natural tomato flavour. Cucumber flavour comes from (E,Z)-nona-2,6-dienal and (E)-non-2-enal. Present at only 0.9 ppb (45 times its threshold), (Z)-non-6-enal gives musk melon its typical aroma. In beer, 0.5 ppb of (E)-non-2-enal is perceived as a strong papery-stale aroma. Aldehydes are also responsible for many fruit aromas. Some flavour differences in varieties of apples were found to be a consequence of quantitative variations in the formation of *trans*-hex-2-enal and *trans*-hex-3-enal as well as of the corresponding alcohols. Benzaldehyde is strongly reminiscent of almonds and is associated with cherry flavour. The odour of citrus comes from aliphatic aldehydes, like decanal, having 8-10 carbon atoms and oxygenated terpenes, such as terpineol and citral.

The off-flavour component of partially hydrogenated vegetable oils and dried milk comes from (E)-non-6-enal. (E,ZZ)-Deca-2,4,7-trienal and (E,E,Z)-deca-2,4,7-trienal are formed by oxidation of linolenic acid and are responsible for the formation of the 'fishy' off-flavour in rancid mackerel oil. The rancid off-flavour in frozen stored cod is attributed to *trans*-hept-4-enal. At concentrations above 2 ppm, *trans*-hept-4-enal produces a rancid note in butter and soyabean oil. But at a level of 1 ppb, *trans*-hept-4-enal confers a creamy flavour to deodourised butter. The *cis* and *trans*-deca-2,4-dienals have been found in a wide variety of foods, including cottonseed oil, soyabean oil, milk fat, beef fat, cooked chicken, tomatoes and rye crisp bread and are believed to impart a desirable deep-fat flavour.

Alcohols

The odour threshold of alcohols is considerably higher than that of the corresponding aldehydes, so they are normally less important to flavour profiles. For example, as the storage time of fruit preserves or jellies is prolonged, the carbonyl content (aldehydes and ketones) decreases due to the formation of corresponding alcohols, this conversion is equivalent to a decrease of the flavour value. *trans*-Hex-3-enol has a green note and occurs in a wide range of higher plants in conjunction with *trans*-hex-3-enal. *trans*-Hex-3-enol was first discovered in fermented tea leaves in 1895. The main component of the volatile constituents of yellow passion fruit is hexan-l-ol. However, the flavour character is not determined by this alcohol, but by trace amounts of sulphur-containing compounds.

Ketones

Although most ketones have relatively high flavour thresholds, some, like the alkan-2-ones of different chain length in dairy foods, are still important to flavour. A compound responsible for a 'metallic' flavour in oxidised butter was shown to be oct-l-en-3-one. A strong blue cheese flavour is imparted to dairy products by the addition of non-8-en-2-one.

Acids

Besides producing a sour taste in the mouth, the volatile acids also can impart an aroma. Butyric and caproic acids interact at individual sub-threshold concentrations to produce a desirable butter flavour. An essential flavour component of Swiss cheese is propionic acid. Both hex-2-enoic and hex-3-enoic acids are important in raspberry flavour. When animal and vegetable oils are heated in the presence of air, alk-2-enoic and alk-3-enoic acids are formed and become an important component of fried food flavour. Several alkyl-branched fatty acids are powerful components of food flavours. An important constituent of the aroma of cranberry is 2-methylbutyric acid. Contributing to the distinct aroma of Turkish tobacco smoke are 2-methylvaleric acid and isovaleric acid. Isovaleric acid has the lowest flavour threshold (0.7 ppm) of all saturated fatty acids and is reminiscent of Limburger cheese. The undesirable odour of mutton is attributed to branched chain and unsaturated fatty acids having 8–10 carbon atoms. (Z)-2-Methylpent-3-enoic acid is used in aroma compositions to impart a sweet, green sharp strawberry character.

Esters

Aliphatic esters in various combinations play a major role in many fruit flavours. Hexyl acetate gives Cox's Orange Pippin apples their strong characteristic aroma. Much of the flavour of Golden Delicious apples comes from hexyl 2-methylbutyrate. Pineapple flavours contain the methyl and ethyl esters of (E)-hex-3-enoic, (Z)-dec-4-enoic and (E) and (Z)-oct-4-enoic acids. Ethyl (E, Z)-deca-2,4-dienoate is the character-impact compound of Bartlett pears. Methyl and ethyl-cinnamates provide sweet, honey notes and are associated with strawberry flavour.

Lactones

Due to their mostly low odour threshold values, averaging around 0.1 ppm, lactones have a high flavour value. Lactones are internally formed esters and in chemical equilibrium with their corresponding acids, 4-hydroxy acids transform into γ-lactones and 5-hydroxy acids transform into δ-lactones. Thus, during storage, the sweet, pineapple aroma of ethyl 5-hydroxyoctanoate and ethyl 5-hydroxydecanoate, changes into an intense coconut-like aroma as these hydroxy esters cleave to expose the carboxylic acid group and cyclise into their corresponding δ-lactones. In many dairy products, δ-lactones impart the distinct impression of sweet cream and milk. A butter-like note is imparted by δ-decalactone. Most δ-lactones are found in animal products, whereas γ-lactones preferentially occur in plants.

Various γ-butyrolactones have been identified in the volatiles of many foodstuffs (chicken, beef, apricot, passion fruit, raspberry, strawberry, raisins, plums, tomatoes, pineapple, citrus, coffee, tea, roasted onions, popcorn, roasted peanuts, cocoa, bread, beer, wine, vinegar and mushrooms), giving many individual flavours but especially a sweet roasted note. Peach flavour contains many lactones: δ-decalactone, γ-hexalactone, γ-heptalactone, γ-octalactone, γ-decalactone and γ-dodecalactone.

Furans

Occurring in the volatiles of all heated foods, oxygenated furans are usually formed from carbohydrates in the Maillard reaction. Furfurals and furanones generally impart caramel-like, sweet, fruity characteristics to foods. Described as burnt and caramel-like, 5-methylfurfural also produces a slight meaty flavour. A rum-like aroma comes from 1-(2-furyl)propan-2-one. Found in beef broth, pineapples and strawberries, 2,5-dimethyl-4-hydroxyfuran-3(2H)-one has a caramel-like, burnt pineapple-like aroma, which at low concentrations changes to a hint of strawberry.

Phenols

Ethyl, vinyl and methoxy-phenols are considered to be important contributors to off-odours in wine. Since volatile phenols are generally not present in grape juices, they must arise from the metabolism of some precursors. Two different pathways are involved: (i) the biochemical degradation of phenolic acids during yeast fermentation, and (ii) the chemical degradation of lignin from the storage barrels.

Lignin also provides phenols in smoked products via the slow burning of wood and makes a major contribution to the aroma of cured meats. Thus, smoked bacon and ham contain phenols arid guaiacols (methoxyphenols) which are responsible for their characteristic smoke flavour.

Many character-impact compounds of spices are phenols, for example, eugenol from cloves (both an alcohol and a phenol) and vanillin from vanilla (both an aldehyde and a phenol).

Terpenoids

Terpenoids are substances derived in nature from the metabolic intermediate, mevalonic acid, which provides the basic structural unit, the isoprene unit. Hemi, mono, sesqui- and di-terpenoids, having one, two, three or four isoprene units, respectively, are well-known, but it is the monoterpenoids that provide the character-impact flavours of many herbs, spices and citrus fruits. The terpenes (hydrocarbons) are found in the essential oils of most plants, but have little flavour of their own. Usually the oxygenated terpenes have flavour threshold values much lower than those of the hydrocarbons. The hydrocarbon terpenes may simply interact with the oxygenated terpenes as a solvent to enhance the ability of the flavour compounds to reach the organoleptic receptors.

Linalool, geraniol, nerol and citronellol are the monoterpene oxygen-containing derivatives that occur most abundantly in nature. Their esters and aldehydes are also common. All the natural compounds derived from linalool and citronellol exist in optically active forms of both enantiomeric series. The optically active forms differ in their odour qualities. (–)-Linalool is a component of basil aroma, whereas its enantiomer, (+)-linalool, is a component of volatiles from coriander. A more oxygenated derivative of linalool, dimethylocta-1,5,7-trien-3-ol, having an aroma similar to that of lime-tree blossoms, has been found in various grapes, wines and teas.

Sulphur-containing compounds

The sulphur group of any compound has a high flavour impact because it binds strongly to the olfactory receptors. For example, thiols have dramatically lower odour thresholds than their analogous alcohols. The potent character-donating constituent of grapefruit, 1-*p*-menthene-8-thiol, a sulphur-containing terpene, has the low threshold of 10^{-7} ppm.

At high concentrations, many sulphur compounds generate a stench aroma. These have been used to detect gas leaks, odourless natural gas is required by law to contain an odourant, such as tributylmercaptan or ethylmercaptan, so that people will recognise when the concentration of natural gas has reached dangerous levels.

Non-Volatile Flavour Compounds

Only a few volatile compounds are detected by the taste buds of the tongue or the inner lining of the mouth. Most receptors in the mouth elicit a response from non-volatile compounds, which must be carried physically via food or saliva to these receptors. Non-volatile compounds, by definition, cannot have an aroma, but they can be broken down to release volatile compounds, such as by the hydrolysis of terpene glycosides or the enzymatic cleavage of glucosinolates.

Amino acids and peptides

The dipeptide, aspartame (N-L-aspartyl-L-phenylalanine methyl ester), is a commercial low calorie sweetener that is 180 times sweeter than sucrose by weight. It has a clean, sweet taste without a bitter or metallic after-taste.

The amino acids alanine and proline are sweet but with a detectable bitter note. The amino acids phenylalanine, isoleucine and tryptophan are bitter. Amino acids and/or peptides formed from the degradation of milk proteins are primarily responsible for the bitterness found in dairy products.

Organic acids

Citric acid gives the tartness to citrus fruits such as oranges and lemons. Citric acid and malic acids give the fresh tartness to apples and tomatoes. In grapes, tartaric and malic acids are the major ones. Dairy products such as yogurt and buttermilk contain lactic acid.

Sugars

In green plants, the main carbohydrate which is translocated from one part of a plant to another is the disaccharide, sucrose. In ripening fruits, sucrose is rapidly converted by an invertase enzyme into glucose and fructose as soon as it enters the fruit. In fruits such as tomatoes, only 5–8 per cent of the fresh weight is solids and half of this is sugars. In storage roots such as potatoes, the sucrose has been converted into starch.

In citrus juices, sugars found in significant quantities are sucrose, glucose and fructose, in orange juice, they occur in the approximate ratio of 2:1:1. The total solids content (sugars represent 63–80 per cent) and the ratio of total sugars to total acids present in citrus juice are so important to the desirable flavour that these values are the primary criteria for determining legal maturity for oranges, grapefruit and tangerines in Florida.

Salts

Salts are ionic compounds that dissociate in water into anionic (–) and cationic (+) species. Cations are primarily responsible for salty taste, with sodium having the lowest threshold. However, table salt (sodium chloride) tastes saltier than other sodium salts, so the anion also exerts an effect on the taste buds. Potassium chloride is sometimes used as a salt replacer in low sodium foods, but it imparts a bitter flavour as well as being salty.

Flavonoids and alkaloids

Most flavonoids and alkaloids are bitter and/or astringent. Both flavonoids and alkaloids contain heterocyclic ring systems, with oxygen being the heteroatom in flavonoids and a basic nitrogen atom being the heteroatom in alkaloids.

Phenols

The compounds responsible for the well-known hot sensation of chilli peppers belong to a family of vanillylamides known as the capsaicinoids. These consist of a phenol, an amide linkage and a long-chain fatty acid of variable lengths. All three of these segments are necessary for the trigeminal nerve endings to be stimulated, that is, a compound must have all three chemical moieties to be perceived as hot.

Large or frequent doses of capsaicinoids reduce the sensitivity of an individual to subsequent usage (adaptation). This has caused problems with reproducibility in sensory evaluations. Capsaicinoids also affect thermoregulation—body temperature actually drops with small doses. This hypothennia is associated with increased perspiration, which is why hot foods are usually eaten in countries where the average temperatures are too high for comfort. Large doses of capsaicinoids, on the other hand, can cause desensitisation and thus allow overheating.

The two families of phenols, gingerols and shogaols, are responsible for the pungency of ginger and have similar structures. In fresh ginger, gingerols are the prominent species, while in commercial oleoresins, the shogaols are the major pungent phenols. The taste threshold pungencies of gingerol (17 ppm) and shogaol (7 ppm) are comparable to that of piperine (10 ppm), which is about 100 times less pungent than the capsaicinoids (0.06 ppm). The higher homologues, gingerols and shogaols, have a lower pungency which follows the same pattern as found among the capsaicinoids.

Flavour Development During Biogenesis

Many flavours, especially those in fruits and vegetables, are the secondary products of various metabolic pathways. Secondary metabolites can be distinguished functionally from primary metabolites, such as proteins, carbohydrates and lipids, in that they do not seem to have any direct physiological function. Secondary metabolites act as an interface between the producing organism and its environment, they may be produced to combat infectious diseases, to attract pollinators and to discourage or encourage herbivores. Secondary metabolites are often synthesised from primary metabolites. For example, alkaloids, flavonoids, phenols and other aromatic compounds can be synthesised from the amino acid primary metabolites phenylalanine, tyrosine and tryptophan.

Fruit flavours

All fruits share a very high proportion of the same volatile compounds. For example, of the 17 esters identified in banana volatiles, only five are not found in apples. Most volatile constituents in fruits contain aliphatic hydrocarbon chains or their derivatives (esters, alcohols, acids, aldehydes, ketones, lactones), with saturated ones predominating in apples, unsaturated ones predominating in pears and branched chains predominating in bananas. These constituents can be viewed as ripening products which develop from two different sources: fatty acids and amino acids.

Esters are by far the largest chemical category of volatiles from fruits. The apple, which has a prominent odour, largely produces and emits esters of relatively low molecular weight. Pear odours are more subtle and contain esters of higher molecular weight. The acidity in fruits is produced by the accumulation of the two citric acid cycie acids, citric and malic. Ripening is associated with a rapid decrease in the enzymes of the citric acid cycle, although more than half of the enzyme activity is lost, citrate actually increases at this time and malic decreases. This has been linked to the production of an nicotinamide-adenine dinucleotide phosphate (NADP)-linked enzyme which decarboxylates malic acid into pyruvate. The increased concentration of pyruvate induces citrate synthase to produce more citrate. This contributes to the increased respiration of carbon dioxide by fruits at the climacteric stage.

Vegetable Aromas

Most vegetable aromas develop during cellular disruption, which releases enzymes that act upon non-volatile precursors. Before the cell walls of the vegetable are broken, there is no aroma, the aroma compounds are chemically bound to precursor handles such as sugars (e.g. terpene glycosides) and amino acids (e.g. cysteine sulphoxides).

FLAVOUR DEVELOPMENT DURING FOOD PROCESSING

Sugar Thermal Breakdown — Caramelisation

When sugars are heated to 100–130°C, any bound water will be released, but without alteration to the molecular structure of the food. At temperatures between 150–180°C, a molecule of water is lost from the sugar molecule, giving an anhydride that can lose further water. This results in the formation of furfural from pentose or 5-hydroxymethylfurfural from hexose sugars. With prolonged high temperatures, caramelised flavours, including many furan derivatives, carbonyl compounds, alcohols and both aliphatic and aromatic hydrocarbons, are formed.

Caramelisation

In candy manufacture, sugars may be burnt intentionally to create flavours. For example, compounds such as maltol, furaneol, norfuraneol, isomaltol, cyclotene and maple lactones are produced during the boiling of maple sap to produce the typical flavour of maple syrup.

Amino Acid Thermal Breakdown

Enzyme activation

The flavour enhancer guanosine 5′-monophosphate (GMP) is rarely detected in raw vegetables. Rather, it is produced during the processing of vegetables from endogenous ribonucleic acid (RNA) which is hydrolysed by enzymes activated at temperatures of 65–75°C. Blanching and steaming of mushrooms (shittake), green beans and green bell peppers result in a high conversion of RNA into GMP, potatoes have an intermediate conversion and cabbage has no conversion of RNA into GMP.

Protein pyrolysis

The thermal decomposition of amino acids and peptides requires temperatures higher than those that are normally encountered during the cooking of foods. Only in surface areas of grilled foods, where localised dehydration allows the temperature to rise significantly above the boiling point of water, will decarboxylation and deamination of amino acids occur with the formation of aldehydes, hydrocarbons, nitriles and amines.

Maillard reaction

This is one of the most important routes to flavour compounds in cooked foods. The French chemist Louis Maillard first described this reaction between reducing sugars and amino compounds when he investigated the coloured compounds (melanoidins) formed in the heating of a solution of glucose and glycine. The Maillard reaction does not require as high a temperature as those associated with sugar caramelisation and protein pyrolysis. Even mixtures of refrigerated sugars and amino acids can show signs of Maillard browning over time. However, Maillard reactions proceed much faster at higher temperatures. Both browning and the formation of flavour compounds in foods generally occur at the high temperatures associated with cooking, evaporation, heat processing and drying. Reaction rates also increase with low moisture levels. Hence, flavour compounds produced by the Maillard reaction tend to be associated with the surfaces of the foods that have been dehydrated by the heat source.

The first step of the Maillard reaction involves the addition of a carbonyl group of a reducing sugar in the open chain form with the amino group of an amino acid or peptide (a primary amino group). The subsequent elimination of water results in a Schiff base. Water is the limiting factor and at this stage, the reaction is reversible. The Schiff's base cyclises to give the corresponding N-substituted aldosylamine. This is converted into the l-amino-l-deoxy-2-ketose by the acid-catalysed Amadori rearrangement. If a ketose, such as fructose, is involved instead of an aldose sugar, then a ketosylamine is formed. The ketosylamine undergoes the Heyns rearrangement to form a 2-amino-2-deoxyaldose. The Amadori and Heyns intermediates themselves do not contribute to flavour, however, they are important precursors of flavour compounds. They are thermally unstable and undergo dehydration and deamination to give a host of degradation products, including furans similar to those obtained in sugar caramelisation.

Strecker degradation

The Strecker degradation is one of the most important flavour reactions associated with Maillard browning. It produces little or no browning of foods itself, because it only involves the oxidative deamination and decarboxylation of an α-amino acid in the presence of a dicarbonyl compound. The Strecker degradation then leads to the formation of an aldehyde containing one fewer carbon atom than the original amino acid and an α-aminoketone. This is an important intermediate in the formation of several classes of heterocyclic compounds, including pryazines, oxazoles and thiazoles.

The aminoketone formed from cysteine is a powerful reducing agent and probably produces hydrogen sulphide by reduction of mercaptoacetaldehyde or cysteine. Alternatively, the break down of the mercaptoimino-enol intermediate formed by the decarboxylation of the cysteine-dicarbonyl condensation product yields hydrogen sulphide, ammonia and acetaldehyde with the regeneration of the original dicarbonyl compound. As hydrogen sulphide is important for the formation of many highly odouriferous compounds in eggs and meats, this emphasises the importance of cysteine in the development of flavours.

The Maillard reaction and associated Strecker degradation are still not fully understood. The subsequent and competing reactions produce a very complex picture, especially as products from one reaction become reactants for another. The amount and type of flavour compounds generated from the Maillard reaction vary with: (i) the type of amino compounds and sugars present in foods, (ii) the pH at which the reactions occur, (iii) the amount of water available, (iv) the presence of any salts that can buffer the pH, and (v) the length of time foods are held at specific temperatures.

Use of Biotechnology to Develop Flavours

Microbes

Fermentation has been practised for the production of food since ancient times. Yeasts have been utilised in brewing alcoholic beverages and in bread making. The major product of yeast metabolism is ethanol, but it also produces simple aliphatic and aromatic alcohols, fatty acid esters, carbonyls, lactones, thio-compounds and some phenolics. The ability of many yeast strains to form high concentrations of lactones has found industrial application. In yeast strains where b-oxidation results in reduced 3-hydroxylation of fatty acids and increased production of 4 and 5-hydroxylations, the cytotoxic effect of free fatty acids in the fermentation broth is reduced and high concentrations of triglycerides in the fermentation broth stimulate the formation of lactones. To increase yields, lactone bioreactors constantly remove volatile flavour products from the fermentation broth as they are produced.

During the ripening process of cheese, a number of enzymatic reactions are catalysed both by microbial enzymes and enzymes already present in raw milk. Milk fat, protein and carbohydrates are degraded to varying extents. These all give rise to a very complex mixture of compounds, some of which contribute to characteristic cheese flavours.

Plants

Through the use of plant tissue culture techniques, especially combined with normal genetic breeding techniques, cell lines of food plants (fruits, vegetables, spices and herbs) can be improved. The plant tissue techniques include: (i) micropropagation of plantlets, (ii) regeneration of plants from callus, (iii) protoplast fusion to produce new hybrids, and (iv) gene transfer.

Although used as much as a colourant than as a flavourant, saffron is one of the most expensive food additives used today. It is very slow-growing, has specific climatic restrictions and has so few stamens per flower. This plant is a good example of how plant tissue culture is being used because normal breeding is inefficient.

Much research has also been conducted to develop *in vitro* production of flavour compounds using suspended plant cell cultures. However, commercialisation of this technique has been hindered by the fact that it is usually cheaper simply to extract the intact plant for the flavour chemicals.

There are several problems associated with the large scale production of flavour compounds *in vitro*:

1. A superior high-yielding cell line is necessary, thus requiring considerable screening of parent lines and the development of analytical techniques for measuring yields.
2. The biochemical pathways of flavour production are not fully understood.
3. The synthesis and/or storage of flavour compounds may be in specialised cells or organs.
4. Culture medium is often expensive, also, because plants produce flavours as secondary metabolites, two media are usually needed.
5. Cytotoxic flavour compounds, which make the culture unstable, must be removed frequently to avoid low yields.
6. New equipment needs to be designed to address problems associated with plant cell shear sensitivity, oxygen transfer and cell aggregation.

Even with all these challenges, plant cell cultures have potential application in the marketplace. Industrial production of shikonin, a naphthoquinone, by a two-stage cell culture process by the Japanese was necessary (and successful) because domestication of the wild shikonin plant, *Lithospermum erthrorhizon*, failed.

Enzymes

In plants and microbes, the only bioconverters are enzymes. Enzymes, either in a crude or a purified form, have traditionally been used as processing aids in the food industry. Enzymes have a high catalytic activity towards a specific substrate and produce end-products under mild controllable conditions. But they do have limitations: (i) they are not stable under extreme conditions, (ii) they have limited substrates, and (iii) water must be present for their activity.

One of the very first *in vivo* usages of enzymes to produce flavours on a large scale is a product known as lipolysed milk fat. This product utilises lipases to liberate fatty acids and has found wide application for the enhancement of butter and cheese characters in dairy products and for flavour development in milk chocolate.

Enzyme modified cheeses (EMC) are products obtained by a controlled proteolytic and/or lipolytic enzyme treatment of a previously manufactured traditional natural cheese. The most important flavour reactions are the liberation of volatile fatty acids from milk fat and the degradation of casein into low molecular weight peptides and amino acids without bitterness development. After thermal inactivation of the enzymes, the EMC product obtained can easily have a flavour intensity 20 times greater than that of natural cheese. EMC is usually used internally in processed cheese manufacturing. In assessing the potential uses of enzymes for the production of flavour compounds, one should consider that in most plant tissues many flavour constituents are bound as glycosides. There is increasing industrial research activity being devoted to the isolation and separation of specific glycosidases from suitable sources. These should soon be available as processing aids to enhance the flavours inherent in many vegetables and fruits.

Chapter 24

Food Additives

INTRODUCTION

Food additives are substances added to food to preserve flavour or enhance its taste, appearance, or other qualities. Some additives have been used for centuries, for example, preserving food by pickling (with vinegar), salting, as with bacon, preserving sweets or using sulphur dioxide as with wines. With the advent of processed foods in the second half of the twentieth century, many more additives have been introduced, of both natural and artificial origin. Food additives also include substances that may be introduced to food indirectly (called 'indirect additives') in the manufacturing process, through packaging, or during storage or transport.

Food additives are utilised in the preparation and processing of almost all types of food in order to give favourable attributes to the food we eat. Very simply, it is a substance which is added to food to enhance its flavour, appearance, or other favourable quality. In fact, the food protection committee of the US national research council defined food additives as 'A substance or a mixture of substances other than a basic food stuff that is present in a food as a result of an aspect of production, processing, storage, or packaging'.

According to US FDA (Food and Drug Administration), a food additive is 'any substance, the intended use of which results or may reasonably be expected to result–directly or indirectly–in its becoming a component or otherwise affecting the characteristics of any food'. Although the term 'food additives' has been used frequently at present, its utilisation has been practiced since ancient times, and probably dating back to much earlier than the hunter-gatherer era. Even though food additives confer much benefit to all sectors, such as the manufacturers, retailers, and customers, utilisation of food additives must be carried out extremely cautiously. Additives, for the most part, are synthetic chemicals. Present day consumers are turning to natural ingredients and bio-based additives due to adverse effects caused by some chemicals. Therefore, plant-derived substances are gaining a foot hold as preservatives, colourants, flavours, and even as antibacterial agents.

Indirect additives, on the other hand, are those entering into food products in small quantities as a result of growing, processing or packaging. Examples of these are lubricating oils from processing equipment or components of packaging material that migrate into food before consumption.

Direct food additives are used in foods for six main reasons:

1. To ensure microbial safety (e.g. against botulism and listeria).
2. To maintain product consistency.
3. To improve or maintain nutritional value.
4. To extend shelf life (e.g. retard the onset of rancidity).
5. To facilitate food processing (e.g. provide leavening or control acidity).
6. To enhance flavour or texture or impart desirable colour.

The differences between food ingredients and additives are mainly that of quantity used in any given formulation. Food ingredients can be consumed alone as food (e.g. sucrose and butter), whereas food additives are used in small quantities relative to the total food consumption but which nonetheless play a large part in the production of desirable and safe food products.

E NUMBERS (INTERNATIONAL NUMBERING SYSTEM) OF FOOD ADDITIVES

Almost all safe-to-use food additives are given 'E numbers' by the European Food Safety Authority. In order to get to this status, the food additive must pass all the safety checks. Following are the general categories of food additives and their E numbers. However, when one food additive has more than one function, it is given only one E number. Chemical compounds and other species are constantly added to the list of safe-to-use food additives as the food additives pass the safety checks. An up to date list of food additives and their E numbers could be obtained from official UK food standards agency web sitehttps://www.food.gov.uk/science/additives/enumberlist#toc-1. The general list of E numbers of food additives is given in Table 24.1. Table 24.2 shows artificial flavouring agents and their flavours and Table 24.3 shows artificial flavour enhancers.

Table 24.1: E numbers of food additives.

Block of numbers	Food additives
E100-E199	Colours
E200-E299	Preservatives
E300-E399	Antioxidants and acidity regulators
E400-E499	Thickeners, stabilisers and emulsifiers
E500-E599	Anticaking agents
E600-E699	Flavour enhancers
E700-E799	Antibiotics
E900-E999	Glazing agents and sweeteners
E1000-E1599	Additional chemicals

Table 24.2: Artificial flavouring agents and their flavours.

Chemical	Odour
Diacetyl, acetylpropionyl, acetoin	Buttery
Isoamyl acetate	Banana
Benzaldehyde	Bitter almond, cherry
Cinnamaldehyde	Cinnamon

(Cont'd...)

Ethyl propionate	Fruity
Methyl anthranilate	Grape
Limonene	Orange
Ethyl decadienoate	Pear
Allyl hexanoate	Pineapple
Ethyl maltol	Sugar, cotton candy
Ethylvanillin	Vanilla
Methyl salicylate	Wintergreen

Table 24.3: Artificial flavour enhancers.

Acid	*Description*
Glutamic acid salts	This amino acid's sodium salt, monosodium glutamate (MSG), is one of the most commonly used flavour enhancers in food processing. Mono- and diglutamate salts are also commonly used
Glycine salts	Simple amino acid salts typically combined with glutamic acid as flavour enhancers
Guanylic acid salts	Nucleotide salts typically combined with glutamic acid as flavour enhancers
Inosinic acid salts	Nucleotide salts created from the breakdown of AMP, due to high costs of production, typically combined with glutamic acid as flavour enhancers
5′-Ribonucleotide salts	Nucleotide salts typically combined with other amino acids and nucleotide salts as flavour enhancers

FUNCTIONS OF DIRECT FOOD ADDITIVES

Direct food additives serve several major functions in foods. Many additives, in fact, are multifunctional. The basic functions are preservation, processing, appeal and convenience and nutrition.

Preservation

Food preservation techniques have advanced in the past 100 years and now include thermal processing, concentration and drying, refrigeration and freezing, modified atmosphere and irradiation. However, the use of chemical preservatives frequently augment these basic preservation techniques and represent the most economical way for food manufacturers to ensure a reasonable shelf-life for the product. Antioxidants and antimicrobial agents perform some of these functions as well.

Processing

Food processors are increasingly using food additives to insure the integrity and appeal of finished products. Emulsifiers maintain mixtures and improve texture in breads, dressings and other foods. They are used in ice cream when smoothness is desired, in breads to increase shelf life and volume and to distribute the shortening and in cake mixes to achieve batter consistency. Stabilisers and thickeners assist in presenting an appealing, consistently-textured product. Sorbitol, a humectant and sweetener, is used to retain moisture and enhance flavour. With the removal of sugar from many foods for dietetic reasons, a bulking agent substitute such as polydextrose is growing in importance.

Appeal and Convenience

The changing eating habits of consumers, partly brought about by the large increase in the percentage of women who work outside the home, is creating a growing need for convenience foods. In many of these types of foods, it is essential that a variety of additives be used to provide the taste, colour, texture, body and general acceptability that are required. This need for convenience, while maintaining aesthetic appeal and taste, is becoming extremely important. Most food additives such as gums, flavouring agents, colourants and sweeteners are included by food processors because consumers in the developed countries demand that food look and taste good as well as being easy and safe to serve.

Nutrition

There have been tremendous advances in knowledge of human nutrition and consumers are increasingly aware of the value of good nutrition. Vitamins, antioxidants, proteins and minerals are added to foods and beverages as supplements in an attempt to ensure proper nutrition for those who do not eat a well-balanced diet. In addition, additives such as antioxidants are often used to prevent deterioration of natural nutrients during processing. Recently there is more importance attributed to disease prevention through proper nutrition, as well as to increasing performance through sport nutrition products. On the other hand the medically based desire for good nutrition through a balanced diet may adversely affect consumer demand for some food additives such as fat substitutes.

TRENDS AND ISSUES RELATED TO FOOD ADDITIVES

While there are many differences in food tastes and preferences among the different regions of the world, the major trends driving the food additive utilisation appear to be very similar in all regions:

1. Concern over safety of processed food.
2. Health consciousness, desire for low-calorie foods.
3. Desire for convenience.
4. Desire by consumers, as well as food manufacturers, for value-added products.
5. Increasing regulatory constraints.
6. Shift from synthetic to natural or semi-natural-based products.
7. Increasing costs of new products in terms of R & D and product commercialisation.
8. Expansion of food service products (fast-food, airline meals, etc.).

New and improved technologies for the most part aim at processing and preserving fruits with minimal use of chemical additives. Aseptic packaging, controlled atmosphere packaging, irradiation and membrane separation/microfiltration processes are typical examples of this trend.

Conversely, microwave heating for both industrial and home use and extrusion represent technologies that are likely to stimulate expanded use of additives such as less volatile flavours more compatible with microwave heating and specialised blends of gums/emulsifiers for the reformulation of innovative extruded food products.

A shift away from commodity to more processed, higher value food products will favour increased use of food additives for processing. Increasingly, sales of ingredient-and-additive blends will dominate in the future. The synergistic effects that enhance the functionality of these materials while reducing the quantity needed will play an ever more significant role in formulated foods. Information on these blends will be scarce because they will be developed in-house by food additive suppliers as well as food manufacturers wishing to maintain confidentiality in order to optimise exclusive commercial benefit.

Other issues affecting the food additive industry include increasing government regulatory activity, increasing R & D and legal expenses and the great length of time needed to perfect, gain approval and market new food additive products.

COLOURS

According to the US FDA, 'A colour additive is any dye, pigment, or substance, which when added or applied to a food, drug or cosmetic, or to the human body, is capable (alone or through reactions with other substances) of imparting colour' . Food colours are used as food additives mainly to yield better sensory effects, specifically appearance contentment. The reasons for adding colours to food are manifold. First, colour may be lost due to the processing and storage conditions of food, and thus food colours are added to compensate such loss of colour. Second, food items with natural colours may show a variation of colour, and thus food colours are added to correct such variations in colour. Third, food colours may be added to further improve the natural colour of the food. Fourth, food colours are added to give colour to food items with no colour.

There are two types of food colours, certified colours and colours exempt from certification. The certified colours are synthetic compounds. They are usually more effective than natural compounds and they do not introduce off-flavours to the foods. Colours derived from natural sources are exempt from certification. These compounds are more expensive than synthetic compounds. Yet, the colours exempt from certification may give off-flavours to the foods.

Health effects of food colourants are a major concern among the consumers and regulatory bodies, and thus, carrying out toxicity studies determining health effects are considered very significant today. A recent study revealed that Allura Red AC lacks genotoxicity after the European Food Safety Authority showed its concern on this matter. In addition to toxicity studies, remedies for the adverse effects of food colourants are being evaluated. For example, Rafati and others demonstrated that the negative effects caused by tartrazine in mice could be mitigated by the simultaneous administration of vitamin E.

Although food colours are added to enhance organoleptic appeal of the foods, naturally occurring food colours such as curcumin and riboflavin possess other beneficial health effects. In fact, curcumin exhibits numerous bioactivities such as antioxidant, antimicrobial, and anticancer. Riboflavin, also, acts as an antioxidant, and it is linked to several health benefits. Numerous strategies have been explored to increase the stability of natural colourants due to beneficial health effects or general lack of toxicity of these compounds. As expected, novel sources of natural colourants are being explored due to the positive attributes of natural colourants. In addition, encapsulation techniques and other innovative methods are being explored in order to improve numerous properties of food colourants as opposed to directly add food colourants in food.

The list of colours usually used in food manufacturing is stated below.

List of colours: Curcumin, Riboflavin, Riboflavin-5'-phosphate, Tartrazine, Quinoline yellow, Sunset Yellow FCF, Orange Yellow S, Cochineal, Carminic acid, Carmines, Azorubine, Carmoisine, Amaranth, Ponceau 4R, Cochineal Red A, Erythrosine, Allura Red AC, Patent Blue V, Indigotine, Indigo Carmine, Brilliant Blue FCF, Chlorophylls and chlorophyllins, Copper complexes of chlorophyll and chlorophyllins, Green S, Plain caramel, Caustic sulphite caramel, Ammonia caramel, Sulphite ammonia caramel, Brilliant Black BN, Black PN, Vegetable carbon, Brown FK, Brown HT, Carotenes, Annatto, Bixin, Norbixin, Paprika extract, Capsanthin, Capsorubin, Lycopene, Beta-apo-8'-carotenal (C30), Ethyl ester of beta-apo-8'-carotenoic acid (C30), Lutein, Canthaxanthin, Beetroot Red, Betanin, Anthocyanins, Litholrubine BK.

PRESERVATIVES

Food preservatives have become an indispensible part of the food industry today. In simple terms, a food preservative is any substance that hinders food deterioration caused by microbes, enzymes, or any other chemical reaction. Millions of people suffer from hunger as a result of lack of enough food and thus, the advantages of using food preservatives in food processing are plenteous. Food preservatives along with other food additives are under strict control by numerous governing bodies.

Most artificial food preservatives impart negative health effects at high doses. For instance, *in vitro* studies have revealed that sodium benzoate and potassium benzoate exhibit genotoxic effects. However, this issue can be dealt with by adhering to the acceptable daily intake (ADI) values of food additives. Interestingly, despite showing adverse effects at toxic levels, some artificial food preservatives show favourable health effects at nontoxic levels.

Natural preservatives are an appealing alternative to artificial preservatives, especially with respect to health effects. A novel trend is to explore and utilise essential oils such as clove essential oil and eugenol extracted from cloves, limonene extracted from citrus fruits, and essential oil extracted from cinnamon as food preservatives of numerous food items including fresh cut produce, juices, and fish. As expected, encapsulated natural food preservatives including thyme essential oil and curcumin have shown favourable properties such as sustained release and enhanced antioxidant and antimicrobial properties. In addition to natural products, fermented milk products have shown promise as food preservatives. The reasons for utilising natural products and nonsynthetic products as food preservatives include imparting health benefits to the consumers and gaining 'clean label' advantage.

Numerous approaches are being taken to find novel food preservatives with ameliorated properties. For instance, peptides have been used successfully as potential food preservatives. Once a peptide food preservative is identified, mass production may be carried out using biotechnology. Combinations of food preservatives have also been studied to discover the combined effect and the possibility of substituting synthetic food preservatives by such combinations. For example, *Cuminum cyminum L.* essential oil and nisin have shown their ability to function as a hurdle against microbes.

Food Preservatives used in Food Manufacturing

Some food preservatives used in food manufacturing are listed below.

- Sorbic acid
- Potassium sorbate
- Calcium sorbate
- Benzoic acid
- Sodium benzoate
- Potassium benzoate
- Calcium benzoate
- Ethyl p-hydroxybenzoate
- Sodium ethyl p-hydroxybenzoate
- Sodium methyl p-hydroxybenzoate
- Sulphur dioxide
- Sodium sulphite
- Sodium hydrogen sulphite
- Sodium metabisulphite
- Potassium metabisulphite
- Calcium sulphite

- Calcium hydrogen sulphite
- Potassium hydrogen sulphite
- Biphenyl, diphenyl
- Nisin
- Natamycin
- Hexamethylene tetramine
- Dimethyl dicarbonate
- Potassium nitrite
- Sodium nitrite
- Sodium nitrate
- Potassium nitrate
- Propionic acid
- Sodium propionate
- Calcium propionate
- Potassium propionate
- Boric acid
- Sodium tetraborate, borax.

ANTIOXIDANTS AND ACIDITY REGULATORS

Antioxidants play a pivotal role in the food industry, combating oxidative stress on oxygen-sensitive species. The antioxidants used in the food industry are either hydrophilic, lipophilic, or amphiphilic, protecting various types of ingredients. Certain antioxidants function also as acidity regulators. Examples include ascorbic acid and citric acid. Acidity regulators are also an essential group of food additives as lowering the pH of the food usually assists to retard microbial attack.

Antioxidants

Although antioxidants are deemed to confer numerous health benefits to the humans, synthetic antioxidants such as butylated hydroxyanisole (BHA) and butylated hydroxytoluene (BHT) have shown negative health effects. On the contrary, some reports have shown chemoprevention properties of those synthetic carcinogenic antioxidants. Again, the issue of toxicity is dealt with by adhering strictly into the ADI published by the governing bodies worldwide including the US FDA. Although the results of synthetic antioxidants are inconsistent, numerous natural antioxidants have the ability to function as nontoxic anticarcinogenic compounds. Examples include ferulic acid, caffeic acid, curcumin, vitamin E, polyphenolic catechins, and carnosol.

As with other food additives, the trend is to utilise and seek for natural food antioxidants. Both pure antioxidants and plant extracts are used and explored these days. Moreover, encapsulation of pure antioxidants and plant extracts showing antioxidant properties is carried out to obtain improved attributes such as improved stability and sustained release of those bioactive compounds. The liposomal encapsulation of the *Schumacheria castaneifolia* methanol extract with antioxidant properties, which may be suitable for applications in the food sector, with high encapsulation efficiencies is an excellent example of encapsulating plant extracts.

Antioxidants used in Food Manufacturing

A list of antioxidants used in food manufacturing is stated below.

- Ascorbic acid, Sodium ascorbate, Calcium ascorbate, Fatty acid esters of ascorbic acid, Tocopherols, Alpha-tocopherol, Gamma-tocopherol, Delta-tocopherol, Propyl gallate, Octyl gallate, Dodecyl gallate, Erythorbic acid, Sodium erythorbate, Tertiary-butyl hydroquinone (TBHQ), Butylated hydroxyanisole (BHA), Butylated hydroxytoluene (BHT), Extracts of rosemary.
- 4-Hexylresorcinol.

Acidity regulators

Acidity regulators such as citric acid, tartaric acid, and phosphoric acid are numbered together with antioxidants in the E numbering system. This approach is very logical as certain acidity regulators, such as citric acid, exhibit antioxidant properties. In fact, citric acid has imparted favourable effects on food, functioning as an acidity regulator and antioxidant simultaneously. What's more, food acidity regulators have shown advantageous combined effects with other food additives on food. Antibrowning effect of citric acid together with ascorbic acid and nitrogen on banana smoothies is an example.

Acidity regulators commonly used in food manufacturing

The list of acidity regulators commonly used in food manufacturing is stated below.

- Sodium lactate, Potassium lactate, Calcium lactate, Citric acid, Sodium citrates, Potassium citrates, Calcium citrates, Tartaric acid [L-(+)], Sodium tartrates, Potassium tartrates, Sodium potassium tartrate, Phosphoric acid, Sodium phosphates, Potassium phosphates, Calcium phosphates, Magnesium phosphates, Sodium malates, Potassium malate, Calcium malates, Metatartaric acid, Calcium tartrate, Adipic acid, Sodium adipate, Potassium adipate, Succinic acid, Triammonium citrate, Calcium disodium ethylene diamine tetra-acetate,
- Calcium disodium EDTA.

THICKENERS, STABILISERS, EMULSIFIERS, AND GELLING AGENTS

Thickeners, stabilisers, emulsifiers, and gelling agents have become an integral part in the current food manufacturing industry. Thickeners increase the volume, change the viscosity, and increase the processability of the food items. Stabilisers, as the name implies, stabilise the food products, sometimes through the utilisation of fillers. Emulsifiers assist in the miscibility of otherwise immiscible substances possible. For instance water-in-oil or oil-in-water emulsions used in the food industry are made utilising emulsifiers. Gelling agents mainly contribute to the viscosity and sensory properties of the food products. In sum, all thickeners, stabilisers, emulsifiers and gelling agents contribute to the stability and palatability of the food product.

This category of food additives also consist of natural and synthetic compounds. In fact, lecithin that assists in emulsification and stabilisation for most food products is mostly extracted from soy bean, and thus it is a natural additive. However, numerous studies are being conducted evaluating the positive effects of synthetic lecithin. Alginate functioning as both a thickener and gelling agent is another natural food additive in this group. Apart from the natural compounds, synthetic emulsifiers such as polysorbates constitute an important component of this group. Although considered food grade, several health concerns have arisen regarding such artificial emulsifiers.

Thickeners-stabilisers-emulsifiers-gelling agents

A list of thickeners-stabilisers-emulsifiers-gelling agents used in food manufacturing are given below:

- Lecithins, alginic acid, sodium alginate, potassium alginate, ammonium alginate, calcium alginate, propane-1-2-diol alginate, agar, carrageenan, processed eucheuma seaweed, locust bean gum, carob gum, guar gum, tragacanth, acacia gum, gum arabic, xanthan gum, karaya gum, tara gum, gellan gum, konjac, soyabean hemicellulose, cassia gum, polyoxyethylene sorbitan monolaurate, polysorbate 20, polyoxyethylene sorbitan mono-oleate, polysorbate 80, polyoxyethylene sorbitan monopalmitate, polysorbate 40, polyoxyethylene sorbitan monostearate, polysorbate 60, polyoxyethylene sorbitan tristearate, polysorbate 65, pectins, ammonium phosphatides, sucrose acetate isobutyrate, glycerol esters of wood rosins, cellulose, methyl cellulose, ethyl cellulose, hydroxypropyl cellulose, hydroxy-propyl methyl cellulose, ethyl methyl cellulose, carboxy methyl cellulose,
- Cross-linked sodium carboxy methyl cellulose.

ANTICAKING AGENTS

As the name implies, the role of anticaking agents is to prevent lumping or caking in food. These agents are added mostly for powders or granulated material. Among the numerous advantages of using anticaking agents include: sustenance of sensory attributes, easiness of packaging, efficient transportation, and simplicity to yield high quality products for consumption. Depending on the food product involved, either water-soluble or organic solvent-soluble anticaking agents are used.

Anticaking agents used in food manufacturing

Anticaking agents frequently used in food manufacturing are stated below:

- Calcium aluminium silicate, calcium phosphate tribasic, calcium silicate, calcium stearate, cellulose, magnesium carbonate, magnesium oxide, magnesium silicate, magnesium stearate, microcrystalline cellulose, propylene glycol, potassium ferrocyanide, trihydrate, silicon dioxide, sodium aluminium silicate, sodium ferrocyanide.
- Decahydrate.

FLAVOURS AND FLAVOUR ENHANCERS

Flavours and flavour enhancers are of extreme importance in the food industry as it is what makes the food sensational. Flavour is perceived by the taste and smell via chemical senses. Also, the chemical irritants perceived in the mouth and throat, temperature and texture are factors affecting the flavour of a food. Now-a-days, both natural and artificial substances are used as food flavours Table 24.2. The basic universally recognised flavours include: sweet, sour, tangy, bitter, umami, hot, that can be perceived through the tongue. On the other hand, the number of sensations that can be perceived through the nose (smell) is limitless. As a result, the food industry is ever growing utilising different combinations of taste and smell. What's more, there is another group of chemical substances that do not impart any flavour in to the food product but enhance the existing flavour in the food Table 24.3. These flavour enhances are highly valued in the food industry as these substances contribute significantly into cost reduction in food manufacturing. Flavours and flavour enhancers frequently used in food manufacturing are stated. Flavours and flavour enhances also are evaluated for their health effects by numerous scientists worldwide. Further, extraction of numerous novel natural flavours is being carried out around the globe as a result of the higher inclination of the customers to such natural compounds. There has been much criticism on the health effects of glutamate—a much consumed flavour enhancer. However, mixed results have been published and there is no evidence to prove that glutamate possesses negative health effects, according to a recent report. Like almost all other food additives, encapsulation, for instance micro-encapsulation and emulsification, is used as means of enhancing the properties of food flavours.

ANTIBIOTICS

Antibiotics are being used in the food industry today to increase the shelf life of numerous food items, especially perishable food items including milk. Although not directly added during food processing, nonvegetarian food may contain a certain amount of antibiotics since antibiotics are frequently used in animal production. However, any antibiotic used for human therapeutic purposes or for animal feed additive are banned for use in the food industry. Tetracycline is a classic example. Maximum permissible amounts of such antibiotic residues have been declared and much emphasis is given to regular monitoring of antibiotic residues in food. Moreover, the antibiotics used in the food industry show slower activity than those used for therapeutic purposes.

Antibiotics used in Food Manufacturing

Antibiotics frequently used in food manufacturing are stated below.

- Nisin, natamycin, subtilin, tylosin phytoncides.

Phytoncides are antibiotics obtained from plants. Examples include: mustard oil, thyme, cinnamaldehyde, eugenol, etc. Antibiotics permitted as food additives are being experimented heavily, especially to engineer more potent variants. Further, encapsulation has become a common technique to enhance the desirable properties of antibiotics. For instance, coated liposomes encapsulating nisin has shown improved sustained release properties beneficial for applications in the food sector.

GLAZING AGENTS AND SWEETENERS

Glazing agents may be either natural or synthetic. They are used mainly for preservation of food items by forming a thin coat around it.

Glazing agents Frequently used in Food Industry

A list of glazing agents frequently used in food industry is stated below.

- Stearic acid, beeswax, candelilla wax, carnauba wax, shellac, microcrystalline wax, crystalline wax, lanolin, oxidised polyethylene wax, esters of colophonium, paraffin.

The most commonly used sweetener used in the food industry is sucrose as it is readily available. Thus, the performance of other sweeteners is frequently measured against that of sucrose. Glucose is also frequently used in the food industry, especially in the manufacturing of confectionaries. However, substitutes for common sugars, natural or artificial, are in high demand due to the prevalence of diabetes mellitus among a significant proportion of people worldwide. Other requirements for sugar substitutes include weight loss, dental care, and reactive hypoglycemia. In addition, using sugar substitutes is cost effective since the sugar substitutes are many times (sometimes more than 100 or even 1000 times) sweeter than sucrose.

Sweeteners Frequently used in Food Manufacturing

A list of sweeteners frequently used in food manufacturing is stated below.

- Erythritol.

- Sorbitol, sorbitol syrup, mannitol, acesulfame K, aspartame, cyclamic acid and its Na and Ca salts, lsomalt, saccharin and its Na - K and Ca salts, sucralose, thaumatin, neohesperidine DC, steviol glycoside, neotame (as a flavour enhancer), salt of aspartame-acesulfame, maltitol, maltitol syrup, lactitol, xylitol.

ADDITIONAL CHEMICALS

The European Food Safety Authority has grouped some food additives as 'additional chemicals' as those chemicals cannot be grouped together with other food additives. These chemicals are numbered from E1000 to E1599. Even though these chemicals may function as other food additives, they have different properties and thus treated differently. For instance, invertase having the number E1103 functions as emulsifiers-stabilisers-thickeners-gelling agents but is in a special category.

Other Chemicals Frequently used in Food Manufacturing

A list of other chemicals frequently used in food manufacturing is stated below.

- Polydextrose, polyvinylpyrrolidone, polyvinylpolypyrrolidone, polyvinyl alcohol, pullulan, basic methacrylate copolymer, oxidised starch, monostarch phosphate, distarch phosphate, phosphated distarch phosphate, acetylated distarch phosphate, acetylated starch, acetylated distarch adipate, hydroxyl propyl starch, hydroxy propyl distarch phosphate, starch sodium octenyl succinate, acetylated oxidised starch, starch aluminum octenyl succinate, triethyl citrate, glyceryl triacetate, triacetin, propan-1-2-diol, propylene glycol, polyethylene glycol.

REGULATIONS OF FOOD ADDITIVES

Food additives are under strict control of numerous governing bodies. In the European Union, the governing bodies are the European Food Safety Authority (EFSA) and the European Commission, Parliament and Council. These bodies are accountable for the safety assessment, which includes toxicological studies and dietary exposure assessment, authorisation which includes maintaining and publishing data bases of food additives permitted to be used in the EU, and control which is involved in legislation and labelling of food additives. The US. Food and drug administration (US FDA) is the main governing body of food additives in USA, and almost all other countries have their own governing bodies of food safety. Food and Agriculture Organisation (FAO) and the World Health Organisation (WHO) work together in the international arena via a Joint Expert Committee on Food Additives (JECFA).

Joint Expert Committee on Food Additives from 1961 has taken initiative of matters regarding the acceptable daily intake (ADI) level. 'ADI is a measure of the amount of a specific substance (originally applied for a food additive, later also for a residue of a veterinary drug or pesticide) in food or drinking water that can be ingested (orally) on a daily basis over a lifetime without an appreciable health risk'. 'ADIs are expressed usually in milligrams (of the substance) per kilogram of body weight per day.'

All of these food additives are used to fine tune the food items to yield a superb food product having sensational attributes. In addition, the preservative effect that the food additives impart is of utmost importance. Further, food safety governing bodies worldwide have set maximum levels to be used in the food industry for all approved food additives. Thus, health risk is at a low level. However, it is advisable to change ones diet time to time so that the subject is not exposed to the same food additives for lengthy periods of time. This practice also may not be essential if the customer pays attention to the recommended daily intake of the ingredients.

SECTION VII

Cleaning and Disinfection, Food Poisoning, Toxicity and HACCP

Chapter 25

Disinfection and Sanitation

INTRODUCTION

Disinfection, other than by heat, is ineffective unless all surfaces have previously been thoroughly cleaned to remove interfering materials. Cleaning is therefore extremely important as part of a two-stage cleaning and disinfection (sanitation) programme. The chapter describes the principles of sanitation, the chemicals and equipment involved, and the programme of events to be followed. For food products of 'low risk' (in terms of stable shelf life and safety), traditional sanitation programmes are adequate and in some cases disinfection may not be required. However, disinfection is essential for 'highrisk' food products, but this cannot be effectively undertaken without due consideration of hygienic design and possible cross-contamination. To ensure continued satisfactory performance of a sanitation programme, routine assessments should be undertaken.

The sanitation is undertaken primarily to remove all undesirable material (food residues, micro-organisms, foreign bodies and cleaning chemicals) from surfaces, in an economical manner and to a level at which any residues remaining are of minimal risk to the quality or safety of the product. Such undesirable material, generally referred to as 'soil', can be derived from normal production, spillages, line-jams, equipment maintenance, packaging or general environmental contamination (dust and dirt).

The products of the food industry fall into two broad categories according to the perceived risk. 'Low-risk' products include 'ambient shelf stable' products and products which require subsequent cooking prior to eating. 'High-risk' products include chilled products with a short shelf life and products which require no cooking prior to consumption.

For low-risk products, correctly-undertaken traditional sanitation programmes are cost-effective, easy to manage and can both increase product quality and reduce the risk of microbial and foreign body contamination. This chapter is intended to provide sufficient practical background knowledge to enable such a thorough sanitation programme to be undertaken.

For high-risk products with intrinsic demands for higher hygiene standards, traditional sanitation programmes have been shown to be unsuitable in some cases. The section on 'Requirements for sanitation of high-risk food production areas' may provide sufficient understanding of cross-contamination issues to ensure successful sanitation programmes which do not result in food product contamination.

SOILS

Throughout the production period, debris builds up on surfaces, requiring subsequent removal and control by sanitation programmes. This debris may result from normal production, spillages, line-jams, maintenance, packaging or general dust and dirt, and may include food residues, micro-organisms and foreign matter. In practical terms, a soil is anything in the wrong place at the wrong time (e.g. peas on a conveyor during production are 'product', but after production or on the floor they are 'soil').

A successful sanitation programme requires knowledge of the nature of the soil to be removed. The product residues are readily observed and may be characterised by their chemical composition (e.g. carbohydrate, fat or protein). In addition, different processing and/or environmental factors affecting the same product soil may lead to a variety of cleaning problems, primarily dependent on moisture levels and temperature. Higher temperatures for product soils usually entail a delay in initiating the sanitation programme (i.e. the drier and more baked the soil becomes, the more difficult it is to remove). Micro-organisms can either be incorporated into the soil or can attach to surfaces and form layers or biofilms. The fundamental means of micro-organism attachment to surfaces are well known. Although attachment to food production surfaces is not well documented, some reviews on this subject have been published.

In other disciplines, biofilms are envisaged as biological growths on surfaces - consisting (sometimes) of higher organisms, a multitude of microbial cells and extracellular polymers - which develop with time into thick biological films. However, in the food processing industry, the time frame for biofilm development is usually relatively short and varies with respect to temperature, nutrient supply and presence of antimicrobial agents. The term biofilm is therefore more associated with the surface attachment and growth of micro-organisms. The type of microbial species present is also extremely important. Relatively high levels of non-spoilage or non-pathogenic micro-organisms on surfaces may be tolerated, but the presence of food pathogens (e.g. *Salmonella* spp. or *Listeria* spp.) would generally be unacceptable.

Research at the Campden Food and Drink Research Association has demonstrated that, given complementary conditions of temperature and a nutrient source, micro-organisms will attach to and grow on a majority of the materials used in food manufacture, including stainless steel, aluminium, high-density nylon, polypropylene, polycarbonate and Polyvinylchloride. Field studies have also demonstrated that surface coverings in excess of 10^7 cells/cm^2 are readily apparent. Therefore, hygienic conditions pertinent to food processing surfaces are not concerned with whether micro-organisms can grow on surfaces or be found in product soils, but rather with whether their numbers can be reduced to a satisfactory level by sanitation programmes. This is especially true for the high-risk environments in which disinfection often plays a crucial role.

SANITATION PRINCIPLES

Soiling of surfaces is a natural process which reduces the free energy available within a system. To undertake a sanitation programme, energy must therefore be added to the soil to reduce both soil particle/soil particle and soil particle/equipment surface interactions. In addition, energy is required to remove micro-organisms remaining after the cleaning phase or to render these non-viable. Within the sanitation programme, the following stages have been identified:

1. The cleaning solution wets and penetrates both the soil and the equipment surface.
2. The cleaning solution reacts with both the soil and the surface to facilitate a number of processes: peptisation of organic materials, dissolution of soluble organics and minerals, emulsification of fats, and the dispersion and removal from the surface of solid soil components.

3. The dispersed soil is prevented from re-depositing back onto the cleansed surface.
4. The disinfectant solution wets residual micro-organisms to facilitate dispersion and surface removal, or the reaction with cell membranes and/or penetration of the microbial cell to produce a biocidal or biostatic action. Dependent on the disinfectant practice chosen, this may be followed by dispersion of the micro-organisms from the surface.

To accomplish these four stages, sanitation programmes utilise a combination of the four major energy factors described below. The proportion of these four factors varies for each sanitation programme, and if the use of one energy source is restricted, this shortfall may usually be balanced by increasing energy inputs from the other factors, as follows:

- Mechanical (or kinetic) energy.
- Chemical energy.
- Temperature (or thermal energy).
- Time.

Mechanical or kinetic energy is used to physically remove soils and may include manual scraping, brushing and wiping, automated scrubbing (physical abrasion) and pressure-jet washing (fluid abrasion). Of these four factors, physical abrasion is regarded as the most efficient in terms of energy transfer, while the efficiency of fluid abrasion and the effect of impact pressure have also been described. In cleaning, chemical energy is used to break down soils to facilitate removal, and to disperse and suspend the soils in solution to aid rinsability. In chemical disinfection, chemicals react with micro-organisms remaining on surfaces after cleaning to reduce their viability or affect their growth rate. The influence of detergency in cleaning and disinfection has been described.

The chemical effects of cleaning and disinfection increase linearly with temperature and approximately double for every 10°C rise. For fatty soils, temperatures above the melting point of the fats are used to break down and emulsify these deposits to aid removal.

For cleaning processes using mechanical, chemical and thermal energies, increasing the duration of action usually increases the efficacy of the process. When extended time periods can be employed in sanitation programmes (e.g. soak-tank operations), other energy inputs can be reduced (e.g. reduced detergent concentration, lower temperature or less mechanical brushing). Alternatively, for soils which are difficult to remove, cleaning efficiency in soak tanks is often improved by using higher temperatures than could be used manually and increasing the duration of soaking.

The retention of soil in cracks and the difficulty of cleaning inaccessible areas mean that routine cleaning operations are never 100% efficient. Therefore, over a course of multiple soiling/cleaning cycles, soil deposits (potentially including micro-organisms) will accumulate. As soil accumulates, cleaning efficiency will decrease and, for a period, soil deposits may grow exponentially (Fig. 25.1). The time scale for such soil accumulation will vary between processing applications and can range from hours (e.g. in heat exchangers) to, typically, several days or weeks. In practice, the build-up of soil is controlled by 'periodic' cleaning. Periodic cleans return the soil accumulation to an acceptable base level (Fig. 25.1) and involve increasing cleaning time and/or energy input (e.g. higher temperatures, alternative chemicals or extensive dismantling of equipment, typically at weekends).

A indicates the curve followed if periodic cleaning returns soil accumulation to an acceptable level (vertical sections on the A curve represent the effects of periodic cleaning), while B represents the situation with routine cleaning alone

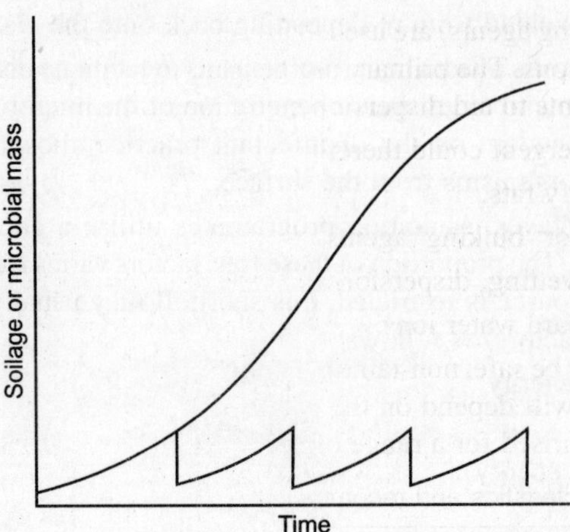

Fig. 25.1: Build-up of soilage and/or micro-organisms in food production areas.

CLEANING CHEMICALS

No single cleaning agent is able to perform all the functions necessary to a successful cleaning programme, and a cleaning solution or detergent is therefore blended from a typical range of characteristic components:

- Water.
- Surfactants.
- Inorganic alkalis.
- Inorganic and organic acids.
- Sequestering agents.

The range and purpose of chemicals used has been extensively documented, and only the principles are outlined below. Potable water is the base ingredient of all 'wet' cleaning systems, and provides the cheapest transport medium for rinsing and dispersing soils. Water has dissolving powers to remove soluble ionic compounds (e.g. salts and sugars), helps to emulsify fats at temperatures above their melting point and, in pressure-jet cleaning, can be used as an abrasive agent. However, water used on its own is a poor 'wetting' agent and cannot dissolve non-ionic compounds.

Organic surfactants (surface-active or wetting agents) are composed of a long nonpolar (hydrophobic) chain or tail and a polar (hydrophilic) head. Surfactants are classified as anionic, cationic or non-ionic, depending on their ionic charge in solution. Anionics and non-ionics are more commonly used than cationic surfactants. Amphipolar molecules aid cleaning by reducing the surface tension of water (thus increasing 'wettability') and by emulsifying fats.

Alkalis are useful cleaning agents, as they are inexpensive, and are able to break down proteins (through the action of hydroxyl ions) and saponify fats. At higher concentrations, alkalis may also be microbicidal. Alkaline detergents may be chlorinated to aid the removal of proteinaceous deposits, but chlorine is not an effective biocide at alkaline pH. The main disadvantages of alkalis are the potential to precipitate hard water ions, the formation of scums with soaps and poor rinsability. Acids have minor detergency properties, although they are very useful in solubilising carbonate and mineral scales (including hard water salts) and proteinaceous deposits. Acids also have microbicidal properties.

Sequestering agents (chelating agents) are used to prevent the precipitation of mineral ions by forming soluble complexes with these ions. The primary use of these agents is in the control of hard water ions, and they are added to surfactants to aid dispersion capacity and rinsability.

A general-purpose food detergent could therefore contain the following elements:

- A strong alkali to saponify fats.
- Weaker alkali 'builders' or 'bulking' agents.
- Surfactants to improve wetting, dispersion and rinsability.
- Sequestrants to control hard water ions.

The detergent should ideally be safe, non-tainting, non-corrosive, stable and environmentally friendly. The choice of cleaning agent will depend on the nature and solubility characteristics of the soil to be removed, and these are summarised for a range of food products in Table 25.1.

Table 25.1: Solubility characteristics and recommended cleaning products for a range of soil types .

Soil types	*Solubility characteristics*	*Recommended cleaning products*
Sugars, organic acids, salt	Water soluble	Mildly alkaline detergent
High protein foods (meat, poultry, fish)	Water soluble, alkali soluble, slightly acid soluble	Chlorinated alkaline detergent
Starchy foods, tomatoes, fruit	Partly water soluble, alkali soluble	Mildly alkaline detergent
Fatty foods (fat meat, butter, margarine, oils)	Water insoluble, alkali soluble	Mildly to strongly alkaline detergent
Heat precipitated water hardness, milk stone, protein scale	Water insoluble, alkali insoluble, acid soluble	Acidic detergent

Chemicals employed during the cleaning stage are responsible for the removal not only of soil but also of the majority of micro-organisms present. Cleaning may remove 2–6 log orders of micro-organisms, and therefore it is vital both to purchase a good-quality formulated cleaning product and to emphasise the importance of ensuring a successful cleaning operation.

Although most microbial contamination is removed in the cleaning phase, sufficient viable micro-organisms may remain on the surface to warrant the application of a disinfectant. Disinfection is undertaken to reduce further the surface population of viable micro-organisms, via removal or destruction, and/or to prevent surface microbial growth during the inter-production period. Heat is the best disinfectant, as it penetrates into surfaces, is non-corrosive, is non-selective to microbial types (higher temperatures are required for spores), is easily measured and leaves no residue. However, for open surfaces, the use of hot water or steam is uneconomical, hazardous or impossible, and reliance is therefore placed on chemical biocides.

This section is therefore restricted to discussion of the factors which control the efficiency of disinfectants. These can be summarised as follows: - interfering substances (primarily organic matter).

- pH
- Concentration
- Contact time.

The efficiency of all disinfectants is reduced in the presence of organic matter for two main reasons: chemical reaction and spatial non-reaction. Organic material may react non-specifically with the disinfectant such that the disinfectant loses its biocidal potency (this is particularly true for oxidative biocides). Other interfering substances (e.g. cleaning chemicals) may react chemically with the disinfectant and destroy its antimicrobial properties, for example, alkaline detergents will disable cationic quaternary ammonium compounds. In a non-reactive way, organic material may form a spatial barrier protecting micro-organisms from the effects of disinfectants (e.g. soil containing micro-organisms may be left in a crevice into which the disinfectant cannot penetrate). It is therefore essential to remove all soil during a comprehensive cleaning phase, and to remove all chemical residues via thorough rinsing, prior to disinfection.

Disinfectants may be affected by the pH of the water used for dilution, and only water within the pH range specified by the manufacturer should be used. For example, chlorine dissociates in water to form HOC1 and the OCI ion. At pH 3–7.5, chlorine is predominantly present as HOC1 or 'free chlorine', which is a very powerful biocide. However, above pH 7.5 the majority of the chlorine is present as the $OC1^-$ ion, which has approximately 1% of the biocidal action of HOC1. Chlorinated alkaline detergents should therefore not be considered biocidal by virtue of the chlorine content alone.

To be effective, disinfectants must find, bind to and traverse microbial cell envelopes before reaching their target site and beginning to undertake the reactions which will subsequently lead to the destruction of the micro-organism. Sufficient contact time is therefore critical to ensure disinfection, and most general-purpose disinfectants are formulated to require at least five minutes to reduce bacterial populations in suspension by five log orders. Five minutes is usually chosen as being representative of the time for which most disinfectants remain on non-horizontal food processing surfaces, although some biocides (including amphoterics and quaternary ammonium compounds) may attach to the surface to prolong contact time, and are claimed by the manufacturers to be 'surface active'. When microbial problems have been associated with a food product, food manufacturers may enhance disinfection by increasing contact time through the use of soak tanks or repeated surface dosing.

The relationship between microbial death and disinfectant concentration is not linear but follows a typical sigmoidal death curve. Microbial populations are difficult to kill at low biocide concentrations, but increasing the concentration leads to a point at which the majority of the population succumbs. Beyond this point, the micro-organisms become more difficult to kill (through resistance or physical protection) and a proportion may survive regardless of increases in concentration. It is therefore important that the disinfectant is used at the concentration recommended by the manufacturer. Changes to this concentration may not enhance effects, application of the disinfectant will never give rise to 'sterile' surfaces.

CLEANING EQUIPMENT

Cleaning and disinfection may be performed manually using simple tools (e.g. brushes or cloths). This form of cleaning is not susceptible to mechanical breakdown or error, is easily directed and is cost-effective for small areas. For operative safety, low levels of chemicals and low temperatures are used, and the major energy input is mechanical (e.g. the effort of the operator). As the area of open surface requiring cleaning and disinfection increases, manual cleaning becomes uneconomical with respect to time and labour, and onlyllight levels of soiling can be removed economically by this method. This is due to the labour cost, which usually represents 75% of the total cost of the sanitation programme. For most food companies, the cost of additional labour resources is prohibitive.

Specialist equipment therefore becomes necessary in the cleaning of larger areas, to rinse surfaces, dispense chemicals and/or provide mechanical energy. Chemicals may be applied as low-pressure mists, foams or gels, while mechanical energy is provided by high- and low-pressure water jets or electrically-powered scrubbing brushes. Alternatively, dismantled equipment and production utensils may undergo manual removal of gross soil, and may then be cleaned and disinfected automatically in tray or tunnel washers. As with soak tank operations, high levels of chemical and thermal energy can be used to cope with the majority of soils.

The differences between the mist, foam and gel techniques reside in varying abilities to maintain detergent/soil/surface contact time. For all three techniques, mechanical energy can be varied by the use of high- or low-pressure water rinses, while temperature effects are minimal for open-surface cleaning.

Mist spraying of chemicals is undertaken using small hand-pumped containers, knapsack sprayers or pressure washing systems at low pressure. Misting 'wets' nonhorizontal surfaces, only small quantities can be applied, as otherwise chemical solutions would quickly run off. This technique results in a useful contact time of ≤5 min. The tendency for aerosols to be formed using this technique (an operative safety hazard) means that only weak chemicals can be applied and the use of misting is therefore limited to light soiling. However, misting is the method most commonly used for applying disinfectants to cleaned surfaces. Foams can be generated and applied by the entrapment of air in high-pressure systems or by the addition of compressed air in low-pressure equipment. Foams work on the principle of forming a layer of bubbles above the surface to be cleaned. The outer film of the bubble holds the cleaning chemical and, as the bubbles collapse, the surface is wetted with fresh chemical solution. The crucial element in foam generation is for the bubbles to collapse at the correct rate: too fast and the contact time will be minimal, too slow and the surface will not be bathed with fresh chemical solution. When the rate is correct, contact times of approximately 15 min are possible on vertical surfaces. The use of thixotropic gels has recently been introduced, these are typically fluid at high and low concentrations but become thick and gelatinous at a concentration of 5–10%. These gels are easily mixed and applied through high- and low-pressure systems, foaming equipment, or portable electric pump units. In contrast to foams, gels physically attach to the surface, and when applied properly (so that the correct 'gelling' properties are obtained) gels will remain surface-bound almost indefinitely.

Foams and gels are more viscous than mists and are less prone to aerosol formation, therefore allowing the use of more concentrated detergents. These techniques are therefore able to cope with higher levels of soils than misting although, in some cases, rinsing of surfaces may require large volumes of water. Foams and gels are popular with operators and management, as a more consistent application of chemicals is possible and it is easier to spot areas which have been 'missed'.

Mists, foams and gels are removed from surfaces by low-pressure hoses operating at mains water pressure or by high-pressure/low-volume systems. Pressure washing systems may be mobile units (in which water is typically pumped at pressures of up to 100 bar [10^7 Pa] through a 15° nozzle), wall-mounted units (serving one or more outlets) or centralised units (where one unit may supply many outlets via a ring main). Water jets confer high mechanical energy, can be used on a wide range of equipment and environmental surfaces, are not limited to flat surfaces, will penetrate into surface irregularities, and are able to mix and apply sanitation chemicals.

Mechanical scrubbers for use on floors, walls and other surfaces include traditional floor scrubbers, scrubber/driers (automats) which vacuum up the cleaning solution, water-driven attachments to high-pressure systems, and electrically-operated smalldiameter brushes. Contact time is usually limited with these techniques (although this time can be increased), but the combination of detergency and high mechanical input allows these systems to tackle most types and levels of soil. As with other automatic techniques, mechanical scrubbers are popular with operators and the only real limitation is that food processing areas have not traditionally been designed for the use of such equipment. However, this can be amended in new or refurbished areas.

SANITATION PROGRAMMES

Sanitation programmes are designed to enable efficient use of water and chemicals, to allow selected chemicals to be used under optimum conditions, to ensure the safety of operators, machinery and products, to be easily managed, and to reduce manual labour and cleaning costs. In this way, an adequate level of sanitation will be achieved economically and with due regard to environmental pollution.

The sanitation programme forms part of a cleaning or sanitation schedule. The schedule should clearly illustrate each stage of the cleaning and disinfection process, all pertinent information on safety, and the key inspection points and means of assessment. A typical cleaning schedule includes the following:

- Description of all chemicals to be used (together with hazard code, in-use concentration, method of preparation, storage conditions and location, and amount for use).
- Information on sanitation equipment (type, use instructions, set parameters (pressure, nozzle type, etc.) maintenance instructions and location).
- Description of the equipment to be cleaned, need for maintenance fitters, and procedures for dismantling and reassembly of equipment.
- Full description of the cleaning process, frequency and requirement for periodic measures.
- Staff requirements and responsibilities.
- Key points for assessment of the sanitation procedure and description of evaluation procedures.

The principle stages involved in a typical sanitation programme are described below.

Step 1: Production Periods

Production staff should be encouraged to operate good cleanliness practices during production and leave their work stations in a reasonable condition (soil left on process lines is wasted product!). Such attention by production staff facilitates the job of the sanitation team, thus improving the quality and safety of the product.

Step 2: Preparation

After production, machinery should be switched off, and electrical and other sensitive systems should be protected from water or chemical ingress. Equipment should be dismantled as required, and unwanted utensils and equipment removed. Dismantled equipment should be stored on racks, tables or soak tanks - not on the floor!

Step 3: Gross Soil Removal

All loosely-adherent or gross soil should be removed manually by brushing, scraping, shovelling or vacuum suction, etc. Wherever possible, soil on floors and walls should be picked up rather than hosed into drains.

Step 4: Pre-rinse

Surfaces should be rinsed from the top downwards with low-pressure cold water, to remove loosely-adherent small debris. Hot water may be used for fatty soils, but too high a temperature may coagulate proteins, making these more difficult to remove.

Step 5: Cleaning

A selection of cleaning chemicals, temperatures and mechanical energy sources should be used to remove adhered soils.

Step 6: Intermediate Rinse

Soil which has been detached and dispersed by cleaning operations, and residues of cleaning chemicals, should be removed from surfaces by rinsing with low-pressure cold water.

Step 7: Disinfection

If necessary, depending on the food product and process involved, chemical disinfectants (or occasionally heat) are applied to remove and/or reduce the viability of remaining micro-organisms to a level of no significant risk.

Step 8: Final Rinse

Disinfectant residues should be removed by rinsing away with low-pressure cold water of known potable quality.

Step 9: Inter-production Cycle Conditions

Procedures should be undertaken to prevent the growth of micro-organisms on product contact surfaces prior to the commencement of the next production process. This may include procedures to control microbial growth (e.g. the removal of excess water and/or equipment drying) or prevent cross-contamination from other sources (e.g. the use of screens when cleaning adjacent production lines).

Step 10: Periodic Practices

Procedures should be undertaken at given time periods (e.g. weekly or monthly) to clean equipment more thoroughly than by daily cleaning. This normally involves additional dismantling of equipment and/or the application of increased cleaning energy. Periodic practices also include the cleaning of areas/items which are usually cleaned less frequently (e.g. ceilings and overhead fittings).

REQUIREMENTS FOR SANITATION OF HIGH-RISK FOOD PRODUCTION AREAS

The requirement to control specific pathogens (particularly *Salmonella* and *Listeria*) in high-risk food production areas has led to the examination of routes of product contamination which, although not specific to such manufacture, are particularly critical during the production of high-risk foods. The two major factors have been identified as hygienic design and cross-contamination.

Hygienic Design

Hygienic design is fundamental to the control of equipment and environmental contamination. Good hygienic design prevents the retention of product outside the main product flow during processing and the retention of product soils (including micro-organisms) after cleaning. Poor hygienic design is often characterised by rough surfaces, crevices and dead spaces, which can retain product residues. Equipment and other environmental surfaces which retain product after cleaning cannot be effectively disinfected (except by heat), and therefore contamination cannot be controlled. The principles of hygienic design are currently being established in Europe through a European Standards Technical Committee (CEN/TC 153) and an independent group, the European Hygienic Design of Equipment Group. Several articles on this subject have also been published.

The areas of hygienic design generally agreed to be of the most common concern for equipment and (where appropriate and using the same principles) environmental surfaces are as follows:

- Construction materials.

- Surface finish
- Joints
- Fasteners
- Drainage
- Internal angles and corners
- Dead spaces
- Bearings and shaft seals
- Instrumentation
- Doors, covers and panels
- Controls.

Hygienic design cannot be examined in full detail but, as an example, the importance of design can be demonstrated for meat slicing machines (Fig. 25.2). Several cases have occurred in the recent past in which *Listeria monocytogenes* has contaminated sliced meat products as a result of inadequate cleaning and disinfection of slicing equipment. This was due to both inadequate dismantling and poor hygienic construction.

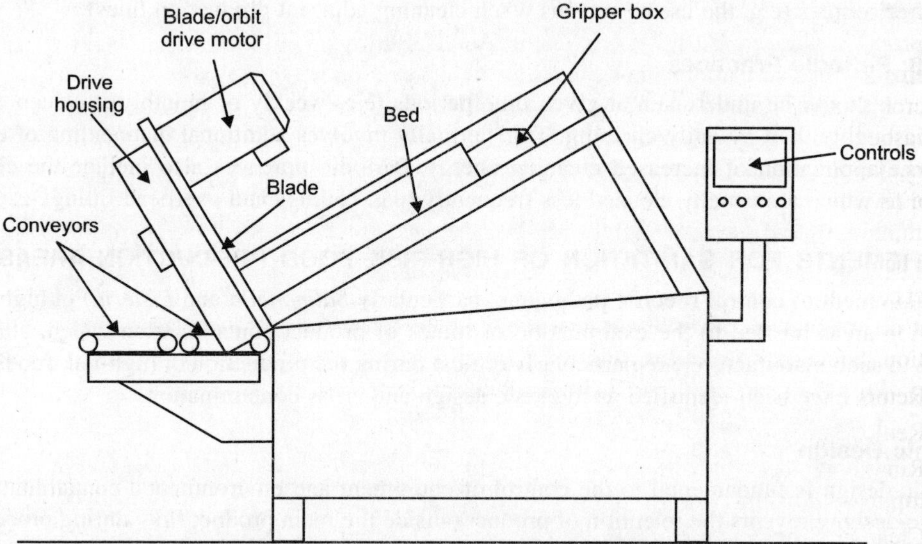

Fig. 25.2: Schematic side elevation of a typical orbital slicing machine.

Metal/metal or metal/plastic joints may be sufficiently tight to prevent the accumulation of product residues, but will allow the entry of micro-organisms which will thus be protected from subsequent sanitation programmes.

The hygiene implications of the design and use of cleaning equipment should be carefully considered and have been described by Holah and others. Smith and others found that cleaning equipment is the most likely source of environmental contamination with *Listeria* spp. and other pathogenic micro-organisms, and that such equipment, by the nature of its use, provides an efficient means of transferring contamination throughout the food processing environment. After use, therefore, cleaning equipment should be thoroughly cleaned, dried and, if appropriate, disinfected. The importance of hygienic design cannot be overstated. Regardless of the quality of the design and execution of the sanitation programme, contamination will never be controlled unless the areas in which soils may be present are exposed. Persons responsible for the management of sanitation programmes in high-risk food production areas must become familiar with the principles of hygienic design to ensure safe and wholesome food products.

Cross-contamination

The potential for cleaning equipment to disperse microbial and physical contamination by the formation of aerosols has been reported, and all cleaning equipment tested was shown to produce viable bacterial aerosols from experimentally contaminated test surfaces.

Given a typical food-contact surface height of 1 m, both high-pressure/low-volume (HPLV) and low-pressure/high-volume (LPHV) techniques were shown to disperse a significant level of aerosol to this height and therefore should not be used during production periods. Reducing water pressure or changing the impact angle made little difference to the degree of aerosol spread, and dispersal to heights of > 1 m was achieved under all test conditions. However, other techniques (including floor scrubbers, mechanically-driven brushes and manual techniques) were acceptable for use in 'clean-as-you-go' operations (which are to be encouraged), as the chance of contaminating products is low when using such methods. After production, HPLV and LPHV techniques may be safely used (and are likely to be the appropriate choice), but sufficient time must be allowed between cleaning and disinfection to ensure that aerosols have settled onto surfaces.

Microbial aerosols can also be generated by automated cleaning and disinfection systems (such as tray washers) and these should not be sited directly in high-risk production areas without physical barriers. Neither manual cleaning stations nor handwashing facilities are thought to produce significant aerosol levels.

To minimise the risks of cross-contamination within the sanitation programme, a sanitation sequence should be established for each processing area. A sanitation sequence determines the order in which the product contact surfaces (equipment) and environmental surfaces (walls, floors, drains, etc.) are sanitised, so that disinfected product contact surfaces are not recontaminated by cleaning aerosols. A typical sanitation sequence would be as follows:

1. Remove gross soil from production equipment.
2. Remove gross soil from environmental surfaces.
3. Rinse equipment and environmental surfaces (usually to a minimum height of 2 m for walls) from top to bottom, and flush to drain.
4. Clean environmental surfaces.
5. Rinse environmental surfaces.
6. Clean equipment.
7. Rinse equipment.
8. Disinfect equipment.
9. Rinse equipment.

If the principles of cross-contamination are understood by cleaning staff and management, it should be possible to undertake a sanitation programme to minimise the level of microbial and physical contamination on all product-contact surfaces within the food processing area prior to the commencement of production.

MONITORING OF SANITATION

Sanitation programmes may be monitored immediately by sensory evaluation, and historically (if the sensory evaluation is satisfactory) by microbiological methods. Sensory evaluations are used as a process control to immediately rectify obvious shortfalls in sanitation, while microbiological assessments are typically used to ensure compliance with microbial standards and optimise sanitation procedures. Methods have been developed to rapidly assess microbial surface populations and/or soil residuals in a time relevant to process control (usually taken as less than 15–20 min). This time scale is sufficient to allow a decision to be made on whether the sanitation programme should be repeated.

Sensory evaluation involves visual inspection of surfaces under good lighting, smelling for product or offensive odours, and feeling for greasy or encrusted surfaces. For some product soils, residues are observed more clearly by wiping the surface with paper tissues. If no product residues are detected, microbiological techniques may be used, these have been extensively reviewed and involve the removal or sampling of micro-organisms from surfaces (using sterile cotton or alginate swabs, sponges or rinses), which are then cultured using standard agar plating methods. Alternatively, micro-organisms may be sampled directly onto self-prepared or commercial ('dip slides') agar contact plates.

A range of rapid techniques is available but most of these are either research tools or are too expensive for routine use, and only the adenosine triphosphate (ATP) technique is regularly used. This technique is based on the assessment of levels of ATP present in animal, plant and microbial cells, via an enzyme-linked system which produces light in proportion to the concentration of ATP present. Surfaces are sampled by swabbing or rinsing, and addition of suitable reagents enables measurement of the level of ATP in approximately 5 min using a luminometer. In the majority of applications, analysis of total ATP is preferred on the assumption that any residues, soil or micro-organisms should have been removed.

Thus, when undertaken correctly - and following a strict sanitation programme determined by the hygiene requirements for the relevant food product - cleaning and disinfection return food production surfaces to a condition of minimum risk for subsequent food production. The acceptable level for numbers of micro-organisms remaining on a surface after cleaning will depend on the food product, the process, the 'risk area', the level of micro-organisms present before cleaning, and the degree of sanitation undertaken.

Given initial levels of 10^5 organisms/cm^2, recent studies in highrisk food production areas have shown reductions of approximately 5 log orders by the sanitation programme, and thus levels of <10 organisms/cm^2 should be obtained. Finally, even the best technical sanitation programme is only as good as the operators. Sanitation staff must therefore be adequately trained, and senior management must take full responsibility for the successful operation of the sanitation programme as, ultimately, failures in the programme usually reflect poor management.

Chapter 26

Food Poisoning

INTRODUCTION

Food poisoning syndrome results from ingestion of water and wide variety of food contaminated with pathogenic micro-organisms (bacteria, viruses, protozoa, fungi), their toxins and chemicals. Food poisoning must be suspected when an acute illness with gastrointestinal or neurological manifestation affect two or more persons, who have shared a meal during the previous 72 hr. The term as generally used encompasses both food-related infection and food-related intoxication.

Some microbiologists consider microbial food poisoning to be different from food-borne infections. In microbial food poisoning, the microbes multiply readily in the food prior to consumption, whereas in food-borne infection, food is merely the vector for microbes that do not grow on their transient substrate. Others consider food poisoning as intoxication of food by chemicals or toxins from bacteria or fungi.

Consumption of poisonous mushroom leads to mycetism, while consumption of food contaminated with toxin producing fungi leads to mycotoxicosis.

Some micro-organisms can use our food as a source of nutrients for their own growth. By growing in the food, metabolising them and producing by-products, they not only render the food inedible but also pose health problems upon consumption. Many of our foods will support the growth of pathogenic micro-organisms or at least serve as a vector for their transmission. Food can get contaminated from plant surfaces, animals, water, sewage, air, soil, or from food handlers during handling and processing.

CLASSIFICATION OF FOOD POISONING

Based on symptoms and duration of onset:

1. Nausea and vomiting within six hours (*Staphylococcus aureus*, *Bacillus cereus*).
2. Abdominal cramps and diarrhoea within 8–16 hr (*Clostridium perfringens, Bacillus cereus*).
3. Fever, abdominal cramps and diarrhoea within 16–48 hr (*Salmonella*, *Shigella*, *Vibrio parahemolyticus*, *Enteroinvasive, E.coli*, *Campylobacter jejuni*).
4. Abdominal cramps and watery diarrhoea within 16–72 hr (Enterotoxigenic *E.coli*, *Vibrio cholerae* O1, O139, *Vibrio parahemolyticus*, NAG vibrios, Norwalk virus).

5. Fever and abdominal cramps within 16–48 hr (*Yersinia enterocolitica*).
6. Bloody diarrhoea without fever within 72–120 hr (Enterohemorrhagic *E.coli* O157:H7).
7. Nausea, vomiting, diarrhoea and paralysis within 18–36 hr (*Clostridium botulinum*)

Based on pathogenesis:

1. Food intoxications resulting from the ingestion of preformed bacterial toxins. (*Staphylococcus aureus*, *Bacillus cereus*, *Clostridium botulinum*, *Clostridium perfringens*).
2. Food intoxications caused by noninvasive bacteria that secrete toxins while adhering to the intestinal wall (Enterotoxigenic *E. coli*, *Vibrio cholerae*, *Campylobacter jejuni*).
3. Food intoxications that follow an intracellular invasion of the intestinal epithelial cells. (*Shigella*, *Salmonella*).
4. Diseases caused by bacteria that enter the blood stream via the intestinal tract. (*Salmonella typhi*, *Listeria monocytogenes*).

BACTERIAL ETIOLOGY OF FOOD POISONING

Food infections by bacteria can be divided into two types:

1. Those in which the food does not ordinarily support the growth of pathogens but merely carries them, e.g. *Salmonella*, *Shigella*, *Vibrio*, etc.
2. Those in which the food can serve as a culture medium for growth of pathogens to numbers that can infect the person.

Food borne infections by bacteria can also be classified as toxicosis and food-infections. In toxicosis, the toxins are released by bacteria such as *Clostridia*, *Bacillus* and *Staphylococcus*. In food-infections, the bacteria are ingested, which later initiate the infection.

Staphylococcus Aureus

Staphylococcus Aureus is gram positive cocci that occurs in singles, pairs, short chains, tetrads and irregular grape like clusters. It is present ubiquitously in the environment. Only those strains that produce enterotoxin can cause food poisoning. Food is usually contaminated from infected food handler. The food handler with an active lesion or carriage can contaminate food.

Incriminated food: Custard and cream filled bakery food, ham, chicken, meat, milk, fish, salads, puddings, piec, etc.

Pathogenesis: If the food is stored for some time at room temperature the organism may multiply in the food and produce toxin. The bacteria produce enterotoxin while multiplying in food. *S. aureus* is known to produce six serologically different types of enterotoxins (A, B, C, C2, D and E) that differ in toxicity. Most food poisoning is caused by enterotoxin A. Isolates commonly belong to phage type III. These enterotoxins tend to be heat stable, with type B being most heat resistant. Low temperature heat inactivated enterotoxin can undergo reactivation in some food. Ingestion of as little as 23 μg of enterotoxin can induce vomiting and diarrhoea. *Staphylococcal* enterotoxins act as superantigens, binding to MHC II molecules and stimulating T cells to divide and produce lymphokines such as IL-2 and TNF-alpha, which induces diarrhea. The toxin acts on the receptors in the gut and sensory stimulus is carried to the vomiting center in the brain by vagus and sympathetic nerves.

Incubation period: Since the ingested food contains preformed toxin, the incubation period is usually 1–6 hr.

Clinical features: The onset is sudden and is characterised by vomiting and diarrhea but no fever. The illness lasts less than 12 hr. There are no complications and treatment is usually not necessary.

Laboratory diagnosis: The presence of a large number of *S. aureus* organisms in a food may indicate poor handling or sanitation, however, it is not sufficient evidence to incriminate a food as the cause of food poisoning. *Staphylococcal* food poisoning can be diagnosed if they are isolated in large numbers from the food and their toxins demonstrated in the food or the isolated *S. aureus* must be shown to produce enterotoxins. Dilutions of food may be plated on Baird-Parker agar or Mannitol Salt agar. Enterotoxin may be detected and identified by gel diffusion.

Bacillus Cereus

Bacillus Cereus is a gram positive aerobic spore bearing bacilli. It is found abundantly in environment and vegetation.

Incriminated food: Commonly associated with rice and vegetables.

Pathogenesis: During the slow cooling, spores germinate and vegetative bacteria multiply, then they sporulate again. Sporulation is also associated with toxin production. The toxin is heat-stable, and can easily withstand the brief high temperatures used to cook fried rice. The short-incubation form is most often associated with fried rice that has been cooked and then held at warm temperatures for several hours. Long-incubation food poisoning is frequently associated with meat or vegetable-containing foods after cooking. The short-incubation form is caused by a preformed heat-stable enterotoxin of molecular weight less than 5000 daltons. The longincubation form of illness is mediated by a heat-labile enterotoxin (molecular weight of approximately 50000 daltons), which activates intestinal adenylate cyclase and causes intestinal fluid secretion.

Incubation period: 1–6 hr in short-incubation form and 8–16 hr in long incubation form.

Clinical features: *B. cereus* causes two types of food-borne intoxications. The 'emetic-type' or the short incubation type has an incubation period of 1 to 6 hr. It is characterised by nausea, vomiting and abdominal cramps and resembles *S. aureus* food poisoning in its symptoms and incubation period. Within 16 hr of eating contaminated fried rice, patients suffer a bout of vomiting that generally lasts for less than a day. The second type is manifested primarily by abdominal cramps and diarrhea with an incubation period of 8 to 16 hr. Diarrhea may be a small volume or profuse and watery. This type is referred to as the 'long-incubation' or diarrheal form of the disease, and it resembles food poisoning caused by *Clostridium perfringens*. In either type, the illness usually lasts less than 24 hr after onset.

Laboratory diagnosis: The short-incubation or emetic form of the disease is diagnosed by the isolation of *B. cereus* from the incriminated food. The long-incubation or diarrheal form is diagnosed by isolation of the organism from stool and food. Isolation from stools alone is not sufficient because 14% of healthy adults have been reported to have transient gastrointestinal colonisation with *B. cereus*.

Clostridium Perfringens

It is a gram positive anaerobic spore bearing bacilli that is present abundantly in the environment, vegetation, sewage and animal feces.

Incriminated food: Food-borne outbreaks of *Clostridium Perfringens* involve meat products that are eaten 1–2 days after preparation. Meats that have been cooked, allowed to cool slowly, and then held for some time before eating are commonly incriminated. Fish pastes and cold chicken too have been incriminated.

Pathogenesis: Spores in food may survive cooking and then germinate when they are improperly stored. When these vegetative cells form endospores in the intestine, they release enterotoxins. The bacterium is known to produce at least 12 different toxins. Food poisoning is mainly caused by Type A strains, which produces alpha and theta toxins. The toxins result in excessive fluid accumulation in the intestinal lumen.

Incubation period: 8–24 hr.

Clinical features: Illness is characterised by acute abdominal pain, diarrhea, and vomiting. Illness is selflimiting and patient recovers in 18–24 hr.

Laboratory diagnosis: Since the bacterium is present normally in the intestine, their isolation from feces may not be sufficient to implicate it. Similarly, isolation from food except in large numbers (>105/g) may not be significant. The homogenised food is diluted and plated on selective medium as well as Robertson cooked meat medium and incubated anaerobically. The isolated bacteria must be shown to produce enterotoxin.

Clostridium Botulinum

It is a gram positive anaerobic spore bearing bacilli that is widely distributed in soil, sediments of lakes and ponds, and decaying vegetation.

Incriminated food: Most cases of botulism are associated with home canned or bottled meat, vegetables and fish. In general, the low and medium acid canned foods are often incriminated. The anaerobic environment produced by the canning process may further encourage the outgrowth of spores.

Pathogenesis: Not all strains of *C.botulinum* produce the botulinum toxin. Seven toxigenic types of the organism exist, each producing an immunologically distinct form of botulinum toxin. The toxins are designated A, B, C1, D, E, F, and G. Lysogenic phages encode toxin C and D serotypes. Food-borne botulism is not an infection but an intoxication since it results from the ingestion of foods that contain the preformed clostridial toxin. If contaminated food has been insufficiently sterilised or canned improperly, the spores may germinate and produce botulinum toxin. The toxin is released only after the death and lysis of cells. The toxin resists digestion and is absorbed by the upper part of the GI tract and then into the blood. It then reaches the peripheral neuromuscular synapses where the toxin binds to the presynaptic stimulatory terminals and blocks the release of the neurotransmitter acetylcholine. This results in flaccid paralysis. Even 1–2 μg of toxin can be lethal to humans.

Incubation period: 12–36 hr.

Clinical features: Common features include vomiting, thirst, dryness of mouth, constipation, ocular paresis (blurred-vision), difficulty in speaking, breathing and swallowing. Coma or delirium may occur in some cases. Death may occur due to respiratory paralysis within 7 days.

Laboratory diagnosis: Spoilage of food or swelling of cans or presence of bubbles inside the can indicate clostridial growth. Food is homogenised in broth and inoculated in Robertson cooked meat medium and blood agar or egg-yolk agar, which is incubated anareobically for 3–5 days at 37°C. The toxin can be demonstrated by injecting intraperitoneally the extract of food or culture into mice or guinea pig.

Enterotoxigenic E. Coli (ETEC)

E. coli are gram negative enteric bacilli that are carried normally in the intestine of humans and animals. Some specific serotypes harbour plasmids that code for toxin production. The enterotoxin production is limited to following O serotypes: O6, O8, O15, O25, O63, O78, O148 and O159.

Incriminated food: Infection is acquired by ingestion of food or water contaminated with ETEC. Contamination of water with human sewage may lead to contamination of foods. Infected food handlers may also contaminate foods. The infective dose is 10^6–10^{10} bacilli.

Pathogenesis: The bacteria colonise the GI tract by means of fimbriae to specific receptors on enterocytes of the proximal small intestine. Enterotoxins produced by ETEC include the LT (heat-labile) toxin and or the ST (heat-stable) toxin. LTs are similar to cholera toxin in structure and mode of action. LTs are holotoxin consisting of A subunit and B subunit. The B subunit of LTs binds to specific ganglioside receptors (GM1) on the epithelial cells of small intestine and facilitates the entry of A subunit where it activates adenylate cyclase. Stimulation of adenylate cyclase causes an increased production of cAMP, which leads to hypersecretion of water and electrolytes into the lumen and inhibition of sodium reasborption.

Incubation period: 16–72 hr.

Clinical features: Sudden onset of watery diarrhea associated with nausea, vomiting, abdominal cramping and bloating is commonly observed. This bacterium is responsible for majority of traveller's diarrhea. The disease is self-limiting and resolves in few days.

Laboratory diagnosis: The sample of feces is cultured on McConkey's agar. The ETEC stains are indistinguishable from the resident *E.coli* by biochemical tests. These strains are differentiated from nontoxigenic *E.coli* present in the bowel by a variety of *in vitro* immunochemical, tissue culture, or DNA hybridisation tests designed to detect either the toxins or genes that encode for these toxins. With the availability of a gene probe method, foods can be analysed directly for the presence of enterotoxigenic *E. coli* in about 3 days. LTs can be detected by Ligated rabbit ileal loop test, morphological changes in Chinese hamster overy cells and Y1 adrenal cells, ELISA, immunodiffusion, coaglutination, etc.

Enterohemorrhagic E. Coli (EHEC)

E. coli are gram negative enteric bacilli that are carried normally in the intestine of humans and animals. EHEC strains have been associated with many serogroups including O4, O26, O45, O91, O111, O145 and O157. The most serotype is O157:H7.

Incriminated food: Cattle appear to be the main source of infection, most cases being associated with the consumption of undercooked beefburgers and similar foods. This disease is often associated with ingestion of inadequately cooked hamburger meat, raw milk, cream and cheeses made from raw milk.

Pathogenesis: EHEC strains may produce one or more types of cytotoxins, which are collectively referred as Shiga-like toxins (SLT) since they are antigenically and functionally similar to Shiga toxin produced by *Shigella dysenteriae*. SLTs were previously known as verotoxin. The toxins provoke cell secretion and kill colonic epithelial cells.

Incubation period: 72–120 hr.

Clinical features: Initial symptoms may be diarrhea with abdominal cramps, which may turn into grossly bloody diarrhoea in a few days. There is however, no fever.

Laboratory diagnosis: Laboratory diagnoses involve culturing the faeces on McConkey's agar or on sorbitol McConkey's agar, where they don't ferment sorbitol. Strains can then be identified by serotyping using specific antisera. SLTs can be detected by ELISA and genes coding for them can be detected by DNA hybridisation techniques.

Vibrio Parahemolyticus

They are straight or curved gram negative halophilic bacilli. In morphology and staining it resembles *V. cholerae* and is actively motile in liquid cultures. It is commonly found in coastal seas, where it has been isolated from marine fauna such as crabs, shrimps, fishes and molluscs.

Incriminated food: Infections are associated with consumption of uncooked or undercooked crabs, prawns, shrimps and other seafoods.

Pathogenesis: No enterotoxin has been demonstrated in the bacterium. The infection is thought to result from invasion of intestinal epithelium.

Incubation period: 7–48 hr.

Clinical features: The clinical infection is characterised by a sudden onset of acute gastroenteritis. Infection may also result in diarrhoea, abdominal pain, vomiting and fever.

Laboratory diagnosis: Homogenised food may be inoculated into TCBS agar or into double strength alkaline peptone water and incubated overnight at 37°C. This bacterium is positive for Kanagawa phenomenon where isolates from human feces show hemolysis on blood agar. Salmonella enteritidis:

These are gram negative rod shaped bacteria that are classified under family enterobacteriaceae. This species does not occur normally in humans but several animals act as reservoirs.

Incriminated food: Most important sources are chicken and poultry. Chicken, duck, turkey and goose may be infected with Salmonella, which then find its way into its feces, eggs or flesh of dressed fowl. Milk and milk products including ice creams have been incriminated.

Pathogenesis: Organism penetrates and passes through the epithelial cells lining the terminal portion of the small intestine. Multiplication of bacteria in the lamina propria produces inflammatory mediators, recruits neutrophils and triggers inflammation. Release of LPS causes fever. Inflammation causes release of prostaglandins from epithelial cells. Prostaglandins cause electrolytes to flow into lumen of the intestine. Water flows into lumen in response to osmotic imbalance resulting in diarrhea.

Incubation period: 12–36 hr.

Clinical features: Sudden onset of abdominal pain, nausea, vomiting and diarrhea, which may be watery, greenish and foul smelling. This may be preceded by headache and chills. Other findings include rostration, muscular weakness and moderate fever. In most cases the symptoms resolve in 2–3 days without any complications.

Laboratory diagnosis: Homogenised food is cultured in selenite F broth and then sub-cultured on deoxycholate citrate agar. Plates are incubated at 37°C overnight and growth identified by biochemical tests and slide agglutination test.

Yersinia Enterocolitica

It is a gram negative psychrophilic rod shaped bacterium that is motile only at temperature below 30°C. *Yersinia enterocolitica* is widely distributed in environment and have been isolated frequently from soil, water and animals. The major animal reservoir for *Y.enterocolitica* strains that cause human illness is pigs, but may also found in many other animals including rodents, rabbits, sheep, cattle, horses, dogs, and cats. Serogroups that predominate in human illness are O:3, O:8, O:9, and O:5.

Incriminated food: Infection is most often acquired by eating contaminated food, especially raw or undercooked pork products. Drinking contaminated unpasteurised milk or untreated water can also transmit the infection.

Pathogenesis: This organism may survive and grow during refrigerated storage. Strains that cause human yersiniosis carry a plasmid that is associated with a number of virulence traits. Ingested bacteria adhere and invade M cells or epithelial cells. They exhibit resistance to complement and phagocytosis. They produce ST only at temperatures below 30°C. The role of ST in the disease process remains uncertain.

Incubation period: 4–7 days.

Clinical features: Disease produced by *Y. enterocolitica* is a typical gastroenteritis characterised by fever, abdominal pain, and diarrhea, which is often bloody. Illness generally lasts from 1 to 2 weeks but chronic cases may persist for up to a year. Apart from gastroenteritis it may also cause pseudoappendicitis, mesenteric lymphadenitis, and terminal ileitis.

Laboratory diagnosis: Suspected food is homogenised in phosphate-buffered saline and inoculated into selenite F broth and held at 4°C for six weeks. The broth is sub-cultured at weekly intervals on DCA or Yersinia selective agar plates. This is termed as cold enrichment technique.

Campylobacter Jejuni

These are small, curved-spiral gram negative bacilli with polar flagella. *Campylobacter jejuni* appear in comma, S-shaped or 'gull-wings/sea-gull' form. Campylobacter are harbored in reproductive and alimentary tracts of some animals.

Incriminated food: Transmission to humans occurs via a fecal-oral route, originating from farm animals, birds, dogs, and processed poultry, with chicken preparation comprising 50–70% of all campylobacter infections. The organism is transmitted to man in milk, meat products and contaminated water. Undercooked poultry and unpasteurised dairy are most often implicated as a source of *C. jejuni*.

Pathogenesis: As few as 500 organisms can cause enteritis. The organism is invasive but generally less so than *Shigella*. Campylobacter produces adenylate cyclase-activating toxins same as of *E. coli* LT and cholera.

Incubation period: Ranges from 2 to11 days.

Clinical features: Patients present with abdominal pain and cramps, diarrhea, malaise, headache, and usually fever. Typically the diarrhoea is watery, but in severe cases bloody diarrhea may occur. Diarrhea may last 2–7 days and the organism may be shed in the patients stool for up to 2 months. Bacteremia is observed in a small minority of cases. The disease is usually self-limiting.

Laboratory diagnosis: The feces may be inoculated in enrichment medium or on selective media such as Campy BAP or Skirrow's medium. The plates are incubated in microaerophilic conditions at 42°C for 2–5 days.

Chapter 27

Food Toxicity and Safety

INTRODUCTION

Until recently, eating food in modern industrialised countries has usually been regarded as a low risk activity, but several highly publicised food safety scares have raised consumer concerns about the safety of our food supplies.

Very few of the foods that we commonly eat have been subject to any toxicological testing and yet they are generally accepted as being safe to eat. However, all chemicals, including those naturally found in foods, are toxic at some dose. Laboratory animals can be killed by feeding them glucose or salt at very high doses and some nutrients such as vitamin A and selenium are hazardous at intakes only a few times greater than normal human requirements. Even very common foods such as pepper have demonstrated carcinogenic activity. Toxicity testing of a food or ingredient can tell us what the likely adverse effects are and at what level of consumption they may occur, but by itself this does not tell us whether it is safe to eat in normally consumed amounts.

'Risk' is the probability that the substance will produce injury under defined conditions of exposure. The concept of risk takes into account the dose and length of exposure as well as the toxicity of a particular chemical, and is a better guide to the safety of a food. Consequently, any attempt to examine the safety of the food supply should not be based on the question 'Is this food or ingredient toxic?' (the answer is always 'yes'), but rather by finding out if eating this substance in normal amounts is likely to increase the risk of illness significantly, i.e. 'Is it safe?'

Risks involved due to food toxicity is shown in Fig. 27.1.

HAZARDOUS SUBSTANCES IN FOOD

Three general classes of hazards are found in foods: (i) microbial or environmental contaminants, (ii) naturally occurring toxic constituents, and (iii) those resulting from intentional food additives or novel foods or ingredients. The most dangerous contaminants are those produced by infestations of bacteria or molds in food, which can produce toxins that remain in the food even after the biological source has been destroyed. Other contaminants, such as pesticide residues or heavy metals, are usually well controlled in modern food supplies but can be significant hazards in particular localities. Naturally occurring toxic

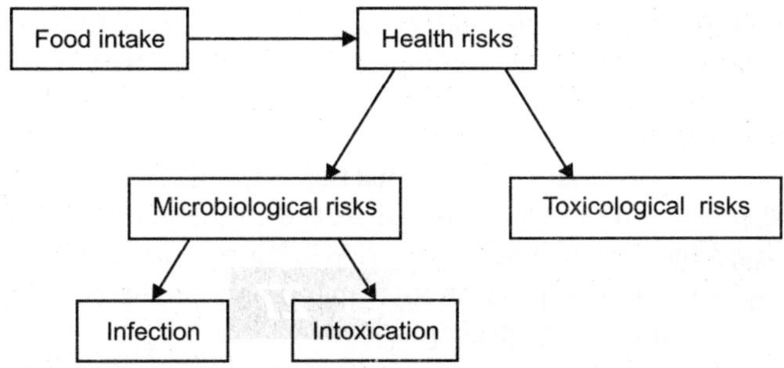

Fig. 27.1: Risks involved due to food toxicity.

constituents are usually present in doses that are too small to produce harmful effects when foods are eaten normally, except in the cases of a typical consumers who may be sensitive to individual ingredients. Food additives or novel foods are generally the least dangerous hazards because their toxicology is well studied and the conditions of use are tightly controlled.

The US Food and Drug Administration (FDA) has ranked the relative importance of health hazards associated with food in the following descending order of seriousness:

1. Microbiological contamination.
2. Inappropriate eating habits.
3. Environmental contamination.
4. Natural toxic constituents.
5. Pesticide residues.
6. Food additives.

This list is very different from that found in public opinion polls, which show that most people rate food additives as one of their major concerns about the safety of the food supply.

MICROBIOLOGICAL CONTAMINATION

Pathogenic Bacteria

Outbreaks of acute gastroenteritis caused by microbial pathogens are usually called food poisoning. They can be caused by foodborne intoxication (where microbes in food produce a toxin that produces the symptom) or foodborne infection (where the symptoms are caused by the activity of live bacterial cells multiplying in the gastrointestinal system). In general the intoxications have a more rapid onset.

The most important pathogens are *Clostridium botulinum*, *Staphylococcus aureus*, *Salmonella* species and *Clostridium perfringens*. The last three organisms account for about 70–80% of all reported outbreaks of foodborne illness, but there are also many others as well as some viral and protozoan agents. The four most frequently identified factors contributing to food poisoning incidents are: improper cooling of food, lapses of 12 hr or more between preparing and eating, contamination by food handlers, and contaminated raw foods or ingredients.

The reported incidence and cost of foodborne illness in most countries is increasing, although it is difficult to measure this exactly. It is estimated that less than 1% of cases are captured in existing notification schemes. Some of the reasons for increasing rates of foodborne illness are: new and emerging pathogens, changes in the food supply (including more intensive animal husbandry and longer shelf life fresh chilled products), ageing populations, and a greater proportion of food eaten away from home. Around 60–80% of foodborne illness arises from the food service industry.

Control of Food Poisoning

The trend in all countries today is to require more formal training of all food handlers and the development of food safety plans wherever food is prepared and served to the public, based on the principles of Hazard Analysis of Critical Control Points (HACCP). HACCP is a preventive approach to quality control, used worldwide in all segments of food production, from primary production, to food manufacture and food service settings. It is based on seven principles:

- Identifying all potential hazards at each step in the food chain and possible preventative actions.
- Determining the critical points in the operation where the hazards must be controlled.
- Establishing limits at each critical control point. Examples of control procedures are washing hands, sanitising food preparation surfaces and tools, cooking food to specific temperature, maximum food storage times.
- Setting up procedures to monitor each critical control point.
- Planning the corrective actions to be taken if a critical limit is exceeded.
- Establishing a recording system to document performance of the process.
- Verifying that the HACCP process is working.

HACCP are discussed in detail in Chapter 28.

Mycotoxins

Molds, or fungi, are capable of producing a wide variety of chemicals that are biologically active. Humans have used some of these as effective antibiotics, but there are also a number of diseases resulting from accidental exposure to fungal products that contaminate food. Some examples are as follows:

Aflatoxins: These are a group of highly toxic and carcinogenic compounds from the common. *Aspergillus* fungus species. They are stable to heat and survive most forms of food processing. Aflatoxin contamination can occur whenever environmental conditions are suitable for mold growth, but the problem is more common in tropical and semitropical regions. Aflatoxins were first recognised in the 1960s in peanuts. On a world-wide basis, maize is the most important food contaminated with aflatoxin.

Patulin is an antibiotic that is produced by the mold *Penicillium caviforme*. It has been implicated as a possible carcinogen from one study in rats although other studies have not confirmed this. Patulin in primarily associated with the apple rotting fungus and so apple juices and some baked goods with fruit can contain patulin.

Fumonisins are carcinogenic mycotoxins from the Fusarium fungus associated with corn. These were first characterised in 1988 and are known to be potent inhibitors of sphingolipid synthesis. Ingestion of fumonisin-affected corn has been shown to be carcinogenic in rats. In 1990 it was reported that use of moldy corn with high levels of fumonisins to make beer in the Transkei of South Africa was associated with a very high incidence of oesphageal cancer.

New Foodborne Diseases

Three of the most serious food pathogens today (*Campylobacter*, *Listeria* and *enterohemorrhagic*, *E. coli*) were unrecognised as causes of illness 45 years ago.

Some of the more important new organisms are:

Campylobacter jejuni was a well-known bacterium in veterinary medicine before it was identified as a human pathogen in 1973. It is now recognised as one of the most important causes of gastroenteritis in humans of similar importance to *Salmonella.* It is present in the flesh of cattle, sheep, pigs and poultry and can be introduced wherever raw meat is handled.

Listeria monocytogenes is a bacterium widely distributed in nature but is unusual in that it grows at refrigeration temperatures (down to 0°C). Listeriosis can cause abortions as well as death in the elderly and those with compromised immune systems, such as people with AIDS. Listeria has been linked to the consumption of contaminated pâtés, milk, soft cheese and undercooked chicken, and is often found in pre-prepared chilled food.

Escherichia coli 0157:H7 is a bacterium that can damage the cells of the colon, leading to bloody diarrhoea and abdominal cramps. Raw or undercooked hamburger meat was a major vehicle of transmission in a number of well publicised outbreaks in the USA in 1993 and contamined metwurst was responsible for a major outbreak of illness in Australia in 1995.

Salmonella typhimurium is a multi-drug resistant strain that has become a major pathogen in the UK in the 1990s. As well as being highly virulent it can survive at low pH and be infectious in very low numbers.

Norwalk virus is found in the faeces of humans and illness is caused by poor personal hygiene among infected food handlers. Symptoms include nausea, vomiting, diarrhoea, abdominal pain and fever. Because it is a virus, it does not reproduce in food, but remains active until the food is eaten.

'Mad cow disease' (or BSE -bovine spongiform encephalopathy) is a slowly progressive and ultimately fatal neurological disorder of adult cattle that results from infection by an unique transmission agent called a prion. Prions seem to be modified forms of normal cell surface proteins. BSE was first confirmed in Britain in 1986, but has now spread to cattle in other countries of Europe, Japan and North America. The same infective agent is also responsible for variant Creutzfeldt Jakob Disease (vCJD), a fatal disease of humans, mostly affecting young adults. By October 2009, it had killed 166 people in Britain and 44 elsewhere, with the number expected to rise because of the disease's long incubation period. Three principal controls have been put in place to keep infected meat out of the food chain: banning slaughter of beef aged over 30 months (before the age at which BSE typically develops), removal of parts of the body with the highest levels of infection (e.g. nervous and bone tissue), and a ban on feeding meat and bonemeal to any farmed livestock. Milk and gelatine products from beef do not appear to be affected.

ENVIRONMENTAL CONTAMINATION

Heavy Metals and Minerals

Selenium is one of the most toxic essential trace elements. The level of selenium in foods usually reflects the levels in the soil and in a few high-selenium areas, such as North Dakota and parts of China, excessive selenium intake has been associated with gastrointestinal disturbances and skin discolouration. In China in the early 1960s, selenium intoxication affected up to fifty per cent of the population in certain villages, with brittle hair, skin lesions and neurological disturbances the main symptoms.

Mercury: Fish can contain 10–1500 mg/kg of organic mercury, and even higher levels when mercury wastes are released into lake waters. Serious poisonings from mercury in fish have occurred in Japan, the most famous being that in Minamata Bay. Another example of widespread mercury intoxication occurred in Iraq in 1971/72 as a result of bread made from wheat treated with mercury-based pesticides.

Most countries have now established maximum permitted levels on mercury in fish in the range of 0.4–1.0 mg/kg. Cadmium is a toxic element that accumulates in biological systems. Chronic exposure at excessive levels can lead to irreversible kidney failure. Plants readily take up cadmium from the soil, and there has been a slow increase in the cadmium levels in soils due to the use of phosphate fertilisers and the affect of air and water pollution. The average food-based cadmium intake is now approximately 10–50 μg per day, which is approaching the provisional tolerable weekly intake. Measures to control cadmium contamination include controls on waste disposal, and developing new crops that accumulate less cadmium.

Criminal Adulteration

Modern food regulations began in the nineteenth century when there widespread examples of adulteration of foods to increase profits. Milk was diluted with water, cocoa with sawdust, and butter with borax. Today standards in the food industry are much higher and risks from illegal adulteration are rare. However, there are still some notorious instances.

In Spain in 1981 there was an outbreak of an apparently new disease characterised by fever, rashes and respiratory problems. Many thousands were hospitalised and over 100 people died. The agent responsible was identified as cooking oil that had been fraudulently sold as pure olive oil but in fact was mostly rapeseed oil intended for industrial uses, which was contaminated with aniline. In China in 2008, at least six children died of acute kidney failure and nearly 300000 fell ill after consuming tainted infant formula. Melamine, a synthetic nitrogenous product found in many industrial goods, was found to have been illegally added to milk-based foods to make them appear higher in protein than they really were.

Packaging Migration

The materials used to package food can sometimes result in contamination of the food itself. At one time the lead used in the solder of metal cans was a significant source of contamination of infant formulae, but this problem has been eliminated by the introduction of non-soldered cans. Bisphenol A (BPA) is an industrial chemical used as the starting material for the production of polycarbonate plastics and synthetic resins. BPA is found in containers that come into contact with foodstuffs such as drinking vessels, baby bottles, and the internal coating on cans for tinned food. BPA belongs to a group of substances that can act in a similar way to some hormones, and studies in laboratory animals suggest that low levels may have an effect on the reproductive system. In 2010, the FDA released a report on the safety of BPA, which raised concern about its potential effects on the brain, behaviour, and prostate gland in fetuses, infants, and young children. Subsequently manufacturers of baby bottles around the world have agreed to move to BPA-free bottles as soon as possible.

Industrial Pollution

Throughout the industrial era, many potentially hazardous substances have been released into the environment and are now widely distributed in the food chain. Among the most important are the polychlorinated biphenyls (PCBs). PCB is a generic term for a wide range of highly stable derivatives of biphenyl that have been used in a vast number of products, including plastics, paints, and lubricants. Although manufacture has now ceased, their stability and lipid solubility has meant that they accumulate in fatty tissue and they have become widespread, particularly in seafood. They can be found at low levels now even in human milk. The health effects of PCBs are not well established, although they are thought to be mild carcinogens. In one incident in Japan in 1978 when rice oil was contaminated with 2000–3000 ppm PCB, growth retardation occurred in young children and the foetuses of exposed mothers.

Radioactive Fallout

The most important dangerous radioisotopes in fall-out are strontium-90 and caesium-137, with half-lives of 28 and 30 years. Strontium is absorbed and metabolised like calcium and stored in bones. Because it is concentrated in milk it is particularly dangerous for infants and children. Since the Nuclear Test Ban Treaty of 1963, the level of radioactive contamination from atmospheric dust has markedly declined, but accidental exposure can still occur, such as that after the Chernobyl disaster, and lead to dangerous food contamination over widespread areas.

Changes during Cooking or Processing

Food is frequently exposed to high temperatures during cooking. In roasting and frying, localised areas of food may be subjected to temperatures that lead to carbonisation and under these circumstances any organic substance is likely to give rise to carcinogens. The major compounds are polycyclic aromatic hydrocarbons (PAH), produced mainly by burning of fats, and heterocyclic amines (HCA) produced from amino acids. Char-broiling or barbecuing is particularly likely to lead to carcinogen formation.

Acrylamide: In 2002 the Swedish National Food Authority announced that acrylamide could be found in starch-containing foods cooked at high temperatures, such as fried or roasted potato products, and cereal-based products including sweet biscuits and toasted bread. In 2010 a WHO expert committee determined that there is evidence that acrylamide can cause cancer in laboratory animals and, while there is currently no scientific evidence which links acrylamide with cancer risk in humans, all food regulatory agencies around the world are promoting a reduction in exposure to acrylamide in food by encouraging new technological strategies aimed at reducing its formation.

Irradiation can be used to sterilise foods, control microbial spoilage, eradicate insect infestations and inhibit undesired sprouting. Despite the great potential of the technology, there has been substantial opposition from consumer groups concerned about the process producing toxic chemicals in foods. Extensive studies have shown the products formed are no different from those produced in normal cooking and over 1300 studies have consistently found no adverse effects from feeding irradiated food to animals or humans. Food irradiation is approved by the WHO and currently more than 30 countries allow some form of use.

NATURAL TOXINS

Many plant species contain hazardous levels of toxic constituents. Intoxications from poisonous plants usually result from the misidentification of plants by individuals harvesting their own foods, but many ordinary foods also contain potential toxicants at less harmful levels.

Inherent Natural Toxins

There are many examples of potentially dangerous toxins in natural food products: cyanogenic glycosides in plants such as almond kernels, cassava and sorghum, alkaloids in herbal teas and comfrey, lathyrus toxin in chick-peas. In Japan the puffer fish, which contains a potentially fatal neurotoxin, is considered a delicacy and is consumed to produce a tingling sensation. However, natural toxicants are a generally accepted hazard because the foods that contain them have been eaten in traditional diets for many generations. We are protected from their harmful effects in three ways: avoidance, removal and detoxification.

Firstly, traditional knowledge has been passed down about which foods are safe and which are not. Thus we know it is safe to eat certain mushrooms and not others.

Secondly, traditional preparation methods have evolved to reduce harmful effects. Specialist chefs prepare puffer fish to remove the parts with the highest toxin concentration. People in South America and Africa use complex chopping and washing procedures in their preparation of cassava that removes much of the cyanide naturally found in the raw product.

Thirdly, the body has numerous detoxification systems, mainly enzymes in the liver, to deal with any toxins we do ingest. So we can still happily eat nutmeg and sassafras, even though both contain the naturally occurring carcinogen safrole.

Abnormal Conditions of the Animal or Plant used for Food

Some foods only become hazardous during particular conditions of growth or storage.

Ciguatera poisoning: This is serious human intoxication, caused by eating contaminated fish, causing gastrointestinal disorders, neurological problems and, in severe cases, death. There are over 400 species of fish that may become ciguatoxic, but almost all of the fatal cases are attributable to barracuda. The poisoning is particularly insidious because it occurs in tropical and subtropical fish that are normally safe to eat, but only when they have been feeding on certain dinoflagellates that produce toxins that accumulate in the flesh.

Paralytic shellfish poisoning: It has been known for many centuries that shellfish can occasionally become toxic. Symptoms include numbness of the lips and fingertips and ascending paralysis, which can lead to death within 24 hr. The poisoning, which primarily affects mussels and clams, occurs when dinoflagellates undergo periods of rapid growth (blooms, or red tides) in areas where the shellfish grow. The toxin cannot be removed by washing or destroyed by heat.

Glycoalkaloids in Potatoes: Solanine is one of a range of heat stable glycoalkaloid compounds found in the green parts of the potato plant that are toxic above concentrations of 20 mg/100g. In normal peeled potatoes there is about 7 mg solanine/100 g. Solanine synthesis can be induced by exposing the tubers to light and also by simple mechanical injury. In very green potatoes, the levels can reach up to 100 mg/100 g. These glycoalkaloids possess anticholinesterase activity which can produce gastrointestinal and neurological disorders, and deaths have occasionally been reported from consumption of excessive amounts of green potatoes.

Enzyme Inhibitors

Protease inhibitors: Substances that inhibit digestive enzymes are widespread in many legume species and trypsin inhibitors are found in oats and maize as well as Brussels sprouts, onion and beetroot. These inhibitors are proteins and therefore are denatured and inactivated by cooking. Thus for humans these substances are not a problem, although feeding raw legumes to animals can result in pancreatic enlargement.

Antivitamins

One of the best known antivitamins is the biotin-binding protein, avidin, in raw egg white. Biotin deficiency induced by eating raw egg white is rare because biotin is well provided in most human diets. The few cases that have been reported involved abnormally large amounts of raw egg white, so the occasional raw egg is perfectly safe. Avidin is inactivated when heated. Other antivitamins, such as the pyridoxine antagonist amino-*D*-proline in flax seeds and a tocopherol oxidase in raw soyabeans, are only of importance in animal feeding.

Mineral-binding agents

Goitrogens: There are a number of glucosinolate and thiocyanate compounds in foods that interfere with normal utilisation of iodine by the thyroid gland and can result in goitres. Goitrogens are widely distributed in cruciferous vegetables such as cabbage, Brussels sprouts and broccoli. The average intake of glucosinolates from vegetables in Great Britain is 76 mg per day and clinical studies have found that intakes of 100–400 mg per day may reduce the uptake of iodine by the thyroid.

There is no evidence that normal consumption of these foods by humans is harmful, but it is possible that eating large amounts of brassica plants might contribute to a higher incidence of goitre in areas where dietary iodine intake is low.

Phytate: In wholemeal cereals can bind minerals and make them less available for absorption. In leavened bread, phytases in the yeast break down the phytate, but in some parts of the Middle East, where unleavened bread is a dietary staple, phytate has been reported to be the cause of zinc deficiency.

Oxalate: Certain plants, including rhubarb, spinach, beetroot, and tea, contain relatively high levels of oxalate. Oxalate can combine with calcium to form an insoluble complex in the gut that is poorly absorbed and high intakes can lower plasma calcium levels. Kidney damage and convulsions can accompany oxalate poisoning. However, the average diet supplies only 70–150mg oxalate per day which could theoretically bind 30–70 mg calcium. Since calcium intakes are usually ten times this amount, food oxalates do not normally have any detrimental effect on mineral balance.

Tannins (polyphenols): These are present in tea, coffee and cocoa as well as broad beans. Tannins inhibit the absorption of iron and in Egypt, in children with low iron intakes, regular consumption of stewed beans has been associated with anaemia. High levels of tea consumption may contribute to low iron status in people with marginal iron intakes.

AGRICULTURAL RESIDUES

Pesticides

The most common agricultural chemicals found in foods are pesticides, albeit at very low levels. The chlorinated organic pesticides (such as DDT and chlordane) were among the first modern pesticides to be used. In general they have low toxicity to mammals and are highly toxic to insects. However they are very stable compounds, which persist in soils, and they are stored in the fat tissue of animals. Because of concern about their effect on the reproduction of certain birds and possible carcinogenic activity, use of these compounds has been restricted.

Surveys of foods show that the levels of organochlorine compounds have been in declining in recent years. Alternative insecticides now in use - such as organophosphates - do not accumulate in the environment. No food poisonings have ever been attributed to the proper use of insecticides on foods, but in 1997 there were 60 cases of food poisoning in India attributed to indiscriminate organophosphate spraying in a kitchen.

Fungicides and Herbicides

Most fungicides and herbicides show very selective toxicity to their target plants and therefore present very little hazard to humans. In addition, most do not accumulate in the environment.

Hormones

The use of hormones, such as bovine somatotrophin (BST), to improve yields of meat and milk has been controversial in many countries. Although low levels of BST can be detected in the milk of treated cows, the hormones are inactive in humans and are digested and inactivated in the stomach when consumed in food. The FDA approved the commercial use of BST in 1993 and later reviews by Canadian authorities and Codex Alimentarius have agreed that there are no health risks to humans. However in several countries BST use is not permitted on animal welfare grounds.

INTENTIONAL FOOD ADDITIVES

Approval Process for Food Additives

Each country has its own legislation to control the approval of additives in foods, but most follow the same general principles that are used by the two main international bodies of experts organised by WHO and the FAO: the Joint Expert Committee on Food Additives (JECFA) and the Codex Alimentarius Committee on Food Additives and Contaminants. The aim of the evaluation of a food additive is to establish an Acceptable Daily Intake (ADI). The ADI is usually expressed in mg/kg of body weight and is defined as the amount of a chemical that might be ingested daily, even over a lifetime, without appreciable risk to the consumer.

The evaluation process consists of a number of steps, as follows:

1. Toxicity testing is carried out in experimental animals usually mice and rats, but other species may also be employed. Three types of testing are performed: (i) acute toxicity studies at high doses to determine the range of possible toxic effects of the chemical, (ii) short-term feeding trials at various doses, and (iii) long-term studies of two years or more to examine the effect of exposures over several generations.
2. From the feeding trials, the level of additive at which observed health effects do not appear in the animals is determined. This is called the 'no observed effect level' (NOEL).
3. The lowest NOEL is divided by a safety factor to derive an exposure level that is regarded as acceptable for humans, the ADI. Most commonly a safety factor of 100 times is used, but for some substances factors of up to 1000 have been used. This safety factor allows for possible differences in susceptibility between experimental animals and humans and also the differences in sensitivity of individual people.

Not all additives have been evaluated for safety using modern testing procedures. Some have been used for many years without apparent harm and in the USA ingredients not evaluated by prescribed testing procedures can be classified as Generally Recognised As Safe (GRAS). This list includes common ingredients such as salt, sugar, seasonings and many food flavourings.

While the 100 fold safety factor is accepted for most additives, in the USA the Delaney Clause prohibits the use in any amount of substances known to cause cancer in animals or humans. When the bill was introduced in 1958, chemicals could be detected down to 100 parts per billion, anything less was considered zero. Improved analytical techniques can now detect substances at parts per trillion and there might be only trivial risks from such minute quantities. The FDA has now changed the interpretation of the clause so that if a food additive increases the chance of developing cancer over a lifetime by less than one case per million of cancer, the threat is considered too small to be of concern.

Artificial Sweeteners

Saccharin is one of the oldest artificial sweeteners, having been used in foods since the last century. Studies in rats have linked high doses (7.5% of the diet by weight) of saccharin with bladder cancer and because of this there have been attempts to ban its use in human foods. However at lower doses, such as one per cent, no adverse effects are found and large epidemiological studies of diabetics who have had lifetime exposure to saccharin have found no increased incidence of cancer in humans.

Cyclamate: Dietary cyclamate appears to promote bladder cancer and induce testicular atrophy in rats although carcinogenicity testing in mice, dogs and primates have all been negative. The US FDA banned the food use of cyclamate in 1969, but in over 50 other countries it is still a permitted sweetener, and there is no good evidence from mutagenicity testing or epidemiological studies that it is a health risk to humans. *Aspartame* is a dipeptide of two amino acids, phenylalanine and aspartic acid. Aspartame is metabolised to phenylalanine and therefore carries a risk for people with phenylketonuria, but for the normal population it is an extremely safe sweetener that is digested like any other protein.

Preservatives

Preservatives are used in foods as antioxidants and to prevent the growth of bacteria and fungi. Most pose no toxicological problems, but a few have generated some concerns.

Sodium nitrite is used as an antimicrobial preservative that is very effective in preventing the growth of *Clostridium botulinum,* as well as acting as a colour fixing agent (to preserve the red colour) in cured meat products such as bacon and ham. Nitrite reacts with primary amides in foods to produce *N*-nitroso derivatives, many of which are carcinogenic. However, the risk to human health from dietary nitrite is difficult to assess. While food additive nitrites are significant, a substantial amount is also produced by bacterial reduction from naturally occurring nitrate in vegetables. In recent years, manufacturers have worked to reduce the levels of nitrite used in cured meats, and have added agents such as ascorbic acid which help to prevent the formation of nitrosamines in the stomach. Sulphur dioxide and its salts (sulphites) are commonly used as inhibitors of enzymic browning, dough conditioners, antimicrobials and antioxidants. Although sulphites have been used for many centuries, with no adverse effect for most consumers, one to two per cent of asthmatics are sensitive to sulphites, and in those individuals the reaction can be fatal.

Colours and Flavours

All colours and flavours approved for use in foods are rigorously evaluated before being approved for use:

Red No 2 (Amaranth): In the early 1970s, data from Russian studies raised questions about Red No. 2's safety. The FDA Toxicology Advisory Committee evaluated numerous reports and decided there was no evidence of a hazard but concluded that feeding it at a high dosage results in a statistically significant increase in malignant tumours in female rats. The FDA ultimately decided to ban the colour, but it is still found in foods in Canada and Europe.

Yellow No 4 (Tartrazine): Food sensitivity to tartrazine can be experienced by a small number of individuals, but claims related to clinical problems such as asthma and hyperactivity are not well supported by scientific studies. Tartrazine is still a permitted additive, but its presence has to be declared in ingredient lists so sensitive individuals can avoid it.

Monosodium Glutamate (MSG): The flavour enhancer MSG is a sodium salt of glutamic acid, one of the most common amino acids. It is present in virtually all foods and found in high levels in tomatoes, mushrooms, broccoli, peas, cheese and soya sauce. Chinese Restaurant Syndrome has been claimed to be caused by foods with a lot of added MSG, but most controlled studies have not demonstrated this effect. Traditional methods for evaluating the safety of colours have not usually considered their potential behavioural effects. New research published in 2007 in the medical journal The Lancet, using a mixture of six permitted colours (sunset yellow, tartrazine, carmoisine, ponceau, quinoline yellow and allura red) at relatively high doses, concluded that there was limited evidence that these colours could effect the activity and attention of children in the general population. However the European Food Safety Authority concluded that uncertainties in the study meant there was insufficient evidence to change current permissions for use of these colours.

NOVEL FOODS

Technology now allows the development of many new ingredients or whole foods that do not have a history of traditional use in the human food supply. Many of these novel foods have been developed to have improved nutritional quality. Recent examples include genetically modified foods, artificial fat substitutes for energy-reduced foods, new algal sources of omega 3 fatty acids, and phytosterols to reduce cholesterol.

Approval Process for Novel Foods

There are significant practical difficulties in assessing the long term safety of modified whole foods or ingredients. Unlike additives, which can be fed at very high doses to assess their toxic effects, it is not possible to feed large amounts of one single food to animals without making their diet nutritionally unbalanced. Animals also prefer a mixture of foods and are likely to refuse to eat if offered a single food in large amounts. These difficulties, and welfare concerns about the use of animal studies that were unlikely to result in meaningful information, led to the development of the concept of 'substantial equivalence', particularly for the assessment of genetically modified (GM) foods.

This type of assessment does not quantify the safety or risk of a food, but aims to determine whether novel foods are as safe as traditional counterparts. For GM foods the process involves assessment and comparison of a wide range of factors including:

- Source and nature of any new protein.
- Stability of any genetic changes.
- Potential toxicity of the new protein.
- Levels of naturally occurring and newly introduced allergens.
- Nutritional composition.
- Levels of anti-nutrients.
- Ability of the food to support normal growth and well being.
- Potential unintended environmental consequences.

Genetically Modified Foods

Modern biotechnology now allows specific individual genes to be identified, copied and transferred into other organisms in a much more direct and controlled way. For example, genes for the enzyme chymosin from beef have been inserted into yeast, and the GM chymosin from these organisms has now widely replaced natural rennet from animals in cheese making. Genetic modification can also allow individual genes to be switched on or off: the gene that controls fruit softening can be repressed to maintain a higher solids content in tomatoes designed for use in tomato paste.

In 2009, 134 million hectares of GM crops were planted worldwide and 77% of all soya is now grown from GM varieties. Most plants have been modified for agricultural purposes: herbicide tolerant soya and canola and insect-resistant corn and cotton now make up the bulk of those crops in North America. There are many future uses planned that will bring more direct consumer benefits: oils with improved fatty acid profiles, rice with higher levels of vitamins, nuts with lower levels of allergens and potatoes that absorb less fat during frying. However, there has been concern expressed about the environmental impacts and safety of these novel foods, in particular related to the issues of allergenicity, toxicity of transgenic food and possible transfer of antibiotic resistance.

Genetic modification usually requires the introduction of the selected gene together with a marker gene. The marker genes are often antibiotic resistance genes that allow selection of the plants that have successfully integrated the new selected gene. Many have expressed concern that when the modified food is eaten the resistance gene might be transferred to bacteria in the gut and acquire resistance to clinically useful antibiotics. Although it has been estimated that the chances of this occurring are extremely small, the use of this method is now being phased out. Most countries have now established stringent approval processes for GM foods including mandatory labelling to inform consumers when foods include GM modified ingredients. Assessments to date have usually found GM foods to be as safe as their normal counterparts and there are likely to be increasing numbers of GM foods in the marketplace in the future.

Fat Substitutes

There are a number of fat substitutes now in use, including *Simplesse* (microcapsules of milk proteins or egg white), *Splendid* (derived from pectin), and *N-oil* (derived from tapioca). In the US *Olestra* - a mixture of heat stable sugar polyesters, that are not digested and yield no energy - has been controversial because it can reduce the absorption of fat soluble vitamins. The FDA approved use of Olestra in a limited range of foods in 1996, but required addition of vitamins A, D and K as well as further monitoring of the health impacts and warning labelling that it may cause abdominal cramping and loose stools. In 2003, after a scientific review of several post-market studies, the FDA concluded that the warning statement was no longer warranted. Olestra is not yet approved in the UK, Europe or Australasia.

Phytosterols

In many countries, plant sterols are now approved to be added to a range of foods to help lower blood cholesterol. They work by reducing the absorption of cholesterol from the gut, but have a side effect of also lowering absorption of carotenoids. A typical daily dose of 2–3 g per day can reduce serum beta-carotene levels by 20–25%. Safety reviews have concluded that since there is no evidence of reduction in serum retinol levels, this effect is not a significant health concern and that advice to maintain adequate fruit and vegetable intakes can ensure adequate carotene intakes.

Nanotechnology

Nanotechnologies are comprised of a range of technologies, processes and materials that involve manipulation of substances at sizes in the nanoscale range (from 1 nm to 100 nm). Food and drinking water naturally comprises particles in the nanometre scale. Humans ingest many millions of organic and inorganic nanoscale particles every day in their food and it is estimated that people inhale around 10 million nanometre scale particles in every breath. Generally, proteins in foods are globular structures 1–10 nm in size and the majority of polysaccharides and lipids are linear polymers with thicknesses in the nanometre range. Milk is an example of an emulsion of fine fat droplets of nanoscale proportions.

It has been claimed that some of the nanomaterials now being used in foods and agricultural products introduce new risks to human health because they may be absorbed more easily. For example, nanoparticles of silver, titanium dioxide, zinc and zinc oxide materials now used in nutritional supplements and food packaging. However it can be concluded that safety cannot be determined from the size alone, and it is novelty and not size which raises concern and which needs to be considered in undertaking risk assessments.

REGULATORY AGENCIES

One of the key roles of all regulatory agencies is risk assessment and management. Risk assessment is a scientific process consisting of four steps:

1. Hazard identification (biological, chemical or physical agents capable of causing adverse health effects).
2. Hazard characterisation (qualitative and quantitative evaluation of the hazards – in including dose-response effects).
3. Exposure assessment (the likely intake of the risk factor from food, taking into account typical dietary patterns).
4. Risk characterisation (estimating the probability and severity of potential adverse effects).

Risk management is the process of weighing policy options in the light of the risk assessment results and selecting appropriate control measures. Control options can include prohibiting certain substances in foods entirely (some carcinogenic herbs, for example), setting maximum permitted levels in foods (e.g. additives, or agricultural residues), through the development of codes of good manufacturing practice, labelling requirements (e.g. warnings about allergens) or by public education about safe use of foods (e.g. in relation to mercury in fish). Risk communication is the process of making the risk management information comprehensible to food producers, policy makers and consumers.

KEY POINTS OF FOOD TOXICITY AND SAFETY

Key points of food toxicity and safety are given below:

- Despite the many potential health risks associated with foods, in practice the degree of risk associated with the modern food supply is extremely low.
- By far the most important hazards of significance are those from biological agents: pathogenic bacteria, viruses, fungi and a few toxic seafoods.
- Trends to larger-scale production, longer distribution chains in the food supply, increased eating away from the home and the emergence of new pathogens means foodborne illness continues to be a significant public health issue.
- The assessment of the safety of food additives is led internationally by Joint FAO/WHO Expert Committee on Food Additives (JECFA), but each individual country still develops and determines their own local regulations and food standards.
- Genetically modified foods, novel foods and nano-materials pose new challenges for traditional safety assessment processes but, as the food supply becomes increasing global, food regulations about food safety are becoming more harmonised internationally.

Chapter 28

Hazard Analysis Critical Control Point

INTRODUCTION

Hazard Analysis Critical Control Point (HACCP) is a food safety system designed to identify and control hazards that may occur in the food production process. The HACCP approach focuses on preventing potential problems that are critical to food safety known as 'critical control points' (CCP) through monitoring and controlling each step of the process. HACCP applies science-based controls from raw materials to finished product. It uses seven principles standardised by the Codex Alimentarius Commission.

HACCP PRINCIPLES

HACCP plans are developed using the seven principles standardised by the Codex Alimentarius Commission. These seven principles are reflected in the HACCP plan steps. They cover repetition of food safety analysis and recording tasks to ensure product safety.

The HACCP plan must include:

- Preventative measures.
- Control limits.
- Monitoring procedures.
- Corrective actions.
- Record keeping.
- Ways to verify that control procedures are followed and areadequate.

Principle 1: Conduct a Hazard Analysis

A hazard analysis is the process of identifying and evaluating hazards. This means looking at agents that might affect a particular food product, or raw ingredient. It looks at how this happens in specific processing operations. A hazard analysis also includes collecting and evaluating information on each hazard. It examines the conditions that lead to hazards being present in food products and looks at how hazards increase.

A food safety risk assessment is then used to decide which hazards could affect food safety. It points out what should be dealt with in the HACCP plan.

Principle 2: Determine the Critical Control Points

A critical control point (CCP) is a point, step or procedure outside of the prerequisite programmes. It is a control measure used to prevent, eliminate, or reduce a hazard to an acceptable level. A CCP should be used at any point in a food safety system where loss of control could result in a health risk.

Correct determination of CCPs is very important for product safety. Decisions about CCPs involve (look at) places in the processing operation to prevent, reduce or eliminate the hazards noted.

A HACCP plan should determine CCPs based on each unique food product. This ensures that resources are focused in food safety risk areas.

Principle 3: Establish Critical Limits

Critical limits are hazard levels or standards that must be set for each CCP. Critical limits must be clearly defined and measurable whenever possible. For example a critical limit for a cooler might be that the temperature is 4°C or lower. Above or below these points, a product or process is unsafe.

Principle 4: Establish Monitoring Procedures

Monitoring means checking to ensure a CCP is under control. It is done by testing, observing, or other means. Methods to monitor each CCP should be put in place. Show that the critical limit(s) are being met. Monitoring procedures should be conducted on-line and should provide immediate results. This enables the facility to take corrective actions immediately if necessary.

Principle 5: Establish Corrective Actions

Corrective actions are taken when CCP monitoring shows that a deviation or loss of control has occurred at a CCP or when results are outside of critical limits. They should be planned out in advance to ensure that problems can be taken care of immediately.

Corrective action must not only be taken when monitoring shows that loss of control has already occurred, but also when production could cause unsafe food in the future. For each CCP, there must be planned, written corrective actions.

The purpose of corrective actions is to:

- Regain control of the hazard.
- Decide how to deal with the affected product.
- Prevent the problem from occurring again.

Principle 6: Establish Verification Procedures

Verification means to check on whether the HACCP system is set up correctly and is being followed. It involves tests, procedures and other means.

Principle 7: Establish Record Keeping and Documentation Procedures

Document all HACCP plans, including the prerequisite programmes. Make sure monitoring and verification records are complete. Check them for accuracy. Activities related to food processing should be documented to prove they are under control. Ensuring adequate and correct documentation will lead to efficient and economical operations. It means that food safety information is on file where staff can find it. It's important to encourage good record keeping by all employees. Records should be legible and completed at the times of checks.

HOW MANY HACCP PLANS ARE NEEDED?

Each food safety system is designed specifically for the facility where it is used. The same is true for HACCP plans. The number of HACCP plans a facility needs depends on:

- Number of products produced.
- Variations between products (e.g. different ingredients or equipment).
- Differences between production processes.

Sometimes it's necessary to group the facility's products into categories. Identify the differences between the categories. It may be necessary to have a different HACCP plan for each category. Similar products, with similar production processes and hazards, can use the same HACCP plan. However, if the facility produces similar products, with differing hazards (e.g. allergens), these products must be separated out. The facility will need to develop a distinct HACCP plan to deal with each different product.

Need for HACCP

In the past few years the food industry has faced new challenges such as the increasing number of emerging pathogenic bacteria (ex. *E. coli* 0157:H7), increasing public concern of chemical contamination of food (ex: lead in food, allergens). HACCP prevents and controls these and other major food safety concerns; minimising food safety risks of the product. HACCP allows food processors to offer a safer product to the consumers, protecting their health and life.

Benefits of HACCP

Although the main goal of HACCP is food protection, there are other benefits acquired through HACCP implementation, such as:

- Increase customer and consumer confidence.
- Maintain or increase market access.
- Improve control of production process.
- Reduce costs through reduction of product losses and rework.
- Increase focus and ownership of food safety.
- Increase business liability protection.
- Improve product quality and consistency.
- Simplify inspections primarily because of the record keeping and documentation.
- It is aligned with other management systems (ISO 22000).

Cost of Implementing and Operating HACCP

The cost of HACCP is dependent on the standard to which they operated prior to developing and implementing the HACCP system. Some of the costs involved during the implementation and maintenance of HACCP are as follows:

Implementation costs

- Consultant fees.

- Investment in new equipment.
- Staff training.
- Structural changes to the plant.
- Staff time in documenting the system.

Operational costs

- Record keeping.
- Product testing.
- Staff training.
- Managerial or supervisory time.

IMPLEMENTATION OF HACCP IN A FOOD PROCESSING PLANT

Food safety is of critical importance to the manufacturers of processed food products. No manufacturer wants to make or sell products which may be responsible for injury, illness, or death of a consumer. In addition, failure to assure the production and distribution of a safe food product can have disastrous economic consequences for a food manufacturer. An unsafe product which has harmed someone can result in legal actions by consumers and/or unwanted publicity that adversely affects a broad range of the company's products. Producing and selling an unsafe product may also result in regulatory actions and in the closure of the business. To avoid such possibilities and to fulfill their commitment to public welfare, food manufacturers devote significant resources to ensuring the production of safe food products. A tool which the food industry is adopting to aid in the production of safe foods is the Hazard Analysis Critical Control Point (HACCP) system.

The HACCP system was introduced to the food processing industry in the early 1970's. HACCP is a systematic approach to hazard identification, assessment and control. HACCP programmes identify the potential hazards which may be associated with a food from growth, through harvesting, processing, storing, and distributing to the consumers' hands.

A well-designed HACCP programme will minimise the risk of developing food safety problems. Because producing safe foods is so important, HACCP programmes must focus strictly on safety so that company management's clear message about food safety is not misunderstood by plant personnel and so that attention to safety does not become diluted by quality concerns.

Many manufacturers made attempts to implement HACCP in their facilities during the 1970's with the intent of assuring food safety. Almost all of those early programmes were discontinued because they failed to achieve any quantifiable objective. This may be due to the fact that these programmes often combined quality and regulatory programmes with HACCP, diluting out the focus on safety.

Such programmes typically had many more 'critical' control points (CCP's) than were needed to assure production of safe foods and were too cumbersome to be sustained over the long haul. Today, most manufacturers are faced with a multitude of safety, quality, and regulatory issues to monitor, but they may lack sufficient resources to monitor all points with the intensity warranted for safety assurance. Thus, unless the safety concerns are separated from quality and regulatory points and given the highest priority, they may not be given adequate attention, resulting in the potential production and release of hazardous food products.

HACCP is a management tool which focuses attention on food safety. A HACCP plan first identifies and assesses all the potential health risks that a particular food may present to the consumer. At this point expertise in food safety must be applied to discriminate between those risks which are significant and those which are so insignificant that they need not be included in the HACCP plan. This evaluation of potential risk must consider all risks associated with ingredients, production practices, and processes as well as storage, distribution, retailing, and consumer storage and use. The controls and monitoring necessary to minimise significant risks are then identified and implemented.

Criteria for selection of CCP's may differ depending on whether we are addressing a processed product, such as a precooked meat item, or a transformed/raw ingredient such as ground beef. In the case of cooked products, it is possible to eliminate pathogens during the cooking process. Thus, the goal in establishing CCP's for biological hazards for cooked products would be to eliminate contaminants and to prevent their reintroduction following cooking. But for a product such as raw ground beef, we cannot eliminate pathogens if present (unless the product is irradiated). The goal of our HACCP plan then is to minimise the possibility of contamination with pathogens and minimise their potential for growth. The individuality of each product and processing system must be considered in HACCP plan development. Thus, each product in a manufacturing plant will have its own HACCP plan tailored to its production system. The purpose of this paper is to present a step-by-step approach to implementing a HACCP programme in a food processing plant using a dry product as an example. Food manufacturers instituting a new HACCP programme will benefit by reviewing and understanding this process. Food manufacturers who already have a HACCP programme will benefit by assuring their programme is focused on safety and comprehensively covers all presented areas.

STEPS IN IMPLEMENTING A HACCP PROGRAMME

1. Gain management commitment. Senior management of a company needs to support food safety and implementation of HACCP in their processing facilities. They need to understand the benefits of HACCP as well as the commitment, costs, and implementation period for such a programme. For effective HACCP implementation, visible management support and commitment are of paramount importance.
2. Identify the HACCP team. After obtaining commitment from senior management, a HACCP team responsible for implementing the programme must be identified. The HACCP team should be multidisciplinary. The team should include, but not necessarily be limited to, members from manufacturing, sanitation, quality control, engineering, and research and development. Knowledge of ingredients, processing systems, potential hazards from operations, equipment, storage, and distribution rests with more than one individual or group. Evaluations of hazards, identification of controls and their limits, and developing the associated monitoring and documentation requires input from various disciplines. The HACCP team should be composed of members capable of providing this information. HACCP is a plant programme from conception to implementation and use. A common misconception is that HACCP is a quality control (QC) programme, and thus, a HACCP team should be staffed solely with QC personnel. With a team composed of QC personnel, the resultant HACCP programme is generally less effective than one which recognises the HACCP role and responsibilities of every person involved in food production. The intent of HACCP is not to increase inspections under the auspices of assuring safety; rather, the intent is to identify hazards and implement proper monitoring and control programmes to assure safety of the finished product by minimising or eliminating potential hazards during processing. The responsibility to monitor and control a particular safety point frequently rests with plant personnel other than QC; QC's role will be one of auditing and verification to assure compliance. For smaller food processors,

where broad expertise may not be available, HACCP experts or process authorities familiar with implementation of HACCP should be consulted. Such experts may be able to assist in identifying the best composition for the HACCP team as well as providing needed expertise in deficient areas.

3. Provide the HACCP team and line workers with training. One or more team member(s) should be trained in the principles of HACCP and its application or implementation. This member can then serve as a resource to other team members. During the early stages of implementation, line workers must also be trained relative to their roles in HACCP application. Since these are the people who actually have control of an operation, they must be included in the process in order to make HACCP work. The training programme should focus on the facility's products and be strongly applications-oriented. Participants should gain sufficient understanding to implement a HACCP programme. The training programme should focus on safety and should differentiate safety concerns from quality concerns and regulatory compliance. Training could be conducted by in-house HACCP experts, an outside HACCP course, or consultants brought in to aid in the implementation of the programme.
4. Utilise the following implementation guidelines. The guidelines prescribed by the National Advisory Committee on Microbiological Criteria for Foods (NACMCF) provide a general approach to implementation of a HACCP programme. Other references also are available which discuss various aspects of HACCP implementation. Adherence to the seven principles of HACCP identified by the NACMCF are recommended in developing the programme.

HACCP principles are already discussed in beginning of this chapter.

It should be noted that the specifics of HACCP are continuing to evolve. Much of the basic HACCP information is being reviewed by such groups as the Codex Committee on Food Hygiene and the NACMCF to address difficulties and to simplify and clarify the tenets. This is encouraging, as the refinements now being made will ultimately serve to improve worldwide understanding and acceptance of HACCP as well as to make implementation easier. While descriptions and various components such as risk assessment techniques may change, the basic tenets will remain the same. The comments below highlight the current NACMCF guidelines while expanding on various areas of the process and providing recommendations that may aid in successful implementation of specific items.

Describe the food and its intended use: Information on the formulation of the food, ingredients used, intended consumer, and any special handling required during ingredient receipt, processing, product storage and distribution, retail display, and consumer use will be important to the HACCP team as it makes its evaluations. Potential hazards of a biological, chemical and physical nature that are associated with the food, its ingredients, and their processing may vary depending upon a product's handling and intended use. Sensitive ingredients historically associated with known hazards must be identified. All of this information is necessary for the team to do a comprehensive evaluation. As an example, we have selected production of a dry product such as a cake mix. The mix is packaged dry into a retail-size box and is stored, distributed, and displayed at room temperature. The consumer will add liquid ingredients, mix, and bake. The primary hazards associated with the product are physical (foreign materials).

Perform a hazard assessment (ingredient and finished product): The perceived safety hazards associated with any step, point, or procedure in the process need to be identified. These would include biological, physical, or chemical hazards. The team should first list all perceived safety hazards without regard to the probability of occurrence or their severity. As noted previously, the primary hazards in our example are physical - foreign material - although there may be chemical hazards such as fungicides applied in the field. The team should then assess the risk associated with each hazard. The risk assessment should be directed at quantifying or qualifying the risk associated with each potential hazard, whether it be of a biological, chemical, or physical nature. Those hazards that would lead to a reasonable probability of an unacceptable consumer health risk need to be prevented, eliminated, or reduced to acceptable levels. Any point or procedure in the process where loss of control may result in an unacceptable health risk is defined as a critical control point (CCP).

Critical control points are differentiated from control points (CP's), which are points where loss of control will not result in an unacceptable health risk. Control points are generally nonsafety points related to product quality or regulatory compliance; while important, they are not regarded as part of a HACCP programme. If a CP is repeatedly violated or several related CP's are simultaneously violated, the situation may warrant placing the affected product on hold.

Role of the HACCP Team

The role of the HACCP team in assessing hazards is to:

1. Assess and recognise potential hazards in ingredients and products based on historical information.
2. Determine if the process contains a controllable step that could eliminate or minimise the hazard.
3. Determine the risk of postprocess contamination or the hazard being reintroduced into the product.
4. Determine the risk of mishandling during storage, distribution, retail display, or by the consumer that may render the product harmful.
5. Determine the presence of a terminal heat treatment that may influence the risk to the consumer.

The above considerations allow the HACCP team to identify areas in which hazards in the food system can be reduced. This analysis may result in changing the form of an ingredient (e.g. fresh to canned), or changing a step in the manufacturing process (e.g. chilled to frozen) to reduce the risk. A modification of this model has been developed for risk assessment of chemical and physical hazards. The HACCP team should determine the method by which it wants to do a hazard analysis.

For ingredients, potential hazards need to be identified. Ideally, the ingredients as delivered to the manufacturer will be free of chemical, physical, and biological hazards. The suppliers of ingredients should be contacted to determine the existence and adequacy of their HACCP programmes. To verify the acceptability of a supplier's HACCP programme, it should be reviewed on paper, the plant may be visited, and the HACCP programme audited. Collaborative studies on analytical tests to verify accuracy may also need to be performed.

If the above are acceptable, an occasional random audit of the supplier's programme is suggested to verify continued acceptability. If the supplier lacks a HACCP programme, control of the hazards associated with the ingredient relies on the following steps: ingredient specifications, letters of guarantee, vendor visits (if possible), vendor record review, and statistical lot acceptance testing for hazards. As the supplier develops a HACCP programme, lot acceptance testing would be replaced by a reduced frequency audit programme. If the supplier lacks an acceptable HACCP programme, the manufacturer needs to establish sufficient controls within his own manufacturing programme to assure product safety. If a significant hazard is determined to exist, a CCP with attendant controls and monitoring should be established.

Select CCP's, enter on the flow diagram: All identified safety hazards determined to be of significance must be controlled at some point in the food processing system. As noted previously, a critical control point is any point, step, or procedure at which control can be applied and a food safety hazard can be prevented, eliminated, or reduced to acceptable levels. If a hazard is identified which cannot be controlled, then the process may need to be redesigned or the product reformulated. CCP's are related to safety and are established only at points where hazards exist which are not controlled at some other point. For example, the cake mix line contains several magnets to remove metal particles; however, a metal detector after packaging serves as the critical control point. Other examples of CCP's include cooking, retorting, chilling, thawing, sifting/scalping, pesticide application during growth of raw material, etc. CCP's are identified on the flow diagram and then entered on the HACCP work sheet. As noted above, a decision tree approach should prove useful in determining whether to establish a CCP at a particular process step.

Establish critical limits: Critical limits on biological, chemical, and physical hazards represent the boundaries of safety and must be defined for each CCP. A CCP may have more than one critical limit. A critical limit is defined as one or more prescribed tolerances that must be met to insure that a CCP effectively controls a health hazard. A critical limit should never be violated. If any one of the critical limits is violated, then the CCP is out of control and the potential for an unacceptable health hazard exists. Examples of critical limits include minimum processing time and temperature, maximum refrigeration holding temperature, minimum hot holding temperature, maximum pesticide application level, maximum screen size on sifter, maximum pH, maximum fill weight, maximum viscosity, etc.

Violating or deviating from a critical limit at a CCP indicates the CCP is out of control. Deviating from the limit should indicate a health hazard could develop; that a product was not produced under conditions assuring safety; or that the safety of the product may be adversely affected by other factors such as raw materials. Outside resources may be necessary to determine the limits of a CCP. These may include, but not be limited to, literature searches, supplier's records/data, regulatory guidelines, and various experts (thermal process authorities, consultants, microbiologists, equipment manufacturers, sanitarians, etc.). Experimental studies may be necessary to fully define the limiting parameters for a CCP.

The critical limits for each CCP should be documented. A column on the HACCP work sheet should note the acceptable critical limits for that CCP. Documentation on how each of the critical limits were derived should be kept as part of the formal HACCP plan. This is particularly important if critical limits were derived from in-house experimental studies.

Establish monitoring requirements: The monitoring methods and procedures for each CCP need to be identified to ensure that the process is within the critical limits and that no safety hazard exists. The method or procedure, the frequency of monitoring, and the accountability for monitoring should be listed on the HACCP work sheet.

Monitoring procedures must be effective to assure safety. Ideally, monitoring of CCP's should be done at the 100% level (i.e. continuously). When it is not possible to monitor the CCP on a continuous basis, the proper interval for monitoring should be established so that food safety is assured. Most monitoring procedures are automated for rapid on-line measurements; time for lengthy analytical testing is generally not available. Microbiological testing is seldom effective as a monitoring procedure for this reason. Chemical and physical measurements, correlated to microbiological results, are preferred due to their timeliness and potential for automation. All supporting documentation on the monitoring methods, accountability, frequency, etc. should be part of the formal HACCP plan and retained by the manufacturer.

Establish corrective action to be taken when there is a deviation identified by monitoring of a CCP: Corrective action should be designed to bring the process back into control (i.e. correct the deviation). All product produced while the CCP was 'out-of-control' should be placed 'on hold.' Generally, this would include all product produced since the last acceptable reading was taken at the monitoring point of the CCP and to the point where the records show the system to be back under control. Disposition of the product involved in the deviation should be determined according to a pre-approved action plan.

This pre-approved plan should be generated or approved by the HACCP team. Examination of any product 'on hold' to determine its acceptability with regard to safety should follow an appropriate attributes sampling plan. This statistical sampling plan will assure sufficient sampling to verify safety or detect a potential hazard. Documentation of the event should be sufficient to identify the disposition of all product involved in the incident and all action taken to correct the incident and prevent reoccurrence. This documentation should be retained by the manufacturer. The corrective action plan or reference where it can be obtained should be noted on the HACCP work sheet. This action plan should be part of the formal HACCP plan.

Establish effective record keeping procedures that document the HACCP plan: Each manufacturing facility should have a formal HACCP plan that effectively documents the HACCP programme for each product. Each product should have its specific HACCP programme tailored to its process. This programme should include adequate documentation, as it relates to safety, on

- The ingredients, their specifications, sourcing, and compliance with specifications.
- The manufacturing process, including identification of CCP's, their limits, and controls.
- Product safety records establishing adequacy of process or formulation, as well as product shelf life.
- Packaging records as they relate to safety.
- Action plans for deviations, product disposition.
- Verification programmes.

Each CCP should be documented. This documentation should include the identification of the CCP, its limits, frequency of monitoring, person accountable for monitoring, and a shift check-off sheet signed or initialed by the accountable party denoting each time the CCP monitoring procedure was checked. An appropriate verification programme should also be in place to audit these sheets.

Establish procedures for verification that the HACCP system is working properly: The purpose of verification is to determine that the HACCP system is operating in accordance with the HACCP plan. Verification uses supplementary information to ensure that the HACCP programme is working.

Examples of verification activities include:

- Checks on the proper functioning and accuracy of CCP monitoring equipment (routine calibration).
- Spot checks of CCP records to verify the adequacy of monitoring and verify HACCP performance.
- Environmental sampling for microbiological pathogens, swabbing of product contact surfaces, and finished product testing for bacteria indicative of insanitary conditions.
- Random collection of ingredient or product samples to verify adequacy of CCP monitoring and control.
- Review of all deviations and dispositions.
- Review of the HACCP plan.

The results of all verification procedures should be documented. The report should include the verification of a functioning HACCP plan, intact and fully completed records and documents associated with CCP's, records verifying proper calibration and operation of all monitoring equipment, and proper handling and documentation of deviations. The HACCP system should also occasionally be verified by an independent auditor (i.e. corporate office, process authority, etc.). This can be done on either a routine or an unannounced basis.

HACCP programme review is recommended whenever there is an ingredient change, product reformulation, manufacturing process or procedure modification, or equipment change. The HACCP team should review the HACCP programme during these events or on a yearly basis, whichever occurs more frequently.

Thus, the HACCP concept, which focuses on food safety, is a systematic approach to hazard identification, assessment, and control. The system offers a rational approach to the control of biological, chemical, and physical hazards in foods; it avoids many weaknesses inherent in the traditional, endproduct inspection approach. The focus of the system is to direct attention to the control of key factors that affect the safety of the food. HACCP is applicable to all parts of the food chain from production through processing to use in the home.

HACCP SYSTEM AND DIFFICULTIES IN ITS IMPLEMENTATION IN FOOD SECTOR

Implementation and adoption of Hazard Analysis and Critical Control Points (HACCP) is a global challenge. The HACCP system is an imperative food safety tool that involves a complex mix of managerial, organisational and technical challenges. Several factors act as barriers to the process of operation such as the knowledge level or available resources for the business comprise of the internal factors whereas external factors include the inaccessibility of government or industry support. The challenges vary from one country to another and from different business sectors. The challenges in implementation of HACCP system are also a barrier which big establishments equipped with fundamental resources, technical specialists and management skills ordeal.

For human beings to lead a healthy life, the food one eats plays a vital role and it is thereby essential to ensure that food we consume is safe and hygienic. In recent years, surveillance and monitoring by a number of countries and researchers indicates that food borne illness is increasing around the world. Globally there are various factors that contribute to the increasing rate of food borne illness. The practice of maintaining the food safety standards from farm to fork is very crucial. Testing the food at the end point is not an advisable way to ensure food safety. The HACCP approach is formulated to prevent hazards before they happen.

In the last decade, the HACCP system has been recognised as a cost-effective procedure for ensuring food safety. Today, this methodology is internationally accepted as a food safety tool which is applied during full food production process. On the other hand, despite the orchestrated efforts of international institutions upsurge HACCP awareness and compliance, only food industries in more developed countries are currently apposite to immediately implement this food safety tool. Researchers have stated various barriers and complications in implementing the system in food plants. HACCP can be defined as a food safety approach whose enactment is quite demanding. In order to cope with the technical barriers of its implementation, it is important to focus on other factors such managerial, organisational and technical resources required for its effective operation. On the other hand, these factors lead to variations in the implementation HACCP from big businesses to small businesses due to distinctions in size of the operations. With this perspective, we seek to understand implementation barriers of HACCP system and gathered world literature reported on this case.

Methodology

The barriers in implementation of HACCP in food industry were reviewed by accessing data published in journals, websites and published data from doctoral thesis and dissertations of post graduate level. The database such as Google search, Google Scholar, PubMed, Science Direct were also used to search the researches related to HACCP implementation in food industry focusing on catering industry. Implementation of HACCP is a key to implementation of food hygiene and safety and prevention from food borne diseases. An understanding of barriers in implementation of HACCP helps to understand the areas where the food industry and government should focus.

Efforts of international institutions in devaluation of HACCP

The system grew out of a need to provide safe food for National Aeronautics and Space Administration (NASA), including the elimination of pathogens, toxins, and foreign objects from food and beverages. The application of HACCP was pioneered, during the sixties, by the Pillsbury Company with the cooperation of NASA, Natick Laboratories of the US Army, and the US Air Force Space Laboratory Project Group. Robert Muller from Pillsbury Company was the inventor of the HACCP standards used by the food industry. The original Pillsbury HACCP procedure has been built up with three components which includes the identification and assessment of all hazards associated with the final foodstuff, the identification of the steps or stages within food production at which these hazards may be controlled, reduced or eliminated: the Critical Control Points (CCPs) and the implementation of monitoring procedures at these CCPs.

In 1993, the European Union issued Council Directive 43/93, established a general requirement for all food business to adopt a risk based food safety management system with the principles of HACCP. However, each country in the EU interpreted the Directive into their national regulations in different ways. This led to widely differing levels of interpretation. Because of that Council Regulation 852/2004, with no option for national amendment, came into force across Europe in January 2004. Under this it was required by all food businesses to implement a system based on HACCP principles. The application of HACCP has been incorporated into Codex guidance texts. Both the United Stated Department of Agriculture (USDA) and the Food and Drug Administration (FDA) has adopted HACCP as the best programme to prevent food borne illnesses. According to the National Advisory Committee on Microbial Criteria for Foods, HACCP is defined as 'a systematic approach to identification, evaluation and control of food safety hazards' and a HACCP plan is 'the written document which is based upon the principles of HACCP and which delineates the procedures to be followed'. World Health Organisation (WHO) has recognised the importance of the HACCP system for the prevention of food borne diseases.

India since 1945 has been a member of Food and Agriculture Organisation (FAO) and Codex Alimentarius Commission. On the other hand, official ordinance regulations on food laws have been fulfilled according to the EU and by the way Indian food business especially export products were obligated to implement HACCP system in food law just like EU member countries. The use of HACCP, based on the internationally accepted seven principles as promoted by the Codex Alimentarius Commission, helped to India gain some recognition in the international markets.

HACCP implementation barriers

Despite huge benefits of HACCP method, the literature suggests that successful implementation has been limited by many factors. The success in developing, installing, monitoring and verifying a successful HACCP system involves a complex mix of factors to address too. Even the big food companies, may face difficult challenges to implement an HACCP system. Therefore a small or medium-sized enterprise (SMEs) may feel that the difficulties of HACCP are insurmountable. Barriers of time, money and skilled personnel have been reported by researchers as common factors preventing HACCP implementation, especially in SMEs. The difficulties vary from country to country or from business sector to business sector, some may be due to internal factors operations, like the knowledge level or available resources or some may be related to external factors, such as the accessibility of government or industry support.

There are 20 potential barriers for implementation of HACCP. The difficulties were expressed with those statements: 'implementation of HACCP impeded by internal budgetary constraints, problems obtaining external funding, current food safety controls considered sufficient, lot of changes to our production processes needed before HACCP could be put in place, the things needing to be done to implement HACCP overwhelmed us, other investments considered more important, lot of changes to our food safety controls needed before HACCP could be, wide-scale upgrading of the plant needed before HACCP could be put in place put in place, scale of operation is too small to have, not sure whether the implementation of HACCP would meet future regulatory requirements, uncertain about the potential benefits of implementing HACCP, HACCP difficult to implement because of internal organisation of the company, concerned that HACCP would reduce our flexibility in production, thought it best to wait and see the experiences of other companies before implementing ourselves, did not really see HACCP as suitable for our plant, not sure whether the implementation of HACCP would meet our customer's requirements, considered that costs of implementing HACCP likely to get cheaper over time, greater priority given to other issues than enhancing our food safety controls, food safety issues not considered sufficiently important to warrant the investment, HACCP goes against all of the ways in which we have traditionally done things'.

Obstacles regarding HACCP implementation are widespread. Food researchers have thereby concluded numerous ways of success to adopt the system in various food industries. The conclusions of the studies together were reported through outcome of a meta-analysis. According to the results, around 50% of the hurdles were associated to training, human resources, planning, knowledge and competence, and management commitments. 10 of the 12 studies investigated in the meta-analysis reported barriers related to worker motivation, awareness, interest, and familiarity with food safety controls. Other barriers were related to poor planning of implementation, excessive documentation, knowledge and competence, external support and lack of resources. The other results of the meta-analysis has shown that among 21 elements, we can allocate seven elements (training, human resources, planning, knowledge and competence, management commitment) representing almost 50% of all identified barriers.

In the catering, food service and retail industries the most common hurdles as presented through various researches have been classified as lack of knowledge, training, high staff turnover, the large variety of products, change in potential demand, variability in workloads, and the large numbers of part time workers. Studies in hospital food services, catering establishments, hotels, kebab houses, takeaways and restaurants, have determined that the basic reason of not developing food safety applications result from the lack of knowledge about these systems. In a study generic HACCP-PRP implementation was quantitatively assessed in 102 small medium enterprises in UK and it was reported that 88% of SMEs believed that the minimal progress in implementing HACCP was due to the lack of time and expertise. Observations have shown that even a large food company, with its resources of money and expertise face significant hurdles in developing a successful HACCP system. Another study shows that the possible factors influencing HACCP implementation in hospital kitchens in Taiwan include gender, age, and job position differences as well as differences in the confidence staff members feel in receiving support from staff in other departments and financial support from the hospital itself. In countries of Central-Europe, studies have shown limited information about HACCP systems. Surveys conducted in these regions (to understand the situation to introduce HACCP methods) show cased the requirement of two basic conditions for successful implementation of HACCP systems. These conditions include a suitable working environment from the hygienic, technical point of view and motivated, satisfied and qualified personnel. Another important barrier for HACCP implementation is expensiveness of the system. A study evaluated the costs and time for full HACCP implementation. According to their study, in the short term, there is lack of correlation in the market requirements for food safety and price improvement hence the cost effectiveness did not always prove positive to the enterprise implementing HACCP.

However, in the long term, this implementation might be the only way to keep plants as suppliers to the food market. It was concluded that for the meat industry, investment in new equipment and microbiological tests of products accounted for most of the implementation and operational costs, respectively. On the other hand, in the seafood industry many companies failed to have a reliable costs and benefits estimation of HACCP implementation beforehand. They concluded that the uncertainty on costs and benefits estimations could be a major restrain for planning HACCP adoption by individual seafood companies. In various studies, time and money were identified as the greatest barriers to improve food safety. Also, lack of financial resources was identified to devote to food safety was the biggest resource barrier.

HACCP implementation requires a complex interrelation among governments, industry and consumers but unfortunately, this responsibility is not always accomplished. Lack of awareness among consumers, lack of trust in food safety legislation and enforcement officers are some of the common issues. In a study, food service managers identified time to establish a HACCP programme, time to run the programme, and labour costs as being the three biggest obstacles. In addition, lack of training funds, time to get used to running the HACCP programme, and union problems were the other identified obstacles. There is a big confusion between prerequisite programmes and HACCP plan, their relations and how they should be managed. The main barrier to implementing a HACCP based food safety management system was the lack of prerequisite programmes.

According to researches, resource management, employee motivation, and employee confidence are the key barriers. Employees are nervous about taking food safety certification examinations and often are not comfortable with the change needed for implementation of a programme like HACCP. Various studies have shown socio-psychological factors, other psychological barriers such as lack of agreement and lack of self- efficacy to influence the implementation of HACCP programmes. Similarly, attitude barriers due to a lack of educative courses, sessions or meetings, make it more difficult for workers to adhere to this system.

In a research work, knowledge of the staff was also found to be important for implementation. 46.6% of respondents claimed to have a good knowledge of HACCP while 6.6% admitted to having a poor knowledge. Another study has demonstrated that an increase in the knowledge of a food handler does not necessarily change their food handling behaviour and is dependent upon their attitude. Constant turnover of employees was also identified as a barrier. 91% of food business directors agreed employees needed more training to improve food safety practices in a study. HACCP can be hindered by lack of time, expertise, training, motivation, commitment and funding in SMEs. It was also found that the availability of sanitation training had a positive relationship to implementing HACCP.

The employment of experienced, technically qualified food staff as the most important factor influencing the implementation of HACCP system while lack of employee training was the biggest employee barrier. Lack of financial resources to devote to food safety was the biggest resource barrier. The survey conducted in small-and medium-scale food producers underlined the lack of knowledge. Only 65% of producers kept any records. Their further results, based on questioning of managers, indicated that the basic lack of hygiene knowledge and understanding could prove to be a major barrier to the effective implementation. Bryan suggested that in the future the number of HACCP principles would increase from seven to ten or more. The ninth HACCP principle, according to him, would be education and training.

In India, the barriers were found similar as reported worldwide. In a research study conducted in four star hotels it was observed that illiteracy, lack in knowledge about HACCP practices acted as a barrier. Along with this lack of adequate HACCP training can also form a barrier. In a study done on flight catering units, reported regular training helped in implantation of HACCP. Street food vendors and small food outlets, fresh juice shops lack adequate facilities like clean water, proper storage facilities, etc. which acts as barriers in HACCP implementation. Also, majority of these vendors and food operators are illiterate and are unaware about HACCP Government should provide adequate aids and regular training to all the food operators for implementation of HACCP.

To sum up, there some common and special barriers of implementing HACCP system for many countries. The difficulties vary from country to country or from business sector to business sector. Especially in India, insufficient funds, illiteracy, and knowledge about HACCP practices are found to be the most encountered barriers to develop HACCP system.

SECTION VIII

Packaging of Food and Allied Products

Chapter 29

Modified Atmosphere Packaging

INTRODUCTION

The normal gaseous composition of air is nitrogen (N_2) 78.08%, oxygen (O_2) 20.96% and carbon dioxide (CO_2) 0.03%, together with variable concentrations of water vapour and traces of inert or noble gases. Many foods spoil rapidly in air due to moisture loss or uptake, reaction with oxygen and the growth of aerobic micro-organisms, i.e. bacteria and moulds. Microbial growth results in changes in texture, colour, flavour and nutritional value of the food. These changes can render food unpalatable and potentially unsafe for human consumption. Storage of foods in a modified gaseous atmosphere can maintain quality and extend product shelf life, by slowing chemical and biochemical deteriorative reactions and by slowing (or in some instances preventing) the growth of spoilage organisms.

Modified atmosphere packaging (MAP) is defined as 'the packaging of a perishable product in an atmosphere that has been modified so that its composition is other than that of air'. Whereas controlled atmosphere storage (CAS) involves maintaining a fixed concentration of gases surrounding the product by careful monitoring and addition of gases, the gaseous composition of fresh MAP foods is constantly changing due to chemical reactions and microbial activity. Gas exchange between the pack head space and the external environment may also occur as a result of permeation across the package material.

Packing foods in a modified atmosphere can offer extended shelf life and improved product presentation in a convenient container, making the product more attractive to the retail customer. However, MAP cannot improve the quality of a poor quality food product. It is, therefore, essential that the food is of the highest quality prior to packing in order to optimise the benefits of modifying the pack atmosphere. Good hygiene practices and temperature control throughout the chill-chain for perishable products are required to maintain the quality benefits and extended shelf life of MAP foods.

GASEOUS ENVIRONMENT

Gases used in MAP

The three main gases used in MAP in Europe are O_2, CO_2 and N_2, carbon monoxide (CO) is used widely in the United States of America (USA). The choice of gas is dependent upon the food product being packed. Used singly or in combination, these gases are used to balance safe shelf life extension with optimal organoleptic properties of the food. Noble or inert gases, such as argon, are in commercial use for products, such as coffee and snack products, however, the literature on their application and benefits is limited. Methylcyclopropene (CMC), an inhibitor of ethylene production, is also being included in some MAP of fruits. Experimental use of sulphur dioxide (SO_2) has also been reported.

Carbon dioxide

Carbon dioxide (CO_2) is a colourless gas with a slight pungent odour at very high concentrations. It is an asphyxiant and slightly corrosive in the presence of moisture. CO_2 dissolves readily in water (1.57 g/kg at 100 kPa, 20°C) to produce carbonic acid (H_2CO_3) that increases the acidity of the solution and reduces the pH. This gas is also soluble in lipids and some other organic compounds. The solubility of CO_2 increases with decreasing temperature. For this reason, the antimicrobial activity of CO_2 is markedly greater at temperatures below 10°C than at 15°C or higher. This has significant implications for MAP of foods, as will be discussed later. The high solubility of CO_2 can result in pack collapse due to the reduction of headspace volume. In some MAP applications, pack collapse is favoured, for example in flow wrapped cheese for retail sale.

Oxygen

Oxygen (O_2) is a colourless, odourless gas that is highly reactive and supports combustion. It has a low solubility in water (0.040 g/kg at 100 kPa, 20°C). Oxygen promotes several types of deteriorative reactions in foods including fat oxidation, browning reactions and pigment oxidation. Most of the common spoilage bacteria and fungi require O_2 for growth. Therefore, to increase the shelf life of foods, the pack atmosphere should contain a low concentration of residual O_2. It should be noted that in some foods a low concentration of O_2 can result in quality and safety problems (e.g. unfavourable colour changes in red meat pigments, senescence in fruits and vegetables and growth of anaerobic food poisoning bacteria), and this must be taken into account when selecting the gaseous composition for a packaged food.

Nitrogen

Nitrogen (N_2) is a relatively unreactive gas with no odour, taste or colour. It has a lower density than air, nonflammable and has a low solubility in water and other food constituents. Nitrogen does not support the growth of aerobic microbes, and therefore, inhibits the growth of aerobic spoilage but does not prevent the growth of anaerobic bacteria. The low solubility of N_2 in foods can be used to prevent pack collapse by including sufficient N_2 in the gas mix to balance the volume decrease due to CO_2 going into solution.

Carbon monoxide

Carbon monoxide (CO) is a colourless, tasteless and odourless gas that is highly reactive and very flammable. It has a low solubility in water but is relatively soluble in some organic solvents. CO is a fungistatic gas and a component of wood smoke, hence, foods have been exposed to this gas for hundreds of years. It has been used in the United States since the 1970s for the shelf-life extension of lettuce and for the MAP of meat and fish since 2002.

Noble gases

The noble gases including helium (He), argon (Ar), xenon (Xe) and neon (Ne) are inert. In combination with other MAP gases they have been found to have a beneficial effect on the shelf life of fresh, meat, ready meals, fresh fruit and vegetables.

Effect of the Gaseous Environment on the Activity of Bacteria, Yeasts and Moulds

Foods can contain a wide range of micro-organisms including bacteria and their spores, yeasts, moulds, protozoa and viruses. While the packaging technologist will generally be concerned with preventing the growth of bacteria, yeasts and moulds in foods, one should be aware that certain pathogenic micro-organisms, while not growing in the food, may survive during the shelf-life period and have the potential, if present in the food, to cause food poisoning or disease in consumers. This section is concerned with the major microbial groups that can be controlled or affected by MAP.

Effect of oxygen

Bacteria, yeasts and moulds have different respiratory and metabolic needs and can be grouped according to their O_2 needs.

Aerobes: They require O_2 for growth and include the ubiquitous Gram-negative spoilage bacteria belonging to the *Pseudomonas* genus. This grouping also includes certain pathogenic bacteria such as *Vibrio parahaemolyticus*. Note that some other *Vibrio* species are classified as facultative aerobes.

Microaerophiles: They grow under low concentrations of O_2. Thus, an environment low in O_2 may be selective for some important pathogens including *Camplobacter jejuni* and *Listeria monocyocytogenes*. Some microaerophilic bacteria, e.g. *Lactobacillus* species, may also require increased levels of CO_2 under low oxygen conditions for optimum growth.

Facultative anaerobes: They generally grow better in O_2 but are also able to grow without it. These include various important genera from the *Enterobacteriacaeae* including pathogenic organisms, such as *Escherichia coli*, *Salmonella* and *Shigella* species, *Staphylococcus aureus*, *Listeria monocytogenes*, *Brochothrix* species, *Vibrio* species, fermentative yeasts and some *Bacillus* species. *Aeromonas hydrophilia* is a new and emerging pathogen that appears to be particularly associated with fish and fish products. Many strains are psychrotrophic and some may grow between 3 and 5°C.

Anaerobes: They are inhibited or killed by the presence of O_2, e.g. the pathogenic bacterium

Clostridium botulinum: The removal of O_2, for example in vacuum packaging, will restrict the growth of aerobic spoilage and pathogenic bacteria and, therefore, extend shelf life. However, as indicated above, there are other micro-organisms including the pathogens *E. coli* and *A. hydrophilia* capable of growth under these conditions.

Effect of carbon dioxide

The antibacterial properties of CO_2 have been known for some time. More recent work has shown that CO_2 is effective against psychrotrophs and has potential for extending the shelf life of food stored at low temperatures. There are several theories regarding the actual mechanism of CO_2 action. In general, CO_2 increases the lag phase and generation time of micro-organisms, and this effect, as would be expected, is enhanced at lower temperatures. There appears to be an array of antimicrobial mechanisms, including CO_2 lowering pH, inhibition of succinic oxidase at CO_2 concentrations greater than 10%, inhibition of certain decarboxylation enzymes and disruption of the cell membrane. The area has also been reviewed by several workers including Daniels and others.

In general, the growth of Gram-negative bacteria is inhibited much more than that of Gram-positive bacteria. The effects of CO_2 are markedly temperature dependent, and it is, therefore, imperative that the integrity of temperature control across the supply chain be maintained to protect the health of the consumer. Of some concern is the observation that germination of spores of *C. botulinum* may be stimulated by CO_2.

CO_2, particularly at low temperatures, is soluble in water and lipids, and adjustment for adsorption is required. A high concentration of CO_2 can lead to defects, e.g. increased drip in fresh meats, and to container collapse. The latter can occur where CO_2 is the major gas present, and where the gas goes into solution in the water and lipid phases of the product. To counteract this effect, an insoluble gas, such as nitrogen or an inert gas, e.g. argon may be added to the gas mix. When CO_2 is required to control the bacterial and mould growth, a minimum of 20% is generally used. Optimal levels appear to be in the region of 20–30%. However, concentrations of 100% CO_2 may be used in bulk packs of meat and poultry.

Effect of nitrogen

Nitrogen is a relatively unreactive gas. It is used to displace air and, in particular, O_2 from MAP. Since air and consequently O_2 have been removed, growth of aerobic spoilage organisms is inhibited or stopped. It is also used to balance gas pressure inside packs, so as to prevent the collapse of packs containing high moisture and fat-containing foods, e.g. meat. Because of the solubility of CO_2 in water and fat, these foods tend to absorb CO_2 from the pack atmosphere. Inert gases function in a similar manner.

Effect of the Gaseous Environment on the Chemical Biochemical and Physical Properties of Foods

Food spoilage can also be caused by chemical and biochemical, including enzyme-catalysed, reactions in food. The packaging technologist should have an awareness of these effects and understand the extent to which modified atmospheres can mitigate them. Of the gases involved in MAP, O_2, because of its reactivity, has been extensively studied. Because of the significance of O_2, this section will largely be concerned with the influence of this gas. However, CO_2, and to a lesser extent CO and ethylene (C_2H_4), have also been investigated. While reference to C_2H_4 is made.

Effect of oxygen

Apart from its effect on micro-organisms, O_2 can promote oxidation of lipids, influence the colour of some food pigments, contribute to enzymic browning and promote off-flavours in some foods. It is important to note that the inclusion of O_2 in a modified atmosphere environment has the potential to have positive and or negative effects on product quality. The resultant effect is largely product dependent.

Lipid oxidation: Lipid or fat oxidation is often called oxidative rancidity and is promoted by O_2. Oxidative rancidity is a major cause of food spoilage. The reaction of O_2 with unsaturated fatty acids in fat-containing foods is a major cause of deterioration of fats or fat-containing foods. Oxidation of unsaturated fat is referred to as autoxidation, since the rate of oxidation increases as the reaction proceeds. Hydroperoxides are the predominant initial reaction products of fatty acids with oxygen. Subsequent reactions control both the rate of reaction and the nature of the products formed. Some of these products, such as acids and aldehydes, are largely responsible for the off-flavour and off-odour characteristics of rancid foods. Removal of O_2 and its replacement with N_2 or CO_2 or mixtures thereof can inhibit the development of rancidity.

Pigment colour in meat: There are three major pigments in meat, oxymyoglobin, myoglobin and metmyoglobin. Consumers value the red colour (oxymyoglobin) of fresh meat as opposed to the purple colour of myoglobin. The colour cycle in fresh meat is reversible and dynamic, with the three pigments, oxymyoglobin (red), myoglobin (purple) and metmyoglobin (brown), being constantly formed and reformed. Brown metmyoglobin, the oxidised or ferric form of the pigment, cannot bind O_2. The purple myoglobin, in the presence of O_2, may be oxygenated to the bright red pigment oxymyoglobin, producing the familiar *bloom* of fresh meat, or it may be oxidised to metmyoglobin, producing the undesirable brown colour of less acceptable fresh meat. Whether the conversion of myoglobin to oxymyoglobin or metmyoglobin is favoured depends on O_2 concentration. Under low O_2 environments, the reduced myoglobin is oxidised to the undesirable brown metmyoglobin pigment. Conversely, high O_2 environments favour the formation of oxymyoglobin.

The red colour of raw cured meat products is due to nitrosylmyoglobin, which is formed by the reaction of myoglobin with nitric oxide (NO). During heating, red nitrosylmyoglobin is converted to pink denatured nitrosohemo-chrome. The red/pink colours of raw and cooked cured meat products are unstable in air and in the light.

Oxygen and light cause the dissociation of NO from the cured meat pigments, resulting in brown/grey discoloration. Hence, MAP under low O_2 levels, and in opaque packages, greatly improves the desirable red/pink colour stability of cured meat products. The use of in-pack O_2 scavenging systems can reduce and maintain residual oxygen at a level that further extends the shelf life of cured meat products. The application of O_2 scavenging technology in food packaging.

Photo-oxidation of chlorophyll: The green colour of chlorophyll changes to brown/grey when oxidised to pheophytin. This is undesirable, e.g. green pasta changing in colour to brown/grey. The photo-oxidation of chlorophyll and loss of desirable green colour can be significantly reduced by MAP under low O_2 levels and in opaque packages.

Oxidative off-flavours: Oxidative off-flavours and off-odours can be caused by numerous oxidative reactions in food and drink products. Oxidative warmed-over flavour is a characteristic off-flavour primarily associated with cooked meats and poultry. Commercially, this affects mainly the chilled ready meals and other cook-chill products. In cooked meats and poultry held at chilled storage temperatures, this stale, oxidised flavour may become apparent within a short time.

Meats, fish, poultry, liquid food, beverage and dairy products, for example, are highly susceptible to oxidative processes, which can initiate a chain of reactions resulting in flavour impairment. This can occur relatively quickly. MAP under low O_2 levels can delay the onset of oxidative off-flavours.

Effects of other MAP gases: Nitrogen is unreactive and has no direct effect on the chemical and biochemical properties of foods. Because of the high solubility of CO_2 and its reaction with water to form carbonic acid, there is potential for some adverse effects on particular foods. These are probably due to the production of localised areas of low pH on or near the food surface. These effects if they do occur, and there is debate whether they occur in practice, may result in the loss of *bloom* in some meats for example. The mechanism is likely to be associated with pH-induced protein changes including denaturation and other changes in conformation, resulting in atypical values for light absorption and reflection from the product surface.

CO can combine with myogloblin to form the bright red compound carboxymyoglobin that is similar in colour to oxymyogloblin. This compound is much more stable than oxymyogloblin and is one of the reasons why CO is toxic. Ironically, this is also one of the factors why this gas is used so extensively in fish, e.g. tuna and beef processing in the United States. CO also retards fat oxidation and the formation of metmyogloblin. The ability of CO to inhibit the browning of cut and physically damaged vegetable tissue has lead to its use in preventing browning in shredded lettuce in particular. Its fungistatic properties have also been employed to inhibit mould growth. Its antifungal properties are enhanced in low O_2 environments. While CO as discussed is approved for use in MAP in the United States, its use in food preservation there is not universally accepted by consumers. Currently, CO is not approved for use in MAP in the European Union.

Physical Spoilage

Physical or physico-chemical changes in food products can cause spoilage, thereby limiting the shelf life. For example, moisture loss in cut fresh vegetables causes wilting and reduction in textural crispness, moisture migration from the filling to the pastry of bakery products can cause a soggy/sticky consistency and syneresis of dairy products results in an undesirable and unsightly separated aqueous layer. Also, some food products are sensitive to chilled temperatures. For example, certain whole tropical fruits are susceptible to chilling injury when exposed to temperatures in the range 0–10°C. Chilling injury causes loss of quality through poor ripening, pitting of the epidermal cells, rotting and development of off-flavours. With the exception of preventing moisture loss and moisture uptake, MAP does not, generally, directly affect physical spoilage.

PACKAGING MATERIALS

Selection of the most appropriate packaging materials is essential to maintaining the quality and safety of MAP foods. Flexible and semi-rigid plastics and plastic laminates are the most common packaging materials used for MAP foods. Plastic materials account for approximately one-third of the total materials demand for food packaging applications and their use is forecast to grow.

Relative ease of forming, light weight, good clarity, heat sealing and strength are some of the properties of plastics that make them suitable as food packaging materials. Advances in polymer processing have enabled the development of plastics that are better suited to particular food packaging applications. However, no single plastic possesses the properties that make it suited to all food packaging applications.

Plastic packaging materialsmay consist of a monolayer formed from a single plastic, but most, if not all, MAP films are multiplayer structures formed from several layers of different plastics. Using coextrusion, lamination or coating technologies, it is possible to combine different types of plastics to form films, semi-rigid sheets or rigid packs. By carefully selecting each component plastic, it is possible to design a material, which possesses the key properties of packaging importance to best match the requirements of the product/package system.

Plastic packaging for MAP applications is most commonly found in the form of flexible films for bags, pouches, pillow packs and top webs in sealed tray systems, or as rigid and semi-rigid structures for base trays, dishes, cups and tubs. Commonly used plastic flexible laminates are produced from polyethylene (PE), polypropylene (PP), polyamide (PA/nylons), polyethylene terephthalate (PET), polyvinyl chloride (PVC), polyvinylidene chloride (PVdC) and ethylene vinyl alcohol (EVOH). Rigid and semi-rigid structures are commonly produced from polypropylene, polyethylene terephthalate, unplasticised polyvinyl chloride and expanded polystyrene (PS).

Main Plastics used in MAP

The following section provides a brief overview of the commonly used plastics for MAP applications. More information on these including properties of packaging importance, definitions and terminology.

Ethylene vinyl alcohol (EVOH)

Polyvinyl alcohol (PVOH) is an excellent gas barrier provided it is dry. In the presence of moisture, PVOH absorbs water, causing the plastic to swell and become plasticised. In this condition, the gas barrier properties of PVOH are greatly reduced. In order to provide greater polymer stability for commercial use, PVOH is copolymerised with ethylene to produce EVOH. The gas barrier properties of EVOH are less than those of PVOH when dry, but EVOH is less sensitive to the presence of moisture, and therefore, it is widely used as a gas barrier layer in MAP applications. This material has good processing properties and is, therefore, suitable for conversion into plastic films and structures. EVOH is always found laminated as a thin film usually in the order of 5 m thickness, sandwiched between hydrophobic polymers, e.g. PE or PP, which protect the polymer from moisture. EVOH also possesses high mechanical strength, high resistance to oils and organic solvents and high thermal stability.

Polyethylene (PE)

The polyethylenes are structurally the simplest group of synthetic polymers and the most commonly used plastic materials for packaging applications. There are several types of PE classified on the basis of density. All are composed of a carbon backbone with a degree of side chain branching that influences density. Low density polyethylene (LDPE) (density, 0.910–0.925 g/cm^3), is generally used in film form whereas high density polyethylene (HDPE) (density, 0.940 g/cm^3), is commonly used for rigid and semi-rigid structures. PEs are characterised as poor gas barriers, but their hydrophobic nature makes them very good barriers to water vapour. Therefore, by itself, PE cannot be used as a packaging material in MAP applications that require a high barrier to gases. PE melts at a relatively low temperature ranging from approximately 100–120°C (dependent on density and crystallinity). A less branched variant called linear low density polyethylene (LLDPE) that offers good heat sealing properties is used as a sealant layer on base trays and lidding films.

Modified PE-based materials that contain interchain ionic bonds are called ionomers. This group of plastics exhibit enhanced heat-sealing properties that enable them to seal more effectively through meat juices, fats and powders. Ionomers also form effective heat seals with aluminium. SurlynR is Dupont's trade name for its range of ionomer materials. A copolymer of ethylene and vinyl acetate, ethylene vinylacetate (EVA), offers enhanced heat-sealing properties over LDPE and is found as a heat seal layer in some MAP applications.

Polyamides (PA)

Polyamides comprise the group of plastics commonly referred to as nylons, which have widespread application in food packaging. Nylons generally have high tensile strength, good puncture and abrasion resistance and good gas barrier properties. Nylons are generally moisture sensitive, due to their hydrophilic nature, and will tend to absorb water from their environment. Moisture in the nylon structure interferes with interchain bonding and adversely affects their properties, including gas barrier. Under conditions of high relative humidity, the gas transmission rate of nylon films generally increases. However, there are commercial nylons that are less affected by moisture. Their relatively high strength and toughness make them ideal materials in vacuum pouches for fresh meat where hard bone ends could puncture other plastic materials. In this application, nylon is generally laminated to PE, which provides the heat-sealing properties.

Polyethylene terephthalate (PET)

Polyethylene terephthalate is the most common polyester used in food packaging applications. PET is a good gas and water vapour barrier, is strong, offers good clarity and is temperature resistant. Crystalline PET (CPET) has poorer optical properties but improved heat resistance melting at temperatures in excess of 270°C. Flexible PET film is used for barrier pouches and top webs as a lidding material for tray packs. CPET is used for dual ovenable pre-formed base trays where its high temperature resistance makes it an ideal container for microwave and convection oven cooking of food.

Polypropylene (PP)

Polypropylene is a versatile polymer that has applications in flexible, rigid and semi-rigid packaging structures. MAP applications are generally for rigid base trays. PP is a good water vapour barrier but a poor gas barrier. Increasing the thickness of the material compensates somewhat for the high gas transmission rate. PP melts at approximately 170°C. It can, therefore, be used as a container for microwaving low-fat food products. It should not be used for microwaving high-fat foods, where temperatures in excess of its melting point could be reached. Foamed PP have been used to provide the structural properties in laminates for MAP thermoformed base trays, where it is combined with an EVOH barrier and a PE heat-sealing layer.

Polystyrene (PS)

Pure polystyrene is a stiff, brittle material and has limited use in MAP applications. Expanded PS (EPS), which is formed from low density blown particles, has been used for many years as a base tray for overwrapped fresh meat, fish and poultry products. Foamed PS has been used as a structural layer for preformed MAP base tray applications. The high gas permeability of foamed PS requires the material to be used in combination with a plastic, such as EVOH, which provides the required gas barrier properties.

Polyvinyl chloride (PVC)

Polyvinyl chloride has a relatively low softening temperature and good processing properties and is, therefore, an ideal material for producing thermoformed packaging structures. Although a poor gas barrier in its plasticised form, unplasticised PVC has improved gas and water vapour barrier properties, which can at best be described as moderate.

Oil and grease resistance are excellent, but PVC can be softened by certain organic solvents. Rigid PVC has very good optical properties and exhibits high gloss and a low haze value. It is a common structural material in MAP thermoformed base trays, where it is laminated to PE to provide the required heat-sealing properties.

Polyvinylidene chloride (PVdC)

Polyvinylidene chloride (a copolymer of vinyl chloride and vinylidene chloride) possesses excellent gas, water vapour and odour barrier properties, with good resistance to oil, grease and organic solvents. Unlike EVOH, the gas barrier properties of PVdC are not significantly affected by the presence of moisture. PVdC effectively heat seals to itself and to other materials.

Exhibiting high temperature resistance, PVdC is suitable for use in packs exposed to hot filling and sterilisation processes. Homopolymers and copolymers of PVdC are some of the best commercially available barrier materials for food packaging applications The above provides a brief introduction to the main plastic materials used in MAP applications.

It should be noted that certain desired properties can be enhanced by further modification of the material. For example, coating a plastic with aluminium (metallisation) can improve the gas and vapour barrier properties and enhance the visual appearance of the material. PP is commonly metallised by passing the film through a *mist* of vapourised aluminium under vacuum. Similar treatments to improve gas and vapour barrier properties include application of a silicon oxide (SiO_x) coating (also referred to as glass coating) to PET film and a diamond-like-carbon (DLC) coating to PET. The former has been used for MAP lidding film with the advantages of providing excellent and stable barrier properties, which are less influenced by the effects of temperature and humidity. To date the main application of the latter has focused on non-MAPs applications, including a barrier coating on PET beverage bottles.

Selection of Plastic Packaging Materials

Several factors must be considered when selecting package materials for MAP applications.

Food contact approval

Packaging materials in contact with food must not transfer components from the packaging to the food product in amounts that could harm the consumer. In Europe, all food contact packaging must comply with EC Directives, which are derived from the framework directive 89/109/EEC and which includes the plastics directive 90/128/EEC. Suppliers must provide evidence to demonstrate that migrant levels from plastics packaging into foods are below the recommended levels and that the plastic material is safe in its intended use.

Gas and vapour barrier properties

Packaging materials for MAP must have the required degree of gas and vapour barrier for the particular food application. Whereas some materials, such as glass and metals (provided they are of sufficient thickness and possess no pores or other imperfections), are a total barrier to gases and vapours, plastic materials are permeable to varying degrees to gases and vapours. These molecules are transported across a plastic package material by a mass transfer process, called permeation. Permeation is defined as 'the diffusional molecular exchange of gases, vapours or liquid permeants across a plastic material which is devoid of imperfections such as cracks and perforations'. Essentially, the gas molecules sorb into one surface of the plastic, are transported through the material by a process of diffusion and desorb on the opposite surface.

The driving force for gas transmission through a plastic film is the partial pressure difference of the gas between both sides of the material, and therefore, the gas concentration difference at the time of measurement should be quoted with the transmission rate value. Relative humidity (RH) is the driving force for water vapour transmission rate (WVTR), and therefore, WVTR values increase with increasing RH. Therefore, RH should always be quoted with WVTR values. RH can also influence the gas transmission rates of hydrophilic plastics and, therefore, should be quoted with gas transmission rate values (although generally gas transmission rates are measured at 0% RH). The barrier properties are primarily dependent on the type of plastic, the permeant gas or vapour and its partial pressure difference across the material and the temperature. As a general rule, the permeability of a synthetic polymer to CO_2 is approximately three to five times higher than the permeability to O_2. No single commercially available plastic provides a total barrier to gases and vapours, and therefore, the materials are selected on the basis of product type, desired shelf life, gas composition, availability and cost.

Optical properties

Good optical properties, such as high gloss and transparency, are essential for bag, pouch and top web materials to satisfy consumer demand for a clear view of the product. To provide attractive appearance and shelf impact, some base tray materials are available in various colours. This also enhances the visual appeal of the product against the tray and helps consumers to identify product ranges and brands on the supermarket shelf. PET, PP and EPS trays are supplied in a range of colours. PVC trays are generally used in their natural form to provide a transparent pack.

Antifogging properties

Condensation (fogging) of water vapour on the inner surface of food packs can occur when the temperature of the pack environment is reduced, resulting in a temperature differential between the pack contents and the packaging material. Fogging of the inner surface of lidding film is a result of light scattering by the small droplets of condensed moisture that leads to poor product visibility and an aesthetically unpleasing appearance of the pack.

This can be overcome by applying antifogging agents to the plastic heat-sealing layer, either as an internal additive or as an external coating. These chemicals decrease the surface energy of the packaging film that enables moisture to spread as a thin film across the under surface of the pack rather than collecting as visible droplets.

Antifogging agents include fatty acid esters. Most lidding materials are available with antifog properties, and commonly treated plastics include LDPE, LLDPE, EVA and PET.

Mechanical properties

Resistance to tearing and puncture and good machine handling characteristics are important in optimising the packaging operation and maintaining pack integrity during forming and subsequent handling and distribution. A further important characteristic of laminates and coextruded films and sheets is the ability of layers to bond effectively together during the packaging operation and during subsequent storage and handling. Certain organic compounds may have an adverse effect on bond strength to the extent that weakened bonds can result in layers peeling apart.

Heat-sealing properties

Effective heat seals are essential for maintaining the desired gas composition within the pack. The ability to form effective heat seals through contamination, such as meat juices, powders, fats and oils, is an advantage in many applications. Heat seal quality is dependent on many factors, including seal material, seal width and machine settings, such as temperature, pressure and dwell time.

MODIFIED PACKAGING ATMOSPHERE MACHINES

The function of MAP machines is to retain the product on a thermoformed or preformed base tray, or within a flexible pouch or bag, modify the atmosphere, apply a top web if required, seal the pack and cut and remove waste trim to produce the final pack. Pack format, presentation, machine performance, versatility and pack costs are essential factors for the packer filler to consider before selecting a machine for a particular product application. The following section provides an overview of the types and operation of MAP machines.

Chamber Machines

For low production throughput, chamber machines are sufficient. These are generally used with preformed pouches, though tray machines are available. The filled pack is loaded into the machine, the chamber closes, a vacuum is pulled on the pack and back flushed with the modified atmosphere. Heated sealing bars seal the pack, the chamber opens, packs are removed and the cycle continues. These machines are generally labour-intensive and cheap, with a simple operation but are relatively slow. Some chamber machines can handle large packages and are suitable for bulk packs.

Snorkel Machines

Snorkel machines operate without a chamber and use pre-formed bags or pouches. The bags are filled and positioned in the machine. The snorkel is introduced into the bag, draws a vacuum and introduces the modified atmosphere. The snorkels withdraw and the bag is heat sealed. Bag in box bulk products and retail packs in large MAP master packs can be produced on these machines.

Form-fill-seal Machines

Form-fill-seal (FFS) machines form pouches from a continuous sheet of roll stock, or form flexible or semi-rigid tray systems comprising a thermoformed tray with a heat-sealed lid. FFS machines may be orientated in a vertical plane or a horizontal plane. Flow wrapping machines are available in both vertical and horizontal formats. The type of format is dependent on the nature of the food product being packed. FFS machines using pre-formed trays or producing thermoformed trays are almost exclusively horizontal machines. This section focuses on horizontal form-fill-seal MAP machines that are used extensively in the food industry.

Thermoformed form-fill-seal tray machines use rollstock film for base web and lidding material. Base film is carried through the machine by clamps, which attach onto the edge of the web and carry it through the forming, filling, evacuation, gas modification, sealing, cutting and discharge stages.

Base trays are produced by applying heat to the base roll stock, which when softened is immediately moulded into the desired shape and size. Forming of the heated, softened sheet can be achieved by applying a vacuum, air pressure, mechanical drawing or a combination of these processes. The softened heated film is normally drawn into the forming mould under the assistance of vacuum applied through evacuation holes located along the base edges and corners of the mould. This process produces a more defined and uniform tray shape. Where deep trays are required, a more uniform distribution of plastic can be achieved by pre-stretching the film, using mechanical devices (plugs) that prevent excessive thinning of the container walls at the base edges and corners.

The tooling for the moulds represents a significant initial capital cost of thermoformed formfill-seal tray machines. Moulds are generally fabricated from either steel or aluminium, the latter being cheaper but less durable than the former. Inserts, called filler plates, can be placed on the base of the die to decrease the forming depth and, therefore, produce shallow trays.

Modification of the Pack Atmosphere

MAP machines use mainly one of two techniques to modify the pack atmosphere.

Gas flushing

This method employs a continuous gas stream that flushes air out of the package prior to sealing. This method is less effective at flushing air out of the pack, and this results in residual oxygen levels of 2–5%. Gas flushing is, therefore, not suited for oxygen-sensitive food products. Generally, gas-flushing machines have a simple and rapid operation and, therefore, a high packing rate.

Compensated vacuum gas flushing

This method uses a two-stage process:

1. Gas flushing stage: The pack is flushed with the modified gas mix.

2. The evacuation stage: A vacuum is pulled on the pack to remove air. Generally, it is not possible to achieve a full vacuum, since reduced pressures will cause water to boil, at which point the vacuum cannot be improved.

The evacuation of air from the pack results in lower residual oxygen levels than that achieved by gas flushing, and, therefore, this method is better suited to packing oxygen sensitive products.

The two-stage process employed by the compensated vacuum method results in a lower packaging rate than that possible with gas flushing.

Sealing

An effective heat seal is critical to maintaining the quality and safety of the packaged product. Film factors (thickness and surface treatments) and plastic composition (resin type, molecular weight distribution and presence of additives) will determine the machine settings for the sealing operation. The correct combination of time, temperature and pressure of the seal bars is necessary to produce a good seal. Insufficient dwell time or temperature can result in ineffective seals that separate at the bond interface. Excessive dwell time or temperature can result in weakness adjacent to the seal area.

Cutting

Packs are discharged as a continuous arrangement of filled and sealed packs from a thermo form fill-seal machine, and, therefore, the final operation is to separate them into individual packs. This can be carried out by two methods – die cutting or a combination of longitudinal and transverse cutting.

Die cutting is achieved in one operation. A shaped blade is forced through the film that is clamped in place by a frame assembly. Transverse cutting separates packs into rows and is carried out by guillotines or punches that are driven through the film that is supported by anvils. This may be carried out in conjunction with longitudinal cutting where circular knives cut through the tray flanges parallel to the length of the film. Regardless of the cutting method, it is important to ensure an even flange remains around the lip of the tray in order to maximise the seal strength. Offset cutting could leave one side of the tray with a thin flange that may open during handling and distribution. Waste trim is either wound onto spindles at the machine discharge or removed by suction into collection bins.

QUALITY ASSURANCE OF MAP

Heat Seal Integrity

The majority of MAP form-fill-seal retail packs are heat sealed. The quality and safety of MAP food will be compromised if the seal integrity is lost during the required life of the pack. A breech of the heat seal will result in a rapid change in the modified atmosphere in the pack headspace. Therefore, the sealing operation constitutes a critical control point and must be monitored during production as part of the quality assurance procedure. It is of key importance that sealing bar temperature, pressure and dwell time are set according to machine manufacturer and packaging supplier specifications and conditions are monitored during machine operation. Seal and pack integrity can be assessed by destructive or nondestructive tests. Destructive tests are based on immersing packs in water and checking for escaping gas bubbles from around the seal. Other test methods measure seal strength by pressurising packs using compressed air until the seal fails. Nondestructive tests are based on measuring changes in pressure generated by packs under vacuum in sealed chambers.

Measurement of Transmission Rate and Permeability in Packaging Films

Accurate determination of the O_2, CO_2 and water vapour permeabilities of plastic-based packaging materials is important for MAP applications. Several methods exist for measuring transmission rate and permeability of gases and vapours across a packaging film. The most common test procedure is based on the isostatic method. In this method, both sides of the test film are maintained at the same total pressure but a constant partial pressure difference is maintained by passing test gas continuously on one side of the film while inert carrier gas continuously removes permeant from the other side of the film. This maintains a very low partial pressure of permeated test gas and establishes a constant gas concentration difference across the film. This is also referred to as the concentration increase method.

MAIN FOOD TYPES

Raw Red Meat

Microbial growth and oxidation of the red oxymyoglobin pigment are the main spoilage mechanisms that limit the shelf life of raw red meats. The packaging technologist in the EU has to maintain the desirable red colour of the oxymyoglobin pigment, by having an appropriate O_2 concentration in the pack atmosphere, and at the same time minimise the growth of aerobic micro-organisms. Technologists in the United States can also use CO to obtain a similar but more lasting effect. Highly pigmented red meats, such as venison and wild boar, require higher concentrations of O_2.

Aerobic spoilage bacteria, such as *Pseudomonas* species, normally constitute the major flora on red meats. Since these bacteria are inhibited by CO_2, it is possible to achieve both red colour stability and microbial inhibition by using gas mixtures containing 20–30% CO_2 and 70–80% O_2. These mixtures can extend the chilled shelf life of red meats from 2–4 days to 5–8 days. A gas/product ratio of 2:1 is recommended.

Red meats provide an ideal medium for the growth of a wide range of spoilage and food poisoning micro-organisms including *E. coli*. Because raw red meats are cooked before consumption, the risk of food poisoning can be greatly reduced by proper cooking. The maintenance of recommended chilled temperatures and good hygiene and handling practices throughout the butchery, MAP, distribution and retailing chain is of critical importance in ensuring both the safety and extended shelf life of red meat products.

Raw Poultry

Microbial growth, particularly growth of *Pseudomonas* and *Achromobacter* species, is the major factor limiting the shelf life of raw poultry. These Gram-negative aerobic spoilage bacteria are effectively inhibited by CO_2. Consequently, the inclusion of CO_2 in MAP at a concentration in excess of 20% can significantly extend the shelf life of raw poultry products. CO_2 concentrations higher than 35% in the gas mixture of retail packs are not recommended because of the risks of pack collapse and excessive drip. Nitrogen is used as an inert filler gas, and a gas/product ratio of 2:1 is recommended. Since pack collapse is not a problem for bulk MAP master packs, gas atmospheres of 100% CO_2 are frequently used.

Since poultry meat provides a good medium for the growth of pathogenic micro-organisms, including some that are not inhibited by CO_2, it is critical that recommended chilled temperatures and good hygiene and handling practices throughout the supply chain are adhered to and that products are properly cooked prior to consumption.

Early research into gas mixes for MAP of poultry meat reported discolouration of the meat at CO_2 concentrations higher than 25%. Even at 15%, the authors sometimes observed a loss of *bloom*. This research is at variance with the lack of problems reported from the commercial use of relatively high levels of CO_2 with meat products, with up to 100% in some products. Gas compositions of 25–50% CO_2 and 50–75% N_2 are used routinely. It would appear that the problems that have been occasionally encountered with high levels of CO_2, e.g. development of greyish tinges on meat, may simply be due to high residual levels of O_2 rather than the concentration of CO_2.

It is recommended that research into the optimal gas composition and package type and size should be conducted for individual food products. Furthermore, headspace gas composition will change during storage due to microbial respiration and gas exchange between the pack headspace and the environment. Therefore, processors should conduct trials to determine the extent to which gas composition changes through the shelf life of the product. The ratio of headspace pack volume to food product volume is also important, as is the types and thickness of the package material and the package design. Shelf-life evaluations must reflect the conditions from manufacture to consumption of the product. It may also be necessary to consider the effect of pack opening on the subsequent shelf life of the product.

Cooked, Cured and Processed Meat Products

The principal spoilage mechanisms that limit the shelf life of cooked, cured and processed meat products are microbial growth, colour change and oxidative rancidity. For cooked meat products, the heating process should kill vegetative bacterial cells, inactivate degradative enzymes and fix the colour. Consequently, spoilage of cooked meat products is primarily due to post-process contamination by micro-organisms, as a result of poor hygiene and handling practices. The colour of cooked meats is susceptible to oxidation, and it is important to have only low levels of residual O_2 in packs. MAP using CO_2/N_2 mixes (gas compositions of 25–50% CO_2 and 50–75% N_2) along with a gas/product ratio of 2:1 is widely used to maximise the shelf life and inhibit the development of oxidative off-flavours and rancidity. Raw cured meat products, e.g. bacon, owe their characteristic pink reddish colour to nitrosyl-myoglobin. This pigment is more stable than oxymyoglobin and is unaffected by high levels of CO_2 but is slowly converted to brown metmyoglobin in air. During cooking, nitrosylmyoglobin is converted to pink denatured nitrosohemo-chrome pigments that are unstable in air.

Processed meat products, such as sausages, frankfurters and beef burgers generally contain sodium metabisulphite, which is an effective preservative against a wide range of spoilage micro-organisms and pathogens. Cooked, cured and processed meat products containing high levels of unsaturated fat are liable to be spoiled by oxidative rancidity, but MAP with CO_2/N_2 mixtures is effective at inhibiting this undesirable reaction.

Potential food poisoning hazards are primarily due to microbial contamination or growth resulting from post-cooking, curing or processing contamination. These can be minimised by using recommended chilled temperatures, good hygiene and handling practices. The low water activity (a_w) and addition of nitrite in cooked, cured and processed meat products inhibit the growth of many food poisoning bacteria, particularly *C. botulinum*. This inhibition may be compromised in products formulated with lower concentrations of chemical preservatives than those used in traditional foods.

The potential effects of any changes in product formulation on the growth and survival of pathogens should always be considered. Cooked meats stored without any added preservatives will be at risk from growth of *C. botulinum* under anaerobic MAP conditions, particularly when held at elevated storage temperatures. It should be noted that many sliced, cooked, cured and processed meat products are vacuum packed for retail sale. However, the shelf life of such products in MAP is similar to that achieved in vacuum packs, and additionally, MAP allows for easier separation of meat slices.

Fish and Fish Products

There has been a very significant increase in the sale of MAP fish products in Europe and particularly in the United Kingdom. Nevertheless, packaging technologists should be aware of a major concern limiting the development of MAP, namely the growth of *C. botulinum*. There is also debate about the cost benefits of MAP, since in some applications only relatively small increases in safe shelf life have been reported. Spoilage of fish results in the production of low molecular weight volatile compounds, therefore, packaging technologists need to consider the odour barrier properties of packaging films and select appropriate high-barrier materials for packaging strong flavoured fresh, smoked and brined fish and fish products.

Spoilage of fish and shellfish results from changes caused by three major mechanisms: (i) the breakdown of tissue by the fish's own enzymes (autolysis of cells), (ii) growth of micro-organisms, and (iii) oxidative reactions. MAP can be used to control mechanisms (ii) and (iii) but has no direct effect on autolysis. Because autolysis is the major cause of spoilage of fish and shellfish stored at temperatures close to 0°C compared with the activities of bacteria, this may explain the reduction in benefits achieved from MAP of fish compared to other flesh products. MAP, while potentially inhibiting oxidative reactions, may be more effective at inhibiting microbial growth.

Oxidative reactions are much more important as shelf life limiters in fish compared with other flesh meat, because seafood has a higher content of polyunsaturated lipids. Storage temperature has a major effect on fat oxidation that occurs even at frozen temperatures. Note that salt addition can accelerate oxidative processes.

Generally, the major spoilage bacteria found on processed fish are aerobes including *Pseudomonas*, *Moraxella*, *Acinetobacter*, *Flavobacterium* and *Cytophaga* species. There are several micro-organisms that are of particular importance when dealing with MAP fish products, these include *C. botulinum*. Use of CO_2 can effectively inhibit the growth of some of these species. The aerobic spoilage organisms tend to be replaced by slower growing, and less odour producing, bacteria, particularly lactic acid bacteria, such as lactobacilli, during storage. Because fish and shellfish contain much lower concentrations of myoglobin, the oxidation status of this pigment is generally less important than that in other meats. Consequently, there is potential to use higher levels of CO_2, e.g. 40%. Because of the high moisture content and the lipid content of some species, N_2 is used to prevent pack collapse. CO is used extensively in the MAP of tuna in the US.

One of the concerns about MAP of fish is that removal of O_2 and its replacement by either N_2 or N_2/CO_2 results in anaerobic conditions that are conducive to the growth of protease negative strains of *C. botulinum*. Because these bacteria can grow at temperatures as low as 3°C and do not significantly alter the sensory properties of the fish, there is the potential for food poisoning that can lead to fatalities. While there is no evidence that CO_2 promotes the growth of psychotropic strains of *C. botulinum*, there are, as discussed previously, some concerns about CO_2 promoting the germination of spores of this organism.

Considerable research has been undertaken to assess, and to control, the risks associated with the growth of *C. botulinum* in MAP of fish and other products. The Advisory Committee on the Microbiological Safety of Food (ACMSF) have recommended controlling factors that should be used singly or in combination to prevent the growth of, and toxin production in prepared chilled food by, psychotropic *C. botulinum*. As far as MAP of raw fish products is concerned, risk can be effectively eliminated if storage temperature is held at 3°C or below and if the shelf life is limited to no more than 10 days. Some fish processors include O_2 in their MAP to further reduce the risk of growth of clostridia. Gas mixtures of 30% O_2, 40% CO_2 and 30% N_2 are used for white non-processed fish, i.e. nonfatty fish. While this will increase the shelf life of some fish and fish products, it would not significantly enhance the shelf life of oily or fatty fish. High, 40%, CO_2 mixes along with 60% N_2 are generally used for smoked and fatty fish. Because of the risks already discussed, it would appear reasonable to aim for a target shelf life of 10–14 days at 3°C.

Fruits and Vegetables

Consumers now expect fresh fruit and vegetable produce throughout the year. MAP has the potential to extend the safe shelf life of many fruits and vegetables. Packaging fresh and unprocessed fruits and vegetables poses many challenges for packaging technologists. As with all products, it is essential to work with the highest quality raw materials, and this is especially true for this product group, often referred to as fresh produce. The quality of fresh produce is markedly dependent on growing conditions, minimising bruising and other damage during harvesting and processing, adherence to good hygienic practices, controlling humidity to prevent desiccation while avoiding condensation to prevent mould growth, and maintaining optimum storage temperatures. Unlike other chilled perishable foods, fresh produce continues to respire after harvesting. The products of aerobic respiration include CO_2 and water vapour. In addition, respiring fruits and vegetables produce C_2H_4 that promotes ripening and softening of tissues. The latter if not controlled will limit shelf life.

Respiration is affected by the intrinsic properties of fresh produce as well as various extrinsic factors, including ambient temperature. It is accepted that the potential shelf life of packed produce is inversely proportional to respiration rate. Respiration rate increases by a factor of 3–4 for every 10°C increase in temperature. Hence, the goal of MAP for fruits and vegetables is to reduce respiration to extend shelf life while maintaining quality.

Respiration can be reduced by lowering the temperature, lowering the O_2 concentration, increasing the CO_2 concentration and by the combined use of O_2 depletion and CO_2 enhancement of pack atmospheres. If the O_2 concentration is reduced beyond a critical concentration, which is dependent on the species and cultivar, then anaerobic respiration will be initiated. The products of anaerobic respiration include ethanol, acetaldehyde and organic acids. Anaerobic respiration, or anaerobiosis, is usually associated with undesirable odours and flavours and a marked deterioration in product quality. While increasing the CO_2 concentration will also inhibit respiration, high concentrations may cause damage in some species and cultivars.

Reducing O_2 concentrations below 5% will slow the respiration rate of many fruits and vegetables. Kader and others have tabulated the minimum O_2 concentration tolerated by a range of fresh produce, while some cultivars of apples and pears can tolerate O_2 concentrations as low as 0.5%, potatoes undergo anaerobic respiration at around 5% O_2. In general, O_2 concentrations below about 3% can induce anaerobic respiration in many species of fresh produce.

Elevated CO_2 can also inhibit respiration. If the gas concentration is too high, then anaerobic respiration is induced with consequent quality problems. CO_2 sensitivity is both species and cultivar dependant, strawberries are able to tolerate 15% CO_2 whereas celery is stressed by CO_2 concentrations above 2%. The tolerance of strawberries to CO_2 can be used to inhibit the growth of the mould *Botrytis cinerea*.

The use of low concentrations of O_2 and elevated levels of CO_2 can have a synergistic effect on slowing down respiration and, indirectly, ripening. While the mechanisms whereby MAP can extend the shelf life of fresh produce are not fully understood, it is known that the low O_2/high CO_2 conditions reduce the conversion of chlorophyll to pheophytin, decrease the sensitivity of plant tissue to C_2H_4, inhibit the synthesis of carotenoids, reduce oxidative browning and discolouration and inhibit the growth of microorganisms. These mechanisms are all temperature dependent. The effects of MAP on the physiology of fruits and vegetables have been the subject of extensive research by various countries of the World.

Packaging technologists should be aware of several major pathogens as far as MAP fresh produce is concerned, in particular, *L. monocytogenes* and *C. botulinum*. As previously discussed, *L. monocytogenes* can grow under reduced O_2 levels and is not markedly inhibited by CO_2. This combined with its ability to grow at temperatures close to 0%C helps explain the concern.

The use of MAP atmospheres containing low concentrations of O_2 and elevated CO_2 concentrations may permit the growth of psychotropic protease-negative strains of *C. botulinum*. However, provided packs are stored at 3°C or below for not more than 10 days, there is unlikely to be a problem with clostridia. Temperature control is critical, since temperature abuse could lead to pack contents becoming toxic.

The environment in which fruits and vegetables are grown may harbour pathogens including *Salmonella* species, enterotoxigenic *E. coli* and viruses. While these micro-organisms may not grow in MAP packs, particularly if the storage temperature is maintained around 3°C, they may survive throughout storage and could cause food poisoning through cross-contamination in the home or due to the consumption of raw or under-processed product. Hygienic preparation, sanitation in chilled-chlorinated water, rinsing and dewatering prior to MAP are now considered as essential treatments to fruits and vegetables prior to packaging to ensure low microbial counts and assure safety. Since there is a risk of anaerobic pathogens, such as *C. botulinum*, growing in MAP packs, a minimum level of O_2 (e.g. 2–3%) is usually recommended to ensure that potentially hazardous conditions are not created.

Equilibrium MAP has been used for fresh produce. Essentially, this involves using knowledge of the permeability characteristics of particular packaging films, along with the respiration characteristics of the product to balance the gas transfer rates of O_2 and CO_2 through the package with the respiration rate of the particular product.

Increasingly, gas packing fresh produce along with $CO_2/O_2/N_2$ gas mixtures is being used. This approach may have benefit in reducing enzymic browning reactions before a passively generated equilibrium modified atmosphere has been established.

Dairy Products

MAP has the potential to increase the shelf life of a number of dairy products. These include fat-filled milk powders, cheeses and fat spreads. In general, these products spoil due to the development of oxidative rancidity in the case of powders and/or the growth of micro-organisms, particularly yeasts and moulds, in the case of cheese.

Whole milk powder is particularly susceptible to the development of off-flavours due to fat oxidation. Commercially, the air is removed under vacuum and replaced with 100% N_2 or N_2/CO_2 mixes and the powder is hermetically sealed in metal cans. Due to the spray drying process, air tends to be absorbed inside the powder particles and will diffuse into the container over time. This typically will raise the residual headspace O_2 content to 1–5% or higher. Because some markets require product with low levels of residual O_2 (<1%), some manufacturers repack the cans after ten days of storage. Obviously, this is both expensive and inconvenient. We have found that use of N_2/CO_2 mixes can be helpful. Use of O_2 scavenging may also be useful.

English territorial cheeses, e.g. Cheddar, have traditionally been vacuum packed. Increasingly MAP is being used with high CO_2 concentration gas mixes. This has the advantage of obtaining a low residual O_2 content and a tight pack due to the CO_2 going into solution. It is important to balance this process using the correct N_2 level in the gas mix so as to avoid excessive pressure being put on the pack seal.

Use of N_2/CO_2 atmospheres have significant potential for extending the shelf life of cottage cheese. The cottage cheese is a high-moisture, low-fat product that is susceptible to a number of spoilage organisms including *Pseudomonas* spp. Use of gas mixtures containing 40% CO_2 balanced with 60% N_2 can increase the shelf life significantly.

Chapter 30

Biodegradable Polymers in Food Packaging

INTRODUCTION

In recent years, there zhas been a marked increase in the interest in use of biodegradable materials in packaging. The principal function of packaging is protection and preservation of food from external contamination. This function involves retardation of deterioration, extension of shelf life, and maintenance of quality and safety of packaged food. Biodegradable polymers are the one which fulfill all these functions without causing any threat to the environment. The belief is that biodegradable polymer materials will reduce the need for synthetic polymer production (thus reducing pollution) at a low cost, thereby producing a positive effect both environmentally and economically.

As well known, synthetic polymer materials have been widely used in every field of human activity during the last decades. These artificial macromolecular substances are usually originating from petroleum and most of the conventional ones are regarded as non-degradable. However, the petroleum resources are limited and the blooming use of non-biodegradable polymers has caused serious environmental problems. In addition, the non-biodegradable polymers are not suitable for temporary use such as sutures. Thus, the polymer materials which are degradable and/or biodegradable have being paid more and more attention since 1970s. Food is the necessity of our day to day life. Now a day's most of the food items are packed. In everyday life, packaging is an important area where biodegradable polymers can be used. The primary factors driving development of the biodegradable packaging market include the increase in crude oil prices, which has narrowed the price differential, consumer demand, the proliferation of convenience packaging, development of new applications for bioplastics, increased economic viability as production ramps up and unit costs decrease, and development of the composting infrastructure for optimal disposal of bioplastic products. Even so, consumer demand for products that are environmentally friendly, safer and nontoxic, as well as, a currently favourable economic scenario leads to the conclusion that biodegradable packaging products will become increasingly popular. In order to reduce the volume of waste, biodegradable polymers are often used. Besides their biodegradability, biopolymers have other characteristics as air permeability, low temperature sealability, availability and low price. Several biopolymers such as starch, cellulose, chitosan, PLA, PCL, PHB, etc. are used for packaging purposes. The current trend in food packaging is the use of blends of different biopolymers like starch-PLA blends, starch-PCL blends, etc. Bottles, jars, vials, drums, pails, cans, barrels, buckets, caps, closures, aerosol parts, packaging films, food containers , disposable cups, coating for all types of packaging, packaging bags, household and institutional refuse bags and film, boxes and baskets, etc. are being manufactured by using biodegradable polymers. Many companies like Novamont, BASF, Biomer, National starch, DuPont, etc. are producing biopolymers.

WHAT ARE POLYMERS?

Polymer materials are solid, non-metallic compounds of high molecular weights. They are comprised of repeating macromolecules, and have varying characteristics depending upon their composition. Each macromolecule that comprises a polymeric material is known as a mer unit. A single mer is called a monomer, while repeating mer units are known as polymers. A variety of materials (both renewable and non-renewable) are employed as feedstock sources for modern plastic materials. Plastics that are formed from non-renewable feedstocks are generally petroleum based, and reinforced by glass or carbon fibres. Renewable resource feedstocks include microbial-grown polymers and those extracted from starch. It is possible to reinforce such materials with natural fibres, from plants such as flax, jute, hemp, and other cellulose sources.

WHAT ARE BIOPOLYMERS?

Biopolymers are long chain compounds made up of long chain molecule subunits. A biopolymer is any organic polymer. Biopolymers have been around for billions of years longer than synthetic polymers like plastics. Well Known biopolymers include starch, proteins and peptides, DNA, and RNA. Together these make up much of our bodies and the majority of the biosphere. These are biodegradable, ecofriendly and are obtained from natural sources. Biopolymers are polymers that are generated from renewable natural sources, are often biodegradable, and not toxic to produce. They can be produced by biological systems (i.e. micro-organisms, plants and animals), or chemically synthesised from biological starting materials (e.g. sugars, starch, natural fats or oils, etc.). Biopolymers are an alternative to petroleum-based polymers (traditional plastics).

Origin and Description of Biobased Polymers

Biobased polymers may be divided into three main categories based on their origin and production:

***Category 1*:** Polymers directly extracted/removed from biomass. Examples are polysaccharides such as starch and cellulose and proteins like casein and gluten.

***Category 2*:** Polymers produced by classical chemical synthesis using renewable biobased monomers. A good example is polylactic acid, a biopolyester polymerised from lactic acid monomers. The monomers themselves may be produced via fermentation of carbohydrate feedstock.

***Category 3*:** Polymers produced by micro-organisms or genetically modified bacteria. To date, this group of biobased polymers consists mainly of the polyhydroxyalkonoates, but developments with bacterial cellulose are in progress.

Starch

Starch is a well–known hydrocolloid biopolymer. It is a low cost polysaccharide, abundantly available and one of the cheapest biodegradable polymers. Starch is produced by agricultural plants in the form of granules, which are hydrophilic. Starch is mainly extracted from potatoes, corn, wheat and rice. It is composed of amylose (poly-α-1, 4-D-glucopyranoside), a linear and crystalline polymer and amylopectin (poly-α-1, 4-Dglucopyranoside and α-1, 6-D-glucopyranoside), a branched and amorphous polymer. Starch has different proportions of amylose and amylopectin ranging from about 10–20% amylase and 80–90% amylopectin depending on the source. Amylose is soluble in water and forms a helical structure. The relative amounts and molar masses of amylose and amylopectin vary with the starch source, yielding to materials of different mechanical properties and biodegradability. As the amylose content of starch increases, the elongation and strength increase too. The stability of starch under stress is not high. The glucoside links start to break at 150°C and above 250°C the granules collapse. Retrogradation, i.e. reorganisation of hydrogen bonds, is observed at low temperatures, during cooling. In its applications starch can be mixed, kept intact, and used in various resins as a filler or melt for blending compounds. In the former form, fillers are starch whiskers used with polymer resins.

Starch is usually used as a thermoplastic. It is plasticised through destructuration in presence of specific amounts of water or plasticisers and heat and then it is extruded. Thermoplastic starch (TPS) has a high sensitivity to humidity. Thermal properties of TPS have been shown to be more influenced by the content of water than the starch molecular weight. TPS thus obtained is almost amorphous. Biodegradation of starch is achieved via hydrolysis at the acetal link by enzymes. The α-1,4 link is attacked by amylases while glucosidases attack the α-1, 6 link. The degradation products are non toxic.

Polylactic Acid

PLA is usually obtained from polycondensation of D- or L-lactic acid or from ring opening polymerisation of lactide, a cyclic dimer of lactic acid. Two optical forms exist: D-lactide and L-lactide. The natural isomer is L-lactide and the synthetic blend is DL-lactide. Other different synthetic methods have been studied too. PLA is a hydrophobic polymer due to the presence of $-CH_3$ side groups. It is more resistant to hydrolysis than PGA because of the steric shielding effect of the methyl side groups. The typical glass transition temperature for representative commercial PLA is 63.8°C, the elongation at break is 30.7% and the tensile strength is 32.22 MPa. Regulation of the physical properties and biodegradability of PLA can be achieved by employing a hydroxy acids comonomer component or by racemisation of D- and L- isomers. A semi-crystalline polymer (PLLA) (crystallinity about 37%) is obtained from L-lactide whereas poly (DL-lactide) (PDLLA) is an amorphous polymer. Their mechanical properties are different as are their degradation times. PLLA is a hard, transparent polymer with an elongation at break of 85–105% and a tensile strength of 45–70 MPa. It has a melting point of 170–180°C and a glass transition temperature of 53°C. PDLLA has no melting point and a T_g around 55°C. It shows much lower tensile strength.

PLA has disadvantages of brittleness and poor thermal stability. PLA can be plasticised to improve the chain mobility and to favour its crystallisation. Plasticisation is realised with oligomeric acid, citrate ester or low molecular polyethylene glycol. High molecular weight PLAs are obtained through ring opening polymerisation. This route allows also the control of the final properties of PLA by adjusting the proportions of the two enantiomers. Other routes are melt/solid state polymerisation, solution polymerisation or chain extension reaction. High molecular weight PLA has better mechanical properties. The rate of degradation of PLA depends on the degree of crystallinity. The degradation rate of PLLA is very low compared to PGA, therefore, some copolymers of lactide and glycoside have been investigated as bioresorbable implant materials. The biodegradability of PLA can also be enhanced by grafting. The graft copolymerisation of L-lactide onto chitosan was carried out by ring opening polymerisation using a tin catalyst. The melting transition temperature and thermal stability of graft polymers increase with increasing grafting percentages. As the lactide content increases, the degradation of the graft polymer decreases.

Poly (Hydroxyalkanoates) (PHAs)

PHAs, of which poly (hydroxybutyrate) (PHB) is the most common, are accumulated by a large number of bacteria as energy and carbon reserves. Due to their biodegradability and biocompatibility these biopolyesters may easily find numerous applications. The properties of PHAs are dependent on their monomer composition, and it is, therefore, of great interest that recent research has revealed that, in addition to PHB, a large variety of PHAs can be synthesised by microbial fermentation. The monomer composition of PHAs depends on the nature of the carbon source and micro-organisms used. PHB is a typical highly crystalline thermoplastic whereas the medium chain lengths PHAs are elastomers with low melting points and a relatively lower degree of crystallinity. A very interesting property of PHAs with respect to food packaging applications is their low water vapour permeability which is close to that of LDPE.

Since 1925, PHB is produced biotechnologically and was attentively studied as biodegradable polyester. The R alkyl substituent group is methyl. PHB is highly crystalline with crystallinity above 50%. Its melting temperature is 180°C. The pure homopolymer is a brittle material. Its glass transition temperature is approximately of 55°C. It has some mechanical properties comparable to synthetic degradable polyesters, as PLA. During storage time at room temperature a secondary crystallisation of the amorphous phase occurs. As a result, stress and elongation modulus increase (E = 1.7 GPa) while the polymer becomes more brittle and hard. Elongation at break is then much lower (10%). Compared to conventional plastics, it suffers from a narrow processability window. PHB is susceptible to thermal degradation at temperatures in the region of the melting point. To make the process easier, PHB can be plasticised, with citrate ester.

PHB resembles isotactic polypropylene (iPP) in relation to melting temperature (175–180°C) and mechanical behaviour. PHBs T_g is around 9°C and the elongation to break of the ultimate PHB (3–8%), which is markedly lower than that of iPP (400%). Incorporation of 3HV or 4HB co-monomers produces remarkable changes in the mechanical properties: the stiffness and tensile strength decrease while the toughness increases with increasing fraction of the respective co-monomer. PHB is degraded by numerous micro-organisms (bacteria, fungi and algae) in various environments. The hydrolytic degradation yields to the formation of 3-hydroxy butyric acid, a normal constituent of blood, nevertheless with a relatively low rate. Different monomers have been grafted onto PHB to prepare biodegradable polymers to be used for wastewater treatments. The grafted monomers were either hydrophilic as acrylic acid or sodium-pstyrene sulphonate, or hydrophobic as styrene or methyl acrylate. The degree of grafting was different according to the monomers, increasing with the following order styrene, sodium-*p*-styrene sulphonate, methyl acrylate and acrylic acid.

Multicomponent polymeric systems containing PHB have been obtained by two ways. The first is a radical polymerisation of an acrylic polymer in the presence of PHB. The second consists in melt mixing PCL with PHB. Peroxide is used in both processes to form intergrafted species responsible for compatibilisation. These methods have been considered as reactive blending. It should be noted that apart from the bacterial synthetic way, other chemical ways have been developed for the production of PHB. The ring opening polymerisation of β-butyrolactone yields to PHB too. Different structures are obtained according to the synthesis route. An isotactic polymer with random stereo sequences is obtained via bacterial process while a polymer with partially stereo regular block is obtained via chemical synthesis. Applications that have been developed from PHB and related materials (e.g. Biopol) can be found in very different areas and cover packaging, hygienic, agricultural, and biomedical products. Recent application developments based on medium chain length PHAs range from high solid alkyd-like paints to pressure sensitive adhesives, biodegradable cheese coatings and biodegradable rubbers. Technically, the prospects for PHAs are very promising. When the price of these materials can be further reduced, application of biopolyesters will also become economically attractive.

Polycaprolactone (PCL)

Poly-ε-caprolactone is a relatively cheap cyclic monomer. A semi-crystalline linear polymer is obtained from ring-opening polymerisation of ε-caprolactone in presence of tin octoate catalyst. PCL is soluble in a wide range of solvents. Its glass transition temperature is low, around –60°C, and its melting point is 60–65°C. PCL is a semi-rigid material at room temperature, has a modulus in the range of low-density polyethylene and high-density polyethylene, a low tensile strength of 23 MPa and a high elongation to break (more than 700%). Thanks to its low T_g, PCL is often used as a compatibiliser or as a soft block in polyurethane formulations. Enzymes and fungi easily biodegrade PCL. To improve the degradation rate, several copolymers with lactide or glycoside have been prepared. PCL is commercially available under the trade names CAPA® (from Solvay, Belgium), Tone® (from Union Carbide, USA) or Celgreen® (from Daicel, Japan) and many others. Possible applications in packaging have been investigated.

Cellulose and Derivatives

Cellulose is the most abundantly occurring natural polymer on earth and is an almost linear polymer of anhydroglucose. It is a linear polymer with very long macromolecular chains of one repeating unit, cellobiose. Cellulose is crystalline, infusible and insoluble in all organic solvents. Because of its regular structure and array of hydroxyl groups, it tends to form strongly hydrogen bonded crystalline micro fibrils and fibres and is most familiar in the form of paper or cardboard in the packaging context. Waxed or polyethylene coated paper is used in some areas of primary food packaging, however the bulk of paper is used for secondary packaging.

Cellulose is a cheap raw material, but difficult to use because of its hydrophilic nature, insolubility and crystalline structure. The cellophane produced is very hydrophilic and, therefore, moisture sensitive, but it has good mechanical properties. It is, however, not thermoplastic owing to the fact that the theoretical melt temperature is above the degradation temperature, and therefore cannot be heat-sealed.

Cellophane is often coated with nitrocellulose wax or PVdC (Poly Vinylidene Chloride) to improve barrier properties and in such form it is used for packaging of baked goods, processed meat, cheese and candies. A number of cellulose derivatives are produced commercially, most commonly carboxy-methyl cellulose, methyl cellulose, ethyl cellulose, hydroxyethyl cellulose, hydroxypropyl cellulose and cellulose acetate. Of these derivatives only cellulose acetate (CA) is widely used in food packaging's (baked goods and fresh produce). CA possesses relatively low gas and moisture barrier properties and has to be plasticised for film production. Many cellulose derivatives possess excellent film-forming properties, but they are simply too expensive for bulk use. This is a direct consequence of the crystalline structure of cellulose making the initial steps of derivatisation difficult and costly. Research is required to develop efficient processing technologies for the production of cellulose derivatives if this situation is to change. Tenite® (Eastman, USA), Bioceta® (Mazzucchelli, Italy), Fasal® (IFA, Austria) and Natureflex® (UCB, Germany) are some of the trade names of cellulose-based polymers.

BLENDS

Starch-polyvinyl Alcohol

TPS and PVOH have excellent compatibility and their blends are of particular interest. TPS and starch can be blended at various ratios to tailor the mechanical properties of the final material. Compared to pure TPS materials, blends present improved tensile strength, elongation and processability. Their biodegradability has been recently investigated. The PVOH content has an important impact on the rate of starch degradation increasing the amount of PVOH will decrease this rate.

Starch-PLA

The mechanical properties of blends of starch with PLA using conventional processes are poor due to incompatibility. An elongation increase can be achieved by using plasticisers or reacting agents during the extrusion process. Coupling agents like isocyanates have been used. The hydroxyl groups of starch could react with the isocyanate group resulting in urethane linkages and compatibilisation of these systems. The effect of gelatinisation of starch was also investigated. It has been shown that in PLA/gelatinised starch blends, starch could be considered as a nucleating agent, resulting in an improvement of crystallinity in PLA blends and a greater superiority of mechanical properties. Another way to improve compatibilisation is to use a compatibiliser. Maleic anhydride can be used for this purpose. An initiator was used to create free radicals on PLA and improved the reaction between maleic acid and PLA. The anhydride group on maleic acid could react with the hydroxyl groups present in starch. Interfacial adhesion between starch and PLA was then significantly improved. The mechanical properties obtained for PLA/starch blends compatibilised with maleic acid are higher than those obtained for virgin PLA/starch blends. A biodegradable PLA-grafted amylose copolymer has been synthesised, to be used as compatibiliser agent in starch/PLA blends.

Starch – PCL

To prepare films by using the film blowing technique, TPS was blended with PCL to adjust the rheological properties of the melt before the process. Novamont (Italy) produces a class of starch blend with different synthetic components. Its trade name is Mater-Bi®. Four grades are available, one of them consists of PCL (Mater-Bi® Z). The highest amount of starch allows the acceleration of the degradation of PCL. The behaviour of some PCL-modified starch blends has been studied. The addition of modified starch leads to an increase of the Young's modulus of PCL and a decrease in tensile strength and elongation at break values. The blend becomes less ductile. Some synthetic polymers with lower biodegradability are used to control the rate of biodegradation according to the applications. The modulus of blends of high-amylose corn starch (25% wt.) and PCL was 50% higher than that of PCL and the tensile strength 15% lower. To increase the mechanical properties of PCL/starch, blends with LDPE were prepared. The biodegradation rate of PCL, which is very low, can be significantly increased by the presence of starch.

PCL/Chitin-chitosan Blends

PCL blends with chitin were prepared as biodegradable composites by melt blending. Increasing the amount of chitin has no effect on the melting or crystallisation temperature. This was attributed to a non miscible blend. Another blending route is solvent casting. The degree of crystallinity of PCL decreases upon blending with chitin. Same results are obtained with PCL/chitosan blends. These blends are expected to have good mechanical properties.

MATERIAL PROPERTIES

Gas Barrier Properties

Many foods require specific atmospheric conditions to sustain their freshness and overall quality during storage. Hence, increasing amounts of our foods are being packed in protective atmosphere with a specific mixture of gases ensuring optimum quality and safety of the food product in question. To ensure a constant gas composition inside the package, the packaging material needs to have certain gas barriers. In most packaging applications the gas mixture inside the package consists of carbon dioxide, oxygen and nitrogen or combinations hereof. The objective of this section is to describe the gas barriers of biobased materials using mineral oil based polymer materials as benchmarks.

Alternatives to presently available gas barrier materials like EVOH and PA6 and an equivalent biobased laminate would be an outer-layer of plasticised chitosan, a protein or starch-derived film combined with PLA or PHA. Notably, the gas barrier properties of PA6 and EVOH are sensitive towards moisture and the LDPE creates a very effective water vapour barrier ensuring that the moisture from the foodstuff does not interfere with the properties of PA6 or EVOH. In the same fashion, PLA and PHA will protect the moisture-sensitive-gas-barrier made of polysaccharide and protein.

Gas barriers and humidity

As many of these biobased materials are hydrophilic, their gas barrier properties are very much dependent on the humidity conditions for the measurements and the gas permeability of hydrophilic biobased materials may increase manifold when humidity increases. Notably, this is a phenomenon also seen with conventional polymers. The gas permeability of high gas barrier materials, such as nylon and ethyl vinyl alcohol, is likewise affected by increasing humidity. Gas barriers based on PLA and PHA is not expected to be dependent on humidity.

Water vapour transmittance

A major challenge for the material manufacturer is the by nature hydrophilic behaviour of many biobased polymers as a lot of food applications demand materials that are resistant to moist conditions. However, when comparing the water vapour transmittance of various biobased materials to materials based on mineral oil, it becomes clear that it is possible to produce biobased materials with water vapour transmittance rates comparable to the ones provided by some conventional plastics. However, if a high water vapour barrier material is required, very few biobased materials apply. Notably, developments are currently focusing on this problem and future biobased materials must also be able to mimic the water vapour barriers of the conventional materials known today.

Thermal and mechanical properties

Next to the barrier properties of the final packaging, the thermal and mechanical properties of the materials are both important for processing and also during the use of the products derived from these materials. Most biobased polymer materials perform in a similar fashion to conventional polymers. This indicates that polystyrene-like polymers (relatively stiff materials with intermediate service temperatures), polyethylene-like polymers (relatively flexible polymers with intermediate service temperatures) and PET-like materials (relatively stiff materials with higher service temperatures) can be found among the available biobased polymers. The mechanical properties in terms of modulus and stiffness are not very different compared to conventional polymers. The modulus of biobased materials ranges from 2500–3000 MPa and lowers for stiff polymers like thermoplastic starches to 50 MPa and lower for rubbery materials like medium chain polyhydroxyalkanoates.

Furthermore, the modulus of most biobased and petroleum derived polymers can be tailored to meet the required mechanical properties by means of plasticising, blending with other polymers or fillers, cross linking or by the addition of fibres. A polymer like bacterial cellulose could for instance be used in materials which require special mechanical properties. In theory, biobased materials can be made having similar strength to the ones we use today.

COMPOSTABILITY

Compostability is another important property required for biopolymers used in food packaging. Notably, the 'composting time' depicted in the figure represents the approximate period of time required for an acceptable level of disintegration of the material to occur. This means that the original material should not be recognisable anymore in the final compost (fraction < 10 mm) nor in the overflow (fraction > 10 mm). The composting time does not reflect the time required for the biodegradation of the materials to be fully completed. The process could subsequently be completed during the use of the compost. The level of technology applied in the composting process highly affects the composting time needed for complete disintegration. Hence, it takes much longer to obtain a mature compost using low technology composting (e.g. passive windrow composting) than using high technology as in an intensively controlled tunnel composting process. Furthermore, the composting time needed for complete disintegration is also affected by the particle size of the material. For example, wood is rapidly composted in the form of sawdust and small chips. A wooden log, however, takes more than one year to be completely disintegrated.

The compostability of the materials are highly dependent on the other properties of the materials, e.g. the first step of the composting is often a hydrolysis or wetting of the material. The rate of this step is very much related to the water vapour transmittance and the water resistance of the material. Hence, the composting rate of a material will be dependent on its other properties.

Manufacturing of Biobased Food Packaging

Engineering of a biobased package or packaging material requires knowledge of the processing and material properties of the polymers. If the properties of the native biopolymer are not identical to the required one, or if the polymer by nature is not thermoplastic, a certain modification of the polymer must take place. For very specific requirements (very low gas permeability or high water resistance) it is unlikely that one polymer will be able to provide all required properties even after modifications. Hence, it is necessary to use multiple materials in a composite, a laminate or co-extruded material.

Possible Products Produced of Biobased Materials

The fundamental repeating chemical units of the biobased materials described so far are identical to those of a significant body of the conventional plastics. Thus, in the broadest sense, poly- saccharides possessing repeating acetal functionality can be regarded as the naturally occurring analogues of the synthetic polyacetals, proteins (repeating peptide functionality) can be compared to the synthetic polyamides while polylactic acid is merely an example of the diverse group of polyesters.

Clearly, however, the gross physical and chemical properties of native biobased materials and their synthetic counterparts are quite different and this is a feature of additional chemical functionality inherent in biobased materials. It should be expected that following requisite processing and product development of biobased materials resulting properties should equal or better those of the conventional alternatives. However, such processing and product development is not always trivial and is unlikely to be cost effective in all cases. It is not surprising, therefore, that the current applications of biobased materials seek not to emulate the properties of conventional plastics, but to capitalise on inherent biodegradability and on other unique properties of these polymers. Biobased plastic applications are currently targeted towards single-use, disposable, short-life packaging materials, service ware items, disposable non-woven's and coatings for paper and paperboard applications. In general, the same shapes and types of food packaging can be made from synthetic and biobased resources. The question is whether the same performance can be achieved by using the biobased materials as with the synthetic ones.

Blown (Barrier) Films

Blown films comprise one of the first product categories to be developed based on mineral oil derived biodegradable polyesters. They have successfully been applied as garbage bags and related applications. Film blowing grades of renewable polymers have been developed based on PLA. Blown films based on these biopolyesters exhibit excellent transparency and cellophane-like mechanical properties. The sealability depends on the degree of crystallinity and good printability can also be achieved. The possibilities of film blowing PHB/V materials are at this time limited due to their slow crystallisation and low melt strength. In many food packaging applications, water vapour barriers as well as gas barriers are required. No single biobased polymer can fulfill both these demands. In this case, the use of co-extrusion can lead to laminates which meet the objectives. Paragon materials which are based on thermoplastic starch can be film blown in a co-extrusion set-up with polymers like PLA and PHB/V as coating materials, resulting in a barrier coating which, for example, proved to be successful in the packaging of cheese. The use of Paragon tie-layers provides the adhesion between the coating and the base layer. In this way, starch-based materials could provide cheap alternatives to presently available gas barrier materials like EVOH and PA6.

Thermoformed Containers

A next class of products is thermoformed containers for food packaging. In order to be able to thermoform a polymer it should be possible to process this material from the melt (extrusion) into sheets and consequently thermoforming these sheets just above the T_g or T_m of the material. Thermoformed products can be found based on PLA and PHB/V. Again, it is possible to produce thermoformed

Foamed Products

Starch-based foams for loose fill applications have been commercially introduced with success some years ago and the market for these products is still growing. Foamed products like trays and clamshells based on starch for food packaging have not yet been introduced commercially. Products based on a molding technique from a slurry phase are close to market introduction. These products are produced form starch base slurries with inorganic and agro fibre based fillers. Other proposed techniques include loose-fill molding, and extrusion transfer molding and expandable bead molding. Foamed products based totally on PLA are still in a developmental phase. In order to be able to use these starch-foamed products in food contact applications coatings should be applied on the starch- based foams. Adhesion between the foam and the coating is of importance.

Paraffin and other oligomer based coatings are proposed next to PLA and PHB/V based coatings. Protein and medium chain length PHA based coatings are close to market introduction. Other proposed techniques include loose-fill molding, foam extrusion, and extrusion transfer molding. Foamed products based totally on PLA are still in a developmental phase. In order to be able to use these starch-foamed products in food contact applications coatings should be applied on the starch-based foams. Adhesion between the foam and the coating is of importance. Paraffin and other oligomer based coatings are proposed next to PLA and PHB/V based coatings. Protein and medium chain length PHA based coatings are close to market introduction.

Coated Paper

It is expected that paper will stay an important biobased packaging material. Paper and board materials have excellent mechanical properties, however, the gas permeabilities are too high for many food applications. The hydrophilic nature of the paper-based materials is a major challenge of these materials when packaging moist foods. To date, the paper-based materials have been coated with a thin layer of synthetic plastic which has provided the materials with the required gas property and water resistance. Alternatively, biobased materials might be used as coating materials thus paving the way for a 100% biobased packaging material. Paper-based materials coated with PE are readily repulpable as the hydrophobic PE is easily removed in the pulping process. Hence, paper-based materials coated with biobased, hydrophobic polymeric materials are, likewise, going to be repulpable.

Additional Developments

To be able to produce a 100% biobased packaging development of biobased additives is needed. Additives used in the production of packaging are plasticisers, UV-stabilisers, adhesives, inks and paints, natural pigments and colorants. So far, few developments have been made in this field and it is suggested to direct research to this area.

To sum up, the food industry has seen great advances in the packaging sector since its inception in the 18th century with most active and intelligent innovations occurring during the past century. These advances have led to improved food quality and safety. While some innovations have stemmed from unexpected sources, most have been driven by changing consumer preferences. The new advances have mostly focused on delaying oxidation and controlling moisture migration, microbial growth, respiration rates, and volatile flavours and aromas. This focus parallels that of food packaging distribution, which has driven change in the key areas of sustainable packaging, use of the packaging value chain relationships for competitive advantage, and the evolving role of food service packaging. Biopolymers have highly influenced the packaging sector greatly. Environmental responsibility is constantly increasing in importance to both consumers and industry.

For those who produce biodegradable plastic materials, this is a key advantage. Biopolymers limit carbon dioxide emissions during creation, and degrade to organic matter after disposal. Although synthetic plastics are a more economically feasible choice than biodegradable ones, an increased availability of biodegradable plastics will allow many consumers to choose them on the basis of their environmentally responsible disposal. The processes which hold the most promise for further development of biopolymer materials are those which employ renewable resource feedstocks. Time is of the essence for biodegradable polymer development, as society's current views on environmental responsibility make this an ideal time for further growth of biopolymers.

Chapter 31

Recent Developments in Food Packaging Based on Nanomaterials

INTRODUCTION

The increasing demand for high food quality and safety, and concerns of environment sustainable development have been encouraging researchers in the food industry to exploit the robust and green biodegradable nanocomposites, which provide new opportunities and challenges for the development of nanomaterials in the food industry. This chapter summarises the recent developments of nanomaterials in food packaging. Two categories of nanomaterials (i.e. inorganic and organic) are included. The synthetic methods, physical and chemical properties, biological activity, and applications in food systems and safety assessments of each nanomaterial are presented. This chapter also highlights the possible mechanisms of antimicrobial activity against bacteria of certain active nanomaterials and their health concerns. It concludes with an outlook of the nanomaterials functionalised in food packaging.

Nanoscience and nanotechnology have become exciting fields of research and development since its introduction by Richard Feynman in 1959. At the heart of research in these fields are the synthesis, characterisation, modelling and applications of new materials with nanometer-scale dimensions, at least one of the three external dimensions ranging from approximately 1 nm to 100 nm, which are called 'nanomaterials'. There are numerous nanomaterials that have been reported in many prior studies, generally divided into the so-called zero-dimensional (e.g. nanoparticles (NPs): quantum dots, nanoclusters and fullerenes), one-dimensional (e.g. nanotubes and nanorods), two-dimensional (e.g. thin films), and three-dimensional (e.g. nanocomposites and nanofibres) nanomaterials.

These materials have exhibited unusual mesoscopic properties, including high surface area, fine particle size, high reactivity, high strength and ductility, which are the reasons that nanomaterials are frequently applied in a diversified range of industrial fields. As the researches of multi-disciplinary areas move along, nanomaterials are advancing with wide applications to electronic, optical and magnetic devices, biology, medicine, energy, defense and so on.

In addition, their developments in food and agriculture industries are nearly similar to their modernisation in medicine delivery and pharmaceutical areas.

In recent years, owing to the unique properties of nanomaterials other than their bulk counterparts mainly covering physical, chemical and biological properties, studies on the synthesis, characterisation, applications and assessments of these materials have promoted the scientific advancement to grow and alter the entire agrifood area. Specifically, many reports have focused on the potential applications of nanomaterials as participants to assure food quality, improve packaging and produce food products with altered function and nutrition.

Packaging is a key component of each stage in the food industry, however, its permeable nature is the major defect in conventional food packaging materials. There are no packaging materials fully resisting water-vapours and atmospheric gases. Moreover, participants along with the food supply chain seek novel, cost-effective, eco-friendly and resourceful food packaging systems to protect and monitor the quality of packaged foods, which is made possible with committed food safety, quality and traceability. As a result, there are several critical factors driving the innovation of food packaging materials to be continuously excavated. On the one hand, food packaging facilitates storage, handling, transport and protection of food from environmental pollution and other influences, and meets the increasing demands of the market, especially related to consumer preference for nutritious and high-quality food products. Some bionanocomposites materials are designed to improve the functional characteristics of general food packaging, such as barrier performance, mechanical strength and thermal stability, and other nanomaterials can incorporate bacteriostatic agents, antioxidants, plant extracts and enzymes to lengthen shelf-life of food products. On the other hand, to date, the majority of materials used in packaging industries are non-biodegradable petroleum-based plastic polymer materials (approximately 8% of the global gas production and fossil feedstock is used to yield synthetic polymers), which in turn, denote a serious problem on the universal environment. The advancement of renewable or green packaging has potentials to reduce the negative environmental impacts caused by the synthetic packaging by using biodegradable or edible materials, plant extracts, and nanocomposite materials. The following two types of materials are in focus: (i) inorganic and metal nanoparticles (nano-clay, montmorillonite nanoparticles, halloysite nanotubes, AgNPs, ZnO-NPs and CuO-NPs, and others), (ii) plant extracts (milk thistle extract, green tea extract, etc.) mixtures incorporated in biopolymers (chitosan, cellulose, starch, etc.).

Furthermore, the enormous potential of nanotechnology has received attention from researchers in multi-disciplinary areas to develop promising and desirable materials in food packaging systems. On the whole, the applications of nanocomposite materials for food packaging reported in the recent three years are divided into three main functions, i.e. improved, smart and active food packaging. Firstly, improved packaging is that the utilisation of nanoparticles in the bionanocomposite materials improves their mechanical and barrier properties, including elasticity, gas barrier characteristics (barrier against oxygen, carbon dioxide, and flavour compounds diffusion) and stability under different temperature and moisture conditions. Secondly, smart (intelligent) packaging performs in terms of information feedback and marketing on real-time quality of packaged food products and also performs as a guard against fraud and fake products and an indicator of the situation of exposure to certain adverse factors such as insufficient temperatures or high oxygen levels. Thirdly, active packaging offers protection and preservation grounded on mechanisms activated by inherent and/or acquired factors (antimicrobial activity, biodegradable activity), and achieves the reduction in loss of food products due to extension of their shelf-life. Though there have been considerable studies on novel nanomaterials applications in food packaging reported every day, most materials are still in the stage of feasibility and demonstration studies, and employments in food packaging field are yet to receive approval concerning their safety issues, which could be caused by the migrations of nanomaterials from packaging to food matrix.

Moreover, the absorption, distribution, metabolism and excretion as well as toxicological assessment of nanoparticles in food intake of humans are important research focuses. Thus, the use of nanomaterials in the food industry opens up multiple possibilities originating from the inherent features of nano-additives, which are either an improvement of the original polymer properties (e.g. barrier or mechanical properties) or introduction of new functionalities (e.g. active and bioactive packaging or sensing and monitoring).

This is an emerging and evolutionary area involving multidisciplinary studies. This chapter summaries the up-to-date developments of nanomaterials applied in the food packaging field, presenting a comprehensive review of various nanostructures and related technologies used to construct functional food packaging systems. The section mainly concentrate on synthesis methods, physical and chemical properties and biological activity, applications in food systems and safety assessments of different types of nanomaterials. This section also highlights the possible mechanism of some characteristics, such as antimicrobial activity against bacteria and improved reduction and stabilisation properties of certain active nanomaterials. In the last part, an outlook of the nanomaterials functionalised in food packaging is included.

INORGANIC AND METAL OXIDE NANOMATERIALS APPLIED IN FOOD PACKAGING

Generally, nanomaterials applied in food packaging can be classified into two categories: inorganic and organic materials. For the former materials, metals and metal oxides and clay nanoparticles incorporated into bionanocomposite films and nanofibres can be considered. Besides common bacteriostatic silver nanoparticles, some of the inorganic agents, like oxidised nanoparticles including CuO, ZnO, TiO_2, MgO and Fe_3O_4, have attracted great interest due to their resistance to the rough processing conditions and enhancement of strong inhibition against foodborne pathogens. As for the other materials like various clays, they could offer resistance to gases and water vapour, and improve the mechanical strength of biopolymers. The second group is organic materials including, but not limited to, phenols, halogenated compounds, quaternary ammonium salts, plastic polymers, plus natural polysaccharide or protein materials such as chitosan, chitin, zein and whey protein isolates, which have lately been highly regarded.

Silver-based Nanoparticles

So far, in all kinds of nanoparticles developed and characterised, silver-based nanoparticles (NPs) have taken an important place due to their inherent feature of antimicrobial activity even in solid-state samples, and have therefore been used as bacteriostatic agents from ancient times. Silver-salts materials also have an inhibition effect on the growth of diverse pathogens affecting human health, such as those in films, catheters, burns, cuts and wounds to protect them from infection. Silver-based particles in nanoscale include silver nanoparticles (AgNPs), silver nanocluster (AgNC) and silver-based alloy materials.

Synthesis methods

AgNPs is one of the most studied and applied antimicrobial agents because of its broad-spectrum antimicrobial activity against micro-organisms. The traditional solvothermal synthesis methods of AgNPs-functionalised packaging materials which usually require physical and chemical preparations of synthesising and immobilising, however, seem to be very expensive and hazardous and not environmentally friendly. This method has been gradually discarded for the tedious and complicated procedure. Interestingly, AgNPs prepared through biological synthesis exhibit high solubility, yield and stability. Additionally, it is simpler, faster, more environmentally friendly and dependable, and is recognised as a green approach to produce AgNPs with well-defined morphology and size under optimal conditions in favour of application in food packaging. Chu and others prepared antimicrobial active poly (lactic acid) (PLA)-based films with alloy of AgNPs and zinc oxide nanoparticles (ZnO-NPs) through a solvent volatilising method. Tao and others developed a convenient and efficient biosynthesis method to synthesise AgNPs-silk/poly (vinyl alcohol) (PVA) bionanocomposite film by blending AgNPs with PVA. Shao and others reported a new green chemistry synthetic method of sodium alginate-AgNPs composite by using sodium alginate as a stabilising agent and ascorbic acid as a reducing agent. Narayanan and Han presented an immobilisation method of borate-stabilised AgNPs as nanofillers in dual-cross-linked polymers comprised of PVA and sodium alginate at different ratios.

Patra and others produced a phyto-mediated biosynthesis of AgNPs through utilising the water extract of watermelon rind under light exposure at room temperature, obtaining prepared AgNPs with an average size of 110 nm and surface plasmon resonance of 425 nm. Azlin-Hasim and others studied the capacity of a layer-by-layer strategy to prepare low-density polyethylene (LDPE) active films with silver nanoparticles coated for food packaging applications. It is found that the green chemistry synthesis for the silver-based nanoparticles is highly effective and displays high potentials.

Physical, chemical properties and biological activity

The physical and chemical properties of nanoparticles are important for their action, efficacy, biodistribution and safety. Accordingly, characterisations of nanomaterial are crucial to evaluate functions of the developed particles. Characterisations are performed using a group of analytical techniques, including transmission electron microscopy (TEM), scanning electron microscopy (SEM), UV-Vis spectroscopy, Fourier transform infrared spectroscopy (FTIR), X-ray diffractometry (XRD), X-ray photoelectron spectroscopy (XPS), dynamic light scattering (DLS), atomic force microscopy (AFM), thermogravimetric analysis (TGA) and differential scanning calorimetric (DSC), to investigate their physical and chemical properties. Those properties include size and size distribution, surface chemistry, particle morphology, coating/capping, particle composition, agglomeration, dissolution rate, thermo-mechanical behaviour, rheological property and particle reactivity in solution. It is equally important that the biological activities of nanomaterials are to be examined for ensuring their claimed antimicrobial property and safety concerns. Tao and others found that PVA film coated by AgNPs-silk showed superior stability, mechanical performance and good antimicrobial activity inhibiting both Gram-positive and Gram-negative bacteria. Arfat and others developed the bionanocomposite films based on fish skin gelatin and bimetallic Ag-Cu nanoparticles (Ag-Cu NPs). The films were characterised to have improved mechanical property and low transparency, thermal stability, yellowness and high antibacterial activity against both Gram-positive and Gram-negative bacteria. Jafari and others studied the effect of chitin nanofibre on the morphological and physical properties of chitosan/silver nanoparticle bionanocomposite films, and concluded that AgNPs had dramatically improved the barrier and mechanical properties, but showed a negative impact on colour properties. Ramachandraiah and others demonstrated a higher antioxidant activity of the biosynthesised AgNPs from persimmon by-products and incorporation in sodium alginate thin films.

Applications in food systems

Because of the aforementioned unique properties, AgNPs have been widely used in the health care industry, house-hold utensils, food storage, environmental and biomedical applications. Herein, it is interesting to emphasise the applications of AgNPs in food systems, including antibacterial, antifungal, antioxidant, anti-inflammatory, antiviral, anti-angiogenic and anti-cancer. Heli and others reported that the exposure of corrosive vapour (ammonia) remarkably reduced the population density of AgNPs embedded into bacterial cellulose, causing a large distance between the residual nanoparticles and a decrease in the UV-Vis absorbance related to the plasmonic properties of AgNPs. This material exhibited colour changes from amber to light amber upon corrosive vapour exposure, and from amber to a grey or taupe colour upon fish or meat spoilage exposure, which opened up an innovative approach and capability in gas sensing to act as a smart packaging for monitoring fish or meat spoilage exposure. Tavakoli and others investigated the effect of nano-silver packaging in increasing the shelf-life of nuts in an *in vitro* model, showing an important effect on extending the shelf-life of nuts with the highest shelf-life of hazelnuts, almonds, pistachios and walnuts extended to 18, 19, 20 and 18 months, respectively.

Deus and others evaluated the effect of an edible film coated with nano-silver on the quality of turkey meat during modified atmosphere and vacuum-sealed packaging for 12 days of storage. Ahmed and others created PLA composite films by loading bimetallic silver-copper nanoparticles and cinnamon essential oil into polymer matrix through compression molding technique, which was utilised in the chicken meat packaging, revealing a new direction of active food packaging to control the pathogenic and spoilage bacteria related to fresh chicken meat.

Safety assessments

On account of gaps in understanding toxicology of nanomaterials, the development of their applications is related to safety concerns. In case of food contact bio-nanocomposite materials, the first steps of consumers' exposures are the migrations of nanoparticles from packaging to food products. Thus, in order to estimate the risk, we need to know the possibilities of nanoparticles released from food contact materials. Gallocchio and others evaluated silver migration from a commercially available food packaging containing AgNPs into chicken meatballs under plausible domestic storage conditions, and tested the contribution of this packaging to restrict food spoilage bacteria proliferation. The results showed that the migration was slow and no significant difference in the analysed bacteria levels between meatballs stored in AgNPs plastic bags and control bags. Tiimob and others tested the release of eggshell-silver tailored copolyester polymer blend film exposed to water and food samples by atomic absorption spectroscopy (AAS) analysis, showing that AgNPs was not released in chicken breast or distilled water until 168 and 72 hr, respectively. Su and others estimated the effects of organic additives (Irganox 1076, Irgafos 168, Chimassorb 944, Tinuvin 622, UV-531 and UV-P) on the release of silver from nanosilver-polyethylene composite films to an acidic food simulant (3% acetic acid) by detection using inductively coupled plasma mass spectrometry (ICP-MS) and found that additives influenced silver release through two synchronous processes: (i) reactions between silver and organic additives promoted release of silver from the composite film to an acidic food simulant, (ii) inhibition or promotion of silver release was influenced by silver oxidation. High humidity and temperature treatment of the prepared films were suggested to markedly enhance silver release by promoting oxidation. Hosseini and others measured the migration of silver from AgNPs polyethylene packaging based on titanium dioxide (TiO_2) into Penaeus semisulcatus by a titration comparison within the other migrations, and found that titration had a superior sensitivity compared to the other migration methods in determining the residues of nanoparticles ($p < 0.05$). Hannon and others determined the silver release from an experimental AgNPs spray coated on the surface of polyester and LDPE packaging material into milk. The test of coating process suggested the process modification has the potential to reduce migration. Becaro and others evaluated the genotoxic and cytotoxic effects of AgNPs (size range between 2 and 8 nm) on root meristematic cells of Allium cepa (*A. cepa*). The related studies often concentrate on the inhibition of growth of harmful bacteria.

Interestingly, Mikiciuk and others reported that the concentration and type of AgNPs solutions had an important effect on probiotic bacteria. These bacteria were isolated from fermented milk products beneficial for the digestive system, including Lactobacillus acidophilus LA-5, Bifidobacterium animalis subsp. lactis BB-12 and Streptococcus thermophilus ST-Y31, which deserves great public attention.

Zinc Oxide Nanoparticles

Zinc oxide (ZnO) has attracted great interest worldwide because of its excellent properties, particularly resulting from the realisation of the development of nanomaterials. Considerable studies of ZnO-NPs have been triggered on the production of nanoparticles using different synthesis methods and on their future applications, attributed to their high luminescent efficiency with a large exciton binding energy (60 meV) and a wide band gap (3.36 eV). ZnO-NPs usually act as antimicrobial and UV-protective agents used in the food packaging area. The increasing focus on ZnO-NPs drives the innovative development of synthesis methods of nanoparticles and their functions.

Synthesis methods

Synthesis methods of zinc oxide have been developing rapidly. Because the synthesis approach determines the properties of nanomaterial, the selection of synthetic methods is a crucial step in the engineering of ZnO-NPs for a decided utilisation. In recent decades, three main approaches have been used for forming ZnO-NPs: physical, chemical and biological methods. Among them, the casting method followed by solvent evaporation is the most common method used in preparation of ZnO nanocomposites with different morphologies. Rokbani and others reported a synthesis method using a combination of ultrasound stimulations and autoclaving to prepare electrospun nanofibres of mesoporous silica doped with ZnO-NPs. Jafarzadeh and others used the solvent casting method to prepare nanocomposite films of nano-kaolin and ZnO nanorod (ZnO-nr) complex embedded into semolina film matrices. Youssef and others prepared a novel bionanocomposites packaging material using carboxymethyl cellulose (CMC), chitosan (CH) and ZnO-NPs by the casting method.

Salarbashi and others developed a soluble soyabean polysaccharide (SSPS) nanocomposite incorporating ZnO-NPs using a solvent-casting method. Shahmohammadi and Almasi obtained bacterial cellulose-based monolayers and multilayer films with 5 wt% ZnO-NPs incorporated by using ultrasound irradiation (40 kHz) during ZnO-BC nanocomposites preparation. Akbariazam and others prepared a novel bionanocomposite of soluble soybean polysaccharide (SSPS) and nanorod-rich ZnO by the casting method.

Physical and chemical properties and biological activity

Compared with traditional antimicrobial agents, metal oxide nanoparticles show higher stability under extreme conditions with antimicrobial activity at low concentrations, and are considered to be non-toxic for humans. Among these metal oxide materials, ZnO-NP is a strong antimicrobial agent. ZnO-NPs exhibited diverse morphologies and showed robust inhibition against growth of broad-spectrum bacterial species. Mizielinska and others studied the effect of UV on the mechanical properties and the antimicrobial activity against tested micro-organisms of PLA/ZnO-NPs films.

They found that a decrease in Q-SUN irradiation to the antimicrobial activity of films with ZnO-NPs against *B. cereus*, whereas Q-UV and UV-A irradiation showed no effect on the mechanical properties of developed nanomaterial. Kotharangannagari and Krishnan studied the shape memory properties of novel biodegradable nanocomposites made of starch, polypropylene glycol (PPG), lysine and ZnO-

NPs. The results showed shape memory properties in the prepared nanocomposites by treating the sample at 25°C and then at 55°C. Furthermore, the mechanical properties showed an increase with increasing of ZnO-NPs content. Babaei-Ghazvini and others investigated the UV-protective property of the prepared biodegradable nanocomposite films incorporated by starch, kefiran and ZnO-NPs, with a function of ZnO-NPs at different contents (1,3, and 5 wt%). The tensile strength and Young's modulus of the specimens were measured and found that they were increased with Zn content up to 3 wt%, whereas elongation at break of the material was decreased. Besides, it is indicated that an increase of T_m following with Zn content increased thermal properties. Mizielinska and others reported a test of change in adhesiveness of fish samples stored in fillets in active coating boxes.

The result showed a decrease of adhesiveness of the fish sample when stored in an active container. Besides, it was found that packaging materials containing ZnO-NPs were more active against cells of psychotropic and mesophilic bacteria than the coatings with polylysine after 144 hr and 72 hr of storage. Calderon and others developed a Zn-ZnO core-shell structure and explored the oxidation capability of carbon supported Zn nanostructures used as oxygen scavenging materials activated by the relative humidity in the environment.

Applications in food systems

ZnO-NPs are recognised as inexpensive with potential antimicrobial properties. So the applications of ZnO-NPs packaging in food systems concentrate on its antibacterial effect, and they are used to prolong the fresh food products' shelf-life. Youssef and others used an innovative carboxymethyl cellulose/chitosan/ZnO bionanocomposite film to enhance the shelf-life of Egyptian soft white cheese. Mizielinska and others compared the impacts of material containing polylysine or ZnO-NPs on the texture of Cod fillets, and found a lowest water loss when the sample was packed with ZnO-NPs, and an increase in the adhesiveness of the fish samples stored in boxes without active coatings, indicating that ZnO-NPs prevented the adhesiveness of food products. Li and others estimated the influences of ZnO-NPs incorporation into PLA films on the quality of fresh-cut apples. It was found that the most weight loss was observed in nano-blend packaging films compared to the PLA film at the end of storage, however, packaging nanomaterial provided a better maintenance of firmness, colour, sensory quality and total phenolic content. It also exhibited a strong inhibition against the growth of micro-organisms.

Beak and others proposed that the synthesised olive flounder bone gelatin/ZnO-NPs film showed antimicrobial activity against *L. monocytogenes* contamination on spinach but with no effect on its quality, mainly including colour and vitamin C content. Suo and others found that ZnO-NPs-coated packaging films increased the occurrence of micro-organism injury, which was helpful to control pork meat in cold storage. Al-Shabib and others prepared Nigella sativa seed extract-zinc nanostructures (NS-ZnNPs) material and found that NS-ZnNPs showed inhibition effects on the biofilm formation of four food pathogens including *C. violaceum* 12472, L. monocytogenes, *E. coli*, PAO1, at their sub-inhibitory concentrations.

Safety assessments

ZnO-NPs are utilised as active materials in food packaging, which might bring a potential risk for consumers contacting with this material. This nanoparticle has been demonstrated in *in vivo* studies that they can access organs through different pathways such as ingestion, inhalation, and parenteral routes. Ansar and others suggested that hesperidin augmented antioxidant defense with antiphlogistic reaction against neurotoxicity induced by ZnO-NPs, and the enzyme activity enhanced the antioxidant potential to reduce oxidative stress. Senapati and others evaluated the immune-toxicity of ZnO-NPs in different ages of BALB/c mice after sub-acute exposure, and found that the aged mice were more susceptible to ZnO-NPs-induced immune-toxicity. Meanwhile, information on the amount of ZnO-NPs contained in food packaging and the impacts of their exposure on intestinal function are still insufficient. Moreno-Olivas and others found that the amount of zinc present in the food was about 100 times higher than the recommended dietary allowance. The effects of ZnO-NP exposure to the small intestine composed of Caco-2 and HT29-MTX cells was investigated in an *in vitro* model. It was found that Fe transport and glucose transport following ZnO NPs exposure were 75% decreased and 30% decreased, respectively. Also, the ZnO-NPs affected the microvilli of the intestinal cells. Zhang and others reported the fate of the packaging material of ZnO-NPs on the coating layer incorporated into PLA-coated paper entering into paper recycling processes. The results of mass balance indicated that 86–91% ZnO-NPs ended up in the material stream, mostly incorporated into the polymer coating, however, 7–16% nanoparticles completed in the desired material stream. Furthermore, the nano-coating showed positive impacts on the quality of recovered fibre. Chia and Leong made a surface modification to decrease the toxicity of ZnO-NPs by silica coating and found a significant decrease on the dissolution of ZnO-NPs. They suggested that the coating offered a possible solution to enhance the biocompatibility of ZnO-NPs, which could broaden the applications such as antibacterial agent in food packaging.

Copper-based Nanoparticles

Copper-based nanoparticles mainly include copper nanoparticles (CuNPs) and copper oxide nanoparticles (CuO-NPs). Most studies focusing on CuO NPs suggest that this material is one of the most-extensively studied metal oxide nanoparticles. The antimicrobial activity is its important feature, thus this material can be used to reduce the growth of bacteria, viruses and fungi. The nano-sized CuO-NPs were allowed to interact with the cell membrane due to their enormous surface area, and then showed an increased antimicrobial effect. CuO-NPs have been applied intensively in chemical engineering and food and biomedical areas, and used as gas sensors, catalysts, water disinfectants, polymer reinforcing agents, and as a material of food packaging, semiconductors, magnetic storage media, solar cells field, emission devices and so on. Consequently, antibacterial activity of CuO-NPs has been widely utilised in the fields of food packaging materials, polymer nanocomposites and water purification.

Synthesis methods

CuO-NPs have potentials for forming antimicrobial nanohybrids. Almasi and others claimed that whether the polymer substrate has already exhibited antimicrobial activity or not, the incorporated CuO-NPs could further increase the activity of the two components contained in the nanocomposite. They have fabricated a novel nanocomposite incorporation into CuO-NPs, bacterial cellulose nanofibres and chitosan nanofibres by a chemical precipitation method. Gu and others introduced a green, facile and low cost biosynthesis of monoclinic CuO-NPs based on an ultrasound method by using the extracts of Cystoseira trinodis as an eco-friendly material. Eivazihollagh and others reported a facile method to synthesise spherical CuNPs *in situ* templated by a gelled cellulose II matrix under the alkaline aqueous conditions. No more than 20 min, the nanocomposite material was harvested in a one-pot reaction. Castro Mayorga and others prepared an active biodegradable nanocomposites of poly(3-hydroxybutyrate-co-3-hydroxy-valerate) (PHBV) melt mixed with CuO-NPs in bilayer structures. This bilayer-structural material was made of an active electrospun fibres mat embedded by PHBV18 (18% valerate) and CuO-NPs, and coating onto a bottom layer of concentration molded PHBV3 (3% mol valerate). Gautam and Mishra synthesised

Cu-NPs material compositing edible bilayer pocket prepared by heat and NaBH4 treated methods to form a heat-sealable casein protein layer laminated with sodium alginate-pectin.

Physical and chemical properties and biological activity

The properties of the CuO-NPs depend on the synthesis method and they are very important for their applications in various areas, such as food packaging research, which rely on their biological activity. Although the specific mechanism of the antimicrobial effect of CuO nanoparticles is little known, their antimicrobial actions on bacterial cells have been proposed. Beigmohammadi and others determined the antimicrobial LDPE packaging films incorporating AgNPs, CuO-NPs and ZnO-NPs in testing of coliform amounts of ultra-filtrated cheese. The results showed the number of surviving coliform bacteria declined to 4.21 log CFU/g after storing for 4 weeks at 4±0.5°C for all three treatments. Almasi and others found that the antimicrobial activity of CuO-NPs against both Gram-negative and Gram-positive bacteria was inhibited after attachment to bacterial cellulose nanofibres, however, a synergistic action presented between chitosan nanofibres and CuO-NPs on the antimicrobial activity was reinforced. Shankar and others evaluated the water vapour permeability, barrier property, UV and thermal stability, and antimicrobial activity of the nanocomposite films. The types of polymers used decided the surface morphology of films. The results showed that the addition of CuO-NPs increased the above-mentioned properties, and the films showed antimicrobial activity against Listeria monocytogenes and *E. coli*.

Applications in food systems

Nanomaterials with various characteristics generated from many polymers constructing copper-based nanocomposites can be used in a variety of applications. The antimicrobial activity of copper-based nanocomposites reveals applications in engineering food packaging, textile industry, medical devices and water decontamination. However, the actual applications in real food samples were little. Gautam and Mishra synthesised copper-based nanocomposite incorporating a pectin layer to enhance its antimicrobial activities. It was applied in packaging coconut oil and then the oxidative stability of oil was investigated during storage.

The results showed that its thermal stability was enhanced due to the nanocomposite addition, and antimicrobial activity of heat-treated nanocomposite film was increased compared to the NaBH4-treated NPs film against the growth of *E. coli*. Li and others prepared chitosan/soy protein isolates nanocomposite film reinforced by Cu nanoclusters, and this material showed the improved elongation at break and tensile strength, and higher water contact angle and degradation temperature and decreased water vapour permeation. Lomate and others developed an LDPE/Cu nanocomposite film in food packaging to extend the shelf-life of peda, which is an Indian sweet dairy product.

Safety assessments

Although copper-based nanocomposites have been applied for diverse purposes, CuO-NPs and copper ions can be released from the packaging materials into the food systems. Little is known on the toxicity of copper-based nanocomposites and more attentions have been concentrated on CuO NPs.

TiO_2 Nanoparticles

Titanium dioxide nanoparticles (TiO_2-NPs), as among the most explored materials, are considered as valuable metal oxide nanomaterials with thermostability and inertia. The material also has the ability to modify the properties of biodegradable films. Besides, this material has many advantages such as being cheap, nontoxic, and photo-stable. It has been emerging as a superior photo-catalyst material for energy and environmental fields, such as air and water purification, antimicrobial, self-cleaning surfaces and water splitting. TiO_2-NPs and their applications in the food packaging area have attracted extensive attentions attributed to their antimicrobial activity.

Synthesis methods

TiO_2-NPs tend to aggregate, which would possibly influence the function of film properties. Changing the surface properties of TiO_2-NPs is an alternative method to solve this problem. In a recent study, several ionic surfactants have been used to non-covalently attach to the surface of TiO_2-NPs, and more innovational nanocomposites have been synthesised to enhance the TiO_2-NPs dispersion behaviour. He and others fabricated biodegradable fish skin gelatin-TiO_2 nanocomposite films by a solvent evaporation method. Li and others proposed a facile and green method to synthesise super-hydrophobic paper by using a layer-by-layer deposition of TiO_2-NPs/sodium alginate multilayers onto a paper surface and then with colloidal carnauba wax adsorbed. Lopez de Dicastillo and others obtained TiO_2 nanotubes by a deposition process of atomic layer covering the electrospun polyvinyl alcohol (PVA) nanofibres at different temperatures to obtain antibacterial nanostructures with a relative high selective area. Nesic and others prepared eco-environmental pectin-TiO_2 nanocomposite aerogels by a sol-gel process and followed by drying under the supercritical conditions. Firstly, pectin was dissolved in water and proper amount of TiO_2 colloid was added, then cross-linking reaction was induced in the presence of zinc ions and tert-butanol. Finally, the gels were subjected to solvent exchange and supercritical CO_2 drying.

Physical and chemical properties and biological activity

Considerable studies indicated that addition of TiO_2-NPs had promoted the suitability of developed films applied in food packaging. The functional properties of these nanomaterials can be tailored by synthesising composites that combine the properties of the individual component to achieve synergistic effects. Xing and others investigated the impact of TiO_2-NPs on the physical and antimicrobial capabilities of polyethylene (PE)-based films. They found that the antimicrobial activity of the films was attributed to the biocidal action of TiO_2-NPs against bacteria. Roilo and others prepared bilayer membranes for food packaging applications by depositing TiO_2-NPs on PLA substrates, cellulose nanofibres and nanocomposite coatings, and found that the addition of TiO_2-NPs reduced the penetrant diffusivity but did not affect gas barrier performances, as well as slightly decreased the optical transparency. Oleyaei and others developed TiO_2-NPs (0.5, 1 and 2 wt%) incorporated into potato starch films. It was found that TiO_2-NPs enhanced the optical transparency, and slightly increased the tensile strength and contact angle, and significantly declined the water vapour permeability properties, and decreased the elongation at break of the film.

Goudarzi and others produced the eco-friendly starch and TiO_2-NPs bio-composites at different TiO_2-NPs contents (1,3, and 5 wt%), and investigated the mechanical, physical, water-vapour permeability (WVP), thermal properties and as well as UV transmittance of the synthesised nanomaterial. They found that hydrophobicity increased, and elongation at break and tensile energy to break increased, while tensile strength, WVP and Young's modulus reduced with increasing TiO_2 content. Abdel Rehim and others prepared the photo-catalytic paper sheets by adding different ratios of TiO_2-NPs/sodium alginate nanocomposite. It was found that biopolymer of sodium alginate reduced the negative effect of the photo-catalyst on paper fibres and increased the adhesion of TiO_2-NPs to them.

Applications in food systems

TiO_2-NPs are antimicrobial agents. When they are irradiated with UV light, many reactive oxygen species are produced that have the ability to kill micro-organisms. Moreover, as nano-additives, TiO_2 can improve the mechanical properties of polymer nanocomposites. Mihaly-Cozmuta and others synthesised three active papers based on cellulose, mainly containing TiO_2, Ag-TiO_2 and Ag-TiO_2-zeolite nanocomposites (P-TiO_2, P-Ag-TiO_2, P-Ag-TiO_2-Z), which aimed at being applied in bread packaging. The efficiency in the bread storage was compared in terms of nutritional parameters (proteins, total fat and carbohydrates), acidity, and change of molds and yeasts. Li and others prepared a novel nano-TiO_2-LDPE (NT-LDPE) packaging. They investigated the effects of NT-LDPE material packaging on the antioxidant activity and quality of strawberries.

Safety assessments

Nanoparticles exhibited an increased surface-to-mass ratio enhancing the reactivity. Moreover, nanoparticles displayed an increased tendency to penetrate the cell membranes and consequently having the potential to transfer through the biological barriers. So far, the health effects of TiO_2-NPs have been explored basically on their uptake by inhalation. It was concluded by the International Agency for Research on Cancer (IARC) that decided based epidemiological studies to assess whether TiO_2 dust causing human cancers was inadequate. Evidence for carcinogenicity in experimental animals was sufficient, which was conducted on account of the induction of respiratory tract tumors in rats after prolonged inhalation. Accordingly, TiO_2-NPs is classified as a Group 2B carcinogen by the IARC. Based on the extensive food-related uses, an increasing attention has been drawn to the risk assessment of TiO_2-NPs applied in food packaging. Ozgur and others evaluated the effect of different amounts of TiO_2-NPs (0.01, 0.1, 0.5, 1, 10 and 50 mg/L) *in vitro* at 4°C for 3 hr on sperm cell kinematics with the velocities of Rainbow trout. Additionally, oxidative stress markers (superoxide dismutase (SOD) and total glutathione (TGSH)) of the sperm cells were tested after their exposure to TiO_2-NPs. The results revealed that a statistical significance ($p < 0.05$) presented in the velocities of sperm cells. When concentration of TiO_2-NPs reached at 10 mg/L, an increased activity of TGSH and SOD ($p < 0.05$) levels were found. Salarbashi and others prepared biodegradable SSPS nanocomposites consisting of varying ratios of SSPS and TiO_2-NPs, and found that TiO_2-NPs existed in plasma membranes of epithelial cell lines after a 10-day exposure to a number of free nanomaterials.

However, anti-cancerous and pro-cancerous activities were not determined because this nanomaterial denoted their neutrality in regards to cancer inhibition or promotion in gastrointestinal tracts. Jo and others evaluated the interactions between TiO_2-NPs and biomolecules including albumin and glucose. They investigated that those biomolecules altered the physical and chemical properties as well as the consequence regarding TiO_2-NPs under physiological conditions. It was found that oral absorption of food grade TiO_2-NPs was slightly higher compared to general grade TiO_2-NPs, however, these nanoparticles were excreted through the feces. Besides, the biokinetics of food grade TiO_2-NPs were extremely relied on their interaction with biomolecules.

Other Metal Oxide and Nonmetal Oxide Nanomaterials

In addition to the metal oxides mentioned above, several other metal oxide and nonmetal oxide nanomaterials also showed an increased potential using as packaging materials, such as MgO-NPs, Fe_3O_4-NPs and iron-based nanoparticles, as well as SiO_2-NPs.

MgO naturally exists as a renewable, colourless, crystalline mineral and is economically produced on a large scale. The use of MgO has been recognised as generally safe even in the food applications by the US Food and Drug Administration (FDA). Swaroop and Shukla produced films by incorporating MgO-NPs in PLA polymer through a solvent casting method, and found 2 wt% amount of MgO-NPs in PLA films exhibited the most observed improvement in the oxygen barrier and tensile strength properties, as well as a superior antibacterial efficacy, whereas, nearly a 25% negative effect was found on water vapour barrier properties.

Ren and others synthesised inorganic materials of magnetic ferroferric oxide nano-particles *in situ* coating on graphene oxide nanosheets (Fe_3O_4@GO) as fillers and then were used to fabricate a PVA nanocomposite film. This material showed a superior barrier capability regarded as a better choice compared to the traditional aluminum films. Shariatinia and Fazli prepared a thickness of 0.13–0.2 mm nanocomposite film made of starch, chitosan, cyclophosphamide, glycerin and Fe_3O_4-NPs. Khalaj and others prepared nanocomposites of the nano-clay containing iron nanoparticles (Fe-NPs)-polypropylene (PP) by a melt interaction. They investigated the morphological, mechanical, gas barrier and thermal properties.

The activities of SiO_2-NPs are related to their average particle size, biocompatibility, high surface area, stability, low toxicity, bad thermal conductivity and supreme insulation. Mallakpour and Nazari developed a facile and fast method to synthesise polymer-based nanocomposite films of PVA and SiO_2-NPs coating on bovine serum albumin (PVA/SiO_2@BSA) using a casting method assisted by sonication. Guo and others investigated the impacts of realistic doses in physiological terms of SiO_2-NP on gastrointestinal function and health, based on an *in vitro* model composed of HT29-MTX and Caco-2 co-cultures representing goblet and absorptive cells, respectively. The results showed that the exposure of SiO_2-NPs was harmful to the brush border membrane and that exposure to the physiologically relevant doses of well-characterised SiO_2-NP for acute (4 hr) and chronic (5 days) time periods eventually led to adverse effects in cells.

Nano-Clay and Silicate Nanoparticles

At the present time, nano-clay has approximately 70% market value all over the world, meaning that it is the most commercially applied nanomaterial. There are various kinds of clay minerals according to their structures and chemistries as well as sources. Based on the layered structures, these materials are categorised into four major classes, i.e. chlorite, montmorillonite (MMT)/smectite, illite and kaolinite. MMT is recognised as the most commonly used in the preparation of nanocomposites among these clays. The widest acceptability in layered clay is obvious since it has high surface reactivity and surface area. As a result, many studies demonstrated that natural biopolymer-layered silicate nanocomposites significantly improved properties in packaging. In spite of this, there were fewer studies of orgnoclays as nanomaterials in food packaging compared to other nano-encapsulation systems.

Synthesis methods

Halloysite nanotubes (HNTs), as a kind of natural nanomaterials belonging to kaolinite, have a hollow tubular-like structure within the inner and outer diameters of 15 nm and 50 nm, respectively. Due to this tubular shape, HNTs have a capability of being loaded by various materials, which have been developed as functional nanocapsules. Biddeci and others prepared a functional biopolymer film by filling a pectin matrix modified with HNTs containing peppermint oil, where HNT surfaces were functionalised with cucurbit uril molecules with the aim to enhance the affinity of the nanofiller towards peppermint oil.

Pereira and others prepared lycopene and MMT-NPs in whey protein concentrate films using the casting/evaporation method. Recently, several agricultural processing wastes have been used to synthesise the nanocomposites as raw materials. Orsuwan and Sothornvit developed a biopolymer film incorporated with banana starch nanoparticles (BSNs) and MMT-NPs, where the BSNs was fabricated using miniemulsion cross-linking to make an enhanced agent.

Oliveira and others used the pectin extracted from pomegranate peels to prepare films with the some amounts of MMT-NPs as reinforcement nanomaterial. Zahedi and others investigated a novel casting method to fabricate a carboxymethyl cellulose (CMC)-based nanocomposite films containing MMT (5 wt%) and ZnO-NPs (1, 2, 3 and 4 wt%) and found addition of ZnO-NPs enhanced the UV-light blocking (from 60% to 99%) of single-layer nano-clay.

Physical and chemical properties and biological activity

Nano-clays, especially MMT, act as crucial fillers in the biodegradation of nanomaterials when incorporated with a polymer, because they are toxin-free, environmentally friendly and safe to be used in food packaging. Besides, their activities to reduce permeability of gases and improve mechanical properties have been confirmed for polymer nanomaterials. Kim and others investigated a potential application of multilayer packaging films for packing food containing waterborne content, which were prepared by dry laminating commercially available PVA/vermiculite nanocomposites. They found a reversible regression of the barrier properties of oxygen presented in the prepared films. Pereira and others characterised the structural and mechanical properties of lycopene/MMT/whey protein concentrate films and found that MMT at the amount of 20 g/kg in the polymeric matrix increased both thermal and mechanical properties. Besides the red colouring ability, lycopene showed no effects on detectable interference in the physical or structural properties. Beigzadeh Ghelejlu and others prepared nano-clay nanocomposite/chitosan active films incorporated with three levels of *Silybum marianum L.* extract (SME) (0.5% v/v, 1% v/v and 1.5% v/v) and MMT (1,3 and 5 wt% of chitosan). The results indicated that the addition of SME and MMT improved the antioxidant properties of the films, but decreased the solubility and WVP and influenced the optical and mechanical properties of films. Notably, plant essential oils have been encapsulated into nano-clay or MMT-NPs to improve the antioxidant and antimicrobial activities of composite materials applied in packaging system, including peppermint, thyme and cinnamon. Khalaj and others found that in the prepared nanocomposite of Fe/MMT/PP-NPs, the intercalation and exfoliation of the clay were affected reversely after the addition of PP-NPs to some extent.

Furthermore, certain homogeneity of uniform distribution of MMT and PP-NPs was observed through TEM and SEM. The melting temperatures increased with clay concentration, however, crystallisation temperature and crystallinity decreased with the clay concentration with NPs compensating the effect of clay. Nano-clays also have prospects in active and intelligent food nano-packaging. Gutiérrez and others developed a nano-clay of MMT containing blueberry extract. They revealed that according to a shift between flavylium and quinoidal forms of anthocyanins in blueberries, the colour was changed following the pH of the system. Thus, addition of blueberry extract could modify the structure of MMT to form novel nano-clays with more active properties.

Applications in food systems

Generally, clays are low-cost, naturally occurring and eco-friendly agents and used in various applications. Clay minerals are used in the fields of agriculture, geology, engineering, construction and process industries. Peter and others investigated the chemical and microbiological characteristics of white bread during the storage in paper packaging modified with Ag/TiO_2-SiO_2-NPs. The results showed good water retention and prolonged shelf-life of bread for 2 days compared to the unmodified packaging. Nalcabasmaz and others developed nanocomposite materials containing 1% nano-clay and 5% poly-beta-pinene (P beta P). They tested the material for packaging sliced salami. The packaged food sample used nanofilms and multi-layered film under different conditions of vacuum, modified atmosphere packaging of 50% CO_2 and 50% N_2 and air, and both stored at 4°C for 90 days. It was found tha. the moisture content and hardness showed no significant changes during storage. The sliced salami stored under vacuum and high CO_2 using the multilayer material displayed the longest storage time of 75 days. Kim and others developed insect-proof HNTs material, which were applied to a LDPE-based film to control Plodia interpunctella (Indian mealmoth) from infesting the food. Peighambardoust and others prepared LDPE-based Films incorporating with organic clay nanoparticle including cloisite 30B, cloisite 20A and cloisite 15A for packaging to decrease the growth of coliform bacteria in ultra-filtrated cheese. The developed films exhibited a decrease of coliform load to 2.05 log CFU/g at the optimum condition, which was corresponding to Japanese industrial standard (JIS Z 2801:2000). Echeverria and others evaluated the future application of active nanocomposite films based on soy protein isolate-MMT loaded with clove essential oil to preserve the muscle fillets of Bluefin tuna stored in refrigerator. They further analysed the possibility of clay in packaging diffusing to the food system. Clay inclined to release the clove oil by extending its antimicrobial activity (especially against *Pseudomonas* spp.) and enhancing antioxidant activity. There were no observed metals (Si and Al) of clay diffused to the muscle of fish. Guimaraes and others evaluated fresh-cut carrots (FCC) coated by MMT-NPs subjected to packaging of passive modified atmosphere.

The use of starch nanoparticles incorporated into coating film together with a modified atmosphere led to the enhanced total antioxidant activity, volatiles, and organic acids maintaining of FCC. Junqueira-Goncalves and others evaluated the effect of addition of MMT-NPs to a lacto-biopolymer coating. They found that the material could improve its water vapour barrier and reduce weight loss, as well as oxygen uptake and the release of carbon dioxide, and improve fruit firmness and reduce mold and yeast load, at last prolong the shelf-life of coated strawberries.

Safety assessments

With nano-clay or MMT-NPs materials attracting more and more attentions worldwide, analyses of risks of these nanomaterials to the lung health of exposed workers have been emerging. Besides, present studies aiming to demonstrate the toxicological actions of nano-clay showed that the structure had resulted in the promotion of cellular uptake and interactions. Han and others presented a study on the degradation and release of nano-clay-loaded LDPE composite for food packaging.

It was found that the toxicity of released nano-clay particles from nano-clay particle-embedded LDPE composites to A594 adenocarcinomic human alveolar basal epithelial cells was degraded. Wagner and others investigated the potential of Cloisite 30B and Cloisite Na+ and their thermally degraded by-products and then induced toxicity in the model of lung epithelial cells of human. Analysis of by-product physical and chemical properties suggested changes happened in structures and functions. Echegoyen and others investigated the migration of nano-clay from food packaging materials to food samples. The results showed that Al-NPs of different sizes and morphologies could migrate into food stimulants with different food stimulants (acetic acid 3% and ethanol 10%), temperatures and times (70°C for 2 hr and 40°C for 10 days) from two commercialised LDPE-based nanocomposite bags analysed by ICP-MS.

ORGANIC BIOPOLYMER-BASED NANOMATERIALS APPLIED IN FOOD PACKAGING

The concept of a bio-based economy is gradually receiving attentions from scientific, societal, and economic aspects, and there is a great deal of driving force to develop strategies for this purpose. The inspiration of producing biopolymer-based materials is to utilise renewable organic sources, including polysaccharides and proteins, aiming at replacing non-renewable fossil sources. There are various organic nanomaterials applied in food packaging, mainly divided into three categories: polymer-based plastics, polysaccharide-based and protein-based nanomaterials, which provide biopolymer matrix for nanocomposite materials.

Polymer-based Nanomaterials

Traditionally, most plastic packaging materials are made from petroleum-based polymers, mainly containing the commodity polystyrene (PS) and polyethylene (PE), which are recognised as not being environmentally friendly. With the development of new polymer materials, the biodegradable polymer-based plastics can provide a viable alternative, such as PVA, polylactic acid (PLA), poly(3-hydroxybutyrate) (PHB) and poly(3-hydroxybutyrate-co-3-hydroxyvalerate) (PHBV) and their biopolymer blends.

PVA

PVA, basically made from polyvinyl acetate through hydrolysis, is easily degraded by biological organisms in water. It has been extensively incorporated into other polymer-based compounds to increase the mechanical properties attributed to its hydrophilic properties and compatible structure, including mechanical performance, solvent resistance, biocompatibility and high hydrophilicity.

Yang and others prepared chitosan/PVA hydrogels containing lignin nanoparticles (LNPs) (1 wt% and 3 wt%) by a freezing–thaw procedure. The study of mechanical, microstructural and thermal characterisations of the nanomaterial showed that the optimal amount of LNPs was at 1 wt%, whereas the agglomerates at higher LNP content were formed and affected the properties. Sarwar and others investigated the impact of Ag-NPs embedded into nanocellulose on the mechanical, physical and thermal properties of PVA-based nanocomposite films. They found that these films had a superior antimicrobial activity against *E. coli* (DH5-alpha) and S. aureus (MRSA). Furthermore, the films showed no cytotoxicity effect on HepG2 and the cell viability was above 90%.

PLA

PLA has drawn more attention resulting from the good biodegradability and being a candidate of substitution for traditional polymers. PLA is mainly produced by condensation polymerisation from lactic acid, derived from fermentation of corn, sugars, tapioca or sugarcane. Among the various biopolymers investigated, PLA exhibits key properties, including biodegradability, renewability and superior mechanical properties, crystallinity and process ability. Aframehr and others investigated the impact of calcium carbonate ($CaCO_3$) nanoparticles on the biodegradability and barrier properties of PLA. The results showed that the barrier properties were increased by loading $CaCO_3$-NPs increasing to 5 wt%. It was also found that the gas permeability of CO_2, O_2 and N_2 were enhanced by increasing temperature but decreased by increasing feeding pressure. Vasile and others prepared the Cu-doped ZnO powder embedded into PLA samples functionalised with Ag-NPs composites by a melt blending process. The results showed an increase of the crystalline degree of PLA when the content of nanoparticle was increased from 0.5 wt% to 1.5 wt%.

PHBV

Polyhydroxyalkanoates (PHAs) have been gradually paid attention recently as biodegradable and biocompatible thermoplastics in packaging applications. The most extensively studied polymer from the PHAs is the poly(3-hydroxybutyrate), PHB, which is partially crystalline with a high rigidity and melting temperature. To decrease the crystallinity, the copolymer obtained with the insertion of 3-hydroxyvalerate (HV) units, named as PHBV, is usually employed with improved handling properties of PHB films. Zembouai and others prepared blends of PLA and PHBV at different PLA/PHBV weight ratios (0/100, 25/75, 50/50, 75/25, 100/0) through a melt compounding process. The formed blends were investigated on the mutual contributions to flammability resistance, thermal stability, rheological behavior and mechanical properties. The results revealed that increasing PLA content in PLA/PHBV blends led to improved properties, such as flammability resistance and thermal stability. Shakil and others developed the sepiolite/PHBV nanocomposite films by using the APTES grafted sepiolite through the solution-casting method. The results provided evidence that the application of biodegradable nanocomposite films would lead to a more efficient water barrier and thermal properties.

Polysaccharide-based Nanomaterials

Starch-based nanomaterials

Aqlil and others investigated a graphene oxide (GO)-filled starch/lignin polymer bionanocomposite. They found that the amount of GO had a strong influence on the mechanical properties and could reduce water vapour permeability and moisture uptake of the prepared film. Shahbazi and others developed starch film incorporated with multi-walled carbon nanotubes with or without hydroxylation and found that the hydrophobic character of the film was greatly improved with incorporation of a nanotube. Oleyaei and others estimated the thermal, mechanical and barrier properties of TiO_2 and montmorillonite on potato starch nanocomposite films. The results showed elongation at break, tensile strength, melting point and glass transition temperature of the films were improved followed the addition of MMT and TiO_2. The visible, UVA, UVB and UVC lights transmittance and water vapour permeability decreased with the increasing amounts of TiO_2 and MMT.

Cellulose-based nanomaterials

Shankar and Rhim prepared nanocellulose material and tested the effects on the properties of agar-based composite films. The crystallinity index of nanocellulose (NC, 0.71) was decreased compared to the micro-crystalline cellulose (MCC, 0.81). The results demonstrated that NC could be used as an enhanced agent for the preparation of biodegradable composites films. Pal and others synthesised reduced graphene oxide and cellulose nanocrystal incorporated into PLA matrix through a modified Hummer's method and an acid hydrolysis. They found that the mechanical property of scaffold was significantly improved. Both tensile strength (23% increase) and elongation at break were increased, which indicated the nanocomposite was ductile compared to unmodified PLA. The distinct anti-bacterial efficacy was observed to inhibit against both Gram-negative *E. coli* and Gram-positive *S. aureus* bacterial strains. Liu and others prepared starch-based nanocomposite films improved by cellulose nanocrystals to control δ-limonene permeability. They found that cellulose nanocrystals amount and aspect ratio were independently controlling δ-limonene permeability through film-structure regulation. Lavoine and others simulated release and diffusion of active substances made of cellulose nanofibre coating to food packaging material through calculating in a mathematical model derived from Fickian diffusion. They found the model was validated for caffeine only.

Chitosan-based nanomaterials

Postnova and others studied approaches in which monolithic hydrogels were prepared through mineralisation of polysaccharide by a method of green sol-gel chemistry, compared with a method through the formation of polyelectrolyte complex. It was found that both approaches were available for the preparation of films with nanoparticles and chitosan bionanocomposites. Liang and others prepared edible chitosan films incorporated with epigallocatechin gallate nanocapsules and characterised their antioxidant properties. It was found that the addition of nanocapsules to chitosan hydrochloride films improved their tensile strength, whereas the percent of elongation at break and lightness was significantly decreased. Buslovich and others developed *in situ* chitosan and vanillin incorporated on packaging films, containing an aqueous/ethanol solution onto a PE surface by an ultrasonic method. The results showed that increased contact surface strongly inhibited the fruit microbial spoilage.

Protein-based Nanomaterials

Zein-based nanomaterials

Zein, a group of prolamins from corn, is a Generally Recognised as Safe (GRAS) food-grade ingredient. With the hydrophobicity of three quarters of the amino acid residues in zein, zein-based nanomaterials have low WVP compared to many other bio-based films. Moreover, zein-based nanomaterials embedded with inorganic AgNC may have advantages such as low toxicity. Aytac and others synthesised thymol (THY)/gamma-Cyclodextrin(gamma-CD) inclusion complex (IC) encapsulated electro-spun zein nanofibrous webs (zein-THY/gamma-CD-IC-NF) as a food packaging nanomaterial and found that zein-THY/gamma-CD-IC-NF (2:1) significantly inhibited the growth of bacteria in meat samples. Rouf and others prepared nanocomposite with the addition of silicate NPs (Laponite) to zein films casting from 70% ethanol solutions. The changes in the surface energy of the films were evaluated using contact angle measurements and showed an increase in surface hydrophobicity. The Young's modulus and tensile strength were increased with increasing nanoparticle concentration. The glass transition temperature was increased and WVP was decreased with only a small amount of Laponite. Oymaci and Altinkaya prepared whey protein isolate (WPI)-based films embedded into zein nanoparticles (ZNPs) coated with sodium caseinate by a casting method. They found that the addition of zein NPs dramatically improved the mechanical and water vapour barrier properties of the WPI with no effect on the elongation of the films. It was also found that both the fractional free volume and hydrophilicity of the WPI films decreased. Gilbert and others prepared a biopolymer-based composite film of hydroxypropyl methyl-cellulose and ZNPs. The results exhibited an increase in tensile strength, a decrease in elongation, and an initial increase followed by gradual decrease in Young's moduli with increasing ZNPs.

Whey protein isolate-based nanomaterials

Qazanfarzadeh and Kadivar prepared WPI-based composite films with different proportions of oat husk nanocellulose (ONC) obtained from acid sulphuric hydrolysis by a solution casting method. They found that the crystallinity increased after acid hydrolysis. The films prepared with 5 wt% ONC showed the highest tensile strength, Young's modulus, solubility and the lowest elongation at break and moisture content. However, WVP and film transparency were decreased with the addition of ONC. Hassannia-Kolaee and others prepared whey protein isolate/pullulan (WPI/PUL) films having different contents of nano-SiO_2 (NS) using a casting method. The results revealed tensile strength of nanocomposite films was enhanced but elongation at break was declined after increasing NS content. Moisture content, water absorption and solubility in water were improved followed as increasing content of NS and the water resistance and barrier properties of the films were also improved. Water vapour permeability of films was decreased with the increasing NS content. Zhang and others developed a chitosan/WPI film incorporated with TiO_2-NPs and found that the nanoparticles improved the compatibility of WPI and chitosan. Nanoparticle incorporation increased the whiteness of chitosan/WPI film, but decreased the transparency. The elongation at break and tensile strength of nanocomposite film were increased by 12.01% and 11.51%, respectively, whereas WVP was decreased by 7.60%.

MECHANISTIC STUDIES OF NANOMATERIALS IN FOOD PACKAGING

Preventing microbial growth in foods is known as a critical function of packaging to meet the challenge of preserving the quality of food products. Accordingly, antimicrobial materials in food packaging are emerging as a promising technology to fulfill the demands. With the applications of antimicrobial agents in food packaging materials, the growth of bacteria is inhibited and thus the shelf-life of food products is prolonged considerably. Antimicrobial materials are grouped into two classes: organic and inorganic materials. Chitosan-based nanoparticles and chitin-based nanoparticles are typical examples of organic materials, which have lately been widely studied. In respect to the organic antimicrobial materials, some noble metals such as Ag-NPs, Cu-NPs and Au-NPs, as well as the oxidised nanomaterials including ZnO, TiO_2 and MgO have attracted much interest because of their resistance to the rough processing conditions and enhancement of strong biocidal impacts against foodborne pathogens.

There are several hypotheses with respect to antimicrobial mechanistic actions of nanomaterials. There was a general consensus that nanomaterials are proved to be an ideal alternative to traditional plastics and they have also served as a potential packaging material to prolong the shelf-life of food products. Because the large surface-to-volume ratio provides more direct interaction to bacterial surfaces, these nanomaterials showed excellent antibacterial properties. Particularly, cationic nanoparticles were firmly attached to the membrane of bacteria with negatively charged outer layers by electrostatic interactions. Disruption of the cell integrity resulted in the leakage of cell contents.

Nanoparticles had intrinsic antibacterial activities to refuse the microbes by mimicking natural course of killing by phagocytic cells, i.e. by producing large quantity of reactive nitrogen species (RNS) and reactive oxygen species (ROS). Besides, nanomaterials could also prevent or overcome biofilm formation. Nanoparticles especially metallic nanoparticles exerted toxic effects by enhancing the natural immunity or mimicking natural immune responses by generating a large quantity of RNS or ROS. Others possibly exerted direct killing effects maybe by directly targeting cellular proteins, DNA or lipids.

Fardioui and others reviewed the antimicrobial mechanisms of ZnO-NPs. They found that the explicit mechanisms were still under debate, but several models were suggested as follows:

1. Electrostatic interactions between cell walls and ZnO-NPs to destroy bacterial cell integrity.
2. Liberation of antimicrobial Zn^{2+} ions regarding accumulation of ZnO-NPs into bacteria cells.
3. ROS formation: Shao and others tested the electronegativity on *S. aureus* and *E. coli* surfaces after AgNPs treatment, and found a possible change in bacterial surface properties. Furthermore, they observed that cell surfaces were strongly distorted after AgNPs treatment. Meanwhile, some nanoparticles were distributed in the bacterial cell surface, which indicated their direct interaction with bacteria and generation of electronic effects and enhancement of reactivity of AgNPs. El Zowalaty and others suggested that the chitosan reacted with proteins on microbial surfaces and caused the leakage of intracellular contents. It also chelated trace metal ions and disrupted the electron transport chain. Furthermore, it interfered with the formation of mRNA and proteins once inside the cell.

CERTAIN ASPECTS OF CONCERNS

In the past decades, nanomaterials in food packaging applications have been developed to enhance the barrier and mechanical properties of traditional and bio-based packaging materials, and/or to provide novel active and smart functionalities. Active and smart packaging materials deliberately incorporate active or smart components, which are intended to release or absorb substances into, onto, or from the packaged food or the surrounding environment, or to provide the intended information of their use conditions. Developments of nanotechnologies are going to increasingly find utilisations in the food packaging area. However, there are gaps in our knowledge on them that put up questions to the scientific community, especially related to toxicity and ecotoxicity. Theoretically, nanoparticles have the potential to migrate to the packed food, but migration assays and risk assessment are still not conclusive. Migrations into food could be considered as the process of mass transfer, in which the low-molecular mass constituents initially existed in the packaging and then released to the packed matrix. Therefore, it was considered as a diffusion process which could be described by Fick's second law. Thus, one of the most important steps during the development of novel food packaging materials is the research of the migration to investigate the probabilities of any undesirable or harmful ingredients migrating to the food products in overall and specific terms.

Briefly, through the investigation, Jokar and others found that many experimental studies had not given a conclusive answer on the possibility of migration of NPs from food packaging materials to the food products. They assumed this could be partially attributed to the lack of suitable analytical methods for the detection of low quantities and small sizes of NPs. They strongly suggested that studies which concluded that no migration occurred add information about the detection limit of the measurements, including both particle mass or number concentration and particle size. Analytical techniques such as single-particle inductively coupled plasma mass spectrometry (SP-ICP-MS) have been gradually playing a role in characterising and quantifying NPs in the food simulants extracts. Besides, it was difficult to conclude the migrations of NPs through predictive models only considering migrations based on diffusion. Generally, three sub-processes in NP migration could be distinguished: (i) diffusion of the molecule into the polymer to food products because of a concentration gradient, (ii) desorption of the molecule from the polymer and subsequent adsorption by the food at the food-packaging interface, (iii) diffusion of the molecule in the food due to a concentration gradient. The food stimulants and test conditions would affect the migration and ingestion actions by electrostatic interactions and chemical or mechanical decomposition and organic additives and treatment of food samples. However, there was a clear lack of data on potential release mechanisms of identified NPs. The question of risk for the consumer associated with migrating NPs from food packaging probably was more complicated than other questions, because there were many influences of physio-chemical characteristics of NPs on gastrointestinal absorption, such as composition, morphology, charge, surface properties and aggregation state and food components. These clearly require more exploration in the future.

In addition to the technical aspects, no regulations on nanotechnology applications have been yet established in a global context mainly because of lack of sufficient and reliable fundamental researches in regard to the safety assessment and migration characters of nanomaterials from packaging to the food system. The FDA considered that evaluations of safety, effectiveness, public health impact, or regulatory status of nanotechnology products should consider any unique properties and behaviors imparted by the application of nanotechnology. The European Commission already edited statutory contents in this direction with technical guidance mentioning nanomaterials, and also recognised active and smart materials and papers to state that new technologies, which are based on engineered materials in nanoparticle sizes that exhibited physical and chemical properties are significantly different from those at a much larger scale. A risk assessment on a case-by-case basis until more is known about the novel technology is needed. On this basis, and taking into account the lack of knowledge about their potential toxicity (oral exposure to nanomaterials had received less attention than the dermal or inhalation pathways), the concept of functional barriers used to prevent migration of contaminants, which were not evaluated by health authorities, could not be applied in the specific case of biopolymer nanocomposites packaging. These statements notably differentiated nano-structure substances from non-nano-structure substances which were authorised for use as a functional barrier, providing that they fulfilled certain standards and the migrations remained below a given limit of detection.

To sum up, the innovation of nanomaterials in the food packaging science has brought many changes in food preservation, storage, distribution and consumption. Thanks to preventing microbial growth in foods by antimicrobial activity of nanomaterials, these changes have extended the shelf-life of foods to certain degrees with better management of spoilage in food products.

Furthermore, the nanotechnology provides numerous choices for cost-effective, eco-friendly, degradable and renewable packaging materials, which have been gaining more attention and acceptance to solve the ecological environment pollutions and food shortage crises by ensuring food reaches the masses. It is pertinent to note that there are some fundamental studies on toxicity and ecotoxicity, migration assays and risk assessment of nanocomposite materials still needed. In this way, it could allow nanomaterials to work better in the food packaging field.

SECTION IX

Food Laws and Food Ethics

Chapter 32

Food Laws and Regulations

INTRODUCTION

Every nation needs an effective food legislation and food control service to promote a safe, honestly presented food supply, and to protect consumers from contaminated, adulterated, and spoiled foods. Generally the food law is divided into two parts: a basic food act and regulations. The Act itself sets out broad principles, while regulations contain detailed provisions. The principles or general provisions to be included in food law are primarily: basic purposes and scope, definitions of basic concepts, inspection, enforcement, biological and chemical contaminants, packaging and labelling, and procedures for the preparation and amendment of the regulations for implementation of the law. Food law is based on scientific studies. Harmonisation of Food Law on the international level is a worldwide trend from the late twentieth century.

Every country needs laws to encourage the production of safe and wholesome foods, and to prohibit the sale of foods that are unsafe or fraudulent. The growing population has placed demands on agriculture for increased production. However, the increase of agricultural production is connected with the wider use of chemicals. Protection of food during transport and storage may require the use of chemicals, too.

The centralised processing of foods in large quantities increases the chances of contamination. There is an increasing demand for convenience foods, foods ready-to-serve or which can be quickly prepared for serving. Because food additives are commonly used in these foods, and because convenience foods are especially susceptible to contamination, strict hygienic and safety precautions are needed. Expansion of the food trade, both within countries and with other nations, needs regulation not only at the national but also at the international level. In past centuries, international trading in food took place with little, if any, government intervention, and it was accepted that the food producers set their own standards and determined the quality of food products offered to consumers.

Many businesses were responsible and took great care to protect the health of consumers. However, some dishonest traders misused the unregulated markets to sell adulterated food. Such abuses led to government involvement and over time to the enactment of food laws and regulations. These laws and regulations, together with food control organisations, ensure the safety of domestically produced, imported, and exported food products.

This chapter discusses the principal requirements of food laws and regulations will be treated.

STRUCTURE OF FOOD LAW

Generally, Food Law may be divided in two parts: (i) a basic food act, and (ii) regulations. The Act itself sets out broad principles, while regulations contain detailed provisions governing the different categories of products coming under the jurisdiction of each set of regulations.

Sometimes food standards, hygienic provisions, lists of food additives, chemical tolerances, and so on are included in basic food control law. For effective administration of and enlightened compliance with the basic food law, detailed provisions are needed. In governments where there is a division between the responsibilities of the legislative and executive branches, the legislative branch enacts the basic law, while detailed regulations are elaborated and promulgated by the executive agency or agencies responsible for administering the law.

Inclusion in the law of detailed specifications about food processing, food standards, hygienic practices, packaging and labelling, food additives, and pesticides may make for difficulties. Prompt revisions of regulations may become necessary because of new scientific knowledge, changes in food processing technology, or emergencies requiring quick action to protect public health. Such revisions can be made much more expeditiously by executive agencies than by legislative bodies.

In some countries food standards are part of the regulations, in other countries they are separate enactments. Regardless of whether they are included in regulations or are separate, they become part of the enforcement structure, and are intended to implement basic food law.

Concerning the principles or general provisions to be included in basic food law, the following points should be stressed:

- Basic purposes and scope of the law.
- Definitions of basic concepts.
- Competence for implementation of the law.
- Inspection and analytical procedures and facilities.
- Enforcement, procedures for enforcement, penalties.
- Regulations for additives, pesticides, contaminants.
- Packaging and labelling.
- Procedures for the preparation and amendment of the regulations for implementation of the law

The basic food law is intended to assure consumers that foods are pure and wholesome, safe to eat, and produced under sanitary conditions. Generally, food law prohibits importation and distribution of food products that are adulterated, or have labels that are false or misleading in any context.

The proper implementing of such a law encourages fair trade practices through compliance with the basic provisions of the food law. This protects the honest manufacturer and dealer against unfair competition. It also stimulates development of the food industry, because quality control along sound scientific lines tends to promote better consumer acceptance of foods.

An important part of the food law is the definition of terms such as food, natural food, imitation food, food additives, adulteration, and food fraud, pesticide residues, food contaminant, and so on.

According to the US Food, Drug, and Cosmetic Act, a food is illegal (adulterated) if:

- It contains added poisonous or deleterious (harmful) substances that may render it injurious to health.

- It contains a natural, poisonous, or deleterious substance which ordinarily renders it injurious to health.
- A raw agricultural product contains residues of pesticides not authorised by the US Environmental Protection Agency (EPA), or in excess of tolerances established by regulations of the US EPA.
- Any part of the food is putrid or decomposed.

Another example of strict definitions is that basic food law should determine the exact content of offenses, which can give rise to penal action. Such offenses may be:

- Deliberate adulteration of food products.
- Production or marketing of foods containing prohibited or unauthorised substances.
- Fraudulent use of labels and trademarks.
- Failure of foods to satisfy standards laid down by law.
- Violation of hygienic requirements, and so on.

FOOD REGULATIONS—WHAT SHOULD BE REGULATED?

As mentioned earlier in this chapter, regulations implement basic food law. Food regulations generally cover the following:

- General regulations.
- Food standards.
- Food hygiene.
- Food additives.
- Pesticides.
- Veterinary drug residues.
- Food packaging and labelling.
- Food advertising.

The general regulations include detailed regulations for guidance of those who enforce food law, regulations concerning official actions, such as making inspections, collecting samples, making decisions about serious infractions, and the disposition of seized lots of food. To this group of general regulations also belong regulations concerning licenses (permits), if firms and/or specific foods must be registered, the regulations should specify conditions and requirements. Regulations concerning imported foods should cover all aspects of the handling of imported foods. It is impossible to make an overview of all the types of regulations, the above example hopefully will give readers an idea about fields covered by general regulations.

Food Standards

In every country, standards are an important part of the regulation of food production and food trade.

Laws and Regulations to Prevent Gross Adulteration and Contamination

Laws and regulations are still needed to prevent gross adulteration and contamination. Although the forms of gross adulteration and contamination of foods (e.g. diluting milk with water, adding foreign matters to spices, use of harmful dyes or chemicals to mask defects of quality, and so on) are rare, in developed countries in particular, the adulteration of fruit juices with lower value fruit varieties, or of instant coffees with cereal and malt-based ingredients have occurred in the late twentieth century.

MICROBIAL CONTAMINATION, HYGIENIC PRACTICE

It is estimated that 80% to 90% of the outbreaks of foodborne illnesses during the 1990s may be attributed to contamination of food by pathogenic bacteria, primarily *Salmonella and Staphylococci*. Proper hygienic practices should be utilised to prevent microbiological contamination and to minimise spoilage of perishable foods, which are most often the vehicles for these contaminants. An adequate supply of safe water is essential for processing food and maintaining sanitary conditions. Codes of hygienic practice have been elaborated by many countries and international organisations (e.g. the Codex Alimentarius Commission of FAO/WHO). Hygienic practices deal with raw materials requirements, processing plant facilities, hygienic operating requirements and practices, health requirements for food handlers, and so on.

Contamination of Foods

Food contamination can come in the form of bacteria, viruses or parasitic organisms. People who become ill as a result of eating contaminated food may experience a variety of symptoms, including fever, abdominal pain, bloating, diarrhea, vomiting and dehydration. Most of these illnesses are short-lived and can be treated with fluids and electrolytes. Because of the extensive nature of the food industry when harvesting, preparing and handling food, contamination has a number of potential sources.

Agricultural contamination

All cultivated or farmed food, whether fruits and vegetables or livestock and seafood, has a high potential for contamination by both biological organisms and chemicals. The sources of these contaminants can be air, dust, water, insects, rodents, equipment, sewage or employees who work hands-on with any of the foods during any stage of the cultivation or processing. Chemical contamination may occur from pesticide or herbicide use. Improper storage of food items also encourages the growth of microbial pathogens. Sanitation techniques, including cleanliness and proper disposal of sewage and waste products, may effectively minimise or eliminate the potential for contamination.

The natural surface flora of plants varies with the plant but usually includes species of *Pseudomonas*, *Alcaligenes*, *Flavobacterium*, and *Micrococcus* and coliforms and lactic acid bacteria. Lactic acid bacterial include *Lactobacillus brevis* and *plantarum*, *Leuconostoc mesenteroides* and *dextranicum*, and *Streptococcus faecium* and *faecalis*. *Bacillus* species, yeasts, and moulds also may be present. The numbers of bacteria will depend on the plant and its environment and may range from a few hundred or thousand per square centimetre of surface to millions. The surface of a well-washed tomato, for example, may show 400 to 700 micro-organisms per square centimetre, while an unwashed tomato would have several thousand. Exposed surfaces of plants become contaminated from soil, water, sewage, air, and animals, so that micro-organisms from these sources are added to the natural flora. Whenever conditions for growth of natural flora and contaminants are present, increases in number of special kinds of micro-organisms take place, especially following harvesting, as will be discussed subsequently. Some fruits have been found to contain viable micro-organisms in their interior. Normal, healthy tomatoes have been shown to contain *Pseudomonas*, coliforms, *Achromobacter*, *Micrococcus*, and *Corynebacterium*, and yeasts have been found inside undamaged fruits. Organisms also have been found in healthy root and tuber vegetables.

From Animals

According to the Centres for Disease Control and Prevention, raw animal products are the most contaminated food sources. This category includes all meats and poultry, dairy products, eggs and shellfish. The actual source of the contamination may come from diseased animals, contaminated feed, water, storage or food processing. For example, hamburger may consist of meat from several different animals, but just one animal could be the source of contamination. Unsanitary conditions in processing plants are also a major cause of the spread of bacteria and viruses.

Sources of micro-organisms from animals include the surface flora, the flora of the respiratory tract, and the flora of the gastrointestinal tract. The natural surface flora of meat animals usually is not as important as the contaminating micro-organisms from their intestinal or respiratory tracts. However, hides, hooves, and hair contain not only large numbers of micro-organisms from soil, manure, feed, and water but also important kinds of spoilage organisms. Feathers and feet of poultry carry heavy contamination from similar sources. The skin of many meat animals may contain micrococci, staphylococci and beta-hemolytic *streptococci*. *Staphylococci* on the skin or from the respiratory tract may find their way onto the carcass and then to the final raw product. The feces and fecal-contaminated products of animals can contain many enteric organisms, including *Salmonella*. Salmonellosis in animals can result in contamination of animal products or by-products and thus contaminate foods derived from them with *Salmonella*.

Pig or beef carcasses may be contaminated with salmonellae. Because of further processing and handling, very few of these organisms result in human salmonellosis. Actually, meat from slaughtered animals is not frequently associated with human salmonellosis. Statistics in recent years have incriminated eggs and egg products much more frequently. Salmonellosis associated with eggs has been reduced because of the pasteurisation of egg products.

Many infectious disease agents of animals can be transmitted to people via foods, but this represents only one of several transmission routes. Many of these diseases have been reduced or eliminated by improvement in animal husbandry, but a listing of agents of animal disease causing infections from foods would include *Brucella*, *Mycobacterium tuberculosis*, *Coxiella*, *Listeria*, *Campylobacter*, beta-hemolytic *streptococci*, *Salmonella*, enteropathogenic *Escherichia coli*, parasites, and viruses.

Animals, from the lowest to the highest forms, contribute their wastes and finally their bodies to the soil and water and to plants growing there. Little attention has been paid to the direct contamination of food plants from this source, except insofar as coliform bacteria or enterococci may be added. Insects and birds cause mechanical damage to fruits and vegetables, introduce micro-organisms, and open the way for microbial spoilage.

From Untreated Sewage

When untreated domestic sewage is used to fertilise plant crops, there is a likelihood that raw plant foods will be contaminated with human pathogens, especially those causing gastrointestinal diseases. The use of 'night soil' as a fertiliser still persists in some parts of the world. In addition to the pathogens, coliform bacteria, anaerobes, enterococci, other intestinal bacteria, and viruses can contaminate the foods from this source. Natural waters contaminated with sewage contribute their micro-organisms to shellfish, fish, and other seafood.

Treated sewage going onto soil or into water also contributes micro-organisms, although it should contain smaller numbers and fewer pathogens than does raw sewage.

From Soil

The soil contains the greatest variety of micro-organisms of any source of contamination. Whenever microbiologists search for new kinds of micro-organisms or new strains for special purposes, they usually turn first to the soil. Not only numerous kinds of micro-organisms but also large total numbers are present in fertile soils, ready to contaminate the surfaces of plants growing on or in them and the surfaces of animals roaming over the land. Soil dust is whipped up by air currents, and soil particles are carried by running water to get into or onto foods. The soil is an important source of heat-resistant spore-forming bacteria.

Modern methods of food handling usually involve washing the surfaces of foods and hence the removal of much of the soil from those surfaces, and care is taken to avoid contamination by soil dust.

From Water

Natural waters contain not only their natural flora but also micro-organisms from soil and possibly from animals or sewage. Surface waters in streams or pools and stored waters in lakes and large ponds vary considerably in their microbial content, from many thousands per millilitre after a rainstorm to the comparatively low numbers that result from self-purification of quiet lakes and ponds or of running water. Groundwaters from springs or wells have passed through layers of rock and soil to a definite level, hence most of the bacteria, as well as the greater part of other suspended material, have been removed. Bacterial numbers in these waters may range from a few to several hundred bacteria per millilitre.

The kinds of bacteria in natural waters are chiefly species of *Pseudomonas*, *Chromobacterium*, *Proteus*, *Micrococcus*, *Bacillus*, *Streptococcus* (enterococci), *Enterobacter*, and *Escherichia*. Bacteria of the last three genera probably are contaminants rather than part of the natural flora. These bacteria in the water surrounding fish and other sea life establish themselves on the surfaces and in the intestinal tracts of the sea fauna.

From Air

Contamination of foods from the air may be important for sanitary as well as economic reasons. Disease organisms, especially those causing respiratory infections, may be spread among employees by air, or the food product may become contaminated.

Total numbers of micro-organisms in a food may be increased from the air, especially if the air is being used for aeration of the product, as in growing bread yeast, although the numbers of organisms introduced by sedimentation from air usually are negligible. Spoilage organisms may come from air, as may those interfering with food fermentations. Mould spores from air may give trouble in cheese, meat, sweetened condensed milk, and sliced bread and bacon.

Treatment of air

It has been pointed out that numbers of micro-organisms in air may be reduced under natural conditions by sedimentation, sunshine, and washing by rain or snow. Removal of micro-organisms from air by artificial means may involve these principles or those of filtration, chemical treatment, heat or electrostatic precipitation. The most frequently used of these methods is filtration through fibres of various sorts, e.g. cotton, fibre glass, etc. or activated carbon.

After the micro-organisms have been removed from air, precautions must be taken to prevent their re-entrance. Positive pressure in rooms keeps outside air away. Filters in ventilating or air-conditioning systems prevent the spread of organisms from one part of a plant to another, and ultraviolet-irradiated air locks at doors reduce the numbers of organisms carried in by workers.

During Handling and Processing

The contamination of foods from the natural sources just discussed may take place before the food is harvested or gathered or during handling and processing of the food. Additional contamination may come from equipment coming in contact with foods, from packaging materials, and from personnel. The processor attempts to clean and 'sanitise' equipment to reduce such contamination and to employ packaging materials that will minimise contamination. The term 'sanitise' is used here rather than 'sterilise' because although an attempt is made to sterilise the equipment, i.e. free it of all living organisms, sterility is seldom attained.

Personnel in food processing plants can contaminate foods during handling and processing. Various workers suggest that human beings shed from 10^3 to 10^4 viable organisms per minute. The numbers and types of organisms shed are closely related to the subjects working environment.

Chapter 33

Food Ethics

INTRODUCTION

Food ethics refers to the moral consequences of food choices, both those made by humans for themselves and those made for food animals. Common concerns are damage to the environment, exploitive labour practices, food shortages for others, inhumane treatment of food animals, and the unintended effects of food policy. Ethical eating is a type of ethical consumerism.

Environmental: Certain methods of food production and certain types of foods have greater environmental impacts than others. The Union of Concerned Scientists advises that avoiding eating beef is one of the two most important actions most people can take to help the environment because of the large amounts of water needed to produce beef, the pollution from fecal, ammonia, carbon dioxide and methane waste associated with raising cows, the physical damage from grazing, and the destruction of wildlife habitat and rainforests to produce land for grazing. Industrially produced meat, such as that from animals raised in Confined Animal Feeding Operations or CAFOs, has 'the greatest impact of any food product on the environment'.

Packaging of commercially produced foods is also an area of concern, because of the environmental impact of both the production of the packaging and the disposal of the packaging. Transportation of commercially produced foods can increase the foods impact on the environment.

Labour practices: Within the food system there are many low-paid occupations. Many farm workers are paid below-minimum wages or work in substandard conditions, especially farm workers in developing countries and migrant workers in industrialised nations. Jobs within food processing catering and food retailing are also often poorly paid and sometimes hazardous.

Distribution of wealth: Since the 1980s, policies promoting global free trade have increased the amount of food exported from poorer countries, which may adversely affect the food available for their own populations. Campaign to reduce levels of food imports, however, may reduce the incomes of farmers in poorer countries, who rely on export sales.

Food availability: Since the 1950s, the food system has become increasingly global and a small number of multi-national corporations now dominate trade in many foodstuffs. One result is that the proportion of industrially processed foods in diets is increasing globally. Public health researchers label these changes the nutrition transition, arguing that, in poorer countries, they are causing increasing rates of non-communicable diseases, such as diabetes.

Policy: Many governmental food policies have unintended consequences.

SPECIFIC FOOD CHOICES

Ethics of eating meat

The question of whether it is right to eat animal flesh is among the most prominent topics in food ethics. People choose not to eat meat for various reasons such as concern for animal welfare, the environmental impact of meat production (environmental vegetarianism), and health considerations. Some argue that slaughtering animals solely because people enjoy the taste of meat is morally wrong or unjustifiable. Vegans often abstain from other animal products for similar reasons.

Ethical vegetarians and ethical vegans may also object to the practices underlying the production of meat, or cite concerns about animal welfare, animal rights, environmental ethics, and religious reasons. In response, some proponents of meat-eating have adduced various scientific, nutritional, cultural, and religious arguments in support of the practice. Some meat-eaters only object to rearing animals in certain ways, such as in factory farms, or killing them with cruelty, others avoid only certain meats, such as veal or foie gras.

Meat

Some ethicists argue that the keeping and killing of animals for human consumption is in itself unethical. Others point out that animal husbandry is 'essential to sustainable farms, which don't rely on fossil fuels and chemicals,' rather using animal waste as fertiliser and animal activity as weed and pest control and using animals to 'convert vegetation that's inedible to humans, and growing on marginal, uncultivated land, into food.'

The method in which food animals are raised and the type of food animal affect the ethics of eating that animal. Farm-raised oysters cause minimal environmental damage and are raised humanely.

Dairy and eggs

Dairy and egg production have ethical consequences, in particular in large-scale industrialised production. Chickens and milk-animals raised in industrial operations are often treated inhumanely.

Small-scale production of eggs, such as by backyard chicken raisers and small diversified farms raising pastured birds or milk-animals, are less ethically fraught but still create some issues for ethicists.

Seafood

Industrial fishing has broad effects with ethical consequences.

Crops

Some foods produced in developing countries are exported in quantities that threaten the ability of local residents to affordably obtain their traditional foods. Western demand for quinoa, a traditional food in Bolivia Peru and Ecuador, has become so high that producers are eating significantly less of the grain, preferring to sell it for import instead and sparking concerns about malnutrition.

FOOD ETHICS IN FOOD POLICY

The ethical issues raised by food production and consumption encompass a very wide range of activities, everything (in the alliterative phrase that has become popular) 'from plough to plate'. That such a broad remit is now receiving attention stems from the realisation that a new attitude to food is called for, one that recognises the importance of a holistic approach.

Following the Second World War, the application of industrial practices to agriculture and food was represented as Taylorism the process by which complex tasks are dispersed into defined specialist activities in the interests of improved efficiency. While such specialisation undoubtedly allows economies of scale, the lack of any overall responsibility for the whole process is a significant drawback.

Consequently, complex regulations have had to be introduced to ensure that adequate standards are observed, particularly in terms of food safety. However, bureaucracy can be extremely cumbersome and, frequently, important issues fall through the net. It would be superfluous to document the regrettable consequences which stemmed from such bureaucratic inadequacies in the case of the outbreak of bovine spongiform encephalopathy, but the epidemic undoubtedly led to a wider appreciation of the hazards of reductionism.

Specifically, the aims here are to:

1. Indicate why ethical analysis of the agricultural and food industries is important.
2. Summarise the ethical theories which underpin ethical analysis.
3. Describe a framework to facilitate ethical analysis.
4. Illustrate the framework using a topical example of a food biotechnology.
5. Demonstrate the relationship between ethical analysis and policy decisions.

Food Ethics

Food ethics is an emerging academic discipline: one of many in the burgeoning field of 'applied ethics'. Other acknowledged branches of applied ethics are: medical, scientific, environmental, legal, educational, political, business, media and social ethics. Each branch attempts to address normative issues by applying ethical theory to the specific circumstances of its particular endeavours.

A number of features distinguish the food and associated agricultural industries from other types of industrial activity, and justify considering food ethics as a discrete and coherent field of academic enquiry. Thus:

1. Food is vital to human survival, in a way in which cars and mobile phones are not.
2. Food production is an organic process, which depends on the exploitation of living resources.
3. Sustainable food supply necessitates ecological and environmental stability and depends on the recycling of essential nutrients, e.g. in the C and N cycles.
4. The ultimate dependence of agricultural productivity on the capture of solar energy by plants involves use of extensive land area, which has implications for the competing claims of other industries and of social amenity.
5. Farming is a way of life which contributes to cultural norms to an extent disproportionate to the numbers actively engaged in it, it also safeguards skills which might prove of inestimable value in the event of military or environmental crisis.

In short, to a greater degree than most other industrial activities, agriculture and food permeate our physical, biological, social and cultural environment, and are likely to do so for the foreseeable future.

Consequently, the associated ethical concerns encompass a correspondingly broad range of issues, such as:

1. The mismatch between global food supplies and human nutritional needs.
2. The impact of agribusiness on rural employment.
3. The consequences of modern agricultural and food biotechnologies for human and animal welfare.
4. The effects of intensive production systems on the sustainability of the global environment.

Ethical issues are crucial in relation to food because these distinctive features mean that the normal checks and balances between producer, retailer and consumer are often inadequate.

Social Contract

If ethical analysis is to be of value, it needs to be instrumental in effecting change, e.g. by reducing hunger, protecting the environment, ensuring food safety or improving farm animal welfare. It needs to take the ethical theories discussed and put them to practical use.

Central to these objectives in democratic societies is the concept of the 'social contract', which may be defined as 'an unwritten agreement between members of a society, which serves as the basis for social cooperation, legal provision and governance'.

According to such a contract, members of a society will concede certain liberties to facilitate a fair and mutually beneficial social structure. This concept might suggest that the focus is on government policy, but many of the issues also directly concern private corporations, which have great influence in shaping food provision on a global scale.

A social contract with respect to food is essential in a democratic society for several reasons. First, a society needs to ensure a supply of safe nutritious food that is universally available, failure to do so is simply inconsistent with the harmony and equity on which a viable democracy depends. Second, the contract needs to take account of issues such as the national economy, the working conditions of farm workers, public sensibilities to the treatment of animals and impacts on the countryside as a social amenity. Moreover, if the 'contractors' are to include all interest groups ('stakeholders'), 'society' needs to be defined in global terms, e.g. taking account of the impacts of biotechnological innovations on the population and economies of less developed countries.

Ultimately, political decisions need to be made as to what is to be enforced or prohibited by law, what is to be encouraged or discouraged (e.g. by fiscal policy or by public education) and whether, and how much, provision is to be made for minority opinions (as in special food labelling requirements for vegetarians).

Broadly speaking, individual ethical judgements on specific issues which have political consequences (e.g. whether to require labelling of a genetically-modified food product) depend on three factors:

1. Acceptance of a set of general ethical principles (such as, 'individuals should be free to choose the type of food they eat').
2. Understanding of relevant evidence and scientific facts (e.g. whether or not there is a significant difference between a genetically-modified food product and the non-genetically-modified product to which it might be claimed to correspond).
3. Adherence to a particular 'world-view' (from the German weltanschauung, meaning 'a particular conception of the nature and purpose of the world', reflected, for example, in an intrinsic preference for either organic food or genetically-modified food).

ETHICAL MATRIX

The ethical matrix is a conceptual tool designed to help decision-makers (as individuals or working in groups) reach sound judgements or decisions about the ethical acceptability and/or optimal regulatory controls for existing or prospective technologies in the field of food and agriculture.

The ethical matrix applies a number of prima facie principles to a set of selected interest groups. The standard principles are: respect for wellbeing, autonomy and fairness, and together they form the columns of the ethical matrix. The rows consist of the 'interest groups' (i.e. affected parties) that are relevant to the issue in question. These might include different groups of people, such as consumers and food producers, but also non-humans, such as farm animals. The arrangement of principles and interest groups in a table, forming the ethical matrix, facilitates easy cross-referencing in deliberation and subsequent reflection on an issue. The ethical matrix was initially designed to facilitate ethical deliberation by those with particular knowledge and/or interest in novel biotechnologies, but who may have little or no formal training in academic ethical theory or have only limited experience in applying such theory to concrete issues. The aim of the ethical matrix is to help users identify ethical issues raised by the use of novel technologies and to arrive at intellectually defensible decisions. However, the ethical matrix does not prescribe any particular decisions.

By Whom and When can the Ethical Matrix be Used

The ethical matrix may be used by a number of groups or individuals in order to structure ethical deliberation, for example on the use of new biotechnologies. A number of organisations can apply the tool, including:

- Governmental advisory committees and/or adhoc working parties.
- Ethics committees at various levels.
- Non-governmental organisations.
- Participants in exercises in public deliberation.
- Commercial companies.

The ethical matrix has also been used by individuals to examine bioethical issues in academic publications, in courses at secondary schools and universities, and in a web-based educational program. The ethical matrix can be used:

- At a strategic level to review ethical dimensions.
- To review the specific ethical impacts of individual technologies (e.g. for a patent or licence application).

Expected Outcomes of Exercises using the Ethical Matrix

Use of the ethical matrix may be expected to result in one or more of the following outcomes:

- Raise awareness of a wide range of ethical issues.
- Encourage ethical reflection.
- Provide a common basis for ethical decision-making.
- Identify areas of agreement between individuals who might nevertheless differ in their overall judgements.
- Clarify the basis of disagreements.
- Make explicit the reasoning that underpins any ethical decisions.

Role of Ethical Matrix

Although the ethical matrix aims to provide a structure for ethical deliberation, it would be wrong to assume that its use could ever enable a committee to arrive at a definitive judgement without applying sound independent ethical reflection and judgement. For the process to be effective, decision-makers must reach a measure of agreement on the interpretation of the principles. Different interpretations of the weights assigned to each of the principles by different people preclude a definitive ethical judgement. Thus, it is not possible to automatically arrive at a unique or prescribed course of action from the use of the ethical matrix. Methodologically, the ethical matrix is a development of the principles encompassed by the common morality, i.e. the ethical code shared by most members of a society in the form of unreflective common sense and tradition. However, because the common morality may only amount to the 'lowest common denominator,' it is likely that real progress in addressing ethical issues will only be made by conscientious, informed dialogue which goes well beyond 'unreflective common sense.'

The aim of the ethical matrix is to select principles that collectively are representative of the two major traditions of ethical theory and thinking of western societies. This means that these traditions, namely, consequentialism and deontology, should be represented by adequate principles.

Essential Features of the Ethical Matrix

There are several ways in which the ethical matrix can be applied to assist decision-making, but all uses share some important common features. In all cases, the ethical matrix offers:

1. A good starting point for ethical deliberation (i.e. a process which entails the careful consideration and discussion of the ethical implications of an issue) which encompasses both:
   - Different perspectives (e.g. stakeholders or affected parties), from which the impact of a proposed novel technology can be assessed.
   - Different concerns, (i.e. ethical principles) according to which the impact of a proposed technology may be differentiated and analysed.
2. However, the possibility of conflicting outcomes in applying the principles to specific cases suggests that it is best to consider the principles as prima facie in nature. This implies that, typically, some principles will need to be assigned more importance, or weight, than others. That is to say, when examining the specifics of a case, a particular principle, although given due consideration in the analysis, may be overridden by another principle that is deemed more important.
3. The weight assigned to particular principles in specific cases usually differs between people using the ethical matrix, and to some extent this is because ethical deliberation entails an appeal to several forms of evidence. 'Evidence' is defined here as 'anything that provides material or information on which a conclusion or proof is based'. Such forms of evidence include, for example:
   - Scientific and economic data.
   - Assessments of the consequences of risk and uncertainty (e.g. reflected in the different ways people apply the Precautionary Principle).
   - Assessments of the intrinsic value of different forms of life (which may reflect peoples' differing world views).
   - Tacit, folk or practical knowledge.
4. Qualitative or quantitative assessments of impacts recorded in the different cells of the ethical matrix (ethical analysis) provide a road map of salient ethical concerns, the different weightings of which underpin the various ethical judgements made.

References

Alford, G., *Food Chemistry*, John Wiley & Sons, New York.

Alouf, D., *Biotechnological Innovations in Food Processing*, Butterworths, London.

Anke, J.T., *Food Engineering Operations*, Marcel Dekker Inc., New York.

Berg, V.T., *Dairy Microbiology*, Applied Science Publishers, London.

Batterman, S.A., *Sampling and Analysis of Food Products*, McGraw-Hill, Tokyo.

Benaim Pinto, C., *Sampling and Analysis of Airborne Micro-organisms*, Prentice Hall, London.

Brown, N.K., *Environmental Microbiology*, Cambridge University Press, Cambridge.

Bradley, S.M., *Food Microbiology*, Academic Press, London.

Budyko, N.P., *Food Processing Waste,* Progress Publishers, Moscow.

Chang, G.D., *Introduction to Environmental Microbiology*, John Wiley & Sons, New York.

Commoner, R.M, *Food Enzymes*, John Wiley & Sons, New York.

Coolingwood, S.A., *Food Flavours,* John Wiley & Sons, New York.

Cox, C.V., *Food Science*, S.P. Medical and Scientific Books, New York.

Daniel, G.L., *Canned Foods and Their Microbiology*, Pergamon Press, Oxford.

Dennis, R.H., *Principles of Food Processing*, Springer, US.

Downe, S.A., *Dairy Microbiology*, John Wiley & Sons, New York.

Dugan, P.R., *Fermentation of Beer*, Plenum Publishing Corporation, London.

Earle, R.L., *Unit Operation in Food Processing*, Butterworth-Heinemann, Ltd., London.

Goldman, M.B., *Treatment of Food Waste*, Gordon and Breach, Science Publishers, New York.

Gould, G.W., *Food Biochemistry*, D. Van Nostrand, New York.

Harding, G.E., *Transport Processes and Unit Operations*, Prentice-Hall, London.

Jatinder, K.S., *Advanced Food Process Engineering*, CRC Press, London.

Krieg, G.M., *Food Engineering and Process Applications,* Heinemann, London.

Lewis, B.B., *Applied Environmental Microbiology*, Elsevier Scientific Publishing Co., Amsterdam.

Lodish, H.K., *Food Processing Technology*, W. H. Freeman and Company, New York.

Miller, M.S., *Food Microbiology*, Prentice-Hall, London.

Park, S.H., *Fundamentals of Food Processing*, Wiley-Blackwell, New York.

Pilar, M.C., *Novel Food Processing Technology*, CRC Press, London.

Riemann, D.L., *Food Processing Technology*, Academic Press, London.

Robert, B.L. and Evison, L.W., *Principles of Food Science*, John Wiley & Sons, New York.

Sengner, J., *Micro-organisms in Food*, John Wiley & Sons, New York.

Smith, P.A., *Encyclopedia of Environmental Microbiology*, John Wiley & Sons, New York.

Tanaka, S.K., *Flavonoids: Dietary Occurrence and Biochemical Activity*, Marcel Dekker, New York.

Wilson, A.L., *Encyclopedia of Food Science*, Academic Press, London.

Index

G

H

I

J

K

L

M

N

T